FIFTH EDITION

UK
GAAP

FIFTH EDITION

UK GAAP

Generally Accepted Accounting Practice in the United Kingdom

Mike Davies, Ron Paterson and Allister Wilson

MACMILLAN

≡II ERNST & YOUNG

Fifth edition published 1997 by
MACMILLAN REFERENCE LTD,
25 Eccleston Place,
London SW1W 9NF, UK.
Companies and representatives throughout the world.

ISBN 0-333-64260-0

Distributed by Macmillan Distribution Ltd, Brunel Road, Houndmills, Basingstoke,
Hampshire RG21 6XS, UK.
Macmillan Reference on the WWW
http://www.macmillan-reference.co.uk

A catalogue record for this book is available from the British Library.

Printed and bound in Great Britain by Clays Ltd, Bungay, Suffolk, UK

Foreword to the fifth edition

Seldom has a comprehensive and authoritative treatise on a country's accepted accounting practice been so readable and easily accessible to a wide audience that it can be recommended not only to accounting practitioners and finance directors but also to students, academics, and users of financial statements, both in the country and overseas.

The authors' success at explaining a complex, technical subject in conversational prose is an impressive achievement. Numerical examples and graphs, as well as extracts from company annual reports, nicely complement the explanations and serve to illustrate applications. The authors supply useful historical background, and they draw on their firm's collective experience to breathe life into dry and sometimes arbitrary accounting standards, Companies Act provisions, and stock exchange rules.

Consonant with the movement toward an international harmonisation of accounting standards, the authors make frequent comparisons with US standards as well as those issued by the International Accounting Standards Committee. In the chapter dealing with the conceptual framework, UK initiatives are compared with a selection of those proposed or adopted in the US, Canada, Australia and New Zealand, as well as with that of the IASC.

The authors' analysis and criticism of particular standards and practices, as well as of the Accounting Standards Board's evolving conceptual framework, do much to stimulate the reader's critical faculty. The controversy stirred by these views is a lively addition to the literature on accounting standards and principles. Throughout the book, the discussion is enriched by the authors' frequent arguments for improved standards and practices.

At the close, the authors helpfully provide a complete set of specimen financial statements for a hypothetical group, as a guide to those concerned with preparing company accounts.

At a time when accounting standards have become so detailed and complicated that they sometimes are not understood even by experts, a work that is at once authoritative and instructive is to be welcomed by all who have a stake in the soundness of company financial reporting.

Since the publication of the first edition of *UK GAAP* in 1989, I have found it to be an indispensable reference work to the norms governing UK financial reporting. Through this foreword, I am pleased to commend the fifth edition to a wide audience.

June 1997

Stephen A. Zeff

Herbert S. Autrey Professor of Accounting

Rice University

Preface to the fifth edition

UK GAAP has developed very significantly since we published the first edition of this book in 1989. Evidence of this can be seen in the progressive expansion of the book itself; this fifth edition is nearly twice the size of the original. The most important factor in this, of course, has been the creation of the Accounting Standards Board in 1990, which has had a profound effect on the shaping of accounting practice, as we have chronicled in each subsequent edition.

In the 1989 Preface to the book, we promised to be forthright in our views as to how accounting practice could be improved. It is well known that since then we have often disagreed with proposals put forward by the ASB, and in particular that we have profound reservations about its draft *Statement of Principles*. The reason for this is not doctrinaire; we simply do not think that this framework provides a good foundation for practical standards that will generate understandable accounts, and this book discusses many examples which explain why that is the case. However, we also compliment the Board on some of its other achievements in enhancing the annual reporting package, such as the development of the cash flow statement and the Operating and Financial Review. More generally, through the distinctive leadership of Sir David Tweedie, the ASB has consistently provided strong advocacy for the best ideals of financial reporting, which we applaud and wholly support, even if we differ as to how these ideals should be advanced.

In 1997, the new factor which may prove to have the most influence on the future development of UK GAAP is the IASC's bid to develop its standards to a level at which they will be accepted throughout the world's capital markets. If a truly global corpus of standards does emerge, it is bound to affect accounting in this country. We continue to record all the developments in this wider arena.

As with all earlier editions, we are indebted to a number of our colleagues in Ernst & Young for their help with the publication of this book, most notably Joanne Brundish, Jan Collins, Matthew Curtis, Carla Jones, Leonie Moffat and Trevor Pijper, but also all the other members of the Technical Services Department, who contributed both directly and indirectly to the book's creation. As authors, however, we continue to take responsibility for all the opinions expressed in the book and the blame for all its faults.

August 1997

Mike Davies
Ron Paterson
Allister Wilson

Detailed contents

CHAPTER 3　　REVENUE RECOGNITION　　　　　　　　　　129

CHAPTER 4   CORPORATE GOVERNANCE AND THE OFR   177

CHAPTER 7   ASSOCIATES AND JOINT VENTURES   421

CHAPTER 8   FOREIGN CURRENCIES   465

CHAPTER 9   FINANCIAL INSTRUMENTS   589

CHAPTER 10   FIXED ASSETS AND DEPRECIATION   623

CHAPTER 13   CAPITALISATION OF BORROWING COSTS   755

CHAPTER 15   CAPITAL INSTRUMENTS   845

CHAPTER 16   OFF BALANCE SHEET TRANSACTIONS   923

CHAPTER 17   LEASES AND HIRE PURCHASE CONTRACTS   979

CHAPTER 20   PENSION COSTS   1105

CHAPTER 26   PROVISIONS   1433

CHAPTER 27   CASH FLOW STATEMENTS 1467

CHAPTER 30   DIRECTORS' REMUNERATION   1615

Chapter 1   The development of UK GAAP

1   DEFINITION OF 'UK GAAP'

1.1   'Principles' or 'practice'

In the UK, the expression 'GAAP' is used more loosely than in most other countries; the reason for this is that GAAP does not have any statutory or regulatory authority or definition, as is the case in, for example, the US, Canada and New Zealand. Consequently, references to GAAP are rarely found in the literature in the UK, and where the expression is used, it is not adequately explained or defined.

There are two instances where the term is used in the Companies Act. In order for a business combination to be treated as a merger, one of the qualifying criteria is that the method 'accords with generally accepted accounting principles or practice'.[1] This is generally taken to mean that the transaction qualifies to be so treated under the relevant accounting standard, but the use of the alternative words 'principles or practice' suggests some doubt on the part of the legislators as to which phrase has general currency. The other arises in the context of realised profits and losses; the Act states that they are 'such profits or losses of the company as fall to be treated as realised in accordance with principles generally accepted, at the time when the accounts are prepared, with respect to the determination for accounting purposes of realised profits or losses'.[2] Although the legislation does not define the term 'principles generally accepted', the Consultative Committee of Accountancy Bodies (CCAB) issued a Technical Release (TR 481) in September 1982 which gave guidance on the determination of realised profits.[3] TR 481 stated that 'principles generally accepted' for the determination of realised profits 'should be considered in conjunction with, inter alia, the legal principles laid down in the new Schedule 8 [now Schedule 4], statements of standard accounting practice ("SSAPs"), and in particular the fundamental accounting concepts referred to in SSAP 2'.[4] This interpretation, however, applies purely to the determination of realised profits;

as will be seen below, it is our view that GAAP should be more widely interpreted.

In one of their Joint Opinions referred to in 2.2 below, Hoffmann and Arden cited the decision in *Odeon Associated Theatres Ltd v Jones (Inspector of Taxes)*[5] as an illustration of the relationship between 'generally accepted accounting principles' and the legal concept of true and fair, and in so doing reached the conclusion that 'the function of the ASC is to formulate what it considers should be generally accepted accounting principles'.[6] Nevertheless, whilst most would agree that the accounting standards represent 'generally accepted accounting principles', what about those areas of accounting which are not addressed in the standards? Furthermore, what about the accounting and disclosure requirements of the Companies Act and Stock Exchange – do they constitute 'generally accepted accounting principles'?

Our view is that GAAP is a dynamic concept which requires constant review, adaptation and reaction to changing circumstances. We believe that use of the term 'principle' gives GAAP an unjustified and inappropriate degree of permanence. GAAP changes in response to changing business and economic needs and developments. As circumstances alter, accounting practices are modified or developed accordingly. The UK's Accounting Standards Board (ASB) recognises this in its *Statement of Aims*, which discusses the Board's ongoing need to issue new accounting standards, or amend existing ones, 'in response to evolving business practices, new economic developments and deficiencies being identified in current practice'.[7] We believe that GAAP goes far beyond mere rules and principles, and encompasses contemporary permissible accounting *practice*.

This is consistent with a description of GAAP laid down by the Auditing Standards Board in the United States in Statement on Auditing Standards No. 69 (SAS 69) – *The Meaning of 'Present Fairly in Conformity with Generally Accepted Accounting Principles' in the Independent Auditor's Report*. SAS 69 states that 'the phrase "generally accepted accounting principles" is a technical accounting term that encompasses the conventions, rules and procedures necessary to define accepted accounting practice at a particular time. It includes not only broad guidelines of general application, but also detailed practices and procedures ... Those conventions, rules, and procedures provide a standard by which to measure financial presentations.'[8] A similar definition of the term 'generally accepted accounting practice' has been incorporated in New Zealand's Financial Reporting Act, which came into effect in 1994.[9]

Accordingly, the boundaries of GAAP extend far beyond the accounting principles contained in accounting standards; UK GAAP includes the requirements of the Companies Act and of the Stock Exchange, as well as any other acceptable accounting treatments not incorporated in the official literature.

1.2   What is 'generally accepted'?

It is often argued that the term 'generally accepted' implies that there must exist a high degree of practical application of a particular accounting practice. However, this interpretation raises certain practical difficulties. For example, what about new areas of accounting which have not, as yet, been generally applied? What about different accounting treatments for similar items – are they all generally accepted?

It is our view that 'generally accepted' does *not* mean 'generally adopted or used'. We believe that, in the UK context, GAAP refers to accounting practices which are regarded as permissible by the accounting profession. The extent to which a particular practice has been adopted is, in our opinion, not the overriding consideration. Any accounting practice which is legitimate in the circumstances under which it has been applied should be regarded as GAAP. The decision as to whether or not a particular practice is permissible or legitimate would depend on one or more of the following factors:

- Is the practice addressed either in the accounting standards, statute or other official pronouncements?

- If the practice is not addressed in UK accounting standards, is it dealt with in International Accounting Standards, or the standards of other countries such as the US?

- Is the practice consistent with the needs of users and the objectives of financial reporting?

- Does the practice have authoritative support in the accounting literature?

- Is the practice being applied by other companies in similar situations?

- Is the practice consistent with the fundamental concept of 'true and fair'?

The aim of this book is to analyse existing UK GAAP on the basis of the above six criteria.

2   ACCOUNTING STANDARDS AND THE CONCEPT OF 'TRUE AND FAIR'

2.1   The introduction of the true and fair concept

The requirement that all financial statements which are prepared for the purpose of compliance with the Companies Act should 'give a true and fair view' was first introduced in the Companies Act 1947.[10] This amended the former requirement of 'true and correct', a change considered necessary on the grounds that there was no clear distinction between the two adjectives when used to describe financial statements. Was it possible for financial statements to be 'true' yet 'incorrect'; or 'untrue' yet 'correct'?

The concept of true and fair was adopted by the EC Council in its Fourth Directive.[11]   In terms of the Directive, annual accounts are defined as a 'composite whole' comprising a balance sheet, profit and loss account and notes; the accounts should be drawn up in accordance with the Directive's detailed provisions and 'give a true and fair view of the company's assets, liabilities, financial position and profit or loss'.[12]   However, to obviate a potential conflict between its detailed provisions and the achievement of truth and fairness, the Directive declared the obligation to give a true and fair view to be overriding. Consequently, where the application of the provisions of the Directive would not be sufficient to give a true and fair view, additional information must be given, and where the application of a provision of the Directive is incompatible with the presentation of a true and fair view, that provision must be departed from (with appropriate disclosure in the notes of the departure).[13]

The provisions of the Fourth Directive were implemented in the UK through the enactment of the Companies Act 1981. Following the consolidation of the various Companies Acts 1948–1983 into the Companies Act 1985, and the subsequent implementation of the Seventh Directive in the 1989 Act, the detailed requirements of the Directive are contained in Schedules 4 and 4A to the 1985 Act, and the requirement that financial statements should give a true and fair view is contained in section 226 for individual companies and section 227 for group financial statements. It is therefore clear that the concept of true and fair is a legal one, and the question as to whether or not a particular company's financial statements comply with sections 226 or 227 can ultimately only be decided by the courts.

It is interesting to note that the IASC has now also adopted the concept of an override in its own accounting standards, after considerable debate. The revised version of IAS 1 – *Presentation of Financial Statements* – now permits an enterprise to depart from another international standard if this is necessary in order to achieve a fair presentation, where compliance with that other standard would have been misleading.

2.2   The interaction of accounting standards and the law

The Companies Act 1989 gave, for the first time in the UK, statutory recognition to the existence of accounting standards. This recognition was achieved through the inclusion of a new section (Section 256) in the Companies Act 1985 and of a new disclosure requirement in Schedule 4 to that Act. The first two sub-sections of Section 256 read as follows:

'(1) In this Part "accounting standards" means statements of standard accounting practice issued by such body or bodies as may be prescribed by regulations.

(2)   References in this Part to accounting standards applicable to a company's annual accounts are to such standards as are, in accordance with their terms, relevant to the company's circumstances and to the accounts.'

In addition, the insertion of Paragraph 36A of Schedule 4 to the Companies Act 1985 resulted in the new requirement for companies to state by way of note to their accounts 'whether the accounts have been prepared in accordance with applicable accounting standards and particulars of any material departure from those standards and the reasons for it shall be given'. (There is an exemption from this requirement for small and medium-sized companies and for certain small and medium-sized groups.)

For twenty years until 1990, the responsibility for developing accounting standards was discharged by the Accounting Standards Committee (ASC). Since then, that function has been fulfilled by the Accounting Standards Board (ASB), having been prescribed by Statutory Regulation as the standard-setting body for the purposes of Section 256(1) of the Companies Act with effect from 20 August 1990.

The ASB's Foreword to Accounting Standards explains the relationship between compliance with the accounting standards and the concept of true and fair. This says that: 'Accounting standards are authoritative statements of how particular types of transaction and other events should be reflected in financial statements and accordingly compliance with accounting standards will normally be necessary for financial statements to give a true and fair view.'[14] It goes on to say that 'because accounting standards are formulated with the objective of ensuring that the information resulting from their application faithfully represents the underlying commercial activity, the Board envisages that only in exceptional circumstances will departure from the requirements of an accounting standard be necessary in order for financial statements to give a true and fair view'.[15]

The meaning of the true and fair requirement, including the legal relationship between accounting standards and the Companies Act, was discussed in two Joint Opinions obtained by the ASC in 1983 and 1984 from Leonard Hoffmann QC (now the Rt. Hon. Lord Justice Hoffmann) and Miss Mary Arden (now The Hon. Mrs Justice Arden). The 1983 opinion states that 'the courts will treat compliance with accepted accounting principles as prima facie evidence that the accounts are true and fair. Equally, deviation from accepted principles will be prima facie evidence that they are not. ... The function of the ASC is to formulate what it considers should be generally accepted accounting principles. Thus the value of a SSAP to a court which has to decide whether accounts are true and fair is two-fold. First, it represents an important statement of professional opinion about the standards which readers may reasonably expect in accounts which are intended to be true and fair. ... Secondly, because accountants are professionally obliged to comply with a SSAP, it creates in the readers an expectation that the accounts will be in conformity with the prescribed standards. This is in itself a reason why accounts which depart from the standard without adequate justification or explanation may be held not to be true and fair.'[16]

This view is supported in the judgment given by Woolf J in *Lloyd Cheyham & Co Ltd v Littlejohn & Co*, in which he stated that 'while they [accounting standards] are not conclusive, ... and they are not as the explanatory foreword makes clear, rigid rules, they are very strong evidence as to what is the proper standard which should be adopted'.[17]

Following statutory recognition of the existence of accounting standards, the ASB requested Miss Mary Arden QC to write a further Opinion which addressed the legal relationship between accounting standards and the true and fair view. The Opinion was issued in April 1993 and published by the ASB as an Appendix to its *Foreword to Accounting Standards*.[18] Whilst this Opinion has been given in the context of the changes in the law discussed above, it is essentially a reiteration of the two previous Joint Opinions. It again explains that 'the immediate effect of the issue of an accounting standard is to create a likelihood that the court will hold that compliance with that standard is necessary to meet the true and fair requirement. That likelihood is strengthened by the degree to which a standard is subsequently accepted in practice. Thus if a particular standard is generally followed, the court is very likely to find that the accounts must comply with it in order to show a true and fair view. The converse of that proposition, that non-acceptance of a standard in practice would almost inevitably lead a court to the conclusion that compliance with it was not necessary to meet the true and fair requirement, is not however the case. Whenever a standard is issued by the Board, then, irrespective of the lack in some quarters of support for it, the court would be bound to give special weight to the opinion of the Board in view of its status as the standard-setting body, the process of investigation, discussion and consultation that it will have undertaken before adopting the standard and the evolving nature of accounting standards.'[19]

Clearly, therefore, although accounting standards have no direct legal authority or effect, it appears highly probable that they will have a very persuasive effect in the courts' interpretation as to whether or not a company's accounts present a true and fair view. This status is further reinforced by the Schedule 4 requirement described above that any departures from accounting standards be explained in the financial statements.

Although the legal standing of accounting standards has grown over the years, however, it is also true that the influence of the law has increasingly encroached on UK GAAP. Until the 1981 Companies Act, the accounting requirements laid down by statute were relatively limited; they comprised the general rules on the scope of accounts for companies and groups, the requirement to give a true and fair view, and a range of disclosure requirements, but they did not concern themselves with the detailed mechanics of accounting or the measurement of assets and liabilities. However, the 1981 Act, and subsequently the 1989 Act, introduced the Fourth and Seventh EC Directives which now specify the format of accounts to be presented and the accounting rules to be followed in considerable detail, and both standard setters and preparers of accounts increasingly find their freedom of action constrained by the law.

The ASB has expressed its intention to consider accounting principles first and the law as a secondary matter, in the following terms: 'In its debates on any accounting topic the Board initially develops its views by considering how its principles of accounting apply to the possible accounting options available for that topic. However, in deciding what is the most appropriate treatment the Board must also consider the environment in which its standards are to be applied. The legislation with which reporting entities must comply forms an important part of that environment. Accordingly, FRSs are drafted in the context of current ... legislation and European Community Directives with the aim of ensuring consistency between accounting standards and the law.'[20]

It is evident, however, that the risk of having its proposals exposed to legal challenge does weigh heavily with the Board. In a sense, the increased legal authority which standards have gained in recent years is proving a two-edged sword, because it makes it more likely that the standards will be subject to judicial interpretation and must be drafted in terms which stand up to that analysis. Increasingly, this has provoked territorial disputes between the accounting and legal professions on who has the right to opine on the interpretation of accounting rules. This rivalry has been described by the Rt. Hon. Lord Justice Hoffmann in the following terms:

'Like many rival tribes, accountants and lawyers have opinions of each other which are largely based on ignorance. The undigested gobbets of company and tax law which most accountants have to learn during training only serve to convince them that lawyers are pedants who try to confine the realities of commerce within an artificial construction of arbitrary rules. Lawyers, curiously enough, tend to think that this is a fair description of accountants. Reading financial statements makes them regard accountants as sophisters, economists and calculators, operating within a closed system capable of producing any desired result and bearing little relationship to the realities of commerce. ... In fact, both professions are deeply engaged in the intolerable wrestle with words and meanings, which give rise to philosophical problems having much in common with each other.'[21]

2.3 The role of International Accounting Standards

The International Accounting Standards Committee (IASC) came into existence in 1973 as a result of an agreement by various accountancy bodies around the world. As at the beginning of 1997, the IASC had members in 88 countries, and its business is conducted by a Board comprising representatives of up to 13 countries and up to four other organisations having an interest in financial reporting.[22] The objectives of the IASC as set out in its constitution are:

(a)   to formulate and publish in the public interest accounting standards to be observed in the presentation of financial statements and to promote their world-wide acceptance and observance; and

(b)   to work generally for the improvement and harmonisation of regulations, accounting standards and procedures relating to the presentation of financial statements.[23]

The Accounting Standards Board's stated approach to International Accounting Standards is as follows: 'FRSs are formulated with due regard to international developments. The Board supports the International Accounting Standards Committee in its aim to harmonise international financial reporting. As part of this support an FRS contains a section explaining how it relates to the International Accounting Standard (IAS) dealing with the same topic. In most cases, compliance with an FRS automatically ensures compliance with the relevant IAS. Where the requirements of an accounting standard and an IAS differ, the accounting standard should be followed by entities reporting within the area of application of the Board's accounting standards.'[24]

When IASs were first issued, they permitted several alternative accounting treatments. The principal reason for this was that the IASC viewed its initial function as prohibiting undesirable accounting practices, whilst acknowledging that there might be more than one acceptable solution to a specific accounting issue. However, in recent years, international accounting standards have been tightened up considerably.

In 1993 the Board of the IASC completed a major project (known as the comparability/improvements project) which had set out to reduce many of the permitted alternative accounting options. This project took four years and culminated in the publication of a package of ten revised international standards which become operative for accounting periods beginning on or after 1 January 1995. Unfortunately, this project was less successful than everyone had hoped it would be, and although the number of permitted alternative options was reduced, they were not eliminated; this means that international standards still incorporate 'benchmark' treatments and 'allowed alternative' treatments.

A much more significant initiative is now in progress, however, the outcome of which will largely determine the course of world harmonisation of accounting and the future role of the IASC; this, in turn, will have a major influence on the future direction of UK GAAP. In 1995, the IASC reached an agreement with the International Organisation of Securities Commissions (IOSCO) that, provided the IASC could complete a core set of upgraded standards to IOSCO's satisfaction by 1999, IOSCO would endorse IASC standards with a view to having them accepted as a sufficient corpus of accounting rules for multinational companies to use for the purposes of cross-border securities issues and listings. This already demanding timetable was subsequently accelerated, so that the present target is to complete the revision of the core standards by March 1998.

Although the outcome of this project cannot be predicted, it raises the stakes considerably for domestic standard-setters. If an accepted international set of standards does emerge, it will inevitably put domestic standards under considerable strain. This may be felt particularly keenly in the US, where foreign registrants are presently required to file accounts reconciled to US GAAP; if this regime were relaxed so as to allow IASC rules to be used instead, the FASB and the SEC might expect to experience considerable pressure from US companies who considered that they should not have to comply with US standards that they perceive to be more demanding; such an attitude is likely to have been reinforced by an FASB publication that claims to have identified 255 differences between US GAAP and IASC standards.[25] Partly for that reason, many observers feel that the SEC is unlikely to allow IOSCO to endorse IASC standards unconditionally unless they correspond closely to existing US standards. At the same time, however, the ASB clearly would not want International standards to be markedly different from UK standards either. As a result, the process of finalising these core international standards is a highly political one, with the major standard-setters of the world all seeking to pull the international consensus in their own direction, knowing that, if they fail, they may be put under pressure to close the gap by amending their domestic standards instead.

This issue has perhaps become the dominant factor affecting the ASB's own work for the time being. In fact, the Board has been very successful to date in influencing several of the IASC's proposed core standards, with the result that they incorporate many of the ASB's own ideas, on subjects such as provisions and contingencies, goodwill and intangible assets, impairment and financial instruments. However, it remains to be seen to what extent these will eventually be converted into standards that achieve global acceptance, and if not, what the effect on UK GAAP will be.

2.4 The experience of other countries

2.4.1 US

To understand the regulation of financial reporting in the US is to understand the workings of the Securities and Exchange Commission (SEC) and it relationship with the US Financial Accounting Standards Board (FASB). Before the 1930s, there were no authoritative or enforceable US standards governing corporate financial reports. Because of the lack of any statutory underpinning, the accounting profession had no authority to establish ground rules which corporations had to follow in their financial statements. However, the abuses in stock exchange practices, the financing of securities and corporate reporting which were revealed after the 1929 stock market crash, led the US Congress to enact the Securities Act of 1933, the Securities Exchange Act of 1934, and several other securities laws. Under this legislation, companies offering new issues of securities for inter-state sale, other than for certain exempted issuers and certain exempted securities, and all companies whose securities are traded publicly, must register and file periodic reports with the Securities and Exchange Commission (SEC). These laws, taken together, emphasise full disclosure by issuers of securities and others acting in the US securities markets and are intended to provide investors with information about the issuer of a security as well as the terms of the security being offered, so that informed decisions on the investment merits of securities can be made and to ensure that fair trading practices prevail in the primary and secondary markets. The SEC, though given wide power to require that full disclosures are made, was not empowered to pass judgement on the quality or merit of an investment.

The SEC was created under the 1934 Act to enforce and administer the federal securities laws subject to the oversight of Congress. Securities involved solely in intrastate transactions are subject to the separate securities laws of the state concerned, but not ordinarily to the federal securities laws. The SEC is composed of five commissioners who are nominated by the President for five-year terms (the persons nominated must be confirmed by Congress in open proceedings), one of whom serves as the chairman. It has a staff of lawyers, accountants, engineers, and financial analysts. Despite its relatively small size (by US federal standards) the SEC has earned a reputation as one of the most ably administered federal regulatory agencies. Its small size has been achieved, in part, through transferring the burden of monitoring compliance with its regulations on to securities issuers and their professional advisers, through severe legal liabilities backed up by vigorous enforcement activities, and through various discretionary powers – principally the sole right to 'accelerate' the effective date of a registration statement – granted by Congress. Though many other federal regulatory agencies are involved in various aspects of financial reporting, particularly in the financial services sector of the US economy, none has the pervasive influence of the SEC.

The US equivalent of a 'true and fair view' is 'fair presentation in conformity with GAAP'. However, the ASC and ASB in the UK have taken rather different approaches to accounting standard setting from that of the FASB in the US. The UK bodies have both adopted a broad fundamental approach which, on the one hand, has allowed a high degree of flexibility, thereby requiring a considerable measure of judgement to be exercised in the application of many of the standards; on the other hand, the looseness (or complete lack) of detailed rules results in similar transactions being accounted for in ways which produce materially different effects. Conversely, some commentators have stated that the FASB has generated a plethora of highly detailed legalistic rules which have, to a large extent, obscured the concept of fair presentation.

used to describe the basis on which financial statements are normally prepared; this encompasses not only specific rules, practices and procedures relating to particular circumstances but also broad principles and conventions of general application, including the underlying financial statement concepts described in Section 1000. More specifically, generally accepted accounting principles comprise the Accounting Recommendations in the *Handbook*; however, for matters not covered by them, the principles that apply are either generally accepted by virtue of their use in similar circumstances by a significant number of entities in Canada, or are consistent with the Recommendations and developed through the exercise of professional judgement, by consulting other informed accountants, where appropriate, and by applying the concepts outlined in Section 1000.[32]

From time to time, the question has been raised as to whether or not the UK should follow the Canadian model of giving accounting standards increased legal backing by incorporating them in the law. As discussed at 3.1.6 below, there has been some movement in that direction as a result of measures included in the Companies Act 1989, but this fell short of the recommendations made by the Dearing Committee.

2.4.3 Germany

The incorporation of the EC Fourth Directive (Accounting Directive), the Seventh Directive (Consolidated Accounts Directive) and the Eighth Directive (Auditor Directive) was achieved in Germany through the enactment on 1 January 1986 of the Accounting Directives Law. One of the most important aspects of this modification of German law was the revision of the Commercial Code, which included the addition of a Third Book containing accounting rules applicable to all businesses.

In terms of the Commercial Code, company financial statements must, in compliance with *required accounting principles* (GoB), present a true and fair view of the net worth, financial position and results of the company.[33] GoB has been interpreted as meaning 'those principles which are not comprehensively codified but which, by application in specific cases, lead to a correct accounting treatment by reference to the objectives of financial statements. They can be determined deductively by making full use of statute and case law, accounting theory, pronouncements of the Institute of German Qualified Accountants as well as accounting practice.'[34] Since the concept of true and fair is relatively new to Germany's Commercial Code, its relationship to GoB is not entirely clear; however, it would appear that the general GoB rule would only be brought into play if, in the preparation of company financial statements, uncertainties in the interpretation and application of the specific rules of the laws and ordinances need to be resolved. Therefore, it seems that GoB will not impose any disclosure requirements additional to those contained in the law, unless the financial statements would otherwise not show a true and fair view.

It is well known that in Germany there is a close inter-relationship between the calculation of profit in the financial statements of individual companies and the calculation of taxable profit. This means that financial statements prepared in accordance with GoB form the basis for the tax computation, resulting in tax-driven balance sheet values. However, this rule need not necessarily apply in the case of group financial statements, where it is permitted for group accounting policies to be different to those followed in individual accounts. Nevertheless, practice shows that many German groups also use tax-driven values in their group financial statements – presumably because of convenience.

More recently, however, legislation has been proposed in Germany to the effect that International Accounting Standards (or indeed other internationally recognised systems such as US GAAP) may be used in consolidated financial statements instead of German law and accounting principles. A similar proposal has been made in France, which would allow French multinational groups to use IASC standards as the sole basis for their consolidated accounts. These are revolutionary changes, and demonstrate the influence of Anglo-American accounting philosophies, at least on those companies which wish to seek access to the international capital markets.

Until recently, German companies have been reluctant to seek listings in the US because of, amongst other things, the onerous disclosure requirements of the US SEC. However, the need to access the US capital markets has begun to be overwhelming, as was the case with Daimler-Benz. Daimler-Benz was the first German company to register with the SEC, with the result that the company's US GAAP figures were somewhat of a revelation to the outside world. The company's registration document included a German GAAP/US GAAP net income reconciliation statement, which revealed that a DM168 million profit under German GAAP for the six months to 30 June 1993 was, in fact, a US GAAP loss of DM949 million. This dispelled the myth of prudent German accounting, and highlighted the gulf in financial reporting practices which exist between two of the world's most industrialised nations.

3   THE DEVELOPMENT OF ACCOUNTING STANDARDS

3.1   The Accounting Standards Committee

Prior to 1970, there were no mandatory requirements in the UK outside company law governing the presentation of financial statements of companies; and even those company law provisions which did exist comprised only the basic minimum, which was inadequate for the purpose of achieving a satisfactory standard of financial reporting. Consequently, accounting practices were varied, inconsistent and sometimes inappropriate; inter-firm and inter-period comparisons were difficult as companies altered accounting treatments and resorted to such practices as 'window-dressing' and 'reserve accounting' to achieve desired results in order to present a picture of profitability and growth. Certain professional accounting bodies (such as the ICAEW) had issued a series of recommendations on accounting principles – but these recommendations were not mandatory.

3.1.1 The creation of the ASC

By 1969 it had become apparent that the basic accounting requirements contained in company law needed the support of more authoritative pronouncements than the recommendations that were being issued. Consequently, the Council of the ICAEW issued a 'Statement of intent on accounting standards in the 1970s',[35] wherein they set out their strategy for the development of accounting standards.

As a result, the ICAEW set up the Accounting Standards Steering Committee in 1970 as the means of implementing this strategy. The Institute of Chartered Accountants of Scotland and the Institute of Chartered Accountants in Ireland became co-sponsors of the Committee almost immediately afterwards; the Chartered Association of Certified Accountants and the Chartered Institute of Management Accountants[36] joined subsequently in 1971 and the Chartered Institute of Public Finance and Accountancy in 1976. With effect from 1 February 1976, the Committee became the Accounting Standards Committee and was reconstituted as a joint committee of these six accountancy bodies who now comprise the Consultative Committee of Accountancy Bodies (CCAB).

3.1.2 The objects and terms of reference of the ASC

The objects of the ASC were 'to define accounting concepts, to narrow differences of financial accounting and reporting treatment, and to codify generally accepted best practice in the public interest. In order to achieve these objects, the ASC was given the following terms of reference:

(a) to keep under review standards of financial accounting and reporting;

(b) to propose to the Councils of each of the CCAB members statements of standard accounting practice and interpretations of such statements;

(c) to publish consultative documents, discussion papers and exposure drafts and submit to the Councils of each of the CCAB members non-mandatory guidance notes with the object of maintaining and advancing accounting standards;

(d) to consult, as appropriate, with representatives of finance, commerce, industry and government, and other bodies and persons concerned with financial reporting; and

(e) to maintain close links with the International Accounting Standards Committee and the accountancy profession in Europe and throughout the world.[37]

3.1.3 The Watts Report

In the light of the eight years' experience gained since its formation, a Review Group was set up in 1978 by the ASC, under the chairmanship of Mr T. R. Watts, to review the standard-setting process and to consider what improvements in that process could be effected. The Review Group submitted a draft consultative document to the ASC in May 1978. The document was adopted by the ASC and published as a basis for public discussion and comment.[38] Following extensive public consultations and debate, the ASC made a number of recommendations in a report to the CCAB which was published in 1981 (the Watts Report).[39] Many of the recommendations of the Watts Report concern fundamental issues which remained unresolved and were consequently revisited by the Dearing Committee (see 3.1.5 below). These included such issues as the need for a conceptual framework; the establishment of a supervisory body to ensure compliance with accounting standards; the application of certain standards only to large companies; a full-time paid ASC chairman; and the need for more resources.

3.1.4 The McKinnon Report

A further review of the standard-setting process was carried out by an ASC working party in 1983. The reasons for the review were:

(a) to develop certain recommendations contained in the Watts Report;

(b) to seek ways by which the standard-setting process could be shortened; and

(c) to consider whether there was a need for alternative or new types of pronouncement.

The findings of this working party were published in a report entitled 'Review of the Standard Setting Process' (the McKinnon Report). However, the report did not address the more fundamental issues raised in the Watts Report, and instead focused on the procedural aspects relating to the development of SSAPs. The report did, nevertheless, recommend that a new category of final pronouncement be introduced, namely the Statement of Recommended Practice (SORP).

3.1.5 The Dearing Report

As the complexities of accounting issues and requirements for more sophisticated levels of financial reporting mounted, the increased demands placed on the ASC clearly indicated that it was unable to fulfil satisfactorily the standard-setting role that it was expected to perform. The ASC had to endure

6 CONCLUSION

UK GAAP incorporates the requirements of accounting standards and UITF Abstracts, of the Companies Act and of the Stock Exchange, together with other accounting practices which are generally accepted by the accounting profession to be permissible. However, as circumstances and environments change, accounting practices require development and adaptation. GAAP, therefore, is a dynamic concept, which is not restricted to the requirements of accounting standards and the law, and is continually undergoing change as circumstances alter.

A major preoccupation for the ASB at present is the international dimension. UK GAAP cannot and should not be left to develop in isolation from accounting practice in the rest of the world, yet these international influences tend to pull in different directions; the preferences of other members of the European Union filter into UK law through the medium of EU Directives, while those of other countries and of the IASC have an impact on UK practice through the operation of the international capital markets. Nevertheless, if the IASC's present endeavour to forge standards that are acceptable to the world's securities regulators proves successful, it may prove to be the most significant influence on UK GAAP (and that of many other countries) for many years to come.

The problem is, however, that highly complicated standards, set at a global level for the benefit of publicly traded multinational companies, are likely to result in accounts that only a dwindling minority of specialised users can comprehend. In addition, such standards are likely to be quite inappropriate for smaller, owner-managed enterprises which constitute the great majority of entities which have to prepare accounts. To date, all the attempts to provide simpler accounts, for either smaller entities or less sophisticated shareholders of larger ones, have amounted to little more than deletion of disclosures from the full accounting package, whereas the problem needs to be addressed at a much more fundamental level. These issues should feature prominently in the ASB's development of its *Statement of Principles* but, as we discuss in Chapter 2, we believe that so far the Board has largely been replicating the work of other standard-setters who have focused on the needs of large listed companies rather than considering the broader uses of financial reporting. Nevertheless, with the task of balancing all these considerations, and with many conflicting political pressures in the background, the ASB has a crucial role in charting the future direction of GAAP in the United Kingdom.

References

1   CA 85, Sch. 5, para. 10(1)(d).
2   *Ibid.*, s 262(3).
3   CCAB, TR 481: *The determination of realised profits and disclosure of distributable profits in the context of the Companies Acts 1948 to 1981*, September 1982.
4   *Ibid.*, para. 4.
5   *Odeon Associated Theatres Ltd v Jones (Inspector of Taxes)* [1971] 1 WLR 442.
6   Leonard Hoffmann QC and Mary H. Arden, The Accounting Standards Committee Joint Opinion, *Legal Opinion on 'True and Fair'*, paras. 9 and 10.
7   *Statement of Aims*, ASB, 1993, para. 2.
8   SAS 69, *The Meaning of 'Present Fairly in Conformity With Generally Accepted Accounting Principles' in the Independent Auditor's Report*, AICPA, January 1992, para. 2.
9   New Zealand: The Financial Reporting Act 1993, s 3.
10   CA 47, s 13(1), re-enacted as CA 48, s 149(1).
11   EC Fourth Directive, Article 2.
12   *Ibid.*, paras. 1–3.
13   *Ibid.*, paras. 4 and 5.
14   *Foreword to Accounting Standards*, ASB, 1993, para. 16.
15   *Ibid.*, para 18.
16   Leonard Hoffmann QC and Mary H. Arden, *op. cit.*, paras. 9 and 10.
17   *Lloyd Cheyham & Co Ltd v Littlejohn & Co* [1987] BCLC 303 at 313.
18   Miss Mary Arden QC, *Accounting Standards Board, The True and Fair Requirement, Opinion*, 21 April 1993.
19   *Ibid.*, para. 10.
20   *Foreword to Accounting Standards*, para. 34.
21   Hoffmann J., Foreword to *Law and Accountancy: Conflict and Co-operation in the 1990s*, Freedman and Power (eds.), 1992.
22   IASC, *Preface to Statements of International Accounting Standards*, para. 1.
23   *Ibid.*, para. 2.
24   *Foreword to Accounting Standards*, para. 36.
25   *The IASC-U.S. Comparison Project: A Report on the Similarities and Differences between IASC Standards and U.S. GAAP*, FASB, November 1996.
26   APB Opinion No. 6, *Status of Accounting Research Bulletins*, Appendix A, paras. 1–3.
27   SEC, Accounting Series Release No. 150.
28   AICPA, *Code of Professional Conduct*, Rule 203–Accounting principles.
29   United States v. Simon, 425 F.2d 796 (2d Cir. 1969), *certiorari* denied 397 U.S. 1006 (1970).
30   See Ross M. Skinner, *Accounting Standards in Evolution*, Holt, Rinehart and Winston, Toronto, 1986, pp. 35–36.
31   CICA, *Handbook*, Volume 1, Section 1500.06.
32   *Ibid.*, Section 1000, paras. .59–.61, *passim*.
33   Commercial Code, Third Book, Second Section, *Supplementary Regulations for Companies*, § 264(2).
34   Jermyn Paul Brooks and Dietz Mertin, *Neues deutsches Bilanzrecht/New German Accounting Legislation*, Düsseldorf: IDW-Verlag GmbH, 1986.
35   The Institute of Chartered Accountants in England and Wales, Occasional Council and Other Pronouncements, *Statement of intent on accounting standards in the 1970s*.
36   At that stage, the Association of Certified Accountants and the Institute of Cost and Management Accountants respectively.
37   ICAEW, *Statement of intent on accounting standards in the 1970s*, p. 1.4.
38   Accounting Standards Committee, *Setting Accounting Standards: A consultative document*.
39   Accounting Standards Committee, *Setting Accounting Standards*.
40   Report of the Review Committee under the chairmanship of Sir Ronald Dearing, *The Making of Accounting Standards*, September 1988, p. ix.
41   This summary of the recommendations has been extracted from the Dearing Report, *ibid.*, pp. 17–45, *passim*.
42   *Ibid.*, para. 10.2.

43 *Ibid.*, para. 11.1.
44 *Ibid.*, p. 44.
45 *Ibid.*, para. 11.3.
46 *Ibid.*, pp. 27–29.
47 *Ibid.*, p. 31.
48 *Ibid.*, p. 33.
49 CA 85, Sch. 4, para. 36A.
50 *Ibid.*, s 246(1)(a).
51 *Ibid.*, s 245B.
52 *Ibid.*, s 245.
53 *Ibid.*, s 245A.
54 Miss Mary Arden QC, *Accounting Standards Board, The True and Fair Requirement, Opinion*, 21 April 1993, para. 12.
55 See, for example: Department of Trade and Industry, *Accounting and Audit Requirements for Small Firms*, London: DTI, 1985; Department of Trade and Industry, *Burdens on Business, Report of a Scrutiny of Administrative and Legislative Requirements*, London: HMSO, March 1985; B. V. Carsberg *et al.*, *Small Company Financial Reporting*, London: Prentice-Hall International, 1985; AICPA, Accounting Standards Division, Committee on Generally Accepted Accounting Principles for Smaller and/or Closely Held Businesses, *Report of the Committee on Generally Accepted Accounting Principles for Smaller and/or Closely Held Businesses*, New York: AICPA, August 1976; Institute of Chartered Accountants of British Columbia, *Task Force on Big GAAP/Little GAAP*, Report to Council, Submitted 30 July 1981.
56 Institute of Chartered Accountants of British Columbia, *op. cit.*, p. 3.
57 *Ibid.*, p. 4.
58 B. V. Carsberg *et al.*, *op. cit.*, p. 83.
59 *Ibid.*, pp. 83–84.
60 TR 690*: Statement by the Accounting Standards Committee on the application of accounting standards to small companies*, February 1988.
61 *Ibid.*, para. 5.
62 *Ibid.*, para. 17.
63 TR 706: *Statement by the Accounting Standards Committee on the definition of 'small company' for the purpose of applying accounting standards*, July 1988, para. 1.1.
64 *Ibid.*, para. 5.1.
65 *Ibid.*, para. 5.2.
66 Consultative Document, *Exemptions from Standards on Grounds of Size or Public Interest*, CCAB, November 1994.
67 *Designed to fit – A Financial Reporting Standard for Smaller Entities*, CCAB, December 1995.
68 Exposure Draft, *The Financial Reporting Standard for Smaller Entities*, ASB, December 1996, Preface.
69 In a similar way, company law has reduced disclosure requirements for small companies, which are now set out in Schedule 8 to the Companies Act, as inserted by *The Companies Act 1985 (Accounts of Small and Medium-sized Companies and Minor Accounting Amendments) Regulations 1997*.
70 CA 85, s 251.
71 *The Companies (Summary Financial Statement) Regulations 1995* (SI 1995/2092).
72 *Ibid.*, Sch 1, para. 2.
73 *Ibid.*, Sch 1, para. 3.
74 *Ibid.*, Sch 1, para. 4.
75 *Ibid.*, Schedules 2 and 3.
76 *Ibid.*, Sch 1, para. 1(1).
77 CA 85, s 251(4) (a).
78 *The Companies (Summary Financial Statement) Regulations 1995* (SI 1995/2092), para. 7 (3) and (4).
79 CA 85, s 251(4) (c) and (d).
80 *Ibid.*, s 251(4) (b).
81 *Summary Financial Statements – The Way Forward*, ICAEW, 1996.
82 As reported in *Inside Track*, ASB, July 1997.
83 SFAC No. 1, *Objectives of Financial Reporting by Business Enterprises*, FASB, November 1978, para. 36.

Chapter 2   The quest for a conceptual framework for financial reporting

1   INTRODUCTION

1.1   What is a conceptual framework?

In general terms, a conceptual framework is a statement of generally accepted theoretical principles which form the frame of reference for a particular field of enquiry. In terms of financial reporting, these theoretical principles provide the basis for both the development of new reporting practices and the evaluation of existing ones. Since the financial reporting process is concerned with the provision of information that is useful in making business and economic decisions, a conceptual framework will form the theoretical basis for determining which events should be accounted for, how they should be measured and how they should be communicated to the user. Therefore, although it is theoretical in nature, a conceptual framework for financial reporting has a highly practical end in view.

1.2   Why is a conceptual framework necessary?

A conceptual framework for financial reporting is, therefore, a theory of accounting against which practical problems can be tested objectively. However, the various standard-setting bodies around the world have too often attempted to resolve practical accounting and reporting problems through the development of accounting standards, without such an accepted theoretical frame of reference. The end result is that the standard-setters have determined the form and content of external financial reports, without resolving such fundamental issues as:

- what are the objectives of these reports?
- who are the users of these reports?
- what are the informational needs of these users?
- what types of report will best satisfy their needs?

Consequently, standards have tended to be produced on a haphazard and 'fire-fighting' approach; evidence of this in the UK may be seen in the way in which the (now defunct) ASC attempted to deal with issues such as off balance sheet finance and the capitalisation of brand names. On the other hand, if an agreed framework existed, the role of the standard-setters would be changed from that of fireman to that of architect, by being able to design external financial reports on the basis of the needs of the user.

Furthermore, in the absence of an agreed conceptual framework, the same theoretical issues are revisited on numerous occasions by different standard-setting working parties, sometimes resulting in the development of standards which are inconsistent with each other, or which are founded on incompatible concepts. For example, inconsistencies exist in UK accounting standards as a result of conflicts between substance vs. form; matching vs. prudence; and whether earnings should be determined through balance sheet measurements or by matching costs and revenue. Some of the present UK standards permit two or more methods of accounting for the same set of circumstances, whilst others permit certain accounting practices to be followed on an arbitrary and unspecified basis. This apparent ambiguity is perhaps indicative of the difficulty involved in determining what is 'true and fair'.

In the US, on the other hand, the FASB has produced a large number of highly detailed accounting rules. Clearly, the proliferation of accounting standards in the US stems from many factors; however, a satisfactory conceptual framework might reduce the need for such a large number of highly detailed standards, since more emphasis could be placed on general principles rather than specific rules.

Nevertheless, it is not only the lack of a conceptual framework which inhibits standard-setters around the world; they must also contend with the politicisation of accounting caused by the conflicting interests of the various groups of users, preparers and auditors. Where proposed accounting standards are thought likely to affect the economic interests of a particular interested party, it is possible that the quality of the accounting standard will suffer. There are several instances where this is evident in the UK. For example, lobbying by the property industry led to the temporary exemption for investment properties from the requirements of SSAP 12; this temporary exemption was originally intended to last for one year, but was extended first for a further year and subsequently for a further 18 months before SSAP 19 became effective, and SSAP 12 was then amended to make the exemption for investment properties permanent. Even in its recent Discussion Paper on the measurement of tangible fixed assets, the ASB is proposing that 'investment properties should continue to be exempted from the requirement to depreciate'[1] – despite the fact that the ASB concedes that there is no conceptual justification for such an exemption.[2]

The only defence that standard-setters can have against such political interference in the standard-setting process is to be able to demonstrate that a proposed accounting practice is derived from a sound theoretical foundation. Otherwise, how does one persuade, for example, an industry lobby that a particular accounting treatment which they perceive as adversely affecting their economic interests is better than one which does not?[3]

An agreed framework is not the panacea for all accounting problems. Nor does it obviate the need for judgement to be exercised in the process of resolving accounting issues. Nevertheless, what it can provide is a framework within which those judgements can be made.

1.3   Early attempts to establish a framework

There have been numerous attempts over the years to define the purpose and nature of accounting. These are to be found in various writings on accounting theory, the authors of which have considered many of the conceptual issues which require resolution in the development of a conceptual framework for financial reporting. Perhaps not surprisingly, most of the earlier studies were carried out by either individual academics or academic committees in the US; for example, the writings in 1940 of Paton and Littleton[4] were intended to present a framework of accounting theory which would be regarded as a coherent and consistent foundation for the development of accounting standards, whilst the studies carried out over the years by various committees of the American Accounting Association have made a significant contribution to accounting theory.[5] In addition to the research carried out by individuals and academic committees, professional accounting bodies around the world have also, from time to time, issued statements which deal with various aspects of accounting theory. These can be seen as the first attempts at developing some form of conceptual framework, some of which are discussed later in this Chapter.

However, there was no corresponding interest in the UK at that time in developing statements on accounting theory. This fact was explained by Solomons in a lecture given by him in 1980, as follows: 'The difference between the ferment in America over accounting principles and the relative apathy that has persisted in Britain until quite recently cannot be explained by any difference in the economic environment. It can only be explained by the difference in the scale of business education there and here, and in particular by the sheer weight of numbers of accounting academics. The American Accounting Association has about 6,000 academic members. In Britain, the Association of University Teachers of Accounting has about 175. Perhaps more importantly, most American practitioners have a university degree in accounting. They have met professors face to face and they do not think of them as troglodytes. Moreover, they know there is a subject called accounting theory; and they think of accounting academics as a distinct branch of the profession with their own contribution to make. It is more a question of quantity than quality. British accounting academics are simply not yet numerous enough to constitute a critical mass.'[6]

The question of the desirability of developing an 'agreed conceptual framework' apparently first received serious consideration by the ASC in 1978 through the publication of its consultative document entitled 'Setting Accounting Standards'[7] (see Chapter 1 at 3.1.3). In that document, the ASC conceded that it had been frequently criticised for failing to develop a conceptual framework, but defended its position by claiming that 'while such a foundation would be a great advantage, it is unavailable at present'.[8] The reasons put forward for this view were based essentially on the premise that since the users of financial statements have different objectives, it would not be possible to develop an acceptable foundation which would be universally accepted.[9] Following this argument, the ASC went on to conclude that 'if an "agreed conceptual framework" is equated with a single undisputed "model", then this is a luxury which evades us at the moment'.[10] Nevertheless, as part of the consultative process, the ASC raised the following two questions on the subject:

1. 'Is it accepted that there is at present no single "model" or "agreed conceptual framework" which can be used as the touchstone for accounting standards?'[11]

2. 'Should the ASC encourage research into the possibility of finding an acceptable "model"?'[12]

Not surprisingly, the written submissions[13] on the consultative document indicated a unanimous 'Yes' in answer to the first question. However, what probably did surprise the ASC was that the second question also received an overwhelming 'Yes'; in fact, a significant number of respondents indicated that they saw the development of a conceptual framework as a matter of great urgency. For example, the Accounting Standards Review Committee of the ICAS stated in its submission that 'it is imperative that work should begin immediately on a conceptual framework rather than that the present practice of producing standards with no theoretical underpinning should continue'.[14]

The ASC's argument that a conceptual framework would not be attainable because the users of financial statements have different objectives was clearly regarded as spurious. This Chapter will highlight the fact that different users should be furnished with different information appropriate to their various objectives, even if it means that in order to achieve this the conceptual framework should incorporate more than one accounting model. Consequently, there is no reason for ruling out an 'agreed conceptual model' by equating it with the unattainable 'single undisputed model'.

2   THE AICPA'S EARLY INITIATIVES IN THE UNITED STATES

2.1   Accounting Research Studies

The Accounting Principles Board (APB) of the AICPA was formed in 1959 to replace the former Committee on Accounting Procedure and the Committee on Terminology. During its existence, the Committee on Accounting Procedure had issued a series of Accounting Research Bulletins (ARBs). In 1953, the first 42 ARBs (eight of which dealt solely with terminology) were revised and restated as a consolidated ARB No. 43 and Accounting Terminology Bulletin No. 1; thereafter, a further eight ARBs were issued. The ARBs were supposedly aimed at the development of generally accepted accounting principles; however, the Committee met with considerable criticism over its failure to deal with contemporary accounting issues (such as leasing and business combinations), which could not be solved from precedents and required the development of accounting principles through pure accounting research.

As a direct response to this, the President of the AICPA set up the Special Committee on Research Program in 1957; in 1958 the Committee recommended the formation of the APB, and the appointment of a director of research with a permanent research staff. The Special Committee also recommended that 'an immediate project of the accounting research staff should be a study of the basic postulates underlying accounting principles generally, and the preparation of a brief statement thereof. There should be also a study of the broad principles of accounting. ... The results of these, as adopted by the [Accounting Principles] Board, should serve as the foundation for the entire body of future pronouncements by the Institute on accounting matters, to which each new release should be related.'[15]

This, therefore, was probably the first mandate given by a professional body for the development of a conceptual framework. The AICPA appointed Maurice Moonitz as its first Director of Accounting Research; Moonitz started work on the postulates study, and appointed Robert Sprouse to work with him on the study of broad accounting principles. The products of the research were contained in Accounting Research Study No. 1 – *The Basic Postulates of Accounting*[16] – and Accounting Research Study No. 3 – *A Tentative Set of Broad Accounting Principles for Business Enterprises* – which were published in 1961 and 1962 respectively.[17]

These studies, however, caused a storm of controversy. Instead of establishing a sound foundation of accounting theory through rigorous argument based on deductive reasoning, Moonitz and Sprouse attempted to persuade the accounting profession to accept a new system of financial reporting based on current values. Furthermore, the realisation principle was discarded on the basis of the assertion that 'profit is attributable to the whole process of business activity, not just to the moment of sale'.[18] This was reflected, for example, in the statement that 'inventories which are readily saleable at known prices with negligible costs of disposal, or with known or readily predictable costs of disposal, should be measured at net realizable value'.[19]

However, the criticism which was levelled at these studies appeared to be based more on the fear of the unknown, rather than on any intellectual shortcomings. Consequently, they were viewed as being too radically different from contemporary generally accepted accounting practice to be accepted, and were rejected by the APB. This resulted in the commissioning of Grady's *Accounting Research Study No. 7 – Inventory of Generally Accepted Accounting Principles for Business Enterprises* – which was published in 1965 and which catalogued the various accounting methods which had been approved by ARBs, APB Opinions or some other precedent.

In all, 15 Accounting Research Studies were published during the life of the APB. However, following the rejection of ARS Nos. 1 and 3, the studies tended to be carried out on an ad hoc basis and without the support of a common foundation. Furthermore, the recommendations contained in the research studies appeared to have been largely ignored in the drafting of the 31 Opinions which the APB issued between 1962 and 1973. Consequently, generally accepted accounting principles in the US were continuing to be formulated without the benefit of research or the foundation of an agreed theoretical framework and, for all intents and purposes, the APB slowly resorted to the position of its predecessor, the Committee on Accounting Procedure.

2.2   APB Statement No. 4

In 1965 the APB made a further attempt to provide a basis for guiding the future development of accounting by establishing a committee to carry out a study which could be used as a basis for understanding the broad fundamentals of accounting. In 1970, the APB approved Statement No. 4 – *Basic Concepts and Accounting Principles Underlying Financial Statements of Business Enterprises*.[20] The statement contained a description of (1) the environment of financial accounting, (2) the objectives of financial statements, (3) the basic features and basic elements of financial accounting and (4) a summary of existing generally accepted accounting principles.

Therefore, it was (on its own admission)[21] a descriptive statement, not prescriptive. For example, assets and liabilities were defined as economic resources and obligations 'that are recognised and measured in conformity with generally accepted accounting principles',[22] which meant that the definitions failed to provide a theoretical basis for the development of generally accepted principles. As a result APB No. 4 was deficient as a theory of accounting and did not respond to the problems which were facing the profession at the time and which had been brought about by the inconsistencies and inadequacies of financial reporting practice.

2.3   The Wheat and Trueblood Committees

In 1971, in response to continued criticism from both within the profession and from the SEC about its inability to establish sound accounting principles, the AICPA announced the formation of two study groups: the *Study Group on Establishment of Accounting Principles*, to be chaired by Francis Wheat, and the *Study Group on Objectives of Financial Statements*, to be chaired by Robert Trueblood. The Wheat Committee published its report in 1972, resulting in the establishment of the Financial Accounting Standards Board (FASB) in 1973 as the successor to the APB. This had the effect of taking the responsibility for setting accounting standards away from the accounting profession and placing it in the hands of an independent body in the private sector. The FASB comprises seven members appointed by the Financial Accounting Foundation (FAF), and is funded by the sale of publications and from contributions made to the FAF. The Board of Trustees of the FAF is appointed by its eight sponsoring organisations, which include, inter alia, the American Accounting Association, the AICPA and two organisations which represent government.

The study carried out by the Trueblood Committee represents the next significant step in the attempt to develop a conceptual framework. In setting the terms of reference of the study group, the Board of Directors of the AICPA stated that the main purpose of the study was 'to refine the objectives of financial statements'.[23] They went on to suggest that APB Statement No. 4 would be a logical starting point for the study, whilst at the same time noting that APB 4 'contains objectives in terms of what is considered acceptable today rather than in terms of what is needed and what is attainable to meet these needs'.[24] The study group was asked to consider at least the following questions:

■   Who needs financial statements?

■   What information do they need?

■   How much of the needed information can be provided by accounting?

■   What framework is required to provide the needed information?[25]

The Trueblood Report[26] was published in October 1973 and developed twelve objectives of financial statements. The principal objective was stated in the following terms: 'the basic objective of financial statements is to provide information useful for making economic decisions'.[27] Having established its twelve objectives of financial statements, the report then discussed seven qualitative characteristics which information contained in financial statements should possess in order to satisfy the needs of users.[28] As will be seen below, the Trueblood Report's objectives of financial statements formed the basis for the development of the FASB's first concepts statement, whilst the qualitative characteristics identified were amongst those discussed in the second concepts statement.

3   THE FASB CONCEPTUAL FRAMEWORK

3.1   Introduction

The Trueblood Committee was at work on its report when the FASB came into existence. Consequently, the Trueblood Report was effectively passed on to the FASB for consideration, thus signalling the beginnings of the FASB's Conceptual Framework Project. The FASB duly considered the report and in June 1974 published a Discussion Memorandum – *Conceptual Framework for Accounting and Reporting: Consideration of the Report of the Study Group on the Objectives of Financial Statements* – which asked for comments on the issues raised.[29]   A public hearing was held during September 1974, and in December 1976 the FASB published its *Tentative Conclusions on Objectives of Financial Statements of Business Enterprises*. In December 1976 the FASB also published a paper – *Scope and Implications of the Conceptual Framework Project* – which summarised its aims for the project, the expected benefits to be derived and the main areas which were expected to be covered.[30]

Following the criticism and eventual replacement of first the Committee on Accounting Procedure, followed by the APB, the FASB was seen by many commentators to be the last opportunity of keeping accounting standard-setting in the private sector. The FASB was clearly aware that accounting standards had to regain the credibility of public opinion which had been lost as a result of the many perceived abuses of financial reporting during the 1960s. The FASB referred to this lack of public confidence, and the possible consequences thereof, as follows: 'skepticism about financial reporting has adverse effects on businesses, on business leaders, and on the public at large. One of these effects is the risk of imposition of government reporting and other regulatory requirements that are not justified – requirements that are not in the public interest because the perceived benefits do not exist or are more than offset by costly interference with the orderly operation of the economy. Skepticism creates adverse public opinion, which may be the antecedent of unjustified government regulation. Every company, every industry stands to suffer because of skepticism about financial reporting.'[31]   The FASB, therefore, saw its conceptual framework project as the means of enhancing the credibility of financial statements in the eyes of the public.

The FASB also recognised that although there had been many attempts by individuals and organisations (such as the American Accounting Association) to develop a theory of accounting, none of these individual theories had become universally accepted or relied on in practice. They therefore expressed a need for a *'constitution,* a coherent system of interrelated objectives and fundamentals that can lead to consistent standards and that prescribes the nature, function, and limits of financial accounting and financial statements'.[32]   The conceptual framework was expected to:

(a)   guide the body responsible for establishing standards;

(b)   provide a frame of reference for resolving accounting questions in the absence of a specific promulgated standard;

(c)   determine bounds for judgement in preparing financial statements;

(d)   increase financial statement users' understanding of and confidence in financial statements; and

(e)   enhance comparability.[33]

To date the FASB has issued six concepts statements, of which one (SFAC No. 4) deals with the objectives of financial reporting by non-business organisations and is beyond the scope of this book, whilst another (SFAC No. 3) dealt with elements of financial statements by business enterprises, and was superseded by SFAC No. 6, which expanded the scope of SFAC No. 3 to encompass not-for-profit organisations. The remaining four are discussed in the sections which follow.

In June 1997 the FASB issued an exposure draft of a further concepts statement which proposes general principles aimed at governing the use of discounting in accounting measurement.[34] This is discussed at 3.6 below.

3.2   The objectives of financial reporting

The first phase of the FASB's conceptual framework project was to develop a statement of the objectives of financial reporting. Clearly, some pioneering work in this area had been done by the Trueblood Committee (see 2.3 above), and this formed the basis of the FASB's first concepts statement. Nevertheless, it was not until 1978 that the FASB finally published this statement.

SFAC No. 1 – *Objectives of Financial Reporting by Business Enterprises* – starts off by making the point that financial reporting includes not only financial statements, but also incorporates other means of communicating financial and non-financial information; this may be achieved, for example, through the medium of stock exchange documents, news releases, management forecasts etc.[35] Having said this, the statement stresses that 'financial reporting is not an end in itself but is intended to provide information that is useful in making business and economic decisions'.[36] This, however, is no new revelation; it is the type of broad generalisation that has characterised numerous previous attempts at establishing a conceptual framework. On the other hand, what it does do is raise all the same issues which the Trueblood Committee had been asked to consider seven years previously, such as: For whom is this information intended? What types of 'business and economic decisions' do they make? What information do they need to enable them to make these decisions? What framework is required to provide this needed information?

components. Investors, creditors, and others who are concerned with assessing the prospects for enterprise net cash inflows are especially interested in that information.'[44]

SFAC No. 1 still recognises the fact that financial reporting should provide information about how the management of an enterprise has discharged its stewardship responsibility.[45] However, it goes on to say that 'earnings information is commonly the focus for assessing management's stewardship or accountability. Management, owners, and others emphasize enterprise performance or profitability in describing how management has discharged its stewardship accountability.'[46]

In other words, the statement is asserting that the measurement of earnings in the income statement should take precedence over the measurement of assets and liabilities in the balance sheet. This is an important principle which should have had an important impact on the principles laid down in the development of future accounting standards. However, as will be seen below, the FASB's subsequent concepts statements have essentially avoided the issue of how to determine net income. Furthermore, more recent statements issued by the FASB tend to suggest an uncertainty as to whether an earnings or balance sheet approach should be followed (for example, SFAS 109 – *Accounting for Income Taxes* – would appear to view the balance sheet as the primary statement).

Interestingly enough, the Accounting Standards Board in the UK is proceeding down a similar road of balance sheet primacy in developing its *Statement of Principles*. As is more fully described at section 5 below, the ASB's Draft *Statement of Principles* adopts a balance sheet approach to recognition, whereby all the elements of financial statements are defined in terms of assets and liabilities, and income recognition is a function of increases and decreases in net assets rather than the completion of acts of performance.

Consequently, despite the general acceptance of the fact that financial reporting should be primarily focused on performance measurement, the conceptual underpinning for financial reporting on both sides of the Atlantic appears to be focusing more and more on the recognition and derecognition of assets and liabilities.

3.3   The qualitative characteristics of accounting information

The FASB's second Concepts Statement – *Qualitative Characteristics of Accounting Information* – examines the characteristics that make accounting information useful to the users of that information. The statement views these characteristics as 'a hierarchy of accounting qualities', which then form the basis for selecting and evaluating information for inclusion in financial reports. The hierarchy is represented in Figure 1 below:[47]

Figure 1

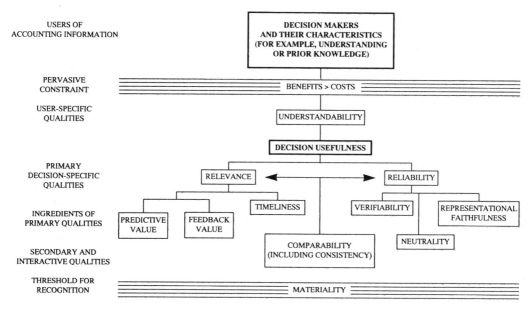

A HIERARCHY OF ACCOUNTING QUALITIES

3.3.1 The decision-makers

The decision-makers (users) appear at the top of the hierarchy against the background of their own specific characteristics. Whilst usefulness for decision-making is the most important quality that accounting information should possess, each decision-maker has to judge what information is useful to his specific decision. This judgement would be based on such factors as the nature of the decision to be made, the information already in his possession or available from other sources, the decision-making process that he employs and his capacity to process all the information that he obtains.

3.3.2 The cost/benefit constraint

Since information should be provided only if the benefits to be derived from that information outweigh the costs of providing it, the cost/benefit constraint pervades the hierarchy. However, the application of this constraint may cause a certain amount of difficulty, since the costs of providing financial information are normally borne by the enterprise (and ultimately passed on to its customers), whilst the benefits are reaped by the users. For this reason, the normal forces of demand and supply will not prevail in the market of financial information, since the external user will almost always view the benefits of additional information as outweighing the costs.

3.3.3   Understandability

The hierarchy depicts understandability as being the key quality for accounting information to achieve 'decision usefulness'. SFAC No. 1 stated that the information provided by financial reporting 'should be comprehensible to those who have a reasonable understanding of business and economic activities and are willing to study the information with reasonable diligence'.[48] Information, whilst it may be relevant, will be wasted if it is provided in a form which cannot be understood by the users for whom it was intended. SFAC No. 1 elaborated on the relationship between useful information and understandability as follows: 'financial information is a tool and, like most tools, cannot be of much direct help to those who are unable or unwilling to use it or who misuse it. Its use can be learned, however, and financial reporting should provide information that can be used by all – nonprofessionals as well as professionals – who are willing to learn to use it properly. Efforts may be needed to increase the understandability of financial information.   Cost-benefit considerations may indicate that information understood or used by only a few should not be provided. Conversely, financial reporting should not exclude relevant information merely because it is difficult for some to understand or because some investors or creditors choose not to use it.'[49]

3.3.4   Relevance and reliability

The qualities that distinguish 'better' (more useful) information from 'inferior' (less useful) information are primarily the qualities of relevance and reliability, with some other characteristics that those qualities imply. SFAC No. 2 identifies relevance and reliability as 'the two primary qualities that make accounting information useful for decision making. Subject to constraints imposed by cost and materiality, increased relevance and increased reliability are the characteristics that make information a more desirable commodity – that is, one useful in making decisions.'[50] However, all this is not new – the qualitative characteristics of relevance and reliability have been discussed in several preceding studies (such as the Trueblood and Corporate Reports). What is new (and probably the most significant aspect of SFAC No. 2), is the recognition of the fact that 'reliability and relevance often impinge on each other'.[51] Consequently, whenever accounting standards are set, decisions have to be made concerning the relative importance of these two characteristics, often resulting in trade-offs being made between them.

For example, one of the most common criticisms made about the various systems of value accounting which have been proposed over the years concerns the high degree of subjectivity involved in assigning values to assets and liabilities. Consequently, for any standard-setting body to propose that the historical cost system be replaced by an income and measurement system based on current values, a decision would have to be made as to the relative weights which should be attributed to presenting information which is both relevant and reliable. The perceived gain in the relevance of the information to the user would have to outweigh the uncertainties concerning the reliability of the current value information.

A   Relevance

The statement defines relevant accounting information as being information which is 'capable of making a difference in a decision by helping users to form predictions about the outcomes of past, present, and future events or to confirm or correct prior expectations'.[52] The statement further describes 'timeliness' as an 'ancillary aspect of relevance. If information is not available when it is needed or becomes available only so long after the reported events that it has no value for future action, it lacks relevance and is of little or no use.'[53] Therefore, in the context of financial reporting, the characteristic of timeliness means that information must be made available to users before it loses its capacity to influence their decisions. However, timeliness alone cannot make information relevant, but a lack of timeliness can result in information losing a degree of relevance which it once had.[54] On the other hand, in many instances there also has to be a trade-off between timeliness and reliability, since generally the more timely the information the less reliable it is.

The hierarchy identifies 'predictive value' and 'feedback value' as the other components of relevance on the basis that 'information can make a difference to decisions by improving decision makers' capacities to predict or by confirming or correcting their earlier expectations'.[55] Predictive value is defined as 'the quality of information that helps users to increase the likelihood of correctly forecasting the outcome of past or present events',[56] whilst feedback value is defined as 'the quality of information that enables users to confirm or correct prior expectations'.[57] Clearly, however, in saying that accounting information has predictive value, it is not suggesting that it is itself a prediction.

B   Reliability

Reliability is the second of the primary qualities, and is ascribed three attributes in the hierarchy. The statement asserts that the 'reliability of a measure rests on the faithfulness with which it represents what it purports to represent, coupled with an assurance for the user, which comes through verification, that it has that representational quality'.[58] This definition gives rise to the three subsidiary qualities of 'representational faithfulness', 'verifiability', and 'neutrality'. Representational faithfulness is an unnecessary piece of jargon introduced into accounting terminology by SFAC No. 2; what it essentially means is that information included in financial reports should represent what it purports to represent. In other words, financial reporting should be truthful. For example, if a group's consolidated balance sheet discloses cash and bank balances, users would be justified in assuming that, in the absence of any statement to the contrary, the financial statements were truthful, and that these represented cash resources freely available to the group; however, if the reality of the situation was that the cash resources were situated in countries which had severe exchange control restrictions, and were, therefore, not available to the group, some might hold the view that the financial statements were not entirely 'representationally faithful'.

It should be noted, however, that there are degrees of representational faithfulness. Because the financial reporting process involves allocations, estimations and subjective judgements, it cannot produce an 'exact' result; consequently, the trade-off between relevance and reliability will often apply, resulting in the presentation of information which is assigned a high degree of relevance, but which sacrifices representational faithfulness. An example of where this might apply is in the context of fair value accounting, where fair values have to be assigned to the separable net assets acquired.

Reliable information should also be verifiable and neutral so that neither measurement nor measurer bias results in the information being presented in such a way that it influences the particular decision being made. Verifiability is a quality of representational faithfulness in that it excludes the possibility of measurement bias, whilst neutrality implies the provision of all relevant and reliable information – irrespective of the effects that the information will have on the entity or a particular user group.

3.3.5 Comparability

The hierarchy lists comparability as an additional quality that financial information should possess in order to achieve relevance and reliability. The quality of comparability includes the fundamental accounting concept of consistency, since the usefulness of information is greatly enhanced if it is prepared on a consistent basis from one period to the next, and can be compared with corresponding information of the same enterprise for some other period, or with similar information about some other enterprise.

3.3.6 Materiality

All the qualitative criteria discussed in SFAC No. 2 are subject to a materiality threshold, since only material information will have an impact on the decision-making process. However, the statement provides no quantitative guidelines for materiality, and it will be a matter of judgement for the providers of information to determine whether or not an item of information has crossed the materiality threshold for recognition. Materiality is closely related to the characteristic of relevance, since both are defined in terms of what influences or makes a difference to an investor or other decision-maker. On the other hand, the two concepts can be distinguished; a decision by management not to disclose certain information may be made because users have no interest in that kind of information (i.e. it is not relevant to their specific needs), or because the amounts involved are too small to make a difference to the users' decisions (i.e. they are not material).

However, if the preparers of financial statements are to decide on what to include in their reporting package, they must have a clear understanding of the users of their reports and their specific information and decision-making needs. In so doing, they should be aware of the types of information likely to influence their decisions (i.e. relevance) as well as the associated magnitude of this information (i.e. materiality).   Consequently, financial reporting will focus generally on information which is regarded as relevant, and specifically on that which is material.   The principal difficulty with this, however, is that the materiality decisions of users vary from class to class and amongst individual users in the same class (see 5.3 below for further discussion of the concept of materiality).

3.3.7   Conservatism

SFAC No. 2 includes an interesting discussion on the convention of 'conservatism' (i.e. prudence).[59] In so doing, it draws a distinction between the 'deliberate, consistent understatement of net assets and profits',[60] and the practice of ensuring that 'uncertainties and risks inherent in business situations are adequately considered'.[61] The statement recognised the fact that, in the eyes of bankers and other lenders, deliberate understatement of assets was desirable, since it increased their margin of safety on assets pledged as security for debts. On the other hand, it was also recognised that consistent understatement was difficult to maintain over a period of any length, and that understated assets would clearly lead to overstated income in later periods when the assets were ultimately realised. Consequently, unwarranted and deliberate conservatism in financial reporting would lead to a contravention of certain of the qualitative characteristics, such as neutrality and representational faithfulness.

3.4   The elements of financial statements

SFAC No. 6 – *Elements of Financial Statements* – was issued in 1985 as a replacement to SFAC No. 3 – *Elements of Financial Statements of Business Enterprises* – having expanded its scope to encompass non-profit organisations. The statement defines ten 'elements' of financial statements that are directly related to the measurement of performance and financial status of an entity. However, the elements are very much interrelated, as six of them are arithmetically derived from the definitions of assets and liabilities.

3.4.1   Assets

Assets are defined as being 'probable future economic benefits obtained or controlled by a particular entity as a result of past transactions or events'.[62] However, the statement then goes on to say that the kinds of items that qualify as assets under this definition are also commonly called 'economic resources'. They are the scarce means that are useful for carrying out economic activities, such as consumption, production and exchange.[63] The common characteristic

those resulting from investments by owners and distributions to owners.'[71] On its own, the term 'comprehensive income' is somewhat meaningless; for example, how does it tie in with the statement in SFAC No. 1[72] that 'the primary focus of financial reporting is information about an enterprise's performance provided by measures of earnings and its components'? Clearly, the FASB was keeping its options open by not defining earnings; in fact, it explained (in a footnote to SFAC No. 6) that whilst 'comprehensive income' is the term used in the statement for the concept that was called 'earnings' in SFAC No. 1, SFAC No. 5 had described earnings for a period as excluding certain cumulative accounting adjustments and other non-owner changes in equity that are included in comprehensive income for a period.[73]

3.4.7 *Revenues, expenses, gains and losses*

SFAC No. 6 identifies the remaining four elements as those which constitute the basic components of 'comprehensive income':

Revenues, which are 'inflows or other enhancements of assets of an entity or settlements of its liabilities (or a combination of both) from delivering or producing goods, rendering services, or other activities that constitute the entity's ongoing major central operations'.[74]

Expenses, which are 'outflows or other using up of assets or incurrences of liabilities (or a combination of both) from delivering or producing goods, rendering services, or carrying out other activities that constitute the entity's ongoing major or central operations'.[75]

Gains, which are 'increases in equity (net assets) from peripheral or incidental transactions of an entity and from all other transactions and other events and circumstances affecting the entity except those that result from revenues or investments by owners'.[76]

Losses, which are 'decreases in equity (net assets) from peripheral or incidental transactions of an entity and from all other transactions and other events and circumstances affecting the entity except those that result from expenses or distributions to owners'.[77]

Therefore, comprehensive income equals revenues minus expenses plus gains minus losses; however, although the statement states that revenues, expenses, gains and losses can be combined in various ways to obtain various measures of enterprise performance,[78] it fails to define net income.

The difficulty surrounding the FASB's definitions of the ten elements is that they are so interrelated, that in attempting to piece them together into a meaningful accounting framework, one gets caught up in a tautology of terms which all lead back to the definitions of assets and liabilities. However, if the primary focus of financial reporting is the measurement of earnings, then surely the starting point should be definitions of earnings and its components, with assets and liabilities being the residuals – rather than the other way around?

Essentially, what the FASB is saying is that assets minus liabilities equals equity and comprehensive income equals changes in equity (excluding transactions with owners), therefore comprehensive income equals the change in net assets. Consequently, the definition of comprehensive income would incorporate items such as capital contributions from non-owners, government grants for capital expenditure and unrealised holding gains. This is all very well, provided that the issues of measurement and capital maintenance have already been settled. However, this is clearly not the case, with the result that the FASB is either restricting itself in the future development of different accounting models for different purposes, or it might have to develop different definitions of the elements of financial statements as different models are developed.

3.5   Recognition and measurement

Throughout the framework project, the FASB had avoided dealing with certain fundamental issues on the basis that they were the 'subject of another project'.[79] The result was the publication in December 1984 of SFAC No. 5 – *Recognition and Measurement in Financial Statements of Business Enterprises* – which attempted to deal with all the previously unresolved issues. However, the statement was somewhat inconclusive – possibly as a consequence of both its self-imposed restrictions discussed above, and the need to reach compromises in order to complete this phase of the project. The statement tends to describe current practices, rather than indicate preferences or propose improvements; for example, in dealing with the issue of measurement attributes, the statement merely states that 'items currently reported in financial statements are measured by different attributes, depending on the nature of the item and the relevance and reliability of the attribute measured'.[80] Then, instead of either prescribing a particular measurement attribute, or discussing the circumstances under which particular attributes should apply, the statement discusses five different attributes which 'are used in present practice' – historical cost, current cost, current market value, net realisable value and present value of future cash flows – and concludes that 'the use of different attributes will continue'.[81] Furthermore, the statement fails to prescribe a particular concept of capital maintenance that should be adopted by an entity, although the FASB bases its discussions on the concept of financial capital maintenance.[82]

The statement defines recognition as 'the process of formally recording or incorporating an item into the financial statements of an entity as an asset, liability, revenue, expense, or the like'.[83] It goes on to discuss four 'fundamental recognition criteria' which any item should meet in order for it to be recognised in the financial statements of an entity. These criteria, which are subject to a cost-benefit constraint and a materiality threshold, are described as follows:

Definitions – the item meets the definition of an element of financial statements.

Measurability – the item has a relevant attribute measurable with sufficient reliability.

Relevance – the information about the item is capable of making a difference in user decisions.

Reliability – the information is representationally faithful, verifiable and neutral.[84]

Although it was probably worth setting out these criteria, they are no more than an encapsulation of certain criteria contained in Concepts Statements 2 and 6.

SFAC No. 5 does make some progress in distinguishing between comprehensive income, earnings and net income. It states that the concept of earnings is similar to net income in present practice, and that a statement of earnings will be much like a present income statement, although 'earnings' does not include the cumulative effect of certain accounting adjustments of earlier periods that are recognised in the current period.[85] However, the statement goes on to say that the FASB 'expects the concept of earnings to be subject to the process of gradual change or evolution that has characterised the development of net income'.[86] Whilst many would agree with the principle that gradual change is the best approach towards gaining general acceptance, one of the problems with SFAC No. 5 is that the FASB does not indicate what it considers to be the desirable direction for this gradual change to follow. Furthermore, the FASB seems to be saying that concepts will evolve as accounting standards are developed – instead of the other way around.

In an evaluation of the FASB's conceptual framework, Professor David Solomons (who, incidentally, was the principal author of SFAC No. 2) came to the following conclusion about SFAC No. 5: 'Under a rigorous grading system I would give Concepts Statement no. 5 an F and require the board to take the course over again – that is, to scrap the statement and start afresh.'[87]

3.6 Using cash flow information in accounting measurements (discounting)

In June 1997 the FASB issued an exposure draft of a proposed new Statement of Financial Accounting Concepts. The purpose of the proposed statement is to provide a framework for using future cash flows as the basis for accounting measurement. It aims to provide general principles governing the use of present value, especially when the amounts of future cash flows and/or their timing are uncertain. The proposals are limited to issues of measurement and do not address recognition questions.

Present values are used to incorporate the time value of money into measurement. In their simplest form, present value techniques capture the amount that an entity demands (or that others demand from it) for money that it will receive (or pay) in the future.[88] The FASB's objective of using present value in an accounting measurement is to capture, to the extent that it is possible, the economic difference between sets of estimated future cash flows. For example, a riskless cash flow of £1,000 due in one day and a risky cash flow of £1,000 due in ten years both have an undiscounted measurement of £1,000. However, no rational entity would be indifferent about which of the two assets it would wish to own. Consequently, the FASB asserts that because present value distinguishes between unlike items that might otherwise appear similar, a measurement based on the present value of estimated future cash flows provides more relevant information for most purposes than a measurement based on the undiscounted sum of those cash flows.[89]

Any combination of cash flows and interest rates could be used to compute a present value, at least in the broadest sense of the term. However, present value is not an end in itself. Simply applying an arbitrary interest rate to a series of cash flows provides limited information to financial statement users and may mislead rather than assist. To provide relevant information in financial reporting, present value must represent some observable measurement attribute of assets or liabilities. The exposure draft identifies two situations which, in the opinion of the FASB, satisfy that requirement. When used in accounting measurements on initial recognition or re-measurement, present value techniques may be used either to estimate fair value or to develop entity-specific measurements:[90]

- the fair value of an asset (or liability) is the amount at which that asset (or liability) could be bought or incurred or sold (or settled) in a current transaction between willing parties — that is, other than in a forced or liquidation sale;

- the entity-specific measurement of an asset (or liability) is the present value of the future cash flows that the entity expects to realise (or pay) through the use (or settlement) and eventual disposition of the item over its economic life. Conceptually, the entity-specific value is that amount at which independent willing parties that share the same information and assumptions about the entity's estimated future cash flows would agree to a transaction. Stated differently, entity-specific value is that amount at which the market would value the cash flows expected by the entity. The assumptions used in an entity-specific measurement reflect the entity's expected use of an asset or settlement of a liability and the role of the entity's proprietary skills in that use or settlement. The FASB's notion of entity-specific measurement is similar to what the ASB refers to as 'value in use' (see 5 below).[91]

The FASB expects to identify one of these two measurement objectives on a project-by-project basis when cash flows are used as the basis for measuring assets or liabilities. The exposure draft focuses on the common elements of all present value measurements and identifies how those elements are used to estimate fair values and entity-specific measurements. Nevertheless, the exposure draft sets out the following four general principles that, in the opinion of the FASB, govern any application of present value techniques in accounting measurements: [92]

■   to the extent that it is possible, estimated cash flows and interest rates should reflect assumptions about all future events and uncertainties that would be considered in deciding whether or not to acquire an asset or group of assets in an arm's-length transaction for cash;

■   interest rates should reflect assumptions that are consistent with those inherent in the estimated cash flows. Otherwise, the effect of some assumptions will be double counted or ignored. For example, an interest rate normally applied to contractual cash flows will reflect expectations about future defaults. That same rate should not be used to discount expected cash flows because they already reflect assumptions about future defaults;

■   estimated cash flows and interest rates should be free from both bias and factors unrelated to the asset or group of assets in question; and

■   estimated cash flows or interest rates should reflect the range of possible outcomes rather than a single most likely, minimum, or maximum possible amount.

According to the FASB, the measurement of liabilities involves different problems than the measurement of assets, including the possibility of different measurement objectives. The exposure draft identifies the following three measurement objectives for liabilities:[93]

■   fair value as assets – the recorded amount of some liabilities is the price at which other entities are willing to hold the entity's liabilities as assets;

■   fair value in settlement – the recorded amount of some liabilities represents the amount that the entity would have to pay a third party to assume the liability; and

■   value in settlement by the entity – the recorded amount of some liabilities represents the amount that the entity expects to pay in settling the obligation (the entity-specific measurement of a liability).

All in all, the exposure draft comes across as no more than an overview of the issues surrounding the use of present values in accounting measurement. In so doing, it leaves the door open to a fairly wide range of practices which can be applied as and when the FASB so decides. This is evidenced, for example, by the statement made in the document that the FASB 'expects to identify one of those two measurement objectives [fair value or value in use] on a project-by-project basis for measuring assets and liabilities'.[94] It is therefore possible that the FASB will be looking to convert this exposure draft into an SFAC in a way that will seemingly provide conceptual support for a fairly wide variety of discounting practices.

3.7   Conclusion

In order to be able to assess the success or failure of the FASB's conceptual framework project, one must refer back to the originally perceived benefits of the project and evaluate whether or not any of them has been achieved (see 3.1 above). Perhaps the acid test may be found in analysing the extent to which the FASB has used the framework in the development of accounting standards. Possibly the best example of where the framework has been used as the basis for an accounting standard is in the development of SFAS 95 – *Statement of Cash Flows*; however, this is clearly the exception. An analysis of the Appendices headed 'Basis for Conclusions' in the more recently issued SFASs, reveals few references to the fact that the members of the FASB have used the concepts statements to guide their thinking – and where reference is made it is generally to broad objectives or qualitative characteristics. On the other hand, it might be argued that the concepts statements have guided the thinking of FASB members without it being expressly stated; however, if this were the case, why is it that the FASB has, for example, issued a statement on reporting comprehensive income (SFAS 130) which seemingly lacks any conceptual integrity and is in conflict with the framework? (See Chapter 22 for further discussion of SFAS 130.)

The weakness of the FASB's conceptual framework project may be attributed to a number of factors; however, the most significant reason will probably be shown to be the Board's failure to deal with the fundamental issues of recognition and measurement. To a certain extent, the FASB has fallen into the same trap as the AICPA did in APB Statement No. 4, in that SFAC No. 5 is a descriptive rather than a prescriptive statement; a statement of accounting concepts should provide a frame of reference for the formulation of financial reporting practice, and not be a description of what current reporting practices are. In the words of Professor Stephen Zeff, 'the FASB's conceptual framework failed to fulfil expectations that it might constitute a powerful intellectual force for improving financial reporting'.[95]

This is not to say that the FASB's project should be rejected out of hand; it contains some outstanding work, particularly in the area of qualitative characteristics. However, a way must be found to address the fundamental issues, without having to resort to compromise solutions; thereafter, a method of implementation will have to be developed which will make whatever transition is necessary acceptable to both the preparers and users of financial reports.

4   UK INITIATIVES

4.1   SSAP 2: Disclosure of accounting policies

SSAP 2[96] does not really set out to form part of a conceptual framework, but its content covers some of the same ground. It was issued in 1971, and although it was not the first accounting standard to be published, it is probably the most fundamental, since its principles pervade financial reporting practice in the UK. The overall objectives of SSAP 2 are to assist in user understanding and interpretation of financial statements by promoting the improvement in the quality of information disclosed. It seeks to achieve this by establishing as generally accepted accounting practice the disclosure in financial statements of clear explanations of the accounting policies followed in the preparation of the financial statements, in so far as these are significant for the purpose of giving a true and fair view.

SSAP 2 develops the standard accounting practice for the disclosure of accounting policies in three stages: first, it describes the four fundamental accounting concepts, it then relates these to the development of accounting bases, and finally it deals with the selection of accounting policies.

4.1.1   *Fundamental accounting concepts*

Fundamental accounting concepts are the broad basic assumptions which underlie the periodic financial statements of business entities. They are practical rules rather than theoretical ideals and are capable of variation and evolution as accounting thought and practice develop.[97]

A   The going concern concept

This concept is applied on the basis that the reporting entity will continue in operational existence for the foreseeable future. This means in particular that the balance sheet and profit and loss account assume no intention or necessity to liquidate or curtail significantly the scale of business operations.[98]

B   The accruals (or matching) concept

In the presentation of the profit and loss account, revenue and profits recognised are matched with the associated costs and expenses incurred in earning them. In order to achieve this, revenues, profits, costs and expenses are accrued (i.e. recognised as they are earned or incurred, not as cash is received or paid), matched with one another in so far as their relationship can be established or justifiably assumed, and dealt with in the profit and loss account for the period to which they relate. However, where the accruals concept is inconsistent with the prudence concept (described below), the latter prevails.[99]

C   The consistency concept

There should be consistency of accounting treatment of like items within each accounting period and from one period to the next.

D   The prudence concept

Under the prudence concept, revenue and profits are not anticipated but are recognised by inclusion in the profit and loss account only when realised in the form of cash or of other assets the ultimate cash realisation of which can be assessed with reasonable certainty. On the other hand, provision is made for all known liabilities whether the amount of these is known with certainty or is a best estimate in the light of the information available.

These four fundamental accounting concepts, together with a fifth concept, have broadly been adopted by the Companies Act 1985 as the accounting principles which should be used in the determination of all items shown in a company's financial statements, although the terms in which they are described are not identical.[100] The fifth principle introduced by the Companies Act is that of 'non-aggregation'. This principle states that 'in determining the aggregate amount of any item the amount of each individual asset or liability that falls to be taken into account shall be determined separately'.[101] For example, compensating inaccuracies in individual amounts should not be lost in one large total, and a group of assets should be valued on an individual asset basis, as opposed to a portfolio basis.

At the same time, though, it is important to recognise that whilst the fundamental accounting concepts are, in theory, firmly entrenched in SSAP 2 and the Companies Act, they are being slowly undermined by recent ASB initiatives. For example, the ASB's recent proposals on the accounting for provisions reflects a fundamentally different interpretation of the prudence concept, as does the suggestion that unrealised gains on financial instruments should be taken to income, particularly when there is no active or liquid market in those instruments and they are not held for trading purposes. The matching concept is similarly under threat, given that the ASB's Draft *Statement of Principles* does not recognise items of deferred expense and income which have traditionally been recognised in the balance sheet as deferred debits and credits (see 5.4.1 below).

4.1.2   Accounting bases

Accounting bases are 'the methods developed for applying fundamental concepts to financial transactions and items, for the purpose of financial accounts, and in particular:

(a)   for determining the accounting periods in which revenue and costs should be recognised in the profit and loss account; and

(b)   for determining the amounts at which material items should be stated in the balance sheet'.[102]

Accounting bases, therefore, are accounting treatments which have evolved in response to the necessity of having to apply the fundamental concepts to areas of practice. However, because of the variety and complexity of types of business and business transactions, there may exist more than one legitimate accounting basis for dealing with a particular item; for example, there are several acceptable accounting bases for the depreciation of fixed assets, each of which is suited to particular types of assets and business circumstances.

4.1.3   Accounting policies

Having established that there exist several recognised accounting bases in respect of individual accounting issues, it is necessary for the management of an entity to select those bases which are most appropriate for their own particular circumstances; those bases selected then become the entity's accounting policies.   Consequently, accounting policies are defined as 'the specific accounting bases selected and consistently followed by a business enterprise as being, in the opinion of management, appropriate to its circumstances and best suited to present fairly its results and financial position'.[103]   Thereafter, the accounting policies selected for dealing with items which are judged material in determining financial position and profit or loss for the year should be disclosed by way of note to the financial statements.[104]

This means, for example, that management should select those bases of depreciating fixed assets which are most appropriate to the types of assets and their use in the business so as to allocate depreciation as fairly as possible to the periods expected to benefit from the use of the assets, and these bases selected should be set out in an accounting policy note to the financial statements. However, this highlights an interesting conflict between SSAP 2 and SSAP 12 – *Accounting for depreciation*. Under SSAP 2, for example, the sum-of-digits and straight-line methods of depreciation are two acceptable accounting bases, each of which is appropriate to a particular pattern of asset use; in the event of management deciding that it would be more appropriate to depreciate an asset using a the sum-of-digits, rather than a straight-line method, this would constitute a change in accounting basis, and therefore a change in accounting policy. SSAP 12, however, states that a change from one method of providing depreciation to another 'does not constitute a change of accounting policy';[105] furthermore, no explanation is given in SSAP 12 for this departure from the principles laid down in SSAP 2.

4.2   The Corporate Report

The first real attempt by the accounting profession in the UK to develop a conceptual framework is to be found in a discussion paper which was issued in 1975 by the then-styled Accounting Standards Steering Committee (later the ASC) and entitled *The Corporate Report*.[106]

The discussion paper deals with 'the fundamental aims of published financial reports and the means by which these aims can be achieved'[107] and uses the term 'corporate report' to mean 'the comprehensive package of information of all kinds which most completely describes an organisation's economic activity'.[108]

It was suggested that this 'comprehensive package' should include more than the 'basic financial statements' (i.e. the balance sheet, profit and loss account and funds statement), and should incorporate additional narrative and descriptive statements.[109]   The discussion paper centres around three main elements: 'the types of organisation which should be expected to publish regular financial information; the main users of such information and their needs; and the form of report which will best meet those needs'.[110]

The discussion paper followed the basic approach that corporate reports should seek to satisfy, as far as possible, the information needs of users.[111]   The committee argued that every economic entity of significant size has an implicit responsibility to report publicly, and concluded that general purpose reports designed for general purpose use are the primary means by which this public accountability is fulfilled.   Users were defined 'as those having a reasonable right to information concerning the reporting entity',[112] a right which arises from the entity's public accountability.

The paper identifies seven user groups[113] as having a reasonable right to information, and discusses the basis of the rights of each group and their information needs.   Not surprisingly, the committee identified a considerable overlap of interest between each of the user groups, including items such as 'evaluating the performance of the entity', 'estimating the future prospects of the entity', 'evaluating managerial performance', 'assessing the liquidity of the entity, its present or future requirements for additional fixed or working capital, and its ability to raise long and short term finance'.[114]

On this basis the committee concluded that 'the fundamental objective of corporate reports is to communicate economic measurements of and information about the resources and performance of the reporting entity useful to those having reasonable rights to such information'.[115]   They went on to say that in order to fulfil this objective and be useful, corporate reports should be relevant, understandable, reliable, complete, objective, timely and comparable[116] (these qualitative characteristics identified were similar to those discussed in the Trueblood Report).

The discussion paper then reviewed the conventional thinking on the aim of published reports together with the then-existing features of published financial statements of UK companies.   The committee also conducted a survey of corporate objectives amongst the chairmen of 300 of the largest UK listed companies, and concluded that 'distributable profit can no longer be regarded as the sole or premier indicator of performance'.[117]   Consequently, it was suggested that there was a need for additional indicators of performance in the corporate reports of all entities.[118]

Part II of the study considers the 'measurement and method' of achieving the above aims. This includes a discussion of the improvement of communication and publication methods of corporate report information, as well as

whilst the remaining cash flows are treated as realised. For example, if the discounted net present value of all expected future cash flows of an entity are £100,000 at the beginning of the year and £115,000 at the end of the year, and if the net cash flows arising during the year were £10,000, then the profit for the year will be £25,000, since this amount could be distributed whilst maintaining the original capital base of £100,000.

Whilst this approach might have some degree of theoretical soundness, it is totally impracticable. Issues such as risk, the determination of discount rates, changes in interest rates and the uncertainty of future cash flows present virtually insurmountable problems. The Sandilands committee rejected present value accounting on the grounds that use of economic value as the basis of valuation of an asset would not meet the needs of users, as it would only be in comparatively few cases that this would represent the value of an asset to a business.[137]

C   *Continuously Contemporary Accounting (CoCoA)*

The current value income model based on exit prices or realisable market values was first advocated by MacNeal in a book published by him in 1939 which dealt, inter alia, with the ethical issue of 'truth' in accounting.[138] MacNeal maintained that financial statements could only present the 'truth' if assets were stated at their current value and the profit and losses accruing from the changes in these values are included in income, and classified as either realised or unrealised. MacNeal did, however, concede that under certain circumstances the use of net realisable values was not appropriate, and that in such cases current replacement costs should be used.

The system known as continuously contemporary accounting (CoCoA) was formally introduced by Chambers in a book which he published in 1966,[139] and the case for exit value accounting was further developed by Sterling.[140] Chambers' theory is based on the premise that entities must be able to choose between alternative courses of action and, because resources are limited, they need to know what resources are available to enable them to engage in exchanges. Consequently, Chambers asserts that this capacity to engage in exchanges is measured by the opportunity cost of holding assets in their existing form, and that this opportunity cost is represented by the current cash equivalent of assets – which Chambers defines as being their current sales value. Initially, Chambers did not apply this principle rigorously and proposed that stocks should be valued at current replacement cost. However, he subsequently amended his view and advocated that exit values should be applied to the valuation of all assets. A difference in the theories of Chambers and Sterling is, for example, that Chambers believes that net realisable values should be based on the assumption that assets are realised in an orderly manner based on sensible adaptations to changing circumstances; Sterling, on the other hand, believes that net realisable values should be based on immediate liquidation prices.

The capital maintenance concept adopted by CoCoA is based on the preservation of the purchasing power of shareholders' equity (using the monetary unit as the unit of measurement, and not the current purchasing power unit used in CPP accounting). Consequently, since all assets (both monetary and non-monetary) are measured at net realisable value, income is defined as the difference between opening and closing equity after maintaining the purchasing power or cash equivalent of such equity. Income for the year, therefore, will comprise (1) the net profit/loss on business operations, (2) the accrued profit/loss arising from the change in the current cash equivalent of assets and (3) the effect on the capital of the entity brought about by the change in the purchasing power of money.

However, despite the widespread publication of his theories, Chambers failed to gain any measure of support for CoCoA outside academic circles. Chambers believed that one of the reasons for this was the lack of empirical evidence that the users of financial statements needed financial information based on net realisable values. Consequently, he set about obtaining this evidence through an empirical survey which he published in 1980.[141] Through carefully designed (but somewhat simplistic) questions, Chambers was able to conclude that his empirical evidence justified the use of net realisable values as the primary basis of measurement.

Chambers' principal survey did, however, produce some anomalous and inconsistent answers, resulting in his having to conduct a supplementary survey of four questions. This highlighted several weaknesses in the formulation of his questions, and cast doubt about the validity of the survey as a whole. These doubts are expressed, for example, in an article by Edward Stamp[142] who stated that 'his questionnaire was inadequate and failed to include necessary questions on valuation, performance measures, and liabilities, that would not have been difficult to frame, even with the constraints imposed by Chambers'.[143] Consequently, these omissions and the style of his research undermine Chambers' claim that his empirical evidence demonstrates that CoCoA provides the best basis for financial reporting.

There is no doubt that there are some compelling theoretical arguments for the presentation of financial statements based on net realisable values; for example, they provide useful information in the assessment of liquidity and financial flexibility. However, net realisable value is unlikely to reflect an asset's 'value to the business', since, for instance, an item of plant might have negligible net realisable value but substantial use value. Therefore, whilst the disclosure of net realisable values might provide useful supplementary information, the arguments in favour of CoCoA as the primary basis of accounting are unconvincing. CoCoA was rejected by the Sandilands committee on the basis that, as a whole, it did not satisfy the information needs of users which they had identified.[144] It is, however, noteworthy that in its discussion document – *Making*

Corporate Reports Valuable – the Research Committee of the ICAS advocated a reporting system based on net realisable values[145] (see 4.6 below).

4.3.3   Cash flow accounting

The principal proponents of cash flow reporting are Lee[146] and Lawson,[147] although there are several other advocates of various approaches to cash flow reporting. Lee's system of cash flow reporting relies heavily on exit value theory and aims to report both actual and potential cash flows. Assets are classified according to their realisability, based on Chambers' principle of orderly liquidation. If a sale price does not exist, assets are to be accounted for as having a zero cash equivalent.[148] Lee has suggested the following four asset classifications for his statement of financial position:

1.   realised assets (e.g. bank balances);

2.   readily-realisable assets (i.e. assets which have a ready market and sale price, such as listed securities, debtors and stocks of finished goods);

3.   non-readily-realisable assets (i.e. assets which do have a market and sale price, but which would not be quickly realised because of the limited nature of the market, such as certain items of plant and work-in-progress); and

4.   not-realisable assets (i.e. assets which have no known sales price and no market, and would therefore be ascribed a zero value, such as highly specialised or obsolete plant).[149]

Liabilities are classified according to maturity, in line with conventional accounting practice.

Lee proposes that, in addition to a 'statement of financial position', the cash flow reporting system should present a 'statement of realised cash flow', a 'statement of realisable earnings' and a 'statement of changes in financial position'.[150] The statement of realised cash flow reports an entity's actual cash inflows and outflows during a particular period; it is noteworthy that the information contained in this statement would be broadly equivalent to that which would be presented in a statement of cash flows under FRS 1 or SFAS 95 (see Chapter 27). The statement of realisable earnings reports periodic profit similar to that provided by a net realisable value accounting system, except that it is described in terms of realised and realisable cash flows. The statement provides an analysis of realised earnings (derived from the entity's operating cash flow), and unrealised earnings (which represent potential cash flows that have accrued during the period as a result of changes in the realisable values of assets, net of the changes in liabilities). The statement of changes in financial position is effectively a conventional funds statement presented on an exit value basis.

Although there are a number of practical accounting and disclosure problems in cash flow reporting, it does have considerable merit. Furthermore, a number of the problems are not unique to cash flow reporting, with equivalent issues remaining unsolved in historical cost accounting. However, one difficulty which does exist is caused by the artificial 12 month reporting period and the necessity to measure 'profitability' over that period and from one period to the next. The principal reason for the development of the accrual basis of accounting was that financial statements prepared on a cash basis (which was probably the oldest form of presentation) provided distorted profit figures from one period to the next. Although the Sandilands committee stated that there was 'much of value in the cash flow accounting principle',[151] it was felt that cash flow accounting would rekindle all the 'old difficulties of assessing the profit or loss for the year when the accounting entity system does not match revenues against costs incurred in their generation'.[152] The committee therefore concluded that the abandonment of the existing concept of the profit and loss account in favour of a cash flow statement would result in the information needs of users not being met. Clearly, however, the committee had not considered the possibility of the presentation of a 'statement of realisable earnings' as advocated by Lee, which would provide a more stable basis for reporting profit than the statement of receipts and payments envisaged by the committee. Lee, however, recognised the problems created by the traditional 12 month reporting period, and suggested that a solution might be found in the use of multi-period aggregates for analysis purposes.

4.3.4   *Current cost accounting (CCA)*

The Sandilands committee recommended the development of a system of current cost accounting which used the monetary unit as the unit of measurement and dealt with the effects of specific price changes (as opposed to changes in the general purchasing power of money) on individual businesses. The committee recommended that the balance sheet should present the 'value to the business' of the company's assets, which was equated with the amount of the loss which would be suffered by an entity if the asset were to be lost or destroyed. Whilst it was stated that the 'value to the business' of an asset might, under certain circumstances, be its net realisable value or economic value, it would normally be based on its replacement cost. Because the committee recommended that financial statements be drawn up in terms of the monetary unit, no adjustment would be made for monetary items.[153] However, it is arguable that current cost accounting does not produce a balance sheet which seeks to be a statement of values of the resources of the company; it simply updates the costs at which they are recorded. This distinction can be illustrated by looking at the financial statements of an oil and gas exploration company. Even on a current cost basis, the carrying value of its principal assets is still based on the (backward-looking) cost of exploration expenditure incurred, not the (forward-looking) value of the oil and gas it has found.

Under the Sandilands system, an entity's 'current cost profit' for a period would be calculated by charging against income 'the value to the business' of assets eliminating the effects of general inflation.[163] In December 1986, SFAS 33 was superseded by SFAS 89 – *Financial Reporting and Changing Prices* – which encourages (but does not require) the disclosure of supplementary information on the effects of changing prices, suggesting similar disclosures to those of SFAS 33 in respect of holding gains and losses.[164] Clearly, therefore, the FASB has adopted the concept of financial capital maintenance, and its commitment to this concept is borne out in Concepts Statement No. 5[165] (see 3.5 above). However, this is not to say that the FASB has found the solution to accounting for the effects of changing prices; SFAS 89 is, in several other respects, a somewhat nebulous and inconclusive standard.

At the time that SSAP 16 was issued, the ASC stated that it was its intention, as far as possible, 'to make no change to SSAP 16 for three years so as to enable producers and users to gain experience in dealing with practical problems and interpreting the information'. However, this statement probably contributed to the eventual demise of the standard, because it was taken as an intention that it would inevitably be revised at the end of the three year period and allowed SSAP 16 to be characterised as 'experimental' or 'provisional'.[166] Over the next few years, there was a continuing decline in the level of compliance with the standard.

In July 1984, the ASC issued a further exposure draft ED 35 – *Accounting for the effects of changing prices*. This restricted the scope of the proposals to public companies which were neither value-based enterprises nor wholly owned subsidiaries, but in respect of these it sought to make CCA a mandatory feature of the primary financial statements (rather than in supplementary statements), declaring that the inclusion of this information was essential to a true and fair view. However, it soon became clear that these proposals could not command general acceptance, and the exposure draft was withdrawn in early 1985.

Soon afterwards, in the face of increasing opposition to the standard, the CCAB bodies voted to make SSAP 16 non-mandatory, and it was later completely withdrawn. The ASC persisted for some months to try to find a viable successor, seeking a more flexible approach and abandoning the proposition that it was essential to a true and fair view in the primary financial statements, but eventually gave up the search. Instead, it published *Accounting for the effects of changing prices: a Handbook*,[167] which was based on various of its earlier pronouncements on the subject together with some of its more recent, hitherto unpublished material. This was its last publication on accounting for changing prices, and although it never completely took the topic off its agenda, there were no further moves to develop a fresh statement on the subject. Interest in the topic among companies in the private sector also remains low; few companies now offer any CCA information to readers of their financial statements.

More importantly, though, it is now becoming increasingly clear that the ASB's current agenda of accounting reform is drawing heavily on MCRV for its inspiration and guidance. It is no coincidence that Sir David Tweedie was a member of the MCRV Committee, and it is not difficult to find similarities between the MCRV conclusions and the ASB's current proposals. One obvious example lies in the Statement of Changes in Financial Wealth, which has been effectively adopted in FRS 3 as the Statement of Total Recognised Gains and Losses.

4.7   The Solomons Report

In May 1987, the Research Board of the ICAEW announced that it had decided to sponsor a project to address the need for guidelines for decisions in financial reporting; the project had been originally inspired by Professor Bryan Carsberg when he was the ICAEW's Director of Research, and Professor David Solomons, a recently retired academic, agreed to carry out the study. One of the reasons for commissioning the work was that respondents to ASC exposure drafts had frequently commented that, until an agreed conceptual framework had been developed, it would be difficult to achieve either consistency in approach towards setting accounting standards, or resolution of certain of the fundamental accounting issues which were being encountered in practice. This was later echoed by the Dearing Committee, which concluded that 'the lack of a conceptual framework is a handicap to those involved in setting accounting standards as well as to those applying them'.[203]

Solomons followed what has become an almost traditional approach to a study of this nature; however, this is perhaps not surprising in view of the fact that he acted as consultant to the FASB on its conceptual framework project and was principal author of SFAC No. 2. He started by examining the purposes of financial reporting, the users of general purpose reports, their needs and how their needs were at present being met. His report then discussed the elements and sub-elements of financial statements and, in so doing, reached a conclusion on the asset and liability vs. the revenue and expense approach to financial accounting, thereby setting the scene for the rest of his study. This concluded that although 'there is no prospect of proving that one of these views is right and the other wrong, it is possible to find reasons for preferring one view to the other, and these Guidelines will be uncompromisingly based on the asset and liability view'.[204]   Solomons' principal argument against the revenue and expense view of income determination was that it 'opens the door to all kinds of income smoothing';[205] he went on to say that 'the revenue and expense view threatens the integrity of the balance sheet and its value as a useful financial statement. Its value is maximized if it can be seen as a statement of financial position; but it can only be that if all the items in it are truly assets, liabilities, and equity, and not other bits left over from the profit and loss account, and if all such items that are capable of being recognised are included in it.'[206]

Having established the fact that he would be following an asset and liability approach, Solomons then set about defining the elements of financial statements on much the same basis as was done in SFAC No. 6 (see 3.4 above). Assets are defined as 'resources or rights incontestably controlled by an entity at the accounting date that are expected to yield it future economic benefits',[207] whilst liabilities are defined as 'obligations of an entity at the accounting date to make future transfers of assets or services (sometimes uncertain as to timing and amount) to other entities'.[208] All the other elements are then derived from these basic definitions; for example, owners' equity comprises net assets and income is the change in net assets.[209]

The Report then ran quickly through the qualitative characteristics of accounting information, giving what might be viewed as a summarised version of SFAC No. 2 (see 3.3 above). Thereafter he focused his attention on the issues of recognition and measurement and the choice of an accounting model for use in preparing general purpose financial statements. In view of the fact that Solomons' guidelines are based on the recognition and measurement of assets and liabilities, it is not surprising that his recognition criteria concentrate on these two elements. Consequently, under Solomons' approach, an item should only be recognised in financial statements if:

'(a) it conforms to the definition of an asset or liability or of one of the sub-elements derived therefrom; and

(b) its magnitude as specified by the accounting model being used can be measured and verified with reasonable certainty; and

(c) the magnitude so arrived at is material in amount'.[210]

Solomons then examined the present historical cost accounting model which is generally accepted in the UK, listing its deficiencies and pointing out that it is not a true historical cost model (as a result, for example, of asset revaluations and the translation of monetary assets and liabilities designated in foreign currencies at closing rates). Thereafter, he sets about devising an improved model for general purpose financial reporting, and listed the following five criteria that such an improved model should possess:

(a) the balance sheet should be a true and fair statement of an entity's financial condition, showing all its assets and liabilities that satisfy the above recognition criteria and conform with the asset and liability definitions;

(b) the entity's assets and liabilities should be carried in the balance sheet at their value to a going concern at the balance sheet date;

(c) profits or losses should mean increases or decreases of real financial capital as compared with the amount at the beginning of the year;

(d) the results shown by the financial statements should be measured consistently and should therefore be comparable from year to year, both in periods of fluctuating prices and stable prices; and

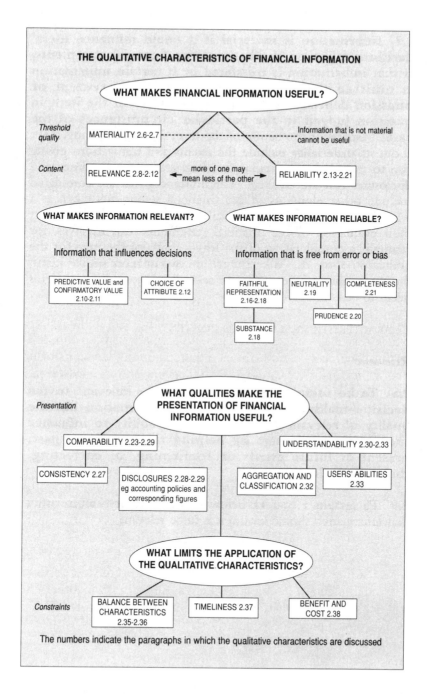

THE QUALITATIVE CHARACTERISTICS OF FINANCIAL INFORMATION

WHAT MAKES FINANCIAL INFORMATION USEFUL?

Threshold quality — MATERIALITY 2.6-2.7 ---- Information that is not material cannot be useful

Content — RELEVANCE 2.8-2.12 ← more of one may mean less of the other → RELIABILITY 2.13-2.21

WHAT MAKES INFORMATION RELEVANT?
Information that influences decisions
PREDICTIVE VALUE and CONFIRMATORY VALUE 2.10-2.11 | CHOICE OF ATTRIBUTE 2.12

WHAT MAKES INFORMATION RELIABLE?
Information that is free from error or bias
FAITHFUL REPRESENTATION 2.16-2.18 | NEUTRALITY 2.19 | COMPLETENESS 2.21
PRUDENCE 2.20
SUBSTANCE 2.18

Presentation
WHAT QUALITIES MAKE THE PRESENTATION OF FINANCIAL INFORMATION USEFUL?
COMPARABILITY 2.23-2.29 | UNDERSTANDABILITY 2.30-2.33
CONSISTENCY 2.27 | DISCLOSURES 2.28-2.29 eg accounting policies and corresponding figures | AGGREGATION AND CLASSIFICATION 2.32 | USERS' ABILITIES 2.33

WHAT LIMITS THE APPLICATION OF THE QUALITATIVE CHARACTERISTICS?
Constraints — BALANCE BETWEEN CHARACTERISTICS 2.35-2.36 | TIMELINESS 2.37 | BENEFIT AND COST 2.38

The numbers indicate the paragraphs in which the qualitative characteristics are discussed

As can be seen from the diagram, the ASB confirms relevance and reliability as the two primary characteristics of accounting information, and again recognises that they are sometimes in conflict, so as to require a trade-off between them. Relevant information is that which influences 'the decisions of users by helping them evaluate past, present or future events or confirming, or correcting, their past evaluations'.[232]   Reliable information is that which is 'free from material error and bias and can be depended upon by users to represent faithfully what it either purports to represent or could reasonably be expected to represent'.[233]

The primary characteristics are supported by two main secondary characteristics: comparability and understandability.   Comparability embraces notions of consistent application of accounting methods throughout an enterprise and through time, as well as the ability to compare one enterprise with another, which implies adequate disclosure of accounting policies – together with changes in policies and the effects of such changes – as well as adherence to accounting standards.[234]   Understandability requires clear presentation of the information, but the chapter comments that it would not be appropriate to omit important but complex information from accounts merely on the grounds that it may be too difficult for certain users to understand.[235]   This way of looking at understandability arguably confuses the ability to interpret a set of accounts with the ability to understand its implications.

The chapter also refers to materiality as a 'threshold quality', i.e. one that needs to be considered first, because if information is immaterial, the other characteristics do not matter.   Material information is information whose omission or misstatement could influence the economic decisions of users taken on the basis of the financial statements.[236]   The important question, however, is against which yardstick information should be judged to be material or immaterial.

The difficulty which arises is that the many different users of the financial statements cannot be consulted by the preparer to discover what is material to them; the preparer must make that assessment on their behalf.   Moreover, some users might have unreasonable expectations of the accuracy of financial statements, and it would not be possible to set materiality at a level which could accommodate their wishes.   According to the ASB, 'aspects of the nature of the item that affect a judgement about its materiality include the events and transactions giving rise to it and the particular financial statement headings and disclosures that are affected.   Circumstances that are considered include other elements of the financial statements taken as a whole and other information available to users that would affect their evaluation of the financial statements: this involves, for example, a consideration of the implications of the item for the evaluation of trends.   Where there are two or more similar items, the materiality of the aggregate as well as the individual items needs to be considered.'[237]

5.4   Chapter 3: The elements of financial statements

The following seven elements are defined in the chapter:

- amounts which should be carried forward under the matching concept (as limited by the prudence concept) because they belong in the profit and loss account of future periods – either deferred costs (such as stock, fixed assets, prepayments) or deferred revenues (such as advances received in respect of future sales, deferred government grants); and

(c) under the prudence concept, what other losses (and corresponding liabilities) have to be accrued in respect of future transactions not yet recognised in the accounting records? Examples might include contingent losses under litigation, or provisions for onerous contractual commitments. (These are relevant to the second part of (a) above, because they provide examples of events that merit recognition in advance of a transaction being carried out.)

Nevertheless, it is now clear that the ASB's proposals for the recognition of gains and losses are very similar to those in the ICAS study *Making Corporate Reports Valuable* (see 4.6 above). The idea that gains and losses arise whenever there is a change in net assets which is not offset by a transaction with owners reflects MCRV's notion of changes in financial wealth. This is borne out by the fact that the ASB has stated in the Draft *Statement of Principles* that 'where an asset changes in value or is disposed of, the gain or loss that is reported is the difference between the new value or the sale proceeds and the value previously reported'.[257] The added implication of this statement is that the ASB's proposed model does not distinguish between realised and unrealised gains and losses. All changes in balance sheet assets and liabilities (excluding transactions with shareholders) are recognised as gains and losses – irrespective of whether or not they are realised. This is justified by the ASB as follows: 'A more useful analysis of the quality of profits than that into realised and unrealised profits is an analysis into those gains and losses that derive from operating activities and those that result from changes in the value of those assets and liabilities that are held on a continuing basis for use in the entity's business.'[258]

A balance sheet-centred approach would, indeed, make a good deal of sense if measurement principles based on an exit-value approach were to be advocated (as in CoCoA and MCRV as discussed at 4.3.2 C and 4.6 above respectively). However, an examination of the measurement chapter of the Draft *Statement of Principles* reveals that this is not the view of the ASB.

5.6   Chapter 5: Measurement in financial statements

This chapter provides a brief summary of the main features of various theoretical measurement approaches. It starts by discussing the features of historical cost accounting, commenting on the way that it has been modified in practice to incorporate asset revaluations. The chapter then contrasts the use of historical costs with the conventional current value systems – namely, entry value (replacement cost), exit value (net realisable value) and value in use (discounted present value of the cash flows expected from continuing use and ultimate sale by the present owner). In so doing, the chapter actively promotes a measurement system based on current values as being superior to historical cost accounting, and concludes that 'practice should develop by evolving in the direction of greater use of current values to the extent that this is consistent with the constraints of reliability and cost'.[259]

However, there are more difficulties associated with current values than merely reliability and cost. The most obvious of these is that current value accounting deals with current opportunities that, by definition, have not yet been realised, whereas historical cost has a grounding in actual events (past transactions). Thus, current values are regarded as particularly subjective items of information. The subjectivity increases as the opportunity moves further into the future, with value in use (requiring estimates of discount rates and the amount and timing of future cash flows) usually considered to be the most subjective of all current value measures. The ASB even acknowledges that there are particular problems of subjectivity and reliability in the case of 'assets that are not regularly dealt with in active markets and when assets are stated at value in use, since the calculation of value in use depends upon expected future returns which may be subject to error and may depend upon subjective judgements'.[260]

Paradoxically, this highlights the most significant advantage of historical cost accounting over current value accounting – namely, that it is based on the actual transactions which the company has undertaken and the cash flows which it has generated. This can be seen as an advantage not just in terms of reliability, but also in terms of relevance, because transactions and their consequent cash flows are the underlying reality of business about which accounts seek to provide information. In contrast, valuation information can be said to lack relevance (as well as reliability) because it does not relate to transactions which the company has undertaken, nor even usually to transactions that it will undertake in the future. There is no reason why current value information (together with underlying assumptions) should not be provided on a supplementary basis (as envisaged in previous studies); however, for financial reporting purposes, the prudent view is that it is neither sufficiently reliable nor relevant to be adopted as the primary basis for measurement.

This view is supported by the findings of an empirical study on the information needs of investors and creditors, published in 1994 by the AICPA Special Committee on Financial Reporting.[261] The study shows that while many users support disclosures of fair value information, they are generally opposed to replacing today's historical cost-based accounting model with a fair value accounting model. This is because users believe that the historical cost-based model provides them with a stable and consistent benchmark that they can rely on to establish historical trends. The study highlighted concern about the subjectivity and potential volatility in reported results of a model based on fair value.

Nevertheless, despite acknowledging the fundamental shortcomings of a measurement system based on current values, the chapter supports the ASB's own perspective about the focus of financial reporting, and ultimately advocates (albeit rather hesitantly) the 'value to the business' measurement model, as advocated by the Solomons Report (see 4.7 above). The ASB describes value to the business as a 'bringing up to date of historical cost, adopting the traditional "cost or less" rule: replacement cost is reduced to net realisable value or value in use where these are lower'.[262] However, despite the ASB's attempt at defining the concept 'value to the business', its real meaning remains as opaque as it did when it was first mentioned in the Sandilands Report, and later in the Solomons Report.

This may be illustrated as follows:[263]

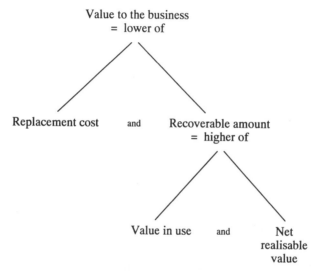

The ASB goes on to say that 'value to the business can be justified as a value that is relevant to economic decision-making',[264] although the chapter is not altogether clear as to why this is so or why it is appropriate for external financial reporting purposes. It is more probable that value to the business is a fundamentally false premise on which to base accounting measurement, and that the ASB is glossing over the most significant weakness in the concept. In reality, the value to the business formula measures deprival value, but not future benefits. What it would cost to replace an asset is irrelevant to measuring its future benefits, and therefore replacement cost cannot be relevant in this context.

Interestingly enough, though, value to the business was the fundamental valuation basis which was promulgated by SSAP 16 – *Current cost accounting* – although SSAP 16 defined recoverable amount as the greater of the net realisable value of an asset and 'the amount recoverable from its further use',[265] without explicitly referring to 'value in use'.

In the case of liabilities, the discussion draft of Chapter 5 which preceded the omnibus version of the Draft *Statement of Principles* devoted considerable space to discussing the concept of 'relief value', which the ASB sees as being the mirror-image equivalent of the value to the business principle. However, this discussion was omitted from the Exposure Draft, with the ASB merely stating that the concept of relief value is an 'unnecessary complication' and that 'the same considerations that support reporting assets at current value suggest that liabilities should also be measured on that basis'.[266] The implication of this statement is that the ASB clearly believes that liabilities should be stated in an entity's balance sheet on some current value basis, and not on the basis of what the entity believes it will ultimately have to pay to settle the liability. This approach would have a dramatic impact on the measurement of both liabilities and provisions, as discussed in Chapter 26 at 2.2.3.

Surprisingly, the ASB devotes little space to discussing the issue of capital maintenance. Presumably, this is because profit is merely a product of balance sheet changes, and once it has been decided on what basis assets and liabilities are to be measured (i.e. 'value to the business'), profit is merely an arithmetical consequence thereof. The ASB does, however, mention in passing a 'real terms capital maintenance system', which is aimed at highlighting 'the extent to which holding gains and losses reflect the effect of general inflation' in situations where general inflation is material factor.[267]

5.7   Chapter 6: Presentation of financial information

Chapter 6 discusses the way in which information should be presented in financial statements in order to meet the objective of providing information about the financial position, performance and financial adaptability of an enterprise that is useful to a wide range of users for assessing the stewardship of management and for making economic decisions.

The chapter identifies the profit and loss account, the statement of total recognised gains and losses, the balance sheet and the cash flow statement as being the four primary financial statements. The important feature of this list is that it is now clear that the ASB views the statement of total recognised gains and losses as a primary statement of performance, and not just a reconciling statement. This is backed up by the statement that 'the gains and losses that are recognised in respect of a period are reported in one of the statements of financial performance, ie the profit and loss account and the statement of total recognised gains and losses'.[268] The chapter goes on to say that 'in assessing the overall financial performance of an entity during a period, all gains and losses need to be considered' and that 'the statements of financial performance report only the gains and losses that arise in the period'.[269]

As stated above, the ASB does not regard the distinction between realised and unrealised gains and losses as being relevant, stating that a more useful analysis of the quality of profits 'is an analysis into those gains and losses that derive from operating activities and those that result from changes in the value of those assets and liabilities that are held on a continuing basis for use in the entity's business'.[270] Consequently, the ASB believes that gains and losses on those assets and liabilities that are held on a continuing basis primarily in order to enable the entity's operations to be carried out, should be reported in the statement of total recognised gains and losses, and not in the profit and loss account, and all other gains and losses are reported in the profit and loss account.

Set out below is a simple illustration of how the ASB's proposed model would work in practice:

Performance measurement based on balance sheet net assets

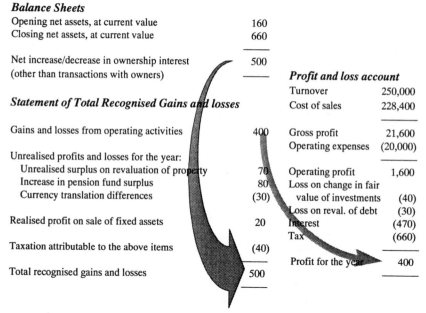

Balance Sheets

Opening net assets, at current value	160
Closing net assets, at current value	660
Net increase/decrease in ownership interest	500
(other than transactions with owners)	

Statement of Total Recognised Gains and losses

Gains and losses from operating activities	400
Unrealised profits and losses for the year:	
Unrealised surplus on revaluation of property	70
Increase in pension fund surplus	80
Currency translation differences	(30)
Realised profit on sale of fixed assets	20
Taxation attributable to the above items	(40)
Total recognised gains and losses	500

Profit and loss account

Turnover	250,000
Cost of sales	228,400
Gross profit	21,600
Operating expenses	(20,000)
Operating profit	1,600
Loss on change in fair	
value of investments	(40)
Loss on reval. of debt	(30)
Interest	(470)
Tax	(660)
Profit for the year	400

This illustrates how total financial performance is measured by reference to changes in balance sheet net assets (other than those which relate to transactions with owners), and that the profit and loss account is relegated to being a subsidiary analysis of gains and losses that derive from operating activities.

5.8   Chapter 7: The reporting entity

Chapter 7 defines the reporting entity as being 'the entity that is the subject of a given set of financial statements'.[271] Whether or not an entity falls under this requirement depends on what the chapter terms 'the demand condition' and 'the supply condition'. The 'demand condition' exists 'if there are potential users with a legitimate interest who rely on such statements as a major source of financial information about the entity', whilst to be able to supply useful financial statements, 'an entity must be a cohesive economic unit, usually resulting from a unified control structure' (the supply condition).[272]

The chapter explores the effect on an entity of its interests in other entities and how this is reflected to give relevant information to users of both its individual and consolidated financial statements. In so doing, it discusses different kinds of investments (from the passive investment to the subsidiary) in the context of the range of different relationships that can exist between the investor and investee (from limited influence to total influence).

The chapter describes control as being 'the highest degree of influence that an investor can have over its investee'[273] and defines control as being 'the power to direct'.[274] It goes on to say that 'to have control, whether of assets or of other entities, an entity must have both of the following abilities:

(a)   the ability to deploy the economic resources, or direct the entities; and

(b)   the ability to ensure that any resulting benefits accrue to itself (with corresponding exposure to losses) and to restrict the access of others to those benefits'.[275]

Chapter 7 then focuses its attention on consolidated financial statements and discusses the main two opposing perspectives for accounting for subsidiaries, namely the proprietary approach and the entity approach. It then looks at changes in the reporting entity in the context of mergers and acquisitions, and ends with a discussion of the inclusion of associates and joint ventures in consolidated financial statements. In so doing, it compares equity accounting with proportional consolidation and rejects proportional consolidation as an acceptable method of incorporating associates into consolidated financial statements.[276] In the case of joint ventures, the chapter suggests that proportional consolidation is acceptable only in cases where 'each venturer has its own separate interest in the risks and rewards that derive either from its particular share of the fixed assets of the venture, or by its having a distinct share of the output or service of the joint venture and, in many cases, of its financing'.[277]

5.9   Overall assessment of the ASB's Draft Statement of Principles

The aim of the ASB in trying to articulate clearly the principles inherent in financial reporting is laudable, but our overall view is that its Draft *Statement of Principles* does not achieve this and that the project therefore needs to start again. Particularly contentious are the aspects of the principles which seek to:

■   supplant the established accounting process, whereby transactions are allocated to accounting periods by reference to the matching and prudence concepts, with recognition tests based on assets and liabilities;

■   phase out historical costs in favour of current values; and

■   elevate the statement of total recognised gains and losses as a performance
    statement and correspondingly diminish the importance of the profit and
    loss account.

More generally, the real purpose of the Draft Statement is unclear: it is neither a
convincing description of the principles that presently underlie accounting
practice, nor is it a persuasive manifesto for change. Many of its supposed
principles seem more like assertions that are designed to correspond to the
ASB's plans for particular projects. At the same time, many of the true
principles of financial reporting are inadequately dealt with or omitted
altogether.

5.9.1 . Recognition tests

The Draft *Statement of Principles* seeks to build accounting around its new
definitions of assets and liabilities and proposed criteria for recognising them in
the balance sheet. This approach would replace the long-established accounting
process in use throughout the world, whereby transactions are allocated to
accounting periods by reference to the matching and prudence concepts. It is
most unlikely to work well in practice.

The fundamental problem is the way in which the Draft *Statement of Principles*
views the accounting process. Assets and liabilities do not form the natural
starting point for devising recognition rules; the real building blocks which
underlie accounting practice are transactions, to which are applied criteria for
revenue and expense recognition, the balance sheet being a result of this
process, not the starting point. The balance sheet provides only a snapshot
which artificially 'freezes' the action of a business which is in fact continuous.
Under the going concern concept, the items in the balance sheet should reflect a
long-term perspective of what are long-term activities, which demands an
allocative approach — this is relevant to topics such as depreciation, pension
cost accounting and so on. Furthermore, the balance sheet can never hope to
capture all the aspects of a company's value: it is simply beyond the reach of
financial reporting to do so. A more realistic ambition is to analyse the
company's transactions so as to measure the further instalment of profit or loss
that it should fairly report as a result of a further year of activity. Empirically,
this is the reality of the accounting process as it has developed to date.

Even though equivalent frameworks elsewhere in the world also suggest a
balance sheet approach, these documents do not correspond to the reality of the
accounting process in those countries. If the (equivalent) approach in the
FASB's concepts were actually applied in the US, for example, the extensive
literature on revenue recognition in that country would be redundant.

To summarise, we consider that the recognition criteria proposed in the Draft
Statement of Principles appear to be a distortion of the real recognition rules
which accountants throughout the world and the ASB itself use and which are in

fact transaction based. Devising rules for accounting based on what assets and liabilities materialise from the transaction may be conceptually 'clean' but in practice, in anything but the most straightforward cases, it simply does not provide the concepts with which to address practical situations. Accounting in real life is essentially an allocative process in which transactions are allocated to appropriate accounting periods. Although the conventions for doing so need to be developed further, it seems likely that this will remain a more workable approach than recognition criteria based on assets and liabilities.

5.9.2   *Historical cost replaced by current values*

The Draft *Statement of Principles* contains a principle that effectively requires historical costs to be replaced by current values if there is evidence that the value has changed to a measurable degree,[278] and more generally says that practice should develop by evolving in the direction of the greater use of current values, based on their supposedly greater relevance than historical costs. This assertion is not backed by any evidence. However, this does not mean that nobody should use current values in appropriate cases, and financial instruments might well be a suitable candidate; but this should not be extrapolated into a general rule for all classes of assets and liabilities. There is no great demand from either users or preparers for such a system. In fact, considerable opposition was expressed by the UK accounting establishment in their responses to the ASB's Draft *Statement of Principles*.

Although the Draft *Statement of Principles* acknowledges that reliability of valuations is a potential constraint, this is obviously not thought to be a serious enough obstacle to prevent the Board from proposing a progressive move to a current value system. For example, reference is made to the development of markets, as a justification for the view that the realisation of profits is becoming of minor importance. In practice, it is unlikely that markets in most business assets will develop to a degree that justifies this posture. Many businesses rely increasingly on the exploitation of assets that are specialised or even unique, and often intangible; it is unrealistic to think that it will be possible to obtain market values for such assets. Indeed, even now the valuations of some supposedly marketable tangible assets often turn out to be based on market transactions that are only hypothetical; the values assigned are really only a capitalisation of future expected earnings. This risks muddling the asset itself with the business in which it is employed, so as to include intangible elements in the amounts disclosed for tangible assets.

However, even supposing support for some form of current value system, the proposals as drafted appear to be a somewhat self-contradictory mix of ideas drawn from various such systems. Thus, the Draft *Statement of Principles* defines a gain as an increase in the excess of assets over liabilities. This means that if the assets and liabilities are measured at current values any increase in these values are gains. This is peculiar, for the document advocates replacement cost as the usual current value to be adopted, but an increase in the cost of replacement of assets is not usually perceived as a gain. This is true even in developed systems such as current cost accounting, under which it is not a gain but an adjustment to maintain the capital of the reporting entity and thereby eliminate gains from historical cost profits.

This is where the Draft *Statement of Principles* lacks coherence – these revaluation movements are to be taken, as gains and losses, to what is said to be a performance statement. This might be more appropriate to a system based on realisable values (as proposed in the ICAS study, *Making Corporate Reports Valuable*), but this is not what is advocated, and even then its relevance in relation to core assets, which in practice will be used in the business rather than sold, is doubtful. The problem really stems from the definition of a gain, which according to the Draft *Statement of Principles* is balance sheet determined. A workable definition of a gain in a current value system is more easily achieved by adopting a profit and loss account focus.

There are circumstances where current values may have their uses and might assist users by being given as supplementary information. For example, such disclosures might be particularly suited to the Operating and Financial Review, which would also give the opportunity to put the valuations in context and explain their inherent subjectivity, perhaps by presenting the valuation information with ranges of outcomes, sensitivities and assumptions. There is a good case for marking to market certain financial instruments, although we see this as a revenue recognition issue, not primarily as a matter of valuation. But it is unlikely that the usefulness of accounts will be improved by removing the fundamental bedrock of historical cost. There is no great user demand for such a move; historical cost accounts are intelligible to users and have an entirely legitimate claim to relevance. In the absence of any obvious demand for current values, we believe that the Board should refrain from imposing the costs of a move towards their greater use. It should at least be incumbent on the Board to prove that any (so far unspecified) benefits are worth the cost and disruption that would inevitably result.

5.9.3 *Statement of total recognised gains and losses (STRGL)*

In the view of many commentators, the proposals for the STRGL would damage the integrity and usefulness of the profit and loss account, to the detriment of financial reporting. The STRGL is meant to assume a much greater significance than it has now, at the expense of the profit and loss account. The promotion in importance of the STRGL is justified in the Draft *Statement of Principles* by the following two assertions:

- that the importance of the distinction between realised and unrealised profits can and should be discarded;

■   that a meaningful split can be made between those gains and losses
      relating to long-term assets and liabilities and operating gains and losses,
      and these should be dealt with in different (and exclusive) performance
      statements.

Existing accounting practice focuses on measuring the further instalment of
profit or loss that a company should report as a result of a further year of
activity. The concept of realisation has an important function in that task,
because it establishes a qualitative threshold that profit must satisfy before it can
be reported. This concept should not be lightly abandoned.

Of course, the definition of what is a realised profit is sometimes problematic
and attempts by the ASB to clarify the interpretation of this term are welcome.
In particular, many would agree that literal interpretations of words such as
'readily convertible into cash', have become outmoded and that a broader
definition is needed, especially to take account of the development of markets in
financial instruments.

5.9.4   *The overall purpose of the Statement of Principles*

Apart from specific reservations about the matters discussed above, there are
also more general concerns about the Draft *Statement of Principles* itself and the
approach that it has taken, since it does not adequately acknowledge the legal
and business context in which accounting is practised and the constraints
thereby placed on it. The objective of financial statements is said to be to
provide information about the financial position, performance and financial
adaptability of an enterprise that is useful to a wide range of users for assessing
the stewardship of management and for making economic decisions. But this
definition is then gradually narrowed.   Assessing the stewardship of
management as an objective is quickly defined out of existence, because it too is
apparently only done to make economic decisions; the wide range of users is
collapsed down to the providers of risk capital – shareholders;   and the
economic decisions to be taken are based on an evaluation of cash generation.
The objective of financial statements, therefore, becomes to predict future cash
flows.

This tenet is the fundamental assumption in an established branch of academic
thought.   As an aid to academic thought and research it is a helpful
simplification.   As the basis for regulatory endeavour, however, it is not
appropriate. Accounts do not, in fact, exist primarily to predict cash flows for
investment decisions; they form a report by the stewards of an enterprise to its
owners, and they sit within a legal and social context that cannot simply be
ignored. They also fulfil a variety of other roles, including the identification of
profits available for dividend; a starting point for the assessment of taxation
(particularly in the light of recent tax cases that have enhanced the importance of
accounting rules); a reference point that can be used for conditions in contracts

with lenders and other parties; the calculation of executive directors' performance bonuses, and so on.

This means that the ASB will not be able to follow the implications of the Draft *Statement of Principles* in practice since there are a variety of other factors, practical and theoretical (such as company law), which it will have to consider in drafting its regulatory proposals. It is thus not an agenda and not all of the guiding influences over the Board's work are discussed. Even the Board's recent proposals on Provisions, Tax and Pension Costs are all at variance with it to some degree. Accordingly, the Draft *Statement of Principles* is left in a vacuum, as an abstraction which cannot fulfil its stated objectives.

There appear to be a number of inconsistencies within the Draft *Statement of Principles*. For example, having asserted that what matters is future cash flow prediction, the Draft *Statement of Principles* then largely ignores this crucial test by repeatedly claiming only that things are or are not 'relevant' to users. Within the context of the framework what this must mean is whether or not these things have predictive value. But this is not put to the test. There is no evidence marshalled, for example, to support the assertion that a historical cost system suffers from a lack of 'relevance' nor that the most important advantage of current values is their relevance to users. This is an absolutely central failing of the Draft *Statement of Principles*. It does not attempt to show that the information it is recommending is the subject of user demand and that users are being disadvantaged by not being in possession of it. This leaves the unfortunate impression that the Draft *Statement of Principles* is in fact a rationalisation of practices which the Board has already decided are superior.

The subliminal message of the Draft *Statement of Principles* as currently drafted is that there are certain fundamental accounting truths which are at present unacceptable to the business community but which through an evolutionary or educational process will become so. This is a difficult position for the ASB to maintain openly, as it implies the Board has insights that others do not possess. The regulatory tradition in the UK has long been that of codifying best practice. This is a good tradition and one which has many safety features, even if it is not as revolutionary as some would like. Many support this tradition and, in their responses to the Draft *Statement of Principles*, urged the Board not to regard accounts as inherently unsatisfactory because they do not measure up to an abstract and rather theoretical benchmark.

At the same time, it is perplexing that the Draft *Statement of Principles* excludes several concepts which the accounting community at large would regard as fundamental. In particular, prudence and accruals are all but ignored, the importance of realised profits is dismissed, the relevance of the going concern concept is not discussed, and historical costs are dismissed as not relevant.

5.10   The reaction of respondents to the ASB's Draft Statement of Principles

The ASB's Draft *Statement of Principles* attracted an unusually large response and considerable criticism when it was published for comment in November 1995. Discussion and debate was stimulated by Ernst and Young's paper – *The ASB's Framework: Time to Decide* – published in February 1996 (which was severely criticised in its turn by the ASB chairman). There was a substantial amount of coverage of the issues in the national and trade press. However, given that the Draft sought to alter the most fundamental of accounting methods and reporting practices, the record 175 responses sent to the ASB should not have been surprising. As a consequence of the responses received, the Draft *Statement of Principles* has been withdrawn for further work by the ASB (see 5.11 below).

A detailed analysis of the responses has been carried out by two UK academics, Professor G. J. Wilkinson-Riddle and Ms L. Holland of De Montfort University.[279] Their paper analyses the responses quantitatively and also includes a qualitative review of them in the light of the common themes that emerged. It concludes that, far from being complacent about accounting regulation, those involved with UK financial reporting are aware that principles are necessary; but are concerned that changes of a fundamental nature do not take place without being practical, coherent, justified and with the informed consent of all those concerned with preparing, auditing and using accounting information.[280]

The following table summarises the 175 respondents' views:[281]

Response Type:	All responses	Number of respondents expressing this view	% of 175 respondents
1	A statement is in principle a good idea	68	39%
2	This SOP is acceptable	12	7%
3	This SOP is not acceptable	134	77%
4	Current values/discounting not acceptable	125	71%
5	Current values/discounting acceptable	9	5%
6	Cash aspects not adequate	12	7%
7	Presentation of SOP inadequate	46	26%
8	Information overload for users	10	6%
9	New concepts not acceptable	12	7%
10	Do not abandon established concepts	82	47%
11	STRGL not viable	51	29%
12	Goodwill treatment inadequate	16	9%
13	Overwhelming practical problems	60	34%
14	Downgrading of P&L not acceptable	71	41%
15	New definitions inadequate	39	22%
16	Recognition/realisation criteria inadequate	39	22%
Total no. of summarised points recorded		786	

It is immediately clear from this table that the vast majority of respondents to the Draft expressed an essentially critical view of the ASB proposals, and it is for this reason that the ASB has announced that its next step 'will be to issue a revised draft of the *Statement of Principles* that addresses the substantive points raised by the comment letters'.[282]

5.11 The ASB's response to the criticism

Having received such an overwhelmingly negative response to its proposals, the ASB faced a dilemma: it wished to pursue its agenda, yet it did not have a mandate to do so on the basis of the Draft *Statement of Principles*. Consequently, in July 1996, the ASB published a paper in an attempt to counter the widespread criticism that it had received.[283] In this paper – *Statement of Principles for Financial Reporting: the way ahead* – the ASB attempted to redeem its position by asserting that criticism of the Draft stemmed largely from 'serious misunderstandings', some of which had been 'expressed by those who apparently had not actually read the draft itself'.[284]

Unfortunately, though, the ASB's paper is not a satisfactory response to the many criticisms which had been levelled at the Draft. For one thing, it trivialises some of the concerns which had been expressed and, in so doing, avoids dealing with them in any satisfactory way. For example, the Board dismisses the criticism of its proposed balance sheet approach by stating that its intention 'is simply to add a measure of discipline to the recording of transactions'.[285] Similarly, the Board side-steps the criticism that had been levelled at the practical issues surrounding the statement of total recognised gains and losses, by merely stating that 'the Board accepts that there should be fuller discussion of the role of the STRGL'.[286]

In any event, the ASB concluded that it would 'not be appropriate to proceed directly to the development of a final document',[287] and that it planned to issue a revised exposure draft in 1997. However, at the time of writing (August 1997), it is not certain that the ASB will be able to keep to that timetable. This leaves the unfortunate impression that, instead, the ASB is already entrenching into several accounting standards (for example, FRS 3 and FRS 5) and proposed standards (for example on provisions) a conceptual approach which has no general agreement and which is still only at an early stage of development and discussion. The danger of this is that the Draft *Statement of Principles* will eventually have to be adopted as final with little or no changes in substance − because to do otherwise will undermine existing accounting standards by removing their theoretical justification.

5.12   Discounting in Financial Reporting

In April 1997 the ASB issued a 'Working Paper' on discounting in financial reporting. The ASB points out that the Working Paper is not a prelude to a future FRS on the topic, and that the decision on whether discounting will be prescribed in any particular circumstance will form part of the development of the relevant Standard. As a result, the Working Paper is described as being 'for the Board's own reference as the Board considers discounting within various projects'.[288]

The ASB states that, in preparing the paper, it has drawn extensively on the research of the FASB in this area (see 3.6 above). It is indeed broadly similar to, but unfortunately no more convincing than, the FASB's equivalent document.

The problem is that the Board has not examined the issue of discounting at a fundamental level. Before looking at specific cases, there is the need to address more general issues. For example, where do interest costs fit into the overall framework of financial reporting? This affects matters such as interest capitalisation and imputed interest, dividends and the distinction between different stakeholders.

Instead, the paper starts with no particular objectives, meanders around the subject of discounting and comes to its conclusions rather abruptly. In fact, the only real conclusion that the paper reaches is that it 'has shown that discounting future cash flows to reflect the time value of money and the effect of the variability of the cash flows is consistent with both historical cost and current value bases of accounting'.[289] However, this comes to the reader of the paper as a bolt from the blue, since there has been no real indication that this was where the paper was leading. This is because the paper is really just a rationalisation of what the ASB wants to do on some of its current projects, such as impairment, provisions and pension liabilities. As a result, the paper includes statements such as: 'discounting is, therefore, a useful tool in accounting measurements'.[290] The paper does devote some time to discussing the issue of risk, but it does so in the context of specific projects such as pensions and provisions.

Moreover, what the paper does not adequately consider is that discounting is not just a balance sheet issue, it affects profit and loss measurement as well whenever cash flows are separated from accruals of income or expenses – for example, the measurement of profit where assets are sold on deferred terms. Furthermore, even in addressing discounting in the context of accounting for environmental liabilities, the paper does not deal with issues such as accounting for abandonment costs, or explain why the balance sheet approach of recognising a discounted liability is preferable to the generally accepted unit of production approach. It is therefore not clear why the ASB believes that entities should be required to record interest on the accretion of a liability in circumstances where no cash is borrowed.

All in all, the ASB's paper adds little to existing knowledge and seems more of a rationalisation of the ASB's current agenda.

6   OTHER INTERNATIONAL FRAMEWORK PROJECTS

The last ten years have seen what might be viewed as a renewed vigour amongst various standard-setting bodies around the world towards seeking an acceptable framework for financial reporting. Each body might have its own reason for doing so, but it is clear that the accounting profession world-wide has come under increasing pressure both as a result of the imprecision of existing accounting standards, and through not being able to respond promptly and effectively to emerging issues, such as off balance sheet finance and asset revaluations. However, as shown throughout this chapter, these recent attempts at developing a framework largely restate the same broad principles that have been repeated over the years, often comprising no more than a précis of previous studies, particularly those of the FASB. The only radically different approach is found in the discussion document issued by the ICAS[291] (see 4.6 above).

6.1   The IASC conceptual framework

In May 1988, the IASC issued an exposure draft – *Framework for the Preparation and Presentation of Financial Statements* – which set out its understanding of 'the conceptual framework that underlies the preparation and presentation of financial statements'.[292]   This was converted without major change into a final statement in September 1989, although it is stressed within the statement that it will be revised from time to time in the light of the Board's experience in working with it.[293]   The statement is not an accounting standard and does not override any specific IAS;[294] it therefore has much the same status as the FASB's concepts statements.

On first reading the IASC Framework statement, one might be forgiven for thinking that it is merely an encapsulation of the FASB's six concepts statements; indeed, it is likely that the IASC, quite understandably, used the FASB project as a basis for its study. This might explain why it contains very much the same basic flaws as there are in the FASB's framework and which are discussed at 3 above. Furthermore, the impression that the statement creates is that the IASC has attempted to justify the status quo; in other words, it appears to have tried to make the proposed framework consistent with current external financial reporting practice. This is evidenced, for example, by the statement in the introduction to the effect that financial statements normally include a balance sheet, a profit and loss statement, a statement of changes in financial position and notes;[295] the statement is then devoted to applying its 'framework' to this traditional financial reporting package, without, for example, following the ICAS approach of considering the possibility of an entirely new package.

The Framework statement begins well, with a lucid exposition of the nature and purposes of financial statements and their qualitative characteristics. However, it then moves into describing the various elements of financial statements and the criteria for their recognition; although this is clearly a difficult area, it has not been dealt with convincingly. Thereafter, the statement loses its impetus altogether and deals with the measurement of these elements in a mere three paragraphs, only noting that a number of possibilities exist, including historical cost, current cost, realisable value and present value.[296]

The fundamental problem with this framework (as with the FASB's framework) is that we do not believe that it is possible to develop general purpose rules on the recognition of elements of financial statements, whilst simultaneously leaving open the questions of how they are to be measured and against what capital maintenance yardstick profit is to be determined. Furthermore, the statement has similar problems to SFAC No. 6 in its definitions of assets and liabilities, with the result that certain traditionally recognised assets and liabilities would be disqualified from appearing in the balance sheet. The statement specifically says that 'the application of the matching concept under this framework does not allow the recognition of items in the balance sheet which do not meet the definition of assets and liabilities';[297] consequent practical effects could include the immediate recognition in income of government grants as they are received, pension cost variations as soon as they are identified, and so on. The effect of this would be to change fundamentally the relationship between the profit and loss account and the balance sheet in the same manner that the ASB has attempted to do in its conceptual framework project.

We do not suggest that any one system is necessarily superior to another, but it is not possible to fit all possible systems of accounting into one framework of rules on the elements of financial statements and their recognition. We believe that lack of clarity on this point has led to constant confusion on accounting concepts, where ideas which belong in discrete methodologies are used interchangeably and lead to a mish-mash that lacks any cohesion. It should be the role of a conceptual framework study to unravel this tangle, but in this respect at least we believe that this document simply compounds the confusion by failing to distinguish the essential features which make different approaches mutually incompatible. We therefore hope that, in considering the applicability of the statement in the course of its future work, the IASC finds it possible to differentiate the features of alternative approaches which require the development of distinct rules on identification and recognition of the individual elements. Unfortunately, though, recent proposals issued by the IASC on matters such as provisions and employee benefits do not encourage one to believe that it has been able to achieve this.

6.2   The CICA financial statement concepts

In December 1988, the CICA *Handbook* Section 1000 – *Financial Statement Concepts* – was issued, describing the concepts underlying the development and use of accounting principles in the general purpose financial statements.[298] It is anticipated that the concepts will be used 'by preparers of financial statements and accounting practitioners in exercising their professional judgment as to the application of generally accepted accounting principles and in establishing accounting policies in areas in which accounting principles are developing'.[299] However, nothing in Section 1000 overrides any specific recommendation in any other Section of the CICA *Handbook*, or any other accounting principle considered to be generally accepted.[300]

In fact, both the form and content of Section 1000 are very similar to the IASC's framework, dealing with the objective of financial statements, qualitative characteristics, elements of financial statements, recognition criteria and measurement in much the same way. The definitions of assets and liabilities are almost identical in the two pronouncements and, although it discusses various measurement bases, Section 1000 also does not establish standards for particular measurement or disclosure issues.[301]

6.3   The New Zealand framework

The 'Framework for Financial Reporting in New Zealand' consists of the Statement of Concepts for General Purpose Financial Reporting, the Framework for Differential Reporting, the Explanatory Foreword to General Purpose Financial Reporting and FRS-2 – *Presentation of Financial Reports*. The

Statement of Concepts became operative for periods commencing on or after
1 January 1995, the Framework for Differential Reporting was effective from
1 February 1994 (and was revised in April 1997), and the Explanatory Foreword
became operative in January 1995. The purpose of FRS-2 is to build on the
Statement of Concepts by establishing a framework for the information to be
presented in general purpose financial reports.

The key elements of this framework that are relevant to this Chapter are as
follows:

6.3.1   Statement of Concepts

The heart of the framework lies in the Statement of Concepts. It covers the
objectives of general purpose financial reporting, the qualitative characteristics
by which the usefulness of financial reports should be measured, the
assumptions underlying the preparation of financial reports, the influences on
the preparation of financial reports, the definition and recognition of the
elements of financial statements and the measurement of the elements.

In discussing the objectives of financial reporting, the Statement acknowledges
that they lie balanced between two roles: an accountability role (providing
information to external parties on the entity's financial and service performance
and its compliance with relevant legal requirements) as well as the more familiar
informative/decision-usefulness role (providing information to external parties
to assist them in making decisions about providing resources to or doing
business with the reporting entity).

The Statement then goes on to describe the qualitative characteristics for general
purpose financial reports in much the same terms as other frameworks –
particularly that of the US, SFAC No. 2 – focusing on relevance,
understandability, reliability and comparability as the primary characteristics.
As do other frameworks, the Statement also acknowledges the trade-offs which
exist between qualitative characteristics. It also discusses the cost/benefit issue,
noting that the benefits derived from information should exceed the cost of
providing it.

The Statement defines the elements of financial statements in essentially the
same way as in most other framework documents, with the definitions of assets
and liabilities providing the building blocks on which the other definitions are
based. Assets are defined as service potential or future economic benefits
controlled by the entity as a result of past transactions or other past events, and
an asset is recognised when it is probable that the service potential or future
economic benefits embodied in the asset will eventuate and the asset possesses a
cost or other value that can be measured with reliability. Liabilities are defined
as present obligations to sacrifice future service potential or future economic
benefits to other entities as a result of past transactions or other past events, and
a liability is recognised when it is probable that the future sacrifice of service

potential or future economic benefits will be required and the liability can be measured with reliability.

A significant point in relation to these recognition criteria is that the term 'probable' is defined as an event being more likely than less likely to occur. Therefore if there is more than a 50% chance of future economic benefits eventuating, and it can be reliably measured, the financial element (e.g. asset or liability) should be recognised.

Like the IASC framework, the Statement only lists the range of possible approaches to the measurement of elements and the choice of capital maintenance concepts. What is noteworthy, though, is that the original Exposure Draft advocated the introduction of a new financial statement – to be termed a Statement of Changes in Financial Wealth – which was not too dissimilar to the statement of total recognised gains and losses found in the UK. However, this proposal has been toned down in the Statement, which now requires that all valuations be recognised in either the statement of financial performance or a new statement of movements in equity.

6.3.2 Differential Reporting

The other aspect of the framework most worthy of comment here is the Framework for Differential Reporting. The purpose of differential reporting is to allow entities which meet specified criteria (defined as 'qualifying entities') to be exempted, in part or in full, from specific financial reporting standards. The Framework sets out the criteria by which entities qualify for differential reporting exemptions. In so doing, it implicitly provides a guide to standard-setters on establishing differential reporting exemptions in respect of future financial reporting standards. Perhaps not surprisingly, the Framework applies only to general purpose financial reports, since special purpose financial reports are tailored to meet the specific information needs of particular users.

An entity is defined as a qualifying entity and will therefore qualify for differential reporting exemptions when it does not have public accountability and:

- at balance sheet date all of its owners are members of the entity's governing body; or
- the entity is not large.

The Framework regards an entity as large if it exceeds any two of the following:

- total revenue of $5.0 million;
- total assets of $2.5 million;
- full time equivalent, paid employees.

These size criteria were amended in April 1997.

Whilst the Institute of Chartered Accountants of New Zealand's work on differential reporting is to be commended, it is unfortunate that a size test has been introduced as one of the qualifying criteria. In our view, the heart of differential reporting lies in the relationship between owners and managers, since the information needs of owner/managers are entirely different from those of external owners, irrespective of the size of the entity. Consequently, there can be little conceptual justification for differential reporting to be governed by size of entity.

6.3.3   Explanatory Foreword

The Explanatory Foreword sets out the context for the statements which follow, explaining the relationship between general purpose financial reports, the Statement of Concepts and Financial Reporting Standards (FRSs). It explains that general purpose financial reports are financial reports which are intended to provide information to meet the needs of external users who are unable to require, or contract for, the preparation of special reports to meet their specific information needs. Again, as is the case in Australia, the distinction between general purpose financial reports and special reports is important in a reporting environment which recognises differential reporting.

7   CONCLUSION

The aims of this Chapter have been twofold: first, we have attempted to provide an outline of the immense amount of energy that has been expended (both on the part of individuals and on the part of specifically constituted committees) in attempting to establish an agreed conceptual framework for financial reporting; second, in so doing, we have highlighted the irreconcilable differences that exist in the various accounting theories that have developed over the years. We see little prospect of general agreement ever being reached on issues such as entry values vs. exit values or the primacy of the balance sheet vs. the profit and loss account. The fact that these differences are irreconcilable is the very reason why we believe that it will not be possible to develop a single generally accepted general purpose accounting model.

However, this does not mean that the search should be abandoned; what it does mean is that an agreed conceptual framework might have to incorporate more than one accounting model so that different users can be furnished with different information appropriate to their various objectives and information needs. This would not necessarily involve supplying less financial information to individual user groups; rather it would mean making sure that each user group has all the information it needs for its investment and other decisions.

That having been said, we believe that historical cost accounting should continue to be the primary basis for UK financial reporting, as it will continue to be in the US. Whilst we do not dispute that users might find current value information about certain assets and liabilities useful, we think that such information should be provided in supplementary form in the operating and financial review, where users would be provided with detailed assumptions, sensitivities and ranges of values. This is because the subjectivity and potential volatility which would necessarily be inherent in the widespread use of current values would seriously undermine the reliability of the financial statements.

We are far from ignorant of the views of analysts and other users regarding the usefulness of current values. However, we are also aware of the fact that users wish to retain the current historical cost model since it provides information that is reliable because the amounts are based on market transactions. The vehicle of disclosure, therefore, should be used so as to offer financial analysts the opportunity to use current values.

We are also well aware of the international dimension to the capital markets and the drive to accounting harmonisation. However, that does not detract from the fact that it is the function of the markets, not accountants, to value companies. Users want a stable, reliable and consistent platform to establish historical trends and on which to base their own predictions about the future. We fully support the provision of current value information where it helps to enhance the decision usefulness of financial reporting; however, we believe that such information should, in the main, be provided on a supplementary basis. There are circumstances in which current value accounting may be appropriate — but only in particular cases, not for the generality of companies.

References

1 Discussion Paper, *Measurement of tangible fixed assets*, ASB, October 1996, para. 6.21.
2 *Ibid.*, para. 6.6.
3 For a full discussion on the politicisation of accounting see: David Solomons, 'The Politicization of Accounting', *Journal of Accountancy*, November 1978, p. 71.
4 W. A. Paton and A. C. Littleton, *An Introduction to Corporate Accounting Standards*, Monograph No. 3, American Accounting Association, 1940.
5 See, for example: American Accounting Association, Executive Committee, 'A Tentative Statement of Accounting Principles Affecting Corporate Reports', *Accounting Review*, June 1936, pp. 187–191; American Accounting Association, Executive Committee, 'Accounting Principles Underlying Corporate Financial Statements', *Accounting Review*, June 1941, pp. 133–139; American Accounting Association, Committee to Prepare a Statement of Basic Accounting Theory, *A Statement of Basic Accounting Theory*, 1966; American Accounting Association, Committee on Concepts and Standards for External Financial Reports, *Statement on Accounting Theory and Theory Acceptance*, 1977. The 1977 report concluded that closure on the debate was not feasible, which is perhaps indicative of the complexity of the problem.
6 David Solomons, 'The Political Implications of Accounting and Accounting Standard Setting', *Being the third Arthur Young Lecture delivered within the University of Glasgow on 22nd October, 1980*, p. 9.
7 ASC, *Setting Accounting Standards: A Consultative document*.

8 *Ibid.*, para. 7.2.
9 *Ibid.*
10 *Ibid.*, para. 7.7.
11 *Ibid.*, p. 47.
12 *Ibid.*
13 ASC, *Submissions on the Accounting Standards Committee's Consultative Document: Setting Accounting Standards*, in two volumes, ASC, 1979.
14 *Ibid.*, Volume I, p. 270.
15 Maurice Moonitz, *The Basic Postulates of Accounting*, Accounting Research Study No. 1, AICPA, 1961, Preface.
16 *Ibid.*
17 Robert T. Sprouse and Maurice Moonitz, *A Tentative Set of Broad Accounting Principles for Business Enterprises*, Accounting Research Study No. 3, AICPA, 1962.
18 *Ibid.*, p. 14.
19 *Ibid.*, p. 27.
20 APB Statement No. 4, *Basic Concepts and Accounting Principles Underlying Financial Statements of Business Enterprises*, AICPA, October 1970.
21 *Ibid.*, para. 3.
22 *Ibid.*, para. 132.
23 Report of the Study Group on the Objectives of Financial Statements, *Objectives of Financial Statements*, AICPA, October 1973, p. 65.
24 *Ibid.*
25 *Ibid.*
26 Report of the Study Group on the Objectives of Financial Statements, *Objectives of Financial Statements*, AICPA, October 1973.
27 *Ibid.*, p. 13.
28 *Ibid.*, pp. 57–60.
29 FASB Discussion Memorandum, *Conceptual Framework for Accounting and Reporting: Consideration of the Report of the Study Group on the Objectives of Financial Statements*, FASB, June 6, 1974.
30 FASB, *Scope and Implications of the Conceptual Framework Project*, FASB, December 2, 1976.
31 *Ibid.*, p. 5.
32 *Ibid.*, p. 2.
33 *Ibid.*, pp. 5 and 6.
34 Proposed Statement of Financial Accounting Concepts, *Using Cash Flow Information in Accounting Measurements*, FASB, June 11, 1997.
35 SFAC No. 1, *Objectives of Financial Reporting by Business Enterprises*, FASB, November 1978, para. 7.
36 *Ibid.*, para. 9.
37 *Ibid.*, para. 24.
38 *Ibid.*, para. 34.
39 *Ibid.*, para. 37.
40 *Ibid.*, para. 24.
41 *Ibid.*, footnote 6.
42 Lucia S. Chang and Kenneth S. Most, *Financial Statements and Investment Decisions*, Miami: Florida International University, 1979.
43 *Ibid.*, p. 33.
44 SFAC 1, para. 43.
45 *Ibid.*, para. 50.
46 *Ibid.*, para. 51.
47 SFAC No. 2, *Qualitative Characteristics of Accounting Information*, FASB, May 1980, Figure 1.
48 SFAC 1, para. 34.
49 SFAC 2, para. 36.
50 *Ibid.*, p. x.
51 *Ibid.*, para. 90.
52 *Ibid.*, p. xi.
53 *Ibid.*, para. 56.

54 *Ibid.*
55 *Ibid.*, para. 51.
56 *Ibid.*, p. xvi.
57 *Ibid.*
58 *Ibid.*, para. 59.
59 *Ibid.*, paras. 91–97.
60 *Ibid.*, para. 93.
61 *Ibid.*, para. 95.
62 SFAC No. 6, *Elements of Financial Statements*, a replacement of FASB Concepts Statement No. 3, FASB, December 1985, para. 25.
63 *Ibid.*, para. 27.
64 *Ibid.*, para. 28.
65 *Ibid.*, para. 35.
66 *Ibid.*, para. 36.
67 *Ibid:*, para. 49.
68 *Ibid.*, para. 66.
69 *Ibid.*
70 *Ibid.*, para. 67.
71 *Ibid.*, para. 70.
72 SFAC 1, para. 43.
73 SFAC 6, p. 1, footnote 1.
74 *Ibid.*, para. 78.
75 *Ibid.*, para. 80.
76 *Ibid.*, para. 82.
77 *Ibid.*, para. 83.
78 *Ibid.*, para. 77.
79 See, for example, SFAC No. 3, *Elements of Financial Statements of Business Enterprises*, FASB, December 1980, para. 58.
80 SFAC No. 5, *Recognition and Measurement in Financial Statements of Business Enterprises*, FASB, December 1984, para. 66.
81 *Ibid.*, paras. 66–70.
82 *Ibid.*, paras. 45–48.
83 *Ibid.*, para. 58.
84 *Ibid.*, para. 63.
85 *Ibid.*, paras. 33 and 34.
86 *Ibid.*, para. 35.
87 David Solomons, 'The FASB's Conceptual Framework: An Evaluation', *Journal of Accountancy*, June 1986, pp. 114–124, at p. 124.
88 Proposed Statement of Financial Accounting Concepts, *Using Cash Flow Information in Accounting Measurements*, FASB, June 1997, para. 13.
89 *Ibid.*, para. 15.
90 *Ibid.*, para. 16.
91 *Ibid.*, paras. 40 to 48.
92 *Ibid.*, para. 50.
93 *Ibid.*, paras. 51 to 54.
94 *Ibid.*, para. 16.
95 Stephen A. Zeff, *Accounting Horizons*, 'A Perspective on the U.S. Public/Private-Sector Approach to the Regulation of Financial Reporting', Vol. 9 No. 1, March 1995, p. 60.
96 SSAP 2, *Disclosure of accounting policies*, November 1971.
97 *Ibid.*, para. 2.
98 *Ibid.*, para. 14.
99 *Ibid.*
100 CA 85, Sch. 4. paras. 9–13.
101 *Ibid.*, para. 14.
102 SSAP 2, para. 15.
103 *Ibid.*, para. 16.
104 *Ibid.*, para. 18.

105   SSAP 12, *Accounting for depreciation*, para. 21.
106   *The Corporate Report*, A discussion paper published for comment by the Accounting Standards Steering Committee, London, 1975.
107   *Ibid.*, para. 0.1.
108   *Ibid.*, para. 0.2.
109   The committee's recommended package of information which should be contained in the annual corporate reports of business enterprises is listed in Appendix 2 of the discussion paper.
110   *The Corporate Report*, para. 0.3.
111   *Ibid.*, para. 1.1.
112   *Ibid.*, para. 1.8.
113   *Ibid.*, para. 1.9. The seven user groups identified were: (a) the equity investor group, (b) the loan creditor group, (c) the employee group, (d) the analyst-adviser group, (e) the business contact group, (f) the government and (g) the public.
114   *Ibid.*, paras. 2.1–2.40.
115   *Ibid.*, para. 3.2.
116   *Ibid.*, para. 3.3.
117   *Ibid.*, para. 4.30.
118   *Ibid.*, para. 4.40.
119   *Ibid.*, para. 6.56.
120   *Ibid.*, paras. 6.56 and 6.57.
121   *Ibid.*, para. 7.4.
122   *Ibid.*, para. 7.15.
123   *Ibid.*, paras. 7.40 and 7.43.
124   Report of the Inflation Accounting Committee, *Inflation Accounting*, Cmnd. 6225, London: HMSO, 1975, (the Sandilands Report).
125   *Ibid.*, p. iv.
126   *Ibid.*, para. 144.
127   *Ibid.*, Chapter 12.
128   SSAP 7 (Provisional), *Accounting for changes in the purchasing power of money*, May 1974.
129   SSAP 7 recommended that the RPI should be used for this purpose.
130   SSAP 7, para. 12.
131   The Sandilands Report, para. 20.
132   *Ibid.*, para. 422.
133   *Ibid.*, paras. 411 and 412.
134   *Ibid.*, para. 415.
135   Edwards and Bell have made significant contributions in the areas of income determination and value measurement — however, it is beyond the scope of this book to provide a detailed analysis of their theories. Their case for income and value measurement based on replacement costs may be found in their classic work: E. O. Edwards and P. W. Bell, *The Theory and Measurement of Business Income*, University of California Press, 1961.
136   The Sandilands Report, para. 453.
137   *Ibid.*, para. 499.
138   Kenneth MacNeal, *Truth in Accounting*, Philadelphia: University of Pennsylvania Press, 1939.
139   R. J. Chambers, *Accounting, Evaluation and Economic Behaviour*, Prentice-Hall, 1966.
140   R. R. Sterling, *Theory of the Measurement of Enterprise Income*, University of Kansas Press, 1970.
141   R. J. Chambers, *The Design of Accounting Standards*, University of Sydney Accounting Research Centre, Monograph No. 1, 1980.
142   Edward Stamp, 'Does the Chambers' Evidence Support the CoCoA System', *Accounting and Business Research*, Spring 1983, pp. 119–127.
143   *Ibid.*, p. 127.
144   The Sandilands Report, para. 510.
145   The Institute of Chartered Accountants of Scotland, *Making Corporate Reports Valuable*, London: Kogan Page, 1988, paras. 6.20–6.23.
146   Lee has published numerous papers on the subject of cash flow accounting, the ideas of which have been drawn together in his book: Tom Lee, *Cash Flow Accounting*, Wokingham, Van Nostrand Reinhold (UK), 1984.

147 Lawson has published widely on the subject of cash flow accounting — see, for example: G. H. Lawson, 'Cash-flow Accounting', *The Accountant*, October 28th, 1971, pp. 586–589; G. H. Lawson, 'The Measurement of Corporate Profitability on a Cash-flow Basis', *The International Journal of Accounting Education and Research*, Vol. 16, No. 1, pp. 11–46.

148 Tom Lee, *op. cit.*, p. 51.

149 *Ibid.*, pp. 51–52.

150 Lee presents a quantified example of his proposed cash flow reporting system, *Ibid.*, pp. 57–72.

151 The Sandilands Report, para. 518.

152 *Ibid.*, para. 517.

153 *Ibid.*, para. 537.

154 For a detailed discussion of the capital maintenance concepts which apply in the Sandilands proposals, see: H. C. Edey, 'Sandilands and the Logic of Current Cost', *Accounting and Business Research*, Volume 9, No. 35, Summer 1979, pp. 191–200.

155 ASC, ED 24, *Current cost accounting*, para. 6.

156 ASC, *Inflation accounting — an interim recommendation by the Accounting Standards Committee*, November 1977.

157 *Ibid.*, para. 4.

158 ED 24, para. 8.

159 *Ibid.*

160 *Ibid.*, para. 9.

161 SSAP 16, *Current cost accounting*, March 1980.

162 *Ibid.*, para. 48.

163 SFAS No. 33, *Financial Reporting and Changing Prices*, paras. 47–56, *passim*.

164 SFAS No. 89, *Financial Reporting and Changing Prices*, paras. 34, 35 and 40–43, *passim*.

165 SFAC 5, paras. 45–48.

166 In January 1983, the Research Board of the ICAEW initiated a research project into the usefulness of current cost accounting. The research was divided into a number of studies designed to investigate the uses made by different interest groups, the benefits and the costs of current cost accounting; the whole project was undertaken under the control of the ICAEW's then Director of Research, Professor Bryan Carsberg. The project was completed in September 1983 and the results were made available to the ASC to assist with its review of SSAP 16. See: Bryan Carsberg and Michael Page (Joint Editors), *Current Cost Accounting: The Benefits and the Costs*, ICAEW, 1984.

167 Accounting Standards Committee, *Accounting for the effects of changing prices: a Handbook*, ASC, 1986.

168 Richard Macve, *A Conceptual Framework for Financial Accounting and Reporting: the possibilities for an agreed structure*, A report prepared at the request of the Accounting Standards Committee, ICAEW, 1981, Preface, p. 3.

169 *Ibid.*, Chapter 6, *passim*.

170 *Ibid.*, p. 52.

171 *Ibid.*, p. 64.

172 *Ibid.*, p. 91.

173 David Solomons, *Guidelines for Financial Reporting Standards*, A Paper Prepared for The Research Board of the Institute of Chartered Accountants in England and Wales and addressed to the Accounting Standards Committee, ICAEW, 1989, (the Solomons Report).

174 Edward Stamp, *Corporate Reporting: Its Future Evolution*, a research study published by the Canadian Institute of Chartered Accountants, 1980, (the Stamp Report), Ch. 1, para. 3.

175 The Corporate Report, paras. 2.22–2.31.

176 Stamp's proposed user groups were as follows: shareholders, management, long- and short-term creditors, analysts and advisers, employees, non-executive directors, customers, suppliers, industry groups, labour unions, government departments and ministers, the public, regulatory agencies, other companies, standard setters and academic researchers. See the Stamp Report, Table 1, p. 44.

177 Edward Stamp, 'First steps towards a British conceptual framework', *Accountancy*, March 1982, pp. 123–130.

178 Stamp's qualitative criteria were ranked (from most important to least important) by the ASC members as follows (*Ibid.*, Figure 2, p. 126): relevance, clarity, substance over form, timeliness, comparability, materiality, freedom from bias, objectivity, rationality, full disclosure, consistency,

isomorphism, verifiability, cost/benefit effectiveness, non-arbitrariness, data availability, flexibility, uniformity, precision, conservatism.

179   The Stamp Report, Chapter 2.

180   *Ibid.*, Chapter 12.

181   ICAS, *Making Corporate Reports Valuable*, para. 0.2.

182   *Ibid.*, Chapter 8.

183   *Ibid.*, paras. 1.1–1.20, *passim.*

184   *Ibid.*, para. 3.6.

185   *Ibid.*, para. 3.11.

186   The Corporate Report, paras. 2.2–2.8.

187   ICAS, *Making Corporate Reports Valuable*, para. 3.12.

188   *Ibid.*, para. 6.36.

189   *Ibid.*

190   *Ibid.*, para. 6.24.

191   The Institute of Chartered Accountants of Scotland, *Making Corporate Reports Valuable — The Literature Surveys*, ICAS, 1988.

192   *Ibid.*, p. 301.

193   ICAS, *Making Corporate Reports Valuable*, paras. 7.12–7.20, *passim.*

194   *Ibid.*, para. 7.21.

195   *Ibid.*, paras. 7.23–7.26, *passim.*

196   *Ibid.*, paras. 7.27–7.32, *passim.*

197   *Ibid.*, para. 7.35.

198   *Ibid.*, para. 7.39.

199   *Ibid.*, para. 5.44.

200   *Ibid.*, para. 7.54.

201   'Melody plc', ICAS, September 1990.

202   The Institute of Chartered Accountants of Scotland, *Making Corporate Reports Valuable, A Feasibility Study: The Post Office*, Stuart MacDonald (Researcher), Pauline Weetman (Editor), ICAS, November 1993.

203   Report of the Review Committee under the chairmanship of Sir Ronald Dearing, *The Making of Accounting Standards*, September 1988, para. 7.2.

204   David Solomons, *Guidelines for Financial Reporting Standards*, p. 17.

205   *Ibid.*, p. 18.

206   *Ibid.*

207   *Ibid.*, p. 20.

208   *Ibid.*, p. 21.

209   *Ibid.*, pp. 23–28.

210   *Ibid.*, p. 43.

211   *Ibid.*, pp. 51–52.

212   *Ibid.*, p. 53.

213   *Ibid.*

214   *Ibid.*, p. 54.

215   *Ibid.*, p. 55.

216   *Ibid.*, p. 56.

217   *Ibid.*, p. 63.

218   *Ibid.*, p. 69.

219   *The Future Shape of Financial Reports*, ICAEW/ICAS, 1991, para. 1-2.

220   *Ibid.*, paras. 3-1 to 3-5.

221   *Ibid.*, para. 4-3.

222   *Foreword to Accounting Standards*, ASB, June 1993, para. 4.

223   Statement of Principles Exposure Draft, *Statement of Principles for Financial Reporting*, ASB, November 1995.

224   *Statement of Principles for Financial Reporting – the way ahead, progress paper on the exposure draft*, ASB, July 1996.

225   Statement of Principles Exposure Draft, *Statement of Principles for Financial Reporting*, para. 1.1.

226   *Ibid.*, para. 1.13.

227   *Ibid.*, paras. 1.5 – 1.7.

228   *Ibid.*, para. 1.6.
229   *Ibid.*, para. 1.9
230   *Ibid.*, para. 1.13.
231   *Ibid.*, p. 41.
232   *Ibid.*, para. 2.8.
233   *Ibid.*, para. 2.13.
234   *Ibid.*, paras. 2.23 – 2.29.
235   *Ibid.*, paras. 2.30 -- 2.33.
236   *Ibid.*, paras. 2.6 – 2.7.
237   *Ibid.*, para. 2.7.
238   *Ibid.*, para. 3.5.
239   *Ibid.*, para. 3.6.
240   *Ibid.*, para. 3.16.
241   *Ibid.*, para. 3.18.
242   *Ibid.*, para. 3.21.
243   *Ibid.*, para. 3.39.
244   *Ibid.*, para. 3.47.
245   *Ibid.*
246   *Ibid.*, para. 3.49.
247   *Ibid.*
248   *Ibid.*, para. 4.1.
249   *Ibid.*, para. 4.5.
250   *Ibid.*, para. 4.6.
251   *Ibid.*, para. 4.7.
252   *Ibid.*, para. 4.8.
253   *Ibid.*, para. 4.11.
254   *Ibid.*, paras. 4.29 and 4.32.
255   *Ibid.*, para. 4.39.
256   *Ibid.*, para. 4.43.
257   *Ibid.*, para. 6.25.
258   *Ibid.*, para. 6.26.
259   *Ibid.*, para. 5.38.
260   *Ibid.*, para. 5.28.
261   The AICPA Special Committee on Financial Reporting, *Meeting the Information Needs of Investors and Creditors*, AICPA, 1994.
262   Exposure Draft, *Statement of Principles for Financial Reporting*, para. 5.22.
263   *Ibid.*, para. 5.23.
264   *Ibid.*, para. 5.22.
265   SSAP 16, *Current cost accounting*, March 1980, para. 43.
266   Exposure Draft, *Statement of Principles for Financial Reporting*, paras. 5.26 – 5.27.
267   *Ibid.*, para. 5.37.
268   *Ibid.*, para. 6.18.
269   *Ibid.*, paras. 6.20 and 6.25.
270   *Ibid.*, para. 6.25.
271   *Ibid.*, para. 7.1.
272   *Ibid.*, para. 7.2.
273   *Ibid.*, para. 7.9.
274   *Ibid.*, para. 7.10.
275   *Ibid.*
276   *Ibid.*, para. 7.38.
277   *Ibid.*, para. 7.41.
278   *Ibid.*, para. 4.7.
279   G. J. Wilkinson-Riddle and L. Holland, *An analysis and discussion of the responses to the ASB's Statement of Principles for Financial Reporting*, Occasional Paper published by The Journal of Applied Accounting Research, July 1997.
280   *Ibid.*, p. 1.
281   *Ibid.*, p. 6.

282 *Statement of Principles for Financial Reporting – the way ahead, progress paper on the exposure draft*, ASB.
283 *Ibid.*
284 *Ibid.*, p. 1.
285 *Ibid.*, p. 6.
286 *Ibid.*, p. 7.
287 *Ibid.*, p. 2.
288 Accounting Standards Board Working Paper, *Discounting in Financial Reporting*, ASB, April 1997, p. 3.
289 *Ibid.*, para. 9.1.
290 *Ibid.*, para 1.6.
291 The Institute of Chartered Accountants of Scotland, *Making Corporate Reports Valuable*, Kogan Page, 1988.
292 Exposure Draft, *Framework for the Preparation and Presentation of Financial Statements*, IASC, May 1988.
293 *Framework for the Preparation and Presentation of Financial Statements*, IASC, September 1989, para. 4.
294 *Ibid.*, para. 2.
295 *Ibid.*, para. 7.
296 *Ibid.*, paras. 99–101.
297 *Ibid.*, para. 95.
298 CICA Handbook, General Accounting, Section 1000, *Financial Statement Concepts*, para. .01.
299 *Ibid.*, para. .02.
300 *Ibid.*, para. .03.
301 *Ibid.*, paras. .53–.58.

Chapter 3   Revenue recognition

1   THE NATURE OF REVENUE

Revenue is generally discussed in accounting literature in terms of inflows of assets to an enterprise which occur as a result of outflows of goods and services from the enterprise. For this reason, the concept of revenue has normally been associated with specific accounting procedures which were primarily directed towards determining the timing and measurement of revenue in the context of the historical cost double-entry system. For example, APB Statement No. 4 defined revenue as the 'gross increases in assets or gross decreases in liabilities recognized and measured in conformity with generally accepted accounting principles that result from those types of profit-directed activities of an enterprise that can change owners' equity'.[1] Consequently, the accounting principles which evolved focused on determining when transactions should be recognised in the financial statements, what amounts were involved in each transaction, how these amounts should be classified and how they should be allocated between accounting periods.

Historical cost accounting in its pure form avoids having to take a valuation approach to financial reporting by virtue of the fact that it is transactions-based; in other words, it relies on transactions to determine the recognition and measurement of assets, liabilities, revenues and expenses. Over the life of an enterprise, its total income will be represented by net cash flows generated; however, because of the requirement to prepare periodic financial statements, it is necessary to break up the enterprise's operating cycle into artificial periods. The effect of this is that at each reporting date the enterprise will have entered into a number of transactions which are incomplete; for example, it might have delivered a product or service to a customer for which payment has not been received, or it might have received payment in respect of a product or service yet to be delivered. Alternatively, it might have expended cash on costs which relate to future exchange transactions, or it might have received goods and services which it has not yet paid for in cash. Consequently, the most important accounting questions which have to be answered revolve around how to allocate the effects of these incomplete transactions between periods for reporting purposes, as opposed to simply letting them fall into the periods in which cash is either received or paid. This allocation process is based on two, sometimes conflicting, fundamental accounting concepts: accruals (or matching), which attempts to move the costs associated with earning revenues to the periods in which the related revenues will be reported; and prudence, under which revenue and profits are not anticipated, whilst anticipated losses are provided for as soon as they are foreseen, with the result that costs are not deferred to the future if there is doubt as to their recoverability.

As a result, the pure historical cost balance sheet contains items of two types: cash (and similar monetary items), and debits and credits which arise as a result of shifting the effects of transactions between reporting periods by applying the accruals and prudence concepts; in other words, the balance sheet simply reflects the balances which result from the enterprise preparing an accruals-based profit and loss account rather than a receipts and payments account. A non-monetary asset under the historical cost system is purely a deferred cost; a cost which has been incurred before the balance sheet date and, by applying the accruals concept, is expected (provided it passes the prudence test) to benefit periods beyond the balance sheet date, so as to justify its being carried forward. Similarly, the balance sheet incorporates credit balances which are awaiting recognition in the profit and loss account but, as a result of the application of the prudence concept, have been deferred to future reporting periods.

It is the aim of this Chapter to suggest broad principles under the existing historical cost accounting system for the recognition of revenues earned from operations. At the same time, though, we are mindful of the fact that the ASB is attempting, through its conceptual framework project to introduce a balance sheet approach to income recognition which would alter radically the basis on which gains and losses are recognised. This is discussed at 4.1 below. However, as discussed in Chapter 2, the ASB's Draft *Statement of Principles* has been withdrawn pending further development; consequently, until such time as the ASB has secured some measure of acceptance of its conceptual framework as a whole, the traditional approach to revenue recognition prevails.

2   REALISED PROFITS

The term 'realised profits' was introduced into UK company legislation in the Companies Act 1980 as a result of the implementation of the Second EC Directive on company law, which provided the basic framework for the co-ordination of national provisions dealing with the maintenance, increase and reduction of the capital of public limited companies.[2] The Directive stated that the amount of a distribution to shareholders may not exceed the amount of the profits at the end of the last financial year plus any profits brought forward and sums drawn from reserves available for this purpose, less any losses brought forward and sums placed to reserve in accordance with the law or the statutes.[3]

As a result, the 1980 Act restricted a company's profits available for distribution to its accumulated realised profits less accumulated realised losses, and in so doing reversed the principle which had been laid down in a number of legal cases which permitted companies to make distributions out of current profits without making good past losses. Nevertheless, it is clear that profit is a function of individual companies and not of groups, and that intra-group transactions are sometimes capable of generating realised and, therefore, distributable profits.

However, the 1980 Act did not define 'realised profits', although a definition was subsequently provided as a result of the implementation of the Fourth EC Directive in the Companies Act 1981. This definition, which was later incorporated into Schedule 4 to the Companies Act 1985, has been amended by the Companies Act 1989, and is now contained in section 262(3) of the Act; it reads as follows: 'References in this Part to "realised profits" and "realised losses", in relation to a company's accounts, are to such profits or losses of the company as fall to be treated as realised in accordance with principles generally accepted, at the time when the accounts are prepared, with respect to the determination for accounting purposes of realised profits or losses.

'This is without prejudice to—

(a) the construction of any other expression (where appropriate) by reference to accepted accounting principles or practice, or

(b) any specific provision for the treatment of profits or losses of any description as realised.'

Whilst the Part of the Act referred to in the above definition is Part VII – Accounts and Audit – the definition is given a slightly wider application through section 742(2) which states that 'references in this Act to "realised profits" and "realised losses", in relation to a company's accounts, shall be construed in accordance with section 262(3)'.

This definition is clearly not concerned with GAAP in its broad sense, but with generally accepted accounting principles for determining realised profits for accounting purposes only. However, it might be argued that such principles do not necessarily exist, since UK accounting principles are directed towards the recognition and disclosure of items in the financial statements of entities in order to present a true and fair view, and not towards the determination of realised profits. Nevertheless, in its technical release on the subject (TR 481), the CCAB indicated that the term 'principles generally accepted' incorporates the legal principles laid down in Schedule 4 of the Companies Act 1985 and the requirements of the SSAPs (particularly the fundamental accounting concepts of prudence and accruals as set out in SSAP 2).[4] TR 481 concluded that 'a profit which is required by statements of standard accounting practice to be recognised in the profit and loss account should normally be treated as a realised profit, unless the SSAP specifically indicates that it should be treated as unrealised'.[5]

The difficulty that arises from this interpretation is that there are a number of areas of profit recognition which are not, as yet, dealt with in accounting standards; furthermore, certain areas which are covered by accounting standards incorporate inconsistencies in approach. For this reason, it is necessary to establish broad principles for the purpose of determining 'realised profit'. Some might hold the view that SSAP 2's definition of the prudence concept does, in fact, provide a basis for recognising realised profits in that it states that 'revenue and profits are not anticipated, but are recognised by inclusion in the profit and loss account when realised in the form either of cash or of other assets the ultimate cash realisation of which can be assessed with reasonable certainty'.[6] However, this definition may be flawed, since the emphasis on 'cash' and 'ultimate cash realisation' would appear to rule out the recognition of barter transactions or even the accrual of investment income on a time basis.

This view has been similarly expressed in the conclusions to a research study on the reporting of profits and the concept of realisation which was carried out by Sir Bryan Carsberg and Christopher Noke.[7] They felt that the concept of realisation should be equated with 'reliability of measurement' – i.e. to ensure that profits are recognised only when they can be said to have occurred with reasonable certainty – and not with 'convertibility to cash'.[8]

In conclusion, therefore, it is not altogether clear whether or not there exists at present a set of principles generally accepted with respect to the determination for accounting purposes of realised profits or losses, as is suggested by the Companies Act. The ASB is, however, attempting to address this through Chapter 4 of its Draft Statement of Principles – *Recognition in financial statements* – by suggesting both general criteria for the recognition of the elements of financial statements, and specific criteria for the recognition of gains and losses in the profit and loss account and the statement of total recognised gains and losses.[9] These are discussed at 4.1 below, although at this stage it is worth noting that the ASB has adopted the position that the analysis of profits into realised and unrealised is not useful.[10]

Furthermore, as discussed more fully at 4.2 below, FRS 5's rules on asset recognition and derecognition will have a direct impact on the timing of revenue recognition in respect of sales of assets (fixed or current) which are recognised in the balance sheet. Again, these rules are not based on any principles of 'convertibility to cash', but instead are dependent on the transferral of all the significant benefits and risks relating to an asset disposed of, and the reliability of the measurement of the monetary amount of the asset received in exchange. It seems on the face of it, therefore, that there is the potential for conflict between SSAP 2 and FRS 5 in this area.

3   THE TIMING OF REVENUE RECOGNITION

Under the historical cost system, revenues are the inflows of assets to an enterprise as a result of the transfer of products and services by the enterprise to its customers during a period of time, and are recorded at the cash amount received or expected to be received (or, in the case of non-monetary exchanges, at their cash equivalent) as the result of these exchange transactions. However, because of the system of periodic financial reporting, it is necessary to determine the point (or points) in time when revenue should be measured and reported. This is governed by what is known as the 'realisation principle', which acknowledges the fact that for revenue to be recognised it is not sufficient merely for a sale to have been made – there has to be a certain degree of performance by the vendor as well. In the US, this principle was formally codified in 1970 in APB Statement No. 4 as follows: 'revenue is generally recognised when both of the following conditions are met: (1) the earning process is complete or virtually complete, and (2) an exchange has taken place'.[11]

The accounting practice which had developed under this principle was essentially as follows:

(a)   revenue from the sale of goods was recognised at the date of delivery to customers;

(b)   revenue from services was recognised when the services had been performed and were billable;

(c)   revenue derived from permitting others to use enterprise resources (e.g. rental, interest and royalty income) was recognised either on a time basis or as the resources were used; and

(d)   revenue from the sale of assets other than products of the enterprise was recognised at the date of sale.[12]

As stated above, revenue is recognised at the amount received or expected to be received as a consequence of the exchange transaction.

Although APB Statement No. 4 did acknowledge that there were certain exceptions to the sales basis of revenue recognition established under the realisation principle (for example, in the case of long-term construction contracts and the mining of precious metals with assured sales prices),[13] many more exceptions have developed in recent years. As a result, no common basis of revenue recognition exists in contemporary financial accounting for all types of exchange transaction; different (and sometimes inconsistent) rules exist for different circumstances. Nevertheless, these rules have been derived from three broad approaches to the recognition of revenue, each of which is appropriate under particular circumstances.

3.1   The critical event approach

In general terms, the operating cycle of an enterprise involves the acquisition of merchandise or raw materials, the production of goods, the sale of goods or services to customers, the delivery of the goods or performance of the services and the ultimate collection of cash; in some cases it might even extend beyond the cash collection stage, for example, if there are on-going after-sales service obligations. The critical event approach is based on the belief that revenue is earned at the point in the operating cycle when the most critical decision is made or the most critical act is performed.[14] It is therefore necessary to identify the event which is considered to be critical to the revenue earning process. In theory, the critical event could occur at various stages during the operating cycle; for example, at the completion of production, at the time of sale, at the time of delivery or at the time of cash collection.

Revenue recognition is subject to a number of uncertainties; these include the estimation of the production cost of the asset, the selling price, the additional selling costs and the ultimate cash collection. However, since these uncertainties fall away at various stages throughout the operating cycle, it is necessary to identify a point in the cycle at which the remaining uncertainties can be estimated with sufficient accuracy to enable revenue to be recognised. In other words, the critical event should not be judged to occur at a point when the prudence concept would preclude recognition by virtue of the uncertainties which still remain.

3.1.1   *The recognition of revenue at the completion of production*

Clearly, the uncertainty surrounding the cost of production is removed when the product is completed; it is therefore necessary to evaluate the remaining uncertainties in order to determine whether or not the completion of production can be used as the critical event for revenue recognition. Where the enterprise has entered into a firm contract for the production and delivery of a product, the sales price will have been determined and the selling costs will have already been incurred. Consequently, provided that both the delivery expenses and the bad debt risk can be satisfactorily assessed, it may be appropriate to report revenue on this basis. An application of this practice is the completed contract method of recognising revenue on construction contracts, in terms of which revenue is recognised only when the contract is completed or substantially completed.

It has also become accepted practice in certain industries to recognise revenue at the completion of production, even though a sales contract may not have been entered into. Normally, this practice would only be adopted in the case of the production of certain precious metals and agricultural commodities, provided that the following criteria are met:

(a)   there should be a ready market for the commodity;

(b)   the market price should be determinable;

(c)   the market price should be stable; and

(d)   selling should not be a major activity of the enterprise and there should be no substantial cost of marketing.

SFAC No. 5 refers to such assets as being 'readily realisable' (since they are saleable at readily determinable prices without significant effort), and acknowledges that revenue may be recognised on the completion of production of such assets, provided that they consist of interchangeable units and quoted prices are available in an active market that can rapidly absorb the quantity held by the enterprise without significantly affecting the price.[15] The accounting treatment for this basis would be to value closing stock at net realisable value (i.e. sales price less estimated selling costs), and write off the related production costs.

An extension of this approach is to be found in the generally accepted accounting practice adopted by many securities dealers and commodity traders of including commodities, futures and options in their financial statements at market value.

3.1.2   *The recognition of revenue at the time of sale*

The time of sale is probably the most widely used basis of recognising revenue from transactions involving the sale of goods. The reason is that, in most cases, the sale is the critical point in the earning process when most of the significant uncertainties are eliminated; the only uncertainties which are likely to remain are those of possible return of the goods (where the customer has the right to do so, thereby cancelling the sale), the failure to collect the sales price (in the case of a credit sale), and any future liabilities in terms of any express or implied customer warranties. However, under normal circumstances, these uncertainties will be both minimal and estimable to a reasonable degree of accuracy, based, inter alia, on past experience.

Nevertheless, the time of sale basis of revenue recognition is not always straightforward. In a large number of cases, a contract for the sale of goods would be entered into after the goods have been acquired or produced by the seller, and delivery takes place either at the same time as the contract, or soon thereafter. However, should revenues be recognised at the time of sale if the sale takes place before production, or if delivery only takes place at some significantly distant time in the future?

From a legal point of view, delivery does not necessarily have to have occurred for a sale to take place. Under the Sale of Goods Act 1979, 'a contract of sale of goods is a contract by which the seller transfers or agrees to transfer the property in goods to the buyer for a money consideration, called the price'.[16] Where, under a contract of sale, title to the goods is transferred from the seller to the buyer the contract is called a sale;[17] where the contract specifies that title to the goods will be transferred at some future date or transfer of title is subject to conditions to be fulfilled in the future, the contract is called an agreement to sell.[18] Consequently, the 'critical event' which determines whether a contract of sale is a 'sale' or whether it is an 'agreement to sell' is the passing of title.

Where the contract of sale contains no conditions as to the passing of title, and the goods are physically capable of immediate delivery to the purchaser, title will pass as soon as the contract is entered into (i.e. at the time of sale), regardless of the time fixed for payment or delivery.[19] However, where the seller is bound to do something to the goods before the purchaser is obliged to take delivery, title will pass as soon as that thing is done and the purchaser has been notified.[20] The passing of title, therefore, is a legal issue (and may be of crucial importance to the parties in certain circumstances, such as liquidation), which is governed by the terms of the contract and can occur at various stages along the earning process. As a result, for revenue recognition purposes, the time of sale is generally taken to be the point of delivery. This, in fact, would appear to be the principle implicit in the conditions for recognition set out in APB Statement No. 4 (see 3 above), where it is stated that revenue from the sales of products is recognised 'at the date of sale, usually interpreted to mean the date of delivery to customers'.[21]

This principle was reinforced by SFAC No. 5 as follows: 'Revenues are not recognized until earned. An entity's revenue-earning activities involve delivering or producing goods, rendering services, or other activities that constitute its ongoing major or central operations, and revenues are considered to have been earned when the entity has substantially accomplished what it must do to be entitled to the benefits represented by the revenues. ... If sale or cash receipt (or both) precedes production and delivery (for example, magazine subscriptions), revenues may be recognised as earned by production and delivery.'[22]

However, the use of the words 'substantially accomplished' in SFAC No. 5 suggest that delivery does not necessarily have to have taken place for revenue to be recognised. Where, for example, delivery is a relatively insignificant part of the earning process, the goods are on hand and available for delivery and there is every expectation that delivery will be made, it may be appropriate to recognise the sale as revenue before delivery takes place. (See 4.3.2 below for discussion of the principles laid down by IAS 18 for determining when to recognise revenue from a transaction involving the sale of goods.)

3.1.3   *The recognition of revenue subsequent to delivery*

Under certain circumstances, the uncertainties which exist after delivery are of such significance that recognition should be delayed beyond the normal recognition point. Where the principal uncertainty concerns collectability, a possible approach would be to record the sale and defer recognition of the profit until cash is received; alternatively, it might be appropriate to defer recognition of the whole sale (and not just the profit) until collection is reasonably assured.

A further example of where it might be appropriate to defer the recognition of revenue beyond the date of delivery is where the enterprise sells its product but gives the customer the right to return the goods (for example, in the case of a mail order business where the customer is given an approval period of, say, 14 days). In such circumstances, revenue should only be recognised on delivery if future returns can be reasonably predicted; if this is not possible, then revenue should only be recognised on receipt of payment for the goods, or on customer acceptance of the goods and express or implied acknowledgement of the liability for payment, or after the 14 days have elapsed – whichever is considered to be the most appropriate under the circumstances.

This area of uncertainty is dealt with in the US under SFAS 48 – *Revenue Recognition When Right of Return Exists* – which states that if an enterprise sells its product but gives the buyer the right to return the product, revenue from the sales transaction is recognised at time of sale only if *all* of the following conditions are met:

(a)   the seller's price to the buyer is substantially fixed or determinable at the date of sale;

(b)   the buyer has paid the seller, or the buyer is obligated to pay the seller and the obligation is not contingent on resale of the product;

(c)   the buyer's obligation to the seller would not be changed in the event of theft or physical destruction or damage of the product;

(d)   the buyer acquiring the product for resale has economic substance apart from that provided by the seller (i.e. the buyer does not merely exist 'on paper' with little or no physical facilities, having been established by the seller primarily for the purpose of recognising revenue);

(e)   the seller does not have significant obligations for future performance to directly bring about resale of the product by the buyer; and

(f)   the amount of future returns can be reasonably estimated.[23]

Revenue which was not recognised at the time of sale because the above conditions were not met, should be recognised either when the return privilege has 'substantially expired', or when all the above conditions are met, whichever occurs first.[24]

The ability to make a reasonable estimate of future returns depends on many factors and will vary from one case to the next. Furthermore, SFAS 48 lists the following factors as being those which might impair a seller's ability to make such an estimate:

(a)   the susceptibility of the product to significant external factors, such as technological obsolescence or changes in demand;

(b)   relatively long periods in which a particular product may be returned;

(c)   absence of historical experience with similar types of sales of similar products, or inability to apply such experience because of changing circumstances; for example, changes in the selling enterprise's marketing policies or its relationships with its customers; and

(d)   absence of a large volume of relatively homogeneous transactions.[25]

These rules should be seen against the background of APB Statement No. 4's requirement that revenue should generally only be recognised when the 'earning process is complete or virtually complete'.[26] The right of return is, therefore, viewed as a significant uncertainty which would preclude recognition under certain circumstances.

3.2   The accretion approach

The accretion approach involves the recognition of revenue during the process of 'production', rather than at the end of a contract or when production is complete.   There are three broad areas of enterprise activity where the application of the accretion approach might be appropriate.

3.2.1   *The use by others of enterprise resources*

The traditional accrual basis of accounting recognises revenue as enterprise resources are used by others; this approach is followed, for example, in the case of recognising rental, royalty or interest income.   However, the question of uncertainty of collection should always be considered (for example, in the case of accrual of interest on third world debt), in which case it might be appropriate to delay recognition until cash is received or where ultimate collection is assured beyond all reasonable doubt.

3.2.2   *Long-term contracts*

The second accepted application of the accretion approach to revenue reporting may be found in the accounting practice for long-term construction contracts. Under certain circumstances, the amount of revenue to be recognised on construction contracts is determined according to the 'percentage-of-completion method', whereby revenue is estimated by reference to the stage of completion of the contract activity at the end of each accounting period. Normally, the main uncertainty which presents difficulty in the application of this approach is the estimation of the total costs, particularly in the early stages of the contract, or where factors such as excavation and the weather may cause added uncertainty. However, the selling price is sometimes uncertain as well, owing to contract modifications which give rise to revenue from 'extras'. (Accounting for long-term contacts is dealt with in detail in Chapter 14.)

3.2.3 Natural growth and 'biological transformation'

Where an enterprise's activity involves production through natural growth or ageing, the accretion approach would suggest that revenue should be recognised at identifiable stages during this process. For example, in the case of growing timber or livestock, there would be market prices available at the various stages of growth; revenue could, therefore, be recognised throughout the production process by making comparative stock valuations and reporting the accretions at each accounting date. This is, in fact, an area which is currently being explored by the IASC in its project on accounting in the agricultural industry. In a Draft Statement of Principles – *Agriculture* – which the IASC issued in December 1996, the Committee is proposing that there should be a blanket application of fair value accounting to all biological assets and agricultural produce throughout their period of growth/ageing, which the Committee refers to as 'biological transformation'.[27]

However, it seems that the IASC has formulated its ideas on a number of unproven assumptions which cast doubt as to the validity of its proposals. These are that:

■ it is assumed that efficient markets exist for all biological assets;

■ it is assumed that there exist active and liquid markets for all the produce of agriculture;

■ it is assumed that biological transformation can be measured with a degree of reliability which is sufficient for incorporation in the accounts; and

■ it is assumed that all sectors of agriculture are sufficiently similar as to be accounted for on the same basis.

We question the validity of these assumptions. For instance, it seems unlikely that there exist active liquid markets for all intermediate agricultural products, such as forests. In any event, even if active and liquid markets do exist, it is doubtful that the risks and volatilities of the markets justify recognising revenue on the basis envisaged by the IASC. This is not to disagree that fair value information concerning biological assets is useful, but we question whether fair valuations will be sufficiently reliable for incorporation in the accounts. In some cases it may even be misleading to do so. It is also likely that the fair value approach proposed by the IASC would place an unnecessary burden on the preparers of accounts to the extent that the costs (including audit costs) would outweigh the benefits.

In any event, under the present historical cost accounting system (including IAS 18), this approach would not be appropriate, since the earning process would be too incomplete, too many significant uncertainties would remain, and a profit could not be regarded as having been realised.

3.3   The revenue allocation approach

The revenue allocation approach is essentially a combination of the critical event and accretion approaches.   One of the difficulties in adopting, for example, the time of sale as the critical event for revenue recognition, is the existence of the uncertainty surrounding after-sale costs (such as customer support service and warranty costs). One way of dealing with these costs could be to make a provision for the future costs to be incurred on the basis of best estimate; alternatively, an approach could be followed whereby revenue is apportioned on the basis of two or more critical events.   Consequently, part of the sale price could be treated as revenue at the point of sale, and the balance could either be recognised on an accretion basis over a warranty period or on the expiration of the warranty.   The recognition of profit by manufacturer/dealer lessors is an example of such an application (see Chapter 17 at 7.6).

4   FUNDAMENTAL RECOGNITION CRITERIA

It is a requirement of the Companies Act 1985 that 'only profits realised at the balance sheet date shall be included in the profit and loss account';[28] in establishing whether or not profits of a company should be treated as 'realised profits', reference should be made to 'principles generally accepted, at the time when the accounts are prepared, with respect to the determination for accounting purposes of realised profits or losses'.[29]   It is unclear as to whether or not generally accepted accounting principles exist for the purposes of determining realised profits for accounting purposes. The only direct reference to realisation in a UK accounting standard is to be found in SSAP 2's definition of prudence; however, this definition would appear to be inadequate, as existing practice indicates that a wider interpretation is being placed on the concept of 'realisation' (see 2 above). For this reason, revenue recognition issues tend to be dealt with on an ad hoc basis, without either a clear definition of the concept of realisation or generally accepted recognition criteria.

However, the ASB is attempting to address this through Chapter 4 of its *Statement of Principles*, which was issued in November 1995 in the form of an exposure draft. As explained at 4.1 below, the effect of the ASB's proposals, if accepted, would alter radically the basis on which revenue would be recognised.

Nevertheless, until such time as the ASB has established clear recognition principles in final form, it is helpful also to examine the authoritative literature which exists internationally. Although this literature has no authority to dictate accounting practice in the UK, it may provide a basis for achieving some consistency in approach towards dealing with practical revenue recognition issues.

4.1 ASB Draft Statement of Principles Chapter 4: Recognition in financial statements

Chapter 3 of the ASB's Draft *Statement of Principles* identifies seven elements of financial statements: these are, assets, liabilities, ownership interest, gains, losses, contributions from owners and distributions to owners. However, because the Draft *Statement of Principles* follows a balance sheet-centred approach, the definitions of the last five elements are dependent on the first two. This means that once assets and liabilities have been defined, the definitions of gains and losses are derived as follows: assets minus liabilities equals ownership interest; gains and losses are increases and decreases in ownership interest, other than those relating to contributions from and distributions to owners. In principle, it does not matter that the definitions of the various elements are so interdependent – as long as workable recognition and measurement rules for assets and liabilities can be devised. However, there is room for doubt on this matter, particularly in the light of the fact that this is where the US Conceptual Framework Project ran into considerable difficulty.

4.1.1 The recognition process

Chapter 4 of the ASB's Draft *Statement of Principles* sets out three stages of the recognition process, all of which are focused on assets and liabilities. These are: initial recognition, subsequent remeasurement and derecognition.[30] As will be seen below, the introduction of 'subsequent remeasurement' in the recognition process provides the first hint of the ASB's balance sheet-focused approach to current value income recognition.

The ASB develops this approach by first establishing recognition criteria for each stage of the recognition process:

An item should be incorporated in the financial statements for the first time (initial recognition) if:

(a) there is sufficient evidence that the change in assets or liabilities inherent in the element has occurred (including, where appropriate, evidence that a future inflow or outflow of benefit will occur); and

(b) it can be measured at a monetary amount with sufficient reliability.[31]

A change in the amount at which an asset or liability is recorded (subsequent remeasurement) should be recorded if:

(a) there is sufficient evidence that the amount of an asset or liability has changed; and

(b) the new amount of the asset or liability can be measured with sufficient reliability.[32]

An asset or liability should cease to be recognised (derecognition) if there is no longer sufficient evidence that the entity has access to future economic benefits or an obligation to transfer economic benefits (including, where appropriate, evidence that a future inflow or outflow of benefit will occur).[33]

This means that whenever a change in an entity's total assets is not offset by an equal change in total liabilities or ownership interest, a gain or loss will arise. It also means, therefore, that the ASB's proposed framework seeks to recognise gains irrespective of whether or not a transaction has occurred. This is borne out by the explanation that 'recognition is triggered where a past event gives rise to a measurable change in the assets and liabilities of the entity',[34] and the identification of two broad classes of past events that may trigger recognition: 'transactions' and 'events other than transactions'.

'Transactions' are described as being 'arrangements under which services or interests in property are acquired by one entity from another'.[35] The ASB goes on to say that 'where a transaction takes place it is necessary to recognise the assets and liabilities acquired. If the transaction is negotiated at arm's length and the consideration is monetary, transactions provide strong evidence of the amount of assets acquired.'[36]

However, initial recognition of assets and liabilities and their subsequent remeasurement may also be triggered by events other than transactions. Usual examples of such events include an adverse court judgement or damage to property as a result of fire. Of course, it is generally accepted in the present accounting framework that these events would trigger the recognition of a provision - although recognition would take place from a profit and loss account perspective as a result of applying the prudence principle. More significantly, though, the ASB then goes on to suggest in its Draft *Statement of Principles* that 'some events that trigger subsequent remeasurement involve the revaluation of the flow of benefits associated with an asset or liability'.[37] The ASB then illustrates this with the example of a change in the value of a freehold property 'where the benefits of occupation are unchanged but the monetary value of those benefits is affected by market price changes'.[38]

4.1.2   *The recognition of gains*

Following the ASB's approach to recognition to its logical conclusion, then, we are led to its proposed rule for the recognition of gains, which is that 'the recognition of gains involves consideration of whether there is sufficient evidence that an increase in net assets (ie in ownership interest) had occurred before the end of the reporting period'.[39]

The implications of this are highly significant when combined with the ASB's vision of a current value measurement system: all increases in net assets (including those brought about by increases in current values) should be recognised as gains (provided that there is sufficient evidence that the change has occurred and it can be measured reliably).

This approach, if implemented, would replace the long-established accounting process in use throughout the world, whereby transactions are allocated to accounting periods by reference to the matching and prudence concepts. However, it is most unlikely to work well in practice.

The fundamental problem is the way in which the Draft *Statement of Principles* views the accounting process. Assets and liabilities do not form the natural starting point for devising recognition rules; the real building blocks which underlie accounting practice are transactions to which are applied criteria for revenue and expense recognition, the balance sheet being a result of this process, not the starting point. Revenue recognition criteria are more demanding than those for recognising assets and liabilities, since they should embody the concept of the revenue having been earned, based on performance by the reporting company.

However matters are made worse by the ASB's proposal that companies should present two statements of financial performance: the profit and loss account and the statement of total recognised gains and losses. This means that some criteria need to be established in order to determine which gains are reported in which statement. A logical solution might be that realised gains are reported in the profit and loss account and unrealised gains are reported in the statement of total recognised gains and losses. However, this is not the view of the ASB. It believes that 'a more useful analysis of the quality of profits than that into realised and unrealised profits is an analysis into those gains and losses that derive from operating activities and those that result from changes in the value of those assets and liabilities that are held on a continuing basis for use in the entity's business'.[40] This means that the ASB's proposed model conveniently avoids having to deal with issues of realisation in revenue recognition. Instead, gains would be taken to the profit and loss account irrespective of whether or not they are realised or a transaction has occurred.

Many would consider these proposed criteria to be a distortion of the real recognition rules which accountants throughout the world and the ASB itself use and which are in fact transactions based. Devising rules for accounting based on what assets and liabilities materialise from the transaction may be conceptually 'clean' but in practice, in anything but the most straightforward cases, it simply does not provide the concepts with which to address practical situations. Accounting in real life is essentially an allocative process in which transactions are allocated to appropriate accounting periods. Although the conventions for doing so need to be developed further, it seems more likely that this will remain a more workable approach than recognition criteria based on determining whether or not there is sufficient evidence that a change in net assets has occurred.

4.2   FRS 5

FRS 5 – *Reporting the substance of transactions* – is a manifestation of the balance sheet approach which the ASB is promulgating in its Draft *Statement of Principles*. Since FRS 5 is concerned with the recognition and derecognition of assets and liabilities, it will necessarily have an impact on the recognition of gains and losses. However, it is unclear as to whether the ASB intended that FRS 5 should alter existing accounting practice in the area of revenue recognition.

FRS 5's rules on asset derecognition deal with the issue of when to remove from the balance sheet assets which have previously been recognised. The rules are designed to determine one of three possible outcomes, and essentially involve a process of determining whether or not a transaction transfers to another party all the significant benefits and risks relating to an asset. FRS 5 anticipates that in the case of most transactions affecting items recognised as assets the situation will be that either the benefits and risks will not be transferred – in which case the asset will continue to be recognised and no sale or disposal will be recorded – or the benefits and risks will be transferred – in which case the asset will cease to be recognised (i.e. a sale or disposal together with the resulting gain or loss will be recorded).

The third possible outcome envisaged by FRS 5 occurs where, although not all of the benefits and risks have been transferred, the transaction is more than a mere financing and has transferred enough of both the benefits and risks to warrant at least some derecognition of the asset. These cases arise where the transaction takes one or more of the following forms:

(a)   where the asset has been subdivided and part of it transferred;

(b)   where the asset is sold for less than its full life; and

(c)   where an asset is transferred for all of its life but some risk or benefit is retained.

FRS 5 states that in these special cases, where the amount of any resulting gain or loss is uncertain, full provision should be made for any probable loss but recognition of any gain, to the extent that it is in doubt, should be deferred.

However, the transfer of the risks and rewards of ownership associated with an asset is not sufficient for revenue to be recognised. It is also necessary to complete the other side of the transaction – namely the recognition of the asset received in exchange for the asset disposed of. The principal rule for recognition of an item as an asset under FRS 5 is that the item can be measured at a monetary amount with sufficient reliability – seemingly irrespective of whether or not the item is readily convertible into known amounts of cash or cash equivalents.

What this means is that FRS 5 has apparently enshrined in UK GAAP what have for some time been the key principles under International Accounting Standards for the recognition of revenue from a transaction involving the sale of goods – namely that the buyer has assumed from the seller the significant risks and rewards of ownership of the assets sold and that the amount of revenue can be measured reliably. However, only time will tell as to whether or not the ASB intended FRS 5 to influence practice in the area of revenue recognition.

4.3   IAS 18

The original version of IAS 18 – *Revenue Recognition* – was issued in 1982 and defined revenue as the 'gross inflow of cash, receivables or other consideration arising in the course of the ordinary activities of an enterprise from the sale of goods, from the rendering of services, and from the use by others of enterprise resources yielding interest, royalties and dividends'.[41] In revising IAS 18 in 1993, the IASC has attempted to retain the approach of the original standard, whilst at the same time create a link between the revised standard and the IASC's conceptual framework.

Consequently, the revised IAS 18 – *Revenue* – now includes the definition of income from the IASC's conceptual framework and states that revenue is income that arises in the course of ordinary activities of an enterprise and is referred to by a variety of different names including sales, fees, interest, dividends and royalties.[42] It goes on to explain that the objective of the revised standard is to prescribe the accounting treatment of revenue arising from the following types of transactions and events:

(a)   the sale of goods;

(b)   the rendering of services; and

(c)   the use by others of enterprise assets yielding interest, royalties and dividends.[43]

The standard then defines 'revenue' as 'the gross inflow of economic benefits during the period arising in the course of the ordinary activities of an enterprise when those inflows result in increases in ownership interest, other than increases relating to contributions from equity participants'.[44] This, in fact, is not too dissimilar from the ASB's Draft *Statement of Principles* which defines 'gains' and 'losses' as increases and decreases in ownership interest other than those relating to contributions from and distributions to owners. However, in distinguishing between 'gains' and 'revenue' in its definition of income, the IASC is able to exclude 'gains' from the scope of IAS 18, thereby avoiding the issue of the recognition of gains which are earned but unrealised.

In any event, though, having established the link between the Framework and IAS 18, the IASC then abandons the Framework and reverts to the old IAS 18 transactions-based critical event approach for the recognition of revenues derived from the sale of goods and the rendering of services, and an accretion approach in respect of revenues derived from the use by others of enterprise resources.

4.3.1 Measurement of revenue

IAS 18 states that the amount of revenue arising on a transaction is usually determined by agreement between the enterprise and the buyer or user of the asset. This means that it is measured at the fair value of the consideration received or receivable taking into account the amount of any trade discounts and volume rebates allowed by the enterprise.[45] The standard defines fair value as 'the amount for which an asset could be exchanged, or a liability settled, between knowledgeable, willing parties in an arm's length transaction'.[46]

Usually, this will present little difficulty as the consideration will normally be in the form of cash or cash equivalents and the amount of revenue will be the amount of cash or cash equivalents received or receivable. However, an issue does arise when the inflow of cash or cash equivalents is deferred, since the fair value of the consideration will then be less than the nominal amount of cash received or receivable. IAS 18 attempts to deal with this by introducing a requirement for the discounting of receivables under these circumstances. Consequently, when an arrangement effectively constitutes a financing transaction, the fair value of the consideration is determined by discounting all future receipts using an imputed rate of interest. The difference between the fair value and the nominal amount of the consideration is recognised as interest revenue.[47]

Although the revised IAS 18 has retained the existing requirement that an exchange of assets or services of a similar nature and value does not give rise to revenue, it has introduced new requirements for exchanges of dissimilar assets or services. As a result, when goods are sold or services are rendered in exchange for dissimilar goods or services, the exchange is regarded as a transaction which generates revenue. The revenue is measured at the fair value of the goods or services received, adjusted by the amount of any cash or cash equivalents transferred. When the fair value of the goods or services received cannot be measured reliably, the revenue is measured at the fair value of the goods or services given up, adjusted by the amount of any cash or cash equivalents transferred.[48]

4.3.2 The sale of goods

IAS 18 lays down the following five criteria which must be satisfied in order to recognise revenue from the sale of goods:

(a) the enterprise has transferred to the buyer the significant risks and rewards of ownership of the goods;

(b) the enterprise retains neither continuing managerial involvement to the degree usually associated with ownership nor effective control over the goods sold;

(c) the amount of revenue can be measured reliably;

(d) it is probable that the economic benefits associated with the transaction will flow to the enterprise; and

(e) the costs incurred or to be incurred in respect of the transaction can be measured reliably.[49]

It is clear that IAS 18 views the passing of risks and rewards as the most crucial of the five criteria, giving the following four examples of situations in which an enterprise may retain the significant risks and rewards of ownership:

(a) when the enterprise retains an obligation for unsatisfactory performance not covered by normal warranty provisions;

(b) when the receipt of the revenue from a particular sale is contingent on the derivation of revenue by the buyer from its sale of the goods;

(c) when the goods are shipped subject to installation and the installation is a significant part of the contract which has not yet been completed by the enterprise; and

(d) when the buyer has the right to rescind the purchase for a reason specified in the sales contract and the enterprise is uncertain about the probability of return.[50]

On closer examination of these examples, though, it is clear that the standard still advocates a critical event approach – despite its attempt to create a link with the IASC's Framework. This is further borne out by the statement in IAS 18 that 'in most cases, the transfer of risks and rewards of ownership coincides with the transfer of legal title or the passing of possession to the buyer'.[51]

It is, therefore, necessary to establish at which point in the earnings process both the significant risks and rewards of ownership are transferred from the seller to the buyer and any significant uncertainties (which would otherwise delay recognition) are removed. For example, the responsibilities of each party during the period between sale and delivery should be established, possibly by examination of the customer agreements. If the goods have merely to be uplifted by the buyer, and the seller has performed all his associated responsibilities, then the sale may be recognised immediately. However, if the substance of the sale is merely that an order has been placed, and the stock has still to be acquired by the seller, then the sale should not be recognised.

IAS 18 does also recognise that under certain circumstances goods are sold subject to reservation of title in order to protect the collectability of the amount due; in such circumstances, provided that the seller has transferred the significant risks and rewards of ownership, the transaction can be treated as a sale and revenue can be recognised.[52] This issue is discussed more fully at 5.2 below.

4.3.3   *The rendering of services*

The principal purpose of the IASC's revision of IAS 18 was to remove the option of being able to use the completed contract method for recognising revenue arising from transactions involving the rendering of services, in the same way as the revision of IAS 11 saw the removal of the completed contract method as an allowed method of accounting for construction contracts. As a result, IAS 18 now requires that when the outcome of a transaction involving the rendering of services can be estimated reliably, revenue is recognised 'by reference to the stage of completion of the transaction at the balance sheet date'[53] (in other words, using the percentage-of-completion method). When the outcome cannot be estimated reliably, revenue is recognised only to the extent of the expenses recognised that are recoverable.[54]

According to IAS 18, the outcome of a transaction can be estimated reliably when all the following conditions are satisfied:

(a)   the amount of revenue can be measured reliably;

(b)   it is probable that the economic benefits associated with the transaction will flow to the enterprise;

(c)   the stage of completion of the transaction at the balance sheet date can be measured reliably; and

(d)   the costs incurred for the transaction and the costs to complete the transaction can be measured reliably.[55]

However, whilst the IASC is to be commended for attempting to relate these criteria back to its Framework's fundamental recognition criterion of reliability of measurement, it is clear that they provide little practical guidance. This fact is borne out by the illustrative examples in the Appendix to IAS 18 which show that, in the case of a transaction involving the rendering of services, the performance of the service is the critical event for revenue recognition.

When it comes to determining the stage of completion of a transaction, IAS 18 suggests three methods that may be used:

(a)   surveys of work performed;

(b)   services performed to date as a percentage of total services to be performed; or

(c)   the proportion that costs incurred to date bear to the estimated total costs of the transaction. Only costs that reflect services performed to date are included in costs incurred to date. Only costs that reflect services performed or to be performed are included in the estimated total costs of the transaction.[56]

For practical purposes, though, when services are performed by an indeterminate number of acts over a specified period of time, the standard permits revenue to be recognised on a straight-line basis over the specified period unless there is evidence that some other method better represents the stage of completion. However, when a specific act is much more significant than any other acts, the standard again reverts to critical event theory requiring that the recognition of revenue be postponed until the significant act is executed.[57]

4.3.4   *Interest, royalties and dividends*

When it is probable that the economic benefits associated with the transaction will flow to the enterprise and that the amount of revenue can be measured reliably, IAS 18 requires that the revenue arising from the use by others of enterprise assets yielding interest, royalties and dividends should be recognised as follows:

(a)   *Interest:* on a time proportion basis that takes into account the effective yield on the asset;

(b)   *Royalties:* on an accrual basis in accordance with the substance of the relevant agreement; and

(c)   *Dividends:* when the shareholder's right to receive payment is established.

The application of the accretion approach under these circumstances would not necessarily be in line with the principle of realised profits as contained in SSAP 2's definition of prudence, since it would sometimes result in the recognition of revenue before it is either 'realised in the form of cash or of other assets the ultimate cash realisation of which can be assessed with reasonable certainty'; nevertheless, such an approach is generally accepted accounting practice in the UK.

4.3.5   *Disclosure*

The revised IAS 18 requires a greater level of disclosure regarding revenue than is generally found in the accounts of UK companies. The new disclosures relate to both revenue recognition policies and amounts of revenue included in the accounts under the different categories of revenue, and are laid down in the standard as follows:

An enterprise should disclose:

(a) the accounting policies adopted for the recognition of revenue including the methods adopted to determine the stage of completion of transactions involving the rendering of services;

(b) the amount of each significant category of revenue recognised during the period including revenue arising from:

(i)   the sale of goods;

(ii) the rendering of services;

(iii) interest;

(iv) royalties;

(v)   dividends; and

(c) the amount of revenue arising from exchanges of goods or services included in each significant category of revenue.[58]

4.4   The US

4.4.1   'The general rule'

Chapter 1 of Accounting Research Bulletin No. 43 (issued in 1953) reprinted the six rules which had been adopted by the membership of the AICPA in 1934. The first of these rules stated that 'profit is deemed to be realized when a sale in the ordinary course of business is effected, unless the circumstances are such that the collection of the sale price is not reasonably assured'.[59] The rule then goes on to state that 'an exception to the general rule may be made in respect of inventories in industries (such as the packing-house industry) in which owing to the impossibility of determining costs it is a trade custom to take inventories at net selling prices, which may exceed cost'.[60] However, it is not entirely clear as to what the 'general rule' actually is. Does the term 'effected' mean that profit is realised when the sale takes place, when delivery takes place, or when title passes?

In addition, a number of further exceptions are created by other authoritative pronouncements. For example, Chapter 11 of ARB 43 (which deals with cost-plus-fixed-fee government contracts) states that 'delivery of goods sold under contract is normally regarded as the test of realization of profit or loss'.[61] Nevertheless, it then goes on to say that 'it is, however, a generally accepted accounting procedure to accrue revenues under certain types of contracts and thereby recognize profits, on the basis of partial performance, where the circumstances are such that total profit can be estimated with reasonable accuracy and ultimate realization is reasonably assured'.[62]

The percentage-of-completion method of recognising revenue on long-term construction contracts is another example of 'an exception to the general rule'. ARB 45 – *Long-Term Construction-Type Contracts* – recognises both the percentage-of-completion and completed contract methods of accounting for long-term contracts. The Bulletin states that: 'in general when estimates of costs to complete and extent of progress toward completion of long-term contracts are reasonably dependable, the percentage-of-completion method is preferable. When lack of dependable estimates or inherent hazards cause forecasts to be doubtful, the completed-contract method is preferable'.[63] It would appear that the criteria to be applied in the selection of method are only broadly similar to those which should be applied in the case of cost-plus-fixed-fee contracts.

APB Statement No. 4 views these practices as exceptions to the realisation principle's exchange rule (see 3 above). However, as will be seen below, there exists a number of other variations to both the general rule laid down in ARB 43 and the realisation principle.

4.4.2   *SFAC No. 5*

As discussed in Chapter 2 of this book, the FASB's Concepts Statement No. 5 – *Recognition and Measurement in Financial Statements of Business Enterprises* – has primarily dealt with recognition issues from the angle of providing reliability of measurement.   However, the broad principle for revenue recognition laid down by SFAC No. 5 is that revenues are not recognised until they are (a) realised or realisable and (b) earned.[64] According to the Statement, revenues are realised 'when products (goods or services), merchandise, or other assets are exchanged for cash or claims to cash', and are realisable 'when related assets received or held are readily convertible to known amounts of cash or claims to cash'.[65] The characteristics of 'readily convertible assets' are that they have '(i) interchangeable (fungible) units and (ii) quoted prices available in an active market that can rapidly absorb the quantity held by the entity without significantly affecting the price'.[66]   Revenues are considered to have been 'earned' when the entity 'has substantially accomplished what it must do to be entitled to the benefits represented by the revenues'.[67]

The most significant difference between the recognition principles laid down in SFAC No. 5 as opposed to APB Statement No. 4 is that whilst the APB interpreted recognition and realisation as being broadly synonymous, SFAC No. 5 uses the terms 'realized' and 'realizability' to focus on conversion and convertibility of non-cash assets into cash or claims to cash.   However, it is doubtful whether SFAC No. 5's revised interpretation of the realisation principle has made any significant progress towards providing a rigorous theory of recognition and measurement. This is highlighted by the fact that SFAC No. 5 provides guidance for applying its recognition criteria and, in so doing, goes on to condone certain existing revenue practices (for example, the percentage-of-completion method and the accrual of certain revenues on a time basis) which clearly are not in accordance with the basic principles laid down in the Statement, since an exchange for cash or claims to cash may not necessarily have occurred.

4.4.3   *FASB Statements and AICPA Statements of Position*

There exist a number of FASB Statements and AICPA Statements of Position which deal with either the recognition of certain forms of revenue, or the recognition of revenue in certain specific industries. These are dealt with under 5 below.

4.5   Summary

As stated at 4.2 above, FRS 5 has had the ostensible effect of introducing a balance sheet approach to revenue recognition. However, to date we see no evidence that this has had any significant effect on the general principles of revenue recognition which are currently enshrined in UK GAAP – namely that the buyer must assume from the seller the significant risks and rewards of ownership of the assets sold and that the amount of revenue must be reliably measurable.

The following table summarises the broad approaches to revenue reporting which would appear to have achieved general acceptance through existing reporting practice. The table indicates the circumstances under which it might be appropriate to apply each of the approaches; nevertheless, it is essential that each situation is considered on its individual merits, with particular attention being paid to the risks and uncertainties which remain at each stage of the earning process and the extent to which the amount of revenue can be measured reliably.

The timing of recognition	*Criteria*	*Examples of practical application*
During production (accretion)	Revenues accrue over time, and no significant uncertainty exists as to measurability or collectability. A contract of sale has been entered into and future costs can be estimated with reasonable accuracy.	The accrual of interest, royalty and dividend income. Accounting for long-term construction contracts using the percentage-of-completion method.
At the completion of production	There should exist a ready market for the commodity which could rapidly absorb the quantity held by the entity; the commodity should comprise interchangeable units; the market price should be determinable and stable; there should be insignificant marketing costs involved.	Certain precious metals and agricultural products.
At the time of sale (but before delivery)	Goods must have already been acquired or manufactured; goods must be capable of immediate delivery to the customer; selling price has been established; all material related expenses (including delivery) have been ascertained; no significant uncertainties remain (e.g. ultimate cash collection, return of goods).	Certain sales of goods (e.g. 'bill and hold' sales). Property sales where there is an irrevocable contract.
On delivery	Criteria for recognition before delivery were not satisfied and no significant uncertainties remain.	Most sales of goods and services. Property sales where there is doubt that the sale will be completed.
Subsequent to delivery	Significant uncertainty regarding collectability existed at the time of delivery; at the time of sale it was not possible to value the consideration with sufficient accuracy.	Certain sales of goods and services (e.g. where the right of return exists). Goods shipped subject to conditions (e.g. installation and inspection/performance).
On an apportionment basis (the revenue allocation approach)	Where revenue represents the supply of initial and subsequent goods/services.	Franchise fees. Sale of goods with after sales service.

5   PROBLEM AREAS

Because of the lack of established generally accepted principles for revenue recognition, coupled with the fact that minimal specific guidance is given in the UK accounting standards as to the timing of revenue reporting, it is necessary to examine specific areas in practice which might be open to inconsistent, controversial or varied accounting practices.   Many of the issues discussed below relate to specific industries which pose their own particular revenue recognition problems; in fact, much of the accounting literature on the subject has been developed (predominantly in the US) in the context of these industries.

5.1   Receipt of initial fees

The practice which has developed in certain industries of charging an initial fee at the inception of a service, followed by subsequent service fees, can present revenue allocation problems.   The reason for this is that it is not always altogether clear what the initial fee represents; consequently, it is necessary to determine what proportion (if any) of the initial fee has been earned on receipt, and how much relates to the provision of future services.   In some cases, large initial fees are paid for the provision of a service, whilst continuing fees are relatively small in relation to future services to be provided; if it is probable that the continuing fees will not cover the cost of the continuing services to be provided, then a portion of the initial fee should be deferred over the period of the service contract such that a reasonable profit is earned throughout the service period.

5.1.1   Franchise fees

The franchise agreements which form the basis of the relationships between franchisors and franchisees can vary widely both in their complexity and in the extent to which various rights, duties and obligations are dealt with in the agreements. For this reason, no standard form franchise agreement exists which would dictate standard accounting practice for the recognition of all franchise fee revenue. Consequently, only a full understanding of the franchise agreement will reveal the substance of a particular arrangement so that the most appropriate accounting treatment can be determined; nevertheless, the following are the more common areas which are likely to be addressed in any franchise agreement and which would be relevant to franchise fee revenue reporting:[68]

(a)   *Rights transferred by the franchisor:* the agreement would give the franchisee the right to use the trade name, processes, know-how of the franchisor for a specified period of time or in perpetuity.

(b)   *The amount and terms of payment of initial fees:* payment of initial fees (where applicable) may be fully or partially due in cash, and may be payable immediately, over a specified period or on the fulfilment of certain obligations by the franchisor.

(c) *Amount and terms of payment of continuing franchise fees:* the franchisee will normally be required to pay a continuing fee to the franchisor – usually on the basis of a percentage of gross revenues.

(d) *Services to be provided by the franchisor initially and on a continuing basis:* the franchisor will usually agree to provide a variety of services and advice to the franchisee, such as:

  ■ site selection;

  ■ the procurement of fixed assets and equipment – these may be either purchased by the franchisee, leased from the franchisor or leased from a third party (possibly with the franchisor guaranteeing the lease payments);

  ■ advertising;

  ■ training of franchisee's personnel;

  ■ inspecting, testing and other quality control programmes; and

  ■ bookkeeping services.

(e) *Acquisition of equipment, stock, supplies etc.:* the franchisee may be required to purchase these items either from the franchisor or from designated suppliers. Some franchisors manufacture products for sale to their franchisees, whilst others act as wholesalers.

In the US, SFAS 45 – *Accounting for Franchise Fee Revenue* – states that franchise fee revenue should be recognised 'when all material services or conditions relating to the sale have been substantially performed or satisfied by the franchisor'.[69] Substantial performance for the franchisor means that:

(a) the franchisor has no remaining obligation or intent (in terms of the franchise agreement, the law or trade practice) to refund any cash received or waive any debts receivable;

(b) substantially all of the initial services of the franchisor required by the franchise agreement have been performed; and

(c) no other material conditions or obligations related to the determination of substantial performance exist.[70]

SFAS 45 also deals with the issue of mixed revenue – i.e. where the initial franchise fee incorporates not only the consideration for the franchise rights and the initial services to be provided by the franchisor, but also tangible assets such as equipment, signs etc. In such cases, the portion of the initial fee which is 'applicable to the tangible assets shall be based on the fair value of the assets and may be recognized before or after recognizing the portion applicable to the initial services. For example, when the portion of the fee relating to the sale of specific tangible assets is objectively determinable, it would be appropriate to recognize that portion when their titles pass, even though the balance of the fee relating to services is recognized when the remaining services or conditions in the franchise agreement have been substantially performed or satisfied.'[71]

In revising IAS 18, the IASC has expanded the Appendix thereto in order to better illustrate the application of the standard in commercial situations. Included in the Appendix is a broad discussion of the receipt of franchise fees, where it is stated that they 'are recognised as revenue on a basis that reflects the purpose for which the fees were charged'.[72] For example, franchise fees for the provision of continuing services, whether part of the initial fee or a separate fee, are recognised as revenue as the services are rendered. When the separate fee does not cover the cost of continuing services together with a reasonable profit, part of the initial fee, sufficient to cover the costs of continuing services and to provide a reasonable profit on those services, is deferred and recognised as revenue as the services are rendered.[73]

In summary, therefore, we suggest that the following basic principles may be applied for the recognition of initial franchise fees:

(a)   first, it is necessary to break down the fee into its various components; for example, fee for franchise rights, fee for initial services to be performed by the franchisor, fair value of tangible assets sold etc. The reason for this is that the individual components may be recognised at different stages; the portion that relates to the franchise rights may be recognised in full immediately, or part of it may have to be deferred (see (b) below); the fee for initial services to be performed should only be recognised when the services have been 'substantially performed' (it is unlikely that substantial performance will have been completed before the franchisee opens for business); and the portion of the fee which relates to tangible assets may be recognised when title passes;

(b)   next, it should be considered whether or not the continuing fee will cover the cost of continuing services to be provided by the franchisor. If not, then a portion of the initial fee should be deferred and amortised over the life of the franchise;

(c)   if the collection period for the initial fees is extended and there is doubt as to the ultimate collectability, revenue should be recognised on a cash received basis; and

(d)   in the event of the franchisor having the option to buy out the franchisee, and there is considered to be a significant probability that he will do so, initial franchise fee revenue should be deferred in full and credited against the cost of the investment when the buy-out occurs.

5.1.2   *Advance royalty/licence receipts*

Under normal circumstances, the accounting treatment of advance royalty/licence receipts is straightforward; under the accruals concept of

SSAP 2, the advance should be treated as deferred income when received, and released to the profit and loss account when earned under the royalty/licence agreement. However, there are certain industries where the forms of agreement entered into are such that advance receipts comprise a number of components, each requiring different accounting treatments.

For example, in the record and music industry, a record company will normally enter into a contractual arrangement with either a recording artist or a production company to deliver finished recording masters over a specified period of time. The albums are then manufactured and shipped to retailers for ultimate sale to the customer. The recording artist will normally be compensated through participating in the record company's sales and licence fee income (i.e. a royalty), although he may receive a non-refundable fixed fee on delivery of the master to the record company.

Example 3.1   Revenue recognition for licensors in the record and music industry

For each recording master delivered by a pop group, THRAG, the group (which operates through a service company) receives a payment of £1,000,000. This amount comprises a non-returnable, non-recoupable payment of £200,000, a non-returnable but recoupable advance of £600,000 and a returnable, recoupable advance of £200,000. The recoupable advances can be recouped against royalties on net sales earned both on the album concerned and on earlier and subsequent albums. This is achieved by computing the total royalties on net sales on all albums delivered under THRAG's service company's agreement with its recording company, and applying against this total the advances and royalties previously paid on those albums.

It is clear that the non-recoupable advance should be recognised in income when received, since it is not related to any future performance; at the other end of the spectrum, recognition of the refundable advance should be deferred and recognised only when recouped. However, the question arises as to whether the non-refundable but recoupable advance on royalties should be recognised immediately or deferred. If one accepts that revenue may be recognised when it is absolutely assured, there is an argument to justify the immediate recognition of the recoupable advance, since it is non-refundable; furthermore, it might be argued that, as far as THRAG is concerned, the earning process is complete, since the group does not have any further performance obligations. Conversely, some might argue that although the advance is non-refundable, it is not earned until it is recouped; furthermore, immediate recognition of royalty advances is likely to lead to a significant distortion of reported income, resulting in there being little correlation between reported income and album sales.

Clearly, therefore, there is no clear-cut answer, and it is our view that either approach is acceptable – i.e. the non-refundable but recoupable advance may be recognised in full as soon as the master is delivered to the recording company or, alternatively, it may be treated as deferred income when received and matched to subsequent album sales, being released to the profit and loss account in the period in which the sales are made. The most important point is that, whichever method is adopted, it is applied consistently. Of course, if the ASB's Draft *Statement of Principles* was to be adopted, its asset/liability approach to the recognition of gains would dictate that all non-returnable advances – whether recoupable or not – would be recognised in income immediately.

It is, perhaps, noteworthy that the deferral approach is supported by the US accounting requirement contained in SFAS 50 – *Financial Reporting in the Record and Music Industry* – which states that where an amount is paid in advance by a licensee to a licensor for the right to sell or distribute records or music, 'the licensor shall report such a minimum guarantee as a liability initially and recognize the guarantee as revenue as the license fee is earned under the agreement. If the licensor cannot otherwise determine the amount of the license fee earned, the guarantee shall be recognized as revenue equally over the remaining performance period, which is generally the period covered by the license agreement.'[74]

Chrysalis is an example of a company which has adopted this approach of deferring the recognition of non-returnable advances against royalties, as illustrated by the following extract:

Extract 3.1: Chrysalis Group PLC (1996)

notes to the accounts

1   ACCOUNTING POLICIES

RECORD ROYALTIES (EXCLUDING RECORD PRODUCER SERVICES AND MUSIC PUBLISHING ROYALTIES) [extract]

Royalty income is included on a receivable basis calculated on sales of records arising during each accounting period as reported by licensees, any unrecouped advances being included in the period in which the licence agreement expires.

Similar recognition principles should be applied in the case of advance fees paid on the sale of film/TV rights. Receipts which are non-refundable and non-recoupable should be recognised immediately, whilst any non-refundable but recoupable royalty advances may either be recognised immediately, or be deferred and recognised as earned; again, the accounting policy selected should be applied consistently.

5.1.3   Loan arrangement fees

The practice of recognising loan arrangement fees as income in the year that the loans are arranged was outlawed in the US through the publication of SFAS 91 – *Accounting for Nonrefundable Fees and Costs Associated with Originating or Acquiring Loans and Initial Direct Costs of Leases* – which requires loan origination fees to be deferred and recognised over the life of the related loan as an adjustment of interest income.[75]   Similarly, direct loan origination costs should be deferred and recognised as a reduction in the yield of the loan.[76]

Since there is no corresponding requirement in the UK, the recognition of arrangement fees on receipt may be regarded as acceptable; however, our preferred approach is that the principles contained in SFAS 91 should equally be applied in the UK. Nevertheless, situations may exist where the lending institution is providing other financial services which are, in themselves, valuable to the borrower and which are covered by the arrangement fee. If this is the case, then it may be argued that the portion of the initial fee which relates to those services should be recognised as income immediately, provided that the interest rate to be charged on the loan is fair and reasonable in relation to the risk involved and that the arrangement fee is not merely an interest prepayment.

The Appendix to IAS 18 includes a series of illustrative examples which relate to financial service fees, pointing out that the recognition of revenue for financial service fees depends on the purposes for which the fees are assessed and the basis of accounting for any associated financial instrument. The examples in the Appendix divide up the types of fees which arise into three categories, distinguishing between:

(a)   those which are an integral part of the effective yield of a financial instrument – in which case the fees are generally treated as an adjustment to the effective yield;

(b)   those which are earned as services are provided – in which case the fees are recognised as revenue either as the services are provided or on a time proportion basis; and

(c)   those which are earned on the execution of a significant act – in which case the fees are recognised as revenue when the significant act has been completed.[77]

Consequently, provided that the arrangement fee is not an integral part of the effective yield of a loan, the fee can be recognised as revenue when the loan has been arranged.

5.1.4   Commitment fees

Commitment fees are fees paid by potential borrowers for a commitment to originate or purchase a loan or group of loans within a particular period of time. According to the ICAEW Industry Accounting and Auditing Guide on banks, 'the fact that a commitment fee may be legally payable at the commencement of a facility should not be allowed to detract from the fact that the fee relates to the provision of a service over a future period of time. Consequently it should usually be accounted for on a time apportionment basis.'[78] This contrasts with the accounting treatment prescribed by SFAS 91, namely that the fee should be deferred until either the commitment is exercised or it expires. If the commitment is exercised, it should normally be recognised over the life of the loan as an adjustment to interest income, and if it expires unexercised it should be recognised in income on expiration.[79]

SFAS 91 does, however, allow the following two exceptions to this general rule:

(a)   if the enterprise's experience with similar arrangements indicates that the likelihood that the commitment will be exercised is remote (i.e. the likelihood is slight that a loan commitment will be exercised prior to its expiration), the commitment fee should be recognised over the commitment period on a straight-line basis as service fee income. If the commitment is subsequently exercised during the commitment period, the remaining unamortised commitment fee at the time of exercise should be recognised over the life of the loan as an adjustment to interest income;[80]

(b)   if the amount of the commitment fee is determined retrospectively as a percentage of the line of credit available but unused in a previous period, then the fee should be recognised as service fee income as of the determination date, provided that:

    (i)   the percentage applied is nominal in relation to the stated interest rate on any related borrowing; and

    (ii)   the borrowing will bear a market interest rate at the date the loan is made.[81]

Applying the criteria set out in the Appendix to IAS 18 (see 5.1.3 above), if it is unlikely that a specific lending arrangement will be entered into, the commitment fee will be recognised as revenue on a time proportion basis over the commitment period.

5.1.5   Credit card fees

It is common practice in the UK for credit card companies to levy a charge, payable in advance, on its cardholders. Although such charges may be seen as commitment fees for the credit facilities offered by the card, they clearly cover the many other services available to cardholders as well. Accordingly, we would suggest that the fees which are periodically charged to cardholders should be deferred and recognised on a straight-line basis over the period the fee entitles the cardholder to use the card.[82]

5.2   Goods sold subject to reservation of title

The Romalpa case,[83] which was decided in 1976, focused attention on the terms of a particular form of sale whereby the seller retains title to the goods sold and, in some cases, the right to other goods produced from them and the ultimate sale proceeds. The appropriate accounting treatment of such sales will depend on the commercial substance of the transaction, rather than its legal form. For example, it may be that the reservation of title is of no economic relevance to either party, except in the event of the insolvency of the purchaser; in other words, the goods are supplied and payment is due on an identical basis to other goods which are sold without reservation of title. In such circumstances, provided there is no significant uncertainty regarding the collectability of the amount due, the sale should be recognised as revenue.

However, the circumstances surrounding the sale might be such that the parties view it as a consignment sale; for example, the purchaser may retain the right to return unsold goods to the seller, and the obligation to pay for the goods might be deferred until such time as the goods are sold to a third party. In such a case it would be inappropriate for the seller to recognise the sale until such time as the purchaser sells the goods and is liable for payment. However, situations of this nature fall within the scope of FRS 5 generally and Application Note A thereof in particular – the details of which are discussed in Chapter 16 of this book.

The accounting treatment of goods sold subject to reservation of title is discussed in a statement of guidance issued by the ICAEW in July 1976 and, although rather out of date, it has never been superseded by a more authoritative document.[84]

5.3 Subscriptions to publications

Publication subscriptions are generally paid in advance and are non-refundable. Nevertheless, since the publications will still have to be produced and delivered to the subscriber, the subscription revenue cannot be regarded as having been earned until production and delivery takes place. Consequently, we recommend that revenue should be deferred and recognised either on a straight-line basis over the subscription period or, where the publications vary in value, revenue should be based on the proportion of the sales value that each publication bears to the total sales value of all publications covered by the subscription. Metal Bulletin is an example of a company which follows such an approach:

Extract 3.2: Metal Bulletin plc (1996)

Statement of Accounting Policies

    (a)   Turnover [extract]

        (i) Subscription revenue is allocated to accounting periods in proportion to the number of issues covered by the subscription published before and after the accounting date. Unappropriated subscription revenue is included with current liabilities.

This accounting policy is a perfect illustration of the difference between the ASB's balance sheet approach to the recognition of gains (as espoused in its Draft *Statement of Principles*), and conventional transactions-based accounting. Metal Bulletin is, quite appropriately, applying the accruals and prudence concepts to allocate the subscription revenue to its profit and loss account as it is earned. Subscriptions received in advance of being earned are carried in the balance sheet as deferred income.

However, the ASB's Draft *Statement of Principles* implicitly denies that such a separate category exists, since it is not acknowledged as one of the elements of financial statements. Instead, the Draft tries to square this circle, using the example of a magazine subscription that has been received in advance by a publisher, by asserting that what is in reality deferred income can be satisfactorily embraced within the definition of a liability.[85]

It does not take much to show that this argument does not stand up. If one was to accept that a balance sheet approach should be followed in accounting for this situation, it would be necessary to consider the nature of the 'liability' involved and measure it appropriately. The publisher's contractual obligation is to provide the magazine, and it would be appropriate to measure such liability at the cost of doing so, not the amount of advance subscriptions received. This would therefore mean recording the profit in the year in which the cash happened to be received, not when the sale was performed, which would be quite inappropriate. It would also mean, for example, that the publisher could boost its immediate reported profits by inducing customers to take out subscriptions for longer periods in advance, such as a five-year subscription at a reduced rate.

5.4   Advertising revenue

The examples in the Appendix to IAS 18 adopt the performance of the service as the critical event for the recognition of revenue derived from the rendering of services. Consequently, media commissions are recognised when the related advertisement or commercial appears before the public. Production commissions are recognised by reference to the stage of completion of the project.[86] We concur with this broad approach which, as illustrated by the following extracts, appears to have been enshrined in UK GAAP:

Extract 3.3: Metal Bulletin plc (1996)

Statement of Accounting Policies

   (a) **Turnover** [extract]

        (ii) Advertisement revenue is brought into account on publication date. All publication expenses are written off at that date.

Extending this principle to media commissions would mean that such revenue should be recognised when the related advertisement or commercial appears before the public. Similarly, production commissions should generally be recognised by reference to stage of completion of the project. This is, in fact, the approach adopted by media group Aegis:

Extract 3.4: Aegis Group plc (1996)

1.   Principal accounting policies

Turnover [extract]

Turnover is recognised when charges are made to clients, principally when advertisements appear in the media. Fees are recognised over the period of the relevant assignments or agreements.

5.5   Software revenue recognition

There are a number of issues relating to the timing of revenue recognition in the software services industry. The issues which arise surround the question of when to recognise revenue from contracts to develop software, software licensing fees, customer support services and data services. However, few of these issues have been addressed in the authoritative literature and, because of the nature of the products and services involved, applying the general revenue recognition principles to software transactions can sometimes be difficult. The result of this has been that in practice software companies have used a variety of methods to recognise revenue, often producing significantly different financial results for similar transactions.

This problem was recognised in the US by the FASB and SEC who encouraged the AICPA to provide guidance on software revenue recognition methods. This culminated in AICPA Statement of Position (SOP) 91–1, which was issued in December 1991. The SOP applies to all entities that earn revenue from licensing, selling, leasing or otherwise marketing computer software. It does not apply to revenue from the sale or licensing of a product containing software that is incidental to the product as a whole, such as software sold as part of a telephone system.

In the absence of any other authoritative literature on the subject, it is useful to examine the relevant issue relating to software revenue recognition in the light of the SOP.

5.5.1 *Software licences with no significant vendor obligations*

The most basic form of licensing arrangement is where a software company gives a customer the right to use a particular software product for a specific period of time. All that the software company has to do is either duplicate a delivery copy from the product master or load a copy of the product on to the customer's system. The question that arises, assuming that the product is deliverable at the time of the signing of the contract, is whether revenue should be recognised at the time of signing the contract or at the time of delivery of the product. The arguments in favour of recognition at the time of signing might suggest that since all costs to develop, produce and market the product have already been incurred, delivery is not a key event in the software company's earnings process. Alternatively, the view might be held that the licensing of a software product is similar to the sale of goods, and that the revenue from the sale of goods is generally recognised on delivery.

It could be argued that the granting of a software licence has no substance until the product is delivered and/or installed and available for use by the customer; consequently revenue should normally only be recognised on delivery. However, it is possible that the 'bill and hold' basis of recognition applicable to sale of goods could be applied to software products. Using this analogy, revenue could be recognised at the point when the product is deliverable, provided that a specific copy of the software product is prepared and assigned to the contract, the software company is obligated to deliver the product at any time which is suitable to the customer, the amount due for the product is billable and payment is not dependent on delivery.

SOP 91–1 provides that if collectability is probable and the vendor has no obligations remaining under the sales or licensing agreement after delivering the software, revenue from the software licensing fee should be recognised on delivery of the software.[87] The SOP goes on to say that if the vendor has insignificant obligations remaining under the sales or licensing agreement after delivering the software, revenue from the software licensing fee should be recognised on delivery of the software if collectability is probable. The remaining obligations should be accounted for either (a) by accruing the remaining costs or (b) by deferring a pro rata portion of revenue and recognising it either ratably as the obligations are fulfilled or on completion of performance.[88]

5.5.2   *Products sold with significant vendor obligations*

Where companies are running well-established computer installations with systems and configurations which they do not wish to change, off-the-shelf software packages are generally not suitable for their purposes. For this reason, some software companies will enter into a customer contract whereby they agree to customise a generalised software product to meet the customer's specific processing needs. A simple form of customisation would be to modify the system's output reports so that they integrate with the customer's existing management reporting system. However, customisation will often entail more involved obligations; for example, having to translate the software so that it is able to run on the customer's specific hardware configuration, data conversion, system integration, installation and testing.

The question which arises, therefore, is on what basis should a software company be recognising revenue where it enters into this type of contract which involves significant contractual obligations? It is our view that the principles laid down in SSAP 9 – *Stocks and long-term contracts* – should be applied in this situation. SSAP 9 defines a long-term contract as 'a contract entered into for the design, manufacture or construction of a single substantial asset or the provision of a service (or of a combination of assets or services which together constitute a single product) where the time taken substantially to complete the contract is such that the contract activity falls into different accounting periods'.[89] The standard requires that 'long-term contracts should be assessed on a contract by contract basis and reflected in the profit and loss account by recording turnover and related costs as contract activity progresses. Turnover is ascertained in a manner appropriate to the stage of completion of the contract, the business and the industry in which it operates. Where it is considered that the outcome of a long-term contract can be assessed with reasonable certainty before its conclusion, the prudently calculated attributable profit should be recognised in the profit and loss account as the difference between the reported turnover and related costs for that contract.'[90]

Consequently, where the software company is able to make reliable estimates as to the extent of progress toward completion of a contract, related revenues and related costs, and where the outcome of the contract can be assessed with reasonable certainty, the percentage-of-completion method of profit recognition should be applied. One company which follows this approach is Logica, a company whose principal activities include the marketing, design, production, integration and maintenance of custom built software and associated hardware systems:

Extract 3.5: Logica plc (1996)

Accounting policies

4 Recognition of profits [extract]

Profit is taken on fixed price contracts while the contract is in progress, having regard to the proportion of the total contract which has been completed at the balance sheet date. Provision is made for all foreseeable future losses.

5 Amounts recoverable on contracts

Amounts recoverable on contracts represent turnover which has not yet been invoiced to clients. Such amounts are separately disclosed within Debtors.

The valuation of amounts recoverable on fixed price contracts is adjusted to take up profit to date or foreseeable losses in accordance with the accounting policy for recognition of profits.

Other amounts recoverable on contracts are valued at the lower of cost or estimated net realisable value.

Cost comprises:

*   professional amounts recoverable valued at the cost of salaries and associated payroll expenses of employees engaged on assignments and a proportion of attributable overheads
*   unbilled expenses incurred and equipment purchased for clients in connection with specific contracts.

On the other hand, where the uncertainties are such that prudence would preclude the accrual of profit, or where the contracts are of a relatively short duration, the completed contract method of accounting should be applied.

SOP 91–1 takes a similar line, stating that where a sales or licensing agreement includes other significant vendor obligations, the agreement should first be examined to determine whether it should be accounted for using contract accounting (i.e. revenues are generally recognised on the basis of percentage of completion) or as a service transaction (i.e. revenue is generally recognised as services are performed).

For agreements with significant vendor obligations beyond delivery of the software that are not accounted for using contract accounting or as service transactions, the SOP states that revenue should not be recognised until all the following conditions are met:

■   delivery has occurred;

■   other remaining vendor obligations are no longer significant; and

■   collectability is probable.[91]

5.5.3   *Post-delivery customer support services*

Often, the software company will provide support services after the product has been delivered to the customer, installed and tested. These services may include a telephone help-line, further customisation, product enhancements, training of new staff etc., and are either included in the cost of the software product or sold separately through a support service contract (which, for example, might be renewable on an annual basis). Even if the contract does not specifically include free product enhancements, customers often enter into service contracts to obtain enhancements at favourable rates, or to ensure that they always have the latest version installed. On the other hand, software companies, to some extent, rely on service contracts as a source of funding of product enhancements; furthermore, the existence of a support service customer base makes it commercially attractive for a company to continue enhancing the product, since a ready market exists for the sale thereof.

It is quite clear that the matching concept would require that the revenue derived from customer support contracts should be deferred and recognised over the period of the contract. This is based on the premise that a liability to perform services is incurred at the inception of the contract, and is discharged over the life of the contract. It might be argued that revenues should be matched with actual costs incurred in rendering the support services; however, it would generally be impracticable to achieve this, and the costs of doing so would probably outweigh the benefits.   Consequently, customer support revenue should normally be recognised on a straight-line basis over the term of the contract. The following extract illustrates what we consider to be an appropriate policy:

Extract 3.6: Total Systems plc (1996)

1.   Accounting policies

Software maintenance

For software covered by maintenance contracts income is credited to the profit and loss account over the period to which the contract relates. Costs associated with these contracts are expensed as incurred.

However, a further problem does exist where the fee for post-delivery customer support services is packaged together with the fee for the product, and is not, therefore, subject to a separate contract. It is our view that the revenue element which relates to the support services should be separated from the initial fee and recognised over time. This should present little difficulty where the price of similar support service contracts is readily available; however, if the software company does not normally sell support contracts separately, it will be necessary to make an allocation based on achieving a reasonable rate of return on the contracts in the light of the costs involved in providing the support service. The selling price of support service contracts is sometimes determined on the basis of a percentage of the selling price of the product which is being supported; under certain circumstances, therefore, this may be a practicable basis of separating the revenue elements where the product and support services are sold as a package.

5.5.4 Data services

Data services companies offer their customers various data processing services such as on-line access to data bases and applications programmes. Normally, the fees charged to customers are made up of three components:

- *subscription fees*, which are, effectively, log-on fees to the data services facilities, and either may or may not include a certain amount of 'free' processing time;

- *usage fees*, which are normally charged either on the basis of the volume of transactions or access time; contracts are often sold subject to a guaranteed minimum usage charge; and

- *data storage fees*, which are charged for storing customer data on the data services company's computer facilities.

The first question which arises is whether non-refundable subscription fee revenue should be recognised immediately the contract is signed or recognised over the period of the contract. The argument in favour of immediate recognition is based on the premise that the subscription fees relate to costs already incurred at the commencement of the contract (e.g. marketing, the installation of data communications devices, data entry etc.), and that future costs are matched with usage fees. The argument against this is that the subscription fees are merely part of the revenue which the data services company receives over the period of the contract, and that (irrespective of the wording of the contract) the customer would, in law, be entitled to claim a refund of a portion of the subscription fees if the data services company failed to provide the processing facilities throughout the duration of the contract.

It is our view that the immediate recognition of the full subscription fee at the inception of the contract would generally not be appropriate, and that the fees should normally be recognised over the period of the contract. However, where there are significant incremental costs incurred at inception, a portion of subscription fee revenue may be recognised to the extent of costs incurred, and the revenues in excess of costs should be deferred and recognised over the term of the contract. In practice, this may be achieved by applying a formula based on a reasonable estimate of associated costs; for example, a policy might be established whereby 25% of subscription fee revenue is recognised at inception to cover associated incremental costs, with the balance of 75% being recognised on a straight-line basis over the term of the contract. However, where the subscription fee includes a portion of 'free' processing time, the fee should be recognised as this time is used up.

Where usage fees are charged on the basis of minimum usage, the question arises as to the basis on which such fees should be recognised. Should the fees be recognised on the basis of an absorption rate which is calculated according to the customer's expected usage during the period, or should they be recognised at the actual rate, with any unused portion being recognised at the expiration of the period? The following example illustrates these two bases:

Example 3.2   Recognition of usage fees for data services

A data services company enters into a 12 month contract to provide a customer with on-line access to a data base at the rate of £60 per hour, subject to a fixed minimum fee of £6,000 (i.e. 100 hours). Unused access time is forfeited at the end of the 12 month period. The company estimates that the customer will only utilise a maximum of 75 hours during the period. The two possible bases of recognising the revenue over the term of the contract are as follows:

* recognised on the basis of the customer's anticipated usage (i.e. revenue would be recognised at the rate of £80 per hour); or
* recognised at the actual rate of £60 per hour, with any unused portion being recognised on the expiration of the contract.

Because of the uncertainty involved in estimating the customer's usage, it is our view that the second of the two options is preferable.

5.6   Film exhibition rights

Revenue received from the licensing of films for exhibition at cinemas and on television should be recognised in accordance with the general recognition principles discussed in this Chapter. Contracts for the television broadcast rights of films normally allow for multiple showings within a specific period; these contracts usually expire either on the date of the last authorised telecast, or on a specified date, whichever occurs first. It is our view that the revenue from the sale of broadcast or exhibition rights may be recognised in full (irrespective of when the licence period begins), provided the following conditions are met:

(a)   a contract has been entered into;

(b)   the film is complete and available for delivery;

(c)   there are no outstanding performance obligations, other than having to make a copy of the film and deliver it to the licensee; and

(d)   collectability is reasonably assured.

Rights for the exhibition of films at cinemas are generally sold either on the basis of a percentage of the box office receipts or for a flat fee. In the case of the percentage basis, revenue should be recognised as it accrues through the showing of the film. Where a non-refundable flat fee is received, we suggest that revenue be recognised on the same basis as described above for television broadcast rights.

In the US, under SFAS 53 – *Financial Reporting by Producers and Distributors of Motion Picture Films* – revenue from a television broadcast contract should only be recognised in full when the licence period begins, and all of the following conditions have been met:

(a)   the licence fee for each film is known;

(b)   the cost of each film is known or reasonably determinable;

(c)   collectability of the full licence fee is reasonably assured;

(d)   the film has been accepted by the licensee in accordance with the conditions of the licence agreement; and

(e)   the film is available for its first telecast.[92]

5.7   The disposal of land and buildings

Unlike the US, there are no laid down rules in the UK for the recognition of the proceeds on disposal of land and buildings. Consequently, the general principles of revenue recognition should be applied in order to determine the point in time at which property sales should be recognised in the profit and loss account. There are two significant points in the earning process which could, depending on the circumstances of the sale, be considered to be the critical event for recognition. The first point is on exchange of contracts, at which time the vendor and purchaser are both bound by a legally enforceable contract of sale; whilst the second possible point of recognition is on completion of the contract. The following extracts illustrate the fact that both approaches are followed in practice:

Extract 3.7: Crest Nicholson Plc (1996)

Accounting Policies

(d)   Income recognition

Profit is recognised on houses when contracts are exchanged and building is substantially complete. Profit is recognised on commercial property developments or units of development when they are substantially complete and subject to binding and unconditional contracts of sale and where legal completion has occurred shortly thereafter. Where the sale price is conditional upon letting, profit is restricted by reference to the space unlet. Profit in respect of construction is recognised when the contract is complete. In the case of contracts that are regarded as long term, profit is recognised during execution provided a binding contract for sale exists and the outcome can be foreseen with reasonable certainty.

Extract 3.8:   Hammerson plc (1996)

1   ACCOUNTING POLICIES

Profits on Sale of Properties [extract]

Profits on sale of properties are taken into account on the completion of contract and receipt of cash.

Although legal title and beneficial ownership do not pass until the contract is completed and the transfer is registered, it is likely that the earnings process is sufficiently complete to permit recognition to take place on exchange of contracts. The reason for this is that the selling price would have been established, all material related expenses would have been ascertained and, usually, no significant uncertainties would remain. If, however, on exchange of contracts there exists doubt that the sale will be ultimately completed, recognition should take place on the receipt of sales proceeds at legal completion.

However, since both approaches appear to be widely used in practice, they should both be regarded as being acceptable accounting practice. Nevertheless, it is important to ensure that, whichever policy is adopted, it is applied consistently, although recognition should always be delayed until completion if significant uncertainties still exist on exchange of contracts. The income recognition policy of Crest Nicholson reproduced above is a good example of the application of this principle.

The illustrative example in the Appendix to IAS 18 states that revenue is normally recognised when legal title passes to the buyer; however, at the same time, it acknowledges that recognition might take place before legal title passes, provided that the seller has no further substantial acts to complete under the contract.[93]

In the US, SFAS 66 – *Accounting for Sales of Real Estate* – lays down rigid rules for the recognition of profit on real estate transactions, and distinguishes between retail land sales (i.e. sales under a property development project) and other sales of real estate. The statement contains extensive provisions which have been developed to deal with complex transactions which are beyond the scope of this book. However, the general requirements for recognising all of the profit on a non-retail land sale are as follows:

Profit should not be recognised in full until all of the following criteria are met:

(a)   the sale is consummated;

(b)   the purchaser's initial and continuing investments are adequate to demonstrate a commitment to pay for the property;

(c)   the vendor's receivable is not subject to future subordination; and

(d) the vendor has transferred to the purchaser the usual risks and rewards of ownership in a transaction that is in substance a sale and does not have a substantial continuing involvement with the property.[94]

A sale is not considered to be consummated until:

(a) the parties are bound by the terms of the contract;

(b) all consideration has been exchanged (i.e. either all monies have been received, or all necessary contractual arrangements have been entered into for the ultimate payment of monies – such as notes supported by irrevocable letters of credit from an independent lending institution);

(c) any permanent financing for which the vendor is responsible has been arranged; and

(d) all conditions precedent to closing the contract have been performed.[95]

SFAS 66 states that these four conditions are usually met 'at the time of closing or after closing, not when an agreement to sell is signed or at a preclosing'.[96]

5.8 Sale and leaseback transactions

A sale and leaseback transaction takes place when an owner sells an asset and immediately reacquires the right to use the asset by entering into a lease with the purchaser. The accounting treatment of any apparent profit arising on the sale of the asset will depend on whether the leaseback is an operating or finance lease. In general terms, if the leaseback is an operating lease, the seller-lessee has disposed of substantially all the risks and rewards of ownership of the asset, and so has realised a profit on disposal. Conversely, if the leaseback is a finance lease, the seller-lessee is, in effect, reacquiring substantially all the risks and rewards of ownership of the asset; consequently, it would be inappropriate to recognise a profit on an asset which, in substance, was never disposed of.[97]

The accounting treatment of the profit arising on sale and leaseback transactions is discussed in Chapter 17 at 7.4.

5.9 Non-monetary/barter transactions

There is currently no authoritative guidance in the UK which deals directly with the accounting for non-monetary transactions. Under IAS 18, when goods or services are exchanged for goods or services which are of a similar nature and value, the exchange is not regarded as a transaction which generates revenue. This is often the case, for example, with exchanges of licence interests in the oil and gas industry. However, when goods or services are exchanged for dissimilar goods or services, the exchange is regarded as a transaction which generates revenue. The revenue is measured at the fair value of the goods or services received, adjusted by the amount of any cash or cash equivalents transferred. When the fair value of the goods or services received cannot be measured reliably, the revenue is measured at the fair value of the goods or services given up, adjusted by the amount of any cash or cash equivalents transferred.[98]

The general principles under US GAAP are similar to IAS 18 and are addressed in APB Opinion No. 29 – *Accounting for Nonmonetary Transactions.* APB 29 states that the basis of accounting for non-monetary transactions is the same as for monetary transactions – i.e. fair values – and a gain or loss is recognised when the book value of the asset given up differs from the fair value recorded for the asset received.[99] However, APB 29 recognises that when neither the fair value of the non-monetary asset received nor the fair value of the non-monetary asset given up can be determined within reasonable limits, the recorded amount of the asset transferred from the enterprise may be the only available measure of the transaction.[100] Furthermore, where the exchange involves 'similar productive assets' – i.e. assets that are of the same general type, that perform the same function or that are in the same line of business – a gain is not recognised.[101]

APB 29 also recognises that the exchange of non-monetary assets may include an amount of monetary consideration. In such cases, the recipient of the monetary consideration has realised a gain on the exchange to the extent that the amount of the monetary receipt exceeds a proportionate share of the recorded amount of the asset surrendered. The portion of the cost applicable to the realised amount should be based on the ratio of the monetary consideration to the total consideration received (i.e. monetary consideration plus the estimated fair value of the non-monetary asset received) or, if more clearly evident, the fair value of the non-monetary asset transferred.

6   CONCLUSION

The growing complexity and variety of business activity have given birth to a variety of forms of revenue-earning transactions which were never contemplated when the point of sale was established several decades ago as the general rule for revenue recognition. Added to this, the gradual move away from strict adherence to the realisation concept has resulted in contemporary generally accepted practice for the recognition of revenue becoming haphazard. Whilst there appears to be a growing practice of recognising revenue during the course of productive activity, it is generally done on the basis of exception, rather than in terms of an established principle.

At the same time, though, instead of bringing order to existing practice, the ASB has proposed a radical new approach to revenue recognition based on changes in balance sheet net assets. This approach, if implemented, would replace the long-established accounting process in use throughout the world, whereby transactions are allocated to accounting periods by reference to the matching and prudence concepts. However, it is most unlikely to work well in practice. Revenue recognition criteria are more demanding than those for recognising assets and liabilities, since they should embody the concept of the revenue having been earned, based on performance by the reporting company. Although the conventions for applying this transactions-based approach need to be developed further, it seems more likely that it will remain a more workable system than recognition criteria based on determining whether or not there is sufficient evidence that a change in net assets has occurred.

References

1   APB Statement No. 4, *Basic Concepts and Accounting Principles Underlying Financial Statements of Business Enterprises*, AICPA, October 1970, para. 134.
2   The Council of the European Communities, *The Second Council Directive on Company Law*, 77/91/EEC.
3   *Ibid.*, Article 15.1(c).
4   CCAB, *The determination of realised profits and disclosure of distributable profits in the context of the Companies Acts 1948 to 1981 (TR 481)*, September 1982, paras. 4–6, *passim*.
5   *Ibid.*, para. 10.
6   SSAP 2, *Disclosure of accounting policies*, November 1971, para. 14.
7   Professor Sir Bryan Carsberg and Christopher Noke, *The reporting of profits and the concept of realisation: A report prepared for the Research Board of the Institute of Chartered Accountants in England and Wales*, London, 1989, p. 41.
8   *Ibid.*, p. 42.
9   Exposure Draft, *Statement of Principles for Financial Reporting*, ASB, November 1995, Chapter 4.
10 *Ibid.*, para. 6.26.
11 APB Statement No. 4, para. 150.
12 *Ibid.*, para. 151.
13 *Ibid.*, para. 152.
14 John H. Myers, 'The Critical Event and Recognition of Net Profit', *Accounting Review* 34, October 1959, pp. 528–532.
15 SFAC No. 5, *Recognition and Measurement in Financial Statements of Business Enterprises*, FASB, December 1984, paras. 83 and 84.
16 Sale of Goods Act 1979, s 2(1).
17 *Ibid.*, s 2(4).
18 *Ibid.*, s 2(5).
19 *Ibid.*, s 18, Rule 1.
20 *Ibid.*, s 18, Rule 2.
21 APB Statement No. 4, para. 151.
22 SFAC No. 5, paras. 83 and 84.
23 SFAS 48, *Revenue Recognition When Right of Return Exists*, FASB, June 1981, para. 6.
24 *Ibid.*
25 *Ibid.*, para. 8.
26 APB Statement No. 4, para. 150.
27 IASC, Draft Statement of Principles, *Agriculture*, IASC, December 1996.
28 CA 85, Sch. 4, para. 12(a).
29 *Ibid.*, s 262(3).
30 Exposure Draft, *Statement of Principles for Financial Reporting*, ASB, para. 4.5.
31 *Ibid.*, para. 4.6.
32 *Ibid.*, para. 4.7.
33 *Ibid.*, para. 4.8.
34 *Ibid.*, para. 4.11.
35 *Ibid.*, para. 4.15.

36 *Ibid.*
37 *Ibid.*, para 4.24.
38 *Ibid.*
39 *Ibid.*, para. 4.29.
40 *Ibid.*, para. 6.26.
41 IAS 18 (Original), *Revenue Recognition*, IASC, December 1982, para. 4.
42 IAS 18, *Revenue*, IASC, Revised 118 1993.
43 *Ibid.*, para. 1.
44 *Ibid.*, para. 7.
45 *Ibid.*, para. 10.
46 *Ibid.*, para. 7.
47 *Ibid.*, para. 11.
48 *Ibid.*, para. 12.
49 *Ibid.*, para. 14.
50 *Ibid.*, para. 16.
51 *Ibid.*, para. 15.
52 *Ibid.*, para. 17.
53 *Ibid.*, para. 20.
54 *Ibid.*, para. 26.
55 *Ibid.*, para. 20.
56 *Ibid.*, para. 24.
57 *Ibid.*, para. 25.
58 *Ibid.*, para. 35.
59 ARB 43, *Restatement and Revision of Accounting Research Bulletins*, AICPA, June 1953, Chapter 1, Section A, para. 1.
60 *Ibid.*
61 *Ibid.*, Chapter 11, Section A, para. 11.
62 *Ibid.*, para. 13.
63 ARB No. 45, *Long-Term Construction-Type Contracts*, AICPA, October 1955, para. 15.
64 SFAC No. 5, para. 83.
65 *Ibid.*
66 *Ibid.*
67 *Ibid.*
68 Based on the AICPA Industry Accounting Guide, *Accounting for Franchise Fee Revenue*, AICPA, 1973.
69 SFAS 45, *Accounting for Franchise Fee Revenue*, FASB, March 1981, para. 5.
70 *Ibid.*
71 *Ibid.*, para 12.
72 IAS 18, Appendix, para. 18.
73 *Ibid.*, Appendix, para. 18(b).
74 SFAS 50, *Financial Reporting in the Record and Music Industry*, FASB, November 1981, para. 8.
75 SFAS 91, *Accounting for Nonrefundable Fees and Costs Associated with Originating or Acquiring Loans and Initial Direct Costs of Leases*, FASB, December 1986, para. 5.
76 *Ibid.*
77 IAS 18, Appendix, para. 14.
78 C. I. Brown, D. J. Mallett and M. G. Taylor, *Banks: An Accounting and Auditing Guide*, Industry Accounting and Auditing Guide published by the ICAEW, 1983, para. 20.2.
79 SFAS 91, para. 8.
80 *Ibid.*, para. 8a.
81 *Ibid.*, para. 8b.
82 This is also the view taken in the US; see SFAS 91 at para. 10.
83 Aluminium Industrie Vaassen B.V. v Romalpa Aluminium Limited [1976] WLR 676.
84 Accounting Recommendation 2.207, *Accounting for goods sold subject to reservation of title*, ICAEW, July 1976.
85 Exposure Draft, *Statement of Principles for Financial Reporting*, ASB, para. 4.30
86 IAS 18, Appendix, para. 12.
87 AICPA, Statement of Position 91–1, *Software Revenue Recognition*, December 12, 1991, para. 32.

88 *Ibid.*, para. 33.
89 SSAP 9, *Stocks and long-term contracts*, Revised September 1988, para. 22.
90 *Ibid.*, paras. 28 and 29.
91 AICPA, SOP 91–1, para. 34.
92 SFAS 53, *Financial Reporting by Producers and Distributors of Motion Picture Films*, FASB, December 1981, para. 6.
93 IAS 18, Appendix, para. 9.
94 SFAS 66, *Accounting for Sales of Real Estate*, FASB, October 1982, para. 5.
95 *Ibid.*, para. 6.
96 *Ibid.*
97 ASC, Guidance Notes on SSAP 21: *Accounting for Leases and Hire Purchase Contracts*, August 1984, paras. 150–156, passim.
98 IAS 18, para. 12.
99 APB Opinion No. 29, *Accounting for Nonmonetary Transactions*, Accounting Principles Board, May 1973, para. 18.
100 *Ibid.*, para. 26.
101 *Ibid.*, paras. 3e and 21b.

Chapter 4   Corporate governance and the OFR

1   THE NEED FOR CORPORATE GOVERNANCE REFORM

A series of spectacular corporate failures and financial scandals in the late 1980s, including BCCI, Polly Peck and Maxwell, heightened concerns about the standard of financial reporting and accountability. These concerns centred around an apparent low level of confidence both in financial reporting and in the ability of auditors to provide the safeguards which the users of company annual reports sought and expected. The factors underlying these were seen as the looseness of accounting standards, the absence of a clear framework for ensuring that directors kept under review the controls in their businesses, and competitive pressures both on companies and on auditors which made it difficult for auditors to stand up to demanding boards.[1] These concerns were heightened by criticisms of the seeming lack of effective board accountability for such matters as directors' remuneration – particularly in the light of an increasing trend in directors being appointed on lucrative rolling contracts, as well as certain well-publicised large compensation payments for loss of office.

In response to these concerns, the Committee on the Financial Aspects of Corporate Governance (the Cadbury Committee) was set up in May 1991 by the Financial Reporting Council, the London Stock Exchange and the accountancy profession, under the chairmanship of Sir Adrian Cadbury. The terms of reference of the Committee were to consider the following issues in relation to financial reporting and accountability and to make recommendations on good practice:[2]

(a)   the responsibilities of executive and non-executive directors for reviewing and reporting on performance to shareholders and other financially interested parties; and the frequency, clarity and form in which information should be provided;

(b)   the case for audit committees of the board, including their composition and role;

(c)   the principal responsibilities of auditors and the extent and value of the audit;

(d)   the links between shareholders, boards and auditors; and

(e)   any other relevant matters.

2   WHAT IS CORPORATE GOVERNANCE?

The Cadbury Report describes corporate governance as 'the system by which companies are directed and controlled. Boards of directors are responsible for the governance of their companies. The shareholders' role in governance is to appoint the directors and the auditors and to satisfy themselves that an appropriate governance structure is in place. The responsibilities of the board include setting the company's strategic aims, providing the leadership to put them into effect, supervising the management of the business and reporting to shareholders on their stewardship. The board's actions are subject to laws, regulations and the shareholders in general meeting.'[3]   Within that overall framework, the specifically financial aspects of corporate governance are the way in which a company's board sets financial policy and oversees its implementation – including the use of financial controls and the process whereby the board reports on the activities and progress of the company to its shareholders.[4]

The overall objective of the Cadbury Committee, therefore, was to help raise the standards of corporate governance and the level of confidence in financial reporting and auditing by setting out clearly what it saw as the respective responsibilities of those involved and what it believed is expected of them.

In this chapter we have reviewed the recommendations of the Cadbury Committee in so far as they impact on the company annual report and accounts. The impact of the Cadbury Report on interim reporting is discussed at 2.2 in Chapter 31.

3   THE CADBURY CODE OF BEST PRACTICE

The Committee's approach was to provide a framework for establishing good corporate governance and accountability. This was done through the Committee's Code of Best Practice (the Code), which it put forward as a benchmark against which companies can be assessed. The full text of the Code, together with corresponding notes, is reproduced as an Appendix to this chapter.

The Code embodies underlying principles of openness, integrity and accountability which, according to the Committee, go together. 'Openness on the part of companies, within the limits set by their competitive position, is the basis for the confidence which needs to exist between business and all those who have a stake in its success. An open approach to the disclosure of information contributes to the efficient working of the market economy, prompts boards to take effective action and allows shareholders and others to scrutinise companies more thoroughly.'[5]

'Integrity means both straightforward dealing and completeness. What is required of financial reporting is that it should be honest and that it should present a balanced picture of the state of the company's affairs. The integrity of reports depends on the integrity of those who prepare and present them.'[6]

'Boards of directors are accountable to their shareholders and both have to play their part in making that accountability effective. Boards of directors need to do so through the quality of the information which they provide to shareholders, and shareholders through their willingness to exercise their responsibilities as owners.'[7]

The Code is aimed at listed companies, but other companies may also benefit from applying it. Although compliance with the Code is recommended, the Committee stressed that it is voluntary and is directed at establishing best practice. The Committee was also of the view that companies should be allowed some flexibility in implementing the Code; this was necessary in order to encourage companies to comply with the spirit of the recommendations. The Code provides a target to which companies can aspire, rather than a straitjacket of rules and regulations. The Committee recognised that if its recommendations were not supported, a legislative or regulatory regime may be necessary to deal with the underlying problems which its report identified.

In response to the Committee's recommendations, the London Stock Exchange has adopted as part of its Listing Rules the requirement for UK incorporated listed companies to include in their annual report and accounts a statement as to whether or not they have complied throughout the accounting period with the Code. This is supplemented by the requirement to report details of, and reasons for, any non-compliance during the period and to have the directors' statement reviewed by the auditors insofar as it relates to objectively verifiable matters in the Code.[8] (A number of examples of companies reporting non-compliance with certain aspects of the Code are shown in the extracts included at 4.1 to 4.4 below.)

During 1995 there were two changes made to the Listing Rules affecting reporting on corporate governance. As a result of these changes the 'statement of compliance' is no longer required to deal with:

- Paragraph 4.6 of the Code, the Stock Exchange having introduced a separate requirement dealing with the directors' going concern statement (see 4.4 below); and

- Paragraphs 3.1 to 3.3 of the Code, the Stock Exchange having introduced a number of new requirements relating to the disclosure of directors' remuneration in the annual reports of companies.

The latter requirements gave effect to the recommendations made by the Study Group on Directors' Remuneration (the 'Greenbury Committee'). This aspect of corporate governance is discussed at 4 in Chapter 30.

At the same time as making the latter change, the Stock Exchange exempted companies with only debt securities or fixed income shares listed from making a statement of compliance. These changes were effective for accounting periods beginning on or after 31 December 1995.[9]

Two aspects of the Code could not initially be complied with as they were the subject of continuing debate. These were the requirements for directors to report on the effectiveness of internal control and that the business is a going concern. The Committee noted that companies would not be able to comply with these points until the necessary guidance had been developed. It recommended that such guidance be developed by the accountancy profession together with representatives of preparers of accounts. Two working parties were set up under the auspices of the Hundred Group of Finance Directors, the ICAEW and the ICAS: the Going Concern Working Group, under the chairmanship of Mr Rodney Baker-Bates and the Internal Control Working Group, under the chairmanship of Mr Paul Rutteman. However, the development of the guidance proved to be a difficult task and it was to be about 2 years after the issue of the Cadbury Report before the working parties produced the necessary guidance to enable the Cadbury jigsaw to be complete.

4   REPORTING ON COMPLIANCE WITH THE CODE

As stated above, we are primarily concerned in this chapter with the impact that the Cadbury Report has on the company annual report and accounts. In effect, this relates to companies incorporated in the UK and listed on the London Stock Exchange which, as stated above, are required to include in their annual report and accounts a statement as to whether or not they have complied throughout the accounting period with the Cadbury Code (save for paragraphs 3.1 to 3.3 and 4.6). A company that has not complied with all or part of the Code must specify the paragraphs with which it has not complied, and (where relevant) for what part of the period such non-compliance continued, and give reasons for the non-compliance.

Set out below is a discussion of each of the points of the Code, giving a commentary and suggested due diligence procedures for directors when considering compliance with the Code. The points which must be covered by the auditors' review are marked with an asterisk, although auditors' review procedures are not discussed.

When assessing compliance with the Code, directors should consider the discussion of the relevant matters in the main body of the Cadbury Report and also the notes to the Code. These notes are not mandatory, but may be regarded as best practice and reflect the spirit of the Code.

4.1 The board of directors

> **1.1** The board should meet regularly, retain full and effective control over the company and monitor the executive management.

Every public company should be headed by an effective board which can both lead and control the business. Within the context of the UK unitary board system, this means a board made up of a combination of executive directors, with their intimate knowledge of the business, and of non-executive directors, who can bring a broader view to the company's activities, under a chairman who accepts the duties and responsibilities which the position entails.[10]

The arrangements whereby boards exercise 'full and effective control' will differ greatly between companies. The level of direct involvement with management below board level will depend on the extent of empowerment of executive management, and the amount of monitoring required will vary accordingly. Nevertheless, effective boards generally share certain characteristics. These will include the openness described above, the board's relationship with executive management, and the effective and timely flow of information both to and from the board.

The frequency of board meetings may also vary considerably between companies, depending, inter alia, on the role of its sub-committees and executive management.

A positive response to this paragraph of the Code depends on compliance with other points in the Code, particularly those concerning the board of directors and non-executive directors. For example, defining those matters specifically reserved for the board and division of responsibilities at the head of the company may be regarded as prerequisites for full and effective control by the board. Directors should therefore consider the impact on the company's compliance with this paragraph of any non-compliance with other parts of the Code.

> **1.2** There should be a clearly accepted division of responsibilities at the head of a company, which will ensure a balance of power and authority, such that no one individual has unfettered powers of decision. Where the chairman is also the chief executive, it is essential that there should be a strong and independent element on the board, with a recognised senior member.

The Committee saw the chairman's role in securing good corporate governance as being crucial. The chairman is primarily responsible for the working of the board, for its balance of membership (subject to shareholders' approval), for ensuring that all relevant issues are on the board's agenda, and for ensuring that all directors are enabled and encouraged to play their full part in its activities.[11]

The Committee stated that the chairman should be able to stand back sufficiently from the day-to-day running of the business to ensure that the board is in full control of the company's affairs and alert to its obligations to shareholders. This contrasts with the role of the chief executive who is actively involved in the implementation of board decisions and the day-to-day management of the company.

Accordingly, the Committee came to the view that the roles of chairman and chief executive should in principle be separate. However, the Committee stopped short of requiring that the roles be split, but introduced a safeguard in cases where they are not. In situations where the chairman is also the chief executive, directors should consider characteristics such as those described below in connection with paragraphs 1.3 and 2.1 of the Code when assessing whether the appropriate checks and balances exist within the board.

There should also be a line of communication to the senior non-executive director, through which the directors can address any concerns about the combined office of chairman and chief executive and its consequences for the effectiveness of the board.

Where the chairman is also the chief executive, it is likely to be appropriate to explain the operation of the checks and balances in the statement of compliance with the Code.

One company which has noted non-compliance with this paragraph of the Code, albeit temporarily, is Sidlaw Group, as shown below:

Extract 4.1: Sidlaw Group plc (1996)

Corporate Governance [extract]

The company has complied throughout the financial year with the provisions of the Cadbury Committee's Code of Best Practice except in respect of the temporary appointment of the Chairman as acting Chief Executive for the period from 8 May to 30 September 1996.

1.3   The board should include non-executive directors of sufficient calibre and number for their views to carry significant weight in the board's decisions.

It is clear that the main thrust of the Cadbury Report centres around the belief that the calibre of the non-executive members of the board is of special importance in setting and maintaining standards of corporate governance. Non-executive directors are expected to bring an independent judgement to bear on issues of strategy, performance, resources (including key appointments), and standards of conduct. As a result, the calibre and number of non-executive directors on a board should be such that their views will carry significant weight in the board's decisions.[12]

The number of non-executives on the board will depend on the particular circumstances of a company. However, because of the importance placed by the Committee on the requirement that non-executive directors should bring independence of judgement to the board's deliberations, the Committee recommended that the majority of non-executive directors should be independent of the company.[13] This means that in order to meet the Committee's recommendations on sub-committees of the board (specifically those concerning the composition of audit committees) all boards will require at least three non-executive directors, of whom at least two should be independent as defined by the Committee (see paragraph 2.2 of the Code). Nevertheless, some smaller listed companies state that they consider that having one or two non-executives is more in keeping with the size of their businesses.

The calibre of non-executives is clearly a matter for consideration by the board as a whole and, where it exists, the nomination committee, prior to appointment or reappointment. Calibre will include breadth and relevance of experience and ability to enable them to discharge their control functions under the Code, particularly those aspects specified in paragraph 2.1 of the Code.

> 1.4* The board should have a formal schedule of matters specifically reserved to it for decision to ensure that the direction and control of the company is firmly in its hands.

Some companies have policies and procedures manuals which specifically cover this point, while others have prepared a list of items to be considered, if appropriate, at each board meeting. Irrespective of the form of such a schedule, it is important that it is formally adopted by the board, that it is circulated to directors and, at least, to executive management and that it is kept up to date.

The schedule might include:

- approval of material acquisitions, disposals, investments, capital projects and other significant transactions;

- authority levels, including the definition of transactions which require multiple board signatures;

- procedures to be followed when decisions are required between board meetings;

- corporate business plan and strategy;

- treasury and risk management policy;
- selection and appointment of non-executive directors and company secretary;
- selection and appointment of senior executives;
- approval of accounts and other reports to shareholders; and
- the establishment of codes of conduct regarding compliance with laws and ethical standards of behaviour.

The existence of a formal schedule will meet the basic requirement of the Code. However, as part of full and effective control, the directors should consider the procedures to ensure that all relevant matters are referred to the board together with adequate information on which to base decisions, and the sanctions available to them where, for example, authority levels are exceeded.

> 1.5*   There should be an agreed procedure for directors in the furtherance of their duties to take independent professional advice if necessary, at the company's expense.

This requirement is in addition to any procedures that enable the directors to consult the company's advisers, and recognises that there may be situations in which a director might wish to take independent advice.

The procedures should be formalised, for example, by board resolution, in the company's articles or in a director's letter of appointment.[14]

> 1.6   All directors should have access to the advice and services of the company secretary, who is responsible to the board for ensuring that board procedures are followed and that applicable rules and regulations are complied with. Any question of the removal of the company secretary should be a matter for the board as a whole.

The company secretary has a key role to play in ensuring that board procedures are both followed and regularly reviewed. The chairman and the board will look to the company secretary for guidance on what their responsibilities are under the rules and regulations to which they are subject and on how those responsibilities should be discharged. All directors should have access to the advice and services of the company secretary and should recognise that the chairman is entitled to the strong and positive support of the company secretary in ensuring the effective functioning of the board.[15] Although the procedures allowing such access may be clearly understood, they should be acknowledged by the board by way of minute or in the letter of appointment for each director.

4.2   Non-executive directors

> 2.1   Non-executive directors should bring an independent judgement to bear on issues of strategy, performance, resources, including key appointments, and standards of conduct.

The Cadbury Committee clearly saw independence of judgement as the essential quality which non-executive directors should bring to the board's deliberations.[16] However, the ability of non-executives to bring such independent judgement will depend on the workings of the board and its committees as well as factors addressed elsewhere in the Code such as their calibre (paragraph 1.3) and independence (paragraph 2.2). It is also dependent on proper and timely briefing and the way they are brought into the debate on significant issues. The non-executives should understand the role they have to play as directors, which may be effected by setting out their responsibilities and duties in their letters of appointment.

The board as a whole should ensure that appropriate procedures are in place to allow the non-executive directors to contribute in the ways set out in the Code, for example through audit, remuneration and nomination committees, as well as at meetings of the full board.

> 2.2   The majority should be independent of management and free from any business or other relationship which could materially interfere with the exercise of their independent judgement, apart from their fees and shareholding. Their fees should reflect the time which they commit to the company.

The Committee made it clear that it is for the board to decide in particular cases whether this definition of independence is met. However, the demonstration of independence will be as important to the shareholder or other observer as compliance with the detailed requirements of the Code.

On fees, the Committee noted that there is a balance to be struck between recognising the value of the contribution made by non-executive directors and not undermining their independence. The demands which are now being made on conscientious non-executive directors are significant and their fees should reflect the time which they devote to the company's affairs. There is, therefore, a case for paying for additional responsibilities taken on, for example, by chairmen of board committees.[17]

Nevertheless, directors should consider the wider issues of independence as well as those set out in the Code. Factors not specifically mentioned in the Code which could impair independence include previous executive involvement with the company and participation in share option schemes. The Committee also saw it as good practice for non-executive service not to be pensionable by the company. Care must also be taken in deciding whether to appoint directors who have significant shareholdings in the company, as this could appear to be inconsistent with the exercise of independent judgement.

Wilson Bowden notes non-compliance with this paragraph of the Code, as shown below:

Extract 4.2: Wilson Bowden plc (1996)

Corporate Governance [extract]

The Board of Wilson Bowden plc continues to endorse the principles of good Corporate Governance. The Board currently comprises seven Executive Directors and four Non-Executive Directors.

On 11th September 1996 Mr Alan Grieve resigned as a Non-Executive Director having served the Company in the capacity for a period of three years. The Board attaches importance to ensuring that Non-Executive Directors have the requisite skills, independence and experience. Mr David Brill was appointed a Non-Executive Director in succession to Mr Grieve on 17th February 1997.

The Group has fully complied throughout the year with the provisions on Corporate Governance contained in the Cadbury Code of Best Practice published in December 1992, except that in the period between the resignation of Mr Grieve and the appointment of Mr Brill it did not have the requisite number of independent Non-Executive Directors.

In this particular case, of the other three non-executive directors, one undertakes special projects for the Board (committing approximately three days a week) and another was senior partner of the group's legal advisers.[18]

Another example is that of Rentokil Initial:

Extract 4.3: Rentokil Initial plc (1996)

Report of the Directors

Corporate governance [extract]

During the year ended 31st December 1996, the company complied in all respects with the provisions of the Code of Best Practice published by the Cadbury Committee on the Financial Aspects of Corporate Governance ("the Code") save that, of the non-executive directors (as shown on page 29), two are also directors of Sophus Berendsen A/S, the company's largest shareholder, and the chairman was a partner in and is currently a consultant to one of the company's legal advisers (paragraph 2.2 of the Code).

> 2.3* Non-executive directors should be appointed for specified terms and reappointment should not be automatic.

This point takes the regular retirement by rotation and re-election of non-executive directors a stage further. It reflects the recommendation in the Cadbury Report that a non-executive director's letter of appointment should set out, inter alia, the term of office. At the end of that term the board and, where applicable, the nomination committee should consider whether reappointment is appropriate, through a similar process to that adopted for the appointment of a new non-executive. This will lead to changes occurring which will help maintain the vitality of the board and enable it to face new challenges.[19]

Directors should be aware that the common provision in a company's articles for the retirement by rotation and re-election of a number of non-executives may well not satisfy the spirit of the Code unless complemented by additional procedures of the nature described in the previous paragraph.

One company which discloses non-compliance with this and the following paragraph (as well as paragraph 4.3 below) is Graseby, as shown below:

Extract 4.4: Graseby plc (1996)

Corporate Governance [extract]

Code of Best Practice

The directors have considered carefully the Code of Best Practice published in 1992 by the Cadbury Committee on the Financial Aspects of Corporate Governance. Graseby had complied with the spirit of the Code for many years before its introduction; in particular, it has long had an audit committee and a remuneration committee. Other than in respect of the particular matters in relation to the audit committee and non-executive appointments previously reported and mentioned below, Graseby continues to comply with the Code.

Audit Committee

The audit committee consists of two non-executive directors (one of whom is the chairman of the committee) and the financial director, who also serves as secretary to the committee. The committee advises the board on the preparation of the group's interim statement and annual accounts, the adequacy of the group's financial information systems and financial controls, and the appointment and remuneration of the auditors and the scope and remit of the audit.

Insofar as the committee includes the financial director, this is a departure from the Code. It is a practice which has been adopted by Graseby for many years, works well and which the board intends to maintain. The non-executive members of the committee enquire of the auditors if there are any matters they wish to raise in the absence of the financial director.

Non-executive appointments

The company does not have a standing nomination committee, which may be considered a departure from the Code. In the case of non-executive appointments to the board, the matter is discussed first by the board as a whole which agrees on the general desirability of an appointment and the broad specification the candidate should meet. Progression of the matter is then delegated to the chairman and the chief executive to look for suitable candidates, sometimes with the assistance of an external agency. The chairman and the chief executive submit a short list, usually consisting of two candidates, to members of the board as a whole. A final decision is taken in a full board meeting after all board members have met the favoured candidate. This practice has served Graseby well and the board intends to continue it. Although non-executive directors are not appointed for a specific term, given the current size of the board they cannot serve for more than four years without submitting themselves for re-election by the shareholders. Graseby's non-executive directors understand that endorsement by the board of their candidacy for re-election is not automatic. Each case is discussed informally by the chairman with other non-executive directors and the chief executive. The chairman then informs the non-executive director concerned of the board's view.

> 2.4* Non-executive directors should be selected through a formal process and both this process and their appointment should be a matter for the board as a whole.

The importance of their distinctive contribution to the board means non-executive directors should be selected with the same impartiality and care as senior executives. Candidates should be considered on merit, based on their ability to discharge the duties of a non-executive. The adoption of a formal selection process will help to ensure that this is carried out.

The Committee considered it good practice for a nomination committee to carry out the selection process and to make proposals to the board. Such a committee should have a majority of non-executive directors on it and be chaired by either the chairman or a non-executive director.[20] A nomination committee is just one formal process that could be adopted and there may be others appropriate in individual circumstances. If an alternative formal process is adopted, the directors should consider whether the circumstances of their company justify a departure from the Committee's view on good practice. The process adopted should be formally approved by the board, which should, of course, also be involved in the final appointment.

4.3   Executive directors

> 3.1 Directors' service contracts should not exceed three years without shareholders' approval.

> 3.2 There should be full and clear disclosure of directors' total emoluments and those of the chairman and highest-paid UK director, including pension contributions and stock options. Separate figures should be given for salary and performance-related elements and the basis on which performance is measured should be explained.

> 3.3 Executive directors' pay should be subject to the recommendations of a remuneration committee made up wholly or mainly of non-executive directors.

As noted earlier, these paragraphs are no longer covered by the compliance statement, following the introduction by the Stock Exchange of more specific requirements in respect of directors' remuneration which gave effect to the recommendations of the Greenbury Committee. These requirements are dealt with at 4 in Chapter 30.

4.4   Reporting and controls

> 4.1   It is the board's duty to present a balanced and understandable assessment of the company's position.

It is well known that both the flexibility allowed to directors through the selection of accounting policies, and the degree of judgement and estimation which underlies the financial reporting process, are significant elements of the expectations gap. The fact that different accounting treatments could be applied to essentially the same facts, means that a company could theoretically report several materially different results of operations and financial positions, each of which could comply with the overriding requirement to show a true and fair view.

Consequently, in order to obviate as far as possible the effects of alternative accounting treatments and presentational techniques, the Committee placed considerable emphasis on the need for shareholders to receive a coherent narrative, supported by figures, of a company's performance and prospects. The Committee recommended that boards should pay particular attention to their duty to present a balanced and understandable assessment of their companies' position, stressing that balance requires that setbacks should be dealt with as well as successes.[21]

With this in mind, and with a view to providing a framework within which directors can discuss the main factors underlying their companies' financial performance and position, the ASB issued in July 1993 a statement of best practice entitled *Operating and Financial Review*. The Operating and Financial Review (OFR) is discussed in detail at 7 below.

> 4.2   The board should ensure that an objective and professional relationship is maintained with the auditors.

The Committee identified the central issue with regard to the audit as being how to ensure its objectivity and effectiveness. The responsibility for maintaining an appropriate relationship rests with both the board and the auditors. An audit committee can play an important part in maintaining such a relationship by providing a forum dedicated to the review of matters within the purview of audit, such as financial statements and internal control.

An audit committee as envisaged by the Code gives the non-executive directors the opportunity to consider, in more detail than is generally possible at board meetings, the important financial aspects of the approach to, and system of, corporate governance. A specific step in the process is for the audit committee to hold a separate meeting with the auditors at least once a year, without executive board members present. This allows discussion to ensure that there are no unresolved issues of concern. The Committee has included this process in its recommendations on audit committees in the notes to the Code, which are discussed further in relation to paragraph 4.3.

> 4.3* The board should establish an audit committee of at least 3 non-executive directors with written terms of reference which deal clearly with its authority and duties.

This paragraph is supported by detailed recommendations in the notes to the Code on the working of audit committees. Directors of companies with audit committees should consider not only whether the requirements of paragraph 4.3 are met, but also if the terms of reference and authorities of the audit committee comply with the more detailed recommendations in the notes. These recommendations are outlined below.

The audit committee should be a formally constituted sub-committee reporting to the board and should meet at least twice a year. It should have written terms of reference dealing with membership, authority and duties. It should have full support to carry out its duties both from within the company and, if necessary, from external advisers. Membership of the committee should be confined to non-executive directors, the majority of whom should be independent. The internal and external auditors and finance director should normally attend audit committee meetings, whilst other members of the board should have the right to attend.

The Cadbury Report also included specimen terms of reference for an audit committee including such matters as constitution, membership, frequency of meetings, authority, duties and reporting procedures.

This is the main area of the Code where companies, particularly smaller companies, note non-compliance with the Code. For example:

Extract 4.5: Frogmore Estates plc (1996)

Report of the directors

11   Corporate Governance [extract]

The company has complied throughout the year to 30th June 1996 with the requirements of the Code of Best Practice published by the Committee on the Financial Aspects of Corporate Governance except that the audit committee consists of two non-executive directors not three as recommended by the Code. The board considers two to be sufficient for the size of the company.

Interestingly, in this situation the company does have three non-executive directors on the board, so it could quite easily comply with this paragraph of the Code if it so wished. In most other situations, companies only have one or two non-executive directors on the board as it is more in keeping with their size of business.

Another example of a company with only two non-executive directors on the audit committee is Graseby (see Extract 4.4 at 4.2 above). However, it also noted non-compliance due to the fact that the finance director was a member of the committee. Not all companies take such a view, for example:

Extract 4.6: Chloride Group PLC (1996)

Directors' report

Corporate governance [extract]

Compliance with code of best practice The Board considers that the company complies with the recommendations of the code of best practice ("the Code") published by the Committee on the Financial Aspects of Corporate Governance, with the exception of the recommendation of the Code that non-executive directors should be appointed for specified terms. The Board does not believe that such a recommendation is necessarily relevant in the present circumstances given the relatively small number of directors, the importance of continuity of service and the fact that the non-executive directors retire by rotation every other year.

For many years a Remuneration Committee and a Funding and Audit Committee have operated – the existence of which is recommended in the Code. The composition and principal responsibilities of all the standing Board Committees are set out on page 10. Specifically the Funding and Audit Committee consists of three non-executive directors together with the Finance Director. This committee holds at least two meetings each year and part of each meeting is reserved for a discussion between the non-executive directors and the external auditors without any executive director in attendance. The Board believes that it is necessary for the Finance Director to work closely with the Funding and Audit Committee in order for him to be fully aware of and to accept responsibility for matters dealt with in this committee.

The Board has not established a Nominations Committee for the selection of non-executive directors, on the basis that the appointment of all directors is a matter involving the entire Board. The establishment of a Nominations Committee is regarded by the Cadbury Committee as good practice but is not a requirement under the Code.

The reason why companies such as Chloride Group do not regard the existence of executive directors on the audit committee as being non-compliance with this paragraph of the Code is that it is only in the notes to the Code where it is stated that membership should be confined to non-executive directors, and the notes do not form part of the Code.

Most non-compliance with this paragraph of the Code arises through the choice of the companies only having one or two non-executive directors. Occasionally, however, a company may find itself in this position following the retirement of one or more non-executive directors from the board but it has not yet found the required replacements. Such non-compliance will need to be disclosed, as illustrated below:

Extract 4.7: The Spring Ram Corporation PLC (1996)

Corporate Governance [extract]

The Group supports the report on the Financial Aspects of Corporate Governance and the Code of Best Practice.

On 16 January 1997 Derek Bucknall and Terry Smith were appointed as Non-Executive Directors to replace Roy Barber and Richard Fortin who left the Board on 15 August 1996. During the intervening period the Company had not completed its recruitment of additional Non-Executive Directors, and therefore had only one Non-Executive Director, albeit one of sufficient calibre for his views to carry significant weight in the Board's decisions as required by paragraph 1.3 of the Code. Save in this respect, the Group was in full compliance with all applicable sections of the Code throughout the period under review and continues to be so.

4.4*   The directors should explain their responsibility for preparing the accounts next to a statement by the auditors about their reporting responsibilities.

The requirement for such an explanation of responsibilities is included in the auditing standard *Auditors' Reports on Financial Statements* (SAS 600). SAS 600 provides example wording for the statement of directors' responsibilities in respect of the accounts. This covers all of the points recommended in the notes to the Code.

Cable and Wireless is an example of a company which has broadly adopted SAS 600's recommended wording in its statement of directors' responsibilities in respect of the accounts:

Extract 4.8:   Cable and Wireless plc (1997)

Directors' responsibilities

in respect of the preparation of financial statements

Company law requires the Directors to prepare financial statements for each financial year which give a true and fair view of the state of affairs of the Company and of the Group and of the profit or loss of the Group for that period. In preparing those financial statements, the Directors are required to:

- select suitable accounting policies and then apply them consistently;
- make judgements and estimates that are reasonable and prudent;
- state whether applicable accounting standards have been followed, subject to any material departures disclosed and explained in the accounts; and
- prepare the financial statements on the going concern basis unless it is inappropriate to presume that the Group will continue in business.

The Directors are responsible for keeping proper accounting records which disclose, with reasonable accuracy at any time, the financial position of the Company and to enable them to ensure that the financial statements comply with the Companies Act 1985. They have general responsibility for taking such steps as are reasonably open to them to safeguard the assets of the Group and to prevent and detect fraud and other irregularities.

It is no longer necessary for the final bullet point to be included since listed companies are required to make a specific statement about going concern. One company which does not make a reference to going concern in its responsibility statement is Marks and Spencer, as shown below:

> *Extract 4.9: Marks and Spencer p.l.c. (1997)*
>
> **DIRECTORS' RESPONSIBILITIES FOR PREPARING THE FINANCIAL STATEMENTS**
>
> The directors are obliged under company law to prepare financial statements for each financial year and to present them annually to the Company's members in Annual General Meeting.
>
> The financial statements, of which the form and content is prescribed by the Companies Act 1985 and applicable accounting standards, must give a true and fair view of the state of affairs of the Company and the Group at the end of the financial year, and of the profit for that period.
>
> The directors are also responsible for the adoption of suitable accounting policies and their consistent use in the financial statements, supported where necessary by reasonable and prudent judgements.
>
> The directors confirm that the above requirements have been complied with in the financial statements.
>
> In addition, the directors are responsible for maintaining adequate accounting records and sufficient internal controls to safeguard the assets of the Group and to prevent and detect fraud or any other irregularities, as described more fully on page 36.

Most companies include such a statement of the directors' responsibilities either on the same page as the audit report, or on the previous page, thus satisfying the requirement that it is 'next to' a statement by the auditors about their reporting responsibilities which are included in the audit report. However, some companies stretch the meaning of 'next to' quite far. In the 1996 annual report of Prudential Corporation, the directors' responsibilities are on pages 37 and 38 whereas the audit report is on page 70. Indeed, it has been known for the statements to be in different documents!

Under SAS 600, where any of the points covered in the example statement are omitted, the auditors are required to include them in their report. It is also worth noting that the directors of Marks and Spencer have included in their responsibilities statement a sentence which confirms that they have, in fact, complied with their statutory obligations. Whilst this is not included in SAS 600's recommended wording, it would seem that the inclusion of such confirmation is desirable in order to bring meaning to the Directors' statement. In any event, the notes to the Cadbury Code recommend that the statement of directors' responsibilities should incorporate various confirmations.[22]

An article on directors' responsibilities statements appeared in the 3 November 1993 issue of the Law Society *Gazette*.[23] The article (which emanated from the Law Society's Committee on Company Law) expressed concern that companies could, if they did not take legal advice on the contents of the statement of responsibilities, run the risk of extending the legal liability of directors 'unnecessarily'. It is, however, difficult to understand how the example statement in SAS 600 could give rise to an extension of directors' liability as it merely summarises the responsibilities imposed on directors by the Companies Act together with their fiduciary duty to safeguard the company's assets.

The article implied that there is some element of shared responsibility between the directors and auditors for the preparation of financial statements, whereas the legal position is that the directors have sole responsibility in this regard. Further, it was implied that the directors are responsible for instructing the auditors to take whatever steps and undertake whatever inspections they consider necessary. In fact, the auditors' responsibilities in company law already require them to perform whatever work they consider necessary; this legal responsibility may neither be added to nor diminished by the directors.

If a company uses the wording suggested in the article, the auditors may be obliged to amend the wording in their audit report to avoid the possibility that a reader of the financial statements could be misled.

The Cadbury Committee recommended the inclusion in the report and accounts of a statement of directors' responsibilities 'so that shareholders are clear where the boundaries between the duties of directors and auditors lie'.[24] Unfortunately, the wording suggested in the *Gazette* appears to confuse rather than clarify in this regard.

It is probably for this reason that a further article on the matter appeared in the 17 December 1993 issue of the *Gazette* which, following discussions between the Auditing Practices Board and the Law Society's Committee on Company Law, took a more measured view of the issue, concluding that 'the directors' responsibility statement and the wording describing the auditors' responsibilities and the basis of their opinion should, in all cases, be considered together so as to avoid inconsistency and yet correctly reflect the legal and factual position'.[25]

> **4.5*** The directors should report on the effectiveness of the company's system of internal control.

Of all the suggestions in the Code, this has proved the most problematic and it was the one that took the longest time to bring into force. The trouble is that it is much harder than it sounds. Superficially, it seems entirely sensible that the directors of a company should be able to comment on how good their control systems are. But on reflection, it soon becomes apparent that this is fraught with difficulty, because there can be no objective yardstick against which to judge the adequacy of internal controls. For one thing, the need for controls depends upon perceived risks, and accordingly their adequacy can only be judged in that context; there is no all-purpose standard of controls that is accepted as necessary in all circumstances. For another, there is a cost/benefit judgement to be made in relation to any system of controls, which means that some managements will legitimately decide to spend more than others on control mechanisms. And since the people who are being asked to report on the adequacy of controls are also those who have had the responsibility of installing them, the requirement is always in danger of becoming a self-fulfilling one – it seems implausible that any board would ever determine that the system they themselves had established was in fact ineffective, unless it had demonstrably broken down to a material degree. Thus the undoubtedly well-intentioned requirement in the Code has proved difficult to deliver in practice.

Initially, the requirement was inoperative pending the issue of guidance for directors on how to implement it, and a working party was established to prepare such guidance. Its terms of reference were drawn from the Cadbury Report, which had recommended that the accountancy profession, in conjunction with representatives of preparers of accounts, should take the lead in:

(a)   developing a set of criteria for assessing the effectiveness of systems of internal control; and

(b)   developing guidance for companies on the form in which directors should report.[26]

In October 1993, the working party, in order to stimulate public debate, published draft guidance for directors in a document entitled *Internal Control and Financial Reporting*.[27] However, the document (which ran to nearly 70 pages) met with widespread opposition and criticism. This led to the working party issuing in August 1994 a revised exposure draft of only seven pages,[28] adopting a much more simplified high level approach than in the first draft. This was converted into a final version (the Guidance)[29] in December 1994, and took effect for financial years beginning on or after 1 January 1995.

As a matter of fact, it does not contain much guidance at all; rather, it waters down the requirements of the Code. Whereas the Code unequivocally called upon the directors to report on the effectiveness of the company's system of internal control, the Guidance has demoted this to an optional extra and requires instead that the directors make a statement covering these four points:

■   acknowledgement by the directors that they are responsible for the company's system of internal financial control;

■   explanation that such a system can provide only reasonable and not absolute assurance against material misstatement or loss;

■   description of the key procedures that the directors have established and which are designed to provide effective internal financial control; and

■   confirmation that the directors (or a board committee) have reviewed the effectiveness of the system of internal financial control.[30]

Although the last of these sounds like the requirement of the Code, it is in fact subtly designed to fall imperceptibly short of it. The distinction is that although the directors will say that they have reviewed the effectiveness of the system, they will not necessarily have to report the results of that review. Whereas the Guidance does go on to say that 'directors may also wish to state their opinion on the effectiveness of their system of internal financial control'[31] (i.e. the actual requirement of the Code), the wording has been constructed to make that actual requirement non-mandatory. Clearly, there was a feeling within the working party that a meaningful report on effectiveness was not deliverable, and this awkward compromise has been the result.

One of the key difficulties with the requirement to report on 'effectiveness', and one of the reasons why it has been watered down by the Guidance, is that the word is difficult to interpret and may be misunderstood. Since controls are not designed to operate in a vacuum, but rather as a response to particular risks, effectiveness can only be interpreted in that same context. Thus, controls may be effective, in the sense that they operate as they were designed to do, and give protection against the risks that the directors have decided should be protected against, while still leaving the business exposed to other significant risks that the directors are content to accept. Business activity is inherently risky and some businesses are inevitably more risky than others; it is not the function of internal control to remove all risk, even if that were possible. However, there is the danger that the readers of any report that confirms the effectiveness of controls might draw the unwarranted conclusion that protection against all material risks has been secured, which is one of the arguments against making such a report.

However, despite the fact that the Guidance has fallen slightly short of the target, the Cadbury Committee contributed a foreword to the Guidance document which accepted that this diluted version will be sufficient to constitute compliance with the Code, at least for the time being. As a result, the requirement of the Code has been changed de facto into the statement containing the four points listed above.

The Guidance has also narrowed down the Code in a second way. The Code called for a statement on the effectiveness of internal control, but as can be seen from the four point requirement listed above the working party has interpreted that as meaning internal financial control, a rather narrower term. Again, however, there is some equivocation on this issue, reflecting a possible lack of consensus in the working party; the Guidance says that 'Directors may wish to and are encouraged to extend the scope of their statement to cover their responsibility for the wider aspects of internal control (rather than just internal financial control) ...'.[32]

According to the Guidance, the distinction between the two terms is this. Internal control is defined as:

'The whole system of controls, financial and otherwise, established in order to provide reasonable assurance of:

(a)   effective and efficient operations;

(b)   internal financial control; and

(c)   compliance with laws and regulations.'[33]

Since internal financial control is element (b) of the above definition, the term obviously excludes the other two elements. It is further defined by the Guidance as:

'The internal controls established in order to provide reasonable assurance of:

(a)   the safeguarding of assets against unauthorised use or disposition; and

(b)   the maintenance of proper accounting records and the reliability of financial information used within the business or for publication.'[34]

As mentioned above, the de facto requirement of the Code as interpreted by the Guidance is that the directors' statement must include these four elements:

■   acknowledgement by the directors that they are responsible for the company's system of internal financial control;

■   explanation that such a system can provide only reasonable and not absolute assurance against material misstatement or loss;

■   description of the key procedures that the directors have established and which are designed to provide effective internal financial control; and

■   confirmation that the directors (or a board committee) have reviewed the effectiveness of the system of internal financial control.

The statement relates to the period of the annual report, but should also take account of material changes in controls up to the date on which it is signed;[35] in practice, we consider that the statement need refer only to the post-balance sheet period by exception, if there has been a material change. The Guidance suggests that the description of the key procedures should address the specific high level procedures used by the company, under five headings:

■   control environment;

■   identification and evaluation of risks and control objectives;

■   information and communication;

■   control procedures; and

■   monitoring and corrective action.[36]

This does describe the key elements of any control system, but there is a danger that a statement which simply follows these headings could become anodyne or boilerplate. For the statement to be of value, the directors must make sure that the description they give really highlights those controls that are particularly important in the context of their own business, rather than dealing only in generalities.

Marks and Spencer provides a good example of this disclosure:

Extract 4.10: Marks and Spencer p.l.c. (1997)

INTERNAL FINANCIAL CONTROL

The Board of Directors has overall responsibility for the Group's systems of internal financial control and for monitoring their effectiveness.

On behalf of the Board, the Audit Committee examines the effectiveness of these systems. This is achieved primarily through a review of the internal audit programme and its findings, reviews of the half year and annual financial statements and a review of the nature and scope of the external audit. Any significant findings or identified risks are closely examined so that appropriate action can be taken.

The annual operating and budgetary plans for each operating area of the Group are reviewed by the relevant Managing Directors prior to submission to the Board for approval. This includes the identification and assessment of the business and financial risks inherent in each operating area. This process is repeated quarterly and compared with actual results for the previous periods and latest forecasts for the balance of the year. The 4-year Group Capital Plan is similarly reviewed and updated by the Capital Expenditure Committee and then the Board. Treasury and risk management policies are reviewed by the Finance Director quarterly and policy changes are approved by the Board.

The Board maintains full control and direction over appropriate strategic, financial, organisational and compliance issues, and has put in place an organisational structure with formally defined lines of responsibility and delegation of authority. There are established procedures for planning and capital expenditure, for information and reporting systems, and for monitoring the Group's businesses and their performances. The Board has delegated to executive management the implementation of the systems of internal financial control within an established framework that applies throughout the Group; these systems are monitored and supported by an independent Internal Audit function which operates internationally.

The systems of internal financial control are designed to provide reasonable, but not absolute, assurance against material misstatement or loss. They include:

– Comprehensive budgeting systems with an annual budget approved by the Board.

– Regular consideration by the Board of actual results compared with budgets and forecasts.

– Quarterly reviews by the Board of year end forecasts.

– Half-yearly reviews by the Board of the Group Capital Plan.

– Clearly defined capital investment control guidelines and procedures set by the Board.

– Regular reporting of legal and accounting developments to the Board.

The Group's control systems address key business and financial risks. The work of the Internal Audit Department is focused on areas of greatest risk as identified by risk analysis and in accordance with an annual audit plan approved each year by the Audit Committee and by the Board. The Board receives a full report from the Chief Internal Auditor each year on the Department's work and findings. The external auditors are engaged to express an opinion on the Financial Statements. They review and test the systems of internal financial control and the data contained in the financial statements to the extent necessary to express their audit opinion. They discuss with management the reporting of operational results and the financial condition of the Group.

The directors, through the Audit Committee, have reviewed the effectiveness of the Group's systems of internal financial control.

One or two companies do go further and express a positive view on the effectiveness of their controls. Guinness is an example:

Extract 4.11: Guinness PLC (1996)

Report of the Directors

Corporate governance [extract]

The Company complies with the Code of Best Practice incorporated in the Report of the Cadbury Committee on The Financial Aspects of Corporate Governance. The Directors acknowledge their ultimate responsibility for ensuring that the Group has in place a system of controls, financial and otherwise, appropriate to the various business environments in which it operates.

These are designed to give reasonable assurance with respect to the reliability of financial information used within the businesses or for publication, and the maintenance of proper accounting records, the safeguarding of assets against unauthorised use or disposition; and that the businesses are being operated efficiently and effectively.

The Group operates within a control framework developed and refined over a number of years and communicated throughout the Group by means of various procedures manuals. These lay down common accounting policies and financial control procedures, in addition to controls of a more operational nature. Of particular importance are those that relate to:

– the definition of the organisation structure and the appropriate delegation of responsibility to operational management;

– the definition of authorisation limits, financial and otherwise;

– the setting of detailed annual budgets and the monthly reporting of actual results against them;

– capital expenditure and investment procedures followed by post-completion appraisals; and

– physical and computer security matters and contingency planning.

Operating units are required to confirm that they comply in all material respects with these procedures.

The Audit Committee comprises five non-executive Directors. The Chairman and Finance Director normally attend the meetings but the Committee also meets with the external auditors without management present. The Committee operates under written terms of reference and its duties include the detailed review of financial statements prior to their recommendation to the Board for approval.

The work of the Group Internal Audit function is overseen by the Audit Committee which approves its plans in advance and reviews the conclusions of its work. Lessons learned are disseminated within the Group as appropriate. Audit plans are drawn up based on an assessment of the control risks in each operating unit and their materiality in a Group context.

The Audit Committee has reviewed the system of internal controls and has reported to the Directors on the result of this review. Accordingly, the Directors are satisfied that the Group continues to have an effective system of internal controls.

It can be seen that not only have Guinness expressed a positive view on the effectiveness of the controls but the statement also deals with the wider aspects of internal control.

The Guidance also says that where control weaknesses have given rise to material losses, contingencies or uncertainties 'which require disclosure in the financial statements or in the auditors' report' (a slightly confusing proviso), the statement should also say what corrective action has been taken or will be taken, or alternatively why no changes are considered necessary.[37] There had previously been a suggestion that control weaknesses had to be reported even if no loss had resulted, but this idea was dropped in the final version of the Guidance.

One company that experienced such circumstances was Wickes. The note that described the problem and its effect on the directors' statement on internal financial control are shown in this extract:

Extract 4.12: Wickes plc (1996)

Notes to financial statements

1 Accounting irregularities

During June 1996 the directors became aware of the existence of serious accounting irregularities within the Group's UK and Continental European retail businesses. Following this discovery the Board instructed Linklaters and Paines and Price Waterhouse to investigate and report to it on the circumstances which gave rise to the inaccuracies in the Group's financial statements. Following an announcement to the London Stock Exchange on 24 June 1996 of the discovery of these accounting irregularities, the Company's shares were suspended. On 27 June 1996 the Board announced that, under the circumstances, it would not be possible to proceed with the payment of the final dividend in respect of the 1995 financial year, originally scheduled to be paid on 4 July 1996.

The results of the Linklaters and Paines and Price Waterhouse investigation were reported to shareholders on 16 October 1996. This investigation concluded that there has been serious mismanagement in relation to certain important areas of the Group's operations, principally in the Buying Department where there was a deliberate misrepresentation of the true basis of certain rebate and contribution arrangements with suppliers. As a result of these irregularities the Group's profits have been considerably overstated in recent years.

The accounting irregularities discovered centred around the nature of the Group's trading arrangements with its suppliers. In many cases amounts receivable from suppliers were recorded as income in the year in which the relevant agreements were entered into, rather than being recorded as income over the period of the supply agreements as they were earned in accordance with their terms. The Linklaters and Paines and Price Waterhouse investigation has confirmed that executives within the Buying Department deliberately implemented an elaborate system to conceal the real terms on which suppliers had made, or had agreed to make, rebate payments or contributions to the Group. The report also concluded that such arrangements were not accounted for in accordance with the Group's accounting policy, approved by the Company's Audit Committee.

The directors originally approved their annual report on the affairs of the Group, together with the financial statements and auditors' report, for the year ended 31 December 1995 on 21 February 1996. On 12 December 1996, revised financial statements were issued to replace the original 31 December 1995 financial statements. The comparative information included within the 1996 financial statement is based on the revised financial statements which are now the statutory financial statements for 1995.

The Group's 1994 and 1995 financial statements included significant amounts of rebate and contribution income which had not been earned. As a result of the material level of correction required, the directors decided to withdraw the 1995 financial statements, dated 21 February 1996. The financial impact of the correction to the Group's original 1995 financial statements is described below. The required correction to the financial statements was calculated based on the review and discussion of correspondence which identified the true nature of the Group's commercial arrangements with its suppliers. In certain cases documentary evidence to support the true nature of the Group's arrangements with its suppliers was incomplete, particularly in relation to the years prior to 1995. Therefore, certain assumptions were required to allocate rebate and contribution income to the years 1992 to 1995. The directors were able to conclude that the revised 1995 Balance Sheet included in the financial statements presented a true and fair view of the state of the Group's affairs as at 31 December 1995, and are satisfied that no material adjustments are necessary to the profit and loss account for the year to 31 December 1995. Whilst they believe that the allocation of rebate and contribution income to the years 1992 to 1994 is reasonable based on the information available, they are unable to conclude that these allocations would not be subject to adjustment if more complete information was available.

The amendments made to the financial statements of the Group as previously issued were as follows:

- the restatement of the contributions receivable from suppliers under the arrangements mentioned above and the associated impact on stocks and tangible fixed assets
- the reversal of the 1995 final dividend, payment of which the Company has cancelled, together with the associated advanced corporation tax
- the tax effect of the restatement of the contributions receivable from suppliers

In addition, the financial statements of the Company as previously issued were revised to include a provision increased to £100 million for permanent diminution in value of the Company's total investment in Wickes Holdings Limited. This diminution in value results from the cumulative effect of the treatment of supplier contributions on the value of certain subsidiary undertakings.

Financial Review

Corporate Governance [extract]

As a result of the irregularities which have been uncovered during the year, and of the consequent substantial disruption to the management of the Group, the Board is unable to confirm that the Company has been in compliance with the Code of Best Practice as recommended by the Cadbury Committee throughout the year in respect of their review of the effectiveness of internal financial controls. With regard to this, the Board has approved new corporate governance procedures and has also considered a risk based assessment of the Company's internal controls. As set out below, the detailed work to review the full effectiveness of the system of internal financial control as required by paragraph 4.5 of the Cadbury Code (as supplemented by the related Guidance for Directors) is now underway.

Internal Financial Control

The Board has overall responsibility for ensuring that the Group maintains a system of internal financial control. The key elements of a system of internal financial control include an organisation structure with clear responsibility and delegation; documented policies for financial reporting, financial risk management and capital expenditure appraisal; preparation of annual budgets and longer term plans and monitoring and reporting of performance against budget. These have been and are in place within the Group. However, the irregularities which caused prior years' profits to be overstated by more than £50 million, indicate that no system can provide absolute protection against material misstatement or loss, particularly where this is caused by deliberate act and confusion.

Nevertheless, the Board is anxious to ensure that the chances of irregularities occurring in future are reduced as far as possible by improving the quality of information at all levels in the Company, creating a more open environment and ensuring that financial analysis is rigorously applied.

Following the irregularities described above, the Board is undertaking a detailed review of the effectiveness of internal financial controls. A framework for a risk based internal control assessment has already been approved by the Board. During 1997 this will be fully developed and priorities given to those areas where above average risks are perceived.

Another company which had to report a breakdown in controls was Pearson:

Extract 4.13: Pearson plc (1996)

Report of the Directors

Corporate governance

Internal financial control – the board of directors has overall responsibility for the Group's system of internal financial control which it exercises through an organisational structure with clearly defined levels of responsibility and authority and appropriate reporting procedures. This structure includes an audit committee, comprising three non-executive directors, which, with the finance director, has reviewed the effectiveness of the internal financial control environment of the Group. The audit committee meets regularly and considers, inter alia, reports from internal and external auditors covering such matters.

On 13 February 1997 we announced the discovery of the breakdown of certain internal controls at Penguin USA, which allowed the unauthorised practice of offering discounts to certain customers in exchange for early payment of invoices. Swift action was taken to stop this irregular practice and to determine how and why the accounting irregularities, which are described in greater detail in the Finance Director's Review on pages 26 to 28 of the Annual Report, were not detected. A thorough review of the Group's control procedures is currently being undertaken in order to ensure, as far as possible, that such an event cannot recur. On the evidence presented so far, both the directors and the auditors believe that the systems and controls in the Group are generally of high quality. However, it must be recognised that no internal control system can provide absolute assurance against misstatement or loss.

The following are the main elements of the Group's control systems:

Financial reporting – there is a comprehensive budgeting system with an annual budget approved by the directors. Monthly trading results and indebtedness are reported against the corresponding figures for the budget and the previous year with corrective action being taken by the directors as appropriate. More detailed financial information, including balance sheets and cash flow statements, is provided quarterly.

Treasury management – the treasury department operates within board approved policies. Major transactions are authorised outside the department at the requisite level and there is an appropriate segregation of duties. Frequent reports are made to the group finance director and quarterly summaries are prepared for the board.

Risk management – the identification of major business risks is carried out in conjunction with operating management and steps are taken to mitigate or eliminate these where possible. In addition the Group provides insurance cover either through its captive insurance subsidiary or externally depending on the scale of the risk in question.

Operating company systems – each operating company maintains financial controls and procedures appropriate to its own business environment and carries out local treasury activities, in both cases conforming to overall standards and guidelines.

Self assessment – each year relevant senior executives and chief executives of operating units are required to confirm in writing compliance with appropriate standards of internal financial control in their respective areas.

Internal audit – the Group has a centralised internal audit department with operations located both in the UK and the US, which reviews systems and procedures in all major operating companies and reports regularly to the operating committee.

In relation to internal control, it is clear that the good intentions within the Cadbury Report have to some extent fallen by the wayside. As envisaged by Cadbury, the reader of a company's annual report was to have been furnished with a report as to whether or not the directors believed its control systems to be operating effectively. However that is seldom what they get under the Guidance which has emerged, and indeed we consider it was unrealistic to think that the original requirement could have been consistently met in any meaningful way. There is therefore a strong possibility that the expectation gap, far from having been narrowed by Cadbury, has in fact been widened further; few lay readers will appreciate the subtlety of the wording of the statement now provided under the Guidance, and they are likely to derive more comfort from it than is warranted by the facts.

Has this aspect of the Code therefore been a waste of time? Not necessarily, in our view. Although the public reporting in relation to internal control has fallen short of its original target, it has achieved a collateral objective; that of raising the profile of internal controls on board agendas, and providing a framework in which they can be discussed, which has provided a mechanism through which companies' systems can be assessed and improved.

> 4.6   The directors should report that the business is a going concern, with supporting assumptions or qualifications as necessary.

As noted at 3 above, this was the other aspect of the Code that companies could not initially comply with until guidance became available. A working party comprising representatives of the Hundred Group of Finance Directors, the ICAEW and the ICAS finally issued its guidance in November 1994.[38] At the same time, the APB issued guidance for auditors reviewing directors' statements on going concern[39] and also issued an auditing standard, SAS 130,[40] which provides guidance to auditors considering, as part of their work in forming their audit opinion, the appropriateness of the going concern basis.

As a result of the necessary guidance being available, in August 1995, the Stock Exchange introduced a separate requirement for listed companies to include in their annual report a statement by the directors that the business is a going concern with supporting assumptions or qualifications as necessary, as interpreted by the guidance for directors. Such a statement is to be reviewed by the auditors before publication.[41] As noted at 3 above, in view of this separate requirement, the statement of compliance with the Code no longer covers this paragraph of the Code.

The guidance for directors recommends a number of procedures relevant to considering going concern under the following categories:[42]

- forecasts and budgets
- borrowing requirements
- liability management
- contingent liabilities
- products and markets
- financial risk management
- other factors

■   financial adaptability

An appendix suggests more detailed procedures under these categories.

When the directors have weighed up the results of the procedures that they have undertaken in order to establish the appropriateness of the going concern basis, there are three basic conclusions that they can reach:

■   they have a reasonable expectation that the company will continue in operational existence for the foreseeable future and have therefore used the going concern basis in preparing the financial statements;

■   they have identified factors which cast some doubt on the ability of the company to continue in operational existence in the foreseeable future but they have used the going concern basis in preparing the financial statements; or

■   they consider that the company is unlikely to continue in operational existence in the foreseeable future and therefore the going concern concept is not an appropriate basis on which to draw up the financial statements.[43]

The guidance envisages that in normal circumstances where the going concern presumption is appropriate the following statement should be made, as illustrated below:

Extract 4.14: Marks and Spencer p.l.c. (1997)

Financial Review [extract]

Going concern

After making enquiries, the directors have a reasonable expectation that the Group has adequate resources to continue in operational existence for the foreseeable future. For this reason, they continue to adopt the going concern basis in preparing the financial statements.

The guidance also illustrates the form of statement where the going concern basis is used despite doubts about going concern.[44]

It can be seen from the above extract that Marks and Spencer has included the statement within its Financial Review; this is in accordance with the guidance which recommends that the statement on going concern should be included in the company's Operating and Financial Review (see 7 below). However, as can be seen from the extracts below, other companies include the statement with the rest of the corporate governance disclosures.

The Cadbury Report emphasises that the directors are not expected to give a guarantee about their company's prospects because there can never be complete certainty about future trading. Therefore the directors are required to state only that they have a 'reasonable expectation' that the company will continue in operation for the foreseeable future. However, the principal area of controversy concerned the meaning of the phrase 'foreseeable future'.

The draft guidance issued by the working party had proposed that the directors should consider at least the period to the next balance sheet date. However, the guidance then went on to state that 'the foreseeable future should extend beyond the next balance sheet date to the extent that the directors are aware of circumstances which could affect the validity of the going concern basis for the company'.[45]

It seems that this guidance was drafted on the basis that most companies would prepare detailed budgets covering the 12 months after the balance sheet date. An alternative would have been to require the directors to look at a period of at least one year from the date that the accounts are signed, but this approach would have been more difficult for some companies as detailed budgets will not always be available. This was the approach taken by the APB when drafting a new auditing standard on the subject. It was clear that a compromise position had to be found. As can be seen from the example statement illustrated in Extract 4.14 above, 'foreseeable future' is an essential element of the decision-making process.

The final guidance produced for directors by the working party discusses 'foreseeable future' and now concludes that it is not possible to specify a minimum period to which directors should pay particular attention in assessing going concern. Stipulating a minimum period would, the working party believes, be artificial and arbitrary. Instead of inventing a 'cut-off point' after which there would be a sudden change in the approach adopted, the working party believes that directors should take account of all information of which they are aware at the time.

However, the working party goes on to state that 'where the period considered by the directors has been limited, for example, to a period of less than one year from the date of approval of the financial statements, the directors should determine whether, in their opinion, the financial statements require any additional disclosure to explain adequately the assumptions that underlie the adoption of the going concern basis'.[46]

In its guidance to auditors reporting on whether the financial statements give a true and fair view, SAS 130 requires that 'if the period to which the directors have paid particular attention in assessing going concern is less than one year from the date of approval of the financial statements, and the directors have not disclosed that fact, the auditors should do so within the section of their report setting out the basis of their opinion, unless the fact is clear from any other references in their report'.[47]

It would therefore appear that one year from the date of approval of financial statements is likely to become the working definition of 'foreseeable future', although information beyond that period cannot be ignored. However, this does not necessarily mean that cash flow forecasts and budgets are needed for the whole of this period – SAS 130 says that it will depend on the circumstances.[48]

Although there is no requirement to do so, some companies do give an indication of the information they have used, and the period that it covers, in making the necessary statement on going concern. For example:

Extract 4.15: Pearson plc (1996)

Report of the Directors

Corporate governance [extract]

Going concern – having reviewed the Group's liquid resources and borrowing facilities and the 1997 and 1998 cash flow forecasts contained in the Group budget for 1997, the directors believe that the Group has adequate resources to continue as a going concern for the foreseeable future. For this reason, the financial statements have, as usual, been prepared on a going concern basis.

Another example is that of Dalgety:

Extract 4.16: Dalgety PLC (1996)

Directors' report [extract]

Going concern

The Directors have reviewed the Group's budget for 1996/97 and projections for the subsequent two years. After taking into account the cash flow implications of these projections, including capital expenditure and reorganisation costs, and after comparing these with the Group's committed borrowing facilities and projected gearing ratios, the directors are satisfied that the Group is a going concern.

4.5 Formats of directors' and auditors' reports on compliance

4.5.1 Reporting by directors

The Cadbury Report recommended that companies should make a statement about their compliance with the Code and give details of, and reasons for, any non-compliance. As noted earlier, this recommendation has now been incorporated in The Listing Rules of the London Stock Exchange. The Report does not give any further guidance on the form of the statement.

Some companies only provide a brief confirmation that the company is in compliance with all aspects of the Code. Although such a statement is adequate in terms of satisfying the requirements of the Stock Exchange, it does not provide great insight into the company's system of corporate governance. Many companies have addressed this point by including in their statement on corporate governance not only a statement of compliance but also a description of the workings of the board and the various committees.

4.5.2 Reporting by auditors

As has already been stated, the Stock Exchange requires the directors' statement on Cadbury compliance to be reviewed by the auditors insofar as it relates to objectively verifiable matters in the Code. The directors' statement that the business is a going concern also has to be reviewed by the auditors. However, the Cadbury Report proposed that auditors should not be required to report formally to shareholders on the findings of their review, but if they identify an area of non-compliance which is not properly disclosed, they should draw attention to it in their report on the accounts.[49] The Stock Exchange rules are silent on whether the auditors should report on their review and whether it should be made public.

Guidance for auditors in this area is contained in APB Bulletin 1995/1, as supplemented by APB Bulletin 1996/3. This guidance states that auditors should always issue a report to the company and that the APB 'strongly recommends that such reports be included in the annual report'.[50] We concur with that recommendation.

Whilst there is no requirement to do so, most companies have adopted the approach of including such a report within the annual report and accounts either:

■   as a separate report by the auditors on corporate governance matters; or

■   as a separate section, with an appropriate heading, in the audit report on the financial statements.

Other companies do not publish the auditors' report on corporate governance matters but the directors make a reference to the auditors' review. A suggested wording for use by directors is included in an Appendix to APB Bulletin 1995/1.

Although the approach adopted is clearly a matter of individual preference, at the same time, we see potential danger in companies remaining silent on the matter of the auditors' review. Where there is neither a report nor a reference to the review, it might beg the question whether the auditors have in fact conducted a review and, if so, whether they have satisfied themselves that the company's statement appropriately reflects compliance with the Code; it could lead to questions at the AGM.

5   CADBURY AND SMALLER QUOTED COMPANIES

Early in 1994 The City Group for Smaller Companies (CISCO) published guidance for smaller quoted companies which is aimed at identifying those areas of the Cadbury Code which may, initially, prove difficult for smaller companies to implement and, wherever possible, suggesting alternative recommendations which are believed feasible and appropriate.[51] The idea behind this is to provide a guide to the measures that all companies (without exception) can reasonably be expected to implement, which is preferable to the option of companies doing nothing.

CISCO defines smaller quoted companies as those not included within the FTSE 350 index, but recognises that many such companies will be able to comply fully with the Cadbury Code.

The areas where alternative recommendations are given relate to the number of non-executive directors and the constitution of audit committees. However, it should be noted that these recommendations do not represent an alternative code, and therefore a listed company that has complied with CISCO's recommendations but not the full Code would still be required to report such non-compliance (with reasons) in its annual accounts.

CISCO's principal alternative recommendations and other refinements are as follows:[52]

- paragraph 1.3 of the Cadbury Code requires companies to appoint non-executives of sufficient calibre and number for their views to carry significant weight in the board's decisions. To meet the Cadbury Committee's recommendations on the composition of sub-committees of the board, boards will require a minimum of three non-executives. CISCO has recommended that there should be at least two and that, to be counted as non-executive directors, the individuals must be truly independent as defined in paragraph 2.2 of the Code;

- in line with the Code requirement that boards should meet regularly, retain full and effective control over the company and monitor the executive management, CISCO suggests that boards should meet not less than six times a year and that the agenda of regular board meetings should always include a report of management accounts from the finance director. It also suggests that whilst it is accepted that any system of corporate governance should not fetter entrepreneurial talent, systems can nevertheless be established where, in relation to certain areas of management, the entrepreneur must always. consult the board as a whole before implementing a decision taken in principle, without compromising commercial effectiveness;

- although the Cadbury Committee recommended that membership of a company's audit committee should be confined to non-executives, CISCO suggests that whilst all non-executives should be members of the audit committee, membership should not be restricted to non-executives. However, CISCO does suggest that a non-executive director should be appointed as chairman of the audit committee and that non-executives should have meetings (at which the executives are not present) with the company's auditors;

- on the question of terms of appointment of non-executives, CISCO makes the point that in a small company the desire to maintain the vitality of the board through the rotation of non-executive directors has to be balanced against the considerable time and effort expended in finding a suitable replacement, and the loss of accumulated knowledge. As a result, CISCO suggests that for smaller companies the term of appointment should normally be for five years and not exceed ten years. It also states that non-executives should neither have share options nor receive any compensation on the termination of their appointment;

■ CISCO recommends that any non-executive who resigns from any quoted company should be entitled to communicate (at the company's expense) with its shareholders giving the reasons for his resignation and raising any matters he considers should be brought to their attention. It suggests further that this procedure could apply where there is fundamental disagreement leading the non-executives to vote against resolutions proposed at board meetings – although in our view this would be a highly unusual course of action to follow; and

■ CISCO's final recommendation is that companies should seek to define the role each non-executive director is expected to fulfil, and the specific objectives of that role, as they should for any other senior appointment, in order to ensure that they receive optimum benefit from the appointment. This should be done before starting the selection or reselection procedure.

It must again be emphasised that CISCO's refined code is not, for Stock Exchange reporting purposes, to be seen as an alternative option to the Cadbury Code. All UK incorporated quoted companies (irrespective of size) are required by the Stock Exchange to include in their annual report and accounts a statement as to whether or not they have complied throughout the accounting period with the Code, and to report details of, and reasons for, any non-compliance.

6   THE CONTINUING DEBATE

In the Cadbury Report, the Committee stated that it would 'remain responsible for reviewing the implementation of the proposals until a successor body is appointed in two years' time, to examine the progress and to continue the ongoing governance review. It will be for our sponsors to agree the remit of the new body and to establish the basis of its support. In the meantime, a programme of research will be undertaken to assist the future monitoring of the Code.'[53]

In fulfilling that latter responsibility the Cadbury Committee:

(a)   set up a Monitoring Sub-Committee;

(b)   encouraged research into a number of projects related to corporate governance; and

(c)   collaborated with the Association of British Insurers in a project to monitor best practice.

The project referred to at (c) led to the publication by the Cadbury Committee in May 1995 of the results of a survey of compliance with best practice.[54] This was based on a sample of almost 700 annual reports, including virtually all of the top

500 listed companies in the UK.[55] The survey was based on annual reports issued up to the end of December 1994; it therefore did not cover compliance or otherwise with paragraphs 4.5 and 4.6 of the Code, guidance for which had only just been issued.[56] The main conclusions of the survey can be summarised as follows:

- Statements of full compliance are most likely to be made by companies in the top 500, whilst the smaller the company, the higher the percentage of statements disclosing limited compliance.

- Although not a requirement of the Code, the majority of companies have split the roles of Chairman and Chief Executive, and where the roles are combined, there is more often than not an independent element of non-executive directors on the board, as recommended in the Cadbury Report. There is a relationship between the size of the company and the number of non-executives on the board, with the larger companies most likely to have three or more. There has been a marked increase in the disclosure of Audit, Nomination and Remuneration Committees since the publication of the Code. The larger the company, the more likely it is to have three or more non-executive directors on the Audit Committee, but there has also been an increase in the disclosure of Audit Committees comprising two non-executives, particularly smaller companies.

- The majority of companies of all sizes have boards on which all or the majority of non-executive directors are independent. The larger the company, the more likely it is to have three or more independent non-executives on the board.

- While larger companies have disclosed compliance with the requirement to have formal terms of appointment for non-executive directors, such disclosure decreases in relation to company size. However, high levels of compliance with both the requirement to have a schedule of matters referred to the board and to have an agreed procedure for independent advice were found in companies of all sizes. There is a higher incidence in all the sample groups of rolling as opposed to fixed-term three-year contracts. The incidence of contracts in excess of three years (either rolling or fixed-term) is very low.[57]

6.1   Hampel Committee

In the event, it was to be almost three years before a successor body was formed, in November 1995, under the chairmanship of Sir Ronald Hampel, Chairman of ICI. The remit of this committee is to 'seek to promote high standards of corporate governance in the interests of investor protection and in order to preserve and enhance the standing of companies listed on the Stock Exchange. The committee's remit will extend to listed companies only.

Against this background the committee will:

(a) conduct a review of the Cadbury code and its implementation to ensure that the original purpose is being achieved, proposing amendments to and deletions from the Code as necessary;

(b) keep under review the role of directors, executive and non-executive, recognising the need for Board cohesion and the common legal responsibilities of all directors;

(c) be prepared to pursue any relevant matters arising from the report of the Study Group on Directors' Remuneration chaired by Sir Richard Greenbury;

(d) address as necessary the role of shareholders in corporate governance issues;

(e) address as necessary the role of auditors in corporate governance issues; and

(f) deal with any other relevant matters.

Without impairing investor protection the committee will always keep in mind the need to restrict the regulatory burden on companies, eg by substituting principles for detail wherever possible.'[58]

The Hampel Committee began its work early in 1996 and a report is expected to be issued in the second half of 1997.

7   THE OPERATING AND FINANCIAL REVIEW (OFR)

In considering the responsibility of boards with respect to financial reports, the Cadbury Committee concluded that what shareholders need from the report and accounts is a coherent narrative, supported by figures, of the company's performance and prospects. As a result, the Committee recommended that boards should pay particular attention to their duty to present a balanced and understandable assessment of their company's position. It went on to say that balance requires that setbacks should be dealt with as well as successes, while the need for the report to be readily understood emphasises that words are as important as figures.[59] The Committee further recognised the advantage to users of accounts of being provided with some explanation of the factors likely to influence their company's future progress, and concluded that the inclusion of an essentially forward-looking Operating and Financial Review (OFR), along the lines of that which was being developed by the ASB, would serve this purpose.[60]

The ASB document to which the Cadbury Committee referred was ultimately published in July 1993 as a Statement of best practice. It has persuasive rather than mandatory force and is not an accounting standard. It is intended that the

OFR should be a discussion of the business as a whole and should give insights into the facts which underlie the figures in the accounts; it should not just repeat these figures in narrative form with no amplification. It should discuss individual aspects of the business in the context of explaining the performance of the business as a whole. The statement requires a consideration of the factors that will affect future performance as well as the year under review. Consequently, although the OFR is a report on the year under review, not a forecast of future results, it should nevertheless draw out those aspects of the year under review that are relevant to an assessment of future prospects.

The essential features of an OFR are as follows:[61]

- it should be written in a clear style and as succinctly as possible, to be readily understandable by the general reader of annual reports, and should include only matters that are likely to be significant to investors;

- it should be balanced and objective, dealing even-handedly with both good and bad aspects;

- it should refer to comments made in previous statements where these have not been borne out by events;

- it should contain analytical discussion rather than merely numerical analysis;

- it should follow a 'top-down' structure, discussing individual aspects of the business in the context of a discussion of the business as a whole;

- it should explain the reason for, and effect of, any changes in accounting policies;

- it should make it clear how any ratios or other numerical information given relate to the financial statements; and

- it should include discussion of:

  - trends and factors underlying the business that have affected the results but are not expected to continue in the future; and

  - known events, trends and uncertainties that are expected to have an impact on the business in the future.

In discussing trends and uncertainties, the OFR should explain their significance to the business, but it is not intended that the OFR should necessarily include a forecast of the outcome of such uncertainties; nor is it suggested that the OFR should contain anything of the nature of a profit forecast.[62] Furthermore, the directors may conclude that, in some cases, a proper discussion of some aspects of the business would require disclosure of confidential or commercially sensitive information. Where the directors decide not to disclose such information, the OFR should ensure that the user is not misled by a discussion that is no longer complete and balanced.[63]

As its title suggests, the OFR consists of two sections: the operating review and the financial review. These are discussed below.

7.1   The operating review

The principal aim of the operating review is to enable the user to understand the dynamics of the various lines of business undertaken – that is, the main influences on the overall results, and how these interrelate. Thus the OFR needs to identify and explain the main factors that underlie the business, and in particular those which either have varied in the past or are expected to change in the future.[64] It should include a discussion of:[65]

- the significant features of the operating performance for the period. This should cover changes in the industry or the environment in which the business operates, developments within the business, and their effect on results. Examples of such changes given by the Statement are as follows:
  - changes in market conditions;
  - new products and services introduced or announced;
  - changes in market share or position;
  - changes in turnover and margins;
  - changes in exchange rates and inflation rates; and
  - new activities, discontinued activities and other acquisitions and disposals;

- the dynamics of the business, discussing the main factors and influences that may have a major effect on future results, whether or not they were significant in the period under review; for example, dependence on major suppliers or customers. The Statement lists the following additional examples of matters that may be relevant:
  - scarcity of raw materials;
  - skill shortages and expertise of uncertain supply;
  - patents, licences or franchises;
  - product liability;
  - health and safety;
  - environmental protection costs and potential environmental liabilities;
  - self insurance;
  - exchange rate fluctuations; and
  - rates of inflation differing between costs and revenues, or between different markets;

- the extent to which the directors have sought to maintain and enhance future income or profits by investment in, for example, capital expenditure, marketing and advertising campaigns and pure and applied research. The Statement lists the following additional examples of activities and expenditure for the enhancement of future profits that may be relevant:

- training programmes;
- refurbishment and maintenance programmes;
- development of new products and services; and
- technical support to customers;

■ the overall return attributable to shareholders, in terms of dividends and increases in shareholders' funds, commenting on the contributions from the operating performance of the various business units and on other items reported as part of total recognised gains and losses;

■ a comparison between profit for the financial year and dividends, both in total and per share terms, indicating the directors' overall dividend policy. Other measures of earnings per share reported should also be discussed; and

■ any subjective judgements to which the financial statements are particularly sensitive.

7.2 The financial review

The principal aim of the financial review is to explain the capital structure of the business, its treasury policy and the dynamics of its financial position – i.e. its sources of liquidity and their application, including the implications of the financing requirements arising from its capital expenditure plans.[66] It should include a discussion of:[67]

■ the capital structure of the business, in terms of maturity profile of debt, type of capital instruments used, currency and interest rate structure. This should include comments on relevant ratios such as interest cover and debt/equity ratios;

■ the capital funding and treasury policies and objectives. These will cover the management of interest rate risk, the maturity profile of borrowings and the management of exchange rate risk. The Statement suggests that the OFR should also discuss the implementation of these policies in the period under review in terms of:

- the manner in which treasury activities are controlled;
- the currencies in which borrowings are made and in which cash and cash equivalents are held;
- the extent to which borrowings are at fixed interest rates;
- the use of financial instruments for hedging purposes; and
- the extent to which foreign currency net investments are hedged by currency borrowings and other hedging instruments;

- the main components of the reconciliation between the actual and standard tax charges where the overall tax charge is different from the standard charge (i.e. the normal UK tax rate applied to the profit before taxation);

- the cash generated from operations and other cash inflows during the period, commenting on any special factors that influenced these. Where segmental cash flows are significantly out of line with segmental profits, this should be indicated and explained;

- the business's liquidity at the end of the period, including comment on the level of borrowings at the end of the period, the seasonality of borrowing requirements and the maturity profile of both borrowings and committed borrowing facilities;

- any restrictions on the ability to transfer funds from one part of the group to meet the obligations of another part of the group where they represent, or might foreseeably come to represent, a significant constraint on the group;

- debt covenants which could have the effect of restricting the use of credit facilities, and where a breach of a covenant has occurred or is expected to occur, the OFR should give details of the measures taken or proposed to remedy the situation;

- the business's ability to remain a going concern as recommended by the Cadbury Committee; and

- the strengths and resources of the business whose value is not fully reflected in the balance sheet – for example, as is the case with intangible assets which have not been capitalised.

7.3 Statement of compliance

As the OFR Statement represents voluntary best practice, directors are not expected to include in the annual report any formal confirmation that they have complied with the principles set out in the Statement – although, clearly, the inclusion of some comment on the extent to which the Statement has been followed may be helpful to the user. However, the Statement suggests that where it is implied, through the use of the words 'operating and financial review' or otherwise, that the directors have endeavoured to follow the principles laid down in the Statement, they should signal any fundamental departure therefrom.[68]

7.4 Disclosures in practice

Although a large proportion of companies include an 'Operating and Financial Review' within their annual report and accounts, the quality of information contained therein has been variable. However, there is evidence that this is improving with experience. Annual surveys by the ICAS Research Committee have assessed the quality of OFRs published by companies in the FT-SE 100, and the most recent survey[69] records that 21 of the companies in question were awarded their highest grade,[70] compared with 16 in the previous year. Interestingly, the researchers also identified a strong trend of convergence between the OFR and the text of the preliminary announcement and predicted that many companies were likely to unite the two before very long.

The 21 companies most highly commended by the ICAS study were as follows:

Arjo Wiggins Appleton	Coats Viyella	Sears
Bass	Grand Metropolitan	Shell Transport & Trading
B.A.T Industries	Imperial Chemical Industries	Siebe
British Steel	Inchcape	TI Group
Burmah Castrol	Reuters	Unilever
Cadbury Schweppes	Royal Bank of Scotland	United Biscuits
Carlton Communications	Scottish Power	Whitbread

The survey also noted that Glaxo had achieved the same standard in the previous year but had been omitted from the survey because it had changed its year end. Readers may wish to refer to the annual reports and accounts of these companies for examples of high quality OFRs that seek to meet the ASB's objectives in this area.

We think that the OFR should be regarded as one of the ASB's most successful innovations. By providing a well-considered framework but allowing scope for experimentation, the Board has encouraged companies to approach the task imaginatively and constructively. Inevitably, some have carried it out better than others, but as the capital markets become more demanding and directors become more aware of their corporate governance responsibilities, balanced, objective and understandable OFRs are increasingly becoming a standard feature of UK GAAP.

APPENDIX: THE CADBURY CODE OF BEST PRACTICE

1   The Board of Directors

1.1   The board should meet regularly, retain full and effective control over the company and monitor the executive management.

1.2   There should be a clearly accepted division of responsibilities at the head of a company, which will ensure a balance of power and authority, such that no one individual has unfettered powers of decision. Where the chairman is also the chief executive, it is essential that there should be a strong and independent element on the board, with a recognised senior member.

1.3   The board should include non-executive directors of sufficient calibre and number for their views to carry significant weight in the board's decisions. (Note 1)

1.4   The board should have a formal schedule of matters specifically reserved to it for decision to ensure that the direction and control of the company is firmly in its hands. (Note 2)

1.5   There should be an agreed procedure for directors in the furtherance of their duties to take independent professional advice if necessary, at the company's expense. (Note 3)

1.6   All directors should have access to the advice and services of the company secretary, who is responsible to the board for ensuring that board procedures are followed and that applicable rules and regulations are complied with. Any question of the removal of the company secretary should be a matter for the board as a whole.

2   Non-Executive Directors

2.1   Non-executive directors should bring an independent judgement to bear on issues of strategy, performance, resources, including key appointments, and standards of conduct.

2.2   The majority should be independent of management and free from any business or other relationship which could materially interfere with the exercise of their independent judgement, apart from their fees and shareholding. Their fees should reflect the time which they commit to the company. (Notes 4 and 5)

2.3   Non-executive directors should be appointed for specified terms and reappointment should not be automatic. (Note 6)

2.4   Non-executive directors should be selected through a formal process and both this process and their appointment should be a matter for the board as a whole. (Note 7)

3   Executive Directors

3.1   Directors' service contracts should not exceed three years without shareholders' approval. (Note 8)

3.2   There should be full and clear disclosure of directors' total emoluments and those of the chairman and highest-paid UK director, including pension contributions and stock options. Separate figures should be given for salary and performance-related elements and the basis on which performance is measured should be explained.

3.3   Executive directors' pay should be subject to the recommendations of a remuneration committee made up wholly or mainly of non-executive directors. (Note 9)

4   Reporting and Controls

4.1   It is the board's duty to present a balanced and understandable assessment of the company's position. (Note 10)

4.2   The board should ensure that an objective and professional relationship is maintained with the auditors.

4.3   The board should establish an audit committee of at least 3 non-executive directors with written terms of reference which deal clearly with its authority and duties. (Note 11)

4.4   The directors should explain their responsibility for preparing the accounts next to a statement by the auditors about their reporting responsibilities. (Note 12)

4.5   The directors should report on the effectiveness of the company's system of internal control. (Note 13)

4.6   The directors should report that the business is a going concern, with supporting assumptions or qualifications as necessary. (Note 13)

NOTES

These notes include further recommendations on good practice. They do not form part of the Code.

1   To meet the Committee's recommendations on the composition of sub-committees of the board, boards will require a minimum of three non-executive directors, one of whom may be the chairman of the company provided he or she is not also its executive head. Additionally, two of the three non-executive directors should be independent in the terms set out in paragraph 2.2 of the Code.

2   A schedule of matters specifically reserved for decision by the full board should be given to directors on appointment and should be kept up to date. The Committee envisages that the schedule would at least include:

     (a)   acquisition and disposal of assets of the company or its subsidiaries that are material to the company;

     (b)   investments, capital projects, authority levels, treasury policies and risk management policies.

The board should lay down rules to determine materiality for any transaction, and should establish clearly which transactions require multiple board signatures. The board should also agree the procedures to be followed when, exceptionally, decisions are required between board meetings.

3   The agreed procedure should be laid down formally, for example in a Board Resolution, in the Articles, or in the Letter of Appointment.

4   It is for the board to decide in particular cases whether this definition of independence is met. Information about the relevant interests of directors should be disclosed in the Directors' Report.

5   The Committee regards it as good practice for non-executive directors not to participate in share option schemes and for their service as non-executive directors not to be pensionable by the company, in order to safeguard their independent position.

6   The Letter of Appointment for non-executive directors should set out their duties, term of office, remuneration, and its review.

7   The Committee regards it as good practice for a nomination committee to carry out the selection process and to make proposals to the board. A nomination committee should have a majority of non-executive directors on it and be chaired either by the chairman or a non-executive director.

8   The Committee does not intend that this provision should apply to existing contracts before they become due for renewal.

9   Membership of the remuneration committee should be set out in the Directors' Report and its chairman should be available to answer questions on remuneration principles and practice at the Annual General Meeting. Best practice is set out in PRO NED's Remuneration Committee guidelines, published in 1992.

10   The report and accounts should contain a coherent narrative, supported by the figures, of the company's performance and prospects. Balance requires that setbacks should be dealt with as well as successes. The need for the report to be readily understood emphasises that words are as important as figures.

11   The Committee's recommendations on audit committees are as follows:

     (a)   They should be formally constituted as sub-committees of the main board to whom they are answerable and to whom they should report regularly; they should be given written terms of reference which deal adequately with their membership, authority and duties; and they should normally meet at least twice a year.

     (b)   There should be a minimum of three members. Membership should be confined to the non-executive directors of the company and a majority of the non-executives serving on the committee should be independent of the company, as defined in paragraph 2.2 of the Code.

     (c)   The external auditor and, where an internal audit function exists, the head of internal audit should normally attend committee meetings, as should the finance director. Other board members should also have the right to attend.

     (d)   The audit committee should have a discussion with the auditors at least once a year, without executive board members present, to ensure that there are no unresolved issues of concern.

     (e)   The audit committee should have explicit authority to investigate any matters within its terms of reference, the resources which it needs to do so, and full access to information. The committee should be able to obtain outside professional advice and if necessary to invite outsiders with relevant experience to attend meetings.

(f) Membership of the committee should be disclosed in the annual report and the chairman of the committee should be available to answer questions about its work at the Annual General Meeting.

Specimen terms of reference for an audit committee, including a list of the most commonly performed duties, are set out in the Committee's full report.

12 The statement of directors' responsibilities should cover the following points:

■ the legal requirement for directors to prepare financial statements for each financial year which give a true and fair view of the state of affairs of the company (or group) as at the end of the financial year and of the profit and loss for that period;

■ the responsibility of the directors for maintaining adequate accounting records, for safeguarding the assets of the company (or group), and for preventing and detecting fraud and other irregularities;

■ confirmation that suitable accounting policies, consistently applied and supported by reasonable and prudent judgements and estimates, have been used in the preparation of the financial statements;

■ confirmation that applicable accounting standards have been followed, subject to any material departures disclosed and explained in the notes to the accounts. (This does not obviate the need for a formal statement in the notes to the accounts disclosing whether the accounts have been prepared in accordance with applicable accounting standards.)

The statement should be placed immediately before the auditors' report which in future will include a separate statement [now developed by the Auditing Practices Board and incorporated in Statement of Auditing Standards 600] on the responsibility of the auditors for expressing an opinion on the accounts.

13 The Committee notes that companies will not be able to comply with paragraphs 4.5 and 4.6 of the Code until the necessary guidance for companies has been developed as recommended in the Committee's report. [Now developed as discussed at 4.4 above.]

14 The company's statement of compliance should be reviewed by the auditors in so far as it relates to paragraphs 1.4, 1.5, 2.3, 2.4, 3.1 to 3.3, and 4.3 to 4.6 of the Code. [Now revised to 1.4, 1.5, 2.3, 2.4 and 4.3 to 4.5 of the Code.]

References

1 The Committee on the Financial Aspects of Corporate Governance, *The Financial Aspects of Corporate Governance*, (The Cadbury Report), December 1992, para. 2.1.
2 *Ibid.*, Appendix 1.
3 *Ibid.*, para. 2.5.
4 *Ibid.*, para. 2.6.
5 *Ibid.*, para. 3.2.
6 *Ibid.*, para. 3.3.
7 *Ibid.*, para. 3.4.
8 *The Listing Rules*, London Stock Exchange, Chapter 12, para. 12.43(j).
9 *Note to subscribers to the Listing Rules Amendment No. 6*, London Stock Exchange, October 1995.
10 The Cadbury Report, para. 4.1.
11 *Ibid.*, para. 4.7.
12 *Ibid.*, para. 4.11.
13 *Ibid.*, para. 4.12.
14 *Ibid.*, para. 4.18.
15 *Ibid.*, para. 4.25.
16 *Ibid.*, para. 4.12.
17 *Ibid.*, para. 4.13.
18 Wilson Bowden plc, Annual Report and Accounts 1996, p. 18.
19 The Cadbury Report, para. 4.16.
20 *Ibid.*, para. 4.30.
21 *Ibid.*, para. 4.50.
22 Note 12 to the Cadbury Code of Best Practice.
23 *Gazette*, 'Directors Responsibilities', Gazette 90/40, 3 November 1993.
24 The Cadbury Report, para. 4.28.
25 *Gazette*, 'Directors responsibilities for financial statements', Gazette 90/46, 17 December 1993.
26 The Cadbury Report, para. 5.16.
27 Internal Control Working Group, *Internal Control and Financial Reporting: Draft guidance for directors of listed companies developed in response to the recommendations of the Cadbury Committee*, October 1993.
28 Internal Control Working Group, *Internal Control and Financial Reporting: Draft guidance for directors of listed companies developed in response to the recommendations of the Cadbury Committee*, August 1994.
29 Internal Control Working Group, *Internal Control and Financial Reporting: Guidance for directors of listed companies registered in the UK*, December 1994.
30 *Ibid.*, para. 8.
31 *Ibid.*
32 *Ibid.*, para. 14.
33 *Ibid.*, para. 2.
34 *Ibid.*
35 *Ibid.*, para. 9.
36 *Ibid.*, para. 11.
37 *Ibid.*, para. 12.
38 Going Concern Working Group, *Going Concern and Financial Reporting: Guidance for directors of listed companies registered in the UK*, November 1994.
39 Bulletin 1994/1, *Disclosures relating to corporate governance (revised)*, APB, November 1994.
40 SAS 130, *The going concern basis in financial statements*, APB, November 1994.
41 *The Listing Rules*, London Stock Exchange, Chapter 12, para. 12.43(v).
42 Going Concern Working Group, *Going Concern and Financial Reporting: Guidance for directors of listed companies registered in the UK*, paras. 24–40.
43 *Ibid.*, para. 47.
44 *Ibid.*, paras. 51 and 52.

45   Going Concern Working Group, *Going Concern and Financial Reporting: Draft guidance for directors of listed companies developed in response to the recommendations of the Cadbury Committee*, May 1993, para. 2.14.

46   Going Concern Working Group, *Going Concern and Financial Reporting: Guidance for directors of listed companies registered in the UK*, para. 20.

47   SAS 130, para. 45.

48   *Ibid.*, para. 47.

49   The Cadbury Report, para. 3.9.

50   Bulletin 1995/1, *Disclosures relating to corporate governance (revised)*, APB, February 1995, para. 46.

51   The City Group for Smaller Companies, *The Financial Aspects of Corporate Governance: Guidance for Smaller Companies*, CISCO, London, 1994.

52   *Ibid.*, 'Refinements for smaller companies', paras. 1–10.

53   The Cadbury Report, para. 1.4.

54   The Committee on the Financial Aspects of Corporate Governance, *Compliance with the Code of Best Practice*, May 1995.

55   *Ibid.*, para. 3.

56   *Ibid.*, paras. 2–6.

57   *Ibid.*, paras. 15–18.

58   FRC PN 34, *Committee on Corporate Governance formed to succeed The Cadbury Committee*, 22 November 1995.

59   The Cadbury Report, para. 4.50.

60   *Ibid.*, para. 4.53.

61   ASB Statement, *Operating and Financial Review*, ASB, July 1993, para. 3.

62   *Ibid.*, para. 4.

63   *Ibid.*, para. 5.

64   *Ibid.*, para. 8.

65   *Ibid.*, paras. 9–22.

66   *Ibid.*, para. 23.

67   *Ibid.*, paras. 25–37.

68   *Ibid.*, para. 38.

69   *Operating and Financial Review: Experiences and Exploration*, Collins and Weetman, ICAS, August 1996.

70   These were those OFRs that could be described as 'a high quality document complying with the spirit of the ASB's proposals and providing a significant addition to the understanding of the annual report'.

Chapter 5   Consolidated accounts

1   THE CONCEPT OF A GROUP

1.1   The objectives of group accounts

Group accounts are designed to extend the reporting entity to embrace other entities which are subject to its control or influence. They involve treating the net assets and activities of subsidiaries held by the holding company as if they were part of the holding company's own net assets and activities; the overall aim is to present the results and state of affairs of the group as if they were those of a single entity.

The basic legal framework for group accounts is to be found in the Companies Act 1985, as amended by the Companies Act 1989. This requires that group accounts are to be in the form of consolidated accounts which 'give a true and fair view of the state of affairs as at the end of the financial year, and the profit or loss for the financial year, of the undertakings included in the consolidation as a whole, so far as concerns members of the company',[1] and that they should comply with the provisions of Schedule 4A with respect to their form and content.[2]

The relevant accounting standard on the subject is FRS 2 – *Accounting for subsidiary undertakings*. This explains that the purpose of consolidated financial statements is to present financial information about a parent undertaking and its subsidiary undertakings as a single economic entity to show the economic resources controlled by the group, the obligations of the group and the results it achieves with those resources.[3] FRS 2 is drafted in terms of the Companies Act, but it applies to all parent undertakings that prepare consolidated financial statements intended to give a true and fair view of the group.[4]

1.2   What is a subsidiary?

The question of the definition of a subsidiary is fundamental to any discussion of group accounts because otherwise it is impossible to say what constitutes the entity which is the subject of the report. The question is also related to the subject of off balance sheet financing, because frequently this hinges on whether the group balance sheet should embrace the accounts of an entity which holds certain assets and liabilities which management may not wish to include in the group accounts (see Chapter 16).

The term used in the legislation is 'subsidiary undertaking'. The definition of this (see 1.2.2 below) is based on the EC Seventh Directive and the same definition has also been adopted by FRS 2.

1.2.1   The EC Seventh Directive

Article 1 of the EC Seventh Directive on Company Law sets out six sets of circumstances under which a parent/subsidiary relationship will be regarded as existing, so as to require the parent to present consolidated accounts, and one further situation requiring consolidation even though such a relationship does not exist. Five of the six sets of circumstances have been incorporated in the UK legislation through the enactment of the Companies Act 1989 and these are discussed at 1.2.2 below. The other two situations contained in the Directive, which were optional and have not been incorporated, are as follows:

(a)   De facto control over appointment of the board

The parent shall consolidate its subsidiary if it is a shareholder or member of it and a majority of the members of the board who have held office throughout the year, the previous year, and up to the time of the issue of the consolidated accounts have *in fact* been appointed solely as a result of the exercise of the parent's voting rights.[5] This is to cater for the situation where, due to the fact that the majority of the shares are widely dispersed, a minority shareholder can exercise de facto control. The Directive allows member states not to implement this part of the definition, or to make it conditional on the holding of at least 20% of the voting rights; the UK government was opposed to this part of the definition at the time of the negotiation of the terms of the directive, and they decided to take advantage of the first of these exemptions.

(b)   Horizontal groups

Consolidated accounts must be prepared for companies which have no shareholding relationship in either of two sets of circumstances. The first is if they are managed on a unified basis under the terms of a contract or provisions in their memorandum or articles of association; the second is if the same people form the majority of the members of the board of both companies during the year and for the period up to the preparation of the accounts.[6] Although the thinking behind the second set of circumstances is easy to understand, it would appear to result occasionally in the consolidation of separate enterprises which were associated with each other only by coincidence and whose combined accounts would have neither meaning nor relevance to anyone. Neither of these provisions has been incorporated in the Companies Act.

1.2.2   The Companies Act

In implementing the Directive, the Companies Act 1989 introduced the term 'subsidiary undertaking' and moved the definition from one based strictly on the form of the shareholding relationship between the companies, nearer to one which reflects the substance of the commercial relationship and in particular who exercises de facto control. The use of the term 'undertaking' also extended the types of entity which may have to be consolidated, in that it not only includes companies or bodies corporate, but also unincorporated associations and partnerships.[7]

Under the Act, a subsidiary undertaking is one in which the parent:

(a)   has a majority of the voting rights; or

(b)   is a member and can appoint or remove a majority of the board; or

(c)   is a member and controls alone a majority of the voting rights by agreement with other members; or

(d)   has the right to exercise a dominant influence through the Memorandum and Articles or a control contract; or

(e)   has a participating interest and either

    (i)   actually exercises a dominant influence over it, or

    (ii)   manages both on a unified basis.[8]

These are discussed further below.

A   Majority of voting rights

This is the main definition based on the power of one entity to control another through the exercise of shareholder voting control. Unlike the old definition of a subsidiary,[9] it concentrates on those shares which can exercise voting power rather than those which are defined in terms of their rights to participate beyond a specified amount in a distribution.

'Voting rights' are defined as 'rights conferred on shareholders in respect of their shares or, in the case of an undertaking not having a share capital, on members, to vote at general meetings of the undertaking on all (or substantially all) matters'.[10]

There are a number of detailed provisions for determining whether or not certain rights are to be taken into account.[11] Paragraph 21 of ED 50, the forerunner of FRS 2, summarised these as follows:

'One example is where rights are only exercisable under certain circumstances; in this case those rights should be taken into account for as long as the particular circumstances continue, or the circumstances are within the control of the holder of the rights. Rights which are normally exercisable but which are temporarily interrupted should continue to be taken into account. Rights should be treated as held by the enterprise on whose behalf a nominee holds them or whose instruction, consent or concurrence is required for their exercise. Fiduciary interests are not taken into account and rights given as security remain the rights of the provider of the security, if the rights are mainly exercisable only in accordance with his instructions or in his interests. Rights of any of its subsidiaries are to be treated as the rights of the parent but rights of a parent should not be attributed to its subsidiaries. The voting rights in an enterprise are to be reduced by any rights held by the enterprise itself.'

B   Control of the board of directors

Essentially this is an anti-avoidance measure, which extends the control concept from control of the company in general meeting to control of the board, to cover situations where the latter exists but not the former.

Whereas previously the right to control the composition of the board only meant the right to appoint or remove a majority in number of the directors, the Companies Act 1989 extended it to mean the right to appoint or remove members of the board entitled to a majority of the voting rights on all (or substantially all) matters at board meetings.[12] This was a further anti-avoidance measure, to cope with the situation where control of the board's decisions is achieved either through the exercise of differential voting rights or a casting vote without having a majority in number of the membership of the board.

However, this change to the criterion could have implications for 'true' 50:50 joint ventures. Where the shareholders in such a joint venture, in order to prevent a deadlock, take it in turns each year to appoint the chairman (with the casting vote), this will mean that the joint venture will be a subsidiary undertaking of each shareholder company every second year. The question then arises, should the undertaking be consolidated, then equity accounted, in alternate years? (Depending on the timing, this could actually mean the undertaking is consolidated for the first part of the shareholding company's year and equity accounted for the remainder, and vice versa in alternate years!) In our view this would clearly be a nonsense and we believe that the appropriate treatment would be not to consolidate on the grounds that there are long-term restrictions which hinder control (see 5.3 below), but to equity account throughout.

Two companies which disclose the fact that they have a subsidiary by virtue of board control are RTZ-CRA and Sema Group, as shown below:

Extract 5.1: The RTZ Corporation PLC – CRA Limited (1996)

27 PRINCIPAL SUBSIDIARY COMPANIES [extract]

Company and country of incorporation	Principal activities	Class of shares held	Proportion of class held %	Group interest %
Namibia				
Rossing Uranium Limited (note c)	Uranium mining	'B'N$1	71.16)	68.58
		'C'N10c	70.59)	

Notes

(c)   The Group holding of shares in Rossing Uranium Limited carries 35.54 per cent of the total voting rights. Rossing is consolidated by virtue of Board control.

Extract 5.2: Sema Group plc (1996)

11. GROUP UNDERTAKINGS [extract]

The principal Group undertakings at 31 December 1996, all of which are engaged in the provision of information technology services, were as follows (all holdings were in ordinary shares):

	Immediate holding company (%)	Country of registration and operation
DIRECT GROUP UNDERTAKINGS		
BAeSEMA Limited	50	England
Sema Group SA	99.8	France
OWNED BY BAeSEMA LIMITED		
Aerosystems International Limited	50	England
OWNED BY SEMA GROUP SA		
TS FM Holdings	40	France

BAeSEMA Limited and TS FM Holdings have been fully consolidated as Group undertakings as defined by the Companies Act 1985. BAeSEMA is consolidated on the basis of a shareholders' agreement which gives the Group control of the Board of directors. TS FM Holdings is consolidated on the basis that it is managed on a unified basis with Sema Group SA.

BAeSEMA's 50% holding in Aerosystems International Limited has been fully consolidated from 1 January 1996 since it is managed on a unified basis with BAeSEMA.

C   Control by contract

Such a contract, which is a feature of German business organisations, is not usually possible under general principles of UK company law, because it would conflict with the directors' fiduciary duty to conduct the affairs of the company in accordance with its own best interests, and is allowed only where the Memorandum and Articles specifically permit it. The Directive provides that this part of the definition applies only where it is consistent with the company law of the country concerned, and for this reason it has been enacted in the UK in a fairly restricted way; it will apply only in cases where the parent company has the right to give directions with respect to the operating and financial policies of the other undertaking which its directors are obliged to comply with whether or not they are for the benefit of that other undertaking, where the undertaking's domestic law and its Memorandum and Articles permit a dominant influence to be exerted through such a contract, and where the contract in question is in writing.[13] This criterion is therefore likely to be of relevance only where a company has a business operation in Germany or another country which adopts the German model.

One company which has disclosed the fact that it had a subsidiary by virtue of a control contract is Sema Group, as shown below:

Extract 5.3: Sema Group plc (1993)

11. GROUP UNDERTAKINGS [extract]

The Group's 50% holding in BAeSEMA Limited, its 50% holding in Sema Group Télécom SA and its 49% holding in Tibet SA have been fully consolidated as Group undertakings as defined by the Companies Act 1989.

BAeSEMA is consolidated on the basis of a shareholders' agreement which gives the Group control of the board of directors. Tibet SA is consolidated on the basis of actual dominant influence exercised by the Group by virtue of a control contract.

D   Control by agreement

This is a more stringent application of the concept of de facto control by a minority investor (see 1.2.1 (a) above), requiring agreement with other shareholders rather than merely their tacit acceptance that control can be exercised. The Directive provides that the member states may introduce more particular requirements for the form and content of such agreements, and the Department of Trade and Industry announced that it intended to draft the legislation so that the agreement must be legally binding but need not be in writing, and that it should include agreements *not* to exercise voting rights as well as those to exercise them in a particular way.[14] Neither of these issues is, in fact, specifically dealt with in the Act; it may, therefore, be that in their absence, oral agreements and agreements not to exercise voting rights are intended to come within the scope of the legislation.

E   Participating interest with dominant influence or unified management

This criterion is one of the member state options contained in the Directive which has been introduced into the legislation in addition to the mandatory definitions set out in A to D above. This part of the Directive has been introduced in a very broad form which is based on a wide definition of 'participating interest', with the clear intention of preventing artificial structures designed to achieve the purposes of off balance sheet finance schemes.

A participating interest in an undertaking is deemed to mean an interest in the shares of the undertaking which is held for the long term for the purpose of securing a contribution to the activities of the investing company by the exercise of control or influence arising from that interest.[15] This is similar to the definition of a related company previously contained in the Companies Act 1985, but is wider in that it includes interests in partnerships and unincorporated associations; it also includes interests which are convertible into interests in shares, such as convertible loan stock, and options to acquire an interest in shares.[16] There is a rebuttable presumption that a holding of 20% or more is a participating interest;[17] however, there is no opposite presumption (as in SSAP 1 – see 2.1 of Chapter 7) that holdings of less than 20% are not participating interests.

Although 'participating interest' is defined in the Act, there is no further definition of the concept of either 'actually exercises a dominant influence' or 'managed on a unified basis' (both are concepts derived from German law); the reason being that the DTI did not want to elaborate on these definitions, since it regarded this as an area to be more appropriately dealt with by means of accounting standards, although ultimately it is a matter of law to be interpreted by the courts. The Act does state, however, that although 'a right to exercise a dominant influence' over another undertaking is defined as 'a right to give directions with respect to the operating and financial policies of that other undertaking which its directors are obliged to comply with whether or not they are for the benefit of that other undertaking' (see D above), this is not to be read as affecting the construction of 'actually exercises a dominant influence'.[18]

In FRS 2, 'dominant influence' is defined as 'influence that can be exercised to achieve the operating and financial policies desired by the holder of the influence, notwithstanding the rights or influence of any other party' and the 'actual exercise of dominant influence' is defined as being 'the exercise of an influence that achieves the result that the operating and financial policies of the undertaking influenced are set in accordance with the wishes of the holder of the influence and for the holder's benefit whether or not those wishes are explicit. The actual exercise of dominant influence is identified by its effect in practice rather than by the way in which it is exercised.'[19]

As explained in FRS 2, 'the effect of the exercise of dominant influence is that the undertaking under influence implements the operating and financial policies that the holder of the influence desires. Thus a power of veto or any other reserve power that has the necessary effect in practice can form the basis whereby one undertaking actually exercises a dominant influence over another. However, such powers are likely to lead to the holder actually exercising a dominant influence over an undertaking only if they are held in conjunction with other rights or powers or if they relate to the day-to-day activities of that undertaking and no similar veto is held by other parties unconnected to the holder.'[20]

Clearly, it will be a matter of judgement and interpretation as to whether these definitions apply to any particular set of circumstances. As FRS 2 explains, 'the full circumstances of each case should be considered, including the effect of any formal or informal agreements between the undertakings, to decide whether or not one undertaking actually exercises a dominant influence over another. Commercial relationships such as that of supplier, customer or lender do not of themselves constitute dominant influence.'[21]

The standard also states that dominant influence can be exercised 'in an interventionist or non-interventionist way. For example, a parent undertaking may set directly and in detail the operating and financial policies of its subsidiary undertaking or it may prefer to influence these by setting out in outline the kind of results it wants achieved without being involved regularly or on a day-to-day basis. Because of the variety of ways that dominant influence may be exercised evidence of continuous intervention is not necessary to support the view that dominant influence is actually exercised. Sufficient evidence might be provided by a rare intervention on a critical matter. Once there has been evidence that one undertaking has exercised a dominant influence over another, then the dominant undertaking should be assumed to continue to exercise its influence until there is evidence to the contrary.'[22]

Where a subsidiary undertaking is so only by virtue of this criterion then FRS 2 requires disclosure of the basis of the parent company's dominant influence.[23] Examples of companies which consolidate subsidiary undertakings which qualify under this criterion are shown in the following extracts:

Extract 5.4: Rentokil Initial plc (1996)

Principal Subsidiary and Associated Undertakings [extract]

The group's 50% interest in Yu Yu Calmic Co Ltd is consolidated as a subsidiary to reflect the group's dominant influence exercised over this company because of its shareholding and its involvement in the management and because the business is conducted under licence from the group.

Extract 5.5: Glaxo Wellcome plc (1996)

Principal subsidiary and associated undertakings [extract]

Subsidiary undertaking	%
Glaxo Saudi Arabia Ltd.	49[a]
Glaxo-Sankyo Co., Ltd.	50[a]

[a] Consolidated as subsidiary undertaking in accordance with section 258(4)(a) of the Companies Act 1985 on the grounds of influence over marketing strategy.

One interesting example is that of Booker which in its 1995 accounts consolidated a subsidiary under this criterion, as indicated below:

Extract 5.6: Booker plc (1995)

Subsidiary and associated undertakings [extract]

Recheio Distribuição SA (40%)5

5   Recheio Distribuição SA is treated as subsidiary on the grounds of Booker plc exercising a dominant influence over the operating and financial policies of that company.

However in the following year the position would appear to have changed:

Extract 5.7: Booker plc (1996)

13.   Fixed asset investments [extract]

Recheio Distribuição SA, in which the group holds a 40% equity interest and which has been consolidated hitherto on the basis of the group exercising dominant control, has been deconsolidated and treated as an associated undertaking effective from 28 December 1996. The change in the status of the investment in Recheio reflects the group's loss of dominant control over the operating and financial policies of that company.

One difficulty which this definition can give rise to is the apportionment of the results and net assets of the subsidiary undertaking between the parent and the minority interests, particularly where the participating interest is in the form of convertible loan stock or options to acquire an interest in shares. This is discussed at 1.3.4 below.

The ASB has defined 'managed on a unified basis' in FRS 2 as being where 'two or more undertakings are managed on a unified basis if the whole of the operations of the undertakings are integrated and they are managed as a single unit. Unified management does not arise solely because one undertaking manages another.'[24]

One company which consolidates subsidiary undertakings which qualify under this criterion is Unilever, as indicated below:

Extract 5.8: Unilever PLC (1996)

Unilever [extract]

The two parent companies, N.V. and PLC, operate as nearly as is practicable as a single entity (the Unilever Group, also referred to as Unilever or the Group). NV and PLC have the same directors and are linked by a series of agreements, including an Equalisation Agreement, which is designed so that the position of the shareholders of both companies is as nearly as possible the same as if they held shares in a single company.

Basis of consolidation [extract]

By reason of the operational and contractual arrangements referred to above and the internal participating interests ... , N.V. and PLC and their group companies constitute a single group under Netherlands and United Kingdom legislation for the purposes of presenting consolidated accounts. Accordingly the accounts of the Unilever Group are presented by both N.V. and PLC as their respective consolidated accounts.

Another example can be seen in Extract 5.2 above.

Questions which have arisen include that of whether more than one party can exercise dominant influence over a single undertaking. We believe that logically, there can only be one *dominant* influence, but there is a more general question of whether an undertaking can be the subsidiary of more than one parent, given that there are five alternative definitions of a subsidiary undertaking relationship, and if it is possible for an undertaking to have two parent companies, should both companies consolidate the undertaking?

On this question, FRS 2 states that 'where more than one undertaking is ... identified as a parent of one subsidiary undertaking, not more than one of those parents can have control as defined in paragraph 6 [of the standard]'.[25] It then suggests that such anomalies might be resolved by taking into account:

(a)   the existence of a quasi subsidiary (see Chapter 16);

(b)   the existence of severe long-term restrictions on the rights of the parent undertaking (see 5.3 below); or

(c)   the existence of a joint venture agreement, whether formal or informal.[26]

In relation to the last of these, the standard states that 'where the tests of the Act identify more than one undertaking as the parent of one subsidiary undertaking it is likely that they have shared control and, therefore, their interests in the subsidiary undertaking are in effect interests in a joint venture and should be treated accordingly [see 4.4 of Chapter 7]. Alternatively, one or more of the undertakings identified under the Act as a parent undertaking may exercise a non-controlling but significant influence over its subsidiary undertaking, in which case it would be more appropriate to treat that subsidiary undertaking in the same way as an associated undertaking rather than to include it in the consolidation.'[27]

1.3 Consolidating partly owned subsidiaries

Various alternative ways of looking at a group become relevant when there are subsidiary companies which are not wholly owned by the holding company; the particular matters which are affected are the elimination of the effects of inter-company transactions, the calculation of minority interests and the treatment of changes in stake in the subsidiary. There are two widely accepted concepts, referred to respectively as the entity concept and the proprietary concept, but the latter has a number of further variants. These are described in turn below.

1.3.1 The entity concept

The entity concept focuses on the existence of the group as an economic unit, rather than looking at it only through the eyes of the dominant shareholder group. It concentrates on the resources controlled by the entity, and regards the identity of owners with claims on these resources as being of secondary importance. It therefore makes no distinction between the treatment given to different classes of shareholders, whether majority or minority, and transactions between the shareholders are regarded as internal to the group.

1.3.2 The proprietary concept

The proprietary concept emphasises ownership through a controlling shareholding interest, and regards the purpose of the production of the consolidated financial statements as being primarily for the information of the shareholders of the holding company. Correspondingly, it makes no attempt to present financial statements which are relevant to the minority shareholders. This is achieved either by treating the minority shareholders as 'outsiders' and reflecting their interests as quasi-liabilities or by leaving them out of the group financial statements entirely, thereby only consolidating the parent's percentage interest in the assets and liabilities of the subsidiary (the 'proportional consolidation' method). This latter version of the concept is the one described in ED 50.[28] The proprietary concept is sometimes referred to as the 'parent company' concept, and there is a variant of it known as the 'parent company extension' concept, which leans more towards the entity concept described above.

1.3.3 Comparison between the different concepts of a group

The distinction between the different methods in practice can best be illustrated by an example:

Example 5.1: Comparison between the different concepts of a group

Assume that company A buys 75% of company B for £1,200 when company B has total net assets with a fair value of £1,000 and a book value of £800. Under the concepts described above, the consolidated balance sheet of company A would incorporate the effects of the acquisition calculated as follows:

	Entity concept £	Proprietary concept £	Parent coy. extension concept £
Net assets of B	1,000	950	1,000
Goodwill	600	450	450
	1,600	1,400	1,450
Minority interest	400	200	250
Investor interest	1,200	1,200	1,200

Under the entity concept, both the tangible net assets and goodwill are reported in the balance sheet at the full amount of their fair value as determined by the transaction involving the majority shareholder. These amounts are then apportioned between the majority and minority shareholders. By way of contrast, the proprietary concept leaves the minority interest unaffected by the transaction of the majority shareholder; it is shown simply as their proportionate share of the book values of the assets of the company. This means that the goodwill is stated at a figure which represents the difference between the cost of the 75% investment (£1,200) and 75% of the fair value of the assets (£750). Perhaps more disturbingly, the assets are carried on a mixed basis which represents 75% of their fair value and 25% of their book value. This feature is eliminated if proportional consolidation is adopted; the minority interest is disregarded altogether, being set against the assets and liabilities of the subsidiary on a line by line basis, so that only the majority investor's share of the subsidiary's assets are consolidated. This would result in consolidation of assets of £750 and goodwill of £450, representing the total of the investment of £1,200. However, the Companies Act does not allow the proportional consolidation approach to be adopted for subsidiary undertakings (although it does allow it to be used for non-corporate joint ventures – see 4.4 of Chapter 7). The feature is also avoided in the parent company extension concept, which includes the assets at the whole amount of their fair value and apportions that between the majority and minority interests, but includes goodwill only as it relates to the majority investor.

The rules contained in the legislation do not permit the use of the entity concept as set out above, because they require that goodwill be calculated by comparing the acquisition cost with the investor's proportionate share of the investee's capital and reserves (after adjusting for fair values); by requiring the assets and liabilities to be included at their fair values, they would also appear to rule out the proprietary concept (although the rules on minority interests do not refer to *adjusted* capital and reserves).[29] The entity method is also ruled out by the international standard on business combinations, IAS 22. This permits either of the other two methods, with the proprietary concept being the preferred approach and the parent company extension method a permitted alternative.[30]

The different concepts are also relevant to the calculation of the adjustments made to eliminate the effects of inter-company transactions. If company A in the above example sold an item of stock to company B for a profit of £100, and company B still held the asset in stock at the year end, it would be necessary to make an adjustment on consolidation to eliminate what was an unrealised profit from the group point of view. Under the proprietary concept, the minority shareholders are regarded as outsiders, and therefore there is a case for saying that 25% of the profit *has* been realised; this would be done by limiting the write-down of stock to £75, all of which is taken off the balance on the group profit and loss account. Under the proportional consolidation method, only 75% of the stock would appear in the consolidated balance sheet in the first place, so the adjustment would simply be to deduct £75 from both the group profit and loss account and from the stock. If the entity concept is followed, as it is the parent which has made the sale, the whole write down of stock of £100 would be charged against the group profit and loss account; no amount would be attributed to the minority interest. Under another approach, the separate entities approach,[31] the adjustment would be effected by apportioning the £100 between the group profit and loss account and the minority interest in the ratio 75:25. In this case the rules in the Companies Act permit inter-company profit eliminations to be made either at their gross amounts or in proportion to the investor's stake in the investee.[32]

A further practical situation where differences between the concepts emerge is when the partly owned subsidiary makes losses which put it into overall deficit. Under the entity concept, the consolidated financial statements would continue to account for these losses and apportion them between the majority and minority interests in proportion to their holdings, even if these created a debit balance for the minority interest in the balance sheet. A proprietary viewpoint would not normally permit the minority interest to be shown as a debit balance, because it could not usually be regarded as a recoverable asset from the point of view of the majority interest, which is the orientation of the financial statements under the proprietary concept. This was the position taken by SSAP 14, which said that 'debit balances should be recognised only if there is a binding obligation on minority shareholders to make good losses incurred which they are able to meet'.[33] FRS 2, on the other hand, has adopted an entity perspective and requires that losses are attributable to the minority interests according to their holdings in loss making subsidiaries, regardless of whether or not this leads to a debit balance or not. Such a debit balance is not regarded as an asset, but the minority share of net liabilities. However, the standard does require the group to make provision to the extent that it has 'any commercial or legal obligation (whether formal or implied) to provide finance that may not be recoverable in respect of the accumulated losses attributable to the minority interest'.[34]

1.3.4   ED 50 and FRS 2

ED 50 discussed these conceptual issues and developed a new concept, called the 'control/ownership concept', which is effectively a variant of the parent company extension concept described above. Under this concept, it is argued that the shareholders of the holding company need information not only on the group as a whole but also on the distinction between what they own and what others own.[35]   In deciding how to deal with the particular matters which are affected by the existence of the minority shareholders, the concept looks at whether 'control' or 'ownership' is the most relevant issue. In respect of questions where control is the most relevant issue, minorities are considered to be within the group, similar in nature to equity, because they are part of the controlled entity. Where ownership is considered to be most important, the minorities are treated as external to the group and regarded as being a liability.[36]

FRS 2 does not contain a detailed discussion of the concepts described above, leaving the conceptual basis of consolidated accounts to be dealt with instead in the proposed chapter on the reporting entity in the ASB's Statement of

Principles (see 5.8 of Chapter 2). However, apart from the treatment of debit balances relating to minority interests (see 1.3.3 above), FRS 2 adopts an approach in respect of minority interests similar to that proposed by ED 50. The practical effects of this approach are as follows.

Where a company becomes a parent of another entity, then as it controls that entity as a whole, all of the net assets of the subsidiary should be restated at fair values and included in the consolidated accounts, not just the proportion owned. Consequently, a minority interest should be recognised at the date of the acquisition based on those fair values. The amount for the minority should not include any share of goodwill arising on the acquisition.[37] In Example 5.1 above, this would result in the same treatment as shown under the parent company extension concept. Thereafter, any profits or losses of the subsidiary are consolidated in full, with an allocation made to the minority interest based on the proportion held by the minority shareholders. As indicated at 1.3.3 above losses continue to be allocated to minority interests even if this leads to a debit balance, although provision should be made to the extent that the parent has any commercial or legal obligation to provide finance that may not be recoverable.[38]

Where dealings in the shares of the subsidiary subsequently take place between the parent company and the minority interests, then as these are ownership issues, they are to be considered as external to the group and accounted for as such. Where the parent is increasing its stake in the subsidiary, then any difference between the consideration paid and the appropriate proportion of the net assets (based on fair values if necessary), i.e. the amount of the minority interest therein, should be treated as goodwill.[39] Where the parent reduces its stake in the subsidiary then a profit or loss should be recorded.[40] These issues are discussed further at 2.6 and 3.4 in Chapter 6 respectively.

The other main area is the elimination of the effects of inter-company transactions. This is regarded as a control issue as transactions between two companies under common control may be arranged without reference to any external party. The minority is, therefore, internal to the group for the calculation of these adjustments and it is not sufficient to adjust only for that part of the transaction which relates to the parent's interest; adjustment for the whole transaction and thus the full amount of any unrealised profit or loss must be made, with a suitable allocation made between the parent and the minority.[41] This is discussed further at 3.4 below.

FRS 2 emphasises that despite the title 'minority interests', there is in principle no upper limit to the proportion of shares in a subsidiary undertaking which may be held as a minority interest while the parent undertaking still qualifies as such under the Companies Act (and the standard).[42] This is due to the fact that the parent/subsidiary relationship is based on the parent having a 'controlling interest', whereas the apportionment of the results and net assets of the subsidiary between the parent and the minority interests is effectively based on their respective equity interests. This will be particularly relevant where the parent/subsidiary relationship is due to the parent having a participating interest and exercising a dominant influence over the subsidiary (see 1.2.2 E above). For example, a company may only have a 45% interest in the ordinary shares of another company but be in a position to exercise dominant influence over it, in which case 55% of the results and net assets of the subsidiary would be attributable to the minority interests.

One area which the standard does not deal with is are those unusual situations which can arise because control and ownership are divorced. There may be difficulties in determining the relevant apportionment particularly where the parent's participating interest is in the form of convertible loan stock or an option to acquire an interest in the shares of the subsidiary. An extreme example of this would be 'the 0% subsidiary' where the participating interest is in the form of an option over all the shares. In our view the apportionment to the minority interests will depend on the particular circumstances. On the one hand, it may be that the minority interests should be attributed 100%; for example, where the option price is yet to be determined or it is based on future results/net assets of the subsidiary, or where it has been agreed between the parties that prior to the exercise of the option all retained profits of the subsidiary are to be distributed to the existing shareholders. On the other hand, it may be that there is a put and call option over the shares, the option price is fixed and it is agreed between the parties that no dividends will be paid to the existing shareholders, in which case no amounts should be attributed to the minority interests; the minority interests should be included at an amount equivalent to the exercise price under the option.

2   HISTORICAL DEVELOPMENT OF RULES ON GROUP ACCOUNTS

2.1   Origins of group accounts

The idea of using a holding company to own further investments in subsidiaries evolved in the US more than 150 years ago, but the preparation of consolidated accounts to portray the results of the group did not become widely established until the early part of this century.

In the UK, groups of companies only became a significant form of business structure around the time of the First World War, and the first time that a company drew up a consolidated balance sheet for its members was when Nobel Industries presented such a statement as at December 1920. At that time there was no reporting requirement for any profit and loss account (even unconsolidated) to be presented, and the first group profit and loss account was not published until 1933, when the Dunlop Rubber Co. included one in its annual accounts. The Stock Exchange made the publication of consolidated accounts a requirement for new issuers in 1939, and the ICAEW published recommendations in 1944[43] which made such accounts best practice for all groups.

2.2 The UK legislative background

The first requirement for group accounts was introduced into the legislation by the Companies Act 1947, which was consolidated soon thereafter into the Companies Act 1948. These basic requirements, having been again consolidated into the Companies Act 1985, remained unchanged until the incorporation into UK law of the EC Seventh Directive on company law, which was one of the principal purposes of the Companies Act 1989. This Directive was issued by the Council of the European Communities in 1983, to establish a financial reporting framework for groups in all member states. The most significant changes were in the definition of a subsidiary, discussed at 1.2.2 above, and in the qualifying conditions for merger accounting, which are covered at 2.1.5 in Chapter 6. Apart from these changes, the impact of the 1989 Act on most groups was relatively minor as, to a large extent, the new rules codified existing practice.

2.3 Accounting standards in the UK

The first general accounting standard on group accounts in the UK was SSAP 14 – *Group accounts* – issued in September 1978. This provided the broad framework to support the basic legal requirements, and dealt in particular with the form which group accounts should take and various miscellaneous matters in relation to the mechanics of the consolidation process. The standard eventually required revision to reflect the new provisions of the Companies Act 1989 and, accordingly, an exposure draft, ED 50 – *Consolidated accounts* – was issued in June 1990. Following the demise of the ASC, the ASB issued its Interim Statement: Consolidated Accounts in December 1990 as a stop-gap measure, and in July 1992 issued FRS 2, *Accounting for Subsidiary Undertakings*, to replace SSAP 14.

There are other standards which deal in more detail with business combinations. These are discussed in Chapter 6.

3 CONSOLIDATION OF SUBSIDIARIES

3.1 Basic principles

It is beyond the scope of this chapter to discuss the detailed mechanics of the consolidation process; there are a number of basic texts which give a full exposition of this subject. The Companies Act 1989 introduced into the legislation some rules relating to the consolidation of subsidiaries,[44] but until then there were no authoritative rules on the subject at a detailed level; SSAP 14 merely stated that 'the method of preparation of consolidated financial statements on an item-by-item basis, eliminating intra-group balances and transactions and unrealised intra-group profit, is well understood ...'.[45]

FRS 2 now defines consolidation as 'the process of adjusting and combining financial information from the individual financial statements of a parent undertaking and its subsidiary undertakings to prepare consolidated financial statements that present financial information for the group as a single economic entity'.[46] This is not as explicit as the definition contained in ED 50 which stated that consolidation was 'a method of accounting under which the information contained in the separate financial statements of a parent and its subsidiaries is presented as though for a single entity. Investments in subsidiaries are eliminated against the subsidiaries' share capital and reserves in accordance with the method of accounting adopted for the business combination. After any necessary consolidation adjustments for such matters as minority interests, intra-group transactions and to obtain consistency of accounting policies, the amounts for assets and liabilities, revenue and expenses in the individual financial statements are added together on a line-by-line basis to form the consolidated accounts.'[47] (Arguably, this was more of a description rather than a definition of a consolidation.) FRS 2 introduces authoritative rules relating to some of these consolidation adjustments and these are referred to below.

3.2 Uniform accounting policies

It is axiomatic that the figures being aggregated in the consolidation process must have been compiled on a consistent basis and therefore that uniform accounting policies should have been adopted by all the members of the group. Of course, local reporting requirements for each subsidiary might dictate that different policies must be used for domestic purposes; the only necessity where this occurs is that appropriate adjustments are made in the course of the consolidation process to eliminate the effects of such differences. FRS 2 endorses this general principle.[48]

The Companies Act does not refer to accounting policies as such in this context, but says that 'where assets and liabilities ... have been valued or otherwise determined by undertakings according to accounting rules differing from those used for the group accounts, the values or amounts shall be adjusted so as to accord with the rules used for the group accounts'.[49] However, this need not be done if the effect is immaterial,[50] or if there are 'special reasons' for leaving them unchanged (in which case disclosure of particulars of the departure, the reasons for it and its effect are to be given).[51] FRS 2 also acknowledges that this may be appropriate in exceptional cases.[52]

Notwithstanding these apparent loopholes in FRS 2 and the Act, the accounts must still give a true and fair view of the group as a whole and it is difficult to imagine that this could be achieved by adding together material figures which have been compiled using profoundly different policies. In practice, however, the relaxation allowed does not seem to be relied on in many cases and groups generally do exert themselves to achieve consistency of policies unless the effect is insignificant.

Although there is no requirement to do so, some companies disclose the fact that adjustments are made to achieve uniform accounting policies, as illustrated below:

Extract 5.9: Allied Domecq PLC (1996)

CONSOLIDATION [extract]

In cases where the statutory accounts of overseas undertakings are prepared on bases inconsistent with group accounting policies, appropriate adjustments are made to conform with the bases adopted in the UK.

Extract 5.10: British Telecommunications plc (1997)

I   Basis of preparation of the financial statements [extract]

Where the financial statements of subsidiary and associated undertakings do not conform with the group's accounting policies, appropriate adjustments are made on consolidation in order to present the group financial statements on a consistent basis.

3.3   Coterminous accounting periods

Since the group is seen as an extension of the parent company in UK law, it is necessary that the period covered by the group accounts corresponds to the accounting reference period of the parent, both in terms of duration and balance sheet date. Once again, this requirement is implicit in the objective that the group accounts should be prepared as if the group were a single entity.

The Companies Act places an onus on the directors of the parent company to ensure that the financial year of each subsidiary is the same as the parent. However, it does acknowledge that there can be good reasons why the individual subsidiaries' own accounts might be drawn up to a different date;[53] for example, in certain countries their year end might be dictated by law, they might choose to adopt a particular accounting period for tax purposes or their trade may be seasonal and have a natural cycle which makes it appropriate to choose a particular reporting date. Another reason could be that they deliberately prepare their accounts to a date shortly before that of the parent (as a materially accurate approximation to the period of the parent) so as to facilitate speedy reporting by the parent of the group results.

Where the period covered by the accounts of an individual member of the group does not correspond to that of the parent, two solutions are possible. The first is for the subsidiary to prepare special accounts solely for the purpose of the consolidation for a period which does match that of the parent. Under the provisions of the Act, such special statements (termed interim accounts) *must* be used if the subsidiary's year end is more than three months before that of the parent; their use is only optional if the year end is no more than three months before that of the parent.[54] One company which has had to use interim accounts is HSBC Holdings, as shown below:

Extract 5.11: HSBC Holdings plc (1996)

1   Basis of preparation [extract]

Accounts of subsidiary undertakings are made up to 31 December, except in the case of Midland Life Limited, which has a year-end of 31 August and for which, therefore, the Group uses interim accounts drawn up to 31 December annually, and Hongkong Bank of Canada, which has a 31 October year-end.

Although, under the Companies Act, the use of interim accounts is only optional if the year end is no more than three months before that of the parent, FRS 2 requires interim accounts to be used in such circumstances unless it is impracticable to do so, in which case the second solution should be adopted.[55] This solution is to use the statutory accounts of the subsidiary for the period last ending before that of the parent. As indicated above such an approach is only possible where the subsidiary's year end is no more than three months before that of the parent. FRS 2 then requires that any changes that have taken place in the intervening period that materially affect the view given by the group's accounts should be taken into account by adjustments in the preparation of the consolidated accounts.[56] In effect, therefore, this means that the group accounts must present (within limits of materiality) the same position as if coterminous year ends had been adopted.

One company which has used interim accounts when statutory accounts made up to within three months of the parent's year end were available is Johnson Fry Holdings, as shown below:

Extract 5.12: Johnson Fry Holdings plc (1996)

Basis of preparation [extract]

The financial statements include the financial statements of the Company and all its subsidiary undertakings made up to 31 December 1996, with the exception of the Pinnacle businesses which changed their year end to 31 October so that audited figures would be available prior to the anticipated sale which was completed on 15 January 1997. In respect of these subsidiary undertakings, audited financial statements to 31 October, together with management accounts covering the remaining two months have been used to draw up these financial statements.

Notwithstanding the preference in FRS 2 for interim accounts to be used, some companies appear to regard the use of such accounts as impracticable as they use the accounts of some of their subsidiaries made up to earlier dates in order to avoid undue delay in the presentation of the group's accounts, as illustrated in the extracts below:

Extract 5.13: Imperial Chemical Industries PLC (1996)

1   Composition of the Group

The Group accounts consolidate the accounts of Imperial Chemical Industries PLC and its subsidiary undertakings, of which there were 380 at 31 December 1996. Owing to local conditions and to avoid undue delay in the presentation of the Group accounts, 68 companies made up their accounts to dates earlier than 31 December, but not earlier than 30 September; 4 subsidiaries made up their accounts prior to 30 September but interim accounts to 31 December were drawn up for consolidation purposes.

Extract 5.14: National Westminster Bank Plc (1996)

(ii)   Basis of consolidation [extract]

To avoid undue delay in the presentation of the Group's accounts, the accounts of certain subsidiary undertakings have been made up to 30 November. There have been no changes in respect of these subsidiary undertakings, in the period from their balance sheet dates to 31 December, that materially affect the view given by the Group's accounts.

FRS 2 requires that, where coterminous year ends are *not* used in respect of any of the group's subsidiaries, there should be disclosure of the name of the subsidiaries involved, the year ends used (and duration of accounting periods, if different from that of the parent) and the reasons for the use of the different dates.[57] The Act contains similar requirements.[58] Given that, as discussed above, the accounts must in any event present materially the same picture as if coterminous years had been used, these requirements seem irrelevant.

The use of the accounts of foreign subsidiaries with non-coterminous year ends also raises the question of what exchange rate should be used for translation purposes. This point is covered in 3.4.1 of Chapter 8.

3.4   Elimination of unrealised profits/losses on inter-company transactions

The reasons for making such an elimination are straightforward; 'no man can make a profit by trading with himself', and when a group is trying to present its results as if it were a single entity, it clearly must not regard internal transactions as giving rise to a realised profit.

In most cases the treatment is uncontentious and entails writing down the value of items of stock (if that is what is involved) held by one group company at the year end which have been purchased from another group company which has made a profit on the deal; the adjusting entry is simply to remove the profit element from the stock valuation and from the balance on the group profit and loss account (net of a deferred tax adjustment if appropriate; the elimination of this profit can be regarded as giving rise to a timing difference, because the group will still be taxed on the profit which is eliminated). This will result in the assets being stated at their cost to the group. Similar adjustments should normally be made where a loss arises on the transfer. However, as indicated in ED 50, where a loss arises on the transfer, this may be indicative of a permanent impairment in value of the asset (or a reduction to net realisable value) and therefore no adjustment should be made. The cost (or written down value) of the asset to the group is then used in calculating the profit or loss with anyone outside the group, so that the full profit or loss to the group is reflected at the point at which the asset is sold to the outside party.[59]

Complications can arise when either the selling or the purchasing company (or both) is not a wholly owned subsidiary, or when one of the parties to the transaction is a subsidiary which is not consolidated. There are essentially two questions: (a) what proportion of the profit in the stock is to be eliminated, and (b) whether, and if so how, to make the elimination against minority interests as well as group shareholders' funds (which has already been discussed to some extent at 1.3.3 above). FRS 2 requires that the whole amount of the profit be eliminated, and that the adjustment be apportioned between the majority and minority interests in proportion to their holdings in the selling company, even if the subsidiary is equity accounted.[60] In Example 5.1 at 1.3.3 above, the parent company was the selling company and therefore *no* amount would be attributed to the minority shareholders; if, on the other hand, the subsidiary had made the profit on selling to the parent, 25% would have been attributed to the minority shareholders.

The Companies Act also contains provisions requiring intra-group profits (and losses) included in the book value of assets to be eliminated in preparing the consolidated accounts. However, where a partly owned subsidiary is involved the Act allows the elimination to be either the whole of the profit (or loss) or the group's interest thereof. These rules do not extend to transactions with subsidiaries which are equity accounted in the group accounts; for example, subsidiaries excluded from consolidation on grounds of different activities.[61] Nevertheless, as indicated above, FRS 2 requires the whole of the profit (or loss) to be eliminated and clarifies that this also applies to transactions with subsidiaries excluded from consolidation on grounds of different activities.[62] It also says that profits and losses arising on transactions with subsidiaries which are excluded for other reasons need not be eliminated except to the extent appropriate if they are equity accounted because significant influence is retained.[63]

The foreign currency complications which can arise from inter-company transactions are dealt with in 3.7.2 of Chapter 8.

4   EXEMPTIONS FROM PREPARING GROUP ACCOUNTS

As well as various rules on exclusion of particular subsidiaries, there are a number of provisions which exempt parent companies from having to present consolidated accounts at all. Previously both SSAP 14[64] and the Companies Act[65] contained provisions that group accounts need not be produced if the reporting company was itself a wholly owned subsidiary, although the Companies Act exemption applied only if it was owned by another British company. This exemption in the legislation was extended by the Companies Act 1989 to companies owned by parents incorporated elsewhere in the EEC, and is not limited to subsidiaries which were wholly owned, although there are provisions which allow minority shareholders to demand the preparation of consolidated accounts.[66] As a result of the creation of the European Economic Area with effect from 1994, the exemption was further extended.[67] The Companies Act also contains provisions to exempt parent companies from having to prepare consolidated accounts if the group falls within certain size limits.[68] FRS 2 repeats the exemptions contained in the legislation.[69] These exemptions are discussed below.

4.1   Intermediate holding companies

As indicated above, intermediate holding companies whose immediate parent undertaking is established in a member state of the European Economic Area (EEA) are exempt from preparing group accounts. The exemption is not confined to wholly owned subsidiaries, but is available where the immediate parent holds more than 50% of the shares in a company. However, minority shareholders have the right to request the preparation of consolidated accounts for a financial year by serving a notice on the company within six months of the end of the previous financial year. The minority in question must hold more than half of the shares in the company not held by the immediate parent or more than 5% of the total shares of the company.[70] The exemption does not apply to companies having shares or debentures listed on a stock exchange in a member state[71] and is subject to the following conditions:

(a)   the company must be included in audited consolidated accounts of a parent undertaking established under the law of a member state of the EEA and which comply with the Seventh Directive. The consolidated accounts must be drawn up to the same date as the company's accounts or an earlier date during the same financial year;[72]

(b)   the following disclosures must be given in the accounts of the company:

   (i)   the fact that the company is exempt from preparing group accounts;[73] and

   (ii)   the name of the parent undertaking which drew up the accounts referred to in (a) above; and

   ■   its country of incorporation, if incorporated outside Great Britain; or

   ■   if it is unincorporated, the address of its principal place of business;[74] and

(c) the accounts referred to in (a) above must be delivered by the company to the registrar together with (if they are not in English) a certified English translation.[75]

This exemption can result in the same set of group accounts being filed by a number of different companies and an example will show that it has some rather surprising effects.

Example 5.2: *Exemption for intermediate parents*

The Company A group has the following structure:

Company A
|
Company B
|
Company C
|
Company D

All the subsidiary undertakings of Company A are 100% owned and all companies prepare their accounts up to the same year end. The effect of the exemption on several different sets of circumstances will be considered as shown by the columns in the following table:

Company	Incorporated in		
	(a)	(b)	(c)
Company A	Great Britain	Netherlands	Netherlands
Company B	United States of America	France	Great Britain
Company C	Great Britain	Great Britain	Great Britain
Company D	Great Britain	Great Britain	Great Britain

(a) Company A and Company C must both prepare group accounts. In the case of Company C, this is because its immediate parent is not incorporated in a member state of the EEA. This structure is, however, unlikely to arise frequently in practice as Company A would not be in the same UK tax group as Company C and Company D.

It would make no difference to the above if Company B were incorporated in the Channel Islands or the Isle of Man as these are not member states of the EEA. Northern Ireland is part of a member state so if Company B were incorporated there, only Company A would have to prepare group accounts.

(b) Company C is exempt from preparing group accounts. If Company B as well as Company A chose to prepare consolidated accounts complying with the Seventh Directive, then Company C could choose to file an English translation of either Company A or Company B's group accounts.

(c) Company B and Company C are exempt from preparing group accounts but both companies must file an English translation of Company A's group accounts. If the Company B (or Company C) group were small or medium-sized (see 4.2 below) it could claim exemption on grounds of size without having to file Company A's accounts. This could reduce duplication of filing to an extent, but it means obtaining a report that in the auditor's opinion the group is entitled to the exemption claimed. Often this will be less costly and time-consuming than translating documents into English. However, this would not be of any assistance if the Company A group contained a public company, a bank or an insurance or financial services company. There is also the drawback that the disclosure requirements are more onerous where the exemption is claimed on grounds of size rather than as an intermediate parent company.

One situation where the exemption may not be available is when a holding company becomes a subsidiary of another EEA company. Under the legislation, the exemption will not be available if the company has not been included in a set of consolidated accounts of the new parent made up to a date which is coterminous or earlier than its own year end. It should be noted that the requirement is not that the *particular accounts* of the company will be included in a set of consolidated accounts of the parent, but that the *company* is included in accounts made up to a date which is coterminous or *earlier* than its own year end.

One other problem with the particular requirements is that other member states may not have actually implemented the Seventh Directive, in which case the UK intermediate holding company will not be able to avail itself of the exemption. Most of the major countries in the EEA have now implemented the Seventh Directive so this will now be less of a problem. However, if the EEA is expanded to encompass other European countries, then it may become more of an issue. It will be necessary, therefore, to check whether a particular member state has embodied the Seventh Directive into its local legislation and, if so, whether there are any transitional provisions delaying the application of the provisions.

Even where the year ends of the UK intermediate holding company and the parent company are the same, problems can arise. The directors of the intermediate holding company have to state in the company's accounts that they are exempt from the obligation to prepare group accounts. However, some of the conditions which have to be met may not have taken place by the time the directors approve their accounts. For example, the consolidated accounts, in which the company is to be included, may not have been prepared and audited; this will be the case if the parent company has a timetable which requires audited accounts of the company to be submitted prior to the audit report on the consolidated accounts being signed. Certainly, the company will still have to file with the registrar the consolidated accounts of the parent. In order to get round these logistical problems, it may be possible for the directors to anticipate these conditions in preparing their accounts, in which case they should only release one set of their audited accounts to the parent company and only file those accounts once they have received the consolidated accounts of the parent. Another possibility would be to submit only an audited consolidation package to the parent company and only prepare their statutory accounts once they have received the consolidated accounts of the parent.

4.2   Small and medium-sized groups

The Companies Act contains provisions such that small and medium-sized groups are exempt from the requirement to prepare consolidated accounts. Where advantage is taken of this exemption, certain disclosures are required in the parent company's accounts concerning its subsidiary undertakings.[76]

To qualify as small or medium-sized, a group must satisfy certain criteria based on the statutory accounts of companies within the group and on the number of employees of the group. The provisions actually include criteria for both small and medium-sized groups although those relating to small groups are redundant for the purposes of the exemption, since any group satisfying them will also satisfy the medium-sized group criteria.

Certain groups may not claim exemption even if they satisfy the criteria. These are groups which contain:

(a)   a public company or a body corporate other than a company (this would include foreign companies) whose constitution allows it to offer its shares or debentures to the public;

(b)   an authorised institution under the Banking Act 1987;

(c)   an insurance company to which Part II of the Insurance Companies Act 1982 applies; or

(d)   an authorised person under the Financial Services Act 1986.[77]

A group qualifies for this exemption if it satisfies at least two of the following three tests:

(a)   its aggregate turnover is not more than £11.2 million net (or £13.44 million gross);

(b)   its aggregate balance sheet total is not more than £5.6 million net (or £6.72 million gross);

(c)   its aggregate number of employees is not more than 250.[78]

It can be seen that there are two sets of financial limits for small or medium-sized groups, one based on aggregate figures from the accounts of group companies before making consolidation set-offs ('gross') and the other on aggregate figures after consolidation set-offs ('net'). If a group satisfies the criteria on either basis, it is exempt from preparing consolidated accounts. The bases can be mixed, i.e. one limit satisfied on a net basis, the other on a gross basis.[79] These financial limits are subject to periodic revision.[80]

The use of the gross basis allows groups to claim exemption from preparing group accounts without having to perform a consolidation exercise to prove their entitlement. Some groups with a significant amount of intra-group trading are likely to have to use the net basis as they may not meet the gross limits.

Unlike the provisions for individual companies filing abbreviated accounts, there is no requirement to adjust the turnover limit in respect of a financial year which is less than or more than 12 months in length.

The Act explains how the aggregate figures should be determined and defines 'balance sheet total' as the total of items A to D if Format 1 is used and the total under the heading 'Assets' if Format 2 is used.[81] All the figures must be taken from statutory accounts.[82] Management accounts are not allowed to be used for this purpose but are permitted, and in some cases required, as a basis for consolidated accounts (see 3.3 above). Some groups may find that, because of the different periods the accounts may cover, consolidated accounts prepared using management accounts give the impression that the group qualifies for the new exemption when this is not in fact the case. In deciding whether the criteria are satisfied, all subsidiary undertakings must be taken into account even if the group is entitled to exclude some of them from consolidation.

The rules for changing an existing status as a small, medium-sized or large group are the same as those for individual companies. This means that an existing status will only change in the second consecutive year in which a group fails to meet (or meets) two out of the three criteria.[83] In the first accounting reference period of the parent company, the group qualifies if it satisfies two out of the three criteria in that year.[84]

4.3   Exemptions contained in FRS 2

As indicated above, FRS 2 repeats the exemptions contained in the Act. Where these exemptions are taken the standard requires that certain disclosures are made in addition to those required by the Act. It requires that the parent's accounts should contain a statement that they present information about it as an individual undertaking and not about its group. The statement should also include or refer to a note giving the grounds on which the parent is exempt from preparing consolidated financial information.[85]

ED 50 had stated that 'in certain circumstances where a parent has made use of an exemption from preparing consolidated accounts, the accounts of the exempt parent alone will not be sufficient to give a true and fair view of the financial position and profit and loss for that period of that parent. Sufficient additional disclosures should be made to enable the parent's accounts to show a true and fair view of its activities and financial position. In some cases such information may best be presented by providing consolidated accounts for the whole group.'[86]   This controversial proposal attracted adverse criticism and was omitted from the standard.

5   EXCLUSION OF SUBSIDIARIES FROM GROUP ACCOUNTS

5.1   Sources of rules on exclusion of particular subsidiaries

Where group accounts are required, there are various circumstances under which it is considered appropriate not to consolidate particular subsidiaries, but instead either to deal with them in some other manner or to exclude them from the group accounts altogether.

Under the Companies Act subsidiaries may be excluded from the consolidated accounts where:

(a)   their activities are sufficiently different from those of the rest of the group;

(b)   there are severe long-term restrictions over the parent's rights;

(c)   they are held with a view to subsequent resale;

(d)   obtaining the information needed would involve disproportionate expense or undue delay; or

(e)   they are immaterial (in aggregate).[87]

FRS 2 only permits subsidiaries to be excluded from consolidation on grounds of criteria (a) to (c) above,[88] although as the standard does not apply to immaterial items exclusion under criterion (e) is also permissible. The ASB took the view that criterion (d) was not an appropriate reason for excluding material subsidiaries.[89] The circumstances under which the three permissible criteria might be applied are discussed in turn below.

5.2   Different activities

The specific rules on this in the Companies Act read as follows:

'Where the activities of one or more subsidiary undertakings are so different from those of other undertakings to be included in the consolidation that their inclusion would be incompatible with the obligation to give a true and fair view, those undertakings shall be excluded from consolidation.

'This ... does not apply merely because some of the undertakings are industrial, some commercial and some provide services, or because they carry on industrial or commercial activities involving different products or provide different services.'[90] In the case of banking and insurance groups, undertakings may not be excluded under the Companies Act on these grounds if their activities are a direct extension of, or ancillary to, the banking or insurance business.[91]

FRS 2 adopts the same approach, stressing that the exclusion is to be applied only in very exceptional cases. It explains that 'the key feature of this exclusion is that it refers only to a subsidiary undertaking whose activities are so different from those of other undertakings included in the consolidation that to include that subsidiary undertaking in the consolidation would be incompatible with the obligation to give a true and fair view. Cases of this sort are so exceptional that it would be misleading to link them in general to any particular contrast of activities. For example, the contrast between Schedule 9 and 9A companies (banking and insurance companies and groups) and other companies or between profit and not-for-profit undertakings is not sufficient of itself to justify non-consolidation. The different activities of undertakings included in the consolidation can better be shown by presenting segmental information rather than by excluding from consolidation the subsidiary undertakings with different activities.'[92]

Where a subsidiary is excluded from consolidation on these grounds, both the Act[93] and FRS 2 require it to be equity accounted.[94] Unlike some of the other exclusions, therefore, this is in essence a different manner of incorporating the company concerned in the group accounts, rather than excluding it altogether.

The previous rules in both UK law and SSAP 14 were not drafted in such a restrictive way. Subsidiaries were frequently not consolidated on the grounds that their accounts were prepared on entirely different bases of accounting from the rest of the group. An obvious example would be a group which owned a subsidiary in the banking or insurance sector which applied substantially different accounting policies from the rest of the group. In fact, there were a number of companies which took a broader view than this, and excluded subsidiaries which they viewed as being in different businesses in less extreme circumstances than those mentioned above; a common example was companies with finance subsidiaries.[95]

FRS 2 and the Companies Act require various general disclosures in respect of subsidiaries excluded from consolidation, which are discussed at 5.5 below. In addition to these general disclosures, the standard requires that, where subsidiaries have been excluded from consolidation because of different activities, their separate accounts should be included in the consolidated accounts. These can be presented in summary form unless the excluded undertakings account for more than 20% of any of the following: the group's operating profits; or its turnover; or its net assets. These amounts should be measured by including the excluded subsidiary undertakings.[96]

Where an excluded subsidiary undertaking is either:

(a)   a body corporate incorporated outside Great Britain which does not have an established place of business in Great Britain; or

(b)   an unincorporated undertaking

the Act requires its latest accounts (or group accounts) to be appended to the accounts delivered to the registrar. However, this does not require the preparation of accounts which would otherwise not be prepared; neither does it require the publication of accounts which would not otherwise be required to be published, but the reason for such accounts not being appended must be explained.[97]   For example, a partnership excluded on these grounds might prepare accounts for its own purposes; however, these would not need to be appended provided the accounts delivered to the registrar contained a note to the effect that the partnership accounts were not appended as they were not required to be published. In the case of foreign companies, this means that, for example, the accounts of a Canadian company would have to be appended but not those of most US companies (since US companies, other than those with a SEC listing, are not required to publish their accounts).

5.3   Operating under severe restrictions

The provisions of the Companies Act which deal with this exclusion state that 'a subsidiary undertaking may be excluded from consolidation where ... severe long-term restrictions substantially hinder the exercise of the rights of the parent company over the assets or management of that undertaking'.[98]   The Act specifies that the rights which are restricted must be rights in the absence of which the company would not be the parent company.

FRS 2 goes further and *requires* subsidiaries to be excluded from consolidation when these circumstances apply. The standard explains that this ground for exclusion ties in with its underlying concept of control as the basis for consolidation. Thus, where the restrictions amount to a loss of control, it would be misleading to continue to include the subsidiary in the consolidation. However, it emphasises that the exclusion should not be applied where only the prospect of restrictions exists, or if the restrictions are minor. The standard refers to the need for them to have 'a severe and restricting effect in practice in the long-term on the rights of the parent undertaking'. It quotes the case of a subsidiary undertaking which is subject to an insolvency procedure in the UK such that control over that undertaking may have passed to a designated official, e.g. an administrator, administrative receiver or liquidator, with the effect that severe long-term restrictions are in force. However, it states that a company voluntary arrangement does not necessarily lead to loss of control. Similarly, in some overseas jurisdictions even formal insolvency procedures may not amount to loss of control.[99]

One company which has not consolidated subsidiaries due to insolvency proceedings is Creston Land and Estates, as shown below:

Extract 5.15: Creston Land and Estates plc (1996)

BASIS OF CONSOLIDATION [extract]

The group accounts consolidate the accounts of the company and all of its subsidiaries except those where severe long term restrictions substantially hinder the exercise of rights over the assets or management of the subsidiary undertaking. Where such restrictions exist a subsidiary undertaking is treated as a fixed asset investment in accordance with Financial Reporting Standard 2.

9   INVESTMENTS HELD AS FIXED ASSETS [extract]

During the year Co-ordinated Land and Estates Limited ("CLE") and its subsidiaries were put into creditors' voluntary liquidation. In addition, British Patent Glazing Limited was put, during the year, into administrative receivership.

Two companies which have invoked this rule in circumstances where insolvency procedures would not appear to have been in progress are shown in the following extracts:

Extract 5.16: Regal Hotel Group plc (1996)

BASIS OF CONSOLIDATION [extract]

The consolidated financial statements incorporate the financial statements of the Company and all of its subsidiaries, with the exception of Bramhope Limited.

11.   INVESTMENTS IN SUBSIDIARIES [extract]

Bramhope Limited ceased to be treated as a consolidated subsidiary undertaking on 25th March 1993 in accordance with Financial Reporting Standard 2.

This was as a result of the severe long term restrictions placed on the Company's control over Bramhope Limited in having to accommodate the wishes of Bramhope's bankers.

Extract 5.17: London and Metropolitan plc (1995)

B)   BASIS OF CONSOLIDATION [extract]

The Company and other Group companies have been released from any financial liability in respect of certain subsidiaries' liabilities and borrowings. As a result of this, the Group has ceased to have any financial interest in the losses of these subsidiaries. As the prospect of the relevant subsidiaries ever making profits is extremely remote and as there are severe long term restrictions on the Group's interest in these subsidiaries, their results have not been consolidated.

34.   GROUP COMPANIES [extract]

For the reasons detailed in the Accounting Policies (Note 2b), the results of Pont Royal SA, Challengerhold Limited, The Bicester Park Development Company Limited and Bettertrade Limited are not consolidated in the Group financial statements.

Summary financial information in respect of subsidiary undertakings not consolidated in the Group accounts is set out below.

	Capital and reserves as at 31 December 1995 £'000	Profit/(loss) for the year ended 31 December 1995 £'000
Pont Royal SA	(19,300)	(6,470)
Challengerhold Limited	(10,578)	155
The Bicester Park Development Company Limited	(15,620)	(1,288)
Bettertrade Limited	(45,498)	(7,603)

During the year ended 31 December 1995 the Group received £144,000 from Challengerhold Limited and £96,000 from The Bicester Park Development Company Limited for the provision of development and project management services to those companies. As at 31 December 1995 there were no balances outstanding between the Group and any of the above companies.

Other circumstances which may justify non-consolidation on these grounds involve political unrest in the country in which the subsidiary is based. An example of this was to be found in the 1991 accounts of Booker set out below:

Extract 5.18: Booker plc (1991)

11 FIXED ASSET INVESTMENTS [extract]

	1991 £m	1990 £m
Attributable net asset value of subsidiary companies not consolidated at 31 December 1991	3.7	3.2
Reduction required under stated accounting policy	1.1	0.9
Balance sheet value 31 December 1991	2.6	2.3
Profit on ordinary activities before taxation attributable to parent company	1.6	1.7
Attributable profit after extraordinary items	1.4	1.2

Consolidation [extract]

Certain subsidiary undertakings operate in countries overseas where the amount of profit that may be remitted is restricted or where freedom of action may be limited. In the opinion of the directors, it would be misleading to consolidate these subsidiaries and the group share of their results is therefore included in profit only to the extent of remittances received. The group's total investment in these subsidiaries is shown as an asset at attributable net asset value either at the date from which this accounting policy was adopted for such companies adjusted for capital subsequently invested or withdrawn, or attributable net asset value at the balance sheet date, whichever is the lower amount.

The reduction to net asset value at the balance sheet date was presumably to recognise a permanent impairment in value.

Another example was in the 1991 accounts of Low & Bonar in respect of its African subsidiaries shown below:

Extract 5.19: Low & Bonar PLC (1991)

(ii) Basis of consolidation [extract]

(b) The accounts of Group companies in Africa are not consolidated as the Directors consider the control of those companies by Low & Bonar PLC significantly impaired by severe long term restrictions.

6. Income from Fixed Asset Investments

	1991	1990
	£000	£000
Income from shares in group companies not consolidated	1,355	683

13. Fixed Asset Investments [extract]

	£000
African interests:	
At 30 November 1990 and 30 November 1991	
— Directors' valuation	2,230

29. Subsidiaries and Associates not Consolidated

	Accounting period	% Owned	Profit after tax £000	1991 Net assets £000	Profit after tax £000	1990 Net assets £000
Subsidiaries						
Bonar Industries (Pty) Ltd	12 months to 30/11/91	100	332	1,769	483	2,253
Bonar (EA) Ltd	12 months to 31/08/91	75	(142)	439	(235)	570
Bonar Colwyn Ltd	12 months to 30/09/91	90	172	1,390	471	1,052
Bonar Plastics Ltd	12 months to 30/09/91	72	41	183	97	169
Bonar Industries (Pyt) Ltd	12 months to 31/08/91	100	203	969	285	1,551
Associate						
Tarpaulin Industries (WA) Ltd	12 months to 30/11/91	40	(9)	254	(13)	274

The required accounting treatment under FRS 2 in these circumstances is to 'freeze' the carrying value of the subsidiary at its equity amount at the time the restrictions came into force, and to carry it as a fixed asset investment. It should not accrue for any trading results thereafter as long as the restrictions remain, unless it is still able to exercise significant influence, in which case it should equity account for the subsidiary as if it were an associate. A provision for permanent impairment in the value of the investment and any inter-company balances may also be needed.[100]

If the restrictions are subsequently removed, the trading results of the subsidiary which accrued during the period when the investment was carried at a frozen amount will need to be accounted for. FRS 2 requires that they be dealt with as a separately disclosed item in the profit and loss account in the year in which control is resumed, along with the release of any previous provision for permanent impairment.[101]

The disclosures required in respect of subsidiaries excluded from consolidation on these grounds are discussed at 5.6 below.

5.4   Held for subsequent resale

The Companies Act allows a subsidiary undertaking to be excluded from the consolidated accounts when 'the interest of the parent company is held exclusively with a view to subsequent resale and the undertaking has not previously been included in consolidated group accounts of the parent company'.[102] This reason cannot be used to justify exclusion of a subsidiary which the parent company has previously consolidated and decides to sell some years after its acquisition; it should be used only for those cases where a group acquires a subsidiary with the intention of selling it on soon thereafter. The Act, however, does not define what is meant by 'held exclusively for subsequent resale'.

FRS 2 supplies such a definition, saying that it is

(a)   an interest for which a purchaser has been identified or is being sought, and which is reasonably expected to be disposed of within approximately one year of its date of acquisition; or

(b)   an interest that was acquired as a result of the enforcement of a security, unless the interest has become part of the continuing activities of the group or the holder acts as if it intends the interest to become so.[103]

As with subsidiaries subject to severe restrictions, FRS 2 goes further than the Act by *requiring* subsidiaries to be excluded when these circumstances apply.[104] Instead, the standard requires that the investment should be carried in the group balance sheet as a current asset, at the lower of cost and net realisable value.[105]

Examples of situations where subsidiaries have been excluded from consolidation as they are held for subsequent resale are shown in the following extracts:

A subsidiary is also described in APB 18 (which deals with equity accounting) as 'a corporation which is controlled, directly or indirectly, by another corporation. The usual condition for control is ownership of a majority (over 50%) of the outstanding voting stock. The power to control may also exist with a lesser degree of ownership, for example, by contract, lease, agreement with other stockholders or by court decree.'[113]

This definition excludes entities which are controlled through significant minority ownership. Hence, entities which qualify as 'subsidiary undertakings' due to a participating interest with dominant influence or unified management (see 1.2.2 E above) would not always be regarded as subsidiaries in the US.

The SEC has a definition of subsidiary, based on control and risk, which is applicable to its registrants. Although the SEC has not developed a list of criteria that provides definitive guidance for determining when an entity should be consolidated, the SEC staff will look to the substance of a parent–subsidiary relationship rather than the legal form of an equity holding. They have cited cases where consolidation of a less-than majority-owned subsidiary has been required when the parent essentially has the ability to control the subsidiary.

The US has also moved towards full consolidation with segmental disclosure as a response to diversified activities. SFAS 94 was issued in October 1987, making it no longer possible to avoid consolidating a subsidiary because of 'nonhomogeneous' operations. The statement explains its reasoning as follows:

'The managerial, operational and financial ties that bind an enterprise into a single economic unit are stronger than the differences between its lines of business. ... Similarly, differences between the varied operations of a group of affiliated corporations that constitutes an economic and financial whole do not preclude including them all in consolidated accounts. Those differences also do not make the equity method a valid substitute for consolidation of majority owned subsidiaries.'[114]

Accordingly, the only grounds for non-consolidation of subsidiaries are where control is likely to be temporary, control does not rest with the majority shareholder or if the subsidiary operates under foreign exchange restrictions, controls or other governmental imposed uncertainties which cast significant doubt on the parent's ability to control the subsidiary.

The FASB is currently undertaking a project involving several groups of issues, one of which is concerned with developing a concept of reporting entity and related conceptual matters and applying these to reach conclusions on the broad issue of consolidation policy and on specific issues of consolidation techniques. In October 1995 it issued an exposure draft – *Consolidated Financial Statements: Policy and Procedures* which proposes that a parent should consolidate all entities that it controls unless control is temporary at the time the entity becomes a subsidiary. For purposes of this requirement, control of another entity is represented by the power to use or direct the use of the individual assets of another entity in essentially the same ways as the controlling entity can use its own assets. Subsequent to public hearings and redeliberations, the FASB has decided to retain most of the basic provisions of the exposure draft but is continuing to deliberate issues relating to transition, definition of control and special purpose entities.

6.2   IASC

The relevant international accounting standard is IAS 27 – *Consolidated Financial Statements and Accounting for Investments in Subsidiaries*. This simply defines a subsidiary as 'an enterprise which is controlled by another enterprise (known as the parent)'. Control is defined as 'the power to govern the financial and operating policies of an enterprise so as to obtain benefits from its activities'.[115]

Control is presumed to exist if the parent owns, directly or indirectly, a majority of the voting rights in the enterprise unless, in exceptional circumstances, it can be clearly demonstrated that such ownership does not constitute control. Control is also considered to exist even when the parent does not own a majority of the voting rights when there is:

(a)   power over more than one half of the voting rights by virtue of an agreement with other investors;

(b)   power to govern the financial and operating policies of the enterprise under a statute or an agreement;

(c)   power to appoint or remove the majority of the members of the board of directors or equivalent governing body; or

(d)   power to cast the majority of votes at meetings of the board of directors or equivalent governing body.[116]

The grounds for non-consolidation of subsidiaries are similar to those in the UK. It is not possible to exclude from consolidation those subsidiaries which undertake dissimilar activities;[117] a subsidiary should only be excluded for consolidation when:

(a)   control is intended to be temporary because the subsidiary is acquired and held exclusively with a view to its subsequent disposal in the near future; or

(b)   it operates under severe long-term restrictions which significantly impair its ability to transfer funds to the parent.[118]

The consolidation procedures required by IAS 27 are principally similar to those required in the UK; the main difference is in the calculation of minority interests. IAS 22 – *Business Combinations* adopts as its benchmark treatment that any minority interest arising on an acquisition should be calculated based on the pre-acquisition carrying amounts of the net assets of the subsidiary, although it does allow the use of fair values as an alternative.[119] As discussed at 1.3.4 above, FRS 2 requires the minority interest to be based on the fair values attributed to the net assets of the subsidiary.

References

1 CA 85, s 227(2)–(3).
2 *Ibid.*, s 227(4).
3 FRS 2, *Accounting for subsidiary undertakings*, ASB, July 1992, para. 1.
4 *Ibid.*, para. 18.
5 EC Seventh Directive, Article 1(1)(d)(aa).
6 *Ibid.*, Article 12.
7 CA 85, s 259(1).
8 *Ibid.*, s 258(1)–(2).
9 CA 85 (original), s 736(1).
10 CA 85, Sch. 10A, para. 2(1).
11 *Ibid.*, paras. 5–8.
12 *Ibid.*, para. 3(1).
13 *Ibid.*, para. 4(1)–(2).
14 Companies Bill, Clause 19, s 258(2).
15 CA 85, s 260(1).
16 *Ibid.*, s 260(3).
17 *Ibid.*, s 260(2).
18 *Ibid.*, Sch. 10A, para. 4(1), (3).
19 FRS 2, para. 7.
20 *Ibid.*, paras. 69–73.
21 *Ibid.*, para. 72.
22 *Ibid.*, para. 73.
23 *Ibid.*, para. 34.
24 *Ibid.*, para. 12.
25 *Ibid.*, para. 62.
26 *Ibid.*, para. 63.
27 *Ibid.*, para. 67.
28 ED 50, *Consolidated accounts*, ASC, June 1990, para. 26.
29 CA 85, Sch. 4A, paras. 9(2) and 17(2).
30 IAS 22, *Business Combinations*, IASC, December 1993, paras. 31–34.
31 R. M. Wilkins, *Group Accounts*, Second edition, London: ICAEW, 1979, p.170.
32 CA 85, Sch. 4A, para. 6(3).
33 SSAP 14, *Group accounts*, ASC, September 1978, para. 34.
34 FRS 2, para. 37.
35 ED 50, para. 28.
36 *Ibid.*, para. 33.
37 FRS 2, paras. 38 and 82.
38 *Ibid.*, paras. 37 and 81.
39 *Ibid.*, paras. 51 and 90.
40 *Ibid.*, paras. 52 and 91.
41 *Ibid.*, paras. 39 and 83.
42 *Ibid.*, para. 80.

43 ICAEW, *Recommendation VII*.
44 CA 85, Sch. 4A.
45 SSAP 14, para. 3.
46 FRS 2, para. 5.
47 ED 50, para. 85.
48 FRS 2, para. 40.
49 CA 85, Sch. 4A, para. 3(1).
50 *Ibid.*, para. 3(3).
51 *Ibid.*, para. 3(2).
52 FRS 2, para. 41.
53 CA 85, s 223(5).
54 *Ibid.*, Sch. 4A, para. 2(2).
55 FRS 2, para. 43.
56 *Ibid.*
57 *Ibid.*, para. 44.
58 CA 85, Sch. 5, para. 19
59 ED 50, para. 36.
60 FRS 2, paras. 39 and 83.
61 CA 85, Sch. 4A, para. 6
62 FRS 2, para. 39.
63 *Ibid.*, para. 83.
64 SSAP 14, para. 19.
65 CA 85 (original), s 229(2).
66 CA 85, s 228.
67 European Economic Area Act 1993, s 2, states that references to the European Economic Community in earlier legislation, such as the Companies Act 1985, is to be interpreted as being to a reference to the European Economic Area.
68 CA 85, ss. 248–249.
69 FRS 2, para. 21.
70 CA 85, s 228(1).
71 *Ibid.*, s 228(3).
72 *Ibid.*, s 228(2)(a).
73 *Ibid.*, s 228(2)(c).
74 *Ibid.*, s 228(2)(d).
75 *Ibid.*, s 228(2)(e)–(f).
76 *Ibid.*, Sch. 5, paras. (1)–(6).
77 CA 85, s 248(4).
78 *Ibid.*, s 249(3).
79 *Ibid.*, s 249(4)
80 In May 1995, the DTI issued a Consultative Document, *Accounting Simplifications*, which indicated that the UK had the option of raising the financial limits by up to 50%.
81 CA 85, s 247(5).
82 *Ibid.*, s 249(5).
83 *Ibid.*, s 249(1)–(2).
84 *Ibid.*, s 249(1)(a).
85 FRS 2, para. 22.
86 ED 50, para. 91.
87 CA 85, s 229(2)–(4).
88 FRS 2, para. 25.
89 *Ibid.*, para. 78(b).
90 CA 85, s 229(4).
91 *Ibid.*, Sch. 9, Part II, para. 1.
92 FRS 2, para. 78(e).
93 CA 85, Sch. 4A, para. 18.
94 FRS 2, para. 30.
95 See earlier editions of the book for examples of companies adopting such a practice.
96 FRS 2, para. 31(d).

97 CA 85, s 243.
98 *Ibid.*, s 229(3)(a).
99 FRS 2, para. 78(c).
100 *Ibid.*, para. 27.
101 *Ibid.*, para. 28.
102 CA 85 s 229(3)(c).
103 FRS 2, para. 11.
104 *Ibid.*, para. 25(b).
105 *Ibid.*, para. 29.
106 *Ibid.*, para. 78(a).
107 CA 85, Sch. 5, para. 15(2).
108 *Ibid.*, para. 15(4).
109 *Ibid.*, para. 17.
110 *Ibid.*, para. 17(2).
111 FRS 2, para. 31.
112 *Ibid.*, para. 32.
113 APB 18, *The Equity Method of Accounting for Investments in Common Stock*, AICPA, March 1971, para. 3.
114 SFAS 94, *Consolidation of All Majority-owned Subsidiaries*, FASB, October 1987, paras. 30 and 31.
115 IAS 27, *Consolidated Financial Statements and Accounting for Investments in Subsidiaries*, IASC, Reformatted November 1994, para. 6.
116 *Ibid.*, para. 12.
117 *Ibid.*, para. 14.
118 *Ibid.*, para. 13.
119 IAS 22, *Business Combinations*, IASC, December 1993, paras. 31–34.

Chapter 6   Business combinations and disposals

1   INTRODUCTION

Chapter 5 deals with the preparation of consolidated accounts by a parent undertaking, but is restricted to issues such as when such accounts should be prepared, what entities should be considered to be part of the group for the purposes of inclusion therein, and how such entities should be dealt with in the consolidated accounts. This chapter deals with those situations where the group structure changes, through entities either joining or leaving the group.

Business combinations is the generic term for the transactions which result in one company joining a group by becoming the subsidiary of another. In accounting terms there are two distinctly different forms of reporting the effects of such an event, referred to in the UK as acquisition accounting and merger accounting respectively.

The two methods of accounting look at business combinations through quite different eyes. An acquisition is seen as the absorption of the target into the clutches of the predator; there is continuity only of the holding company, in the sense that only the post-acquisition results of the target are reported as earnings of the group, and the comparative figures remain those of the holding company (and any previously held subsidiaries). In contrast, a merger is seen as the uniting of the interests of two formerly distinct shareholder groups, and in order to present continuity of both entities there is retrospective restatement to show the group as if the companies had always been together, by combining the results of both companies pre- and post-combination and also by restatement of the comparatives. The difficulty for accountants, however, has been how to translate this difference in philosophy into criteria which permit particular transactions to be categorised as being of one type or the other.

There have been several successive attempts to distinguish between the circumstances when each of these methods is appropriate, culminating in the issue of FRS 6 – *Acquisitions and mergers* – in September 1994. In addition, the Companies Act, which incorporates the requirements of the EC Seventh Directive, also sets forth qualifying conditions for merger accounting.

FRS 2 – *Accounting for subsidiary undertakings* – which is the general accounting standard on consolidated accounts in the UK, also deals with some aspects which are relevant to business combinations, and there are currently two further accounting standards which deal in detail with business combinations. SSAP 22 – *Accounting for goodwill* – was issued in December 1984, and FRS 7 – *Fair values in acquisition accounting* – was published in September 1994. These, and their predecessors, are all explained in this chapter at 2 below.

The other possible change in the composition of a group involves the disposal of a group company. There is no specific accounting standard in the UK dealing with this issue. It is generally covered in FRS 2, although SSAP 22 is also of some relevance. Again, the changes to the Companies Act as a result of the EC Seventh Directive also had some implications. The issues relating to disposals are dealt with at 3 below.

The chapter also deals with some issues relating to group reorganisations at 4 below. These involve the restructuring of the relationships between companies in a group by, for example, setting up a new holding company, changing the direct ownership of a subsidiary within the group, or transferring businesses from one company to another because of a process of divisionalisation. In principle, most of such changes should have no impact on the consolidated financial statements (provided there are no minority interests affected), because they are purely internal and cannot affect the group when it is being portrayed as a single entity. However, all such transactions can have a significant impact on the financial statements of the individual companies in the group.

2   BUSINESS COMBINATIONS

2.1   Historical development of rules on the criteria for mergers and acquisitions

2.1.1   ED 3

In the UK, the first pronouncement on the subject was ED 3, issued by the ASC in 1971. In the event, ED 3 was never proceeded with, and was eventually withdrawn nearly ten years later. One of the reasons why the ASC did not persist with it was that there was a school of thought which held that merger accounting was in fact contrary to company law; this is because the mechanics of the method require the shares issued by the holding company as consideration for the shares of the subsidiary to be recorded at their nominal value rather than their fair value, and this was thought to be in possible contravention of the Companies Act rules on share premium account. This legal doubt was eventually confirmed in a tax case, *Shearer v Bercain,*[1] in 1980, and this prevented any further progress towards an accounting standard until the law was amended to facilitate merger accounting by introducing variations to the rules on share premium account (described as 'merger relief').

2.1.2 Merger relief

In order to be able to record shares issued at their nominal value, and the cost of an investment in a subsidiary acquired in exchange for these shares at the same amount, it is necessary to satisfy the requirements of what is now section 131 of the Companies Act 1985. This is the part in the Act which was originally introduced in the Companies Act 1981 to remove the obstacle to merger accounting which was revealed in the case of *Shearer v Bercain,* as discussed above.

The section broadly relieves companies from the basic requirement to set up a share premium account in respect of equity shares issued in exchange for shares in another company in the course of a transaction which results in the issuing company securing at least a 90% holding in the equity shares of the other company. (This paraphrases the words in the Act, and the precise wording should be referred to in order to ensure that any particular transaction falls within its terms.) In addition there are further provisions with a similar purpose which apply to shares issued in the course of a group reconstruction.

The rules on merger relief and those on merger accounting are frequently confused with each other. However, not only are they based on the satisfaction of different criteria, they in fact have quite distinct purposes. Merger accounting is a form of financial reporting which applies to business combinations, but although the merger relief provisions were brought in to facilitate it, merger relief is purely a legal matter to do with the maintenance of capital for the protection of creditors and has very little to do with accounting per se. Moreover, merger relief may be available under transactions which are accounted for as acquisitions, rather than mergers, and the two are not interdependent in that sense.

There are some differences of legal opinion as to whether merger relief is in fact *compulsory* when the conditions of section 131 are met, or whether it is optional. The Act says that where the conditions are met, then section 130 does not apply to the premiums on the shares issued. Section 130 is the basic requirement to set up a share premium account where shares are issued at a premium and therefore some people argue that the effect of this relief is simply to make section 130 optional rather than mandatory, but others take the view that it makes it illegal to set up a share premium account. The most common treatment adopted by those who qualify for merger relief but account for the transaction as an acquisition has in fact been to regard the issue as having taken place at fair value, but to record a 'merger reserve' rather than a share premium account, and to use this as a home for the write-off of goodwill emerging on the acquisition (see 2.5.2 C below).

On the other hand, some companies record the transaction in their individual company financial statements based on the nominal value of the shares issued, the merger reserve only arising in the consolidated financial statements where it is used for writing off the goodwill on the acquisition. One company which adopts such a treatment is Glynwed International, as indicated below:

Extract 6.1: Glynwed International plc (1996)

1. ACCOUNTING POLICIES

Acquisitions [extract]

In the Company accounts, where advantage can be taken of the merger relief rules, shares issued as consideration for acquisitions are accounted for at nominal value.

It is possible, however, that such a treatment is no longer allowed since the issue of FRS 4 – *Capital instruments* – by the ASB in December 1993. Paragraphs 11 and 45 of that standard require the net proceeds received on the issue of shares to be credited to shareholders' funds, based on the fair value of the consideration. This appears to remove the 'nominal value' option except where the shares have been issued as part of a business combination that is accounted for as a merger, although paragraph 3 of Appendix I to the standard which deals with legal requirements might suggest otherwise as it states that nothing in the standard affects the availability of merger relief under section 131 of the Act. Similarly, Appendix I to FRS 6 states that the requirements of that standard do 'not deal with the form of accounting to be used in the acquiring or issuing company's own accounts and in particular does not restrict the reliefs available under sections 131–133 of the Companies Act'.[2]

2.1.3   ED 31

Once the legal obstacle was removed, the ASC was able to continue the development of an accounting standard to distinguish between the two types of business combination, and ED 31 – *Accounting for acquisitions and mergers* – was issued in October 1982. The exposure draft put forward a new concept as the guiding principle as to what was a merger – that no material resources should leave the group.[3] This contrasted with the philosophy pursued by ED 3, which was based on a notion of 'continuing ownership in a continuing business'.[4]

2.1.4   SSAP 23

ED 31 was eventually converted into a standard – SSAP 23 – issued by the ASC in April 1985. It continued to use the principle of 'no material resources leaving the group' as its central point of reference for defining a merger, and laid down the following detailed criteria for permitting a business combination to be treated as a merger:

(a)   the business combination results from an offer to the holders of all equity shares and the holders of all voting shares which are not already held by the offeror; and

(b)   the offeror has secured, as a result of the offer, a holding of (i) at least 90% of all equity shares (taking each class of equity separately) and (ii) the shares carrying at least 90% of the votes of the offeree; and

(c)   immediately prior to the offer, the offeror does not hold (i) 20% or more of all equity shares of the offeree (taking each class of equity separately), or (ii) shares carrying 20% or more of the votes of the offeree; and

(d)   not less than 90% of the fair value of the total consideration given for the equity share capital (including that given for shares already held) is in the form of equity share capital; not less than 90% of the fair value of the total consideration given for voting non-equity share capital (including that given for shares already held) is in the form of equity and/or voting non-equity share capital.[5]

The standard made merger accounting *optional* when the criteria were met, whereas under ED 31, satisfaction of the criteria was expressed as leading to the *mandatory* use of merger accounting.

The SSAP 23 rules, therefore, depended very much on the form of the transaction being undertaken, and many of its critics were concerned about the ease with which it was possible to vary the form in order to bring a transaction within these rules. For example, the '20% prior holding' rule could be circumvented by selling any holding in excess of that limit to a third party (such as a merchant bank) immediately before making the offer and then acquiring it again in the course of the general offer. Also, cash consideration could, in theory at least, be disguised as equity by issuing redeemable preference shares (which could be brought within the equity definition by giving them theoretical rights to participate beyond a specified amount in a distribution) as part of the consideration and then redeeming them a short time later, so that in substance the consideration was in cash.

A more widespread ploy was the use of 'vendor rights' or 'vendor placings' as a means of coming within the merger criteria although still offering cash to the vendors. This involved offering shares to the vendor in exchange for his shares in the company being acquired, but with a side arrangement where, if the vendor preferred to receive cash, the shares would be placed either with the acquirer's own shareholders (vendor rights) or with third parties (vendor placings) and the proceeds passed on to the vendors.

2.1.5   Companies Act 1989

The implementation of the EC Seventh Directive on Company Law in the Companies Act 1989 to some extent restricted the ability of UK companies to apply merger accounting. Article 20 of the Directive sets out the qualifying conditions for merger accounting, and this disqualifies transactions where the consideration includes a cash payment exceeding 10% of the nominal value of the shares issued to effect the business combination. Although this looked superficially similar to the rule in SSAP 23 that at least 90% of the fair value of the consideration must be in the form of equity share capital, there were two important differences.

The first is that the Seventh Directive refers to the *nominal* value of the shares issued, rather than their *fair* value in setting the 10% limit. Since shares cannot be issued at a discount, this limit would never be wider than the SSAP 23 equivalent, and would often be much narrower; the extent of this restriction depended on how much higher was the fair value of the predator's shares compared with their nominal value.

The other difference is that the Seventh Directive rule is expressed in terms of the 10%, and refers to cash, whereas the SSAP 23 equivalent required at least 90% to be in the form of equity. Other forms of consideration, such as loan stock, are not addressed directly by either rule and would be dealt with differently as a result. Thus it would have been possible for a substantial part of the consideration to be in the form of loan stock without breaching the Seventh Directive limit, whereas this would have breached the SSAP 23 rule if it exceeded 10% in value of the total consideration. However, in drafting the Companies Act, the DTI extended the restriction on cash to cover any form of consideration other than equity, so that loan stock will not qualify.

The conditions laid down in the Act which have to be met before merger accounting can be applied are as follows:

'(a)   that at least 90% of the nominal value of the relevant shares in the undertaking acquired is held by or on behalf of the parent company and its subsidiary undertakings,

(b)   that the proportion referred to in (a) was attained pursuant to an arrangement providing for the issue of equity shares by the parent company or one or more of its subsidiary undertakings,

(c)   that the fair value of any consideration other than the issue of equity shares given pursuant to the arrangement by the parent company and its subsidiary undertakings did not exceed 10% of the nominal value of the equity shares issued, and

(d)   that adoption of the merger method of accounting accords with generally accepted accounting principles or practice.'[6]

'Relevant shares' are defined as being those carrying unrestricted rights to participate both in distributions and in surplus assets on a winding up.[7]

2.1.6 ED 48

In answering some of the criticisms made against SSAP 23 (see 2.1.4 above), the ASC in February 1990 issued ED 48 – *Accounting for acquisitions and mergers* – which abandoned the principle of 'no material resources leaving the group' for determining what is a merger and when merger or acquisition accounting should be used. Instead, the ASC proposed a series of subjective tests designed to identify whether or not a merger had taken place in substance. These were very similar to those eventually proposed by the ASB in FRED 6 and subsequently converted into FRS 6.

2.1.7 FRED 6

The ASB replaced the ASC six months later and the subject was not progressed for some time. However, in May 1993 the ASB published FRED 6 – *Acquisitions and mergers*. As mentioned above, the proposals of this exposure draft were developed from those in ED 48 and, although no major changes were proposed, the ASB sought to remove some of the subjectivity which would have been required in applying ED 48. The overall approach of FRED 6, therefore, was based on the belief that merger accounting should only be applied to those rare business combinations that can properly be regarded as mergers in substance, and that, except for such rare cases, business combinations are more appropriately accounted for as acquisitions.

2.1.8 FRS 6

FRED 6 was converted into a standard in September 1994. The accounting practices set out in FRS 6 were to be adopted in respect of business combinations first accounted for in accounts relating to periods beginning on or after 23 December 1994.[8] Since it would clearly be impracticable to restate accounts for previous business combinations that had taken place in earlier years, the standard did not require retrospective application for previous periods.

A 'business combination' is defined in FRS 6 as 'the bringing together of separate entities into one economic entity as a result of one entity uniting with, or obtaining control over the net assets and operations of, another'.[9] The standard applies not only when an entity becomes a subsidiary undertaking of a parent company but also where an individual company or other reporting entity combines with a business other than a subsidiary undertaking.[10]

FRS 6 defines a merger as 'a business combination that results in the creation of a new reporting entity formed from the combining parties, in which the shareholders of the combining entities come together in a partnership for the mutual sharing of the risks and benefits of the combined entity, and in which no party to the combination in substance obtains control over any other, or is otherwise seen to be dominant, whether by virtue of the proportion of its shareholders' rights in the combined entity, the influence of its directors or otherwise'.[11] It is thus regarded not as the augmentation of one entity by the addition of another, but as the creation of a new reporting entity from the parties to the combination. An acquisition is defined as any other business combination that is not a merger.

The standard sets out the following five criteria that a business combination must meet for it to be accounted for as a merger, at the same time emphasising that merger accounting must also be allowed by companies' legislation (see 2.1.5 above). In aggregate, these criteria are very restrictive and in interpreting them the parties to the merger are considered to be not just the business of each entity that is combining but also the management of the entity and the body of its shareholders. Merger accounting is considered by the ASB not to be appropriate where any of the parties does not have an established independent track record as a result of it being a recent divestment from a larger entity.[12] It is unclear why this should be the case.

(a)　no party to the combination is portrayed as either acquirer or acquired, either by its own board or management or by that of another party to the combination.[13]

If the terms of a share for share exchange indicate that one party has paid a premium over the market value of the shares acquired, this is evidence that that party has taken the role of acquirer unless there is a clear explanation for this apparent premium other than its being a premium paid to acquire control.[14]

It is necessary to consider all the circumstances surrounding the transaction in interpreting the nature of the combination.[15]

(b)　all parties to the combination, as represented by the boards of directors or their appointees, participate in establishing the management structure for the combined entity and in selecting the management personnel, and such decisions are made on the basis of a consensus between the parties to the combination rather than purely by exercise of voting rights;[16]

It is necessary to consider not only the formal management structure of the combined entity but also the identity of all persons involved in the main financial and operating decisions and the way in which the decision making process operates in practice within the combined entity.[17]

Also, although it is only necessary to consider the decisions made in the period of initial integration and restructuring at the time of the combination, both the short term and long term consequences of decisions made in this period need to be considered.[18]

(c)   the relative sizes of the combining entities are not so disparate that one party dominates the combined entity by virtue of its relative size;[19]

A party would be presumed to dominate if its ownership interest in the combined entity is more than 50% larger than that of each of the other parties to the combination (although this presumption is rebuttable).[20] This means that if any party obtains a 60% interest in the combined entity, the combination probably cannot be accounted for as a merger.

(d)   under the terms of the combination or related arrangements, the consideration received by equity shareholders of each party to the combination, in relation to their equity shareholding, comprises primarily equity shares in the combined entity, and any non-equity consideration, or equity shares carrying substantially reduced voting or distribution rights, represents an immaterial proportion of the fair value of the consideration received by the shareholders of that party. Where one of the combining entities has, within the period of two years before the combination, acquired equity shares in another of the combining entities, the consideration for this acquisition should be taken into account in determining whether this criterion has been met.[21]

For the purpose of this criterion, the consideration should not be taken to include the distribution to shareholders of:

(i)   an interest in a peripheral part of the business of the entity in which they were shareholders and which does not form part of the combined entity; or

(ii)   the proceeds of the sale of such a business, or loan stock representing such proceeds.

A peripheral part of the business is one that can be disposed of without having a material effect on the nature and focus of the entity's operations.[22] However, interpretation of what is a peripheral part of an entity would necessarily be a fairly subjective judgement.

(e)   no equity shareholders of any of the combining entities retain any material interest in the future performance of only part of the combined entity.[23] In particular, therefore, any earn-out arrangements or similar performance related schemes would mean the combination could not be interpreted as a merger.[24]

For the purposes of these criteria, any convertible shares or loan stock should be regarded as equity to the extent that they are converted into equity as a result of the business combination.[25] Equity and non-equity shares are defined in identical terms to those set out in FRS 4 (see 2.2.2 of Chapter 15).

FRS 6 states that in applying these criteria, it is necessary to consider the substance and not just the form of the arrangements, and to take account of all relevant information related to the combination.[26] It also discusses each of the criteria in more detail, providing examples of situations which might indicate whether or not the particular criterion is met.[27] Failure to meet any of the five criteria is to be regarded as meaning that the definition of a merger has not been met and thus merger accounting is not to be used for the business combination. Conversely, where a business combination meets these criteria, acquisition accounting is not permitted. In reality, however, merger accounting remains voluntary in the sense that it would be very easy for any company not wishing to use the method to 'fail' one of the very restrictive criteria.

It is clear that most business combinations which had been accounted for as mergers in previous years would not meet the criteria laid down by FRS 6. Merger accounting has become a much more rare occurrence as most business combinations will have to be regarded as acquisitions. Indeed, when it exposed FRED 6, the ASB also suggested an alternative approach of prohibiting the use of merger accounting entirely other than for certain group reconstructions, but did not, in the event, take this more extreme step.

It may be just as well that they did not do so because since the standard was issued there have been a number of instances where merger accounting has been applied.[28] The main use of merger accounting nowadays, however, is for combinations made within a group, i.e. group reconstructions (see 4 below).

2.2 Acquisitions: basic principles

When Company A acquires Company B, it has to consolidate B's trading results from the effective date of acquisition onwards. Similarly, it thereafter includes B's assets and liabilities in its consolidated balance sheet, eliminating the share capital and reserves of B at the acquisition date against the cost of A's investment in B's shares. In contrast to merger accounting, the pre-acquisition results and reserves of B are completely eliminated from the consolidated financial statements, rather than brought in retrospectively. The Companies Act 1989 has enshrined this principle in the law.[29]

FRS 2 defines the date of acquisition in terms of when control passes; it states that 'the date for accounting for an undertaking becoming a subsidiary undertaking is the date on which control of that undertaking passes to its new parent undertaking'.[30] This is a matter of fact and cannot be artificially backdated or otherwise altered. It then explains when such a date might be under various circumstances: 'Where control is transferred by a public offer, the date control is transferred is the date the offer becomes unconditional, usually as a result of a sufficient number of acceptances being received. For private treaties, the date control is transferred is generally the date an unconditional offer is accepted. Where an undertaking becomes ... a subsidiary undertaking as a result of the issue or cancellation of shares, the date control is transferred is the date of issue or cancellation. The date that control passes may be indicated by the acquiring party commencing its direction of the operating and financial policies of the acquired undertaking or by changes in the flow of economic benefits.' It also states that 'the date on which the consideration for the transfer of control is paid is often an important indication of the date on which a subsidiary undertaking is acquired or disposed of. However, the date the consideration passes is not conclusive evidence of the date of the transfer of control because this date can be set to fall on a date other than that on which control is transferred, with compensation for any lead or lag included in the consideration. Consideration may also be paid in instalments.'[31]

2.3 Acquisitions: measuring the fair value of the consideration

In order to account for the acquisition, the acquiring company must first measure the cost of what it is accounting for, which will normally represent both the cost of the investment in its own balance sheet and the amount to be allocated between the identifiable net assets of the subsidiary and goodwill in the consolidated financial statements. Both the law and accounting standards have for some time specified that the cost is to be based on the fair value of the consideration given if acquisition accounting is used, but until the publication of FRS 7, there was no standard which elaborated on how this was to be determined, although there had been a number of previous initiatives to produce one.

In July 1990, the ASC issued an exposure draft, ED 53 – *Fair value in the context of acquisition accounting* – having published a Discussion Paper two years earlier on the topic;[32] the main proposals of the exposure draft dealt with monetary items, securities and other non-monetary assets given as consideration together with deferred and contingent consideration.[33]

In April 1993 the ASB published a Discussion Paper – *Fair values in acquisition accounting* – which limited its discussion on the fair value of purchase consideration to deferred and contingent consideration in terms which were more consistent with the ASB's draft Statement of Principles, as most commentators had been supportive of the proposals in ED 53 relating to ascertaining the fair values of other elements of the purchase consideration. An exposure draft, FRED 7,[34] was published in December 1993 and its proposals in respect of determining the cost of acquisition were similar to those contained in ED 53. This was converted into FRS 7 nine months later, without substantial change. The accounting practices set out in FRS 7 were to be adopted in respect of business combinations first accounted for in accounts relating to periods beginning on or after 23 December 1994.[35] Since it would clearly have been impracticable to restate accounts for previous business combinations that had taken place in earlier years, the standard did not require retrospective application for previous periods.

The basic requirement of FRS 7 is that 'the cost of acquisition is the amount of cash paid and the fair value of other purchase consideration given by the acquirer, together with the expenses of the acquisition … . Where a subsidiary undertaking is acquired in stages, the cost of acquisition is the total of the costs of the interests acquired, determined as at the date of each transaction.'[36] This latter aspect of acquiring a subsidiary in stages is discussed further at 2.6 below. Issues relating to the first part of the requirement are discussed at 2.3.1 to 2.3.6 below.

2.3.1   Cash and other monetary consideration

The purchase consideration may comprise cash or other monetary items, including the assumption of liabilities by the acquirer. FRS 7 states that the fair value of such items 'is normally readily determinable as the amount paid or payable in respect of the item'.[37] However, when settlement is deferred, fair values are to be obtained by discounting to their present value the amounts expected to be payable in the future, using an appropriate discount rate (see 2.3.4 below).

The effect of discounting future obligations is to reduce the amount of goodwill recognised on the acquisition (or increase the amount of any negative goodwill) and also to reduce post-acquisition profits. This is because the amount of consideration given is deemed to be smaller. It is then augmented by notional interest charges in the post-acquisition profit and loss account to bring the carrying value of the obligation up to the settlement value by the due date.

2.3.2   Capital instruments

The purchase consideration may comprise capital instruments issued by the acquirer, including shares, debentures, loans and debt instruments, share warrants and other options relating to the securities of the acquirer.

Where such instruments are quoted on a ready market, FRS 7 states that 'the market price on the date of acquisition would normally provide the most reliable measure of fair value'. Where the acquisition arises out of a public offer, 'the relevant date is the date on which the offer or, where there is a series of revised offers, the successful offer becomes unconditional, usually as a result of a sufficient number of acceptances being received'. However, 'where, owing to unusual fluctuations, the market price on one particular date is an unreliable measure of fair value, market prices for a reasonable period before the date of acquisition, during which acceptances could be made, would need to be considered'.[38] Unfortunately, unlike ED 53, FRS 7 gives no guidance as to what a reasonable period might be. ED 53 observed that the period chosen would depend on both specific conditions and also general market conditions.[39] However, it advised that usually a period of 10 dealing days prior to the date of acquisition would be appropriate. It may be that in the absence of anything more specific in FRS 7, this could be taken as a guide, although obviously the specific circumstances would have to be taken into account. The purpose of this is to take some sort of average price so that the value of the consideration given is not distorted by a transient fluctuation.

For other securities, a suitable market price might not exist; this might be due to the fact that the securities are not quoted, or if they are quoted, the market price is unreliable owing, for example, to the lack of an active market in the quantities involved. Where this is the case, the fair value should be estimated by taking into account items such as:

(a)   the value of similar securities that are quoted;

(b)   the present value of the future cash flows of the instrument issued;

(c)   any cash alternative to the issue of securities; and

(d)   the value of any underlying security into which there is an option to convert.[40]

Where it is not possible to value the consideration given by any of the above methods, the best estimate of its value may be given by valuing the entity acquired.[41]

Many British companies have always used the price ruling at the date at which the offer became unconditional; one company which explicitly says that this in its policy is Travis Perkins, as shown below:

Extract 6.2: Travis Perkins plc (1996)

Accounting Policies

(b)   Basis of preparation [extract]

The cost of any acquisition represents the cash value of the consideration and/or the market value of the shares issued on the date the offer became unconditional, plus expenses.

Sometimes, shares are issued by the acquirer which rank fully for dividends which are to be paid in respect of a period before the acquisition took place. In these circumstances, some companies apportion the subsequent dividend into two components when it is paid, with a 'pre-acquisition' element added to the cost of the investment in the subsidiary (and therefore increasing the goodwill) and leaving only the post-acquisition element to be taken out of the profit and loss account. One company which has adopted such a treatment is MEPC (see Extract 6.20 below). FRS 7 does not deal with this specific issue. In our view such a treatment is inappropriate where the cost of the investment in the acquired subsidiary is recorded at the (cum div) fair value of the securities issued as consideration; this is because the fair value of the securities will already reflect the fact that the shareholders are entitled to the dividend and therefore the dividend cost is double-counted. This is not the case where merger relief has been taken (see 2.1.2 above) and the cost of the investment is recorded at the nominal value of the shares issued as consideration. One example of this is to be found in the 1989 financial statements of BICC, as shown in the following extract:

Extract 6.3: BICC plc (1989)

11   ORDINARY DIVIDENDS

	1989		1988	
	Per share p	**Amount £m**	Per share p	Amount £m
Interim payable	**5.75**	**15.1**	4.75	11.2
Final proposed	**13.25**	**36.0**	11.25	26.7
	19.00	**51.1**	16.00	37.9
Pre-acquisition proportion relating to shares issued for acquisitions		**(2.2)**		(0.9)
		48.9		37.0

15   INVESTMENTS [extract]

BICC plc issued 7.6m ordinary shares in 1988 and 2.6m ordinary shares in 1989 for the share capital of Ceat Cavi Industrie Srl. 22.1m were also issued in 1989 to acquire Manshine Ltd, a company formed in connection with the acquisition of BRIntic Corporation, and 0.7m ordinary shares were issued for the share capital of Syntek Ltd and Cruickshank and Partners Ltd.

...

Having taken advantage of the merger relief provisions under s 131, Companies Act 1985, the investment in these companies is recorded at the nominal value of the shares issued as consideration, plus costs, including the pre-acquisition proportion of dividend and related advance corporation tax in respect of the shares issued in the year.

2.3.3   Non-monetary assets

The purchase consideration may comprise non-monetary assets, including securities of another entity. FRS 7 states that for such consideration 'fair values would be determined by reference to market prices, estimated realisable values, independent valuations, or other available evidence'.[42] This is not as specific as the proposal in ED 53 which focused on the value of the sacrifice made by the acquirer by giving up such assets, and invoked a concept similar to that of 'deprival value' which was used as the basis of valuations in current cost accounting. The loss suffered by the acquirer was the alternative proceeds he could have received for the asset, unless he could make good his loss by replacing the asset, in which case it was the cost of such replacement. In the absence of anything more specific in FRS 7, the deprival value principle seems a sensible one to adopt.

Two companies which have had to address this issue are George Wimpey and Tarmac when they swapped their respective construction and housing businesses. George Wimpey has regarded the consideration given as being the equivalent of the book values of the net assets of the construction business, as seen below:

Extract 6.4: George Wimpey PLC (1996)

26   Asset Exchange with Tarmac plc

On 1 March 1996, George Wimpey PLC acquired Tarmac's Housing division, McLean Homes, by exchange of Wimpey's Construction and Minerals divisions. The Group has used acquisition accounting to account for the acquisition. Goodwill arising on consolidation has been written off direct to reserves. The impact of this acquisition on the consolidated net assets was as follows:

	Book Cost of Assets Acquired	Revaluation	Provisions	Reassessment of Fair Values of Net Current Assets	Fair Value of Assets Acquired
Net assets acquired from Tarmac:					
Tangible assets and fixed asset investments	6.1	0.3	–	–	6.4
Net current assets	316.7	–	–	(14.1)	302.6
Provisions	–	–	(1.2)	–	(1.2)
Cash at bank and in hand	2.2	–	–	–	2.2
Borrowings and inter-company debt	(51.1)	–	–	–	(51.1)
Total net assets	273.9	0.3	(1.2)	(14.1)	258.9

Consideration:	
Net assets of Construction and Minerals divisions	
Tangible assets and fixed asset investments	335.7
Net current assets	(7.1)
Cash at bank and in hand	43.9
Borrowings and inter-company debt	(35.3)
Provisions	(27.0)
Minority interests	(13.6)
Total net assets	296.6
Professional fees and other costs of the transaction	4.2
Goodwill arising on asset exchange	41.9

Provisions acquired from Tarmac relate mainly to rental provisions for void property which existed at the date of acquisition. Of this provision, £0.2 million had been utilised at 31 December 1996. The fair value adjustment to net current assets mainly results from a reassessment of the net realisable value of work in progress and land.

This can be contrasted with Tarmac which has regarded the consideration given for the Wimpey business acquired as being an estimate of the fair value of the housing division given in return as shown below:

Extract 6.5: Tarmac plc (1996)

29   Acquisitions and divestments [extract]

Exchange of businesses with George Wimpey PLC

On 1st March 1996 the Group's UK and US private sector housing business ('the Housing Division') was exchanged for the world-wide minerals and construction businesses of George Wimpey PLC ('Wimpey'). The effects of this exchange on the net assets of the Group are summarised below:

| | **Wimpey businesses acquired** | | | | **Housing Division divested** |
| | Fair value adjustments in respect of: | | | | |
	Book value £m	Revaluation of assets acquired £m	Accounting policy alignment £m	Fair value £m	£m
Tangible assets	334.6	13.3	–	347.9	6.1
Associated undertakings	1.1	(1.1)	–	–	–
Stocks	30.9	(0.4)	–	30.5	397.4
Debtors	183.2	(38.6)	–	144.6	58.8
Cash, less overdrafts	36.5	–	–	36.5	(53.5)
Creditors, deferred liabilities and provisions	(249.2)	(18.8)	(9.5)	(277.5)	(130.1)
Inter-group loans	(29.2)	–	–	(29.2)	4.5
Equity minority interests	(13.6)	(5.3)	–	(18.9)	–
Net assets	294.3	(50.9)	(9.5)		
Fair value of assets exchanged				233.9	283.2
Professional fees and other costs of transaction				(7.5)	7.1
				226.4	290.3
Directors' estimate of fair value of Housing Division, as divested				291.0	291.0
Goodwill arising on acquisition of Wimpey businesses, written off directly to reserves				64.6	
Unrealised profit on disposal of Housing Division					0.7

The £9.5 million accounting policy alignment adjustment represents additional environmental and restoration provisions, which remain substantially unutilised at the year end.

The revaluation of assets acquired within the above table incorporates the adjustment of book values to those achieved on subsequent divestments of US businesses, an independent valuation of mineral reserves (note 12) and a reassessment of the realisable values of amounts recoverable on contracts and other net current assets.

It is interesting to note from the above extracts that both parties to the transaction considered that the fair value of the assets acquired was less than the corresponding book value. Indeed, they also disagreed as to what the book values were.

2.3.4 Deferred consideration

The term 'deferred consideration' is not used in FRS 7 but was stated in the ASB's Discussion Paper to denote consideration, payable in cash, shares or other securities, which is determined precisely at the time of the acquisition either in value or as a number of shares, but where the payment is delayed for a defined period.

The standard only discusses the situation where settlement of cash consideration is deferred, in which case 'fair values are obtained by discounting to their present value the amounts expected to be payable in the future. The appropriate discount rate is the rate at which the acquirer could obtain a similar borrowing, taking into account its credit standing and any security given.'[43]

Deferred consideration in a form other than cash is not discussed in FRS 7; it is unclear why this should be the case. However, it may be that where such consideration is payable in shares, or other securities, then the acquirer is regarded as having issued a capital instrument as part of the consideration at the time of the acquisition and therefore the fair value should be determined following the principles set out for capital instruments discussed at 2.3.2 above. The standard also does not deal with how deferred consideration payable in shares should be dealt with, but in our view it should be dealt with in a similar manner to contingent consideration which is to be satisfied by shares (see 2.3.5 below).

Although many companies refer to deferred consideration in their accounts, such consideration is in reality contingent consideration under FRS 7.

2.3.5 Contingent consideration

The terms of an acquisition may provide that the value of the purchase consideration, which may be payable in cash, shares or other securities at a future date, depends on uncertain future events, such as the future performance of the acquired company. FRS 7 quotes the example of an 'earn out', 'where consideration payable to the vendor takes the form of an initial payment, together with further payments based on a multiple of future profits of the acquired company. By its nature, the fair value of such contingent consideration cannot be determined precisely at the date of acquisition.'[44]

The standard requires that 'where the amount of purchase consideration is contingent on one or more future events, the cost of acquisition should include a reasonable estimate of the fair value of amounts expected to be payable in the future. The cost of acquisition should be adjusted when revised estimates are made, with consequential corresponding adjustments continuing to be made to goodwill until the ultimate outcome is known.'[45]

For this calculation, therefore, goodwill can remain open for several periods after the acquisition. This is in contrast to the normal rule that fair values and thus goodwill should not be adjusted after the first full period following the one in which the acquisition took place (see 2.4.2 below).

Although the ASB's Discussion Paper proposed that if such amounts were to be payable in cash or by the issue of a debt instrument, they were to be discounted to their present value,[46] FRS 7 does not specifically state this to be the case. However, it is arguable that such amounts by their nature are 'deferred' and therefore any amount payable in cash should be discounted, and if payable by the issue of a loan instrument, the fair value of such an instrument would reflect a discounted value. Similarly, the ASB Discussion Paper proposed that if such amounts were payable in shares, then the fair value of contingent consideration should be based on its expected value.[47] Again, FRS 7 is silent on this issue.

Although, as the standard comments, by its nature the fair value of contingent consideration cannot be determined precisely at the date of acquisition, acquiring companies should provide for a reasonable estimate of the outcome. Usually, an indication of the likely amounts payable should be available since in drawing up the terms of the agreement the parties will have had to consider closely the likely outcomes.

In some cases it will be clear that at least a certain amount is very likely to be payable, and in these circumstances it would seem appropriate to provide for that amount. This is more likely to be the case in those situations where the contingent consideration is based on the target company maintaining a level of profits which it is currently earning (either for a particular period or as an average over a set period) or achieving profits which it is currently budgeting.

Examples of companies making full provision for contingent consideration are shown in the following extracts:

Extract 6.6: T&N plc (1996)

24 Acquisitions [extract]

On 12 July 1996 the Group acquired the trade, fixed assets and stock of Cummins Engine Company's piston ring business in the United States. The consideration is contingent on the profits of the business during 1997 and therefore has not yet been finally determined. The maximum consideration of £6.5m has been provided in these accounts, this being the current best estimate of the amount which will be payable.

Extract 6.7: TT Group plc (1995)

21. Acquisitions [extract]

Satisfied by:	Comment	Linton and Hirst Fair value £000	Other Fair value £000	Total Fair value £000
Cash consideration		14,704	6,222	20,926
Cash costs		269	33	302
Contingent consideration	(f)	1,680	82	1,762
Issue of loan notes by subsidiary		–	36	36
Creditors and other accruals		17	–	17
		16,670	6,373	23,043

Comments

(f) Contingent consideration of £1,680,000 in respect of Linton and Hirst is due for payment in April 1996 following the achievement of profits before taxation of more than £2,500,000 for the year ended 31 December 1995. Costs relating to this contingent consideration have been included in accruals. Other contingent consideration of £82,000 in respect of Scorpio Power Systems represents the element of a bonus agreement covering the next three years which is virtually certain to be paid unless the vendors cease to be employees.

Clearly, TT Group had to provide in full for the contingent consideration in respect of the Linton and Hirst acquisition as the profit target related to the year just past (it effectively was no longer contingent). T&N on the other hand provided in full on the basis that it was the current best estimate of the amount payable. Another company which has made provision on the basis of its current expectations is Cookson Group, as shown below:

Extract 6.8: Cookson Group plc (1995)

19 Acquisitions, disposal and termination of operations [extract]

On 2 May 1995 the Group completed the acquisition of MPM Enterprises, Inc. The initial consideration was £41.9m with additional consideration payable dependent on the average earnings of the acquired business during the three years ending in June 1998. The maximum additional amount payable is $85m. Based on management's current expectations of the level to which the relevant profit targets will be met, additional consideration of $30m has been accrued as at 31 December 1995.

However, occasionally the terms of the agreement may be such that it is impossible to say whether, and if so how much, additional consideration will be paid, and in that case companies may have no option but to deal with the matter by disclosure, rather than by provision. Where consideration is only payable on profits which are in excess of those currently being earned or budgeted for by the target company, then it may be more appropriate to disclose only the contingent consideration. FRS 7 is clear, however, that even 'where it is not possible to estimate the total amounts payable with any degree of certainty, at least those amounts that are reasonably expected to be payable would be recognised'.[48]

One company which has not made any provision for contingent consideration but merely gave disclosure of its existence was Tibbett & Britten Group:

Extract 6.9: Tibbett & Britten Group plc (1995)

24 DEFERRED CONSIDERATION ON ACQUISITION

Under the terms of the agreement for the acquisition of Metra Media Transport BV a further consideration of up to £1,005,000 may be payable to the vendors in 2000, subject to the continuance of an agreed minimum level of business during the five years starting 2 July 2000.

Under the terms of the acquisition of Transportes y Distribuciones Martinez, SA (Tradismasa) a further consideration of up to £133,000 may be payable to the vendors in the years to 1997. Such payments are contingent upon the levels of profits achieved by Tradismasa in 1996.

Due to the degree of uncertainty, the directors consider a provision for these amounts to be inappropriate.

Under the terms of the acquisition of Eskimo-Iglo Tiefkühllogistik AG ("TKL") in Austria further consideration of up to £7,995,000 (ATS 125 million) may be payable to the vendors for the remaining 30% of the shareholding in TKL in instalments on 1 January 1997, 1998, 1999 and 2000. Such payments are contingent upon the cumulative levels of profit achieved by TKL in the five years 1995 to 1999.

The 1996 accounts show that the company was correct not to provide any consideration in respect of the Tradismasa acquisition as no amount has been paid and provision is still not made in respect of the others.

Since the corresponding adjustment is to goodwill (which under SSAP 22 is generally taken to reserves with no impact on earnings) the different treatments will only affect the profit and loss account to the extent that an interest charge is recognised on a discounted cash liability or a debt instrument; the main effect will be on the balance sheet. What that effect is will depend on whether the further consideration will be in the form of cash or shares. Where it is the former, the consideration will reduce both the net assets of the group and its equity; where it is the latter, the net assets and the total equity will be unaffected. As explained in FRS 7, 'where contingent consideration is to be satisfied by the issue of shares, there is no obligation to transfer economic benefits and, accordingly, amounts recognised would be reported as part of shareholders' funds, for example as a separate caption representing shares to be issued. In the analysis of shareholders' funds, amounts would be attributed to equity and non-equity interests depending on the nature of the shares to be issued, in accordance with FRS 4 "Capital Instruments". When the shares are issued, appropriate transfers would be necessary between any amounts then held in shareholders' funds in respect of their issue and called up share capital and share premium.'[49]

In some situations the acquirer has an option to issue either shares or cash; because there is no obligation to transfer economic benefits then this future consideration is not a liability. Accordingly, the standard states that the expected future consideration should be accounted for as a credit to shareholders' funds (as explained above) until an irrevocable decision regarding the form of consideration has been taken. Where the vendor has the choice, then the expected future consideration represents an obligation to the vendor and should be accounted for as a liability until the shares are issued or the cash is paid.[50]

FRS 7 also discusses the situation where acquisition agreements may require payments to be made in various forms, for example as non-competition payments or as bonuses to the vendors who continue to work for the acquired company. The standard states that 'in such circumstances, it is necessary to determine whether the substance of the agreement is payment for the business acquired, or an expense such as compensation for services or profit sharing. In the first case the expected payments would be accounted for as contingent purchase consideration; in the other case the payments would be treated as expenses of the period to which they relate.'[51]

2.3.6   Acquisition expenses

FRS 7 takes a deliberately restrictive view as to what acquisition expenses should be treated as part of the cost of the acquisition in order to avoid the danger of overstating the cost of acquisition. The standard requires that only 'fees and similar incremental costs incurred directly in making an acquisition should, except for the issue costs of shares and other securities that are required by FRS 4 "Capital Instruments" to be accounted for as a reduction in the proceeds of a capital instrument, be included in the cost of acquisition. Internal costs and other expenses that cannot be directly attributed to the acquisition should be charged to the profit and loss account.'[52] Costs which may be capitalised include 'incremental costs such as professional fees paid to merchant banks, accountants, legal advisers, valuers and other consultants'; they do not include 'any allocation of costs that would still have been incurred had the acquisition not been entered into – for example, the costs of maintaining an acquisitions department or management remuneration'.[53]

The Companies Act also allows 'such amount (if any) in respect of fees and other expenses of the acquisition as the company may determine' to be included in arriving at the cost of the acquisition.[54]

2.3.7   Pre-acquisition dividends

Although it has no bearing on the determination of the fair value of the consideration given under FRS 7, one question which sometimes arises is how the acquiring company should account for dividends received from the subsidiary out of its pre-acquisition profits. The rules on this are less than clear. The traditional view was that this was, in effect, a return of the capital paid to acquire the company and was not in any sense a profit, and that accordingly it should be applied to reduce the cost of the investment in the acquiring company's balance sheet. This view was supported by some rather arcane wording that used to be in paragraph 15(5) of Schedule 8 to the Companies Act 1948, but this was changed in the Companies Act 1981.[55]

The more widely accepted view of the law is now that the question of whether or not pre-acquisition dividends have to be written off against the cost of the investment has to be subdivided into two sub-questions:

(a) does the receipt of the dividend constitute a realised profit in the financial statements of the holding company? and

(b) does provision for permanent impairment have to be made against the cost of the investment?

Of the two questions set out above, (a) is the more straightforward, provided it can be accepted that the receipt of the dividend can properly be described as a profit at all; the issue of whether it is realised is generally not in question. However, the one which really requires interpretation is (b). Because both the law and normal accounting practice require provision to be made only for *permanent* diminution in the value of a fixed asset, it is possible to advance the view that, provided the investment will eventually recover the value which has been removed from it by making the distribution (by earning further profits, say) then it is unnecessary to write it down and hence the dividend to the holding company can be passed on to its own shareholders.

Following this approach would allow an acquiring company to distribute immediately all the pre-acquisition profits shown in the subsidiary's balance sheet provided that it could foresee that the subsidiary would earn an equivalent amount of profits in the future. Even if this is good law, it is questionable whether it is good accounting. There is a strong argument that the receipt of a pre-acquisition dividend *is* a partial return of the purchase price and the true and fair way to account for it is to deduct it from the cost of the investment rather than to call it a profit, which was the conclusion favoured by Accountants Digest No. 189 on SSAP 23.[56]

It should of course be pointed out that the above discussion is based on the premise that the cost of the investment in the holding company's books does represent the fair value of the subsidiary. There may be circumstances where it does not, such as when merger relief has been taken or if the subsidiary was not purchased in an arm's-length transaction, and obviously this could require a different view to be taken. In such a case there would seem to be no reason to write down the value of the investment unless the effect of the dividend was to reduce the underlying value of the subsidiary below its carrying amount in the financial statements of the holding company.

Appendix I to FRS 6 does address the topic but does not come out with a firm conclusion. It states that 'where a dividend is paid to the acquiring or issuing company out of pre-combination profits, it would appear that it need not necessarily be applied as a reduction in the carrying value of the investment in the subsidiary undertaking. Such a dividend received should be applied to reduce the carrying value of the investment to the extent necessary to provide for a diminution in value of the investment in the subsidiary undertaking as stated in the accounts of the parent company. To the extent that this is not necessary, it appears that the amount received will be realised profit in the hands of the parent company.'[57]

It may be, however, that the answer to question (b) above will be affected by the ASB's proposals on measuring the impairment of fixed assets (see 4.4 of Chapter 10).

2.4 Acquisitions: measuring the fair value of the net assets acquired

2.4.1 Basic principles

The central requirement to bring in the assets of the subsidiary in the group accounts at their fair value rather than their book value in the subsidiary's accounts has been laid down in accounting standards for many years. However, until FRS 7, no standard elaborated in much detail on how this should be done.

The Companies Act takes a similar approach; it states that 'the identifiable assets and liabilities of the undertaking acquired shall be included in the consolidated balance sheet at their fair values at the date of the acquisition'.[58] The Act defines such assets and liabilities as those which are capable of being disposed of or discharged separately without necessarily disposing of a business of the undertaking.

The purpose of the fair value allocation is simply to establish a realistic starting point for the consolidation of the subsidiary's assets and results. The book values in the subsidiary's own financial statements are of no direct relevance for this purpose, because they do not stem from transactions of the reporting entity (the acquiring group), and in effect they are based on the original cost of what are second-hand assets from the group's point of view. The fair value exercise is an attempt to account fairly for the acquisition transaction by asking what the acquiring group has spent, and what it has got for its money.

Of course, the purchase price for most acquisitions is not settled on the basis of an analysis of the individual assets and liabilities of the target company; it is based instead on factors such as the earnings and cash flows which can be brought to the acquiring group. In that sense the purchase allocation exercise is an artificial one rather than portraying the results of a real analysis which has formed part of a business decision. Nevertheless such an allocation has to take place if the group is to be able to present consolidated financial statements, and the hypothetical nature of the allocation does not render it invalid.

The two basic questions which need to be answered in carrying out such an exercise are:

(a)   what assets and liabilities have been acquired? and

(b)   what values should be placed on them?

The answers to these questions depend on whether the exercise should be carried out based on the perspective of the acquiring company or not.

A   *Acquirer's perspective – ED 53*

ED 53 proposed that 'the fair values of the identifiable assets and liabilities should represent estimates, based on the perspective of the acquiring company, of the amount it would have cost that company had there been direct acquisition of those items individually in their current location and condition'.[59] This meant that the acquirer's intentions regarding the future use of assets or the incurring of future costs were allowed to be taken into account. This was a key point because it was on the basis of this perspective that provision could be made in the fair value exercise for, for example, reorganisation costs. FRS 7 has not retained this 'acquirer's perspective'.

B   *Neutral perspective – FRS 7*

The key to the approach adopted by the ASB in FRS 7 is that 'the identifiable assets and liabilities to be recognised should be those of the acquired entity that existed at the date of the acquisition'.[60] The standard defines identifiable assets and liabilities as those 'that are capable of being disposed of or settled separately, without disposing of a business of the entity'.[61] It indicates that these may include items that were not previously recognised in the accounts of the acquired company, such as pension surpluses or deficiencies and contingent assets.[62] It also indicates that identifiable liabilities include items such as onerous contracts or commitments that existed at the time of acquisition, whether or not the corresponding obligations were recognised as liabilities in the accounts of the acquired company.[63] Although these items were not recognised in the accounts of the acquired company, the ASB would nevertheless see them as assets and liabilities. The key point is that they existed at the date of the acquisition; they merely had not been recognised.

However, items such as provisions for reorganisation costs expected to be incurred as a result of the acquisition are not permitted; this is because they are not liabilities of the acquired company at the date of acquisition.[64] The perspective of the acquirer, the acquiring company management's intention to undertake a programme of reorganisation, is not relevant. In the acquired company at the time of acquisition there is no such programme contemplated which would justify provision – only if the acquired entity was already committed to the reorganisation, and unable realistically to withdraw from it, would it be regarded as pre-acquisition.

In Appendix III to FRS 7, the ASB explains that it takes the view that 'under its draft Statement of Principles, management intent is not a sufficient basis for recognising changes to an entity's assets or liabilities. It is events, not intentions for future actions, that increase or decrease an entity's assets and liabilities. When intentions are translated into actions that commit the entity to particular courses of action, the accounting should then reflect any obligations or changes in assets that arise from those actions. In relation to acquisition accounting, the Board concluded that events of a post-acquisition period that resulted in the recognition of additional liabilities or the impairment of existing assets of an acquired entity should be reported as events of that period rather than of the pre-acquisition period.'[65]

FRS 7 says that its general principles will result in the following being treated as post-acquisition items:

(a) changes resulting from the acquirer's intentions or future actions;

(b) impairments, or other changes, resulting from events subsequent to the acquisition; and

(c) provisions or accruals for future operating losses or for reorganisation and integration costs expected to be incurred as a result of the acquisition, whether they relate to the acquired entity or to the acquirer.[66]

The recognised assets and liabilities are to be measured at fair values that reflect the conditions at the date of the acquisition.[67]

The requirements of FRS 7 for attributing fair values to particular categories of assets and liabilities are discussed at 2.4.3 below. FRS 7 defines 'fair value' as 'the amount at which an asset or liability could be exchanged in a transaction in an arm's length transaction between informed and willing parties, other than in a forced or liquidation sale'.[68]

Although most of the detailed rules are based on the perspective outlined above, there are occasions (for example, deferred tax) where they do not seem to be in accordance with the principle that they should not be affected by the acquirer's intentions.

One area where the judgement of the acquirer is still specifically important is in the choice of accounting policies to be used in recognising and measuring the assets and liabilities which have been acquired. Although FRS 7 sets out the general principles already discussed and sets out further specific rules which are discussed below, it allows that subject to these, fair values should be determined in accordance with the acquirer's accounting policies for similar assets and liabilities. One particular area where this will be important is in the discretion allowed to reporting entities in the calculation of cost. For example, a property development company which does not capitalise interest into the cost of its developments may acquire a company which does. (Rather surprisingly, the standard appears to imply that the fair value of development stocks should be calculated with reference to cost rather than market value.) In that case, the fair value of the acquired company's developments should be calculated according to the acquirer's policies i.e. excluding interest. The post-acquisition profit shown on disposal of the developments will therefore be higher in the hands of the acquirer than it would have been in the hands of the acquired company. Fair values are thus not independent of the acquirer's choices.

2.4.2   *The use of hindsight*

The fact that the fair value process is inevitably, to some degree, a rationalisation of the price paid after the event means that an accounting issue arises: how much hindsight can the acquirer impute into the values assigned, or must the allocation be based solely on the information which he had at the time when he was making his bid? There is a theoretical argument for the latter, which is that if he was unaware of a particular matter, such as the fact that there was a deficiency in the pension fund of the target, then it cannot have influenced the acquisition price and thus should not feature in any allocation of that price.

Whatever the merits of that view in theory, however, it cannot be used in practice. If the acquirer was only able to assign values to items that he knew about at the time of the acquisition, the exercise would in many cases be completely impossible, because, as noted above, most acquisitions are not primarily based on an assessment of the value of the assets and liabilities of the target company. It is therefore necessary to allow the acquirer a reasonable period of time in which to investigate the assets and liabilities which have been acquired and make a reasoned allocation of values to them. The remaining question is, how much time should be allowed?

The ASC originally suggested that, as a practical matter, the date to be used as the limit of the hindsight period should in fact be the date on which the acquiring company has to present the first consolidated financial statements which incorporate the acquired subsidiary. However, many commentators viewed this as an unrealistically tight deadline. ED 53, therefore, relaxed this proposal to say that if accounts are approved within the first six months after the date of the acquisition, and if there has been insufficient time to complete the fair value exercise, then a provisional allocation should be made for the purpose of these accounts which may be amended (with an adjustment to goodwill) in the next accounts if any of the valuations is found to be inaccurate.

In its Discussion Paper the ASB noted that 'several of those who commented on ED 53 argued that the time limit proposed by ED 53 was too inflexible for groups to be able to deal adequately with major and complex acquisitions. Concern was also expressed that, for listed companies, it was inappropriate to define this limit by reference to the publication of subsequent interim accounts.'[69] Accordingly, the ASB proposed to extend the period even further, notwithstanding the fact that its proposed restrictions on fair value adjustments should simplify the exercise.

FRS 7 now requires that adjustments to the fair values of assets and liabilities should be fixed, if possible, by the date at which the accounts for the first full financial year following the acquisition are approved by the directors. If that is not possible, however, provisional valuations should be made. These should be amended, if necessary, in the next financial statements for the first full financial year following the acquisition, with a corresponding adjustment to goodwill. [70]

Thereafter, adjustments should be recognised as profits or losses when identified. The only circumstances in which a retrospective adjustment to the goodwill calculation could be regarded as appropriate would be if the original allocation was regarded as a fundamental error which required to be dealt with as a prior year adjustment under FRS 3. [71] This would probably be the case only if the original allocation was based on a complete misinterpretation of the facts which were available at the time; it would not apply simply because new information had come to light which changed the acquiring management's view of the value of the item in question.

As indicated at 2.4.1 B above, the recognised assets and liabilities are to be measured at fair values that reflect the conditions at the date of the acquisition. So whatever period of hindsight is used, therefore, it is important that the allocation reflects conditions as they existed at the date of the acquisition, rather than being affected by subsequent events. There is a parallel to be drawn here with the accounting treatment of post-balance sheet events; only those events which provide further evidence of conditions as they existed at the acquisition date should be taken into account.

A number of extracts in this chapter make it clear that the fair value assessment is provisional and therefore it may be that further adjustments will be required in the following year.

2.4.3 Requirements for individual assets and liabilities

The requirements of FRS 7 for each class of asset or liability are set out below.

A   Non-monetary assets

FRS 7 states that, 'where similar assets are bought and sold on a readily accessible market, the market price will represent the fair value. Where quoted market prices are not available, market prices can often be estimated, either by independent valuations, or valuation techniques such as discounting estimated future cash flows to their present values. In some cases, where quoted market prices are not available, subsequent sales of acquired assets may provide the most reliable evidence of fair value at the time of the acquisition.' [72]

An important factor which this fails to address is whether the market price is intended to be a buying price or a selling price, and this confusion pervades much of the standard. Also, although the passage cited above might suggest that market values, if available, are to be used for all non-monetary assets, it is clear that this is not always to be the case. For example, it is not envisaged that stocks of finished goods are included at their sales value, but on the other hand, the discussion of investments implies that a sales price is being discussed. In contrast, FRED 7 contained a more understandable general rule, which was not carried through to the standard, that non-monetary assets were to be measured at the lower of replacement cost and recoverable amount.[73] It is not clear what the ASB intended by making that change, particularly since some of the more detailed discussion continues to reflect the terms of the exposure draft.

Where the value of an asset is impaired due, for example, to lack of profitability, underutilisation or obsolescence, such that the replacement cost is not recoverable in full, the fair value is the estimated recoverable amount.[74] 'Recoverable amount' is described as 'the greater of the net realisable value of an asset and, where appropriate, the value in use', which is in turn defined as 'the present value of the future cash flows obtainable as a result of an asset's continued use, including those resulting from the ultimate disposal of the asset'.[75] This is similar to the 'value to the business' rule for valuing assets advocated in the ASB's draft Statement of Principles (see 5.6 of Chapter 2). The recoverable amount should reflect the condition of the asset on acquisition but not any impairments resulting from subsequent events.[76] The standard emphasises that where acquired assets that had not been impaired before acquisition are subsequently disposed of for a reduced price (for example, as part of a post-acquisition reorganisation of the enlarged group), any losses resulting from their disposal are to be treated as post-acquisition losses, not as adjustments to the fair values as at the acquisition date.[77]

FRS 7 contains more detailed provisions for particular types of non-monetary asset as follows:

- Tangible fixed assets

'The fair value of a tangible fixed asset should be based on:

(a) market value, if assets similar in type and condition are bought and sold on an open market; or

(b) depreciated replacement cost, reflecting the acquired business's normal buying process and the sources of supply and prices available to it.'

The fair value should not exceed the recoverable amount of the asset.[78]

The standard also suggests that in some circumstances, the historical cost of an asset updated by the use of price indices may be the most reliable means of estimating replacement cost. Where prices have not changed materially, or where no relevant price indices are available, it would be acceptable to use a carrying value based on historical cost as a reasonable proxy for fair value.[79]

Examples of fair value adjustments in respect of tangible fixed assets are illustrated in the following extracts:

Extract 6.10: Johnston Press plc (1996)

14 Fixed Assets Investments [extract]

b)   On 1 July 1996 the Company acquired the newspaper interests of Emap plc. The consideration of £213,309,000 was paid wholly in cash. The fair value of the assets acquired (as outlined below) was £199,177,000 and the resulting goodwill of £14,132,000 was written off to Reserves.

	Book value £'000	Revaluations £'000	Provisions £'000	Fair value to Group £'000
Fixed assets				
Intangible	458	175,772[f]	–	176,230
Tangible	21,722	(5,588)[a]	(384)[b]	15,750
Current assets				
Stocks	1,154	–	–	1,154
Debtors	18,969	–	(635)[c]	18,334
Cash	28	–	–	28
Total assets	42,331	170,184	(1,019)	211,496
Creditors				
Bank overdrafts	191	–	–	191
Trade creditors	3,622	–	–	3,622
Other creditors	293	–	–	293
Taxes and social security costs	2,698	–	(135)	2,563
Accruals	4,040	–	944[d]	4,984
Provisions - deferred taxation	1,901	–	(1,235)[e]	666
Total liabilities	12,745	–	(426)	12,319
Net assets	29,586	170,184	(593)	199,177

The fair value accounting adjustments are:

[a] Revaluation of properties and plant by professional valuers;

[b] Additional depreciation in respect of plant and machinery to align to Group policy;

[c] Additional provision for bad debts;

[d] Additional creditors to provide for empty properties and other items;

[e] Taxation provision on fair value adjustments;

[f] Valuation of titles.

Extract 6.11: Scottish Television plc (1996)

29 ACQUISITIONS [extract]

On 18 October 1996, the Company declared its offer for Caledonian unconditional and the results of Caledonian have been consolidated from this date using the acquisition method.

The book values of the assets and liabilities of Caledonian immediately prior to the acquisition and the fair value adjustments required in recognition of the change of ownership are as follows:

	Book value prior to acquisition £m	Revaluations £m	Accounting policy alignment £m	Fair value £m
Intangible assets	64.5	(8.5)**(a)**	–	56.0
Tangible assets	18.5	(7.3)**(b)**	–	11.2
Stocks	0.6	–	(0.2)**(c)**	0.4
Debtors	11.5	(0.2)**(d)**	–	11.3
Cash	1.4	–	–	1.4
Creditors	(12.2)	(1.3)**(e)**	–	(13.5)
Net assets acquired	**84.3**	**(17.3)**	**(0.2)**	**66.8**

Consideration	
Cash	53.4
Assumption of liabilities	67.6
Loan notes	0.8
Total consideration	**121.8**
Fair value of net assets acquired above	(66.8)
Goodwill	**55.0**

Fair value adjustments

a)   The directors have derived the value of the intangible assets owned by Caledonian using discounted cash flow valuations and are supported by a comparative view of the transaction values of similar properties within the newspaper industry. The main intangible assets together with the values attributed may be summarised as follows:

	Book value £m	Fair value £m	Adjustment £m
The Herald	60.5	50.0	(10.5)
Evening Times	–	6.0	6.0
Scottish Farmer	4.0	–	4.0
Totals	**64.5**	**56.0**	**(8.5)**

b) Caledonian's freehold land and buildings have been adjusted to open market value. The open market value has been assessed by Fuller Peiser Property Consultants. This resulted in a reduction of book value by £5.4 million. Caledonian's plant and machinery has been adjusted to market value in accordance with information received from manufacturers. This has resulted in a reduction in book value of £1.7 million. Obsolete equipment has been written down by £0.2 million. Tangible fixed assets have therefore been written down by £7.3 million in aggregate.

c) Group policy is not to recognise a value for stocks of engineering and electrical stores. Stocks have been written down by £0.2 million to align the Caledonian accounting policy with that of the Group.

d) The fair value of debtors has been reduced by £0.2 million in respect of potential bad debts not previously provided and credit notes issued post acquisition in respect of pre acquisition sales.

e) The fair value of creditors falling due within one year has been increased by £1.3 million to reflect the estimated costs of repairing the buildings to meet minimum health and safety standards, to allow for a number of contractual arrangements entered into by previous management which are regarded as onerous and for additional taxation liabilities.

f) The actuarial value of liabilities arising under the pension arrangements committed to by Caledonian has been reassessed in accordance with assumptions generally used by the Group in determining such liabilities. This valuation indicated that the assets of the Caledonian pension funds exceeded the actuarial liabilities by £0.9 million at the date of acquisition. In accordance with accounting standards, this excess has been recognised as an asset on acquisition and is included in Caledonian's book value prior to fair value adjustments.

It can be seen from the above extracts that these companies have incorporated plant and machinery at valuation as well as properties. It is fair to say that although most companies will make adjustments to include properties at a valuation very few companies make similar adjustments for plant and machinery. However, that is not to say that no fair value adjustments are made in respect of such assets. It can be seen from Extract 6.10 above that in addition to having a valuation adjustment in respect of plant and machinery, Johnston Press also has an adjustment to align the depreciation policy in line with that of the group. Other examples of companies making similar fair value adjustments to tangible fixed assets to align depreciation policies are Stagecoach and Bernard Matthews.[80]

Arguably such adjustments to reflect the acquirer's depreciation methods or lives are not necessary to align the accounting policies of the two companies as they both had policies to depreciate the assets over their useful service lives. If the target company were to change its depreciation methods or asset lives to that adopted by its new parent, then SSAP 12 would not allow these to be dealt with by way of prior year adjustment as a change in accounting policy (see Chapter 10 at 3.8 and 3.9).

Another company which has made an adjustment to reflect its own accounting policies is FKI, as shown below:

Extract 6.12: FKI plc (1996)

28 Acquisitions during the year [extract]

On 19 April 1995 the Group acquired the whole of the ordinary share capital of Amdura Corporation at a price of $2.30 per ordinary share. In addition all issued and outstanding preferred shares of Amdura were cancelled and converted into a right to receive cash, an amount of $2,500 plus any accrued but unpaid dividends and for the purchase of all outstanding stock options under Amdura's 1992 Stock Option Plan.

The acquisition has been accounted for using the acquisition method of accounting.

The following table sets out the book values of the identifiable assets and liabilities acquired and their fair value to the Group:

	Book value £'000	Accounting policy alignment £'000	Fair value adjustments £'000	Fair value to Group £'000
Fixed assets				
Intangible assets	9,187	(9,187)	–	–
Tangible assets	25,034	(3,683)	–	21,351
Current assets				
Stocks	30,187	123	(893)	29,417
Debtors	16,963	–	–	16,963
Cash at bank and in hand	1,031	–	–	1,031
Total assets	82,402	(12,747)	(893)	68,762
Liabilities				
Loans and overdrafts	(19,920)	–	–	(19,920)
Trade creditors	(10,652)	–	–	(10,652)
Other creditors and accruals	(15,123)	–	–	(15,123)
Post retirement provisions	(2,360)	–	(315)	(2,675)
Net assets acquired	34,347	(12,747)	(1,208)	20,392
Total consideration including expenses				41,492
Goodwill				21,100

The accounting policy alignments relate to the following:

- elimination of goodwill of £8,678,000 and other intangible assets of £509,000 capitalised under US accounting principles. Other intangibles include trade marks, customer lists and non compete agreements.

- the write off of drawings of £3,683,000 included within tangible fixed assets. FKI does not capitalise such assets in its accounts.

- increase in valuation of stocks of £123,000 as a result of applying first-in, first out basis of valuation on all stocks.

The fair value adjustments relate to the following:

- reduction in the value of stocks of £404,000 by adopting an SSAP 9 basis of accounting and excluding certain overheads that are not considered to be attributable to production.

- reduction in the value of stocks at one operating site of £489,000 following a complete physical inventory of all stocks at all sites.

- increase in the provision for post-retirement benefits of £315,000 following an actuarial valuation of all post retirement benefit schemes performed by qualified actuaries.

The Group obtained independent external valuations of the properties acquired. The valuations obtained did not differ significantly from the carrying book values of £8,001,000 and therefore no adjustment was made.

In addition to the above adjustments the Group costs of rationalisation and reorganisation of the acquired business of £1,237,000 have been charged to the profit and loss account. The movement in the provision for such costs is disclosed in note 23.

It can be seen that in this situation the difference in accounting policy was not in respect of differences in depreciation policy but in whether the policy was to capitalise the particular type of asset or not.

One company which made no fair value adjustment in respect of tangible fixed assets, but possibly should have, was Wace Group:

Extract 6.13: Wace Group PLC (1996)

22. ACQUISITION [extract]

On 31 January 1996 the Group completed the purchase of the trade, assets and goodwill of Hallmark Cards Inc.'s greetings cards manufacturing facility in Rathfarnham. Dublin. On the same date the Group and Hallmark also entered into a five year supply agreement for the manufacture of greetings cards for Hallmark brands in the UK and Eire. The acquisition has been accounted for using acquisition accounting and has been consolidated into the Group balance sheet as follows:

	Book value at acquisition	Fair value adjustments: Revaluation	Fair value at acquisition
	£000	£000	£000
Tangible fixed assets	4,576	–	4,576
Stock	1,207	(108)	1,099
Pension surplus	–	1,396	1,396
Deferred taxation	–	(823)	(823)
Pre-acquisition reorganisation provision	(661)	–	(661)
Net assets	5,122	465	5,587
Goodwill arising			351
Total cost of acquisition			5,938
Satisfied by			
Cash consideration			5,783
Cash costs			155
			5,938

The principal adjustments reflect the Group's estimate of the net realisable value of certain work in progress and the recognition of the surplus on the pension scheme. The provision for deferred tax relates to the pension surplus and the freehold property included in tangible fixed assets.

The value of the surplus as at 31 January 1996 of I£1,346,000 was advised by the scheme's actuaries, Mercer Limited, based on their last actuarial valuation performed as at 1 January 1996 which reported a surplus of I£1,220,400. The valuation used the projected unit cost method and the principal assumptions used were that investment returns would be 2.5 per cent higher than the growth in annual salaries and 3.5 per cent higher than the growth in state pensions: no allowance was made for increases in pensions in the course of payment which were valued using a yield of 8.5 per cent. The actuarial value of the assets at 31 January 1996 I£6,706,400 which on a continuance basis represented 125 per cent of the benefits accrued to the members of the scheme. The surplus will be amortised over the expected working lives of the members.

25. POST BALANCE SHEET EVENTS [extract]

On 21 February 1997 the Group exchanged contracts to sell and lease back the land and buildings at Rathfarnham Dublin acquired with the purchase from Hallmark. Completion is scheduled to take place on 30 June 1997. The contractual consideration is I£6.5m which compares with an anticipated carrying value at the date of disposal of I£3.4m. The Group also completed the disposal of a property at Market Road London on 14 February 1997 for a consideration of £1.85m which is the carrying value within properties for resale at 31 December 1996.

It can be seen that the consideration for the property under the sale and leaseback arrangement is approximately double the carrying value of the property acquired as part of the acquisition which might suggest that the value at the date of acquisition was also greater than the book value at that date.

■ Intangible assets

FRED 7 said that intangible assets, such as patent rights and licences, that are permitted by other accounting standards to be recognised separately from purchased goodwill should be valued at current replacement cost, which is normally their estimated value in the market. The exposure draft gave no further indication as to how this proposal was to apply in practice. It was unclear whether it meant that unless other accounting standards specifically permitted their recognition (such as SSAP 13 on research and development) then no fair values could be attributed – although that would not have been consistent with its reference to patent rights and licences. FRS 7 is even more abbreviated saying only that, 'where an intangible asset is recognised, its fair value should be based on its replacement cost, which is normally its estimated market value'.[81]

The main issue is to what extent assets such as brand names or newspaper titles can be regarded as part of the identifiable assets as defined. The recognition of such assets has become more frequent in recent years, and it is commonly the case that they are carried in the balance sheet without amortisation, subject only to write-down if they become permanently impaired.

Examples of companies recognising such intangible assets (and making fair value adjustments to the items already recognised) are Johnston Press and Scottish Television (see Extracts 6.10 and 6.11 above).

The distinction between such items and goodwill probably rests on whether or not they can be regarded as identifiable assets, i.e. assets which can be identified and sold without necessarily disposing of the business as a whole. There is no doubt that such assets can be very valuable; the real test is whether the business would remain if they were disposed of. This might depend on the facts of each individual case, because in some cases the right to sell particular brands might be the very essence of a business, while in others the ownership of such rights might be more incidental to the main activities.

The ASB's Discussion Paper on goodwill proposed that intangible assets arising on an acquisition should be subsumed within purchased goodwill rather than being accounted for separately. However, most commentators disagreed with that approach so FRED 12 proposes that such intangible assets should be recognised separately as long as a reliable value can be placed on such assets. This is discussed further in Chapter 10 at 1.3.2 and 1.3.3.

One further area of interest is the interplay between the acquiring company's own accounting policy for intangibles and the requirements of FRS 7. For example, a computer software development company may base its own accounting policy on the treatments permitted by SFAS 86 (the US standard on the topic). This is very much more prescriptive, and restrictive, about the capitalisation of software development costs than the more general rules in SSAP 13. In particular, all expenditures are written off until technological feasibility, strictly evidenced by a working model, has been established. If such a company buys another software company, the target may have several valuable products on the brink of commercial realisation – this may indeed be the reason for the acquisition. However, despite the value of such products, there would appear to be no requirement for the acquiring company to attempt to ascribe a fair value to them. FRS 7 refers only to situations where an intangible is recognised – if the accounting policies of the acquirer do not call for recognition, there is no need to include any amount in respect of the software products in the fair value exercise. This would enhance post-acquisition profits.

One company which has made a fair value adjustment on the basis that its own accounting policy is not to recognise the intangible assets recorded by the target company is Graseby, as shown below:

Extract 6.14: *Graseby plc (1996)*

12   Business acquisition[extract]

On 31st July 1996 the group completed the first stage of the acquisition from Minnesota Mining and Manufacturing Company (3M) of its worldwide infusion therapy business (3MJT), whose principal operations are located in the US. The net assets acquired and the consideration given, which was discharged wholly by cash, are given below:

	Net assets acquired	Fair value adjustment	Accounting policy alignment	Purchase consideration	Adjusted net assets
Tangible fixed assets	1,056	–	–	–	1,056
Patents	1,279	–	(1,279)	–	–
Stocks	2,960	(17)	(43)	–	2,900
Debtors	4,264	–	–	–	4,264
Creditors	(327)	–	–	–	(327)
Provisions	(187)	(1,464)	–	–	(1,651)
Taxation	–	–	323	–	323
Total net assets	9,045	(1,481)	(999)	–	6,565

Purchase consideration
- Payable to vendor   8,979
- Professional fees and associated costs   1,243

                                                                  10,222

Goodwill   3,657

The fair value adjustments relate primarily to provisions created for the cost of dealing with certain warranty problems associated with the installed product base.

All amounts are expressed in £000 unless otherwise stated

Another example is FKI as shown in Extract 6.12 above.

■   Stocks and work in progress

FRS 7 requires that 'stocks including commodity stocks, that the acquired entity trades on a market in which it participates as both a buyer and a seller should be valued at current market prices'.[82]

However, 'other stocks, and work-in-progress, should be valued at the lower of replacement cost and net realisable value. Replacement cost is for this purpose the cost at which the stocks would have been replaced by the acquired entity, reflecting its normal buying process and the sources of supply and prices available to it – that is, the current cost of bringing the stocks to their present location and condition.'[83] For example, for a business purchasing in wholesale markets the replacement cost would be the wholesale price.

On the other hand, the replacement cost of manufactured stocks and work-in-progress would normally be the current cost of manufacturing based, for example, on current standard costs where these are employed. The standard does indicate that in practice, where there is a short manufacturing cycle, replacement cost may not be materially different from historical cost.[84]

This aspect of the standard is significantly different from the proposal in ED 53 whereby such stock was to be valued including profit earned to date, which would thus have been pre-acquisition from the point of view of the acquiring group and hence would not appear in its results when the stock was subsequently sold; FRS 7 is only taking account of input price changes during the period the stock is held.

For long-term maturing stocks, replacement cost would be based on market values if stocks at similar stages are regularly traded in the market. In other situations, a surrogate for replacement cost may be the historical cost of bringing such stock to its present location and condition, including an amount representing an interest cost in respect of holding the stock.[85] For long-term contracts, the standard envisages that no fair value adjustments will be made, other than those that would normally result from assessing the outcome of the contract under SSAP 9, or reflecting the changeover to the acquirer's accounting policies.[86]

Another issue which FRS 7 addresses is the effect of incorporating stocks at their net realisable value. The standard states that where an acquirer reaches a judgement about the value of slow-moving or redundant stocks that differs from that of the management of the acquired company, any material write-down of the carrying value of stocks in the acquired company's books before or at the time of the acquisition needs to be justified by the circumstances of the acquired company before acquisition. If exceptional profits appear to have been earned on the realisation of stocks after the date of the acquisition, the fair values should be re-examined and, if necessary, an adjustment made to these values and a corresponding adjustment to goodwill.[87] This is clearly aimed at ensuring that acquirers do not make excessive provisions against the carrying value of stock, but then sell the stock at prices which give rise to a profit.

Although the standard appears to be very strict about write-downs, it is nevertheless the case that the acquirer can genuinely have a view about the value of slow moving or redundant stocks that differs from that of the management of the acquired entity. Existing management, particularly if the company has been going through a hard time with poor profitability, may have actively resisted write-downs in the value of the stock. The acquiring management may feel less accountable for the levels of such stock and feel able to take a much more critical look at its value.

One company which would appear to have had a significantly different view of the value of stock compared to that of the existing management is Kingfisher in relation to its acquisition of part of Norweb Retail, as indicated below:

Extract 6.15: Kingfisher plc (1997)

28 Acquisitions [extract]

On 24 November 1996, Comet Group PLC completed the purchase of a substantial part of Norweb Retail, a division of Norweb plc. Details of the net assets acquired are given in the following table:

£ millions	Book value at acquisition	Revaluation adjustments	Fair value to the Group
Tangible fixed assets	23.2	(3.2)	20.0
Stocks	55.2	(25.2)	30.0
Provision for reorganisation	(22.0)	–	(22.0)
Warranty provision	(4.2)	–	(4.2)
	52.2	(28.4)	23.8
Goodwill written off to reserves			1.2
Net cost of acquisition satisfied wholly in cash			25.0

The revaluation adjustments are made to reflect the fair value of the net assets acquired.

The provision for reorganisation of £22.0m relates to the closure of the Norweb high street stores which had been a commitment prior to acquisition. A further post acquisition provision has been charged in this year's profit and loss account of £8.7m relating to the reorganisation of the combined portfolio of out of town stores.

Although there are other examples of companies making fair value write-downs in respect of the net realisable values of stocks acquired the impact is not as great as that in the extract above. It is also fair to say that there do not appear to be many examples whereby adjustments are made to increase book values of stocks, although this may be due to the fact that replacement cost is not materially different from book values given the current low levels of inflation.

Where adjustments have been made to reduce the carrying value of stocks, an interesting question which then arises is where the new management turns the company around and generates a profit on the now written-down stock. Such a profit would be disclosable (see 2.8.2 below) but as discussed, FRS 7 also entertains the idea that the profit should not be taken, but that the fair values should be re-opened and the goodwill figure adjusted instead. It appears necessary, therefore, to assess what would have been the value of the stock in the target company, with the old management and prospects. The acquiring management may feel that the value of the stock was low, justifying its fair value exercise write-down. If the profits on the disposal of the stock have then been generated because of the new management's efforts in finding new outlets or uses for that stock then it is consistent with the philosophy of FRS 7 that those profits should be taken post-acquisition.

A further issue which arises in the context of the fair value of stocks is the calculation of cost. The accounting policy adopted for the identification of stock cost can legitimately differ as between the acquirer and the acquired company. Mention has already been made of the choice as to whether interest is capitalised into cost. In the context of stocks, issues such as the level of overheads to be costed into stocks are legitimate bases of difference as between companies. Application of the costing basis adopted by the acquiring company may result in quite legitimately lower stock carrying values being adopted by the acquiring company, and thus higher post-acquisition profits being reported. Thus, although the standard quite rightly directs attention to unusual post-acquisition profits being made on acquired stock, there can be acceptable reasons why such profits are not inappropriate.

Examples of companies of making fair value adjustments due to different policies in respect of determining the cost of stocks are shown in the following extracts:

Extract 6.16: Persimmon plc (1996)

15 Acquisitions [extract]

On 26 February 1996 the company acquired the whole of the issued share capital of Ideal Homes Holdings Limited for a total consideration of £177,572,000. The consideration was satisfied by cash and the acquisition expenses amounted to £2,373,000. The acquisition has been accounted for by the acquisition method of accounting.

The consolidated assets and liabilities of Ideal Homes Holdings Limited acquired are set out below:

	Book value £'000	Revaluations £'000	Other adjustments £'000	Accounting policy alignment £'000	Fair value £'000
Tangible fixed assets	1,627	(480)	(336)	–	811
Investments	9,546	–	(1,000)	–	8,546
Stock	173,380	–	(3,917)	(3,437)	166,026
Debtors	13,217	–	(510)	–	12,707
Deferred tax	–	–	7,000	–	7,000
Total assets	197,770	(480)	1,237	(3,437)	195,090
Creditors	(41,733)	–	(1,307)	–	(43,040)
Net assets	156,037	(480)	(70)	(3,437)	152,050
Goodwill					27,895
Total cost of assets acquired					179,945

The book value of the assets and liabilities shown above have been taken from the management accounts of the acquired business at the date of acquisition.

The fair value adjustments above principally arise for the following reasons:

a.   Revaluations representing the restatement of certain of the long leasehold properties acquired to their estimated market values.

b.   Other adjustments principally representing the:

- write down of fixed assets following a physical verification exercise and assessment of the realisable value of certain assets

- write down of investments following a review of the underlying net assets and assessment of their realisable value

- write down of stock following an assessment of the realisable value of work in progress and strategic land

- write down of debtors following an assessment of the estimated recoverable value

- recognition of unprovided amounts in respect of onerous contracts and other liabilities

- recognition of a deferred tax asset in respect of trading losses acquired

c.   Accounting policy realignments, which align the accounting policies of the acquired group with those adopted by Persimmon. being principally the write-off of capitalised selling costs and ground rents which were both carried in stocks.

Extract 6.17: Premier Farnell plc (1996)

23. ACQUISITIONS AND DISPOSALS [extract]

(i) Acquisition of Premier

On 11th April 1996 the Group acquired Premier Industrial Corporation ("Premier") for a consideration of £1,877.2 million. Details of the acquisition, including the fair value adjustments made to the assets and liabilities acquired are set out below:

	Book value at acquisition £m	Accounting policy alignment £m	Other £m	Fair value £m
Tangible fixed assets	43.2	(2.0)	4.9[a]	46.1
Intangible assets	8.5	(8.5)[1]	–	–
Investments	2.0	–	(2.0)	–
Stock	127.3	(20.8)[2]	–	106.5
Debtors - due within one year	92.5	(3.4)	(1.2)	87.9
- due after one year	13.7	–	40.4[b]	54.1
Creditors	(57.7)	(2.1)	(2.7)	(62.5)
Corporate and deferred taxes	(7.1)	(3.7)[3]	(18.0)[b]	(28.8)
Provisions	–	–	(4.6)[c]	(4.6)
Net cash	82.0	–	–	82.0
	304.4	(40.5)	16.8	280.7

Consideration		
Shares		923.7
Cash including costs		953.5
		1,877.2
Goodwill written off (note 21)		1,596.5

Accounting policy alignment

[1]write-off of goodwill

[2]adjustments required to reflect UK GAAP eliminate overheads from stock valuation and adopt stock provisioning in accordance with Group accounting practice.

[3]write-off of deferred tax assets in accordance with UK GAAP

Accounting policy alignments also reflect the adoption of Group policies in respect of fixed asset capitalisation, catalogue costs, sales returns and holiday pay.

Other

[a] revaluation of land and buildings.

[b] actuarial valuation of pension surplus in accordance with FRS7 and SSAP24 and recognition of corresponding deferred tax provision.

[c] actuarial valuation of post-retirement obligation.

Other adjustments also reflect the write-down of investments to net realisable value and the recognition of liabilities existing at the acquisition date.

■ Investments

FRS 7 says that 'quoted investments should be valued at market price, adjusted if necessary for unusual price fluctuations or for the size of the holding'.[88]

Little guidance is given as to how these values, or adjustments to them, are to be determined. As noted above, it is not clear whether the market price is that for a purchase or a sale and thus whether the adjustment for an unmarketable size of holding is intended to be made upwards or downwards. Rather confusingly, the standard comments that the adjustments for large holdings may be to reflect either a lower realisable value representing the difficulties of disposal or a higher value for a holding representing a substantial voting block.[89]

No specific guidance is given on the treatment of unquoted investments which therefore fall to be valued at the amount they could be exchanged at in an arm's length transaction between informed and willing parties. The standard does briefly discuss the valuation of unquoted instruments in the context of valuing capital instruments given as part of the consideration (see 2.3.2 above). Similar considerations would apply in the valuation of unquoted investments acquired.

One company which made a significant adjustment in respect of investments was Granada Group:

Extract 6.18: Granada Group PLC (1996)

25   Acquisition of businesses [extract]

	Book value	Fair value adjustment	Fair value to Group
a Summary of the effect of the acquisition of Forte			
Tangible fixed assets	3,908.3	4.7	3,913.0
Investments	177.9	117.2	295.1
Stocks	29.6	(1.4)	28.2
Debtors	182.7	(8.1)	174.6
Creditors	(439.3)	(173.2)	(612.5)
Cash and cash equivalents	228.0	–	228.0
Corporation tax	(61.5)	–	(61.5)
Deferred taxation	(49.7)	–	(49.7)
Finance lease obligations	(517.6)	–	(517.6)
Borrowings	(981.8)	–	(981.8)
Minority interests	(63.5)	–	(63.5)
Net assets acquired	2,413.1	(60.8)	2,352.3
Shares issued			1,911.9
Cash paid (excluding share issue costs)			2,084.0
Fair value of consideration			3,995.9
Goodwill			(1,643.6)
			2,352.3

No indication is given in the accounts as to what the fair value adjustment was. However, the major investments held by Forte were its associates, The Savoy Hotel and ALPHA Airports Group, both of which are quoted.

An example of a company making adjustments in respect of unquoted investments is United Utilities, as shown below:

Extract 6.19: United Utilities PLC (1996)

Financial review [extract]

Acquisition of Norweb [extract]

The consideration was offset by the realisation of £300 million in cash on the disposal of Norweb's investments in the National Grid and the Pumped Storage Business. These proceeds exceeded our expectations at the time of the acquisition.

The investments in the National Grid and Pumped Storage Business were revalued upward by £199.6 million, net of £48 million tax provisions, reflecting the net proceeds received on disposal.

It can be seen that the investments have been valued at amounts subsequently realised, rather than the values which were expected to be realised at the time of the acquisition. This is consistent with the guidance in the standard in respect of businesses held for resale (see G below).

B   Monetary assets and liabilities

The standard states that 'the fair value of monetary assets and liabilities, including accruals and provisions, should take into account the amounts expected to be received or paid and their timing. Fair value should be determined by reference to market prices, where available, by reference to the current price at which the business could acquire similar assets or enter into similar obligations, or by discounting to present value.'[90]

Short-term monetary items, such as trade debtors and creditors, will be recognised at the amount expected to be received or paid on settlement or redemption. It is unlikely that these will require to be discounted. However, the fair values of certain long-term monetary items may be materially different from their book values. This is designed to deal with the situation, say, where the acquired company has long-term debt with a fixed rate of interest that no longer reflects current rates. Another example is a material long-term debtor where the delay in settlement is not compensated for by an interest charge reflecting current rates.

FRS 7 does not specify a discount rate which is appropriate for all situations. It states that 'the choice of interest rate to be applied to long-term borrowings would be affected by current lending rates for an equivalent term, the credit standing of the issuer and the nature of any security'. (The reference to the issuer suggests that the interest rate is to be specific to the acquired company, not that of the acquirer, which is consistent with the standard's general approach.) 'For long-term debtors (after any necessary provisions had been made) the interest rate would be based on current lending rates.'[91]

The differences between fair values arrived at by discounting and the total amounts receivable or payable in respect of the relevant items represent discounts or premiums on acquisition and are dealt with as interest income or expense by allocation to accounting periods over the term of the monetary amounts at a constant rate based on their carrying amounts, along the lines of FRS 4.[92]

Example 6.1:   Effect of discounting long-term loans

A company, X plc, acquires another, Y plc on 1 January 19X4. Y has a fixed rate bank loan of £10,000 taken out when interest rates were higher. It is committed to a rate of 10% pa on this borrowing which is due for repayment in two years. Interest is payable annually in one year and two years' time and the principal is to be repaid with the final interest payment. If it took a two year loan out at the time of the acquisition, it would be able to obtain a rate of only 6%.

Under FRS 7 the fair value of the loan is :

$$[£1,000 \div 1.06] + [£11,000 \div (1.06 \times 1.06)]$$
$$= £10,733$$

The acquired loan would therefore be recorded at this figure.

The accounting should therefore be as follows. The profit and loss account charge for the first period will be £1,000, the coupon, reduced by a debit to the carrying value of the loan of £356. This gives a 'correct' charge of £644 for the period being £10,733 x 6%. The carrying value of the loan is then £10,377.

The charge for the second period will be £1,000, the coupon, reduced by a debit to the carrying value of the loan of £377. This gives a 'correct' charge of £623 for the period, being £10,377 x 6%. The carrying value of the loan is then the amount repayable.

	Cash flows £	Interest charge £	Carrying value in the balance sheet £
At 1 January 19X4			10,733
At 31 December 19X4	(1,000)	644	10,377
At 31 December 19X5	(11,000)	623	0

Where debt instruments are quoted, market values at the date of acquisition will be used instead of present values. However, the standard states that where a reduced pre-acquisition market value on an acquired company's debt reflected the market's perception that it was at risk of being unable to fulfil its repayment obligations, the reduction would not be recognised in the fair value allocation if the debt was expected to be repaid at its full amount[93] (presumably as a result of having been acquired). In contrast to the choice of interest rate discussed above in this case it seems that the credit rating of the *acquiring* company is to be reflected in the value attached to such items, which seems to depart from the standard's general approach on this occasion.

One possible difficulty with this requirement is the extent to which the principle of discounting should be applied to some of the other requirements for attributing fair values of particular assets or liabilities. For example, if provisions are to be made in respect of deferred taxation or for environmental liabilities should these be discounted? Although there may be a theoretical argument for this, we do not believe that this was intended by the ASB. It would clearly be anomalous for the deferred tax relating to the acquired company to be discounted, but the rest of the group's deferred tax not to be discounted. It may be, however, in assessing a provision for environmental liabilities that it could be based on discounted amounts.

Examples of companies making fair value adjustments for monetary assets or liabilities based on market values or by discounting amounts receivable or payable are few and far between. This could be due to the fact that companies have floating rate debt and therefore the existing book value will be equivalent to the fair value, or any adjustments may not be material. One company making a fair value adjustment in respect of loan capital is MEPC, as shown below:

Extract 6.20: MEPC plc (1996)

6 Acquisitions [extract]

The major acquisitions during the year were the purchase of the net assets of North American Properties Unit Trust (NAPUT) on 1 February 1996 the consideration being satisfied by the issue of 11,976,952 ordinary shares at 406p and the balance by cash, and Caledonian Land Limited (previously Caledonian Land plc) on 31 August 1996 for a cash consideration.

The impact of the acquisitions on the consolidated net assets (using an exchange rate of £1=US $1.5309 for NAPUT) was:

	Net assets on acquisition £m	Revaluation adjustments £m	Adjusted net assets £m
Attributable net assets:			
Investment properties	244.9	(1.8)	243.1
Properties acquired for disposal	38.9	–	38.9
Debtors	4.9	(0.1)	4.8
Cash	9.9	–	9.9
Loan capital	(107.3)	(8.0)	(115.3)
Creditors	(16.0)	–	(16.0)
Minority interests	(3.3)	0.6	(2.7)
	172.0	(9.3)	162.7
Consideration			
Issue of shares			48.6
Cash, acquisition costs (£2.5m) and capitalised dividends (£0.8m)			114.1
			162.7

(a) Loan capital consolidated at acquisition of NAPUT has been revalued to market value as at the date of acquisition.

Another example is shown in Extract 6.26 below.

Most fair value adjustments relating to monetary assets, such as debtors, are due to reassessments of their recoverable amount or to align accounting policies for bad debt provisions; for example, see Extracts 6.10, 6.11 and 6.16 above.

C Contingencies

Both contingent assets and liabilities should be measured at fair values where these can be determined. For this purpose reasonable estimates of the expected outcome may be used.[94] The treatment of contingent assets is an example of the situation whereby assets are recognised as part of the fair value exercise when they are not normally recognised in accounts when no acquisition is involved; SSAP 18 only allows recognition of contingent assets when their realisation becomes reasonably certain. Although the treatment in FRS 7 seems imprudent at first sight, it is in fact designed to *exclude* from post-acquisition profits any windfall gains from transactions or events which took place before the acquisition was made. In effect, the acquirer has made an investment in a speculative asset.

On a practical note, acquiring managements will often be reluctant to recognise contingent assets. The details surrounding them will often be hazy and managements will be reluctant to threaten post-acquisition profits with the possibility of a write down of the contingent asset if the gain does not in the event materialise – from their point of view there is downside but no upside. An example of a contingent asset, however, would be the need to reflect expected receipts under an 'earn-out' arrangement in respect of a company previously disposed of from the acquired group.

Certain contingent assets and liabilities that crystallise as a result of the acquisition are also to be recognised as part of the fair value exercise, provided that the underlying contingency was in existence before the acquisition. An example is where the acquired company has previously entered into a contract that contains a clause under which obligations are triggered in the event of a change in ownership.[95]

One company which made a fair value adjustment in respect of a contingent asset was GKN in its 1994 accounts, as shown below:

Extract 6.21: GKN plc (1994)

23 ACQUISITIONS [extract]

The fair value adjustments made include:

(c) a debtor for the net cash received in June 1994 amounting to £112 million arising from an arbitration award against the Arab Organisation for Industrialisation (AOI) following the termination of a joint venture between AOI and Westland Helicopters Limited to manufacture Lynx helicopters under licence. This receipt was secured as a result of actions initiated by Westland prior to acquisition and has accordingly been referred back to 31st March 1994. A further final net receipt of £51 million was negotiated in August 1994 and has been treated as a post acquisition exceptional profit (see note 4). These items, taken together with the net £15 million received by Westland in December 1993, give a total net receipt of £178 million from the reward.

An example of a company that has provided for contingent liabilities is TI Group, as shown below:

Extract 6.22: TI Group plc (1996)

1   ACQUISITIONS AND DISPOSALS [extract]

Fair value of net assets acquired - Forsheda

	Book values prior to acquisition £m	Provisional fair value adjustments		Provisional fair values to TI Group £m
		Conformity with TI accounting policies £m	Legal & environmental issues £m	
Fixed intangible assets principally goodwill	8.7	(8.7)	–	–
Fixed tangible assets	27.7	(0.9)	–	**26.8**
Stocks	12.4	(0.6)	–	**11.8**
Debtors	21.3	(0.4)	–	**21.2**
Creditors	(19.5)	0.2	(6.4)	**(25.7)**
Pensions and other post-retirement obligations	(6.2)	0.1	–	**(6.1)**
Deferred taxation	(4.7)	–	–	**(4.7)**
Net cash/(debt)	19.2	–	–	**19.2**
Net assets	58.9	(10.0)	(6.4)	**42.5**

The fair value adjustments to achieve conformity with TI accounting policies mainly relate to the write off of intangible assets (principally goodwill) harmonising fixed asset lives and alignment of accounting methods for making provisions for slow moving inventory and doubtful debtors.

Provisions were created in respect of five specific legal and environmental issues. The amounts provided are provisional and are based on best estimates. They will be reviewed at the end of 1997 and any amounts not expected to be utilised will be written back to goodwill and not through the profit and loss account.

It would appear that TI Group has been prudent in making its best estimates of the provisions for the legal and environmental liabilities because it seems only to expect amounts to be written back when it reassesses the provisional amounts in 1997. Other examples are shown in Extract 6.5 above and Extract 6.26 below.

D   Pensions and other post-retirement benefits

FRS 7 requires that the fair value of a deficiency in a funded pension or other post-retirement benefits scheme, or accrued obligations in an unfunded scheme, should be recognised as a liability of the acquiring group. To the extent that it is reasonably expected to be realised, a surplus in a funded scheme should be recognised as an asset.[96] The assets or liabilities which are recognised are in substitution for any existing prepayments or provisions that have accumulated in the accounts of the acquired company under the requirements of SSAP 24 or UITF 6.

This is another example where assets or liabilities are to be recognised as part of the fair value exercise which would otherwise not be allowed in the absence of an acquisition; in most situations SSAP 24 does not allow the immediate recognition of surpluses or deficiencies of pension schemes, but requires them to be recognised systematically over the average remaining service lives of the employees. Essentially this requirement is based on the fact that a pension fund represents an off balance sheet resource (which may be positive or negative, depending on the solvency of the fund), and that post-acquisition results will be distorted unless recognition is given to the existence of this asset or liability at the time of the acquisition.

A change from the exposure draft is the introduction of the proviso regarding the recognition of assets through use of the phrase 'to the extent that it is reasonably expected to be realised'. As was indicated when FRED 7 was published, this was an area which the ASB could not agree upon. A minority of the members disagreed with giving instant recognition to a pension surplus and would have preferred to spread it forward over the average service lives of the employees.[97] The wording above appears to have been the compromise reached, but like many compromises it is far from satisfactory, because it is unclear what it means.

The explanation section of FRS 7 states that 'the fair value attributed to a surplus in a funded scheme would be determined taking into account not only the actuarial surplus of the fund, but also the extent to which the surplus could be realised in cash terms, by way of reduction of future contributions or otherwise, and the time-scale of such potential realisations',[98] but this still does not clarify the issue, because it introduces a vague test of recoverability that has no equivalent in SSAP 24 itself. It further states that 'a pension asset ... would be recognised only insofar as the acquired entity or the acquirer was able to benefit from the existing surplus',[99] but it remains unclear in what circumstances the acquired entity or acquirer will not benefit from such a surplus.

FRS 7 says that changes in pension or other post-retirement arrangements following an acquisition should be accounted for as post-acquisition items.[100] An example is the cost of improvements to benefits granted to members of an acquired scheme as part of harmonising remuneration packages in the enlarged group. This is consistent with accounting for any changes affecting the pension arrangements of the acquirer's own workforce. The cost of these changes should therefore be dealt with in accordance with SSAP 24 or UITF 6 by being spread forward over average service lives.

One company which has made an adjustment to incorporate a pension surplus is BICC, as shown below:

Extract 6.23: BICC plc (1996)

19   Acquisitions [extract]

	Consideration and costs £m	Fair value of assets acquired £m	Goodwill £m
British Rail Infrastructure companies	53	30	23
BTCC Phillips Inc minority interest	7	1	6
	60	31	29

On 3 April 1996 the Group acquired three British Rail Infrastructure companies The total consideration including expenses was £33m of which £32m was paid on completion. On 29 March 1996 the Group acquired the outstanding minority interest in its Canadian subsidiary BICC Phillips Inc for £7m. The Group has used acquisition accounting to account for these purchases. Adjustments have been made to reflect the fair value of assets of the British Rail Infrastructure companies acquired as follows:

	Net tangible assets acquired £m	Fair value adjustments £m	Fair value of assets acquired £m
Fixed assets	16	–	16
Stocks	8	–	8
Debtors	79	31	110
Creditors	(70)	–	(70)
Provisions, including deferred taxation	(2)	(20)	(22)
Net borrowings	(12)	–	(12)
	19	11	30

Fair value adjustments, which include, principally, recognition of the pension fund surplus, related deferred taxation and provisions for known liabilities, are provisional estimates which will be revised if necessary in 1997.

Other examples are shown in Extracts 6.11 and 6.13 above. Interestingly, Scottish Television has included the adjustment as part of the book values rather than as a fair value adjustment.

One company which does not appear to have made any fair value adjustment in respect of a pension surplus is United Utilities. No reference is made to pensions in the discussion of fair value adjustments yet the pensions note discloses the following:

Extract 6.24: United Utilities PLC (1996)

23   Pensions [extract]

Most employees of NORWEB plc who joined prior to 1 October 1991 are members of the ESPS, a defined benefit scheme. This scheme is now closed to new employees.

The latest full actuarial valuation of NORWEB's section of the ESPS was carried out by Bacon & Woodrow, consulting actuaries, as at 31 March 1995. The attained age method was used for the valuation and the principal actuarial assumptions adopted for average annual growth rates were investment returns 9 per cent, salary increases (exclusive of merit awards) 6.5 per cent and pensions increases 5 per cent.

The total market value of NORWEB's share of the net assets of the ESPS at 31 March 1995 was £662.3 million.

The valuation showed that the actuarial value of the assets of NORWEB's section of the ESPS as at 31 March 1995 represented 112.8 per cent of the actuarial value of the accrued benefits. This is within the statutory maximum. The accrued benefits include all benefits for pensioners and other former members as well as benefits based on service completed to date for active members, allowing for future salary rises. In deriving the pension cost, the surplus remaining after benefit improvements is being spread over the future working lifetime of the members.

It would seem from the above that there may have been a pension surplus at the date of acquisition. Although the fair values in respect of Norweb were reassessed in the following year, pensions was not one of the areas adjusted.[101]

Examples of companies making an adjustment to reflect a pension deficit or actuarial liability re other post-retirement benefits are shown in Extracts 6.12 and 6.17 above.

E   Taxation

FRS 7 says that deferred tax assets and liabilities recognised in the fair value exercise should be determined by considering the enlarged group as a whole.[102]

Although no specific guidance is given by the standard, the recognition of deferred tax in the context of a fair value exercise falls into two areas. First of all there will be existing timing differences within the acquired company which will give rise to a potential liability to deferred tax which will need to be considered. In addition, the adjustments made as a result of the fair value exercise may lead to quasi-timing differences which will also require provision for deferred tax. The difference between the fair values assigned and the tax base values of the assets and liabilities acquired are in fact not strictly timing differences within the SSAP 15 definition; however, differences between accounting profits and taxable profits will arise in subsequent periods as items pass through the profit and loss account and therefore it is necessary to treat them as such in order to avoid distorting post-acquisition earnings. Arguably, however, not all fair value adjustments are to be regarded as timing differences; as FRED 7 proposed, it is only those that would be timing differences under SSAP 15 if reflected in the accounts of the acquired company.

Although not specifically addressed by FRS 7, where assets or liabilities are recognised in respect of pension schemes and post-retirement benefits, then the deferred tax implications should be accounted for in accordance with SSAP 15 (as amended in December 1992) - see Chapter 21 at 1.2.6. This should obviously be based on the accounting policy of the acquirer for such differences. One company which has made full provision in respect of the tax implications of incorporating a pension surplus as part of the fair value exercise is Premier Farnell, as shown in Extract 6.17.

The standard also requires that the benefit to the group of any tax losses attributable to an acquired entity at the date of acquisition should be recognised in accordance with the requirements of SSAP 15.[103] Again, application of this principle may result in deferred tax assets being recognised on acquisition that were previously unrecognised in the acquired company's accounts because SSAP 15 did not allow it. One company which has made a fair value adjustment to reflect a deferred tax asset in respect of losses is Persimmon, as shown in Extract 6.16.

It can be seen that FRS 7 requires that the deferred tax to be recognised should be determined on an overall group basis; similarly, losses can be recognised if they benefit the group. This seems to be at odds with the standard's general approach that assets and liabilities recognised as part of the fair value exercise should not reflect increases or decreases resulting from the acquirer's intentions for future actions. The ASB's Discussion Paper had proposed an approach for deferred tax which did not take account of the acquirer's different plans for capital expenditure or post-acquisition group relief arrangements, but reflected only the acquired company's plans etc. However, the ASB has recognised that it would be extremely difficult, if not impossible, for such an approach to work in practice. The partial provision approach of SSAP 15 has to be based on future intentions and these can only be those of the reporting entity, therefore it has to be done on an overall group basis.

F   Provisions

The most significant impact of FRS 7 has been on the area of provisions, particularly reorganisation or rationalisation provisions and provisions for future trading losses of the acquired companies.

■   Reorganisation or rationalisation provisions

As indicated at 2.4.1 B above, FRS 7 states that the assets and liabilities that are to be fair valued are to be those of the acquired company and should not include 'provisions or accruals … for reorganisation and integration costs expected to be incurred as a result of the acquisition, whether they relate to the acquired entity or to the acquirer'.[104] Only if the acquired entity was already committed to the course of action in question, and unable realistically to withdraw from it would it be regarded as pre-acquisition.

In practice this had been one of the areas of fair value accounting which prior to FRS 7 had given rise to a great deal of controversy, and alleged abuse. The ability to provide for costs of reorganisation programmes without having to charge these costs in the profit and loss account is a very attractive opportunity, and one which has understandably tempted some companies to be enthusiastic in their estimation of these provisions.

Clearly, the ASB has adopted a restrictive approach, with the costs of any such reorganisations or rationalisation being treated as post-acquisition costs. By doing this the ASB has really only moved the goalposts, because although provisions for such costs can no longer bypass the profit and loss account as part of the goodwill calculation, such one-off provisions are still made but highlighted in the profit and loss account as exceptional items (see Extract 6.42 below). The ASB is trying to address such big bath provisions by developing a standard on provisions and contingencies (see Chapter 26 at 3.2). The disclosure requirements of FRS 6 in respect of such items are discussed at 2.8.2 below.

It might be thought that it is possible to get around the FRS 7 rules by getting the vendor to commit itself, prior to the formal acquisition date, to a particular course of action to reorganise or restructure the business so that the costs can be regarded as being pre-acquisition costs. However, the standard emphasises that where provisions for future costs were made by the acquired company shortly before the acquisition took place, particular attention has to be paid to the circumstances in order to determine whether obligations were incurred by the acquired company before the acquisition. Only if the acquired company was demonstrably committed to the expenditure whether or not the acquisition was completed would it have a liability at the date of acquisition. If obligations were incurred as a result of the influence of the acquirer, it would be necessary to consider whether control had passed to the acquirer at an earlier date and, consequently, whether the date of acquisition pre-dated such commitments.[105] The ASB's earlier Discussion Paper had, in fact, proposed an anti-avoidance measure whereby decisions taken before the date of acquisition either at the request of, or during negotiations with, the acquirer would be deemed to be post-acquisition.[106] These proposals were not well supported, so the standard does not include such prescriptive anti-avoidance measures.

The only situation where a high level of commitment to the proposed expenditures need not be demonstrated is where the provisions were made outside the context of the acquisition process. In this case they should not be excluded from the fair value exercise – they can reasonably be said to be liabilities of the acquired entity (at least under current accounting standards - see Chapter 26 at 3.2 for a discussion of the ASB's proposals in this area). That this possibility is entertained by the standard is clear from the disclosure required of those reorganisation provisions included in the liabilities of the acquired entity made in the twelve months up to the date of acquisition (see 2.8.2 below).

In general, however, for reorganisation provisions to be accepted as part of the fair value exercise, a very high standard of prior commitment to the expenditure has to be demonstrated.

Examples of companies who have reflected pre-acquisition reorganisation provisions as part of the book values of the net assets acquired without making any adjustments thereto are Kingfisher and Wace Group, as shown in Extracts 6.15 and 6.13. In the former example, the note discloses that a further post-acquisition provision has been charged to the profit and loss account. Extract 6.26 below shows an example of a company making a fair value adjustment to an existing pre-acquisition reorganisation provision. However, there were also further reorganisation costs in respect of the acquisition charged to the profit and loss account.

■   Provisions for future operating losses

For the same reasons as for reorganisation provisions, FRS 7 requires that the assets and liabilities that are to be fair valued are to be those of the acquired company and should not include provisions for future operating losses.[107] The future trading results of the subsidiary do not represent one of its identifiable assets or liabilities, and they must be consolidated with those of the rest of the group from the date of acquisition. Thus the effect on the acquisition price of whatever future results were anticipated will fall to be dealt with as part of goodwill, positive or negative.

■   Other provisions

Although FRS 7 takes a restrictive view in setting up provisions for reorganisation costs or for future losses, this does not mean that it does not allow any provisions to be set up as part of the fair value exercise. An acquired company may have certain commitments which are not reflected as liabilities in its own accounts which nevertheless should form part of the identifiable liabilities to be recognised as part of the acquisition. Paragraph 38 of the standard states that 'identifiable liabilities include items such as onerous contracts and commitments that existed at the time of acquisition, whether or not the corresponding obligations were recognised as liabilities in the financial statements of the acquired entity'.

It is clear that the possibility under the FRS of recognising as liabilities of the acquired entity such items as onerous contracts and commitments, and thus bringing them into the fair value exercise, will provide some scope for reflecting the affairs of an acquired company more fully than if the fair value exercise were limited to items just recognised by the acquired company. FRS 7 does not define what it regards as an onerous contract, nor does it give any examples. FRED 14 – *Provisions and contingencies* – proposes to define an onerous contract as 'a contract entered into with another party under which the unavoidable costs of fulfilling the terms of the contract exceed any revenues expected to be received from the goods or services supplied or purchased directly or indirectly under the contract and where the entity would have to compensate the other party if it did not fulfil the terms of the contract'.[108] The only example of an onerous contract quoted in FRED 14 is vacant leasehold property. An example of a company making provision in respect of vacant properties as part of the fair value exercise is Johnston Press, as shown in Extract 6.10 above.

Some might argue that examples of onerous contracts could include leases at an unfavourable rental or for an excessive amount of space; and contracts to provide services in an area of business which is unprofitable. It has been argued by some commentators that provision for leases, the rentals for which at the date of acquisition are above present market rents, should not be made as part of the fair value exercise. This is because under SSAP 21 such operating leases are not reflected as liabilities.[109] However, the counter argument to this is that FRS 7 requires fair value adjustments to be made for other items such as contingencies and pensions which would not otherwise be allowed by the relevant accounting standards in these areas (see C and D above). Also, much of the guidance in other areas in the standard require fair values to be based on market conditions at the acquisition date. In our view such leases can be regarded as onerous leases and provision made for the excess over market rates.

An interesting example of a company making provision for onerous contracts is United Utilities in respect of its acquisition of Norweb, as shown below:

Extract 6.25: United Utilities PLC (1996)

Financial review [extract]

Acquisition of Norweb [extract]

Provision was made for gas and electricity contracts of £173.2 million mainly in relation to long term power purchase agreements, where the recent collapse in gas prices and reduced capacity costs resulted in onerous conditions compared to prices available in November 1995, the date the fair valuation was made. The provisions are of a long term nature and, in any event, will not be utilised prior to 1998. Also included is a small element relating to short term take or pay gas purchase contracts.

The fair value adjustments will be reviewed again during the course of 1996/97 and amended as necessary in the light of subsequent events.

This seems to suggest that the contracts only became onerous after the acquisition in which case it is questionable as to whether such an adjustment should have been made. As can be seen from the above extract, the fair value adjustments were to be reviewed the following year and although subsequent adjustments were made, none of them related to these contracts.[110]

Other examples of companies making provisions for onerous contracts are shown in Extracts 6.11 and 6.16 above.

One company which has made significant fair value adjustments to reflect various provisions is Rentokil Initial in respect of its acquisition of BET, as can be seen from the following extract:

Extract 6.26: Rentokil Initial plc (1996)

29   Acquisitions [extract]

The group purchased 15 companies and businesses during the year as set out on page 63 for a total consideration of £2,230.3m of which £2,221.7m was in respect of the acquisition on 29th April 1996 of BET Public Limited Company. The total adjustments required to the balance sheet figures of companies and businesses acquired in order to present the net assets of those companies and businesses at fair values in accordance with group accounting principles were £260.8m, of which £259.7m related to BET, details of which are set out on pages 58 and 59 together with the matching adjustment to goodwill. All of these businesses have been accounted for as acquisitions.

BET acquisition

	Book value	Revaluations	Consistency of accounting policy	Other	Fair value
	£m	£m	£m	£m	£m
Tangible fixed assets	609.2	(24.1)	(22.9)	–	562.2
Investments	33.0	(3.4)	(18.3)	(1.0)	10.3
Stock	35.0	(3.3)	–	–	31.7
Debtors	372.5	12.4	(0.6)	–	384.3
Creditors	(472.1)	(61.4)	(6.0)	–	(539.5)
Provisions					
– Vacant property	(20.7)	–	–	(47.5)	(68.2)
– Environmental	(4.4)	–	–	(49.9)	(54.3)
– Subsidiary	–	–	–	(33.0)	(33.0)
– Pre-acquisition restructuring	(1.8)	–	–	(5.0)	(6.8)
Taxation	(108.2)	3.5	–	–	(104.7)
Net debt	(130.5)	–	–	–	(130.5)
	312.0	(76.3)	(47.8)	(136.4)	51.5
Minority interests	(1.7)	0.8	–	–	(0.9)
Net assets acquired	310.3	(75.5)	(47.8)	(136.4)	50.6
Special dividend to BET shareholders					38.2
Adjusted assets					88.8
Goodwill					2,132.9
Consideration					2,221.7

Satisfied by	
Shares issued	1,653.2
Cash (including special dividend paid of £38.2m and deducting cash received from exercise of share options of £18.0m)	568.5
	2,221.7

The book values of the assets and liabilities shown on page 58 have been taken from the management accounts of BET at the date of acquisition (at actual exchange rates at that date). The fair value adjustments set out on page 58 are provisional figures which will be finalised in the 1997 financial statements following professional property valuations as at the date of acquisition and on final review of judgemental areas.

Revaluation adjustments in respect of tangible fixed assets comprise the revaluation of certain freehold properties and the write-off of obsolete or impaired plant and machinery and fixtures and fittings.

Revaluations of investments and stock reflect the write-down to estimated realisable value. The adjustment to debtors includes establishing an asset (£16.9m) to reflect the pension fund surplus arising from actuarial valuations, offset by various write-downs to reflect estimated realisable value.

The revaluations of creditors relate to liabilities which were not fully reflected in the balance sheet of BET's business on acquisition. These include adjustments to provisions for insurance claims, liabilities under onerous contracts and the reassessment of legal claims. An adjustment of £5.6m has been made in order to reflect a market coupon on the BET US $ bond.

A net deferred tax asset of £10.7m for expected tax relief on fair value adjustments has been recognised partially offset by tax liabilities of £7.2m.

The book values acquired included provisions for reorganisation and restructuring costs amounting to £1.8m. These provisions related to reorganisations established by BET in the year prior to acquisition, which were reviewed and increased by £5.0m. This increase relates to irrevocable reorganisations commenced by BET management before the acquisition.

The fair value adjustments for alignment of accounting policies reflect the restatement of assets and liabilities in accordance with the policies of the group including the removal of capitalised security alarm installation costs (£14.3m), the write-off of capitalised container and vehicle refurbishment costs in distribution companies, provision for the group's share of deferred consideration payable by an associated company for the acquisition of a business (£18.3m), provision for outstanding holiday pay entitlements of employees and the alignment of general bad debt provisioning policy.

Additional provision has also been made for vacant property costs relating to future net rental outgoings of the substantial number of vacant and sub-let properties owned and leased by BET. Environmental provisions were also made for the estimated costs of remediation on BET sites. Provision has also been made for major regulatory and taxation problems in a subsidiary.

It can be seen from the above that most of the provisions made by Rentokil Initial are not to reflect new liabilities, but are reassessments of provisions and creditors which were already recorded within the books of BET. It will be interesting to see when these provisional fair values are reviewed in 1997 as to whether the company has been over-enthusiastic in making these provisions.

G   *Businesses held exclusively with a view to subsequent resale*

This is another area where the detailed rules of the standard seem to be at odds with its general approach that the fair value exercise should not reflect the acquirer's intentions for future actions. It requires that 'where an interest in a separate business of the acquired entity is sold as a single unit within approximately one year of the date of acquisition, the investment in that business should be treated as a single asset for the purposes of determining fair values. Its fair value should be based on the net proceeds of the sale, adjusted for the fair value of any assets or liabilities transferred into or out of the business, unless such adjusted net proceeds are demonstrably different from the fair value at the date of acquisition as a result of a post-acquisition event. This treatment should be applied to any business operation, whether a separate subsidiary undertaking or not, provided that its assets, liabilities, results of operations and activities are clearly distinguishable, physically, operationally and for financial reporting purposes, from the other assets, liabilities, results of operations and activities of the acquired entity.'[111]

Where the business has not yet been sold by the time of approval of the first set of accounts after the date of acquisition, the fair value of the interest in the business is based on the estimated net proceeds of sale and carried as a current asset, provided that:

'(a)   a purchaser has been identified or is being sought; and

(b)   the disposal is reasonably expected to occur within approximately one year of the date of acquisition.'[112]

This is based on the requirement of FRS 2, that a subsidiary which is reasonably expected to be disposed of with approximately one year of acquisition is to be included in the consolidated balance sheet as a current asset at the lower of cost and net realisable value; its results and assets and liabilities should not be consolidated (see 5.4 of Chapter 5). However, the principle has been extended to other business operations that are not subsidiaries.

The fair value to be attributed will normally be the actual realised amount as this is considered to be the most reliable evidence of fair value at the date of acquisition (or if the sale has not yet been completed, at the estimated sales proceeds). The net proceeds, which should take into account any costs of disposal (including incremental costs such as professional fees), should be discounted to obtain the net present value at date of acquisition, if material.[113]

This appears inconsistent with the general approach of FRS 7, as it depends on the acquirer's intentions for the business operation. However, in an appendix to FRED 7 the ASB said that it 'rejects that interpretation because it believes that the resale value of a business in an arm's length transaction would normally provide the most reliable evidence of its fair value, and should be used unless specific post-acquisition events occur during the holding period that require a profit or loss on disposal to be recorded'.[114]

The overall objective is therefore to produce a neutral impact on the group's results (apart from any interest effect, if discounting is applied). Accordingly, any initial estimate of fair value should normally be adjusted to actual net realised value within the period allowed for completing the investigation of fair values (see 2.4.4 below). However, it will be appropriate for a post-acquisition profit or loss on disposal to be recognised and for the fair values at acquisition to be different from the net realised value where:

(a)   the acquirer has made a material change to the acquired business before disposal;

(b)   specific post-acquisition events occur during the holding period that materially change the fair value of the business from the fair value estimated at the date of acquisition; or

(c)   the disposal is completed at a reduced price for a quick sale.[115]

One company which included businesses held for resale as part of the net assets acquired (and having provisionally revalued them upwards in the year of acquisition reduced the values the following year) was Reckitt & Colman, as illustrated in Extracts 6.39, 6.40 and 6.41 at 2.8.2 below.

2.4.4   *Subsequent amendments to fair value*

FRS 7 says that the fair value exercise should be completed, if possible, by the date on which the first post-acquisition accounts of the acquirer are approved by the directors, although if this is not possible, a provisional allocation of fair values is allowed which must be finalised in the next year (see 2.4.2 above). Otherwise, the only circumstances in which a retrospective adjustment to the goodwill calculation could be regarded as appropriate would be if the original allocation was regarded as a fundamental error which required to be dealt with as a prior year adjustment under FRS 3. This would probably be the case only if the original allocation was based on a complete misinterpretation of the facts which were available at the time; it would not apply simply because new information had come to light which changed the acquiring management's view of the value of the item in question.

2.4.5   *'Push-down accounting'*

The term 'push-down accounting' relates to the practice of incorporating, or 'pushing-down', the fair value adjustments which have been made by the acquiring company into the financial statements of the acquired subsidiary, including the goodwill arising on the acquisition. Such a practice is used in the US, where it has been required in certain situations by the Securities and Exchange Commission.[116] It is argued that the acquisition, being an independently bargained transaction, provides better evidence of the values of the assets and liabilities of the subsidiary than those previously contained within its financial statements, and therefore represents an improved basis of accounting.

There are, however, contrary views, which hold that the transaction in question was one to which the reporting entity was not a party, and there is no reason why it should intrude into the entity's own accounting records.

Whatever the theoretical arguments, it is certainly true that push-down accounting can be an expedient practice, because it obviates the need to make extensive consolidation adjustments in each subsequent year, based on parallel accounting records. But in fact most of the adjustments which push-down accounting would entail would fall foul of the Companies Act valuation rules or of other accounting standards. It is possible, by using the alternative valuation rules, to revalue fixed assets directly in the subsidiary's financial statements, and where this constitutes a major part of the fair value adjustments then this can be a worthwhile move; however, most of the other adjustments discussed in 2.4.3 above could not be made directly in the subsidiary's financial statements.

2.5 Acquisitions: accounting for goodwill

2.5.1 Introduction

Once the fair values of both the consideration given and the net assets acquired have been measured, the difference between the two represents purchased goodwill which remains to be accounted for. How to account for it is a subject on which widely differing opinions are held, and this is evidenced both by the time which it originally took the ASC to develop a standard on the subject and by the fact that the eventual standard permitted a choice between two alternative methods: amortisation through the profit and loss account and immediate write-off direct to reserves. (The ASC subsequently changed its stance and issued an exposure draft which proposed to eliminate such a choice, as discussed below.)

The choice between these (and other) treatments depends to some extent on what goodwill is perceived to be in the first place. Some view it as an asset like any other, which has been acquired at a cost, and which needs to be accounted for in the same way as any other asset. The other main camp is occupied by those who do not regard goodwill as a real asset in the first place, but more in the nature of a consolidation difference which emerges as part of the accounting process and has to be dealt with in the least damaging manner possible. This divergence of view underlies much of the disagreement about the treatment of goodwill when it arises.

Those people who view goodwill as an asset say that it has been acquired at a cost, and, as would be done in the case of any other asset, this cost should be capitalised initially in the balance sheet, and charged to revenue over its economic life. At this point, the next divergence of view arises, because the fact that it is both intangible and not separately identifiable means that its economic life is very difficult if not impossible to determine.

Some people respond to this difficulty by taking the view that goodwill does not necessarily have a finite life at all and therefore should not be written off until there is evidence that its value has been impaired. They would maintain that any period of amortisation would be completely arbitrary. Others would take the view that such an approach would be impracticable because it is impossible to detect falls in value of the original goodwill other than in fairly extreme circumstances; they would therefore support the amortisation approach as the most practical way of eliminating the asset from the financial statements on a systematic basis, even if the choice of amortisation period is difficult to determine.

Those who do not regard goodwill as a real asset in the first place tend to favour eliminating goodwill directly against reserves in the year of acquisition. They would say that the financial statements should deal solely with identifiable items which arise from an acquisition; to try to deal with goodwill using normal accounting principles would be a futile attempt to account for the unaccountable. Goodwill in their eyes is simply a product of the accounting process and should be eliminated by an accounting entry, not reported as the consumption of an identifiable resource.

The ASB in developing its own proposals for goodwill has dispensed with these traditional views of goodwill and has decided that purchased goodwill is neither an asset nor is it an immediate loss in value, but is a bridge between the cost of the investment shown as an asset in the acquirer's own balance sheet and the identifiable assets and liabilities reflected in its consolidated balance sheet.[117] It is finalising a standard that builds on that premise (see B below)

A   The development of SSAP 22

The ASC first considered this matter in a Discussion Paper published in 1980.[118] This adopted the view that goodwill was an asset, rather than simply a consolidation difference and should be accounted for as such. It recommended that it should be carried as a fixed asset in the balance sheet and subjected to annual amortisation, and written down to its recoverable amount to recognise any permanent impairment in value which became evident. It rejected the notion that it could be carried as a permanent asset, without amortisation. (This had already been ruled out by the EC Fourth Directive, and subsequently by the EC Seventh Directive.)

Two years later, however, when the Committee issued an exposure draft (ED 30) on the subject, it had retreated from the attempt to mandate a single treatment; either amortisation through the profit and loss account or immediate elimination through reserves was to be permitted, provided the policy was applied consistently.[119] This choice was maintained in the eventual accounting standard, SSAP 22, which was issued at the end of 1984, but by now the direct write-off treatment had become the preferred one.[120]

As well as permitting two different treatments, which are based on different philosophical views on the nature of goodwill, SSAP 22 (unlike ED 30) even allows the same company to choose between the different methods to be applied in relation to different acquisitions. One company which adopts such a policy is Chloride Group, as shown below:

> *Extract 6.27: Chloride Group PLC (1997)*
>
> **Goodwill**
>
> The treatment of goodwill arising on consolidation (representing the excess of the fair value of the consideration given over the fair value of the separable net assets acquired) depends on the circumstances surrounding each individual acquisition. Goodwill is either written off directly against reserves, or alternatively, is capitalised and amortised over an appropriate period.

There have also been instances of companies who have started accounting for goodwill under one policy and changed to the alternative policy soon thereafter; most commonly this involves changing from amortisation to direct write-off (perhaps after adequate reserves have been built up to absorb the write-off), but there have been some instances of companies who have moved in the opposite direction.

This extreme form of flexibility of approach has led to substantial criticism of the standard, whose only real effect has therefore been to outlaw the practice of carrying goodwill as a permanent asset without amortisation, and some would say that even this consequence can be avoided by assigning value to some other form of intangible asset rather than goodwill, as discussed at 2.4.3 A above, and contending that it has an infinite life and need not be amortised.

B   *Proposals to amend SSAP 22*

(a)   ED 47

In view of the criticism received, the ASC reconsidered its stance in relation to goodwill and issued ED 47 – *Accounting for goodwill* – which proposed that goodwill should be recognised as a fixed asset and should be amortised through the profit and loss account; the option of writing it off immediately to reserves was not to be allowed. The ASC had therefore turned full circle since issuing its initial views on the matter in the Discussion Paper published in 1980.

ED 47 met with widespread disapproval, particularly from preparers of financial statements, the main objection being that in many cases management spent heavily to maintain and enhance the value of goodwill. Companies, therefore, did not believe it appropriate to be forced to make an annual amortisation charge in those cases where the value of goodwill had not been reduced but had been maintained or even increased. However, the existing option of writing goodwill off immediately against reserves also attracted criticism.

There was clear support from preparers of financial statements for a method whereby purchased goodwill is capitalised, but is not subject to automatic annual amortisation charges, although an annual review for impairment would be necessary.

(b)   ASB Discussion Paper

In December 1993 the ASB published a Discussion Paper – *Goodwill and intangible assets* – which suggested six possible approaches to accounting for goodwill, classified between two main categories based on either capitalisation or elimination in reserves. These were as follows:[121]

(i)   Capitalisation and predetermined life amortisation

Purchased goodwill is capitalised, then amortised over a predetermined finite life subject to a maximum of, for instance, 20 years. Its amortised carrying value is assessed each year for recoverability.

(ii)   Capitalisation and annual review

Purchased goodwill is capitalised, then written down through the application of systematic annual review procedures to estimate the required annual amortisation charges. There may be years when the annual charge is zero.

(iii) Combination of (i) and (ii) above

(i) would be the method used for most acquisitions, but (ii) should be used for those special circumstances where the goodwill has an indeterminate life expected to be greater than 20 years.

(iv)   Immediate write-off reserve

Purchased goodwill is eliminated against reserves immediately on acquisition.

(v)   Separate write-off reserve

Purchased goodwill is transferred to a separate goodwill write-off reserve immediately on acquisition and carried in the balance sheet as a 'dangling debit'.

(vi)   Variant of (v): Separate write-off reserve with recoverability assessment

Purchased goodwill is transferred to a separate goodwill write-off reserve immediately on acquisition and the balance in this reserve is assessed for recoverability at each year-end. Losses reducing the recoverable amount below the balance in the write-off reserve are charged to the profit and loss account.

The paper discussed the rationale, related conceptual issues, practical advantages and disadvantages of each of these methods.[122] However, the ASB had not yet reached a consensus on the appropriate method to use, although two of the possible approaches did have support amongst members of the ASB.[123] These were:

■   Capitalise and amortise (maximum life of 20 years) unless purchased goodwill has an indeterminate life believed to be greater than 20 years, in which case it would be capitalised and subjected to a rigorous annual review to determine whether the amount had diminished (i.e. method (iii) above); and

- Eliminate immediately on acquisition by transfer to a separate reserve which would be included in the balance sheet after striking a sub-total of all other items in shareholders' funds. There would be no further accounting for this balance except on disposal or closure of the related business (i.e. method (v) above).

As was probably to be expected no overall consensus emerged in the responses to the Discussion Paper. The most favoured individual option was the second approach supported by ASB members, but more commentators preferred one of the capitalisation methods. Accordingly, the ASB developed proposals based on the first approach supported by members of the ASB.

In June 1995 a Working Paper was issued for subsequent debate at a public hearing held later that year.[124] These proposals received broad support from the majority of respondents to the Working Paper, although a significant minority were against them. As a result, the ASB issued FRED 12 – *Goodwill and intangible assets* – a year later in June 1996.

(c) FRED 12

As indicated earlier, the ASB has decided that purchased goodwill is neither an asset nor is it an immediate loss in value, but has rationalised its proposals by saying that it is a bridge between the cost of the investment shown as an asset in the acquirer's own balance sheet and the identifiable assets and liabilities reflected in its consolidated balance sheet.

FRED 12 proposes the following treatment in respect of goodwill:

- Positive purchased goodwill is to capitalised and classified as an asset on the balance sheet (notwithstanding the fact that the ASB has said it is not an asset).[125] As with SSAP 22, internally generated goodwill is not allowed to be recognised.[126]

- Negative goodwill is also to be recognised on the balance sheet, immediately below positive goodwill.[127] The ASB's Working Paper had not discussed the topic of negative goodwill and in our view the proposal borders on the absurd; our preference would be for it to be shown as a deferred credit in the balance sheet.

- Positive goodwill is to be amortised systematically over its useful life where this is believed to be less than twenty years or when its value is not capable of continued measurement in future.[128] It establishes a rebuttable presumption that the useful life of goodwill is limited and does not exceed 20 years, and requires 'valid and disclosed grounds' where this presumption is rebutted.[129] A straight-line method of amortisation should be used unless another method can be demonstrated to be more appropriate.[130] It is thought unlikely that a less conservative method than straight-line will be justifiable. It is also stated that methods that aim to produce a constant rate of return, such as the 'reverse sum of the digits' method are not appropriate for amortising goodwill.[131] In amortising goodwill no residual value is to be assumed.[132]

■ Positive goodwill which is considered to have a useful life in excess of 20 years and whose value is expected to be capable of reliable measurement in future, is to be amortised over its economic life, but will be subject to detailed annual impairment tests.[133]

■ Positive goodwill is not to be amortised if its useful life is indefinite and its value is expected to be capable of reliable measurement in future, but will be subject to detailed impairment tests.[134] As the Companies Act requires goodwill to be amortised, the 'true and fair override' provisions would need to be invoked to justify non-amortisation and therefore disclosures under UITF Abstract 7 – *True and fair view override disclosures* – would be necessary.

■ Negative goodwill is not to be amortised but is to be written back through the statement of total recognised gains and losses as the difference between the value of the investment and the values of the identified net assets diminishes.[135] Negative goodwill would only be taken to the profit and loss to the extent that there is any remaining balance when the investment to which it relates is sold (see 3.3 below).[136] We are not convinced that the ASB has made a sufficiently convincing case for this lack of symmetry between positive and negative goodwill.

■ Positive goodwill which is not being amortised or which is being amortised over a period in excess of 20 years is to be subject to an annual impairment test, comprising a comparison of the carrying value of the goodwill and its recoverable amount, being its value in use.[137] Other positive goodwill is also to be subject to the same test but only:

(i) at the end of the first full financial year following the acquisition; and

(ii) in subsequent periods if there are indications of impairment.[138]

Since introducing this impairment test within FRED 12, the ASB had proposed a similar test for tangible fixed assets in its Discussion Paper – *Impairment of tangible fixed assets* – issued in April 1996 and as the process is essentially the same has now proposed to set out the requirements in a single standard. Accordingly, FRED 15 – *Impairment of fixed assets and goodwill*– which was issued in June 1997, embraces goodwill (and intangibles). The FRED 15 impairment test (which is virtually unchanged from the FRED 12 proposal) is discussed at 4.4 of Chapter 10. If a standard on goodwill comes out before a standard based on FRED 15 then it will contain rules for impairment reviews which will be withdrawn once the impairment standard is published.[139]

The exposure draft also proposes numerous disclosures, most of which relate to the fact that the goodwill is being capitalised as an asset, which is subject to amortisation and impairment rules.

FRED 12 proposes transitional arrangements whereby the accounting practices discussed above are to apply only to goodwill first accounted for in accounting periods beginning on or after a certain date or to goodwill previously capitalised in earlier periods. Goodwill which has been written off to reserves under SSAP 22 will not need to be resurrected as an asset and will be subject to the existing disclosure requirements for goodwill.[140]

2.5.2 *Immediate write-off: which reserve?*

Until the ASB develops a revised standard, the rules in SSAP 22 apply; consequently, companies have the option to write off goodwill directly to reserves. However, SSAP 22 does not specify which reserve should be the destination of goodwill write-offs, and a variety of practice has grown up, perhaps founded more on expediency than on any principle. The debate is complicated by the fact that, while the classification of reserves in a *company* balance sheet has particular legal significance because of the rules on distributions, this is not true in relation to the reserves in a *group* balance sheet; however, some of the arguments which have developed on the issue have not always recognised this fact. The more common possibilities are discussed below.

A   Profit and loss account

This is the most straightforward option, and has been quite widely used in practice. It can also be seen as the most conservative, since it has the greatest impact on the group's apparent ability or intention to make distributions, but as described above, this effect is more cosmetic than real because distributions are determined by the reserves of individual companies, not groups.

B   Capital reserve

There is no statutory requirement to maintain such a reserve (unlike 'capital redemption reserve', which is discussed at F below), but in fact this category is used voluntarily in a wide range of circumstances, not all of them either rational or systematically and consistently applied. Where such a reserve exists, however, it intuitively seems a natural home for charging goodwill which has arisen on what is perceived to be a 'capital' transaction.

Sometimes, the capital reserve will have arisen on other acquisition transactions in the form of 'negative goodwill' (which is discussed further at 2.5.5 below), and in this sense it will be consistent to take positive goodwill to the same place so that the balance on this reserve represents the total effect of charging and crediting goodwill directly to reserves. There is no prohibition in SSAP 22 in netting off these items in reserves. However, it should be noted that if the amount of positive goodwill exceeds that of the negative goodwill, a debit balance on the reserve will arise and it will take on the character of a 'goodwill write-off reserve', which is discussed further at G below.

C   *Merger reserve*

Again, this term has no statutory meaning and there is no requirement to maintain such a classification. However, a practice has grown up of creating such a reserve in circumstances where share premium relief has been claimed on an issue of shares under section 131 of the Companies Act 1985, yet the shares issued have still been recorded at their fair value rather than their nominal value, generally because acquisition accounting is being used for the transaction in respect of which the shares were issued. In other words, it is a voluntarily created substitute for a share premium account where section 131 gives relief from the need to set up such an account, but unlike a share premium account it is not subject to statutory restrictions on its application or distribution. (This does not necessarily imply that it can be distributed, because it is arguable that the issue of shares at a premium does not give rise to a realised profit unless the consideration received on issue of the shares has been realised in a subsequent sale.) Even if the cost of the subsidiary is recorded in the acquiring company's balance sheet based on the nominal amount of the shares issued, it will still be necessary to create a merger reserve on consolidation; this is because SSAP 22 requires goodwill to be the difference between the fair value of the consideration given and the aggregate fair values of the net assets acquired.[141]

Since this reserve arises on an acquisition, it automatically becomes available as a possible home for writing off goodwill at the same time as the goodwill itself emerges, and it has been widely used for this purpose. However, there is no exact relationship between the quantum of goodwill and the amount available on this reserve, although the amounts which arise under each category will tend to be higher or lower as the general level of share prices rises or falls. This means that the reserve may not be large enough to absorb the amount of goodwill, and the directors will have to decide whether to leave a net debit balance on this reserve or to absorb the excess elsewhere.

An example of the use of such a reserve category is to be found in the 1993 accounts of Tomkins:

Extract 6.28: Tomkins PLC (1993)

19   RESERVES [extract]

The Group:	Share premium £ million	Merger reserve £ million	Capital reserve £ million	Profit & loss account £ million	Total £ million
At 2 May 1992	24.3	3.2	142.8	200.0	370.3
Retained profit for the year	–	–	–	43.4	43.4
Net premium on shares issued	50.1	–	–	–	50.1
Capitalisation issue	(14.1)	–	–	–	(14.1)
Premium on shares issued in part consideration	–	390.8	–	–	390.8
Net premium on loan stock issued	–	–	636.9	–	636.9
Goodwill written off	–	(394.0)	(352.4)	–	(746.4)
Foreign exchange translation	–	–	–	(2.3)	(2.3)
Scrip dividends	–	–	–	1.1	1.1
At 1 May 1993	**60.3**	**–**	**427.3**	**242.2**	**729.8**

It can be seen from the above extract that the merger reserve was insufficient to write off all of the goodwill and that Tomkins chose to write off the balance against capital reserve. Granada Group on the other hand decided to leave the resulting debit balance which assumes the appearance of a 'goodwill write-off reserve', as illustrated below:

Extract 6.29: Granada Group PLC (1996)

24   Reconciliation of movements in shareholders' funds [extract]

a Group	Share capital £m	Share premium £m	Revaluation reserve £m	Merger reserve £m	Profit and loss account £m	Total 1996 £m
Balance at 30 September 1995	163.6	163.3	139.5	(416.4)	533.7	583.7
Retained profit for period for equity shareholders	–	–	–	–	172.8	172.8
Other finance costs of non-equity shares	–	–	–	–	(1.2)	(1.2)
Adjustments in respect of shares for dividend scheme	–	–	–	–	6.8	6.8
Shares issued in the period (net)	67.4	4.7	–	1,845.2	–	1,917.3
Share issue costs	–	(85.5)	–	–	–	(85.5)
Currency adjustments	–	–	–	–	(8.5)	(8.5)
Net movement on goodwill	–	–	–	(1,563.0)	(34.6)	(1,597.6)
Transfers	–	–	23.8	–	(23.8)	–
At 28 September 1996	**231.0**	**82.5**	**163.3**	**(134.2)**	**645.2**	**987.8**

It is not only goodwill arising on the particular acquisition that has given rise to the merger reserve which can be written off against the reserve, but also goodwill on other acquisitions; indeed, British Gas in its 1989 financial statements transferred £29m of goodwill which arose in respect of a prior year acquisition from retained profits to a merger reserve arising on an acquisition in 1989, thereby eliminating the merger reserve.[142]

D   Revaluation reserve

Unlike the previous two categories, this is a statutory reserve and there are legal rules on how it may be reduced; these would appear to prohibit writing off goodwill to this reserve.

The Companies Act 1989 amended the rules contained in Schedule 4 to the Companies Act relating to revaluation reserves so that such reserves can only be reduced by way of capitalisation or 'to the extent that the amounts transferred to it are no longer necessary for the purposes of the valuation method used'.[143] The Act effectively extends these provisions to consolidated financial statements by requiring that 'group accounts shall comply so far as practicable with the provisions of ... Schedule 4 ... as if the undertakings included in the consolidation ("the group") were a single company'.[144] However, companies were not required to reinstate any previous reductions of the revaluation reserve as a result of having written off goodwill, even though such reductions were arguably illegal.[145] Nevertheless we consider that it is preferable for companies to reinstate the revaluation reserve.

One company which previously adopted the treatment of writing off goodwill against revaluation reserve was Grand Metropolitan and it reinstated the revaluation reserve, as shown in the following extract from its 1991 accounts:

Extract 6.30: Grand Metropolitan Public Limited Company (1991)

25   Reserves [extract]

	Share premium £m	Revaluation £m	Goodwill £m	Profit and loss £m	Total £m
At 30th September, 1990	451	1,253	(2,193)	3,382	2,893
Exchange adjustments	–	3	–	(18)	(15)
Retained profit for the year	–	–	–	214	214
Unrealised profit on sale of tenanted pub estate	–	–	–	23	23
Premiums on share issues, less expenses	70	–	–	–	70
Goodwill acquired during the year	–	–	(278)	–	(278)
Transfer of goodwill on disposal	–	–	235	(235)	–
Realisation of reserves on disposal	–	(395)	–	395	–
At 30th September, 1991	521	861	(2,236)	3,761	2,907

Reserves have been reclassified to identify goodwill arising on acquisitions. Goodwill is stated net of £426m of special reserve which, with shareholder and Court approval, was created in 1988 by a transfer from the share premium account. Aggregate goodwill written off, net of disposals, is £2,662m (1990 - £2,619m).

E   Share premium account

Again, this is a statutory reserve, and it is clear that it may not be used as a home for goodwill being written off. Nevertheless a practice has grown up of using this reserve indirectly by applying to the court for release of the reserve under the provisions of the Companies Act which deal with the reduction of capital. The effect of this is that the court may agree that the share premium account can be cancelled and another reserve substituted for it; the court will normally impose restrictions on the distributability of that new reserve, but will permit it to be used to absorb the goodwill write-off. As with some other reserves, the subsequent write-off can sometimes exceed the amount of the reserve created by the cancellation of the share premium account, and the remaining debit balance then assumes the appearance of the 'goodwill write-off reserve' discussed at G below. One such example is to be found in the 1987 financial statements of Blue Arrow:

Extract 6.31: Blue Arrow PLC (1987)

17   Reserves [extract]

The Group	Share premium account £000	Merger reserve £000	Capital reserve £000	Revaluation reserve £000	Profit and loss account £000
At 1 November 1986	28,669	–	–	830	5,315
Cancellation and reclassification	(28,669)	–	28,669	–	–
Premium on shares issued during the year	812,009	14,509	–	–	–
Expenses of issue	(33,042)	–	(8)	–	–
Retained profit for the year	–	–	–	–	13,480
Goodwill arising on consolidation written off	–	(14,509)	(856,256)	–	–
Currency exchange adjustments	–	–	–	(1,213)	–
At 31 October 1987	778,967	–	(827,595)	(383)	18,795

In accordance with the provisions of Section 131 of the Companies Act 1985, the Company has transferred to Merger Reserve the premium arising on the issue of shares as consideration for subsidiaries acquired during the year. The Group has applied this Merger Reserve to write down the goodwill arising on consolidation.

A Special Resolution was passed at an Extraordinary General Meeting of the Company held on 9 March 1987, whereby the whole amount then standing to the credit of the Company's Share Premium Account was cancelled and a capital reserve of an identical amount was created, against which goodwill arising on consolidation could be written off.

The confirmation of the Court was obtained in accordance with the Companies Act 1985 on 6 April 1987.

Total group reserves therefore showed a negative figure of some £30m, which, when set against share capital of £35m, reduced shareholders' funds to £5m. Subsequent to the year-end, the company once again applied to the court to have their new share premium account cancelled in order to allow most of the debit balance on capital reserve to be eliminated.

F   Capital redemption reserve

This, like share premium account, is a statutory reserve and is therefore subject to similar restrictions on its use; it may not be applied directly as a home for a goodwill write-off, although there seems no reason in principle why, as with share premium account, the company could not apply to the court to have its capital reduced and create a reserve against which goodwill could be offset by that means.

G   'Goodwill write-off reserve'

This term refers to a practice which some companies have applied, of simply setting up a new reserve category within shareholders' funds as the destination for goodwill write-offs, so that in effect the goodwill simply becomes a debit balance carried within equity. Some doubts have been expressed as to the propriety of such a move, but it does not seem to offend any particular legal provision, and indeed was one of the methods proposed in the ASB's Discussion Paper. It does, in fact, have the merit that it is evident from the disclosure how much goodwill has been charged to reserves (assuming no other reserves have been used), whereas under some of the other treatments discussed it is difficult to trace this after the year in which the write-off has been made.

One example of a negative goodwill reserve is shown below:

Extract 6.32: Guinness PLC (1996)

Group Balance Sheet [extract]

	Notes	1996 £m	1995 £m
EQUITY			
Capital and reserves			
Called up share capital	21(B)	483	506
Share premium account	21(B)	590	569
		1,073	1,075
Other reserves	22(A)	2,141	2,069
Goodwill	22(B)	(1,298)	(1,298)
Shareholders' funds		**4,152**	**4,286**
Minority interests		95	111
Total equity		**4,247**	**4,397**

T & S Stores also has a goodwill write-off reserve, but shows a sub-total of shareholders' funds before and after such reserve, as shown below:

Extract 6.33: T & S Stores Plc (1996)

Balance Sheets [extract]

	Notes	Group 1996 £'000	1995 £'000
CAPITAL AND RESERVES - EQUITY INTERESTS			
Called up share capital	17	**3,598**	3,257
Share premium account	18	**17,366**	6,229
Capital reserve	18	**47,700**	47,700
Profit and loss account	18	**47,112**	40,654
TOTAL SHAREHOLDERS' FUNDS			
BEFORE GOODWILL WRITE OFF		**115,776**	97,840
Goodwill written off	18	**(90,519)**	(78,339)
TOTAL SHAREHOLDERS' FUNDS	20	**26,102**	23,416

This presentation is very similar to treating the goodwill as a dangling debit.

H   Conclusion

In the present climate, therefore, there is a wide range of possible homes in which goodwill may be accommodated, and there appears to be no definite guiding principle that can be laid down which makes any one more appropriate than the others. Although the most straightforward treatment would be to use the profit and loss account balance, there is no particular reason why companies have to do so, and those who have large amounts of goodwill to dispose of may consider this to be an unattractive option.

2.5.3   Effect on realised profits of writing off goodwill

This subject is dealt with in Appendix 2 to SSAP 22, which starts by making it clear that the question is often irrelevant because the distribution rules in the Companies Act depend on profits realised in the financial statements of individual companies, not groups, whereas most goodwill is written off only on consolidation. Nevertheless, goodwill can also arise in the financial statements of a single company (for example, where it acquires an unincorporated business), so the question cannot be ignored.

The appendix acknowledges that the elimination of goodwill by the direct write-off approach leaves an unanswered question as to whether realised reserves have been diminished. There will be some circumstances when it is clear that the charge should be to realised reserves, such as when the value of the goodwill has been permanently impaired, but the appendix concludes that the mere decision to take goodwill to reserves does not imply that this has happened; the reason for taking it there is usually one of policy as to the exclusion of goodwill from the balance sheet, not to recognise that any loss has been suffered.

However, the appendix goes on to say that goodwill should not be regarded as having an infinite life, and that at some time its elimination must be regarded as having reflected a realised loss. It therefore suggests that, if the goodwill is originally written off against an unrealised reserve, it may be appropriate to make an annual transfer between that reserve and realised reserves to amortise the amount of the goodwill, thus simulating the effect on reserves which would have been achieved had the company followed a policy of amortisation in the profit and loss account.

Such a process necessarily involves taking a view on the economic life of the goodwill, and although this would have to have been taken anyway if a policy of amortisation in the profit and loss account had been followed, one of the reasons for using the reserve route in the first place is that such an estimate cannot readily be made. There is therefore a slight element of self-contradiction in the treatment.

An example of such a treatment can be found in the 1987 financial statements of Johnson Fry, as shown in the extract reproduced below. As the extract shows, the transfer has been made only in respect of the goodwill (described as 'Purchased goodwill') carried in the holding company's accounts (presumably for the reason mentioned above, that the matter is of no relevance in the context of the group reserves):

Extract 6.34: Johnson Fry PLC (1987)

20. Reserves [extract]

The movement on reserves during the year was as follows:

Group	Share premium £	Other reserves (arising on application of Section 131 Companies Act, 1985) £	Other reserves £	Retained profits £
Beginning of year	–	–	–	513,890
Retained earnings for the year	–	–	–	538,017
				1,051,907
Premium on allotments made:				
on placing	933,436	–	–	–
on acquisitions and investments	375,039	939,126	–	–
	1,308,475			
Costs of issue	(183,862)			
	1,124,613			
Applied on capitalisation:				
December 1986 (4:1)	(324,167)			
September 1987 (1:1)	(495,615)			
	(819,782)	–	–	–
Purchased goodwill:				
- written off	–	–	(230,000)	–
- amortisation	–	–	21,000	(21,000)
Goodwill eliminated on consolidation	–	(1,675,741)	–	–
End of year	£304,831	£(736,615)	£(209,000)	£1,030,907

Events may take place which mean that the amortisation period has to be varied, or the whole amount remaining in the unrealised reserve has to be transferred immediately. This would happen most obviously if the business to which the goodwill relates were to be sold, but it might also apply if it became clear that the value of the goodwill had been permanently impaired.

It should also be noted that in the case of a public company, writing off goodwill to reserves can have an impact on the company's distributable reserves even though it might have no impact on its realised reserves. This is because of the additional restriction on distributions for public companies which prevent their net assets from being reduced below the total of their share capital and non-distributable reserves.[146] The goodwill write-off will bring this restriction into consideration if it exceeds the company's unrealised profits and distributable reserves.

2.5.4   Amortisation

A   Period of amortisation

Where goodwill is to be amortised, it will be necessary to make an estimate of the useful economic life which is to be the basis of the charge. This is a particularly problematical decision, because the asset to be amortised may be regarded as unidentifiable in the first place[147] and it may therefore be impossible to determine when its life can be thought to have ended.

The Discussion Paper published by the ASC in 1980 recommended that goodwill should be amortised in the profit and loss account over a period based on the P/E ratio of the company acquired.[148] In the subsequent exposure draft, this suggestion was dropped, and reference was instead made to 'the number of years during which the acquiring company may reasonably foresee super-profits resulting from the purchased goodwill which exists at the time of purchase'.[149] It went on to say that this would suggest a relatively short period, such as 10 years or less, and recommended that in any event a maximum of 20 years should be imposed by the proposed standard. In fact, SSAP 22 does not lay down any definitive rule on the matter, although it does discuss the issue to some extent in Appendix 1 in rather nebulous terms.

The EC Fourth and Seventh Directives take a comparatively short period, five years, as their basic rule, but permit member states to extend this to the useful economic life of the asset if this is thought to be longer; the UK has embodied this option in the Companies Act in implementing both Directives.[150] At the other extreme, US GAAP imposes a maximum period for the amortisation of goodwill of 40 years,[151] and this has become widely adopted as the norm in practice in that country for most companies, although a shorter period is required in certain cases. The international standard states that the period should not exceed five years unless a longer period, not exceeding 20 years, can be justified.[152]

It is difficult to generalise about UK practice, because relatively few companies choose the amortisation approach in the first place, but those that do seem to gravitate towards a period somewhere between these two extremes, say from 10 to 20 years. There have been some instances of companies choosing to use 40 years, but in the main such a duration seems to be regarded as implausibly long.

ED 47 proposed that the amortisation period should be determined by identifying and evaluating the factors that gave rise to the goodwill such as 'customer awareness, reputation for quality, marketing and distribution skills, technical know-how, established business connections, management ability, level of workforce training and the like'.[153] It can be seen that these are equally as nebulous as those included in Appendix 1 to SSAP 22. The exposure draft suggested that the following criteria may be relevant in determining the life of such advantages:

(a)   the foreseeable life of the business or industry;

(b)   expected changes in products, markets or technology;

(c)   the expected future period of service of key individuals or groups of employees;

(d)   expected future demand or other economic factors which may affect current advantages;

(e)   legal, regulatory or contractual factors affecting the useful life.[154]

In determining the life, the effects of subsequent expenditure or other circumstances affecting the company after the acquisition were not to be taken into account; the reason being that this would have the effect of capitalising non-purchased goodwill.[155]

However, ED 47 suggested that the life should not exceed 20 years except in rare circumstances where the directors can justify that it should be longer, but in any event the life should not exceed 40 years.[156]

The ASB's Discussion Paper suggested a maximum of 20 years so as to be consistent with the majority of the international community, but sought views on whether any other period would be appropriate. As indicated earlier, FRED 12 establishes a rebuttable presumption that the useful life of goodwill is limited and does not exceed 20 years. However, it does allow for the useful life to be regarded as indefinite.

B   Method of amortisation

SSAP 22 does not specify which amortisation method should be used; therefore, companies are free to choose whichever method they consider appropriate in the circumstances subject to the overriding proviso that it is 'systematic'. US GAAP requires the straight-line method to be used unless the directors can justify that another systematic basis is more appropriate[157] and this is probably the most common practice adopted in the UK. One unusual method was that adopted by Charterhall, as illustrated below:

Extract 6.35: Charterhall PLC (1989)

INTANGIBLE ASSETS [extract]

Goodwill

On the acquisition of subsidiaries and businesses, the purchase consideration is allocated over the underlying net tangible assets, significant intangible assets and goodwill. Goodwill arising on the acquisition of subsidiaries has been capitalised and is amortised (after taking account of the anticipated impact of inflation on future earnings) through the Profit and Loss Account over a period not exceeding 40 years, estimated by the Directors to be the useful economic life.

On the acquisition of associated companies which are deemed non-core activities, goodwill is written off to Reserves.

10. INTANGIBLE ASSETS [extract]

	Goodwill
	£'000
Cost	
At 1 July, 1988	10,232
Additions	49,120
At 30 June 1989	59,352
Amortisation	
At 1 July, 1988	44
Charge for the year	138
At 30 June 1989	182
Net book value	
At 30 June, 1989	**59,170**
At 30 June, 1988	10,188

By taking account of the effect of inflation on future earnings, such an approach will result in a rising amortisation charge similar to the use of the 'annuity method' for fixed assets (see Chapter 10 at 3.7.4).

ED 47 proposed to take a similar approach to that in the US by requiring the straight-line method to be used unless another systematic basis gave a more realistic allocation, but with the additional proviso that any alternative method had to be more conservative than the straight-line method.[158]

The ASB's Discussion Paper did not discuss any methods of amortisation. However, the FRED 12 proposal discussed earlier effectively follows the approach in ED 47 and would not allow the method adopted by Charterhall.

2.5.5 *Negative goodwill*

Negative goodwill arises when the fair value of the net assets taken over in an acquisition transaction exceeds the fair value of the consideration given. On the face of it, the acquiring company has bought the business cheaply. This may have been the case for various reasons. The vendor may have been in a weak bargaining position relative to the acquirer; the assets may be of special value to the acquirer but this is not reflected in the acquisition price; or there may be an expectation of poor trading results which means that the business as a whole is at present worth less than is indicated by the values of the separable net assets.

There are a number of possible approaches which could be applied when accounting for negative goodwill. One is to say that, even if the separable net assets are worth more than the value of the business as a whole, they did not cost the acquirer that much, and that accordingly the negative goodwill should be applied to reduce the separable assets to their cost to the acquiring company. This is the approach followed in the US, where negative goodwill is eliminated by proportionately writing down the value of the fixed assets of the acquired company other than any marketable securities which it possesses; only when these have been written down to zero is it permissible to recognise negative goodwill, which is then classified as a deferred credit and amortised to the profit and loss account over the period expected to be benefited, with a maximum of forty years.[159] The effect of this is to recognise the negative goodwill in the profit and loss account, but this is done on a conservative basis by associating it with the cost of the items which have the longest lives.

Another approach is to try to identify why the negative goodwill arose, and to account for it based on that analysis. The ASC Discussion Paper on the subject issued in 1980 addressed the matter in these terms:

'... negative goodwill may arise as a consequence of the expectations of future losses (or reduced profits) or alternatively may just represent a bargain purchase by the acquiror. The logical treatment of negative goodwill which is related to future losses or reduced profits would be to amortise the capital reserve over the expected period of such losses or profits by crediting it to the profit and loss account (as the provision is progressively realised over this period). UK and Irish examples of this treatment in practice are rare but not unknown. Negative goodwill which arises due to a bargain purchase should, on the same basis, in principle be credited to the profit and loss account in the year in which the acquisition is made. However, because of the impracticability of defining the exact proportion of a transaction which represents a bargain purchase in all but exceptional circumstances, and because it would be imprudent so to treat negative goodwill which did not represent a bargain, the panel does not recommend this treatment.'[160]

The document went on to recommend 'that negative goodwill should generally be treated as the exact reverse of positive goodwill ... viz. it should be passed through the profit and loss account, spread over the periods which are expected to benefit from the acquisition. Any such transfer should be separately disclosed. However, to ensure that only amounts which have been realised (as demonstrated by the use or realisation of the other assets concerned) are credited to the profit and loss account, the accumulated amount written off negative goodwill should never exceed the aggregate of:

(a)   the total depreciation charged for assets of that investee since acquisition by the group; together with

(b)   any element of the proceeds on disposal of assets by the investee which corresponds to a surplus at the date of acquisition of the fair value of those assets over their book value.'[161]

This was the foundation of the proposals on negative goodwill in the exposure draft which preceded SSAP 22, which contained the following requirements:

'Any excess of the fair value of the separable net assets over the fair value of the consideration given (negative goodwill) which arises as a result of a bargain purchase should be carried to reserves representing unrealised profits, from which it may be transferred to reserves of realised profits as the relevant assets are depreciated or sold. However, negative goodwill which represents an amount specifically set aside for future losses and/or costs taken into account in arriving at the purchase price should be set up as a provision in the balance sheet and released to the profit and loss account over the period in which the losses or costs are, or are expected to be, incurred, provided that at the time of the acquisition the directors of the acquiring company can foresee on reasonable evidence that losses or costs are likely to be incurred by the acquired company and that provision for those losses or costs is necessary in accordance with the prudence concept.'[162]

Under this approach, some forms of negative goodwill (if they were thought to represent provisions for costs or losses) would eventually be reported in earnings, and some would not, because they would simply be dealt with within reserves. This was in contrast to the Discussion Paper, which had recommended that both types of negative goodwill should be dealt with in the profit and loss account. This disparity of approach did not find favour with commentators on the exposure draft, and when SSAP 22 was published the required treatment had again changed. Provisions for costs or losses were to be treated as liabilities to be set up as part of the fair value exercise, rather than regarded as an element of negative goodwill.[163]   The standard requires that all negative goodwill be compulsorily taken to reserves. In contrast to the position for positive goodwill, there is no alternative which allows the option of amortisation into the profit and loss account, which is arguably a conceptually inconsistent approach.

ED 47 proposed that negative goodwill be treated as the converse of positive goodwill; i.e. credited systematically through the profit and loss account over a suitable period. This period was to be decided based on the particular circumstances which gave rise to the negative goodwill.[164]   The ASC had changed tack slightly on the reasons why such negative goodwill arises; it now suggested that there were two basic reasons:

(a) where a bargain purchase has been made for whatever reason; e.g. forced sale, negotiating skills or market imperfections;

(b) where disadvantages exist which are part of the business but are not attributable to any particular assets or class of asset; e.g. a badly motivated workforce, unfavourable customer perceptions.[165]

Like the factors on which the useful life of positive goodwill was to be assessed, these are rather nebulous and the only guidance given in the exposure draft was that, 'in many circumstances, the average life of the fixed assets may provide a suitable period over which the credit should be taken',[166] although previously it had stated such an approach as being relevant 'where the negative goodwill arises from some disadvantage which relates generally to all the assets of the enterprise'.[167] It does seem though that the ASC did not envisage negative goodwill arising as a result of a bargain purchase being credited to profit and loss account in the year of purchase, which its earlier Discussion Paper suggested, but in such a way that 'accounts for the progressive realisation of the profit on the purchase'.[168]

The treatment of any negative goodwill which has yet to be credited to profit and loss account was also dependent on the distinction between these two reasons; negative goodwill arising because of a bargain purchase was to be included as a deferred credit under 'Accruals and deferred income', whereas negative goodwill arising because disadvantages exist was to be included under 'Provisions for liabilities and charges'.[169] It would appear, therefore, that the ASC considered that it was possible to distinguish between these two reasons having previously considered that it was impracticable to define 'the exact proportion of a transaction which represents a bargain purchase in all but exceptional circumstances'.[170]

The ASB did consider whether the approach adopted in the US and that now preferred by the IASC for negative goodwill should have any bearing on its proposals for fair value accounting, but decided that it should not and that the requirements of the existing accounting pronouncements should remain.[171] The ASB's Discussion Paper did not deal with the topic of negative goodwill at all. However, as indicated earlier, FRED 12 proposes that negative goodwill is to be treated as a negative asset and that it is not to be amortised but is to be written back through the statement of total recognised gains and losses as the difference between the value of the investment and the values of the identified net assets diminishes.[172] Negative goodwill would only be taken to the profit and loss to the extent that there is any remaining balance when the investment to which it relates is sold (see 3.3 below).[173] Nevertheless, it is possible that this proposal will again change before the standard is finalised.

The EC Seventh Directive bears more than a passing resemblance to ED 30 (which was the ASC's current published thinking when the Directive was being finalised). It says that 'a negative consolidation difference may be transferred to the consolidated profit and loss account only:

(a)   where that difference corresponds to the expectation at the date of acquisition of unfavourable future results in that undertaking, or to the expectation of costs which that undertaking would incur, in so far as such an expectation materialises; or

(b)   in so far as such a difference corresponds to a realised gain'.[174]

However, this does not dictate that such a treatment must be applied, it simply restricts any transfers to the profit and loss account to those which fit these criteria. Indeed, the provisions introduced into the legislation by the Companies Act 1989 make no reference as to how such a negative consolidation difference is to be accounted for.

2.6   Step-by-step acquisitions

2.6.1   Background

So far, this chapter has discussed acquisitions which result from a single purchase transaction, or at least a series of related transactions which occur over a relatively short period of time. However, in practice some subsidiaries are acquired in a series of steps which take place over an extended period, during which the underlying value of the subsidiary is likely to change, both because of the trading profits (or losses) which it retains and because of other movements in the fair values of its assets and liabilities. The accounting problems which this creates are therefore how to establish the fair values of the net assets acquired, and how to measure its pre-acquisition reserves.

2.6.2   Example

The problem can be illustrated by the following example, which is based on that in the ASC Discussion Paper on fair value accounting.[175]

Example 6.2:   Step-by-step acquisitions

Company A acquires an 80% holding in Company B as a result of four separate transactions over a number of years, as set out in the table below. At the time of these transactions, the fair values of the net assets of B were as shown, and for the purpose of this illustration, the consideration paid was exactly proportionate to the share of the net assets, at fair value, which was thereby being acquired.

Transaction number	Holding acquired %	Total value of investee £m	Price paid £m	Cumulative holding %	Cumulative price paid £m
1	10	10	1.00	10	1.00
2	20	13	2.60	30	3.60
3	21	15	3.15	51	6.75
4	29	20	5.80	80	12.55
	80		12.55		

As the above table shows, Company B was merely an unconsolidated investment after transaction 1, became an associate as a result of transaction 2 and a subsidiary as a result of transaction 3, while transaction 4 resulted in the minority interest being reduced from 49% to 20%.

The accounting choices which are available are of two sorts; when to make the initial calculation of fair values for the purposes of determining goodwill, and whether to make a revised calculation when each successive change in the size of the holding takes place. As stated at 3.1 of Chapter 7, SSAP 1 requires that the investment in an associate should be analysed at the time of acquisition between the investor's share of the underlying separable net assets (at fair value, if possible) and goodwill, so the answer to the first question above is that this calculation should be made after transaction 2; however, if Company A is unable to get the information on fair values which is required for that exercise, it may be possible to carry it out only after transaction 3. The more significant question is whether each further purchase of shares thereafter should lead to a recalculation of the goodwill equation.

If the exercise were first carried out after transaction 2, and reperformed after each subsequent increase in the shareholding, the calculations would be as follows:

After transaction 2	£m
Cost of investment	3.60
Share of assets at fair value (30% of £13m)	3.90
Capital reserve on consolidation	0.30

Note that, in this particular example (because all purchases take place at the underlying asset value), the capital reserve in fact represents the increase in reserves attributable to the 10% stake held by Company A during the period when its value grew from £10m to £13m. However, it has been beyond the scope of normal consolidation accounting entries to treat this as part of the group's post-acquisition reserves.

After transaction 3	£m
Cost of investment	6.75
Share of assets at fair value (51% of £15m)	7.65
	0.90
Less: post-acquisition share of reserves of associate (30% of (£15m – £13m))	0.60
Capital reserve on consolidation	0.30

	£m	£m
After transaction 4		
Cost of investment		12.55
Share of assets at fair value (80% of £20m)		16.00
		3.45
Less: post-acquisition share of reserves		
of associate (30% of (£15m – £13m))	0.60	
of subsidiary (51% of (£20m – £15m))	2.55	
		3.15
Capital reserve on consolidation		0.30

Although the accounting set out above may be appropriate in principle, it can give rise to difficulties in practice. One of these is that, once the shareholding crosses the 50% threshold, the assets of the investee will be consolidated on a line-by-line basis and it is thereafter difficult (and arguably inappropriate) to ascribe new fair values to them when further shares have been acquired, so as to reduce the size of the minority interest. If, in the above example, Company B owned a single investment property (and nothing else) which was appreciating in value throughout the period during which Company A's stake was changing, the accounting consequences would be as follows:

Example 6.3:   Step-by-step acquisitions: consolidating the assets concerned

	£m
After transaction 2	
Cost of investment as before	3.60
Represented by:	
Share of associate's assets at fair value (30% of £13m)	3.90
Capital reserve on consolidation	(0.30)
	3.60

	£m
After transaction 3	
Cost of investment as before	6.75
Represented by:	
Investment property	15.00
Minority interest (49% of £15m)	(7.35)
	7.65
Post-acquisition reserves (as before)	(0.60)
Capital reserve on consolidation	(0.30)
	6.75

The post-acquisition reserves would in fact represent Company A's 30% share of the revaluation reserve arising from the uplift in the value of the property from £13m to £15m.

	£m
After transaction 4	
Cost of investment as before	12.55
Represented by:	
Investment property	20.00
Minority interest (20% of £20m)	(4.00)
	16.00
Post-acquisition reserves (as before)	(3.15)
Capital reserve on consolidation	(0.30)
	12.55

In order to achieve this accounting, it is necessary to revalue the investment property in the consolidated accounts following transaction 4. (This also takes place implicitly following transaction 3, but is not obvious because an investment property appears in the consolidated balance sheet in substitution for an investment in an associate.) However, if the assets were not investment properties, there has until now been no compulsion for the group to revalue its assets in this way, and the ASC Discussion Paper on fair value mentioned two other possibilities, which are discussed below:

The first of these is that they may retain the asset at £15m, in which case the consolidated financial statements after transaction 4 will show the following:

	£m
Cost of investment (as before)	12.55
Represented by:	
Property	15.00
Minority interest (20% of £15m)	(3.00)
	12.00
Post-acquisition reserves (as after transaction 3)	(0.60)
Goodwill on consolidation[*]	1.15
	12.55

[*]This can be analysed as follows:

	£m
Cost of 29% acquired	5.80
Minority interest: 29% of £15m	(4.35)
	1.45
Capital reserve existing after transaction 3	(0.30)
	1.15

The defect with this treatment is that it overstates goodwill by attributing to it an amount which is in reality attributable to the property. Conversely, the cost of the property to the group is understated and gains on any subsequent valuation or on disposal which are measured by reference to that cost will be overstated.

The ASC Discussion Paper therefore offered a further alternative which involves accounting for the property on a 'mixed' basis that takes account of the cost of the different transactions. Applying this approach to transaction 4 would give the following result:

	£m
Cost of investment (as before)	12.55
Represented by:	
Property	16.45
Minority interest (20% of £15m)	(3.00)
	13.45
Post-acquisition reserves (as after transaction 3)	(0.60)
Capital reserve on consolidation	(0.30)
	12.55

This is achieved by applying the cost of the transaction 4 investment of £5.8m to increase the asset by 29% of £5m (the increase in the stake of the uplift in value since the previous transaction) and applying the remainder to reduce the minority interest. Whatever the theoretical case for this treatment, it seems to produce figures which have little meaning or usefulness.

2.6.3   FRS 2 requirements

There is no ideal solution to this problem of accounting for step-by-step acquisitions; each of the approaches shown in the above example would appear to have some defects. In theory, the best treatment (and the one recommended in the ASC Discussion Paper) would appear to be to recalculate fair values whenever there has been a significant change of stake as shown in the first of the treatments in the example. However, in practice companies seldom made any further adjustments to the fair values of the net assets of their subsidiaries after majority control has been secured. The 'mixed' treatment shown above is also unlikely to have been applied in practice.

The ASB reconsidered this issue in FRS 2 and effectively adopted the treatment recommended by the ASC Discussion Paper, although there are some differences due to the implications of the Companies Act provisions on acquisition accounting.

A   Investment becoming a subsidiary

The standard states that the Companies Act requires that 'the identifiable assets and liabilities of a subsidiary undertaking should be included in the consolidation at fair value at the date of its acquisition, that is the date it becomes a subsidiary undertaking. This requirement is also applicable where the group's interest in the undertaking that becomes a subsidiary undertaking is acquired in stages.'[176] As explained by the standard, 'the effect of the Schedule 4A paragraph 9 method of acquisition accounting is to treat as goodwill, or negative goodwill, the whole of the difference between, on the one hand, the fair value, at the date of its identifiable assets and liabilities and, on the other hand, the total acquisition cost of the interests held by the group in that subsidiary undertaking. This applies even where part of the acquisition cost arises from purchases of interests at earlier dates.'[177]

The effect of this on Example 6.3 above would appear to be as follows:

Example 6.4:   Step-by-step acquisitions: consolidating the assets concerned

After transaction 3

In consolidating the subsidiary there is a difference between the fair value of the net assets at the date of becoming a subsidiary and the aggregate cost of the investment, being:

	£m
Investment property	15.00
Minority interest (49% of £15m)	(7.35)
	7.65
Cost of investment	6.75
Difference	0.90

FRS 2 indicates that this difference is negative goodwill in terms of the Companies Act. However, as the consideration paid was exactly proportionate to the share of net assets, at fair value, which was thereby being acquired, there was in fact no goodwill. This difference is equivalent to:

	£m
Post-acquisition reserves of associate (as before)	0.60
Capital reserve on consolidation (as before)	0.30
	0.90

The post-acquisition reserves represent Company A's 30% share of the revaluation reserve arising from the uplift in the value of the property from £13m to £15m which will be reflected in the group's reserves. However, in other situations these post-acquisition reserves may have been reflected in the group retained profits. Such reserves become reclassified as part of goodwill, in this case negative goodwill.

However, FRS 2 indicates that, in special circumstances (such as an associate becoming a subsidiary), 'not using fair values at the dates of earlier purchases, while using an acquisition cost part of which relates to earlier purchases, may result in accounting that is inconsistent with the way the investment has been treated previously and, for that reason, may fail to give a true and fair view. ... In the rare cases where the Schedule 4A paragraph 9 calculation of goodwill would be misleading, goodwill should be calculated as the sum of the goodwill arising from each purchase of an interest in the relevant undertaking adjusted as necessary for any subsequent diminution in value. Goodwill arising on each purchase should be calculated as the difference between the cost of that purchase and the fair value at the date of that purchase of the identifiable assets and liabilities attributable to the interest purchased. The difference between the goodwill calculated on this method and that calculated on the method provided by the Act is shown in reserves.'[178] When such a 'true and fair override' is used, it will be necessary to disclose the particulars of the departure, the reasons for it and its effect as required by the Act.[179]

An example of a company using the 'true and fair override' was THORN EMI in its 1995 accounts, as shown below:

Extract 6.36: THORN EMI plc (1995)

30. Purchase of businesses [extract]

   TOEMI - On 3 October 1994, THORN EMI plc increased its shareholding in TOEMI from 50 to 55 per cent. TOEMI became a consolidated subsidiary on this date, having previously been accounted for as an associated company.

   The transaction was effected by a redemption of shares owned by the joint venture partner, Toshiba Corporation, and funded by TOEMI's cash reserves in which the Group already had a 50 per cent beneficial interest. The indirect cost to the Group was therefore Yen 3.75 billion (£24.1m).

   The Companies Act 1985 normally requires goodwill arising on the acquisition of a subsidiary undertaking to be calculated as the difference between the total acquisition cost of the undertaking and the fair value of the Group's share of the identifiable assets and liabilities at the date it became a subsidiary undertaking.

   FRS 2 recognises that, where an investment in an associated undertaking is increased and it becomes a subsidiary undertaking, in order to show a true and fair view goodwill should be calculated on each purchase as the difference between the cost of that purchase and the fair value at the date of that purchase.

   If goodwill had been calculated in accordance with the basis set out in the Companies Act 1985, £61.2m of the Group's share of the retained earnings of TOEMI would have been reclassified as goodwill and in total negative goodwill of £63.9m would have been recognised.

A number of other companies have adopted a similar method to calculate goodwill but have not given the 'true and fair override' disclosures, presumably on the basis that the effect was not material.

B   Increased investment in existing subsidiary

Where a group increases its holding in the equity of a subsidiary undertaking, the standard requires that the net identifiable assets and liabilities of that subsidiary undertaking should be revalued to fair value and goodwill arising on the increase in interest should be calculated by reference to those fair values. This revaluation is not required if the difference between net fair values and carrying amounts of the assets and liabilities is not material.[180] Companies which have normally adopted the practice of comparing the consideration paid with the carrying value of the minority interest acquired and regarded the difference as goodwill, will need to reconsider their treatment.

Although the legislation contains certain detailed acquisition accounting rules which refer to fair values,[181] it does state that they apply 'where an undertaking becomes a subsidiary undertaking of the parent company';[182] they would, therefore, appear not to apply to acquisitions of shares in a company after it has become a subsidiary.

An example of a company making fair value adjustments in these circumstances is Glaxo Wellcome, as shown in the following extract:

Extract 6.37: Glaxo Wellcome plc (1996)

23 Acquisitions and Disposals [extract]

Acquisitions

Nippon Glaxo Limited

In December 1996 the Group redeemed the 50 per cent equity interest in Nippon Glaxo Limited previously held by its joint venture partner, Shin Nihon Jitsugyo Co. Ltd. ("SNJ"), thereby increasing the Group's interest to 100 per cent. SNJ is the family company of the then president and vice-president of Nippon Glaxo Limited, who relinquished these positions on the redemption. The cost of the redemption was Yen 68 billion (£343 million) comprising consideration of Yen 67 billion (£339 million) and redemption expenses of Yen 1 billion (£4 million). The consideration was paid in cash, Yen 54 billion on 25th December 1996 and Yen 13 billion on 10th January 1997.

Previously Nippon Glaxo Limited had been consolidated as a subsidiary undertaking in accordance with Section 258(4)(a) of the Companies Act 1985 and a minority interest of 50 per cent had been accounted for. The redemption eliminates the minority interest.

The fair value of the net assets of Nippon Glaxo Limited at the date of redemption exceeded the book value by £39 million, comprising adjustments of £42 million in respect of the value of land and £3 million for additional liabilities. Consolidated Group net assets have therefore been increased by £39 million, with the 50 per cent attributable to the Group's pre-existing interest added to reserves and 50 per cent added to minority interests. Goodwill on consolidation is calculated as the difference between the cost of redemption and the adjusted value of the minority interest.

Burroughs Wellcome (India) Limited

In February 1996 the Group purchased an additional 19 per cent equity interest in Burroughs Wellcome (India) Limited, increasing its holding to 51 per cent. From that point Burroughs Wellcome (India) Limited has been consolidated as a subsidiary undertaking, having previously been accounted for as an associated undertaking.

Goodwill arising on acquisitions in the year

	Book values £m	Fair value adjustments £m	Net assets acquired £m	Cost of acquisition £m	Goodwill £m
Nippon Glaxo Limited	85	20	105	343	238
Burroughs Wellcome (India) Limited	7	–	7	15	8
	92	20	112	358	246

It is unclear why there should have been a fair value adjustment to reflect additional liabilities, because as the company was an existing subsidiary all liabilities would normally already have been provided.

Although it may be possible to incorporate fair value adjustments for valuation of fixed assets, some of the fair value adjustments required by FRS 7 discussed at 2.4.3 above would fall foul of the Companies Act valuation rules or of other accounting standards. For example, one fair value adjustment might be to incorporate a pension scheme surplus, but this would not be allowed by SSAP 24, so clearly there are limitations as to the fair value adjustments which can be made in this sort of situation.

2.7   Mergers

2.7.1   Basic principles

In contrast to acquisition accounting, merger accounting involves retrospective restatement of the consolidated financial statements to show the reporting entity as if the combining companies had always been members of the group.[183] This means that the effective date of the combination has no significance other than for the purposes of various disclosures; both pre- and post-combination results of the subsidiary are combined with those of the holding company in showing the results for the period of the combination, and it is therefore of little significance whether it took place at the beginning or the end of the year. Similarly, the comparative figures and any historical summaries should be restated to consolidate the results of the new subsidiary retrospectively, which will usually mean that the earnings trend will be significantly different from what it would have been had acquisition accounting been applied.

In the balance sheet, the assets and liabilities of both companies are combined on the basis of their book values, with adjustments made only to eliminate any differences in accounting policies between the two.[184] Thus, there is no equivalent of the requirement under acquisition accounting to attribute fair values to the net assets of the subsidiary so as to reflect their cost to the group; merger accounting seeks to portray continuity of both of the combining entities, not that of the holding company, and therefore makes no amendment to the values at which the assets of either are included other than to harmonise accounting policies.

These basic principles are also embodied in the legislation following changes made by the Companies Act 1989.[185]

2.7.2   Equity eliminations

The cost of the investment will normally be carried at the nominal value of the shares of the holding company which have been issued to effect the combination, together with the fair value of any other consideration given. (The ability to record these shares at nominal rather than fair values on issue depends on qualifying for merger relief under section 131 of the Companies Act 1985, which is discussed under 2.1.2 above.)

As well as combining the assets and liabilities of the companies concerned, it will be necessary to eliminate the share capital of the subsidiary against the cost of the investment as stated in the balance sheet of the holding company. This is in principle a straightforward exercise, but when the two amounts do not equate to each other, the question arises of what to do with the difference, positive or negative.

FRS 6 requires the difference to be shown as a movement on other reserves in the consolidated accounts and also to be shown in the reconciliation of shareholders' funds.[186] It also emphasises that such a difference is not goodwill.[187] The Companies Act also requires such difference to be shown as a movement in consolidated reserves.[188] However, neither the standard nor the legislation specify any particular reserve.

Where the cost of the investment is less than the nominal value of the share capital of the subsidiary, the elimination of these two amounts will leave a residual credit in shareholders' funds in the consolidated balance sheet; this is generally classified as some form of capital reserve.

Where the reverse situation applies, the net debit has to be eliminated against consolidated reserves in some way and choices have to be made as to the order in which the group's reserves should be applied for this purpose. There are no particular rules on the matter in any authoritative document, but the normal practice is to apply these first against the most restricted categories of reserves,[189] and subsequently if any excess remains, against the group's retained earnings. Where the reserves are in the subsidiary concerned then, in effect, this is equivalent to the partial capitalisation of the reserves of the subsidiary; if they had had a bonus issue out of their own reserves prior to the merger, to make their share capital equal to the consideration shares offered by the new holding company, no consolidation difference would have emerged.

Apart from the effects of dealing with any imbalance as discussed above, there is no other elimination of the reserves of the subsidiary, which are combined with those of the holding company, in contrast to the treatment under acquisition accounting. However, some of the subsidiary's reserves may need to be reclassified in order to make sense in the context of the group financial statements.

FRS 6 requires that any existing balance on the share premium account or capital redemption reserve of the new subsidiary undertaking should be brought in by being shown as a movement on other reserves.[190] This is because they do not relate to the share capital of the reporting entity. Again, this difference should be shown in the reconciliation of movements in shareholders' funds.[191] Such a difference should probably be taken to the same reserve as that on the elimination of the share capital of the subsidiary, because in reality the distinction between share capital and share premium can be seen to be somewhat arbitrary in this context.

2.7.3 Expenses of the merger

One other question which sometimes arises in this context is how to account for the expenses of the merger. Although in the past there may have been good arguments for various treatments, FRS 6 requires that *all* merger costs should be charged through the profit and loss account at the effective date of the merger as costs of a fundamental reorganisation or restructuring under FRS 3 (see Chapter 22 at 2.6.3).[192]

However, some of these costs may be regarded as share issue expenses and therefore qualify to be written off against the share premium account of the holding company (if such an account exists). FRS 6 does not prohibit the subsequent charging of such costs to the share premium account by means of a transfer between reserves.[193]

2.7.4 Non-coterminous accounting periods

Particular practical problems in accounting for the merger can arise in the frequent circumstances that the accounting periods of the combining companies do not match each other. Although this can also create problems when acquisition accounting is used, the requirement in merger accounting to restate the consolidated financial statements retrospectively makes the difficulties particularly severe.

Company law dictates that the financial statements of the group must give a true and fair view in respect of the accounting period of the holding company, so this will require the period used by the subsidiary to be made to conform to that of its parent rather than the other way round. Naturally, the parent can change its own accounting reference date, but this can only be done for the future, not retrospectively. It will therefore be necessary to try to draw up financial statements for the subsidiary at each of the relevant balance sheet dates of the holding company.

The easiest part of the process will be to make sure that the subsidiary prepares a balance sheet at the next balance sheet date of the holding company, to allow a consolidated balance sheet at that date to be prepared. The difficult part will be to recreate balance sheets at the dates previously used by the parent, which will be necessary not only for the purposes of comparative figures for the balance sheet but also in order to allow the profit and loss account and cash flow statement of the current and comparative periods (together with any historical periods disclosed) to be drawn up.

Quite often it might prove impossible to draw up financial statements at these earlier dates with the same degree of accuracy that would be attainable in normal circumstances, because it is not possible after the event to institute normal year-end procedures such as stock counts and so on. It may therefore be necessary to make estimates of what such financial statements would have shown if they had been drawn up at that time, by relying on management information or by extrapolation between the reporting dates which were used (with allowance for seasonal or other relevant factors).

Another treatment which may be found appropriate would be to use non-coterminous years for the comparative figures, with the result that there will be the need to deal with the effects of either a 'gap' or an overlapping period as an adjustment to reserves. This was the solution chosen by Belhaven when it merger accounted for its acquisition of Garfunkels Restaurants, as explained in the following extract:

Extract 6.38: Belhaven plc (1987)

BASIS OF CONSOLIDATION [extract]

The accounting year end of Belhaven plc has been changed and the results are therefore presented for a nine-month period to December 31, 1987. The comparative figures combine the results of Belhaven plc for the year to March 31, 1987 and the audited results of Garfunkels Restaurants plc for the year to December 28, 1986, and the Balance Sheets of the two Groups as at these dates. The results for Garfunkels for the three months to March 31, 1987 are dealt with as a movement in reserves (Note 21).

A particular problem can arise when a company is incorporated specially for the purpose of acting as the new holding company of a merging group. Because, as noted above, the accounting reference period of the group must by law be that of the holding company, this may result in the inadvertent creation of an accounting period which is not the one which the group would have preferred. Moreover, unless the company has been in existence for two years, arguably its statutory accounts should not be able to deal with the results of the group for the current and comparative periods, because strictly they should only go as far back as the date of incorporation of the holding company. One solution to this might be to present the information for the more relevant chosen period in supplementary pro-forma form. However, it appears that in practice some companies do not go to such trouble and just produce accounts for the period they wish, as if the company had always been in existence. This was the approach adopted in the 1996 accounts of Securicor Group.

The best solution to the problem, however, would be to ensure that the new holding company has an accounting reference date which suits that of the group, and has been in existence long enough to allow a full set of group accounts for the chosen period to be presented.

2.7.5 *Dividends of the subsidiary*

Since the profit and loss accounts of both the combining companies will be aggregated retrospectively, it will be necessary to consider how to deal with the dividends of the subsidiary paid before the date of the combination. Essentially, the pre-merger dividends of both the parent and the subsidiary will be combined and shown as distributions in the consolidated profit and loss account, although it would be helpful to distinguish them either on the face of the profit and loss account or in a note. However, after the date of the merger, the only dividends shown will be those of the parent (those of the subsidiary will by then be inter-company payments and will thus be eliminated on consolidation).

2.8   Disclosure requirements relating to business combinations

Until FRS 6 was issued, most disclosures relating to business combinations in group accounts arose from the requirements of SSAPs 22 and 23, although there were disclosure requirements in a number of other accounting standards as well. In publishing FRS 6, the ASB took the opportunity to consolidate most of the requirements into a single standard as well as introducing some additional ones. These requirements are considered at 2.8.1 to 2.8.3 below.

The Companies Act contains a number of detailed disclosure requirements. Many of these duplicate those contained in the standards, but there are a few additional matters in the legislation and these are considered at 2.8.4 below.

2.8.1   *All business combinations*

The following information should be disclosed in respect of all business combinations occurring in the financial year, whether they be acquisitions or mergers:

(a)   the names of the combining entities (other than the reporting entity);

(b)   whether the combination has been accounted for as an acquisition or a merger;

(c)   the date of the combination.[194]

Taking both the requirements of the Companies Act (see 2.8.4 below) and the standard together, details must be given for all combinations, even small ones. There is no explicit materiality limitation – all entities must be named and the date of acquisition given.

FRS 2 requires that where an undertaking becomes a subsidiary undertaking other than as a result of a purchase or exchange of shares then the circumstances should be disclosed.[195]

2.8.2   *Acquisitions*

FRS 6 requires the disclosures set out below in (a) to (k) to be given for each material acquisition, and in aggregate for other acquisitions that are material in total but not individually.[196]

(a)   the composition and fair value of the consideration given by the acquiring company and its subsidiary undertakings should be disclosed. The nature of any deferred or contingent consideration should be stated. For contingent consideration, the range of possible outcomes and principal factors affecting the outcome should be given.[197]

Examples of disclosures in respect of contingent consideration are given at 2.3.5 above.

(b)   a table should be provided showing, for each class of assets and liabilities of the acquired entity:

   (i)   the book values recorded in the acquired entity's books immediately before the acquisition and before any fair value adjustments;

   (ii)   the fair value adjustments, analysed into

   ■   revaluations,

   ■   adjustments to harmonise accounting policies, and

   ■   any other significant adjustments.

   The reasons for the adjustments must be given; and

   (iii)   the fair values at date of acquisition.

   The table should include a statement of the amount of goodwill (positive or negative) arising on the acquisition.[198]

It may be necessary to modify the disclosures given in the fair value table where a business is acquired, rather than a company, because the acquiring company may be unable to give all the required information as it may not have access to the book values of the assets and liabilities recorded by the previous owner. However, we would recommend that where a business is acquired a full fair value table should be provided if at all possible. Extracts 6.10, 6.13, 6.14 and 6.15 above show examples of companies giving full fair value tables in respect of businesses acquired.

(c)   also in the table above, there must be separately identified any provisions for reorganisation and restructuring costs included in the liabilities of the acquired entity (and any related asset write downs) made in the twelve months up to the date of acquisition.[199]

As already discussed at 2.4.3 F above, the creation of reorganisation provisions has been made much more difficult by FRS 7. However, there may still be circumstances where they can be made and will feature in the liabilities recognised for the acquired entity. Although, strictly speaking, this requirement does not call for separate disclosure of reorganisation and similar provisions set up in the context of the fair value exercise rather than by the management of the acquired entity within the twelve months prior to the date of acquisition, there appears to be no reason why the disclosure of the two elements of any provisions should be different. It may be best therefore to disclose all such provisions in the fair value table required, whenever made. Extracts 6.13, 6.15 and 6.26 show examples of companies giving disclosure of pre-acquisition reorganisation provisions.

(d)   where fair values are determined on a provisional basis only, that fact has to be stated and the reasons given. Subsequent material adjustments to these provisional fair values (and corresponding adjustments to goodwill) should be disclosed and explained.[200]

Extracts 6.22, 6.25 and 6.26 show examples of companies giving disclosure in respect of provisional fair values. One company which has made subsequent adjustments to provisional fair values is Reckitt & Colman. In its 1994 accounts Reckitt & Colman gave the following disclosures in respect of its acquisition of the L&F household products business:

Extract 6.39: Reckitt & Colman plc (1994)

27   ACQUISITION OF BUSINESSES [extract]

On 31 December 1994 the group purchased the L&F household products business ('L&F Household') of Eastman Kodak Company ('Kodak'). The purchase consideration, including fees and costs of £8.40m associated with the acquisition, amounted to £1,001.90m, payable in cash, of which £1.25m was paid in 1994 and $989.50m on 3 January 1995. The remaining cost of acquisition has been or will be paid during 1994. The value of these assets and the consequent adjustment to the consideration is subject to agreement with Kodak. The net assets of all acquisitions were:

	Book value	Revaluation of assets/ (liabilities)	Other	Fair value of assets/ (liabilities) acquired
	£m	£m	£m	£m
L&F Household:				
Intangible fixed assets	–	635.99	–	635.99
Tangible fixed assets	59.45	44.04	–	103.49
Current assets/(liabilities)				
Stocks	31.99	–	–	31.99
Debtors	40.20	–	13.00	53.20
Businesses and brands held for disposal	11.60	77.10	(8.80)	79.90
Creditors	(44.39)	–	(2.46)	(46.85)
Provisions for liabilities and charges/liabilities due after more than one year	(41.86)	(4.40)	(4.01)	(50.27)
	56.99	752.73	(2.27)	807.45
Other businesses acquired	1.09	–	–	1.09
All acquisitions	58.08	752.73	(2.27)	808.54

Subsequent adjustments were made the following year and the 1995 accounts contained the following disclosure in respect of these adjustments:

Extract 6.40: Reckitt & Colman plc (1995)

25 ACQUISITION OF BUSINESSES [extract]

On 31 December 1994 the group purchased the L&F household products business (L&F Products) which was provisionally valued in the 1994 accounts. In accordance with FRS 7, an adjustment has been made in the 1995 accounts for amendments to that provisional fair value, now that the investigation for determining such a value has been completed. The difference has been taken as an adjustment to goodwill on acquisition. Amended and provisional values of net assets acquired are as follows:

	Amended value 1995 £m	Provisional value 1994 £m
L&F Products:		
Intangible fixed assets	**636.0**	636.0
Tangible fixed assets	**72.6**	103.5
Current assets/(liabilities)		
Stocks	**29.4**	32.0
Debtors	**53.2**	53.2
Businesses and brands held for disposal	**31.9**	79.9
Creditors	**(49.8)**	(46.9)
Provisions for liabilities and charges/liabilities due after more than one year	**(47.1)**	(50.3)
	726.2	807.4
Goodwill	**279.9**	194.5
Cost of acquisition	**1,006.1**	1,001.9
L&F Products: amount paid in year	**1,004.8**	1.3
Other businesses acquired: amounts paid relating to prior year acquisitions	**1.6**	10.8
Effect on cash flow	**1,006.4**	12.1

The company obviously felt that this gave adequate disclosure and explanation of the adjustments that were made. However, the matter was brought to the attention of the Financial Reporting Review Panel and it concluded that the disclosure was insufficient. In the Panel's view this second stage of disclosure requires a similar level of disclosure and explanation as is given in the year of acquisition under (b) above and should include an analysis of the adjustments and an explanation of the reasons for them. Accordingly, Reckitt & Colman included the following disclosure in its 1996 accounts:

Extract 6.41: Reckitt & Colman plc (1996)

24. Acquisition of businesses

a)   Fair value adjustments in 1995 Annual Accounts (see Note 25 of the 1995 Annual Accounts)

As a result of an enquiry by the Financial Reporting Review Panel, the note on the fair value adjustments that were made in the 1995 accounts has been reissued in order to give full disclosure and reason for these adjustments. The figures themselves are unchanged.

On 31 December 1994 the group purchased the L&F household products business (L&F Products) which was provisionally valued in the 1994 accounts. In the initial period post acquisition communications between the acquired L&F business and Reckitt & Colman were specifically prohibited by a "hold separate" decree issued by the Federal Trade Commission (FTC). This gave rise to one of the issues referred to in Note i). The acquisition was also conditional on the disposal of certain businesses in the US as required by the FTC.

In accordance with FRS 7 an adjustment was made in the 1995 accounts for amendments to that provisional fair value.

The difference was taken as an adjustment to goodwill on acquisition. Amended and provisional values of net assets acquired were as follows and the explanations for those changes are given in the notes below:

	Amended value 1995 £m	Adjustments Total	Adjustments Revaluation	Adjustments Other	Provisional value 1994 £m
L&F Products					
Intangible fixed assets	636.0				636.0
Tangible fixed assets	72.6	(30.9)	(30.9)i		103.5
Current assets/(liabilities):					
Stocks	29.4	(2.6)		(2.6)ii	32.0
Debtors	53.2				53.2
Businesses and brands held for disposal	31.9	(48.0)	(48.0)iii		79.9
Creditors	(49.8)	(2.9)		(2.9)ii	(46.9)
Provisions for liabilities and charges					
due after more than one year	(47.1)	3.2		3.2ii	(50.3)
	726.2	(81.2)	(78.9)	(2.3)	807.4
Goodwill	279.9iv	85.4			194.5
Cost of Acquisition	1,006.1	4.2			1,001.9

Note i) - The adjustments to the provisional fair values of the tangible assets arose because the initial calculations, carried out by external appraisal consultants, were based on US fair value accounting and included inappropriate elements of future cash flow as a basis of their valuation. As some of these cash flows were brand-related the plant was inappropriately overvalued. This anomaly was not identified until later in 1995 when full control and access to the business was gained (see introductory paragraph for an explanation of this).

Note ii) - Small adjustments in drawing up the definitive disposal balance sheet.

Note iii) - A more detailed investigation into the businesses held for disposal was completed subsequent to the date of signing the annual accounts. The businesses and brands held for disposal comprised parts of the acquired operation in both the US and Germany, and these were immediately placed for sale following the acquisition. As a result of the tight timetable for the completion of the 1994 accounts, the value of the businesses held for disposal had not been fully evaluated when the 1994 accounts were completed and this meant that the provisional fair value of the businesses held for disposal had been overstated by some £48m in the 1994 accounts against their estimated worth as at the end of 1995.

Note iv) - The goodwill adjustment is a reflection of the amended fair values mentioned above.

It can be seen that not only does this give more explanation about the adjustments, it also gives more detailed explanation as to why the fair value adjustments were provisional in the first place.

(e)   any exceptional post-acquisition profit or loss that is determined using the fair values recognised on acquisition should be disclosed in accordance with FRS 3, and identified as relating to the acquisition.[201] The explanatory note in the standard gives three examples:

(i)   profits or losses on the disposal of acquired stocks where the fair values of stocks sold lead to abnormal trading margins after the acquisition;

(ii)   the release of provisions in respect of an acquired loss making long-term contract that the acquirer makes profitable; and

(iii) the realisation of contingent assets or liabilities at amounts materially different from their attributed fair values.[202]

This is a new and rather onerous disclosure requirement but it is not clear what it was intended to achieve or that it adds much of use to the existing FRS 3 disclosures about exceptional items. It would seem that it is necessary to ascertain whether any exceptional items arising in the period are calculated using fair values that were ascribed in a fair value exercise (regardless of how far in the past those fair values were ascribed). If so, the disclosure must be given that the exceptional item relates to an acquisition – it does not appear to be strictly necessary to identify which one, although that may be felt to be helpful disclosure. The identification of the exceptional items must be given, as for the rest of these disclosures, separately for each material acquisition and in aggregate for the rest.

(f)   movements on provisions or accruals for costs related to acquisitions should be disclosed and analysed between the amounts used for the specific purpose for which they were created and amounts released unused.[203]

It is probably the case that the ASB is intending through the use of the wording adopted that provisions should not be used for anything other than the purpose for which they were established (although this is not actually stated). It is again worth stressing that this disclosure must be given for each material acquisition separately. It is therefore necessary that any provisions maintained must be analysed by acquisition, so that any individually material movement relating to an acquisition provision established in a material acquisition can be disclosed separately.

(g)   as required by FRS 3, in the period of acquisition the post-acquisition results of the acquired entity should be shown as a component of continuing operations in the profit and loss account (other than those which are also discontinued in the same period). Where an acquisition has a material impact on a major business segment, this should be disclosed and explained.[204]

(h)   where it is not practicable to determine the post-acquisition results of an operation, an indication of its contribution to turnover and operating profit should be given, or, if even that is not possible, that fact and the reasons for it should be explained.[205]

Although (g) and (h) appear to duplicate FRS 3 requirements, the information is now required for each material acquisition separately and only in aggregate for others. The requirements of FRS 3 are discussed further at 2.5 of Chapter 22.

One way of giving this disclosure is for the material acquisition to be identified on the face of the profit and loss account, as shown below:

Extract 6.42: Granada Group PLC (1996)

Consolidated profit and loss account [extract]

Note	For the 52 weeks ended 28 September 1996	Total before exceptional items £m	Exceptional items (note 7) £m	Total after exceptional items 1996 £m	1995 £m
1	Turnover:				
	Continuing operations	2,611.7	–	2,611.7	2,381.2
	Acquisitions - Forte	1,205.2	–	1,205.2	–
		3,816.9	–	3,816.9	2,381.2
	Depreciation on tangible assets	184.6	–	184.6	132.3
2	Staff costs	884.8	43.8	928.6	528.4
3	Net other operating costs	2,070.6	33.4	2,104.0	1,332.4
		3,140.0	77.2	3,217.2	1,993.1
	Operating profit:				
	Continuing operations	444.4	(3.6)	440.8	388.1
	Acquisitions - Forte	232.5	(73.6)	158.9	–
1	Total operating profit	676.9	(77.2)	599.7	388.1

Alternatively the information can be disclosed by way of note, as shown below:

Extract 6.43: Rentokil Initial plc (1996)

29 Acquisitions [extract]

From the dates of acquisition to 31st December 1996 the acquisitions contributed £1,334.6m to turnover (BET £1,331.7m), £116.9m to profit before interest (BET £116.1m) and £85.2m to profit after interest (BET £84.6m). BET contributed £138.6m to the group's net operating cash flows, paid £31.5m in respect of interest, £15.5m in respect of taxation and utilised £114.2m for capital expenditure. In its last financial year to 30th March 1996, BET made a profit after tax and minority interests of £101.8m.

(i)   in accordance with FRS 1, the cash flow statement should show the amount of cash paid in respect of the consideration, showing separately any balances of cash and overdrafts acquired. In addition, a note to the cash flow statement should show a summary of the effects of acquisitions indicating how much of the consideration comprised cash.[206]

(j)   in accordance with FRS 1, material effects on amounts reported under each of the standard headings reflecting the cash flows of the acquired entity in the period should be disclosed, as far as is practicable.[207]

Although (i) and (j) appear to duplicate FRS 1 requirements, the disclosures must be given for each material acquisition and in aggregate for the remainder. The requirements of FRS 1 are discussed further at 2.7.1 of Chapter 27.

(k)   in financial statements following the acquisition, the costs incurred in the period in reorganising, restructuring and integrating the acquisition should be shown. Such costs are those that:

(i)   would not have been incurred had the acquisition not taken place; and

(ii)   relate to a project identified and controlled by management as part of a reorganisation or integration programme set up at the time of acquisition or as a direct consequence of an immediate post-acquisition review.[208]

These costs, whether relating to a fundamental restructuring or not, are to be disclosed separately from other exceptional items.[209] The point of this disclosure requirement appears to be to ensure that the costs of reorganisation are still disclosed even though they do not feature any longer in the fair value exercise. The disclosure, however, appears to be voluntary since it will be easy for managements who feel burdened by the disclosure requirements to 'fail' the test of having set up the programme of reorganisation at the time of acquisition or in an immediate post-acquisition review. Nevertheless, where reorganisation or restructuring costs are incurred most companies are giving disclosure (see for example Extracts 6.12 and 6.15 above).

As these costs may extend over more than one period, it is suggested in the explanation section of the standard that 'for major acquisitions, therefore, management may wish to state in the notes to the financial statements the nature and amount of such costs expected to be incurred in relation to the acquisition (including asset write-downs), indicating the extent to which they have been charged to the profit and loss account'.[210] An illustrative example of how such information might be shown is included in Appendix IV to the standard. As this is not a requirement of the standard, companies do not appear to be bothering with such disclosure other than giving disclosure under (k) above.

It should be emphasised again that the disclosures discussed in (a) to (k) above are to be given for each material acquisition, and in aggregate for other acquisitions that are material in total but not individually. Most of the extracts to which reference has been made generally have been in situations when there has been only one material acquisition. Where a company is acquisitive, then it may be that separate disclosures will need to be given for a number of acquisitions in the year. Indeed, Stagecoach Holdings in its 1996 accounts has given disclosures in respect of 5 acquisitions.[211]

The disclosure requirements discussed at (d), (e), (f) and (k) above do not necessarily apply to the period in which the acquisition is made, but in future accounting periods following the acquisition. Since FRS 6 is only mandatory for acquisitions first accounted for in accounting periods beginning on or after 23 December 1994 then these requirements do not apply to earlier acquisitions. However, it may be some information may still be required in respect of such acquisitions as a result of the old (less onerous) requirements of SSAP 22, as follows:

(a)   movements on provisions related to acquisitions should be disclosed and analysed between the amounts used and the amounts released unused or applied for any other purpose. Sufficient details should be given to identify the extent to which provisions have proved unnecessary;[212]

(b)   where there are subsequent material adjustments to previous provisional fair values, with a consequent adjustment to goodwill, those adjustments should be disclosed and explained.[213]

Although FRS 6 superseded most of the disclosure requirements contained in SSAP 22, some of that standard's provision are still applicable and require the following disclosures:

(a)   the accounting policy followed in respect of goodwill;[214]

(b)   the amount of goodwill recognised as a result of each separate acquisition made during the year (where material). The fair value of the consideration and the amount of purchased goodwill arising on each acquisition should be separately disclosed. The disclosure should identify the method of dealing with the goodwill arising and whether it has been set off against merger reserve or other reserves or has been carried forward as an intangible asset;[215]

(c) where the amortisation treatment has been applied, the period selected for amortising the goodwill in question, and movements on the goodwill account during the year.[216]

The above disclosure requirements of SSAP 22 also apply to acquisitions of associates. However, the disclosure requirements of FRS 6 do not. This means that there is no longer a requirement to give a fair value table on the acquisition of an associate.

FRS 6 has also clarified and extended the disclosures to be given in respect of pre-acquisition performance (which used to be required under paragraph 13(4) of Schedule 4A to the Companies Act 1985). For each material acquisition the profit after taxation and minority interests of the acquired entity should be given for :

(a) the period from the beginning of the acquired entity's financial year to the date of acquisition, giving the date on which this period began; and

(b) its previous period.

There is no requirement to give this information in aggregate for other acquisitions.[217] The information is not only required when a material subsidiary is acquired but also if a material unincorporated business has been acquired.

The standard extends the pre-acquisition information to be given in the context of substantial acquisitions, i.e. those where:

(a) for listed companies, the combination is a Class I or Super Class I transaction under the Stock Exchange listing rules; or

(b) for other entities, either

(i) the net assets or operating profits of the acquired entity exceed 15 per cent of those of the acquiring entity, or

(ii) the fair value of the consideration given exceeds 15 per cent of the net assets of the acquiring entity;

and in any other exceptional cases where disclosure is necessary to give a true and fair view. For the purposes of (b) above, net assets and profits should be those shown in the accounts for the last financial year before the date of the acquisition; and the net assets should be augmented by any purchased goodwill eliminated against reserves as a matter of accounting policy and not charged to the profit and loss account.[218] About a year after the standard was issued the Stock Exchange Listing Rules were amended deleting all reference to Class I transactions. In order to maintain the status quo, the UITF issued Abstract 15 - *Disclosure of substantial acquisitions.* Accordingly, for the purposes of (a) above, the reference to Class I transactions should be interpreted as meaning those transactions in which any of the ratios set out in the Stock Exchange Listing Rules defining Super Class I transactions exceeds 15%.[219] The required information is:

(a) the summarised profit and loss account and statement of total recognised gains and losses of the acquired entity for the period from the beginning of its financial year to the effective date of acquisition, giving the date on which this period began. The summarised profit and loss account should show, as a minimum, the analysis of turnover, operating profit and those exceptional items falling under paragraph 20 of FRS 3; profit before taxation; taxation and minority interests; and extraordinary items; and

(b) the profit after tax and minority interests for the acquired entity's previous financial year.

This information should be shown on the basis of the acquired entity's accounting policies prior to the acquisition.[220] An example of such disclosure is shown below:

Extract 6.44: Premier Farnell plc (1996)

23. ACQUISITIONS AND DISPOSALS [extract]

(i) Acquisition of Premier

The summarised profit and loss account and statement of total recognised gains and losses for Premier from the beginning of its financial year on 1st June 1995 to 10th April 1996 are set out below:

	1st June 1995 to 10th April 1996 £m
Summarised profit and loss account	
Turnover	472.3
Operating profit	90.3
Exceptional items	(12.9)
Profit before interest	77.4
Interest	3.1
Profit before tax	80.5
Tax	(34.7)
Profit after tax	45.8
Dividends	(24.6)
Retained profit	21.2

Statement of total recognised gains and losses

Retained profit for the period	21.2
Currency translation adjustment	(0.3)
Total recognised gains since last annual report	20.9

Exceptional items include costs incurred by Premier in connection with the acquisition in April 1996.

The profit after tax achieved by Premier in the year ended 31st May 1995 was £68.4 million.

The information shown above has been prepared on the basis of Premier's accounting policies prior to the acquisition.

As noted above, this new disclosure requirement is effectively an extension of the now repealed Companies Act requirement to disclose information about the pre-acquisition results of acquired subsidiaries and therefore seems of questionable relevance as it is to be based on pre-acquisition accounting policies and values which do not reflect the terms of the acquisition transaction.

2.8.3 Mergers

FRS 6 requires that for each business combination accounted for as a merger (other than group reconstructions), the following information should be disclosed:[221]

(a) an analysis of the principal components of the current year's profit and loss account and statement of total recognised gains and losses into:

    (i) amounts relating to the merged entity for the period after the effective date of the merger, and

    (ii) for each party to the merger, amounts relating to that party for the period up to the date of the merger;

(b) an analysis similar to (a) (ii) for the previous year;

(c) the composition and fair value of the consideration given by the issuing company and its subsidiary undertakings;

(d) the aggregate book value of the net assets of each party to the merger at the date of the merger; and

(e) the nature and amount of significant accounting adjustments made to the net assets of any party to the merger to achieve consistency of accounting policies, and an explanation of any other significant adjustments made to the net assets of any party to the merger as a consequence of the merger; and

(f) a statement of the adjustments to consolidated reserves.

The analysis of the profit and loss account in (a) and (b) above should show as a minimum the turnover, operating profit and exceptional items, split between continuing operations, discontinued operations and acquisitions; taxation and minority interests; and extraordinary items.

An example of these disclosures is shown below:

Extract 6.45: United News & Media plc (1996)

29. Business merger As explained in the accounting policies, on 8 February 1996, United and MAI announced plans for the merging of their respective businesses. The merger was to be effected by way of offers made by United for the whole of the issued share capital of MAI, being 332,718,123 ordinary shares of 5 pence each and 120,956.330 preference shares of 5 pence each, for a consideration of 242,090,550 ordinary shares of 25 pence each, the fair value of which amounted to £1,560.3 million. These offers became unconditional on 2 April 1996. The merger has been accounted for using the merger accounting principles set out in Financial Reporting Standard 6. Accordingly the financial information for the current period has been presented, and that for the prior periods restated, as if MAI had been owned by United throughout the current and prior accounting periods.

The book value of net assets at the time of the merger together with adjustments arising from the alignment of accounting policies were

	£m
United	
Book value of net assets at time of merger	238.0
Merger adjustment (note 24)	(73.0)
Restated net assets at time of merger	165.0
MAI	
Book value of net assets at time of merger	224.6
Merger adjustment (note 24)	(27.7)
Restated net assets at time of merger	196.9

An analysis of contribution to the profit attributable to shareholders made by the combining groups in the period prior to the merger date on 2 April 1996, the principal components of the profit and loss accounts and statements or total recognised gains and losses is as follows:

Profit and loss account	United pre merger £m	MAI pre merger £m	Combined post merger £m	Total £m
Turnover				
Continuing operations	268.8	196.9	1,451.8	1,917.5
Acquisitions	2.7	–	18.3	21.0
Discontinued operations	6.8	14.6	30.8	52.2
	278.3	211.5	1,500.9	1,990.7
Operating profit				
Continuing operations	21.4	23.5	129.6	174.5
Acquisitions	0.7	–	(18.1)	(17.4)
Discontinued operations	0.2	4.0	6.9	11.1
	22.3	27.5	118.4	168.2
Income from interests in associated undertakings	1.9	3.9	(47.1)	(41.3)
Income from other fixed asset investments	0.6	–	1.6	2.2
Total operating profit	24.8	31.4	72.9	129.1
Merger expenses	–	–	(31.0)	(31.0)
Profit on the disposal of fixed asset investments	–	11.6	–	11.6
Profit on sales and closure of businesses	–	–	138.0	138.0
Profit on ordinary activities before interest	24.8	43.0	179.9	247.7
Net interest expense	(4.0)	(1.0)	(8.9)	(13.9)
Profit before tax	20.8	42.0	171.0	233.8
Tax	(6.8)	(14.0)	(55.1)	(75.9)
Profit after tax	14.0	28.0	115.9	157.9
Minority interest	–	(0.2)	(5.3)	(5.5)
Profit for the year	14.0	27.8	110.6	152.4
Total recognised gains and losses				
Profit for the year	14.0	27.8	110.6	152.4
Exchange gains	–	–	1.4	1.4
	14.0	27.8	112.0	153.8

The equivalent analysis for the year ended 31 December 1995 is as follows

Profit and loss account	United £m	MAI £m	Total £m
Turnover			
Continuing operations	1,032.9	768.2	1,801.1
Discontinued operations	37.7	52.6	90.3
	1,070.6	820.8	1,891.4
Operating profit			
Continuing operations	111.2	89.1	200.3
Discontinued operations	3.9	12.8	16.7
	115.1	101.9	217.0
Income from interests in associated undertakings	0.9	12.9	13.8
Income from other fixed asset investments	3.3	–	3.3
Total operating profit	119.3	114.8	234.1
Loss on sales and closure of businesses	(2.9)	–	(2.9)
Profit on ordinary activities before interest	116.4	114.8	231.2
Net interest expense	(11.9)	(4.0)	(15.9)
Profit before tax	104.5	110.8	215.3
Tax	(34.3)	(36.0)	(70.3)
Profit after tax	70.2	74.8	145.0
Minority interest	(1.5)	1.4	(0.1)
Profit for the year	68.7	76.2	144.9

Total recognised gains and losses			
Profit for the year	68.7	76.2	144.9
Exchange losses	(0.5)	–	(0.5)
	68.2	76.2	144.4

24. Merger adjustments The merger adjustments reflect the alignment of accounting policies following the merger:

(a)   Intangible assets - in previous periods publishing rights and titles had been stated at directors' valuation. These are now stated at fair value on acquisition and are not revalued. The effect of this restatement is a debit adjustment to the revaluation reserve of £73 million. The comparative figures for 1995 have been restated.

(b)   Consolidation - on acquisition of subsidiary undertakings, businesses or associated undertakings the purchase consideration is allocated between underlying assets on a fair value basis. Any goodwill arising is written off direct to reserves. Previously in MAI the goodwill relating to certain associates was amortised over its expected economic life. The effect of this restatement is a debit adjustment to goodwill of £27.7 million. The comparative figures for 1995 have been restated.

23. Share premium account and reserves [extract]

Group	Share premium account £m	Merger reserve £m	Revaluation reserve £m	Other reserves £m	Goodwill reserve £m	Profit and loss account £m	Total £m
At 1 January 1996 as previously reported:							
United	205.6	–	80.2	467.3	(826.5)	236.3	162.9
MAI	60.7	–	–	30.2	(237.4)	340.2	193.7
Consolidation adjustment	–	(37.1)	–	–	–	–	(37.1)
Merger adjustment	(60.7)	60.7	(73.0)	–	(27.7)	–	(100.7)
As restated	205.6	23.6	7.2	497.5	(1,091.6)	576.5	218.8

The consolidation adjustment represents the difference between the nominal value of 25 pence of the shares issued to former MAI shareholders and the nominal value of 5 pence of the MAI shares acquired.

Many of these disclosures have their origin in the previous disclosure requirements in SSAP 23, updated for the impact of FRS 3. In our view, these original disclosure requirements were needed to compensate for the fact that merger accounting was very easily available under SSAP 23 for business combinations which, in substance, were acquisitions. This information would seem to be irrelevant in the context of a true merger.

Group reconstructions that are accounted for by using merger accounting are exempted from the disclosure requirements in the FRS, but must still give the information required by companies legislation.

2.8.4 Companies Act

As indicated at 2.8.1 above, some of the above disclosure requirements which are contained in FRS 6 are duplicated in the Companies Act,[222] but in many cases the standard has extended the information required by the legislation.

However, the Act requires the names of subsidiaries acquired, and whether they have been accounted for as acquisitions or mergers, even if they do not significantly affect the figures shown in the group accounts.[223] This was an issue noted by the Financial Reporting Review Panel in its findings in respect of the 1990 financial statements of Williams Holdings.[224]

The Act also requires disclosure of the cumulative amount of goodwill resulting from acquisitions in that and earlier years which has been written off otherwise than in the consolidated profit and loss account for that or any earlier year. This figure would be net of any goodwill attributable to subsidiaries or businesses which had been disposed of.[225] It would also not include any goodwill which was being amortised and arguably any goodwill against which a provision for impairment had been made.

Any information required by the Companies Act need not be given in respect of an undertaking established under the law of a country outside the UK or an undertaking which carries on business outside the UK if the directors consider it would be prejudicial to the business of the undertaking or any other group member. However, this is subject to the agreement of the Secretary of State.[226]

Disclosure of the cumulative amount of goodwill is also not required in respect of any undertaking acquired prior to 23 December 1989, where the necessary information is unavailable, or cannot be obtained without unreasonable expense or delay. Any company taking advantage of this exemption must disclose that it has done so.[227]

Companies have generally met the requirement to disclose the cumulative amount of goodwill written off by including a footnote within the reserves note along the following lines:

> *Extract 6.46: Granada Group PLC (1996)*
>
> **24   Reconciliation of movements in shareholders' funds** [extract]
>
> The cumulative amount of any goodwill written-off resulting from acquisitions made in the current and earlier financial years, net of any goodwill attributable to subsidiary undertakings or businesses subsequently disposed of, is £3,060.4 million (1995: £1,462.8 million).

As goodwill is defined in terms of the fair value of any consideration given, the figure to be disclosed should not be net of any merger relief that has been taken under section 131 of the Companies Act (see 2.1.2 above). Ferguson International failed to do this in its 1995 accounts and as a result the Financial Reporting Review Panel required it to correct the disclosure in its 1996 accounts.[228]

One drawback with such disclosures is that it is not always evident from the financial statements which reserves have been affected by the goodwill write-offs. This may be why some companies have changed their policy in respect of goodwill written off, by reconstituting a goodwill write-off reserve. One company which did this was Grand Metropolitan (see Extract 6.30 at 2.5.2 D above); even then some footnote disclosure was required because the 'goodwill' reserve was net of a special reserve created as a result of a share premium reduction scheme.

Some companies have only disclosed the goodwill which has accumulated from a particular date. For example:

> *Extract 6.47: APV plc (1996)*
>
> **23 RESERVES** [extract]
>
> (v) The cumulative goodwill write off on acquisitions less goodwill realised on disposals from 1 January 1987 to 31 December 1996 was £166.8 million (1995 – £168.6 million).

Such a treatment will be acceptable as long as the figure disclosed is not materially different from that which would have been disclosed if the company had gone back further and included all acquisitions.

As indicated above, an exemption is available in respect of acquisitions made prior to 23 December 1989, in which case certain disclosures are required. GEC has made use of this exemption and makes the necessary disclosure, as shown below:

Extract 6.48: The General Electric Company p.l.c. (1996)

23 Goodwill [extract]

Goodwill written off in respect of acquisitions of businesses which were in the Group at 31st March, 1996 made since 23rd December 1989, amounted to £1,160 million (1995 £515 million). Information to calculate the amount of goodwill written off in respect of businesses acquired prior to that date is either unavailable or it would be costly to obtain.

One company which discloses the cumulative amounts of both positive and negative goodwill is Commercial Union, as shown below:

Extract 6.49: Commercial Union plc (1996)

30. Profit and loss account [extract]

The cumulative amounts of positive and negative goodwill charged or credited to consolidated profit and loss account, attributable to subsidiary undertakings acquired after 1 January 1968 and not subsequently sold, are £458m and £22m respectively. Similar information relating to subsidiary undertakings before 1968 is not readily available.

These are presumably disclosed separately because strictly the amount of goodwill which is required to be disclosed under the Companies Act is that relating to positive goodwill; the legislation does not use the term 'negative goodwill', but 'negative consolidation difference'. Also, the Companies Act only refers to acquisitions of subsidiaries, so strictly the amount disclosed should not include amounts relating to associates and unincorporated businesses. Cable and Wireless discloses separately the amount relating to associates, as shown below:

Extract 6.50: Cable and Wireless plc (1997)

26   RESERVES [extract]

The cumulative amount of goodwill resulting from acquisitions during the year ended 31 March 1997 and prior years, net of goodwill written back through the profit and loss account amounted to £818m (1996 - £957m). Of this amount £352m (1996 - £646m) related to associated undertakings.

A notable example is Guinness, which not only discloses the aggregate amount, but shows the movements and analyses them between the various acquisitions that the company has made, as shown in the following extract:

Extract 6.51: Guinness PLC (1996)

23. RESERVES AND GOODWILL [extract]

(B) GOODWILL

	Year of acquisition	1 January 1996 £m	Additions £m	Disposals £m	31 December 1996 £m
Distillers	1986	284	–	–	284
Schenley	1987	92	–	–	92
Asbach	1991-92	112	–	–	112
Cruzcampo Group	1991	325	–	–	325
Glenmore	1991	5	–	–	5
MH	1994	104	–	–	104
Other		379	–	–	379
		1,298	**–**	**–**	**1,298**

A provision of £146m has been made against the value of the goodwill arising on the acquisition of the Group's interest in LVMH as set out in Note 5.

The £2m disposal of goodwill arising on acquisition of the Group's interest in LVMH reflects goodwill attributable to the RoC beauty products business, the sale of which was completed by LVMH in December 1993.

As indicated at 2.8.3 above, group reconstructions that are accounted for by using merger accounting are exempted from the disclosure requirements in FRS 6, but must still give (in addition to the information outlined at 2.8.1 above) the following information which is required by companies legislation:

(a)   the composition and fair value of the consideration given by the issuing company and its subsidiary undertakings;[229] and

(b)   an explanation of any significant adjustments made to the assets and liabilities of the undertaking acquired, together with a statement of any resulting adjustment to the consolidated reserves (including the re-statement of the opening consolidated reserves).[230]

3   DISPOSALS

3.1   Basic principles

The other possible change in the composition of a group involves the disposal of a group company. In principle the results of the company being disposed of should continue to be consolidated as part of the group results until the effective date of disposal, and the gain or loss on disposal should be determined by comparing the carrying value of the subsidiary's net assets at that date with the sales proceeds obtained. There are, however, a number of aspects which need to be considered, which are discussed more fully below.

3.2   Effective date of disposal

FRS 2 defines the date of disposal in terms of when control passes; it states that 'the date for accounting for an undertaking ceasing to be a subsidiary undertaking is the date on which its former parent undertaking relinquishes its control over that undertaking'.[231] These provisions are discussed further at 2.2 above.

One complication which can arise is when a decision has been taken before a year-end to dispose of a subsidiary after the year-end and a loss is expected to emerge. Under FRS 3, if a decision has been made to sell an operation, any consequential provision should reflect the extent to which obligations have been incurred that are not expected to be covered by the future profits of the operation or the disposal of the operation. Such a provision can only be made in respect of a proposed sale if the company is demonstrably committed to the sale; this should be evidenced by a binding sale agreement. In these circumstances, provision should be made for the loss which is anticipated, and this should also take account of the trading results which are expected to arise up to the date of disposal, which will either be trading losses which increase the amount of the loss on disposal or trading profits which go to mitigate it. The effective date of 'deconsolidation' will be the balance sheet date in the sense that the group financial statements for the following period will not be impacted by the results of the subsidiary being disposed of, except to the extent of any difference between the amount provided and the actual results until the date of disposal.

This then gives rise to questions of presentation of the 'deconsolidated' subsidiary, both in the balance sheet and in the profit and loss account. In the balance sheet, the straightforward treatment would be to continue to consolidate the company on a line-by-line basis as normal. However, an alternative treatment sometimes adopted in the past was to show the net assets as one line in the balance sheet, possibly with a summarised balance sheet shown by way of note. Arguably, the former treatment is the one required by the Companies Act; at the balance sheet date it is still a subsidiary which must be consolidated (none of the grounds for non-consolidation applies) and the Act requires line-by-line consolidation. This is also reinforced by the fact that FRS 2 requires consolidation up to the date of disposal.

In the profit and loss account, similarly, it is possible to continue to consolidate the results of the subsidiary in question as normal. Again, this is arguably what is required by the Companies Act. Where a provision for losses up to the date of actual disposal has been made at the balance sheet date, the question arises of whether, and if so how, to show the actual results in the consolidated financial statements of the following year. Frequently companies used to show only the net effect of any over or under provision. However, a strict application of the rules on the effective date of disposal would require the results to continue to be consolidated until that date as normal, and to show an offsetting release of the provision made at the previous year-end.

FRS 2 requires that the consolidated profit and loss account should include the results of a subsidiary undertaking up to the date of its disposal.[232] In addition, FRS 3 indicates that the results of discontinued operations should be shown under the statutory format headings with the utilisation of the provision analysed as necessary between the operating loss and the loss on sale.[233] It would seem therefore that a strict application of the rules is required and the alternative treatment is no longer possible.

3.3   Goodwill of subsidiaries disposed of

Where a subsidiary has been acquired and then disposed of (particularly if the period of ownership was relatively short), it is necessary to keep sight of what has happened to any goodwill, positive or negative, which arose on the acquisition. If it has been taken to reserves, then there is a danger that it will bypass the profit and loss account altogether and result in a misstatement of the gain or loss on disposal because the goodwill has not been taken into account.

3.3.1   UITF 3

The UITF considered this matter in December 1991 and it issued Abstract 3 – *Treatment of Goodwill on Disposal of a Business*. The UITF determined that goodwill should be taken into account in the calculation of the gain or loss on disposal. UITF 3 states that 'the amount included in the consolidated profit and loss account in respect of the profit or loss on disposal of a previously acquired business, subsidiary or associated undertaking should be determined by including, if material, the attributable goodwill where it has previously been eliminated against reserves as a matter of accounting policy and has not previously been charged in the profit and loss account'.[234]

It can be seen that it is not only on the disposal of a subsidiary that any goodwill has to be taken into account, but also on the disposal of a business or an associate undertaking. In addition, the principle also applies to closures of businesses and to negative goodwill.[235]

UITF 3 requires the amount of the goodwill included in the calculation to be separately disclosed as a component of the profit or loss on disposal, either on the face of the profit and loss account or in a note to the financial statements.[236]

Although the principle of including the goodwill in the calculation is a straightforward one, it can be difficult to apply in practice unless the subsidiary in question has been sold in exactly the same form as it was purchased. If the business of the subsidiary has been integrated with that of the rest of the group, or reorganised in any other way, then it is not necessarily the case that the sale of the company automatically means that the goodwill which was acquired with it has also been sold.

The UITF recognised this problem. However, it considered that the disclosure requirements of the Companies Act and SSAP 22 relating to goodwill (see 2.8.4

above and 3.6 below) effectively require companies to maintain records that would normally enable an appropriate estimate or apportionment to be made of the purchased goodwill attributable to the disposal. Nevertheless, it accepted that 'there may be cases where it is genuinely impractical to make a reasonable estimate of the purchased goodwill attributable to a disposal, for example, where a disposal relates to a business that was part of a group acquired many years ago and subsequently restructured'. In such situations where it is not possible to ascertain the goodwill, or make a reasonable estimation, this fact and the reason should be explained.[237]

A supplementary issue which the UITF considered was whether the amount of the goodwill brought into the calculation should be the gross amount that has been eliminated against reserves or whether some allowance should be made for any notional amortisation during the period of ownership. The UITF concluded that, 'if there has been no charge in the profit and loss account in respect of the premium paid on acquisition, the gross attributable amount should be brought into the calculation'.[238] This is to ensure that none of the goodwill bypasses the profit and loss account.

Approximately one year after issuing the Abstract, the UITF had noted that a small minority of companies were applying it in an unsatisfactory manner and therefore felt obliged to issue a statement emphasising the way in which it should be applied.[239] There were two approaches noted, as follows:

(a)   some companies had been presenting the goodwill debit in the profit and loss account separately from, rather than as part of, the profit or loss on disposal. Although the Abstract requires disclosure of the amount of goodwill included in the calculation, the UITF emphasised that it clearly indicates that the goodwill element should be included *as part of* the profit or loss on disposal, and not distanced from it as a separate item. Where the item is presented as two components there should be, in addition, a single sub-total showing the profit or loss on disposal. The UITF also stated that a caption such as 'loss on disposal of subsidiary' should not be used to describe an item that does not take into account any related goodwill.

(b)   some companies were crediting, in the profit and loss account, before the deduction of dividends, an amount equal to the goodwill element of the profit or loss on disposal, thereby mitigating the impact on the bottom line of the profit and loss account. The UITF stated that while it is acceptable to show dividends are paid out of accumulated reserves, this should not be done in such a way that implies (e.g. by the striking of a sub-total) that the profit for the period is calculated after crediting the goodwill release.

Regarding (b) above, the ASB emphasised that for the purposes of FRS 3, the credit adjustment arising on a disposal should be shown in the reconciliation of movements of shareholders' funds; it should not be included in the profit and loss account for the year (unless it is extended to include a full appropriation account) nor in the statement of recognised gains and losses.

Examples of disclosures meeting the requirements of UITF 3 are shown below:

Extract 6.52: Norcros p.l.c. (1997)

Group profit and loss account [extract]

	Continuing operations 1997 £m	Discontinued operations 1997 £m	Total 1997 £m	*Continuing operations 1996 £m*	*Discontinued operations 1996 £m*	*Total 1996 £m*
Net profit on disposal of businesses						
- Net tangible assets	–	**47.5**	**47.5**	–	*12.0*	*12.0*
- Goodwill previously written off against reserves	–	**(1.7)**	**(1.7)**	–	*–*	*–*
	–	**45.8**	**45.8**	–	*12.0*	*12.0*

Extract 6.53: APV plc (1996)

6 Disposal of businesses [extract]

	1996 £m	1995 £m
Continuing operations		
Profit on disposal of Australasia Catering Equipment and Retail Bakery businesses	**8.0**	–
Profit on disposal of the UK Refrigeration & Freezer business	**(0.3)**	12.2
Other profit less losses on disposal of businesses	–	0.7
	7.7	12.9

(i) The Australasia Catering Equipment and Retail Bakery businesses were sold in March 1996 for a consideration of £18.6 million. The profit on disposal of these businesses was generated as follows:

	£m	£m
Consideration		**18.6**
Net assets sold		
Fixed assets	**(1.0)**	
Stock	**(7.1)**	
Debtors	**(1.4)**	
Creditors	**1.3**	
Pension surplus		**0.4**
Goodwill adjustment		**(2.0)**
Disposal costs and provisions for future expenditure		**(0.8)**
Profit on disposal of Australasia Catering Equipment and Retail Bakery businesses		**8.0**

Although UITF 3 only deals with the treatment of goodwill on the disposal and closure of businesses, some companies have extended the principle to situations where goodwill has become permanently impaired, as illustrated below:

Extract 6.54: Saatchi & Saatchi Company PLC (1993)

GOODWILL

Goodwill, including any additional goodwill arising from the contingent capital payments disclosed in Note 22, is written off directly to reserves in the year in which it arises. A charge is recognised in the Group's profit and loss account in respect of any permanent diminution in value of acquisition goodwill.

CONSOLIDATED PROFIT AND LOSS ACCOUNT [extract]

	Note:	Total Year ended 31 Dec 1993 £ million	Total Year ended 31 Dec 1992 £ million
TRADING PROFIT		36.8	34.2
Write down of goodwill reserves	4	–	(600.0)
OPERATING PROFIT (LOSS)		36.8	(565.8)

4. EXCEPTIONAL ITEMS [extract]

The write down of goodwill reserves in 1992 arose from a review of the cost of acquired goodwill and assessment of permanent diminution in value.

Extract 6.55: Thorntons PLC (1993)

CONSOLIDATED PROFIT AND LOSS ACCOUNT [extract]

	Notes	1993 £000	£000	1992 £000	£000
Operating profit			*9,354*		*10,591*
Profit on property disposals			*–*		*148*
			9,354		*10,591*
Exceptional items:					
Provision for restructuring of French business	*4*	*7,630*		*–*	
Goodwill on French acquisition written off		*5,405*		*–*	
		13,035		*–*	
UK reorganisation		*140*		*630*	
Property write-downs less disposal profits		*–*		*194*	
			13,175		*824*
			(3,821)		*9,767*

3.3.2   FRS 2

The ruling made by the UITF in Abstract 3 has been reinforced by FRS 2. The standard requires that where a subsidiary undertaking is disposed of, the gain or loss should be calculated 'by comparing the carrying amount of the net assets of that subsidiary undertaking attributable to the group's interest before the cessation with any remaining carrying amount attributable to the group's interest after the cessation together with any proceeds received. The net assets compared should include any related goodwill not previously written-off through the profit and loss account.'[240]

3.4   Partial disposals

When part of the investment in a subsidiary is sold, but a sufficient number of the shares are held for it to retain subsidiary or associate status, it is necessary to consider how to account for the disposal in the consolidated financial statements. When more than 50% of the shares are retained, all the assets and liabilities remain consolidated on a line-by-line basis, so the accounting entries affect only the consolidated reserves and the minority interest. The calculation of the gain or loss on sale will be achieved by comparing the sale proceeds with the consolidated net asset value (including any related goodwill) attributable to the shares sold at the date of the disposal, as in the following example:

Example 6.5: Partial disposal of shares in a subsidiary

Company A has a 100% investment in Company B, based on an original investment of £4,000. No goodwill arose on this transaction. Company B has subsequently earned profits of £6,000 which it has retained. The balance sheets of the companies and of the group show the following immediately before the sale:

	Company A £000	Company B £000	Consolidated £000
Investment in B	4		
Other net assets	20	10	30
	24	10	30
Share capital	10	4	10
Reserves	14	6	20
	24	10	30

Company A sells 40% of its shares in Company B to a third party for £7,000. It will compute its gain on this transaction (ignoring any taxation payable on the gain), in its own profit and loss account and in that of the group, thus:

	Own accounts £000	Group accounts £000
Sale proceeds	7.0	7.0
40% of investment/net assets	1.6	4.0
Gain on sale	5.4	3.0

The balance sheets will now show the following:

	Company A £000	Company B £000	Consolidated £000
Investment in B	2.4		
Other net assets	27.0	10.0	37.0
	29.4	10.0	37.0
Minority interest			4.0
Share capital	10.0	4.0	10.0
Reserves	19.4	6.0	23.0
	29.4	10.0	37.0

The same basic principles apply where only an associate holding is retained, the only difference being that the balance sheet will carry the underlying assets of Company B on one line. If Company A had sold 60% of its holding for £11,000, the effect on the profit and loss accounts and balance sheets (again ignoring the effects of any taxation payable) would have been as follows:

	Own accounts	Group accounts
	£000	£000
Sale proceeds	11.0	11.0
60% of investment/net assets	2.4	6.0
Gain on sale	8.6	5.0

The balance sheets would now show the following:

	Company A	Company B	Consolidated
	£000	£000	£000
Investment in B	1.6		4.0
Other net assets	31.0	10.0	31.0
	32.6	10.0	35.0
Share capital	10.0	4.0	10.0
Reserves	22.6	6.0	25.0
	32.6	10.0	35.0

The above approach is that which is required by FRS 2.[241] It might be thought that such an approach is inconsistent with the treatment of intra-group transactions under the standard (see 3.4 of Chapter 5). However, as explained by the ASB, 'where the group disposes of part of its interest in a subsidiary undertaking it transacts directly with third parties and a profit or loss for the group is reported in the consolidated financial statements. This can be contrasted with the treatment of intra-group transactions where no profit or loss arises for the group as a whole because the transaction involves only undertakings included in the consolidation and under common control and does not directly involve any third party.'[242]

3.5   Deemed disposals

An undertaking may cease to be a subsidiary undertaking, or the group may reduce its proportional interest in that undertaking, other than by actual disposal. These deemed disposals may arise for a number of reasons:

(a)   the group does not take up its full allocation in a rights issue;

(b)   the subsidiary undertaking declares special scrip dividends which are not taken up by the parent so that its proportional interest is diminished;

(c)   another party exercises its options or warrants; or

(d)   the subsidiary undertaking issues shares to third parties.

FRS 2 says that the accounting for deemed disposals and direct disposals should be the same; in respect of both, the profit or loss should be calculated as described in 3.3.2 above.[243]

Example 6.6: *Dilution in the holding of an investment in a subsidiary undertaking*

Company H owns 800,000 £1 shares in Company S which has a share capital of £1,000,000 and net assets of £2,500,000, the balance of £1,500,000 being retained profits. Company H has owned its investment since the formation of Company S, and therefore has consolidated 80% of its profits (£1,200,000). Its share of Company S's net assets is therefore £2,000,000.

Company S issues 1,000,000 shares to third parties for cash of £3,000,000 thereby increasing its net assets to £5,500,000. The share capital and reserves of Company S and the amounts attributable to Company H (40%) are now as follows:

	Company S	Attributable to Company H
	£	£
Share capital	2,000,000	800,000
Share premium account	2,000,000	800,000
Profit and loss account	1,500,000	600,000
Total	5,500,000	2,200,000

Company H has increased its share of net assets from £2,000,000 to £2,200,000. This gain of £200,000 should be included in Company H's consolidated profit and loss account. However, its share of Company S's distributable reserves has actually declined from £1,200,000 to £600,000. It could be argued that Company H should reclassify its group reserves by making a transfer of £800,000 from retained profits to some other reserve, reflecting the fact that these profits have been replaced by a share of Company S's share premium account, which is not distributable. This may be the preferable route particularly if Company S is now to be treated as an associate of Company H. However, FRS 2 does not give any guidance on this issue.

An example of a company recognising a profit through the profit and loss account in respect of a deemed disposal is shown in the following extract from the 1995 accounts of Courts:

Extract 6.56: Courts Plc (1995)

5   Exceptional credit

	1995 £'000	1994 £'000
Profit on deemed disposal of interest in Courts (Mauritius) Ltd	550	–
Profit arising on sale of shares in Courts (Singapore) Ltd	–	9,428
	550	9,428

3.6   Disclosure requirements relating to disposals

SSAP 22 requires the following information to be disclosed in respect of each material disposal of a previously acquired business or business segment:

(a)   the profit or loss on the disposal;

(b)   the amount of the purchased goodwill attributable to the business or business segment disposed of and how it has been treated in determining the profit or loss on disposal;

(c)   the accounting treatment adopted and the amount of the proceeds in situations where no profit or loss is recorded on a disposal because the proceeds have been accounted for as a reduction in the cost of the acquisition.[244]

For businesses which were acquired before 1 January 1989, if it is impossible or impracticable to ascertain the attributable goodwill, then this fact should be stated and the reason for non-disclosure given.[245]

As indicated at 3.3.1 above, UITF 3 requires the amount of the goodwill included in the calculation to be separately disclosed as a component of the profit or loss on disposal, either on the face of the profit and loss account or in a note to the financial statements. (Although the UITF has ruled on this issue, the disclosure requirement of SSAP 22 described at (b) above still remains.)

In addition, the Companies Act requires that where there has been a disposal of a material subsidiary during the financial year, disclosure should be made of the name of the subsidiary and of its results up to the date of disposal.[246] However, a similar exemption to that in respect of business combinations indicated at 2.8.4 above applies if disclosure is thought to be prejudicial.

FRS 2 has repeated the requirements of the Act, but has extended them such that the name of each material undertaking which ceases to be a subsidiary undertaking, together with any ownership interest retained, should be disclosed. Where this arises other than by way of disposal of at least part of the interest held by the group, the circumstances in which the undertaking ceased to be a subsidiary undertaking should be explained.[247]

In addition, FRS 1 requires disclosure of the effects of disposals of subsidiaries on the cash flow statement and FRS 3 requires separate disclosure of the aggregate results of discontinued operations during the period. These are discussed at 2.7.1 of Chapter 27 and 2.3 of Chapter 22 respectively.

4   GROUP REORGANISATIONS

4.1   Introduction

Group reorganisations involve the restructuring of the relationships between companies in a group by, for example, setting up a new holding company, changing the direct ownership of a subsidiary within the group, or transferring businesses from one company to another because of a process of divisionalisation. In principle, most of such changes should have no impact on the consolidated financial statements (provided there are no minority interests affected), because they are purely internal and cannot affect the group when it is being portrayed as a single entity. However, all such transactions can have a significant impact on the financial statements of the individual companies in the group, and this is described for each of the main types of transaction in the sections which follow. All the examples given assume that all the subsidiaries are owned 100% by the parent company.

4.2 Setting up a new top holding company

Reorganisations of this type may take place, for example, to introduce a public company over the top of an existing group as a vehicle for flotation, or to improve the co-ordination of diverse businesses. It involves H becoming the new holding company of A, as shown in the diagram below, and this may be achieved either by the shareholders subscribing for shares in H and then H paying cash for A or, more usually, by H issuing its own shares to the shareholders of A in exchange for the shares in A.

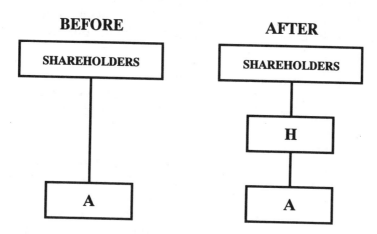

This type of reorganisation will qualify as a 'group reconstruction' under FRS 6 which is defined as any of the following arrangements:

(a) the transfer of a shareholding in a subsidiary undertaking from one group company to another;

(b) the addition of a new parent company to a group;

(c) the transfer of shares in one or more subsidiary undertakings of a group to a new company that is not a group company but whose shareholders are the same as those of the group's parent; and

(d) the combination into a group of two or more companies that before the combination had the same shareholders.[248]

FRS 6 has not exempted group reconstructions from its provisions but states that merger accounting may be used for group reconstructions, even though there is no business combination meeting the definition of a merger, provided:

(a)   the requirements of the Companies Act for merger accounting are met (see 2.1.5 above);

(b)   the ultimate shareholders remain the same, and the rights of each such shareholder, relative to the others, are unchanged; and

(c)   no minority's interest in the net assets of the group is altered by the transfer.[249]

It can be seen that under FRS 6 the use of merger accounting for group reconstructions is to be optional. However, because of condition (a) above, if the new holding company pays cash for the subsidiary, then merger accounting will not be possible as the Companies Act provisions will not be met. Merger accounting is only permitted under the legislation where the shares are acquired by means of a share for share exchange and the fair value of any consideration other than equity shares does not exceed 10% of the nominal value of the equity shares issued.[250]

Therefore if H pays cash for A, it should (in theory at least) account for the transaction as an acquisition, which involves attributing fair values to A's assets, consolidating only the post-acquisition results of A and possibly freezing A's pre-acquisition reserves from being distributed to H's shareholders in the future (see 2.3.7 above for a discussion of the treatment of pre-acquisition dividends). All these consequences are usually undesirable when the sole intention is to insert a new holding company at the top of the group, and it is relatively unlikely that this means of effecting the transaction will be chosen. In any event, H could have difficulty in financing such a transaction, and A could not provide the necessary finance (e.g. by any kind of loan or guarantee) because UK company law does not permit a company to provide financial assistance for the purchase of its own shares.[251]

It is therefore more likely that the transaction will be effected by the exchange of shares. In this case the transaction will qualify for merger accounting (subject to all the provisos in FRS 6 set out above) and hence the consolidated financial statements may continue to carry the assets and liabilities of A at their previous book values and all profits before and after the merger can continue to be consolidated (although there are possible problems if H does not have the same accounting period and has not been in existence long enough – see 2.7.4 above). Also, the transaction will qualify for merger relief under section 131 of the Companies Act, so the investment in A can be recorded by H at the nominal value of the shares issued by H (although as indicated at 2.1.2 above, this may only be possible under FRS 4 if merger accounting is adopted); the reserves of A will be 'frozen' as a result of the transaction only to the extent that the nominal value of H's shares exceeds that of A's shares.

Where the option of using merger accounting is not taken, or cannot be taken because cash is involved, it would seem that acquisition accounting needs to be used, although as FRS 6 states 'acquisition accounting would require the restatement at fair value of the assets and liabilities of the company transferred, and the recognising of goodwill, which is likely to be inappropriate in the case of a transaction that does not alter the relative rights of the ultimate shareholders'.[252] (In the US, the basic rules on acquisition accounting do not apply to a transfer of assets or an exchange of shares between companies under common control.)[253]

4.3 Changing direct ownership of a company within a group

4.3.1 Subsidiary moved 'up'

This involves a 'grandson' subsidiary being moved up to become a 'son', as shown in the diagram below. Such a change might be made say, to allow B to be disposed of while C is retained, or because B and C are in different businesses and the group wishes to restructure itself so that the different businesses are conducted through directly owned subsidiaries.

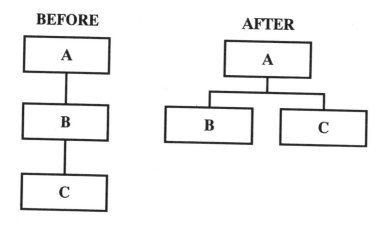

This result could be achieved either by B transferring its investment in C to A as a dividend in specie, or by A paying cash (or a cash equivalent) to B for the investment in C. It is not possible to effect this transaction by a share for share exchange, because an allotment by a holding company (A) to its subsidiary (B) is void.[254]

If the mechanism used is to be a dividend in specie then B must have sufficient distributable profits. If B has previously revalued its investment in C then the amount of that revaluation may be treated as a realised profit in deciding whether the dividend is legal and in accounting for the dividend; for example, if B's balance sheet is as follows:

	£
Investment in C (cost £100)	900
Other net assets	100
	1,000
Share capital	100
Revaluation reserve	800
Profit and loss account	100
	1,000

On the face of it, B cannot make a distribution of more than £100. However, if it makes a distribution in kind of its investment in C, the revaluation reserve can be treated as realised.[255]

Where the transaction is effected as a dividend in specie then the problem of how A accounts for it also arises. It will need to reflect its new investment in C at a value, but two questions then arise; what value to place on it, and whether the transaction gives rise to a realised profit. The legal position on both of these points is unclear. On the first question, a range of possible values would appear to be possible – the value might for example be agreed between the parties, it could be at current fair value, it could be the carrying value previously recorded in B's financial statements or it might even be nil. In practice, it might be convenient to use B's carrying value, but it cannot be said with certainty that this is the right answer. On the second issue, it may appear that A has realised a profit by being given a valuable asset (subject to the need to write down its investment in B), but it might be contended with some justification that this is not realised, since in substance nothing has changed – A still owns the same two subsidiaries as it did before. Where it is sufficiently significant (e.g. in relation to a proposed distribution), it may be advisable to seek legal advice on these points.

If A pays cash to B in exchange for its investment in C, the transaction is on the face of it straightforward. B will have to record a gain or loss on sale if the purchase price differs from the value at which it carried its investment in C, although frequently the transfer may be made on such terms that no gain or loss is recorded. However, there is a danger that a transfer at a price which does not fully reflect the true value of C (i.e. made at less than an arm's-length price) will be regarded as having given rise to a distribution, and if the transaction is made to facilitate B's leaving the group, it could also be regarded as financial assistance which may be illegal – there are therefore various possible legal pitfalls which must be borne in mind.

Regardless of the value at which these transactions take place, there should be no effect on the group financial statements, because the group as a whole is in no different position from before; it has made neither an acquisition nor a disposal.

4.3.2 Subsidiary moved 'down'

This involves a 'son' becoming a 'grandson' as shown in the diagram below. Such a change might be made, say, if A is a foreign holding company but B and C are UK companies who will form a UK tax group as a result of the reorganisation.

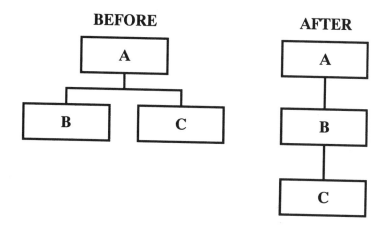

This reorganisation could be achieved either by B paying cash to A or by B issuing its shares to A in exchange for the shares in C. As in the previous two examples, there should be no effect on the group financial statements as a result of the reorganisation.

The accounting in the case of a cash transaction is relatively straightforward, following the principles described above in 4.3.1. However, if C is sold at an amount greater or smaller than its carrying value, the issue of whether A should recognise a gain or loss will again arise; as with the question discussed in 4.3.1 above, the law on this is unclear. The question of whether B has effectively made a distribution is again unlikely to arise; in the context of this transaction it could arise only if the transfer were made at a price which was in excess of the fair value of C, which is in practice unlikely.

In the case of a share-for-share exchange, the provisions of section 132 of the Companies Act 1985 become relevant. This section is designed to give partial relief from the requirement to set up a share premium account in the circumstances of a group reconstruction involving the issue of shares. It requires a share premium account of the 'minimum premium value' to be established; this is the amount by which the book value of the investment (or cost, if lower) exceeds the nominal value of the shares issued. The effect of this is to preserve the book value of the investment (any amount by which the investment had been revalued would effectively be reversed, but the investment could also be revalued again). The operation of the section is illustrated in the following example:

Example 6.7

The balance sheets of A and its direct subsidiaries B and C are as follows:

	A £	B £	C £	Group £
Investment in B	200			
Investment in C	100			
Other net assets	300	275	300	875
	600	275	300	875
Share capital	500	200	100	500
Profit and loss account	100	75	200	375
	600	275	300	875

B then issues 50 £1 shares to A in exchange for A's investment in C, which is shown in A's balance sheet at a cost of £100. The minimum premium value is therefore £50. The resultant balance sheets would be:

	A £	B £	C £	Group £
Investment in B	300			
Investment in C		100		
Other net assets	300	275	300	875
	600	375	300	875
Share capital	500	250	100	500
Share premium		50		
Profit and loss account	100	75	200	375
	600	375	300	875

Care must be taken in this situation to avoid issuing shares at a discount; this means that it must be possible to demonstrate that C is worth at least the nominal value of the shares issued by B.

If B were to prepare group accounts then the accounting considerations are similar to those discussed at 4.2 above.

4.3.3 Subsidiary moved 'along'

This involves a 'grandson' subsidiary being moved along to become another 'grandson' but under a different 'son', as shown in the diagram below. It would be achieved by C paying cash or other assets to B rather than issuing shares, because otherwise the resulting holding of B in C would probably negate the desired effect of the transaction.

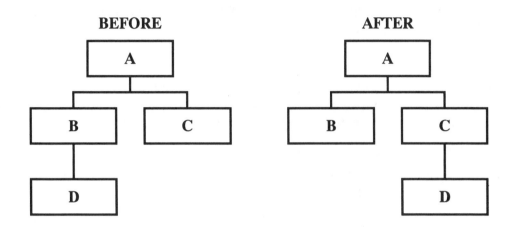

The accounting considerations are similar to those under 4.3.1 above, and once again there can be no effect on the group financial statements, because when the group is looked upon as a single entity there has been no change. The question of an effective distribution cannot arise because the purchaser is not the holding company. As above, if the transaction is a prelude to B leaving the group, or is intended to facilitate it, and C pays less than fair value then problems of financial assistance can arise. If C were to prepare group accounts then the accounting considerations are similar to those discussed at 4.2 above where the new holding company pays cash.

Although C cannot issue shares directly to B as it might negate the desired effect of the transaction, it may, however, be possible to achieve the same effect by utilising a combination of the reorganisations outlined at 4.3.1 and 4.3.2 above.

4.4 Divisionalisation of an existing group

The term 'divisionalisation' in this context is used to signify the transfer of the assets and trades of a number of subsidiaries into one company so that the businesses are brought together. It is a means of rationalising and simplifying the group and can result in a saving of administration costs. Transactions of this type are usually effected for a cash consideration, which is often left outstanding on inter-company account as the shell company has no requirement for cash.

In principle the accounting treatment is straightforward. However, one complication which can arise is that there might be an apparent need to write down the investment in the shell company to reflect an impairment in its value, depending on the price at which the assets were transferred. This will typically arise where the shell company was originally purchased at a price which included goodwill, but the business is then transferred to another company at a price which reflects only the value of the net tangible assets; this will mean that, although the goodwill still exists, the business to which it relates is now in another company, and although the group as a whole is unaffected, the value of the investment in the shell company now falls short of its cost. This issue is discussed in Chapter 11 at 2.2.1.

4.5 Demergers

In this context, this refers to splitting up an existing group of companies into two or more separate groups of companies, in order to separate their different trades, possibly as a prelude, say, to floating off one of the businesses.

This could be achieved in a number of ways:

(a) Company A transfers its shareholdings in a subsidiary, B, to its shareholders as a dividend in specie.

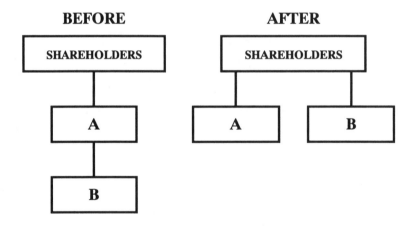

(b)   Company A transfers a trade to another company, C (usually formed for the purposes of the demerger) and in exchange C issues shares to the shareholders of A.

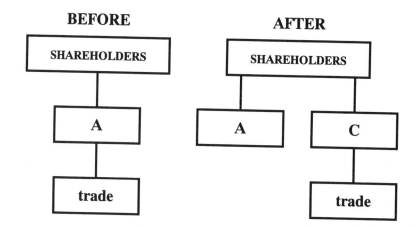

(c)   Company A transfers its shareholding in a subsidiary, B, to another company, C; in return, shares in C are issued to some or all of the shareholders in A.

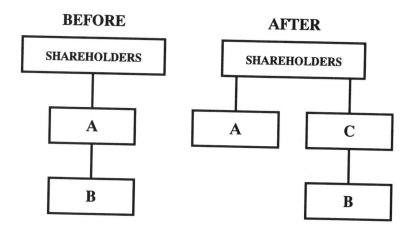

Whichever route is adopted, the transaction involves a distribution by A to its shareholders. This is less obvious in the second and third examples outlined above, but it is as though A had distributed the assets or shares in question to its own shareholders, which they then exchange for shares in C. Similar accounting issues arise in each case; for the purposes of illustration, an example is shown below of a transaction of type (c) above.

Example 6.8

B is a subsidiary of A and is to be demerged from the group. The form of the transaction is that a new company, C, is to be formed which will issue shares to the shareholders of A in exchange for A's investment in B. The balance sheets before the demerger are as follows:

	A £	B £	A group £
Investment in B	500		
Other net assets	1,200	800	2,000
	1,700	800	2,000
Share capital	1,000	500	1,000
Profit and loss account	700	300	1,000
	1,700	800	2,000

C is to issue 500 £1 ordinary shares to the shareholders of A in exchange for the shares in B held by A. In effect this amounts to a distribution of £500 by A to its shareholders so that, in the A group financial statements the company's net assets are reduced by £500 and the group's net assets by £800 (i.e. the net asset value of B). In the financial statements, the usual treatment is to disclose these amounts as movements on retained earnings, along the following lines:

Profit and loss account	Group £	Company £
Balance at 1 January 19X1	1,000	700
Demerger of B	(800)	(500)
Profit for the year	350	350
Balance at 31 December 19X1	550	550

From C's point of view, the questions which arise are whether its shares are being issued at a premium and if so whether share premium relief should be taken. As this part of the transaction amounts to a merger of C with B, the answers to both questions are yes. However, if the demerger was of an unincorporated business, then merger relief would not be available, since it applies only to share exchanges and not to issues of shares in exchange for assets; this contrasts with group reconstruction relief, which is available for both – see 4.3.2 above. The same point applies to a transaction of type (b) above.

It also seems logical to use merger accounting for this kind of transaction and it is likely to be a 'group reconstruction' under FRS 6; merger accounting can therefore be adopted provided all the conditions are met. Although this is likely to be the case for the demerger transaction itself, in many cases it is likely to have been preceded by a number of other internal transactions involving transfers of subsidiaries or businesses around the group some of which may have been for shares and others for cash or on inter-company account.

One example of a demerger was ICI's bioscience interests to Zeneca in 1993. However, as disclosed in Zeneca's accounts merger accounting has been applied even though all the conditions laid down for merger accounting were not met, the 'true and fair override' being used:

Extract 6.57: Zeneca Group PLC (1993)

2 BASIS OF CONSOLIDATION AND PRESENTATION OF FINANCIAL INFORMATION [extract]

The transfer of ZENECA Limited to the Company has been accounted for in accordance with the principles of merger accounting set out in Statement of Standard Accounting Practice No. 23 (SSAP 23) and Schedule 4(A) to the Companies Act 1985. The financial statements are therefore presented as if ZENECA Limited and its subsidiaries had been owned and controlled by the Company throughout.

ZENECA Limited was created through an internal reorganisation within ICI which resulted in the transfer to it of ICI's bioscience activities with effect from 1 January 1993. The bioscience interests included both subsidiaries, some of which were themselves subject to reorganisation prior to transfer, and certain unincorporated business activities of ICI. These transactions have been accounted for in these group accounts using the principles of merger accounting as if ZENECA Limited had been in existence throughout. This is not in accordance with SSAP 23 and Schedule 4(A) to the Companies Act 1985 as the transfer of the unincorporated business activities and the reorganisation of certain subsidiaries prior to transfer to ZENECA Limited do not meet all the conditions laid down for merger accounting.

The directors consider that to apply acquisition accounting to any part of the reorganisation of the Zeneca businesses, with consequent adjustments to the fair values of the related assets and liabilities and the reflection of post reorganisation results only within ZENECA Group PLC's accounts, would fail to give a true and fair view of the Group's state of affairs and results for the shareholders since they have had a continuing interest in the Zeneca businesses both before and after the demerger. Due to the number and complexity of transactions involved, it is not practicable to quantify the effect of this departure.

Although this demerger preceded FRS 6, such preliminary transactions would also not have met the conditions laid down in FRS 6 (given that one of the conditions for group reconstructions is that it is allowed by the Companies Act).

As far as ICI's accounts are concerned, the businesses transferred to Zeneca have been consolidated up to the date of demerger and shown as discontinued operations. As indicated above, a demerger involves a distribution to the shareholders. ICI dealt with this as follows:

Extract 6.58: Imperial Chemical Industries PLC (1993)

10 DIVIDENDS

	1993	1992	**1993**	1992
	pence per			
	£1 share		**£m**	**£m**
Interim, paid 4 October 1993	**10.5p**	21p	**76**	150
Second interim, to be confirmed as final, payable 28 April 1994	**17.0p**	34p	**123**	243
	27.5p	55p	**199**	393

Demerger dividend – This comprises the net assets of Zeneca at date of demerger. The resolution to give effect to the demerger, which was passed at the Extraordinary General Meeting of the Company on 28 May 1993, approved a dividend of £464,566,941 on the Ordinary Shares of £1 each in the Company: this was the holding value of Zeneca Limited by the Company.   **363**

			562	393

23 RESERVES [extract]

The cumulative amount of goodwill resulting from acquisitions during 1993 and prior years, net of goodwill attributable to subsidiary undertakings or businesses demerged or disposed of prior to 31 December 1993, amounted to £609m (1992 £1,700m, reduced by £69m following a detailed review to identify all such goodwill). Goodwill in respect of Zeneca businesses which were demerged totalled £1,011m.

It can be seen that ICI has charged as the demerger dividend in the consolidated profit and loss account the amount of the net assets of businesses demerged, although noting the dividend approved by the shareholders which was based on the carrying amount of the investment in the parent's books. Although not a disposal or closure of a business, it is arguable that the demerger dividend should also have included the goodwill attributable to the businesses demerged based on the requirements of UITF 3 (see 3.3.1 above). Such an approach was adopted by Pearson in respect of its demerger of Royal Doulton in 1993, as shown below:

Extract 6.59: Pearson plc (1993)

B DIVIDENDS

			1993 £m	1992 £m
Interim paid	5.375p	(5.375p)	29.4	29.3
Final proposed	7.625p	(6.625p)	42.1	36.2
Dividends per ordinary share 13.0p (12.0p)			71.5	65.5
Demerger dividend *in specie* (see note 19)			111.8	–
			183.3	65.5

20 Notes on the company balance sheet [extract]

The company demerger dividend in specie of £134.2 million is the historical cost of the investment in Royal Doulton.

The group demerger dividend in specie of £111.8 million is the net assets of Royal Doulton at the date of demerger and goodwill written back on disposal.

The amount of goodwill included within the group demerger dividend is £10m; not included is demerger expenses of £2.2m which is included within loss on sale of businesses.[256]

4.6 Capital contributions

One form of transaction which is sometimes made within a group is a 'capital contribution', where one company injects funds in another (usually its subsidiary) in the form of a non-returnable gift. Whenever capital contributions are made, complex tax considerations can arise and should be addressed.

Capital contributions have no legal status in the UK – certainly the term is not used anywhere in the Companies Acts. This has led to uncertainty over the appropriate accounting treatment in the financial statements of both the giver and the receiver of the capital contribution.

Until recently there has been no reference to capital contributions in accounting standards. However, the Application Notes in FRS 4 – *Capital instruments* – deal with the treatment from the standpoint of a subsidiary receiving the contribution.

4.6.1 Treatment in the financial statements of the paying company

In the most common situation, where the contribution is made by a company to one of its subsidiaries, the treatment is relatively straightforward; the amount of the contribution should be added to the cost of the investment in the subsidiary. However, it will not be possible to regard it as part of the purchase price of shares in the subsidiary, so it should be classified as a separate item when the cost of the investment is analysed. As with any fixed asset, it will be necessary to write down the investment whenever it is recognised that its value has been permanently impaired; this should be considered when subsequent dividends are received from the subsidiary which could be regarded as having been met out of the capital contribution and hence representing a return of it.

Where the contribution is made to a fellow-subsidiary, it will not be possible to regard it as an asset of any kind; it is neither an investment in the other company, nor can it be treated as a monetary receivable, since by definition there is no obligation on the part of the recipient to return it. Accordingly, the only available treatment to the paying company in these circumstances will be to write it off in the profit and loss account of the period in which the payment is made.

4.6.2 *Treatment in the financial statements of the receiving company*

The Application Notes in FRS 4 state that a subsidiary should include capital contributions received from its parent within shareholders' funds, and in the year in which a contribution is received, it should be reported in the reconciliation of movements in shareholders' funds. No indication is given as to where in shareholders' funds it is to be included, but the most common treatment would appear to be to credit the amount received to a separate reserve with a suitable title, such as 'capital contribution', or 'capital reserve'.

Notwithstanding this, it is generally considered that the contribution can be regarded for distribution purposes as a realised profit, and accordingly is available to be paid out by way of dividend. However, where the contribution received is in the form of a non-monetary asset it is doubtful whether this should be the case. Where a contribution is regarded for distribution purposes as a realised profit, it may be appropriate to reclassify the reserve to which the contribution was originally taken as part of the profit and loss account balance.

Where the contribution is received from a fellow-subsidiary, then it could be argued the contribution should be credited to the profit and loss account in the year of receipt as it is not a transaction with the company's shareholder.

There is no compelling reason why there need be symmetry of treatment between the accounting used by the giving and receiving companies, although this will usually be the case; it would, for example, be theoretically possible for the giving company to charge the contribution made to the profit and loss account, while the recipient credited the contribution directly to shareholders' funds. Whatever treatment is adopted, the whole effect of the transaction will be eliminated from the consolidated financial statements.

5 COMPARISON WITH US AND IASC PRONOUNCEMENTS

5.1 US

The main standards in the US in this area are APB Opinion 16 – *Business Combinations* – and APB Opinion 17 – *Intangible Assets* – both of which were issued by the AICPA in 1970. In addition there are several interpretations issued by the AICPA and the FASB, a number of EITF consensuses and various SEC rulings dealing with the topic.

Notwithstanding the volume of literature in the US and the fact that the original standards are nearly 30 years old, the requirements in respect of business combinations are similar to those of FRSs 6 and 7; any significant differences are noted in the discussions below. The main area of difference, however, is in respect of the accounting for goodwill.

These differences may become fewer in the future because in August 1996 the FASB added to its agenda a project to reconsider APBs 16 and 17. This was because there was a continued need for interpretation on the part of the EITF and the FASB (notwithstanding the volume of existing interpretative literature) and because of the opportunity it presents for further international harmonisation, particularly in view of the work being carried out by the ASB and the IASC.

The project is to focus on what constitutes a business combination, the determination of when the pooling-of-interests method (merger accounting) and the purchase method (acquisition accounting) should be applied (including issues such as the need for two separate and distinct methods of accounting for business combinations or whether to narrow the differences in accounting results between those methods), the income statement recognition and timing of purchase accounting (fair value) adjustments, and the accounting for goodwill and other intangible assets.[257] In June 1997 the FASB issued a Special Report – *Issues Associated with the FASB Project on Business Combinations* – which sought comments on a number of questions posed about the project.

The main differences between the present US requirements and those in the UK are discussed below.

5.1.1 The pooling-of-interests method

As in the UK, the purchase method (acquisition accounting) and the pooling-of-interests method are both acceptable in accounting for business combinations, although not as alternatives in accounting for the same business combination. As in the UK, a business combination either qualifies for the pooling-of-interests method or must be accounted for as a purchase.[258]

A 'pooling-of-interests' is a business combination where two or more previously independent common shareholder groups exchange voting common stock and combine their resources, talents and risks to form a new entity to carry on in combination the previous businesses and to continue their earnings streams. Neither shareholder group withdraws nor invests resources but, in effect, they mutually exchange risks and benefits.[259]

The general concept of a pooling is supported by a series of detailed rules in APB 16 designed to prevent what is really a purchase from qualifying for pooling accounting. A business combination must meet all of the following criteria to be accounted for as a pooling of interests:

A   *Attributes of the combining companies*

(a)   Each of the combining companies is autonomous and has not been a subsidiary or division of another company within two years before the plan of combination is initiated.

(b)   Each of the combining companies is independent of the others, and in particular does not hold investments in the others.[260]

B   *Manner of the combination*

(a)   The combination is effected in a single transaction, or in accordance with a specific plan, within one year after the plan is initiated.[261]

(b)   The issuing company offers and issues only common stock with rights identical to those of the majority of its outstanding voting common stock in exchange for substantially all (90% or more) of the voting common stock interest of the other company.[262]

(c)   No change in the equity interests of the voting common stock of any combining company may be made in contemplation of a pooling-of-interests either within the two years prior to the merger being initiated or between the dates the merger is initiated and consummated.[263]

(d)   The ratio of the interest of an individual common stockholder to those of other common stockholders in a combining company remains the same as a result of the exchange of stock.[264]

(e)   The voting rights to which the common stock ownership interests in the resulting combined entity are entitled are exercisable by the stockholders; the stockholders are neither deprived of nor restricted in exercising those rights.[265]

(f)   The entire plan of combination must be resolved by the consummation date. Thus, the combined entity may not agree to contingently issue additional shares or distribute other consideration at a later date to the former owners of the combining company.[266]

C   *Absence of planned transactions*

(a)   Stock issued in a pooling must remain outstanding outside the combined entity without arrangements for any of the entities involved to use their financial resources to buy out former stockholders or induce others to do so.[267]

(b)   The combined company must not enter into other financial arrangements for the benefit of the former stockholders of a combining company, such as the guarantee of loans secured by stock issued in the combination, which in effect negates the exchange of equity securities.[268]

(c)   The combined company may not intend or plan to dispose of a significant part of the assets of the combining companies within two years after the combination other than disposals in the ordinary course of business.[269]

Although these conditions were intended to limit the use of the pooling-of-interests method, it continues to be used widely today in the US.[270]

5.1.2   Application of pooling-of-interests method

When applying the pooling-of-interests method, the recorded assets and liabilities of the separate companies should be combined in the financial statements. Adjustments may have to be made to eliminate differences in accounting policies adopted by the separate enterprises. The consolidated financial statements should report results of operations for the period in which the combination occurs as though the companies had been combined as of the beginning of the period.[271]

Notes to the financial statements should disclose details of the effects of a business combination which is to be accounted for by the pooling method consummated before the issuance of but after the date of the financial statements. The details including revenue, net income and earnings per share should be disclosed as if the consummation had occurred at the date of the financial statements.[272]

5.1.3   The purchase method

As in the UK, if a business combination does not meet the pooling-of-interests criteria, it must be accounted for under the purchase method. The purchase method under APB 16 is very similar in outline to acquisition accounting under UK GAAP.[273] However, some differences do exist between them.

The purchase method follows principles normally applicable under historical cost accounting when recording acquisitions of assets for cash, by exchanging other assets, or by issuing shares. Acquiring assets in a group requires ascertaining the cost of the assets as a group and then allocating the cost to the individual assets that comprise the group. Like FRS 7 in the UK, APB 16 provides guidance on determining the cost of a group and on assigning a portion of the total cost to each individual asset acquired on the basis of its fair value. A difference between the sum of the assigned costs of the tangible and identifiable intangible assets acquired less liabilities assumed and the cost of the group is evidence of unspecified intangible values – i.e. goodwill.

5.1.4 Acquisition date

The rule in FRS 2 is not the same as that in the US, where the normal date of acquisition is the date on which assets are received and other assets are given or securities are issued – in other words, when consideration passes. In the US, the parties are allowed to designate the end of an accounting period as being the effective date, provided it is between the dates on which the business combination is initiated and consummated. However, where the effective date is before the date on which the consideration passes, US GAAP requires that the purchase price be adjusted for imputed interest on the amount of the consideration outstanding between these dates.[274] This is to prevent what would in effect be double counting during this period, because the acquiring company would be both recognising the profits from the new subsidiary and also continuing to enjoy the use of the funds which were to be paid to the vendors.

5.1.5 The cost of the acquired enterprise

Cash and other assets distributed, securities issued unconditionally and amounts of contingent consideration that are determinable (i.e. where the outcome of the contingency is determinable beyond reasonable doubt) at the date of acquisition should be included in determining the cost of an acquired enterprise and recorded at that date.[275]

Contingent consideration is usually recorded when the contingency is resolved and consideration is issued or becomes issuable.[276] As noted above it is only recorded at the date of acquisition if the outcome of the contingency is determined beyond reasonable doubt.

The cost of an acquired company is measured by the fair values of assets distributed (e.g. marketable securities). In the case of quoted equity securities, the market price for a reasonable period before and after the date the terms of the acquisition are agreed to and announced should be considered in determining the fair value of securities issued.[277] In other words, the date of measurement of the value of the shares should not be influenced by the need to obtain shareholder or regulatory approval.[278]

The fair value of a debt security is its present value. A premium or discount should be recorded for a debt security issued with an interest rate fixed materially above or below the effective rate or current yield for an otherwise comparable security.[279]

The issue of additional securities or other consideration at the resolution of contingencies based on earnings results in an addition to the cost of an acquired company and consequently to the goodwill also. This additional element should be amortised over the remaining life of the goodwill.[280]

5.1.6 *Recording fair values of identifiable assets and liabilities*

A General approach

APB 16 requires an acquiring company to allocate the cost of an acquired company to all identifiable assets acquired and liabilities assumed in a business combination by reference to their fair values at date of acquisition.[281] The concept of fair value differs from that in FRS 7. Under APB 16, it is appropriate to take account of the acquirer's intentions when identifying and allocating fair values to the assets acquired and liabilities assumed. For example, it is appropriate to recognise as liabilities the costs of a plan to exit an activity of an acquired company or to terminate the employment, or relocate, employees of an acquired company provided certain conditions are met.

The rules for attributing fair values to specific assets and liabilities are set out below.

B Tangible fixed assets

The fair values of tangible fixed assets should be determined as follows:

Assets such as land and natural resources at appraised values;[282]

Plant and equipment that is to be:

- used, at current replacement cost for similar capacity unless the expected future use of the assets indicates a lower value to the acquirer. Replacement cost may be determined directly if a used asset market exists for the assets acquired. Otherwise, it should be approximated from replacement cost new less estimated accumulated depreciation;

- sold, at fair value less cost to sell.[283]

C Intangible assets

Identifiable intangible assets (except goodwill) that can be identified and named, including contracts, patents, franchises, customer and supplier lists, and favourable leases should be included at appraised values.[284]

D Inventories

The fair values of inventories should be determined as follows:[285]

Finished goods at estimated selling price less any future anticipated costs and less a reasonable profit allowance for the selling effort of the acquiring company;

Work in progress at estimated selling price less any future costs to completion and less a reasonable profit allowance for the completing and selling effort of the acquiring company;

Raw materials at current replacement costs.

E   *Investments*

Marketable securities at current net realisable values.[286] Non-marketable securities at appraised values.[287]

F   *Monetary assets and liabilities*

Receivables at their present values based on appropriate current interest rates and after making provisions for bad debts.[288]

All liabilities (including notes and accounts payable, long-term debt), and accruals (e.g. accruals for warranties, vacation pay, deferred compensation) at their present value determined at appropriate current interest rates. Similarly, other liabilities and commitments (including unfavourable leases, contracts and commitments and plant closing expense incident to the acquisition) at present values of amounts to be paid determined at appropriate current interest rates.[289]

G   *Businesses sold or held exclusively with a view to subsequent resale*

The allocation of purchase price to assets to be sold is addressed in EITF 87-11. The guidance is more detailed but consistent with the approach used in FRS 7 in the UK.

H   *Pre-acquisition contingencies*

Amounts that can be reasonably estimated for contingencies in existence at the date of acquisition that are probable should be recorded as part of the fair value exercise.[290]

I   *Pensions and OPEBs*

The requirements in SFAS 87 and SFAS 106 are similar to those in FRS 7. However, the measurement of such assets or liabilities should reflect the effect of:

■   any changes in assumptions based on the purchaser's assessment of relevant future events;

■   changes to benefit plans of the acquired entity in compliance with the conditions of the business combination. If improvements were not a condition of the combination, credit granted for prior service should be treated as a plan amendment (i.e. impacting post-acquisition earnings).

■   terminating or curtailing the acquired entity's benefit plans, if those actions are expected.[291]

J   *Deferred taxation*

Under SFAS 109, a deferred tax liability or asset should be recognised for differences between the assigned values and the tax bases of the assets and liabilities recognised in a purchase business combination except, inter alia, goodwill.

If the tax benefits of an acquired entity's operating loss or tax credit carryforward for financial reporting are not recognised at the acquisition date (i.e. a valuation allowance is made under SFAS 109), subsequent recognition should:

■ first be applied to eliminate any goodwill and other non current intangible assets related to the acquisition; and

■ next be recognised as a reduction of the tax expense.[292]

K   *Provisions for reorganisations and future losses*

APB 16 permits consideration of the acquirer's intentions when identifying and allocating fair values to the assets acquired and liabilities assumed. For example, it is appropriate to recognise as liabilities the costs of a plan to exit an activity of an acquired company or to terminate the employment, or relocate, employees of an acquired company provided the following conditions are met:

■ as of the acquisition date, management begins to assess and formulate a plan;

■ as soon as possible after the acquisition date, management completes its assessment of which activities are to be ceased or which employees are to be affected and commits itself to the plan;

■ the plan identifies the actions to be taken to complete the plan, including the method of disposition and location of activities or the number, function and location of employees who are to be made redundant or relocated; and

■ actions required by the plan will begin as soon as possible after the plan is finalised and the period of time to complete the plan indicates that significant changes are unlikely.[293]

5.1.7   *The allocation period*

An allocation period is permitted for the management of the acquiring company to conduct an investigation of the assets and liabilities which have been acquired. The duration of this is not an absolute period of time, although it should usually not extend beyond one year from the acquisition date; the period in fact ends 'when the acquiring enterprise is no longer waiting for information which it has arranged to obtain and which is known to be available and obtainable'. Adjustments should be made to fair values (if necessary) when uncertainties existing at the date of acquisition have been resolved prior to the close of the 'allocation' period. The exceptions to this rule are adjustments resulting from economic events that clearly occurred subsequent to the acquisition date and adjustments to deferred tax, which should be accounted for in accordance with SFAS 109 and EITF 93-7.[294]

5.1.8 *Accounting for goodwill*

Unlike the UK, positive goodwill must be amortised on a straight line basis over its estimated useful life not exceeding 40 years. In most cases the useful life will be less than 40 years. An accelerated method of amortisation should be used for goodwill when the amount assigned to goodwill includes costs for identifiable intangibles whose fair values are not determinable and the benefits expected to be received from those intangibles decline over the expected life of the factors which are the basis for those intangibles. It is generally inappropriate to lengthen the period of amortisation once established at acquisition.[295]

Negative goodwill should be allocated to reduce proportionately the values assigned to non-current assets in determining their fair values. Any remainder should be classified as a deferred credit and amortised to income over a period estimated to be benefited but not in excess of 40 years.[296]

5.1.9 *Disclosures in respect of acquisitions*

The disclosure requirements in the US are less onerous than those in the UK. The disclosures required are:[297]

(a) name and brief description of the acquired entity:

(b) method of accounting;

(c) period for which results of operations of the acquired entity are included in the income statement of the acquiring company;

(d) cost of the acquired entity and, if applicable, the number of shares of stock issued or issuable, and the amount assigned to the issued and issuable shares;

(e) description of the plan for amortisation of acquired goodwill, the amortisation method, and the period;

(f) contingent payments, options, or commitments specified in the acquisition agreement; and

(g) the results of the period (unless the acquisition was at or near the beginning of the period) and of the immediately preceding period on a pro forma basis as though the companies had been combined throughout those periods. Such pro forma information should be given after taking account of fair value adjustments.

5.2   IASC

The relevant international standard is IAS 22 – *Business Combinations*. The original standard was issued in November 1983, but was revised in 1993, the revised version being effective for accounting periods beginning on or after 1 January 1995. This covers not only those areas dealt with in FRSs 6 and 7 but also the accounting for goodwill. Some consequential changes were made following the issue of a revised version of IAS 12 – *Income Taxes* – in October 1996 (see Chapter 21 at 5.2). These changes prohibited discounting of deferred tax assets and liabilities resulting from business combinations and conformed the guidance in IAS 22 re taxation balances to the guidance in IAS 12. These changes become operative for accounting periods beginning on or after 1 January 1998.

As a result of its recent exposure draft on impairment of assets (E55) and its approval of an exposure draft on intangible assets (see Chapter 10 at 7.2) the IASC has approved the publication of an exposure draft proposing to revise IAS 22 in respect of the accounting for positive goodwill such that the accounting will be similar to that proposed by FRED 12, i.e. goodwill is to be amortised over its economic life as before, but there will be a rebuttable presumption that the maximum life is 20 years. Goodwill being amortised over a period in excess of 20 years is to be subject to an annual impairment test based on E55. The IASC, however, does not appear to contemplate goodwill having an indefinite life as is done in FRED 12. It is also proposed that the benchmark treatment for negative goodwill (see 5.2.3 below) should be eliminated and certain changes made to the allowed alternative treatment.

The main differences between the present IASC requirements and those in the UK are dealt with below.

5.2.1   Uniting of interests

As in the UK, IAS 22 draws a distinction between an acquisition and a uniting of interests (merger). A uniting of interests is defined as 'a business combination in which the shareholders of the combining enterprises combine control over the whole, or effectively the whole, of their net assets and operations to achieve a continuing mutual sharing in the risks and benefits attaching to the combined entity such that neither party can be identified as the acquirer'.[298]

The criteria to be satisfied before a combination can be accounted for as a uniting of interests are similar to the criteria in FRS 6, although they are not phrased quite as prescriptively. IAS 22 states that in order to achieve a mutual sharing of the risks and benefits of the combined entity:[299]

(a)   the substantial majority, if not all, of the voting common shares of the combining enterprises must be exchanged or pooled;

(b)   the fair value of one enterprise is not significantly different from that of the other enterprise; and

(c)   the shareholders of each enterprise maintain substantially the same voting rights and interest in the combined entity, relative to each other, after the combination as before.

However, IAS 22 comments that the likelihood of a mutual sharing of the risks and benefits of the combined entity diminishes and the likelihood that an acquirer can be identified increases when:[300]

(a)   the relative equality in fair values of the combining enterprises is reduced and the percentage of voting common shares exchanged decreases;

(b)   financial arrangements provide a relative advantage to one group of shareholders over the other shareholders; and

(c)   one party's share of the equity in the combined entity depends on how the business which it previously controlled performs subsequent to the business combination.

If the combination is one of the exceptional cases in which an acquirer cannot be identified then it should be accounted for as a uniting of interests ('merger' or 'pooling-of-interests'). The way in which such accounting should be done is consistent with the method required by FRS 6.[301]

5.2.2 *Acquisitions*

The prescribed treatments under IAS 22 are in general very similar to those specified by FRS 7. The cost of acquisition is thus defined as 'the amount of cash or cash equivalents paid or the fair value, at the date of exchange, of the other purchase consideration given by the acquirer in exchange for control over the net assets of the other enterprise, plus any costs directly attributable to the acquisition'.[302]

One difference between the UK and the International standard is in the treatment of contingent consideration. IAS 22 states that where the acquisition agreement provides for an adjustment to the purchase consideration contingent on one or more future events, the amount of the adjustment should be included in the cost of acquisition as at the date of acquisition if the adjustment is probable and the amount can be measured reliably.[303] This is less prescriptive than FRS 7.

The other main difference in acquisition accounting as defined by IAS 22 is that the fair values of identifiable assets and liabilities are determined by reference to their intended use by the acquirer.[304] Thus, IAS 22 allows that unfavourable contracts and plant closure expenses *incidental to* the acquisition should be valued at the present values of amounts to be disbursed in discharging the obligation.[305] Many of the guidelines contained in IAS 22 for determining the fair values of particular assets and liabilities[306] are similar to those in FRS 7, although clearly the application of them will differ as a result of this difference in approach. Inventories, however, are to be fair valued on a similar basis to that used in the US (see 5.1.6 D above)

5.2.3 Accounting for goodwill

Unlike the predominant UK practice to date, positive goodwill is capitalised as an asset and amortised (generally, on a straight line basis) over its economic useful life. This should not exceed 5 years, unless a longer period (which cannot exceed 20 years) can be justified.[307] The standard sets out factors to be considered for determining the life of goodwill similar to those that had been proposed in ED 47 (see 2.5.4 A above).[308]

For negative goodwill, IAS 22 lays down a benchmark treatment which is the same as that adopted in the US (see 5.1.8 above), but any excess should be released over a period not exceeding 5 years unless a longer period (which cannot exceed 20 years) can be justified.[309] However, the standard allows an alternative treatment whereby it is all taken to deferred income.[310]

5.2.4 Disclosures

For uniting of interests the disclosure requirements are similar to those for mergers under FRS 6.[311] Again, like the US, the disclosure requirements of IAS 22 are not as onerous as those in FRS 6.[312]

6 CONCLUSION

It is now more than 10 years since the first detailed accounting standards relating to business combinations, dealing with the accounting for goodwill and for acquisitions and mergers, were issued in the UK, and although they soon came under attack we still do not have revised standards on all of these related topics. In 1990 the ASC issued exposure drafts which proposed to revise these standards by changing the existing distinction between mergers and acquisitions and, most controversially of all, to require the amortisation of goodwill against earnings, together with proposals to introduce rules on fair value accounting. However, it was to be a further three years before the ASB published its own thoughts on these thorny topics.

By issuing FRSs 6 and 7, the Board has narrowed down some of the contentious issues. Merger accounting is now very rare, and therefore all the attention is now focused on acquisition accounting. FRS 7 has certainly reduced some of the more significant abuses, but it has to be said that it is not a very convincing standard at a conceptual level and shows signs of the haste with which it was finalised. A number of issues have been ducked, notably the treatment of intangible assets and negative goodwill, while certain others have been dealt with in a rather vague and inconsistent way.

Although we now have accounting standards on these matters, we are still awaiting a resolution of the other significant aspect of acquisition accounting, that of goodwill. The ASB is poised to finalise a standard based on FRED 12, but we remain unconvinced that goodwill is 'capable of reliable measurement in future' or that its useful life can be estimated except, perhaps, over a very short period.

Because of the assumptions and allocations that are necessary in any attempt to measure goodwill, we doubt that the proposed impairment test will be able to identify a reduction in 'value' with sufficient reliability. Despite its apparent science and complexity, this is a subjective test of the continuing worth of the business, and we are sceptical about an approach which depends solely on such judgements.

References

1 *Shearer (Inspector of Taxes) v. Bercain (Ltd.)*, (1980) 3 All E.R. 295.
2 FRS 6, *Acquisitions and mergers*, ASB, September 1994, Appendix I, para. 15.
3 ED 31, *Accounting for acquisitions and mergers*, ASC, October 1982, para. 3.
4 ED 3, *Accounting for acquisitions and mergers*, ASC, January 1971, para. 1.
5 SSAP 23, *Accounting for acquisitions and mergers*, ASC, April 1985, para. 17.
6 CA 85, Sch. 4A, para. 10.
7 *Ibid.*, para. 10(2).
8 FRS 6, para. 38.
9 *Ibid.*, para. 2.
10 *Ibid.*, para. 4.
11 *Ibid.*, para. 2.
12 *Ibid.*, para. 58.
13 *Ibid.*, para. 6.
14 *Ibid.*, para. 61.
15 *Ibid.*, para. 62.
16 *Ibid.*, para. 7.
17 *Ibid.*, para. 64.
18 *Ibid.*, para. 66.
19 *Ibid.*, para. 8.
20 *Ibid.*, para. 68.
21 *Ibid.*, para. 9.
22 *Ibid.*, para. 10.
23 *Ibid.*, para. 11.
24 *Ibid.*, para. 76.
25 *Ibid.*, para. 12.
26 *Ibid.*, para. 56.
27 *Ibid.*, paras. 60–77.
28 For example, Lloyds-TSB Group, Royal SunAlliance and United News & Media.
29 CA 85, Sch. 4A, para. 9.
30 FRS 2, *Accounting for subsidiary undertakings*, ASB, July 1992, para. 45.
31 *Ibid.*, para. 85.
32 ASC Discussion Paper, *Fair value in the context of acquisition accounting*.
33 ED 53, *Fair value in the context of acquisition accounting*, ASC, July 1990, paras. 58-65.

34 FRED 7, *Fair values in acquisition accounting*, ASB, December 1993.
35 FRS 7, *Fair Values in Acquisition Accounting*, ASB, September 1994, para. 30.
36 *Ibid.*, para. 26.
37 *Ibid.*, para. 77.
38 *Ibid.*, para. 78.
39 ED 53, para. 58.
40 FRS 7, para. 79.
41 *Ibid.*
42 *Ibid.*, para. 80.
43 *Ibid.*, para. 77.
44 *Ibid.*, para. 81.
45 *Ibid.*, para. 27.
46 ASB Discussion Paper, *Fair values in acquisition accounting*, ASB, April 1993, para. 12.4
47 *Ibid.*
48 FRS 7, para. 81.
49 *Ibid.*, para. 82.
50 *Ibid.*, para. 83.
51 *Ibid.*, para. 84.
52 *Ibid.*, para. 28.
53 *Ibid.*, para. 85.
54 CA 85, Sch. 4A, para. 9(4).
55 CA 81, s 40(3).
56 Accountants Digest No. 189, *A Guide to Accounting Standards – SSAP 23 Accounting for acquisitions and mergers*, Summer 1986.
57 FRS 6, Appendix I, para. 16.
58 CA 85, Sch. 4A, para. 9(2).
59 ED 53, para. 68.
60 FRS 7, para. 5.
61 *Ibid.*, para. 2.
62 *Ibid.*, para. 35.
63 *Ibid.*, para. 38.
64 *Ibid.*, para. 39.
65 *Ibid.*, Appendix III, para. 14.
66 *Ibid.*, para. 7.
67 *Ibid.*, para. 6.
68 *Ibid.*, para. 2.
69 ASB Discussion Paper, *Fair values in acquisition accounting*, para. 5.5
70 FRS 7, paras. 23–24.
71 *Ibid.*, para. 25.
72 *Ibid.*, para. 43.
73 FRED 7, para. 13.
74 FRS 7, para. 47.
75 *Ibid.*, para. 2.
76 *Ibid.*, para. 47.
77 *Ibid.*, para. 48.
78 *Ibid.*, para. 9.
79 *Ibid.*, para. 51.
80 See Stagecoach Holdings plc, Report and Accounts 1996, pp. 47–49 and Bernard Matthews plc, Report and Accounts 1996, p. 31.
81 FRS 7, para. 10.
82 *Ibid.*, para. 11.
83 *Ibid.*, para. 12.
84 *Ibid.*, paras. 53 and 54.
85 *Ibid.*, para. 55.
86 *Ibid.*, para. 56.
87 *Ibid.*, para. 57.
88 *Ibid.*, para. 13.

89 *Ibid.*, para. 58.
90 *Ibid.*, para. 14.
91 *Ibid.*, para. 61.
92 *Ibid.*, para. 62.
93 *Ibid.*, para. 63.
94 *Ibid.*, para. 15.
95 *Ibid.*, para. 37.
96 *Ibid.*, para. 19.
97 FRED 7, Appendix III, para. 35.
98 FRS 7, para. 71.
99 *Ibid.*, para. 72.
100 *Ibid.*, para. 20.
101 United Utilities PLC, Annual Report & Accounts 1997, p. 48.
102 FRS 7, para. 21.
103 *Ibid.*, para. 22.
104 *Ibid.*, para. 7.
105 *Ibid.*, para. 40.
106 ASB Discussion Paper, *Fair values in acquisition accounting*, paras. 2.10–2.12. It was also suggested that there should be a rebuttable presumption that a decision taken within six months before the acquisition should be deemed to be post-acquisition.
107 FRS 7, para. 7.
108 FRED 14, *Provisions and contingencies*, ASB, June 1997, para. 2.
109 A. Lennard and S. Peerless, *Accountancy*, January 1995, p.129.
110 United Utilities PLC, Annual Report & Accounts 1997, p. 48.
111 FRS 7, para. 16.
112 *Ibid.*, para. 17.
113 *Ibid.*, paras. 65 and 66.
114 FRED 7, Appendix III, para. 33.
115 FRS 7, para. 69.
116 Staff Accounting Bulletin No. 54, SEC, Washington, 1983.
117 FRED 12, *Goodwill and intangible assets*, ASB, para.22.
118 ASC Discussion Paper, *Accounting for goodwill*, 1980.
119 ED 30, *Accounting for Goodwill*, October 1982, para. 56.
120 SSAP 22, paras. 39 and 41.
121 ASB Discussion Paper, *Goodwill and intangible assets*, ASB, December 1993, paras. 1.5 and 1.6.
122 *Ibid.*, sections 4–7.
123 *Ibid.*, para. 8.1.
124 *Goodwill & Intangible Assets - working paper for discussion at public hearing*, ASB, June 1995.
125 FRED 12, para. 6.
126 *Ibid.*, para. 7.
127 *Ibid.*, para. 7.
128 *Ibid.*, paras. 14 and 15.
129 *Ibid.*, para. 12.
130 *Ibid.*, para. 18.
131 *Ibid.*, para. 78.
132 *Ibid.*, para. 17.
133 *Ibid.*, paras. 16 and 21.
134 *Ibid.*
135 *Ibid.*, paras. 38 and 39.
136 *Ibid.*, para. 39.
137 *Ibid.*, para. 22.
138 *Ibid.*, para. 20.
139 FRED 15, *Impairment of fixed assets and goodwill*, ASB, Preface.
140 FRED 12, para. 58.
141 SSAP 22, para. 36.
142 British Gas plc, Annual Report and Accounts 1989, p. 35.
143 CA 85, Sch. 4, para 34(3).

144 *Ibid.*, Sch. 4A, para. 1.
145 SI 1990/355, article 9.
146 CA 85, s 264.
147 SSAP 22, paras. 26 and 27.
148 ASC Discussion Paper, *Accounting for goodwill*, paras. 8.1–8.7.
149 ED 30, para. 30.
150 CA 85 contains no specific rules on the treatment of consolidation goodwill. However, the application of Sch. 4A, para. 1(1) of the Act means that the present rules contained in the Companies Act will apply.
151 APB 17, *Intangible Assets*, AICPA, August 1970, para. 29.
152 IAS 22, *Business Combinations*, IASC, Revised 1993, para. 42.
153 ED 47, paras. 4 and 51.
154 *Ibid.*, para. 17.
155 *Ibid.*, para. 16.
156 *Ibid.*, para. 52.
157 APB 17, para. 30.
158 ED 47, para. 50.
159 APB 16, *Business Combinations*, AICPA, August 1970, para. 91.
160 ASC Discussion Paper, *Accounting for goodwill*, paras. 11.2–11.4.
161 *Ibid.*, para. 11.5.
162 ED 30, para. 58.
163 SSAP 22, para. 14.
164 ED 47, para. 56.
165 *Ibid.*, para. 30.
166 *Ibid.*, para. 56.
167 *Ibid.*, para. 31.
168 *Ibid.*, para. 33.
169 *Ibid.*, paras. 32 and 33.
170 ASC Discussion Paper, *Accounting for goodwill*, paras. 11.2–11.4.
171 FRED 7, Appendix III, paras. 50–53.
172 *Ibid.*, paras. 38 and 39.
173 *Ibid.*, para. 39.
174 EC Seventh Directive, Article 31.
175 ASC Discussion Paper, *Fair value in the context of acquisition accounting.*
176 FRS 2, para. 50.
177 *Ibid.*, para. 89.
178 *Ibid.*
179 CA 85, s 228(6).
180 FRS 2, para. 51.
181 CA 85, Sch. 4A, para. 9.
182 *Ibid.*, para. 7(1).
183 FRS 6, paras. 16 and 17.
184 *Ibid.*, para. 17.
185 CA 85, Sch. 4A, para. 11.
186 FRS 6, para. 18
187 *Ibid.*, para. 41.
188 *Ibid.*, paras. 11(5)–(6).
189 However, it is probably not permissible to use reserve categories which would not have been available as a destination for goodwill if acquisition accounting had been applied; see the discussion on this topic at 2.5.2.
190 FRS 6, para.18.
191 *Ibid.*
192 *Ibid.*, para. 19.
193 *Ibid.*, para. 51.
194 *Ibid.*, para. 21.
195 FRS 2, para. 49.
196 FRS 6, para. 23.

197 *Ibid.*, para. 24.
198 *Ibid.*, para. 25.
199 *Ibid.*, para. 26.
200 *Ibid.*, para. 27.
201 *Ibid.*, para. 30.
202 *Ibid.*, para. 85.
203 *Ibid.*, para. 32.
204 *Ibid.*, para. 28.
205 *Ibid.*, para. 29.
206 *Ibid.*, para. 33. The requirement of FRS 6 is based on the original FRS 1 and has been interpreted in a way which is consistent with FRS 1 (Revised 1996).
207 *Ibid.*, para. 34. Again, the requirement of FRS 6 is based on the original FRS 1 and has been interpreted in a way which is consistent with FRS 1 (Revised 1996).
208 *Ibid.*, para. 31.
209 *Ibid.*, para. 86.
210 *Ibid.*, para. 87.
211 Stagecoach Holdings plc, Report and Accounts 1996, pp. 47–49.
212 FRS 6, para. 49.
213 *Ibid.*, para. 50.
214 SSAP 22, para. 43.
215 *Ibid.*, paras. 44 and 47.
216 *Ibid.*, para. 45.
217 FRS 6, para. 35.
218 *Ibid.*, para. 37.
219 UITF 15, para. 3.
220 FRS 6, para. 36.
221 *Ibid.*, para. 22.
222 CA 85, Sch. 4A, para. 13.
223 *Ibid.*, para. 13(2).
224 FRRP PN 5, 28 January 1992.
225 CA 85, para. 14.
226 *Ibid.*, para. 16.
227 SI 1990/355, article 9.
228 FRRP PN 35, 13 December 1995.
229 CA 85, Sch. 4A, para. 13(3).
230 *Ibid.*, para. 13(6).
231 FRS 2, para. 45.
232 *Ibid.*, para. xxii.
233 FRS 3, *Reporting financial performance*, ASB, October 1992, para. 18.
234 UITF 3, *Treatment of Goodwill on Disposal of a Business*, December 1991, para. 7.
235 *Ibid.*, para. 12.
236 *Ibid.*, para. 10.
237 *Ibid.*, para. 11.
238 *Ibid.*, para. 9.
239 Information Sheet No. 6, UITF, 17 December 1992.
240 FRS 2, para. 47.
241 *Ibid.*, para. 52.
242 *Ibid.*, para. 91.
243 *Ibid.*, para. 87.
244 SSAP 22, para. 52.
245 *Ibid.*, paras. 53 and 55.
246 CA 85, Sch. 4A, para. 15.
247 FRS 2, para. 48. Para. 49 appears to contain a similar requirement.
248 FRS 6, para. 2.
249 *Ibid.*, para. 13.
250 CA 85, Sch. 4A, para. 10(c).
251 *Ibid.*, s 151 *et seq.*

252 FRS 6, para. 78.
253 APB 16, para. 5 and AIN–APB 16, *Business Combinations: Accounting Interpretations of APB Opinion No. 16*, AICPA, March 1973, para. 39.
254 CA 85, s 23.
255 *Ibid.*, s 276.
256 Pearson plc, Report and Accounts 1993, pp. 51 and 67.
257 FASB Status Report No. 287, FASB, 22 April 1997, p. 3.
258 APB 16, paras. 42 and 43.
259 *Ibid.*, para. 45.
260 *Ibid.*, para. 46.
261 *Ibid.*, para. 47a.
262 *Ibid.*, para. 47b.
263 *Ibid.*, para. 47c.
264 *Ibid.*, para. 47e.
265 *Ibid.*, para. 47f.
266 *Ibid.*, para. 47g.
267 *Ibid.*, para. 48.
268 *Ibid.*, para. 48b.
269 *Ibid.*, para. 48c.
270 FASB Special Report, *Issues Associated with the FASB Project on Business Combinations*, FASB, June 1997, p. 2.
271 APB 16, paras. 51-56.
272 *Ibid.*, para. 65.
273 *Ibid.*, paras. 66-68.
274 *Ibid.*, para. 93.
275 *Ibid.*, para. 78.
276 *Ibid.*, para. 79.
277 *Ibid.*, para. 74.
278 EITF 95-19, *Determination of the Measurement Date for the Market Price of Securities Issued in a Purchase Business Combination.*
279 *Ibid.*, para. 72.
280 *Ibid.*, para. 80.
281 *Ibid.*, para. 68.
282 *Ibid.*, para. 88f.
283 *Ibid.*, para. 88d.
284 *Ibid.*, para. 88e.
285 *Ibid.*, para. 88c.
286 *Ibid.*, para. 88a.
287 *Ibid.*, para. 88f.
288 *Ibid.*, para. 88b.
289 *Ibid.*, paras. 88g, h and i.
290 SFAS 38, *Accounting for Preacquisition Contingencies of Purchased Enterprises*, FASB, September 1980, para. 5.
291 SFAS 87, *Employers' Accounting for Pensions*, FASB, December 1985, para. 74 and SFAS 106, *Employers' Accounting for Postretirement Benefits Other than Pensions*, FASB, December 1990, paras. 86 and 87.
292 SFAS 109, *Accounting for Income Taxes*, FASB, February 1992, para. 30.
293 EITF 95-3, *Recognition of Liabilities in Connection with a Purchase Business Combination.*
294 SFAS 38, paras. 4 and 5.
295 APB 17, para. 30.
296 APB 16, para. 91.
297 *Ibid.*, paras. 95 and 96.
298 IAS 22, para. 9.
299 *Ibid.*, para. 16.
300 *Ibid.*, para. 17.
301 *Ibid.*, paras. 61-67.
302 *Ibid.*, para. 22.

303 *Ibid.*, para. 52.
304 *Ibid.*, para. 38.
305 *Ibid.*, para. 39.
306 *Ibid.*
307 *Ibid.*, paras. 40-42.
308 *Ibid.*, para. 44.
309 *Ibid.*, para. 49.
310 *Ibid.*, para. 51.
311 *Ibid.*, para. 74.
312 *Ibid.*, paras. 70-73.

Chapter 7

Associates and joint ventures

1 INTRODUCTION

Traditionally, investments in companies which did not satisfy the criteria for classification as subsidiaries were carried at cost, and the revenue from them was recognised only on the basis of dividends received. However, during the 1960s it was recognised that there was a case for an intermediate form of accounting, since there was a growing tendency for groups to conduct part of their activities by taking substantial minority stakes in other companies and exercising a degree of influence over their business which fell short of complete control. Mere recognition of dividends was seen to be an inadequate measure of the results of this activity (and one which could be manipulated by the investor, where he could influence the investee's distribution policy). Moreover, since it was unlikely that the investee would fully distribute its earnings, the cost of the investment would give an increasingly unrealistic indication of its underlying value.

This intermediate form of accounting, equity accounting, was first used by the Royal Dutch Shell group in 1964, and subsequently recognised in UK accounting literature by the issue of SSAP 1 – *Accounting for associated companies* – in 1971. Although the standard has been revised a number of times since then and further revision is being considered, the basic rules are little changed. The essence of it is that it requires a modified form of consolidation of the results and assets of investees in the investor's financial statements when the investor is able to exercise 'significant influence', but not control, over the management of the investee. Rather than full scale consolidation on a line by line basis, equity accounting involves incorporation of the investor's share of results and assets of the investee in one line in the investor's profit and loss account and balance sheet.

As a result of changes made by the Companies Act 1989, the legislation also requires associated undertakings (see 2.2 below) to be equity accounted (previously the Companies Act only permitted such treatment);[1] it also permits unincorporated joint ventures to be proportionally consolidated (see 4.4 below).

In view of these changes to the legislation and the fact that many companies now enter into joint ventures, the ASB has embarked on producing a revised standard on the topic. In July 1994 it issued a Discussion Paper[2] and this was followed by FRED 11 – *Associated and joint ventures* – in March 1996. However, a final revised standard has not yet been published, principally due to concerns about joint ventures and the use of proportional consolidation. The ASB is consulting with the IASC and other standard setting bodies and intends to publish a further exposure draft before finalising a standard.

2   THE DEFINITION OF AN ASSOCIATE

2.1   SSAP 1

The present definition of an associated company in SSAP 1 says that it is 'a company not being a subsidiary of the investing group or company in which the interest of the investing group or company is for the *long term* and, having regard to the disposition of the other shareholdings, the investing group or company is in a position to exercise a *significant influence* over the company in which the investment is made'.[3] The various elements of the definition shown above in italics are discussed further below.

'Long term' is not defined in the standard; however, it is defined in FRS 2 (in relation to subsidiaries) as 'held other than exclusively with a view to subsequent resale',[4] and this should be regarded as a persuasive interpretation in relation to associates. As discussed in 5.4 of Chapter 5, this should be interpreted as relating to the intention at the time of acquisition, not subsequently; if the interest is not reasonably expected to be disposed of within approximately one year of the date of acquisition of the interest, then the interest is held for the long term. Thus, in our view an investment should not cease to be an associate merely because the investor decides that he is no longer going to keep it for the long term but will dispose of it when a suitable opportunity arises; it should continue to be equity accounted for until the effective date of disposal. However, there are examples of companies adopting a contrary view. For example, Redland in its 1995 accounts reclassified an associate at its year end, as shown below:

Extract 7.1: Redland PLC (1995)

9   Investments [extract]

Group

Shares in associates	Listed overseas £ million	Unlisted £ million	Total £ million
Group's share of net assets other than goodwill:			
At 1st January 1995	8.0	177.2	185.2
Foreign currency adjustments	0.1	(1.3)	(1.2)
Additions	0.5	5.7	6.2
Disposals	–	(102.9)	(102.9)
Transfer to debtors of investment held for resale (see note below)	–	(35.4)	(35.4)
Retained profit	1.2	11.9	13.1
At 31st December 1995	9.8	55.2	65.0

Since the end of the year, the Group's investment in Terca Brick Industries NV has been sold for £71 million.

Presumably therefore in its 1996 accounts Redland did not equity account for this investment up to the date of its disposal in March 1996.

Another company which has also ceased to equity account for one of its associates is The Rank Group, as shown below:

Extract 7.2: The Rank Group Plc (1996)

14   OTHER INVESTMENTS [extract]

	Group 1996 £m	Group 1995 Pro forma £m	Company 1996 £m
Balances at 31 December 1995	–	–	–
Transferred from associated undertakings (note 13)	432	–	–
Revaluation adjustment (b)	498	–	–
Additions	1	–	1
Balances at 31 December 1996	931	–	1

(a)   The investment in the Rank Xerox companies has been transferred from associated undertakings. The Directors now consider that the investment is no longer held for the long term and that the Group's role in the management of the Rank Xerox companies and Fuji Xerox has been reduced. Accordingly it is no longer appropriate to account for the investment as an associate.

(b)   The Group's investment in the Rank Xerox companies was revalued by the Directors to £930 million, the value implied by the transaction in 1995 with Xerox Corporation (in which the Group secured £620 million for a 40% share of the interest held at that time). The Directors believe that this gives a fairer reflection of the value of the investment.

(c)   In 1996, dividends receivable from the Rank Xerox companies were £49m gross (£39m net of Advance Corporation Tax). Details of the Rank Xerox companies are given on pages 86 and 87.

(d)   The historical cost of the Group's interest in the Rank Xerox companies is £15m. At 1 January 1996, the date on which the Group ceased to equity account for this interest, the total book value was £432m.

In addition to the investment no longer being held for the long term it would appear from the above extract that there also was a change in the relationship between the company and its investee and it may have been this factor which added more weight to the decision that the investee no longer fulfilled the definition of an associate. It can be seen from the above extract that not only did the investee cease to be an associate but it was revalued, a treatment that SSAP 1 does not allow for associates except in the investor's company accounts.[5]

'Significant influence' is described as involving participation in the financial and operating policy decisions of the investee (including dividend policy), but not necessarily control of these policies. One indication of such participation is representation on the board, but this is not a conclusive test.[6] SSAP 1 goes on to say that interests of 20% or more in the equity voting rights of the investee give rise to the presumption that the investor will have such influence over it, while those of a smaller amount do not; however, either of these presumptions is rebuttable (the latter requiring concurrence of the investee), because the real test is whether influence exists, not whether a particular percentage holding has been achieved.[7] The ability to exercise influence through a minority stake obviously depends on the degree of influence or control exercised by the other shareholders; if they have the ability to act jointly, or if there is a majority shareholder, then a minority investor could only exercise influence with their consent and could otherwise find his attempts to exercise influence frustrated by their controlling interest.

It should be noted that it is not necessary that significant influence is in fact exercised; the test is whether the investor has the ability to exercise it if he wants to. Thus, he may be entirely happy with the way that the investee is being managed and content to take no active part, but if he is in a position to intervene so as to inhibit the management from moving in a direction with which he disagrees, then the SSAP 1 test is met.

Although the SSAP refers to associated *companies* (not *undertakings*, as in the Companies Act definition referred to below), there is no real distinction because 'company' is broadly defined in the standard, and is not confined to corporate enterprises.[8]

One company which has an interest in another company of greater than 20% but which is not regarded as an associated company is United News & Media, as shown below:

Extract 7.3: United News & Media plc (1996)

12. Fixed asset investments [extract]

The overall 29.9% interest in HTV has not been treated as an associated undertaking since the group did not participate in the direction of its investment during the year, had no board representation and did not exercise significant influence.

Another is British Aerospace, as shown below:

Extract 7.4: British Aerospace Public Limited Company (1996)

12. Fixed asset – investments [extract]

Orange plc

Included within investments of the Group is a 21.91% (Company 1.71%) interest in the ordinary share capital of Orange plc, a company registered in England and Wales. Of the remaining shares, 48.22% are controlled by Hutchison Whampoa Ltd. In view of this shareholding structure the investment is not accounted for as an associated undertaking.

Loans in the Group and Company at 31st December, 1995 represented bonds of £207 million issued by Orange plc which bore interest at 7.2% to maturity. On 2nd April, 1996 Orange plc was admitted to the London Stock Exchange following an initial public offering at 205p per share. Orange plc used part of the proceeds of the offering to repay £194 million of bond capital, together with accumulated interest. The remaining bonds, together with accumulated interest, were converted to ordinary shares in Orange plc at a conversion price of 205p per share. Subsequent to the flotation the Group's and Company's investment in Orange plc has been revalued at a Directors' valuation based upon this offer price, valuing the Group's holding at £538 million and the Company's holding at £42 million. The market value of the Group's investment at 31st December, 1996 was £493 million.

In the Group the investment has, in total, been revalued by £542 million (the carrying value prior to the revaluation was negative £4 million). Of this revaluation £514 million has been recognised in the statement of total recognised gains and losses. The other £28 million offsets goodwill previously written off directly to reserves and does not, therefore, pass through the statement of total recognised gains and losses.

(Like The Rank Group in Extract 7.2 above British Aerospace has included its investment at a valuation.)

These can be contrasted with the Royal Bank of Scotland which has regarded companies in which it has an interest as low as 10% as being associates:

Extract 7.5: The Royal Bank of Scotland Group plc (1996)

20   Interests in associated undertakings [extract]

The principal associated undertakings are:

	Total issued share and loan capital at 30th September 1996	% held	Share of results based on accounts made up to	Nature of business
Banco de Comercio e				
Industria, S.A.	31.1m ordinary shares of Es 1,000	12.8	30th September*	Banking
(incorporated in Portugal)	Es 17.5m loan capital	–		
ICCH Limited	6.75m £1 ordinary shares	10.0	31st July*	Clearing house
(registered in England)				holding company
Inter-Bank On Line				
System Limited	6.1m £1 ordinary shares	24.1	30th September*	Technology
(registered in Scotland)				
Linea Directa Aseguradora S.A.	1,200.0m 5 Ptas	50.0	30th September*	Insurance
(registered in Spain)				
Newton Management Limited	5.9m 10p ordinary shares	–	30th September*	Fund
(registered in England)	18.3m 50p A ordinary shares	33.1		management
P.T. Bank Multicor	1.2m shares of Rp 50,000	24.0	30th September*	Banking
(incorporated in Indonesia)	Rp 23,400.0m loan capital	–		
Privilege Insurance Holdings Limited	2.5m £1 ordinary shares	60.0	30th September	Insurance
(registered in England)	27.5m £1 preference shares	100.0		
The Scottish Agricultural	2.0m £1 ordinary shares	33.3	31st March	Agricultural
Securities Corporation p.l.c.				lending
(registered in Scotland)				
Travellers Cheque Associates Limited	0.5m £1 ordinary shares	10.0	30th June*	Issuing sterling
(registered in England)				travellers cheques

* Incorporating unaudited interim accounts.

Banco de Comercio e Industria, S.A. operates in Portugal, Linea Directa Aseguradora S.A. operates in Spain and P.T. Bank Multicor operates in Indonesia. The UK is the principal area of operation for the other associated undertakings. Dividends receivable from the associated undertakings (excluding tax credits) totalled £4 million (1995 - £5 million).

Where the equity shareholdings are less than 20%, associated undertakings are accounted for as such due to significant influence being exercised through representation on the board of directors and participation in financial and operating policy decisions.

Mr P.J. Wood, a director of the company, has an interest in Privilege Insurance Holdings Limited.

2.2 The Companies Act 1985

The Act defines associated undertakings in similar terms to SSAP 1, as an undertaking in which a participating interest is held and over which significant influence is exercised.[9] A participating interest in an undertaking is an interest in the shares of the undertaking which is held for the long term for the purpose of securing a contribution to the activities of the investing company by the exercise of control or influence arising from that interest.[10] This includes interests in partnerships and unincorporated associations; it also includes interests which are convertible into interests in shares, such as convertible loan stock, and options to acquire an interest in shares.[11] Again the Act picks up the SSAP 1 assertion that a holding of 20% of the shareholders' or members' voting rights is presumed to confer significant influence (but not the contrary presumption).

2.3 ED 50

ED 50 was published in June 1990 and proposed to amend both SSAPs 1 and 14. In the event, although the ASB's Interim Statement: Consolidated Accounts made limited amendments to both standards, only the revision of SSAP 14 has been progressed further (resulting in its replacement by FRS 2) and the revision of SSAP 1 remains incomplete. ED 50 sought to change the definition of associates in SSAP 1 to bring it more in line with the Companies Act.[12]

Participating interest was to have the same meaning as in the Act and significant influence to be effectively the same as in SSAP 1, although further amplification of the ways it might be exercisable was given along the lines of that contained in IAS 28 (see 6.2.1 below).[13]

2.4 ASB Discussion Paper

The ASB's Discussion Paper defined associated undertakings in similar terms to that contained in the Companies Act.[14] However, it proposed that significant influence will only be exercised if the following conditions are met:[15]

'(a) The investor must exercise influence over the operating and financing policies of the investee that is sufficient for it to fulfil its role as a partner in the business of that entity. This means that in the area of their mutual interest the investee will generally implement policies that are consistent with the strategy of the investor.

(b) The investor must reasonably expect to benefit, at least in the long term, from the economic benefits accumulated by the economic activities of its investee. In the long run the value of a business consists of the cash flows it generates. Through its influence over the financial policy of the investee, particularly with respect to dividend policy and investment decisions, the investor, therefore, must have the ability to secure access in the long run to its share of these cash flows if it is to benefit (other than by disposing of its interest) from any increases in the value of the investee. This condition does not imply that the investor must always press for the highest possible dividend; a long-term interest in the future cash flows of the investee may be equally compatible with favouring a policy of re-investment.

(c)   The investor's interest must provide it with some protection from changes in the operating and financial policies of the investee that would significantly affect the benefits it expects or the risks to which it is exposed.'

Associated undertakings could either be 'joint ventures' (which are defined – see 4.4 below) or associates (which are any associates which are not joint ventures). The ASB regarded associated undertakings (as defined) as being a form of strategic alliance whereby the investor acts as a partner in the business of the investee and it is only in such situations that equity accounting should be used. However, in the light of comments received on the Discussion Paper the ASB has had to revise its approach.

2.5   FRED 11

FRED 11 defines an associate as 'an entity (other than a subsidiary) in which another entity (the investor) has a participating interest and over whose operating and financial policies the investor exercises a significant influence'.[16] This is again consistent with the Companies Act. A participating interest is also defined in similar terms to the Act and the definition of an 'interest held on a long term basis' is the same as that contained in FRS 2. The exposure draft also defines what is meant by the 'exercise of significant influence' as being 'the exercise of a degree of influence by an investor over the operating and financial policies of its investee that results in the following conditions being fulfilled:[17]

'(a)   The investor is actively involved and is influential in the direction of its investee through its participation in policy decisions covering all aspects of policy relevant to the investor, including decisions on strategic issues such as:

   (i)   the expansion or contraction of the business, participation in other entities, changes in products, markets and activities of its investee; and

   (ii)   determining the balance between dividend and reinvestment.

(b)   Over time, the investee generally implements policies that are consistent with the strategy of the investor and avoids implementing policies that are contrary to the investor's interests.'

The ASB has backed off from the idea that the investor acts as a partner in the business of the investee but that the investor uses the associate as a medium through which it conducts a part of its activities through its direct involvement in the operating and financial policies of the associate; the participation in such policy decisions being with a view to gaining economic benefits from the activities of the investee. The ASB explains that the investor's long-term interest in the future cash flows of its investee is compatible with a policy of reinvestment by the investee; the investor may not, therefore, always press its investee to follow a strategy of paying high dividends.[18] It also explains that condition (b) above does not mean that an investor does not exercise significant influence just because the investee has acted contrary to the investor's interest (it may have done so unwittingly). However, what it does mean is that if the investee persistently implements policies that are inconsistent with the investor's strategy then the investor does not exercise significant influence.[19]

The proposed definition is narrower than that in SSAP 1. Whereas SSAP 1 only requires the investor *to be in a position* to exercise significant influence, FRED 11 proposes that it should be *actively involved* through participation in policy decisions on strategic issues. The ASB considers that in practice, this difference 'may have a limited effect because the best evidence that an entity is in a position to exercise significant influence is that it is actually exercising such influence'.[20] However, in our view the requirement for an active involvement and influence in policy decisions is too restrictive, providing scope for strategic investments not to be equity accounted.

The proposed definition in FRED 11 goes on to say that 'significant influence is usually exercised through nomination to the board of directors (or its equivalent). It may also be exercised in other ways that allow the investor to participate effectively in policy-making decisions. The existence of significant influence presupposes an agreement or understanding, formal or informal, between the investor and its investee. Once an investor has fulfilled the above conditions for exercising significant influence, it should be regarded as continuing to exercise significant influence until an event or transaction takes away its ability to do so.'[21]

The proposed definition then states that 'it is unlikely that an investor can exercise significant influence unless it has a substantial basis of voting power. A holding of 20 per cent or more of the voting rights in another entity suggests, but does not ensure, that the investor exercises significant influence over that entity. The presumption of the exercise of significant influence at the 20 per cent threshold is rebutted if the investor does not fulfil the criteria for the exercise of significant influence set out above. For the purpose of applying this presumption, the shares held by the parent and its subsidiaries in that entity should be aggregated.'[22] The 20% threshold contained in SSAP 1 and the Companies Act is clearly subordinated to the substance of the relationship. As explained by the ASB 'the presumption should not to be taken as setting a threshold at 20 per cent that divides investments that are associates from those that are not. The decisive feature in identifying investments that are associates is the actual nature of the relationship between investor and investee rather than the level of voting rights or ownership interests held. The actual nature of the relationship usually becomes clear after an investment is acquired but arrangements (such as the number of board members the investor may nominate and the proposed decision-taking process) may be used to evaluate the relationship before the record is established. It is, however, the actual nature of the relationship that should be reflected where this develops differently from earlier relationships.'[23]

3 THE ACCOUNTING TREATMENT OF ASSOCIATES

3.1 Equity accounting under SSAP 1

The basic approach of equity accounting involves adding the investor's share of post-acquisition profits to the cost of the investment and deducting dividends received so that the carrying value of the investment reflects the cost plus post-acquisition retained earnings of the investee. This approach was modified slightly in the 1982 revision of SSAP 1, so as to require the investment to be analysed into three components:

(a)   the investing group's share of the net assets other than goodwill of the associate stated, where possible, after attributing fair values to the net assets at the time of acquisition of the interest;

(b)   the investing group's share of any goodwill in the associated company's own financial statements; and

(c)   the premium paid (or discount) on the acquisition of the interests in the associated companies insofar as it has not already been written off or amortised.[24]

SSAP 1 does not specifically state how the goodwill is to be accounted for, but this is currently governed by SSAP 22, which applies the same rules to goodwill arising on the acquisition of associates as it does to goodwill emerging on the consolidation of subsidiaries. Consequently, such goodwill must be dealt with either by immediate elimination in reserves, or by amortisation in the profit and loss account.[25] The result of this change is that, assuming the former of these two options is adopted, the carrying value of the associate will represent the investor's share of its net assets (after attributing fair values at the date of acquisition).

The attribution of fair values can be problematical in practice because, again, the investor only has influence, not control, over the investee and cannot therefore insist on receiving the same degree of information that could be demanded from a subsidiary. It may therefore be that the exercise will have to be confined to the most significant items, such as the revaluation of major property assets, and this will often be acceptable on grounds of materiality. It should not be forgotten also that the subsequent share of the investee's profits recognised by the investor should also reflect any material adjustments based on this fair value allocation (such as adjustments to depreciation). This point is not specifically addressed in the standard, but it follows from the proposition that equity accounting is a modified form of consolidation and that the same general principles therefore apply. Similarly, adjustments should be made, where material, to bring the accounting policies of the associate into line with those of the investor.

The following example illustrates why such fair value adjustments are necessary:

Example 7.1:   Attributing fair values to the assets of associates

Company A buys a 40% stake in Company B for £2,000,000. Company B is an investment company and its only asset is a portfolio of investments with a book value of £3,000,000 but a fair value of £5,000,000.

If Company A did not apply fair value accounting to the analysis of its stake in Company B, it would record its share of the net assets of B at £1,200,000 and goodwill of £800,000, which, depending on its accounting policy for goodwill, would probably be written off to reserves. The proper treatment in this particular case would be to attribute all of its investment in B to the underlying portfolio of investments and to recognise no goodwill. (Tax effects have been ignored in this example for the sake of simplicity.)

If one year later, Company B sells its portfolio for £6,000,000, it will report a pre-tax profit of £3,000,000, of which Company A's share will be £1,200,000. However, A must make an adjustment to this figure to eliminate the £800,000 fair value adjustment which reflected the pre-acquisition gain made by B, but not recorded in its own books at that time, and therefore record a profit of only £400,000.

The presentation of the figures relating to the associate in the investor's financial statements is relatively straightforward. In the profit and loss account, the share of the associate's pre-tax results are shown as one line, and the share of its tax charge similarly shown as an element of the investor's own tax charge.

In the balance sheet, the investment in the associate should again be shown as one line within fixed assets (analysed between shares and any loans), and any material inter-company trading balances should be shown in current assets or liabilities. The investor's financial statements should also include its share of any reserve movements of the associate, such as a revaluation surplus (but obviously with regard to any fair value adjustment).

Where the associate is very material in relation to the investor, SSAP 1 suggests that the notes to the investor's financial statements should contain summarised profit and loss account and balance sheet information to indicate the scale and nature of the figures which underlie the 'one line' inclusion of the associate.[26] It is not particularly common to do this, but some companies do give such supplementary information in respect of their associates.[27] However a number of companies have adopted the practice of showing the amount of their share of the turnover derived from the operations of associates.[28] This is generally done as shown in the following extract:

Extract 7.6: GKN plc (1996)

CONSOLIDATED PROFIT AND LOSS ACCOUNT [extract]

	Notes	BEFORE EXCEPTIONAL ITEMS £m	EXCEPTIONAL ITEMS £m	1996 TOTAL £m	1995 TOTAL £m
Sales					
Subsidiaries:					
continuing operations		**2862.6**	–	**2862.6**	2602.8
discontinued operations		**10.4**	–	**10.4**	290.8
	2	**2873.0**	–	**2873.0**	2893.6
Share of associated companies:					
continuing operations	2	**464.0**	–	**464.0**	411.1
		3337.0	–	**3337.0**	3304.7

The profit and loss account then continues with 'Operating profit', a note showing all of the format headings (including the 'true' group turnover) making up that number.

One interesting example is Lonrho which, rather than adopting the treatment adopted by GKN and other companies, has chosen to invoke the true and fair override provisions of the Companies Act and consolidate the associates' turnover:

Extract 7.7: Lonrho Plc (1996)

Consolidated profit and loss account [extract]

	Note	1996 Before exceptional items £m	1996 Exceptional items £m	1996 Total £m	1995 Before exceptional items £m	1995 Exceptional items £m	1995 Total £m
	1,2						
Turnover (including associates)							
– continuing operations		**2,070**		**2,070**	2,043		2,043
– discontinued operations							
– Metropole		**76**		**76**	68		68
		2,146		**2,146**	2,111		2,111

Basis of accounting [extract]

The consolidation of the turnover of associates is not in accordance with the Statement of Standard Accounting Practice No.1; however, the Directors consider that this presentation is necessary in order for the accounts to show a true and fair view. The contribution of associates to the Group's results is significant and the Directors consider that exclusion of turnover of associates could distort the measurement of the Group's performance.

3.2 Equity accounting under FRED 11

The ASB's Discussion Paper raised the possibility of accounting for associated undertakings by proportional consolidation but rejected it. Instead it proposed that they should continue to be equity accounted but in an expanded manner ('the expanded equity method').[29] This received almost universal support and therefore has been taken up in FRED 11. The exposure draft proposes a definition of the 'equity method' as being 'a method of accounting that brings an investment into its investor's financial statements initially at its cost, identifying any goodwill arising. The carrying amount of the investment is adjusted in each period by the investor's share of results of its investee, which the investor recognises in its profit and loss account, the investor's share of any relevant gains or losses, which the investor recognises in its statement of total recognised gains and losses, and any other changes in the investee's net assets, including distributions to its owners, for example by dividend.'[30]

To apply the equity method of accounting, the investor's share in its investee needs to be calculated. Where the investor is a group, its share of the associate is the aggregate of the holdings of the parent and its subsidiaries in that entity (amounts held by other associates or joint ventures are ignored).[31] Where the investee is corporate, the investor's share is usually calculated at its proportional holding of ordinary shares in that entity because this is the basis of its entitlement to dividends and other distributions and of its liability to contributions. In some cases the arrangements for sharing dividends and other distributions and the liability to make contributions may be more complicated; for example, they may depend on the nature of the distribution to be made or the way the underlying cash flows arise. In these cases, it is proposed that the substance of the respective rights held need to be assessed to establish the most appropriate measure of the investor's interest.[32]

The exposure draft then proposes that the same principles should be applied in calculating the amounts to be included by the equity method for associates as in the consolidation of subsidiaries. Accordingly, the following rules are proposed:[33]

(a) When an entity acquires an investee, fair values should be attributed to its underlying assets and liabilities and the consideration paid in acquiring it. Depreciation should be based on these fair values. The difference between the investor's share of these fair values and the consideration paid is goodwill arising on the acquisition. The investee's assets used in calculating the goodwill arising on its acquisition should not include any goodwill carried in the balance sheet of the investee.

(b) Where profits and losses resulting from transactions between the investor and its associate are included in the carrying amount of assets in either entity, the part relating to the investor's share should be eliminated. Where the transaction provides evidence of impairment of any similar assets held by the investor, this should be taken into account.

(c) In arriving at the amounts to be included by the equity method, the same accounting policies as those of the investor should be applied.

(d) Where the period end of the associate differs from that of the investor, the entity should be included on the basis of financial statements prepared to the investor's period end.

It is recognised in the exposure draft that, whereas an investor controls its subsidiaries, thus providing access to the information necessary for such procedures, it only exercises significant influence over its associates. Therefore, in making the relevant adjustments described above where access to information is limited, estimates may be used. However it cautions that where the information available to the investor is extremely limited, the investor's relationship with the investee should be reassessed because this may mean that the investor's influence is not significant.[34]

Where the use of coterminous accounting periods is not practicable, the exposure draft proposes slightly different rules from those presently in SSAP 1 (see 4.1 below).

Where an associate itself has subsidiaries, associates or joint ventures, the results and net assets to be taken into account by the equity method are the results and net assets of that entity's group, including that group's interest in its associate and joint ventures.[35]

The main impact of FRED 11 is that rather than showing the share of the associate's pre-tax results as one line, the investor should include its share of the associate's operating results as part of the group's operating activities and all format headings occurring after operating profit, including those required by FRS 3 (see 2.6.3 of Chapter 22), should include the appropriate share of similar items relating to the associate (with separate disclosure where material).[36] The exposure draft emphasises that the investor's share of the associate's turnover should not be included in the group turnover, but indicates that a total combining the amounts may be shown on a pro-forma basis. However, if this is done then any segmental analysis of turnover (see 2.2.5. of Chapter 19) should also include the associate's turnover, but distinguishing amounts for the group itself from amounts relating to the associate.[37]

4   OTHER PARTICULAR ISSUES

4.1   Non-coterminous periods

The rules about the accounting period of the investee are somewhat confused. SSAP 1 contains the slightly odd requirement that the financial statements of the investee which are used as the source of figures to be equity accounted are to be either coterminous with the investor's accounting reference period or 'made up to a date which is either not more than six months before, or shortly after, the date of the financial statements of the investing group'.[38] It seems rather strange that the standard appears to tolerate a difference in year end of six months in one direction from the investor's year end, but a short but unspecified period in the other direction. If the overall objective is to give a true and fair view of the results for the investor's own financial year, any non-matching of the associate's year can presumably only be accepted on the grounds that the effect is not material, in which case the detail of the SSAP 1 rule seems of questionable relevance.

The standard goes on to say that where the associate's year end is before that of the investor, 'care should be taken to ensure that later information has not materially affected the view shown by the financial statements of the associated company'.[39] It is not entirely clear what action is suggested where it is felt that subsequent events have materially changed this view; the same paragraph goes on to say that the financial statements should disclose the circumstances where the effect of using non-coterminous year ends is material, but a better solution would presumably be to use the updated information which showed that the effect was material to amend the figures incorporated in the financial statements. The international accounting standard deals with this problem by saying that 'adjustments are made for the effects of any significant events or transactions between the investor and the associate that occur between the date of the associate's financial statements and the date of the investor's financial statements'.[40]

Some companies, indeed, make such adjustments, as indicated in the following extracts:

Extract 7.8: United News & Media plc (1996)

Investments [extract]

Investments in companies where the group exercises significant influence are included as associates under the equity method of accounting. The figures included in the financial statements are based on audited accounts, adjusted where necessary by reference to management accounts for the period up to 31 December.

Extract 7.9: Pearson plc (1996)

C Partnerships and associated undertakings [extract]

The figures included in the financial statements have been based on audited accounts, adjusted where necessary by reference to unaudited management accounts for the subsequent period to 31 December.

Of course, it can be difficult to ensure that the associate provides up-to-date information when the investor has only a minority stake in it. A holding company is usually able to tell its subsidiary to change its year end to coincide with its own, but the various investors in an associate may all have different year ends, and none of them has the control which is needed in order to dictate when the associate's year end should be, nor can they necessarily demand the production of interim accounts for their own purposes (although this can sometimes give an indication of whether or not they do, in fact, exercise significant influence). There can, therefore, be very significant practical difficulties in obtaining information for a period which corresponds to that of the investor, and this can be compounded when the associate has a Stock Exchange listing, which means that only published information can be disclosed in the financial statements of the investor. Nevertheless the fundamental requirement to give a true and fair view of the results of the investor group for its own financial year remains, and cannot be satisfied by incorporating results for an entirely different period. Fortunately, however, the effect will rarely be material to the group.

FRED 11 proposes that the associated undertaking should be included on the basis of interim financial statements prepared to the investor's period end unless this is impracticable. Where this is the case, the exposure draft proposes that 'the entity should be included on the basis of financial statements prepared for a period ending not more than three months before the investor's period-end. Where using these financial statements would release restricted, price-sensitive information, financial statements prepared for a period that ended not more than six months before the investor's period-end may be used. Any changes that take place between the entity's period end and its investor's that materially affect the view given by the investor's financial statements should be taken into account by adjustment.[41]

4.2   Deficiency of assets

When an associate makes post-acquisition losses, to the extent that it has a deficiency of assets in its balance sheet, the question arises of whether the investor should continue to account for these results, and thus carry its investment at a negative amount. The position taken by SSAP 1 on the subject is that in these circumstances 'it will usually be supported by its shareholders (either by way of loans or by way of an agreement, either formal or informal, to support it)'. The standard goes on to say that 'in these circumstances, the investing group should reflect its share of the deficiency of net assets in its consolidated financial statements'.[42]

Examples of companies which reflect net liabilities in respect of an associate are shown below:

Extract 7.10: Sidlaw Group plc (1996)

14 **Investments** [extract]

	Group	
	1996	1995
	£000	£000
Associated undertakings	–	–

18 **Creditors due after one year** [extract]

	Group	
	1996	1995
	£000	£000
Losses of associated undertaking	1,026	1,021

Extract 7.11: Williams Holdings PLC (1996)

19 **Provisions for liabilities and charges** [extract]

	Investment in Newmond PLC £m
Group	
At 1st January 1996	–
Acquired	22.9
At 31st December 1996	22.9

The cost of investment in Newmond PLC was £58.4m. The group's share of the net liabilities has been estimated at £22.9m, which is shown above. Goodwill of £81.3m has been written off to reserves on the transaction.

FRED 11 proposes that the investor should take account of any deficiency in net assets of its associated undertakings; the only exception being where there is sufficient evidence that an event has irrevocably changed the relationship between the investor and the associate, marking its irreversible withdrawal from the associate.[43] Such evidence is stated to include 'a public statement by the investor that it is withdrawing, with a demonstrable commitment to the process of withdrawal, or evidence that the direction of the operating and financial policies of the investee are to be determined by the investee's creditors, including its bankers, rather than the equity shareholders'.[44]

4.3   Investor not preparing group financial statements

A company which has no subsidiaries, but which has an investment in an associate, has a particular problem because of the requirements of the Companies Act that only realised profits can be included in the profit and loss account.[45] Since it does not produce group financial statements, its profit and loss account will be a company profit and loss account, and the only income 'realised' from the associate in that context will be dividends received/

receivable. For that reason, SSAP 1 suggests that it should equity account only by producing a supplementary pro-forma profit and loss account in addition to the company profit and loss account or 'by adding the information in supplementary form to its own profit and loss account ... in such a way that its share of the profits of the associated companies is not treated as realised ...'.[46] An example of such a presentation is shown below:[47]

Example 7.2:   *Unconsolidated profit and loss account incorporating associate's results*

	£'000	£'000
Turnover		2,000
Cost of sales		1,400
		600
Gross profit		600
Distribution costs	175	
Administrative expenses	125	
		300
Profit on ordinary activities before taxation		300
Tax on profit on ordinary activities		85
Profit on ordinary activities after taxation		215
Aggregate amount of dividends proposed		80
Amount set aside to reserves		135

Supplementary statement incorporating results of associated companies:

	£'000
Share of profits less losses of associated companies	50
Less tax	15
Share of profits less losses of associated companies	35
Profit on ordinary activities after taxation (as above)	215
Profit attributable to members of the investing company	250
Aggregate amount of dividends proposed	80
Net profit retained (£35,000 by associated companies)	170

Similar considerations apply in relation to the balance sheet. Where a group balance sheet is not presented, and as the company balance sheet will normally carry the investment at cost, SSAP 1 suggests either that a separate pro-forma balance sheet should be given, presenting the associate on an equity accounting basis, or that the information should be added in supplementary form to the company balance sheet.[48] The situation arises only relatively seldom, because most companies who have equity stakes in associates also have subsidiary companies and have the obligation to present consolidated financial statements.

Companies which are exempt from preparing consolidated accounts do not need to include such information. The supplementary information relating to the profit and loss account is also not required to be given by companies which 'would be exempt, if they had subsidiaries'.[49] This is presumably meant to cover those companies which would meet the small/medium-sized criteria (see 4.2 of Chapter 5). If that is the case, it is unclear why the balance sheet information is still required. However, they may be required to disclose some information about the associates under the Companies Act.[50]

FRED 11 proposes to continue the requirements and exemptions contained in SSAP 1 (but drafted in such a way that exempts disclosure of all information).[51]

4.4   Joint ventures

Most of the discussion in SSAP 1 is in terms which describe the associate as a company; however, it is made clear that the same principles apply to investments in unincorporated bodies, such as partnerships. Frequently, such forms are used for the conduct of joint ventures. However, the nature of these vehicles gives rise to some further considerations.

The first is that the nature of the relationship with the investee might mean that there is some other, more appropriate form of presentation rather than one line equity accounting. For example, the investor may have a direct interest in certain assets which it has contributed to the venture, and the only other asset or liability to be recognised might be its entitlement or obligation to receive or pay sums under the profit sharing agreement and, in these circumstances, it may be appropriate to reflect these items directly in its balance sheet. Alternatively, it might be appropriate to reflect directly in its own financial statements its proportional share of the assets and liabilities of the investee by a form of proportional consolidation; such a treatment is frequently applied in such industries as oil and gas and construction.

The Companies Act contains provisions which permit proportional consolidation for certain joint ventures[52] and the following points are worth noting:

(a)   the Act restricts proportional consolidation to unincorporated joint ventures. Incorporated joint ventures will therefore generally be equity accounted as associated undertakings;

(b)   the Act requires that the joint venture should be managed 'jointly with one or more undertakings not included in the consolidation' but otherwise places no restriction on the type of non-corporate joint venture which may be proportionally consolidated;

(c) the Act permits proportional consolidation in group accounts but contains no provisions allowing such a treatment in individual company accounts. It could be inferred from this that the intention of the legislation is that such a treatment is not permitted. However, it is arguable that proportional consolidation ought to be adopted in individual accounts on the basis that there is, in effect, a direct interest in a proportion of the assets, liabilities, income and expenditure of the joint venture; and

(d) the Act contains no detailed description of the proportional consolidation method, stating merely that 'the provisions of this Part relating to the preparation of consolidated accounts apply, with any necessary modifications, to proportional consolidation under this paragraph'.

One company which uses proportional consolidation for its joint ventures and partnerships is John Mowlem, as illustrated below:

Extract 7.12: John Mowlem & Company PLC (1996)

Joint ventures and partnerships

The Group's share of the results and net assets of non-incorporated construction joint ventures is proportionately consolidated in the Group profit and loss account and balance sheet.

Certain disclosures are required in relation to joint ventures which are proportionally consolidated (see 5.6 below).

Another consideration which should be borne in mind when there is an investment in an unincorporated investee is that the investor is likely to have joint and several liability for the liabilities of the investee, and this may need to be reflected in its financial statements, either as a contingent liability or even as a provision if it appears likely that it will be called on to meet this obligation without recovery from its fellow investors.

The ASB supplemented the general description of a joint venture by including a definition in its Interim Statement: Consolidated Accounts as follows:

'A joint venture is an undertaking by which its participants expect to achieve some common purpose or benefit. It is controlled jointly by two or more venturers. Joint control is the contractually agreed sharing of control.'[53]

In its Discussion Paper, the ASB defined a joint venture as 'an entity that, as a result of a contractual arrangement, is jointly controlled by the reporting entity and other venturers with a view to benefit. The contractual arrangement may take different forms but will cover matters such as the activities, duration, policies and procedures of the joint venture, the allocation of assets and liabilities, the decision-making process, capital contributions and sharing of output, income, expenses or results of the joint venture.'[54] The Discussion Paper proposed that joint ventures, whether corporate or non-corporate, should be accounted for under the expanded equity method as for associates and should not be proportionally consolidated.[55] However, jointly controlled operations or jointly controlled assets that did not by themselves constitute a 'business' would not amount to a joint venture; such joint activities were to fall outwith the scope of any revised standard.[56]

Although these proposals were the single most popular option among those commenting, there was significant opposition. Commentators argued strongly that an accounting standard should recognise that joint ventures were commercially distinct from associates. Accordingly, FRED 11 proposes that joint ventures should either be equity accounted or proportionally consolidated depending on the circumstances. The exposure draft defines a joint venture as 'an entity that, as a result of a contractual arrangement, is jointly controlled by the reporting entity and other venturers (excluding any subsidiary of the reporting entity)'. The key relationship in the definition is 'joint control' and a reporting entity 'jointly controls a venture with other entities if none of the entities alone can control that entity but all together can do so and decisions on financial and operating policy essential to the activities, economic performance and financial position of that venture require each venturer's consent. The requirement for an entity's consent does not have to be set out in the joint venture agreement provided that the joint venture works in practice on the basis of securing the consent of each venturer to all major strategy decisions. Day-to-day management can be delegated by the venturers collectively to one of the venturers or another entity.'[57]

It is proposed that most joint ventures will be equity accounted as for associates. This is because it is usually the case that the venturers share in common the benefits, risks and obligations of their joint venture.[58] However, proportional consolidation will be required for joint ventures where each venturer has its own separate interest in the benefits, risks and obligations of the venture. A joint venture of this type is seen as a framework within which each venturer carries out its own activities consistent with its own business strategy and achieves a result that may be substantially independent of the results achieved by the other venturers.[59] The exposure draft suggests that such joint ventures will be of two broad types:

(a) a joint venture whose particular role is to contribute a product or service at a specified stage in the venturer's business. The purpose of such a joint venture is to carry out a stage in the venturer's own business rather than to perform as a business in its own right; and

(b) a joint venture within which the venturer has a distinct and separate share, such that the benefits, risks and obligations of that part accrue solely to the venturer and its share of any output or profit relates wholly to certain assets in the joint venture that are distinct and identifiable.[60]

We support the concept that most joint ventures should be equity accounted, for the reasons given, and that there are some circumstances when proportional consolidation is more appropriate. We have difficulty in applying the exceptional circumstances described in the FRED to joint ventures commonly found in practice, however, because the first example described is not a 'venture' and the second is not 'joint' (there is no sharing of assets).

There are two concepts that are fundamental to the distinction:

- joint control as distinguished from actual control of specific assets that are managed jointly within a larger project; and

- a separate business as distinguished from part of each venturer's business.

Using this classification, two types of 'joint venture' can be distinguished:

- 'true' joint ventures where there is both joint control of assets and a separate business venture, which should be equity accounted; and

- other 'arrangements' which fail to meet either of the two essential elements.

The 'other arrangements' fall into two categories:

(a) jointly managed assets or operations, where the venturers retain control of their own assets which are used within a joint project to produce a product which is sold externally (aircraft manufacture is an example) or used by each venturer; and

(b) jointly controlled assets which produce a product (or provide a service) which is sold by or on behalf of each venturer or distributed to each venturer for use or sale (a shared production/ transport facility in the oil industry is an example).

The appropriate accounting would seem to be separate recognition of the venturer's own assets, liabilities, expenses and share of output/turnover and profit for (a) and proportional consolidation for (b). Both examples in the exposure draft fit into this analysis, although one would be proportionally consolidated and one recognised in the venturer's own accounts.

4.5   Loss of associate status

It is possible that the investee might cease to be an associate without any change having taken place in the investment held by the investor, either because the investor's stake has been diluted by the issue of shares by the investee to other parties or because the other shareholders now act together to prevent the investor from exercising influence over the investee. In the latter circumstance, the investment should not be restated to its original cost, but rather frozen at the amount of its equity value at the time when the influence was lost, and this figure should in effect be treated as equivalent to cost in the group financial statements. (The real cost should continue to be shown as such in the investor's own balance sheet.) The 'frozen' carrying value should be kept under review to see whether there has been any permanent impairment in value for which provision has to be made, and one reason for such a write-down might be the receipt of dividends paid out of profits which had been earned by the investee (and accounted for by the investor) during the period when significant influence was exercised. This is the treatment required by SSAP 1 whenever an investment ceases to be an associate.[61]

However, we believe that a different treatment might be required in the first of the two sets of circumstances outlined above, namely where the investor's stake has been diluted because the associate has issued shares to another party. In these circumstances the investor should, in our view, adjust the carrying value of his investment and recognise a gain or loss depending on whether the shares were issued to the third party at a value which was higher or lower than the asset value of the associate as reflected in the financial statements of the investor. The remaining amount should then be 'frozen' and accounted for as above. This is illustrated by the following example:

Example 7.3:   Dilution in the holding of an investment in an associate

A company owns 200,000 £1 shares in an associated company which has a share capital of £1,000,000 and net assets of £2,500,000. The associate issues 600,000 shares to a third party for cash of £1,800,000.

The accounting will be as follows:

	£
Carrying value of associate	
before the transaction – 20% of £2,500,000	500,000
after the transaction – 12.5% of £4,300,000	537,500
Gain	37,500

FRS 2 discusses such 'deemed' disposals in the context of subsidiaries and requires a gain or loss to be calculated in such a manner.[62] This issue is discussed further at 3.5 of Chapter 6.

SSAP 1 does not deal with the situation where a company has ceased to be an associate because significant influence over it has been lost, and circumstances again change so that the investor's ability to exercise influence is restored; in particular, how should the investor account for the share of the associate's results earned during the period when the investee was not regarded as an associate because of the absence of influence? Our recommendation is that these results should be accounted for as a separately disclosed item in the results for the year in which the investee again becomes an associate. This would be consistent with the treatment required by FRS 2 in relation to subsidiaries that were previously subject to severe restrictions which were subsequently lifted (see 5.3 of Chapter 5).

FRED 11 proposes rules relating to the disposal of an associate which encompass an investment ceasing to be an associate because it no longer fulfils either of the two elements of the definition; the holding of a participating interest and the exercise of significant influence.[63] Where an investment in an associate is disposed of in stages then processes similar to those contained in FRS 2 for subsidiaries are to be followed (see 3.3. to 3.5 of Chapter 6).[64] Where an investor continues to hold an investment in its former associate then the initial carrying amount for the interest retained is to be the proportion retained of the final net amount recorded under the equity method for that investment on the date it ceased to be an associate. This amount should be reviewed and written down, if necessary, to its recoverable amount.[65]

The ASB's Discussion paper stated that the Board expected that implementation of its revised definition of associated undertaking would cause certain interests which presently qualify as associated companies under SSAP 1 to cease to do so. It was proposed that such former associated companies should be treated as investments and prior years should be adjusted to reflect this. Such investments are likely to be fixed asset investments and would therefore be included at purchase price, market value or directors' valuation.[66] Nevertheless, the ASB recommended that they should be carried at either market value or directors' valuation, with any difference between this amount and the original purchase price included in a revaluation reserve.[67] However, FRED 11 does not contain any specific proposals or discussion as to what is to happen in such circumstances.

4.6   Elimination of unrealised profits on transactions with associates

The issue of elimination of unrealised profits (and losses) on transactions between companies within a group is discussed at 3.4 of Chapter 5. SSAP 1 effectively extends such adjustments to transactions between a group member and an associate of the group by requiring that 'adjustments similar to those adopted for the purpose of presenting consolidated financial statements should be made to exclude from the investing group's consolidated financial statements such items as unrealised profits on stocks transferred to or from associated companies'.[68]   As indicated at 3.4 of Chapter 5, FRS 2 contains specific requirements relating to transactions within a group. ED 50 proposed similar requirements where profits or losses have arisen on transactions between the group and its associate or joint venture. It proposed that an adjustment be made for the group's share of that profit or loss. Where the associate or joint venture is equity accounted, this adjustment should be taken in the consolidated profit and loss account against either the group or the associate according to which of them recorded the profit on the transaction; the adjustment in the balance sheet should be made against the asset which was the subject of the transaction if it is held by the group or else against the amount recorded for the associate. Where the joint venture has been proportionally consolidated the adjustment should be made against the relevant items in the consolidated accounts.[69]

This treatment should be contrasted with that required when an inter-company transaction takes place involving a company which is not a wholly owned subsidiary. In such a situation, FRS 2 requires elimination of *all* of the profit or loss and this to be attributed between the majority and minority shareholders in the *selling* company.[70] Therefore, if a parent sells an asset to a 51% subsidiary all of the profit will be eliminated; no amount would be attributed to the minority shareholders. However, if the parent sold the asset to a 50% associate then under ED 50 only that portion would have to be eliminated.

The treatment proposed by ED 50 was adopted by Tesco in its 1990 accounts, as shown in the following extract:

Extract 7.13: Tesco PLC (1990)

Note 9

Investments [extract]

b) The group has one associated company, Shopping Centres Limited, whose main activity is property investment in which the group participates on a 50:50 basis. This company operates and is incorporated in the United Kingdom.

An amount of £6.3m representing the unrealised 50% element of the profit on the sale of three of the group's properties to Shopping Centres Limited in the year 1988/89 has been offset against the cost of the investment.

This treatment can be contrasted with that adopted by Storehouse in its 1990 accounts, as shown below:

Extract 7.14: Storehouse PLC (1990)

12   Investment in Related Companies [extract]

The Group owns 50 per cent of the issued share capital of Oppidan Estates Limited (Oppidan), the parent company of a group which operates principally in the UK as a property development and investment group in association with London & Edinburgh Trust PLC (LET).

At 31 December 1989 the company had commitments to purchase a further £97.6 million of properties from Storehouse and LET under the joint venture agreement. At 31 March the company had commitments to purchase £49.7 million of properties from Storehouse and LET.

As part of the joint venture agreement between Storehouse and LET, the Group has sold properties to Oppidan with a book value of £96.5 million for £120.4 million. LET have themselves sold properties to Oppidan at a market value of £49.0 million.

Half of the profit on this sale by Storehouse has been accounted for as an exceptional item and the balance recorded as deferred income and will be released to the profit and loss account over an extended period.

Tesco has adopted the same treatment as it did before in its 1997 accounts:

Extract 7.15: Tesco PLC (1997)

Note 12   Fixed asset investments [extract]

b) The Group's associated undertakings are:

	Business	Share of equity and preference share capital	Country of incorporation
Shopping Centres Limited	Property investment	50%	Registered in England
BLT Properties Limited	Property investment	50%	Registered in England

BLT Properties Limited was formed during the year. An amount of £1m representing the unrealised 50% element of the profit on the sale of seven of the group's properties to BLT Properties Limited has been offset against the cost of the investment.

Another treatment that has been adopted is that by Grand Metropolitan which would appear to have taken the unrealised profit directly to reserves:

Extract 7.16: Grand Metropolitan Public Limited Company (1991)

16   Inntrepreneur Estates Ltd [extract]

On 28th March the group and Courage merged their tenanted pub estates into a joint venture company called Inntrepreneur Estates Ltd (IEL) which is incorporated in England. The group has a 50% shareholding in the IEL share capital and IEL has been treated as an associate within these financial statements.

25   Reserves [extract]

	Share premium £m	Revaluation £m	Goodwill £m	Profit and loss £m	Total £m
At 30th September, 1990	451	1,253	(2,193)	3,382	2,893
Exchange adjustments	–	3	–	(18)	(15)
Retained profit for the year	–	–	–	214	214
Unrealised profit on sale of tenanted pub estate	–	–	–	23	23
Premiums on share issues, less expenses	70	–	–	–	70
Goodwill acquired during the year	–	–	(278)	–	(278)
Transfer of goodwill on disposal	–	–	235	(235)	–
Realisation of reserves on disposal	–	(395)	–	395	–
At 30th September, 1991	521	861	(2,236)	3,761	2,907

One interesting example is that of Smiths Industries which has chosen to eliminate *all* of the profit having previously only eliminated its share of the profit, as shown in the following extract:

Extract 7.17: Smiths Industries plc (1996)

6 Exceptional items	**1996**	1995
	£m	£m
Unrealised profit elimination relating to associated company	**(9.1)**	–

Following the increase in the Company's interest in Japan Medico Co. Ltd to 50%, the opportunity has been taken to review the basis of eliminating the intercompany profit on stock held by associates. It has been decided to adopt the more prudent approach of eliminating all such profit and as a result £9.1m has been charged as an exceptional item in arriving at cost of sales.

As indicated at 3.2 above, FRED 11 proposes that where profits and losses resulting from transactions between the investor and its associate (or joint venture) are included in the carrying amount of assets in either entity, the part relating to the investor's share should be eliminated.[71] No indication is given as to how this is to be effected, but presumably it is envisaged that it will be done in the manner suggested in ED 50.

FRED 11 proposes that such an adjustment is also to apply to transfers of assets or liabilities to set up a joint venture or to acquire an initial stake in an associate.[72] This is an area where present treatment is diverse. The adjustment made by Grand Metropolitan would appear to have been made in such a situation.

One company which has recognised a profit in the profit and loss account, and has therefore not made any adjustment, is Bridon, as shown below:

Extract 7.18: Bridon plc (1996)

9. INVESTMENTS

	Group		Company	
SHARES IN ASSOCIATED UNDERTAKINGS	**1996 £000**	1995 £000	**1996 £000**	1995 £000
At 1 January	**607**	614	**–**	–
Additions	**4,460**	–	**4,460**	–
Share of retained profits	**163**	12	**–**	–
Dividends received	**(21)**	–	**–**	–
Goodwill written off	**(2,786)**	–	**–**	–
Exchange difference	**(75)**	(19)	**–**	–
At 31 December	**2,348**	607	**4,460**	–

The shares in associated undertakings comprise a 41% interest in the ordinary share capital of PT Bripindo Utama, a company incorporated in Indonesia, and a 30% interest in the ordinary share capital of The Rope Company Limited, a company incorporated in the United Kingdom, acquired in 1996 (note 23).

23. SALE OF BUSINESSES [extract]

	1996 £000	1995 £000
Fixed assets	**2,669**	–
Stocks	**2,039**	–
Finance leases	**(78)**	–
Profit on disposal of tangible fixed assets	**200**	–
Sale consideration	**4,830**	–

The sale of businesses comprises £170,000 in respect of the automotive products business of Birkmyre Pty Limited in Australia and £4,660,000 in respect of the marine rope division sold to The Rope Company Limited. The latter sale was satisfied by a 30% shareholding in The Rope Company Limited and an unsecured loan note for £260,000, repayable on 1 December 1999 bearing interest at 1.5% above bank base rate.

Another company which has recognised a profit, but in circumstances where it would appear that cash consideration was received, some of which was reinvested in the company to which the businesses were sold, is Williams Holdings, as shown below:

Extract 7.19: Williams Holdings PLC (1996)

25   Acquisition and disposal of subsidiary and associated companies [extract]

	Disposals 1996 £m
Fixed assets	96.2
Investments	0.7
Stocks	46.3
Debtors	87.0
Cash	23.4
Bank overdrafts	–
Loans and finance leases	(2.8)
Creditors	(80.4)
Deferred tax	(12.9)
Provisions for liabilities and charges	7.6
	165.1
Profit on disposal before tax	97.1
Goodwill	165.3
Cash consideration	427.5
Cash acquired (sold)	(23.4)
	404.1

Disposals are shown before the costs of reinvestment in Saia Burgess Holdings (Jersey) Ltd of £7.0m and Newmond PLC of £58.4m.

22   Acquisitions [extract]

In addition, investments in two associated companies have been made in the year. £58.4m of the proceeds arising on the disposal of the UK Building Products businesses was reinvested in Newmond PLC, the parent company used in the management buy-out. The group's share of net liabilities of Newmond PLC has been estimated at £22.9m.

Of the disposal proceeds £360m related to the businesses sold to Newmond in which the company took a 26% stake.

One company which has not recognised any profit (although this may just be because book values seem to equate to fair values of the assets concerned) where it has contributed net assets to a new associate is P&O, as shown below:

Extract 7.20: The Peninsular and Oriental Steam Navigation Company (1996)

12　Other investments [extract]

The formation of P&O Nedlloyd on 31 December 1996 has resulted in P&O Containers Ltd ceasing to be a P&O subsidiary. The carrying value of the Group's interest in the separately identifiable net assets before and after the transaction is the same. The net assets of P&O Containers Ltd contributed on formation, together with attributable goodwill historically deducted from reserves, have been compared with the fair value of the Group's interest in the business acquired. This resulted in neither a gain nor loss and had no effect on reserves (note 17). Set out in the table below are the Group's share of P&O Nedlloyd's opening balance sheet, after deducting goodwill, based on estimates prepared within the Group and the P&O Containers Ltd's assets contributed on formation on 31 December 1996. The P&O Nedlloyd balance sheet is provisional because completion accounts have not been finalised at the date of this report.

	Provisional P&O Nedlloyd net assets	Group share of P&O Nedlloyd net assets	P&O Containers' net assets on formation
Ships	867.4	433.7	446.2
Other fixed assets	437.8	218.9	354.4
Net working capital	(3.0)	(1.5)	20.7
Net borrowings	(353.2)	(176.6)	(354.3)
Corporate tax	0.4	0.2	0.2
Provisions	(32.6)	(16.3)	(8.9)
Minority interests	(11.0)	(5.5)	(5.4)
	905.8	452.9	452.9

5　DISCLOSURE REQUIREMENTS REGARDING ASSOCIATES

Most disclosures relating to associates in group financial statements arise from the requirements of SSAP 1. Many of the requirements of the Companies Act 1985 duplicate those in the standard, but there are a few additional ones in the legislation. Where a company has acquired or disposed of an associate during the year, certain disclosures may also be required by SSAP 22 – *Accounting for goodwill*. The disclosure requirements are considered below.

5.1　Profit and loss account

The following should be disclosed:

(a)　the investor's share of:

    (i)　pre-tax profits less losses;

    (ii)　tax relating thereto;

    (iii)　extraordinary items (if material and extraordinary in the context of the group);

    (iv)　net profits less losses retained;[73]

(b)   if they are of major significance in relation to the results of the investing group, these details of an individual associate's results:

   (i)   total turnover;

   (ii)   total depreciation charge;

   (iii) total profits less losses before tax;

   (iv)   the amount of such profits attributable to the investing group;[74] and

(c)   any amount written off goodwill relating to the investment in an associate.[75]

5.2   Balance sheet

The following should be disclosed:

(a)   the investor's share of net assets other than goodwill;

(b)   the individual or aggregate amount of;

   (i)   any premium or discount on acquisition;

   (ii)   the investor's share of any goodwill in the associate's own accounts;[76]

(c)   loans to or from the associate;[77]

(d)   debtors and creditors resulting from trading with the associate;[78]

(e)   the investor's share of post-acquisition reserves and movements therein, and any tax effect of distribution of these if they relate to overseas associates;[79] and

(f)   if they are of major significance in relation to the financial position of the investing group, details of an individual associate's tangible and intangible assets and liabilities.[80]

5.3   Notes

It is necessary to disclose the following information about associates by way of note:

(a)   their names;

(b)   the proportion of the number of the issued shares of each class held by the investing group (and by the parent company);

(c)   an indication of the nature of the associate's business;[81]

(d)   details concerning non-coterminous year ends, if material;[82]

(e)   details and reasons where the presumption that a 20% stake confers significant influence which justifies associate status, or the converse presumption, is rebutted;[83]

(f)   restrictions on ability of the associate to distribute profits;[84] and

(g)   their country of incorporation, if outside Great Britain.[85]

An example of a comprehensive note which shows disclosures relating to associated companies is to be found in the financial statements of Sainsbury:

Extract 7.21: J Sainsbury plc (1997)

Note 4   Investment in Associated Undertakings

The Company's principal Associated Undertakings are:-

	Share of Allotted Capital	Share of Profit Before Tax	
		1997 **£m**	1996 £m
Giant Food Inc. (Food Retailing - US)			
125,000 Voting Common Stock of $1 each	50%		
11,779,931 Non-Voting Common Stock of $1 each	19.8%	17	18
Breckland Farms Limited (Pig Farming - UK)			
200,000 "B" Ordinary Shares of £1 each			
141,532 1% Redeemable Preference Shares of £1 each	50%	1	1
(other shareholder, Pauls plc)			
Hampden Group PLC (DIY Retailing - UK)			
4,470,000 Ordinary Shares of 10p each	29.7%	1	–
		19	19

Summary of movements	Group	Company
	£m	£m
Shares		
At 10th March 1996	98	7
Purchase of Giant Food Inc. shares (Note 5)	20	–
Exchange adjustments to reserves (Note 15)	(5)	–
At 8th March 1997	113	7
Share of Post Acquisition Reserves		
At 10th March 1996	10	
Share of retained profit for the year	6	
Other adjustments to reserves (Note 15)	5	
At 8th March 1997	21	
Long Term Capital Advances		
At 10th March 1996	6	5
Additions in period	7	8
At 8th March 1997	13	13
Total Net Investment 8th March 1997	147	20
9th March 1996	114	12

The Group's investment in shares in Associated Undertakings at 8th March 1997 represented £265 million (1996: £224 million) in respect of the cost of shares, less goodwill of £150 million set off against reserves (1996: £129 million), less accumulated exchange adjustments of £2 million (1996: additions of £3 million). The Company's investment in shares in Associated Undertakings at 8th March 1997 represented cost of shares of £7 million (1996: £7 million).

At 8th March 1997 the market value of shares listed on a recognised US stock exchange was £241 million (1996: £206 million) and on a recognised UK stock exchange of £4 million (1996: £4 million).

The proportion of the profits of the Associated Undertakings attributable to the Group and the reserves included in the Group Balance Sheet are taken from the audited accounts produced within three months of the balance sheet date.

The investment in Breckland Farms Limited is held directly by J Sainsbury plc. Investments in Giant Food Inc. and Hampden Group PLC are held by Subsidiaries.

Giant Food Inc. has been classified as an Associated Undertaking in view of the proportion of voting stock held.

5.4   Acquisitions/disposals

As indicated at 3 above, SSAP 22 applies the same rules to goodwill arising on the acquisition of associates as it does to that arising on the acquisition of subsidiaries. The standard requires a number of disclosures to be made in respect of acquisitions and disposals during a period and these apply equally to associates as they do to subsidiaries. These are discussed at 2.8.2 and 3.6 of Chapter 6.

5.5 Stock Exchange requirements

The Stock Exchange requires listed companies to disclose in their annual report the following information in respect of all associated undertakings:

(a)   the principal country of operation;

(b)   particulars of issued capital and debt securities; and

(c)   the group's percentage interest (direct or indirect) of each class of security.[86]

However, the Stock Exchange in May 1997 issued proposals to delete these requirements on the basis that they effectively duplicate disclosures required by accounting standards or the Companies Act.[87]

5.6 Proportionally consolidated joint ventures

In relation to a joint venture which is proportionally consolidated (see 4.4 above), the Companies Act requires the following disclosures to be given:

(a)   its name;

(b)   its principal place of business;

(c)   the factors on which joint management is based;

(d)   the proportion of the capital of the joint venture held by the group; and

(e)   where the financial year end of the joint venture did not coincide with that of the parent company of the reporting group, the date of its last year end (ending before the financial year end of the parent company).[88]

An example of disclosures relating to proportionally consolidated joint ventures is that of Taylor Woodrow shown below:

Extract 7.22: Taylor Woodrow plc (1996)

Particulars of Principal Joint Ventures

Name of joint venture (*Interests held by subsidiary undertakings)	Address of principal place of business	Taylor Woodrow plc interest in joint venture capital
Construction		
Costain Building & Civil Engineering Limited/Taylor Woodrow Civil Engineering Limited Jubilee Line Extension 104 Joint Venture*	345 Ruislip Road, Southall Middlesex UB1 2QX	50%
Translink Joint Venture*	Terminal Sub Project, Beachborough Folkestone, Kent CT19 4QU	20%
Housing		
Harrington Park Joint Venture*	Level 1, 96 Phillip Street, Parramatta, New South Wales 2150, Australia	50%
Taylor Woodrow/Kenco Limited* (a limited partnership)	7120 South Beneva Road, Sarasota, Florida 34238-2150, USA	39%

The above joint ventures are managed jointly through management boards on which subsidiary undertakings of the group and the other joint venturers are represented in accordance with the respective interests held in the joint ventures.

5.7 FRED 11

The ASB's Discussion Paper proposed to retain most of the present disclosure requirements of SSAP 1 but to require also that the amounts included in the profit and loss account and balance sheet should be expanded by providing additional information in respect of associates and joint ventures. The Discussion Paper proposed four levels of disclosure of such additional information depending on whether the interests are material or substantial, both individually and in aggregate. Interests were to be deemed to be substantial individually or in aggregate where the investor's share exceeded 15% of the following for the investor group (excluding amounts for the associates or joint ventures): gross assets, gross liabilities, turnover or results.[89]

Many commentators believed that the proposed disclosures were excessive so the ASB has curtailed its original proposals in developing FRED 11. The exposure draft now proposes the following levels of disclosures:

5.7.1   All equity accounted associates and joint ventures

Where the amounts included by equity accounting under any profit and loss account heading is material, then this should be indicated on the face of the profit and loss account with reference to a note setting out the amounts included.[90] Similar disclosure is required in respect of amounts included in the statement of total recognised gains and losses.[91]

5.7.2   Aggregate interests exceeding a 15% threshold

Additional disclosures are to be given where the aggregate of the investor's interests in its equity accounted associates and joint ventures exceeds 15% of any of the following for the investor group (excluding any amounts for associates and joint ventures): gross assets, gross liabilities, turnover or operating results (on a three-year average).[92] The additional disclosures to be made are the aggregate of the investor's share of the following:

(a)   turnover (if turnover is not already shown as a memorandum item);

(b)   debt analysed in accordance with FRS 4 (see 2.2.7 of Chapter 15), showing how much is with recourse to the investor and how much is without recourse;

(c)   assets and liabilities analysed by major balance sheet heading (i.e. those designated by Roman numerals in the Companies Act formats, except of fixed assets which need not be analysed further). Further analysis should be given where this is necessary to understand the nature of the total amounts shown.

5.7.3   Individual interest exceeding a 25% threshold

Where the investor's interest in an individual associate or joint venture exceeds 25% of any of the following for the investor group (excluding any amounts for associates and joint ventures): gross assets, gross liabilities, turnover or operating results (on a three-year average), condensed financial information should be included showing its profit and loss account and its balance sheet, the latter in as much detail as under 5.7.2 (c) above. If there is only one such associate or joint venture which accounts for nearly all of the amounts that make up the investor's aggregate interests in equity accounted entities, only aggregate information need be given with a note explaining this and identifying the single individually substantial associate or joint venture.[93]

5.7.4   Proportionally consolidated joint ventures

A note should disclose any material aggregate amounts proportionally consolidated in the venturer's balance sheet, profit and loss account, statement of total recognised gains and losses and cash flow statement.[94] The proposed disclosures outlined at 5.7.3 above also applies to any individual proportionally consolidated joint venture.

6 COMPARISON WITH US AND IASC PRONOUNCEMENTS

6.1 US

The principal pronouncement in the US which deals with this topic is APB 18 – *The Equity Method of Accounting for Investments in Common Stock*. Like SSAP 1 in the UK, this requires equity accounting to be followed by an investor whose investment in voting stock gives it the ability to exercise significant influence over operating and financial policies over an investee,[95] including investments in corporate joint ventures.[96] Equity accounting will also be appropriate in accounting for investments in unincorporated joint ventures and partnerships; however, circumstances and industry practice may determine that the investor accounts on a pro-rata basis for its share of the assets, liabilities, revenues and expenses.[97]

Unlike the UK (see 4.3 above), the equity method of accounting should be used even where the investing company does not have any subsidiaries and therefore does not prepare consolidated accounts.[98]

The method of equity accounting in the US is similar to that in the UK, the main difference being that the share of the post-tax profits or losses is included as a single line item whereas in the UK the share of the pre-tax results is included in arriving at the group's profit before tax and the share of the associate's tax is included within the group's tax charge.

Another area where there is a difference is where the associate has a deficiency of net assets. The basic rule in the US is that 'the investor ordinarily shall discontinue applying the equity method when the investment (and net advances) is reduced to zero and shall not provide for additional losses unless the investor has guaranteed obligations of the investee or is otherwise committed to provide further financial support for the investee. If the investee subsequently reports net income, the investor shall resume applying the equity method only after its share of that net income equals the share of net losses not recognized during the period the equity method was suspended.' This rule is complicated further by the additional requirement that the investor should 'provide for additional losses when the imminent return to profitable operations by an investee appears to be assured. For example, a material, non-recurring loss of an isolated nature may reduce an investment below zero even though the underlying profitable operating pattern of an investee is unimpaired.'[99] The effect of this is the apparently odd one that a US investor would provide for a loss of an investee which was going to be reversed, but not for one which was to be perpetuated; presumably the distinction is simply that in the latter case the investor would be more likely simply to abandon the investment, and need not therefore provide for a loss which would never be suffered.

Many of the changes proposed by the ASB under FRED 11 will create further differences between the US and the UK. However, the FASB is undertaking a project on Unconsolidated Entities where it is intended to address presentation and other issues relating to investments in noncontrolled corporations and partnerships, including joint ventures.

6.2 IASC

6.2.1 Associates

The relevant international pronouncement which deals with this topic is IAS 28 – *Accounting for Investments in Associates*. The definition of an associate in IAS 28 is similar to that in SSAP 1. However, the IAS definition elaborates further on the ways in which significant influence might be exercisable; it states that this will usually be evidenced in one or more of the following ways:

(a) representation on the board of directors or equivalent governing body of the investee;

(b) participation in policy-making processes;

(c) material transactions between the investor and the investee;

(d) interchange of managerial personnel; or

(e) provision of essential technical information.[100]

This wording is based on the equivalent requirement in the US.[101]

Where an investor does not have any subsidiaries, IAS 28 permits associates either to be equity accounted or to be carried at cost (or valuation).[102]

Like the US, the main difference in equity accounting under the international standard is that the share of the post-tax profits or losses is included as a single line item whereas in the UK the share of the pre-tax results is included in arriving at the group's profit before tax and the share of the associate's tax is included within the group's tax charge.

The other area where there is a slight difference in approach is where the associate has a deficiency of net assets. The approach is similar to the equivalent basic rule in the US (see 6.1 above).[103]

As with the US, many of the changes proposed by the ASB under FRED 11 will create further differences between IAS 28 and the UK.[104]

6.2.2 Joint ventures

The IASC has issued a standard, IAS 31 – *Financial Reporting of Interests in Joint Ventures*. The standard defines a joint venture as 'a contractual arrangement whereby two or more parties ('venturers') undertake an economic activity which is subject to joint control'. Joint control is the contractually agreed sharing of control (i.e. the power to govern the financial and operating policies of an economic activity so as to obtain benefits from it) over an economic activity.[105]

Under the IASC standard, the accounting for interests in joint ventures depends on whether they are interests in:

(a)   jointly controlled operations;

(b)   jointly controlled assets; or

(c)   jointly controlled entities.

A jointly controlled operation is one which involves the use of assets and other resources of the venturers, rather than the establishment of an entity separate from the venturers themselves.[106] In respect of its interest in a jointly controlled operation, a venturer should recognise in both its own and its consolidated financial statements:

(a)   the assets that it controls and the liabilities that it incurs; and

(b)   the expenses that it incurs and its share of the income that it earns from the sale of goods or services by the joint venture.[107]

Some joint ventures involve the joint control and/or ownership of assets, but without the establishment of an entity separate from the venturers themselves. Joint ventures of this type are particularly common in extractive industries. For example, a number of oil companies may jointly control and operate an oil pipeline.[108]

In respect of its interest in jointly controlled assets, a venturer should recognise in both its own and its consolidated financial statements:

(a)   its share of the jointly controlled assets, classified according to the nature of the assets;

(b)   any liabilities which it has incurred; and

(c)   its share of any liabilities incurred jointly with the other venturers.[109]

A jointly controlled entity, as its name implies, is a separate legal entity in which each venturer has an interest.[110] In its consolidated financial statements, a venturer should include its interest in a joint venture entity by means of proportional consolidation.[111] This should be carried out either:

(a)   on a line-by-line basis (i.e. the venturer includes its share of the assets, liabilities, income and expenditure of the entity in the similar items in its own consolidated accounts); or

(b)   on an aggregated basis (i.e. the venturer includes separate line items for its share of the total assets, liabilities, income and expenditure of the entity in its own consolidated accounts).[112]

This is irrespective of whether the entity is a corporate body or not. IAS 31 also permits, but strongly discourages, the use of equity accounting for jointly controlled entities in consolidated financial statements.[113] It expresses no preference for the treatment of jointly controlled entities in a venturer's individual financial statements.[114]

The above requirements of IAS 31 principally differ from the ASB's proposals under FRED 11 in the following respects:

(a)   FRED 11 requires a joint venture to be an 'entity'; the effect of this being that jointly controlled operations and jointly controlled assets are not joint ventures under FRED 11, but they are under the IAS 31 definition of a joint venture;

(b)   FRED 11 requires most joint ventures to be equity accounted, whereas IAS 31 only allows such a treatment, preferring instead proportional consolidation.

7   CONCLUSION

Equity accounting for associates has been a feature of UK accounting for over 25 years since the issue of SSAP 1 in 1971. Although the standard has been revised a number of times since then, the basic rules are little changed. It is recognised that the standard needs to be revised in view of changes made in the legislation and the fact that many companies now enter into joint ventures. To this end the ASB published its proposals for a revised standard with FRED 11 in March 1996 almost two years after its earlier Discussion Paper on the topic. The main feature of the proposals is that 'significant influence' will be defined in a more restrictive way.

The implementation of the proposals will cause certain interests which presently qualify as associates to cease to do so. The proposals seem to be based on a concern that some companies, following a failed takeover bid, have been unjustifiably taking credit for their share of profits of investees without subsequently being able to gain access to them. Although we agree that it is inappropriate to equity account in such cases, we think that the existing SSAP 1 already precludes it. A more frequent abuse of the standard actually lies in the other direction where companies, particularly in start-up situations, sometimes argue that they should not equity account for an investment (which is often loss-making) because they claim not to have significant influence. By restricting the criteria to active and actual influence, the ASB's proposals run the risk of lending support to such arguments.

The delay in issuing a final revised standard would suggest that FRED 11 had not really resolved how best to deal with joint ventures. Hopefully the discussions between the ASB and the IASC and other standard setting bodies will result in a successful conclusion and a revised standard being finalised in the near future.

References

1   CA 85, Sch. 4A, para. 22.
2   ASB Discussion Paper, *Associates and Joint Ventures*, ASB, July 1994.
3   SSAP 1, *Accounting for associated companies*, ASC, Amended December 1990, para. 13.
4   FRS 2, *Accounting for subsidiary undertakings*, ASB, July 1992, para. 10.
5   SSAP 1, para. 25.
6   *Ibid.*, para. 13.
7   *Ibid.*, paras. 14 and 15.
8   *Ibid.*, para. 11.
9   CA 85, Sch. 4A, para. 20.
10 *Ibid.*, s 260(1).
11 *Ibid.*, s 260(3).
12 ED 50, *Consolidated accounts*, ASC, June 1990, para. 82.
13 *Ibid.*, para. 83.
14 ASB Discussion Paper, *Associates and Joint Ventures*, para. 3.3.
15 *Ibid.*, para. 3.7.
16 FRED 11, *Associates and joint ventures*, ASB, March 1996, para. 2.
17 *Ibid.*
18 *Ibid.*, para. 36.
19 *Ibid.*, para. 37.
20 *Ibid.*, Appendix III, para. 7.
21 *Ibid.*, para. 2.
22 *Ibid.*
23 *Ibid.*, para. 38.
24 SSAP 1, para. 26.
25 SSAP 22, *Accounting for goodwill*, ASC, Revised 1989, paras. 3, 39 and 41.
26 SSAP 1, paras. 23 and 30.
27 See, for example, Guinness PLC, Report and Accounts 1996, pp. 48 and 54; Henly's Group plc, Annual Report and Accounts 1996, pp. 38 and 39; and Countryside Properties PLC, Annual Report and Accounts 1996, p. 34.
28 See, for example, BICC plc, Annual Report and Accounts 1996, p. 34; Cookson Group plc, Annual Report 1996, p. 52; and Powell Duffryn plc, Annual Report and Accounts 1997, p. 31.
29 ASB Discussion Paper, *Associates and Joint Ventures*, Section 4.
30 FRED 11, para. 2.
31 *Ibid.*, para. 11.
32 *Ibid.*, para. 46.
33 *Ibid.*, para. 10.
34 *Ibid.*, para. 47.
35 *Ibid.*, para. 11.
36 *Ibid.*, para. 12.
37 *Ibid.*, para. 13.
38 SSAP 1, para. 36.
39 *Ibid.*, para. 37.
40 IAS 28, *Accounting for Investments in Associates*, IASC, Reformatted 1994, para. 16.
41 *Ibid.*, para. 10.
42 SSAP 1, para. 33.
43 FRED 11, para. 21.

44 *Ibid.,* para. 51.
45 CA 85, Sch. 4, para. 12(a).
46 SSAP 1, para. 24.
47 Example taken from Accountants Digest No. 126, *An Accountants Digest Guide to Accounting Standards – Accounting For Associated Companies*, p. 41.
48 SSAP 1, para. 35.
49 *Ibid.,* para. 24.
50 CA 85, Sch. 5, paras. 7–9.
51 FRED 11, para. 23.
52 CA 85, Sch. 4A, para. 19.
53 *Interim Statement: Consolidated Accounts*, ASB, December 1990, para. 33.
54 ASB Discussion Paper, *Associates and Joint Ventures*, para. 3.11.
55 *Ibid.,* para. 4.12.
56 *Ibid.,* paras. 3.16 and 3.17.
57 FRED 11, para. 2.
58 *Ibid.,* para. 8.
59 *Ibid.,* para. 9.
60 *Ibid.,* para. 45.
61 SSAP 1, para. 43.
62 FRS 2, paras. 47 and 87.
63 FRED 11, para. 18.
64 *Ibid.,* para. 19.
65 *Ibid.,* para. 20.
66 ASB Discussion Paper, *Associates and Joint Ventures*, para. 5.21.
67 *Ibid.,* paras. 5.22 and 5.23.
68 SSAP 1, para. 39.
69 ED 50, para. 115.
70 FRS 2, para. 39.
71 FRED 11, para. 10.
72 *Ibid.,* para. 49.
73 SSAP 1, paras. 19–22.
74 *Ibid.,* para. 23.
75 *Ibid.,* para. 32.
76 *Ibid.,* para. 26.
77 *Ibid.,* paras. 27 and 28.
78 *Ibid.,* para. 29.
79 *Ibid.,* para. 31.
80 *Ibid.,* para. 30.
81 *Ibid.,* para. 49.
82 *Ibid.,* para. 37.
83 *Ibid.,* para. 38.
84 *Ibid.,* para. 40.
85 CA 85, Sch. 5, Part II, para. 22(3).
86 *The Listing Rules*, London Stock Exchange, Chapter 12, para. 12.43(g).
87 Consultative document, London Stock Exchange, May 1997.
88 CA 85, Sch. 5, Part II, para. 21.
89 ASB Discussion Paper, *Associates and Joint Ventures*, para. 4.18.
90 FRED 11, para. 12.
91 *Ibid.,* para. 13.
92 *Ibid.,* paras. 24 and 25.
93 *Ibid.,* para. 28.
94 *Ibid.,* para. 27.
95 APB 18, *The Equity Method of Accounting for Investments in Common Stock*, AICPA, March 1971, para. 17.
96 *Ibid.,* para. 16.
97 AIN-APB 18, *The Equity Method of Accounting for Investments in Common Stock: Accounting Interpretations of APB Opinion No. 18*, AICPA, November 1971–February 1972, para. 2.

98 APB 18, para. 14. This paragraph has, in fact, been deleted by SFAS 94, but the principle has not been changed.
99 *Ibid.*, para. 19(j).
100 IAS 28, para. 5.
101 APB 18, para. 17.
102 IAS 28, para. 14.
103 *Ibid.*, para. 22.
104 See FRED 11, Appendix II for a discussion of the differences.
105 IAS 31, *Financial Reporting of Interests in Joint Ventures*, IASC, Reformatted 1994, para. 2.
106 *Ibid.*, para. 8.
107 *Ibid.*, para. 10.
108 *Ibid.*, paras. 13–15.
109 *Ibid.*, para. 16.
110 *Ibid.*, para. 19.
111 *Ibid.*, para. 25.
112 *Ibid.*, para. 28.
113 *Ibid.*, paras. 32–33.
114 *Ibid.*, para. 41.

Chapter 8   Foreign currencies

1   THE DEVELOPMENT OF AN ACCOUNTING STANDARD IN THE UK

1.1   Background

A company can engage in foreign currency operations in two ways. It may enter directly into transactions which are denominated in foreign currencies, the results of which need to be translated into the currency in which the company reports. Alternatively, it may conduct foreign operations through a foreign enterprise, normally a subsidiary or associated company, which keeps its accounting records in a foreign currency and, in order to prepare consolidated financial statements, will need to translate the financial statements of the foreign enterprise into its own reporting currency.[1] Accounting for these translation processes has been one of the most significant problem areas in financial reporting in recent years.

Essentially, there were four distinct methods which could be used in the translation process:

(a) *current rate method* – all assets and liabilities are translated at the current rate of exchange, i.e. the exchange rate at the balance sheet date;

(b) *temporal method* – assets and liabilities carried at current prices are translated at the current rate of exchange, e.g. cash, debtors, creditors, investments at market value. Assets and liabilities carried at past prices, e.g. property, investments at cost, prepayments, are translated at the rate of exchange in effect at the dates to which the prices pertain;

(c) *current/non-current method* – all current assets and current liabilities are translated at the current rate of exchange. Non-current assets and liabilities are translated at historical rates, i.e. the exchange rate in effect at the time the asset was acquired or the liability incurred; and

(d) *monetary/non-monetary method* – monetary assets and liabilities, i.e. items which represent the right to receive or the obligation to pay a fixed amount of money, are translated at the current rate of exchange. Non-monetary assets and liabilities are translated at the historical rate.

There was no consensus either in the UK or internationally on the best theoretical approach to adopt. In essence, the arguments surround the choice of exchange rates to be used in the translation process and the subsequent treatment of the exchange differences which arise. The fact that foreign exchange rates have become increasingly volatile has only magnified the effects of using different approaches. As a result of these problems, the subject of foreign currency translation had been on the agenda of the ASC since the early 1970s.

1.2   SSAP 6

When SSAP 6[2] was issued in April 1974, although dealing mainly with extraordinary items and prior year adjustments, it gave recognition to the problem by stating: 'At a time of frequent movement of foreign currency exchange rates, the accounting treatment of foreign currency transactions and conversions and the distinguishing of items that are extraordinary present many problems. These problems are currently under study with a view to the issue of a separate accounting standard. In the meantime, the accounting policies adopted should be disclosed and explained in accordance with Statement of Standard Accounting Practice No. 2 Disclosure of accounting policies.'[3]

1.3   ED 16

The first pronouncement by the ASC on the treatment of the problems was in ED 16[4] issued in September 1975. This did not require any particular method of translation to be adopted other than to require foreign currency borrowings to be translated at closing rates of exchange.[5] It mainly set out how exchange differences were to be dealt with; namely, in the profit and loss account as part of the ordinary activities of the business except:

(a)   differences arising from extraordinary items, which were themselves to be treated as extraordinary items;

(b)   differences arising on translation of fixed assets, which were to be treated as if they were revaluations of fixed assets, i.e. taken direct to reserves unless they represented losses not covered by gains on the same items held in reserves or gains on items where losses had previously been taken to profit and loss account; and

(c)   exchange losses arising on the translation of foreign currency net borrowings, which could be taken to reserves to offset gains arising in (b) above which had also been taken to reserves.[6]

The ASC acknowledged that this was just a temporary measure by stating: 'The subject is one in which conflicting opinions are strongly held and it must be expected that some time will elapse before a standard is issued which will describe the method or methods of accounting to be applied.'[7]

1.4   ED 21

The next step by the ASC was to issue ED 21[8] in September 1977. This limited the options of accounting methods by permitting the use of either the closing rate or temporal methods.[9]

If the closing rate method were to be used, exchange differences would be treated in the same way as required by ED 16, except that the differences which were to be dealt with in the profit and loss account as part of the ordinary activities of the business were now to be treated as a quasi-extraordinary item, i.e. as a separate item after the profit for the year from ordinary operations.[10]

If the temporal method were to be used then all exchange differences would be reported as part of the profit from ordinary operations unless they arose from items which would themselves be treated as extraordinary.[11]

The main comments received on ED 21 were that:[12]

(a)   there was a lack of clarity in the distinction between the treatment of exchange differences in individual companies and differences arising on consolidation;

(b)   two methods of translation should not be allowed when the closing rate was so widely adopted in the UK;

(c)   the occasions when the cover concept could be applied were not clear;

(d)   the different treatment given to current assets as opposed to fixed assets was not supported;

(e)   support for the use of the closing rate and the average rate for translating the profit and loss account was evenly divided;

(f)   the net investment concept in ED 21 was inadequately developed;

(g)   there was strong support for keeping exchange differences out of operating profit but little support for displaying them as quasi-extraordinary items; and

(h)   the global concept for offsetting gains and losses on exchange was thought to be imprudent.

1.5   ED 27

The reason why ED 16 and ED 21 permitted the use of either the closing rate or the temporal method was that the latter method was the only method which could be used in the USA. Following the implementation of SFAS 8 in the USA it gradually became evident that when consolidated accounts are drawn up in a relatively weak currency, such a method produces results which do not seem to make commercial and economic sense. As a result the FASB decided to review its existing standard, SFAS 8.[13] In Canada, the Canadian Institute of Chartered Accountants (CICA), which had published its standard on foreign currencies in 1978,[14] advocating the use of the temporal method, suspended it in 1979 pending further study. Conscious of the need for international harmonisation in this field, there then followed a long period of consultation between the ASC, the FASB and the CICA.

So it was that the ASC issued ED 27 in October 1980. This was based on the closing rate/net investment concept and proposed an approach to translation which is related to the cash flow consequences of exchange movements. Exchange differences which give rise to cash flows, i.e. those resulting from business transactions, are reported as part of the profit or loss for the period. Other exchange differences which do not give rise to cash flows, because they result from retranslations of the holding company's long-term investment in the foreign subsidiary, are reported as reserve movements. ED 27 also introduced another version of the cover concept where a foreign currency loan has been used to finance the purchase of an investment in a foreign subsidiary.

1.6   SSAP 20

The majority of commentators supported the principles set out in ED 27 and so it eventually formed the basis of SSAP 20. However, since the exposure draft was issued the Companies Act 1981 had been enacted. The accounting rules contained in the Act had certain ramifications on the treatment of exchange differences and these had to be resolved. It was not, therefore, until April 1983 that SSAP 20 was finally issued.

The ASB has embarked on a project dealing with financial instruments which impinges on many of the areas covered by this chapter, particularly in relation to forward currency contracts, currency swaps and currency options as well as extending the disclosures in respect of foreign currencies. It may well be that at the end of the day some amendment to SSAP 20 will be necessary as a result. The ASB's proposals for financial instruments are covered in Chapter 9.

2   REQUIREMENTS OF SSAP 20

2.1   Objectives of translation

SSAP 20 states that 'the translation of foreign currency transactions and financial statements should produce results which are generally compatible with the effects of rate changes on a company's cash flows and its equity and should ensure that the financial statements present a true and fair view of the results of management actions. Consolidated statements should reflect the financial results and relationships as measured in the foreign currency financial statements prior to translation.'[15] It will be seen when looking at the requirements of the standard that in certain situations these objectives conflict.

2.2   Definitions of terms

The main definitions of terms which are contained in SSAP 20 are as follows:[16]

A *foreign enterprise* is a subsidiary, associated company or branch whose operations are based in a country other than that of the investing company or whose assets and liabilities are denominated mainly in a foreign currency.

A *foreign branch* is either a legally constituted enterprise located overseas or a group of assets and liabilities which are accounted for in foreign currencies.

Translation is the process whereby financial data denominated in one currency are expressed in terms of another currency. It includes both the expression of individual transactions in terms of another currency and the expression of a complete set of financial statements prepared in one currency in terms of another currency.

A company's *local currency* is the currency of the primary economic environment in which it operates and generates net cash flows.

An *exchange rate* is a rate at which two currencies may be exchanged for each other at a particular point in time; different rates apply for spot and forward transactions.

The *closing rate* is the exchange rate for spot transactions ruling at the balance sheet date and is the mean of the buying and selling rates at the close of business on the day for which the rate is to be ascertained.

A *forward contract* is an agreement to exchange different currencies at a specified rate. The difference between the specified rate and the spot rate ruling on the date the contract was entered into is the discount or premium on the forward contract.

The *net investment* which a company has in a foreign enterprise is its effective equity stake and comprises its proportion of such foreign enterprise's net assets; in appropriate circumstances, intra-group loans and other deferred balances may be regarded as part of the effective equity stake.

Monetary items are money held and amounts to be received or paid in money and, where a company is not an exempt company, should be categorised as either short-term or long-term. Short-term monetary items are those which fall due within one year of the balance sheet date. (An exempt company is essentially a bank or an insurance company.)

2.3   Individual companies

As indicated in 1.1 above a company can either enter directly into foreign currency transactions or it may conduct foreign operations through a foreign enterprise. The standard therefore requires that the procedures to be adopted when accounting for foreign operations should be considered in two stages, namely the preparation of the financial statements of the individual company and the preparation of the consolidated financial statements.

The first stage to be considered is the preparation of the financial statements of an individual company. The procedures to be followed should be applied to each company within a group prior to the preparation of the consolidated accounts. The general requirements of SSAP 20 are as follows.

2.3.1   Recording of transactions

Generally, all foreign currency transactions entered into by a company should be translated into its local currency at the exchange rate ruling on the date the transaction occurs. An average rate for a period is acceptable if rates do not fluctuate significantly during the relevant period. Where the transaction is to be settled at a contracted rate then that rate should be used.[17]

2.3.2   Retranslation of monetary/non-monetary assets and liabilities at balance sheet date

At the balance sheet date, monetary assets and liabilities denominated in foreign currencies resulting from unsettled transactions should be translated using the closing rate. Again, where the transaction is to be settled at a contracted rate then that rate should be used.[18]

Non-monetary assets should not be retranslated but should remain translated at the rate ruling when they were originally recorded.[19]

2.3.3   Treatment of exchange differences

Exchange differences will arise when transactions are settled at exchange rates which are different from those used when the transactions were previously recorded. They will also arise on any unsettled transactions at the balance sheet date if the closing rate differs from those used previously.[20]   All exchange differences should be included as part of the profit or loss for the period from ordinary activities, unless they arise as a result of events which themselves are treated as extraordinary, in which case they should be included as part of such items. This treatment should be adopted for all monetary items irrespective of whether they are short-term or long-term and irrespective of whether the exchange differences are gains or losses.[21]

The rationale for the above treatment is that the exchange differences have already been reflected in cash flows, in the case of settled transactions, or will be in the future in the case of unsettled transactions.[22] This is consistent with the

The method used for translating the financial statements of a foreign enterprise should only be changed when the financial and other operational relationship changes and renders the method used inappropriate.[26]

2.4.3 Closing rate/net investment method

For most investing companies in the UK where foreign operations are carried out by foreign enterprises it is normally the case that the foreign enterprises operate as separate or quasi-independent entities.[27] The day to day operations of the foreign enterprise will be based in its local currency, are likely to be financed wholly or partly in its own currency, and will not be dependent on the reporting currency of the holding company. The foreign enterprise will be managed so as to maximise the local currency profits attributable to the holding company. Consequently, the financial statements of the foreign enterprise expressed in its local currency will be the best available indicator of its performance and value to the group. In order to preserve the inherent relationships included in these local currency financial statements it is therefore necessary to use a single rate of exchange when translating the financial statements in the preparation of the consolidated financial statements.[28]

A   Balance sheet

The standard therefore requires that under the closing rate/net investment method the balance sheet of the foreign enterprise should be translated into the reporting currency of the investing company using the rate of exchange at the balance sheet date, i.e. the closing rate.[29]

B   Profit and loss account

The profit and loss account of the foreign enterprise under this method should be translated at the closing rate or at an average rate for the period.[30] In our view the use of the closing rate is preferable as this will achieve the objective of translation of reflecting the financial results and relationships as measured in the foreign currency financial statements prior to translation.[31] The use of an average rate is justified by SSAP 20 on the grounds that it reflects more fairly the profits or losses and cash flows as they arise to the group throughout an accounting period.[32] Although the standard allows a choice as to which rate is used it does require that the one selected is applied consistently from period to period.[33]

C   Treatment of exchange differences

Exchange differences will arise under the closing rate/net investment method if the exchange rate used for translating the balance sheet differs from that ruling at the previous balance sheet date or at the date of any subsequent capital injection or reduction.[34] Exchange differences will also arise where an average rate is used for translating the profit and loss account and this differs from the closing rate.[35] The standard requires that both such exchange differences should be recorded as a movement on reserves.[36] As paragraph 19 of SSAP 20 explains: 'If exchange differences arising from the retranslation of a company's net investment in its foreign enterprise were introduced into the profit and loss account, the results from trading operations, as shown in the local currency financial statements would be distorted. Such differences may result from many factors unrelated to the trading performance or financing operations of the foreign enterprise; in particular, they do not represent or measure changes in actual or prospective cash flows. It is therefore inappropriate to regard them as profits or losses and they should be dealt with as adjustments to reserves.'

Example 8.5

A UK company owns 100% of the share capital of a German company which was set up ten years ago in 19W1 when the exchange rate was £1=DM4. It uses the closing rate method for incorporating the accounts of the subsidiary in its consolidated accounts for the year ended 31 December 19X1. The exchange rate at the year end is £1=DM2 (19X0: £1=DM3). The profit and loss account of the subsidiary for that year and its balance sheet at the beginning and end of the year in local currency and translated into sterling are as follows:

Profit and loss account

	DM	£
Sales	35,000	17,500
Cost of sales	(33,190)	(16,595)
Depreciation	(500)	(250)
Interest	(350)	(175)
Profit before taxation	960	480
Taxation	(460)	(230)
Profit after taxation	500	250

Balance sheets	19X0 DM	19X1 DM	19X0 £	19X1 £
Fixed assets	6,000	5,500	2,000	2,750
Current assets				
Stocks	2,700	3,000	900	1,500
Debtors	4,800	4,000	1,600	2,000
Cash	200	600	67	300
	7,700	7,600	2,567	3,800
Current liabilities				
Creditors	4,530	3,840	1,510	1,920
Taxation	870	460	290	230
	5,400	4,300	1,800	2,150
Net current assets	2,300	3,300	767	1,650
	8,300	8,800	2,767	4,400
Long-term loans	3,600	3,600	1,200	1,800
	4,700	5,200	1,567	2,600
Share capital	1,000	1,000	250	250
Retained profits	3,700	4,200	1,317	2,350
	4,700	5,200	1,567	2,600

The movement in retained profits is as follows:

	£
Balance brought forward	1,317
Profit for year	250
Exchange difference	783
	2,350

The exchange difference of £783 is the exchange difference on the opening net investment in the subsidiary and is calculated as follows:

Opening net assets at opening rate	– DM4,700 at DM3=£1	= £1,567
Opening net assets at closing rate	– DM4,700 at DM2=£1	= £2,350
Exchange gain on net investment		£ 783

This exchange gain should be shown as a movement on reserves and should not be reflected in the profit and loss account.

If the company were to have adopted a policy of translating the profit and loss account at an average rate of exchange and the appropriate weighted average rate was DM2.5=£1 then the profit and loss account would have been as follows:

	DM	£
Sales	35,000	14,000
Cost of sales	(33,190)	(13,276)
Depreciation	(500)	(200)
Interest	(350)	(140)
Profit before taxation	960	384
Taxation	(460)	(184)
Profit after taxation	500	200

The difference between the profit and loss account translated at an average rate, i.e. £200, and at the closing rate, i.e. £250, would be recorded as a movement in reserves.

Examples of accounting policies of companies using this method of translation are illustrated below:

Extract 8.6: Racal Electronics Plc (1997)

4   FOREIGN CURRENCIES [extract]

The accounts of overseas subsidiary and associated companies, and assets and liabilities denominated in foreign currencies held by United Kingdom companies, have been translated at the rates ruling on 31 March 1997. Exchange differences arising on the retranslation of these accounts at the beginning of the year, and differences on long term foreign currency loans which relate to investments in overseas companies, are dealt with as a movement in reserves.

The translation loss of £596 which is shown in the profit and loss account represents the exchange loss on monetary items during the year and is calculated as follows:

	Opening monetary items	Closing monetary items
	DM	DM
Debtors	4,800	4,000
Cash	200	600
Creditors	(4,530)	(3,840)
Taxation	(870)	(460)
Long-term loans	(3,600)	(3,600)
	(4,000)	(3,300)

			£	£
Opening monetary items at opening rate	– DM(4,000) at DM3	= (1,334)		
Opening monetary items at closing rate	– DM(4,000) at DM2	= (2,000)		
			(666)	
Change in monetary items at average rate	– DM700 at DM2.5	= 280		
Change in monetary items at closing rate	– DM700 at DM2	= 350		
			70	
Total exchange loss				(596)

Examples of accounting policies of companies using this method of translation are illustrated below:

Extract 8.8: Reuters Holdings PLC (1996)

FOREIGN CURRENCY TRANSLATION [extract]

Where it is considered that the functional currency of an operation is sterling the financial statements are expressed in sterling on the following basis:

a. Fixed assets are translated into sterling at the rates ruling on the date of acquisition as adjusted for any profits or losses from related financial instruments.
b. Monetary assets and liabilities denominated in a foreign currency are translated into sterling at the foreign exchange rates ruling at the balance sheet date.
c. Revenue and expenses in foreign currencies are recorded in sterling at the rates ruling at the dates of the transactions.
d. Any gains or losses arising on translation are reported as part of profit.

Extract 8.9: Babcock International Group PLC (1997)

FOREIGN CURRENCIES [extract]

Where it is considered that an overseas undertaking is more dependent on sterling than its own reporting currency the Financial Statements of the undertaking are consolidated using the temporal method, thereby treating all transactions as though they had been entered into by the undertaking itself in sterling.

2.4.5 Foreign equity investments financed by borrowings

We have already seen in 2.3.7 above that where a company has used foreign currency borrowings to finance, or provide a hedge against, its foreign equity investments the standard allows the exchange differences on the borrowings to be taken to reserves rather than the profit and loss account.

A similar provision for consolidated accounts is contained in paragraph 57 of the standard. This is because under the closing rate method exchange differences on the net investment in foreign enterprises are taken to reserves and not reflected in the profit for the year. It would therefore be inappropriate for exchange differences on group borrowings which have been used to finance the investments or provide a hedge against the exchange risk associated with the investments to be taken to the profit and loss account. As the group is covered in economic terms against any movement in exchange rates then the exchange differences on the borrowings should be taken to reserves to offset the exchange differences on the net investments in the foreign enterprises.[42]

Where foreign currency borrowings of the group, therefore, have been used to finance, or provide a hedge against group equity investments then, subject to the conditions set out below, the exchange differences arising on the related foreign currency borrowings may be offset against the exchange differences arising on the retranslation of the net investments as a movement on reserves so that they are not reported as part of the profit or loss for the period.[43]

The conditions to be fulfilled are:

(a)   the relationships between the investing company and the foreign enterprises concerned justify the use of the closing rate method for consolidation purposes;

(b)   exchange gains or losses arising on foreign currency borrowings are offset only to the extent of the exchange differences arising on the net investments in foreign enterprises in that particular period;

(c)   the foreign currency borrowings should not exceed the total amount of cash that the net investments are expected to generate, whether from profits or otherwise; and

(d)   the accounting treatment should be applied consistently from period to period.[44]

The last three conditions are similar to those contained in paragraph 51 of the standard relating to the offset procedures for individual companies. The first condition is necessary as it is only when the closing rate method is used that the financial statements would not otherwise reflect the fact that the group is covered in economic terms against movements in exchange differences. Where a foreign enterprise is consolidated using the temporal method then, as all exchange differences are taken to the profit and loss account, any exchange differences on related borrowings should also be taken to the profit and loss account.

Although the general principles of paragraph 57 of the standard are the same as those used in the offset procedures for individual companies there are a number of differences in detail. These will normally require the calculations used in the individual companies' financial statements to be reversed on consolidation and the amount recalculated for the purposes of the consolidated financial statements:

(a)   in the individual companies' financial statements *all* equity investments are included in the calculation, whereas for the consolidated financial statements investments which are consolidated using the temporal method are excluded;

(b)   in the individual companies' financial statements it is the exchange difference on the carrying value of the investment which is included in the calculation, whereas for the consolidated financial statements it is the exchange difference on the underlying net assets which is included; and

(c)   in the individual companies' financial statements only borrowings of the company can be included in the calculation, whereas in the consolidated financial statements borrowings of any group company can be included.

The only situation in which there will be no need to recalculate the amount of the offset is where the provisions of paragraph 51 of the standard have been applied in the investing company's financial statements to a foreign equity investment which is neither a subsidiary nor an associated company. This is because paragraph 58 of the standard allows the amount of the offset in the individual company's financial statements to be carried forward to the consolidated financial statements, since the exchange risk is hedged in both the company and the group. It should be borne in mind, however, that this does not mean that all such equity investments throughout the group can be retranslated at closing rates and the resulting exchange differences used in the offset process.

Example 8.7

A UK company is preparing its financial statements for the year ended 31 December 19X1. It has two wholly owned subsidiaries:

(i) A Japanese company which it acquired a number of years ago at a cost of ¥500m. It incorporates the financial statements of the subsidiary in its consolidated financial statements using the closing rate method. During 19X0 the company borrowed ¥1,000m repayable in ten years' time in 19Y0, to provide a hedge against the investment, which was then considered to be worth in excess of ¥1,500m. The net assets of the subsidiary at 31 December 19X0 were ¥1,200m.

(ii) A French company which it set up on 1 February 19X1 at a cost of FFr10m. It is going to incorporate this subsidiary in its consolidated financial statements using the temporal method. The exchange loss for the period is £41,081. It partially financed the acquisition of the shares by borrowing FFr8m repayable in 19X6.

In addition, the UK company has a 10% investment in a US company which it acquired in 19X0 at a cost of US$2m, financed by means of a US dollar loan of the same amount. At 31 December 19X1 none of the loan has been repaid.

The relevant exchange rates are:

	£1=¥	£1=FFr	£1=US$
31/12/X0	235		1.48
1/2/X1		9.25	
31/12/X1	225	10.00	1.88

Using the provisions of paragraphs 51, 57 and 58 of the standard the treatment in the company and consolidated financial statements would be as follows:

Company financial statements			Profit/loss for year £	Reserves £
Investment in Japanese company				
31/12/X0 – ¥500m	@ 235	= £2,127,660		
31/12/X1 – ¥500m	@ 225	= £2,222,222		
Exchange gain		£ 94,562		94,562
¥1,000m Loan				
31/12/X0 – ¥1,000m	@ 235	= £4,255,319		
31/12/X1 – ¥1,000m	@ 225	= £4,444,444		
Exchange loss		£ (189,125)	(94,563)	(94,562)
Investment in French company				
1/2/X1 – FFr10m	@ 9.25	= £1,081,081		
31/12/X1 – FFr10m	@ 10.00	= £1,000,000		
Exchange loss		£ (81,081)		(81,081)
FFr8m Loan				
1/2/X1 – FFr8m	@ 9.25	= £864,865		
31/12/X1 – FFr8m	@ 10.00	= £800,000		
Exchange gain		£ 64,865		64,865
Investment in US company				
31/12/X0 – US$2m	@ 1.48	= £1,351,351		
31/12/X1 – US$2m	@ 1.88	= £1,063,830		
Exchange loss		£ (287,521)		(287,521)
US$2m Loan				
31/12/X0 – US$2m	@ 1.48	= £1,351,351		
31/12/X1 – US$2m	@ 1.88	= £1,063,830		
Exchange gain		£ 287,521		287,521
Net exchange loss			(94,563)	(16,216)

The exchange loss on the ¥1,000m loan taken to reserves has had to be restricted as a result of condition (a) of paragraph 51 of the standard.

It can be seen that where an exchange gain arises on a foreign loan and it is taken to reserves under paragraph 51 then it is possible to have a net exchange loss being taken to reserves as the exchange loss on the investment can exceed the exchange gain on the related loan.

Consolidated financial statements			Profit/loss for year £	Reserves £
Net investment in Japanese company				
31/12/X0 – ¥1,200m	@ 235	= £5,106,383		
31/12/X1 – ¥1,200m	@ 225	= £5,333,333		
Exchange gain		£ 226,950		226,950
¥1,000m Loan				
31/12/X0 – ¥1,000m	@ 235	= £4,255,319		
31/12/X1 – ¥1,000m	@ 225	= £4,444,444		
Exchange loss		£ (189,125)		(189,125)
Investment in French company				
Exchange loss (as given)			(41,081)	
FFr8m Loan				
1/2/X1 – FFr8m	@ 9.25	= £864,865		
31/12/X1 – FFr8m	@ 10.00	= £800,000		
Exchange gain		£ 64,865	64,865	
Investment in US company				
31/12/X0 – US$2m	@ 1.48	= £1,351,351		
31/12/X1 – US$2m	@ 1.88	= £1,063,830		
Exchange loss		£ (287,521)		(287,521)
US$2m Loan				
31/12/X0 – US$2m	@ 1.48	= £1,351,351		
31/12/X1 – US$2m	@ 1.88	= £1,063,830		
Exchange gain		£ 287,521		287,521
Net exchange gain			23,784	37,825

In the consolidated financial statements all of the exchange loss on the ¥1,000m loan can be taken to reserves as it is less than the exchange gain on the net investment in the Japanese subsidiary. The exchange gain on the FFr8m loan has to be taken to the profit/loss for the year as the temporal method is used and therefore condition (a) of paragraph 57 of the standard is not met. It can be seen that the same treatment is adopted for the US$ investment and loan as in the company financial statements as a result of paragraph 58.

2.4.6　Associated companies

As indicated in 2.4.1 above, the provisions of the standard relating to consolidated financial statements apply to the incorporation of the results of all foreign enterprises, including associated companies. The definition of associated companies and the required accounting treatment are dealt with in SSAP 1[45] and are discussed in Chapter 7.

When incorporating the results of foreign associated companies, therefore, the closing rate/net investment method should normally be used. In view of the fact that the investing company only has significant influence over the associated company and does not control it, it is unlikely that the affairs of the associated company are so closely linked with those of the investing company that the use of the temporal method will be appropriate. The requirements of the closing rate/net investment method have been explained in 2.4.3 above.

2.4.7 Foreign branches

The provisions of the standard relating to consolidated financial statements also apply to the incorporation of the results of foreign branches, not only in the consolidated financial statements but also in the financial statements of an individual company.[46] The definition of a foreign branch contained in the standard is such that it includes not just a legally constituted enterprise located overseas but also a group of assets and liabilities which are accounted for in foreign currencies.[47]

The reason for this wide definition was to cater for the situation where a company had international assets such as ships or aircraft which earn revenues in a foreign currency, normally US dollars, financed by borrowings in the same currency and to allow the use of the closing rate/net investment method. If this had not been done, then under the provisions of the standard it would have been necessary for such assets to be translated at historical rates, the borrowings to be translated at closing rates and any exchange difference thereon taken to the profit or loss for the year. The cover method contained in paragraphs 51 and 57 of the standard would not have applied as these provisions only deal with borrowings which finance equity investments and not other types of non-monetary assets.

A   Possible situations

In addition to the situation referred to above, the statement issued by the ASC on the publication of the standard also quoted the following as being examples of situations where a group of assets and liabilities should be accounted for under the closing rate/net investment method:

(a)   a hotel in France financed by borrowings in French francs;

(b)   a foreign currency insurance operation where the liabilities are substantially covered by the holding of foreign currency assets.[48]

B   Treatment

The results of a foreign branch should be incorporated in the financial statements in the same way as foreign subsidiaries are included in the consolidated financial statements, i.e. the closing rate/net investment method should normally be used.[49] The use of this method is explained in 2.4.3 above.

However, in many cases the operations of a branch are a direct extension of the trade of the investing company and its cash flows have a direct impact upon those of the investing company in which case the temporal method is required to be used. It should not automatically be assumed, therefore, that the closing rate/net investment method is the correct method to use and careful consideration should be given to the factors referred to in 2.4.4 above.

Hardy Oil & Gas adopts such a treatment in respect of its foreign currency assets and liabilities in both subsidiaries and branches, as is illustrated in its accounting policy below:

Extract 8.10: Hardy Oil & Gas plc (1996)

E   Foreign currencies

Transactions of UK companies in foreign currencies are translated at the rates prevailing at the date of each transaction. Monetary assets and liabilities in foreign currencies are retranslated at the rates of exchange prevailing at the balance sheet date.

Exchange gains and losses resulting from the translation to year end rates of the opening net assets of foreign subsidiaries, branches, and any related loans, are treated as movements in reserves. The trading results of overseas subsidiaries are translated into sterling at the year end rate of exchange. All other exchange differences are dealt with through the profit and loss account.

2.5   Disclosures

2.5.1   Requirements of SSAP 20

The standard requires the following disclosures to be made in the financial statements:

(a)   the methods used in the translation of the financial statements of foreign enterprises, i.e. closing rate method or temporal method. Where the closing rate method is used it should also be stated whether the closing rate or an average rate has been used to translate the profit and loss account;[50]

(b)   the net amount of exchange gains and losses on foreign currency borrowings less deposits charged or credited to the profit and loss account.[51] It should be noted that exchange differences on deposits have to be taken into account; it is not just the exchange differences on borrowings;

(c)   the net amount of exchange gains and losses on foreign currency borrowings less deposits offset in reserves under the provisions of paragraphs 51, 57 and 58 of the standard;[52]

(d) the net movement on reserves arising from exchange differences.[53] This will normally be the exchange differences on the net investments of those subsidiaries translated using the closing rate method.

There is no requirement for exchange differences taken to profit and loss account, other than those referred to in (b) above, to be disclosed. This is because the ASC considered 'that such disclosure is not necessarily helpful since it is influenced by the extent to which the company's trade is conducted in foreign currencies and the extent to which the company covers its exchange risk by entering into forward exchange contracts. Moreover, an agreement to settle a transaction in a foreign currency reflects only one aspect of the pricing or purchasing decision involved in normal trading. In any case a small difference may disguise a significant gain and significant loss and disclosure of the net figure will not indicate the risks inherent in trading in foreign currencies.'[54]

2.5.2 Examples of disclosures

Examples of disclosures of the methods used have been illustrated earlier in the chapter in giving extracts of accounting policies used. A good example of an accounting policy for foreign currencies which covers most of the various aspects is that of Reckitt & Colman:

Extract 8.11: Reckitt & Colman plc (1996)

Foreign currency translation

Transactions denominated in foreign currencies are translated at the rate of exchange on the day the transaction occurs or at the contracted rate if the transaction is covered by a forward exchange contract.

Assets and liabilities denominated in a foreign currency are translated at the exchange rate ruling on the balance sheet date or if appropriate at a forward contract rate. Exchange differences arising in the accounts of individual undertakings are included in the profit and loss account except that, where foreign currency borrowings have been used to finance equity investments in foreign currencies, exchange differences arising on the borrowings are dealt with through reserves to the extent that they are covered by exchange differences arising on the net assets represented by the equity investments.

The accounts of overseas subsidiaries and associated undertakings are translated into Sterling on the following basis:

Assets and liabilities at the rate of exchange ruling at the year-end date except for tangible fixed assets of undertakings operating in countries where hyper-inflation exists which are translated at historical rates of exchange.

Profit and loss account items at the average rate of exchange for the financial year. An inflation adjustment is charged in arriving at local currency profits of undertakings operating in hyper-inflation countries before they are translated to reflect the impact of the hyper inflation on the undertakings' working capital requirements.

Exchange differences arising on the translation of accounts into Sterling are recorded as movements on reserves.

(The particular problem of hyper-inflation is discussed in 3.4.9 below.)

The requirements to disclose those exchange differences taken to reserves are usually met in one of two ways:

(a)   Show both types of exchange difference separately.

Extract 8.12: Reckitt & Colman plc (1996)

22.   Reserves [extract]

	Group Profit and loss £m	Parent Profit and loss £m
Net exchange gain on foreign currency borrowings*	28.7	28.7
Exchange differences arising on translation of net investments in overseas subsidiary undertakings	(132.8)	(86.0)

*Net exchange gain on foreign currency borrowings is stated after deducting UK corporation tax of £13.3m (1995, £nil) in accordance with current accounting practice. Such tax effects have arisen as a result of recent changes in UK tax legislation.

(b)   Show a net figure but disclose that relating to borrowings by way of a note.

Extract 8.13: Bunzl plc (1995)

18.   Movements on reserves [extract]

	Share premium account £m	Revaluation reserve £m	Merger reserve £m	Profit and loss account £m
Currency translation movement	–	0.5	–	0.4

Currency (losses)/profits of £(0.2)m (1994: £1.7m) relating to foreign currency exchange contracts and borrowings to finance investment overseas have been included within the currency translation movement in the profit and loss account.

One company which disclosed exchange differences on borrowings being taken to reserves and to the profit and loss account was Daily Mail and General Trust in its 1993 accounts, as shown below:

Extract 8.14: Daily Mail and General Trust plc (1993)

4   Foreign Exchange Difference [extract]

The foreign exchange difference of £4.0 million (1992 £Nil) arises on the retranslation into sterling of the Group's net US dollar liabilities at the rate of exchange prevailing at the end of the year, ie £1=$1.5055. The calculation of the Group's dollar debt is compared with the book value of its dollar net assets (adjusted to include goodwill arising on acquisitions). This treatment does not reflect the economic value of those net assets.

27.   Reserves [extract]

(iii)   As permitted by SSAP 20, an exchange gain of £5.3 million arising on the retranslation of overseas investments has been offset in reserves against a loss of £9.3 million on the retranslation of a US dollar denominated liability. The resulting unmatched difference of £4.0 million has been charged against operating profit (Note 4).

2.5.3 FRED 13

As mentioned earlier, the ASB has embarked on a project dealing with financial instruments. In April 1997, it issued FRED 13 – *Derivatives and other financial instruments: Disclosures*. This contains a number of proposed disclosures relating to the foreign currency aspects of a company's financial instruments. See 3 of Chapter 9 for a discussion of the proposed disclosures.

3 PROBLEM AREAS

3.1 Individual companies

3.1.1 Date of transaction

The basic requirement of paragraph 46 of SSAP 20 is that transactions should be recorded at the rate ruling at the date the transaction occurred. No guidance is given in the standard as to what that date should be. SFAS 52 gives some help by defining the transaction date as being the date at which a transaction is recorded in accounting records in conformity with generally accepted accounting principles.[55] The following example illustrates the difficulty in determining the transaction date:

Example 8.8: Establishing the transaction date

A UK company buys an item of stock from a German company. The dates relating to the transaction, and the relevant exchange rates, are as follows:

Date	Event	£1=DM
24 February 1988	Goods are ordered	2.99
4 March 1988	Goods are shipped from Germany and invoice dated that day	3.00
7 March 1988	Invoice is received	3.05
8 March 1988	Goods are received	3.07
17 March 1988	Invoice is recorded	3.10
31 March 1988	Invoice is paid	3.12

In our view the date of the transaction should be when the company should recognise an asset and liability as a result of the transaction. This will normally be when the risks and rewards of ownership of the goods have passed to the UK company.

It is unlikely at the date the goods are ordered that all the risks and rewards of ownership of the goods have passed to the UK company and therefore this date should not be used as the date of the transaction.

If the goods are shipped free on board (f.o.b.) then as the risks and rewards of ownership pass on shipment then this date should be used.

If, however, the goods are not shipped f.o.b. then the risks and rewards of ownership normally pass on delivery and therefore the date the goods are received should be treated as the date of the transaction.

The dates on which the invoice is received and is recorded are irrelevant to when the risks and rewards of ownership pass and therefore should not be considered to be the date of the transaction. In practice, it may be acceptable that as a matter of administrative convenience that the exchange rate at the date the invoice is recorded is used, particularly if there is no undue delay in processing the invoice. If this is done then care should be taken to ensure that the exchange rate used is not significantly different from that ruling on the 'true' date of the transaction.

It is clear from SSAP 20 that the date the invoice is paid is not the date of the transaction because if it were then no exchange differences would arise on unsettled transactions.

Most companies do not indicate in their accounting policies what is meant by the date of transaction. One company which does is Racal Electronics:

Extract 8.15: Racal Electronics Plc (1997)

4 FOREIGN CURRENCIES [extract]

United Kingdom exports in foreign currencies are converted at the rates relative to the period of shipment.

3.1.2   Use of average rate

As indicated in 2.3.1 above, rather than using the actual rate ruling at the date of the transaction 'if the rates do not fluctuate significantly, an average rate for the period may be used as an approximation'.[56] For companies which engage in a large number of foreign currency transactions it will be more convenient for them to use an average rate rather than using the exact rate for each transaction. If an average rate is to be used, what guidance can be given in choosing and using such a rate?

(a)   Length of period
      As an average rate should only be used as an approximation of actual rates then care has to be taken that significant fluctuations in the day to day exchange rates do not arise in the period selected. For this reason the period chosen should not be too long. We believe that the maximum length of period should be one month and where there is volatility of exchange rates it will be better to set rates on a more frequent basis, say, a weekly basis, especially where the value of transactions is significant.

(b)   Estimate of average rate
      The estimation of the appropriate average rate will depend on whether the rate is to be applied to transactions which have already occurred or to transactions which will occur after setting the rate. Obviously, if the transactions have already occurred then the average rate used should relate to the period during which those transactions occurred; e.g. purchase transactions for the previous week should be translated using the average rate for that week, not an average rate for the week the invoices are being recorded.
      If there is no time delay between the date of the transaction and the date of recording and the rate is therefore being set for the following period then

the rate selected should be a reasonable estimate of the expected exchange rate during that period. This could be done by using the closing rate at the end of the previous period or by using the actual average rate for the previous period. We would suggest that the former be used. Although a forward rate could be used, it should be remembered that forward rates are *not* estimates of future exchange rates but are a function of the spot rate adjusted by reference to interest differentials (see 3.3.1 A below). Whatever means is used to estimate the average rate, the actual rates during the period should be monitored and if there is a significant move in the exchange rate away from the average rate then the rate being applied should be revised.

(c)   Application of average rate
We believe that average rates should only be used as a matter of convenience where there are a large number of transactions. Even where an average rate is used we would recommend that for large one-off transactions the actual rate should be used; e.g. purchase of a fixed asset or an overseas investment or taking out a foreign loan. Where the number of foreign currency transactions is small it will probably not be worthwhile setting and monitoring average rates and therefore actual rates should be used.

3.1.3   Dual rates or suspension of rates

One practical difficulty in translating foreign currency amounts is where there is more than one exchange rate for that particular currency depending on the nature of the transaction. In some cases the difference between the exchange rates can be small and therefore it probably does not matter which rate is actually used. However, in other situations, such as was the case with the South African rand, the difference can be quite significant. In these circumstances, what rate should be used? SSAP 20 is silent on this matter, but some guidance can be found in SFAS 52. It states that 'the applicable rate at which a particular transaction could be settled at the transaction date shall be used to translate and record the transaction. At a subsequent balance sheet date, the current rate (closing rate) is that rate at which the related receivable or payable could be settled at that date.'[57] Companies should therefore look at the nature of the transaction and apply the appropriate exchange rate. If there are doubts as to whether funds will be receivable at the more favourable rate then it may be necessary on the grounds of prudence to use the less favourable rate.

Another practical difficulty which could arise is where for some reason exchangeability between two currencies is temporarily lacking at the transaction date or at the subsequent balance sheet date. Again SSAP 20 makes no comment on this matter but SFAS 52 requires that the first subsequent rate at which exchanges could be made shall be used.[58]

3.1.4 Monetary or non-monetary

As discussed in 2.3.2 above, SSAP 20 generally requires that monetary items denominated in foreign currencies be retranslated using closing rates at each balance sheet date and non-monetary items should not be retranslated. Monetary items are defined as 'money held and amounts to be received or paid in money'.[59] The only examples of such items given in the standard are the obvious ones such as 'cash and bank balances, loans and amounts receivable and payable'.[60] Examples of non-monetary items given are equally obvious: 'plant, machinery and equity investments'.[61] Further examples of non-monetary items are those items listed in SFAS 52 as accounts to be remeasured using historical exchange rates when the temporal method is being applied.[62] Even with this guidance there are a number of particular items where the distinction may not be that clear.

A Deposits or progress payments paid against fixed assets or stocks

Companies may be required to pay deposits or progress payments when acquiring fixed assets or stocks from overseas. The question then arises as to whether such payments should be retranslated as monetary items or not.

Example 8.9

A UK company contracts to purchase an item of plant and machinery for US$10,000 on the following terms:

Payable on signing contract (1 December 19X1)	– 10%
Payable on delivery (22 December 19X1)	– 40%
Payable on installation (11 January 19X2)	– 50%

At 31 December 19X1 the company has paid the first two amounts on the due dates when the respective exchange rates were £1=US$1.82 and £1=US$1.83. The closing rate at its balance sheet date, 31 December 19X1, is £1=US$1.88.

	(i) £	(ii) £
First payment – US$1,000	549	532
Second payment – US$4,000	2,186	2,128
	2,735	2,660

(i) If the payments made are regarded as progress payments then the amounts should be treated as non-monetary items and included in the balance sheet at £2,735. This would appear to be consistent with SFAS 52 which in defining 'transaction date' states: 'A long-term commitment may have more than one transaction date (for example, the due date of each progress payment under a construction contract is an anticipated transaction date).'[63]

(ii) If the payments made are regarded as deposits, and are refundable, then the amounts should probably be treated as monetary items and included in the balance sheet at £2,660 and an exchange loss of £75 recorded in the profit and loss account.

In practice, it will often be necessary to consider the terms of the contract to ascertain the nature of the payments made in order to determine the appropriate accounting treatment.

B   *Debt securities held as investments*

Companies may acquire or invest in overseas debt securities which have a fixed term of redemption, e.g. a US treasury bond or loan stock of an American company.

Example 8.10

A UK company invests in US$1m 8% Treasury bonds at a cost of US$950,000 on 30 June 19X1 when the exchange rate was £1=US$1.75. The bonds are redeemable at par on 30 June 19X6. At the company's year end, 31 December 19X1, the closing rate of exchange is US$1.88.

In our view whether the investment is a monetary item or not depends on the company's intention for realising the investment.

(i) If the company intends holding the investment to the redemption date and is amortising the difference between cost and redemption value over the period to redemption we believe that the carrying amount is in the nature of a monetary item and therefore should be retranslated at the closing rate:

Cost	$950,000		
Amortisation – $50,000 ÷ 10	5,000		
	$955,000	@ £1=US$1.88 =	£507,979

If the company does not adopt a policy of amortising the difference between cost and redemption value over the period to redemption then we believe the investment should not be retranslated as it is not being accounted for as if it were a monetary item.

(ii) If the company does not intend to hold the investment until the redemption date but intends to sell it beforehand then the investment should be regarded as a non-monetary item and recorded at a cost of £542,857 and no exchange difference taken to profit and loss account. If the investment is written down because the market value at the year end is lower than cost or is revalued upwards because the market value is greater than cost then the investment should be translated using the rate of £1=US$1.88 as this is the rate relevant to the measurement date of the item.

C   *Foreign currency loans convertible into equity shares*

Occasionally companies in the UK have issued bonds (or debentures), expressed in a foreign currency (usually US dollars), which are convertible into a fixed number of ordinary shares of the UK company at the holder's option. The terms of the bonds normally require the company to redeem the bonds at a fixed amount (expressed in the foreign currency) at the end of their term. The holders and/or the company may also have the option of redeeming the bonds at an agreed amount (expressed in the foreign currency). The question then arises – do the bonds represent a monetary liability to be translated at closing rates or, because they may never be repaid in cash if they are converted for shares, do they represent a non-monetary item which should not be retranslated at closing rates?

Example 8.11

A UK company issues US$100m 6% convertible bonds on 30 June 19X0 when the exchange rate was £1=US$1.53. The share price at that date was £3.00 per share and the conversion terms are based on a share price of £3.27. The bonds are expressed as being convertible into shares at a share price of £3.27 per share and at a fixed exchange rate of £1=US$1.53. Assuming full conversion, therefore, the maximum number of shares which would be issued would be 19,987,607. (The conversion terms could have been expressed as 'convertible into shares at a fixed price of US$5.00' or as 'convertible into 1,000 shares for each US$5,000 of bonds held'; the number of shares to be issued would effectively be the same.) The bonds are only redeemable in 20 years' time on 30 June 19Z0.

How should the company account for these bonds in its accounts for the year ended 31 December 19X0 and the year ended 31 December 19X1? The exchange rates at the balance sheet dates are £1=US$1.48 and £1=US$1.88 respectively. No bonds have been converted by 31 December 19X1.

	Option 1 £m	Option 2 £m	Option 3 £m	Option 4 £m
Accounts for 31 December 19X0				
Issue price	65.4	65.4	65.4	65.4
Exchange loss taken to p/l account	2.2	–	2.2	2.2
Balance sheet liability	67.6	65.4	67.6	67.6
Accounts for 31 December 19X1				
Exchange gain taken to p/l account	(14.4)	–	(2.2)	(2.2)
Exchange gain deferred	–	–	–	(12.2)
Balance sheet liability	53.2	65.4	65.4	53.2

Option 1
It could be argued that until such time as the bonds have been converted they are monetary liabilities of the company and therefore should be retranslated at the closing rate of exchange at each year end. The fact that the company may never actually pay any cash if all the bondholders exercise their right of conversion is irrelevant. At the time of conversion the bondholder will assess whether it is beneficial to convert his holding into shares with regard to the then sterling amount of the bond using the exchange rate at that time. It is therefore this value which the company should treat as having received in return for the issue of shares.

Option 2
It could be argued that as the terms are likely to be set so that it is probable that conversion will take place during the term of the bond then as no cash will actually be paid by the company the bonds should not be treated as a monetary liability. They should, therefore, not be retranslated at closing rates of exchange at each balance sheet date but should be translated at the historical rate of US$1.53. The company should treat the amount received on the issue of the bonds as being the amount received on the issue of the shares.

Option 3

This is a variation of option 2 above. The difference is that until conversion has taken place some recognition should be given to the fact that the bonds may be redeemed and if the bonds translated at closing rate gives a greater liability than that using the historical rate then, on the grounds of prudence, a loss should be recognised. Gains would only be recognised to the extent that they matched losses previously taken to profit and loss account.

Option 4

This is a variation of option 1 above. The difference is that as the bonds may be converted into shares and not repaid in cash it is considered that they may not ultimately be a monetary item and therefore some recognition of this fact should be given. This is done by not recognising any gains in the profit and loss account except to the extent that they offset previously recognised losses. On the grounds of prudence any excess gains would be treated as a deferred credit as they may not ultimately be realised if the bonds are converted.

Under FRS 4, convertible bonds should be accounted for by reference to their current form, i.e. as liabilities; the finance cost should be calculated on the assumption that the debt will never be converted (see Chapter 15 at 2.2.2). Accordingly, it would be inconsistent, if for translation purposes, any allowance were made for the possible conversion of the bond. In our view, convertible bonds should now be treated no differently from normal borrowings for translation purposes and therefore option 1 should be adopted.

It would appear that such bonds are commonly treated as monetary items as they are retranslated at closing rates of exchange. However, frequently the cover method (see 2.3.7 and 2.4.5 above) is applied and the exchange differences on the bonds are taken to reserves and not reflected in the profit or loss for the year. LASMO in fact used to translate its convertible bonds at the fixed rate of exchange but changed its accounting policy in 1987:

Extract 8.16: London & Scottish Marine Oil PLC (1987)

1   Restatement of prior years

In the past, the liability under the $9\frac{1}{4}$ per cent Convertible Bonds Due 1999 (which are denominated in US dollars, and are convertible into ordinary shares at the option of the bond holders) was translated into sterling at the fixed exchange rate contained in the conditions of the Bonds. To reflect more accurately the liability prior to conversion, the liability has been translated at the exchange rate current at the balance sheet date. Prior years have been restated to reflect the above.

3.1.5   Treatment of exchange differences

The general rule of SSAP 20 is that all exchange differences on monetary items should be recognised as part of the profit or loss for the year.[64] Apart from the possible treatment of gains on long-term monetary items (see 2.3.6 above) and the treatment of exchange differences on borrowings financing, or hedging against, foreign equity investments (see 2.3.7 above), are there any other circumstances where it is possible for exchange differences not to be taken as part of the profit or loss for the year?

A   *Capitalisation of exchange differences*

On many occasions where a UK company is acquiring an asset (other than an equity investment) from overseas it finances the acquisition by means of a foreign loan. The general rules of SSAP 20 require the asset to be translated at historical rates and for the loan to be translated at closing rates.[65] Consequently, exchange differences on the loan are taken to profit and loss account with no offsetting exchange difference on the asset. One means of avoiding this situation is if the asset and liability can be regarded as a foreign branch, as discussed in 2.4.7 above. However, it will not always be possible to regard them as such and therefore consideration has to be given to any other way in which the exchange differences on the loan need not be taken to the profit or loss for the year.

In our view the only other possible circumstance is where the asset is still in the course of production. The Companies Act 1985 requires assets to be included at their purchase price or production cost.[66] Production cost can include indirect overheads attributable to the production of the asset to the extent that they relate to the period of production[67] (see 2 of Chapter 10 for a fuller discussion of these requirements). One of the overheads that the Companies Act 1985 specifically allows to be included is interest on borrowings.[68] It is often argued that exchange differences on foreign borrowings are really part of the interest cost of the foreign borrowing. A UK company may take out a borrowing in a 'hard' currency, e.g. Swiss francs, rather than in sterling so as to benefit from the low interest rate. However, as this lower interest charge is likely to be offset by exchange losses on the borrowing then these losses should be treated as part of the interest cost of the borrowing. Indeed, paragraph 68 of the standard suggests that exchange differences on borrowings should be disclosed as part of 'other interest receivable/payable and similar income/expense' in the profit and loss account. As a result we believe that exchange differences on foreign currency loans should be capitalised as part of the cost of the asset when interest costs on the same borrowings are being capitalised. Capitalisation of borrowing costs is discussed more fully in Chapter 13. Where such a treatment is being adopted then similar disclosure to that of the interest costs shown in 4.2 of that chapter should be given for the exchange differences on the borrowings. However, as it is possible to adopt a policy of not capitalising borrowing costs, then even if the interest costs are not being capitalised we believe it is acceptable to capitalise the exchange differences on the borrowings which arise during the period of production.

B   *Hedging transactions – deferment of exchange differences*

The only specific reference which SSAP 20 makes to hedging is in respect of foreign currency borrowings providing a hedge against its foreign currency equity investments.[69] It also allows transactions to be recorded at the rate specified in a related forward contract,[70] which is another way of hedging. A further method by which companies may hedge against a foreign currency exposure is by matching foreign currency debtors in one currency with creditors

Example 8.13

On 31 March 19X1 a UK company wishes to enter into a forward contract to buy US$1m in six months' time. Ignoring any profit which the bank would take on the transaction the rate under contract would be calculated as if the bank had on 31 March 19X1:

(i)   sold the company an amount of US dollars at the spot rate on that date, which would yield a total of US$1m in six months' time;

(ii)   placed the amount of US dollars in (i) above on deposit for the company; and

(iii)   lent the company the amount of sterling in (i) above repayable, with interest, in six months' time.

At 31 March 19X1 the spot rate is £1=US$1.888 and the US dollar and sterling interest rates are 7%p.a. and 8.75%p.a. respectively.

The amount of US dollars which the bank would 'sell' to the company would be US$966,184. Interest on the 'deposit' at 7%p.a. for six months would be US$33,816 which would mean that the company would be entitled to US$1m in six months' time.

The amount of sterling 'lent' to the company would be £511,750. Interest on this loan at 8.75%p.a. for the six months would be £22,389 and therefore the company would have to pay £534,139 at the end of the six months.

This cost of £534,139 for the US$1m gives an exchange rate of £1.872.

Normally, forward contract rates are not quoted as single figures in the UK but are quoted as being either at a discount or premium on the spot rate. To arrive at the contract rate a discount is *added* to the spot rate and a premium is *deducted* from the spot rate.

B   Reasons for companies taking out forward contracts

In most situations companies enter into a forward contract to protect themselves from the risks of exchange rate variations. This will normally be done to hedge:

(a)   a future commitment or transaction which will require the purchase or sale of foreign currency; or

(b)   an existing foreign currency monetary asset or liability; or

(c)   an investment in a foreign enterprise, such as an overseas subsidiary; or

(d)   the results of a foreign enterprise.

In the first two situations a company is hedging the transaction to fix the amount of cash in sterling terms which will be required, whereas in the other two situations a company is hedging to offset the effect of translating the investment or results of the foreign enterprise.

In addition, companies may also enter into a forward contract by way of speculation in the hope that they can make a profit out of doing so.

In our view the accounting for forward contracts should be based on the economic rationale for the company entering into the contract in the first place and therefore will be different in each of these situations. We will now look at how this can be done by considering examples of each of these situations.

C   *Forward contracts taken out to hedge future commitments or transactions*

Example 8.14

On 30 September 19X0 a UK company contracts to buy an item of plant and machinery from a US company for US$500,000, with delivery on 31 January 19X1 and payment due on 31 March 19X1. In order to hedge against the movements in exchange rates it enters into a forward contract on 30 September 19X0 to buy US$500,000 in six months' time. The premium on such a contract is US$0.02 and based on the spot rate of £1=US$1.63 gives a contracted rate of £1=US$1.61.

The relevant spot rates are:

	£1=US$
31 December 19X0	1.88
31 January 19X1	1.77
31 March 19X1	1.89

How should the company account for these transactions in its financial statements for the years ended 31 December 19X0 and 31 December 19X1?

There are two basic methods:

(i) Record the asset and the liability at 31 January 19X1 at £310,559 being US$500,000 translated at the contracted rate of £1=US$1.61. No exchange loss would be recognised on the forward contract in either year and no exchange gain on the liability to the supplier would be recognised in the year ended 31 December 19X1. This treatment is straightforward and reflects the fact that the company has eliminated all currency risks by entering into the forward contract.

It could however be argued that such a treatment is not allowed by SSAP 20. Paragraph 46 of the standard only refers to *trading* transactions being translated at rates specified in related forward contracts. Trading transactions are not defined in SSAP 20 and a narrow interpretation would preclude capital transactions, such as the purchase of fixed assets, from being so treated. However, it would appear that some companies adopt a wider interpretation, as indicated in 3.3.1 D below. We concur with such an interpretation.

(ii) The forward contract and the acquisition of the asset are accounted for as two separate transactions. The asset and the liability to the supplier are initially recorded at 31 January 19X1 at £282,486 (US$500,000 @ 1.77). An exchange gain on the amount due to the supplier up to the date of payment of £17,936, being £264,550 (US$500,000 @ 1.89) less £282,486, is recognised in the profit and loss account for the year ended 31 December 19X1.

The exchange difference on the forward contract up to the transaction date is not recognised in the profit and loss account but is deferred and included in the recorded amount of the asset. Thereafter, any exchange difference on the contract is matched against the exchange difference on the liability to the supplier. Accordingly, although there is an exchange loss on the contract at 31 December 19X0 of £40,792, being £306,749 (US$500,000 @ 1.63) less £265,957 (US$500,000 @ 1.88) this is not recognised in the profit and loss account but is deferred. In 19X1 there is an exchange gain on the contract up to the date of the transaction on 31 January 19X1 of £16,529, being £282,486 (US$500,000 @ 1.77) less £265,957. Again, this is not recognised in the profit and loss account. This gain together with the loss previously deferred is included in recording the asset. Accordingly, the asset is recorded at £306,749 (£282,486 + £40,792 − £16,529). This is equivalent to the asset being recorded at the spot rate ruling when the forward contract was entered into.

Following the transaction date there is an exchange loss on the forward contract of £17,936 which should be taken to the profit and loss account. It can be seen that this will offset the exchange gain on the amount due to the supplier in the same period and therefore reflects the fact that the company had hedged its exposure to exchange differences.

In addition to the exchange difference on the forward contract, recognition has to be given to the premium on the contract, i.e. the difference between the contracted amount translated at the contracted rate and translated at the spot rate when the contract was taken out. In this case the premium is £3,810 being £310,559 (US$500,000 @ 1.61) less £306,749 (US$500,000 @ 1.63). As this premium essentially represents an interest cost (see Example 8.13 above) over the period of the contract then this should be amortised over that period as a finance charge. Accordingly, £1,905 would be charged to the profit and loss account in the year ended 31 December 19X0 and £1,905 in the following year. This second method is that suggested by SFAS 52.[77]

We believe that both of these methods are acceptable but would recommend that companies adopt the approach suggested in SFAS 52 as outlined in (ii) above. However, it should be borne in mind that where an exchange loss on the forward contract arises it should not be deferred if it would lead to recognising losses in later periods.[78] An alternative treatment allowed by SFAS 52 for the premium or discount on a contract which hedges a future commitment or transaction is to include that proportion of the premium or discount which relates to the commitment period, i.e. up to the date of the transaction, as part of the transaction.[79]

It should be noted that the treatment discussed in the second method in the above example is only allowed by SFAS 52 if the contract is designated as a hedge and the foreign currency commitment is firm.[80] Accordingly, if in the above example the company had not contracted for the plant and machinery at 30 September 19X0 but it was only their intention at that date to enter into such contract then the US standard would not have allowed deferral of any of the exchange differences on the forward contract prior to contracting for the plant. We believe that in the UK it is unnecessary for such a stringent test to be applied and the treatment can be applied where a company has a reasonable expectation of entering into the transaction.

One company which refers to forward contracts taken out to hedge future commitments is Amstrad, as shown in the extract below:

Extract 8.18: Amstrad plc (1996)

d) Foreign currencies [extract]

Foreign currency contracts existing at the year end which are in excess of trading commitments and on which a gain or loss has arisen at the year end are recognised as part of the loss on ordinary activities for the year.

Another example is Grand Metropolitan, as shown in Extract 9.1 in Chapter 9.

D   *Forward contracts taken out to hedge an existing foreign currency monetary asset or liability*

Example 8.15

Suppose the UK company in the previous example enters into the same forward contract. However, this time it does so because it has an existing loan of US$500,000 which is due for repayment on 31 March 19X1 and wishes to hedge against any further exchange risk.

How should the forward contract and the loan be treated in the financial statements for the years ended 31 December 19X0 and 31 December 19X1?

There are three basic methods:

(i) Translate the loan at the contracted rate of £1=US$1.61, i.e. £310,559. The difference between this amount and the recorded amount at 30 September 19X0 based on the spot rate at that date, i.e. £306,749, is written off in the profit and loss account for the year ended 31 December 19X0 along with the previous exchange differences on the loan. No amounts are recorded in the profit and loss account for the year ended 31 December 19X1.

(ii) Again, translate the loan at the contracted rate. However, as the difference of £3,810 (£310,559 less £306,749) represents the premium on the contract then it is deferred and amortised over the period of the contract. Accordingly, £1,905 is charged in the profit and loss account for the year ended 31 December 19X0 and £1,905 in the following year.

It has been suggested that the treatment of the loans in each of these methods is not allowed by SSAP 20 as loans are not trading transactions.[81] However, we believe this to be a narrow interpretation of the standard and it would appear that companies do translate loans at rates specified in forward contracts (see Extract 8.19 below).

(iii) Treat the loan and the forward contract as two separate transactions. The loan is translated at the closing rate at 31 December 19X0 and the exchange difference thereon is taken to profit and loss account. This exchange difference will include an exchange gain of £40,792 for the period from 30 September 19X0 to 31 December 19X0, being £306,749 (US$500,000 @ 1.63) less £265,957 (US$500,000 @ 1.88). The forward contract should also be regarded as a foreign currency transaction on which an exchange difference arises. SSAP 20 does not make this clear. However, it is clear from SFAS 52 that a forward contract is a foreign currency transaction.[82] Accordingly, an exchange loss of £40,792 on the contract should be recognised in the profit and loss account for the year ended 31 December 19X0. This will offset the gain on the loan and therefore the results will not be affected by exchange differences from 30 September 19X0, which was the purpose of taking out the contract. In the profit and loss account for the year ended 31 December 19X1 a further exchange gain of £1,407, being £265,957 less £264,550 (US$500,000 @ 1.89) will be recognised on the loan offset by an equivalent exchange loss on the forward contract. As in method (ii) the premium on the contract would be amortised over the period of the contract. This method is that required by SFAS 52.[83]

We believe that all three methods are acceptable but would recommend that companies adopt method (iii). However, it would appear that at least some companies are translating loans at contracted rates, as the following extract shows:

Month	Month end	Average for month	Average for quarter	Average for year
June 19X0	1.53			
July 19X0	1.49	1.51		
August 19X0	1.49	1.49		
September 19X0	1.45	1.47	1.49	
October 19X0	1.41	1.43		
November 19X0	1.43	1.43		
December 19X0	1.48	1.44	1.43	
January 19X1	1.51	1.51		
February 19X1	1.55	1.53		
March 19X1	1.61	1.59	1.54	
April 19X1	1.66	1.63		
May 19X1	1.63	1.67		
June 19X1	1.61	1.63	1.64	1.53

Average of month end rates – 1.53
Average of quarter end rates – 1.54

The results of the subsidiary for each of the 12 months to 30 June 19X1 and the translation thereof under each of the above methods (using monthly figures where appropriate) are shown below:

Month	US$	(e) quarterly £	(e) monthly £	(f) quarterly £	(f) monthly £
July 19X0	1,000		671		662
August 19X0	1,100		738		738
September 19X0	1,200	2,276	828	2,215	816
October 19X0	2,000		1,418		1,399
November 19X0	4,000		2,797		2,797
December 19X0	10,000	10,811	6,757	11,189	6,944
January 19X1	5,000		3,311		3,311
February 19X1	1,300		839		850
March 19X1	1,350	4,752	839	4,968	849
April 19X1	1,300		783		798
May 19X1	1,400		859		838
June 19X1	1,400	2,547	870	2,500	859
Total	31,050	20,386	20,710	20,872	20,861

Method (a)	US$31,050 @ 1.48= £20,980
Method (b)	US$31,050 @ 1.57= £19,777
Method (c) – monthly	US$31,050 @ 1.53= £20,294
Method (c) – quarterly	US$31,050 @ 1.54= £20,162
Method (d)	US$31,050 @ 1.53= £20,294

It can be seen that by far the simplest methods to use are the methods (a) to (d).

In our view methods (a) and (b) should not be used as it is unlikely in these times of volatile exchange rates that they give appropriate weighting to the exchange rates which have been in existence throughout the period in question. They are only going to give an acceptable answer if the exchange rate has been static or steadily increasing or decreasing throughout the period.

Method (c) based on quarter end rates has similar drawbacks and therefore should not normally be used.

Method (c) based on month end rates and method (d) are better than the previous methods as they do take into account more exchange rates which have applied throughout the year with method (d) being preferable as this will have taken account of daily exchange rates. Average monthly rates for most major currencies are likely to be given in publications issued by the government, banks and other sources and therefore it is unnecessary for companies to calculate their own. The work involved in calculating an average for the year, therefore, is not very onerous. Method (d) will normally give reasonable and acceptable results when there are no seasonal variations in items of income and expenditure.

Where there are seasonal variations in items of income and expenditure then this will not be the case. It can be seen from the above example that because more than 60% of the results arise in the winter months when the US dollar has been stronger in relation to sterling compared to during the whole of the period, method (d) has deflated the results shown by method (f), which is more accurate. In these situations appropriate exchange rates should be applied to the appropriate items. This can be done by using either of methods (e) or (f) preferably using figures and rates for each month. Where such a method is being used care should be taken to ensure that the periodic accounts are accurate and that cut-off procedures have been adequate, otherwise significant items may be translated at the wrong average rate.

Where there are significant one-off transactions then it is likely that actual rates at the date of the transaction should be used to give a more accurate weighting. Indeed, SFAS 52 requires that for revenues, expenses, gains, and losses the exchange rate at the date on which these elements are recognised should be used or an appropriately weighted average.[97]

Most companies do not indicate how they have applied an average rate, but merely state that the results are translated at average rates or weighted average rates. Two companies which are more specific in their accounting policies on the use of average rates are Allied Domecq and Boots, as illustrated below:

Extract 8.28: Allied Domecq PLC (1996)

FOREIGN CURRENCIES [extract]

The profits of overseas subsidiary and associated undertakings are translated at weighted average rates each month.

Extract 8.29: The Boots Company PLC (1997)

Foreign currencies [extract]

The results and cash flows of overseas subsidiaries are translated into sterling on an average exchange rate basis, weighted by the actual results of each month.

3.4.4 *Change from closing rate to average rate or vice versa*

By allowing companies the choice of using either the closing rate or an average rate for the period in translating the results of foreign enterprises, the question then arises – can a company change the method used by switching from closing rate to an average rate or vice versa?

Paragraph 17 of the standard states that the use of either method is permitted 'provided that the one selected is applied consistently from period to period'. It could be argued that this means that once a company has chosen a particular method no change should be made on the grounds of consistency. However, in view of the arguments expressed in paragraph 17 about the use of each of the methods it would seem possible that a company could justify changing from one method to the other on the grounds that it was adopting a better method.

If a change is made, it could be argued either that it is a change in accounting policy needing a prior year adjustment under FRS 3[98] and therefore the previous year's profit and loss account changed to the new basis, or that it is only a refinement of the existing policy which would not require a prior year adjustment. A refinement of an accounting policy is normally one that seeks to give a more accurate estimation in pursuit of the same basis of measurement; for example, a provision for stock obsolescence. This is not the case here, and in view of the conceptual differences of each method discussed in paragraph 17 of SSAP 20 we believe that this suggests a change in accounting policy. This would also appear to be required by paragraph 17 when it says that the method should be applied consistently from period to period.

A number of companies did change from the closing rate method to the average rate method in 1985/86. This was probably due to the dramatic weakening of the US dollar from January/February 1985 to the autumn of that year. In particular, the exchange rate moved from £1=US\$1.08 at the end of February to £1=US\$1.24 at the end of March. Companies were finding that, in addition to depressing their reported results, they were having to reassess their expected results due to the change in the exchange rate. They were also finding that figures previously reported in their interim announcements could be remarkably different when the annual figures were being translated at the closing rate. This particular problem is discussed in 3.4.11 below.

Since then more companies have changed to using average rates. Most major companies now use the average rate method.

3.4.5   To which reserve should exchange differences be taken?

SSAP 20 requires that exchange differences arising from the retranslation of the net investment at the closing rate should be recorded as a movement on reserves; however, it does not specify the category of reserves to which they should be taken. A number of companies take them to retained profits. Many companies in addition to showing such exchange differences as movements on retained profits also show them as movements on other reserves such as revaluation reserves and capital reserves. However, this is likely to be as a result of items dealt with in 3.4.6 below.

One company which has taken the exchange differences to a separate currency translation reserve is Scholl, as shown below:

Extract 8.30: Scholl PLC (1996)

21   Reserves [extract]

	Foreign currency translation reserve £000
Group	
At 1st January 1996	4,867
Loss on translation	(6,594)
At 31st December 1996	(1,727)

3.4.6   Post-acquisition capital or revaluation reserves

As indicated above, SSAP 20 does not specify the reserve to which the exchange difference arising from the retranslation of the net investment at the closing rate should be taken. Normally, they should be taken to only one category of reserve. However, the foreign enterprise may have a non-distributable capital reserve which arose after the company was acquired by the investing company. Alternatively, it may have revalued some assets since it was acquired and therefore has a revaluation reserve. As these reserves will not be reported as part of retained profits in the consolidated financial statements the question then arises – if exchange differences are normally taken to retained profits, should

This is based on the view that one of the objectives of SSAP 20 is to produce results which are compatible with the effects of rate changes on a company's cash flow; that is why exchange differences on monetary items are normally recognised as part of the profit or loss for the year. Exchange rate changes in this instance have ultimately caused the company to receive less cash and therefore should be reflected at some time in arriving at the profit or loss for the year. It could also be argued in this particular case that not to do so would mean that the company has reported more profits in the consolidated profit and loss account than has actually been realised, contrary to the requirements of the Companies Act 1985.[101]

The treatment suggested in option (iii) above is that which is required by SFAS 52 upon the sale or upon complete or substantially complete liquidation of an investment in a foreign entity.[102] Indeed, under US GAAP if a partial sale takes place then the relevant proportion of the accumulated exchange difference should be included in the gain/loss on sale.[103] Similar requirements are contained in the international standard, IAS 21.[104] In the above example if 25% of the shares in the subsidiary had been sold then £(19,882) would have been included in the calculation of the gain/loss on sale.

However, under FRS 3, as the original exchange differences would have been reflected in the statement of total recognised gains and losses when they arose then they should not be recognised again in the year of disposal in either the profit and loss account or the statement of recognised gains and losses (see Chapter 22 at 2.9.1). Accordingly, option (iii) is unacceptable and in our view option (ii) is preferable to option (i).

It would appear that in practice most companies do not include the cumulative exchange differences in the profit and loss account in the year of disposal, and no transfer between reserves is generally required as the exchange differences are already in retained profits.

3.4.8 Change from closing rate/net investment method to temporal method or vice versa

As indicated in 2.4.2 above, the method used for translating the financial statements of a foreign enterprise should normally only be changed when the financial and other operational relationship changes and renders the method used inappropriate. Where this is the case, therefore, it must be remembered that, as it is a change in the circumstances which has given rise to the change in method, this is not a change in accounting policy and therefore a prior year adjustment under FRS 3 is inappropriate. How should the change, therefore, be accounted for?

SSAP 20 does not deal with this situation; however, guidance can be sought from SFAS 52.

A   Change from closing rate/net investment method to temporal method

SFAS 52 states that the translated amounts of non-monetary assets at the end of the period prior to the change should become the accounting basis for those assets for the current and future periods.[105]   There is therefore no need to translate these assets at the historical rates that applied when the assets were acquired. The cumulative exchange differences that have been taken to reserves in prior periods should not be taken to the profit and loss account in the year of change but should remain in reserves. SFAS 52 actually requires these exchange differences to remain in equity.[106]

B   *Change from temporal method to closing rate/net investment method*

SFAS 52 states that the adjustment attributable to restating non-monetary assets, previously translated at historical rates, at closing rates should be reported in the cumulative translation adjustments component of equity.[107]   This adjustment should, therefore, be treated as a reserve movement.

3.4.9   *Hyper-inflation*

One particular problem with the use of the closing rate/net investment method is when it is applied to a foreign enterprise which operates in a country where a very high rate of inflation exists. Consider the following example:

Example 8.24

On 30 June 19X0 a UK company sets up a subsidiary in Brazil. On that date the subsidiary acquires property for 10,000 Cruzados. Ignoring depreciation on the property, this asset would be included in the group financial statements at 30 June 19X0 and 30 June 19X6, as follows:

	Cruzados	Exchange rate	£
30 June 19X0	10,000	£1=0.123Cr	81,301
30 June 19X6	10,000	£1=21.18Cr	472

This example illustrates the 'disappearing assets' problem and it is for this reason that SSAP 20 says that in these circumstances 'it may not be possible to present fairly in historical cost accounts the financial position of a foreign enterprise simply by a translation process'.[108]   The other impact is that profits may be inflated (either from high interest income on deposits in a rapidly depreciating currency or from trading operations at unrealistic levels of profitability) whilst a significant exchange loss is taken direct to reserves. The standard suggests, therefore, that the local currency financial statements should be adjusted where possible to reflect current price levels before the translation process is undertaken. No indication is given as to whether this restatement should be done based on specific price changes (current cost principles) or general price changes (current purchasing power principles), so either would appear to be acceptable.

SSAP 20 does not define what 'a very high rate of inflation' is; in addition, it is not that clear as to when and how the guidance in the standard should be applied in practice.

A   UITF 9

As a result of this uncertainty the UITF considered the matter and in June 1993 issued Abstract 9 – *Accounting for Operations in Hyper-inflationary Economies* – which became effective for accounting periods ending on or after 23 August 1993.

The UITF agreed that adjustments are required where the cumulative inflation rate over three years is approaching, or exceeds, 100% and the operations in the hyper-inflationary economies are material.[109] Although this sounds high, this is equivalent to an annual inflation rate of 26% compounded over that period. This is similar to what SFAS 52 regards as a highly inflationary economy.[110]

Countries which have recently had three-year cumulative inflation of 100% or more include:[111]

Afghanistan	Honduras	Mongolia	Tanzania
Algeria	Iran	Mozambique	Turkey
Belarus	Jamaica	Nigeria	Ukraine
Brazil	Kazakhstan	Poland	Uruguay
Ecuador	Latvia	Romania	Venezuela
Estonia	Lithuania	Russia	Zaire
Ghana	Madagascar	Rwanda	Zambia
Guinea-Bissau	Malawi	Sudan	
Haiti	Mexico	Suriname	

Information on inflation rates in various countries is available in *International Financial Statistics*, published monthly by the International Monetary Fund.

Although SSAP 20 suggests that the local currency financial statements should be adjusted to reflect current price levels, the UITF recognised that the lack of reliable and timely inflation indices can pose a major practical problem. Accordingly the UITF regards two methods as being acceptable to eliminate the distortion caused by hyper-inflation:

(a)   adjust the local currency financial statements to reflect current price levels before the translation process (as suggested by SSAP 20). This includes taking any gain or loss on the net monetary position through the profit and loss account; or

(b)   use a relatively stable currency (not necessarily sterling) as the functional currency of the foreign operations. If the transactions of the operation are not recorded initially in that stable currency, then they must be remeasured into the stable currency by applying the temporal method (see 2.4.4

above). These remeasured financial statements are then translated into sterling using the closing rate method.[112]   This is effectively the same treatment as required by SFAS 52 which regards the reporting currency of the investing company (the US dollar) as if it were the functional currency of the foreign enterprise.[113]

We can see the effect of using these two methods on the 'disappearing assets' problem illustrated above in the following example:

Example 8.25

(a)   Adjusting for current price levels

The relevant consumer price indices at 30 June 19X0 and 30 June 19X6 are 100 and 23,436 respectively. The asset would therefore be included in the group financial statements at 30 June 19X6 as follows:

10,000 Cruzados x 23,436/100 = 2,343,600 Cruzados @ £1=21.18Cr = £110,652.

(b)   Remeasuring using a stable currency

The US dollar is regarded as the relevant stable currency. The asset is remeasured using a historical rate of exchange for US dollars at 30 June 19X0 of US$1=0.053Cr. This produces a cost for the asset of US$188,679. This is then translated into sterling at the US dollar exchange rate at 30 June 19X6 of £1=US$1.53 which gives an amount of £123,320.

Two companies which follow the former method are Lonrho and Unilever, as illustrated in the following extracts:

Extract 8.31: Lonrho Plc (1996)

Consolidation of Group companies [extract]

Results of subsidiaries and associates operating in hyper-inflationary economies are adjusted to reflect current price levels in those countries concerned.

Extract 8.32: Unilever PLC (1996)

Foreign currencies [extract]

In preparing the consolidated accounts, the profit and loss account, the cash flow statement and all movements in assets and liabilities are translated at annual average rates of exchange. The balance sheet, other than the ordinary share capital of NV and PLC, is translated at year-end rates of exchange. In the case of hyper-inflation economies, the accounts are adjusted to remove the influences of inflation before being translated.

On the other hand, two companies which adopt the latter method are Courtaulds and GKN, as shown below:

Some companies go further than Guinness in that they, in giving their segmental disclosures, restate all the comparative figures based on the current year's exchange rates.[120]

Although this extra disclosure can only help a user of financial statements it must be remembered that this mathematical effect of different exchange rates ignores the economic effect of the changes in the exchange rates on the actual trading results of the foreign enterprises. SFAS 52 states that the Financial Accounting Standards Board when preparing the standard 'considered a proposal for financial statement disclosure that would describe and possibly quantify the effects of rate changes on reported revenue and earnings. This type of disclosure might have included the mathematical effect of translating revenue and expenses at rates that are different from those used in a preceding period as well as the economic effects of rate changes, such as the effects on selling prices, sales volume, and cost structures.' The Board rejected requiring such disclosures 'primarily because of the wide variety of potential effects, the perceived difficulties of developing the information, and the impracticality of providing meaningful guidelines'. However, the Board encouraged management to give extra disclosure of 'an analysis and discussion of the effects of rate changes on the reported results of operations. The purpose is to assist financial report users in understanding the broader economic implications of rate changes and to compare recent results with those of prior periods.'[121]

3.4.12 Branches

We have discussed previously the application of the provisions of SSAP 20 in relation to branches and we have seen that the definition of a foreign branch is a very wide one in that it includes a group of assets and liabilities which are accounted for in foreign currencies. This was mainly to cater for international assets which are financed by foreign borrowings, since the cover method could not be used as it is only applicable to equity investments. In many cases, therefore, the reason for regarding assets and liabilities as a foreign branch will be to allow exchange differences on the related borrowing to be taken to reserves rather than to the profit and loss account.

Once a company has decided that a particular category of assets and liabilities should be regarded as a foreign branch consideration should be given as to which assets and liabilities should be included. In our view the minimum which can be included is the international asset itself, e.g. aircraft, ship or oil and gas interest, and the related borrowing. However, we recommend that, in addition, any trading balances, e.g. debtors and creditors, should also be included. In particular, as the branch should not be an integral part of the company's business and its cash flows should not have an impact upon those of the rest of the company in order to justify the use of the closing rate/net investment method, the bank account through which most of the cash flows of the branch will flow should be considered to be part of the branch assets and liabilities.

It should be borne in mind that the exchange difference which is taken to reserves is on the net investment in the branch. As such this amount can be a net exchange gain or loss and the exchange difference on the borrowings included in the branch can exceed the corresponding exchange difference on the branch assets. There is, therefore, no restriction on the exchange differences on the borrowings taken to reserves as there would be if the provisions of the cover method applied.

3.5   Cover method

We have looked at the basic requirements of the cover method in 2.3.7 above and 2.4.5 above as it is applied in individual companies' financial statements and consolidated financial statements respectively. There are, however, a number of problem areas resulting from the provisions of the standard which we believe have to be addressed. Many of these problem areas are relevant to both sets of financial statements. Until recently, the main focus of attention in this area has generally been in relation to the external financial reporting aspects of the consolidated financial statements. However, due to the introduction of a new tax regime for foreign exchange differences in 1995 the focus has shifted to the position in individual companies since taxation is assessed on individual companies not groups.

3.5.1   What are 'foreign currency borrowings'?

By adopting the cover method companies can take some, if not all, of the exchange differences arising on the foreign currency borrowings to reserves. Borrowings are not defined in the standard, so what should be regarded as borrowings?

The statement issued by the ASC on the publication of the standard in commenting on these provisions referred to 'loans'[122] but even then we do not believe that this term should be interpreted too literally.

The Stock Exchange, in requiring disclosure of indebtedness in listing particulars of listed companies, includes within this category loan capital, term loans, bank overdrafts, liabilities under acceptances (other than normal trade bills), acceptance credits and hire purchase commitments.[123] In our view all of these items can be regarded as borrowings for the purpose of the standard although it is unlikely that liabilities under hire purchase contracts, or finance leases, will have been taken out with a view to providing a hedge against foreign equity investments. Normal trade creditors and trade bills should not be regarded as borrowings, although it has been suggested that extended credit from a supplier could be included as the economic effects are the same as for a straightforward loan.[124]

3.5.2 Borrowings taken out before or after the investment

The provisions of the standard apply to borrowings which have been used to finance, or provide a hedge against, its foreign equity investments. Accordingly, the provisions not only apply to borrowings taken out at the same time as the investment is made but also to borrowings which have been taken out before the investment is made and to borrowings which are taken out after the investment is made. How should the provisions be applied, therefore, in the first accounting period when the investment holding period has been different from the period for which the borrowing has been in place?

A   Borrowings taken out before the investment

Example 8.29

A UK company is intending to invest in a US company so on 1 May 19X1 it borrows US$500,000, repayable in five years' time, which it places in a US$ deposit account in the meantime. On 31 May 19X1 it purchases all of the shares of the US company at a cost of US$800,000 using the US$500,000 in the deposit account and the balance paid out of its sterling bank account. How should the company apply the cover method in its financial statements for the period to 31 December 19X1?

The relevant exchange rates are:

	£1=US$
1 May 19X1	1.66
31 May 19X1	1.63
31 December 19X1	1.88

		Option (i)		Option (ii)	
		P/L account	Reserves	P/L account	Reserves
Exchange differences		£	£	£	£
Investment					
US$800,000	@ 1.63 = £490,798				
	@ 1.88 = £425,532				
			(65,266)		(65,266)
Deposit					
US$500,000	@ 1.66 = £301,205				
	@ 1.63 = £306,748				
		5,543		5,543	
Borrowing					
US$500,000	@ 1.66 = £301,205				
	@ 1.63 = £306,748				
			(5,543)	(5,543)	
	@ 1.88 = £265,957		40,791		40,791
		5,543	(30,018)	nil	(24,475)

Option (i) is based on the view that as the borrowings were used to finance the purchase of the investment all of the exchange difference on the borrowings can be offset against the exchange differences as long as the criteria of the standard are met. However, in our view this ignores the fact that for the period prior to purchasing the investment the borrowing was effectively matched against the deposit. Therefore our preference would be for the exchange difference on the borrowing for the period up to purchasing the investment to be taken to profit and loss to offset the exchange difference on the deposit as shown in option (ii).

We also believe that such a treatment should be adopted if the proceeds of the borrowings had been placed in a sterling deposit account as the company would have been uncovered during that period. The effect of exchange differences would have impacted on the cash flow of the company as it would have been required to pay an extra £5,543 out of its sterling bank account to purchase the investment. Accordingly, the exchange difference should be taken to profit and loss account.

Problems also arise when borrowings are taken out as a hedge against existing foreign investments.

B   *Borrowings taken out after the investment*

Example 8.30

A UK company has an equity investment in a German company which it acquired in 19W1 at a cost of DM500,000 when the exchange rate was £1=DM5.00. Up until 19X1 the UK company has had no foreign borrowings so the investment has been carried in the company's financial statements at its historical sterling cost of £100,000. On 30 April 19X1 the company considered the investment to be worth DM1,000,000 and in order to provide a hedge against the investment borrowed DM1,000,000, repayable in three years' time, and used the proceeds to reduce its sterling overdraft. How should the company apply the cover method in its financial statements for the year ended 31 December 19X1?

The relevant exchange rates are:

	£1=DM
31 December 19X0	2.86
30 April 19X1	2.98
31 December 19X1	2.96

		P/L £	Reserves £
Option (i)			
Exchange differences			
Investment – DM500,000	@ 5.00 = £100,000		
	@ 2.96 = £168,919		
	—————		68,919
Borrowing – DM1,000,000	@ 2.98 = £335,570		
	@ 2.96 = £337,838		
	—————		(2,268)
			—————
			66,651
			—————

		P/L £	Reserves £
Option (ii)			
Exchange differences			
Investment – DM500,000	@ 5.00 = £100,000 @ 2.86 = £174,825		
			74,825
	@ 2.96 = £168,919		(5,906)
Borrowing – DM1,000,000	@ 2.98 = £335,570 @ 2.96 = £337,838		
		(2,268)	
		(2,268)	68,919
Option (iii)			
Exchange differences			
Investment – DM500,000	@ 5.00 = £100,000 @ 2.98 = £167,785		
			67,785
	@ 2.96 = £168,919		1,134
Borrowing – DM1,000,000	@ 2.98 = £335,570 @ 2.96 = £337,838		
		(1,134)	(1,134)
		(1,134)	67,785

Option (i) regards all of the exchange gain on the investment which is recognised in this accounting period as being available for offset against the exchange loss on the total borrowing. This would appear to meet the conditions laid down in paragraphs 51 and 57 of the standard.

Option (ii) regards only the exchange difference arising on the investment during the year as being available for offset. As this is a loss, and a loss has also arisen on the borrowing, then under the conditions of the above paragraphs the exchange loss on the borrowings must be taken to profit and loss for the year.

Neither of these options, although acceptable under the standard, reflects the rationale for taking out the borrowings in the first place which was to hedge the exchange risk on the investment from the date it was decided to do so, i.e. 30 April 19X1. To achieve this, the exchange differences on the investment available for offset should be those which arise during the same period as the borrowing has been in existence.

Option (iii) is done on this basis and it can be seen that only half of the exchange loss on the borrowings can be offset against the exchange difference on the investment. This is due to the fact that the investment is recorded at the original cost of DM500,000 whereas the borrowing is twice that amount. In order for the company to reflect fully the rationale behind their decision they should incorporate the investment at its valuation of DM1,000,000. If this were done, then all of the exchange loss on the borrowing could be taken to reserves.

It can be seen from option (iii) in the above example that the carrying amount of the investment can have implications for the amount of exchange differences on the borrowings which can be taken to reserves under the cover method. Under the recently introduced tax regime, individual companies may make an election to match a foreign currency borrowing against shares in a foreign currency subsidiary, so that no taxable loss or gain on the borrowing results. However, to achieve such a result it is necessary that the translation of the carrying amount of the subsidiary gives rise to exchange differences which exceed those on the borrowings. Thus in the above example, the UK company would need to incorporate the investment at its valuation at 30 April 19X1 to ensure such a result on an ongoing basis (assuming all the conditions of paragraph 51 of SSAP 20 are met). If under its hedging strategy the company were to increase the amount of foreign currency borrowings because the underlying value of the subsidiary had increased, then it would be necessary to incorporate further valuations at the time the borrowings were increased in order to ensure that no exchange differences on the borrowings have to be taken to the profit and loss account.

3.5.3   Repayment of borrowings

Similar problems also arise when a company repays a foreign currency borrowing which has provided a hedge against a foreign equity investment.

A   Treatment of exchange differences

Example 8.31

A UK company has an equity investment in a Swiss company which it acquired for a cost of SFr3m when the exchange rate was £1=SFr3.00. It financed the acquisition by borrowing SFr3m. In the financial statements up to 30 April 19X1 the cover method has been applied. On 31 March 19X2 the company took advantage of the strong pound and decided to repay the borrowings in full. The company has no other foreign borrowings. How should the company apply the cover method in its financial statements for the year ended 30 April 19X2?

The relevant exchange rates are:

	£1=SFr
30 April 19X1	2.46
31 March 19X2	2.58
30 April 19X2	2.61

		Option (i)		Option (ii)	
		P/L	Reserves	P/L	Reserves
		£	£	£	£
Exchange differences					
Investment					
SFr3,000,000	@ 2.46 = £1,219,512				
	@ 2.58 = £1,162,791				
			(56,721)		(56,721)
Borrowing					
SFr3,000,000	@ 2.46 = £1,219,512				
	@ 2.58 = £1,162,791				
		56,721			56,721
		56,721	(56,721)	nil	nil

Option (i) is based on the view that as there are no borrowings at the year end then the cover method does not apply and the matching should be considered as having ceased at the beginning of the accounting period. As the exchange gain on the loan has arisen on a settled transaction it should be reported as part of the profit or loss for the year. However, it could be argued that this does not comply with condition (c) of paragraph 51 of the standard which requires the accounting treatment adopted to be applied consistently. Again, such a treatment does not reflect the fact that the company had hedged its investment up to 31 March 19X2 and it is only after that date that it has not been covered. Accordingly, we believe that option (ii) should be followed.

Another problem which arises when such borrowings are repaid is – how should the related investment which is no longer hedged subsequently be accounted for in the financial statements of the investing company?

B   *Subsequent treatment of investment*

Example 8.32

In the above example, how should the investment be included in the balance sheet at 30 April 19X2 and at subsequent year ends?

Option (i) – The investment should be retained at the exchange rate ruling at the final date of repaying the loan, i.e. £1,162,791 (£1=SFr2.58). No further retranslation should take place until another borrowing is taken out to provide a hedge. This method regards the investment as being a currency asset only during the period there are related currency borrowings. This would appear to be the method suggested by other commentators.[125] It does mean, however, that the figure for the investment in future periods is rather meaningless as it represents neither the historical cost in sterling terms nor the currency amount at closing rates. It does not even necessarily represent the actual sterling cost of the investment, as not all of the investment may have been financed by borrowings and the borrowings may have been repaid at different dates.

Option (ii) – The investment is translated at the closing rate of £1=SFr2.61 and included at £1,149,425 and is retranslated each year at closing rates. This is based on the view that the company *has* used foreign currency borrowings to finance the investment and therefore the provisions of paragraph 51 can still be applied. It also means that the accounting treatment for this investment is being applied consistently from period to period. Even if it were considered that such a policy was not in accordance with the standard then it would be possible for the company to adopt such a treatment by retaining a nominal borrowing in the foreign currency!

Option (iii) – The investment is retained at the rate ruling at the beginning of the period, i.e. £1,219,512 (£1=SFr2.46). This is based on the same premise as option (i) in the previous example.

Option (iv) – The investment should be restated at the historical rate ruling at the date of purchase, i.e. £1,000,000 (£1=SFr3.00). This is based on the view that the company no longer has a hedge against its investment and should account for it as if this had always been the case. The financial statements will, therefore, reflect the effect on net equity of choosing to finance the investment for the period it was so financed only by including the net exchange difference on the borrowing in reserves.

In our view all of the above options are acceptable, but the one chosen should be consistently applied.

3.5.4   Goodwill on consolidation

We have already discussed in 3.4.10 above the question of whether or not goodwill on consolidation, which arises on the acquisition of a foreign enterprise and is capitalised and amortised, is a currency asset. We indicated that our preference was to treat it as a currency asset. Where the investment is financed by foreign currency borrowings the question then arises, can the exchange differences arising on the goodwill be used in the offset process under the provisions of paragraph 57 of the standard?   Indeed, if the company has chosen to write off goodwill on consolidation immediately to reserves, can any of the exchange differences on the related borrowing be taken to reserves in the consolidated financial statements?

Example 8.33

A UK company acquired all the equity share capital of a German company for DM3m on 30 September 19X1. The acquisition was financed by taking out a loan of DM3m which is repayable over ten years commencing 31 March 19X2. As the net assets of the German company are negligible, all of the purchase price is represented by goodwill. The company has applied the cover method in its own financial statements for the period ended 31 December 19X1. The relevant exchange rates at 30 September 19X1 and 31 December 19X1 are £1=DM3.00 and £1=DM2.96 respectively.

Accordingly, the investment and the loan are both included in the company's financial statements at £1,013,514 and an exchange gain on the investment of £13,514 and a corresponding exchange loss on the loan are taken to reserves.

If the company chooses to capitalise the goodwill on consolidation and treat it as a currency asset and translate it at closing rate then, ignoring any amortisation of the goodwill for the three months to 31 December 19X1, an exchange gain of £13,514 on the goodwill will arise and be taken to reserves in the consolidated financial statements. Can the company apply the cover method under paragraph 57 of the standard and take the exchange loss on the loan to reserves?

It would appear that the answer to this question is no.

Paragraph 57 of the standard only allows the exchange difference on the borrowing to be taken to reserves to the extent that it is offset by the exchange difference on the net investment which is taken to reserves and the definition of the net investment contained in the standard refers to the net assets of the foreign enterprise.[126] As the goodwill only arises on consolidation and is not included in the balance sheet of the foreign enterprise then it could be argued that the goodwill is not part of the net assets of the foreign enterprise. This view is supported by the statement issued by the ASC on the publication of SSAP 20 which indicated that any goodwill element contained in the carrying amount of the investment in the investing company's financial statements would not be available for offset on consolidation when applying the cover method provisions of paragraph 57 of the standard.[127]

However, we believe that in such circumstances the company should be able to apply the cover method provided that condition (c) of paragraph 57 is met.

The goodwill is being regarded as a currency asset which is retranslated at closing rates. This treatment is required by SFAS 52[128] and, in our view, more logical as the value of the foreign company as a whole is likely to be based on the expected future earnings stream expressed in the foreign currency and the goodwill relates to a business which operates in the economic environment of that currency. Not to take into account the exchange differences arising on the goodwill in applying the cover method ignores the economic reality that the group is covered against movements in exchange rates.

What if the company had chosen to write off the goodwill to reserves immediately?

Again, it could be argued that the cover method cannot be applied. No asset is being recognised in the financial statements and therefore there can be no exchange differences arising thereon against which the exchange difference on the loan can be offset. However, most companies who choose a policy of writing off goodwill immediately do so as a matter of policy, not because of the fact that the goodwill has suddenly become worthless and it could be argued that the treatment of exchange differences on borrowings should not be affected by the choice of accounting policy for goodwill. We believe, therefore, there is a case to say that such goodwill, which would have been included in the consolidated balance sheet had a policy of capitalisation and amortisation been followed, can be taken into account when applying the cover method.

Examples of companies which take goodwill into account when applying the cover method are TI Group and United News & Media, as illustrated below:

Extract 8.37: TI Group plc (1996)

22   RESERVES [extract]

Currency translation included within total recognised gains and losses comprised negative movements in respect of overseas investments, inclusive of goodwill, of £130.1m (1995 £17.2m positive) and positive movements of £27.2m (1995 £7.2m negative) in respect of foreign currency financing of those investments.

Extract 8.38: United News & Media plc (1996)

Foreign currencies [extract]

Differences arising on the restatement of investment, including goodwill, in foreign subsidiary undertakings and related net foreign currency borrowings and from the results of those companies at average rate, are taken to reserves, and are reported in the statement of total recognised gains and losses.

3.5.5 All investments/borrowings?

Companies may have more than one foreign currency investment which have been financed, or are hedged by, more than one foreign currency borrowing. The question may then arise, can a company apply the cover method for some investments/borrowings and not apply it for others?

Example 8.34

On 30 September 19X1 a UK company acquires all the equity share capital of two foreign companies as follows:

(i)   A German company at a cost of DM3m financed by a loan of DM3m repayable in five years' time.

(ii) A US company at a cost of US$1,630,000 financed by a loan of US$1,630,000 repayable in five years' time.

The company wishes to apply the cover method to the German investment and related loan but not to apply it to the US investment and related loan in its financial statements for the year ended 31 December 19X1. Is such a treatment possible under SSAP 20?

The relevant exchange rates are:

	£1=DM	£1=US$
30 September 19X1	3.00	1.63
31 December 19X1	2.96	1.88

The effect of such a treatment is as follows:

		P/L account £	Reserves £
Exchange differences			
Investments			
– DM 3,000,000	@ DM3.00 = £1,000,000		
	@ DM2.96 = £1,013,514		
	———————		13,514
– US$1,630,000	@ US$1.63 = £1,000,000		
	@ US$1.63 = £1,000,000		
	———————		–
Loans			
– DM 3,000,000	@ DM3.00 = £1,000,000		
	@ DM2.96 = £1,013,514		
	———————		(13,514)
– US$1,630,000	@ US$1.63 = £1,000,000		
	@ US$1.88 = £ 867,021		
	———————	132,979	–
		————	————
		132,979	–
		————	————

It can be seen that by applying the cover method to the German investment/loan only the exchange gain on the US$ loan has been taken to profit and loss account whereas the exchange loss on the DM loan has been taken to reserves offset by a corresponding exchange gain on the net investment. It would appear that this is allowed by SSAP 20, as paragraph 51 states that the equity investments *may* be denominated in foreign currencies. It must be emphasised, however, that where exchange losses on the investments are arising but are not being recognised consideration has to be given as to whether a provision for permanent diminution in value is necessary. Paragraph 57 in dealing with the consolidated financial statements is equally permissive as it states that the exchange differences on the borrowings *may* be offset as reserve movements. If in the above example the net assets of the US company at the date of acquisition were equivalent to the price paid then although an exchange loss of £132,979 would be taken to group reserves, the company could continue to take the exchange gain on the loan to the profit and loss account.

It has been suggested that the final condition of paragraphs 51 and 57 requires companies to apply the cover method to all matched investments.[129] The final condition requires companies to apply the same accounting policy from *period to period* and therefore this suggestion seems to be a rather broad interpretation of the provisions. Nevertheless, we believe it is preferable for companies to adopt the same policy for all matched investments.

3.5.6   Must currencies be the same?

All of the previous examples which we have considered have been based on situations where the investment and the related borrowing have been expressed in the same foreign currency. The provisions of the standard actually make no reference to the currencies of the borrowings or the investments, and consequently it is not necessary for this to be the case. ED 27 included such a restriction but this was removed 'since a number of commentators considered it to be unacceptably rigid, particularly having regard to the wide variety of loan arrangements available and to the multi-currency nature of many of them. Since the alternative of a complete offset of currencies would allow too much freedom and carry the risk of imprudent accounting, a compromise solution has been adopted. The offset is now permitted only to the extent that the underlying foreign currency borrowings do not exceed the amount of cash expected to be generated by the net investments, either from profits or otherwise. ASC considers that this restriction should ensure that offset is permitted only when there is genuine cover for the related exchange gains and losses, whilst at the same time recognising the realities of treasury management.'[130]   Specific problems relating to this compromise solution are addressed at 3.5.8 and 3.5.9 below.

An illustration of the cover method provisions where the currencies are not the same can be seen in the following example:

Example 8.35

On 1 January 19X1 a UK company acquires an equity investment in a Dutch company at a cost of DFl 4,700,000 and finances the acquisition by borrowing 73,400,000 Belgian francs repayable in seven years' time. Based on the exchange rates at that date both amounts are equivalent to £1,000,000. By applying the cover method in SSAP 20 the amounts of the investment and the borrowing in the financial statements for each of the years ended 31 December up until 19X6 would be as follows:

| | Investment | | Borrowing | |
	£1=DFl	£	£1=BF	£
31 December 19X1	4.25	1,105,882	75.6	970,899
31 December 19X2	4.45	1,056,180	80.8	908,416
31 December 19X3	4.13	1,138,015	73.4	1,000,000
31 December 19X4	3.99	1,177,945	72.4	1,013,812
31 December 19X5	3.25	1,446,154	59.5	1,233,613
31 December 19X6	3.34	1,407,186	62.0	1,183,871

The treatment of exchange differences under the cover method would be as follows:

	Investment Reserves	Borrowing	
		Reserves	P/L account
	£	£	£
31 December 19X1	105,882	–	29,101
31 December 19X2	(49,702)	49,702	12,781
31 December 19X3	81,835	(81,835)	(9,749)
31 December 19X4	39,930	(13,812)	–
31 December 19X5	268,209	(219,801)	–
31 December 19X6	(38,968)	38,968	10,774
	407,186	(226,778)	42,907

In 19X1 as both the investment and the borrowing are showing exchange gains then none of the exchange gain in the borrowing can be offset in reserves and therefore all of the gain must be taken to the profit and loss account.

In 19X2 although there is a total exchange gain on the borrowing of £62,483, only £49,702 can be offset in reserves as that is the extent of the exchange loss on the investment. The balance of £12,781 has to be taken to the profit and loss account.

Similarly, in 19X3 the exchange loss which is capable of being offset is limited. No account can be taken of the previous exchange gains on the investment which are sitting in reserves. It is only the exchange difference arising in the year which can be used in the offset process. It can be seen from the figures for 19X2 and 19X3 that this applies whether or not the exchange difference on the borrowing is a gain or a loss.

In 19X4 and 19X5 all of the exchange loss on the borrowing can be offset in reserves. In 19X6 the exchange gain on the borrowing is restricted as it was in 19X2.

It can be seen from the above example that when the cover method contained in SSAP 20 is used in circumstances where the investment and borrowings are in different currencies it can lead to inconsistent treatment of the exchange differences on the borrowing. In the above example in three of the years part of the exchange difference is taken to reserves and part to the profit and loss account. In two of the years all of the difference is taken to reserves and in the other year all of the difference is taken to profit and loss account. In our view this makes a nonsense of the consistency concept.

Another weakness of the cover method when different currencies are involved can be illustrated by the following example:

Example 8.36

A UK company has a Spanish subsidiary. At 31 December 19X0 the net assets of the subsidiary are Ptas222m. On 1 January 19X1 the company decides to double its investment in the Spanish company by investing a further Ptas222m and borrows 2,980,000 Swiss francs repayable in five years' time.

The relevant exchange rates are as follows:

	£1=Ptas	£1=SFr
31 December 19X0 and 1 January 19X1	222	2.98
31 December 19X1	196	2.40

Using the cover method, the financial statements would reflect the following treatment for the resulting exchange differences:

Exchange gain on investment

Ptas444m	@ 222 = £2,000,000	
	@ 196 = £2,265,306	
	———	£265,306

Exchange loss on borrowing

SFr2,980,000	@ 2.98 = £1,000,000	
	@ 2.40 = £1,241,666	
	———	(241,666)

Net gain taken to reserves	£ 23,640

The cover method allows all of the exchange difference on the investment to be used in the offset process. However, the result of the decision to finance the extra investment by the Swiss loan has been:

Gain on increased investment of Ptas222m	£132,653
Loss on Swiss loan	(241,666)
	£(109,013)

Although a net loss has arisen as a result of the decision no loss is reflected in the profit and loss account.

The above examples demonstrate that the cover method of SSAP 20 does not produce sensible results which reflect the economic substance of the transactions when different currencies are involved.

In our view proper cover can only exist if the risk of exposure to currency movements is removed. This can only happen if the borrowings, which are providing the hedge, are in the same currency as the investment. One of the arguments put forward by the ASC for removing the restriction of having the same currency was that it was too rigid 'particularly having regard to the wide variety of loan arrangements available and to the multi-currency nature of many of them'.[131] We consider the fact that companies can borrow in most of the major foreign currencies means that having a requirement for the same currency would not be too rigid because they can arrange to have the borrowings in the currency they want in order to provide effective cover against their investments.

Another criticism of the cover method in SSAP 20 is that 'the position taken by the ASC is that if there is a gain on a net investment and a loss on borrowings, then ex-post facto there has been cover; if there has been a gain on both or a loss on both, then there has been no cover. The basic flaw here is that cover by its very nature – to remove the risk – is a matter of premeditated intent. Evidence of this intent is a key feature of SFAS 52's approach to cover.'[132]

SFAS 52 requires that exchange gains and losses on transactions that are designated as, and are effective as, economic hedges of a net investment in a foreign entity shall not be included in the profit and loss account but shall be reported in the same manner as the translation adjustments relating to the net investment.[133] Ordinarily, a transaction that hedges a net investment should be denominated in the same currency as the net investment. SFAS 52 recognises that it may not be practical or feasible for this to be the case and, therefore, in these situations allows the hedging transaction to be in a currency which generally moves in tandem with the currency of the net investment.[134]

3.5.7 Pooled basis?

Where companies have a number of investments financed by a number of borrowings, how should the cover method be applied? Should it be applied on a pooled basis, i.e. by aggregating all the investments and all the borrowings and comparing the net exchange difference on each; or should it be done on an individual basis if specific borrowings can be identified or on a currency by currency basis?

Depending on how it is done different treatments are likely to arise. We can see this from the following example:

Example 8.37

A UK company has two wholly owned foreign subsidiaries, a Canadian company and a Japanese company. The net investments in these subsidiaries at 31 December 19X0 are C$4.5m and ¥300m respectively. The original investments in these companies were financed by borrowings of C$3m and ¥400m respectively. How should the company apply the cover method in its consolidated financial statements for the year ended 31 December 19X1?

The relevant exchange rates are:

	£1=C$	£1=¥
31 December 19X0	2.05	235
31 December 19X1	2.45	229

		(i) P/L account £	(i) Reserves £	(ii) Reserves £
Exchange difference on investments				
Canadian company				
– C$4.5m	@ 2.05 = £2,195,122			
	@ 2.45 = £1,836,735			
			(358,387)	(358,387)
Japanese company				
– ¥300m	@ 235 = £1,276,596			
	@ 229 = £1,310,044			
			33,448	33,448
				(324,939)
Exchange difference on borrowings				
Canadian dollar loan				
– C$3m	@ 2.05 = £1,463,415			
	@ 2.45 = £1,224,490			
			238,925	238,925
Japanese yen loan				
– ¥400m	@ 235 = £1,702,128			
	@ 229 = £1,746,725			
		(11,149)	(33,448)	(44,597)
				194,328
		(11,149)	(119,462)	(130,611)

Method (i) has applied the cover method by regarding the investments/borrowings as being in two separate pools of currencies. As a result, that part of the loss on the yen loan which has not been covered by exchange gains on the yen investments has been taken to the profit and loss account.

Method (ii) has taken a global approach and as there are sufficient net losses on the investments to offset the net gains on the borrowings then all of the exchange differences can be offset to reserves.

It has been suggested that SSAP 20 requires an aggregate basis as illustrated in method (ii). The reason is that companies usually manage their treasuries on a pool basis and finance groups of investments with the basket of loans, often in different currencies.[135] In our view companies are permitted to apply the cover method on an individual basis or a currency by currency pool basis, as illustrated in method (i) above. We believe that such a basis is preferable as it is only when the currencies are the same that proper cover exists.

The global approach will have the same effect where all the investments in each particular currency exceed the amount of the borrowings in each particular currency. However, where there may be a shortfall of investments in any particular currency when compared to borrowings in the same currency, the global approach has the effect of regarding the excess borrowings as providing a hedge against investments in different currencies.

Whichever method is used it should be applied consistently from period to period.

3.5.8 What is meant by condition (b) of paragraph 51 and condition (c) of paragraph 57?

These conditions require that the foreign currency borrowings used in the offset process should not exceed the total amount of cash that the investments are expected to be able to generate, whether from profits or otherwise. As explained in 3.5.6 above the reason for this condition was to allow the cover method to be used when different currencies were involved. No guidance is given in the standard as to how such amount of cash should be determined. How should these conditions therefore be applied?

Example 8.38

A UK company acquires an equity investment in a Dutch company at a cost of DFl 4m on 1 January 19X1. During 19X0 the company had taken out a loan of 13 million French francs repayable in five years' time with a view to investing in a French company. However, this investment was never made and the company was left with the loan. In preparing its financial statements for the year ended 31 December 19X1 the company wishes to regard the French franc loan as providing a hedge against the Dutch investment and apply the cover method. How should this be done?

The relevant exchange rates are:

	£1=DFl	£1=FFr
31 December 19X0		10.85
1 January 19X1	3.99	
31 December 19X1	3.25	9.46

Exchange differences

Investment – DFl 4m	@ 3.99 = £1,002,506	
	@ 3.25 = £1,230,769	
Exchange gain	—————	£228,263
Loan – FFr13m	@ 10.85 = £1,198,157	
	@ 9.46 = £1,374,207	
Exchange loss	—————	£(176,050)

By just applying condition (a) of paragraph 51 of the standard it would seem that all of the exchange loss on the loan can be taken to reserves as there are sufficient exchange gains on the investment available for offset.

However, what about condition (b)? How should the amount of cash which the investment is expected to generate be determined?

(i) It could be argued that it should be calculated as being the amount that would be raised if the investment were sold immediately.

If this is equivalent to its book value at the year end, i.e. £1,230,769, then as the loan exceeds this amount it could be argued that the cover method cannot be applied and therefore all of the exchange loss on the loan of £176,050 should be taken to the profit and loss account and the investment should be recorded at the historical rate; i.e. £1,002,506. Alternatively, it could be argued that a proportion of the loan can be used in the offset process to the extent that it is covered by the value of the investment. This means that FFr11,643,074 (£1,230,769 @ £1=FFr9.46) can be used in the process. The exchange loss on this amount is £157,675 and it is this amount which can be taken to reserves. The remainder of the exchange loss on the loan of £18,375 would be taken to the profit and loss account. We believe the latter approach is the more appropriate treatment.

What if the amount at which the investment could be sold is in excess of its book value? It may be that the investment is now worth DFl 4.5m which is equivalent to £1,384,615. It would appear that in these circumstances all of the exchange loss on the borrowing can be offset in reserves, even although the financial statements do not reflect the fact that the borrowings are covered. On the grounds of prudence, we believe it would be preferable to use the carrying value of the investment.

(ii) It could be argued that it is not necessary to consider an immediate sale of the investment, particularly as it is unlikely that such a course of action is the intention of the investing company, but that regard should be given to future profits which will result in further dividends being received or an increase in the amount ultimately received when the investment is sold. No guidance is given at all in the standard as to the period over which profits are to be taken into account. In view of the impracticalities of forecasting future dividend streams and ultimate sale proceeds, we believe that companies in applying these provisions should consider the cash proceeds which would be received from the immediate sale of the investment as in (i) above. If a future sale and future dividends have to be taken into account then consideration should also be given to the future interest expense which will be incurred on the borrowing.

Where the currencies are the same, in most situations condition (b) of paragraph 51 and condition (c) of paragraph 57 are irrelevant. This is because of the requirement that exchange differences on the borrowings can only be offset in reserves to the extent that there are corresponding exchange differences on the related investment. This ensures that full cover will only arise if the carrying value of the investment is at least equivalent to the amount of the borrowings. If the investment will not generate cash equivalent to the amount of the borrowings then provision should be made against the carrying value of the investment. This means that the amount of exchange differences on the net investment will correspondingly be less and therefore the exchange differences on the borrowings which exceed that amount will have to be taken to the profit and loss account.

However, even where the currencies are the same, problems can arise in the year the conditions are not met.

3.5.9 *What should happen in the year of change of the above conditions not being met?*

A   *Investment making losses*

Example 8.39

A UK company has a wholly owned Japanese subsidiary which it set up several years ago at a cost of ¥1,000m. Up until 19X0 the subsidiary was profitable and on 1 January 19X1 the company borrowed ¥1,000m repayable in four years' time to provide a hedge against its investment. During 19X1 the subsidiary began to make losses such that at 31 December 19X1 the net assets of the subsidiary had been reduced to ¥1,000m. In its financial statements for the year ended 31 December 19X1 the company applied the cover method and exchange losses of £1,234,043 were offset in reserves. At that date, exchange gains on the investment included in the company and consolidated reserves were £1,875,000 and £2,500,000 respectively. In the year to 31 December 19X2 the subsidiary has made further losses of ¥400m but it is now considered that the losses have been stemmed and that the subsidiary will break even in the next three years. The results of the subsidiary are translated using closing rates. Assuming that the net asset value at 31 December 19X2 is considered to be the cash expected to be generated by the investment, how should the cover method be applied in the financial statements for the year ended 31 December 19X2?

The relevant exchange rates are:

	£1=¥
31 December 19X1	235
31 December 19X2	229

Exchange differences

Investment – ¥1,000m	@ 235 = £4,255,319	
	@ 229 = £4,366,812	
	————	£111,493
Loan – ¥1,000m	@ 235 = £4,255,319	
	@ 229 = £4,366,812	
	————	£(111,493)

As the exchange loss on the loan is matched by the exchange gain on the investment it would appear that none of the exchange loss on the loan need be taken to profit and loss account. However, as the cash expected to be generated from the investment is only ¥600m then this condition has to be considered. The possible effects of this on the cover method are as follows:

(a) Abandon the cover method with retrospective effect.

It could be argued that as the amount of the loan exceeds the cash expected to be generated then the cover method cannot be applied and therefore this year's exchange loss on the loan should be reflected in the profit and loss account for the year. The previous exchange losses on the loan cannot be taken through the profit or loss account for the year as a result of FRS 3, but if necessary should be transferred to retained profits. In the company financial statements the investment should be translated at historical rates and the exchange gains of £1,875,000 on the investment reversed. This reflects the position which would have been shown if the cover method had not been applied. A prior year adjustment is inappropriate as it is a change in circumstances which has given rise to the cover method not being used.

(b) Abandon the cover method for the current year and thereafter.

As in (a), this year's exchange loss on the loan should be reflected in the profit and loss account. However, as the company was hedged last year, the company's financial statements should still reflect that fact. The investment would not be restated at historical rates but a provision of £1,635,232 would be made against last year's carrying value for the investment to reduce it to ¥600m @ £1=229, i.e. £2,620,087.

(c) Apply the cover method for the current year but abandon it thereafter.

The calculation of exchange differences is based on opening figures for the investment and the loan. At that time the cash expected from the investment was sufficient to meet the loan, and accordingly the cover method can still be applied and therefore all of the exchange loss on the loan can be taken to reserves. However, provision would have to made in the company's financial statements to reduce the retranslated cost of investment of £4,366,812 to its recoverable amount of £2,620,087.

(d) Apply the cover method to the amount recoverable.

This treatment considers that in applying the cash restriction the loan is effectively split into two parts: (i) an amount equivalent to the cash expected to be generated and (ii) the excess over this amount. The first part is still considered to hedge the investment and the cover method can still be applied to that part. The second part is no longer providing a hedge against any investment and therefore any exchange differences relating to this part must be taken to profit and loss account. In this example, therefore, the treatment would be as follows:

Exchange gain on investment (as above)		£111,493
Exchange loss on restricted loan		
¥600m	@ 235 = £2,553,191	
	@ 229 = £2,620,087	
		(66,896)
Net exchange gain taken to reserves		£ 44,597

The exchange loss on the remainder of the loan, of £44,597, would be taken to the profit and loss account. In the company's financial statements a provision of £1,746,725 would be made to reduce the retranslated cost of investment to its recoverable amount as in (c) above.

In our view all of these treatments are acceptable under the standard but we believe that method (d) is preferable as this recognises that the company is still hedged to a certain extent.

B   Respective currency movements

We indicated earlier that the reason for condition (b) of paragraph 51 and condition (c) of paragraph 57 of the standard was to allow the cover method to be used when different currencies were involved. Although companies may decide to invest in one currency and borrow in another with the expectation or hope that they will generally move in tandem in relation to sterling, this will not always be the case. In any period some currencies will strengthen in relation to sterling and others will weaken and of those that move in the same direction the extent to which they strengthen or weaken can be markedly different. As a result, the cash restriction conditions may become relevant where they have not been before.

Example 8.40

On 1 January 19X0 a UK company invests in a German company at a cost of DM3,540,000. How should the company apply the cover method in its financial statements for the year ended 31 December 19X0 if it financed the investment with (a) a loan of 3,990,000 Dutch guilders or (b) a loan of 290 million Japanese yen ?

The relevant exchange rates are:

	£1=DM	£1=DFl	£1=¥
1 January 19X0	3.54	3.99	290
31 December 19X0	2.86	3.25	235

	(a) £	(b) £
Exchange gain on investment		
DM3,540,000 @ 3.54 = £1,000,000		
@ 2.86 = £1,237,762		
	237,762	237,762
Exchange loss on loan		
(a) DFl 3,990,000 @ 3.99 = £1,000,000		
@ 3.25 = £1,227,692		
	(227,692)	
(b) ¥290m @ 290 = £1,000,000		
@ 235 = £1,234,043		
		(234,043)
	10,070	3,719

It can be seen that in both cases that the hedging has been successful and the cover method can be applied.

We now look at the position in the financial statements for the following year, 19X1. The relevant exchange rates at the year end are £1=DM2.97=DFl 3.33=¥229.

	(a)	(b)
	£	£

Exchange loss on investment
DM3,540,000   @ 2.86 = £1,237,762
                @ 2.97 = £1,191,919

	(a)	(b)
	(45,843)	(45,843)

Exchange difference on loan
(a) DFl 3,990,000 @ 3.25 = £1,227,692
                   @ 3.33 = £1,198,198

	29,494	

(b) ¥290m   @ 235 = £1,234,043
               @ 229 = £1,266,376

		(32,333)

It can be seen that in the case of the DFl loan condition (a) of paragraph 51 of the standard is met and therefore it would appear that the cover method can be applied. However, if the book value of the investment is considered to be the recoverable amount of the investment then condition (b) has to be considered as the book value of £1,191,919 is less than the amount of the loan which is £1,198,198.

This is due to the fact that although both currencies have weakened in relation to sterling the DM has weakened more than the DFl.

In the case of the yen loan the cover method cannot be applied as there are exchange losses on both the investment and the loan. This is because the currencies have moved in opposite directions in relation to sterling with the yen continuing to strengthen. Again, consideration has to be given to the effect of condition (b) as this loan is even more clearly not covered by the amount of the investment.

The possible treatments of condition (b) are those which were considered in the previous example. In the case of the DFl loan in this example, adopting either of methods (a), (b) or (d) will have the curious effect of actually improving the results shown in the profit and loss account as all or part of the exchange gain on the loan will be reflected therein.

3.6   Intra-group long-term loans and deferred trading balances

3.6.1   General requirement

SSAP 20 requires that all monetary items are translated at closing rates[136] and the resulting exchange differences are taken to profit and loss account.[137] This requirement is equally valid for amounts due to or from other companies within the group.[138] Any exchange differences on these inter-company accounts would be reflected, initially, in the profit and loss account of the group company which was exposed to the currency risk. On consolidation, such exchange differences would normally remain in the profit and loss account in the same way as exchange differences on monetary items resulting from transactions with third parties.

In certain circumstances, however, a holding company may decide to finance a subsidiary with loan capital rather than equity share capital with the intention of providing long-term capital for the subsidiary. This may be done for a variety of reasons: there may be tax advantages in so doing; the subsidiary may be restricted in paying dividends but not interest payments; or it may be easier to recover loans rather than equity in the event of nationalisation of the subsidiary.

Whatever the reason, the substance of the transaction is to provide long-term finance for the subsidiary and therefore the question arises of why the financial statements should show a different result by including exchange differences on the loan in the profit and loss account when exchange differences relating to the equity finance would be taken to reserves.

3.6.2 *Paragraphs 20 and 43*

Paragraph 20 of SSAP 20 recognises this and the fact that companies may finance subsidiaries by deferring trading balances as follows: 'Although equity investments in foreign enterprises will normally be made by the purchase of shares, investments may also be made by means of long-term loans and inter-company deferred trading balances. Where financing by such means is intended to be, for all practical purposes, as permanent as equity, such loans and inter-company balances should be treated as part of the investing company's net investment in the foreign enterprise; hence exchange differences arising on such loans and inter-company balances should be dealt with as adjustments to reserves.'

The definition of 'net investment' in paragraph 43 of the standard states that 'in appropriate circumstances, intra-group loans and other deferred balances may be regarded as part of the effective equity stake'.

3.6.3 *How permanent is permanent?*

It can be seen from the above that this treatment for the exchange differences should be applied where such inter-company accounts are intended to be, for all practical purposes, as permanent as equity. How should this be interpreted?

It could be argued that if it is planned or intended to repay the inter-company amount at any time while the company is a subsidiary then it is not as permanent as equity and the exchange differences should be taken to the profit and loss account. The amount should only be considered as permanent as equity if it will be repaid only when the holding company disinvests entirely from the subsidiary. This would mean that even if a company had financed a subsidiary by providing it with a loan which was due to be repaid in twenty or thirty years' time and the intention was that this would be repaid at that time then the exchange differences on the loan during that period should be recorded in the profit and loss account. This is because the exchange differences will ultimately be reflected in cash flows.

However, it is recognised that in such circumstances this would be unrealistic and therefore a shorter timespan should be considered. It has been suggested by other writers that if there is no intention to repay the amount within the foreseeable future then the inter-company account can be regarded as permanent as equity.[139]

The term 'foreseeable future' is used in paragraph 12 of SSAP 15 – *Accounting for deferred taxation* – and, although not defined, is often taken to mean a period of approximately three to five years.[140] It has been suggested that this same criterion is used in considering whether an inter-company account is as permanent as equity.[141]

It is probably easier to regard a long-term loan which is not repayable until twenty or thirty years as being as permanent as equity. What if the loan is a short-term one which is continually rolled over? In our view, if the intention is that the loan will continue to be rolled over so that it is effectively a long-term one which is not repayable in the foreseeable future, then the loan can be regarded as permanent as equity. However, we believe that if the intention is that the loan will only be rolled over until such time as the subsidiary can repay the loan, then the loan should not be regarded as permanent as equity.

The standard also allows deferred trading balances to be regarded as permanent as equity.[142] As well as including balances arising from purchase and sale of goods and services these could also include interest payments and dividend payments which have not been paid for in cash but are accumulated in the inter-company account.

In our view, such balances should only be regarded as permanent if cash settlement is not made or planned to be made in the foreseeable future. If a subsidiary makes payment for purchases from its parent company, but is continually indebted to the parent company as a result of new purchases, then in these circumstances, as individual transactions are settled, no part of the inter-company balance should be regarded as permanent. Accordingly, such exchange differences should be taken to profit and loss account.

3.6.4   *What happens in year of change?*

It may happen that a company will decide that its subsidiary requires to be refinanced and instead of investing more equity capital in the subsidiary decides that an existing inter-company account, which has previously been regarded as a normal monetary item, should become a long-term deferred trading balance and no repayment of such amount will be requested within the foreseeable future. How should the company treat the exchange differences relating to the inter-company account in the consolidated financial statements in the year it was so designated?

Example 8.41

A UK company has a wholly owned US subsidiary whose net assets at 31 December 19X0 were US$2,000,000. These net assets were arrived at after taking account of a liability to the UK parent of £500,000. Using the closing exchange rate of £1=US$1.48 this liability was included in the US company's balance sheet at that date at US$740,000. On 30 June 19X1 the company decided that in order to refinance the US subsidiary it would regard the liability of £500,000 as a long-term liability which would not be called for repayment in the foreseeable future. Consequently, the company thereafter regarded such loan as being part of its net investment in the subsidiary. In the year ended 31 December 19X1 the US company made no profit or loss other than any exchange difference to be recognised on its liability to its parent company. The relevant exchange rate at that date was £1=US$1.88.

The financial statements of the subsidiary in US$ and translated using the closing rate are as follows:

Balance sheet	31 December 19X1		31 December 19X0	
	US$	£	US$	£
Assets	2,740,000	1,457,447	2,740,000	1,851,351
Amount due to parent	940,000	500,000	740,000	500,000
Net assets	1,800,000	957,447	2,000,000	1,351,351
Profit and loss account				
Exchange difference	(200,000)			

The normal treatment would be for this exchange loss to be translated at the closing rate and included in the consolidated profit and loss account as £106,383. As the net investment was US$2,000,000 then there would have been an exchange loss taken to reserves of £287,521, i.e. £1,351,351 less £1,063,830 (US$2,000,000 @ £1=1.88).

However, as the company now regards the amount due as being as permanent as equity it has to be included in the net investment. The question then arises as to when this should be regarded as having happened and how the exchange difference on it should be calculated. The only guidance given in SSAP 20 is in paragraph 16 which states that when applying the closing rate/net investment method, exchange differences arise if the rate ruling at the balance sheet date differs from the rate ruling at the date of subsequent capital injection. In this case there has been no capital injection as such, merely a 'redesignation' of a previous inter-company balance.

One treatment would be to regard the 'capital injection' as having taken place at the beginning of the accounting period and, therefore, the net investment increased at that date to US$2,740,000. The exchange loss on this amount is £393,904, i.e. £1,851,351 less £1,457,447, and this amount should be taken to reserves. Accordingly, all of the exchange loss included in the subsidiary's profit and loss account would be taken to reserves on consolidation. This has the merit of treating all of the exchange loss for this year consistently in the same way and it could be argued that this treatment is necessary as none of the exchange loss has any impact on the prospective cash flows of the group.

An alternative treatment would be to regard the 'capital injection' as having occurred when it was decided to redesignate the inter-company account and to take the exchange difference arising on the account up to that date to the profit and loss account. Only the exchange difference arising thereafter would be taken to reserves. At 30 June 19X1 the subsidiary would have translated the inter-company account as US$805,000 (£500,000 @£1=1.61) and therefore the exchange loss up to that date was US$65,000. Translated at the closing rate this amount would be included in the consolidated profit and loss account as £34,574. Accordingly, £71,809 (£106,383 less £34,574) would be taken to reserves.

This amount represents the exchange loss on the 'capital injection' of US$805,000. Translated at the closing rate this amounts to £428,191 which is £71,809 less than the original £500,000. This treatment has the merit of treating the inter-company account up to the date of redesignation consistently with previous years and taking the same exchange difference to reserves which would have been taken if a capital injection had taken place at 30 June 19X1. For these reasons we believe that this treatment is preferable to the former treatment although both treatments are acceptable.

Suppose, instead of the inter-company account being £500,000, it was denominated in dollars at US$740,000. In this case the parent company would be exposed to the exchange risk; what would be the position?

The subsidiary's net assets at both 31 December 19X0 and 19X1 would be:

Assets	US$2,740,000
Amount due to parent company	740,000
Net assets	US$2,000,000

As the inter-company account is expressed in US dollars, there will be no exchange difference thereon in the subsidiary's profit and loss account.

There will, however, be an exchange loss in the parent company as follows:

$$US\$740,000 \quad @ \; 1.48 = £500,000$$
$$@ \; 1.88 = £393,617$$
$$£106,383$$

Again, in the consolidated financial statements as the inter-company account is now regarded as part of the equity investment some or all of this amount can be taken to reserves. If the treatment of regarding this as happening at the beginning of the period is adopted then all of the exchange loss would be taken to reserves. This gives the same result as when the account was expressed in sterling.

If the alternative treatment is adopted then the position would be:

$$\$740,000 \quad @ \; 1.48 = £500,000$$
$$@ \; 1.61 = £459,627$$
$$£40,373$$
$$@ \; 1.61 = £459,627$$
$$@ \; 1.88 = £393,617$$
$$£66,010$$

The exchange loss up to 30 June 19X1 of £40,373 would be taken to the profit and loss account and the exchange loss thereafter of £66,010 would be taken to reserves. This is different from when the account was expressed in sterling because the 'capital injection' in this case is US$740,000 whereas before it was effectively US$805,000.

3.6.5 Is such a treatment allowed in the company financial statements?

We saw in the above example that when the inter-company account was expressed in US dollars an exchange difference arose in the parent company and how this would be treated in the consolidated financial statements. What about the parent company financial statements? Is a similar approach allowed?

Some people take the view that SSAP 20 does not permit exchange differences on loans and deferred trading balances which are considered to be as permanent as equity to be taken to reserves in the parent company's own financial statements.[143] This is because the standard only refers to such treatment when discussing the closing rate/net investment method and in defining the net investment in the foreign enterprise.[144] As a result, it is only relevant to consolidated financial statements. No allowance is made in the provisions of SSAP 20 dealing with the financial statements of individual companies for such a treatment. These provisions require all exchange differences on monetary items to be taken to the profit and loss account (except in circumstances which are not relevant here).[145] The parent company's financial statements should therefore reflect in the results the effect of the parent company being exposed to exchange risk on its inter-company account as it is a monetary item.

Another view is that the parent company's financial statements should reflect the fact that in substance the inter-company account is not a monetary item.[146] If the account is intended to be as permanent as equity then the financial statements of the parent company should effectively show the same results and financial position as if it were an equity investment. One of the objectives of SSAP 20 is to produce results which are compatible with the effects of exchange rate changes on a company's cash flows.[147] As there is no intention for the inter-company account to be repaid until disinvestment or at least in the foreseeable future then there will be no effect on the company's cash flows as no repayments are being made. Accordingly, no exchange differences relating to the inter-company account should be reflected in the profit and loss account. We believe that this is the approach which companies should be adopting.

3.6.6 If so, how should loans be translated?

Example 8.42

Suppose in the previous example the inter-company account of US$740,000 initially arose when the exchange rate was £1=US$1.25. The possible treatments would be:

(a) Translate at closing rate

The reason for this treatment is to reflect the fact that the inter-company account is a monetary item and as such should be retranslated at closing rate. However, as the exchange differences will not impact on cash flows they should not all be taken to the profit and loss account for the year but some or all of them should be taken to reserves as explained in 3.6.4 above. It could be argued that as paragraph 20 of the standard refers to exchange differences being taken to reserves that this is the treatment required by the standard.

(b) Translate at historical rate ruling when account originally arose

As the account is considered to be as permanent as equity then it should be translated as such. Equity investments should be included at the historical rate of exchange (unless they have been financed or hedged by foreign borrowings). The account would therefore be included in the parent company balance sheet at £592,000, i.e. US$740,000 @ £1=US$1.25. The difference between this and the previously recorded amount of £500,000, or the amount when it was regarded as permanent, of £459,627, should be treated as a reserve movement.

(c) Retain at the rate ruling when the account was considered to be permanent

The reason for this treatment is that the decision during the year is a change in circumstance. Accordingly, the nature of the account only changed on 30 June 19X1 and it is this date which is relevant for determining the historical rate of exchange. The account would therefore be translated as £459,627 and no further exchange difference would be recorded. (If the former treatment referred to in 3.6.4 above is adopted on consolidation then a consistent treatment in the parent company's financial statements would be to retain the account at the amount included in the previous balance sheet, i.e. £500,000.)

All previous exchange differences relating to the account should not be reversed as they arose when the inter-company account was considered to be a monetary amount.

In our view method (c) is preferable as this would be the amount included if it were an equity investment; however, all three methods are probably acceptable.

3.6.7   UK subsidiary with loan from overseas parent company

The previous sections have dealt with a UK parent considering that an amount due by a foreign subsidiary is as permanent as equity. What about the opposite situation where an amount is owed by a UK company to its overseas parent company, expressed in the foreign currency? Can similar treatments be adopted where the overseas parent company considers the amount due by the UK company as permanent as equity so that exchange differences on the inter-company account do not need to be reflected in the UK company's profit or loss for the year in its own financial statements?

SSAP 20 does not deal with this specific point. It could be argued that if there is no intention that such an amount will be repaid then any exchange differences will have no effect on the cash flows of the UK company and, therefore, they should not be reflected in the profit and loss account. To adopt similar treatments to those referred to above would reflect the substance of the transaction.

We believe, however, that the UK company has to translate the inter-company account at closing rate and take the exchange differences arising thereon to the profit and loss account. This is because the amount will be shown as a liability in the balance sheet and cannot be shown as equity until such time as shares are issued to the parent company or the parent company writes off the inter-company account as a capital contribution.

account for forward contracts which are designated as a hedge against anticipated future transactions rather than just those which are the subject of a firm commitment.

4.2   Cover method

4.2.1   Criticisms

We have looked at a number of problem areas relating to the use of the cover method in 3.5 above. In our view there are three main criticisms which can be made against the provisions of SSAP 20 in respect of borrowings which have been used to finance, or provide a hedge against, equity investments.

A   Use is optional

First, by stating that the equity investments *may* be denominated in foreign currencies [154] the standard allows companies to choose whether or not they wish to apply the cover method provisions. As a result comparability between different companies is unlikely to be achieved. This also applies to the provisions relating to consolidated financial statements as exchange differences *may* be offset as reserve movements.[155]

B   Cover may not exist when borrowings are in different currencies

Second, the absence of a requirement that borrowings be in the same currency as the investment means that cover may not exist. Different currencies may move in different directions in relation to sterling or to a different extent in the same direction in relation to sterling. Accordingly, companies cannot be assured that they will always be covered. In order to eliminate the exchange risk completely it is necessary for the borrowings to be in the same currency as the investment.

C   It can lead to inconsistent treatment from period to period

Third, by allowing borrowings to be in different currencies from the investments then the exchange differences on the borrowings will not necessarily be treated the same way each year. In those periods in which the criteria contained in SSAP 20 are met exchange differences will be taken to reserves, and in periods in which they are not met exchange differences will either all be taken to profit and loss account or some will be taken to reserves and the rest to profit and loss account.

4.2.2   Solution

We believe that SSAP 20 should be amended along similar lines to that contained in SFAS 52.[156]

A   Designation requirement

Exchange differences on transactions (including borrowings) that are designated, and are effective, as economic hedges of an equity investment or the net investment in a foreign enterprise should be taken to reserves and should not be taken to the profit and loss account, commencing from the designation date. Such treatment will ensure that the accounting for the exchange differences reflect the economic rationale of the decision taken by the company.

B   Same currency requirement with exception for use of tandem currency

The transaction which hedges the equity investment or the net investment in the foreign enterprise should be denominated in the same currency as the investment. Where it is not practical or feasible for the currency to be the same then the hedging transaction may be in a currency which generally moves in tandem with the currency of the hedged investment. Such a requirement will recognise that an effective hedge can only arise where the currencies are the same.

4.3   Conclusion

We believe that the reporting of foreign currency transactions would be significantly improved if SSAP 20 were amended as suggested above and greater comparability of results between companies within the UK and internationally would be achieved. As all of the suggestions are compatible with the existing provisions of SSAP 20 we would recommend that companies adopt such treatments presently.

5   RELATED COMPANIES ACT REQUIREMENTS

There are a number of requirements of the Companies Act 1985 which have to be considered when accounting for foreign exchange transactions. The main implications are considered below.

5.1   Realised profits

Most companies in the UK when preparing their financial statements have to comply with the accounting requirements of Schedule 4 of the Companies Act 1985.

5.1.1   Schedule 4, paragraph 12

Paragraph 12 of Schedule 4 requires that items in a company's financial statements shall be determined on a prudent basis and only profits which are realised at the balance sheet date can be included in the profit and loss account. However, what is meant by realised profits?

5.1.2   Section 262(3)

Section 262(3) of the Companies Act 1985 states that realised profits should be interpreted as 'such profits of the company as fall to be treated as realised profits for the purposes of those accounts in accordance with principles generally accepted with respect to the determination for accounting purposes of realised profits at the time when those accounts are prepared'.

The main reference to realised profits by the accountancy profession in the UK is in SSAP 2 when defining the concept of prudence. This states 'revenue and profits are not anticipated, but are recognised by inclusion in the profit and loss account only when realised in the form either of cash or of other assets the ultimate cash realisation of which can be assessed with reasonable certainty'.[157]

The normal requirement for exchange differences in the financial statements of a company is that they are taken to the profit and loss account. As a result the ASC in considering this treatment for exchange differences had to give some guidance as to whether exchange gains were to be regarded as realised or not and whether the treatment of such gains required by the standard was consistent with the provisions of paragraph 12.

SSAP 20 identifies three categories of exchange gains which have to be considered.

5.1.3 Settled transactions

First, those arising on settled transactions. As such exchange gains have already impacted on the cash flows of the company then they are clearly realised in cash terms and, therefore, their inclusion in the profit and loss account does not conflict with paragraph 12.

5.1.4 Short-term monetary items

Second, those arising on short-term monetary items. A short-term monetary item is defined in SSAP 20 as one which falls due within one year of the balance sheet date.[158] The statement issued by the ASC at the time the standard was issued said that such exchange gains could be regarded as realised in accordance with the prudence concept contained in SSAP 2, as their ultimate cash realisation can normally be assessed with reasonable certainty. Accordingly, their inclusion in the profit and loss account is not considered to be in conflict with paragraph 12.[159]

5.1.5 Long-term monetary items

Third, those arising on long-term monetary items. It is generally considered that such gains are probably unrealised. The ASC recognised this potential conflict with paragraph 12 but still decided that exchange gains on such items should be taken to the profit and loss account. It considered that a symmetrical treatment of exchange gains and losses was necessary to show a true and fair view of the results of a company involved in foreign currency operations. This treatment acknowledges that exchange gains can be determined no less objectively than exchange losses and it would be illogical to deny that favourable movements in exchange rates had occurred whilst accounting for adverse movements. As there will probably be some interaction between currency movements and interest rates then the profit and loss account will reflect the full impact of the currency involvement.[160] So how was the conflict resolved?

One way would have been to invoke the true and fair view override allowed by what is now section 226 of the Companies Act 1985. However, as the problem was with one of the accounting principles contained in Schedule 4 it was decided to invoke paragraph 15 of that schedule.[161]

This paragraph specifically permits a departure from the accounting principles where there are special reasons and it is considered that the need for a symmetrical treatment constitutes a special reason. As a result, companies which have taken exchange gains on long-term monetary items need to disclose the particulars of the departure, the reasons for it and its effect in a note to the financial statements. An example of such disclosure is as follows:

> The profit and loss account includes gains on translation of long-term monetary items. The inclusion of these gains represents a departure from the statutory requirement that only realised profit may be included in the profit and loss account. The directors consider that this accounting treatment, which is in accordance with SSAP 20, is necessary in order to give a true and fair view. The unrealised gains included for the year amounted to £10,000 (19X1–£5,000) and the cumulative amount included at 31 December 19X2 is £15,000.

A   Problem areas

In 3.2 above we considered a number of problem areas in relation to exchange gains on long-term monetary items which will also be relevant in deciding whether it is necessary to invoke paragraph 15 and give the necessary disclosures, in particular the amount of the exchange gains which are involved.

(a)   Past exchange losses

It could be argued that past exchange losses on a long-term monetary item should be ignored and that all of the exchange gain in the current year is unrealised and therefore disclosure is required of the full amount. This would appear to be an ultra cautious view.[162]

Our view is that past exchange losses should be taken into account and that disclosure is only required to the extent that the exchange gain exceeds the net losses previously recognised. Any exchange gain up to the amount of the past losses is effectively a reversal of a provision for losses no longer required. This would appear to be the approach taken by other writers.[163]

Accordingly, if the exchange gain is less than the past exchange losses no disclosure is required under paragraph 15.

(b)   Settled or unsettled transactions

As the exchange gain in question relates to an unsettled long-term monetary item then in considering the effect of past exchange losses we

borrowings as unrealised because they are covered by foreign currency assets, then it may be appropriate for the directors of the company to seek legal advice.

5.3 Disclosure

There are a number of provisions of the Companies Act which have to be considered in relation to disclosure within a company's financial statements.

5.3.1 Basis of translation

A   Schedule 4, paragraph 58(1)

Paragraph 58(1) of Schedule 4 requires that 'where sums originally denominated in foreign currencies have been brought into account under any items shown in the balance sheet or profit or loss account, the basis on which those sums have been translated into sterling shall be stated'.

B   SSAP 20, paragraph 59

This effectively extends the requirement of paragraph 59 of the standard so that disclosure of the method of translating monetary and non-monetary items by individual companies is given. Paragraph 59 only requires the method used in translating the financial statements of foreign enterprises to be disclosed.

5.3.2 Treatment of exchange differences in profit and loss account

A   Formats

The profit and loss formats contained in Schedule 4 set out the headings of income and expenditure which a company should use in preparing its profit and loss account. It will therefore be necessary for companies to consider under which heading exchange differences reported as part of the profit or loss for the year should be included. Distinction is effectively made in the formats between operating income and expenditure and other income and expenditure. Accordingly, the nature of each exchange difference will have to be considered.

B   SSAP 20, paragraph 68

Guidance is given in paragraph 68 of the standard. Gains or losses arising from trading transactions should normally be shown as 'other operating income or expense' while those arising from arrangements which may be considered as financing should be disclosed separately as part of 'other interest receivable/payable and similar income/expense'. The amounts included do not have to be separately disclosed; however, it should be borne in mind that the standard requires the net exchange difference on foreign currency borrowings less deposits to be disclosed.

5.3.3 Reserve movements

A   Schedule 4, paragraph 46

Paragraph 46 of Schedule 4 requires the following information to be disclosed about movements on any reserve:

(a)   the amount of the reserve at the date of the beginning of the financial year and as at the balance sheet date respectively;

(b)   any amounts transferred to or from the reserve during that year; and

(c)   the source and application respectively of any amounts so transferred.

B   SSAP 20, paragraph 60

These requirements are unlikely to have any major impact as paragraph 60 of the standard requires the net movement on reserves arising from exchange differences to be disclosed.

5.3.4 Movements on provisions for liabilities and charges

A   Schedule 4, paragraph 46

The requirements referred to above in respect of reserve movements apply equally to movements on provisions for liabilities and charges, e.g. a provision for deferred tax. Accordingly, it will be necessary to disclose separately the net movement on the provision which arises from exchange differences.

5.3.5 Movements on fixed assets

A   Schedule 4, paragraph 42

Paragraph 42 of Schedule 4 requires, inter alia, disclosure of movements on fixed assets resulting from:

(a)   acquisitions of any assets during the year;

(b)   disposals of any assets during the year; and

(c)   any transfer of assets of the company to and from another category of asset during the year.

Similarly, movements on provisions for depreciation or diminution in value have to be shown.

As a result of these requirements, where fixed assets are translated at closing rates it will be necessary to disclose separately the net movements arising on the cost or valuation of the fixed assets and on any related provision resulting from exchange differences.

5.4 Alternative accounting rules

5.4.1 Schedule 4, Part II, section C

Section C of Part II of Schedule 4 allows companies to include assets in the balance sheet at amounts based on valuations or current costs rather than being included at amounts based on historical costs. Where this is done there are a number of requirements which have to be followed, e.g. disclosure of comparable figures based on historical costs.

The question then arises – does the process of translating assets at closing rates constitute a departure from the normal historical cost rules and the requirements of Section C apply?

It could be argued, particularly where the cover method is being used and investments are translated at closing rates or where a tangible asset is regarded as part of a branch and translated at closing rates, that items do have a sterling historical cost and if they are included at an amount other than that cost then it must be a departure.

5.4.2 SSAP 20, paragraph 66

Paragraph 66 of SSAP 20, however, makes it clear that this is not the view taken by the standard. The translation process by itself merely translates the historical cost expressed in foreign currency at a closing rate of exchange. It does not result in a valuation of the asset or express it at its current cost. Accordingly, if it is thought that the provisions of SSAP 20 do result in a departure from the historical cost rules then it would appear that the provisions of the Companies Act are being breached. This is because the alternative accounting rules only allow assets to be included at a valuation, normally a market value, or at current cost.

6 COMPARISON WITH US AND IASC PRONOUNCEMENTS

6.1 US

6.1.1 General comment

The equivalent standard in the US is SFAS 52 – *Foreign Currency Translation*. Prior to the issue of the respective exposure drafts of both SSAP 20 and SFAS 52 there was a long period of consultation between the standard setting bodies of the two countries, together with that of Canada.

Accordingly, the requirements of SSAP 20 and SFAS 52 are both based on the same conceptual theory in that they both advocate the use of the closing rate/net investment method when dealing with the financial statements of foreign enterprises whose functional currency is different from that of the reporting currency of the holding company. Nevertheless, there are a number of differences between the two standards, of which the main ones are outlined below.

6.1.2   *Main differences*

A   *Results of foreign enterprises*

Where the closing rate/net investment method is being used, SFAS 52 requires the revenues, expenses, gains, and losses of foreign enterprises to be translated at the exchange rates ruling when those elements are recognised or at an appropriate weighted average rate for the period.[170]

SSAP 20, on the other hand, allows a choice of translating the results of the foreign enterprise either at the closing rate of exchange or at an average rate for the period.[171]

B   *Cover method*

The cover method in SFAS 52 can only be applied where the investment which is being hedged is consolidated or equity accounted.[172]   However, the hedging transaction is not restricted to being a foreign currency borrowing but can be any foreign currency transaction which provides a hedge.[173]   SFAS 52 requires such a transaction to be designated as, and effective as, an economic hedge of the net investment in the foreign enterprise. If a transaction is designated a hedge then all exchange differences until such time it is no longer designated must be taken to reserves.[174]   In order that the hedge is effective the transaction has to be in the same foreign currency as the investment or, if this is impossible to arrange, in a foreign currency which moves in tandem with that of the investment.[175]

The cover method in SSAP 20 can be applied in individual companies' financial statements to investments which are carried at cost. However, the cover method only applies to foreign currency borrowings. The method may or may not be applied to such borrowings which provide a hedge as long as the treatment is applied consistently from period to period. The borrowings need not be in the same foreign currency as the investment but the exchange difference taken to reserves is restricted to the offsetting exchange difference on the investment.[176]

C   *Forward exchange contracts*

SFAS 52 contains detailed requirements in respect of forward exchange contracts, including agreements that are essentially the same as forward exchange contracts.[177]   The accounting for such contracts depends on whether they are taken out as a hedge against a foreign currency exposure or are merely speculative. Where the contract is a hedge then any exchange gain or loss on the contract is accounted for separately from the discount or premium on the contract. The accounting for these amounts will depend on whether the contract is a hedge against:

(a)   a net investment in a foreign enterprise; or

(b)   a foreign currency commitment; or

(c)   other foreign currency exposures.

Where the forward contract is speculative then no separate accounting recognition is given to the discount or premium on the contract.

The requirements of SFAS 52 in respect of such contracts are dealt with in 3.3.1 above.

SSAP 20 contains very little guidance on accounting for forward exchange contracts. It allows, but does not require, companies to record transactions and monetary assets and liabilities using the forward rate specified in any related or matching forward contract.[178]

D   Hyper-inflation

SFAS 52 defines a highly inflationary economy as one that has cumulative inflation of approximately 100% or more over a three year period. Where a company has an investment in a foreign enterprise in a highly inflationary economy then the financial statements of the enterprise have to be remeasured as if its functional currency were the reporting currency, i.e. effectively translated using the temporal method.[179]

SSAP 20 gives no guidance as to what it means by 'a very high rate of inflation'. It suggests that where a company has an investment in a foreign enterprise which operates in a country with a high rate of inflation then the financial statements should be adjusted where possible to reflect current price levels before the translation process takes place.[180] However, UITF 9 now effectively defines hyper-inflation in similar terms to that in SFAS 52 but requires the financial statements of the foreign enterprise either to be adjusted for inflation first or to be prepared using a strong currency (not necessarily the reporting currency) as the functional currency.

E   Disclosure

SFAS 52 requires the net exchange gain or loss included in net profit to be disclosed.[181] It also requires the translation adjustments which result from translating the foreign enterprise's financial statements to be classified separately within other comprehensive income. Accordingly, the cumulative exchange differences will be disclosed.[182]

SSAP 20 does not require the net exchange gain or loss included in net profit to be disclosed. It does, however, require the net exchange gain or loss on borrowings less deposits included in net profit to be disclosed.[183]

SSAP 20 only requires the translation adjustments which result from translating the foreign enterprise's financial statements to be taken to reserves and for the movement in reserves during the period to be disclosed.[184] They do not have to be taken to a separate reserve and therefore the cumulative exchange differences will not be apparent from the financial statements.

F   *Disposal of investment*

SFAS 52 and FASB Interpretation 37 require that where all or part of an investment in a foreign enterprise is sold, or it is substantially liquidated, then the cumulative exchange differences included within other comprehensive income relating to the part which is sold or liquidated shall be included in the net profit for the period as part of the gain or loss on sale or liquidation.[185]

SSAP 20 contains no provisions as to what should happen to the cumulative exchange differences when the investment is sold or liquidated. However, under FRS 3, as the original exchange differences would have been reflected in the statement of total recognised gains and losses when they arose then they should not be recognised again in the year of disposal in either the profit and loss account or the statement of recognised gains and losses (see Chapter 22 at 2.9.1).

6.2   IASC

6.2.1   *General comment*

The relevant international standard is IAS 21 – *The Effects of Changes in Foreign Exchange Rates*. The original standard on this topic was issued in July 1983, but a revised version was published in December 1993 and is effective for accounting periods beginning on or after 1 January 1995. Although the revised standard follows the same general approach as SSAP 20, nevertheless there are a number of differences, of which the main ones are outlined below.

6.2.2   *Main differences*

A   *Results of foreign enterprises*

IAS 21 adopts a similar approach to that taken by SFAS 52 as discussed in 6.1.2 A above in that income and expense items of foreign enterprises are to be translated at the rates ruling at the dates of the transactions (or at an average rate that approximates the actual rate).[186]

As indicated earlier in 6.1.2 A above SSAP 20 allows a choice of translating the results of foreign enterprises either at the closing rate or at an average rate for the period.

B   *Cover method*

IAS 21 does not deal with hedge accounting for foreign currency items, other than the requirement for exchange differences arising on a foreign currency liability accounted for as a hedge of a net investment in a foreign entity to be taken to reserves as part of equity.[187] Other aspects of hedge accounting, including the criteria for the use of hedge accounting, are no longer covered in IAS 21 as they are being dealt with in the IASC's project on financial instruments (see Chapter 9 at 4.2).[188]

C   *Forward exchange contracts*

IAS 21 regards an unperformed foreign exchange contract as being like any other type of foreign currency transaction.[189] Again it no longer deals with forward contracts in any detail as they are being dealt with in the project on financial instruments.

As indicated earlier in 6.1.2 C above SSAP 20 contains little guidance in this area and allows companies to use the forward rate in recording transactions and translating monetary items, including long-term items.

D   *Hyper-inflation*

IAS 21 requires the financial statements of an enterprise that reports in the currency of a hyper-inflationary economy to be restated in accordance with the international standard, IAS 29 – *Financial Reporting in Hyperinflationary Economies* – before the translation process is undertaken.[190] It also requires the income and expense items of such enterprises to be translated at the closing rate of exchange.[191]

SSAP 20 only recommends that a similar approach is adopted 'where possible', although as indicated at 6.1.2 D above, UITF 9 requires the financial statements of the foreign enterprise either to be adjusted for inflation first or to be prepared using a strong currency (not necessarily the reporting currency) as the functional currency.

E   *Disclosure*

IAS 21 requires the amount of exchange difference taken to profit and loss account to be disclosed.[192] SSAP 20 only requires the net exchange gain or loss on borrowings less deposits included in net profit to be disclosed.

IAS 21 also requires disclosure of the following:

(a)   When the reporting currency is different from that of the country in which the enterprise is domiciled the reason for using that different currency. The reason for any change in reporting currency should also be disclosed.[193]

(b)   When there is a change from using the temporal method to the closing rate method or vice versa:

    (i)   the nature of the change in classification;

    (ii)   the reason for the change;

(iii) the impact of the change in classification on shareholders' equity; and

(iv) the impact on net profit or loss for each prior period had the change in classification occurred at the beginning of the earliest period presented.[194]

(c) The method selected to translate goodwill and fair value adjustments arising on the acquisition of a foreign entity.[195]

F   *Disposal of investment*

IAS 21 adopts a similar approach to that taken by SFAS 52 as discussed in 6.1.2 F above in that on the disposal of a foreign entity, the cumulative amount of the exchange differences which have been deferred or taken to equity and which relate to that foreign entity are to be included as part of the gain or loss on disposal.[196]

SSAP 20 contains no provisions as to what should happen to the cumulative exchange differences when the investment is sold or liquidated. However, under FRS 3, as the original exchange differences would have been reflected in the statement of total recognised gains and losses when they arose, then they should not be recognised again in the year of disposal in either the profit and loss account or the statement of recognised gains and losses (see Chapter 22 at 2.9.1).

References

1 SSAP 20, *Foreign currency translation*, ASC, April 1983, para. 1.
2 SSAP 6, *Extraordinary items and prior year adjustments*, ASC, April 1974.
3 *Ibid.*, para. 6.
4 ED 16, *Supplement to extraordinary items and prior year adjustments*, ASC, September 1975.
5 *Ibid.*, para. 17.
6 *Ibid.*, paras. 15 and 16.
7 *Ibid.*, para. 5.
8 ED 21, *Accounting for foreign currency transactions*, ASC, September 1977.
9 *Ibid.*, para. 30.
10 *Ibid.*, paras. 32–34.
11 *Ibid.*, para. 35.
12 ED 27, *Accounting for foreign currency translations*, ASC, October 1980, para. 92.
13 SFAS 8, *Accounting for the translation of foreign currency transactions and foreign currency financial statements*, FASB, October 1975.
14 CICA Handbook, Section 1650, *Translation of foreign currency transactions and foreign currency financial statements*.
15 SSAP 20, para. 2.
16 *Ibid.*, paras. 36–44.
17 *Ibid.*, para. 46.
18 *Ibid.*, para. 48.

19 *Ibid.*, para. 47.
20 *Ibid.*, para. 7.
21 *Ibid.*, paras. 49 and 50.
22 *Ibid.*, para. 8.
23 *Ibid.*, para. 28.
24 *Ibid.*, para. 52.
25 *Ibid.*, para. 13.
26 *Ibid.*, para. 14.
27 *Ibid.*, para. 21.
28 ED 27, para. 98.
29 SSAP 20, para. 16.
30 *Ibid.*, para. 54.
31 *Ibid.*, para. 2.
32 *Ibid.*, para. 17
33 *Ibid.*
34 *Ibid.*, para. 16.
35 *Ibid.*, para. 54.
36 *Ibid.*, paras. 53 and 54.
37 *Ibid.*, para. 22.
38 *Ibid.*, para. 23.
39 Accountants Digest No. 150, *A guide to accounting standards – foreign currency translation*, Winter 1983/84, p. 9.
40 SSAP 20, para. 24.
41 *Ibid.*, para. 22.
42 *Ibid.*, para. 30.
43 *Ibid.*, para. 51.
44 *Ibid.*
45 SSAP 1, *Accounting for associated companies*, ASC, Amended December 1990.
46 SSAP 20, para. 52.
47 *Ibid.*, para. 37.
48 Technical Release 504, *Statement by the Accounting Standards Committee on the publication of SSAP 20: Foreign currency translation*, April 1983, para. 24.
49 SSAP 20, para. 52.
50 *Ibid.*, para. 59.
51 *Ibid.*, para. 60.
52 *Ibid.*
53 *Ibid.*
54 TR 504, para. 28.
55 SFAS 52, *Foreign currency translation*, FASB, December 1981, para. 162.
56 SSAP 20, para. 46.
57 SFAS 52, para. 27.
58 *Ibid.*, para. 26.
59 SSAP 20, para. 44.
60 *Ibid.*, para. 6.
61 *Ibid.*, para. 5.
62 SFAS 52, para. 48.
63 *Ibid.*, para. 162.
64 SSAP 20, para. 49.
65 *Ibid.*, paras. 46 and 47.
66 CA 85, Sch. 4, paras. 17 and 22.
67 *Ibid.*, para. 26(3).
68 *Ibid.*
69 SSAP 20, para. 51.
70 *Ibid.*, para. 46.
71 SFAS 52, paras. 21 and 132.
72 *Ibid.*, para. 133.
73 *Ibid.*, para. 21.

74 Accountants Digest No. 150, p. 6.
75 C. A. Westwick, *Accounting for Overseas Operations*, Aldershot: Gower, 1986, p. 18.
76 SSAP 20, para. 42.
77 SFAS 52, paras. 17, 18 and 21.
78 *Ibid.*, para. 21.
79 *Ibid.*, para. 18.
80 *Ibid.*, para. 21.
81 Accountants Digest No. 150, p. 5.
82 SFAS 52, para. 17.
83 *Ibid.*, paras. 17 and 18.
84 *Ibid.*, paras. 18 and 20.
85 *Ibid.*, para. 20.
86 *Ibid.*, para. 19.
87 CA 85, Sch. 4, para. 50(5).
88 SFAS 52, para. 17.
89 Issue No. 90-17, *Hedging Foreign Currency Risks with Purchased Options*, EITF.
90 SFAS 80, *Accounting for Futures Contracts*, FASB, August 1984.
91 See Issue No. 91-4, *Hedging Foreign Currency Risks with Complex Options and Similar Transactions*, EITF.
92 SFAS 52, para. 28.
93 *Ibid.*, para. 139.
94 *Ibid.*, para. 27.
95 *Ibid.*, para. 138.
96 SSAP 20, para. 18.
97 SFAS 52, para. 12.
98 FRS 3, *Reporting financial performance*, ASB, October 1992, paras. 29 and 62.
99 SFAS 52, para. 13 and SFAS 130, *Reporting Comprehensive Income*, FASB, June 1997, paras. 17 and 29.
100 CA 85, Sch. 4, para. 33.
101 *Ibid.*, para. 12.
102 SFAS 52, para. 14.
103 FASB Interpretation No. 37, *Accounting for Translation Adjustments upon Sale of Part of an Investment in a Foreign Entity*, FASB, July 1983, para. 2.
104 IAS 21, *The Effects of Changes in Foreign Exchange Rates*, IASC, Revised 1993, para. 37.
105 SFAS 52, para. 46.
106 *Ibid.*
107 *Ibid.*
108 SSAP 20, para. 26.
109 UITF 9, *Accounting for Operations in Hyper-inflationary Economies*, June 1993, para. 5.
110 SFAS 52, para. 11.
111 Based on information published by the International Monetary Fund, *International Financial Statistics*, Volume XLIX, Number 16, April 1997. Countries which are close to the highly inflationary criteria are Burundi, Chad, Colombia, Hungary, Myanmar, Sierra Leone and Zimbabwe. There may be additional countries with cumulative inflation of 100% or more because the cited source only includes inflation data for approximately 80 countries and not all those countries have reported data for 1996 so it may be that other countries need to be considered as having a hyper-inflationary economy.
112 UITF 9, para. 6.
113 SFAS 52, para. 11.
114 UITF 9, para. 7.
115 *Ibid.*, para. 8.
116 SSAP 22, *Accounting for goodwill*, Revised July 1989, para. 41.
117 SSAP 20, para. 43.
118 TR 504, para. 21.
119 SFAS 52, para. 101.
120 See, for example, The Weir Group PLC, Report & Accounts 1996, p. 33.
121 SFAS 52, para. 144.

122 TR 504, paras. 18 and 19.
123 The London Stock Exchange, *The Listing Rules*, Chapter 6, para. 6.E.15(a).
124 Westwick, *op. cit.*, p. 22.
125 Touche Ross & Co., *Financial Reporting and Accounting Manual*, Fourth Edition, London, Dublin and Edinburgh: Butterworths, 1994, p. 339, and N. Spinney, *The Accountant's Magazine*, May 1983, p. 178.
126 SSAP 20, para. 43.
127 TR 504, para. 21.
128 SFAS 52, para. 101.
129 Accountants Digest No. 150, p. 7.
130 TR 504, para. 18.
131 *Ibid.*
132 D. Hegarty, *Accountancy*, November 1983, p. 147.
133 SFAS 52, para. 20.
134 *Ibid.*, para. 130.
135 Accountants Digest No. 150, p. 7.
136 SSAP 20, para. 48.
137 *Ibid.*, para. 49.
138 *Ibid.*, para. 12.
139 See Westwick, *op. cit.*, p. 99 and J. Carty, *Foreign Currency Accounting – A practical guide for 1982 financial statements*, pp. 21 and 22.
140 SSAP 15, *Accounting for deferred tax*, ASC, Amended December 1992, appendix, para. 4.
141 Carty, *op. cit.*, pp. 21 and 22.
142 SSAP 20, para. 20.
143 See Accountants Digest No. 150, p. 16 and Westwick, *op. cit.*, p. 99.
144 SSAP 20, paras. 20 and 43.
145 *Ibid.*, paras. 46–51.
146 Touche Ross, *op. cit.*, p. 333.
147 SSAP 20, para. 2.
148 Westwick, *op. cit.*, p. 101.
149 Accountants Digest No. 150, p. 15.
150 SFAS 52, para. 25.
151 *Ibid.*, para. 12.
152 SSAP 20, paras. 46 and 48.
153 *Ibid.*, para. 42.
154 *Ibid.*, para. 51.
155 *Ibid.*, para. 57.
156 SFAS 52, paras. 20, 128 and 130.
157 SSAP 2, para. 14(d).
158 SSAP 20, para. 44.
159 TR 504, para. 10.
160 *Ibid.*, para. 11.
161 *Ibid.*, para. 12.
162 Westwick, *op. cit.*, p. 77.
163 *Ibid.* and Accountants Digest No. 150, p. 32.
164 CA 85, s 264.
165 TR 504, para. 32.
166 *Ibid.*, para. 33(a).
167 *Ibid.*, para. 32.
168 SSAP 20, para. 36.
169 *Ibid.*, para. 53.
170 SFAS 52, para. 12.
171 SSAP 20, para. 54.
172 This is due to the definition of 'foreign entity' in SFAS 52, para. 162.
173 SFAS 52, para. 20(a).
174 *Ibid.*
175 *Ibid.*, para. 130.

176 SSAP 20, paras. 51 and 58.
177 SFAS 52, paras. 17–20.
178 SSAP 20, paras. 46 and 48.
179 SFAS 52, para. 11.
180 SSAP 20, para. 26.
181 SFAS 52, para. 30.
182 *Ibid.*, paras. 13 and 31.
183 SSAP 20, para. 60(a).
184 *Ibid.*, paras. 54 and 60(b).
185 SFAS 52, para. 14 and FASB Interpretation No. 37, para. 2.
186 IAS 21, para. 30(b).
187 *Ibid.*, para. 19.
188 *Ibid.*, para. 2.
189 *Ibid.*, para. 8(c).
190 *Ibid.*, para. 36.
191 *Ibid.*, para. 30(b).
192 *Ibid.*, para. 42(a).
193 *Ibid.*, para. 43.
194 *Ibid.*, para. 44.
195 *Ibid.*, para. 45.
196 *Ibid.*, para. 37.

Chapter 9   Financial instruments

1   INTRODUCTION

1.1   Background

The development of sophisticated financial markets, which permit companies to trade in previously uninvented contracts and thereby transform their risk profile, is perhaps the new factor in business life that poses the most searching challenge to traditional financial reporting practices. The IASC, in its newsletter of December 1996, commented on the issue in these terms:

'At the roots of the need for change in accounting for financial instruments are fundamental changes in international financial markets. ... An enterprise can substantially change its financial risk profile instantaneously, requiring careful and continuous monitoring. ... Alternatively, an enterprise may use derivatives as speculative tools to multiply the effects of changes in interest, foreign exchange or security or commodity prices, thus multiplying the gains if prices move advantageously or, alternatively, multiplying the losses if they move adversely. ... Accounting for financial instruments has not kept pace with information needs of financial market participants.

'Existing accounting practices are founded on principles developed when the primary focus of accounting was on manufacturing companies that combine inputs (materials, labour, plant and equipment, and various types of overheads) and transform them into outputs (goods or services) for sale. Accounting for these revenue-generating processes is concerned primarily with accruing costs to be matched with revenues. A key point in this process is the point of revenue realisation – the point at which a company is considered to have transformed its inputs into cash or claims to cash (i.e., financial instruments).

'These traditional realisation and cost-based measurement concepts are not adequate for the recognition and measurement of financial instruments. Recognising this, many countries have moved part way to embrace fair value accounting for some financial instruments. ...'[1]

This was the forerunner of the IASC Discussion Paper published in March 1997 (see 4.2.3 below) and it lays down the challenge very cogently. Do we need a new approach to accounting if we are to cope with the particular characteristics of financial instruments? And indeed, does this approach in turn imply that we should now abandon traditional accounting methods for other areas of business activity as well? The IASC authors felt able to distinguish the two issues, but in the UK some of the thinking behind the financial instruments proposals is visibly affecting the ASB's work in other areas. However, the more immediate issue is how to improve the recognition, measurement and disclosure of financial instruments themselves, which is the subject matter of this chapter.

The ASB means to address the subject in two stages, by developing first a disclosure standard and then a standard that deals with recognition and measurement issues. It published a comprehensive Discussion Paper[2] on the topic in July 1996, which set out its long-term aims for both stages of the project, and in April 1997 it issued FRED 13, a proposed standard on disclosure.[3] This was later modified, in July 1997 by a further exposure draft proposing a different regime for banks and similar institutions.[4] The Discussion Paper envisaged that the recognition and measurement rules would apply only to listed companies and other public interest entities but that most of the disclosure requirements would apply to all entities; however by the time FRED 13 had been developed the scope of the proposed disclosure requirements had been limited to publicly traded companies, banks and insurance companies. The Board's proposals on measurement are dealt with in 2 below and those on disclosure are covered in 3.

1.2   What is a financial instrument?

1.2.1   *Definition*

The ASB has adopted the same definitions as have been used by the IASC in its equivalent project. The main terms used are defined as follows:

A *financial instrument* is any contract that gives rise to both a financial asset of one entity and a financial liability or equity instrument of another entity.

A *financial asset* is any asset that is:

(a)   cash;

(b)   a contractual right to receive cash or another financial asset from another entity;

(c)   a contractual right to exchange financial instruments with another entity under conditions that are potentially favourable; or

(d)   an equity instrument of another entity.

A *financial liability* is any liability that is a contractual obligation:

(a)   to deliver cash or another financial asset to another entity; or

(b)   to exchange financial instruments with another entity under conditions that are potentially unfavourable.

An *equity instrument* is any contract that evidences an ownership interest in an entity, i.e. a residual interest in the assets of the entity after deducting all of its liabilities.[5]

1.2.2   Examples of financial instruments

The Discussion Paper cites the following as examples of financial instruments:[6]

(a)   cash, including foreign currency;

(b)   deposits, debtors, creditors, notes, loans, bonds, and debentures to be settled in cash;

(c)   unconditional lease obligations;

(d)   shares including ordinary shares, preference shares and deferred shares;

(e)   warrants or options to subscribe for shares of or purchase shares from the issuing entity;

(f)   obligations of an entity to issue or deliver its own shares, such as a share option or warrant;

(g)   derivative instruments such as forward contracts, futures, swaps and options that will be settled in cash or another financial instrument. An example of the latter is an option to purchase shares; and

(h)   contingent liabilities that arise from contracts and, if they arise, will be settled in cash – an example is a financial guarantee.

In fact, in terms of the definitions quoted at 1.2.1 above, many of these are actually examples of financial *assets* or *liabilities*, not financial *instruments*; for example, cash or debtors cannot be described as contracts, which is an essential element of the definition, although they may arise from such contracts. The ASB paper tends to use the terms loosely rather than strictly as they are defined, which sometimes makes its proposals difficult to interpret.

Even the central definition of a financial instrument itself is capable of more than one interpretation. It is stated to be 'a contract that gives rise to both a financial asset of one entity and a financial liability ... of another entity' but it is not clear whether this means contracts that *only* have that result, such as a loan instrument, or whether it is also meant to include contracts that create financial assets and liabilities in the course of a wider transaction, such as the sale of goods on credit. The ASB paper sometimes does appear to use the term in that wider sense, but this would imply that virtually *all* contracts (other than barter transactions) would fall within the definition of a financial instrument, which is probably not what most readers would expect. This is an aspect of the project that must be clarified before any standard is finalised.

The Discussion Paper does make it clear that the following are *not* financial instruments:[7]

(a)   physical assets, such as stock, property, plant and equipment;

(b)   intangible assets, such as patents and trademarks;

(c)   prepayments for goods or services, since these will not be settled in cash or another financial instrument;

(d)   obligations to be settled by the delivery of goods or the rendering of services, such as most warranty obligations;

(e)   income taxes (including deferred tax), since these are statutory rather than contractual obligations;

(f)   forwards, swaps and options to be settled by the delivery of goods or the rendering of services;

(g)   contingent items that do not arise from contracts, for example a contingent liability for a tort judgment; and

(h)   the minority interest that arises on consolidating a subsidiary that is not wholly-owned.

The overall scope of the proposals in the Discussion Paper therefore seems to embrace the following, which is rather different from the definition of financial instruments quoted above:

■   cash;

■   other monetary assets and liabilities, insofar as they have arisen as a result of a contract rather than by some other means;

■   derivatives to be settled by the exchange of monetary assets or liabilities, but not those to be settled by the delivery of commodities or other physical assets;[8] and

■   shares, both in the reporting entity and in other entities, and derivatives giving rights over such shares.

1.2.3   *Instruments scoped out of the project*

There is a further list of items which, although regarded as falling within the definition of a financial instrument, are proposed to be excluded from the scope of the project, mostly because they are the subject of other standards or statutory rules that the ASB does not wish to disturb at this stage.[9] These are:

(a)   assets and liabilities arising under operating leases. (This makes it clear that assets and liabilities under finance leases are to be so included.);

(b)   assets and liabilities relating to pensions and other post-retirement benefits;

(c)   shares in subsidiaries and associates;

(d)   obligations to employees under employee share option and employee share schemes;

(e)   financial instruments held by insurance companies; and

(f)   equity shares of the reporting entity, and warrants and options over such shares. (This makes it clear that non-equity shares as defined by FRS 4 (see Chapter 15 at 2.2.2) are to be included within the scope of the project.)

2   THE ASB'S MEASUREMENT PROPOSALS

2.1   Current values

2.1.1   *The Board's conclusion*

The ASB has taken the view that all financial instruments held by listed and other public interest entities should be carried in the balance sheet at current values, with one minor exception. This is that movements in the value of the reporting entity's own liabilities that are attributable to changes in its own creditworthiness should be ignored. The Board intends eventually to develop an accounting standard which reflects that conclusion, but in the meantime wishes to improve the disclosure given about financial instruments, as discussed in 3 below.

The Board sees it as necessary to use current values for *all* financial instruments because any more restricted application of current values would result in asymmetries and anomalies. In its Discussion Paper, it explicitly considered four 'half-way house' options but rejected them all. These were:

■   To require current values to be used only by more sophisticated companies which actively managed their treasury exposures. This was rejected as an untenable distinction for several reasons,[10] although at the same time it is noteworthy that the Board has implicitly made a similar proposal by saying that the eventual measurement rules should apply only to listed and other large companies.

■   To distinguish between different instruments based on management's intent for holding them. The ASB has always been suspicious of management intent as the basis for any accounting distinction, and was quick to reject it in this context.[11] Again, however, the distinction does resurface elsewhere in the Discussion Paper; for example, at least one of the categories of gains and losses taken to the statement of total recognised gains and losses rather than to the profit and loss account (see 2.2 below) depends on management intent.

■   To require current value accounting to be used only for derivatives and not for other financial instruments. The Board also dismissed this because it did not represent a meaningful distinction in the context of modern treasury management practices – it is often possible to construct the same exposure from a synthesis of various financial instruments, which may involve either derivatives or non-derivatives, and it does not seem sensible that the accounting treatment should differ depending on which particular cocktail is employed.[12]

■   To limit current value accounting to derivatives and those other instruments that they are designed to hedge. This is essentially the basis put forward by the FASB (see 4.1 below), and is less easy to dismiss. It adopts the point of view that conventional accounting still works adequately for traditional forms of finance, and it is only necessary to accommodate the impact of the newly burgeoning derivatives industry. However, in the end the ASB has rejected this as well because it considers that it introduces at least as many difficulties as it resolves.[13]

2.1.2   *How to determine current values*

Any requirement to use current values presupposes that reliable valuations can be obtained. The Board is optimistic on this point, perhaps excessively so in relation to certain instruments such as non-marketable securities or those for which the market is thin. It puts forward the following principles for guidance:

'(a)   For short-term financial instruments, such as trade debtors and creditors, and for instruments, such as floating rate borrowings, whose payments are reset to market rates at frequent intervals, historical cost (i.e. the principal amount due adjusted, in the case of assets, for bad debts) will normally approximate to current value and can be used as a surrogate.

(b)   The current value of a deposit without a specified maturity is the amount payable on demand at the balance sheet date.

(c)   In other cases, where a quoted price is available, it should be used (bid price for an asset and offer price for a liability, although active market participants may use mid-market price where this reflects the price that they can achieve). Where more than one quoted price is available, the price in the most active market for transactions of the relevant size should be used.

(d)   Otherwise the entity should estimate current value based on either the quoted price of a similar instrument (adjusted to take account of the differences) or valuation techniques such as discounted cash flow analysis and accepted option pricing models. The rate used to discount future cash flows should be a risk-adjusted rate, where practicable the prevailing market rate of interest for an instrument with substantially the same terms and characteristics including remaining term, currency, time for which the interest rate is fixed, prepayment risk and, for an asset, creditworthiness of the debtor. Alternatively, an entity may discount at a rate that reflects only some of these factors and make a separate adjustment to reflect the others (particularly changes in the creditworthiness of a debtor). Changes in the entity's own creditworthiness should not be taken into account.

(e)   The method chosen should be applied consistently from year to year.

(f)   The method and assumptions used should not generally produce a gain or loss on issue/acquisition of the instrument.'[14]

2.2   The disposition of gains and losses

The Discussion Paper states that 'the Board believes that resolving the ... issue of where the gains and losses are reported is essential to measuring all instruments at current value'.[15] The ASB's tentative solution to this issue is that all gains and losses should be reported in the profit and loss account with the exception of the following, which should go to the statement of total recognised gains and losses:

(a)   Changes in the value of the reporting entity's long-term fixed rate debt and non-equity shares (except to the extent that it reflects a change in the entity's creditworthiness). Similarly, any gain or loss on early redemption of the borrowing is to be reported in the statement of total recognised gains and losses, not the profit and loss account.[16]

It should be noted that the interest cost on fixed rate debt in the profit and loss account is to remain unaffected by this valuation, which is anomalous and contrary to the ASB's general philosophy on the treatment of revalued items. For example, it contrasts with the treatment of a revalued fixed asset, where the subsequent depreciation charge is based on the revalued amount, not on the historical cost.[17] The difference can be illustrated in the following example:

Example 10.1   Treatment of interest on fixed rate borrowing

A company borrows £1m at a fixed rate of 12% for five years. At the end of the first year, interest rates fall to 8% and remain at that level for the rest of the five year term.

Following the ASB's proposals, the profit and loss account would show a finance cost of £120,000 for each of the five years whereas the balance sheet would show the liability at each year end of the remaining cash flows discounted at 8%, giving rise to the figures in the table below. As this shows, the gains and losses in the statement of total recognised gains and losses net out to zero over the term of the loan (all figures in £000s).

Year	P&L charge	STRGL movement	Total charge	Opening loan balance	Closing loan balance
1	120	132	252	1,000	1,132
2	120	(29)	91	1,132	1,103
3	120	(32)	88	1,103	1,071
4	120	(34)	86	1,071	1,037
5	120	(37)	83	1,037	1,000
Total	600	–	600		

If, on the other hand, the treatment was consistent with that used for depreciating a revalued fixed asset, the accounting treatment would be rather different. In year 1, the interest payment of £120,000 would again all be charged to the profit and loss account and, the loan would again be revalued to £1,132,000 with the increase of £132,000 being charged to the STRGL. In years 2 to 5, the interest payment of £120,000 would be divided between the profit and loss account (based on 8% of the outstanding balance) and a 'repayment' element that would reduce the balance sheet amount of the loan (the remainder). The latter element would bring the balance back to £1m at the end of the 5 year term. This is summarised below.

Year	P&L charge	STRGL charge	Total charge	Opening balance	'Repayment' element	Closing balance
1	120	132	252	1,000		1,132
2	91		91	1,132	29	1,103
3	88		88	1,103	32	1,071
4	86		86	1,071	34	1,037
5	83		83	1,037	37	1,000
Total	468	132	600			

The result this time would therefore be that only £468,000 of the £600,000 interest paid would be charged in the profit and loss account, with the remaining £132,000 charged to the STRGL. The treatment proposed in the Discussion Paper effectively 'recycles' this charge back through the profit and loss account so as to restore the interest expense to a historical cost basis.

The ASB notes that this latter treatment may be more conceptually attractive but also that it may be regarded as counter-intuitive, since it portrays the company as having a variable interest loan whereas in fact it is contracted to pay a fixed rate. Accordingly, it has opted for the former treatment for the time being. This, however, is a fundamental issue which is not confined to the revaluation of debt. If the profit and loss account consequences of marking all instruments to market are too disturbing for even the Board to accept, then it must call into question whether the proposal is well founded.

(b)   Changes in the value of interest rate derivatives, to the extent that they serve to 'convert' a borrowing from fixed to floating or vice versa.[18]

(c) Changes in the value of fixed interest rate debt investments to the extent that they 'match-fund' a borrowing (i.e. that they are in the same currency and have a similar maturity and interest basis as the borrowing).[19]

(d) Differences arising on the retranslation of a net investment in an overseas operation (as already required by SSAP 20 – see Chapter 8 at 2.4.5), and, to the extent that a derivative or borrowing serves to mitigate the translation risk on the investment, exchange differences on that derivative or borrowing.[20]

(e) Changes in the value of long-term strategic investments.[21]

It should be noted that items (b) to (d) all require judgments to be made as to the effectiveness or otherwise of a hedge, and therefore introduce some of the issues that the ASB considered that it was avoiding by proposing that all financial instruments be carried at current values rather than adopting one of the approaches it dismissed as 'halfway houses'. Furthermore, item (e), in requiring some investments to be designated as long-term strategic investments, depends on an expression of management intent which the Board was again anxious to avoid. We agree with the Board that resolving the issue of where to report gains and losses is critical to the whole marking to market basis of the future standard, but these proposals are far from convincing and must call the whole approach into question.

2.3 Hedging issues

The most difficult issue that remains to be resolved is whether some form of hedge accounting should be allowed and if so what it should be. Hedge accounting can be described as an exception routine whereby separate transactions are linked with each other for accounting purposes because one of them is designed to offset exposures arising on the other. This might take a number of forms:

■ it may link transactions that would otherwise fall in different accounting periods; for example, a company that has ordered a fixed asset from a foreign supplier for delivery in the next financial year might take out a forward contract this year to buy the required amount of foreign currency so as to fix the sterling cost of the asset;

■ it may link items that might in any case have been reported within the same period but in a way that affects their classification in the accounts, such as items taken to the statement of total recognised gains and losses rather than the profit and loss account as discussed under 2.2 above.

The ASB's discussion of hedging implicitly accepts the second of these as legitimate and focuses on the first. Some ASB members take the view that inter-period hedge accounting should not be allowed at all, but others believe that at least some manifestations of it should be permitted. Possible scenarios in which this might be applied are illustrated below:

Example 10.2   Hedging of contracted but unrecognised items

A company has an obligation to buy a certain minimum quantity of raw materials in the following financial year for a price denominated in US dollars under a take-or-pay contract. In order to fix the sterling cost of the materials it takes out a forward contract to buy dollars at the requisite time.

If no hedge accounting were permitted, the ASB's proposals would require the forward contract to be valued at the year end and the resulting gain or loss to be recognised in the profit and loss account for the period which had ended. Furthermore, in the following financial year, the purchase of the raw materials would be recorded at the spot rate for dollars ruling at the date of purchase and that amount would be recorded as the cost of the stock; any further gain or loss on closing out the forward contract would be taken to the profit and loss account. This distinction affects both the timing of recognition of the gain or loss (when the stock is purchased or when it is sold) and its classification (as a financial item or as part of cost of sales). Obviously, if the hedged item were a fixed asset rather than stock these differences would be accentuated.

Alternatively, if hedge accounting were permitted, the gain or loss on valuing the forward contract at the year end would be deferred to be matched with the transaction in the next period which it was designed to hedge. This would be consistent with SSAP 20, which presently (if rather vaguely) allows purchases to be recorded at the rate specified in a matching forward contract. Some members of the ASB would continue to permit such a treatment, whereas others would not.

Example 10.3   Hedging of future transactions

The scenario is the same as in the previous example, except that no contract exists at the year end which requires the reporting entity to purchase the minimum quantity of raw materials. However, it fully expects to make the purchase and indeed these raw materials are essential to its business. The raw materials are only available from the US, so there is an inevitable currency risk involved in the purchase.

Some of those who would have permitted hedge accounting in the first set of circumstances would not permit it in this case. In the previous scenario, the obligation was a contractual one and would have been recognised in the balance sheet and revalued to its current value were it not for what the ASB regards as a present accounting 'anomaly' in that future firm commitments are not necessarily recognised in the balance sheet. However, under this new scenario there is no contractual obligation at the balance sheet date, so this argument does not apply.

Others, however, would still permit hedge accounting so long as the requirement to purchase the raw materials could be regarded as a 'commercial commitment'. This is a notoriously difficult concept to pin down. The Discussion Paper talks of it in terms of the need for a business to continue in business for at least the short term because the costs of immediate shut-down would be prohibitive, and would therefore permit necessary purchases to support continued operations for that short term period as falling within the meaning of the expression 'commercial commitment'. This is clearly a far-fetched way of looking at healthy businesses in real life, although it is possible to sympathise with the ASB's objective in trying to limit the future period during which forecast transactions could be hedged; otherwise, there would be little to stop the company saying that it will hedge its expected dollar purchases of the next five years and rolling forward the gains and losses on forward contracts that cover the whole of that period.

The Discussion Paper also considered the possibility of hedging of existing assets or liabilities that were not carried at current value; however, if the ASB succeeds in its broader objective of requiring all financial instruments to be marked to market, then the relevance of this category will largely fall away.

3   THE ASB'S DISCLOSURE PROPOSALS

As noted earlier in this chapter, although the ASB's long term objective is to resolve the measurement issues that arise on financial instruments, its more immediate aim is to improve their disclosure. The Discussion Paper contained a number of recommended disclosures which were to be regarded as best practice pending the development of a standard on the subject. This was superseded in April 1997 by the publication of FRED 13, whose proposals are set out below.

The proposed disclosures fall into two categories: narrative disclosures, which may be either included in the accounts or relegated, with an appropriate cross reference, to the Operating and Financial Review (or equivalent statement); and numerical disclosures to be included in the notes to the accounts. In the ASB's Discussion Paper, the narrative disclosures were to be separate from the accounts and non-mandatory, but the exposure draft proposes to make them compulsory. On the other hand, the exposure draft limits its requirements to publicly traded companies, banks and insurance companies,[22] whereas the Discussion Paper intended its disclosures to apply to all companies.

As mentioned in 1 above, FRED 13 was modified in relation to banks and similar institutions by the publication on 24 July 1997 of a further exposure draft.[23] This disapplied most of the requirements in the original exposure draft so far as banks were concerned and substituted a different set of proposals. Most significantly, it acknowledged the need for different disclosures as between banks' trading and non-trading activities – a distinction that had until then been largely rejected in other recent proposals. It may be expected that companies outside the financial sector will now redouble their arguments that a similar distinction is appropriate in their case.

It is beyond the scope of this book to address the requirements of specialised industry sectors, so the banks' supplement to FRED 13 is not discussed further here. However, one consequence of the publication of this supplement was to change most of the paragraph references in the original exposure draft (by inserting many new paragraphs). Since the ASB has not published a full version of the revised exposure draft, our footnote references to FRED 13 retain the original numbering for ease of reference.

Many of FRED 13's disclosure requirements apply not only to financial instruments but also to certain commodity contracts: those for the delivery of gold; and those which, as a matter of market practice, are normally settled financially rather than resulting in the physical delivery of the commodity that the contract provides for.[24] However there is a 'commercially prejudicial' exemption which allows disclosure to be omitted in exceptional cases. This applies where the market in the commodity is illiquid and dominated by very few participants, and if disclosure of the commodity positions would be likely to move the market significantly and prejudice the reporting entity's interests. If this exemption is taken, this fact must be disclosed, with an explanation of the reasons.[25]

The financial instruments exempted from the scope of FRED 13[26] are slightly different from those proposed to be scoped out by the Discussion Paper as listed at 1.2.3 above. The main differences are these:

■ The Discussion Paper proposed to exclude shares in subsidiaries and associates. FRED 13 broadens this so as to exclude all interests in subsidiaries, quasi-subsidiaries, associates, partnerships and joint ventures and any other intra-group financial instruments, but brings back in any such interests that are held exclusively for resale.

■ FRED 13 also scopes out equity minority interests in subsidiaries and quasi-subsidiaries.

■ The Discussion Paper excluded financial instruments held by insurance companies; FRED 13, on the other hand, scopes out obligations arising on insurance contracts other than financial guarantees and guaranteed investment contracts.

■ FRED 13 also scopes out 'those take-or-pay or similar executory contracts that are financial instruments', although it does not explain this category further.

3.1 Narrative disclosures

FRED 13 says that entities should discuss their objectives, policies and strategies in using financial instruments by reference to the matters set out below.

First of all, they should describe the major financial risks that they face and their use of financial instruments in managing each of these risks, distinguishing between instruments that they trade in and other instruments.[27] This description might usefully subdivide risks under such headings as interest rate risk, currency risk and commodity price risk.

The Explanation section to the exposure draft suggests that this would usually include:

■ An explanation of how the entity incurs market price risk, cash flow risk and credit risk and management's attitude to these risks. This would entail a description of the particular markets that represent the primary source of exposure to the entity;

- A description of the entity's risk management and treasury policies, how its treasury activities are controlled (including how limits are set) and, for entities trading in financial instruments, information about market price risk and the adequacy of capital resources to support the level of activity;

- The nature of, and purposes for which, the main types of instruments are used (such as financing, risk management or hedging, speculation/trading); and

- An explanation of how the year end figures relate to these policies. If the year end position is unrepresentative of the position during the year, this should be explained and quantified.

The FRED also calls for post balance sheet information to be given showing how major financial risks have changed. In particular it calls for disclosure of the purpose and effect of major financing transactions undertaken up to the date of approval of the accounts; and the effect of any significant changes in the entity's exposures or changes in price risks on its positions up to 'a suitably practicable date' before the approval of the accounts. It also asks for some disclosure of the potential impact of interest rate changes.[28]

Entities should then disclose their objectives and policies for using the various kinds of financial instruments, and any changes in these policies from the previous year.[29] This should explain their policies, with quantification where appropriate, on:

(a) the fixed/floating split, maturity profile and currency profile of borrowings;

(b) the extent to which foreign currency debtors and creditors are hedged to the functional currency of the business unit concerned;

(c) the extent to which foreign currency net investments are hedged by currency borrowings and other instruments; and

(d) any hedging of future transactions (both those that are contractually committed and those that are not).[30]

Although predating FRED 13, GrandMet's and BOC's 1996 accounts disclose significant information about their respective approaches to interest rate and foreign currency risks, as shown in the following extracts. GrandMet's is contained in the notes to its accounts, while BOC's is dealt with in its Finance and Treasury Review.

Extract 9.1: Grand Metropolitan Public Limited Company (1996)

19 Net borrowings and risk management [extract]

(ii) Interest risk management

The group's underlying borrowings are predominantly fixed rate. The group uses interest rate swaps to manage the level of floating rate debt to a pre-defined proportion of net borrowings. In addition, where appropriate, the group uses forward rate agreements to manage short term interest rate exposures.

At 30th September 1996, the group had a portfolio of US dollar denominated interest rate swaps with an aggregate notional principal of £1,867m, which have been entered into at various times during the last five years. £640m of these contracts have the effect of fixing the rate of interest. Of these, £160m were in operation at the year end at a weighted average rate of 6.3% for a weighted average term of 1.9 years. The remaining £480m are forward starting, the earliest starting in April 1998 and the latest maturing in August 2004. These have the effect of fixing the rate of interest at a weighted average rate of 7.4% for a weighted average term of 3.8 years. £1,140m of the US dollar interest rate swaps have the effect of converting fixed to variable rate for a weighted average term of 5.9 years from the year end. In addition, £87m of the US dollar interest rate swaps adjust the payment dates and the basis of the interest calculations on existing floating rate debt. The group also has sterling denominated interest rate swaps fixing £150m of debt at a rate of 8.6% with a weighted average maturity of 3.0 years, and further sterling denominated swaps that effectively convert £1,200m of fixed rate borrowings to floating rate, with a weighted average maturity of 2.6 years.

At 30th September 1996, after taking account of interest rate swaps (current and forward starting), and currency and cross currency interest rate swaps (see below), the group's net borrowings were largely denominated in US dollars. Approximately two-thirds of the group's net borrowings bear fixed rate interest, with a weighted average interest rate of 7.5% and weighted average term of 10.2 years.

(iii) Exchange risk management

The group hedges its exposure to gains and losses on the translation of foreign currency net assets using foreign currency borrowings, currency swaps, and cross currency interest rate swaps. These swaps have the same effect as depositing sterling and borrowing, for example, US dollars. At 30th September 1996, over 80% of the group's capital employed was denominated in US dollars and, including the impact of currency swaps, the group had net borrowings denominated in US dollars of £2,304m, thereby hedging approximately 50% of the US dollar denominated capital employed.

The group hedges the translation of a proportion of its future profits denominated in US dollars using currency option cylinders which limit the translation exposure of the group's US dollar profits before tax to movements in the dollar/sterling exchange rate. For those profits hedged, the group is only exposed to exchange rate movements within a specified range. The impact of exchange rate movements outside that range is taken by the counterparty to the hedge. At 30th September 1996, these options limited the exchange impact on approximately 60% of the estimated US dollar profits before tax for the year ending 30th September 1997 to within the range £1=$1.46 to £1=$1.61. At 5th December 1996, the date of signing the accounts, further transactions had increased the proportion hedged to 80% with an approximate range of £1=$1.50 to £1=$1.60.

The group hedges approximately 80% of its estimated foreign currency transactional cash flows over an 18 month timeframe using foreign exchange contracts.

At 30th September 1996, as a result of the translational and transactional exposure cover outlined above, the group had outstanding gross foreign exchange contracts equivalent to approximately £2,780m (1995 – *£3,800m*) and cross currency interest rate swaps equivalent to £714m (1995 – *£nil*). Of the total, approximately 45% (1995 - *40%*) were to sell US dollars. They have maturities ranging to November 1999, but the majority mature within 18 months of the balance sheet date.

Extract 9.2: The BOC Group plc (1996)

Funding

The Group has borrowings in a wide range of currencies, although 80 per cent of the net debt is denominated in US dollars, Australian dollars, Japanese yen, sterling and South African rand. Foreign currency investments are hedged wherever possible by borrowing in the same currency, either by means of direct borrowings or the use of other hedging instruments such as currency swaps.

The Group maintains a mix of floating and fixed rate debt. At present, there is a 50:50 balance. As well as medium and long-term borrowings, the Group has substantial short-term borrowings, principally in the form of commercial paper. It is the Group's policy that all outstanding commercial paper is backed up by committed medium-term borrowing facilities. To achieve this, the Group maintains substantial medium-term committed facilities with a group of strong relationship banks.

Borrowings are managed with the objective to ensure that the average life of Group debt is maintained in excess of five years. During the year, the Group was able to take advantage of opportunities in the bond markets to strengthen the balance sheet by issuing medium-term bonds to replace short-term commercial paper thereby extending the maturity of its net debt.

Managing currency risk

The Group's currency risk is managed in a non-speculative manner by selectively hedging known individual business transactions and by borrowing in the currency of investment revenues where practicable and cost-effective. This has been carried out by means of forward contracts and currency swaps. The Group does not enter into any leveraged derivative transactions.

FRED 13 also includes a reminder that SSAP 2 requires disclosure of all significant accounting policies, and suggests this extensive list of matters that might require to be disclosed in relation to financial instruments:

(a) the methods used to account for derivative financial instruments, the types of derivative financial instruments accounted for under each method and the criteria that determine the accounting method used;

(b) the basis for recognising, and ceasing to recognise, financial instruments and the treatment of financial instruments not recognised;

(c) the basis of measurement applied to financial assets and liabilities on initial recognition and subsequently;

(d) the basis for recognising and measuring income and expenses (and gains and losses), including the recognition of income and expenses arising from financial instruments used for hedging purposes;

(e) the basis on which provisions are recognised for losses arising from financial instrument exposures that have not been recognised; and

(f) policies on offsetting.[31]

It is also suggested that these further policies may be relevant where financial instruments are carried at cost:

(a) the treatment of premiums and discounts on monetary financial assets;

(b)   the treatment of changes in the estimated amount of determinable future cash flows associated with a monetary financial instrument, such as a debenture indexed to a commodity price;

(c)   the treatment of declines in the fair value of financial assets below their carrying amount; and

(d)   the treatment of restructured financial liabilities.[32]

Where hedge accounting has been applied, yet more detailed policies are suggested:

(a)   the circumstances in which a financial instrument is accounted for as a hedge;

(b)   the nature of the special recognition and measurement treatment applied to the instrument;

(c)   the method used to account for an instrument that ceases to be designated as a hedge;

(d)   the method used to account for the hedge when the underlying item or position matures, is sold, extinguished or terminated; and

(e)   the method used to account for the hedge of a future transaction when that transaction is no longer likely to occur.[33]

The above list goes far beyond the level of detail disclosed by even the most conscientious companies. Reuters includes this accounting policy to describe some of its treasury activities and how financial instruments are accounted for, and most companies do not have an accounting policy note devoted to treasury activities at all.

Extract 9.3: Reuters Holdings PLC (1996)

ACCOUNTING POLICIES

TREASURY

Reuters receives revenue and incurs expenses in more than 50 currencies and uses financial instruments to hedge a substantial portion of its net cash flow. Profits and losses from hedging activities are matched with the underlying cash flows being hedged. Those relating to trading cash flows are reported as part of profit and those relating to Reuters capital expenditure programme are adjusted against the cost of the assets to which they relate.

Reuters uses financial instruments to hedge a portion of its interest receivable. Profits and losses on financial instruments are reported as part of profit for the period to which they relate.

3.2   Numerical disclosures

FRED 13 also asks for the following note disclosures to be given in the accounts:

Interest rate and currency profile

(a) An analysis of borrowings by major currency, further subdivided between those at fixed and those at floating rates. This analysis is after taking account of non-optional derivatives such as interest rate and currency swaps whose effect is to 'alter' the interest basis or currency of the borrowings (it is noteworthy that the ASB has chosen to avoid the word 'hedge' in this context). The analysis may also be net of cash and liquid resources, unless these are particularly material, and it should be capable of being traced back to the various items in the balance sheet.[34]

(b) The above analysis should exclude the effect of optional derivatives, convertible debt and other instruments that cannot be adequately reflected in it because they have unusual terms or conditions – generally those that do not provide a sufficiently close hedge to be easily incorporated in the analysis. Instead, these should be dealt with in a separate summary that explains their terms and conditions.[35] This might include such elements as the notional principal amounts involved, the rates of interest and the period for which the instrument is operative.[36]

(c) For fixed rate debt, the weighted average interest rate and weighted average period for which rates are fixed are both to be disclosed.[37]

Tesco and BG provide examples of the disclosures required by (a), (b) and (c) above:

Extract 9.4: Tesco PLC (1997)

Note 19 Financial instruments [extract]

Analysis of interest rate exposure and currency of net debt

The interest rate exposure and currency of group net debt as at 22 February 1997 after swaps was:

Currency	Total £m	Floating rate debt £m	Fixed rate debt £m	Weighted average interest rate 22 February 1997 %	Weighted average time for which rate is fixed Years
Sterling	638	436	202	9.2	6
French franc	138	30	108	6.7	4
Other	(27)	(27)	–	–	–
Net debt at 22 February 1997	**749**	**439**	**310**	**8.3**	**6**
% of net debt		59%	41%		
Net debt at 24 February 1996	813	682	131	9.5	6

The interest rate exposure of the group has been further managed by the purchase of interest rate caps with an aggregate notional principal of £70m (1996 – nil) and an average strike rate of 8.14% for the period to October 2001. The current value of these contracts, if realised, would generate a gain of £1m.

Extract 9.5: BG plc (1996)

16 Borrowings [extract]

The following table analyses the currency and interest rate composition of the Group's debt portfolio after taking account of currency and interest rate swaps.

Currency	Fixed rate weighted average period years	Fixed rate weighted average interest rate %	Fixed borrowings £m	Floating borrowings £m	1996 Total £m	1995 Total £m
Sterling	5.2	8.0	3,076	677	3,753	3,463
US$	2.9	7.1	245	75	320	352
ITL	0.25	7.5	21	–	21	–
Cdn$	–	–	–	–	–	418
			3,342	752	4,094	4,233

Tate & Lyle presents similar information in this note, but without explicitly listing the amounts of its floating rate borrowings:

Extract 9.6: *Tate & Lyle Public Limited Company (1996)*

32 Currency and Interest Rate Exposure of Borrowings

After taking into account the various interest rate and currency swaps entered into by the Group, the currency and interest rate exposure of the borrowings of the Group as at 28th September 1996 was:

	Total net borrowings £ million	Fixed rate net borrowings £ million	Fixed rate gross borrowings £ million	Average interest rate (%) of fixed rate gross borrowings	Average years to maturity of fixed rate gross borrowings
Sterling	150.9	126.2	126.2	11.1%	4.4
United States	478.6	191.1	221.0	6.6%	4.2
Canadian Dollars	70.5	37.5	37.5	5.9%	2.8
Australian Dollars	16.1	–	–	–	–
Exchange Rate Mechanism currencies	123.5	(10.2)	7.4	4.5%	4.1
Others	(5.5)	–	–	–	–
Total/average	834.1	344.6	392.1	7.9%	4.2

The analysis of average interest rates and years to maturity is on fixed rate gross borrowings and after adjustments for interest rate swaps. The interest rate exposure is further protected by interest rate caps on £10 million at 10% until June 1998, US$50 million at 6.72% until July 1999 and US$28.5 million at 6.65% until December 1999. The Group also has a BFr 1,000 million collar at 6.03% floor/7% cap commencing in January 1997 for two years.

The average sterling interest rate of 11.1% reduces to 7.2% if the amortisation of the premium on redemption of the Guaranteed Bonds referred to in Note 18 is excluded.

The Group has also entered into two flexible chooser caps which give the right to fix two six-month settings over a two year period. The first is for FFr 200 million at 6% and runs for two years from October 1996 and the second is for FFr 300 million at 6% and runs for two years from January 1997.

Subsequent to the year end the Group entered into a US$200 million interest rate cap at 9.5% until October 2000 and into a US$150 million interest rate cap at 9.5% until November 2000.

(d)   For floating rate debt, the interest basis is to be given.[38] This appears to mean identifying the benchmark rate (such as LIBOR) that the debt is based on, but not the particular margin over that rate that is payable, and it must be questionable whether this is really useful information that warrants disclosure. The exposure draft regards 'floating rate debt' as that for which the interest rate is reset at least annually, and to be consistent with this definition it says that fixed rate debt which is within a year of maturity should be included with floating rate debt for the purposes of the required disclosures.[39] This must be questionable, however, because it may give a misleading impression of the company's borrowing strategy.

(e)   If the entity holds significant interest-bearing investments (including finance lease receivables), it should give similar analyses to those described above in relation to debt (excluding any liquid resources netted off against debt under (a) above).[40]

(f)   The entity's net assets (before deducting any debt) should be analysed according to its main functional currencies and these amounts compared with the currencies of its debt. This should distinguish those net assets that are matched by currency borrowings from those that are not, and if there are material unmatched assets and liabilities they are to be further analysed according to the main functional currencies of the operations that hold them. For this purpose, matching borrowings are both those that are held within an operation whose net assets are measured in a particular functional currency and those that are related to it under the cover method of SSAP 20 (see Chapter 8 at 3.5), and should also take account of non-optional derivatives that provide a hedge.

This analysis is apparently meant to be show the manner in which SSAP 20 has been applied, so that the resulting disclosures explain the currency exposures that lead to translation differences in both the profit and loss account and the statement of total recognised gains and losses. However, neither the wording of the requirement nor the illustrative example in the Appendix to the FRED seem to achieve this successfully. The problem seems to be in the presumption that there is a total population of exchange differences that can be analysed into 'matched' and 'unmatched' categories, but SSAP 20 does not really work like this. Apart from anything else, exchange differences on the net investment in a foreign entity are taken to the statement of total recognised gains and losses whether or not they are financed by foreign currency borrowing, so they do not have to be 'matched' in any sense.[41] It therefore seems that this requirement will have to be substantially reconsidered before the standard is finalised.

Tesco discloses this analysis of its net assets and borrowings by currency, which corresponds to part of FRED 13's proposed requirement:

Extract 9.7: Tesco PLC (1997)

Note 19 Financial instruments [extract]
Currency analysis of net assets

		Financing		Net investment	
Currency	Net assets before financing £m	Effect of currency swaps £m	Gross debt £m	1997 £m	1996 £m
Sterling	**4,531**	**62**	**(797)**	**3,796**	3,562
French franc	**132**	**(55)**	**(86)**	**(9)**	–
Other	**121**	**(7)**	**(11)**	**103**	26
Total	**4,784**	**–**	**(894)**	**3,890**	3,588

The currency swaps are shown above at year end value which is equal to their current value.

Other significant financial instruments outstanding at the year end are £64m nominal value forward foreign exchange contracts hedging the cost of currency denominated purchases. On a mark-to-market basis these contracts show a loss of £1m.

Liquidity

(g)   Entities should disclose a maturity profile of the carrying amount of borrowings into those maturing in: 1 year or less; 1–2 years; 2–5 years; and after 5 years.[42] (This is similar to the existing requirement of FRS 4 (see 2.2.10 (d) of Chapter 15).) In addition, FRED 13 asks for disclosure of material committed but undrawn borrowing facilities, distinguishing those that expire within one year from those that extend beyond that term.[43] This disclosure might also go on to explain the purpose and period for which the facilities are committed and whether they are subject to annual review.[44]

British Petroleum and Bass are among a growing number of companies which disclose the extent of unutilised facilities:

Extract 9.8: The British Petroleum Company p.l.c. (1996)

20 Finance debt [extract]

At 31 December 1996 the group had substantial amounts of undrawn borrowing facilities available including £1,183 million (£2,035 million) which was covered by formal commitments.

Extract 9.9: Bass PLC (1996)

19 Borrowings [extract]

Facilities committed by banks amount to £1,265 million (1995 £1,215 million) of which £353 million (1995 £258 million) was utilised at 30 September 1996 and £391 million (1995 £376 million) was in support of the outstanding US dollar commercial paper.

Chloride gives this note about the borrowing powers imposed by its Articles:

Extract 9.10: Chloride Group PLC (1997)

24 BORROWINGS [extract]

The company's articles of association limit the external borrowings of the company and its subsidiary undertakings to an amount equal to twice the share capital and consolidated reserves.

Fair values

(h)   For each category of financial assets and liabilities, including amounts not recognised in the balance sheet, the total of the category's fair value compared to its book value. Those financial assets and liabilities that are not traded on organised markets in a standard form are to be shown separately,[45] and where fair values have had to be estimated in the absence of quoted prices, the methods used and assumptions underlying the estimates have to be disclosed.[46] If it is not practicable to estimate the values of some items reliably, it will be permissible instead to disclose the book values of such items, the reasons why estimating their value is impracticable, and information about the main characteristics that affect their value; however, this is not meant to be an easy loophole to avoid disclosure – FRED 13 makes it clear that this alternative is only available in rather extreme circumstances.[47] Where the fair value of any item is not materially different from its book value – as will generally be true for floating rate debt, or short term debtors and creditors – the book value may be used as a surrogate for the fair value.[48]

FRED 13 is not prescriptive about how financial assets and liabilities should be categorised for the purposes of the above disclosures, but the classification should take account of the nature of the item and the purpose for which it is held, which should tie in with the discussion of the use of these instruments given in the narrative section of the annual report. A typical categorisation might be between items held or issued for trading; borrowings; instruments held to manage the interest basis or currency profile of borrowings; and instruments used to hedge future transactions.[49] It is also suggested that optional and non-optional derivatives need to be shown separately.[50]

As with some of the other disclosure requirements of FRED 13, this proposal reflects the ASB's views as to the eventual measurement rules for financial instruments. Those who do not necessarily agree that it is appropriate to mark all instruments to market may be less easily persuaded about the relevance of disclosing such values.

British Telecom discloses this information about the fair values of its financial instruments in its 1997 accounts:

Extract 9.11: British Telecommunications plc (1997)

23. Financial instruments and risk management [extract]

(d)   Fair value of financial instruments

The following table shows the carrying amounts and fair values of the group's financial instruments at 31 March 1997 and 1996. The carrying amounts are included in the group balance sheet under the indicated headings, with the exception of derivative amounts related to borrowings, which are included in debtors or other creditors as appropriate. The fair values of the financial instruments are the amount at which the instruments could be exchanged in a current transaction between willing parties, other than in a forced or liquidation sale.

	Carrying amount		Fair value	
	1997	1996	**1997**	1996
	£m	£m	**£m**	£m
Non-derivatives:				
Assets				
Cash at bank and in hand	**26**	121	**26**	121
Short-term investments *(i)*	**2,974**	2,568	**2,974**	2,568
Liabilities				
Short-term borrowings *(ii)*	**221**	13	**221**	13
Long-term borrowings, excluding finance leases *(iii)*	**2,953**	3,620	**3,168**	3,874
Derivatives relating to borrowings (net) *(iv):*				
Assets	–	16	–	61
Liabilities	**11**	–	**7**	–

(i)   The fair values of listed short-term investments were estimated based on quoted market prices for those investments. The carrying amount of the other short-term deposits and investments approximated to their fair values due to the short maturity of the instruments held.

(ii)   The fair value of short-term borrowings approximated to carrying value due to the short maturity of the instruments.

(iii)   The fair value of the group's bonds, debentures, notes and other long-term borrowings has been estimated on the basis of quoted market prices for the same or similar issues with the same maturities where they existed, and on calculations of the present value of future cash flows using the appropriate discount rates in effect at the balance sheet dates, where market prices of similar issues did not exist.

(iv)   The fair value of the group's outstanding foreign currency and interest rate swap agreements was estimated by calculating the present value, using appropriate discount rates in effect at the balance sheet dates, of affected future cash flows translated, where appropriate, into pounds sterling at the market rates in effect at the balance sheet dates.

The exposure draft is rather confusing about the extent to which debit and credit balances may be netted off for the purposes of this disclosure. It says that financial assets and liabilities should generally be shown in separate categories, except that derivatives held or issued for the same purpose (such as hedging interest exposures) would be grouped together even if this involved netting off debits and credits.[51] But it also says that the fair values of unrecognised assets and liabilities should be offset only if they do not constitute separate assets and liabilities, which requires the entity to be able to enforce a legal right to make a net settlement even if any of the counterparties became insolvent.[52] The combined effect of these strictures is not easy to interpret.

Non-equity shares

(i)   For the purposes of the various analyses disclosed, entities will have to decide whether or not their non-equity shares should be included with debt. This is to be determined on the basis of whether the shares 'behave' more like debt or like equity, which in turn is to be resolved by considering whether the value of the shares moves more in sympathy with that of debt instruments or equity instruments. Thus a redeemable preference share might be classified as debt for the purposes of the analysis, but if it also included a conversion right into equity (particularly one that was likely to be exercised in the not-too-distant future) then it could be more appropriate to exclude it from the analyses of debt. Non-equity shares which are excluded from the analyses are to be 'shown adjoining the analyses and cross-referred to the information required by FRS 4 that explains their equity characteristics'[53] (see Chapter 15 at 2.2.10 (b)).

It seems unnecessarily complicated, however, to require non-equity shares to be subdivided into quasi-debt and quasi-equity categories in a way that has not been done in FRS 4. Given that FRS 4 already requires extensive details to be given as to the terms of all non-equity shares, it is really not necessary to confuse the issue by including some of the non-equity shares in the analysis of debt as well.

Instruments held or issued for trading

(j)   Entities should disclose the fair values at the balance sheet date of financial assets and financial liabilities that are held or issued for trading. If these amounts are materially unrepresentative of the position that obtained during the year, then average amounts for the year are also to be disclosed. The net gain or loss from trading included in the profit and loss account is also to be disclosed, analysed by type of financial instrument 'and also in such other way as is consistent with the entity's management of its financial instrument trading activities'.[54]

Hedges of future transactions

(k)   The ASB's distrust of hedge accounting is evident from the extent of the required disclosures where instruments have been accounted for as hedges of future transactions. FRED 13 calls for disclosure of

    (i)   a description of the future transactions, including the period of time until they are expected to occur, divided between those which are contracted for and those that are uncontracted;

    (ii)   a description of the instruments used to hedge them;

(iii) the amount of gains or losses on the hedging instruments, analysed between those used to hedge contracted and uncontracted exposures, and also between gains and losses that have been recognised but carried forward in the balance sheet and those that have not been recognised. It is also necessary to disclose the amount of these gains that are not expected to be recognised in the profit and loss account of the following year; and

(iv) the amount of gains or losses recognised in the profit and loss account that arose in previous years but were carried forward to the current year as a hedge. There should also be disclosure of any gains or losses recognised in the profit and loss account on instruments that were previously designated as a hedge but were reclassified during the year so as to lose that designation.[55]

These requirements are worded in language that reflects the ASB's views on hedge accounting; in particular, they ask for the disclosure of 'gains' and 'losses' on hedging instruments. From the point of view of the companies who use them, however, these are not gains and losses at all, but simply constitute an element of the cost of the item being hedged, and there is a significant risk that they will be misinterpreted as a result. There might even be a danger that some companies could curtail a prudent financial strategy of hedging commercial exposures through a reluctance to disclose such 'gains' and 'losses' in case they are wrongly thought to be indulging in a speculative activity. This shows that disclosure requirements are not as neutral as they may seem, but are bound up in the measurement issues that the ASB will eventually be returning to.

Market price risk

(l) FRED 13's final set of proposed disclosures is non-mandatory, to encourage experimentation in an admittedly difficult area. It calls for additional numerical disclosures to explain the magnitude of market price risk for all financial instruments and also for commodity contracts, physical commodity positions and other items that carry financial risk. The manner in which this is done should reflect the way (or ways) in which the entity manages its risk exposures, and be accompanied by narrative explanation that puts the figures in context.[56]

This disclosure should also be accompanied by

(i) an explanation of the method or modelling technique used and the key parameters and assumptions underlying the data provided;

(ii) an explanation of the limitations that may cause the information not to reflect fully the overall market price risk of the entity, including a description of leverage, option or prepayment features that may increase market price risk; and

(iii) the reasons for material changes in the amount of reported market price risk when compared with information reported in the previous period.[57]

The explanation section of the exposure draft gives a number of suggestions as to how market price risk might be evaluated and presented, but notes that each has its shortcomings and thus a combination of approaches might be more helpful.[58]

This seems a very ambitious suggestion given the already far-reaching nature of the proposed mandatory disclosures, and it seems unlikely that many companies would respond to this particular challenge.

4   COMPARISON WITH US AND IASC PRONOUNCEMENTS

4.1   US

In the United States, the FASB has been working on a complex project on financial instruments since 1986. Several pronouncements have been issued to date: SFAS 105, SFAS 107 and SFAS 119 deal with disclosure issues, while a further standard dealing with matters of recognition and measurement is in the course of preparation. These are described briefly in 4.1.2 and 4.1.3 below.

4.1.1   Definition

In 1990, the FASB issued its first standard under its financial . instruments project; this was SFAS 105, dealing with off balance sheet exposures and concentrations of credit risk. Its definition of financial instruments is rather different from that used by the ASB and IASC. SFAS 105 defines a financial instrument as

- cash,

- evidence of an ownership interest in an entity, or

- a contract that both:

    a. imposes on one entity a contractual obligation
       (1) to deliver cash or another financial instrument to a second entity, or
       (2) to exchange financial instruments on potentially unfavourable terms with the second entity, [and]

    b. conveys to that second entity a contractual right
       (1) to receive cash or another financial instrument from the first entity or
       (2) to exchange other financial instruments on potentially favourable terms with the first entity.[59]

This is a complex definition, but in fact it seems to describe the intended subject matter of the standard rather more successfully than the ASB/IASC definition does (see 1.2 above).

As the standard notes, the definition is recursive but not circular, because although it contains the term being defined (financial instrument) itself, it requires a chain of contractual obligations that ultimately ends in the delivery of cash or an ownership interest in an entity. The standard also emphasises that, when it talks about contractual rights and obligations, it includes conditional as well as unconditional rights and obligations.[60]

4.1.2 Disclosure requirements

SFAS 105 requires note disclosure of the details of instruments that expose the entity to off balance sheet risk of accounting loss – that is, those where the potential for loss exceeds the amount of assets on the balance sheet or goes beyond the amount of disclosed liabilities. The standard requires quantification of credit risk – the worst-case position that would result if the counterparty to each such instrument completely failed to honour its contractual obligations – together with details of security held to mitigate such risks.[61] On the other hand, market risk – the risk of loss through movements in market prices – is dealt with by narrative discussion rather than any attempt to quantify such loss; no worst-case can generally be measured in respect of such risks.[62]

The next standard on disclosure followed in 1991. This was SFAS 107, which requires disclosure to be made of the fair value of financial instruments, except for any where it is impracticable to do so.[63] In the latter case, entities must say why it is impracticable and also give other information relevant to an assessment of the instrument's value, such as its carrying amount, effective interest rate and maturity.[64]

In 1994, the FASB issued a third disclosure standard, SFAS 119, extending the scope of the previous two (mainly to require more disaggregation) and focusing primarily on derivatives, in particular futures, forward, swap and option contracts. It requires a distinction to be made between derivatives held or issued for trading purposes and those used for other purposes, with different disclosure requirements for each.

Where an entity uses derivatives for trading purposes, the standard requires it to disclose not just their fair value at the end of the year, but also their average fair value during the year. In addition, detailed disaggregated disclosure is to be given of the net gains and losses arising from trading in derivatives during the year.[65]

Entities that use derivatives for purposes other than trading must describe their objectives for holding or issuing them and their strategies for pursuing these objectives, explaining the classes of derivatives used. They must also give a full description of the accounting policy used in respect of these derivatives. Where the derivatives are used to hedge anticipated transactions, they must also disclose details of these transactions, the classes of derivatives used to hedge them, the amounts of hedging gains and losses deferred, and the transactions or events that will lead to these deferred gains or losses being recognised in earnings.[66]

4.1.3　Recognition and measurement requirements

In June 1996, the FASB issued an exposure draft[67] of a standard which proposed rules for the recognition and measurement of derivatives, with particular reference to hedging. This clearly built upon the ground laid down in SFAS 119.

The exposure draft proposes that all derivatives should be measured and included in the balance sheet at fair value. However, the change in value is to be reported differently in the accounts depending on the function that the derivative fulfils:

- If the derivative is designated as a hedge of a net investment in a foreign entity, the change in value of the derivative is reported in comprehensive income (broadly equivalent to the UK concept of total recognised gains and losses).

- If the derivative is designated as a hedge of a forecast transaction, the change in value is again included in comprehensive income, but then channelled through the profit and loss account in the period when the hedged transaction was predicted to be reported there.

- Otherwise the change in fair value of the derivative is to be reported in the profit and loss account. If it is designated as a hedge of an existing asset, liability or firm commitment, however, the change in value of the hedged item is also to be reported in the profit and loss account to the extent that it offsets the change in value of the derivative.

This differs from the ASB's proposal in a number of respects. Most importantly, its scope is confined to derivatives and those things that they hedge, whereas the ASB proposes that all financial instruments be included in the balance sheet at fair value; however, the FASB has made no secret of the fact that it hopes eventually to arrive at the ASB's position. The US standard has a much more developed view on hedging than the ASB has yet formed; at this stage, the ASB is still looking for inspiration on the subject. The FASB's use of a statement of comprehensive income is also very different from UK practice in the statement of total recognised gains and losses, because it envisages 'recycling' some gains and losses through the profit and loss account, which is contrary to the ASB's philosophy in the UK.

4.2 IASC

4.2.1 Introduction

The IASC has been conducting a project on financial instruments for several years in conjunction with the Canadian Institute of Chartered Accountants. Two attempts were made to deal comprehensively with the issue, in two successive exposure drafts (E40 in 1991 and E48 in 1994). However, the IASC then decided to lower its sights in the same way as other standard setters and converted E48 into a standard dealing with disclosure issues alone; IAS 32 was published in March 1995, and is summarised in 4.2.2 below. Two years later, however, the Steering Group published a Discussion Paper dealing extensively with the measurement and recognition issues and making proposals for a comprehensive standard on financial assets and liabilities. This is summarised in 4.2.3 below.

4.2.2 IAS 32 – Financial Instruments: Disclosure and Presentation

IAS 32 came into force for accounting periods beginning on or after 1 January 1996. Its main definitions are the same as those subsequently used by the ASB (see 1.2 above). The standard does not apply to interests in subsidiaries, associates or joint ventures, or to obligations arising under post-employment benefits, employee stock option or purchase plans or insurance contracts, but it is intended to be applied by all companies, whereas FRED 13 is designed to be mandatory only for listed companies, banks and insurance companies.[68]

IAS 32's distinction between debt and equity depends on whether or not the issuer has a contractual obligation to deliver cash or another financial asset to the holder of the instrument (or to exchange another financial instrument with him on potential unfavourable terms), regardless of the legal form of the instrument.[69] On this analysis, redeemable preference shares are regarded as liabilities rather than equity instruments. The classification of finance costs between interest and dividends in the income statement is consistent with the analysis of the instruments in the balance sheet.[70] While there is obvious conceptual merit in such an approach, it runs into conflict with the law in the UK; accordingly, while FRED 13 proposes that redeemable preference shares be included with debt for the purposes of the various analyses it requires, they remain classified as non-equity shares for balance sheet purposes.

The standard also differs from UK practice and FRED 13 by requiring 'split accounting' (as described in 2.2.2 of Chapter 15) for hybrid instruments such as convertible bonds. In other words, the proceeds of issue of such a bond have to be allocated between the amount that represents a straight financial liability and the element which represents an equity instrument.[71]

In presenting related amounts in the balance sheet, IAS 32 requires the reporting entity to net off a financial asset against a financial liability only when it has a legally enforceable right of set-off and intends to settle the two amounts either on a net basis or simultaneously.[72] Under FRED 13, the question of management intent is regarded as irrelevant to such questions.

For each class of financial asset, financial liability and equity instrument (whether recognised on the balance sheet or not) the standard requires enterprises to disclose:

(a)   information about the extent and nature of the financial instruments, including significant terms and conditions that may affect the amount, timing and certainty of future cash flows; and

(b)   the accounting policies and methods adopted, including the criteria for recognition and the basis of measurement applied.[73]

For financial assets and liabilities, they should also disclose information about their exposure to interest rate risk, including contractual repricing or maturity dates, whichever dates are earlier, and their effective interest rates where applicable.[74] Estimates of their fair value must also be given, except if this is impracticable, in which case that fact must be disclosed together with information about the principal characteristics of the item that are relevant to its fair value.[75]

In relation to assets, information about credit risk must be disclosed, including the maximum exposure to credit risk (ignoring any collateral) if other parties fail to perform their obligations under financial instruments, together with any significant concentrations of credit risk.[76] Where any asset is carried at an amount above its fair value, the enterprise must disclose both its fair value and book value and the reason for management's belief that the latter will be recovered.[77] FRED 13 does not require such disclosures.

One particular set of disclosures is required when the reporting entity has used financial instruments to hedge anticipated future transactions. In such a case, it must disclose details of both the hedging instruments and the anticipated transactions, including details of when they are expected to occur, and the amount of any deferred or unrecognised gains or losses and when they are likely to be recognised in the profit and loss account.[78]

4.2.3   *Discussion Paper – Accounting for Financial Assets and Financial Liabilities*

This elegantly reasoned Discussion Paper was published by the IASC in March 1997, and it represents the most radical approach to accounting for financial instruments yet proposed. In concept, its main proposals are very simple: all financial assets and liabilities should be recognised as soon as the reporting entity becomes a party to the contractual provisions that they entail;[79] thereafter they should be stated at fair value in the balance sheet;[80] and all movements in fair value thereafter should be reported in income.[81]

The Steering Group has therefore rejected the more limited approach that had been proposed in E48. That exposure draft had suggested that fair value accounting should not be applied to those instruments that were intended to be held for the long term or to maturity, but this was no longer thought to be a worthwhile distinction. The scope of the proposals has also broadened slightly; pension and insurance obligations are no longer to be exempted, although it is conceded that they both deserve further study before a standard can be finalised. The eventual standard is meant to apply to all enterprises (and not just listed companies and similar bodies, as proposed by the ASB in the UK).

In another change from E48, the Discussion Paper proposes a 'financial components' approach to recognition and derecognition, to deal with cases where the rights attaching to financial instruments are split up, such as in the transfer of receivables with recourse. E48 had proposed to allow derecognition when substantially all the risks and rewards of ownership were transferred, but the Steering Group now advocates decomposing the instrument into its component parts in such a case.[82]

The Discussion Paper takes a very restrictive view of hedge accounting. With two minor exceptions, it proposes that no special treatment should be accorded to financial instruments that are designated as hedges of other exposures; they should all still be carried at fair value and gains or losses reported in income. The first exception is for currency hedges of foreign investments which would continue to be reported in reserves to offset the translation difference on the foreign investments. The second relates to hedges of anticipated transactions; provided certain conditions are met, the gain or loss may be reported in 'other comprehensive income' (the equivalent of the UK statement of total recognised gains and losses) and thereafter recycled through the profit and loss account when the effects of the hedged transaction themselves are reported there.[83]

These proposals represent the views of the Steering Group and not necessarily those of the IASC Board, and it remains to be seen whether they will be converted into a standard. If they are, it would put the IASC in the unusual position of having gone beyond the approach taken by any domestic standard-setter (apart from the CICA, which has provided much of the impetus for the project).

5   CONCLUSION

It is clear that the subject of accounting for financial instruments is likely to remain one of the most difficult regulatory challenges for the next few years. Perhaps unusually, there seems to be a high degree of consensus among the major standard-setters – that marking all financial instruments to market can be the only ultimate solution – but this is a controversial view that may meet with considerable resistance. Also unusually, the IASC is in the uncomfortable position of proposing a standard that has not yet commanded acceptance in any individual country, and could end up out on a limb as a result.

The arguments for mark-to-market accounting seem cogent, and the IASC has assembled them very persuasively in its Discussion Paper. But they are nonetheless revolutionary; by the authors' own admission, they require the adoption of a new capital maintenance concept ('current-market-rate-of-return') for measuring financial instruments.[84] And this will simply introduce a new inconsistency, unless it is applied to the measurement of other items in the accounts as well, which would be an even more radical proposal. The ASB equivalent goes slightly less far, but would still represent a fundamental change to existing practice.

The ASB's disclosure proposals in FRED 13 are somewhat less controversial, and should achieve their aim of making companies' treasury activity more transparent. However, even these are ambitious and sometimes contentious. They require significant interpretation and some of them need to be reconsidered before a standard can be finalised. Even when they are eventually implemented, it will take time for both preparers and users of accounts to get used to working with them in practice. Despite the seeming urgency of the whole issue, therefore, we think that the regulation of accounting for financial instruments is a project that cannot be hurried.

References

1   *IASC Update*, IASC, December 1996.
2   Discussion Paper, *Derivatives and other financial instruments*, ASB, July 1996.
3   FRED 13, *Derivatives and other financial instruments: Disclosures*, ASB, April 1997.
4   FRED 13 Supplement – *Derivatives and other financial instruments: Disclosures by banks and similar institutions*, ASB, July 1997.
5   *Derivatives and other financial instruments*, para. 1.2.2.
6   *Ibid.*, para. 1.2.11.
7   *Ibid.*, para. 1.2.12.
8   The discussion paper says (at para. 1.3.5) that the ASB is minded to include commodity-based derivatives where the market practice is to close out the contract by monetary settlement rather than by the physical delivery of the commodity.
9   *Derivatives and other financial instruments*, para. 1.4.1.
10   *Ibid.*, Summary of issues and the Board's initial conclusions, paras. 14 and 15.
11   *Ibid.*, paras. 16 and 17.
12   *Ibid.*, paras. 18–21.
13   *Ibid.*, paras. 22–25.
14   *Ibid.*, Appendix, para. A6.
15   *Ibid.*, para. 2.5.3.
16   *Ibid.*, para. 3.5.1(b) and (c).
17   SSAP 12, *Accounting for Depreciation*, ASC, December 1977, para. 16.
18   *Derivatives and other financial instruments*, para. 3.5.1(d).
19   *Ibid.*

20 *Ibid.*, para. 3.3.21.
21 *Ibid.*, para. 3.5.1(b) and (c).
22 FRED 13, para. 4.
23 FRED 13 Supplement – *Derivatives and other financial instruments: Disclosures by banks and similar institutions*, ASB, July 1997.
24 FRED 13, para. 27.
25 *Ibid.*, para. 28.
26 *Ibid.*, para. 6.
27 *Ibid.*, para. 7.
28 *Ibid.*, para. 53.
29 *Ibid.*, para. 8.
30 *Ibid.*, para. 54.
31 *Ibid.*, para. 49.
32 *Ibid.*, para. 50.
33 *Ibid.*, para. 51.
34 *Ibid.*, para. 10.
35 *Ibid.*, para. 11.
36 *Ibid.*, para. 58.
37 *Ibid.*, para. 12.
38 *Ibid.*
39 *Ibid.*, paras. 59 and 60.
40 *Ibid.*, paras. 13 and 14.
41 *Ibid.*, paras. 15 and 16.
42 *Ibid.*, para. 17.
43 *Ibid.*, para. 18.
44 *Ibid.*, para. 65.
45 *Ibid.*, para. 19.
46 *Ibid.*, para. 20.
47 *Ibid.*, paras. 74 and 75.
48 *Ibid.*, para. 21.
49 *Ibid.*, para. 68.
50 *Ibid.*, para. 69.
51 *Ibid.*, para. 69.
52 *Ibid.*, paras. 31 and 70.
53 *Ibid.*, para. 22.
54 *Ibid.*, para. 23.
55 *Ibid.*, paras. 24–26.
56 *Ibid.*, para. 29.
57 *Ibid.*, para. 30.
58 *Ibid.*, paras. 86–88.
59 SFAS 105, *Disclosure of Information about Financial Instruments with Off-Balance-Sheet Risk and Financial Instruments with Concentrations of Credit Risk*, FASB, March 1990, para. 6.
60 *Ibid.*, footnote 1.
61 *Ibid.*, para. 18.
62 *Ibid.*, para. 17.
63 SFAS 107, *Disclosures about Fair Value of Financial Instruments*, FASB, December 1991, para. 10.
64 *Ibid.*, para. 14.
65 SFAS 119, *Disclosure about Derivative Financial Instruments and Fair Value of Financial Instruments*, FASB, October 1994, para. 10.
66 *Ibid.*, para. 11.
67 Exposure draft, *Accounting for Derivative and Similar Financial Instruments and for Hedging Activities*, FASB, June 1996.
68 IAS 32, *Financial Instruments: Disclosure and Presentation*, IASC, March 1995, para. 1.
69 *Ibid.*, para. 19.
70 *Ibid.*, para. 30.
71 *Ibid.*, para. 23.
72 *Ibid.*, para. 33.

73   *Ibid.*, para. 47.
74   *Ibid.*, para. 56.
75   *Ibid.*, para. 77.
76   *Ibid.*, para. 66.
77   *Ibid.*, para. 88.
78   *Ibid.*, para. 91.
79   Discussion Paper, *Accounting for Financial Assets and Financial Liabilities*, Chapter 3, para. 3.1.
80   *Ibid.*, Chapter 4, para. 2.1 and Chapter 5, para. 3.1.
81   *Ibid.*, Chapter 6, para. 5.1.
82   *Ibid.*, Chapter 3, paras. 4.1 and 9.1–5.
83   *Ibid.*, Chapter 7, para. 4.39.
84   *Ibid.*, Chapter 6, para. 2.4.

Chapter 10   Fixed assets and depreciation

1   INTRODUCTION

1.1   Background

The broad principles for accounting for fixed assets are generally well understood in the UK. The cost of fixed assets should be capitalised when they are acquired, subsequently depreciated through the profit and loss account over their working lives, and written down if at any time the carrying value is seen not to be fully recoverable. When a fixed asset is sold or scrapped, the difference between the written down value and any proceeds is recorded as the gain or loss on disposal. But there are many complications in applying these simple principles in practice. When should a fixed asset initially be recognised? How should its cost be measured? How should it be depreciated? When should it be regarded as not fully recoverable? Worse, a new and confusing dimension is added to these and other problems if management decides to revalue the asset rather than continuing to carry it on the basis of its historical cost.

Up till now, accounting standard setters in the UK have developed standards on these subjects in a rather piecemeal and incomplete way. There are standards dealing with depreciation (SSAP 12 – *Accounting for depreciation*), some revaluations (SSAP 19 – *Accounting for investment properties*), and some intangibles (SSAP 13 – *Accounting for research and development* and SSAP 22 – *Accounting for goodwill*). The old ASC had projects in hand to deal more comprehensively with the subject, which led to the issue of two exposure drafts[1] shortly before its demise, but the ASB did not finalise these projects when it took over. The Board now has separate projects on the measurement of tangible fixed assets; impairment of fixed assets; and on goodwill and intangible assets. To date it has produced a Discussion Paper on the first, and exposure drafts on the remaining two.[2]

In addition, company law deals with certain accounting practices and valuation rules as they relate to fixed assets. The statutory requirements cover depreciation, permanent and temporary diminutions in value, the components of the cost of an asset, whether purchased or self-constructed, and the bases of valuation of fixed assets.

1.2   The meaning of fixed assets

The Companies Act 1985 defines fixed assets as those which are intended for use on a continuing basis in the company's activities and any assets which are not intended for such use are taken to be current assets.[3] This is not by itself a very helpful definition, particularly when it is applied to such assets as investments – to what extent and in what sense is an investment intended for 'use' in a business? The balance sheet formats give further information as to what is intended as a fixed asset: intangible assets including development costs and goodwill, tangible fixed assets and investments, including shares in subsidiary and associated undertakings. The full balance sheet formats for fixed assets are given in 6.3 below.

The definition says that fixed assets must be intended for use on a continuing basis, but this is not normally interpreted to mean that individual items should be transferred out of fixed assets when a decision to dispose of them has been made; the definition refers more to the nature of the item and its original function when it was acquired. Nevertheless, one or two companies have a policy of making such a transfer, such as those appearing in the accounts of Wolseley and Central Transport Rental Group.

Extract 10.1: Wolseley plc (1996)

Accounting policies

Real property awaiting disposal

Real property awaiting disposal is transferred to current assets at the lower of book written down value and estimated net realisable value. Depreciation is not applied to real property awaiting disposal, but the carrying value is reviewed annually and written down through the profit and loss account to current estimated net realisable value if lower.

Extract 10.2: Central Transport Rental Group plc (1996)

Accounting policies

q) Transfer of operating assets to current assets

The operating asset fleet is reviewed at each year end to identify those units which it is considered will not provide sufficient returns in the future or no longer meet the specification requirement to warrant their continued inclusion in the operating fleet. These units are written down to their estimated market values and transferred to Current Assets – Assets held for sale.

The practices of property companies in moving properties between fixed and current categories are discussed further in 5.3.6 below.

The ASB proposes to define tangible fixed assets as:

'Assets that have physical substance and are held for use in the production or supply of goods and services, for rental to others, or for administrative purposes on a continuing basis in the reporting entity's activities.'[4]

This builds upon the Companies Act definition but is much more specific. In contrast, the Board's definition of intangible assets in FRED 12 is:

'Non-monetary fixed assets that do not have physical substance but are identifiable and are controlled by the entity through legal rights or physical custody.'[5] 'Identifiable' assets and liabilities are further defined as those 'that are capable of being disposed of or settled separately, without disposing of a business of the entity'.[6] This therefore really means 'separable', rather than identifiable, although the wording is similar to that in the Companies Act.[7]

The notion of maintaining physical custody over something that has no physical substance seems rather strange, and in fact FRED 15 modifies the definition slightly, saying only 'custody'.[8] FRED 12 explains that it means such things as maintaining the benefits of technical or intellectual knowledge by keeping them secret. The requirement to maintain control through legal rights or physical custody, however, means that pseudo-assets such as portfolios of clients or highly trained staff could not be recognised as assets.

As is discussed in part 1 of Chapter 11, investments are difficult to define and the distinction between fixed and current asset investments is also difficult to make. However, this chapter does not consider investments further, and confines itself to tangible and intangible fixed assets. Investment properties are dealt with in this Chapter, but other investments, both fixed and current, are discussed in Chapter 11, while the particular issue of capitalisation of interest (which is not confined to fixed assets) is covered by Chapter 13. Two specific categories of intangible assets, goodwill and development expenditure, are considered in Chapters 6 and 12 respectively.

1.3 Criteria for recognition of fixed assets

1.3.1 Criteria for tangible fixed assets

The ASB's projects on tangible fixed assets do not yet include specific proposals on recognition criteria. However, they may be expected to follow the general approach of the Board's draft *Statement of Principles*, which has proposed the following recognition tests:

'An element should be recognised if:

(a) there is sufficient evidence that the change in assets or liabilities inherent in the element has occurred (including where appropriate, evidence that a future inflow or outflow of benefit will occur); and

(b)   it can be measured at a monetary amount with sufficient reliability.'[9]

Elements of financial statements are assets, liabilities, equity, gains and losses. Of these, 'assets' is the element which is relevant to this discussion, and they are defined in the *Statement of Principles* as 'rights or other access to future economic benefits controlled by an entity as a result of past transactions or events'.[10]

1.3.2   Criteria for intangible fixed assets

FRED 12 has rather more practical guidance on the recognition of intangible assets. Essentially it falls into three parts:

■   Intangible assets bought separately should be capitalised at cost.[11]

■   Intangible assets obtained in the course of acquiring a business should be recognised separately from goodwill if their value can be measured reliably on initial recognition.[12] The draft explains that this does not necessarily require there to be a market value, but also allows the use of valuation methods based on factors such as notional royalties or multiples of turnover.[13]

■   Internally developed intangible assets should be recognised only if they have a readily ascertainable market value.[14] Here the proposal is much more restrictive, because it requires there to be an active market in that particular asset; it says that the item must belong to a homogeneous population of assets that are equivalent in all material respects, such as cable television operating licences, import quotas and EU milk quotas. This therefore rules out the possibility of recognising unique intangibles such as brands, publishing titles and patented drugs if they are home-grown rather than acquired.

However, the ASB clearly considers that assets such as brands *can* be separately recognised if they are obtained as part of an acquisition, even though questions might be raised as to whether they are really 'identifiable' in the sense of being capable of disposal while retaining the business to which they relate.

Guinness, Cadbury Schweppes and WPP Group all provide examples of acquired brands that have been capitalised:

Extract 10.3: Guinness PLC (1996)

Accounting Policies

Brands

The fair value of businesses acquired and of interests taken in associated undertakings includes brands, which are recognised where the brand has a value which is substantial and long term. Acquired brands are only recognised where title is clear, brand earnings are separately identifiable, the brand could be sold separately from the rest of the business and where the brand achieves earnings in excess of those achieved by unbranded products.

Amortisation is not provided except where the end of the useful economic life of the acquired brand can be foreseen. The useful economic lives of brands and their carrying value are subject to annual review and any amortisation or provision for permanent impairment would be charged against the profit for the period in which it arose.

Notes to the Group Accounts

12. ACQUIRED BRANDS AT COST

The amount stated for brands represents the cost of acquired brands. Brands are only recognised where title is clear, brand earnings are separately identifiable, the brand could be sold separately from the rest of the business and where the brand achieves earnings in excess of those achieved by unbranded products.

The cost of the brands is calculated at acquisition, as part of the fair value accounting for businesses acquired, on the basis of after tax multiples of pre-acquisition earnings after deducting attributable capital employed.

The acquired brands which have been recognised include Bell's, Dewar's, Johnnie Walker, Old Parr and White Horse Scotch whisky, Gordon's and Tanqueray gin and Asbach brandy.

The acquired brands of MH which have been recognised as part of the investment in MH are set out in Note 13(A).

The Directors have reviewed the amounts at which brands are stated and are of the opinion that there has been no impairment in the value of the brands recognised, that all brands recognised could be sold for amounts substantially greater than those recognised in the balance sheet and that the end of the useful economic lives of the brands cannot be foreseen.

13. INVESTMENT IN MH

(A) Group's interest in MH [extract]

The attributable share of MH's net assets includes brands, at cost, of £403m (1995 £472m), with the decrease in value of £69m being attributable to exchange rate movements. MH brands which have been recognised include Hennessy cognac and Moët & Chandon, Dom Pérignon, Mercier, Veuve Cliquot Ponsardin and Pommery champagnes.

Extract 10.4: Cadbury Schweppes p.l.c. (1996)

Accounting Policies

n)   Intangibles

Intangibles represent significant owned brands acquired since 1985 valued at historical cost. No amortisation is charged as the annual results reflect significant expenditure in support of these brands and the values are reviewed annually with a view to write down if a permanent diminution arises.

Notes on the Accounts

12 Intangible Assets

	1996 £m	1995 £m
Cost at beginning of year	1,689	522
Exchange rate adjustments	(142)	35
Addition	–	1,132
	1,547	1,689

Extract 10.5: WPP Group plc (1996)

Accounting policies

4   Intangible fixed assets

Intangible fixed assets comprise certain acquired separable corporate brand names. These are shown at a valuation of the incremental earnings expected to arise from the ownership of brands. The valuations have been based on the present value of notional royalty savings arising from ownership of those brands and on estimates of profits attributable to brand loyalty. The valuations are subject to annual review. No depreciation is provided since, in the opinion of the directors, the brands do not have a finite useful economic life.

Notes to the accounts
12 Intangible fixed assets

	1996 £m	1995 £m	1994 £m
Corporate brand names	350.0	350.0	350.0

Corporate brand names represent the directors' valuation of the brand names J. Walter Thompson and Hill and Knowlton which were originally valued in 1988, and Ogilvy & Mather acquired in 1989 as part of The Ogilvy Group, Inc. These assets have been valued in accordance with the Group's accounting policy for intangible fixed assets. In the course of their annual review the directors consulted their advisers, The Henley Centre and HSBC Samuel Montagu.

A prominent but isolated example of recognition of 'homegrown' brand names, was Ranks Hovis McDougall:

Extract 10.6: Ranks Hovis McDougall PLC (1991)

ACCOUNTING POLICIES

Intangible assets The accounting treatment for additions to goodwill is considered on an individual basis and elimination against reserves has been selected as appropriate for the current year.

Brands, both acquired and created within the Group, are included at their 'current cost'. Such cost, which is reviewed annually, is not subject to amortisation.

NOTES TO THE ACCOUNTS

13   Intangible assets

	The Group £m	The Company £m
Brands		
At 1 September 1990	588.0	–
Revaluation	20.0	–
At 31 August 1991	608.0	–

The Group has valued its brands at their 'current use value to the Group' in conjunction with Interbrand Group plc, branding consultants.

This basis of valuation ignores any possible alternative use of a brand, any possible extension to the range of products currently marketed under a brand, any element of hope value and any possible increase in value of a brand due to either a special investment or a financial transaction (e.g. licensing) which would leave the Group with a different interest from the one being valued.

In 1992 the company was acquired by Tomkins PLC. Interestingly, however, Tomkins decided not to attribute any value to the brands in allocating the purchase price to the assets acquired.

1.3.3   The brands debate: which intangible assets are capable of being accounted for?

No one would deny that intangible assets are of real economic value to businesses, and in certain industry sectors, they are of overwhelming importance to the success of the enterprise. The debate is not on that issue; it is on whether it is within the compass of our present accounting model to capture and convey useful information about such assets. By their nature, many intangible assets have characteristics which cause accounting difficulty. Some of these characteristics are described below.

A   Separability

As noted above, one element of the definition of intangible assets in FRED 12 is that they must be identifiable, meaning that they must be capable of separate disposal without disposing of the business to which they relate. The stipulation that assets to which fair values may be assigned following an acquisition must be separable in this way has its origins in SSAP 22 – *Accounting for goodwill*. Paragraph 13 of that standard reads as follows:

'In deciding whether a particular asset falls into the category of separable net assets, the test is whether that asset could be identified and sold separately without disposing of the business as a whole. For example an asset may be an essential part of a company's manufacturing operations, and it may be that the asset would be of very little value other than in its present use; but it could be sold separately or bought from its manufacturers, whereas goodwill could not be – it could only be either acquired or sold as part of the process of acquiring or selling the business as a whole. Separable net assets may include identifiable intangibles such as those specifically mentioned in the balance sheet formats in the Companies Act 1985, i.e. "concessions, patents, licences, trade marks and similar rights and assets"; other examples include publishing titles, franchise rights and customer lists. (This list of examples is not intended to be comprehensive.) Identifiable intangibles such as these form part of the separable net assets which are recorded in an acquiring company's accounts at fair value, even if they were not recorded in the acquired company's accounts.'

The standard goes on to define separable net assets as 'those assets (and liabilities) which can be identified and sold (or discharged) without necessarily disposing of the business as a whole. They include identifiable intangibles.'[15]

The Companies Act 1989 introduced a similar concept into the law, but used the word 'identifiable' rather than 'separable', otherwise retaining the same definition.[16]

The characteristic of 'separability', however, is not generally applied as a criterion for recognition of an asset. Moreover, the above definition is not a very illuminating one and causes confusion in practice; for example, some might argue that the brand of a one-brand company was not separable because without it there would be no business left, whereas if it belonged to a company with a hundred brands then it would be separable – however, this may not be logical because the same asset is involved in each case.

Possibly what SSAP 22 really meant by its definition of separability is that the asset must be distinguishable from goodwill. It may not be intended to establish a general principle of separability as a characteristic of an asset; it simply seeks to disqualify assets which are too much like goodwill, by setting a test which goodwill itself could not satisfy. Unfortunately it does so in terms which permit differences of opinion on whether certain assets, such as brands, are truly separable.

There is, however, a broader aspect of separability which may be relevant to the debate; this is the question of whether the asset is a discrete asset, in the sense that the boundaries between it and other assets can be clearly and unequivocally drawn. In the case of intangible assets, discreteness is particularly hard to establish because of the essential woolliness of an intangible asset. It is possible to establish it in some individual cases, if it represents a right to a particular stream of income which is independent of any other asset; an example would be a copyright giving rise to a stream of royalty income. However, where it is something which is used in combination with other assets to achieve income for the business, then it is very hard to say where the boundaries of the asset lie. Thus brands, which may be an important asset of a business, are used in combination with both the tangible assets of the business and the other intangible assets, such as a skilled workforce, an established distribution network, customer lists and so on. It is very difficult, if not impossible, to put a value on any of these intangible elements individually in a meaningful way. Moreover, if elements are valued individually there is a danger that their joint contribution to the profitability of the business will be arbitrarily assigned to one of these individual elements or even double-counted by being assigned to more than one element; furthermore, if the value of the elements is derived from the value of the business as a whole it would appear that all that is being done in reality is a valuation of goodwill.

B   *Maintenance or substitution?*

A related difficulty in accounting for such intangibles is that it is often difficult to determine whether the asset originally recorded is being maintained or whether a new asset is being gradually substituted for it. This enters into the question of how to account for the asset in subsequent years; must the original asset be written down as it erodes, even if a very similar asset grows up to replace it at the same time as a result of management's efforts in nurturing the valuable aspects of the business? The question of whether the asset is the same one or a different one can take on a metaphysical air. For example, if a customer list is bought, does it have to be written off if the customers on the list change, even if the new ones are as valuable as the old ones? That is a relatively concrete example; it may be even more difficult to determine whether a brand remains the same asset over time as it is subtly reshaped to meet new market opportunities. It is tempting to take the pragmatic view that substitution does not matter so long as overall value is maintained, but conventional accounting requires disaggregated assets and liabilities reflected in accounts to be measured individually, not as part of a shifting portfolio of varying components. However, it should also be admitted that similar arguments are sometimes put forward to justify non-depreciation of tangible assets as well, on the basis that continual refurbishment restores the fabric of the asset and removes the need to record any depreciation. (See 3.2 below.)

C   *Uncertainty of cost of creation*

A third difficulty, again on the same theme, is that when assets of the nature under discussion are created, it is generally not as the result of specific expenditure on that particular asset but as the by-product of expenditures made in the general conduct of the business. A well-trained workforce is built up over a period, not just as a result of expenditure on training, but because successful management and employment strategies of all kinds are in operation. The value of a brand is made not simply by inventing a desirable product with a consumer-seductive name, but by building market share by the skilful exploitation of the product in a whole host of ways. Joint or by-product costing is not a new technique for accountants, but it would be tested beyond the limit if it had to address how to determine the cost of intangible assets developed as a result of the general operations of the business.

D   Conclusion

These are just a few of the issues that make it very difficult to accommodate a comprehensive range of intangible assets within our familiar accounting framework. This view was supported by a 1989 research study from the London Business School. The authors concluded that 'the present flexible position, far from being neutral, is potentially corrosive to the whole basis of financial reporting and that to allow brands – whether acquired or homegrown – to continue to be included in the balance sheet would be highly unwise'.[17]

A major complicating factor in this debate has been a widespread disagreement and misunderstanding of what a balance sheet is intended to portray. To those people who see the balance sheet as trying to give an indication of the value of the company's assets, the inclusion of brands at a current value makes eminent sense. However, when it is recognised that the balance sheet is derived from the transactions of the company, and is a repository of unexpired costs and revenues, then it is hard to argue that the valuation of brands fits in to this framework. If the balance sheet were to become a statement of value, many more changes would be needed to the historical cost system than the mere valuation of brands.

The debate has not really advanced very much in recent years. FRS 7 rather ducked the issue in relation to acquired brands, saying only that '*where* [emphasis added] an intangible asset is recognised, its fair value should be based on its replacement cost, which is normally its estimated market value', but did not resolve the question of when such assets should be recognised. FRED 12 appears to be more positive on the subject, by saying that 'an intangible asset acquired as part of the acquisition of a business should be recognised separately from goodwill if its value can be measured reliably on initial recognition',[18] but this glosses over the fact that brands do not qualify to be counted as intangible assets in terms of the definition unless they are regarded as separable, and the draft does not discuss this issue. In respect of homegrown brands, however, FRED 12 is much clearer: they should not be recognised. But altogether, the topic of brand accounting remains an area of some controversy.

2   COST

2.1   Basic requirement

The Companies Act requires that, subject to any provision for depreciation or diminution in value, the amount to be included in respect of any fixed asset shall be its purchase price or production cost.[19] (The alternative of carrying assets at a valuation is discussed in 5 below.)

2.2   Purchase price

The Companies Act defines 'purchase price' as to include any consideration, whether in cash or otherwise, given by the company in respect of that asset.[20] In addition, according to the Act, 'the purchase price of an asset shall be determined by adding to the actual price paid any expenses incidental to its acquisition'.[21]

'Purchase price' has been interpreted by some as prohibiting the deduction of capital grants received from the cost of the asset, one of the treatments permitted by SSAP 4[22] (this is discussed more fully in Chapter 18 at 3.1.1).

'Expenses incidental to its acquisition' are those costs which have been incurred as a direct consequence of the purchase of the asset and are necessary in order to make it available for use. For example, in the case of an item of plant or equipment, these costs could include site preparation, delivery and handling charges, installation costs and professional fees.

2.3   Production cost

The definition in the Act of the production cost of any asset (fixed or current) says that it:

'shall be determined by adding to the purchase price of the raw materials and consumables used the amount of the costs incurred by the company which are directly attributable to the production of that asset.

In addition there may be included in the production cost of an asset –

(a)   a reasonable proportion of the costs incurred by the company which are only indirectly attributable to the production of that asset, but only to the extent that they relate to the period of production; and

(b)   interest on capital borrowed to finance the production of that asset, to the extent that it accrues in respect of the period of production.'[23]

There are a number of problems that arise from this legal definition of production cost. These include the meanings of 'directly' and 'indirectly' attributable costs and 'period of production', which are discussed further below. Capitalisation of interest is dealt with in Chapter 13.

2.4   Directly and indirectly attributable costs

Directly attributable costs will include, in addition to the costs of raw materials and consumables referred to in the definition, direct labour, direct expenses and sub-contracted work. There is no further indication in the Act as to what is meant by indirectly attributable costs, but these will generally be regarded to be overheads.

The ASB's Discussion Paper on the *Measurement of tangible fixed assets* does not elaborate on what indirect costs might be included. ED 51 did not offer very much on the subject either, but it did say that administrative and other general overheads should not be included as part of the cost of a fixed asset unless they can be reasonably attributed to its purchase or to bringing it to its working condition.[24] In addition, Appendix 1 to that exposure draft specifically sanctioned the capitalisation of production overheads and, in the case of buildings, of overheads that are indirectly attributable to the production of the building to the extent that they relate to the period of production.

More specific guidance about the treatment of overheads might be drawn from the rules relating to stocks and work in progress contained in SSAP 9. As noted in 2.3 above, the legal definition of production cost applies to both fixed and current assets. SSAP 9 requires the cost of stocks to include the costs of conversion and these include production overheads and any other overheads attributable in the particular circumstances of the business to bringing the product or service to its present location and condition.[25] The practical problems of identifying production overheads as part of the costs of conversion of current assets, stock and work in progress, are discussed in Appendix 1 to SSAP 9. This describes how overheads should be classified by function rather than whether the overhead varies with time or volume. It goes into such details as how the costs of central service departments, such as the accounts department, should be allocated between the functions of production, marketing, selling and administration and how only those that relate to the production function should be included in the costs of conversion and hence in work in progress.[26]

In principle these overheads can also be allocated to the function of producing assets for the enterprise's own use. However, because of the likely scale of production of fixed assets relative to total operations, few enterprises will allocate any part of such central costs to the construction of their own assets. Exceptions could include major manufacturing or construction concerns where some items of plant and machinery or buildings are self-constructed; companies, often part of a group, that build properties for own use or for investment; and industries where there are many outlets, such as multiple retailers, restaurant or hotel chains where there may be significant administration costs associated with acquiring, building and refurbishing property. Such organisations may employ suitably qualified professional personnel, for example architects, surveyors and lawyers. These costs may, in part at least, be incurred before there has been any development work on the asset itself, and the circumstances in which they may be capitalised are described in 2.5 below.

Companies' accounts rarely disclose policies on the capitalisation of overheads, and it is not easy to determine which costs are actually being included. British Telecommunications gives a policy that includes the capitalisation of overheads as part of the cost of self-constructed assets, but even here it is not entirely clear what costs are covered by the policy:

Extract 10.7: British Telecommunications plc (1997)

VIII   Tangible fixed assets [extract]

(a) Cost

Cost in the case of network services comprises expenditure up to and including the last distribution point and includes contractors' charges and payments on account, materials, direct labour and related overheads.

2.5   The period of production

As indicated in 2.3 above, indirectly attributable costs and interest can only be included in production cost to the extent that they relate to the period of production. However, there is no guidance in the Act to help determine when the period of production either commences or finishes.

Defining when the period finishes is usually the more significant of the two issues, and it is this that the ASB's Discussion Paper addresses. The paper endorses the practice of continuing to capitalise costs during an initial commissioning period where this is necessary to bring the asset up to its full operating capability; however, it distinguishes this from the case where the asset is fully operational but is not yet achieving its targeted profitability because demand is still building up. In the latter case, the production period has finished and no further costs should be capitalised.[27]

A frequent example of the latter practice can be found in the property industry, where it is common to continue to capitalise interest on properties which have been constructed but are not yet fully let. The argument has been that the asset being constructed is not simply the physical structure of the building but a fully tenanted investment property, and the production period correspondingly includes not simply the construction period but also the letting period. Examples of such policies appear in the accounts of MEPC, British Land and Hammerson:

Extract 10.8: MEPC plc (1996)

Notes to the accounts

1   Accounting policies

Properties [extract]

A property ceases to be treated as being in the course of development at the earliest of:

(1) the date when the development becomes fully let and income producing

(2) the date when income exceeds outgoings

(3) a date up to three years after completion to allow for letting.

Extract 10.9: British Land plc (1997)

Accounting policies

Properties [extract]

A property ceases to be treated as a development either nine months after practical completion or when two-thirds of the anticipated gross income becomes receivable, which ever is the earlier.

Extract 10.10: Hammerson plc (1996)

Notes to the Accounts

1   ACCOUNTING POLICIES

Cost of Properties [extract]

A property is regarded as being in the course of development until substantially let and income producing or until income exceeds outgoings.

As can be seen, these interpretations vary substantially. However, it would appear that the ASB's proposals would prohibit the practice of extending the production period beyond the date of practical completion of the physical asset.

Determining the commencement of the period of production is usually less contentious. However, it is noteworthy that, in 1997, BAA changed its definition so as to delay the date of commencement of a project until planning permission has been obtained and a firm decision to proceed has been taken (see Chapter 13).

2.6   Abnormal costs and cost inefficiencies

The ASB's Discussion Paper follows the approach taken by IAS 16 that costs arising from inefficiencies should be excluded from the production cost of an asset.[28] Such inefficiencies might include the effects of production delays or a wastage of materials. This is similar to the position taken by SSAP 9, where costs that would not be incurred under 'normal operating conditions' are excluded from the costs of conversion of stock.[29]

The argument behind this position is that such costs do not add anything to the value of the asset. However, it could be argued that 'value' is not immediately relevant when it comes to determining which costs should initially be capitalised in the balance sheet. Arguably, the total cost to the enterprise of the asset should be established, after which it becomes possible to assess whether there has been an impairment in value (see 4 below) – if there has been, the carrying value of the asset should be reduced to its recoverable amount. This might be a more logical approach, and would still comply with the Companies Act definition of 'production cost'.

Deciding what is an inefficiency that is to be excluded from the cost is not straightforward. The ASB distinguishes such inefficiencies from scenarios where 'the technical difficulties encountered in construction may be greater than foreseen, or estimates of the construction time may have been over-optimistic';[30] cost overruns arising from such events should still be capitalised. The difference, as the ASB sees it, is that these costs are necessary to the asset's construction, whereas cost inefficiencies are not. Nevertheless, this is likely to be a difficult distinction to make in practice.

In support of this approach, the actual principle that the ASB proposes is that:

■ costs should be capitalised only to the extent that they relate to an enhancement of the future economic benefits of the tangible fixed asset, but

■ cost inefficiencies should not be capitalised.[31]

However, this guidance is not as clear as it might be. It would be more coherent simply to say that the necessary costs incurred in creating the asset should be capitalised.

2.7   Improvements and repairs

It is often difficult to decide whether expenditure on improvements and repairs is capital or revenue in nature and whether such expenditure should be capitalised as part of the original asset or as a separate category of fixed asset.

The ASB's approach to this relies on the principle advanced above in relation to the capitalisation of initial expenditure on an asset, that 'costs should be capitalised only to the extent that they relate to an enhancement of the future economic benefits of the tangible fixed asset'.[32] The Discussion Paper goes on to say that the key to assessing this is 'to determine the period over which the economic benefits arising from the expenditure are expected to last:

■ if this period is less than one year, the future economic benefits will not be enhanced and the expenditure should not be capitalised

■   if this period is more than one year and the expenditure is material, the future economic benefits of the asset will be enhanced and the expenditure should be capitalised'.[33]

In our view, this is a poor approach, and one that could lead to much inappropriate capitalisation of repairs; essentially it means that all material repairs whose effects will be felt for more than a year are to be regarded as capital expenditure. In practice, *all* repairs are intended to enhance the future benefits of an asset, otherwise they would not be undertaken, and the arbitrary one-year cut off will eliminate only the most minor repairs. The proposed principle is misguided, and this aspect of the Discussion Paper needs to be completely reconsidered.

The ASB might usefully examine the proposals in ED 51, which addressed this problem rather more sensibly. It defined expenditure that can be capitalised and added to the gross carrying amount of the asset as that which increases the expected future benefits from the asset *beyond its previously assessed standard of performance*.[34] The words in italics and their interpretation may provide the essential part of the definition that is presently lacking from the ASB's paper.

Examples of such benefits given by ED 51 in its explanation included:

(a)   a significant prolongation in the fixed asset's estimated useful life beyond that conferred by repairs and maintenance;

(b)   an increase in its capacity;

(c)   a substantial improvement in the quality of output or a reduction in previously assessed operating costs; or

(d)   a substantial increase in the open market value of the fixed asset.[35]

These examples were based on the equivalent suggestions contained in IAS 16, except for the last one, which was unique to ED 51. However, although the definition and examples are helpful in assessing whether expenditure is capital, there are still a number of ambiguities which would need to be clarified.

First, the exposure draft referred to the 'previously assessed standard of performance' but it is not clear whether or not this meant the standard assessed when the asset was originally brought into use. This would imply, for example, that no repairs to a building should be capitalised unless they actually extended its originally assessed life or capacity, which could be unnecessarily restrictive. An alternative interpretation would be that it refers to an assessment made at the time the work is undertaken: however, this might be too broad a definition because, as mentioned above, almost any repair will increase the standard of performance of the asset, otherwise it would not be undertaken.

Second, the definition refers only to expenditure which can be included in the gross carrying amount, but it is not clear as to whether the 'gross carrying amount' refers to total assets or just to the asset on which money is being spent. It is reasonable to assume that it means the former, as otherwise it would exclude capitalisation of items that have a different life to the one being repaired.

An important consideration in legislating for this area is to avoid the risk of double-counting, by continuing to carry forward the book value of an asset (or part of an asset) that has been replaced, while also capitalising the cost of its replacement. This means that the treatment of repairs must have regard to the accounting treatment of the original asset and its subsequent depreciation.

3 DEPRECIATION

3.1 Introduction

This section deals with the general principles of depreciation and with depreciation as it applies to assets carried at historical cost. The specific problems of depreciation of assets carried at valuation are dealt with in 5.3.2 below.

Depreciation is defined in SSAP 12 as follows:

'Depreciation is the measure of the wearing out, consumption, or other reduction in the useful life of a fixed asset whether arising from use, effluxion of time or obsolescence through technological or market changes.'[36]

This looks upon depreciation as a measure of consumption, not a means of valuation. Fixed assets are seen as costs that will be consumed over the period expected to benefit from their use and which should therefore be matched to the appropriate revenues. However, depreciation is often portrayed as a measure of loss of value,[37] which would therefore only be charged if the value of an asset at the end of an accounting period was less than the carrying value at the beginning of the accounting period. The purpose of depreciation is sometimes also thought of as being to provide a provision for replacement, but this aim is not supported by SSAP 12 and was specifically considered and rejected in the US.[38]

In comments to the ASB on possible future revisions to SSAP 12, the ICAEW has highlighted the ongoing confusion between the allocation and valuation objectives of depreciation, and asked for this to be clarified. It stated its preference for an allocation approach, but noted that depreciation was 'often seen as a measure of loss of value, not least by the management of many companies unwilling to provide depreciation on certain assets'.[39] Some of the arguments frequently raised against depreciation are discussed at 3.2 below.

The ASB's Discussion Paper has supported the view that depreciation is a measure of consumption and rejected the idea that it is designed to reflect a change in value. It proposes to define depreciation in terms very similar to the existing SSAP 12 definition, as follows:

'Depreciation is the measure of the wearing out, consumption, or other reduction in the useful economic life of a tangible fixed asset whether arising from use, effluxion of time or obsolescence through either changes in technology or demand for the goods and services produced by the asset.'[40]

3.2 Arguments against depreciation

Ever since SSAP 12 was published, there has been some resistance to the requirement to apply depreciation to particular types of asset. Often, the arguments rely at least to some extent on the view that it makes no sense to apply depreciation to an asset whose value is not currently declining, taking the position that depreciation is a valuation technique rather than a measure of consumption. Other arguments often depend on the assertion that the asset in question has an unlimited life.

3.2.1 *Investment properties*

The first group to mount opposition to the standard was the property industry, who gained an initial exemption from the standard, and later secured a new standard specifically designed for properties held for investment. SSAP 19, which was published in 1981, requires such properties to be carried at the current market valuation without provision for depreciation, except in the case of leasehold properties where the lease has fewer than 20 years remaining.

An investment property is defined as an interest in land and/or buildings:

(a)   in respect of which construction work and development have been completed; and

(b)   which is held for its investment potential, any rental income being negotiated at arm's length.[41]

Excluded from this definition are properties owned and occupied by a company for its own purposes and properties let to and occupied by other companies in the same group.[42] It should also be noted that this definition is not confined to properties held by property companies. Charities are, however, exempted from SSAP 19.[43]

Lobbying by the property industry and others had first of all led to a temporary exemption for investment properties when SSAP 12[44] was published in December 1977. This was originally intended to last for one year, but was progressively extended. ED 26[45] was issued by the ASC in September 1980, with the objective that it should form the basis of an additional section to SSAP 12, dealing specifically with the accounting for investment properties, but in fact it led ultimately to the publication of a separate standard. The ASC published a statement together with ED 26 setting out this reasoning for a special accounting treatment for investment properties:

'It is ... persuasively argued that a different treatment is required for a fixed asset which is not held for "consumption" in the business operations of an enterprise but is held as a disposable investment. In such a case the current value of the investment, and changes in that current value, are of prime importance rather than a calculation of systematic annual depreciation.

'The argument therefore proceeds:

(a) the financial statements of enterprises holding investments are more helpful to users of financial statements if the investments are accounted for at current values rather than on the basis of a cost or valuation established some time in the past; and

(b) depreciation is only one element which enters into the annual change in the value of a property and as the use of a current value places the prime emphasis on the values of the assets, it is not generally useful to attempt to distinguish, estimate and account separately for the element of depreciation; and

(c) depreciation, although not separately identified, will be taken into account in dealing with changes in current values.'[46]

While the position of the property industry was being considered, it was necessary also to consider the EU Fourth Directive, enacted in the UK in 1981, which made depreciation a legal requirement. A compromise was eventually reached based on the proposition that to depreciate investment properties would lead to the accounts not giving a true and fair view, and it was therefore necessary to invoke the 'true and fair override'.[47] Although the standard was issued shortly after the Fourth Directive was enacted in the UK, the rules in SSAP 19 relating to revaluation deficits were inconsistent with those in the Companies Act (see 5.3.4B below) until the ASB made a limited amendment to the standard in July 1994 to bring it into line with the Act.[48]

In its 1996 Discussion Paper, the Board considered the whole issue more fully, and examined a number of arguments that have frequently been advanced to justify non-depreciation of investment properties:

- the tenant is required to maintain the property to a specified standard

- the valuation of an investment property takes account of depreciation

- depreciation reduces distributable reserves

- there are practical difficulties in measuring depreciation

■ investment properties play a fundamentally different role from owner-occupied properties and for this reason it is appropriate to adopt a different accounting treatment.

The paper dismissed the first four of these, but the Board was divided on the merits of the last issue. In the event, however, no change to the existing exemption has been proposed, although further comment on the whole question was invited.

3.2.2   Other tangible assets that are said not to depreciate

The need to depreciate various other assets has also been a source of continual argument since SSAP 12 was published. This is manifested by the number of companies that avoid charging it on at least some of their properties. This practice began with brewers, but it has now been extended to a number of other industries. In 1978 the finance directors of some of the major brewers met with members of the ASC in order to present their case that licensed premises did not have to be depreciated. Their argument rested on a number of points, of which the most important was that brewers have to maintain their premises to high standards in order to attract and retain custom. Every year a proportion of the premises would be refurbished and the costs charged to revenue.

However, the brewers did not succeed in gaining an exemption from the requirements of SSAP 12. Instead, it was acknowledged that the combination of very long life and high residual value meant that there was not a significant amount of depreciation to be charged. When SSAP 12 first came to be revised, this argument had become so well established that it was incorporated into the exposure draft of the proposed new standard.[49] It was not included in the revised standard because, as the ASC statement accompanying the revised version of SSAP 12 stated,[50] 'a significant number of commentators expressed concern that the proposal could be open to misinterpretation or misuse. It was believed that it might represent a loophole in the standard, permitting non-depreciation of many types of property, in addition to freehold land and investment properties.' The statement went on to point out that the general principle of SSAP 12 should be applied in all cases but that there may be circumstances where it would not be appropriate to charge depreciation.

Notwithstanding this, the practice remains widely adopted by brewers and has since spread to hotels, High Street retailers and banks, among others. Examples of each of these follow:

Extract 10.11: Allied Domecq PLC (1996)

Accounting Policies

DEPRECIATION [extract]

No depreciation is provided on land, or on licensed and certain other properties, which are freehold or held on lease for a term of or exceeding 100 years unexpired. It is the group's policy to maintain the licensed estate in such condition that the value of the estate is not impaired by the passage of time. As a consequence, any element of depreciation would, in the opinion of the directors, be immaterial.

Extract 10.12: Friendly Hotels plc (1996)

Accounting policies

Depreciation – Tangible fixed assets

It is group policy not to provide depreciation on freehold and long leasehold premises. The premises are maintained to a high standard and the directors consider that the lives of the premises are so long and their residual value so great that depreciation is not necessary except for short leasehold premises under 21 years unexpired.

Where any permanent diminution of property value is incurred, a provision is made in the profit and loss account. The directors' estimate of residual values is based on prices prevailing at the time of acquisition or subsequent independent valuation.

Burton is one among a number of retailers with a similar policy in respect of its High Street shops:

Extract 10.13: The Burton Group plc (1996)

1 **Accounting policies**

d **Depreciation**

Depreciation is calculated so as to allocate the cost of tangible fixed assets over their estimated useful economic lives. No depreciation is charged on non-industrial freehold and long leasehold properties, other than rack-rented properties, because the directors consider that the economic lives of these properties and their residual values, excluding inflation, are such that depreciation is not significant. The residual values of the properties are regularly reviewed in order to identify any permanent diminution in value which would be charged to the profit and loss account. Rack-rented long leasehold properties are those held on leases providing for rent reviews every five years. ...

Lloyds TSB Group is typical of the clearing banks in not depreciating its branch properties:

Extract 10.14: Lloyds TSB Group plc (1996)

NOTES TO THE ACCOUNTS

2 Accounting policies

i Tangible fixed assets [extract]

Land is not depreciated. Leasehold premises with unexpired lease terms of 50 years or less are depreciated by equal annual instalments over the remaining period of the lease. Freehold and long leasehold buildings are maintained in a state of good repair and it is considered that residual values, based on prices prevailing at the time of acquisition or subsequent valuation, are such that depreciation is not significant. ...

For a number of years the major supermarket operators generally followed a practice of non-depreciation in respect of their stores. However, in 1994 falling values of their stores brought the realisation that these assets were not really of the same character as pubs and hotels, and it has since become normal in that sector to follow a traditional approach to depreciation. Tesco discloses the following policy:

Extract 10.15: Tesco PLC (1997)

Accounting policies

Fixed assets and depreciation

Fixed assets include amounts in respect of interest paid, net of taxation, on funds specifically related to the financing of assets in the course of construction.

Depreciation is provided on an equal annual instalment basis over the expected useful working lives of the assets, after they have been brought into use, at the following rates:

Land premiums paid in excess of the alternative use value on acquisition – at 4% of cost.

Freehold and leasehold buildings with greater than 40 years unexpired – at 2.5% of cost.

Leasehold properties with less than 40 years unexpired are amortised by equal instalments over the unexpired period of the lease.

Plant, equipment, fixtures and fittings and motor vehicles – at rates varying from 10% to 33%.

Another category of assets which is generally not depreciated is the infrastructure assets of certain public utilities:

Extract 10.16: Thames Water Plc (1997)

d **Tangible fixed assets** comprise:

- Infrastructure assets (being mains and sewers, impounding and pumped raw water storage reservoirs and sludge pipelines);

- Landfill sites; and

- Other assets (including properties, overground plant and equipment)

i **Infrastructure assets** comprise a network of systems. Expenditure on infrastructure assets relating to increases in capacity or enhancements of the network is treated as additions. Expenditure on maintaining the operating capability of the network in accordance with defined standards of service is charged as an operating cost and is classified as infrastructure renewals expenditure.

No depreciation is charged on infrastructure assets because the network of systems is required to be maintained in perpetuity and therefore has no finite economic life.

Another practice which has grown up among companies which exploit mineral deposits is to depreciate their deposits only over the last portion of the life of the minerals being extracted. An example is to be found in the accounts of Tarmac:

Extract 10.17: Tarmac plc (1996)

Principal Accounting Policies

Depreciation [extract]

Depreciation is based on historic cost or revaluation, less the estimated residual values, and the estimated economic lives of the assets concerned. Freehold land is not depreciated. Mineral reserves are amortised over their estimated commercial life where this is less than ten years. Other tangible assets are depreciated in equal annual instalments over the period of their estimated economic lives. ...

Similar policies are followed by several other companies in the same industry, including Alfred McAlpine, Redland and RMC Group, although the life chosen by the last two is 20 rather than 10 years. The argument advanced to support such a treatment is generally that the value of the deposits does not tend to diminish appreciably until the deposits are nearly exhausted – again a valuation perspective of depreciation rather than a consumption view. In some respects this is similar to the SSAP 19 rule, that leasehold properties should be depreciated at least over the last 20 years of their lives, presumably on the same argument that the value does not decline significantly until then. Redland's policy reflects this way of thinking:

Extract 10.18: Redland PLC (1996)

Notes to the Accounts

1 Accounting policies

Tangible fixed assets [extract]

ii) Depreciation is provided on mineral bearing land to reflect the diminution in economic values as a result of mineral extraction. As a result, no provision is made where the remaining life is judged to be in excess of 20 years since the amount is not material. No depreciation is provided on other freehold land.

An ICAEW report to the ASB on SSAP 12 commented on this practice as follows: 'Because mineral reserves are valued on a net present value basis, in practice there would be little difference between the values of a mine with, say, 20 years' reserves as compared with a mine with 60 years' reserves of the same mineral. Consequently, it is argued that any loss in value of a mine occurs in the last 20 (or 15 or 10) years of its life, and therefore no depreciation is necessary until that point. Some people express this slightly differently (but achieve the same result) by asserting that they are using the annuity method of depreciation [see 3.7.4 below] and that accordingly depreciation is weighted heavily towards the final years of the life of the mine. This again highlights the need to reassess the role of depreciation – i.e. is it an allocation of cost or recognition of decline in value?'[51] The report concluded that the ASB should consult with companies in the industry and consider giving specific guidance on this matter.

Another version of the same argument is to be found in Granada's accounts in relation to motorway service areas:

Extract 10.19: Granada Group PLC (1996)

Accounting policies

4 Depreciation [extract]

... Motorway service areas held subject to short leaseholds are not depreciated whilst their value is maintained or increased. Depreciation thereafter is provided on a straight line basis over the residual period of the lease.

Although it does not seek to change the approach to depreciation taken by SSAP 12, the ASB's Discussion Paper on the *Measurement of tangible fixed assets* takes a dim view of most of the above arguments for non-depreciation. It says that 'although the life of many buildings is extended by regular maintenance, few can be regarded as having a limitless life ...'. It also makes clear its view that an increase in value of the property does not excuse the absence of depreciation. However, there can be little doubt that the argument on this issue will continue.

In our view, non-depreciation is entirely appropriate where it can be shown that the life of the asset is truly unlimited, or that the eventual residual value achieved by the present owner will not be less than the present carrying amount (bearing in mind that SSAP 12 requires the residual value to be determined in terms of prices ruling at the date of acquisition or revaluation, and not at the end of each year). However, we are more sceptical about arguments that depend on the fact that the value of an asset with a finite life has not yet started to decline.

It is also sometimes argued that assets not currently in use, for example ships that have been laid up, do not need to be depreciated. This argument is based on a view of depreciation as part of the cost of using an asset, to be matched against the revenue earned by it. However, depreciation is more usually viewed as an allocation of the cost of an asset over its useful life, so it should normally continue to be charged while the asset is not used. The lack of use may affect the asset's estimated useful life or be symptomatic of circumstances that affect its residual value (for example, it may be caused by a major slump in the world shipping markets), either of which may affect the amount of depreciation being charged. It might be argued that where an asset has not been used in a particular year its useful economic life has effectively been extended; but in that case depreciation will still need to be charged, albeit at a reduced rate.

If the asset is being depreciated using the unit of production method, then it might seem appropriate not to depreciate it when it is not in use. However, the unit of production method is sometimes applied with an assumed minimum amount of production, which means that a charge is still made in periods of no activity. Once again this may be a sign that there is a problem with the recoverable amount of the asset; there may, for example, be a decline in demand for the product (see 4.4 below).

3.2.3 Intangible assets

Intangible assets are often argued to have an unlimited life which renders amortisation irrelevant. This is exemplified in the following extracts:

Extract 10.20: Daily Mail and General Trust plc (1996)

Accounting policies

4. Intangible fixed assets

Publishing rights, titles and certain other intangible assets are stated at fair value as explained in note 13 to the accounts. These assets are valued by management on the basis of cashflow projections, and the values attributed represent the economic value of the assets to the Group at the date of acquisition. Since these assets have no finite life, amortisation is not provided unless there is a permanent diminution in their values, which are re-assessed annually.

Extract 10.21: WPP Group plc (1996)

ACCOUNTING POLICIES

4   Intangible fixed assets

Intangible fixed assets comprise certain acquired separable corporate brand names. These are shown at a valuation of the incremental earnings expected to arise from the ownership of brands. The valuations have been based on the present value of notional royalty savings arising from ownership of those brands and on estimates of profits attributable to brand loyalty. The valuations are subject to annual review. No depreciation is provided since, in the opinion of the directors, the brands do not have a finite useful economic life.

FRED 12 acknowledges that some intangible assets can indeed last indefinitely, such that amortisation is not necessary. However, it establishes a rebuttable presumption that the useful lives of intangibles are limited and do not exceed 20 years, and requires 'valid and disclosed grounds' where this presumption is rebutted. It also makes it clear that an intangible asset that depends on legal rights that have a finite life must itself be assumed to be limited to that life unless renewal of the legal rights is assured.[52]

3.3   The requirements of the Companies Act

The Companies Act requires any fixed asset that has a limited useful economic life to be depreciated over that life, on a systematic basis, down to its residual value (if any).[53] Depreciation is to be based on the carrying value; on the purchase price or production cost under the historical cost rules,[54] and on the revalued amount if the alternative accounting rules are being followed.[55] Depreciation of revalued assets is dealt with in 5.3.2 below.

3.4   SSAP 12

SSAP 12 was originally published in 1977 (following ED 15, which was published in January 1975). Subsequently, in 1982 the ASC issued a Discussion Paper on SSAP 12 dealing with a number of new issues including the effect of revaluations on depreciation, supplementary depreciation and the estimation of useful lives.[56] This was followed by ED 37 in April 1985 and finally by a revised version of SSAP 12 in January 1987.

The main requirements of the standard are discussed below.

3.4.1   Scope

The standard covers all fixed assets except for the following:

(a)   investment properties (see 3.2.1 above);

(b)   goodwill (see Chapter 6);

(c)   development costs (see Chapter 12);

(d)   investments (see Chapter 11).

3.4.2 Definitions

The following are the definitions in paragraphs 10 to 13 of SSAP 12:

Depreciation is the measure of the wearing out, consumption, or other reduction in the useful life of a fixed asset whether arising from use, effluxion of time or obsolescence through technological or market changes.

The *useful economic life* of an asset is the period over which the present owner will derive economic benefits from its use.

Residual value is the realisable value of the asset at the end of its useful economic life, based on prices prevailing at the date of acquisition or revaluation, if this has taken place, and after taking account of realisation costs.

Recoverable amount is the greater of the net realisable value of an asset and, where appropriate, the amount recoverable from its further use.

3.4.3 Accounting treatment

Provision for depreciation is the allocation of the cost or revalued amount of an asset, less its residual value, as fairly as possible to the periods expected to benefit from its use, i.e. over its useful economic life.[57]

There is to be consistency of treatment between the profit and loss account and the balance sheet, so that if an asset is carried at a revalued amount the depreciation must be based on this. Split depreciation is not permitted; the whole of the depreciation charge must go through the profit and loss account. Similarly, supplementary depreciation in excess of that based on the carrying value of the asset is not allowed.[58]

3.4.4 Asset lives

Asset lives must be realistically assessed and the same life must be used in historical cost accounts and on any accounts which reflect the effects of changing prices. They should be regularly reviewed.[59]

The standard goes on to point out that if asset lives are regularly reviewed, no material distortions to future results or financial position should arise when they are revised; the net book amount should be written off prospectively over the remaining useful life of the asset. However, if future results would be materially distorted then the adjustment to accumulated depreciation should be made through the profit and loss account for the current year, generally as an exceptional item.

3.4.5 Permanent diminutions

Immediate provision should be made for permanent diminutions in value. The carrying value should be written down to the estimated recoverable amount, which should then be written off over the remaining useful life of the asset. The provision should be made through the profit and loss account for the period. If the reasons for making the provision cease to apply, the provision should be written back to the extent that it is no longer necessary.

Two reasons for a permanent diminution are suggested: obsolescence or a fall in demand for a product.[60]

3.4.6   Depreciation on revalued assets

Depreciation is to be based on the revalued amounts and the remaining life of the asset at the time of the valuation. It is not permitted to write back to the profit and loss account any depreciation charged prior to the revaluation, except to the extent that it represents a provision for diminution in value now no longer necessary.[61]

3.5   Useful economic life

The useful economic life of an asset must be assessed before its residual value and depreciation can be calculated.

It should be noted that the useful economic life is the period over which the present owner will benefit and not the total potential life of the asset; the two will not always be the same. For example, a company may have a policy of replacing all of its cars after three years, so this will be their estimated useful life for depreciation purposes.

Secondly, the standard requires that asset lives be estimated on a realistic basis and reviewed regularly. Regular review will mean that the initial estimate of the life, which is often performed without actual experience of the asset in question, can be reassessed in the light of experience.

Despite this injunction, many companies tend to use quite a broad brush in estimating asset lives, often based on perceived norms rather than a close analysis of their own expectations. As a result, companies often have a material proportion of assets still in use but fully depreciated. This became so commonplace that ED 37 introduced a requirement that fully depreciated assets be reinstated if it was considered necessary in order for the accounts to give a true and fair view.[62] However, it was not clear what kind of circumstances were envisaged and the requirement was dropped from the revised standard.

One company which discloses the amount of its fully depreciated assets is British Steel, as shown in the following extract:

Extract 10.22: British Steel plc (1997)

10. Tangible fixed assets [extract]
(i) Included above are fully depreciated assets with an original cost of £1,055m (1996: £931m) which are still in use. In addition, there are fully depreciated assets with an original cost of £127m (1996: £605m) which are permanently out of use and pending disposal, demolition or reapplication elsewhere in the business.

An example of a company that explicitly states that it regularly reviews asset lives is ICI. As a result the accounting policy note cannot give the period over which the assets are depreciated, except as global averages, as illustrated below:

Extract 10.23: Imperial Chemical Industries PLC (1996)

Accounting policies

DEPRECIATION

The Group's policy is to write-off the book value of each tangible fixed asset evenly to its residual value over its estimated remaining life. Reviews are made annually of the estimated remaining lives of individual productive assets, taking account of commercial and technological obsolescence as well as normal wear and tear. Under this policy it becomes impracticable to calculate average asset lives exactly; however, the total lives approximate to 26 years for buildings and 18 years for plant and equipment. Depreciation of assets qualifying for grants is calculated on their full cost.

Companies often charge a full year's depreciation in the year of acquisition, regardless of when the assets were acquired, but many also depreciate their assets on a monthly basis for management accounts purposes and carry the same figures into their annual accounts. At the opposite extreme, one or two commence depreciation only in the following year; GKN is an example, as shown in the following extract:

Extract 10.24: GKN plc (1996)

3 OPERATING PROFIT [extract]

Depreciation is not provided on freehold land. In the case of buildings and computers, depreciation is provided on valuation or original cost. For all other categories of asset, depreciation is provided on the written down value at the beginning of the financial year. Except in special cases, depreciation is not charged on fixed assets capitalised during the year and available for use but a full year's depreciation is charged on fixed assets sold or scrapped during the year.

The effect of charging a full year's depreciation in the year of disposal is in fact only one of classification in the profit and loss account, because it changes the gain or loss reported on sale by an equal and opposite amount. GKN's practice of providing no depreciation in the first year is probably convenient, and is unlikely to create a material distortion in practice, but in principle depreciation should be charged from the date the asset is brought into use.

3.6 Residual values

Both the standard and the Act require residual values to be taken into account when calculating depreciation on an asset. The original SSAP 12 stated in its explanatory note that where residual value was likely to be small in relation to cost it was convenient to regard it as nil.[63] This was partly a recognition of the problems in determining the residual values – as the explanatory note to the original standard said, the precise assessment of residual value is normally a difficult matter.[64]

The standard contains a definition of residual value, given in 3.4.2 above. When assets are being carried at historical cost the residual value must be based on prices prevailing at the time of purchase. For example, if an asset has an estimated useful life of six years, the company should look at the net realisable value of a six year old equivalent asset as at the date of purchase rather than considering how much the asset will be worth in six years' time. Other factors to be taken into account will include location (in the case of property), the risk of obsolescence and the planned maintenance policy. This obviously makes an accurate assessment of residual value difficult.

Basing residual values on prices prevailing at the time of purchase means that it is not permitted to anticipate inflationary holding gains, and this has always been contentious. During periods of price increases, and other things being equal, a company that has calculated the residual value in accordance with the requirements of the standard will provide more depreciation than is necessary to reduce the carrying value to the actual residual value, which will result in a profit on disposal of the asset being reported.

3.7   Depreciation methods

Depreciation methods are not prescribed in SSAP 12, which merely states that the depreciable amount of the asset should be allocated 'as fairly as possible to the periods expected to benefit from their use. The depreciation methods used should be the ones which are the most appropriate having regard to the types of asset and their use in the business.'[65] A change from one method of providing depreciation to another is only permitted if the new method will more fairly present the enterprise's results and financial position. A change of method is not a change in accounting policy.[66]

Paragraph 8 in the explanatory note section of SSAP 12 states:

'There is a range of acceptable depreciation methods. Management should select the method regarded as most appropriate to the type of asset and its use in the business so as to allocate depreciation as fairly as possible to the periods expected to benefit from the asset's use. Although the straight line method is the simplest to apply, it may not always be the most appropriate.'

This is not altogether helpful, as no further guidance is given as to what 'fair' means in this context, nor as to the circumstances in which the straight line method is not appropriate. Nevertheless, the straight line method is overwhelmingly the most popular among large companies.

The other methods most commonly found in practice are reducing balance, sum of the digits (or 'rule of 78'), annuity and unit of production.

3.7.1   Straight line method

The asset is written off in equal instalments over its estimated useful life. The method is easy to apply, and also allows revisions to estimates to be made easily.

Example 10.1   Straight line depreciation

An asset costs £8,000 and has a residual value of nil. Depreciation is to be provided at 25% on a straight line basis.

		£
Year 1	Cost	8,000
	Depreciation at 25% of £8,000	2,000
	Net book value	6,000
Year 2	Depreciation at 25% of £8,000	2,000
	Net book value	4,000
Year 3	Depreciation at 25% of £8,000	2,000
	Net book value	2,000
Year 4	Depreciation at 25% of £8,000	2,000
	Net book value	–

3.7.2   Reducing balance method

The same percentage of the asset's net book value is written off annually.

Example 10.2   Reducing balance depreciation

An asset costs £8,000. Depreciation is to be provided at 25% on the reducing balance.

		£
Year 1	Cost	8,000
	Depreciation at 25% of £8,000	2,000
	Net book value	6,000
Year 2	Depreciation at 25% of £6,000	1,500
	Net book value	4,500
Year 3	Depreciation at 25% of £4,500	1,125
	Net book value	3,375

Under this method, the carrying value of the asset is never completely written off.

It is argued in favour of this method that the depreciation charge complements the costs of maintaining and running the asset. In the early years these costs are low and the depreciation charge is high, while in later years this is reversed.

3.7.3 Other reducing balance methods

A Double declining balance

This method is sometimes applied in the US, where it has corresponded to tax allowances on assets. The method involves determining the asset's depreciation on a straight line basis over its useful life. This annual amount is multiplied by an appropriate factor (it does not have to be doubled) to give the first year's charge and depreciation at the same percentage rate is charged on the reducing balance in subsequent years.

Example 10.3   Double declining balance depreciation

An asset costs £6,000 and has a life of ten years, which means that, calculated on the straight line basis, the annual depreciation charge would be £600. On the double declining balance method (assuming a factor of two), the depreciation charge for the first year would be £1,200 and depreciation would continue to be charged at 20% on the reducing balance thereafter.

B Sum of digits

This is another form of reducing balance method, but one that is based on the estimated life of the asset and which can therefore easily be applied if the asset has a residual value. If an asset has an estimated useful life of four years then the digits 1, 2, 3, and 4 are added together, giving a total of 10. Depreciation of four-tenths, three-tenths and so on, of the cost of the asset, less any residual value, will be charged in the respective years. The method is sometimes called the 'rule of 78', 78 being the sum of the digits 1 to 12.

Example 10.4   Sum of the digits depreciation

An asset costs £10,000 and is expected to be sold for £2,000 after four years. Depreciation is to be provided over four years using the sum of the digits method.

		£
Year 1	Cost	10,000
	Depreciation at $^4/_{10}$ of £8,000	3,200
	Net book value	6,800
Year 2	Depreciation at $^3/_{10}$ of £8,000	2,400
	Net book value	4,400
Year 3	Depreciation at $^2/_{10}$ of £8,000	1,600
	Net book value	2,800
Year 4	Depreciation at $^1/_{10}$ of £8,000	800
	Net book value	2,000

C   Reducing percentage

Another method which is sometimes used, and may represent an approximation to one of the previous methods, is to set predetermined proportions of the asset which are to be written off in each year of the asset's life. An example of a company using this method for certain of its assets is RMC Group.

Extract 10.25: RMC Group p.l.c. (1996)

Accounting Policies

DEPRECIATION AND DEPLETION

Depreciation is calculated to write off the cost of tangible fixed assets over their expected useful lives using the straight line basis, except as referred to below. ...

Commercial vehicles in the United Kingdom are depreciated over a period of 5 to 8 years on a reducing percentage basis, which reflects value consumed. ...

3.7.4   Annuity method

This is a method where account is taken of the cost of capital notionally invested in the asset. Notional interest and depreciation combined will give an approximately constant charge to revenue: depreciation is therefore low in the early years when the capital invested is high.

BOC applies this method to certain of its production plants, as illustrated below:

Extract 10.26: The BOC Group plc (1996)

5 Tangible fixed assets [extract]

(a) No depreciation is charged on freehold land or construction in progress. Depreciation is charged on all other fixed assets on the straight line basis over the effective lives except for certain tonnage plants where depreciation is calculated on an annuity basis over the life of the contract.

These 'tonnage plants' are built to supply specific long-term fixed contract customers.

As mentioned at 3.2 above, some argue that such a method is appropriate for assets such as mineral reserves, because it reflects the fact that the value of the asset (on a net present value basis) tends to decline only as the end of its life approaches. Perhaps a more powerful way of expressing the argument would be that, if the asset generates cash flows evenly over a long period, it is in that respect analogous to a lease receivable, and the annuity method of depreciation mirrors the accounting treatment which SSAP 21 requires in relation to leases, where a growing proportion of the revenue stream is allocated to write off the capital balance over the life of the lease. There is some merit in that argument, but to apply it consistently it would be necessary to consider all the items in the balance sheet and see how the cost of capital should influence their accounting treatment, not just certain selected assets.

3.7.5　Unit of production method

Under this method, the asset is written off in line with its estimated total output. By relating depreciation to productive capacity it reflects the fact that the useful economic life of certain assets, principally machinery, is more closely linked to its usage and output than to time. Vickers discloses such a policy in relation to the tooling for the production of its Rolls-Royce cars:

> Extract 10.27: Vickers P.L.C. (1996)
>
> **ACCOUNTING POLICIES**
>
> **Tangible assets** [extract]
>
> Motor car tooling is amortised on a per unit basis which takes into account actual production of each model and a conservative estimate of future production to the end of the model lives.

This method is also normally used in extractive industries, for example, to amortise the costs of development of productive oil and gas facilities,[67] as shown in the following extract:

> Extract 10.28: The British Petroleum Company p.l.c. (1996)
>
> **ACCOUNTING POLICIES**
>
> **Depreciation**
>
> Oil and gas production assets are depreciated using a unit-of-production method based upon estimated proved reserves. ...

3.7.6　Choice of depreciation method

Each of the various methods of calculating depreciation has its adherents who believe that conceptually it gives the 'best' answer in a given accounting context. In most circumstances the straight line method will give perfectly acceptable results. For certain assets where economic life is more linked to usage than to time, the unit of production method is preferable. As well as the extractive industries mentioned above, this could also apply to vehicles and aircraft. However, a complicating factor here, particularly in the case of aircraft, is that there may be many component parts, each of which has a separate life which may be measured by mileage or hours of service.

3.8　Changes in method of providing depreciation

As noted in 3.7 above, a change from one method of providing depreciation to another is only permitted if this will give a fairer presentation of an enterprise's results and financial position. The standard does not permit such a change to be dealt with as a prior year adjustment but requires it to be dealt with prospectively through the accounts as it states that 'such a change does not ... constitute a change of accounting policy; the net book value of the asset should be written off over the remaining life, commencing with the period in which the change is made'.[68] This accounting treatment, which can also be necessitated by a change in estimated life, is described in 3.9 below.

In our view there is a possible conflict between the above treatment required by SSAP 12 and the treatment which would be suggested by SSAP 2 – *Disclosure of accounting policies* – and FRS 3. According to SSAP 2, 'depreciation of fixed assets' is an accounting base[69] and this presumably means charging or not charging depreciation. If this is the case, a particular method of depreciation would appear to be an *accounting policy* in terms of SSAP 2. Accounting policies are defined in SSAP 2 as 'the specific accounting bases selected and consistently followed by a business enterprise as being, in the opinion of the management, appropriate to its circumstances and best suited to present fairly its results and financial position'.[70] But for the specific requirement of SSAP 12, a change from one method of charging depreciation to another could, therefore, be a change in accounting policy which would require a prior year adjustment.[71]

3.9 Changes in estimated life

The position under the original standard was unambiguous. When there was a revision of life of an asset, the unamortised cost was to be charged to revenue over the remaining life of the asset. There have always been those, however, who have argued that this was an incorrect approach as it meant that future depreciation charges would always be wrong; future accounting periods would, in effect, be 'penalised' (if the revised life was shorter) for the past errors in estimation.

The present standard requires a similar treatment, but now permits, in certain circumstances, the adjustment to accumulated depreciation to be made through the profit and loss account for the year. This means that such revisions are to be dealt with neither as changes in accounting policy, nor as fundamental errors, either of which would require a prior year adjustment.

Example 10.5   Change in life

A company purchases an asset in 19X1 costing £1,200. The original estimate of its useful life is ten years. At the beginning of 19X4 the remaining life is assessed as being three years and therefore the total life is revised to six years. Depreciation is being provided on a straight line basis.

Year	19X1 £	19X2 £	19X3 £	19X4 £	19X5 £	19X6 £
Depreciation charge						
– on prospective write off basis	120	120	120	280	280	280
– on cumulative catch up basis	120	120	120	440	200	200
Difference in effect on profit and loss account charge	–	–	–	160	(80)	(80)

The cumulative adjustment is only permitted through the current year's results if future results would be materially distorted. It is important to note that the adjustment could be a debit or a credit, i.e. could result from the lengthening as well as shortening of asset lives.

Since an adjustment is made only when the effect on the future years concerned would otherwise be to create a material distortion, it is obvious that the adjustment itself must be an even greater distortion of the results of the year in which it is made. For this reason it would seem necessary to disclose the adjustment as an exceptional item. In some circumstances, the need to make the change might itself be attributed to an exceptional item such as a restructuring, as is illustrated in the following extract:

Extract 10.29: Thorntons PLC (1996)

7. Costs of restructuring UK operations

Costs relating to the fundamental restructuring of the retail operations of the UK business have been treated as exceptional costs after arriving at operating profit. Exceptional operating charges relate primarily to UK manufacturing restructuring costs.

	Exceptional operating charges 1996 £000	Non-operating exceptionals 1996 £000	Total 1996 £000	Total 1995 £000
Accelerated write-down of assets (see (a) below)	136	3,314	3,450	–
Asset write-offs	–	2,039	2,039	–
Redundancy	1,015	768	1,783	643
Occupancy costs	55	3,761	3,816	–
Stock write-off	450	–	450	–
Other restructuring costs	619	653	1,272	132
	2,275	10,535	12,810	775

(a) The cost of the accelerated write-down of retail assets included in non-operating exceptionals arises from the decision to depreciate shop fittings over four years and leasehold improvements over five years rather than together over seven years. The accelerated cost has arisen from the restructuring of the retail business.

In addition to this backlog effect, Thorntons also quantified the effect on the depreciation charge for the current year within the fixed assets note.

The usual treatment, however, should be the prospective write off over the remaining life of the asset, as has been adopted by J D Wetherspoon in this extract:

Extract 10.30: J D Wetherspoon plc (1996)

2 Accounting adjustments

The Directors decided that, with effect from 1 August 1995, all freehold buildings would be depreciated to residual value over a life of fifty years and leasehold buildings over the lease term (or fifty years or less). In prior periods, such properties were not depreciated. Additionally, it was decided that major renovations to trading properties would henceforward be depreciated over six years, whereas previously they were depreciated over three years. UK generally accepted accounting principles do not allow the previous years' figures to be restated and hence the comparative figures have not been adjusted. Had they been, the depreciation charge in 1995 would have been £1.6 million greater than the figure shown in Note 7.

It must be pointed out that changing the life of an individual asset will only in unusual circumstances have a material effect on the accounts. If the class of asset continues to be replaced with equivalent assets (which have the new, revised life), then the annual depreciation charge will soon be the same whether or not there was an adjustment to accumulated depreciation in the year of review, although the cumulative catch up is likely to be a material adjustment in that year's results.

There is no reason why the life of an asset should not be reassessed in exactly the same way when it has been fully depreciated or written down to a nominal amount, although regular review of asset lives will prevent this happening. This is despite the fact that the requirement to reinstate fully depreciated assets was not included in the revised version of SSAP 12, as mentioned in 3.5 above.

3.10 Treatment of minor items

Some types of business may have a very large number of minor fixed assets such as tools, cutlery, containers or sheets and towels. There are practical problems in recording them on an asset-by-asset basis in an asset register; they are difficult to control and frequently lost. The main consequence is that it becomes very difficult to provide depreciation on them.

There are a number of ways in which companies attempt to deal with the problems of depreciating minor assets. The items may be written off to the profit and loss account (the company will probably have a minimum value for capitalising assets), they may be capitalised at a fixed amount, a treatment which is permitted in the Act, or the company may have some other form of policy that writes them off when they are used up but without having to identify them individually.

Marks and Spencer's accounts include a policy which describes the write off to revenue of minor items:

Extract 10.31: Marks and Spencer p.l.c. (1997)

Accounting policies

Repairs and renewals

Expenditure on repairs, renewals and minor items of equipment is written off in the year in which it is incurred.

Some other companies capitalise their minor items at a fixed amount, for example, when they are originally provided, as a form of capital 'base stock'; additions are not capitalised and depreciation is not charged. This is permitted under the accounting rules in the Companies Act, which state that tangible fixed assets may be included at a fixed amount provided that their overall value is not material to assessing the company's state of affairs and their quantity, value and composition are not subject to material variation.[72]

Although this is a common accounting practice, it does not strictly conform to the requirement of SSAP 12 that all assets be depreciated, and companies that do apply such a policy do so on the basis that the constant loss and replacement of stock items does lead to a materially constant amount. It is only acceptable as an accounting policy on the grounds of materiality. In periods of inflation the difference between the carrying value of these assets and their actual cost could quickly become very marked, in which case the policy may have to be modified.

Another issue of this kind that sometimes arises is the treatment of a pool of circulating assets that pass back and forward to customers. Cadbury Schweppes discloses this approach to returnable containers

Extract 10.32: Cadbury Schweppes p.l.c. (1996)

Accounting Policies

(k) Tangible fixed assets

… Returnable containers are included in fixed assets at cost. Depreciation is charged to reflect estimated loss or breakage rates in each market. …

Notes on the Accounts

13 Tangible Fixed Assets [extract]

Plant and equipment also includes returnable containers of £38m (1995: £45m) whose value at most recent purchase price would be £56m (1995: £65m).

In 1996, Brammer fell foul of the Financial Reporting Review Panel because it had been carrying a pool of instruments that were rented out to customers as stock in its balance sheet rather than as fixed assets. The 1994 accounts read as follows:

Extract 10.33: Brammer plc (1994)

Accounting Policies

Stock

Stock of rental instruments is valued at the lower of amortised cost and net realisable value, net realisable value being the present value of the net anticipated future rental income.

This was amended in the 1995 accounts as follows:

Extract 10.34: Brammer plc (1995)

Accounting Policies

Change of accounting policy – rental inventory

... the company has agreed with the Financial Reporting Review Panel that rental inventory, previously classified as current assets, should be reclassified as fixed assets. As a result of effecting this change:

- proceeds from the disposal of previously rented instruments is excluded from turnover and included in profit on sale of fixed assets in the profit and loss account.

- rental inventory is classified as fixed assets and is valued at cost less depreciation on a straight line basis over the expected economic lives of the assets (generally 2 to 6 years) taking account of estimated residual values, less any necessary provision for permanent diminution in value.

- the depreciation charge for the year on rental inventory is added back to operating profit in arriving at net cash inflow from operating activities in the cash flow statement.

The accounts carrying value of rental inventory is unchanged and, accordingly, the change of classification does not affect the profit for the year in any year or the shareholders' equity at the end of any year. The figures in the 1994 consolidated profit and loss account, balance sheet and cash flow statement have been reclassified as a result of this change.

---

4 IMPAIRMENT

4.1 Introduction

Provisions for impairment of fixed assets, or permanent diminutions in their value, are not yet covered in any depth by UK accounting standards or the law. SSAP 12 refers to the treatment of permanent diminutions in the case of assets carried at cost, but specifically excludes revalued assets when covering the profit and loss account treatment of provisions.[73] The statutory accounting rules in Schedule 4 also require provisions for diminution in value to be made in appropriate circumstances, and require certain disclosures, but do not otherwise go into any detail on the subject. However, the ASB is developing a standard which will deal comprehensively with the subject and radically change existing practice.

This section covers impairment both in general and as it applies to assets carried at historical cost. The specific problems relating to assets carried at valuation are dealt with in 5.3.4 below.

4.2   Companies Act requirements

The Act requires provisions for diminution in value to be made in respect of any fixed asset if the reduction in value is expected to be permanent.

The provisions are to be made through the profit and loss account.[74] Provisions no longer required are to be written back, again through the profit and loss account.[75] In either case, amounts not shown in the profit and loss account must be disclosed in the notes to the accounts.[76] It should also be noted that, except in the circumstances of a revaluation of all assets (see 5.3.6 below), the Act requires any provision to be treated as a realised loss for distribution purposes whether it is considered to be permanent or temporary.

4.3   SSAP 12 and permanent diminutions

SSAP 12 requires provisions to be made, if at any time there is a permanent diminution in value, to write the net book amount of the asset down to its estimated recoverable amount. This should then be written off over the remaining useful life of the asset. If the reasons for making the provision cease to apply it should be written back to the profit and loss account.[77]

Provisions for permanent diminutions in value of assets (and any reversals) should be charged (or credited) in the profit and loss account for the period.[78]

Although the ASB is now developing a standard on the subject, there is presently little further guidance on impairment testing in UK accounting literature except for one industry sector; detailed guidance for oil and gas companies has been issued in an industry SORP, dealing with the annual ceiling test carried out on the carrying value of their interests in particular pools or fields. The ceiling test should determine whether the carrying value (whether determined under full cost or successful efforts methods), less any provisions for abandonment costs and deferred production or revenue-related taxes, is covered by the anticipated future net revenue attributable to the company's interests.[79] The rules laid down in the SORP for the purposes of the test are as follows:

(a)   future net revenues are the estimated revenues from production of commercial reserves less operating costs, production or revenue-related taxes (including UK petroleum revenue tax), insurance and royalties, future development costs and abandonment costs. General financing costs and taxation on profits (including UK corporation tax) should not be deducted in the calculation of future net revenues;

(b)   prices and cost levels used should be those ruling at the date as at which the ceiling test is applied; and

(c)   estimates of future net revenues and costs should not be discounted.[80]

As can be seen from the section which follows, this approach is significantly different from that now proposed by the ASB.

4.4 FRED 15

In April 1996 the ASB published a Discussion Paper on *Impairment of tangible fixed assets* and subsequently broadened its scope, to cover goodwill and intangible assets as well, in an exposure draft issued in June 1997. FRED 15 takes a radically new approach to the subject; it does not explicitly differentiate between temporary and permanent impairment, it measures recovery of assets at a post-tax profit level; and it introduces discounting into the measurement process.

The proposed standard says that a detailed review will be needed only if there are 'indications of impairment'. These are said to include:

■ operating losses or negative operating cash flows in the current year, which have also occurred in the past or are expected to recur in the future;

■ a significant decrease in the market value of a fixed asset;

■ obsolescence or physical damage to the fixed asset;

■ a significant adverse change in the business or in the market in which the asset is used;

■ a significant adverse change in the statutory or other regulatory environment in which the business operates;

■ a significant adverse change in any 'indicator of value' (such as multiples of turnover) used to measure the fair value of an asset on acquisition;

■ a forthcoming reorganisation of the business;

■ a major loss of key employees;

■ a significant increase in market rates of interest or other market rates of return which materially affect the asset's recoverable amount.[81]

The last of these is particularly noteworthy, because it highlights how radical this proposed change to practice is. Assets will in future be judged to be impaired if they are no longer expected to earn a current market rate of return. This means that an upward move in general interest rates may give rise to a write-down in fixed assets even though they will generate the same cash flows as before and, correspondingly, a decline in interest rates will lead to the reversal of any such write-down. Implicitly, therefore, this imports the 'current-market-rate-of-return' capital maintenance concept that has been controversially proposed by the IASC for financial instruments (see Chapter 9 at 5).

If it is concluded that there are indications of impairment, then the next stage is to test the carrying value of the assets concerned against their recoverable amount, which is defined as the higher of net realisable value and value in use (i.e. the present value of expected future cash flows generated by using the asset), and write off any excess.[82] At this stage, an aggregation issue arises; cash flows can seldom be associated with individual assets so as to permit such a comparison. The proposed standard therefore requires a more indirect test, involving the cash flows of 'income-generating units' (the smallest segments of the business for which substantially independent income streams can be identified). These cash flows have to be forecast, discounted to their present value, and the resulting figure compared to the carrying value of the net assets of the segment concerned.

If that comparison shows that the carrying value exceeds the present value of the forecast cash flows, the excess has to be eliminated, first against the goodwill assigned to the segment, next against any other intangible asset, and thereafter against the tangible assets. The reduced carrying value of the assets should then be written off over their remaining life (which should first be reassessed).[83]

Although the income-generating units are meant to be those whose income streams are largely independent of each other, the exposure draft also requires them to embrace all the assets of the company, including central assets such as the head office. Accordingly, such central assets have to be apportioned across the units in some way.[84] This contrasts with the treatment of such assets for the purposes of segmental reporting, where they would be left unallocated rather than assigned to segments in an artificial way. Similarly, goodwill is also to be allocated to income-generating units, except that if more than one income-generating unit was acquired in the same acquisition, they can still be combined for the purposes of the assessing the recoverability of the assets including the goodwill.[85]

FRED 15 says that the cash flows to be assessed should take account of all costs including central overheads and tax, and use an after-tax interest rate that 'the market would expect on an equally risky investment'.[86] The exposure draft says that this may be estimated by reference to (for example):

- the rate implicit in market transactions of similar assets;

- the weighted average cost of capital of a listed company with similar risk profiles;

- the weighted average cost of capital of the reporting company but only if adjusted for the particular risks associated with the income generating unit in question.[87]

This guidance as to the choice of rate seems rather more theoretical than practical. However, irrespective of the rate chosen, this approach is radically different from present practice. Under existing rules, companies generally assess the recoverability of their assets at an operating profit level, or even a gross profit level, and do not employ discounting.

We are not convinced that this really improves financial reporting. In other contexts, the ASB has been anxious to stop companies masking sub-standard performance by pre-emptive provisions (see Chapter 26); yet this is close to what is being proposed here. Under these proposals, no company should ever report a sub-standard rate of return on its assets employed; if it does, it will mean that it has not adequately provided for impairment in the past. Moreover, for all their apparent science, the calculations made under this methodology will be highly subjective, and we doubt if this will provide better information for the users of accounts.

It is also debatable whether this method complies with company law, because it involves assessing assets for impairment on a portfolio basis rather than individually. In contrast, the Act requires that 'in determining the aggregate amount of any item the amount of each individual asset or liability that falls to be taken into account shall be determined separately'.[88]

The approach is also inconsistent with generally accepted practice for depreciation which, except when annuity-based methods are used, does not take account of the time value of money. As FRED 15 specifies, once assets have been written down to the present value of their forecast future cash flows they will continue to be depreciated as normal; however, this will produce incoherent numbers because of the combination of the two approaches. It would be more consistent simply to think of impairment as accelerated depreciation and to provide for it on an undiscounted basis. All in all, we think present GAAP is superior to the methodology proposed by FRED 15.

5 REVALUATIONS

5.1 Introduction

5.1.1 Background

The incorporation of revalued assets into historical cost accounts was widespread during the 1970s when the United Kingdom was suffering from unprecedented levels of inflation. In the following decade the ICAEW annual surveys of published accounts identified a movement away from the practice of revaluation, but more recent research has shown that some 60% of large companies still include at least some of their assets at a valuation.[89]

Rank provides one example of a company that has recently reverted to a historical cost basis:

Extract 10.35: The Rank Group Plc (1996)

Accounting Policies

1 BASIS OF PREPARATION

Changes in accounting policy [extract]

Land and buildings are stated on the historical cost basis. Previously they had been revalued on a rolling cycle and the valuation incorporated in the accounts. The effect of this change, which has been shown as a prior year adjustment, has been to reduce the profit for the year ended 31 December 1995 by £4 million and to reduce Shareholders' funds at that date by £186 million. The directors believe that this change facilitates analysis of returns in the Group's business segments.

Although this change was attributed to a desire to clarify historical segmental returns, it is noteworthy that the change was accompanied by a £334 million write-down of fixed assets to their recoverable amount, of which £186 million was taken as a prior year adjustment as shown in the above extract and the remaining £148 million reported as a provision for permanent diminution in the profit and loss account. Under the previous year's policy (as shown in this extract from the 1995 accounts), the whole amount of the impairment would have been charged against earnings:

Extract 10.36: The Rank Group Plc (1995)

Accounting Policies

VIII LAND AND BUILDINGS [extract]

Any revaluation deficit, calculated by reference to the previous carrying value, is recorded in the revaluation reserve to the extent that it is considered to be a temporary diminution in value. To the extent that any such diminution is considered to be permanent, it is charged to the profit and loss account.

SSAP 12 requires the profit and loss account charge for depreciation on revalued assets to be based on carrying amount. Similarly, FRS 3 measures the gain or loss on disposal of a revalued asset by reference to its revalued amount. Accordingly, a company that revalues its depreciable assets will show a lower earnings per share as a result. Revaluations also affect the comparability of balance sheet ratios such as the return on capital. However, most major companies include at least some of their fixed assets at revalued amounts.

SSAP 12 encourages revaluations of tangible fixed assets on the grounds that they give 'useful and relevant information to users of accounts', and this paragraph goes on: 'This statement does not prescribe how frequently assets should be revalued but, where a policy of revaluing assets is adopted, the valuations should be kept up to date.'[90] In spite of this wording (which is in the explanatory notes and so does not form part of the standard itself), the valuations of property in many companies' accounts have tended to be undertaken at infrequent intervals and may often be some years out of date. Valuations are presently permitted on an asset-by-asset basis; they do not have to cover all of the assets in a particular class and in practice rarely do so.

Companies usually do not disclose a policy on revaluations and the current situation of ad hoc valuations may mean that in fact they often do not have one; they need give no reasons as to why certain assets have been revalued and others left at historical cost. Finally, it is rarely clear as to exactly which basis of valuation has been used. The Companies Act is vague; 'market value' and 'current cost', the two permitted bases for the valuation of tangible fixed assets, would permit a number of different interpretations (see 5.2 below).

In summary, many accounts include valuations of some assets, almost always confined to land and buildings, but there is no overall rationale for the inclusion of revalued assets in the first place. This has made it very difficult to develop a systematic and consistent approach to the accounting problems which result from their inclusion: how to account for permanent and temporary diminutions in value, depreciation and disposals.

5.1.2 ED 51

In May 1990, the ASC published ED 51 – *Accounting for fixed assets and revaluations* – which sought to impose some order on the diversity of practice described above. As well as dealing with the issues of how to account for revaluations once the decision has been made to incorporate them (described in more detail at 5.3 below), it addressed the basic question of whether assets should be revalued at all and what restrictions should be placed on a company's freedom to incorporate valuations in its accounts.

The stance taken by the exposure draft was essentially a pragmatic one. It accepted that the incorporation of valuations in historical cost accounts has little, if any, conceptual validity. Nevertheless, it acknowledged that the practice had become widespread, and that there was little purpose in trying either to prohibit it or to make it compulsory. Accordingly, ED 51 proposed certain ground rules to impose greater consistency on the practice where companies had chosen to adopt it.

The exposure draft proposed, first of all, that a decision should be made in relation to each class of assets as to whether that class is to be carried at historical cost or at a valuation.[91] In other words, it sought to prohibit piecemeal valuations where some assets within a class are carried at cost while others are carried at a valuation. For this purpose, a class of assets was defined as a category 'having a similar nature or function in the business of the enterprise and which comprises one or more items each of which is shown in the financial statements as a single item without further subdivision. For the purpose of this definition, subdivision by reference to the geographical location of fixed assets should be ignored.'[92]

As well as restricting piecemeal valuations, ED 51 proposed to require valuations to be kept up to date. It did not specifically call for annual valuations, but proposed that valuations which were more than five years old should not be used.[93] In addition, however, it required more frequent valuations if values had moved significantly since the date of the previous valuation. A continuous 'rolling' basis of valuation was also permissible.[94] The purpose of these proposals was clear; irrelevant, outdated valuations should not be presented in company accounts.

5.1.3   ASB Discussion Paper on valuations

In March 1993, the ASB published a Discussion Paper entitled *The role of valuation in financial reporting*. This put forward a different set of possibilities and invited comment. The scope of the paper was not confined to fixed assets, but extended to other items in the balance sheet as well. It suggested that current values should be used for the following categories of assets, only the first of which is relevant to this chapter:

■   properties, excluding fixed assets specific to the business;

■   quoted investments; and

■   stock of a commodity nature and long-term stock where a market of sufficient depth exists.[95]

However, these proposals were not really explored in any depth. The question of what makes fixed assets 'specific to the business', was not adequately explained. More importantly, it was not established why it would be appropriate to revalue some fixed assets and not others; the paper discussed valuations only in nebulous terms and without any clarity of purpose. It did not even discuss where the other side of the revaluation entry should go, saying only that 'the Board will need to consider how gains and losses should be allocated between the profit and loss account and the statement of total recognised gains and losses'.[96]

5.1.4   ASB Discussion Paper on the Measurement of tangible fixed assets

The ASB's Discussion Paper of October 1996 picks up where ED 51 left off more than six years before. Like that earlier draft, it does not propose to make valuations compulsory, but seeks to ban out of date valuations from the balance sheet and to require any policy of valuation to be applied to a whole class of assets rather than on a selective basis. A class, however, is defined in a more accommodating way than was proposed in ED 51; the proposed definition is 'a category of tangible fixed assets having a similar nature or function in the business of the entity. Assets used within different geographical segments and classes of business may be treated as separate classes of asset.' This therefore allows quite small classifications to be used, which may impose less consistency on valuation policy than was originally intended.

Like ED 51, the proposals also require valuations to be kept up to date, suggesting a full external valuation every three to five years, with less formal interim valuations in the intervening years. A 'rolling' basis would again be permitted.

Unlike the ASB's earlier Discussion Paper on valuations, this paper tries to explain the benefits of using a valuation approach, at least for non-specialised properties. It asserts that:

(a)   the demand from potential users tends to cause the current value of non-specialised property to diverge from historical cost to a greater extent than that of most specialised assets. Balance sheets with up-to-date non-specialised property values therefore provide useful information on a company's asset base;

(b)   non-specialised properties represent a store of value affecting the financial position and adaptability of an entity and therefore up-to-date values give more relevant information than historical values about the assets available as security for borrowings and the asset base used to generate earnings. They also make possible the calculation of a more realistic gearing ratio;

(c)   changes in value of non-specialised properties can have potentially major effects on profit measurement on disposal. However, where values are kept up-to-date, gains and losses are recognised in the year in which they occur rather than when they are realised. One potential effect is that the opportunity for purchasers to make profits from understated values is much reduced:

(d)   an established market normally exists for non-specialised property and therefore, in the majority of cases when compared with more specialised assets, a reliable market value can be obtained at a reasonable cost.

These are rather unconvincing arguments. Taking them one by one,

(a)   no evidence has been summoned to support the paper's assertion that the values of non-specialised assets diverge more from historical cost than those of specialised assets. Common sense suggests that the reverse is more likely to be true.

(b)   relevance is said to follow from the fact that non-specialised properties represent a 'store of value' affecting the financial position and adaptability of an entity. Yet most such assets are properties such as factory units, warehouses, offices and retail outlets. They are actually a necessary input for production that must be paid for, not items which can be disposed of to realise that value without disrupting the business. This 'store of value' appears to boil down to the assets' potential use as security for borrowings, hardly a major argument in favour of the inclusion of valuations in accounts.

(c)   current values are thought to be superior because they alter reported profits on disposal by dealing with revaluation movements through the statement of total recognised gains and losses. This obviously depends entirely on one's point of view on the merits of historical cost accounting, and it does not acknowledge the difference in quality between revaluation surpluses and realised profits. In addition, this argument is expressed solely in relation to non-specialised assets carried at valuation, whereas carrying specialised assets at depreciated replacement cost is to be permitted; an increase in the cost of replacing an asset cannot realistically be seen as an economic gain for the reporting entity.

(d) it is said to be an advantage of valuations of non-specialised assets that there are usually established markets in which reliable market values can be obtained at reasonable cost. However, this is not always true. During the worst of the property slump, in 1990 to 1992, valuers were not always able to provide reasonably accurate valuations because of the thinness of the property market. At times the only valuations which could be obtained were 'deathbed' valuations which could hardly have been regarded as being relevant. Moreover, many non-specialised properties are actually sold as businesses, not as assets, and the problems (and unreliability) of these valuations are not addressed in the Discussion Paper at all – see the discussion of Queens Moat Houses at 5.2.5 below. In any case, the cheapness of these valuations is not an argument for their relevance, but an admission of the difficulties and obstacles of obtaining reliable valuations of specialised assets.

Altogether, the supposed advantages of valuations that have been advanced in this paper are less than compelling.

5.1.5   SSAP 19

SSAP 19 requires investment properties to be included in the balance sheet at their open market value. They should not be depreciated except for leasehold property which should be depreciated at least over the last twenty years of the lease period.[97]

The standard does not require the valuations to be carried out by qualified or independent valuers, but recommends that 'where investment properties represent a substantial proportion of the total assets of a major enterprise (e.g. a listed company) the valuation thereof would normally be carried out:

a) annually by persons holding a recognised professional qualification and having recent post-qualification experience in the location and category of the properties concerned; and

b) at least every five years by an external valuer'.[98]

Some property companies have no stated policy on the frequency of independent valuations; however, most have regular valuations. Examples of companies having a stated policy on the subject are shown below:

Extract 10.37: *Raglan Property Trust plc (1997)*

(c) Investment properties [extract]

Investment properties are shown at their open market value based on annual valuations. Such valuations are undertaken by independent valuers at least once every three years and by the directors in consultation with independent valuers in the interim periods.

Extract 10.38: *Liberty International Holdings PLC (1996)*

Investment properties [extract]

Completed investment properties are professionally valued on an open market basis by external valuers at the end of each financial year. Surpluses and deficits arising during the year are reflected in the revaluation reserve. Permanent diminutions in the value of an investment property are charged in the profit and loss account.

Some property companies have annual external valuations and include a copy of the valuer's report in their annual report and accounts.[99]

5.2   Bases of valuation

5.2.1   General principles

The main influence on accounting for revaluations is the Companies Act 1985; the Alternative Accounting Rules in Part C of Schedule 4 of the Act give the statutory bases and rules regarding revaluations. In addition to historical cost, the Act recognises the following bases of valuation for the various classes of fixed asset:

(a)   tangible fixed assets may be included at market value or current cost;[100]

(b)   intangibles, except goodwill, may be included at current cost;[101]

(c)   investments may be included at market value or at directors' valuation.[102]

In each case 'market value' is at the date of the asset's last valuation; in other words, the Act does not require the value to be as of the date of the accounts. Current cost, however, implies a value as at the balance sheet date.

The three bases listed above (current cost, market value and directors' valuation) are not explained further in the Act and they are discussed further below. It is important to appreciate, however, that these are not three distinct and mutually exclusive valuation bases: on the contrary, they overlap with each other.

Current cost is a valuation *concept* developed in relation to current cost accounting, which is generally defined as shown in this diagram:[103]

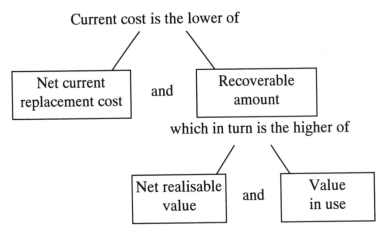

Each of these three elements still requires a *method* of valuation to measure what the relevant amount is. 'Market value' may be appropriate in determining replacement cost and/or net realisable value, depending on the manner in which the enterprise would replace and/or dispose of the asset in question, and there are a number of different valuation methods which are designed to arrive at some form of market value. Similarly, 'directors' valuation' is not a basis as such, but simply permits the directors to adopt whatever basis seems to them appropriate in the circumstances of the company, subject to disclosure of the basis used and the reasons for choosing it. Accordingly, in exercising that judgement, they may be trying to assess the replacement cost of the asset in question and they may be aiming to estimate its market value for that purpose. It can therefore be seen that the three apparently different 'bases' are in fact pitched at different levels of description and the application of all three is substantially intertwined.

The ASB uses the model shown in the above diagram as its conceptual basis for valuation, although calling the resulting amount 'value to the business' rather than 'current cost'. In fact, it can be argued that *neither* term properly describes the model; 'current cost' really only refers to the net current replacement cost leg of the diagram, whereas 'value to the business', in any normal meaning of the words, would address the amount the entity expected to recoup from its existing asset; that is, its recoverable amount. The true significance of the model is that it reflects the greatest loss the entity could suffer if, hypothetically, it were to be deprived of the asset. This 'deprival value' is the foundation of current cost accounting, in which its function is to measure the cost of replacing resources as they are consumed in the profit and loss account, not the value of those that remain in the balance sheet.

This is a fundamental distinction, but one which has never been properly unravelled by UK standard setters. Measuring consumption in the profit and loss account is a backwards-looking exercise, designed to match costs (albeit current costs in this context) against revenues. Replacement cost is an entry value, and movements in it are not gains and losses but rather adjustments to the (physical) capital that must be maintained before any profit can be achieved. If the desire is to measure value in the balance sheet it is necessary to concentrate on forward-looking measures – exit values – and forget about cost-based measures. Under this approach, movements in value can be regarded as gains and losses.

Modified historical cost accounting, the ad hoc practice of spasmodic revaluations that has grown up in the UK, is a muddle of the two approaches. In seeking to impose some order upon it, the ASB Discussion Paper on the *Measurement of tangible fixed assets* invokes the 'value to the business' model and asserts that it is relevant because it 'considers an asset in terms of the opportunities available to the owner in relation to the asset, ie to replace, hold or sell'.[104] However, this statement does not bear much scrutiny. The only opportunities an owner has in relation to an existing asset are to hold it or sell it. The possibility of buying another asset, whether as a replacement or not, does not add to these two choices in relation to the existing asset, and consequently it cannot affect its value. The truth is that the model properly belongs only in a current cost system.

The mechanics associated with different approaches to the valuation of assets are discussed below.

5.2.2   *Valuation of land and buildings*

A   *General principles*

As discussed above, 'market value' is not defined further in the Act, and it can have a number of different meanings as can be seen in this section.

In 1974 a joint working party of members of the ICAEW and the Royal Institution of Chartered Surveyors (RICS) was set up; this resulted in the issuance by the RICS of guidance notes on the valuation of properties for the purposes of company accounts. At this time the ICAEW issued an accounting recommendation[105] which stated that these notes contained the acceptable bases for valuation and the circumstances in which they should be used. The RICS guidance notes have been regularly updated and were reissued in 1990 as 'Statements of Asset Valuation Practice' (SAVPs) and more recently embodied in the RICS *Appraisal and Valuation Manual*, but the ICAEW has never revised its original statement. However, much of the relevant guidance is now picked up in the ASB's Discussion Paper on the *Measurement of tangible fixed assets*. The main possibilities are discussed below.

B   *Open market value*

Under the RICS *Appraisal and Valuation Manual*, 'open market value' (OMV) is defined as the best price at which the sale of an interest in property would have been completed unconditionally for cash consideration on the date of valuation assuming:

(a)   a willing seller;

(b)   that, prior to the date of valuation, there had been a reasonable period (having regard to the nature of the property and the state of the market) for the proper marketing of the interest, for the agreement of the price and terms and for the completion of the sale;

(c)   that the state of the market, level of values and other circumstances were, on any assumed date of exchange of contracts, the same as on the date of valuation;

(d)   that no account is taken of any additional bid by a prospective purchaser with a special interest; and

(e)   that both parties to the transaction had acted knowledgeably, prudently and without compulsion.[106]

Such a valuation does not assume that the property will be confined to its existing use, and is therefore generally used in relation to investment properties. Its relevance to other kinds of property is discussed further below.

C   *Existing use value*

The RICS defines 'existing use value' (EUV) in terms of the above definition of open market value but with two extra conditions:

(f)   the property can be used for the foreseeable future only for the existing use; and

(g)   that vacant possession is provided on completion of the sale of all parts of the property occupied by the business (save that, solely where the property is owned by a public or other non-profit-making body for the delivery of a service, it is to be assumed that the property will continue to be occupied or let for its existing use).[107]

The RICS Manual explains that, where a property is fully developed for its most beneficial use, its EUV is likely to be the same as its OMV with vacant possession.[108] However, there will be occasions where the two diverge. On the one hand, OMV may exceed EUV because the latter does not admit the possibility of putting a higher value on a property because it could be redeployed to a more valuable use. Less usually, OMV may fall short of EUV, for example because the present owner enjoys some benefits that could not be passed on in a sale, such as planning consents that are personal to the present occupier.

The manual also explains that EUV has been developed specifically for financial reporting purposes. The concept behind it is that of net current replacement cost, i.e. 'the cost of purchasing, at the least cost, the remaining service potential of the asset at the balance sheet date'.[109] The ASB Discussion Paper proposes that EUV should be the basis on which owner-occupied non-specialised properties should be valued, although the amount of any difference between the two bases should be disclosed if it is material.[110]

D Valuations that include trading potential

This is a particular variant of EUV which is customarily applied to certain types of property and is based upon their earning capacity, essentially valuing them more as businesses than physical assets. Such properties, which can include hotels, public houses, cinemas, theatres, petrol stations, betting shops or specialised leisure and sporting facilities, are sold on the open market as fully operational business units at prices based directly on trading potential. The valuation will therefore include all of the assets of the business as a going concern, including fixtures and fittings and the value of the trading potential. The report may not distinguish between the various elements that make up the valuation.

Surprisingly, the ASB's Discussion Paper on the *Measurement of tangible fixed assets* scarcely mentions this basis. However, it was briefly discussed in SSAP 22, in these terms: 'this trading potential is sometimes thought of as goodwill, but such a basis of valuation would normally exclude any goodwill which is personal to the present owner or management and which would not pass with the property on a sale with vacant possession. This practice is acceptable in certain limited categories of business. Where it is followed, the assets concerned should be disclosed separately and the notes to the accounts should make clear that this practice has been followed and that the amount at which the assets concerned are stated does not exceed their open market value, having regard to the trading potential of the business. This treatment is not dealt with in part 3 of the standard as it concerns the treatment of other assets, not of goodwill.'[111]

The paragraph quoted above conveys an impression of some disquiet on behalf of the ASC, because it is clear that the valuation does include some intangible elements, whether attributable to goodwill which is not specific to the present occupier, or to some more particular asset, such as a gaming or liquor licence. It is arguable that such intangible assets should be split out from the valuation and accounted for separately, since even if they are not capable of being disposed of separately from the land and buildings they may well have a different useful life from the bricks and mortar and hence justify a different period of amortisation from the life attributed to the building for depreciation purposes. However, this allocation may not be easily derived and it does not generally seem to be made in practice.

As a matter of fact, assets that are valued using this basis are frequently not depreciated at all, for the reasons discussed at 3.2.2 above, which highlights a further paradox. The ASB's Discussion Paper on *Measurement of tangible fixed assets* insists that depreciation should be charged on such assets, but has taken a more relaxed view in relation to intangible assets, which may be left at their original amount unless found to be impaired. Yet where this basis is used, any valuation of the property is likely to include a substantial intangible element, and this only accentuates the contrast between the Board's approaches to the depreciation of tangible and intangible assets.

The problem for the valuer is in distinguishing between the value of the trading potential which runs with the property and the value of goodwill which has been created in the business by the present owner and which may be transferable on sale. The relevant RICS Guidance Note states that only the former should be included in the valuation,[112] but this will inevitably be difficult to distinguish in practice.

Trading potential valuations can also cause problems in respect of fixtures and fittings. The trading potential valuation will include those so-called landlord's fixtures and fittings that are necessary for the business to function. For example, a hotel's valuation would have to include beds, bed linen and other necessary furnishings. A valuation may also be performed on the hotel in its current condition, i.e. including fixtures and fittings that have been added by the existing owner over and above this basic level. However, part or all of either category of fixtures and fittings may have been purchased by the current owner and included in the accounts, probably at cost, as a separate category of fixed asset.

E   *Estimated Realisation Price and Estimated Restricted Realisation Price*

The ASB paper tends to equate EUV with replacement cost and OMV with net realisable value. This is perhaps understandable in the sense that EUV reflects the present owner's circumstances whereas OMV is a more general measure of value, but the RICS does not differentiate these two bases in terms of purchase or sale transactions. In any case, any distinction based on buying and selling prices would have to include acquisition costs in the former and deduct disposal costs from the latter, but this is not a feature of the definitions of either OMV or EUV.

A nearer equivalent to net realisable value would seem to be what the RICS calls 'Estimated Realisation Price', or ERP, although again disposal costs would have to be deducted. This is defined as 'an opinion as to the amount of cash consideration before deduction of costs of sale which the Valuer considers, on the date of the valuation, can reasonably be expected to be obtained on future completion of an unconditional sale of the interest in the subject property assuming:

(a)   a willing seller;

(b)   that completion will take place on a future date specified by the Valuer to allow a reasonable period for proper marketing (having regard to the nature of the property and the state of the market);

(c)   that no account is taken of any additional bid by a prospective purchaser with a special interest; and

(d)   that both parties to the transaction will act knowledgeably, prudently and without compulsion.'[113]

The main difference between this and OMV is that ERP assumes that marketing of the property only starts at the date of the valuation, for completion in the future, whereas OMV is based on a hypothetical completion on the valuation date in respect of a property that has already been marketed.

A further basis is referred to by the RICS manual as 'Estimated Restricted Realisation Price' (ERRP), which amends condition (b) above so as to remove the assumption of a reasonable period for proper marketing. This therefore equates to a forced sale basis, which may be appropriate when a company's accounts are being prepared on a break-up basis because it is no longer a going concern.

5.2.3   Depreciated replacement cost of land and buildings

Some specialised buildings do not have a readily obtainable market value because they are usually sold only as part of the businesses in which they are used; it will, therefore, be necessary for these to be incorporated on the basis of their depreciated replacement cost (DRC). Since this is strictly an application of current cost rather than open market value in terms of the Act, it would imply that such a valuation would have to be updated annually, although it is unlikely that this interpretation has been widely applied in the past.

The RICS defines specialised properties, to which a DRC basis should be applied, as:

'those which, due to their specialised nature, are rarely, if ever, sold on the open market for single occupation for a continuation of their existing use, except as part of a sale of the business in occupation. Their specialised nature may arise from the construction, arrangement, size or location of the property, or a combination of these factors, or may be due to the nature of the plant and machinery and items of equipment which the buildings are designed to house, or the function, or the purpose for which the buildings are provided.'

The RICS Manual goes on to give the following examples of properties that meet this definition:

- oil refineries and chemical works where, usually, the buildings are no more than housings or cladding for highly specialised plant;

- power stations and dock installations where the building and site engineering works are related directly to the business of the owner, it being highly unlikely that they would have a value to anyone other than a company acquiring the undertaking;

■   properties of such construction, arrangement, size or specification that there would be no market (for a sale to a single owner occupier for the continuation of existing use) for those buildings;

■   standard properties in particular geographical areas and remote from main business centres, located there for operational or business reasons, which are of such an abnormal size for that district that there would be no market for such buildings there;

■   schools, colleges, universities and research establishments where there is no competing market demand from other organisations using these types of property in the locality;

■   hospitals, other specialised health care premises and leisure centres where there is no competing market demand from other organisations wishing to use these types of property in the locality; and

■   museums, libraries, and other similar premises provided by the public sector.[114]

Depreciated replacement cost is defined as 'the aggregate amount of the value of the land for the existing use or a notional replacement site in the same locality, and the gross replacement cost of the buildings and other site works, from which appropriate deductions may then be made to allow for the age, condition, economic or functional obsolescence and environmental factors etc; all of these might result in the existing property being worth less to the undertaking in occupation than would a new replacement.'[115]

Depreciated replacement cost is a rather unsatisfactory basis; it is represented as a valuation of property, but in circumstances where, by definition, no evidence of value can be found. It has obvious relevance within the context of current cost accounting, where the objective is to measure profit against the current cost of resources consumed, but much less relevance outside that context. It is particularly odd that increases in the cost of replacing assets should be regarded as gains, to be reported in measuring the company's performance in the statement of total recognised gains and losses. Moreover, a DRC valuation is often likely to give a higher valuation than one done on an open market basis (see the example quoted in 5.2.5 below). For this reason, it is necessary to ensure that the property really is so specialised that an open market value cannot be obtained. In addition, it is necessary to be satisfied that the potential profitability of the business is adequate to support the value derived on a depreciated replacement cost basis, or whether a lower figure should be adopted,[116] although of course the latter course would mean that the basis of valuation had become something else again.

Guinness values its breweries and distilleries using depreciated replacement cost, as illustrated below:

Extract 10.39: Guinness PLC (1996)

Accounting Policies

Tangible fixed assets and depreciation [extract]

In the case of distilleries, breweries and related specialised properties, valuations are principally on a depreciated replacement cost basis.

5.2.4 Valuations of other assets

Apart from investments, which is discussed in Chapter 11, few companies carry any assets other than property at valuation. Most cases fall into one of two groups: a few companies carrying all, or almost all, of their assets on a basis that accords with the principles of current cost accounting and those that carry certain intangible assets at valuation. As noted at 1.3.2 above, FRED 12 proposes particularly restrictive rules on the latter practice.

5.2.5 The comparability and reliability of valuations

Although the valuation bases described above are the ones most commonly found in practice and should be the only ones that are incorporated into company accounts, there are yet others that may be encountered, such as fire insurance values or valuations for bank security purposes. It is always necessary to establish the basis and purpose of any valuation as the different methods may come up with widely different values.

Westwick, in his book on property valuations, quotes a series of valuations and these clearly demonstrate the dangers of using the values prepared for one purpose for any other purpose. These were performed by Richard Ellis on a very substantial food preparation factory. This particular building was a borderline case; arguments could have been put forward for valuing it on an open market value or by depreciated replacement cost. The former value came to £3.5 million, the latter to £6.5 million. The fire insurance value, the gross replacement cost of the building, was highest; this amounted to £8.4 million. The lowest, which was the forced sale value, amounted to £3 million.[117]

Controversy about the reliability of valuations was fuelled in 1993 by the publication of a succession of valuations of the hotels operated by Queens Moat Houses. The *Financial Times* summarised the salient facts in an article in November:

'The two firms of chartered surveyors under scrutiny for valuing Queens Moat Houses' assets at figures that differed by nearly £500m used the same basis to prepare their figures, the company said yesterday. Both Weatherall Green & Smith and Jones Lang Wootton compiled their valuations on an open market, willing seller basis ... Weatherall produced a final valuation of £1.35bn for the 1992 accounts. Within four months, Jones had submitted an alternative figure of £861m based on the same financial information.'

The article also went on to describe earlier valuations: 'QMH ... said Weatherall had prepared a 1991 valuation of £2bn and a draft valuation for 1992 of £1.86bn. The latter was presented to banks in April this year and did not take into account the changed circumstances of the group. At the board's request, Weatherall supplied a revised figure in May of £1.35bn, qualified because it was based on unaudited financial information.'

When the accounts were eventually issued, the properties were included at a valuation of £732 million, which meant that £1,342 million had to be written off the previous year's valuation. The fixed assets note contained the following footnote:

Extract 10.40: Queens Moat Houses P.L.C. (1992)

Notes to the Accounts

12 Tangible fixed assets [extract]

The group's properties were valued as at 31st December 1992 by Jones Lang Wootton, Chartered Surveyors, on an open market existing use basis as fully operational business units. The valuations were carried out in accordance with the Statements of Asset Valuation Practice and Guidance Notes published by the Royal Institution of Chartered Surveyors. The group has revalued its property assets as at 31 December 1992 on the basis of these independent professional valuations.

As explained in the directors' report, the current directors consider that they do not have a sufficient understanding of the 1991 property valuation to enable them to provide a full explanation for the decline in the property values from 31 December 1991 to 31 December 1992 of £1,341.5 million, of which £537.6 million has been charged to revaluation reserve (note 21) and £803.9 million charged as an exceptional item in the profit and loss account (note 6).

In March 1994, the Royal Institution of Chartered Surveyors published the report of a working party (the Mallinson Report) responding to recent criticisms of their profession. This said that 'valuers need to be able to demonstrate to clients that, although there are many valuers who will make different judgements, all work within a common body of knowledge, application and expression. Differences will therefore be as narrow as possible, and where they occur they will be reasonable and explicable, not perverse or chaotic.'[118] The report went on to make 43 detailed recommendations aimed at improving the practices of the valuation profession.

5.3 Accounting for revaluations

When an asset is revalued the Companies Act states that the 'profit or loss' on revaluation must go to a separate reserve, the revaluation reserve.[119] Under FRS 3, this means that the revaluation surplus or deficit is reported in the statement of total recognised gains and losses.[120]

The revaluation reserve shall be reduced if amounts standing to its credit are, in the opinion of the directors, 'no longer necessary for the purposes of the valuation method used'.[121] Amounts may be released to the profit and loss account only if they were previously charged to that account or if they represent realised profits.[122] This permits transfers from revaluation reserve for the depreciation which has been charged through the profit and loss account on the revaluation surplus and for the surplus realised on the sale of a revalued asset. It also allows a company to change its policy from one where assets are revalued and to write back the reduction in the carrying value against the surplus. The Act also states that the revaluation reserve can be capitalised in a bonus issue, but apart from all these specified uses, the balance on the reserve shall not be reduced.[123] The use of the word 'reduced' is not ideal, given that the Act permits the balance on the reserve to be either a debit or a credit, but presumably the intention is that credits should not be released from the reserve except in one of the ways permitted by the Act.

5.3.1 Accounting for revaluation surpluses

The accounting treatment of a surplus arising on the revaluation of a depreciated asset is uncontroversial; the following example provides an illustration:

Example 10.6   Revaluation of fixed assets

On 1 January 19X1 a company acquires an asset for £1,000. The asset has an economic life of ten years and is depreciated on a straight line basis. The residual value is assumed to be nil. At 31 December 19X4 the asset is valued at £1,200. The accepted accounting treatment is as follows:

	£
Fixed assets	
Cost or valuation	
At 1 January 19X4	1,000
Surplus on revaluation	200
At 31 December 19X4	1,200
Depreciation	
At 1 January 19X4	300
Provided during the year	100
Surplus on revaluation	(400)
At 31 December 19X4	–
Net book value	
At 31 December 19X4	1,200
At 31 December 19X3	700
Revaluation surplus	
	£
Revaluation reserve	600
Retained profits	–
Profit or loss for year	–
	600

The treatment is based on the view that the revaluation establishes a new base of a *used* asset and, accordingly, the surplus to be taken to the revaluation reserve is the difference between the valuation and the net book value at the date of the valuation. In addition, no depreciation should be added back to retained profits, or the profit and loss account, as it was correct to charge depreciation in previous years. This is supported by paragraph 22 of SSAP 12. It is also consistent with the Companies Act, which states that the amount of the profit to be credited to the revaluation reserve is to be 'after allowing, where appropriate, for any provisions for depreciation or diminution in value made otherwise than by reference to the value so determined'.

5.3.2   *Depreciation of revalued assets*

As indicated in 3.4.6 above, depreciation is to be based on the revalued amount and the remaining life of the asset at the time of the valuation. The estimated residual value to be taken into account should be based on prices prevailing at the date of the valuation.[124]

SSAP 12 requires the whole of the depreciation charge to be passed through the profit and loss account.[125] This represents an amendment to the original SSAP in order to outlaw the practice of 'split depreciation', whereby depreciation in the balance sheet was based on the asset's carrying amount but only the portion that related to depreciation on historical cost was passed through the profit and loss account; the balance being charged directly to the revaluation reserve.

This practice of split depreciation may be argued to be permitted by the Companies Act (whether by accident or design) as the depreciation rules require that the provision be based on the carrying amount but does not specify that the whole charge must pass through the profit and loss account.[126]

Nobes states that the arguments in favour of split depreciation are:

(a)   a consistent charge for depreciation can be maintained over the life of an asset, irrespective of ad hoc revaluations;

(b)   connected to this, the depreciation charge is more objective than if it can be drastically altered at the whim of management; and

(c)   the total charge against profit over the life of an asset is its cost, whereas with revalued depreciation the charge exceeds cost.[127]

Split depreciation is also consistent with the usual treatment of impairment of revalued assets, where only that part of the diminution below depreciated historical cost is passed through the profit and loss account.

The ASB Discussion Paper on *Measurement of tangible fixed assets* dismisses the case for split depreciation, saying that 'the purpose of charging depreciation to the profit and loss account is to show the cost of the economic benefits consumed during the period. Depreciation based on current value reflects the cost that the entity would have avoided if it had not used the asset. Hence depreciation measured at current prices represents the best measure of the operating cost of using the asset in question.' Curiously, this argument strongly *supports* split depreciation if 'cost' in the three sentences quoted above is taken to mean historical cost! Obviously, however, the Board's mindset throughout the above passage is rooted in current cost, so much so that it does not appear to have noticed that the word 'current' is implied rather than explicitly stated.

Although SSAP 12 prohibits the practice of split depreciation, it does not make any reference to the accounting treatment of the revaluation reserve relating to the asset which is being depreciated. The usual treatment is shown in the following example:

Example 10.7   Effect of depreciation on revaluation reserve

On 1 January 19X1 a company acquires an asset for £1,000. The asset has an economic life of ten years and is depreciated on a straight line basis. The residual value is assumed to be £nil. At 31 December 19X4 the asset is valued at £1,200. The company accounts for the revaluation as shown in Example 10.6 above, with £600 being credited to the revaluation reserve. At 31 December 19X4 the economic life of the asset is considered to be the remainder of its original life, i.e. six years, and its residual value is still considered to be £nil. In the year ended 31 December 19X5 and later years depreciation charged to the profit and loss account is £200 p.a.

The usual treatment is to transfer £100 p.a. from the revaluation reserve to retained profits within the reserves note. This avoids the revaluation reserve being maintained indefinitely even after the asset ceases to exist, which does not seem sensible. The transfer is to retained earnings and not to the profit and loss account for the year; the latter treatment would be tantamount to allowing split depreciation (prohibited by SSAP 12) and would also fall foul of FRS 3, which does not permit amounts which have previously been reported in the statement of total recognised gains and losses to pass subsequently through the profit and loss account.[128] The treatment is also sanctioned by para. 34(3) of Schedule 4 to the Companies Act which allows amounts to be transferred to the profit and loss account if the amount has previously been charged there or is a realised profit. A transfer is possible because the amount of £100 is a realised profit in terms of s 275(2) of the Companies Act.

ED 51, although not dealing primarily with depreciation, supported this treatment by proposing that 'a transfer should be made each period from the revaluation reserve to the profit and loss account reserve of an amount equal to the difference between depreciation for the period calculated on the basis of the historical cost of fixed assets carried at a valuation and the actual depreciation charge based on the revalued amounts in respect of those fixed assets'.[129]

5.3.3   Disposal of revalued assets

The measurement of profit when a revalued asset is disposed of was a subject that the ASC wrestled with in five different sets of proposals during its life,[130] always without resolution. The issue was whether it should be based on the carrying amount in the balance sheet, with the revaluation surplus on that asset transferred as a reserve movement to realised reserves, or on the depreciated historical cost, in which case the revaluation surplus would be treated as part of the calculation of profit on disposal. The ASB finally resolved the matter in favour of the former treatment with the issue of FRS 3.

The following example illustrates these alternative treatments:

Example 10.8   Disposal of revalued assets

The asset which was revalued at £1,200 in Example 10.7 above is sold for £1,300 on 31 December 19X6. The annual depreciation charge for 19X5 and 19X6 is £200 and the company has made an annual transfer from revaluation reserve to realised reserves of £100, which represents the annual depreciation on the revaluation surplus. For the purposes of this example taxation has been ignored. The carrying value and the depreciated historical cost of the asset at the date of sale are as follows:

	Carrying value £	Historical cost £
Cost or valuation		
At 31 December 19X6	1,200	1,000
Depreciation		
At 1 January 19X6	200	500
Charge for year	200	100
At 31 December 19X6	400	600
Net book value at 31 December 19X6	800	400

The profit on disposal based on the balance sheet carrying value is £500; based on depreciated original cost it is £900 as shown below.

	(i) £	(ii) £
Profit on trading activities	1,000	1,000
Profit on sale of revalued asset	500	900
Retained profit for the financial year	1,500	1,900
Retained profits		
Opening balance	6,000	6,000
Retained profit for the financial year	1,500	1,900
Transfer from revaluation reserve – realised on sale	400	–
Transfer from revaluation reserve – depreciation	100	100
Closing balance	8,000	8,000
Revaluation reserve		
Opening balance	500	500
Transfer to profit and loss account – realised on sale	–	(400)
Transfer to retained profits – realised on sale	(400)	–
Transfer to retained profits – depreciation	(100)	(100)
Closing balance	–	–

Method (i) is the approach required by FRS 3.[131] It can be seen that this method is consistent with the treatment required by SSAP 12 in relation to any excess depreciation resulting from the revaluation of assets in that the amount included in the profit and loss account is based on the (revalued) carrying amount of the asset.

5.3.4 *Downward valuations and provisions for permanent impairment*

A *General properties*

There are in principle three ways in which a fall in the valuation of an asset might be reflected in a company's accounts; these are shown in the following example which, for simplicity, ignores depreciation:

Example 10.9 Downward valuations

On 1 January 19X1 a company acquires an asset for £1,000. At 31 December 19X2 it is valued at £1,200 giving rise to a revaluation reserve of £200. At 31 December 19X4 it is revalued at £900. The three possible methods are as follows:

	(i) £	(ii) £	(iii) £
Valuation			
At 1 January 19X4	1,200	1,200	1,200
Deficit on valuation	(300)	(300)	(300)
At 31 December 19X4	900	900	900
Revaluation reserve			
At 1 January 19X4	200	200	200
Deficit on valuation	(300)	(200)	–
Transfer to realised reserves	–	–	(200)
At 31 December 19X4	(100)	–	–
Charge to profit and loss account	–	100	300

(i)   Under this method the whole deficit is charged to the revaluation reserve. This treatment is based on the fact that under the alternative accounting rules contained in the Companies Act surpluses and *deficits* arising on the revaluation of an asset can be dealt with through the revaluation reserve.[132] This is supported by SSAP 19 (see 5.3.4B below). There is no statutory bar to an overall debit balance arising on the revaluation reserve.

(ii)   Under this method the downward movement is split, with previous valuations being reversed while the deficit below depreciated historical cost is charged to the profit and loss account. This means that only the element that represents a diminution in historical cost terms is reflected in the profit and loss account.

(iii)   Under this method the whole deficit is charged to the profit and loss account; the release of any previous revaluation above cost is dealt with as a reserve movement. This method is based on the view that the £1,200 valuation became the new substitute for cost when it was incorporated in the accounts in 19X2 and that the original cost is now irrelevant so far as future accounting for the asset is concerned. This method would be consistent with the treatment of depreciation and of sales of revalued assets under SSAP 12 and FRS 3.

In the above example, there has so far been no discussion of whether the fall in value is a provision for permanent diminution in value of the asset or whether it should be regarded as a downward revaluation. The accounting profession has not found it easy to distinguish between the two, mainly because of the obscurity of the conceptual reasoning behind including revaluations in historical cost accounts in general – never mind downward valuations. However, it is possible to attempt to draw the following distinction.

A provision for permanent impairment in value must be made whenever it can be foreseen that the carrying value of an asset will not be recovered in full, either through profitable use or through disposal. It is not an option whether to recognise it or not; if a loss is foreseen, prudence demands that it be provided for. A downward revaluation, however, arises when a company voluntarily decides that its policy is to carry a class of assets at a valuation rather than at historical cost, and the asset in question is found to have a lower value than was previously recorded. The fact that its revalued amount is less than its carrying value does not necessarily imply that a permanent impairment needs to be recognised; for one thing, it may be demonstrable that the fall in value is only a temporary one; but more importantly, the valuation basis, which might often be replacement cost, may say nothing about the amount to be recovered through future use or sale of the asset. Indeed the normal situation when assets are valued under current cost accounting principles is that the replacement cost of an asset is less than its recoverable amount.

If it is possible to distinguish these two different scenarios, then the question of which of the three methods is appropriate becomes easier to answer. On this analysis, method (i) is appropriate only in cases where the diminution in value is expected to be temporary. Where the diminution is considered to be indicative of a permanent impairment in value of the asset, it is inconsistent with the accounting concept of prudence not to provide for at least that part below depreciated historical cost in the profit and loss account (method (ii)). The more stringent method (iii) is seldom found in practice (although it used to be the disclosed policy of Rank – see Extract 10.36 above), but it would also be an allowable treatment, and indeed was proposed by the ASC in ED 51.[133]

The ASB's Discussion Paper on the *Impairment of tangible fixed assets* sought to address this issue. It tried to establish a theoretical distinction between losses associated with operating activities, that should be reported in the profit and loss account, and holding losses, that should be taken to reserves and reported in the statement of total recognised gains and losses. The former category was further explained as those losses which reflected a reduction in the quantum of the service potential of the asset, such as those occasioned by physical damage or obsolescence. Unfortunately, the Board then found great difficulty in applying its own distinction; it cited five hypothetical examples of falling asset values, but confessed itself unable to categorise them in accordance with its own conceptual approach.[134] As a result the eventual proposal in the Discussion Paper, which the Board itself described as 'somewhat arbitrary', was that:

- any impairment that is caused by an obvious reduction in the quantum of the service potential of an asset should be recognised in the profit and loss account;

- other impairment of revalued assets should be recognised in the statement of total recognised gains and losses until the carrying value reaches the level of depreciated historical cost;

- further impairment of revalued assets should be recognised in the profit and loss account, as should impairment of assets that are not revalued.[135]

This subsequently became the basis of FRED 15.[136] What this boils down to, unless a company feels able to identify an obvious reduction in the quantum of the service potential of an asset, is support for method (ii) in the Example discussed above, which is probably the most sensible approach. It does, however, remain inconsistent with the treatment of depreciation and disposal of revalued assets, so the whole conceptual basis of this area of accounting remains unsatisfactory.

In its later Discussion Paper on the *Measurement of tangible fixed assets*, the ASB touched once more on the difficulty of differentiating downward valuations from impairments. It again proposed that 'a loss on revaluation should be recognised in the statement of total recognised gains and losses until the carrying value reaches the level of depreciated historical cost', but this time it took a slightly different approach to further losses. The paper proposed that 'further revaluation losses should be recognised in the profit and loss account, unless it can be demonstrated that there has been no impairment in the income-generating unit to which the tangible fixed asset belongs, in which case the further losses may be recognised in the statement of total recognised gains and losses'.[137] This therefore brings in the aggregation problem discussed in 4.4 above; under this proposal, it would seem that even definite losses on individual assets need not be channelled through the profit and loss account if the assets belong to a segment that remains profitable in overall terms. This seems a very dubious proposition.

The Companies Act also requires that any permanent diminution in value of a revalued asset should be measured by reference to the asset's revalued amount rather than its historical cost.[138] However, this again depends on a determination that a provision for permanent diminution has been made, rather than a downward revaluation, which should be debited to the revaluation reserve in terms of the Act.

FRED 15 also deals with the reversal of impairment write-downs which are subsequently found to have been unnecessary. It says that they should be credited to the profit and loss account to the extent that the original impairment loss (adjusted for subsequent depreciation) was recognised there, with any further credit being taken to the statement of total recognised gains and losses.[139]

B   Investment properties

The original SSAP 19 effectively adopted a portfolio approach and required only overall deficits on revaluation to be charged to profit and loss account, as opposed to deficits on individual properties. The Companies Act, on the other hand, requires permanent deficits below historical cost on individual properties to be charged to profit and loss account but permits temporary valuation deficits to be included in revaluation reserve even if this results in a negative reserve.[140] The original SSAP 19 made no reference to the distinction between temporary and permanent deficits.

For many years after the introduction of SSAP 19, the property market remained generally buoyant so the conflict between SSAP 19 and the Companies Act probably did not have any significant impact on accounts. However, with the slump in the market at the end of the 1980s, the conflict became more of an issue. This was heightened by rules contained in FRS 3: first, a disposal of a property with an underlying revaluation surplus could unmask a deficit on other properties, resulting in an overall revaluation deficit on revaluation reserve which arguably under SSAP 19 then needed to be taken to the profit and loss account; second, if a net deficit on the revaluation reserve had been charged to the profit and loss account under the original SSAP 19, then FRS 3 would require any subsequent surpluses on revaluation to be taken to the statement of total recognised gains and losses and not to the profit and loss account.

As a result of these difficulties, the ASB took steps to amend SSAP 19 in July 1994, and the conflict between SSAP 19 on the one hand, and the Companies Act and FRS 3 on the other, has now been removed.

SSAP 19 as amended now allows companies to have a deficit on their investment property revaluation reserve.

5.3.5   Other uses of the revaluation reserve

Where the revaluation reserve has been reduced by making a bonus issue, further problems arise. To the extent that the revaluation reserve no longer exists, it could be argued that such amount can no longer be used for making any transfers which a company normally makes between revaluation reserve and retained profits, or for writing off that part of a permanent diminution in the value of an asset which the company could have charged to revaluation reserve. If all of the revaluation reserve has been capitalised then no such transfers or write-offs could be made. In most situations only some of the reserve will have been capitalised and, therefore, under this approach it will be necessary to:

(a)   decide that specific revaluation surpluses have been capitalised and, therefore, no transfers or write-offs can be made in respect of the assets to which the surpluses related. However, transfers and write-offs in respect of other assets can continue; or

(b)   decide that a proportion of each revaluation surplus has been capitalised and, therefore, a proportion still remains. Accordingly, a proportion of the amount of the transfers or write-offs which would have been made can be made; or

(c)   continue to make the transfers or write-offs until the remaining surplus has been extinguished.

All three methods are probably acceptable.

On this subject, a footnote in the ASB's Discussion Paper on the *Impairment of tangible fixed assets* confirms that the question of whether impairments of revalued assets can be charged to the statement of total recognised gains and losses rather than the profit and loss account is unaffected by whether or not the revaluation reserve has already been used for some other purpose.[141]

5.3.6   Transfers of properties between current assets and fixed assets

A   *Reclassifications from investment property to trading property*

Property companies sometimes transfer properties from their investment portfolio to their trading portfolio. The question then arises as to what should happen to the revaluation surplus/deficit which had previously been recognised when the property was regarded as an investment property. A few companies reflect these reclassifications in their group accounts as if they were transactions with third parties, and treat them as having become realised.

There may be an argument for saying that the property has realised its investment potential on becoming a trading property. Also, such transfers are usually between two distinct companies (i.e. an investment and a trading company) so the profit is realised in the transferor company. However, it is difficult to reconcile a treatment as realised in the group accounts, as opposed to an individual company's accounts, with the notion that consolidation is intended to represent the group as a single economic entity. Nevertheless, such profits at least do not distort the profit and loss account in the year of transfer since they are dealt with as a realisation of the revaluation reserve by a transfer between reserves.

An alternative treatment is to leave the property at its valuation on transfer but not to treat the accumulated valuation surplus as realised. If this treatment is adopted, interest capitalised on any subsequent development should be based on cost (see 3.3.6 of Chapter 13).

Another approach is to reverse any revaluation surplus/deficit relating to a property transferred and include it in trading property at the lower of cost and net realisable value; this will ensure consistency in the accounting treatment of all trading properties. For example:

Extract 10.41: Daejan Holdings PLC (1991)

(g)   Properties [extract]
   (ii) Trading and Development Properties
      These properties are stated at the lower of cost and net realisable value. In the case of properties acquired from other Group companies any profit in the transferor company is eliminated on consolidation until realised by the Group.

This is an issue which the UITF briefly considered in 1992 but did not pursue.

B   *Reclassifications from trading property to investment property*

On a reclassification from trading property to investment property, the basis of valuation in the accounts will change from the lower of cost and net realisable value to open market value. As discussed in A above, such transfers are usually between two separate companies, but any intra-group profit should be eliminated on consolidation, to avoid distorting the profit and loss account.

In view of the slump in the property market at the end of the 1980s, the question became not so much one of whether any profit should be recognised or eliminated, but whether a transfer should be recorded at the carrying amount in the previous balance sheet or at an amount equivalent to the lower of cost and net realisable value at the date of the transfer. Trafalgar House adopted the former treatment in its 1991 accounts, as shown in the following extract:

Extract 10.42: Trafalgar House Public Limited Company (1991)

12 Tangible fixed assets [extract]

	Properties			
		Leaseholds		
	Freeholds	Long	Short	Total
Reclassification from current assets	111.4	44.0	–	155.4
Deficit on valuation	(50.5)	(17.5)	–	(68.0)

Properties reclassified from current assets were valued on 30th September 1991 on the basis of open market value by independent firms of chartered surveyors (£78.1), and by internal qualified surveyors (£9.3m).

14 Developments for sale [extract]

On 1st October 1990 certain commercial properties in the UK were transferred to tangible fixed assets (Note 12).

The deficit on revaluation of £68.0 million was taken to revaluation reserve.

This issue is one which the UITF did take up. In July 1992 it issued Abstract 5 – *Transfers from Current Assets to Fixed Assets*. The UITF was concerned, particularly in the economic climate of the time, that there was a 'possibility that companies could avoid charging the profit and loss account with write-downs to net realisable value arising on unsold trading assets. This could be done by transferring the relevant assets from current assets to fixed assets at above net realisable value, as a result of which any later write down might be debited to revaluation reserve.'[142]

The UITF agreed that in respect of such transfers, the current asset accounting rules should be applied up to the effective date of transfer, which is the date of management's change of intent. Consequently, the transfer should be made at the lower of cost and net realisable value, and accordingly an assessment should be made of the net realisable value at the date of transfer. If this is less than its previous carrying value the diminution should be charged in the profit and loss account, reflecting the loss to the company while the asset was held as a current asset.[143]

Further to the issue of UITF 5 (and after the intervention of the Financial Reporting Review Panel), Trafalgar House adopted the requirements of the abstract in its 1992 accounts and restated its 1991 comparatives accordingly.

5.3.7 Distributable profits and revaluations of fixed assets

A revaluation surplus is not a realised profit and may only be transferred to the profit and loss account on realisation.[144] It is not available for distribution.[145]

In order to determine a company's profits available for distribution all provisions for depreciation or diminution in value of assets are normally to be treated as realised losses,[146] except to the extent that the depreciation has been increased because of a previous upward revaluation of the asset.[147] The legislation implies that such provisions include downward revaluations of fixed assets, which have been taken to the revaluation reserve on the basis that the fall in value does not reflect a permanent impairment.[148] This means that even where such a temporary diminution in value of a fixed asset has been taken to revaluation reserve, then as the loss is defined by reference to the provision against the asset, not the reserve to which it has been written off, such a loss will normally be regarded as a realised loss. However, an exception is made for a provision in respect of a diminution in value of a fixed asset appearing on a revaluation of *all* of the fixed assets other than goodwill of the company.[149]

The directors are not required to formally revalue all fixed assets and incorporate these revaluations into the accounts in order to take advantage of the exception; the value only has to be 'considered', and this does not imply that the book amount of the asset has to be altered.[150] The Act states that fixed assets that have not actually been revalued are to be treated as if they had, if the directors are satisfied that the aggregate value of all fixed assets is not less than the amount at which they are currently stated in the company's accounts.[151] Thus a downward valuation of a fixed asset need not be treated as a realised loss if the directors are satisfied that the company's fixed assets are worth, in total, not less than their net book value.

This exception can only be taken if the following note disclosure is made:[152]

(a)   that the directors have considered the value of some of the fixed assets of the company, without actually revaluing those assets;

(b)   that they are satisfied that the aggregate value of those assets at the time in question is or was not less than the aggregate amount at which they are being stated in the company's accounts; and

(c)   that the relevant items are accordingly stated in the relevant accounts on the basis that a revaluation of all of the company's fixed assets which was deemed to have taken place included the assets that have suffered a diminution in value.

An example of such a note is to be found in the accounts of Berisford:

Extract 10.43: Berisford plc (1996)

Accounting policies

Investments

a) Subsidiary entities

In the accounts of the Company investments in subsidiary entities are valued at cost plus the Group's share of post-acquisition retained profits and other reserves, less losses and any goodwill arising on acquisition.

21 Reserves [extract]

(i) The Directors have revalued the Company's investments in subsidiary entities at 28 September 1996 in the manner set out in the accounting policies note [quoted above]. The Directors have considered the value of the remaining fixed assets and are satisfied that these are worth, in total, not less than the aggregate amount at which they are stated in the Company's accounts. Accordingly, in accordance with Section 275 of the Companies Act 1985 the aggregate provision does not fall to be classified as a realised loss and therefore distributable reserves of the Company are £33.8m (1995 £21.6m) as analysed [below]:

	1996 £m	1995 £m
Profit and loss account	(42.2)	(26.0)
Provisions against investments in subsidiary entities	235.4	240.3
Excess of provisions over surpluses on revaluation of investments in subsidiary entities	(159.4)	(192.7)
Distributable reserves	33.8	21.6

The note must be repeated in subsequent accounts for as long as advantage is to be taken of the exemption as these may become 'relevant accounts', i.e. those on which a distribution is to be based.[153] Berisford has avoided showing the debit balance on profit and loss account on the face of the balance sheet by setting it off against larger credit balances on share premium account and revaluation reserve to produce a single figure for 'reserves'. Strictly, however, this does not comply with the Companies Act formats, which require each of these figures to be disclosed on the face of the balance sheet.

6 DISCLOSURE

6.1 Introduction

There are disclosure requirements for fixed assets in both the Companies Act and accounting standards. These requirements are dealt with here in the order in which they are usually encountered in a company's annual report: directors' report, balance sheet and profit and loss account, accounting policies and notes to the accounts. The additional disclosure requirements for revalued amounts are dealt with in 6.6 below.

6.2 Directors' report

The market value of 'interests in land' (taken to mean land and buildings)[154] should also be disclosed if it differs substantially from the amount at which the assets are carried in the balance sheet and if, in the directors' opinion, the difference is of such significance that it should be brought to the attention of the members or debenture holders. The difference should be quantified 'with such degree of precision as is practicable'.[155]

This disclosure is seldom seen in practice, except perhaps when the property market has moved significantly up or down. An example of this was seen in the 1993 accounts of Lloyds Bank:

Extract 10.44: Lloyds Bank Plc (1993)

Directors' Report [extract]

PREMISES

The directors have reviewed the current value of premises and are of the opinion that, compared with the balance sheet amount, there is a shortfall of £162 million, of which £155 million relates to UK premises and £7 million to overseas premises. The directors are of the opinion that this shortfall, an average of some 13 per cent, will not prove to be permanent and no adjustment has been made in the balance sheet.

6.3　Balance sheet and profit and loss account

There are various statutory disclosures with regard to the balance sheet and profit and loss account.

The statutory formats require that fixed assets be disclosed under the headings shown here.[156] Companies' accounts usually include only the net book amounts of intangible and tangible assets and investments on the face of the balance sheet, with the information required by the Arabic numerals relegated to the notes.

As is permitted by the Act, the format categories with Arabic numerals are frequently modified to suit the circumstances of the business. Allied-Domecq, for example, has two main categories of 'Production and other properties' and 'Licensed properties'. The former is analysed between 'properties' of various kinds, 'plant and machinery' and 'vehicles, casks and sundry equipment'; the latter between 'properties' and 'furniture, fittings and equipment'.[157]

> I　Intangible assets
> 　1. Development costs
> 　2. Concessions, patents, licences, trademarks, and similar rights and assets
> 　3. Goodwill
> 　4. Payments on account
> II　Tangible assets
> 　1. Land and buildings
> 　2. Plant and machinery
> 　3. Fixtures, fittings, tools and equipment
> 　4. Payments on account and assets in course of construction
> III　Investments
> 　　[with various sub-classifications]

If profit and loss account Formats 2 or 4 are chosen, then 'depreciation and other amounts written off tangible and intangible fixed assets' must be shown, either on the face of the profit and loss account or in the notes.[158]

If Formats 1 or 3 are chosen, the equivalent information must be given in the notes to the accounts.[159]

If a provision for permanent diminution in value of any fixed asset has been made then it must be disclosed in the notes to the accounts if it is not shown in the profit and loss account.[160]

As discussed in Chapter 22, the gain or loss on sale of fixed assets is one of the three specified exceptional items which is required to be shown after operating profit in the profit and loss account.[161]

6.4　Accounting policies

SSAP 12 requires that disclosure be made, for each major class of depreciable asset, of the depreciation method used and the useful economic lives or the depreciation rates used.[162] This is usually given in the accounting policies note.

Certain categories of asset, for example plant and machinery, will probably include items depreciated at a variety of rates. It is usual to disclose a range of lives and/or rates in order to satisfy the disclosure requirements.

Bass gives a very comprehensive description of its accounting policies on fixed assets and depreciation, as shown in the following extract:

Extract 10.45: Bass PLC (1996)

ACCOUNTING POLICIES

Fixed assets and depreciation

i) Intangible assets

No value is attributed to trademarks, concessions, patents and similar rights and assets, including hotel franchises and management contracts.

ii) Tangible assets

Freehold and leasehold properties including related licences are stated at cost or valuation less depreciation where relevant. All other fixed assets are stated at cost.

iii) Interest

Interest paid in respect of certain major projects is capitalised to the extent that it relates to the period prior to the project becoming operational.

iv) Revaluation reserve

Surpluses and deficits, to the extent that any deficit is regarded as temporary, arising from the professional valuations of properties are taken direct to the revaluation reserve. Where a permanent diminution in value of an individual property is identified, the deficit is eliminated first against any revaluation reserve in respect of that property with any excess being charged to the profit and loss account. Valuation surpluses or deficits realised on sale are transferred from the revaluation reserve to the profit and loss account reserve.

v) Depreciation

Freehold land and licences are not depreciated.

Hotels and public houses held as freehold or with a leasehold interest in excess of 50 years are maintained, as a matter of policy, by a programme of repair and refurbishment such that their residual values are at least equal to book values. Having regard to this, it is the opinion of the directors that depreciation on any such property, as required by the Companies Act 1985 and accounting standards, would not be material.

Leasehold hotels and public houses are amortised over the unexpired term of the lease when less than 50 years.

Other freehold and leasehold properties are written off over 50 years, with the exception of breweries and maltings which are written off over 25 years, from the later of the date of acquisition and latest valuation.

Other tangible fixed assets are depreciated over their estimated useful lives, namely:

Plant and machinery	4-20 years
Information technology equipment	3-5 years
Equipment in retail outlets	3-10 years
Vehicles	3-10 years

6.5 Notes to the accounts

The note disclosures with regard to cost and depreciation of fixed assets are based on the requirements of the Companies Act and SSAP 12. The requirements of the Act cover all fixed assets; SSAP 12 excludes investments and some intangibles (see 3.4.1 above). For each of the categories of fixed asset shown in the statutory formats (see 6.3 above) the Companies Act requires the following to be disclosed:

(a)   the appropriate amounts at the beginning of the financial year and as at the balance sheet date, based either on historical cost (purchase price or production cost) or alternative accounting rules;[163]

(b)   all movements during the year, including revaluation surpluses and deficits, acquisitions, disposals and transfers.[164] Other movements that might also be reflected in the carrying value of the asset, such as exchange differences, will also be disclosed in the note; and

(c)   the cumulative amount of depreciation as at the beginning and end of the financial year on the appropriate basis of cost or valuation, the depreciation charge for the period and adjustments in respect of disposals or for other reasons.[165]

In addition to the information noted in 6.4 above, SSAP 12 requires that, for each major class of depreciable asset, the following is disclosed:

(a)   total depreciation charged for the period;[166] and

(b)   the gross amount of depreciable assets and the related accumulated depreciation.[167]

Companies will generally comply with these requirements by including separate notes for each major category of fixed asset: i.e. intangible fixed assets, tangible fixed assets and investments. An example of such a note for tangible fixed assets is illustrated below:

Extract 10.46: Reckitt & Colman plc (1996)

10. Fixed assets – tangible assets [extract]

	Freehold land £m	Properties £m	Plant and equipment £m	Total £m
Cost:				
At 31 December 1995	**39.5**	**191.2**	**493.1**	**723.8**
Additions during the year	0.5	13.0	66.6	80.1
Disposals during the year	(6.5)	(13.2)	(43.2)	(62.9)
Exchange adjustments	(2.9)	(16.5)	(44.4)	(63.8)
At 4 January 1997	**30.6**	**174.5**	**472.1**	**677.2**
Accumulated depreciation:				
At 31 December 1995		**(54.8)**	**(251.1)**	**(305.9)**
Provided during the year		(7.6)	(43.0)	(50.6)
Disposals during the year		7.1	31.4	38.5
Exchange adjustments		5.2	22.7	27.9
At 4 January 1997		**(50.1)**	**(240.0)**	**(290.1)**
Net book amounts:				
At 31 December 1995	**39.5**	**136.4**	**242.0**	**417.9**
At 4 January 1997	**30.6**	**124.4**	**232.1**	**387.1**

	1996 £m	1995 £m
The net book amount of properties comprise:		
Freehold buildings	**120.7**	133.2
Long leaseholds	**3.4**	2.8
Short leaseholds	**0.3**	0.4
	124.4	136.4

It can be seen from the above extract that separate disclosure is given of the gross amount of depreciable assets as required by SSAP 12, by distinguishing freehold land from 'properties'. An alternative is to show these as a single amount of freehold property and to disclose the amount of freehold land included, so that the depreciable amount (that relating to the buildings) can be deduced, as illustrated below:

Extract 10.47: The Weir Group PLC (1996)

7 Tangible Assets [extract]

The value of freehold land included in freehold land and buildings amounted to £8,054,000 at cost and £1,190,000 at valuation (1995 £8,249,000 at cost and £1,297,000 at valuation).

Gleeson discloses the depreciable amount of its fixed assets more directly, as a footnote to the fixed assets note, as shown below:

Extract 10.48: M J Gleeson Group plc (1996)

11 Tangible fixed assets [extract]

	Owner occupied property £000	Plant and machinery £000
Cost or valuation at 30th June 1996:		
At cost	3,405	16,952
At professional valuation in 1992	6,240	–
	9,645	16,952
Depreciable amount thereof	5,485	16,952

SSAP 12 also requires that where there has been a change in the depreciation method used, the effect, if material, should be disclosed in the year of change. The reasons for the change should also be disclosed.[168]

The Companies Act requires the carrying amount of 'land and buildings' to be analysed between that held under freehold and long and short leaseholds.[169] Long leases are those with more than 50 years unexpired as at the balance sheet date.[170] This is normally achieved either by splitting the 'land and buildings' category in the fixed asset note into the three sub-categories or by making separate note disclosure as illustrated in the extract of Reckitt & Colman shown above.

6.6   Additional disclosures for items carried at valuation

The Companies Act requires that where assets have been included in the accounts at amounts based on a valuation then the items affected and the basis of valuation adopted should be disclosed in a note to the accounts.[171] In the case of each balance sheet item affected, disclosure should be made of either:

(a)   the comparable amounts based on historical costs; or

(b)   the differences between the amounts in (a) above and the amounts actually included in the balance sheet.[172]

The comparable amounts are the gross amounts and cumulative provisions for depreciation or diminution in values and should relate to *all* of the assets covered by the balance sheet item.[173]

Most major companies would appear to adopt the former method of disclosure. A good example of disclosure is that of Blue Circle, as illustrated below:

Extract 10.49: *Blue Circle Industries PLC (1996)*

12 Tangible assets [extract]

| | Land and buildings | | | | | |
	Freehold £m	Long lease £m	Short lease £m	Plant and machinery £m	Assets under construction £m	Total £m
Group						
Net book value at 31 December 1996	370.9	3.1	3.0	526.4	63.0	966.4
Net book value at 31 December 1995	409.8	3.1	3.2	535.4	45.0	996.5
Historical cost at 31 December 1996	481.1	3.8	4.4	1,132.6	63.0	1,684.9
Accumulated historical depreciation	125.9	0.8	1.9	627.6	–	756.2
Net historical cost at 31 December 1996	355.2	3.0	2.5	505.0	63.0	928.7

It can be seen from the above extract that almost all of the categories of tangible fixed assets have been affected by valuations and Blue Circle has, therefore, included the disclosure as part of its fixed asset table; in most situations, it will only be land and buildings which are affected by valuations and disclosure will generally be given by way of footnote.

Although the Act requires the amounts to be disclosed to deal with all the assets included in the balance sheet item affected by valuations, some companies disclose the comparable historical cost information for only the assets which have been revalued. Where such an approach is taken then it is necessary to disclose the gross amount and accumulated depreciation for the revalued assets which are included in the balance sheet so that the total figures, in historical cost terms, can be deduced. This is shown in the following extract:

Extract 10.50: Imperial Chemical Industries PLC (1996)

13   TANGIBLE FIXED ASSETS [extract]

	Group			
	Land and buildings		Plant and equipment	
	1996	1995	**1996**	1995
	£m	£m	**£m**	£m
Revalued assets included in tangible fixed assets:				
At revalued amount	**78**	78	**80**	80
Depreciation	**(26)**	(23)	**(71)**	(69)
Net book value	**52**	55	**9**	11
At historical cost	**41**	41	**95**	94
Depreciation	**(22)**	(19)	**(88)**	(86)
Net book value	**19**	22	**7**	8

For all items (other than listed investments) that are carried at valuation, the Companies Act also requires the years in which the assets were valued and the amounts at which they were valued to be disclosed.[174] An example of this disclosure is given by the following extract from the notes to Delta's accounts:

Extract 10.51: Delta plc (1996)

17 Tangible assets [extract]

Analysis of cost or valuation of land and buildings	£ million
At professional valuation in:	
1994 and earlier years	39.3
1995	38.0
1996 (iv)	12.7
At cost	16.6
At 28 December 1996	**106.6**

(iv) The revaluations which were made in 1996 comprise: UK £8.6 million and overseas £4.1 million valued on an existing use basis, these valuations having been carried out by Henry Butcher & Co., International Asset Consultants, in accordance with the RICS appraisal and valuation manual.

The information in this extract is generally the only information given by companies in respect of past valuations, despite the fact that, as mentioned earlier, the Companies Act also strictly requires the basis of valuation to be disclosed.[175] However, some companies do give more information than the statutory minimum, for example by disclosing the names and professional qualifications of valuers in respect of valuations that took place in previous years, as illustrated in the following extract:

Extract 10.52: Sears plc (1997)

9. Fixed tangible assets [extract]

The majority of the Group's properties were professionally valued by Messrs Healey & Baker, Chesterton and Jones Land Wootton as at 31st January 1993. The basis for valuation was open market value for existing use or, for those properties not occupied by the Group, open market value. Freeholds and leaseholds which expire more than 25 years after the date of valuation are included at 31st January 1993 valuations amounting to £392.5 million. The remaining properties are included at cost or at their previous valuation less depreciation if the period to expiry had fallen to less than 25 years by 31st January 1997.

Where fixed assets (other than investments) have been revalued during the year, then the Companies Act also requires disclosure of the names or qualifications of the persons making the valuation and the bases used by them.[176] An excellent example of such disclosure is shown below:

Extract 10.53: Taylor Woodrow plc (1996)

11 Valuation of Properties

The investment properties of the group were valued at £385.9m as at 31 December 1996 by the following valuers, on an open market basis:

		Equivalent
Canada – Stewart, Young Hillesheim & Atlin Limited	C$144.1m	£61.3m
Gibraltar – a team member who is a Fellow of the Royal Institution of Chartered Surveyors	£1.4m	£1.4m
Sultanate of Oman – Cluttons	RO4.2m	£6.4m
United Kingdom – Knight Frank	£315.1m	£315.1m
United Kingdom – a team member who is an Associate of the Royal Institution of Chartered Surveyors	£1.7m	£1.7m

Investment property valuations in Gibraltar, the Sultanate of Oman and the United Kingdom were undertaken by Chartered Surveyors (external unless noted as team members) in accordance with the Appraisal and Valuation Manual of the Royal Institution of Chartered Surveyors.

The valuations of fixed asset properties as at 31 December 1994 were made by the following valuers, on an open market for existing use basis, and those valuations, as adjusted for sales, amounted to £43.3m:

		Equivalent
Australia – J L W Advisory Services Pty. Limited	A$3.3m	£1.5m
Canada – Stewart, Young Hillesheim & Atlin Limited	C$3.4m	£1.4m
Denmark –ADBO ApS	DKr11.8m	£1.2m
Gibraltar – a team member who is a Fellow of the Royal Institution of Chartered Surveyors	£0.5m	£0.5m
United Kingdom – Knight Frank	£38.7m	£38.7m

Fixed asset property valuations in Gibraltar and the United Kingdom were undertaken by Chartered Surveyors (external unless noted as team members) in accordance with the Statements of Asset Valuation Practice and Guidance Notes of the Royal Institution of Chartered Surveyors.

In addition, SSAP 12 requires, in the year of valuation, disclosure of the effect of the revaluation on the depreciation charge, if material.[177] Such disclosure is very rarely seen in practice. This could be due to the fact that most revaluations relate to property and, therefore, any effect is immaterial due to the long lives of the properties (if indeed depreciation is being charged at all on the properties). In addition, assuming that the revaluation is carried out as at the end of the year, it will be the following year before there is any impact on the depreciation charge.

The revaluation reserve itself should be included as a separate sub-heading in the position shown in the formats, but need not be so called.[178] The treatment for tax purposes of amounts credited or debited to the revaluation reserve must be disclosed in a note to the accounts.[179]

6.7   Disclosures for investment properties

6.7.1   Disclosures required by SSAP 19

The carrying value of investment properties and the investment revaluation reserve should be shown prominently in the financial statements.[180] The following details concerning the valuation should also be given:

(a)   the basis of the valuation;

(b)   the names or qualifications of the valuers; and

(c)   if the valuation was made by an officer or employee of the company or group owning the property, the financial statements should disclose this fact.[181]

SSAP 19 refers to an 'investment revaluation reserve'[182] but in practice this term is seldom used in property company accounts. Most companies prefer just 'revaluation reserve', although some take advantage of the freedom allowed by the Companies Act to change this particular heading[183] with headings such as 'property revaluation reserve' and 'unrealised capital account'.

SSAP 19 requires that the carrying value of investment properties and the investment revaluation reserve be 'displayed prominently in the accounts'.[184] This means that if assets other than investment properties are revalued, the revaluation reserve should be split to show the amount relating to investment properties as opposed to other revalued assets. In practice, such splits are seldom seen.

6.7.2   Balance sheet classification

Many companies with investment properties adapt the Companies Act balance sheet headings, often by splitting tangible fixed assets into two categories, one for investment properties and one for other tangible fixed assets. Where appropriate, the former figure should be analysed between completed investment properties and properties under development, since investment properties by definition do not include properties in the course of development. Some companies give this analysis on the face of the balance sheet, others in the notes to the accounts. The latter figure is usually analysed in the notes to the accounts between the headings shown above, although this is not strictly necessary where the total of other tangible fixed assets is immaterial.[185]

6.7.3 Disclosure on use of 'true and fair override'

The company law requirement to depart from the usual legal rules if to follow them would lead to the accounts not showing a true and fair view (the 'true and fair override') was referred to in 3.2.1 above, as was the reliance on this requirement as a basis for SSAP 19. When the 'true and fair override' is used, the Companies Act requires disclosure of 'particulars of the departure, the reasons for it and its effect' in a note to the accounts.[186] In December 1992 the UITF issued Abstract 7 – *True and fair override disclosures* – which interprets the Companies Act disclosure requirement as follows:[187]

(a)   'Particulars of any such departure' – a statement of the treatment which the Act would normally require in the circumstances and a description of the treatment actually adopted;

(b)   'the reasons for it' – a statement as to why the treatment prescribed would not give a true and fair view;

(c)   'its effect' – a description of how the position shown in the accounts is different as a result of the departure, normally with quantification except (i) where quantification is already evident in the accounts themselves, or (ii) whenever the effect cannot reasonably be quantified, in which case the directors should explain the circumstances.

The disclosure required by UITF 7 should either be included, or cross-referenced, in the note stating compliance with accounting standards (as required by the Companies Act).[188]

Examples of such disclosures are illustrated below:

Extract 10.54: Hammerson plc (1996)

Basis of accounting

The financial statements are prepared under the historical cost convention as modified by the revaluation of investment properties and in accordance with all applicable accounting standards. The financial statements are in compliance with the Companies Act 1985 except that, as explained below, investment properties are not depreciated.

Depreciation [extract]

In accordance with Statement of Standard Accounting Practice No. 19, no depreciation is provided in respect of freehold properties or leasehold properties with over 20 years to expiry. This is a departure from the requirements of the Companies Act 1985 which requires all properties to be depreciated. Such properties are not held for consumption but for investment and the directors consider that to depreciate them would not give a true and fair view. Depreciation is only one amongst many factors reflected in the annual valuation of properties and accordingly the amount of depreciation which might otherwise have been charged cannot be separately identified or quantified. The directors consider that this policy results in the accounts giving a true and fair view.

Extract 10.55: Land Securities PLC (1997)

1   Accounting Policies [extract]

The financial statements have been prepared under the historical cost convention modified by the revaluation of properties and in accordance with applicable accounting standards. Compliance with SSAP 19 "Accounting for Investment Properties" requires a departure from the requirements of the Companies Act 1985 relating to depreciation and amortisation and an explanation of this departure is given in (e) below.

(e)   DEPRECIATION AND AMORTISATION [extract]

In accordance with SSAP 19, no depreciation or amortisation is provided in respect of freehold or leasehold properties held on leases having more than 20 years unexpired. This departure from the requirements of the Companies Act 1985, for all properties to be depreciated, is, in the opinion of the Directors, necessary for the financial statements to give a true and fair view in accordance with applicable accounting standards, as properties are included in the financial statements at their open market value.

The effect of depreciation and amortisation on value is already reflected annually in the valuation of properties, and the amount attributed to this factor by the valuers cannot reasonably be separately identified or quantified. Had the provisions of the Act been followed, net assets would not have been affected but revenue profits would have been reduced for this and earlier years.

The above extracts can be contrasted with the disclosure which is given by MEPC, as shown below:

Extract 10.56: MEPC plc (1996)

Depreciation and amortisation [extract]

In accordance with Statement of Standard Accounting Practice No 19 investment properties are revalued annually and the aggregate surplus or deficit is transferred to a revaluation reserve, and no depreciation or amortisation is provided in respect of freehold investment properties and leasehold investment properties with over 20 years to expiry. This treatment may be a departure from the requirements of the Companies Act concerning the depreciation of fixed assets. However, these properties are not held for consumption but for investment and the Directors consider that systematic annual depreciation would be inappropriate. The accounting policy adopted is therefore necessary for the accounts to give a true and fair view. Depreciation or amortisation is only one of many factors reflected in the annual valuation and the amount which might otherwise have been shown cannot be separately identified or quantified.

It can be seen that MEPC has not said that there is a departure from the Companies Act requirement but that there *may* be a departure. It is unclear why this should be the case but it may be because any depreciation would have been immaterial and therefore there would be no departure from the requirements of the Companies Act. Another company which has not categorically stated that there is a departure is Slough Estates.[189]

The extracts shown above say that the effect of the departure cannot reasonably be quantified. Most property companies say this, but Wilson Bowden is an exception, as shown below

---

Extract 10.57: Wilson Bowden plc (1996)

Principal Accounting Policies

Depreciation [extract]

In accordance with SSAP 19, (i) investment properties are revalued annually and where a deficit is considered to be permanent this is charged to the profit and loss account, otherwise the aggregate surplus or deficit is transferred to a revaluation reserve, and (ii) no depreciation or amortisation is provided in respect of freehold investment properties and leasehold investment properties with over twenty five years to run.

The requirement of the Companies Act 1985 ('the Act') is to depreciate all properties, but that requirement conflicts with the generally accepted accounting principle set out in SSAP 19. The Directors consider that, as these properties are not held for consumption but for investment, to depreciate them would not give a true and fair view and that it is necessary to adopt SSAP 19 in order to give a true and fair view.

If this departure from the Act had not been made the profit for the financial year would have been reduced by depreciation on the revalued properties of £93,000 (1995 reduced by £94,000).

---

7   COMPARISON WITH US AND IASC PRONOUNCEMENTS

7.1   US

As in the UK, there is no accounting standard in the US that covers all aspects of accounting for fixed assets, but a number of standards cover different parts of the subject. An important item in the cost of assets constructed for a business's own use or resale, the capitalisation of interest, is covered by SFAS 34.[190] There are also industry-specific standards such as SFAS 67[191] which deals with the costs of constructing buildings for real estate developers.

There is no general standard on depreciation in the US equivalent to SSAP 12, although some aspects are covered in ARBs 43 and 44 (revised).[192] There are, however, a number of standards that deal with detailed aspects of the subject.[193] Disclosure is dealt with by paragraphs 4 and 5 of APB 12.

Depreciation is defined in ARB 43 as follows:

'A system of accounting which aims to distribute the cost or other basic value of tangible capital assets, less salvage (if any), over the estimated useful life of the unit (which may be a group of assets) in a systematic and rational manner. It is a process of allocation, not of valuation.'[194]

In 1995 the FASB issued an important statement on impairment of fixed assets, SFAS 121.[195] This is similar in some respects to the ASB proposals (which were to some extent modelled on it), but there are also some important differences.

Like the ASB proposals (discussed at 4.4 above), SFAS 121 first requires companies to consider whether there are 'indications of impairment'. However, unlike the UK version, the US approach assesses this on the basis of the *un*discounted future cash flows of the business segment concerned; if this test shows no shortfall, nothing further requires to be done. If there is a shortfall on this test, then the asset has to be written down to its fair value, which may be either an externally determined market value or an internal calculation based on *discounted* future cash flows. This switch from an undiscounted basis for triggering the recognition of impairment to a discounted basis for measuring it can obviously produce some anomalous results.

Another important difference between the two approaches is that once an impairment write-down has been recorded under the US standard, it cannot subsequently be reversed even if conditions improve.[196] In contrast, an impairment provision made in the UK is reversed if the need for it has gone away.

Under usual conditions, revaluations of fixed assets are not permitted in US accounts. In APB 6 it is stated: 'Property, plant and equipment should not be written up by an entity to reflect appraisal, market or current values which are above cost to the entity.'[197]

The US position on accounting for investment properties contrasts starkly with that in the UK. No special treatment is allowed for investment properties and, as indicated above, revaluations are generally not permitted.[198] Real estate companies tend to have unclassified balance sheets with all properties shown under the same heading. Some give supplementary current value information.

7.2   IASC

IAS 16 – *Accounting for property, plant and equipment* – covers cost, carrying value (including improvements and repairs, recoverable amount and revaluations), disposals and disclosure, while depreciation is covered by both IAS 16 and IAS 4.[199] As the title shows, the standard deals only with tangible fixed assets; as yet, there is no international standard on intangibles, although as discussed below a proposed standard has now been exposed.

The benchmark treatment under IAS 16 is to carry fixed assets at historical cost.[200] However, it also permits them to be carried at revalued amounts as an allowed alternative, so long as the valuations are kept materially up to date.[201] It requires that an entire class of assets be revalued, where the valuation approach is followed, rather than allowing piecemeal valuations of individual assets.[202]

The gain or loss on disposal of revalued assets is to be measured by reference to the revalued amount of the asset, not its original cost,[203] but (perhaps inconsistently), write-downs of revalued assets are to be charged against the revaluation reserve to the extent that there is a surplus held there in relation to the asset in question, and only thereafter charged as an expense.[204]

IAS 16 also contains requirements on depreciation, which broadly correspond to those in SSAP 12. These duplicate similar requirements in IAS 4 – *Accounting for Depreciation* – which has been retained because it covers intangible assets as well as property, plant and equipment, and therefore cannot be withdrawn at this stage.

The IASC published E55, a proposed standard on *Impairment of Assets*, in May 1997. This is very similar to FRED 15 (see 4.4 above), but differs in the following main respects:

■   FRED 15 proposes that all the assets of an entity, including goodwill and corporate assets such as the head office, should be allocated to individual income generating units for the purposes of the impairment test. E55, however, says that such assets should only be allocated to such units where this can be done on a reasonable and consistent basis and otherwise should be included in a second impairment test at a higher level of aggregation (perhaps at the level of the whole enterprise);[205]

■   FRED 15 seeks to measure impairment on an after-tax basis, whereas E55 does so on a pre-tax basis, dealing with tax as a separate issue;[206]

■   E55 deals with all impairments of revalued assets by taking the write-down first against the revaluation reserve relating to that asset and only thereafter (when the value falls below depreciated historical cost), charging it to the profit and loss account.[207] FRED 15, however, seeks to distinguish impairments that reflect a 'clear reduction in the quantum of service potential' from other impairments and says that the former should always be charged in the profit and loss account.

IAS 25 on accounting for investments permits investment properties to be classified either as property or as long-term investments.[208] If classified as property, they must be depreciated in accordance with IAS 16.[209] If classified as long-term investments they may be either revalued or retained at cost.[210]

Other requirements of IAS 25 which are relevant to investment properties are:

(a) if revaluations are used, a policy for the frequency of revaluations should be adopted and an entire category of long-term investments should be revalued at the same time;[211]

(b) provision must be made for permanent diminutions in the value of long-term investments. This must be done for each investment individually;[212]

(c) increases in value on a revaluation should be credited to revaluation reserve. Any reduction below cost on an individual investment should be charged to profit and loss account. A subsequent reversal of such a decrease should be credited to profit and loss account;[213]

(d) if short-term investments are carried at the lower of cost and market value, revaluations should be reversed on a reclassification from long-term to short-term;[214]

(e) the accounts should disclose:

   (i)   the accounting policies for determining the carrying amount of investments and the treatment of revaluation surpluses on the disposal of revalued investments;

   (ii) the fair value of investment properties if treated as long-term investments and not revalued;

   (iii) for long-term investments carried at valuation:

   - the policy for the frequency of revaluations;

   - the date of the latest revaluation; and

   - the basis of revaluation, stating whether an external valuer was used;

   (iv) movements on revaluation surplus and the nature of such movements; and

   (v)   for enterprises whose main business is the holding of investments, an analysis of the portfolio of investments.[215]

In 1989, the IASC issued an exposure draft, E32 – *Comparability of Financial Statements* – which proposed to amend, inter alia, the requirements of IAS 25. The main change proposed was to make the preferred treatment for investment properties that they should be measured at cost and depreciated in accordance with IAS 4 (which has since been superseded by the revision to IAS 16). However, the alternative treatment of dealing with such assets as long-term investments carried at valuation was still to be allowed, provided additional information was given.[216] The only change to the provisions dealing with the accounting for revaluations of such assets was that on disposal of a revalued asset any revaluation surplus remaining in the revaluation reserves relating to the disposed asset should be transferred to retained earnings (and not to income as presently allowed).[217] These proposals were endorsed in a statement of intent published by the IASC in July 1990,[218] but have never been implemented.

The IASC published an exposure draft on intangible assets in June 1995,[219] but at its July 1997 meeting the IASC approved a further exposure draft to replace it. This follows a similar approach to FRED 12 in most respects; in particular, it sets fairly restrictive criteria for the recognition of intangible assets. The IASC's benchmark treatment is to carry intangibles on the basis of historical cost, but like FRED 12 it allows revaluation as an alternative, provided there is an ascertainable market value for the intangible in question. There are, however, a number of differences, as discussed below:

■ The definition of intangible assets in both exposure drafts requires them to be 'identifiable'. However, in the UK exposure draft this is defined to mean 'capable of being disposed of or settled separately, without disposing of a business of the entity', whereas in the IASC version it has a less narrow and more literal meaning;

■ The IASC version embraces research and development expenditure within its scope, whereas FRED 12 leaves that issue to SSAP 13. This is because the IASC rejects a 'deferred cost' perspective for including items in the balance sheet although it has to use rather tortuously worded recognition criteria to continue to allow the same expenditure to be capitalised from a balance sheet perspective; and

■ The IASC exposure draft is consistent with FRED 12 in imposing a presumption that intangibles have a maximum life of 20 years. Although this presumption can be rebutted if adequate evidence to support a longer life exists (and is disclosed), the possibility of an indefinite life is not acknowledged.

8 CONCLUSION

In principle, accounting for fixed assets should not pose many conceptual difficulties. The essential purpose is to allocate the cost of assets which provide enduring benefits against the revenues of the periods which enjoy these benefits. However, that straightforward objective does not always prove easy to achieve.

One of the main factors which complicates the issue is the widespread but piecemeal practice of incorporating revaluations in what are otherwise historical cost accounts. This immediately poses accounting questions about how to treat the revaluation surplus subsequently, but more seriously it also confuses the objectives of traditional accounting for fixed assets; it gives support to the view that the balance sheet is intended to portray the value of the assets employed and therefore that depreciation should also be designed to meet that end, or at least that the maintenance of value can justify the absence of depreciation.

Unfortunately, we do not believe that the ASB is succeeding in unravelling these issues very convincingly. The approach for intangible assets that it is proposing does depend on the view that maintenance of value can justify non-amortisation, but the Board rejects such an argument in relation to operational tangible assets and accepts it only on pragmatic grounds for investment properties. It has been unable to develop a consistent approach for revalued assets as between depreciation and disposals on the one hand and impairment on the other. And by proposing to require impaired assets to be measured on a discounted basis it has introduced a fresh inconsistency, since depreciation methods typically do not take account of the time value of money. We regret to say that we are not confident that these various proposals will improve the accounting treatment of fixed assets.

References

1 ED 51, *Accounting for fixed assets and revaluations*, ASC, May 1990 and ED 52, *Accounting for intangible fixed assets*, ASC, May 1990.
2 Discussion Paper, *Measurement of tangible fixed assets*, ASB, October 1996, FRED 15, *Impairment of fixed assets and goodwill*, ASB, June 1997 and FRED 12, *Goodwill and intangible assets*, ASB, June 1996.
3 CA 85, s 262(1).
4 FRED 15, para. 2.
5 FRED 12, para. 2.
6 *Ibid.*
7 CA 85, Sch 4A, para. 9(2).
8 FRED 15, para. 2.
9 Draft *Statement of principles for financial reporting*, ASB, November 1995, para. 4.6.
10 *Ibid.*, para. 3.5.
11 FRED 12, para. 8.
12 *Ibid.*, para. 9.
13 *Ibid.*, para. 69.
14 *Ibid.*, para. 11.
15 SSAP 22, *Accounting for goodwill*, ASC, Revised July 1989, para. 27.
16 CA 85, Sch 4A, para. 9(2).
17 Barwise, Higson, Likierman and Marsh, *Accounting for Brands*, 1989, p. 8.
18 FRED 12, para. 9.
19 CA 85, Sch. 4, para. 17.

20 CA 85, s 262(1).
21 *Ibid.*, Sch. 4, para. 26(1).
22 SSAP 4, *Accounting for government grants*, ASC, Revised July 1990, para. 25.
23 CA 85, Sch. 4, paras. 26(2) and 26(3).
24 ED 51, para. 11.
25 SSAP 9, *Stocks and long-term contracts*, ASC, Revised September 1988, para. 19.
26 *Ibid.*, Appendix 1, paras. 4–7.
27 *Measurement of tangible fixed assets*, para. 1.10.
28 *Ibid.*, paras. 1.4–1.6.
29 SSAP 9, Appendix 1, para. 1.
30 *Measurement of tangible fixed assets*, para. 1.6.
31 *Ibid.*
32 *Ibid.*, para. 1.24.
33 *Ibid.*, para. 1.25.
34 ED 51, para. 76.
35 *Ibid.*, para. 19.
36 SSAP 12, *Accounting for depreciation*, ASC, revised January 1987, para. 10.
37 This view was to an extent supported by the definition in the original version of SSAP 12, at para. 15 which ran (in part): 'depreciation is the measure of the wearing out, consumption or other loss of value of a fixed asset...'.
38 ARB 43, para. 7. Note that this consolidates the earlier ARB 33 that dates from 1947, but has not been superseded.
39 FRAG 2/92, ICAEW, 1992, para. 16.
40 *Measurement of tangible fixed assets*, para. 5.16.
41 SSAP 19, *Accounting for investment properties*, ASC, November 1991, para. 7.
42 *Ibid.*, para. 8.
43 *Ibid.*, para. 9.
44 SSAP 12, *Accounting for depreciation*, ASC, December 1977, para. 22.
45 ED 26, *Accounting for investment properties – an addition to SSAP 12 'Accounting for depreciation'*, ASC, September 1980.
46 *Statement by the Accounting Standards Committee on the publication of ED 26 'Accounting for investment properties'*, paras. 7 and 8.
47 CA 85, s 228(5).
48 *Amendment to SSAP 19 'Accounting for investment properties'*, ASB, July 1994, para. 7.
49 ED 37, *Accounting for depreciation*, ASC, March 1985, para. 25, stated, 'In certain very restricted instances it may not be appropriate to charge depreciation in respect of what would normally be a depreciable asset. This would arise only where the asset is maintained to such a standard that:
    a) the estimated residual value is equal to or greater than its net book amount, or
    b) its estimated useful economic life is either infinite or such that any depreciation charge would be insignificant.'
50 Technical Release 648, *Statement on the publication of SSAP 12 (Revised) Accounting for depreciation*, para. 10.
51 FRAG 2/92, para. 47.
52 FRED 12, para 13.
53 CA 85, Sch. 4, para. 18.
54 *Ibid.*
55 *Ibid.*, para. 32.
56 ASC, *A review of SSAP 12 – Accounting for depreciation*, paras. 3.1–3.4, 6.1–6.2 and 4.1–4.6.
57 SSAP 12, para. 15.
58 *Ibid.*, para. 16.
59 *Ibid.*, para. 17.
60 *Ibid.*, paras. 19 and 20.
61 *Ibid.*, para. 22.
62 ED 37, para. 20.
63 Original SSAP 12, para. 4.
64 *Ibid.*
65 SSAP 12, para. 15.

66 *Ibid.*, para. 21.
67 See the SORP on *Accounting for oil and gas exploration and development activities*, Oil Industry Accounting Committee, December 1987, paras. 62–65 and 84–87.
68 SSAP 12, para. 21.
69 SSAP 2, *Disclosure of accounting policies*, ASC, November 1971, para. 13.
70 *Ibid.*, para. 16.
71 FRS 3, *Reporting of financial performance*, ASB, December 1992, paras. 29 and 62.
72 CA 85, Sch. 4, para. 25.
73 SSAP 12, para. 20.
74 CA 85, Sch. 4, para. 19(2).
75 *Ibid.*, para. 19(3).
76 *Ibid.*, paras. 19(1) and (2). The use of the word 'shown' makes the wording ambiguous, but it is generally considered to mean that the provisions must be made through the profit and loss account and either disclosed on the face of the profit and loss account or in the notes to the accounts.
77 SSAP 12, para. 19.
78 *Ibid.*, para. 20.
79 SORP on *Accounting for oil and gas exploration and development activities*, para. 66.
80 *Ibid.*, para. 67.
81 FRED 15, para. 8.
82 *Ibid.*, para. 11.
83 *Ibid.*, para. 17.
84 *Ibid.*, para. 34.
85 *Ibid.*, para. 37.
86 *Ibid.*, para. 38.
87 *Ibid.*, para. 40.
88 CA 85, Sch 4, para. 14.
89 *Company Reporting*, October 1995.
90 SSAP 12, para. 5.
91 *Ibid.*, para. 81.
92 *Ibid.*, para. 53.
93 ED 51, para. 84.
94 *Ibid.*, para. 86.
95 *The role of valuation in financial reporting*, ASB, March 1993, para. 34.
96 *Ibid.*, para. 10.
97 SSAP 19, paras. 10 and 11.
98 *Ibid.*, para. 6.
99 See for example Land Securities PLC, Report and Financial Statements 1997, p. 39.
100 CA 85, Sch. 4, para. 31(2).
101 *Ibid.*, para. 31(1).
102 *Ibid.*, para. 31(3).
103 *Accounting for the effects of changing prices: a Handbook*, ASC, 1986, paras. A1.3 and A1.4. In fact, the same diagram is often used to describe the alternative term 'value to the business'.
104 *Measurement of tangible fixed assets*, para. 4.11.
105 (S20) 2.205, *Valuation of company property assets and their disclosure in directors' reports or accounts of companies*.
106 RICS *Appraisal and Valuation Manual*, RICS, September 1995, Practice Statement 4, para. 4.2.1.
107 *Ibid.*, para. 4.3.1.
108 *Ibid.*, para. 4.3.10.
109 *Ibid.*, para. 4.3.2.
110 *Measurement of tangible fixed assets*, para. 4.21.
111 SSAP 22, para. 15.
112 See Guidance Note 7, *Trading-Related Valuations and Goodwill*, RICS, for further guidance on this subject.
113 RICS *Appraisal and Valuation Manual*, Practice Statement 4, para. 4.5.1.
114 *Ibid.*, Definitions.
115 *Ibid.*, Practice Statement 4, para. 4.8.1.
116 *Ibid.*, para. 4.8.5.

117 C. A. Westwick, *Property Valuations and Accounts*, ICAEW, 1980, pp. 57–58.
118 *Report of the President's Working Party on Commercial Property Valuations*, Foreword.
119 CA 85, Sch. 4, para. 34(1).
120 FRS 3, para. 13.
121 CA 85, Sch. 4, para. 34(3). Until amended by the CA 89, this read '... for the purpose of the accounting policies adopted by the company', which was capable of wider interpretation.
122 *Ibid.*, para. 34(3)(a).
123 *Ibid.*, paras. 34(3A) and (3B).
124 SSAP 12, para. 13.
125 *Ibid.*, para. 16.
126 CA 85, Sch. 4, paras. 32(1) and (3).
127 C. Nobes, *Depreciation Problems in the Context of Historic Cost Accounting*, p. 26.
128 FRS 3, para. 56.
129 ED 51, para. 96.
130 ASC Discussion Paper, *A review of SSAP 6 – Extraordinary items and prior year adjustments*, para. 2.11, ASC Discussion Paper, *A review of SSAP 12 – Accounting for depreciation*, paras. 7.2 and 7.3, ED 16, *Supplement to 'Extraordinary items and prior year adjustments'*, ASC, September 1975, para. 14, ED 36, *Extraordinary items and prior year adjustments*, ASC, January 1985, para. 26 and ED 51, para. 80.
131 FRS 3, para. 21.
132 CA 85, Sch. 4, para. 34(1).
133 ED 51, para. 79.
134 *Impairment of tangible fixed assets*, paras. 5.8–9.
135 *Ibid.*, para. 5.10.
136 FRED 15, para. 52.
137 *Measurement of tangible fixed assets*, para. 2.23.
138 CA 85, Sch. 4, para. 32.
139 FRED 15, para. 55.
140 CA 85, Sch. 4, paras. 19 and 34.
141 *Impairment of tangible fixed assets*, footnote to para. 5.10.
142 UITF 5, *Transfers from Current Assets to Fixed Assets*, July 1992, para. 2.
143 *Ibid.*, para. 5.
144 CA 85, Sch. 4, para. 34(3).
145 *Ibid.*, s 263(3).
146 *Ibid.*, s 275(1).
147 *Ibid.*, s 275(2).
148 This inference can be drawn from the wording of s 275(1), which reads 'a provision ... other than one in respect of a diminution in value of a fixed asset appearing on a revaluation of all the fixed assets...', which suggests that diminutions identified by revaluations constitute provisions as defined by para. 88 of Sch 4.
149 CA 85, s 275(2).
150 See D. Foster, *Accounting Requirements*, Butterworths Company Law Guide, Second edition, 1990, p. 340, para. 12.88, where this interpretation is given.
151 CA 85, s 275(5).
152 *Ibid.*, s 275(6).
153 'Relevant accounts' are defined in *Ibid.*, ss. 270–273.
154 Interpretation Act 1978, Sch. 1.
155 CA 85, Sch. 7, para. 1(2).
156 *Ibid.*, Sch. 4, para. 8, balance sheet formats.
157 Allied Domecq PLC, Report & Accounts 1996, p. 51.
158 CA 85, Sch. 4, para. 8, profit and loss account formats.
159 *Ibid.*, note (17) on the profit and loss account formats.
160 *Ibid.*, paras. 19(1) and 19(2).
161 FRS 3, para. 20.
162 SSAP 12, paras. 25(a) and (b).
163 CA 85, Sch. 4, paras. 42(1)(a) and 42(2).
164 *Ibid.*, para. 42(1)(b).

165 *Ibid.*, para. 42(3).
166 SSAP 12, para. 25(c).
167 *Ibid.*, para. 25(d).
168 *Ibid.*, para. 26.
169 CA 85, Sch. 4, para. 44.
170 *Ibid.*, para. 83(1).
171 *Ibid.*, paras. 33(1) and (2).
172 *Ibid.*, para. 33(3).
173 *Ibid.*, para. 33(4).
174 *Ibid.*, para. 43(a).
175 *Ibid.*, para. 33(2).
176 *Ibid.*, para. 43(b).
177 SSAP 12, para. 26.
178 CA 85, Sch. 4, para. 34(2).
179 *Ibid.*, para. 34(4).
180 SSAP 19 (amended), para. 15.
181 *Ibid.*, para. 12.
182 *Ibid.*, para. 13.
183 CA 85, Sch. 4, para. 34(2).
184 SSAP 19 (amended), para. 15.
185 CA 85, Sch. 4, para. 3(4).
186 CA 85, s 228(6).
187 UITF 7, *True and fair override disclosures*, December 1992, para. 4.
188 *Ibid.*, para. 7.
189 See Slough Estates plc, Annual Report 1996, p. 51.
190 SFAS 34, *Capitalization of Interest Cost*, FASB, October 1979.
191 SFAS 67, *Accounting for Costs and Initial Rental Operations of Real Estate Projects*, FASB, October 1982.
192 ARB No. 43, *Restatement and Revision of Accounting Research Bulletins*, Chapter 9 and ARB No. 44 (Revised), *Declining-balance Depreciation*.
193 These include ARB 43, Chapter 9A which discusses whether assets should be depreciated more quickly to compensate for inflation and rejects the idea, and a number of statements that deal with depreciation methods approved by the Internal Revenue and the timing differences that may result, including ARB 44 (Revised) – *Declining Balance Depreciation* and APB 1 – *New Depreciation Guidelines and Rules*.
194 ARB 43, Chapter 9, para. 5.
195 SFAS 121, *Accounting for the Impairment of Long-Lived Assets and for Long-Lived Assets to Be Disposed Of*, FASB, March 1995.
196 *Ibid.*, para. 11.
197 APB 6, para. 17. This continues: 'This section is not intended to change accounting practices followed in connection with quasi-reorganizations or reorganizations. This section may not apply to foreign operations under unusual conditions such as serious inflation or currency devaluation. However, when the accounts of an enterprise with foreign operations are translated into US currency for consolidation, such write-ups normally are eliminated. Whenever appreciation has been recorded in the books, income shall be charged with depreciation computed on the written-up amounts.'
198 APB Opinion No. 6, *Status of Accounting Research Bulletins*, October 1965, para. 17.
199 IAS 4, *Depreciation Accounting*, IASC, October 1976.
200 IAS 16, *Property, Plant and Equipment*, IASC, revised November 1993, para. 29.
201 *Ibid.*, para. 30.
202 *Ibid.*, para. 36.
203 *Ibid.*, para. 61.
204 *Ibid.*, para. 40.
205 E55, *Impairment of assets*, IASC, May 1997, para. 59.
206 *Ibid., para. 45.*
207 *Ibid.*, footnote to para. 41.
208 IAS 25, para. 45.
209 IAS 16, para. 5. Prior to this revised standard, depreciation of property was dealt with in IAS 4.

210 IAS 25, para. 47.
211 *Ibid.*
212 *Ibid.*
213 *Ibid.*, para. 48.
214 *Ibid.*, para. 51(a).
215 *Ibid.*, para. 55.
216 E32, *Comparability of Financial Statements*, IASC, January 1989, para. 203.
217 *Ibid.*, para. 220.
218 Statement of Intent, *Comparability of Financial Statements*, IASC, July 1990.
219 E50, *Intangible Assets*, IASC, June 1995.

Chapter 11   Investments

1   INTRODUCTION

Investments come in so many different forms, and may be held for such different purposes, that it can be difficult to formulate a precise definition of them. Although not directly relevant to financial reporting, the Financial Services Act 1986 includes the following in its definition of an investment:

- shares and stock in the share capital of a company;

- debentures, including debenture stock, loan stock, bonds, certificates of deposit and other instruments creating or acknowledging indebtedness including those issued by public bodies;

- warrants or other instruments entitling the holder to subscribe for any of the above;

- certificates or other instruments which confer property rights in respect of the above, rights to acquire, dispose of, underwrite or convert an investment, and rights (other than options) to acquire investments other than by subscription;

- units in collective investment schemes including shares in or securities of an open-ended investment company;

- options to acquire or dispose of currency, gold or silver, or any investment as defined in the Act, including other options;

- futures;

- contracts for differences and similar instruments;

- long-term insurance contracts; and

- rights and interests in any of the above.[1]

Each of these is further described in some detail by the Act.

In 1990, the ASC published an exposure draft on the subject, ED 55 – *Accounting for investments*, although it has never been progressed further. Its definition of investments was at the other end of the spectrum; whereas the Financial Services Act is highly specific, ED 55's definition was very general. It defined an investment simply as 'an asset that is characterised by its ability to generate economic benefits in the form of distributions and/or appreciation in value'.[2] This was a slight variant of the equivalent in the international accounting standard on the subject, which says that 'an investment is an asset held by an enterprise for the accretion of wealth through distribution (such as interest, royalties, dividends and rentals), for capital appreciation or for other benefits to the investing enterprise such as those obtained through trading relationships'.[3]

Although they would otherwise fall within the above definition, investment properties were excluded from the scope of ED 55 because they are dealt with in a separate accounting standard, SSAP 19. They are similarly excluded from the scope of this chapter, but are discussed in Chapter 10.

As mentioned above, enterprises may hold investments for a variety of different purposes. For example, an investment may be held:

- as a short-term store of wealth, perhaps by a seasonal business during the part of the year when its stocks are low, or by any enterprise for a period pending investment in operational assets;

- as a trading asset, by an enterprise whose business entails dealing in investments for profit;

- as a means of exercising control or influence over another enterprise which becomes its subsidiary or associated undertaking as a result;

- as a trade investment, to form a long-term but less influential relationship with another enterprise in a similar line of business;

- as a means of building up resources to meet long-term obligations, as in the case of a pension fund or an insurance company;

- as a means of hedging against some obligation of the enterprise, where the investment and the obligation have certain risk-related characteristics in common;

- as part of a managed portfolio of investments, in order to allow members of the enterprise to spread their risk without having to invest directly in the underlying components of the portfolio, as in the case of investment trusts and unit trusts.

Schedule 4 to the Companies Act addresses accounting for investments at a general level, but does not apply to banking and insurance companies, which are governed by separate schedules of their own. There are also some particular provisions for investment companies in Schedule 4 itself.[4] It is beyond the scope of this book to discuss detailed requirements for companies in specialised industries, and accordingly this chapter will confine itself to the general requirements for accounting for investments.[5]

In the absence of any accounting standard, the Companies Act remains the only source of rules on accounting for investments. As indicated above, the ASB has never progressed ED 55; however, its current project on financial instruments (which is dealt with in Chapter 9) is broad enough to embrace almost all investments within its scope and this is likely to form the basis of accounting for investments in the future. The present statutory requirements are discussed in 2 below, together with an indication of how these might change in the future.

2 REQUIREMENTS FOR ACCOUNTING FOR INVESTMENTS

2.1 Classification

The formats in Schedule 4 to the Companies Act 1985 indicate that investments may be classified as either fixed asset investments or current asset investments. The available categories within each are shown opposite:[6]

The Act does not have a particular rule for distinguishing between fixed and current asset *investments*. It is necessary to apply the general rule that a fixed asset is one which is intended for use on a continuing basis in the company's activities and a current asset is one not intended for such use.[7] However, this is an unhelpful distinction for investments which, by their nature, are not intended for *use* in a company's activities at all, whether on a continuing basis or otherwise.

B	**Fixed assets**
III	Investments
	1. Shares in group undertakings
	2. Loans to group undertakings
	3. Participating interests
	4. Loans to undertakings in which the group has a participating interest
	5. Other investments other than loans
	6. Other loans
	7. Own shares
C	**Current assets**
III	Investments
	1. Shares in group undertakings
	2. Own shares
	3. Other investments

ED 55 proposed a more practical test for distinguishing between fixed and current asset investments. It defined a fixed asset investment as one 'which is intended to be held for use on a continuing basis in the activities of the enterprise. An investment should be classified as a fixed asset only where an intention to hold the investment for the long term can clearly be demonstrated or where there are restrictions as to the investor's ability to dispose of the investment.'[8] A current asset investment was the 'default' category; in other words it was defined, as in the Companies Act, as one which fails to meet the criteria for classification as a fixed asset investment.[9]

ED 55's definition therefore built on the Companies Act definition, but tried to make more sense of it. It elaborated on its own definition by saying that the category of fixed asset investments would comprise:

(a)   equity shareholdings in or loans to subsidiaries and associates;

(b)   investments arising from other trading relationships;

(c)   investments that either cannot be disposed of or cannot be disposed of without a significant effect on the operations of the enterprise; and

(d)   investments that are intended to be held for use on a continuing basis by enterprises whose objective is to hold a portfolio of investments to provide income and/or capital growth for their members.[10]

It emphasised that the fact that an investment is held for a lengthy period does not mean that it is to be accounted for as a fixed asset investment; it must be held for reasons which bring it within the definition.

This approach contrasts with that used in IAS 25, which defines a current investment as 'an investment which is by its nature readily realisable and is intended to be held for not more than one year',[11] and leaves all other investments to be classified as long-term investments. However, the international standard is not constrained by the terms of the Companies Act, which in distinguishing between a current and a fixed asset places emphasis on the purpose for which the asset is held rather than its liquidity.

2.2   Accounting rules

2.2.1   *Fixed asset investments*

The general statutory rule for the valuation of a fixed asset applies, namely that it should be included at its purchase price (production cost is an irrelevant alternative for an investment).[12] Purchase price includes any expenses incidental to its acquisition,[13] which will normally only include relatively minor dealing costs and stamp duty, but in the context of a contested takeover of a public company, the incidental costs may be very significant indeed.

Where the alternative accounting rules are invoked, fixed asset investments may be carried either at their market value determined at the date of their last valuation or at a directors' valuation.[14] The latter may be on any basis which appears to the directors to be appropriate in the circumstances of the company, so long as details of the basis and the reasons for adopting it are disclosed in a note to the accounts. One common practice is to include investments in subsidiary and/or associated undertakings in the balance sheet of the parent company at their net asset value, as shown in this extract:

> *Extract 11.1: Kwik-Fit Holdings plc (1997)*
>
> Statement of Accounting Policies
>
> **Investment in subsidiary undertakings**
>
> The Company accounts for its investments in subsidiary undertakings by the equity method, whereby the original cost of the investments is adjusted for the movement in underlying net assets applicable to the investments since their date of acquisition with an adjustment to the Company's revaluation reserve.

ED 55 proposed to tighten up the basic requirements of the Companies Act by removing the possibility of a historical valuation which is neither the original purchase price nor the current value of the asset. Unless a company wished to carry its investments at historical cost, ED 55 required annual valuations.[15] Moreover, it proposed that the revalued amount should be treated as if it were cost for all subsequent purposes. This meant that if any decline in value was expected to be a permanent one, then the whole amount of the write-down (compared to its previously revalued amount) was to be charged to the profit and loss account.[16]

This proposal was inconsistent with the requirements of IAS 25, which requires that amounts written off revalued assets should first be charged against any revaluation surplus existing in respect of the asset, and only thereafter should any remaining write-off be charged to the profit and loss account.[17] The logic of the ED 55 proposal was not really explained. There may be some argument for following this approach in relation to operational assets (based on some notion of maintaining capital based on operating capability), but it is difficult to see any merit in it for investments which, by definition, are not consumed in operations for which such a capital maintenance concept may be relevant. Furthermore, a difficulty remains of distinguishing between a provision for permanent diminution in value and a downward revaluation, as is discussed more fully in 5.3.4 of Chapter 10.

Where a revalued investment is subsequently sold, ED 55 again required the gain or loss on disposal to be calculated as the difference between the proceeds and the (revalued) carrying amount prior to disposal. Any net surplus previously credited to and retained in the revaluation reserve was to be released to the profit and loss account as a reserve transfer.[18] The gain or loss on disposal was normally to be dealt with in the profit and loss account, but an exemption from this requirement was proposed for investment companies as defined in the Companies Act,[19] since their articles prohibit them from distributing gains on disposal of such investments and as a result they customarily deal with both gains and losses in reserves.[20] These proposals have now been adopted in FRS 3, which requires the gain or loss on the sale of all revalued assets to be measured by reference to their revalued amount rather than their historical cost, and also allows the exemption for investment companies described above.[21] FRS 3, however, does not address the question of how to deal with the permanent impairment of revalued assets.

Investments are not excluded from the depreciation rules of the Act (although they are excluded from the provisions of SSAP 12), but these usually do not apply because most investments have an indefinite life. However, for investments such as dated gilts, bonds or redeemable preference shares that are to be held to maturity it is common to amortise the premium or discount to redemption over their term; this treatment was proposed by ED 55.[22] The amortisation should be systematic and designed to recognise the constant yield earned on the investment or an approximation to it, although in practice a straight line basis may meet this requirement within bounds of materiality.[23]

The Post Office discloses such a policy, as shown in this extract:

Extract 11.2: The Post Office (1997)

ACCOUNTING POLICIES AND GENERAL NOTES

G   INVESTMENTS [extract]

(ii) Other investments held as fixed assets are stated in the balance sheet on the basis of cost adjusted so as to amortise to redemption value over the period to maturity. If sold before maturity, the difference between the proceeds and the amortised value is taken to the profit and loss account in the year of realisation.

Glaxo Wellcome discloses a policy of recognising income on this basis for such investments if they are to be held to redemption, although it is not entirely clear why such a condition should apply to investments held as current assets, as shown in this policy:

Extract 11.3: Glaxo Wellcome plc (1996)

2 ACCOUNTING POLICIES AND DEFINITIONS

Current asset investments: [extract]

… In the case of securities acquired at a significant premium or discount to maturity value, and intended to be held to redemption, cost is adjusted to amortise the premium or discount over the period to maturity of the security. …

A policy of amortising premiums or discounts is most frequently applied to gilts, but is equally relevant to other types of redeemable security, such as deep discounted bonds. In the case of more complex securities which have a number of redemption options at different dates and different prices it will be appropriate to exercise prudence in determining the amount of income to be recognised in order to avoid the danger of reporting income which is not subsequently received.

Fixed asset investments are also subject to the statutory requirement to write them down to reflect any permanent diminution in their value. Such a provision is to be charged in the profit and loss account and is to be released if it is subsequently found to be unnecessary, with disclosure of the amounts in each case.[24] As well as these requirements, which apply to all fixed assets, the Act specifically allows provision to be made against the value of fixed asset investments even where their fall in value is not expected to be permanent.[25]

In addition, the ASB intends to include certain investments within the scope of its general standard on impairment of fixed assets. The relevant exposure draft, FRED 15, says that it will apply to those investments that are not covered by its project on financial instruments, which therefore means investments in subsidiaries, associates, and joint ventures.[26]

A more detailed discussion of both FRED 15 and the operation of the valuation rules for fixed assets is contained in Chapter 10. However, one particular issue which frequently arises is how a holding company should deal with investments in subsidiaries whose value has been impaired, either as a result of trading losses or following a group reconstruction.

If a subsidiary company makes losses then its net asset value may fall below the amount at which the investment is stated in the company's balance sheet. A provision must be made if there has been a permanent reduction in profitability which has resulted in a real reduction in value and there is no prospect of an improvement in fortunes in the foreseeable future. As described above, it is quite common for holding companies to carry investments in subsidiaries at net asset value, with the result that temporary diminutions are taken to revaluation reserve. However, where the diminution is expected to be permanent then it should be charged to the profit and loss account.

A common form of group reconstruction involves the transfer to another group company of the tangible assets and trade of a subsidiary. If the original purchase price included an element of goodwill, the remaining shell may have a carrying value in the parent company's balance sheet in excess of its net worth. It could be argued that as the subsidiary is now a shell company a provision should be made against the carrying value to reduce it to its net worth. However, in such a reorganisation there has been no real loss either to the holding company or to the group, and as a result companies frequently conclude that it would be inappropriate to make a provision. Nevertheless, the impairment in carrying value should always be recognised if the assets and/or the trade transferred are themselves sold outside the group. It is only possible to argue that the loss need not be recognised as long as there is a matching gain elsewhere in the group which has also not been recognised.

Signet Group has taken a different approach to this problem, applying a true and fair override and transferring the excess amount to goodwill, as shown in this extract:

Extract 11.4: Signet Group plc (1997)

26 Intangible assets and investments (held as fixed assets) [extract]

True and fair override on divisionalisation of subsidiary undertakings

As part of a rationalisation of the Group, the trades and net assets of two subsidiary undertakings were transferred into the Company in previous years. The consideration for this divisionalisation was based upon the book value of the subsidiary undertakings' net assets, and took no account of goodwill inherent in these businesses. This resulted in an apparent overvaluation of investments held in the Company's books, though there was no overall loss to the Group. Schedule 4 to the Companies Act 1985 requires that, where such overvaluation is expected to be permanent, the investment should be written down accordingly. The directors consider that as the substance of the transaction was merely to reorganise the Group's operations, such a treatment would fail to give a true and fair view and the diminution in value of the investments has instead been re-allocated to goodwill.

The effect on the Company's balance sheet of this departure from the requirements of Schedule 4 is to recognise goodwill of £64,090,000 (1996: £65,975,000), net of amortisation of £11,310,000 (1996: £9,425,000).

As discussed more fully in Chapter 9, the ASB's long-term proposals on financial instruments entail valuing all investments at market value, without differentiating between fixed and current asset investments[27] (but excluding shares in subsidiaries and associates[28]). Movements in value would normally be dealt with in the profit and loss account, but two exceptions are proposed, for which the movements would be reported in the statement of total recognised gains and losses. These are:

- 'Long-term, strategic holdings of shares'.[29] This category is not defined further but is distinguished from 'shares that are held for trading in the short term or as a readily disposable store of value'. This therefore carries overtones of a fixed/current split.

- 'Debt investments that match-fund a borrowing'.[30] These are holdings of fixed interest securities that have similar maturities and interest bases to fixed interest rate debt. The implicit argument is that, since they provide a hedge to the interest rate exposure on the debt, and since movements in the value of the debt are taken to the statement of total recognised gains and losses, the offsetting gains and losses on the investments should be taken there as well.

2.2.2 Current asset investments

The valuation rules for current asset investments in the Companies Act again dictate that the investment should initially be recorded at its purchase price, including any incidental expenses.[31] A current asset investment must be written down to its net realisable value if it is less than its purchase price, but that write-down should again be reversed if the reasons for it cease to apply.[32] If the alternative accounting rules are adopted, a current asset investment may be revalued to its current cost.[33]

ED 55 proposed to distinguish between 'readily marketable' investments and others. An investment was to be regarded as readily marketable if it was one 'for which an active market exists, which is both open and accessible, and for which a market value (or some other indicator from which a value may be calculated) is quoted openly'.[34] The purpose of the distinction was to ensure that those investments thus classified were capable of being readily disposed of at the stated value. The exposure draft proposed that such investments, if they were held as current assets, should be marked to market; in other words, they should be carried in the balance sheet at their current market value and all movements in that value between one balance sheet date and the next should be included in the profit and loss account as a component of income from investments.[35] Current asset investments that were not readily marketable were to be valued in accordance with the Companies Act rules as set out above.

Marking to market is commonly applied by companies whose business involves dealing in investments, but is not generally used by most other companies. The Post Office discloses such a policy in relation to gilts, as shown in this extract:

Extract 11.5: The Post Office (1997)

ACCOUNTING POLICIES AND GENERAL NOTES

G   INVESTMENTS [extract]

(iii) Investments held as current assets are stated at market value at the balance sheet date and the difference between cost and market value is taken to the profit and loss account. This treatment is a departure from UK accounting rules which stipulate that unrealised profits be credited to a revaluation reserve. In the opinion of the Board Members, the treatment adopted is necessary to present a true and fair view. All such investments are readily marketable Government securities. The accounting treatment adopted represents a fairer reflection of the investment return.

ED 55 argued that this treatment is the most appropriate for measuring the results of the enterprise because it reflects the success or failure of the decision to invest in all its readily marketable current asset investments during the year – not simply those which management has chosen to sell before the year end. An analogy was drawn between this treatment and that required by SSAP 20 in respect of foreign currency balances, where profits are recognised on all such balances, not simply those converted into sterling at the end of the year. It is argued that gains arising on marking to market can be regarded as realised profits, because, as with the foreign currency balances, they could readily have been converted into cash at the end of the year had management chosen to do so. However, the exposure draft limited the proposal to those investments which are readily marketable, because only they are capable of being readily disposed of at their stated value, and to those which are current assets, because fixed assets are by definition not intended to be disposed of at all.

Where the holding in an otherwise readily marketable investment is so large that it could not be disposed of without a material effect on the quoted market price, the exposure draft said that the price used should be adjusted to reflect the proceeds that could realistically be expected from gradual disposal of the investment in the ordinary course of business.[36] This was seen as a controversial suggestion, because it may be argued that the practice of marking to market is only justified where the investment in question could have been instantaneously liquidated at a reliable market price, and that if this could not be done because the holding is a very large one, then the practice should not be applied. ED 55 asked for specific comment on this issue.

The ASB's proposals on financial instruments go much further. They say that *all* investments should be marked to market, even those held as fixed assets, those which are not readily marketable, and those which are large holdings (except that certain gains and losses are proposed to be dealt with in the statement of total recognised gains and losses rather than the profit and loss account, as explained in 2.2.1 above). The implicit logic is not that these gains and losses could have been instantaneously realised, but simply that it is necessary to use market values for financial assets in order to reflect the performance of the company for the period.

Marking to market involves a departure from the requirements of the Companies Act as discussed above. The difficulty is not so much that any appreciation in value does not represent a realised profit – the determination of realised profits allows some room for interpretation by accounting rules – but rather that the balance sheet valuation rules in Schedule 4 do not allow valuations unless the other side of the entry is taken to a revaluation reserve under the alternative accounting rules. ED 55 sought to justify this departure on the basis that it was necessary to depart from these rules in order to give a true and fair view, but this was a controversial proposition, because the true and fair override can only be invoked in 'special circumstances' and it may be argued that the mere decision to hold readily marketable investments as a current asset does not give rise to circumstances which are sufficiently special to warrant the departure. This legal difficulty has probably been one of the factors that has prevented the ASB from picking up the project and turning ED 55 into a standard. It remains to be seen, however, how the ASB will be able to reconcile its own more far-reaching proposals for financial instruments with the law.

Companies which are not required to prepare their accounts under Schedule 4 to the Act are not subject to this legal obstacle. This category includes banks, which are also among those most likely to be engaging in investment dealing activities where marking to market is most appropriate. Schedule 9 to the Companies Act explicitly recognises the practice.[37]

Coats Viyella discloses accounting policies for fixed and current asset investments which follow the orthodox measurement rules described above:

> *Extract 11.6: Coats Viyella Plc (1996)*
>
> **Statement of accounting policies**
>
> **Investments**
>
> Fixed asset investments are stated at cost unless, in the opinion of the Directors, there has been a permanent diminution in value, in which case an appropriate adjustment is made.
>
> Listed current asset investments are stated at the lower of cost or market value, and other current asset investments are stated at the lower of cost and estimated net realisable value.

2.2.3 Other matters relevant to all investments

One issue which sometimes arises is the treatment of reclassifications of investments from current assets to fixed assets or vice versa, since the rules governing their measurement are not the same. Under UITF 5, current assets which are transferred to fixed assets should continue to be accounted for under the appropriate rules for current assets up to the date of transfer, and therefore transferred at the amount that is appropriate under these rules.[38] This rule was devised to prevent companies avoiding a write-down of current assets to net realisable value by redesignating them as fixed assets. The Abstract does not deal with transfers in the opposite direction, from fixed to current assets.

Where a company has an investment which has been built up over a period at different prices, it is not necessary for the actual purchase price to be assigned to the specific securities acquired in each transaction; instead it is permissible to use one of the methods suggested by the Act for 'fungible assets' (which are most commonly used for valuing stock – see 3.1 and 3.2 of Chapter 14). These allow costs to be assigned on the basis of FIFO, LIFO, weighted average or any other similar method rather than using the actual cost, but with the proviso that the replacement cost or most recent purchase price of the holding should be disclosed if it is materially different from the balance sheet amount.[39] ED 55 sought to narrow this down by requiring the average purchase price to be used for the purposes of accounting for any subsequent partial disposals.[40] ED 55 also said that each investment within a category should accounted for separately, rather than on a portfolio basis.[41] This is in any event a Companies Act requirement.[42]

ED 55 proposed that an investment transaction should be accounted for as of the date on which the risks and rewards of ownership pass from the seller to the purchaser.[43] This will generally be the date on which the trade was made, rather than the subsequent settlement date (a view now supported by the ASB, but not by the IASC, in their respective financial instruments projects). It also said that if an investment was acquired with an accrued entitlement to interest or a fixed dividend, its cost should be based on its purchase price excluding the amount of the accrued interest or dividend.[44] There is no equivalent discussion in the law.

2.2.4 *Income recognition*

ED 55 proposed that all income from investments should be recognised in the profit and loss account when it became receivable.[45] This implies a normal accruals basis for interest and fixed rate dividends, while in the case of dividends on equity securities the amount due should be recognised when it is declared or, in the case of quoted securities, on the ex-dividend date; in practice, a cash basis of accounting for such income may produce materially the same results. However, it suggested an exception for the case of intra-group dividends, where frequently decisions on such dividends are made after the year end but before the accounts are finalised; it said that the parent company could recognise such dividends from subsidiary undertakings provided they were declared before the date of approval of its own financial statements.[46]

2.2.5 *Investments held for hedging purposes*

ED 55 did not purport to set rules to govern the accounting treatment of investments held to hedge obligations of the enterprise, since this is a highly complex matter. However, it avoided inadvertently frustrating the aims of hedging by giving an exemption from its requirements where to apply them 'would not properly reflect the economic substance of the hedge'.[47] As explained in Chapter 9, the ASB means to address this issue in its current project on financial instruments, but has not so far determined its position.

2.3   Disclosure requirements

The Act requires various disclosures to be made in relation to investments. In respect of fixed asset investments, the following must be shown:

(a)   the appropriate amounts at the beginning of the financial year and as at the balance sheet date, based either on historical cost or alternative accounting rules.[48] Where investments are carried at valuation, equivalent historical cost information must be disclosed;[49]

(b)   all movements during the year, including revaluation surpluses and deficits, acquisitions, disposals and transfers.[50] Such movements would also include exchange differences; and

(c)   the cumulative amount of provisions for depreciation or diminution in value as at the beginning and end of the financial year on the appropriate basis of cost or valuation, the provision for the period and adjustments in respect of disposals or for other reasons.[51] Systematic depreciation will not apply to most investments since they will not have a finite life and hence will not be depreciated: however, it will apply to dated securities where they are being amortised to their eventual redemption price. The need to provide for permanent diminution in value can of course apply to any investment.

This information has to be disclosed in respect of each type of investment included in the balance sheet formats (see 2.1 above). Consequently, these disclosures can become quite complicated, particularly where a company has associated undertakings. One approach is that of P & O, as shown below:

Extract 11.7: The Peninsular and Oriental Steam Navigation Company (1996)

12. Other Investments [extract]

| | Associates | | | Other investments | | |
	shares £m	reserves £m	loans £m	listed £m	unlisted £m	Total £m
Group						
At 1 January 1996	110.1	(15.7)	29.6	0.3	63.3	187.6
Exchange movements	(5.8)	(3.7)	(1.6)	–	1.9	(9.2)
Additions	14.6	–	7.3	–	14.0	35.9
Transfer on formation of P&O Nedlloyd	452.9	–	32.5	–	–	485.4
Transfer on acquisition as subsidiaries	0.5	33.8	(7.1)	–	–	27.2
Share of retained profits for year	–	(4.9)	–	–	–	(4.9)
Surplus on valuation	–	0.7	–	–	–	0.7
Provisions	(0.9)	–	(3.7)	–	(0.1)	(4.7)
Disposals/repayments	(3.5)	1.2	(3.9)	–	(61.2)	(67.4)
On formation of P&O Nedlloyd	(2.2)	(1.1)	(0.1)	–	–	(3.4)
At 31 December 1996	565.7	10.3	53.0	0.3	17.9	647.2

(a) The net book value of shares in associates and other investments in the Group is stated after deducting provisions totalling £17.8m (1995 £17.2m).

The Act requires these disclosures in respect of both fixed and current asset investments:

(a) the amount relating to listed investments;[52]

(b) the aggregate market value of listed investments, if different from the book value, and the stock exchange value if it is less than the market value thus disclosed;[53]

(c) various details where the investment is 'significant', i.e. where it is either 20% or more of the nominal value of the shares of that class in the investee, or it represents more than 20% of the investor's own assets. The details to be disclosed are:

(i) the name of the investee;

(ii) its country of incorporation (if outside Great Britain). For unincorporated investees the address of the principal place of business has to be disclosed; and

(iii) a description and the proportion of each class of shares held.[54]

In addition, the statutory formats for the profit and loss account contain separate headings for the following:

- Income from shares in group undertakings
- Income from participating interests
- Income from other fixed asset investments
- Other interest receivable and similar income
- Amounts written off investments.

There are also various statutory disclosure requirements concerning investments in subsidiary and associated undertakings when group accounts are not prepared, which are beyond the scope of this chapter but are listed in Chapter 28 at 3.1.3.

Two examples of balance sheet notes are shown below: on current asset investments in an extract from the accounts of Pearson, and on fixed asset investments in an extract from the accounts of TI Group:

Extract 11.8: Pearson plc (1996)

15 Current asset investments [extract]

	Valuations		Book values	
	1996	1995	1996	1995
	£m	£m	£m	£m
Listed abroad	–	16.1	–	–
Unlisted	7.9	9.8	7.9	8.3
	7.9	25.9	7.9	8.3

Listed investment valuations are at middle market quotation and unlisted investments are at directors' valuations. If all investments were realised at valuation there would be no liability for taxation.

Extract 11.9: TI Group plc (1996)

14 INVESTMENTS

	Associated Undertakings £m	Other Participating Interests £m	Own Shares £m	Total £m
The Group				
Shares at valuation				
At 31st December 1995	**45.2**	**4.6**	**1.3**	**51.1**
Exchange rate adjustments	**(6.6)**	**(0.5)**	–	**(7.1)**
Additions	**5.0**	–	**1.8**	**6.8**
Conversions to subsidiary undertakings and disposals	**(2.2)**	**(3.1)**	**(0.5)**	**(5.8)**
Movement during year	**(1.7)**	–	–	**(1.7)**
At 31st December 1996	**39.7**	**1.0**	**2.6**	**43.3**

Associated undertakings

The principal associated undertakings are:

	Country of Operation	Number of Shares in Issue	Nominal Value of Share Capital in Issue	% held	Class of Share
Messier-Dowty International Ltd	UK	50,000,000	£50m	50	Ordinary
Valti SA	France	600,000	FF60m	20	Ordinary
John Crane (Japan) Inc	Japan	144,000	¥144m	49	Ordinary
Korea Bundy Corp	South Korea	252,000	Kw1,260m	39	Ordinary

The interest in associated undertakings is shown in the Group balance sheet at a valuation being the proportion of net assets attributable to TI at the date of acquisition, plus TI's share of post-acquisition earnings which at 31st December 1996 amounted to £4.6m (1995 £8.4m).

Messier-Dowty

The Group's principal associated undertaking is Messier-Dowty International Ltd, established on 1st January 1995 as a 50:50 joint venture between TI Group and SNECMA of France by combining the Dowty and Messier aircraft landing gear businesses which operate primarily in Canada, France and the UK.

For 1996, Messier-Dowty's total sales were £247.2m (1995 £248.1m) including £10.3m (1995 £9.7m) to TI Group, depreciation was £10.7m (1995 £10.8m) and profit before taxation was £18.3m (1995 £17.2m). Sales by TI Group to Messier-Dowty were £25.3m (1995 £21.0m).

At 31st December 1996 Messier-Dowty's consolidated summary balance sheet comprised:

	£m
Fixed assets	**71.1**
Net current assets excluding net cash	**67.4**
Other creditors falling due after more than one year	**(22.6)**
Net borrowings	**(55.6)**
Total shareholders' funds	**60.3**

TI Group's investment in Messier-Dowty:

	£m
At 31st December 1995	36.6
80% share of Messier-Dowty's profit after tax	9.9
Dividends received	(11.4)
Exchange rate adjustments	(5.3)
At 31st December 1996	**29.8**

Other associated undertakings

The Group purchased the remaining shares in Bundy Tubing Co (Australia) Pty Ltd (Bundy Asia Pacific) in October 1996, from which time it has been accounted for as a subsidiary.

The Group increased its investment in Korea Bundy Corp from 15% to 39% in October 1996, from which time it has been accounted for as an associated undertaking.

Sales between TI Group and its other associated undertakings in 1996 amounted to £2.0m (1995 £1.6m), mainly to John Crane Japan. Sales by other associated undertakings to TI Group were not material to either party in either year.

Other participating interests

	Country of Operation	Number of Shares in Issue	Nominal Value of Share Capital in Issue	% held	Class of Share
Tube Investments of India Ltd	India	24,623,093	Rs246m	4	Ordinary

Other participating interests are all listed companies stated at Directors' valuation with a market value at 31st December 1996 of £1.5m (1995 £2.7m). The investment in Usui Bundy Tubing was sold in December 1996; TI Group retained the rights to use the name 'Bundy' in Japan.

Own shares

The TI Group Employee Share Trust was established in 1995 with the purpose of holding shares in the Company for subsequent transfer to employees under various incentive schemes. In accordance with UITF 13 the Trust's accounts have been incorporated into the Company and Group accounts.

At 31st December 1996 the Trust held 541,611 shares in the Company (1995 340,000) with a market value of £3.2m (1995 £1.6m). Dividends on the shares have been waived. Costs of administration are included in the profit and loss account as they accrue.

The Company	£m
Shares at cost	
At 31st December 1995	1,211.7
Acquisitions	25.9
Disposals	(37.4)
Exchange rate adjustments and other movements	(7.2)
At 31st December 1996	**1,193.0**

Provisions for diminution in value included in the above at 31st December 1996 amounted to £65.4m (1995 £94.0m). A list of the Group's principal subsidiaries, associated undertakings and other participating interests is set out on pages 64 and 65.

Insofar as marking to market invokes the 'true and fair override' (see 2.2.2 above), it will also be necessary to disclose particulars of the departure from the valuation rules of Schedule 4 to the Companies Act, the reasons for the departure and its effect on the financial statements.[55]

3   COMPARISON WITH US AND IASC PRONOUNCEMENTS

3.1   US

In the US, SFAS 107, *Disclosures about Fair Value of Financial Instruments*, was issued in 1991. It requires all entities to disclose the fair value of financial instruments where practicable. The definition of financial instruments will include most investments, although equity investments in consolidated subsidiaries are specifically exempted. Where disclosure of the fair value is impracticable, the reason for this has to be disclosed, together with information pertinent to estimating the fair value, such as the carrying amount, effective interest rate and maturity of the financial instrument.

The question of how to account for marketable equity investments and all debt securities is addressed by SFAS 115 – *Accounting for Certain Investments in Debt and Equity Securities* – issued in 1993 to supersede SFAS 12.[56] This requires that such investments be classified as falling into one of three categories and accounted for as follows:

(a)   *Held-to-maturity securities* (debt securities whose owner has both the positive intent and the ability to hold them to maturity) are carried at amortised cost.

(b)   *Trading securities* (debt and equity securities that are bought and held principally for resale in the near term) are carried at fair value and the resulting gains and losses included in earnings.

(c)   *Available-for-sale securities* (the rest) are also carried at fair value but the gains and losses included in a separate component of shareholders' equity, not in earnings.

The statement also adds several further disclosure requirements.

SFAS 115 does not apply to investments in associates and subsidiaries, nor to securities whose fair value is not readily determinable, broadly those that are not quoted on an exchange. There are also certain exemptions for companies in industries which have specialised accounting practices relating to investments.

3.2   IASC

3.2.1   IAS 25

The international standard IAS 25 – *Accounting for Investments* – was issued in March 1986 and is fairly accommodating in its requirements. It permits current asset investments to be carried either at market value or at the lower of cost and market value, and in the former case it permits movement in value to be taken either to the profit and loss account or to owners' equity. Long-term investments may similarly be carried at either cost or valuation, and gains and losses on disposal of revalued assets can be measured against either their original cost or their revalued amount.[57]

3.2.2   E32

In January 1989, the IASC issued E32, which proposed changes to reduce the options available in a large number of its standards, including IAS 25. The main changes proposed were that it would be the preferred treatment to carry current asset investments at market value, with the lower of cost and market basis as the allowed alternative, and to carry long-term investments at cost, with revalued amounts as the allowed alternative. However, since then the IASC has embarked on a wide-ranging project on financial instruments, and since this bears heavily on the subject of investments the Committee decided not to implement the proposals on investments in E32.

3.2.3   E48

The IASC published E48 – *Financial Instruments* – in January 1994, replacing an earlier exposure draft, E40, which had been issued over two years earlier. The exposure draft is a long and complex one and its scope is very wide. It seeks to establish a comprehensive framework of accounting rules for financial assets and liabilities from the point of view of both the issuer and the holder. Accordingly, it deals with accounting for investments since these represent financial assets from the point of view of the holder, but its coverage is much wider.

Different measurement rules are proposed for financial assets depending on whether they are held (a) for the long term or to maturity, (b) as hedges or (c) for other purposes. The 'Benchmark' treatment for each is described below.

Financial assets held for the long term or to maturity should continue to be carried at the amount initially recognised (i.e. cost), or recoverable amount if lower.[58] As an exception to cost, if the asset is to be settled through scheduled payments of fixed or determinable amounts, it should be remeasured at each balance sheet date at the amount of the scheduled future payments discounted at the rate of interest inherent in the initially recognised amount.[59]

Gains and losses in the fair value of a financial asset accounted for as a hedge should be recognised in income at the same time as the corresponding loss or gain from a change in the fair value of the hedged position is recognised in income.[60]

Financial assets held for other purposes should be marked to market; that is, they should be remeasured at fair value at each balance sheet date and the gain or loss recognised in income as it arises.[61]

E48 has not been progressed, however, and has been overtaken by a further discussion paper, which is discussed below.

3.2.4 Accounting for Financial Assets and Financial Liabilities

This discussion paper was published by the IASC's Steering Committee on Financial Instruments in March 1997. It takes the most simple, but also radical, approach to investments that could be imagined; they should all be marked to market and all gains and losses recognised in the profit and loss account. No variations in treatment are proposed for investments held for different purposes, nor is there any differential approach for unmarketable securities. As more fully discussed in Chapter 9 at 4.2.3, the proposals are very controversial and it remains to be seen whether they will be converted into a standard.

4 CONCLUSION

ED 55 has never been progressed, largely because of the legal obstacles within the EU Fourth Directive that appear to rule out mark-to-market accounting for most UK companies. However, there is now a clear trend among standard setters internationally towards the increased use of this treatment, and if this gains widespread acceptance there may well be some relaxation of these legal prohibitions. The issue may then become how far to take the approach. The IASC's project on financial instruments proposes the most complete version of it, but many may regard it as too extreme, particularly when it involves reporting in the profit and loss account unrealised gains on the revaluation of unmarketable securities that are held for the long term. The future direction of this subject, therefore, is likely to depend on the degree to which the IASC's bold move commands acceptance.

References

1   Financial Services Act 1986, Sch. 1, para. 1.
2   ED 55, *Accounting for investments*, ASC, July 1990, para. 54.
3   IAS 25, *Accounting for Investments*, IASC, March 1986, para. 3.
4   CA 85, Sch. 4, Part V.
5   For recommendations on accounting by Investment Trusts, see the SORP on *Financial Statements of Investment Trust Companies*, The Association of Investment Trust Companies, December 1995. For recommendations on accounting for securities in the financial statements of banks, see the SORP on *Securities*, British Bankers Association and Irish Bankers' Federation, September 1990.

6   CA 85, Sch. 4, para. 8, balance sheet formats.
7   *Ibid.*, s 262(1).
8   ED 55, para. 55.
9   *Ibid.*, para. 56.
10   *Ibid.*, para. 24.
11   IAS 25, para. 3.
12   CA 85, Sch. 4, para. 17.
13   *Ibid.*, para. 26(1).
14   *Ibid.*, para. 31(3).
15   ED 55, para. 63.
16   *Ibid.*, para. 68.
17   IAS 25, para. 48.
18   ED 55, para. 69.
19   CA 85, s 266 and Sch. 4, para. 73.
20   ED 55, para. 70.
21   FRS 3, *Reporting financial performance*, ASB, December 1992, paras. 21 and 31.
22   ED 55, para. 74.
23   *Ibid.*, para. 42.
24   CA 85, Sch 4, paras. 19(2) and (3).
25   *Ibid.*, para. 19(1).
26   FRED 15, *Impairment of Fixed Assets and Goodwill*, ASB, June 1997, paras. 4 and 5.
27   ASB Discussion Paper, *Derivatives and other financial instruments*, ASB, July 1996, para. 3.5.1(a).
28   *Ibid.*, para. 1.4.1(c).
29   *Ibid.*, para. 3.3.21.
30   *Ibid.*, para. 3.5.1(d).
31   CA 85, Sch 4, para. 22.
32   *Ibid.*, para. 23.
33   *Ibid.*, para. 31(5).
34   ED 55, para. 57.
35   *Ibid.*, paras. 60 and 66.
36   *Ibid.*, para. 61.
37   CA 85, Sch. 9, Part 1, paras. 33 and 34.
38   UITF 5, *Transfers from current assets to fixed assets*, UITF, July 1992, para. 5.
39   *Ibid.*, para. 27.
40   ED 55, para. 71.
41   *Ibid.*, para. 65.
42   CA 85, Sch. 4, para. 14.
43   ED 55, para. 76.
44   *Ibid.*, para. 64.
45   *Ibid.*, para. 73.
46   *Ibid.*, para. 41.
47   *Ibid.*, para. 59.
48   CA 85, Sch. 4, paras. 42(1)(a) and 42(2).
49   *Ibid.*, para. 33(3).
50   *Ibid.*, para. 42(1)(b).
51   *Ibid.*, para. 42(3).
52   *Ibid.*, para. 45(1).
53   *Ibid.*, para. 45(2).
54   *Ibid.*, Sch. 5, paras. 7 and 8.
55   CA 85, ss 226(5) and 227(6).
56   SFAS 12, *Accounting for Certain Marketable Securities*, FASB, December 1975.
57   IAS 25, paras. 46–50.
58   *Ibid.*, paras. 85, 100 and 113.
59   *Ibid.*, para. 92.
60   *Ibid.*, para. 150
61   *Ibid.*, paras. 162 and 163.

Chapter 12

Research and development

1 INTRODUCTION

1.1 Possible accounting treatments of research and development expenditure

There are essentially four possible methods of accounting for research and development expenditure. These are as follows:

(a) charge all costs to expense when incurred; or

(b) capitalise all costs when incurred; or

(c) capitalise costs when incurred providing specified conditions are fulfilled and charge all others to expense; or

(d) accumulate all costs in a special category distinct from assets and expenses until the existence of future benefits can be determined.

Each of the above is considered in turn.

1.1.1 Charge all costs to expense when incurred

This is the required treatment in the US (see 5.1 below). The five factors offered by the FASB as support for its requirements to expense all expenditure immediately were as follows:[1]

(a) *uncertainty of future benefits*

The primary reason offered by the FASB for expensing research and development costs was the uncertainty associated with such costs. It was argued that research and development projects have considerable risk, i.e. a large probability of failure and consequently all such costs should be expensed. As support for this argument, the FASB cited one study of a number of industries which found that an average of less than 2% of new product ideas and less than 15% of product development projects were commercially successful.

(b) *lack of causal relationship between expenditure and benefits*

The FASB cited in its statement three research studies that generally failed to find a significant connection between research and development expenditure and increased future benefits by subsequent sales, earnings or share of industry sales. However, the fact that the three studies cited failed to find a causal relationship between expenditure and benefits does not mean that such a relationship does not exist. If this was the case, then companies would be much more reluctant to incur such expenditure.

(c) *research and development does not meet the accounting concept of an asset*

The FASB argued that to be an asset the expenditure would need to be subject to reasonable measurement. They stated that 'the criterion of measurability would require that a resource not be recognised as an asset for accounting purposes unless at the time it is acquired or developed its future economic benefits can be identified and objectively measured'.[2] However, this could be argued in relation to practically any asset at the time it is acquired.

(d) *matching of revenues and expenses*

The FASB argued that because of the uncertainty of future benefits of research and development expenditure there was an insufficient cause and effect relationship to justify the carrying forward of research and development expenditure to future periods.

(e) *relevance of resulting information for investment and credit decisions*

The FASB stated that APB Statement No. 4 indicates that certain costs are immediately recognised as expenses because allocating them to several accounting periods is considered to serve no useful purpose. The FASB went on to state that 'the relationship between current research and development costs and the amount of resultant future benefits to an enterprise is so uncertain that capitalisation of any research and development costs is not useful in assessing the earnings potential of the enterprise'.[3]

1.1.2 Capitalise all costs when incurred

Enterprises undertake research and development expenditure in the hope of future benefits. Hence, it could be argued that if future benefits were unlikely then the expenditure would not be incurred. Whilst this may be the case for some projects, it is undoubtedly not so for all such expenditure. One could, however, perhaps argue that since future benefits will be gained from some of the expenditure, then an enterprise should capitalise all such costs and match the total costs to the future benefits derived from some of them.

However, a meaningful method of amortisation would be impossible to achieve since the expenditure would be carried out at different points in time and also the period of benefit would be extremely difficult to determine.

1.1.3   Capitalise costs when incurred if certain conditions are met

A prerequisite of this treatment is the establishment of conditions that must be fulfilled before research and development costs may be capitalised. Furthermore, once such conditions are established they must be capable of being applied by all enterprises. If the specified conditions are not met, then costs are to be expensed.

1.1.4   Accumulation of costs in a special category

At a future date such costs could then be either transferred to assets if future benefits could reasonably be established or written off if it were reasonably established that no significant future benefits would arise.

This treatment would draw attention to the uncertainty surrounding the expenditure and would also delay the decision of whether to capitalise or expense. However, such accumulated costs would arguably serve little purpose insofar as analysts and other users are concerned.

1.1.5   Which treatment should be adopted?

SSAP 13 – *Accounting for research and development* – states that the choice of an appropriate accounting treatment for research and development centres around the application of fundamental accounting concepts 'including the "accruals" concept by which revenue and costs are accrued, matched and dealt with in the period to which they relate and the "prudence" concept by which revenue and profits are not anticipated but are recognised only when realised in the form either of cash or of other assets the ultimate cash realisation of which can be established with reasonable certainty. It is a corollary of the prudence concept that expenditure should be written off in the period in which it arises unless its relationship to the revenue of a future period can be assessed with reasonable certainty.'[4]

It was on the basis of this argument that the existing UK practice was formulated although, as is explained below, SSAP 13 has adopted an approach which is somewhat of a hybrid of the various options available.

1.2   Development of accounting standards in the UK

1.2.1   ED 14

As a result of the different accounting treatments that were being adopted by companies in practice, the ASC issued ED 14 – *Accounting for Research and Development* – in January 1975. Although the exposure draft made a distinction between pure and applied research and development expenditure, it proposed that all research and development expenditure should be written off as incurred to the profit and loss account, with very minor exceptions. The exposure draft received widespread criticism, particularly from the aerospace industry, with the bulk of such criticism being concerned with the treatment of development expenditure. It was pointed out that the design and development stage of a new aircraft took at least five years prior to the delivery of the first production aircraft to a customer, and that sales of a successful aircraft then continued for at least ten years with delivery of spares continuing well beyond that point.[5]

1.2.2   ED 17

Owing to the criticism received, ED 14 was withdrawn and replaced by ED 17 – *Accounting for research and development–revised* – which was issued in April 1976. Whilst still proposing that pure and applied research expenditure be expensed in the year in which it was incurred, it recognised that some development expenditure could be clearly matched to future benefits which were reasonably certain. Consequently, the exposure draft concluded that such expenditure should be capitalised provided certain criteria were met. This exposure draft was more favourably received. However, a number of commentators made the point that 'where companies wished to write off development expenditure, even though the projects fulfilled the conditions in ED 17 which would justify carrying forward the expenditure, they should be permitted to do so provided the treatment was disclosed in notes to the accounts'.[6]

1.2.3   SSAP 13

Consequently, when SSAP 13 was issued in December 1977, although the standard contained essentially the same requirements as those of ED 17, it did not *require* companies to defer development expenditure but, where certain criteria were fulfilled, *allowed them the choice* between immediate write off or capitalisation.[7]

1.2.4   ED 41

Since the issue of SSAP 13, the Fourth EC Company Law Directive was enacted in UK company law, following which the ASC embarked on a policy of reviewing its existing accounting standards. (The relevant requirements of the Companies Act which relate to research and development expenditure are discussed at 3 below.) As a result, ED 41 – *Accounting for research and development* – was issued in June 1987. The principal change to SSAP 13 proposed by ED 41 related to the disclosure of the amount of research and development costs charged to the profit and loss account in the current period.

The exposure draft also proposed that deferred research and development expenditure be disclosed under intangible fixed assets in the balance sheet, rather than deferred expenditure, as it was classified under the original SSAP 13.[8] The exposure draft also intended to continue the requirement of

SSAP 13 that development expenditure once written off should not be reinstated even though the uncertainties which led to its being written off no longer applied.[9] However, such a treatment arguably conflicts with the Companies Act requirements relating to fixed assets. Paragraph 19(3) of Schedule 4 to the Companies Act requires any provisions against the value of a fixed asset to be released when the reasons for its creation cease to apply.

1.2.5 SSAP 13 (Revised)

SSAP 13 (Revised) – *Accounting for research and development* – was issued in January 1989, following essentially the line taken by ED 41. The main changes between the standard and the exposure draft were as follows:

(a) although the standard requires the amount of research and development costs charged to the profit and loss account to be disclosed, certain enterprises are exempt from this disclosure; and

(b) the requirement that development expenditure once written off should not be reinstated even though the uncertainties which led to its being written off no longer apply, was deleted in the revised standard, presumably in view of the apparent conflict with the Companies Act referred to at 1.2.4 above.

1.2.6 FRED 12

As discussed in Chapter 10, the ASB is developing a standard on accounting for goodwill and intangibles and in June 1996 issued FRED 12 – *Goodwill and Intangibles*. However, this proposes that any research and development costs accounted for under SSAP 13 are to be excluded from any standard based on that exposure draft.[10] As discussed at 5.2 below, this was also the original intention of the IASC in developing its own standard on intangible assets, but it has since decided to incorporate research and development costs within such a standard. If an international standard comes out on this basis then it may be that the ASB will adopt a similar approach.

2   REQUIREMENTS OF SSAP 13

2.1   Definitions

Research and development expenditure is defined in SSAP 13 as 'expenditure falling into one or more of the following broad categories (except to the extent that it relates to locating or exploiting oil, gas or mineral deposits or is reimbursable by third parties either directly or under the terms of a firm contract to develop and manufacture at an agreed price calculated to reimburse both elements of expenditure):

(a) *pure (or basic) research:* experimental or theoretical work undertaken primarily to acquire new scientific or technical knowledge for its own sake rather than directed towards any specific aim or application;

(b) *applied research:* original or critical investigation undertaken in order to gain new scientific or technical knowledge and directed towards a specific practical aim or objective;

(c) *development:* use of scientific or technical knowledge in order to produce new or substantially improved materials, devices, products or services, to install new processes or systems prior to the commencement of commercial production or commercial applications, or to improving substantially those already produced or installed.'[11]

The definitions of the different types of research and development used in the standard are based on those used by the Organisation for Economic Co-operation and Development (OECD).[12]

However, as paragraph 4 of the standard states, 'the dividing line between these categories is often indistinct and particular expenditure may have characteristics of more than one category. This is especially so when new products or services are developed through research and development to production, when the activities may have characteristics of both development and production.' For example, a project may start out as basic research, the results of which may lead to the development of new products or systems, particularly in, say, the pharmaceutical industry.

It can be seen that the standard specifically excludes from the definition:

(a) expenditure incurred in locating and exploiting oil, gas and mineral deposits. However, development of new surveying methods and techniques as an integral part of research on geographical phenomena should be included in research and development;[13] and

(b) research and development expenditure which is reimbursed by a third party. Any such expenditure which has not been reimbursed at the balance sheet date should be dealt with as contract work in progress.[14]

2.2 Accounting

The accounting treatment of research and development prescribed by SSAP 13 is as follows:

2.2.1 Fixed assets

The cost of fixed assets acquired or constructed in order to provide facilities for research and development activities over a number of accounting periods should be capitalised and written off over their useful life through the profit and loss account.[15] The depreciation so written off should be included as part of the expenditure on research and development.[16] Where an asset is used in the course of the development activities, however, the depreciation thereon can be regarded as part of the overhead costs to be included as part of development costs, if such costs are to be deferred (see 2.2.3 below).

2.2.2 *Pure and applied research*

Expenditure on pure and applied research (other than the cost of fixed assets used for the purpose of research activities) should be written off in the year of expenditure through the profit and loss account.[17] SSAP 13 states the reason for this as being because such expenditure can be regarded as part of a continuing operation required to maintain a company's business and its competitive position; in general, no one particular period rather than any other will be expected to benefit and therefore it is appropriate that these costs should be written off as they are incurred.[18] In any event, the Companies Act does not allow pure or applied research to be treated as an asset (see 3.1 below).

2.2.3 *Development expenditure*

The standard proposes a different treatment for development expenditure, the reason being that the development of new products or services is distinguishable from pure and applied research. Expenditure on such development is normally undertaken with a reasonable expectation of specific commercial success and of future benefits arising from the work, either from increased revenue and related profits or from reduced costs. On these grounds it may be argued that such expenditure, to the extent that it is recoverable, should be deferred to be matched against the future revenue.[19] Consequently, the standard allows such expenditure to be deferred, but only if certain conditions are met.

The standard requires that development expenditure should be written off in the year of expenditure except in the following circumstances when it *may* be deferred to future periods:

(a) there is a clearly defined project; and

(b) the related expenditure is separately identifiable; and

(c) the outcome of such a project has been assessed with reasonable certainty as to:

  (i) its technical feasibility, and

  (ii) its ultimate commercial viability considered in the light of factors such as likely market conditions (including competing products), public opinion, consumer and environmental legislation; and

(d) the aggregate of the deferred development costs, any further development costs, and related production, selling and administration costs is reasonably expected to be exceeded by related future sales or other revenues; and

(e)   adequate resources exist, or are reasonably expected to be available, to enable the project to be completed and to provide any consequential increases in working capital.[20]

Where these circumstances exist, the standard permits (but does not require) development expenditure to be deferred to the extent that its recovery can reasonably be regarded as assured.[21] However, if a policy of deferral is adopted, it should be consistently applied to all development projects that meet the above criteria.[22]

The development costs should be amortised and the amortisation should commence with the commercial production or application of the product, service, process or system and should be allocated on a systematic basis to each accounting period, by reference to either the sale or use of the product, service, process or system or the period over which these are expected to be sold or used.[23]

The deferred development expenditure should be reviewed at the end of each accounting period and, where the circumstances that justified the deferral no longer apply, or are considered doubtful, the expenditure, to the extent that it is considered irrecoverable, should be written off immediately. This should be done on a project by project basis.[24]

2.3   Disclosure

The disclosure requirements of SSAP 13 are as follows:

(a)   the accounting policy on research and development expenditure should be stated and explained (as, in any event, required by SSAP 2);[25]

(b)   the total amount of research and development expenditure charged in the profit and loss account should be disclosed, analysed between the current year's expenditure and amounts amortised from deferred expenditure.[26] It is emphasised that the amounts disclosed should include any amortisation of fixed assets used in the research and development activity;

(c)   movements on deferred development expenditure and the amount carried forward at the beginning and the end of the period should be disclosed;[27] and

(d)   deferred development expenditure should be disclosed under intangible fixed assets in the balance sheet.[28]

However, the information contained in (b) above need only be given by:[29]

(a)   public companies (as defined in section 1 of the Companies Act 1985) or holding companies that have one or more public companies as a subsidiary;

(b) banking and insurance companies (as defined in section 744 of the Companies Act), and preparing accounts in accordance with Schedules 9 or 9A thereto, or holding companies that have one or more banking and insurance companies as a subsidiary; and

(c) private companies (and other enterprises) which do not satisfy the criteria, multiplied in each case by ten, for defining a medium-sized company under section 247 of the Companies Act.

At present, this means that enterprises with any two of the following fall outside the exemption and will have to give the additional disclosures:

(i)   turnover exceeding £112m,

(ii)   total assets exceeding £56m,

(iii) average number of employees exceeding 2,500.

2.4   Current reporting practice

Most major companies which incur research and development costs adopt a policy of writing off the expenditure as it is incurred. One company which adopts such a policy is SmithKline Beecham, as illustrated below:

Extract 12.1: SmithKline Beecham plc (1996)

Accounting Policies [extract]

Research and development expenditure

Laboratory buildings and equipment used for research and development are included as fixed assets and written off in accordance with the Group's depreciation policy. Other research and development expenditure is written off in the year in which it is incurred.

Consolidated profit and loss account [extract]

	1996 Total £m	1995 Total £m
Sales		
Continuing operations	**7,925**	7,011
Cost of goods sold	**(2,718)**	(2,399)
Gross profit	**5,207**	4,612
Selling, general and administrative expenses	**(2,807)**	(2,739)
Research and development expenditure	**(764)**	(653)
Trading profit		
Continuing operations	**1,636**	1,220

It is noteworthy that SmithKline Beecham has disclosed the research and development charge for the year as a separate item in the body of its profit and loss account, as opposed to disclosing the amount in the notes, which is the route which most companies have taken. Furthermore, it can be seen that, in compliance with SSAP 13, the company treats its fixed assets which are used in research and development activities in the same way as any other fixed asset.

One company which adopts the policy of deferring certain development costs is Grampian Holdings, as illustrated below:

Extract 12.2: Grampian Holdings plc (1996/97)

Accounting Policies [extract]

Intellectual Property and Research and Development

Expenditure is charged as incurred, with the exception of intellectual property and development expenditure on an individual project where the future recoverability can be foreseen with reasonable assurance. Any expenditure carried forward is amortised in line with the expected sales from the related project subject to a maximum amortisation period of the licence, generally five years.

Notes to the Accounts

4. **Profit before interest and taxation** [extract]

		1996/97	1995
		£000	£000
a)	This is stated after charging (crediting)		
	Research and development:		
	Charged during the period	**428**	486
	Amortised during the period	**2,160**	1,744

10. **Intangible Fixed Assets**

	Intellectual Property and Development Expenditure		
	Cost	Amortisation	Net book Value
	£000	**£000**	**£000**
At 1 January 1996	14,660	(6,207)	8,453
Exchange rate adjustments	(177)	95	(82)
Additions	2,051	–	2,051
Charge for the year	–	(2,160)	(2,160)
At 31 January 1997	16,534	(8,272)	8,262

---

3   REQUIREMENTS OF THE COMPANIES ACT 1985

3.1   Accounting

The accounting treatment for research and development costs required by SSAP 13 is in effect backed up by the requirements of the Companies Act 1985. The Act permits a company's balance sheet or profit and loss account to include an item representing or covering the amount of any asset or liability, income or expenditure not otherwise covered by any of the items listed in the formats set out in Schedule 4 to the Act, but prohibits the treatment of costs of research as an asset.[30] Paragraph 20(1) of Schedule 4, however, states that development costs which are included under fixed assets in the balance sheet formats may only be included in a company's balance sheet in 'special circumstances'. There is no explanation in the Act as to what the 'special circumstances' might be, but it is reasonable to assume that the circumstances under which development expenditure may be deferred in accordance with SSAP 13 satisfy the requirements for 'special circumstances' for Companies Act purposes; this is because ED 41 stated that the DTI had confirmed that the recommended practice concerning deferral of development expenditure satisfied the term.[31]

As deferred development costs are to be treated as fixed assets, then all of the Companies Act requirements relating to fixed assets apply to such costs (see Chapter 10).

3.2 Disclosure

3.2.1 Financial statements

Where an amount is included in a company's balance sheet in respect of development costs the following information must be given in a note to the accounts:

(a) the period over which the amount of those costs originally capitalised is being written off; and

(b) the reasons for capitalising the development costs in question.[32]

The disclosure requirements relating to fixed assets generally will also apply.

3.2.2 Directors' report

The directors' report should contain an indication of the activities (if any) of the company and its subsidiary undertakings in the field of research and development.[33] However, in practice this frequently results in a fairly minimal statement on the subject being given, for example:

Extract 12.3: Amersham International plc (1997)

Report of the Directors [extract]

Research and development   Group policy is to invest in product innovation and process improvement at a level designed to enable it to be a market leader in any business in which it competes. It is also Group policy to seek out new business opportunities by exploiting its skills and technological base.

Extract 12.4: B.A.T Industries p.l.c. (1996)

Directors' report [extract]

Research and development

The Group's activities are concentrated on the development of new products, new processes, quality improvement of existing products and cost reduction programmes in the tobacco industry.

…

Research is also undertaken into various aspects of the science and behavioural science related to smoking, including continued significant funding of independent studies.

A good example of disclosure is that of Glaxo Holdings, which devotes three pages of its annual report to meeting the requirement.[34] However, this is only to be expected from a company which states in its mission statement that it 'is a research-based company whose people are committed to fighting disease by bringing innovative medicines and services to patients throughout the world and to the healthcare providers who serve them'.[35]

3.3   Distributable profits

The Companies Act only allows distributions to be made out of a company's net realised profits.[36] In determining such net realised profits, any amount shown in respect of development costs, which is included as an asset in the balance sheet, is to be treated as a realised loss.[37] However, this will not apply if:

(a)   there are special circumstances in the company's case justifying the directors in deciding that the amount shown in respect of development costs is not to be treated as a realised loss; and

(b)   the note to the accounts required by paragraph 20 of Schedule 4 to the Companies Act (reasons for showing development costs as an asset) states that the amount is not to be so treated and explains the circumstances relied upon to justify the decision of the directors to that effect.[38]

4   PROBLEM AREAS

4.1   What activities should be included within research and development?

Although the definition of research and development is very broad, there are difficulties in determining what types of activity constitute 'research and development'. SSAP 13 states that research and development activity is distinguished from non-research based activity by the presence or absence of an element of innovation. If the activity departs from routine and breaks new ground it should normally be included; if it follows an established pattern it should normally be excluded.[39]

Examples of activities that would normally be included in research and development are as follows:[40]

(a) experimental, theoretical or other work aimed at the discovery of new knowledge, or the advancement of existing knowledge;

(b) searching for applications of that knowledge;

(c) formulation and design of possible applications for such work;

(d) testing in search for, or evaluation of, product, service or process alternatives;

(e) design, construction and testing of pre-production prototypes and models and development batches;

(f) design of products, services, processes or systems involving new technology or substantially improving those already produced or installed; and

(g) construction and operation of pilot plants.

Examples of activities which should not be included are as follows:[41]

(a) testing and analysis either of equipment or product for purposes of quality or quantity control;

(b) periodic alterations to existing products, services or processes even though these may represent some improvement;

(c) operational research not tied to a specific research and development activity;

(d) cost of corrective action in connection with break-downs during commercial production;

(e) legal and administrative work in connection with patent applications, records and litigation and the sale or licensing of patents;

(f) activity, including design and construction engineering, relating to the construction, relocation, rearrangement or start-up of facilities or equipment other than facilities or equipment whose sole use is for a particular research and development project; and

(g) market research.

Although the above items are not normally to be included within 'research and development' and accounted for as such under SSAP 13, this does not mean that all costs of such activities will invariably be charged to the profit and loss account as incurred. This may be appropriate for certain of the costs (such as (a) or (b) above), but for some of the other costs it may be possible to regard them as part of the cost of a fixed asset (such as (f) above).

4.2   What costs should be included within the category of research and development?

Having decided which activities are to be included as research and development it is then necessary to determine what costs are to be included as the cost of those activities. SSAP 13 does not give guidance on the types of costs which can be included. However, guidance can be sought from both SFAS 2 in the US and IAS 9 as these identify the elements of costs which should be included (see 5.1 and 5.2 below). It must be remembered, however, that where development expenditure is to be deferred as an intangible asset, the accounting rules for fixed assets under Schedule 4 to the Companies Act must be taken into account.

4.3   Availability of choice between immediate write off and capitalisation of development expenditure

As indicated at 2.2.3 above, it is possible for a company to choose a policy of either writing off, or deferring and amortising, development expenditure which fulfils all the conditions laid down in paragraph 25 of SSAP 13. In view of this choice, is it possible for a company to change from a policy of writing off such expenditure to one of deferring and amortising or vice versa? We believe that a change of policy will normally be acceptable; furthermore, it will be necessary to restate comparative figures to reflect the new policy in accordance with FRS 3 (see Chapter 22 at 2.14). However, where a change from a policy of writing off such expenditure to one of deferring and amortising is contemplated, care should be taken to ensure that all the conditions which require to be fulfilled were applicable at the time the expenditure was incurred. If the conditions were not met at that time, then the costs should not be capitalised under the new policy but should remain written off; this is because such costs would not have been capitalised if the new policy had been in force at the time the expenditure was incurred.

4.4   Elimination of uncertainty in respect of development expenditure

4.4.1   *Expenditure previously not capitalised*

The last three conditions for deferral laid down in paragraph 25 of SSAP 13 effectively mean that development expenditure should only be deferred if it can be shown to be recoverable with sufficient certainty (see 2.2.3 above). However, what happens if a company has not capitalised development expenditure because the conditions were not met, but at a later date the uncertainties which led to its write-off no longer apply?

The original SSAP 13 (and ED 41) made it clear that such expenditure could not be reinstated as an asset; however, the revised SSAP 13 is silent on the matter. Nevertheless, we believe that in such circumstances the expenditure should not be reinstated as an asset.

4.4.2 *Deferred expenditure previously capitalised and subsequently written down*

Paragraph 29 of SSAP 13 requires deferred development expenditure to be reviewed annually and to be written down to its recoverable amount (see 2.2.3 above). What happens if at a later date the uncertainties which gave rise to that write-down no longer apply?

Again, SSAP 13 is silent on this issue; however, consideration in this instance has to be given to the requirements of the Companies Act relating to provisions for diminutions in value of fixed assets. These require that where the reasons for which any provision was made have ceased to apply to any extent, then the provision shall be written back to the extent that it is no longer necessary.[42] These requirements of the Companies Act do not apply to the situation discussed at 4.4.1 above as no asset was recorded in the first instance.

5 COMPARISON WITH US AND IASC PRONOUNCEMENTS

5.1 US

The principal standard in the US which deals with this issue is SFAS 2 – *Accounting for Research and Development Costs* – which was issued in October 1974.[43] The statement defines 'research' and 'development' as follows:

'*Research* is planned search or critical investigation aimed at discovery of new knowledge with the hope that such knowledge will be useful in developing a new product or service (hereinafter "product") or a new process or technique (hereinafter "process") or in bringing about a significant improvement to an existing product or process.'

'*Development* is the translation of research findings or other knowledge into a plan or design for a new product or process or for a significant improvement to an existing product or process whether intended for sale or use. It includes the conceptual formulation, design, and testing of product alternatives, construction of prototypes and operation of pilot plants. It does not include routine or periodic alterations to existing products, production lines, manufacturing process, and other on-going operations even though those alterations may represent improvements and it does not include market research or market testing activities.'[44]

It can be seen that no distinction is made between 'pure' and 'applied' research as is done in SSAP 13, and that a more detailed definition of 'development' is given.

Like SSAP 13, SFAS 2 provides examples of those activities that would normally be included in research and development and those that would not.[45] In addition, however, SFAS 2 identifies elements of costs which shall be identified with the research and development activities; these are as follows:

(a)   materials, equipment and facilities;

(b)   personnel;

(c)   intangibles purchased from others;

(d)   contract services; and

(e)   indirect costs.[46]

The main difference between SSAP 13 and SFAS 2 is that SFAS 2 requires that all research and development costs encompassed by the statement should be charged to expense when incurred, for the reasons discussed at 1.1.1 above. Furthermore, SFAS 2 requires all enterprises to disclose the amount expensed whereas SSAP 13 exempts certain enterprises from disclosing such information (see 2.3 above).

It should be noted that SFAS 2 encompasses research and development costs incurred in the process of creating a software product. SFAS 86 – *Accounting for the Costs of Computer Software to be Sold, Leased, or Otherwise Marketed* – specifically states that 'all costs incurred to establish the technological feasibility of a computer software product to be sold, leased or otherwise marketed are research and development costs'. Those costs shall be charged to expense when incurred as required by SFAS 2.[47] Technical feasibility is established upon completion of a detailed program design or, in its absence, completion of a working model.[48]

5.2   IASC

The relevant international standard is IAS 9 – *Research and Development Costs*. The original standard on this topic was issued in July 1978, but a revised version was published in December 1993 and is effective for accounting periods beginning on or after 1 January 1995. The requirements of this revised standard are broadly similar to those of SSAP 13, with one exception; IAS 9 specifically requires that development costs *must* be recognised as an asset when they meet the criteria in paragraph 17 of IAS 9 and it is probable that these costs will be recovered.

The definitions of 'research' and 'development' contained in IAS 9 are as follows:[49]

'*Research* is original and planned investigation undertaken with the prospect of gaining new scientific or technical knowledge and understanding.'

'*Development* is the application of research findings or other knowledge to a plan or design for the production of new or substantially improved materials, devices, products, processes, systems or services prior to the commencement of commercial production or use.'

Like SFAS 2, no distinction is made between 'pure' and 'applied' research.

IAS 9 also identifies the costs which should be included within research and development costs as follows:

(a) the salaries, wages and other related costs of personnel engaged in research and development activities;

(b) the costs of material and services consumed in such activities;

(c) the depreciation of property, plant and equipment to the extent that they are used for such activities;

(d) a reasonable allocation of overhead costs, other than general overheads, related to such activities; and

(e) other costs, such as the amortisation of patents and licences, to the extent that they are used for such activities.[50]

The standard provides that research costs should be expensed in the period in which they are incurred. Development costs should also be charged as an expense of the period in which they are incurred unless certain criteria are met (similar to those conditions laid down in SSAP 13), in which case they should be capitalised as an asset and accounted for in the same manner as required by SSAP 13.[51]

Like SFAS 2, IAS 9 requires all enterprises to disclose the amount of research and development expenditure charged as an expense to be disclosed, whereas SSAP 13 exempts certain enterprises from disclosing such information (see 2.3 above).

As discussed more fully in Chapter 10 at 7.2, the IASC is developing a standard on intangible assets. The original exposure draft, E50 – *Intangible Assets*, issued in June 1995 intended to scope out research and development from its proposals.[52] However, at its July 1997 meeting the IASC approved a revised exposure draft which embraces research and development expenditure within its scope, whereas FRED 12 leaves that issue to SSAP 13. This is because the IASC rejects a 'deferred cost' perspective for including items in the balance sheet although it has to use rather tortuously worded recognition criteria to continue to allow the same expenditure to be capitalised from a balance sheet perspective.

References

1   SFAS 2, *Accounting for Research and Development Costs*, FASB, October 1974, paras. 39–50.
2   *Ibid.*, para. 44.
3   *Ibid.*, para. 50.

4   SSAP 13, *Accounting for research and development*, ASC, Issued December 1977, Revised January 1989, para. 1.
5   Letter dated 15 August 1975 from the Society of British Aerospace Companies Ltd to the Technical Director of ICAEW.
6   Technical Release 264, *Statement by the Accounting Standards Committee on the publication of SSAP 13 Accounting for research and development*.
7   Original SSAP 13, para. 21.
8   ED 41, *Accounting for Research and Development*, ASC, June 1987, para. 33; Original SSAP 13, para. 28.
9   *Ibid.*, para. 29.
10 FRED 12, *Goodwill and Intangible Assets*, ASB, June 1996, para. 5.
11 SSAP 13, para. 21.
12 *Ibid.*, para. 2.
13 *Ibid.*, para. 18.
14 *Ibid.*, para. 17.
15 *Ibid.*, para. 23.
16 *Ibid.*, para. 16.
17 *Ibid.*, para. 24.
18 *Ibid.*, para. 8.
19 *Ibid.*, para. 9.
20 *Ibid.*, para. 25.
21 *Ibid.*, para. 26.
22 *Ibid.*, para. 27.
23 *Ibid.*, para. 28.
24 *Ibid.*, para. 29.
25 *Ibid.*, para. 30.
26 *Ibid.*, para. 31.
27 *Ibid.*, para. 32.
28 *Ibid.*
29 *Ibid.*, para. 22.
30 CA 85, Sch. 4, para. 3(2).
31 ED 41, Preface, para. 1.5.
32 CA 85, Sch. 4, para. 20(2).
33 *Ibid.*, Sch. 7, para. 6(c).
34 Glaxo Wellcome plc, Annual Report & Accounts and Form 20-F 1996, pp. 13–15.
35 *Ibid.*, p. 8.
36 CA 85, s 263.
37 *Ibid.*, s 269(1).
38 *Ibid.*, s 269(2).
39 SSAP 13, para. 5.
40 *Ibid.*, para. 6.
41 *Ibid.*, para. 7.
42 CA 85, Sch. 4, para. 19(3).
43 See also, for example, SFAS 7, *Accounting and Reporting by Development Stage Enterprises*, FASB, June 1975 and SFAS 68, *Research and Development Arrangements*, FASB, October 1982.
44 SFAS 2, para. 8.
45 *Ibid.*, paras. 9 and 10.
46 *Ibid.*, para. 11.
47 SFAS 86, *Accounting for the Costs of Computer Software to be Sold, Leased, or Otherwise Marketed*, FASB, August 1985, para. 3.
48 *Ibid.*, summary.
49 IAS 9, *Research and Development Costs*, IASC, December 1993, para. 6.
50 *Ibid.*, para. 12.
51 *Ibid.*, paras. 16–29.
52 E50, *Intangible Assets*, IASC, June 1995, para. 2.

Chapter 13

Capitalisation of borrowing costs

1   INTRODUCTION

1.1   The development of the practice of capitalisation

A point of contention in determining the initial measurement of a tangible fixed asset is whether borrowing costs incurred during the period of construction of an asset should or should not be capitalised. This issue was referred to in company law for the first time in 1981, with the Companies Act 1981 permitting the inclusion of interest in the production cost of an asset.[1]

Since then, the practice of capitalising borrowing costs has become increasingly common in the UK in industries which have major fixed asset developments, such as property, retail and hotels. However, there is still no UK accounting standard on the subject, so capitalisation remains optional, and accounting treatments varied and inconsistent. For that reason, the ASB has now put the subject on its agenda, and has addressed it as part of its current project on the measurement of tangible fixed assets.[2]

In the US, the capitalisation of borrowing costs received renewed attention in the early 1970s, following the increased use of borrowed funds to finance business operations, coupled with a sharp rise in interest rates. Prior to that, it was predominantly the public utility companies which capitalised borrowing costs, with most other companies accounting for interest cost as a current period expense. In 1971, the Accounting Principles Board set up a committee to consider the subject; however, although the committee prepared a comprehensive working paper setting out the principal issues to be considered, its activities were terminated before a pronouncement could be issued. In 1974, the SEC became concerned about the growing popularity of interest capitalisation, when it noted an increase in the number of non-utility registrants that were adopting a policy of capitalising interest as part of the cost of certain assets. This was causing inconsistency between those companies whose earnings were boosted by capitalisation and others which expensed interest costs as incurred. In 1974, the SEC imposed a moratorium[3] on companies adopting or extending a policy of interest capitalisation (public utilities[4] and registrants covered by AICPA Guides *Accounting for Retail Land Sales* and *Audits of Savings and Loan Associations* were excluded from the moratorium). Shortly thereafter, the FASB agreed to consider the subject, and added the project to its technical agenda. This ultimately led to the publication in 1979 of SFAS 34 — *Capitalisation of Interest Cost* — which made capitalisation of interest compulsory for certain assets requiring a period of time to get them ready for their intended use.[5]

In March 1984, the IASC published IAS 23 — *Capitalisation of Borrowing Costs* — which provided a more flexible approach to the issue than does SFAS 34. Under this original version of IAS 23, capitalisation was optional, but certain rules were laid down if a policy of capitalisation was adopted.[6] However, as part of its Improvements Project, the IASC proposed that the flexibility currently contained in IAS 23 should be reduced and that borrowing costs which meet certain specified criteria should be recognised as an asset. These proposals were contained in Exposure Draft E39 — *Capitalisation of Borrowing Costs* — and bore a number of close similarities to the underlying principles and requirements of SFAS 34. Nevertheless, an eleventh hour change of heart on the part of the Board of the IASC saw the revised version of IAS 23 — *Borrowing Costs* — issued in 1993 with an entirely different approach. Under the revised IAS 23 the 'benchmark treatment' for borrowing costs is that they should be recognised as an expense in the period in which they are incurred regardless of how the borrowings are applied.[7] However, the IASC did not go so far as to ban the capitalisation of borrowing costs altogether, and the revised IAS 23 incorporates capitalisation as an 'allowed alternative treatment'.

Thus, there is currently a major difference in approach between the UK, US and International standards. In the UK, capitalisation is permitted under the Companies Act, but there are no rules laid down as to how it should be applied (although the ASB has indicated that it does not support this present situation);[8] in the US, capitalisation is mandatory under certain prescribed conditions, subject to certain exemptions; whilst IAS 23 prefers interest to be expensed but allows capitalisation within a framework of rules.

1.2 Arguments for and against capitalisation

The arguments for and against capitalisation are evenly balanced, and this was clearly evidenced by the fact that SFAS 34 was only adopted by a margin of four votes to three.[9] However, in general terms, proponents of the view that borrowing costs should be capitalised under prescribed conditions usually advance the following arguments:[10]

(a) borrowing costs incurred as a consequence of a decision to acquire an asset are not intrinsically different from other costs that are commonly capitalised. If an asset requires a period of time to bring it to the condition and location necessary for its intended use, the borrowing costs incurred during that period as a result of expenditures on the asset are a part of the cost of acquiring the asset;

(b)   a better matching of income and expenditure is achieved, in that interest incurred with a view to future benefit is carried forward to be expensed in the period or periods expected to benefit. Consequently, the failure to capitalise the borrowing costs associated with the acquisition of assets will reduce current earnings as a consequence of the acquisition of assets;

(c)   this method results in greater comparability between companies constructing assets and other companies buying similar completed assets, as well as between the costs of those assets paid for in stages and those paid for on completion within an individual company. This is because the purchase price of completed assets acquired will normally include interest, as the vendor needs to take into account all his costs, including interest, in pricing the asset; and

(d)   although tangible fixed asset costs are higher as a result of capitalising interest, and therefore are more likely to exceed the recoverable amount of the asset, the accounts are more likely to reflect the true success or failure of the project. If interest costs are not capitalised, the recoverable amount of the asset may exceed its book value and the fact that the initial decision to proceed with the project was poor would not become apparent from the accounts.

On the other hand, proponents of the view that borrowing costs should always be charged to income, regardless of how the borrowings are applied, generally advance the following arguments to support their view:[11]

(a)   it is illogical to treat financing costs as a period expense in normal circumstances, then to treat them as a direct cost of an asset during its period of construction and to revert to treating them as a period expense once the asset is complete even though financing costs are probably continuing to be incurred in respect of the asset. This is because the nature of interest does not change because of the use to which the funds are put; it remains a period cost of financing the business, and its treatment should not change merely as a result of the completion of a tangible fixed asset;

(b)   borrowing costs are incurred in support of the whole of the activities of the enterprise. Any attempt to associate borrowing costs with a particular asset is necessarily arbitrary;

(c)   capitalisation of borrowing costs results in the same type of asset having a different carrying amount, depending on the method of financing adopted by the enterprise. Limiting capitalised interest to interest on borrowings would preclude the equity-funded enterprise from capitalising interest, even though it incurs an economic cost of the same order as an enterprise that has borrowed funds. In other words, it is inconsistent to allow debt funded entities to include interest costs in the cost of an asset, whilst prohibiting equity funded entities from reflecting similarly the cost of capital in the cost of an asset;

(d) treating borrowing costs as a charge against income results in financial statements giving more comparable results from period to period, thus providing a better indication of the future cash flows of an enterprise. Interest costs fluctuate with the borrowing levels and rates which give rise to them, not with asset acquisition; and

(e) capitalisation leads to higher tangible fixed asset costs, which are more likely to exceed the recoverable amount of the asset. Although the impairment review proposed by the ASB and IASC may identify such irrecoverable amounts, these reviews will apply to business units that will usually be much wider than individual tangible fixed assets, and it may be argued that they should be regarded as a 'long stop' rather than as the principal means of ensuring that individual assets are not overstated.

1.3 The accounting alternatives

There are essentially three possible methods of accounting for borrowing costs; these are as follows:[12]

(a) account for interest on debt as an expense of the period in which it is incurred;

(b) capitalise interest on debt as part of the cost of an asset when prescribed conditions are met; and

(c) capitalise interest on debt and imputed interest on shareholders' equity as part of the cost of an asset when prescribed conditions are met.

In drafting SFAS 34, the FASB considered these three methods and concluded that alternative (b) should be adopted, whilst in its revision of IAS 23 the Board of the IASC opted for alternative (a) as the 'benchmark treatment' and alternative (b) as an 'allowed alternative treatment'. In the UK, the ASB has not yet reached agreement on whether the capitalisation of interest should be mandatory or prohibited.[13]

In arriving at its conclusions on SFAS 34, the FASB considered the possibility of capitalising interest, not just as a cost of acquiring assets, but also as a cost of holding assets. However, this idea was rejected on the grounds that under the present accounting model, costs are not added to assets subsequent to their readiness for use; therefore, consideration of such a proposal would require a comprehensive re-examination of this fundamental principle.[14]

1.3.1 Account for interest on debt as an expense of the period in which it is incurred

This was the approach favoured by the three dissenting FASB members, who held the view that 'interest cost, like dividends, is more directly associable with the period during which the capital giving rise to it is outstanding than the material, labor, and other resources into which capital is converted'.[15] It was therefore being suggested that interest should not be allocated to assets in the way that other costs are; the reasoning being that the financing structure of an enterprise is used to finance all its activities, and any allocation of particular sources of finance to particular assets is arbitrary. A decision to discontinue a particular project will not usually result in immediate repayment of any borrowings allocated as financing it, since the borrowings will normally continue to finance the remaining activities. As a cost of obtaining finance, interest should be expensed as incurred over the period of availability of the finance. The dissenting FASB members also held the view that capitalisation misstated the calculation of the return on a company's total capital employed — a computation often made by users of financial statements.

Conversely, the majority members of the FASB argued that an enterprise which is funded wholly by equity capital is not the same as one which has borrowed funds; and, similarly, an enterprise that is making substantial expenditures for asset construction differs from one which is not. They therefore maintained that 'those who assert that comparability among enterprises would be greater if all interest cost were expensed would create an illusion of comparability that may disguise the differences in facts'.[16]

1.3.2 Capitalise interest on debt as part of the cost of an asset when prescribed conditions are met

This alternative was both adopted by SFAS 34 and sanctioned by IAS 23 as an 'allowed alternative treatment'. The FASB experienced some difficulty in reconciling capitalisation based on cost of capital (see 1.3.3 below) with the historical cost convention, and it was this that led to their conclusion that the capitalisation rate should be based on rates of interest on outstanding borrowings. In arriving at this conclusion, the FASB put forward the following argument:

'In the present accounting framework, the cost of a resource is generally measured by the historical exchange price paid to acquire it. However, funds are an unusual kind of resource in that, although an enterprise obtains funds from various sources, only borrowed funds give rise to a cost that can be described as a historical exchange price. Although a historical exchange transaction may occur when equity securities are issued, that transaction is not the basis generally advocated for measuring the cost of equity capital. It is generally agreed that the use of equity capital entails an economic cost, but in the absence of a historical exchange price, the cost of equity capital is not reliably determinable. The Board concluded, therefore, that the cost of financing expenditures for a qualifying asset should be measured by assigning to the asset an appropriate proportion of the interest cost incurred on borrowings during the period of its acquisition.'[17]

It then remained to be determined exactly which borrowings should be used as a basis for the capitalisation rate. The FASB adopted the concept of borrowings which could have been avoided in the absence of expenditure on the asset as being most consistent with the arguments quoted above. It also concluded that interest capitalised should not exceed interest incurred for similar reasons.

1.3.3 Capitalise interest on debt and imputed interest on owners' equity in respect of qualifying assets during their production period

This method is based on the premise that an asset must be financed during its production period and that finance has an associated cost. The FASB developed the argument as follows:

'Financing has a cost. The cost may take the form of explicit interest on borrowed funds, or it may take the form of a return foregone on an alternative use of funds, but regardless of the form it takes, a financing cost is necessarily incurred. On the premise that the historical cost of acquiring an asset should include all costs necessarily incurred to bring it to the condition and location necessary for its intended use, the Board concluded that, in principle, the cost incurred in financing expenditures for an asset during a required construction or development period is itself a part of the asset's historical acquisition cost.'[18]

Some FASB members were of the opinion, therefore, that there is a valid conceptual argument for measuring the cost of financing the acquisition of certain assets on the basis of the enterprise's cost of capital, which would include imputed interest on equity capital, as well as interest on borrowed capital. Nevertheless, in view of the fact that, in the present accounting framework, the cost of a resource is generally measured by the historical exchange price paid to acquire it, all the FASB members agreed that recognition of the cost of equity capital does not conform to this framework.[19] Perhaps fortunately, this obviated the necessity of having to resolve the issue of how to account for the credit corresponding to the imputed interest.

2 A COMPARISON BETWEEN THE UK, US AND IASC

2.1 The current UK position

As already mentioned, there is no UK accounting standard on capitalisation of interest, which remains optional but is an increasingly common practice. ED 51 — *Accounting for fixed assets and revaluations* — which was issued by the former Accounting Standards Committee in 1990, dealt with the capitalisation of borrowing costs in a somewhat cursory manner, proposing that enterprises should be allowed to choose whether or not they capitalise borrowing costs on projects that take a substantial period of time to be brought into use for their intended purpose.[20]

In October 1996 the ASB published a Discussion Paper entitled *Measurement of tangible fixed assets* in which it indicated that it does not support either this position or the current situation whereby the capitalisation of interest is optional.[21] Consequently, for reasons of consistency of reporting, the ASB is proposing that capitalisation should be either mandatory or prohibited. At the same time, though, the members of the ASB are not yet agreed on which treatment to require. For this reason, as part of the ASB consultative process, respondents to the Discussion Paper were asked to give their views on which option they preferred.[22] At the time of writing, it is still not known what the final position of the ASB will be.

Our view is that, because of the necessarily arbitrary and inconsistent results that it gives, capitalisation should be prohibited. However, should the ASB ultimately require that capitalisation be mandatory, it is important that it ensures that companies apply the policy consistently. In other words, companies should be required to capitalise interest on all qualifying assets throughout their period of construction, even if doing so results in the initial measurement of the cost of an asset exceeding its recoverable amount. Any excess which arises should then be dealt with by way of an impairment write-down, and not indirectly through the cessation of interest capitalisation during the period of construction (see 3.5.1 below).

It is noteworthy that British Land is an example of a company which has a policy of interest capitalisation in respect of development properties, but which only applies the policy when the directors consider it prudent to do so:

Extract 13.1: British Land Company PLC (1997)

Accounting Policies

Properties [extract]

(III) DEVELOPMENT PROPERTIES are stated at the lower of cost and net realisable value. The cost of properties in course of development includes attributable interest and other outgoings net of rental income provided the directors consider it prudent having regard to the development potential of the property.

Whilst this policy is perfectly acceptable (and, indeed, prudent) under current UK GAAP, if the ASB decides to opt for mandatory capitalisation it will have to decide also whether or not such an approach should continue to be permitted.

In the case of long-term contracts, interest is referred to in Appendix 1 to SSAP 9 in the following terms, which would appear to discourage rather than encourage capitalisation:

'In ascertaining costs of long-term contracts it is not normally appropriate to include interest payable on borrowed money. However, in circumstances where sums borrowed can be identified as financing specific long-term contracts, it may be appropriate to include such related interest in cost, in which circumstances the inclusion of interest and the amount of interest so included should be disclosed in a note to the financial statements.'[23] (See also Chapter 14 at 7.3.5.)

The Companies Act 1985 permits the inclusion in the production cost of an asset of:

'(a)   a reasonable proportion of the costs incurred by the company which are only indirectly attributable to the production of that asset; and

(b)   interest on capital borrowed to finance the production of that asset, to the extent that it accrues in respect of the period of production;

provided, however, in a case within paragraph (b) above, that the inclusion of the interest in determining the cost of that asset and the amount of the interest so included is disclosed in a note to the accounts'.[24]

The wording of (b) above raises the question as to whether or not capitalisation can only take place where there have been specific borrowings made for the financing of a specific asset. For example, if a company has held a vacant piece of land for several years, and now begins to develop it using internally generated financial resources without incurring any additional borrowings, can it, nevertheless, capitalise other unrelated borrowing costs despite the absence of 'capital borrowed to finance the production of that asset'? The answer appears to be that in practice companies apply a more liberal interpretation to this provision, and capitalise interest costs irrespective of whether or not they relate to incremental or specific borrowings (this issue is discussed further in 3.3.1 below).

However, the words 'interest on capital borrowed ...' in (b) above clearly indicate that actual borrowings must have been incurred before capitalisation can take place. This would, therefore, appear to rule out the capitalisation of 'notional interest' (see 3.3.2 below).

It is noteworthy that Sainsbury's has adopted the accounting policy whereby 'interest incurred on borrowings to finance specific property developments is capitalised net of tax relief', thereby placing a strict interpretation on the application of paragraph 26(3)(b) of Schedule 4 to the Companies Act.[25]

Companies listed on The Stock Exchange must also disclose the amount of interest capitalised during the year and give an indication of the amount and treatment of any related tax relief.[26]

2.2 US

SFAS 34's stated objectives of capitalising interest are: '(a) to obtain a measure of acquisition cost that more closely reflects the enterprise's total investment in the asset and (b) to charge a cost that relates to the acquisition of a resource that will benefit future periods against the revenues of the periods benefited.'[27] The standard makes capitalisation of interest compulsory for certain assets requiring a period of time to get them ready for their intended use. These are referred to as 'qualifying assets'. Since its introduction, SFAS 34 has been amended by two subsequent standards: SFAS 58[28] and SFAS 62.[29]

2.2.1 Qualifying and non-qualifying assets

Qualifying assets are defined as follows:

(a) assets that are constructed or otherwise produced for an enterprise's own use (including assets constructed or produced for the enterprise by others for which deposits or progress payments have been made);[30]

(b) assets intended for sale or lease that are constructed or otherwise produced as discrete projects (e.g. ships or real estate developments);[31] and

(c) investments accounted for by the equity method 'while the investee has activities in progress necessary to commence its planned principal operations provided that the investee's activities include the use of funds to acquire qualifying assets for its operations'.[32]

The following are non-qualifying assets:

(a) inventories that are 'routinely manufactured or otherwise produced in large quantities on a repetitive basis';[33]

(b) assets that are in use or ready for their intended use;[34]

(c) assets not in use which are not being prepared for use;[35]

(d) assets that are not included in the consolidated balance sheet of the parent company and consolidated subsidiaries;[36] and

(e) investments accounted for by the equity method after the planned principal operations of the investee begin.[37]

Land that is not undergoing activities necessary to get it ready for its intended use is not a qualifying asset. If activities are undertaken for the purpose of developing land for a particular use, the expenditures to acquire the land qualify for interest capitalisation while those activities are in progress.[38]

2.2.2 Capitalisation rate

The amount to be capitalised is the interest cost which could theoretically have been avoided if the expenditure on the qualifying asset were not made. This is determined by applying an interest rate (the 'capitalisation rate') to the average amount of accumulated expenditure for the asset during the financial year. The capitalisation rate must be based on borrowings outstanding during the year. The borrowings used may be specific borrowings used to finance the qualifying asset. Alternatively, a weighted average rate of interest on other borrowings may be used, provided that the borrowings are selected with the objective in mind of capitalising that part of the interest cost which could theoretically have been avoided in the absence of expenditure on the qualifying asset. Also, with this objective in mind, it follows that interest capitalised must not exceed the interest cost incurred by the enterprise.[39] In consolidated financial statements, this limitation would be based on the total borrowing costs incurred by the parent company and its consolidated subsidiaries.[40]

The expenditure to which the capitalisation rate is applied is not necessarily the same as the amount capitalised for the asset in question. If a significant part of the amount capitalised relates to costs which have effectively been financed interest-free by third parties (e.g. retention money) that part must be excluded from the expenditure on which interest is capitalised.[41]

2.2.3   Capitalisation period

Generally, the period during which interest should be capitalised is defined in terms of the following three conditions:

(a)   expenditures for the asset must have been made;

(b)   activities that are necessary to get the asset ready for its intended use are in progress; and

(c)   interest cost is being incurred (including the imputation of interest on certain types of payables in accordance with APB Opinion No. 21 — *Interest on Receivables and Payables*).

The capitalisation period begins when all three conditions are present and continues as long as they remain present. The capitalisation period ends when the asset is substantially complete and ready for its intended use.[42]

If an asset is completed in parts and each part is capable of being used independently while work continues on the other parts, then capitalisation should cease on each part when it is substantially complete and ready for use.[43]

Interest capitalisation is not discontinued merely because it is necessary to write the asset down to a value below cost. In that case, the provision is increased to take account of the capitalised interest.[44]

2.2.4   Disclosure

The financial statements must disclose the total interest cost incurred and the amount capitalised during the financial year.[45]

2.3 IASC

In common with many of the other earlier international standards, the original version of IAS 23 issued in 1984 allowed a choice of treatments. In this case, the choice was between adopting a policy of capitalising or of not capitalising borrowing costs in respect of 'assets that take a substantial period of time to get them ready for their intended use or sale'.[46] This meant that capitalisation was optional — even if the criteria for capitalisation were met. However, for those enterprises which did adopt a policy of capitalisation, the standard was broadly similar to the US position discussed in 2.2 above, although IAS 23 was somewhat less specific.

E32, which was issued by the IASC in January 1989 under its improvements project, proposed to amend, inter alia, the requirements of IAS 23. The main change proposed was that the benchmark treatment for borrowing costs would be that they should be recognised as an expense when incurred, although the alternative treatment of capitalising such costs would still be allowed when certain criteria were met, and provided certain information was given.[47]

However, in July 1990 the IASC published a Statement of Intent[48] which set out its decisions following its review of the comments received on E32. One of the issues on which the IASC agreed to make substantive changes to the proposals in E32 related to IAS 23. These proposed changes were subsequently published in Exposure Draft E39 — *Capitalisation of Borrowing Costs.*[49]

E39 followed a substantially US GAAP approach, proposing that borrowing costs had to be recognised as part of the cost of an asset if it took a substantial period of time to get the asset ready for its intended use or sale; in all other circumstances they were to be recognised as an expense.[50] However, the Board of the IASC had a last minute change of heart and reverted to the approach which had originally been proposed in E32.

2.3.1 The revised IAS 23

The revised IAS 23 was issued in December 1993 (effective 1 January 1995) with the 'benchmark treatment' that borrowing costs should be recognised as an expense in the period in which they are incurred regardless of how the borrowings are applied.[51] However, the IASC did not go so far as to prohibit the capitalisation of borrowing costs altogether, and the revised standard incorporates capitalisation as an 'allowed alternative treatment'.[52] Under the allowed treatment, borrowing costs that are directly attributable to the acquisition, construction or production of a qualifying asset are included in the cost of that asset. Such borrowing costs are capitalised when it is probable that they will result in future economic benefits to the enterprise and the costs can be measured reliably. In the case of enterprises which follow this treatment, the requirements of the revised standard are as follows:

A   Qualifying assets

IAS 23 defines a qualifying asset as 'an asset that necessarily takes a substantial period of time to get ready for its intended use or sale'.[53] Examples of qualifying assets are stocks that require a substantial period of time to bring them to a saleable condition, manufacturing plants, power generation facilities and investment properties. Stocks that are routinely manufactured, or otherwise produced in large quantities on a repetitive basis over a short period of time, and assets that are ready for their intended use or sale when acquired are not qualifying assets. In the case of equity accounted investments, the IASC considered whether or not the investor should look through to the investee's activities when applying the proposed revised Standard. However, it decided that this could involve an element of double-counting, since the investee itself would apply the Standard.[54] Accordingly, in contrast to the original IAS 23, the revised standard states that 'other investments' should not be qualifying assets.[55]

It is noteworthy that the revised standard also reflects a change in thinking in the case of routinely manufactured stocks. Unlike the original IAS 23, distinction is now made between stocks that require a substantial period of time to bring them to a saleable condition (such as whisky and plantations), and stocks that are routinely manufactured or otherwise produced in large quantities on a repetitive basis over a short period of time. Previously, the original standard implied that borrowing costs should not be capitalised on stocks which take a long time to mature.

B   Borrowing costs eligible for capitalisation

Borrowing costs are interest and other costs incurred by an enterprise in connection with the borrowing of funds.[56] These may include:

(a)   interest on bank overdrafts and short-term and long-term borrowings;

(b)   amortisation of discounts or premiums relating to borrowings;

(c)   amortisation of ancillary costs incurred in connection with the arrangement of borrowings;

(d)   finance charges in respect of finance leases; and

(e)   exchange differences arising from foreign currency borrowings to the extent that they are regarded as an adjustment to interest costs.[57]

However, the fundamental requirement for capitalisation under IAS 23 is that the borrowing costs must be 'directly attributable to the acquisition, construction or production of a qualifying asset'.[58] In determining which costs satisfy this criterion, the standard starts from the premise that directly attributable borrowing costs are those that would have been avoided if the expenditure on the qualifying asset had not been made — which is very much in line with the strict interpretation of the requirements in the UK as laid down in the

Companies Act (see 2.1 above). Nevertheless, IAS 23 concedes that practical difficulties arise in identifying a direct relationship between particular borrowings and a qualifying asset and in determining the borrowings which could otherwise have been avoided; for example, in the case of an enterprise with a group treasury function that uses a range of debt instruments to borrow funds at varying rates of interest and lends those funds on various bases to other enterprises in the group. (Some might argue that it is for this very reason that capitalisation of borrowing costs should always be recognised as an expense when incurred.)

In any event, though, the standard makes allowance for the difficulties which arise in practice and concedes that the exercise of judgement is required. Consequently, to the extent that funds are borrowed specifically for the purpose of obtaining a qualifying asset, the amount of borrowing costs eligible for capitalisation on that asset should be determined as the actual borrowing costs incurred on that borrowing during the period, less any investment income on the temporary investment of those borrowings.[59]

On the other hand, to the extent that funds are borrowed generally and used for the purpose of obtaining a qualifying asset, the amount of borrowing costs eligible for capitalisation should be determined by applying a capitalisation rate to the expenditures on that asset. The capitalisation rate should be the weighted average of the borrowing costs applicable to the borrowings of the enterprise that are outstanding during the period, other than borrowings made specifically for the purpose of obtaining a qualifying asset. The amount of borrowing costs capitalised during a period should not exceed the amount of borrowing costs incurred during that period.[60]

It is noteworthy that, where funds are borrowed generally, the amount of borrowing costs which may be capitalised is limited to the gross amount of borrowing costs incurred, and that this amount is not reduced by interest income earned. In our view this is the correct approach, since to deduct interest income in determining the amount to be capitalised would, in these circumstances, produce illogical results. For example, retail groups are likely to have substantial amounts of excess cash available for short-term investment, and to attempt to establish a relationship between the interest earned on these funds and the interest paid on project finance would seem to be a misapplication of the principles of interest capitalisation.

C   *Commencement of capitalisation*

IAS 23 requires that capitalisation should commence when:

(a)   expenditures for the asset are being incurred;

(b)   borrowing costs are being incurred; and

(c)   activities that are necessary to prepare the asset for its intended use or sale are in progress.[61]

The standard goes on to state that the activities necessary to prepare an asset for its intended use or sale encompass more than the physical construction of the asset. They also include technical and administrative work (such as activities associated with obtaining permits) prior to the commencement of physical construction. However, such activities exclude the holding of an asset when no production or development that changes the asset's condition is taking place. For example, borrowing costs incurred while land is under development are capitalised during the period in which activities related to the development are being undertaken. However, borrowing costs incurred while land acquired for building purposes is held without any associated development activity do not qualify for capitalisation.[62]

D   Suspension of capitalisation

IAS 23 states that capitalisation should be suspended during extended periods in which active development is interrupted. However, the standard distinguishes between extended periods of interruption (when capitalisation would be suspended) and periods of temporary delay (when capitalisation is not normally suspended).[63]

E   Cessation of capitalisation

The standard requires that capitalisation should cease when substantially all the activities necessary to prepare the qualifying asset for its intended use or sale are complete.[64] An asset is normally ready for its intended use or sale when the physical construction of the asset is complete even though routine administrative work might still continue. If minor modifications, such as the decoration of a property to the purchaser's specification, are all that are outstanding, this indicates that substantially all the activities are complete.

Furthermore, when the construction of a qualifying asset is completed in parts and each part is capable of being used while construction continues on other parts, capitalisation should cease when substantially all the activities necessary to prepare that part for its intended use or sale are completed.[65] An example of this might be a business park comprising several buildings, each of which is capable of being fully utilised while construction continues on other parts.

F   Disclosure

Under IAS 23 the following disclosures are required to be made:

(a)   the accounting policy adopted for borrowing costs;

(b)   the amount of borrowing costs capitalised during the period; and

(c)   the capitalisation rate used to determine the amount of borrowing costs eligible for capitalisation.[66]

3   ISSUES ARISING IN PRACTICE

3.1   Qualifying assets

In the UK, the range of assets on which companies have capitalised interest covers both fixed assets and stock. Specific examples of the types of assets included are property developments, ships, aircraft, maturing whisky stocks and tobacco, and the policy of capitalising interest is fairly widespread in the UK — particularly in the case of the property industry. One notable exception, however, is Land Securities, which makes it clear in its accounting policies that all interest is expensed:

Extract 13.2: Land Securities PLC (1997)

Notes to the Financial Statements

1   Accounting Policies

(d)   PROPERTIES [extract]

Additions to properties include costs of a capital nature only; interest and other costs in respect of developments and refurbishments are treated as revenue expenditure and written off as incurred.

Guinness is an example of a company which has adopted the policy of capitalising financing costs in respect of its whisky and other spirit stocks:

Extract 13.3: Guinness PLC (1996)

Accounting policies

Stocks

Stocks are stated at the lower of cost and net realisable value. Cost includes raw materials, duties where applicable, direct labour and expenses and the appropriate proportion of production and other overheads, including financing costs in respect of whisky and other spirit stocks during their normal maturation period.

The Companies Act is drawn sufficiently widely to permit interest to be included in the production cost of any fixed or current asset,[67] but in practice capitalisation only takes place where the production period is sufficiently long for borrowing costs to be significant in relation to the total production cost.

However, as described in 2.2.1 above, the US definition of qualifying assets is narrower than this. In particular, capitalisation of interest on stocks which are routinely manufactured or otherwise produced in large quantities on a repetitive basis is not permitted in the US. The reason given by the FASB for this was that they considered that 'the informational benefit does not justify the cost of so doing'.[68] This principle could also be applied to maturing whisky or tobacco stocks, on the basis that, although an individual batch of whisky or tobacco may be held in stock for a significant period, there is a constant flow of product into and out of stock; hence, the effect on earnings of capitalising interest on such items usually would not be significant in the long run. In addition, some commentators argued that the ageing of such stocks is not part of the production process.[69]   However, interpretational difficulties of the phrase 'routinely manufactured or otherwise produced in large quantities on a repetitive basis'[70] may lead companies to capitalise interest in these situations.

IAS 23, on the other hand, specifically includes 'inventories that require a substantial period of time to bring them to a saleable condition' amongst its examples of qualifying assets, whilst inventories that are routinely manufactured or otherwise produced in large quantities on a repetitive basis over a short period of time are not qualifying assets.[71]

In the case of equity accounted investments, SFAS 34 regards them as being qualifying assets as long as the investee has activities in progress necessary to commence its planned principal operations and provided that the investee's activities include the use of funds to acquire qualifying assets for its operations. Conversely, the IASC has taken the view that capitalising interest in respect of investments could involve an element of double-counting, since the investee itself would apply the standard. Consequently, investments fall outside the IAS 23 definition of qualifying assets.

In the light of these differing requirements, it is noteworthy that RTZ-CRA capitalises interest on investments in mining associates during the development period of the mines, and whilst this clearly complies with SFAS 34 it is unclear as to whether or not it follows a strict application of the Companies Act:

Extract 13.4: The RTZ Corporation PLC and CRA Limited (1996)

NOTES TO THE 1996 ACCOUNTS

10 FIXED ASSET INVESTMENTS [extract]

(a) The Group's investments in associated companies includes, where appropriate, entry premiums on acquisition plus interest capitalised by the Group during the development period of the relevant mines. At 31 December 1996, this capitalised interest less accumulated amortisation amounted to US$39 million (1995 - US$43 million).

3.2   Period of production

Problems are frequently encountered in defining the capitalisation period — when to start, when to suspend and when to stop capitalising. Many companies give no indication of their interpretation of the capitalisation period despite the fact that difficulties can arise at virtually every stage in the production period.

3.2.1 Commencement of capitalisation period

Property developments provide a good illustration of the sort of difficulties which can arise in defining the commencement of the capitalisation period. There are a number of possible stages in the development which might be relevant to such a definition:

■ the decision to develop a site;

■ earliest purchase of part of the development site;

■ completion of purchase of the entire development site;

■ vacant possession of the entire site;

■ activities necessary in order to obtain planning permission are in progress;

■ when planning permission has been obtained;

■ entering into a building contract; and

■ commencement of building work (or of site preparation).

In deciding which of these factors is most appropriate, the particular circumstances of the individual development need to be considered carefully. The US principles described in 2.2.3 above are also a good guide. For example, the first factor listed above (decision to develop) would not usually be appropriate because it would generally occur before expenditures had been made on the development. However, there are circumstances where the decision date could be appropriate. For example, where the company decides to purchase a property adjacent to an existing investment property and redevelop both sites together, it could be appropriate to start capitalising interest from the date of the decision provided the decision was acted upon promptly.

Land awaiting development often causes difficulties. Given that there must be a period of production, the mere holding of a land bank would not seem to be sufficient justification for capitalisation. This view has been reinforced by the IASC in its revised version of IAS 23, which states that 'borrowing costs incurred while land acquired for building purposes is held without any associated development activity do not qualify for capitalisation'.[72] In the light of this, it is noteworthy that Slough Estates appears to have a policy of interest capitalisation in respect of land held for development:

Extract 13.5: Slough Estates plc (1996)

Accounting Policies

Capitalisation of interest [extract]

Interests costs incurred in funding land for or under development and construction work in progress are capitalised during the period of development.

Companies tend not to define the beginning of their capitalisation period in their financial statements. In the case of property developments, this may well be because the basis for selecting a commencement date depends very much on the nature of the individual development.

Nonetheless, the important factor to bear in mind when selecting the appropriate commencement date is that the Companies Act only permits capitalisation of interest during a period of production,[73] and therefore it is necessary that the company has embarked on the production of a specific asset.

However, as discussed at 2.3.1 C above, this is an area in which the IASC has attempted to provide additional guidance. Under the revised IAS 23, one of the conditions for the commencement of capitalisation is that 'activities that are necessary to prepare the asset for its intended use or sale are in progress'.[74] It then goes on to say that 'the activities necessary to prepare an asset for its intended use or sale encompass more than the physical construction of the asset. They also include technical and administrative work (such as activities associated with obtaining permits) prior to the commencement of physical construction. However, such activities exclude the holding of an asset when no production or development that changes the asset's condition is taking place.'[75]

3.2.2   End of capitalisation period

The general principle is that capitalisation should cease when the qualifying asset is ready for its intended use or sale. Nevertheless, there are a number of practical difficulties in isolating a particular point in time when this event occurs. In revising IAS 23, the IASC attempted to address this by providing limited guidance in this area. It states that an asset is normally ready for its intended use or sale when the physical construction of the asset is complete even though routine administrative work might still continue. It explains further that if minor modifications, such as the decoration of a property to the purchaser's or user's specification, are all that are outstanding, this indicates that substantially all the activities are complete.[76]

Under US GAAP the capitalisation period ends when the asset is 'substantially complete and ready for its intended use'.[77] The words 'substantially complete' are used to prohibit continuation of capitalisation in situations in which completion of the asset is intentionally delayed.

The question as to when capitalisation should cease also arises in the case of qualifying assets that are constructed in stages or parts. Again, the only real guidance is to be found in the revised IAS 23, which distinguishes between the situation where a qualifying asset is completed in parts and each part is capable of being used while construction continues on other parts, and the situation where the qualifying asset needs to be complete in its entirety before any part can be used. Not surprisingly, the standard states that in the former case capitalisation in respect of each part should cease when substantially all the activities necessary to prepare that part for its intended use or sale are completed,[78] while in the latter case capitalisation should only cease when substantially all the activities necessary to prepare the entire asset for its intended use or sale are complete. An example of a part that is usable while construction continues on other parts of an asset is a business park comprising several buildings that can be used individually. On the other hand, an example of an asset that needs to be complete before it can be used is an industrial plant involving several processes which are carried out in sequence at different units within the same site, such as a steel mill.

As with commencement of capitalisation, many UK companies give little or no indication as to how the end of their capitalisation period is defined.

However, the following are examples of companies which do have an accounting policy which refers to the end of the capitalisation period:

Extract 13.6: Daily Mail and General Trust plc (1996)

Accounting Policies

13 Interest

Loan interest and financing costs incurred on major property developments are capitalised, net of taxation, until the earlier of:

(a)   the date on which the property becomes substantially let and income producing;

(b)   the date when income exceeds outgoings including development interest; and

(c)   a date not later than two years after practical completion, as certified by the architects.

Extract 13.7: Slough Estates plc (1996)

Accounting Policies

Capitalisation of interest

Interest costs incurred in funding land for or under development and construction work in progress are capitalised during the period of development. A property is regarded as being in the course of development until substantially let or the expiration of a period varying from 6 months to 2 years from the issue of the Architect's certificate of practical completion, whichever is the earlier. Interest costs incurred in funding major construction programmes for the Utilities Division are capitalised during the period of construction.

Extract 13.8: MEPC plc (1996)

Accounting policies

Properties [extract]

A property ceases to be treated as being in course of development at the earliest of:

(1) the date when the development becomes fully let and income producing

(2) the date when income exceeds outgoings

(3) a date up to three years after completion to allow for letting.

These are fairly typical of the accounting policies of property development companies. Generally speaking, developments are not regarded as ready for their intended use until a reasonable period of time has been allowed to find tenants, i.e. until they are (or ought to be) income-producing. However, the US standard would not allow this treatment, as capitalisation would have to cease on each part of the development as it became substantially complete and ready for use.[79]

3.2.3 *Interruptions and delays during development*

It is sometimes argued that capitalisation of interest should be suspended when interruptions or delays occur during development, since interest incurred during an interruption or delay does not add to the value of the development. Whilst this is true, it is also true that delays and interruptions add to the *cost* of a development. It therefore seems more appropriate to continue to capitalise interest even though a write down may be necessary. If the development is abandoned completely, then the interest costs should be written off together with other abortive expenditure incurred on the development.

Nevertheless, both IAS 23 and SFAS 34 specifically state that capitalisation should be suspended during extended periods in which active development is interrupted.[80] The argument for this approach is that borrowing costs incurred during an extended period when the activities that are necessary to prepare an asset for its intended use or sale are interrupted are costs of holding partially completed assets, and therefore do not qualify for capitalisation. However, neither standard requires suspension of capitalisation where there are brief interruptions in activities, interruptions that are externally imposed, and delays that are inherent in the asset acquisition process.[81]

3.3   Determination of amount to be capitalised

3.3.1 *Borrowings and capitalisation rate*

Few companies give any indication of their method of calculating interest to be capitalised. However, it seems likely that there is a wide divergence in methods used, as literature[82] on the subject discusses a variety of possible methods of calculation including:

(a) rate of interest on borrowings specifically taken out to finance the development;

(b) weighted average rate of interest. This could be based on:

    (i) all borrowings; or

    (ii) selected borrowings, e.g. as in SFAS 34 where the borrowings are selected as representing avoidable interest costs (see 2.2.2 above);

(c) highest rate of interest;

(d) rate of interest on most recent borrowings;

(e) market capitalisation rate. This is a measure of the rate of return investors could earn elsewhere and could be either a general rate or specific to a particular industry; and

(f) total interest charge as a percentage of total funds available, including shareholders' funds. This method assumes that finance has been provided pro rata by shareholders and lenders so, in effect, interest is capitalised only on that part of the asset presumed to have been financed out of borrowings.

Of the above, we prefer methods (a) or (b)(ii) using a selection of borrowings intended to represent those which would have been avoided in the absence of expenditure on the qualifying asset. Note that these methods assume that the asset is financed entirely by borrowings. Method (f), on the other hand, assumes that the asset is financed by a combination of borrowings and shareholders' funds, but only accounts for the cost of borrowings. We do not believe that any strong arguments can be advanced in favour of methods (c) to (e), although these methods might fit the circumstances of a particular case at a given point in time.

The Companies Act wording quoted in 2.1 above appears only to permit method (a) in that it refers to capital borrowed to finance the production of *that* asset. It could be argued that capitalisation can only take place where specific borrowings can be identified with specific assets. However, it is not reasonable or practicable to take such a strict line. This would mean, for example, that a company which chose not to repay a particular borrowing because it was needed to finance a development would not be able to capitalise the interest on that borrowing. In practice, therefore, a more liberal interpretation is applied.

The following example illustrates the application of the preferred methods (contrasted with method (f)):

Example 13.1: Calculation of capitalisation rate

On 1 April 19X1 a company engages in the development of a property which is expected to take five years to complete, at a cost of £6,000,000. The balance sheets at 31 December 19X0 and 31 December 19X1, prior to capitalisation of interest, are as follows:

	31 December 19X0	31 December 19X1
	£	£
Development property	—	1,200,000
Other assets	6,000,000	6,800,000
	6,000,000	8,000,000
Loans		
8% debenture stock	2,500,000	2,500,000
Bank loan at 10% p.a.	—	2,000,000
Bank loan at 12% p.a.	1,000,000	1,000,000
	3,500,000	5,500,000
Shareholders' equity	2,500,000	2,500,000

The bank loan at 10% was taken out on 31 March 19X1 and the total interest charge for the year ended 31 December 19X1 was as follows:

	£
£2,500,000 x 8%	200,000
£2,000,000 x 10% x 9/12	150,000
£1,000,000 x 12%	120,000
	470,000

Expenditure was incurred on the development as follows:

	£
1 April 19X1	600,000
1 July 19X1	400,000
1 October 19X1	200,000
	1,200,000

(a) If the bank loan at 10% p.a. is a new borrowing taken out specifically to finance the development, then the amount of interest to be capitalised is:

	£
£600,000 x 10% x 9/12	45,000
£400,000 x 10% x 6/12	20,000
£200,000 x 10% x 3/12	5,000
	70,000

(b) If all the borrowings would have been avoided but for the development then the amount of interest to be capitalised is:

$$\frac{\text{Total interest expense for period}}{\text{Weighted average total borrowings}} \quad \text{x Development expenditure}$$

i.e.

$$\frac{470,000}{3,500,000 + (2,000,000 \times 9/12)} = 9.4\%$$

	£
£600,000 x 9.4% x 9/12	42,300
£400,000 x 9.4% x 6/12	18,800
£200,000 x 9.4% x 3/12	4,700
	65,800

If the 8% debenture stock was irredeemable then as the borrowings could not have been avoided the above calculation would be done using the figures for the bank loans and their related interest costs only.

If method (f) is used then the interest rate to be applied would be:

$$\frac{\text{Total interest expense for period}}{\text{Weighted average total borrowings + weighted average shareholders' equity}}$$

i.e.

$$\frac{470,000}{5,000,000 + 2,500,000} = 6.27\%$$

Accordingly, a lower amount of interest would be capitalised reflecting the fact that part of the development is financed by shareholders' equity.

As mentioned above, few companies give any indication of their method of calculating interest to be capitalised. However, exceptions to this include Safeway and MEPC, who state the following:

Extract 13.9: Safeway plc (1997)

Statement of Accounting Policies

Tangible fixed assets [extract]

Interest costs relating to the financing of freehold and long leasehold developments are capitalised at the weighted average cost of the related borrowings up to the date of completion of the project.

Extract 13.10: MEPC plc (1996)

Accounting policies

Properties [extract]

An amount equivalent to interest and other outgoings less rental income attributable to properties in course of development is transferred to the cost of properties. For this purpose the interest rate applied to funds provided for property development is arrived at by reference, where appropriate, to the actual rate payable on borrowings for development purposes and, in regard to that part of the development cost financed out of general funds, to the average rate paid on funding the assets employed by the Group.

In its Discussion Paper on the measurement of tangible fixed assets, the ASB identifies three possible rates that an entity could use for determining the amount of interest to be capitalised:[83]

■   the entity's weighted average cost of capital;

■   the actual rate incurred on specific borrowings; or

■   the weighted average of the borrowing costs applicable to the borrowings that are outstanding during the period.

The Discussion Paper then argues that 'conceptually, the rate of interest directly attributable to bringing the asset into working condition for its intended use is the entity's weighted average cost of capital'.[84] However, the Discussion Paper then concedes that this approach would appear to be inappropriate, since it would lead to the capitalisation of notional interest relating to the cost of capital which, in turn, neither meets the definition of a loss or the definition of an asset.[85] As already stated above, in developing SFAS 34, the FASB also rejected this approach – although for different reasons.

Having rejected the approach based on cost of capital, the Discussion Paper then examines the other two possible approaches, and concludes that they are both appropriate, depending on the particular circumstances and nature of borrowings. The Paper argues that, in some circumstances, the borrowing cost borne by an entity as a result of incurring expenditure on a tangible fixed asset can readily be identified – for example, where the entity has borrowed funds specifically for the purpose of financing the construction of an asset. In this case, the Paper suggests that it would be appropriate to capitalise the actual rate incurred on the specific borrowings. However, the Paper goes on to say that in many circumstances such a direct relationship will not exist – for example, where the funds used to finance the construction of a tangible fixed asset form part of the general borrowings of the entity, which include a variety of different debt instruments with varying interest rates. In this case, the Paper suggests that it would be more appropriate to capitalise the weighted average of the borrowing costs applicable to the borrowings outstanding during the period.[86]

Consequently, it appears that the ASB's current thinking on the subject of capitalisation rate favours a mixed approach, in line with IAS 23: where the entity has borrowed funds specifically for the purpose of financing the construction of a tangible fixed asset, the ASB is proposing that the amount of interest that should be capitalised is the actual interest incurred on the borrowings during the period, net of investment income earned on the funds in the event they are temporarily invested until expenditure on the asset is incurred.[87] However, where the funds used to finance the construction of a tangible fixed asset form part of the general borrowings of the entity, the ASB is proposing that the amount of interest capitalised should be determined by applying a capitalisation rate to the expenditure on that asset. In this latter case, the capitalisation rate should be the weighted average of the borrowing costs applicable to the borrowings of the entity that are outstanding during the period, excluding borrowings of the entity that are specifically for the purpose of constructing other tangible fixed assets.[88]

3.3.2 Limitation on interest capitalised

We have seen in 2 above that the amount of borrowing costs capitalised during a period should not exceed the total amount of borrowing costs incurred by the enterprise in that period. However, if a company has received interest income during the period, the question arises as to whether the maximum amount which should be capitalised is the net interest incurred after deducting such interest, or the gross interest incurred. As stated above, the ASB is proposing that, where a company has borrowed funds specifically for the purpose of financing the construction of a tangible fixed asset, investment income earned on the funds should be deducted.

This proposed approach is consistent with IAS 23, which states that to the extent that funds are borrowed specifically for the purpose of obtaining a qualifying asset, the amount of borrowing costs eligible for capitalisation on that asset should be determined as the actual borrowing costs incurred on that borrowing during the period less any investment income on the temporary investment of those borrowings.[89] This is because the financing arrangements for a qualifying asset may result in an enterprise obtaining borrowed funds and incurring associated borrowing costs before some or all of the funds are used for expenditures on the qualifying asset. In such circumstances, the funds are often temporarily invested pending their expenditure on the qualifying asset. Consequently, in determining the amount of borrowing costs eligible for capitalisation during a period, any investment income earned on such funds is deducted from costs incurred.[90]

To the extent that funds are borrowed generally and used for the purpose of obtaining a qualifying asset, the ASB's Discussion Paper mirrors IAS 23's requirement that the amount of interest capitalised during a period should not exceed the amount of borrowing costs incurred during that period.[91]

However, in the US, interest earned is not offset against interest cost in determining either capitalisation rates or limitations on the amount of interest cost to be capitalised, except in situations involving the acquisition of qualifying assets financed by the proceeds of tax-exempt borrowings if those funds are externally restricted to finance the acquisition of specified qualifying assets or to service the related debt.[92] The provisions in SFAS 34 for determining the amount of interest cost to be capitalised deal solely with the interest cost incurred and the rates applicable to borrowings outstanding. Temporary or short-term investment decisions are not related to the determination of the acquisition cost of the asset or to the allocation of that cost against revenues of the periods benefited by the asset.

3.3.3   Gross or net of tax relief

Some companies capitalise interest net of the related tax relief whilst others capitalise gross. The argument usually advanced in favour of capitalising net is that the tax relief should follow the accounting charge which gives rise to it.[93] Against this, it can be argued that it is not usual to account for assets net of tax effects. Where capital allowances are received in respect of the costs of fixed assets, the tax benefit is reflected in the tax charge in the profit and loss account. Provision is made under SSAP 15 for this timing difference only if it is likely that it will reverse in the foreseeable future. If no provision is necessary, then the full benefit is reflected in the profit and loss account. Capitalisation of interest also creates a timing difference which should be accounted for in accordance with SSAP 15. Consequently, of the two treatments, we consider the arguments in favour of capitalisation gross to be the stronger.

Nevertheless, capitalisation net of tax relief would seem to be the more common treatment, although not all companies explain which treatment they have adopted — in spite of The Stock Exchange requirement to give 'an indication of the amount and treatment of any related tax relief'.[94] This issue is not addressed in the ASB's Discussion Paper.

3.3.4   Compounding

Another question which frequently arises in practice is whether interest should be capitalised on a compound basis. On the face of it, the basis should be compound because the cost of the asset is the amount being funded, and capitalised interest is part of the cost. However, where it is only interest on specific borrowings which is being capitalised, consideration should be given as to whether interest is actually suffered on a compound basis under the terms of the borrowings, since this may not be the case where interest is paid as it falls due.

Example 13.2: Capitalising interest on a compound basis

The facts are as in Example 13.1 above (see 3.3.1 above) with the 10% bank loan representing a loan specifically financing the development. In addition to the £1,200,000 expended on the development in 19X1, a further £800,000 is incurred on 1 January 19X2. All interest falls due on 30 June and 31 December each year and is paid on the due dates. Interest incurred on the bank loan in 19X2 is, therefore, £200,000.

If interest is capitalised on a compound basis, amounts capitalised in 19X1 and 19X2 will be as follows:

19X1: (as before) £70,000
19X2: (£1,200,000 + £70,000 + £800,000) x 10% = £207,000

The interest capitalised in 19X2 therefore exceeds the interest incurred on the specific borrowing. This results purely from capitalising interest on a compound basis when it is not actually suffered on a compound basis. In cases such as this, interest should not be capitalised on a compound basis.

If the interest was not paid half-yearly but was rolled-up and payable when the loan was to be repaid then it would be likely that interest would be required to be compounded. If it were to be compounded on an annual basis then the charge for 19X2 would have been £215,000 and therefore the interest could be capitalised on a compound basis.

Where the borrowings taken into account in determining the capitalisation rate include bank overdrafts then it would be appropriate to capitalise interest on a compound basis. Any interest paid is likely to be financed out of the bank overdrafts and therefore interest will be incurred on a compound basis.

3.3.5 Accrued costs

In principle, costs of a qualifying asset which have only been accrued but have not yet been paid in cash should be excluded from the amount on which interest is capitalised. It should be noted that the effect of applying this principle is often merely to delay the capitalisation of interest since the costs will be included once they have been paid in cash. In most cases it is unlikely that the effect will be material as the time between accrual and payment of the cost will not be that great. However, the effect is potentially material where a significant part of the amount capitalised relates to costs which have been financed interest-free by third parties for a long period. An example of this is retention money which is not generally payable until the asset is completed.

3.3.6 Asset not previously held at cost

An asset may appear in the financial statements prior to the capitalisation period on a basis other than cost, i.e. it may have been written down below cost or revalued above cost. The question then arises as to whether the calculation of interest to be capitalised should be based on cost or book value. In these circumstances, cost should be used as this is the amount that the company or group has had to finance. In the case of an asset previously written down, the circumstances giving rise to the provision may still be present (see 3.5.1 below).

3.4   Group financial statements

3.4.1   *Borrowings in one company and development in another*

A question which often arises in practice is whether it is appropriate to capitalise interest in the group financial statements on borrowings where the borrowings appear in the financial statements of a different group company from that carrying out the development. Based on the preference already stated, capitalisation in such circumstances would only be appropriate if the amount capitalised fairly reflected the interest cost of the group on borrowings from third parties which could theoretically have been avoided if the expenditure on the qualifying asset were not made.

Although it may be appropriate to capitalise interest in the group financial statements, the company carrying out the development should not capitalise any interest in its own financial statements as it has no borrowings (see 3.3.2 above). If, however, the company has intra-group borrowings then interest on such borrowings may be capitalised.

3.4.2   *Qualifying assets held by investments accounted for using the equity method*

The circumstances in which capitalisation would be permitted in the US for such assets are described in 2.2.1 above. In the UK, property developments are often carried out as joint ventures, frequently through the medium of associated undertakings. In such cases, the joint venture may be financed principally by equity and the joint venture partners may have financed their participating interests by borrowings. It is not appropriate to capitalise interest in the associate on the borrowings of the partners as the interest charge is not a cost of the associate. Neither would it be appropriate to capitalise interest in the individual (as opposed to group) financial statements of the investing companies because the qualifying asset does not belong to them. The asset which the investing companies have is a participating interest, which is not in the course of production. However, the question does arise as to whether an adjustment may be made in the investor's group financial statements to capitalise interest on the borrowings financing the participating interest when the associated undertaking is equity accounted.

Example 13.3

A company has a 50% investment in an associated undertaking whose balance sheet at 31 December 19X1 is as follows:

	£'000	£'000
Share capital		100
Share premium		900
		1,000
Borrowings: 10% loan		1,000
		2,000
Expenditure on development	1,600	
Capitalised interest	100 *	
		1,700
Cash		300
		2,000

* £1,600,000 x 10% restricted to actual interest incurred of £100,000.

The cost of the investment was £500,000 which was financed by a borrowing at 9% p.a. The investing company could, therefore, capitalise additional interest of £27,000 (being £600,000 x 50% x 9%) in its group financial statements (recognising that only 50% of the development expenditure not funded by borrowings is funded by the investing company).

Capitalisation in these circumstances appears to be justified on the basis that the borrowings are effectively financing the company's share of the development. It would have been possible for a similar result to be shown if the investing companies had decided to finance the associated undertaking with borrowings and only a nominal amount of equity. As shown in Extract 13.4 at 3.1 above, RTZ-CRA capitalises interest on investments in mining associates during the development period of the mines, and therefore appears to be applying this principle in practice. Nevertheless, it is worth noting that, in revising IAS 23, the IASC decided that investments in enterprises should not be qualifying assets (see 2.3.1 above).

Where the qualifying assets are held by an investment which is not effectively an interest in a joint venture or consortium it is unlikely that an adjustment should be made in the group financial statements. This is because the interest in the investing company would probably not have been avoided if the investee had not incurred the costs on the qualifying asset.

3.5   Other issues

3.5.1   *Provisions for diminution in value*

Care is needed to ensure that interest capitalisation does not result in assets being carried at too high a value. This may, for example, arise in the following circumstances:

(a)   assets which had been written down prior to the capitalisation period (see 3.3.6 above for a discussion of the basis for the amount to be capitalised in these circumstances); and

(b)   delays and interruptions during development may increase costs to the extent that a provision becomes necessary.

If interest is regarded as an intrinsic cost of the asset, then logic would dictate that interest capitalisation should not cease merely because a provision becomes necessary (see 3.2.3 above for the rationale for this). In determining the amount of the provision, all future costs, *including interest*, to be incurred to completion should be taken into account.

Nevertheless, there are in fact a number of companies which have seemingly adopted the policy of only capitalising interest to the extent that the cost of the qualifying asset does not become greater than its open market value (see, for example, Extract 13.1 above). However, as discussed at 2.1 above, if the ASB ultimately decides to opt for mandatory capitalisation it will have to decide also whether or not such an approach should continue to be permitted.

3.5.2   *Change of policy*

When interest is capitalised for the first time, FRS 3 requires that a prior year adjustment be made as this is a change of accounting policy. In theory, the adjustment should be made in respect of all assets still held which would, during their period of production, have satisfied the criteria adopted for capitalisation. However, this can create considerable difficulty in the case of fixed assets which were produced many years ago; accordingly, some compromises may have to be made in calculating the prior year adjustment; nevertheless it should be possible to produce a materially accurate figure.

Interestingly enough though, in revising IAS 23 the IASC appears to have anticipated this potential difficulty by introducing the following transitional provisions: 'When the adoption of this Standard constitutes a change in accounting policy, an enterprise is encouraged to adjust its financial statements in accordance with International Accounting Standard IAS 8, Net Profit or Loss for the period, Fundamental Errors and Changes in Accounting Policies. Alternatively, enterprises following the allowed alternative treatment should capitalise only those borrowing costs incurred after the effective date of the Standard which meet the criteria for capitalisation.'[95]

During the property slump of the late 80s/early 90s a number of UK property companies changed their policy with regard to borrowing costs from one of capitalisation to one of annual expense. In a number of cases this resulted in substantial asset write-downs by way of prior year adjustment. Trafalgar House is an example of a company which made such a change:

Extract 13.11: Trafalgar House Public Limited Company (1991)

NOTES TO THE ACCOUNTS

1   Accounting policies

Comparative figures have been restated to reflect the changes in accounting policies for fixed asset investments and developments for sale and for changes in presentation.

14   Developments for sale [extract]

From 1st October 1990 the Group's policy in regard to the inclusion of financing charges in the costs of residential developments was changed so as to include interest only in respect of certain long term developments; the amount of such interest at 30th September 1991 was nil.

24   Reserves [extract]

Developments for sale include financing charges on commercial developments and certain long-term residential developments. This is a change from the previous accounting policy of including financing charges on all developments. Adjustments to the Group's reserves as at 30th September 1990 have been made in respect of finance charges of £41.7m previously included in residential developments for sale.

It is interesting to note that Trafalgar House's change in policy was effected in two stages, thereby affording the company a second opportunity of reducing the impact of property write-downs on the profit and loss account – as revealed by the following extract from the company's 1993 accounts:

Extract 13.12: Trafalgar House Public Limited Company (1993)

Notes to the Accounts

1   **Changes in accounting policies and in presentation** [extract]

Changes in accounting policies

Financing charges on developments are now charged to the profit and loss account as incurred except where these relate to major long term commercial developments. Previously, related financing charges were included in the cost of commercial developments and certain long term residential developments. The accounting policy has been changed because the directors consider that the new policy reflects the current trend of accounting practice in the property industry.

The effect of the change of accounting policy for financing charges on developments has been to reduce the opening carrying value of development properties and therefore to decrease the amount of the required write down. Accordingly, the loss for the current year has been reduced by £21.2 million.

BAA provides an example of a company which has recently refined its policy on interest capitalisation so that interest is now only capitalised once planning permission has been obtained and a firm decision to proceed has been taken. In previous years, BAA's accounting policy was stated rather loosely as applying when 'the borrowing finances tangible fixed assets in the course of construction'. This is now more tightly described, as shown in the following extract:

Extract 13.13: BAA plc (1997)

Financial review [extract]

Interest capitalisation policy

For many years, BAA has followed a policy of capitalising interest on borrowings which finance its capital projects. The announcement of further delays to the Terminal 5 enquiry at Heathrow has led the Board to reconsider the application of its policy on interest capitalisation. Following a detailed review, the Board has refined its definition of the period of production to commence only when planning permission has been obtained and a firm decision to proceed has been taken.

As a result, interest of £40m, representing interest in the pre-production phase which was capitalised in earlier years, has been charged as an exceptional interest charge. If the previous method of calculating interest to be capitalised had been applied in 1996/97, then a further £13m would have been capitalised, which would have represented an increase in earnings per share of 1.2 pence. Even if the old basis had been used, the directors confirm that there would be no need, at today's date, to write down any fixed assets as a result of impairment in value.

Accounting policies

Interest [extract]

Interest payable is charged as incurred except where the borrowing finances tangible fixed assets in the course of construction. Such interest is capitalised once planning permission has been obtained and a firm decision to proceed has been taken until the asset is complete and income producing and is then written off by way of depreciation of the relevant asset.

BAA's disclosures are to be commended on two counts: first, the company has not been selective in refining its policy – that is, it has not just applied the refined policy to the Terminal 5 project, and kept the old policy for everything else and, second, the company is to be commended for clarifying that the policy refinement is not being used as a surrogate for an impairment problem.

3.5.3 *Exchange differences as a borrowing cost*

Borrowings in one currency may have been used to finance a development the costs of which are incurred primarily in another currency, e.g. a Swiss franc loan financing a sterling development. This may have been done on the basis that, over the period of the development, the interest cost, after allowing for exchange differences, was expected to be less than the interest cost of an equivalent sterling loan. In these circumstances, there is a good argument for capitalising the interest cost and the exchange difference. In fact, SSAP 20 — *Foreign currency translation* — suggests that gains or losses arising from arrangements which may be considered as financing should be disclosed separately as part of

'Other interest receivable/payable and similar income/expense'.[96] This approach would also be consistent with IAS 23, which defines borrowing costs as including exchange differences arising from foreign currency borrowings to the extent that they are regarded as an adjustment to interest costs.[97]

On the other hand, accounting practice in the US would be different. This is because US GAAP focuses more narrowly on interest costs, rather than on the broader concept of total borrowing costs; consequently, whilst SFAS 34 does not address the issue directly, in practice items such as foreign currency differences relating to borrowed funds would not be included in the total amount of interest cost incurred available for capitalisation.

3.5.4 Assets produced by others

According to the Companies Act 1985, the production cost of an asset 'shall be determined by adding to the purchase price of the raw materials and consumables used the amount of the costs incurred by the company which are directly attributable to the production of that asset'.[98] Interest may be included in production cost as described in 2.1 above. This could be interpreted as meaning that interest may only be capitalised on assets produced by the company itself rather than assets produced by others for the company, because if the assets are produced entirely by others the production costs are not incurred by the company.

However, this interpretation would rule out capitalisation on most development and construction projects which hardly seems logical given that the rationale for capitalising interest is strongly dependent on the view that it is an integral part of cost. Not surprisingly, therefore, a wider interpretation of the Companies Act is used in practice, as can be seen, for example, from the following extracts:

Extract 13.14: The Peninsular and Oriental Steam Navigation Company (1996)

Accounting policies

Ships and other fixed assets [extract]

Interest incurred in respect of payments on account of assets under construction is capitalised to the cost of the asset concerned.

Extract 13.15: British Airways Plc (1997)

NOTES TO THE ACCOUNTS

1   ACCOUNTING POLICIES

Tangible fixed assets [extract]

a   CAPITALISATION OF INTEREST ON PROGRESS PAYMENTS

Interest attributed to progress payments made on account of aircraft and other assets under construction is capitalised and added to the cost of the asset concerned. Interest capitalised in respect of progress payments on those aircraft which subsequently become subject to extendible operating lease arrangements is carried forward and written off over the initial lease period.

SFAS 34 does, in fact, make it clear that qualifying assets include 'assets constructed or produced for the enterprise by others for which deposits or progress payments have been made',[99] although both the ASB's Discussion Paper and IAS 23 are silent on this point.

3.5.5   Depreciation

It is sometimes argued that capitalised interest should be written off faster than the depreciation rate of other costs of a development on the basis that it is less tangible. Certainly this is a conservative approach, but it is not a rational one. The basis for capitalising interest in the first place depends strongly on the view that it is an integral part of cost so there is no reason to treat it separately for depreciation purposes.

3.5.6   Interest capitalisation and 'creative accounting'

Critics of the standard of UK corporate reporting have, from time to time, stated that interest capitalisation is not a prudent policy. It has even been suggested, or at least implied, that it was a contributing factor to the recent financial difficulties of many companies within the property sector. Apparently, it was felt by some that the capitalisation, rather than the expensing, of interest had in some way hidden the high debt service costs within the property sector.

Many such comments can be rebutted quite simply. Certainly, it should always be possible to determine the extent of the interest capitalised and this is required to be shown in UK accounts by law. This does require a reader of the accounts to look at the notes as well as the primary statements, but he should be doing this anyway to obtain a full view of the reported results and financial position of a company.

Some would argue that the combination of capitalisation and the need to consider the end value of the properties concerned will actually produce a worse, and arguably more prudent, result than if interest had been expensed. The reasons for this are twofold:

(a)   First, capitalisation clearly increases the risk that project costs will exceed value, particularly if the market falls.   However, this does no more than reflect the real financial success or failure of a project as measured against the original assessment of the development's viability, which will always have an interest cost factored into it.

(b)   Second, if interest is regarded as an intrinsic cost of the project, future interest to the end of the production period should be taken into account in determining whether any accounting provision is necessary.   If interest is not capitalised, such future interest will normally be expensed in future periods and will therefore be recognised later.

Thus, although both policies will produce the same aggregate result over the life of a development, a policy of capitalisation should actually accelerate the recognition of losses.   One would have thought that such a result was entirely in keeping with the overriding concept of accounting prudence; perhaps the opponents of capitalisation have not quite grasped this point.   Certainly, from the point of view of a company's bankers, the proper application of capitalisation is likely to give an earlier warning of covenant and cash flow problems.

4   DISCLOSURE

4.1   Balance sheet and related notes

If interest is included in the production cost of an asset, the Companies Act 1985 requires disclosure of 'the amount of the interest so included'.[100]   This presumably means the cumulative amount of capitalised interest as opposed to the amount capitalised during the year.   If the asset in question is a fixed asset, then it would seem that the disclosure ought to continue beyond the production period and presumably the amount disclosed should be net of any depreciation or provision for diminution in value.   Such disclosure is useful because it shows the cumulative effect on the financial statements of the decision to capitalise interest.   In practice, it seems that most property companies do, in fact, show the cumulative capitalised interest content of completed stock and fixed assets.

Where interest is being capitalised on a tangible fixed asset (which must by definition be in a period of production) it is likely that the asset to which it relates will have to be disclosed separately from other tangible fixed assets as the balance sheet formats require 'payments on account and assets in course of construction' to be disclosed.[101]

4.2   Profit and loss account and related notes

The Companies Act requires the interest on certain categories of borrowing to be disclosed.[102]   This information is normally given in a note to the financial statements.   Interest capitalised is usually shown as a deduction from interest incurred within this note. For companies capitalising net of tax relief, a similar presentation is often used for the tax note. For example:

Interest payable	19X2 £'000	19X1 £'000
On bank loans and overdrafts and other loans repayable within five years	1,000	750
On other loans	700	900
	1,700	1,650
Interest capitalised on development properties	(800)	(600)
	900	1,050

Tax on profit on ordinary activities	19X2 £'000	19X1 £'000
Corporation tax at 31%	2,500	2,000
Deferred tax	500	250
Tax relief attributable to capitalised interest	248	186
	3,248	2,436

Companies capitalising gross generally disclose the tax relief on capitalised interest in narrative form, for example:

Interest payable	19X2 £'000	19X1 £'000
On bank loans and overdrafts and other loans repayable within five years	1,000	750
On other loans	700	900
	1,700	1,650
Interest capitalised on development properties	(800)	(600)
	900	1,050

Tax on profit on ordinary activities	19X2 £'000	19X1 £'000
Corporation tax at 31%	2,500	2,000
Deferred tax	500	250
	3,000	2,250

The above charge is net of tax relief attributable to capitalised interest of £248,000 (19X1: £186,000).

4.3 Accounting policy

The following information should be clear from the accounting policy of a company capitalising interest (some of the information is already required, as indicated in the footnotes):

(a)   the classes of assets on which interest is capitalised;[103]

(b)   the method of calculation, e.g. whether specific borrowings are used and, if not, the basis of selection of the borrowings used in the calculation;

(c)   whether capitalisation is gross or net of tax relief;[104] and

(d)   how the capitalisation period is defined.

Nevertheless, many companies capitalising interest give rather less information than the above. However, MEPC is an example of a company which does give good disclosure of all of the above information:

Extract 13.16: MEPC plc (1996)

Accounting policies

Properties [extract]

The Group's properties are valued annually for the Board. The bases of valuation of investment and development properties are described in note 13.

Investment properties are included at cost and valuation. Development and trading properties are included at the lower of cost and net realisable value.

No account is taken of any surplus arising on the valuation of development or trading properties; deficits on trading properties are charged to the profit and loss account. All other surpluses or deficits against book value are transferred to the revaluation reserve except for those deficits expected to be permanent, which are included in the profit and loss account and then transferred to other reserves.

Where properties are transferred from the investment portfolio to the development portfolio, "cost" is deemed for this purpose to be book value at the date of transfer.

Net gains or losses on disposal of investment properties are calculated by reference to book value at date of disposal.

An amount equivalent to interest and other outgoings less rental income attributable to properties in course of development is transferred to the cost of properties. For this purpose the interest rate applied to funds provided for property development is arrived at by reference, where appropriate, to the actual rate payable on borrowings for development purposes and, in regard to that part of the development cost financed out of general funds, to the average rate paid on funding the assets employed by the Group.

A property ceases to be treated as being in course of development at the earliest of:

(1) the date when the development becomes fully let and income producing

(2) the date when income exceeds outgoings

(3) a date up to three years after completion to allow for letting.

Taxation [extract]

Where a transfer of an amount equivalent to interest and other outgoings attributable to properties in the course of development is made and tax relief is receivable for the cost of such interest and other outgoings, the tax relief so claimed is treated as a reduction of development cost.

5   CONCLUSION

There is still no UK accounting standard on the subject of capitalisation of borrowing costs, so capitalisation remains optional, and accounting treatments varied and inconsistent. For that reason, the ASB has now put the subject on its agenda, and has addressed it as part of its current project on the measurement of tangible fixed assets.

At the same time, though, the Discussion Paper's consideration of the subject can hardly be regarded as rigorous. It is therefore debatable whether any decision should be made on whether or not to capitalise interest without a proper discussion of the nature of finance costs and how they fit within the structure of financial reporting by a company to its stakeholders. The ASB needs to address the fundamental issue as to whether or not the capitalisation of borrowing costs is a conceptually sound basis of accounting in the first place.

In so doing, the ASB will need to take cognisance of the fact that there is a valid conceptual argument for measuring the cost of financing the acquisition of qualifying assets on the basis of the entity's cost of capital – which would include imputed interest on equity capital as well as interest on borrowings. At the same time it must be recognised that the capitalisation of the cost of equity capital does not conform to the present historical cost accounting framework, under which the cost of a resource is measured by reference to historical exchange prices. Nevertheless, to only permit the capitalisation of interest on borrowed capital is an incomplete approach which suffers from arbitrariness and a lack of even-handedness.

Conversely, it may be argued that the capitalisation of borrowing costs into most types of property development is an entirely logical and appropriate policy. Interest is a development cost and is no different in this respect to the concrete, bricks and land. The ASB will, therefore, need to decide whether or not the arguments in favour of capitalisation of borrowing costs outweigh the disadvantages of allowing an accounting practice which often produces arbitrary results.

However, in the absence of a proper debate, the only reasonable conclusion would be not to permit the capitalisation of interest at all.

References

1   CA 85, Sch. 4, para. 26(3)(b).
2   ASB Discussion Paper, *Measurement of tangible fixed assets,* October 1996.

matched with the physical flow of goods with reasonable accuracy. In any event, even in the case of businesses which do not deal in perishable goods, this would reflect what would probably be a sound management policy. Consequently, in practice where it is not possible to value stock on an actual cost basis, the FIFO method is generally used since it is most likely to approximate the physical flow of goods sold, resulting in the most accurate measurement of cost flows. For example, Laura Ashley discloses a comprehensive FIFO stock policy:

Extract 14.2: Laura Ashley Holdings plc (1997)

Accounting Policies

Stocks and work in progress

Stocks are valued at the lower of cost and net realisable value. Cost is determined on a first in, first out basis.

The cost of Group manufactured products includes all direct expenditure and attributable overheads based on a normal level of activity. Net realisable value is the price at which stocks can be sold in the normal course of business after allowing for the costs of realisation and, where appropriate, the cost of conversion from their existing state to a finished state. Provision is made where necessary for non-current and defective stocks.

3.2 Cost flow assumptions which disregard the physical flow of goods

3.2.1 Weighted average

This method, which is suitable where stock units are identical or near identical, involves the computation of an average unit cost by dividing the total cost of units by the number of units. The average unit cost then has to be revised with every receipt of stock, or alternatively at the end of predetermined periods. The justification for this approach is that 'it is illogical to distinguish between similar stock items merely because different levels of cost existed at the time they were purchased or produced'.[18] In practice, weighted average would appear to be less widely used than FIFO as it involves more clerical effort, and its results are not very different from FIFO in times of relatively low inflation, or where stock turnover is relatively quick.

Nevertheless, there are certain businesses which hold large quantities of relatively homogeneous stock for which the weighted average method of stock valuation is the most appropriate. For example:

Extract 14.3: The Rugby Group PLC (1996)

Notes on the accounts

1   ACCOUNTING POLICIES

Stocks

Stocks are valued at the lower of cost and net realisable value after making due allowance for obsolete and slow moving items. Cost is based upon "First in, First out" or "Weighted Average" valuation methods and includes, where appropriate, a proportion of production overheads. Development land has been valued at its cost of acquisition and development.

However, given that the group has applied both the FIFO and weighted average bases to the valuation of its stocks, it would, perhaps, have been useful to know which basis has been applied to which stocks.

3.2.2   LIFO (last-in, first-out)

This method is, as its name suggests, the opposite to FIFO and assumes that the most recent purchases or production are disposed of first; in certain cases this could represent the physical flow of stock (e.g. if a store is filled and emptied from the top). This is in an attempt to match current costs with current revenues so that the profit and loss account excludes the effects of holding gains. Essentially, therefore, LIFO is an attempt to achieve something closer to replacement cost accounting for the profit and loss account, whilst disregarding the balance sheet. Consequently, the period-end balance of stock on hand represents the earliest purchases of the item, resulting in stocks being stated in the balance sheet at amounts which usually bear little relationship to recent cost levels. For this reason, LIFO is ordinarily not permitted to be used under SSAP 9[19] despite the fact that it is specifically allowed under the legislation.[20] However, since the balance sheet value of stock merely represents a deferred cost, and bears no relationship to the stock's worth to the firm, we do not see any conceptual difficulty in using LIFO in an historical cost accounting framework which is profit and loss oriented. The difficulty which does arise is that LIFO distorts the calculation of working capital ratios and makes inter-firm comparisons difficult. The simple solution to this would be to report current stock valuations as supplementary information (in any event, the Companies Act requires a company to disclose the difference between the replacement cost or most recent purchase price of stocks and their book value, where this difference is material).[21]

LIFO has not been widely used in the UK, principally because the Inland Revenue has never permitted its use for tax purposes. The position is different in the US, where the Internal Revenue Codes of 1938 and 1939 officially recognised LIFO as an acceptable method for the computation of tax, provided that it was used consistently for tax and financial reporting purposes. Therefore, if LIFO is used by individual companies in a group for tax purposes, it must also be used for reporting purposes in the financial statements of those companies as well as in the group financial statements.

Some companies have used LIFO as a method of attempting to solve the problem of accounting for changes in price levels, even to the extent of viewing it as a substitute for the cost of sales adjustment under SSAP 16.[22] Although this does achieve a measure of success in that the profit and loss account reflects current costs of sales, it does not fully adjust income for general price changes (although neither did the SSAP 16 cost of sales adjustment); in addition, there is the danger that the profit and loss account can be seriously distorted if stock quantities fall and cause very old costs to be included in cost of sales.

The revision in 1993 of IAS 2 had the effect of setting down the FIFO and weighted average cost formulas as the 'benchmark treatments' for determining the cost of inventories,[23] although LIFO was, at the eleventh hour, retained as an 'allowed alternative treatment'[24] (see 6.2.2 below).

3.2.3 Base stock

This is another valuation method which is permitted by the legislation[25] but not approved by SSAP 9 (using the same reasoning as for LIFO).[26] Under this method a fixed quantity of stock is stated at a fixed price and any amount over the fixed quantity is valued using more usual methods, such as FIFO. The philosophy behind this method is that any on-going business must hold a certain minimum quantity of stock at all times; this base level of stock is then viewed as being more in the nature of a fixed asset, rather than stock to be sold or consumed. The fixed quantity is taken to be that level of stock which must always be held to maintain normal operating levels. The base stock method is not permitted for tax purposes in either the UK or US, and is rarely seen in practice. It is important to note that the use of the base stock method would only be permitted by the Companies Act 1985 in the case of 'assets of a kind which are constantly being replaced where—

(a) their overall value is not material to assessing the company's state of affairs; and

(b) their quantity, value and composition are not subject to material variation'.[27]

The revision in 1993 of IAS 2 saw the elimination of the base stock cost formula as a permitted method of costing (see 6.2.2 below).

3.3   Illustration of the effect of different cost flow assumptions

The following example illustrates the practical effect of the FIFO, weighted average and LIFO cost flow assumptions:

Example 14.1

Company A's stock transactions for the three months ended 31 March 19X1 were as follows:

	Units	Unit cost	Unit selling price
		£	£
Stock on hand: 1 January 19X1	60	30	
January purchases	90	45	
January sales	(40)		60
February purchases	55	60	
February sales	(45)		100
March purchases	60	75	
March sales	(75)		130
Stock on hand: 31 March 19X1	105		

The company maintains its stock records on the perpetual system, and all purchases are made on the first day of the month.

The value of cost of sales for the three months ended 31 March 19X1 and closing stock at that date under various costing methods are as follows:

	FIFO	Weighted average	LIFO
	£	£	£
Sales	16,650	16,650	16,650
Cost of sales	(6,450)	(7,805)	(9,825)
Gross profit	10,200	8,845	6,825
Stock at 31 March 19X1	7,200	5,845	3,825

The above example illustrates that, under the historical cost framework, accounting for stock is merely a cost allocation process, and that stock disclosed in the balance sheet is no more than a deferred cost. Therefore, it is necessary to decide how much of the cost of goods available for sale during the period should be written off, and how much should be deferred. In this example, the total costs of £13,650 are allocated/deferred according to the three costing methods illustrated.

Clearly, the extent of the divergence in results under the three methods illustrated above is a function of the rate of price changes. In times of rising prices, FIFO tends to overstate profit because earlier and lower unit costs are matched with current prices, whilst valuing period-end stocks at the most recent costs which are the more realistic measures of current cost. Conversely, LIFO more realistically reflects profit by matching the most recent unit costs with current selling price, whilst valuing period-end stocks at the oldest and, therefore, less realistic unit costs.

An interesting example of a company which attempted to overcome this difficulty is Cookson. Until 1993, the company used the base stock and LIFO methods to value certain of its commodity stocks for profit and loss account purposes, whilst stating these stocks in the balance sheet at a FIFO valuation. The difference between the base stock/LIFO and FIFO valuations was included in reserves.

Extract 14.4: Cookson Group plc (1992)

Notes to the accounts

1 Accounting policies

Accounting convention

The accounts on pages 28 to 46 are prepared in accordance with the Companies Act 1985 and under the historical cost convention as modified by the revaluation of certain tangible fixed assets. Other than as stated below for certain of the Group's stocks, the Group accounts have been prepared in accordance with applicable accounting standards, including Financial Reporting Standard No. 3.

Stocks

All stocks are stated in the Group balance sheet at the lower of cost and net realisable value on the first in first out (FIFO) method. Cost comprises expenditure directly incurred in purchasing or manufacturing stocks together with, where appropriate, attributable overheads based on normal activity levels.

The valuation of stocks for the Group profit and loss account differs, for certain Group subsidiaries, from that required by Statement of Standard Accounting Practice No 9. An explanation and quantification of this departure from SSAP 9 is given in note 11 on page 38.

---

11 Stocks

	1992 £m	1991 £m
Raw materials	76.9	64.5
Work in progress	38.3	30.3
Finished goods	97.4	85.2
Total stocks	212.6	180.0

Certain metals and minerals stocks held by Group subsidiaries are valued in the profit and loss account on the Base Stock or, for certain overseas subsidiaries, the last in first out (LIFO) method. As market prices of the materials involved can fluctuate widely over a period, and because these companies are processors and not traders, the effects of such variations in stock values are not operating profits or losses. The use of the Base Stock and LIFO methods, together with covering arrangements for quantities in excess of Base Stock levels, causes the profit and loss account to be charged with the current cost of the materials consumed. The stock valuation for the balance sheet is at the lower of cost and net realisable value on the first in first out (FIFO) method. The difference between the Base Stock or LIFO valuations, where these methods are used, and the FIFO valuation is included in reserves. This amounted to a charge of **£4.1m** in 1992 (1991: £7.5m).

The directors believe that this method of accounting is more appropriate for these stocks than that required by Statement of Standard Accounting Practice No 9.

The above approach previously followed by Cookson may be compared with that which would be followed under current cost accounting, since the difference between the base stock/LIFO and FIFO methods included in reserves is broadly similar to a current cost reserve. Nevertheless, some might argue that the company's balance sheet presentation of stocks amounts to a form of reserve accounting which is contrary to UK GAAP, and that, under existing rules, the amounts at which stocks are stated in the balance sheet and profit and loss account should be the same.

In any event, in 1993 Cookson decided to discontinue this differential approach to stock valuation and adopt a more conventional FIFO policy in conformity with SSAP 9. This change in policy was described in the company's 1993 accounts in the following terms:

Extract 14.5: Cookson Group plc (1993)

Notes to the accounts

20 PRIOR YEAR ADJUSTMENTS [extract]

(c) Stock valuation

In previous years the valuation of certain stocks for the Group profit and loss account differed from that required by Statement of Standard Accounting Practice No. 9 (SSAP 9). These stocks were valued in the profit and loss account on the Base Stock or, for certain overseas subsidiaries, the Last In First Out (LIFO) method. As the market prices of the materials in question could fluctuate widely over a period, and because these companies were processors and not traders, the effects of such variations in stock values were not operating profits or losses. The use of the Base Stock and LIFO methods, together with covering arrangements for quantities in excess of Base Stock level, caused the profit and loss account to be charged with the current costs of the materials consumed.

In recent years, as a result of the combined effects of changes in some of the products concerned, in procurement and also in the composition of the Group, the Directors believe that it is no longer warranted to apply policies for these stocks which differ from that required by SSAP 9. Accordingly all Group stocks are now valued on the basis explained in the Accounting Policies in Note 1 and in accordance with SSAP 9.

The results for 1992 have been restated in the Group profit and loss account, reducing the operating profit for that year by £3.7m. Had the previous policy been applied for 1993, the effect on the results would have been negligible.

---

4 THE DEVELOPMENT OF SSAP 9 (REVISED)

4.1 The original SSAP 9

SSAP 9 was originally issued in 1975 because, as the preamble to the standard stated, 'no area of accounting has produced wider differences in practice than the computation of the amount at which stocks and work in progress are stated in financial accounts'.[28] The standard commenced by stating the basic requirement that stocks and work in progress should normally be stated at the lower of cost and net realisable value.[29] It made it clear that production overheads must be included in stock by requiring that 'such costs [of stocks and work in progress] will include all related production overheads, even though these may accrue on a time basis'.[30] Furthermore, it emphasised that the approach previously taken by some companies of excluding certain overheads from stocks on the grounds of prudence was unacceptable, by stating that 'in so far as the circumstances of the business require an element of prudence in determining the amount at which stocks and work in progress are stated, this needs to be taken into account in the determination of net realisable value and not by the exclusion from cost of selected overheads'.[31]

In relation to contracting work in progress SSAP 9 required a different treatment only in respect of those contracts which extend for more than one year.[32] Any work in progress in respect of contracts lasting less than one year had to be accounted for on the normal basis, i.e. at the lower of cost and net realisable value. This immediately gave rise to a conceptual problem in that activities which are identical in nature were required to be accounted for in different ways because of an artificial distinction based on an arbitrary duration. The difference in treatment arose from the requirement to include 'attributable profit'[33] within the balance sheet figure for long-term contract work in progress. In arriving at this balance sheet figure one also had to deduct any foreseeable losses and progress payments received and receivable.[34] This latter rule ensured that for the most part long-term contract work in progress was stated at the lower of: (i) cost plus attributable profit and (ii) net realisable value.

The reason why a different treatment is required for long-term contracts is that if the basic rule of accounting for stocks was applied to them this would result in an annual profit and loss account reflecting the outcome only of contracts completed during the year, which, in a contracting company, might bear no relation to the company's actual level of activity for the year. Obviously, if a company operated at the same level of activity over the years on contracts of similar size and duration there would be no real difference in the results reported each year under the percentage of completion and the completed contracts methods. However, in practice this is not the way things happen in any contracting industry and therefore attributable profit has to be accrued on uncompleted contracts in order to present a consistent view of the results of the company's activities during the period.

4.2   The need for revision

One of the accounting rules introduced by the Companies Act 1981 in its implementation of the EC Fourth Directive was that current assets are to be stated at the lower of their cost and net realisable value. This principle has been carried through to the Companies Act 1985 via paragraphs 22 and 23 of Schedule 4, which state that 'the amount to be included in respect of any current asset shall be its purchase price or production cost. If the net realisable value of any current asset is lower than its purchase price or production cost, the amount to be included in respect of that asset shall be the net realisable value.' However, this resulted in a conflict with SSAP 9, which required long-term work in progress in the balance sheet to include attributable profit. The legislation was not outlawing the inclusion of the attributable profit in the profit and loss account, merely the inclusion of it within the value of a current asset. Nevertheless, there was scope within the legislation to depart from the detailed accounting rules if this was necessary to give a true and fair view and if full details of the departure, including its effect, were given in a note to the accounts (the 'true and fair override').[35]

In so doing, there were essentially two approaches followed by companies to fulfil the requirement to disclose the details and effect of the departure from the statutory valuation rules:

Extract 14.6: The Plessey Company plc (1988)

16 Stocks [extract]

In accordance with the provisions of SSAP 9, attributable profit amounting to £36.6m (1987 – £35.0m) has been included in the value of long term contract work-in-progress. The directors are of the opinion that this departure from statutory valuation rules is necessary to enable the accounts to give a true and fair view.

Extract 14.7: The Peninsular and Oriental Steam Navigation Company (1987)

18 Stocks [extract]

To enable the accounts to give a true and fair view, attributable profit is included in long term work in progress. This is a departure from the statutory valuation rules but is required by section 228 of the Companies Act 1985. Work in progress is stated net of progress payments of £1,366.2m (1986 £1,090.8m) which cannot be allocated between the related cost and profit.

Representatives of the Department of Trade and Industry (DTI) had made it clear that they were unhappy with the use of the true and fair override in such a general way as it was intended that it only be used in very rare circumstances.

4.3   SSAP 9 (Revised)

As a result of the DTI's objections, a working party was set up by the ASC to review SSAP 9. This resulted in ED 40 being published in November 1986, and ultimately in the release of SSAP 9 (Revised) in September 1988. There were effectively no changes to the accounting and disclosure requirements contained in the original standard in respect of stocks and work in progress. The changes made, therefore, were only in respect of long-term contracts and were two-fold: one concerned the presentation of long-term contract balances within the balance sheet and was designed to meet the DTI's objections, while the other was a revision to the definition of a long-term contract and was intended to remove the problems associated with the arbitrariness of the twelve month rule within the definition in the original standard.

The requirements of SSAP 9 (Revised) in respect of stocks and work in progress are dealt with in 6 below; long-term contracts are dealt with in 7 below.

5   THE REQUIREMENTS OF THE COMPANIES ACT 1985

The legal requirements of accounting for and disclosure of stocks within a company's financial statements are included along with most other legal accounting requirements in Schedule 4 to the Companies Act 1985. There is no specific mention made in the legislation of long-term contracts. This is because the legislation treats all current assets in the same way and is the principal reason why SSAP 9 was revised.

5.1   Lower of cost and net realisable value

Paragraphs 22 and 23 of Schedule 4, which apply to all current assets and not just stocks, are very similar to paragraph 26 of SSAP 9 and provide that current assets should be stated at the lower of their purchase price or production cost and net realisable value.

5.2   Stock included at a fixed amount

As discussed at 3.2.3 above in the context of the base stock method of costing stock, paragraph 25 of Schedule 4 provides that stocks of raw materials and consumables which are constantly being replaced may be included at a fixed quantity and value provided that the overall value of such stocks is not material to the company's balance sheet and that their quantity, value and composition are not subject to material variation.

5.3   Determination of purchase price or production cost

The rules that apply in determining the cost of an asset are set out in paragraph 26 of Schedule 4, as follows:

(a)   the purchase price of an asset should include any expenses incidental to the acquisition of that asset, e.g. customs duties;

(b)   the production cost of an asset should include, in addition to the cost of the raw materials and consumables, any other directly attributable production costs, e.g. direct labour costs;

(c)   in the case of current assets, distribution costs may not be included in production costs;

(d)   in addition to the costs at (b) above there may be included some costs 'which are only indirectly attributable to the production of that asset'. Most commonly these would be costs that vary with time rather than production, e.g. rent, rates and insurance; and

(e)   'Interest on capital borrowed to finance the production' may also be included in stock. Capitalisation of interest is discussed in Chapter 13.

Any costs that fall to be included under (d) and (e) above can only be included to the extent that they accrue during the period of production, and the amount of any interest included must be separately disclosed.

5.4   Costing method and replacement cost

Paragraph 27 of Schedule 4 provides that stocks may be stated using FIFO, LIFO, weighted average or any other method similar to any of those, but whichever method is chosen, it must be appropriate to the circumstances of the company. However, where any item of stock is valued by one of these methods rather than at actual cost, the difference between the amount at which it is included in the financial statements and its replacement cost or most recent actual purchase price or production cost is required to be disclosed if that difference is material. A strict interpretation of the paragraph could require some meaningless disclosures to be given. However, in practice, if an amount is disclosed it is usually the total replacement cost of stocks. For example:

Extract 14.8: The British Petroleum Company p.l.c. (1996)

Notes on accounts

17 Stocks

		£ million
	1996	1995
Petroleum	**2,407**	2,144
Chemicals	**272**	315
Other	**64**	43
	2,743	2,502
Stores	**266**	312
	3,009	2,814
Replacement cost	**3,039**	2,966

In fact, BP provides considerably more replacement cost information in its 1996 accounts, thereby affording the reader the opportunity to gain a better appreciation of the group's performance. For example, in addition to a discussion in the Financial Review of the 1996 results in terms of replacement cost profits, the group prepares its profit and loss account in such a way as to show its operating profit for the year on both a replacement cost and historical cost basis, thereby illustrating the effects of stock holding gains and losses on the group results:

Extract 14.9: The British Petroleum Company p.l.c. (1996)

Group income statement

			£ million
For the year ended 31 December	Note	**1996**	1995
Turnover	1	**44,731**	36,106
Replacement cost of sales		**36,325**	28,648
Production taxes	2	**823**	673
Gross profit		**7,583**	6,785
Distribution and administration expenses	3	**3,704**	3,768
Exploration expenditure written off		**203**	177
		3,676	2,840
Other income	4	**516**	570
Replacement cost operating profit	5	**4,192**	3,410
Loss on sale or termination of operations	6	**(175)**	(3)
European refining and marketing joint venture implementation costs	6	**(341)**	–
Refinery network rationalisation costs	6	**–**	(965)
Replacement cost profit before interest and tax	5	**3,676**	2,442
Stock holding gains (losses)	5	**402**	2
Historical cost profit before interest and tax		**4,078**	2,444
Interest expense	7	**411**	498
Profit before taxation		**3,667**	1,946
Taxation	8	**1,107**	829
Profit after taxation		**2,560**	1,117
Minority shareholders' interest		**8**	(5)
Profit for the year		**2,552**	1,122
Distribution to shareholders	9	**1,102**	850
Retained profit for the year		**1,450**	272
Earnings per ordinary share	10	**45.5p**	20.2p

BP then takes this further by basing the segmental information of its result on a replacement cost basis, as explained in the following accounting policy note:

> ### Extract 14.10: The British Petroleum Company p.l.c. (1996)
> **Accounting policies**
>
> **Replacement cost**
>
> The results of individual businesses and geographical areas are presented on a replacement cost basis. Replacement cost operating results exclude stock holding gains or losses and reflect the average cost of supplies incurred during the year, and thus provide insight into underlying trading results. Stock holding gains or losses represent the difference between the replacement cost of sales and the historical cost of sales calculated using the first-in first-out method.

Clearly, therefore, BP provides substantially more replacement cost information than virtually any other major UK company. However, this is perhaps a function of the industry in which BP operates, since it can be strongly argued that results prepared on a replacement cost basis provide a more meaningful means of assessing the underlying performance of a company in the oil industry.

5.4.1 Most recent actual purchase price or production cost

It should be noted that paragraph 27(5) of Schedule 4 permits the use of the most recent actual purchase price or production cost rather than replacement cost if the former appears more appropriate to the directors of the company — although such disclosure is likely to have most relevance in the cases of companies which value their stocks on bases other than FIFO and is, therefore, rarely seen in practice.

5.5 Current cost

Paragraph 31 of Schedule 4 allows stocks to be included at their current cost. However, this treatment is rarely seen in practice, as almost all companies prepare their statutory financial statements under the historical cost convention. One notable exception to this is BG plc which prepares its primary accounts under current cost principles, and provides historical cost information on a supplementary basis. The company's auditors report on both sets of information, giving a 'true and fair' opinion on the current cost accounts and a 'properly prepared in accordance with the accounting policies' opinion on the supplementary historical cost information.[36]

Other companies which are subject to price regulation generally prepare their primary financial statements for shareholders on an historical cost basis, with the regulatory accounts being filed separately and made available on request. However, a significant number of such companies still append supplementary current cost information to their historical cost accounts.

6   STOCKS

6.1   The accounting and disclosure requirements of SSAP 9 (Revised)

6.1.1   *Suitable analysis of stocks*

Stocks should be stated in financial statements at 'the total of the lower of cost and net realisable value of the separate items of stock or of groups of similar items'.[37] (The constituents of cost are dealt with at 6.3.1 below.)

Stocks should be sub-classified on the face of the balance sheet or in the notes thereto, so as to indicate the amounts held in each of the main categories in the standard balance sheet formats contained in Schedule 4 to the Companies Act 1985.[38] These sub-headings are as follows:

- raw materials and consumables
- work in progress
- finished goods and goods for resale
- payments on account.[39]

In practice, most companies follow these classifications strictly and present stock as a note to the financial statements, as follows:

Extract 14.11: Smiths Industries plc (1996)

Notes to the Accounts

	Consolidated		Company	
	1996 £m	1995 £m	1996 £m	1995 £m
17 Stocks				
Stocks comprise:				
Raw materials and consumables	51.4	44.0	5.2	5.6
Work in progress	53.9	53.1	24.4	20.4
Finished goods	56.7	47.6	8.0	7.1
	162.0	144.7	37.6	33.1
Less: Payments on account	11.3	8.5	5.1	3.7
	150.7	136.2	32.5	29.4

The application of these classifications should, however, be done in conjunction with the requirements of Schedule 4, paragraph 3(3), which states that 'in preparing a company's balance sheet or profit and loss account the directors of the company shall adapt the arrangement and headings and sub-headings ... in any case where the special nature of the company's business requires such adaptation'.[40]

It is therefore the responsibility of the directors to ensure that the classifications used are appropriate to the nature of the company's business. Although variations are rarely found in practice, J. Bibby & Sons presents an example of a company which has analysed its stocks by segment as well as category:

Extract 14.12: J. Bibby & Sons PLC (1996)

   Notes to the accounts

		1996 £000's	1995 £000's
8	**Stocks**		
	Industrial	**41,079**	40,157
	Materials Handling	**29,751**	31,900
	Capital Equipment	**58,870**	58,948
		129,700	131,005
	Raw materials	**21,318**	17,553
	Work in progress	**10,726**	8,336
	Finished goods	**76,530**	85,184
	Residual interests in equipment	**21,126**	19,932
		129,700	131,005

In the opinion of the Directors, the replacement cost of stocks is not materially different from the value of stock as listed above.

6.1.2 Accounting policies

SSAP 9 requires that the accounting policies that have been applied to stocks should be stated and applied consistently within the business from year to year. In practice, the degree of detail given varies quite considerably, with some policies being comprehensive and informative, and others less so. For example:

Extract 14.13: British Steel plc (1997)

Presentation of accounts and accounting policies

VIII Stocks

Stocks of raw materials are valued at cost or, if they are to be realised without processing, the lower of cost and net realisable value. Cost is determined using the 'first in first out' method. Stocks of partly processed materials, finished products and stores are individually valued at the lower of cost and net realisable value. Cost of partly processed and finished products comprises cost of production including works overheads. Net realisable value is the price at which the stocks can be realised in the normal course of business after allowing for the cost of conversion from their existing state to a finished condition and cost of disposal. Provisions are made to cover slow moving and obsolescent items.

Extract 14.14: Booker plc (1996)

Principal accounting policies

Valuation of stocks

Stocks, stores and work-in-progress are valued at the lower of cost and net realisable value. Cost includes, where appropriate, production and other direct overhead expenses.

Extract 14.15: Sears plc (1997)

Accounting policies

Stocks and work in progress

Stocks and work in progress are stated at the lower of cost and net realisable value.

Nevertheless, we believe that the accounting policy for stock should at least provide the following level of detail of information (where applicable):

Stocks

Stocks are stated at the lower of cost incurred in bringing each product to its present location and condition, and net realisable value, as follows:

Raw materials, consumables and
goods for resale   –   purchase cost on a first-in, first-out basis.

Work in progress and finished goods   –   cost of direct materials and labour plus attributable overheads based on a normal level of activity.

Net realisable value is based on estimated selling price less any further costs expected to be incurred to completion and disposal.

6.2   Comparison with US and IASC pronouncements

6.2.1   *US*

In the US, accounting for stocks is governed by Chapter 4 of Accounting Research Bulletin No. 43.[41] As with SSAP 9, ARB 43 recognises that the matching concept is the main principle underlying the accounting for stocks. The underlying principles of the bulletin are as follows:

(a)   stocks should normally be stated at the lower of cost or market ('market' as used here follows a formula reflecting current replacement cost as well as net realisable value).

Depending on the character of the stock, in certain circumstances the rule of lower of cost or market may be applied to the total of stock (see 6.3.2 below); and

(b)   the basis of stating stocks and the cost flow assumption used should be disclosed and should be consistently applied. The assumption made on the flow of costs should be that which most clearly reflects periodic income. As discussed at 3.2.2 above, the LIFO method of costing is permitted – seemingly on the basis of fiscal considerations.

In certain circumstances, principally where there is an organised and liquid market at fixed prices (e.g. precious metals) with little or no selling costs, stocks may be stated at market value, even where this is greater than cost.

6.2.2   IASC

IAS 2, which was revised in December 1993 (effective 1 January 1995), has similar requirements to both SSAP 9 and ARB 43, Chapter 4. The principal rule is that 'inventories should be measured at the lower of cost and net realisable value'.[42]

In January 1989, the IASC issued an exposure draft, E32 — *Comparability of Financial Statements* — which proposed to amend, inter alia, the requirements of IAS 2. The main change proposed in respect of IAS 2 was that the base stock method should no longer be permitted, although LIFO would continue to be an allowed alternative.[43]

However, many commentators on E32 argued that the use of LIFO should not be permitted because:

(a)   fiscal considerations unique to particular countries do not provide an adequate conceptual basis for selecting appropriate accounting treatments; and

(b)   it is inconsistent to retain LIFO in an historical cost context as a partial attempt to account for the effects of changing prices without introducing other changes to provide a more comprehensive method of inflation accounting.[44]

These arguments persuaded the Board of the IASC to revise its proposals with respect to LIFO. Consequently, the IASC's Exposure Draft E38 (which was ultimately converted to the revised version of IAS 2) proposed that FIFO and weighted average cost should be the only formulas permitted.[45]

At its meeting in June 1992, the IASC Board reviewed the comment letters on E38 and agreed the substance of the provisions to be included in the revised IAS on inventories. In general, it was agreed that these should follow the proposals in E38 and, in particular, the Board confirmed that the revised standard should not permit the use of the LIFO and base stock cost formulas.[46] However, despite all this, the IASC Board had a last-minute change of heart and decided to retain LIFO as an 'allowed alternative treatment', although the base stock formula was eliminated as a permitted method.

Consequently, the stated preference or 'benchmark treatment' in the revised IAS 2 is for using either FIFO or weighted average as the assumption on cost flows, with LIFO as the allowed alternative treatment.[47]   However, where the LIFO cost formula is used, disclosure must be given of the difference between the amount of the stocks as disclosed in the balance sheet and either (a) the lower of the amount arrived at in accordance with either the FIFO or weighted average methods and net realisable value, or (b) the lower of current cost at the balance sheet date and net realisable value.[48]   The only exception to the benchmark and allowed alternative treatments applies in the cases of stocks of items which are not ordinarily interchangeable and goods or services which are produced and segregated for specific projects; in these situations, costs should be assigned on the basis of specific identification.[49]

The remainder of the revised standard describes how to arrive at historical cost and net realisable value as well as the disclosure to be made in financial statements, and follows the principles contained in SSAP 9.

6.3   Problem areas

6.3.1   *Constituents of cost*

Both SSAP 9 and the Companies Act 1985 require that stocks should be stated in the balance sheet at the lower of cost and net realisable value. Both SSAP 9 and the Companies Act 1985 also require that the purchase price of stocks shall be determined by adding to the actual purchase price paid any incidental expenses of acquisition, together with both directly and indirectly attributable overheads.[50]

SSAP 9 states that:

'The determination of profit for an accounting year requires the matching of costs with related revenues. ...

'In order to match costs and revenue, 'costs' of stocks should comprise that expenditure which has been incurred in the normal course of business in bringing the product or service to its present location and condition. Such costs will include all related production overheads, even though these may accrue on a time basis.

'The methods used in allocating costs to stocks need to be selected with a view to providing the fairest possible approximation to the expenditure actually incurred in bringing the product to its present location and condition.'[51]

SSAP 9 at paragraph 17 defines cost as being 'that expenditure which has been incurred in the normal course of business in bringing the product or service to its present location and condition'. Paragraph 17 goes on to say that 'this expenditure should include, in addition to cost of purchase, such costs of conversion as are appropriate to that location and condition'. Cost of purchase comprises 'purchase price' and 'any other directly attributable costs', and 'cost of conversion' includes 'other overheads, if any, attributable in the particular circumstances of the business to bringing the product or service to its present location and condition'.[52]

The term 'present location and condition' is not defined or explained in SSAP 9 and is therefore a matter of interpretation and judgement depending on the particular facts and circumstances surrounding the business in question. For example, in the context of a retail company, the particular circumstances of the business are that 'present location and condition' may be interpreted to mean positioned on the stores' shelves and ready for sale – i.e. point of sale. Safeway is an example of a company which adopts this approach:

Extract 14.16: Safeway plc (1997)

Statement of Accounting Policies

Stocks

Stocks are stated at the lower of cost and net realisable value. For stocks at retail stores, cost is calculated by reference to selling price less appropriate trading margins.

Cost of sales and distribution costs

Cost of sales represents the purchase cost of goods for resale and includes the cost of transfer to the point of sale.

Distribution costs represent the cost of holding goods at the point of sale, selling costs and the costs of transferring goods to the customer and include store operating expenses.

Appendix 1 to SSAP 9 incorporates ten paragraphs which deal with further practical considerations in respect of the allocation of overheads. Paragraph 10 of the Appendix reinforces the point that the allocation of all attributable overheads to the valuation of stock is a mandatory requirement of SSAP 9, and that even the prudence argument cannot be used as a reason for omitting selected overheads from allocation. Paragraph 10 reads as follows:

'The adoption of a conservative approach to the valuation of stocks and long-term contracts has sometimes been used as one of the reasons for omitting selected production overheads. In so far as the circumstances of the business require an element of prudence in determining the amount at which stocks and long-term contracts are stated, this needs to be taken into account in the determination of net realisable value and not by the exclusion from cost of selected overheads.'

This means that overheads should be allocated to the cost of stock on a consistent basis from year to year, and should not be omitted in anticipation of a net realisable value difficulty. Once overheads have been allocated, the carrying value of stock should then be reviewed in order to ensure that it is stated at the lower of cost and net realisable value.

For the most part there are few problems over the inclusion of direct costs in stocks. Problems tend to arise, however, over certain overheads and with regard to the question of how overheads are to be incorporated into stock valuation.

A   Distribution costs

By law, distribution costs may not be included in the cost of stocks (see 5.3 above). However, SSAP 9 defines cost as 'that expenditure which has been incurred in the normal course of business in bringing the product or service to its present location and condition'.[53] As a result, a company which includes in stock the cost of transporting goods from its factory to its warehouse in accordance with the standard may not be complying with the law. In practice, however, the costs of such transport are not likely to be material and the company can take advantage of paragraph 86 of Schedule 4 to the Companies Act 1985 which provides that immaterial amounts may be disregarded for the purposes of any provision of Schedule 4. Where such costs are material it may be necessary for the company to invoke the 'true and fair override'.[54] However, an alternative and perhaps more reasonable view might be that the 'distribution costs' referred to in paragraph 26 of Schedule 4 are costs of distribution to customers, and that therefore the costs of transporting goods to a warehouse would not fall within the meaning of the prohibition.

B   Selling costs

SSAP 9 states that normally only purchase and production costs should be included in the cost of stocks. However, in certain specific circumstances the standard recognises that it might be appropriate to include other types of cost in stock:

'Where firm sales contracts have been entered into for the provision of goods or services to customer's specification, overheads relating to design, and marketing and selling costs incurred before manufacture may be included in arriving at cost.'[55]

Although ordinarily such costs should be expensed in the period in which they are incurred, the matching concept requires, that in the above circumstances they should be deferred and matched against their related revenues.

IAS 2 specifically cites selling costs as one of the examples of costs which should be excluded from the cost of inventories and recognised as expenses in the period in which they are incurred.[56]

C   Storage costs

Storage costs are not costs which would normally be incurred in bringing a product to its present location and condition. However, where it is necessary to store raw materials or work in progress prior to a further processing or manufacturing stage, the costs of such storage should be included in production overheads. In addition, the costs of storing maturing stocks, such as whisky, should be included in the cost of production.

Storage costs were specifically addressed by the IASC in its revision of IAS 2, which now states that such costs should be excluded from the cost of stocks, unless they are necessary in the production process prior to a further production stage.[57]

D   *General/administrative overheads*

SSAP 9 makes it clear that the costs of general, as opposed to functional, management are not normally costs of production and should therefore be excluded from the value of stock.[58]   However, the standard recognises that in smaller organisations there may not be a clear distinction of management functions and that 'in such organisations the cost of management may fairly be allocated on suitable bases to the functions of production, marketing, selling and administration'.[59]   Overheads relating to service departments, such as accounts and personnel departments, should be allocated to the main functions of production, marketing, selling and administration on a basis which reflects the amount of support supplied by the service department to the particular main function.   SSAP 9 states that 'problems may also arise in allocating the costs of central service departments, the allocation of which should depend on the function or functions that the department is serving.   For example, the accounts department will normally support the following functions:

(a)   production — by paying direct and indirect production wages and salaries, by controlling purchases and by preparing periodic financial statements for the production units;

(b)   marketing and distribution — by analysing sales and by controlling the sales ledger;

(c)   general administration — by preparing management accounts and annual financial statements and budgets, by controlling cash resources and by planning investments.

Only those costs of the accounts department that can be allocated to the production function fall to be included in the cost of conversion.'[60]

IAS 2 adopts a similar approach to that of SSAP 9, stating that costs other than production overheads 'are included in the cost of inventories only to the extent that they are incurred in bringing the inventories to their present location and condition'.[61]   Consequently, administrative overheads which are not clearly related to production should be excluded from the cost of stocks.[62]

E   *Allocation of overheads*

SSAP 9 states that the overheads to be included in stock must be allocated on the basis of a company's normal level of activity.[63]   Unfortunately 'normal' is not defined although the standard does give some guidance as to the factors to be considered:

'(a)   the volume of production which the production facilities are intended by their designers and by management to produce under the working conditions (e.g. single or double shift) prevailing during the year;

(b)   the budgeted level of activity for the year under review and for the ensuing year;

(c)   the level of activity achieved both in the year under review and in previous years'.[64]

In practice, a normal level of activity is established by reference to the budgeted or expected level of activity over several years; however, during a start-up period, and until normal operating conditions are reached, the actual level of activity will generally be taken as normal. The reason for this is that it would arguably be unreasonable to expense to the profit and loss account start-up costs which are expected to result in future revenues. It has been suggested that the overhead recovery rate in a start-up period 'should be based on the level of activity which obtains when the plant is working at normal production capacity';[65] but this is unlikely to be done in practice as the first year's results will be depressed through the recognition of non-recurring costs involved in the start-up.

No matter how overheads are being allocated to stock, it is necessary to ensure that only 'normal' costs are being included and that 'abnormal' costs, e.g. excess scrap and the cost of excess facilities, are being expensed as period costs. This occurs automatically as a result of using standard costing, assuming that the standards are regularly reviewed and variances are properly analysed and appropriately dealt with. However, where a standard costing system is not in place, it is necessary for an exercise to be carried out to ensure that no such abnormal costs have been included in closing stock. It is important to bear in mind that this exercise should be carried out on all cost categories, including direct costs.

The overheads to be included based on the normal level of activity should be applied by reference to the most significant direct cost. Thus if a process is particularly capital intensive the overheads should be applied to stock by an overhead recovery rate based on direct machine hours, while if labour costs are more significant the recovery rate should be based on direct labour hours. In practice a recovery rate based on direct labour hours has often been used because, historically speaking, labour has been regarded as the key limiting factor on the level of production.

In computing the costs to be allocated via the overhead recovery rate, costs such as distribution and selling must be excluded, together with cost of storing raw materials and work in progress, unless it is necessary that these latter costs be incurred prior to further processing.

IAS 2 is more specific on this issue and states that the allocation of fixed production overheads should be based on the normal capacity of the production facilities, although the actual level of production may be used if it approximates normal capacity. 'Normal capacity' is defined as being the production expected to be achieved on average over a number of periods or seasons under normal circumstances, taking into account the loss of capacity resulting from planned maintenance. Consequently, the proportion of overhead allocated to a unit of production is not increased as a consequence of low production or idle plant, and overheads which are not allocated are recognised as an expense in the period in which they are incurred. Furthermore, in periods of abnormally high production, the proportion of overhead allocated to a unit of production is decreased so that stocks are not measured above historical cost.[66]

6.3.2 *Net realisable value*

As already discussed, it is the basic rule of accounting for stocks that they are stated at the lower of their cost and net realisable value. SSAP 9 defines net realisable value as follows:

'*Net realisable value:* the actual or estimated selling price (net of trade but before settlement discounts) less:

(a) all further costs to completion; and

(b) all costs to be incurred in marketing, selling and distributing.'[67]

Appendix 1 to SSAP 9 identifies the following situations where net realisable value might be less than cost:

'(a) an increase in costs or a fall in selling price;

(b) physical deterioration of stocks;

(c) obsolescence of products;

(d) a decision as part of a company's marketing strategy to manufacture and sell products at a loss;

(e) errors in production or purchasing'.[68]

In addition it points out that when a company has excess stocks on hand the risk of situations (a) to (c) above occurring increases and must be considered in assessing net realisable value. A provision will also be required for losses on commitments made for both the future purchases and sales of stocks.

SSAP 9 requires that the comparison of cost and net realisable value should be done on an item by item basis or by groups of similar items.[69] In the US, ARB 43 states that 'depending on the character and composition of the inventory, the rule of *cost or market, whichever is lower* may properly be applied either directly to each item or to the total of the inventory (or, in some cases, to the total of the components of each major category). The method should be that which most clearly reflects periodic income.'[70] The reasoning behind allowing the comparison to be done on an overall basis in certain circumstances, is that 'the reduction of individual items to *market* may not always lead to the most useful result if the utility of the total inventory to the business is not below its cost. This might be the case if selling prices are not affected by temporary or small fluctuations in current costs of purchase or manufacture. Similarly, where more than one major product or operational category exists, the application of the *cost or market, whichever is lower* rule to the total of the items included in such major categories may result in the most useful determination of income.'[71]

This highlights an important difference in approach between the UK and US. Net realisable value, as it would be applied in the UK, depends on the ultimate selling price of a completed product. Thus, a whisky distiller, for example, would not write down his stock of grain because of a fall in the grain price, so long as he expected still to sell the whisky at a profit. However, the US definition of market is partly based on *replacement cost*, so a different result might follow unless stocks are looked at in aggregate.

The following example illustrates the different effects that can be achieved by applying the 'lower of cost and net realisable value' rule to individual items, groups of items and to the total stock:

Example 14.2:   *Alternative methods of applying the lower of cost and net realisable value rule*

| | Value of stock at: | | Application of rule to: | | |
	Cost £	Net realisable value £	Individual items £	Major groups £	Total stock £
Group 1					
Item A	2,000	3,000	2,000		
Item B	4,000	2,500	2,500		
Item C	5,000	3,000	3,000		
TOTAL	11,000	8,500	7,500	8,500	
Group 2					
Item D	1,000	1,500	1,000		
Item E	8,000	16,000	8,000		
Item F	10,000	6,000	6,000		
TOTAL	19,000	23,500	15,000	19,000	
TOTAL STOCK	30,000	32,000	22,500	27,500	30,000

The valuation of £30,000 which arises from the application of the rule to the total of stock is not acceptable in the UK, as it results in what are regarded as realised losses being offset against what are regarded as unrealised gains. The valuation of £27,500 which results from the application of the rule to groups of similar items is acceptable, provided the individual items within the groups are sold together — because the stock is effectively being regarded as consisting of two major lines. The valuation of £22,500 is, of course, acceptable as it is the result of the strictest application of the rule.

The comparison of cost and net realisable value of finished goods is normally straightforward where there are established selling prices for the finished goods. Where a provision is required in respect of finished goods, the carrying value of any related raw materials, work in progress and spares must also be reviewed to see if any further provision is required.

Where the selling price of finished goods varies with the price of raw materials and there has been a fall in the price of the raw materials then some provision may be required in respect of any stock of the finished goods (as well as possibly being required in respect of stocks of the raw materials and any forward purchase contracts).

Often raw materials are bought in order to make different product lines. In these cases it is normally not possible to arrive at a particular net realisable value for each item of raw material based on selling price. Therefore, current replacement cost might be the best guide to net realisable value in such circumstances. If current replacement cost is less than historical cost, however, a provision is only required to be made if the finished goods into which they will be made are expected to be sold at a loss. No provision should be made just because the anticipated profit will be less than normal.

6.3.3 The valuation of high volumes of similar items of stock

Practical problems in the valuation of stock arise in the case of businesses which have high volumes of various line items of stock. This situation occurs almost exclusively in the retail trade where similar mark-ups are applied to all stock items or groups of items, and the selling price is marked on each individual item of stock (e.g. in the case of a supermarket). In such a situation, it may be time-consuming to determine the cost of the period-end stock on a more conventional basis; consequently, the most practical method of determining period-end stock may be to record stock on hand at selling prices and then convert it to cost by removing the normal mark-up. Not surprisingly, this method of stock valuation is known as the 'retail method'.

However, a complication in applying the retail method is in determining the margin to be applied to the stock at selling price to convert it back to cost. Since different lines and different departments may have widely different margins, it is normally necessary to subdivide stock and apply the appropriate margins to each subdivision. Furthermore, where stocks have been marked down to below original selling price, adjustments have to be made to eliminate the effect of these markdowns so as to prevent any item of stock being valued at less than both its cost and its net realisable value. In practice, however, companies which use the retail method, tend to apply a gross profit margin computed on an average basis, rather than apply specific mark-up percentages. This practice is, in fact, acknowledged by IAS 2 which states that 'an average percentage for each retail department is often used'.[72]

Marks & Spencer is an example of a company which applies the retail method:

Extract 14.17: Marks and Spencer p.l.c. (1997)

Accounting policies

STOCKS

Stocks are valued at the lower of cost and net realisable value using the retail method.

It is noteworthy that Appendix 1 to SSAP 9 states that this method 'is acceptable only if it can be demonstrated that the method gives a reasonable approximation to the actual cost'.[73]

6.3.4   Marking to market

The practice has developed, principally among commodity dealing companies, of stating stock at market value and also taking into account profits and losses arising on the valuation of forward contracts ('marking to market'). This represents a departure from the statutory valuation rules in that stocks are being stated at more than cost, but this is generally justified as being necessary in order to show a true and fair view. SSAP 9 does not specifically deal with this issue; in fact it is difficult to come to any conclusion other than that the requirement in the standard that stocks should be included at the lower of cost and net realisable value has, in this instance, been dispensed with. Advocates of marking to market would argue, however, that this is a specialised development to which the generality of SSAP 9 should not apply and which was not envisaged when SSAP 9 was being originally developed. Unfortunately the problem of marking stock at market value was not addressed when SSAP 9 was revised. However, as discussed at 6.2.1 above, there is support for this practice under US GAAP.

It is our opinion that, despite the departure from the standard, marking to market is acceptable in certain circumstances. We would suggest that appropriate criteria might be that:

(a)   the company's principal activity is the trading of commodities and/or marketable securities;

(b)   the nature of the business is such that the commodities traded do not alter significantly in character between purchase and sale;

(c)   the commodities are or can be traded on an organised terminal or futures market; and

(d)   the market is sufficiently liquid to allow the company to realise its stock and forward contracts at prices close to those used in their valuation.

7   LONG-TERM CONTRACTS

7.1   The accounting and disclosure requirements of SSAP 9 (Revised)

As has been discussed in 4.2 above, the need for the ASC's revision in 1988 of SSAP 9 arose principally as a result of the conflict which existed between the original statement and the Companies Act regarding the balance sheet measurement of long-term contract balances. At the same time it was decided to redefine 'long-term contract' so as to remove the problems associated with the arbitrariness of the twelve month rule within the definition in the original standard.

7.1.1   Definition

The original SSAP 9 defined a long-term contract as 'a contract entered into for manufacture or building of a single substantial entity or the provision of a service where the time taken to manufacture, build or provide is such that a substantial proportion of all such contract work will extend for a period exceeding one year'.[74] This definition had an illogical practical result in that two contracts which were identical in all respects except for duration had to be accounted for differently: a 51-week contract had to be treated as short term, whilst a 53-week contract had to be treated as long term. A possible solution to this anomalous situation might have been that if a company was substantially engaged in long-term contracts, then *all* contracts should be accounted for as long term on the percentage of completion basis — even if there were some which lasted for less than a year. Conversely, if a company was substantially engaged in short-term contracts, then *all* contracts should be accounted for as short term on the completed contracts basis — even if some contracts extended for more than a year. However, such an approach would not have been in compliance with the original SSAP 9, and would probably only have been acceptable on grounds of materiality.

SSAP 9 (Revised) removed the arbitrary nature of this one-year rule whilst, at the same time, retaining one year as one criterion which might distinguish a long-term contract. The revised definition is as follows: a *long-term contract* is 'a contract entered into for the design, manufacture or construction of a single substantial asset or the provision of a service (or of a combination of assets or services which together constitute a single project) where the time taken substantially to complete the contract is such that the contract activity falls into different accounting periods. A contract that is required to be accounted for as long-term by this accounting standard will usually extend for a period exceeding one year. However, a duration exceeding one year is not an essential feature of a long-term contract. Some contracts with a shorter duration than one year should be accounted for as long-term contracts if they are sufficiently material to the activity of the period that not to record turnover and attributable profit would lead to a distortion of the period's turnover and results such that the financial statements would not give a true and fair view, provided that the policy is applied consistently within the reporting entity and from year to year.'[75]

The practical impact of this revised definition is that short-term contracting businesses will probably be able to account for all their contracts as short term (even if some contracts extend for more than a year), and long-term contracting businesses will be able to account for all their contracts as long term (even if some are for less than a year). However, if a business is clearly in both the short-term and long-term contracting businesses, criteria must be established for distinguishing between such contracts, and appropriate accounting policies must be established and applied consistently.

However, it should be noted that whilst the revised definition of a long-term contract does eliminate the rigid one-year rule, it does create a new area of potential controversy with regard to the accrual of profit on short-term contracts. This is discussed at 7.3.4 below.

7.1.2 Turnover, related costs and attributable profit

Long-term contracts should be:

(a)   assessed on a contract by contract basis; and

(b)   reflected in the profit and loss account by recording turnover and related costs as contract activity progresses.[76]

The standard fails to lay down a method for determining turnover and merely states that 'turnover is ascertained in a manner appropriate to the stage of completion of the contract, the business and the industry in which it operates'.[77] SSAP 9 then states that 'where it is considered that the outcome of a long-term contract can be assessed with reasonable certainty before its conclusion, the prudently calculated attributable profit should be recognised in the profit and loss account as the difference between the reported turnover and related costs for that contract'.[78]   Based on this requirement, it would appear that the attributable profit is merely the balancing figure once 'turnover' and 'related costs' have been determined. One would therefore have expected SSAP 9 to define 'related costs' and require companies to disclose an accounting policy for the determination of 'related costs'. Instead it defines 'attributable profit' and requires an accounting policy which sets out how it has been ascertained. As a result, either turnover or related costs will be the balancing figure.

'Attributable profit' is defined as 'that part of the total profit currently estimated to arise over the duration of the contract, after allowing for estimated remedial and maintenance costs and increases in costs so far as not recoverable under the terms of the contract, that fairly reflects the profit attributable to that part of the work performed at the accounting date. (There can be no attributable profit until the profitable outcome of the contract can be assessed with reasonable certainty.)'[79]

This definition, however, raises the question as to whether or not a company is required to book a loss in the early years of an overall profitable contract merely because the high cost work of the contract is being carried out in the earlier years. In our view, this was clearly not the intention of SSAP 9 – provided that the overall profitability of the contract can be assessed with reasonable certainty.

See 7.3 below for further discussion of the problems associated with determining profit and turnover.

7.1.3 Accounting policies

SSAP 9 requires that companies must disclose their accounting policies in respect of long-term contracts, in particular the method of ascertaining both turnover and attributable profit. These policies must be applied consistently within the business and from year to year.[80]

Current reporting practice reflects a wide variety in the amount of detail given by companies in their accounting policies for turnover and profit recognition. BICC discloses fairly comprehensive policies:

Extract 14.18: BICC plc (1996)

Principal accounting policies

4 Turnover

Turnover represents amounts invoiced to outside customers, except in respect of contracting activities where turnover represents the value of work carried out during the year including amounts not invoiced. Turnover is recognised on property developments when they are subject to substantially unconditional contracts for sale. Turnover excludes value added and similar sales-based taxes.

5 Profit recognition on contracting activities

Profit on individual contracts is taken only when their outcome can be foreseen with reasonable certainty, based on the lower of the percentage margin earned to date and that prudently forecast at completion, taking account of agreed claims. Full provision is made for all known or expected losses on individual contracts, taking a prudent view of future claims income, immediately such losses are foreseen. Profit for the year includes the benefit of claims settled on contracts completed in prior years.

7.1.4 *The financial statement presentation of long-term contracts*

In order to solve the conflict between the original SSAP 9 and the Companies Act, the revised standard requires that long-term contracts should be disclosed in the financial statements as follows:

'(a) the amount by which recorded turnover is in excess of payments on account should be classified as "amounts recoverable on contracts" and separately disclosed within debtors;

(b) the balance of payments on account (in excess of amounts (i) matched with turnover; and (ii) offset against long-term contract balances) should be classified as payments on account and separately disclosed within creditors;

(c) the amount of long-term contracts, at costs incurred, net of amounts transferred to cost of sales, after deducting foreseeable losses and payments on account not matched with turnover, should be classified as "long-term contract balances" and separately disclosed within the balance sheet heading "Stocks". The balance sheet note should disclose separately the balances of:

   (i)   net cost less foreseeable losses; and

   (ii) applicable payments on account;

(d) the amount by which the provision or accrual for foreseeable losses exceeds the costs incurred (after transfers to cost of sales) should be included within either provisions for liabilities and charges or creditors as appropriate.'[81]

The 'amounts recoverable on contracts' represent the excess of the value of work carried out to the balance sheet date (which has been recorded as turnover) over cumulative payments on account. 'The amount and realisability of the balance therefore depend on the value of work carried out being ascertained appropriately. The balance arises as a derivative of this process of contract revenue recognition and is directly linked to turnover. In substance, it represents accrued revenue receivable and has the attributes of a debtor.'[82]

SSAP 9 is unclear as to what the circumstances are under which it would be appropriate to classify the provision or accrual for foreseeable losses within creditors, and it is our view that, under normal circumstances, these amounts should be included in the balance sheet within provisions for liabilities and charges.

7.1.5 Illustrative examples of the disclosure of long-term contracts

The following example is based on Appendix 3 to SSAP 9, and serves to illustrate the financial statement disclosure requirements of SSAP 9 as they apply to the various circumstances which might arise in respect of long-term contracts.

Example 14.3: *Application of the principles of SSAP 9 to long-term contracts*

The following assumptions apply to each of the contracts, and in each case the company's summarised profit and loss account for the year ended 31 October 19X9 and a balance sheet as at that date is illustrated:

(1) This is the first year of the contract.
(2) The company has only one contract.
(3) All payments on account have actually been received in the form of cash.
(4) All costs incurred have been paid in cash.
(5) All the information is as at the balance sheet date, 31 October 19X9.
(6) Share capital is minimal and is ignored.
(7) Any necessary finance is provided by bank overdraft.

Contract 1

	£'000
Turnover	145
Cost of sales	110
Payments on account	100
Costs incurred	110

Financial statement presentation of Contract 1 (SSAP 9, para. 30):

SUMMARISED PROFIT AND LOSS ACCOUNT for the year ended 31 October 19X9

	£'000
Turnover	145
Cost of sales	110
Gross profit on long-term contracts	35

SUMMARISED BALANCE SHEET as at 31 October 19X9

	£'000
Current assets	
Debtors	
Amounts recoverable on contracts [145 - 100]	45
Current liabilities	
Overdraft	10
Net current assets	35
Profit and loss account	35

Contract 2

	£'000
Turnover	520
Cost of sales	450
Payments on account	600
Costs incurred	510

Financial statement presentation of Contract 2 (SSAP 9, para. 30):

SUMMARISED PROFIT AND LOSS ACCOUNT for the year ended 31 October 19X9

	£'000
Turnover	520
Cost of sales	450
Gross profit on long-term contracts	70

SUMMARISED BALANCE SHEET as at 31 October 19X9

Current assets	
Stocks (Note 1)	—
Cash	90
	90
Current liabilities	
Payments on account [600 - 520 - 60]	20
Net current assets	70
Profit and loss account	70

Note 1
Long-term contract balances

Net cost [510 - 450]	60
less: payments on account	(60)
	—

Contract 3

	£'000
Turnover	380
Cost of sales	350
Payments on account	400
Costs incurred	450

Financial statement presentation of Contract 3 (SSAP 9, para. 30):

SUMMARISED PROFIT AND LOSS ACCOUNT for the year ended 31 October 19X9

	£'000
Turnover	380
Cost of sales	350
Gross profit on long-term contracts	30

SUMMARISED BALANCE SHEET as at 31 October 19X9

Current assets	
Stocks	
Long-term contract balances (Note 1)	80
Current liabilities	
Overdraft	50
	30
Profit and loss account	30

Note 1

Long-term contract balances	
Net cost [450 - 350]	100
less: payments on account [400 - 380]	20
	80

Contract 4

	. £'000	
Turnover	200	
Cost of sales	250	
Payments on account	150	
Costs incurred	250	
Provision for foreseeable losses	40	(not included in cost of sales above)

Financial statement presentation of Contract 4 (SSAP 9, para. 30):

SUMMARISED PROFIT AND LOSS ACCOUNT for the year ended 31 October 19X9

	£'000
Turnover	200
Cost of sales [250 + 40]	290
Gross (loss) on long-term contracts	(90)

SUMMARISED BALANCE SHEET as at 31 October 19X9

Current assets	
Debtors	
Amounts recoverable on contracts [200 - 150]	50
Current liabilities	
Overdraft	100
Net current (liabilities)	(50)
Provisions for liabilities and charges	
Provision for foreseeable losses on contracts	(40)
	(90)
Profit and loss account	(90)

(Note that the provision for foreseeable losses of 40 is not offset against the debit balance of 50 included in debtors.)

Contract 5

	£'000	
Turnover	55	
Cost of sales	55	
Payments on account	80	
Costs incurred	100	
Provision for foreseeable losses	30	(not included in cost of sales above)

Financial statement presentation of Contract 5 (SSAP 9, para. 30):

SUMMARISED PROFIT AND LOSS ACCOUNT for the year ended 31 October 19X9

	£'000
Turnover	55
Cost of sales [55 + 30]	85
Gross (loss) on long-term contracts	(30)

SUMMARISED BALANCE SHEET as at 31 October 19X9

Current assets	
Stocks	
Long-term contract balances (Note 1)	—
Current liabilities	
Overdraft	20
Payments on account [80 - 55 - 15]	10
Net current (liabilities)	(30)
Profit and loss account	(30)

Note 1

Long-term contract balances	
Net cost (after deducting foreseeable losses) [100 - 55 - 30]	15
less: payments on account	(15)
	—

7.2   Comparison with US and IASC pronouncements

7.2.1   *US*

In the US, accounting for contracting activity is governed by Accounting Research Bulletin No. 45 — *Long-Term Construction-Type Contracts* — issued in 1955. ARB 45 allows both the percentage of completion and the completed contract methods of accounting for long-term contracts, although it expresses a preference for the former 'when estimates of costs to complete and extent of progress toward completion of long-term contracts are reasonably dependable'.[83] It is emphasised under both methods that full provision must be made for anticipated losses.

7.2.2   *IASC*

The 1993 revision of IAS 11 — *Construction Contracts* — saw the removal of the completed contract method as an allowed method of accounting for construction contracts. IAS 11 now requires that when the outcome of a construction contract can be reliably estimated, revenue and expenses associated with the construction contract should be recognised by reference to the stage of completion of the contract activity at the balance sheet date.[84]

The stage of completion of a contract may be determined in a variety of ways, including: the proportion that contract costs incurred for work performed to date bear to the estimated total contract costs; surveys of work performed; or completion of a physical proportion of the contract work.[85] However, IAS 11 states that when the stage of completion is determined by reference to the contract costs incurred to date, only those contract costs that reflect work performed are included in costs incurred to date. Examples of contract costs which are excluded are: contract costs that relate to future activity on the contract, such as costs of materials that have been delivered to a contract site or set aside for use in a contract but not yet installed, used or applied during contract performance, unless the materials have been made specially for the contract; and payments made to subcontractors in advance of work performed under the subcontract.[86]

In the case of a fixed price contract, the outcome of a construction contract can be estimated reliably when all the following conditions are satisfied:

(a)   total contract revenue can be measured reliably;

(b)   it is probable that the economic benefits associated with the contract will flow to the enterprise;

(c)   both the contract costs to complete the contract and the stage of contract completion at the balance sheet date can be measured reliably; and

(d)   the contract costs attributable to the contract can be clearly identified and measured reliably so that actual contract costs incurred can be compared with prior estimates.[87]

In the case of a cost plus contract, the outcome of a construction contract can be estimated reliably when the following conditions are satisfied:

(a)   it is probable that the economic benefits associated with the contract will flow to the enterprise; and

(b)   the contract costs attributable to the contract, whether or not specifically reimbursable, can be clearly identified and measured reliably.[88]

When the outcome of a construction contract cannot be measured reliably, revenue should be recognised only to the extent of recoverable costs incurred and costs should be recognised as an expense in the period when incurred.[89] In both instances, when it is probable that total contract costs will exceed total contract revenue, the expected loss should be recognised as an expense immediately.[90] The amount of the loss is determined irrespective of whether or not work has commenced on the contract, the stage of completion of the contract, or the amount of profits expected to arise on other contracts which are not treated as a single construction contract.[91]

The revised IAS 11 also introduced the following new disclosures to be given by enterprises in respect of construction contracts:

(a)   the amount of contract revenue recognised as revenue in the period;

(b)   the methods used to determine the contract revenue recognised in the period; and

(c)   the methods used to determine the stage of completion of contracts in progress.[92]

In the case of contracts in progress at the balance sheet date, an enterprise should disclose each of the following:

(a)   the aggregate amount of costs incurred and recognised profits (less recognised losses) to date;

(b)   the amount of advances received; and

(c)   the amount of retentions.[93]

In addition, an enterprise should present:

(a)   the gross amount due from customers for contract work as an asset for all contracts in progress for which costs incurred plus recognised profits (less recognised losses) exceed progress billings (i.e. the net amount of costs incurred plus recognised profits, less the sum of recognised losses and progress billings); and

(b)   the gross amount due to customers for contract work as a liability for all contracts in progress for which progress billings exceed costs incurred plus recognised profits (i.e. the net amount of costs incurred plus recognised profits, less the sum of recognised losses and progress billings).[94]

7.3   Problem areas

7.3.1   *How much profit?*

Although SSAP 9 requires the accrual of attributable profit into long-term contract balances, it does not give adequate guidance on how the amount is actually to be computed. The following example illustrates difficulties which may arise under certain circumstances:

Example 14.4: Calculation of attributable profit

Halfway through its 19X1 financial year a company commences work on a contract that will last for 24 months. The total sales value is £1,200 and this is to be invoiced in total on completion of the contract. The total expected costs are £600 and these will be incurred evenly throughout the contract. Everything goes according to plan for the rest of the financial year. During the following financial year, 19X2, the company runs into problems on this contract and incurs additional costs of £100 which will not be recovered from the customer. At the end of that year the company is reasonably certain that costs to complete will still be the planned £150. Future experience bears this out.

Using the definition of attributable profit in paragraph 23 of SSAP 9, the profit taken could be calculated as follows:

	19X1 £	19X2 £	19X3 £
Total expected profit on contract	600	500	500
Percentage of contract completed	25%	75%	100%
∴ total profit to be attributed	150	375	500
Less: profit already taken	—	150	375
Attributable profit for the period	150	225	125

Some might hold the view that the above does not reflect the results of 19X2 and 19X3 fairly, however, as it effectively defers inefficiencies of 19X2 into 19X3. The additional costs in 19X2 are an unfortunate incident occurring in that year which, while impacting on the overall profitability of the contract, do not affect the costs to complete at the end of that year and should consequently be expensed in 19X2. A fairer allocation of profits might be as follows:

	19X1 £	19X2 £	19X3 £
Turnover (being sales value of work done)	300	600	300
Cost of sales	150	*400	150
Attributable profit	150	200	150

* Comprises anticipated cost of sales of £300 and the additional costs of £100.

Paragraph 9 of SSAP 9 states that 'any known inequalities of profitability in the various stages of a contract' should be taken into account in calculating the attributable profit. It then goes on to confirm the latter treatment illustrated in the above example, by detailing the procedures which should be followed in order to take the inequalities into account. The procedures are 'to include an appropriate proportion of total contract value as turnover in the profit and loss account as the contract activity progresses. The costs incurred in reaching that stage of completion are matched with this turnover, resulting in the reporting of results that can be attributed to the proportion of work completed.'[95] As the above example shows, it is in fact desirable that such inequalities be taken into account, as otherwise there may not be a proper matching of costs and revenues.

In the above example the inequality was an inefficiency which had to be taken into account by being written off as a period expense. Some inequalities have to be taken into account in a different way, however. For example, where a contract is split into various stages with each stage having a separate price established, it may be necessary to allocate the total contract price over all the stages to as to reflect the 'real' profit on each stage. Obviously, where each stage's price reflects the relative value of that particular stage, this is not a problem and no adjustment is required; however, where there has been a payment in advance (or 'front-end loading') some adjustment will be necessary or profit will be taken in advance and not over the duration of the contract as it is earned.

7.3.2 How much turnover?

SSAP 9 states that it deliberately does not define turnover because of the different methods used in practice to determine it.[96] It does require, however, that the means by which turnover is ascertained be disclosed. Although there are a wide variety of methods used, whichever is selected the amount should represent an appropriate proportion of total contract value.[97] The following example illustrates some of the more common methods of computing turnover:

Example 14.5: Determination of turnover

A company is engaged in a long-term contract with an expected sales value of £10,000. It is the end of the accounting period during which the company commenced work on this contract and they require to compute the amount of turnover to be reflected in the profit and loss account for this contract.

Scenario (i)   An independent surveyor has certified that at the period-end the contract is 55% complete and that the company is entitled to apply for cumulative progress payments of £5,225 (after a 5% retention). In this case the company would record turnover of £5,500 being the sales value of the work done. (If it is anticipated that rectification work will have to be carried out to secure the release of the retention money then this should be taken into account in computing the attributable profit — it should have no bearing on the amount of turnover to be recorded.)

Scenario (ii)   No valuation has been done by an independent surveyor as it is not required under the terms of the contract. The company's best estimate is that the contract is 60% complete. There is no real difference here from the first scenario. The value of the work done and, therefore, the turnover to be recognised is £6,000.

Scenario (iii) The company has incurred and applied costs of £4,000. £3,000 is the best estimate of costs to complete. The company should therefore recognise turnover of £5,714, being the appropriate proportion of total contract value, and computed thus:

$$\frac{4,000}{7,000} \times 10,000 = 5,714$$

If the costs incurred to date included, say, £500 in respect of unapplied raw materials, then the turnover to be recognised falls to £5,000 being:

$$\frac{costs\ incurred\ and\ applied}{total\ costs} \quad \frac{(4,000-500)}{7,000} \times 10,000 = 5,000$$

There are, however, other ways than cost of measuring work done, e.g. labour hours. The use of cost will tend to lead to an overstatement of progress (because materials are usually acquired upfront), and the use of labour hours might lead to a more realistic basis for computing turnover.

Note that in each of the above scenarios the computation of the amount of turnover is quite independent of the question of how much (if any) profit should be taken. This is as it should be, because even if a contract is loss-making the sales price will be earned and this should be reflected by recording turnover. In the final analysis, any loss arises because costs are greater than revenue, and costs should be reflected through cost of sales. In view of the different results that can arise from the use of different methods, the importance of disclosing the particular method used is highlighted.

The above example applies only to fixed-price contracts. Where a contract is on a cost-plus basis, it is necessary to examine the costs incurred to ensure they are of the type and size envisaged in the terms of the contract. Only once this is done and the recoverable costs identified can the figure be grossed up to arrive at the appropriate turnover figure.

7.3.3 Approved variations and claims

Appendix 1 to SSAP 9 states that 'where approved variations have been made to a contract in the course of it and the amount to be received in respect of these variations has not yet been settled and is likely to be a material factor in the outcome, it is necessary to make a conservative estimate of the amount likely to be received and this is then treated as part of the total sales value. On the other hand, allowance needs to be made for foreseen claims or penalties payable arising out of delays in completion or from other causes.'[98]

Due to the extended periods over which contracts are carried out and sometimes to the circumstances prevailing when the work is being done or due to be done, it is quite normal for a contractor to submit claims for additional sums to a customer. Such claims arise 'from circumstances not envisaged in the contract' or 'as an indirect consequence of approved variations'[99] and their outcome can be crucial in determining whether the related contract will be profitable. Because their settlement is by negotiation (which can in practice be very protracted), they are subject to a very high level of uncertainty; consequently, no credit should be taken for them until they have been agreed at least in principle. In the absence of an agreed sum, the amount to be accrued should be prudently assessed.

In practice, few companies give any indication as to how variations and claims are dealt with in their accounts; however, those companies which do deal with this matter in their accounting policies generally state that revenues derived from claims and variations on contracts are recognised only when they have been either received in cash or certified for payment.

7.3.4 Should profits be accrued on short-term contracts?

In discussing the revised definition of a long-term contract at 7.1.1 above, it was mentioned that the new definition creates a new area of potential controversy with regard to the accrual of profit on short-term contracts. This arises as a result of the last sentence of the definition, which states that 'some contracts with a shorter duration than one year should be accounted for as long-term contracts if they are sufficiently material to the activity of the period that not to record turnover and attributable profit would lead to a distortion of the period's turnover and results such that the financial statements would not give a true and fair view, provided that the policy is applied consistently within the reporting entity and from year to year'.[100]

The implication of this requirement is that even if a company is purely involved in short-term contracting work and has adopted the completed contract method, if it has a material amount of uncompleted short-term contracts at the year-end, they should be accounted for as long-term contracts — i.e. turnover should be recorded and profit accrued. Since many contracting companies are likely to be in this position, it seems that, on the face of it, most short-term contracts will have to be accounted for as long term — irrespective of the accounting policy adopted. Our view, however, is that this could hardly have been the standard's intention. Consequently, we believe that the crucial factor in applying this definition is to ensure that whatever policy is applied, it is used on a consistent basis. If contracts with a shorter duration than one year are accounted for as long-term contracts, this should be a stated accounting policy, and not applied only when it is expedient to do so.

7.3.5   *Inclusion of interest*

Paragraph 26(3)(b) of Schedule 4 to the Companies Act 1985 states that 'there may be included in the production cost of an asset interest on capital borrowed to finance the production of that asset, to the extent that it accrues in respect of the period of production'.[101] Appendix 1 to SSAP 9 deals with this issue in the context of long-term contracts, and states that 'in ascertaining costs of long-term contracts it is not normally appropriate to include interest payable on borrowed money. However, in circumstances where sums borrowed can be identified as financing specific long-term contracts, it may be appropriate to include such related interest in cost, in which circumstances the inclusion of interest and the amount of interest so included should be disclosed in a note to the financial statements.'[102]

It is our view that, provided that all the criteria for capitalisation of interest costs are met (e.g. qualifying assets, period of production, etc.), it is perfectly acceptable to do so. This is, in fact, the position adopted by IAS 11, which states that costs that may be attributable to contract activity in general and can be allocated to specific contracts also include borrowing costs when the contractor adopts the allowed alternative treatment in IAS 23.[103] (See Chapter 13 for a detailed discussion of the circumstances under which interest may be capitalised.)

References

1 SSAP 9, *Stocks and long-term contracts*, Revised September 1988, para. 16.
2 Accounting Research Bulletin No. 43, AICPA, June 1953, Chapter 4, *Inventory Pricing*, Statement 1.
3 IAS 2, *Inventories*, IASC, Revised 1993, paras. 4 and 16.
4 SSAP 9, para. 22.
5 See, for example, SSAP 9, para. 1; ARB 43, Chapter 4, Statement 2; and Eldon S. Hendriksen, *Accounting Theory*, p. 299.
6 SSAP 9, para. 3.
7 The term 'stocks' as used in this Chapter, includes 'manufacturing work-in-progress'.
8 This basic rule is entrenched in the UK, US and IASC pronouncements on stock: SSAP 9, para. 26; ARB 43, Chapter 4, Statement 5; IAS 2, para. 6.
9 SSAP 9, para. 17.
10 *Ibid.*

11 *Ibid.*, para. 18.
12 *Ibid.*, para. 19.
13 *Ibid.*, para. 3.
14 IAS 2, para. 7.
15 *Ibid.*, para 10.
16 ARB 43, Chapter 4, Statement 3.
17 SSAP 9, para. 4.
18 Accountants Digest No. 158, *A Guide to Accounting Standards — Valuation of Stocks and Work in Progress*, Summer 1984, p. 7.
19 SSAP 9, Appendix 1, para. 12.
20 CA 85, Sch. 4, para. 27(2)(b).
21 *Ibid.*, Sch. 4, para. 27(3). This requirement does not apply if stocks are valued at actual cost.
22 SSAP 16, *Current cost accounting*. This statement was withdrawn in April 1988.
23 IAS 2, para. 21.
24 *Ibid.*, para. 23.
25 CA 85, Sch. 4, para. 25.
26 SSAP 9, Appendix 1, para. 12.
27 CA 85, Sch. 4, para. 25(2).
28 SSAP 9 (Original), *Stocks and work in progress*, May 1975.
29 *Ibid.*, para. 1.
30 *Ibid.*, para. 3.
31 *Ibid.*, Appendix 1, para. 10.
32 *Ibid.*, para. 22.
33 *Ibid.*, para. 27.
34 *Ibid.*
35 CA 85, Sch. 4, para. 15.
36 BG plc, Annual Report and Accounts 1996, p. 36.
37 SSAP 9, para. 26.
38 *Ibid.*, para. 27.
39 *Ibid.*; CA 85, Sch. 4, Balance Sheet Formats.
40 *Ibid.*, para. 3(3).
41 ARB 43, Chapter 4, *Inventory Pricing*.
42 IAS 2, para. 6.
43 E32, *Comparability of Financial Statements*, IASC, January 1989, para. 29.
44 IASC, *Insight*, October 1991, p. 9.
45 E38, para. 19.
46 IASC, *Update*, June 1992.
47 IAS 2, paras. 21–24.
48 *Ibid.*, para. 36.
49 *Ibid.*, paras. 19 and 20.
50 CA 85, Sch. 4, para. 26; SSAP 9, paras. 17 to 19.
51 SSAP 9, paras. 1, 3 and 4.
52 *Ibid.*, paras. 18 and 19(c).
53 *Ibid.*, para. 17.
54 See CA 85, Sch. 4, para. 15. The company's directors will have to explain in the financial statements that their policy represents a departure from the statutory valuation rules, but has been applied in order to comply with SSAP 9 and is necessary to give a true and fair view. The full particulars and effects of the departure will also have to be given.
55 SSAP 9, Appendix 1, para. 2.
56 IAS 2, para. 14.
57 *Ibid.*, para. 14.
58 SSAP 9, Appendix 1, para. 5.
59 *Ibid.*, para. 6.
60 *Ibid.*, para. 7.
61 IAS 2, para. 13.
62 *Ibid.*, para. 14(c).
63 SSAP 9, Appendix 1, para. 8.

64 *Ibid.*
65 Accountants Digest No. 158, p. 12.
66 IAS 2, para. 11.
67 SSAP 9, para. 21.
68 *Ibid.*, Appendix 1, para. 20.
69 *Ibid.*, para. 26.
70 ARB 43, Chapter 4, Statement 7.
71 *Ibid.*, para. 11.
72 IAS 2, para. 18.
73 SSAP 9, Appendix 1, para. 14.
74 SSAP 9 (Original), para. 22.
75 SSAP 9, para. 22.
76 *Ibid.*, para. 28.
77 *Ibid.*
78 *Ibid.*, para. 29.
79 *Ibid.*, para. 23.
80 *Ibid.*, para. 32.
81 *Ibid.*, para. 30.
82 *Ibid.*, Appendix 3, para. 5.
83 Accounting Research Bulletin No. 45, *Long-Term Construction-Type Contracts*, AICPA, October 1955, para. 15.
84 IAS 11, *Construction Contracts*, IASC, Revised 1993, para. 22.
85 *Ibid.*, para. 30.
86 *Ibid.*, para. 31.
87 *Ibid.*, para. 23.
88 *Ibid.*, para. 24.
89 *Ibid.*, para. 32.
90 *Ibid.*, para. 36.
91 *Ibid.*, para. 37.
92 *Ibid.*, para. 39.
93 *Ibid.*, para. 40.
94 *Ibid.*, paras. 42–44.
95 SSAP 9, para. 9.
96 *Ibid.*, Appendix 1, para. 23.
97 *Ibid.*, para. 9.
98 *Ibid.*, Appendix 1, para. 26.
99 *Ibid.*, Appendix 1, para. 27.
100 *Ibid.*, para. 22.
101 CA 85, Sch. 4, para. 26(3)(b).
102 SSAP 9, Appendix 1, para. 21.
103 IAS 11, para. 18.

Chapter 15   Capital instruments

1   INTRODUCTION

The accounting treatment of capital instruments – shares and debt securities – by their issuer was not historically regarded as presenting significant problems in the UK. However, the substantial development of innovative forms of finance during the 1980s made the accounting profession ask whether the conventional framework for distinguishing share and loan capital, together with the Companies Act disclosure requirements, remained adequate. With the further development of financial derivatives in recent years this aspect of financial reporting has become increasingly complex.

The traditional distinction between shares and debt is clear. The issue of shares creates an ownership interest in a company, remunerated by dividends, which are accounted for as a distribution of profits, not a charge made in arriving at it. Loan finance, on the other hand, is remunerated by interest, which is charged in the profit and loss account as an expense. In general, lenders will rank before shareholders in priority of claims over the assets of the company, although in practice there may also be differential rights between different categories of lenders and classes of shareholders. The two forms of finance also have different tax implications, both for the investor and the investee.

In economic terms, however, the distinction between share and loan capital can be less clear-cut than the legal categorisation would suggest. For example, a redeemable preference share could be considered to be, in substance, much more like debt than equity, while on the other hand many would argue that a bond which will be converted into ordinary shares deserves to be thought of as being more in the nature of equity than of debt, even before conversion has occurred.

The fact that instruments which are otherwise similar in substance can have different tax and accounting consequences, because of their form, has encouraged the development of a number of complex forms of finance which exhibit characteristics of both equity and debt. The accounting profession has not always found it easy to decide how to balance competing considerations of substance and form in accounting for these instruments, especially since the fundamental distinction between debt and equity is rooted in form to begin with.

Many of these questions have been answered by FRS 4 – *Accounting for Capital Instruments* – which was issued in December 1993. This standard lays down a framework for distinguishing between shares and debt, and also between sub-categories of each. In addition, it prescribes how these instruments and their associated finance costs are to be measured, and lays down detailed requirements for the disclosure of their terms. This chapter analyses the standard and explains how it is applied in practice.

As explained in Chapter 9, the ASB has embarked upon a more fundamental re-examination of this subject under the umbrella of its financial instruments project (which looks at assets as well as liabilities). This may eventually transform the whole approach to accounting for share and loan capital, but the Board has acknowledged that any such changes lie a number of years ahead. This chapter refers to some of these longer-term proposals in passing, but otherwise confines itself to the accounting rules for capital instruments as they stand at present.

2   FRS 4

2.1   The development of FRS 4

2.1.1   TR 677

In 1987 the Technical Committee of the ICAEW published TR 677 – *Accounting for complex capital issues*. This Technical Release carried no mandatory status, but was issued as a discussion paper on which comment was invited. It was not subsequently developed into any more authoritative statement and has now been superseded by FRS 4.

TR 677 was a relatively brief document and, despite its title, dealt with relatively simple forms of financing instrument and discussed them only superficially. It put forward the following 'general principles':

(a)   When equity or loan capital is raised the amount of capital shown in the balance sheet should increase by the net proceeds of this issue after deducting proper expenditure incurred with third parties in the course of the issue. Such expenditure incurred may be allowed to be written off to share premium account.

(b)   Where the cost of repaying loan capital is greater than the proceeds of the issue the difference should be charged through the profit and loss account by instalments, calculated on an appropriate basis, over the period from the date of issue to the date of repayment.

(c)   Unless there are good economic reasons for taking another approach, the total charge to the profit and loss account in any year should be based on the effective annual rate throughout the whole period of the loan. Where the date or the amount of the repayment is uncertain, the amount of the charge in the profit and loss account should be related to best estimates available each time financial statements are prepared.

(d)   Cash proceeds received on the issue of options to subscribe for the company's own shares should be treated as capital.

(e)   Where a transaction has a number of constituent parts the accounting treatment of each should be considered separately, but having regard to the true commercial effect of the transaction taken as a whole.

(f)   The financial statements should disclose sufficient information about a complex capital issue for a reader to appreciate its nature and impact. In particular, where instruments, or parts of instruments, representing complex capital issues are quoted in the market, disclosure of market value at each balance sheet date may be useful.

An Appendix to the Technical Release discussed how these principles should be applied to various instruments.

2.1.2   UITF 1

The UITF published its first Abstract in July 1991.[1] This dealt with a relatively narrow topic: the accounting treatment of 'supplemental interest' on a convertible bond. Where a convertible bond was issued on terms which entitled the holder to receive an additional amount of backdated interest if he redeemed the bond, the UITF ruled that this supplemental interest had to be accrued from the outset. This outlawed the practice of ignoring the supplemental interest on the argument that conversion was likely to occur and hence that the supplemental interest would not become payable. The requirement was subsequently incorporated in FRS 4 and UITF 1 has been withdrawn.

2.1.3   The ASB Discussion Paper

In December 1991, the ASB published a Discussion Paper on capital instruments as the forerunner of the exposure draft of an accounting standard.[2] The paper addressed a wide range of issues, including the distinction between debt and equity and the measurement principles governing each category, together with their classification and disclosure in the balance sheet and profit and loss account.

2.1.4   FRED 3

One year later, in December 1992, the Board published the exposure draft of a standard on capital instruments, FRED 3.[3] This was based on the main proposals which had been set out in the earlier Discussion Paper, redrawn in the form of a draft standard, and it was subsequently converted into FRS 4 without substantial amendment.

There was a subsequent consultation on one additional matter: the appropriate accounting treatment when debt is renegotiated. Companies in financial difficulties sometimes reach an agreement with their lenders which allows them to reduce or defer their future payments of principal or interest under the debt. In these circumstances, the ASB proposed that the renegotiated debt should be stated at its fair value (based on discounting the rescheduled payments to their net present value) with a corresponding gain being recognised in the profit and loss account.[4] However, commentators criticised this proposal on the grounds that it was imprudent; in particular they noted that the amount of the reported gain would be inflated because the discount rate used in valuing the debt would reflect the collapse of the company's own credit rating, which seemed perverse. As a result of these comments, the matter was not dealt with in the eventual standard, although the general issue will re-emerge within the Board's financial instruments project.

2.1.5   UITF 8

In March 1993, the UITF published its eighth Abstract, dealing with the repurchase of debt.[5] This provided that, where a company purchased its own debt at a price which differed from the carrying amount of the liability on its balance sheet, it should account for the difference as a profit or loss in the year of repurchase. As with UITF 1, this requirement was incorporated in FRS 4 and the Abstract has been withdrawn.

2.1.6   FRS 4

FRS 4 was issued in December 1993. As mentioned above, it contained only minor changes from the exposure draft, and it incorporated the requirements of UITFs 1 and 8, as a result of which these two Abstracts were withdrawn. The main features of the standard are summarised in the next section, while its application to particular types of capital instrument is dealt with in 4 below. The standard itself contains a set of Application Notes which illustrate how the rules are to be applied in practice. FRS 4 came into effect for accounting periods ending on or after 22 June 1994. Its requirements are discussed in 2.2 below.

As more fully discussed in Chapter 9, in July 1996 the ASB published a wide-ranging discussion paper on *Derivatives and other financial instruments*, proposing a radical new approach to the recognition and measurement of share and loan capital (as well as other financial items) and also suggesting substantial new disclosure requirements. This was to be progressed in two stages, with disclosure taking precedence, and in April 1997 the Board duly published FRED 13 as the draft of a standard requiring these disclosures. The recognition and measurement proposals are less immediate, and the approach in FRS 4 is likely to remain in force at least until 1999 or 2000.

2.2 The requirements of FRS 4

2.2.1 The definition of capital instruments

The standard defines capital instruments as 'all instruments that are issued by reporting entities as a means of raising finance, including shares, debentures, loans and debt instruments, options and warrants that give the holder the right to subscribe for or obtain capital instruments. In the case of consolidated financial statements the term includes capital instruments issued by subsidiaries except those that are held by another member of the group included in the consolidation.'[6]

FRS 4 discusses the accounting treatment of capital instruments only from the issuer's point of view; it does not say how investors should account for such instruments. In addition, three particular classes of capital instrument are excluded from the scope of the standard:

(a)   warrants issued to employees under employee share schemes;

(b)   leases;

(c)   equity shares issued as part of a business combination that is accounted for as a merger.[7]

The first of these involves complex matters which the Board did not wish to address in this standard, although the UITF has since addressed certain issues concerning employee share schemes – see 4.7 below. The remaining two were already the subject of rules from other sources – see Chapters 17 and 6. FRS 4 also has a minor exemption for investment companies allowing them to charge finance costs to capital in certain circumstances,[8] the details of which are beyond the scope of this book.

2.2.2 The distinction between debt and share capital

The first main issue which the standard discusses is how to distinguish an instrument between debt and share capital (or minority interests in the case of instruments issued by a subsidiary). The ASB bases the distinction on the definition of a liability which it is developing under its *Statement of Principles*. This says that 'liabilities are an entity's obligations to transfer economic benefits as a result of past transactions or events',[9] so the Board's criterion is to classify all instruments which contain an obligation to transfer economic benefits as debt.[10] This applies equally whether the obligation is unconditional or merely contingent. This means that (for example) convertible debt has to be shown as a liability, rather than classifying it as shares on the argument that it is likely to be converted into shares in the future. It also applies to subordinated debt; even if debt is subordinated to the claims of all other creditors, that is not sufficient to make it equivalent to share capital, and it should therefore continue to be classified as debt.

Applying the above approach might be expected to result in redeemable preference shares being shown as debt. However, the standard does not go this far; any instrument which is part of the company's share capital must remain in the share capital section of the balance sheet. This may seem to be preferring form to substance, but the Board argues that shares should always be treated differently, because payments made under them are subject to legal restrictions and (more to the point) to classify them as liabilities would be in breach of the format requirements of the Companies Act.[11]

Nevertheless, FRS 4 does require shareholders' funds to be subdivided into equity and non-equity components, so that shares which have more of the character of debt are distinguished from pure equity shares. For this purpose, the standard has had to distinguish between these two categories and has done so by defining non-equity shares and making equity shares the residual category. The definition of non-equity shares is somewhat complex; they are defined as shares possessing any of the following characteristics:

(a)   any of the rights of the shares to receive payments (whether in respect of dividends, in respect of redemption or otherwise) are for a limited amount that is not calculated by reference to the company's assets or profits or the dividends on any class of equity share;

(b)   any of their rights to participate in a surplus in a winding up are limited to a specific amount that is not calculated by reference to the company's assets or profits and such limitation had a commercial effect in practice at the time the shares were issued or, if later, at the time the limitation was introduced; or

(c)   the shares are redeemable either according to their terms, or because the holder, or any party other than the issuer, can require their redemption.[12]

Some aspects of the definition are not particularly intuitive. A participating preference share, whose holder receives a dividend which is both partly fixed and partly variable, might be thought to be an equity share because the overall amount of the dividend is not limited; however, the relevant Application Note to FRS 4 says that they are non-equity shares, on the argument that the fixed element of the dividend is for a limited amount. This result suggests another way of looking at non-equity shares, as those whose holders enjoy a degree of priority over the equity shareholders, in the sense that they are entitled to receive certain amounts (provided they are available) without regard to the results of the company.

The standard similarly calls for shares issued by subsidiaries, and therefore shown as minority interests in the consolidated balance sheet, to be analysed into equity and non-equity categories. Arjo Wiggins Appleton provides an example of this disclosure:

Extract 15.1: Arjo Wiggins Appleton p.l.c. (1996)

19. Minority interests	**1996** **£m**	1995 £m
Equity interests	**2.3**	3.0
Non-equity interest	**1.1**	1.3
	3.4	4.3

The non-equity minority interest relates to Arjomari-Prioux S.A.'s holding of 100,000 Class B shares of FFR 100 each, fully paid, in the capital of Arjo Wiggins S.A., which carry a right to a priority dividend. The company has an option to acquire these shares at their par value, plus accrued interest, in the event of liquidation of Arjo Wiggins S.A., or if the total shareholding of Arjomari-Prioux S.A. in the Company falls to below 5%.

The minority interests in the Group's profit and loss account relate entirely to equity interests.

FRS 4 goes further than it was able to do with shares of the reporting entity by saying that shares held by minorities are sometimes equivalent to debt from the group's point of view and should therefore be shown as such. This would apply if any member of the group had an obligation to transfer economic benefits to the minority shareholder, for example if the parent company guaranteed the redemption of these shares.[13] Arjo Wiggins Appleton is also in this position:

Extract 15.2: Arjo Wiggins Appleton p.l.c. (1996)

13 Borrowings [extract]

During the year, the Group raised £364.7 million through the issue, by a subsidiary undertaking, of cumulative redeemable preference shares, denominated in sterling and French francs, to a consortium of banks. In accordance with FRS 4 'Capital instruments', these preference shares are classified as unsecured bank loans in the Group accounts, as the Company has undertaken to purchase the shares, in the event of the subsidiary failing to make the expected payments, and has, accordingly, provided guarantees. The consolidated balance sheet as at 31 December 1996 includes borrowings of £341.9 million in respect of these shares, the reduction being due to the retranslation of the French franc tranche.

Sometimes, however, such a guarantee will be subordinated to such a degree that the rights of the holder of the shares in the subsidiary are no greater than those of a preference shareholder of the parent. If this is the case, FRS 4 allows the shares to remain in minority interests.[14] Grand Metropolitan shows an example of this:

> **Extract 15.3: Grand Metropolitan Public Limited Company (1996)**
>
> **27 Minority interests – non-equity**
> Non-equity minority interests of £390m *(1995 – £349m)* comprise £354m of 9.42% and £36m of 7.973% cumulative guaranteed preferred securities issued by subsidiaries. The holders of these securities have no rights against group companies other than the issuing entity and, to the extent prescribed by the guarantee, the company. The guarantee in relation to these securities has been structured so as to place the holders of the securities in the same position in relation to the company as are the holders of the most senior preference shares of the company. To the extent that payments due under the guarantee are not made because the company has insufficient distributable profits, the company has covenanted that it will not make any distribution on any share capital which ranks junior to these securities.

One potentially controversial matter is the classification of hybrid instruments which have characteristics of both debt and equity, such as convertible debt. As discussed in 4.2.4 below, in the years before the standard was issued some companies had developed the practice of showing certain convertible debt instruments in their balance sheet under share capital, on the argument that conversion into equity was highly probable. The standard takes a contrary view. Although it concedes that it is not certain that such instruments will result in the transfer of economic benefits, and therefore fall within the definition of a liability, it takes the view that any future conversion should not be anticipated, and that accordingly hybrid instruments should be classified according to their present form, although disclosed separately from other liabilities on the face of the balance sheet.[15]

An alternative approach would have been to split hybrid instruments into their debt and equity components, as has been proposed by the IASC[16] (see 5.2 below). The ASB's earlier Discussion Paper invited comments on two variants of this, described in an Appendix to the Discussion Paper as 'split accounting' and the 'imputed interest approach'.[17]

These attempt to recognise the substance of the convertible bond as a hybrid instrument with debt and equity elements – a combination of straight debt and an option or warrant – and account separately for each of the two components.

The steps involved in split accounting are as follows:

1   The net proceeds received from the issue of convertible debt are analysed between the amount that represents the liability and the amount in respect of the conversion rights. These two components are thereafter accounted for entirely separately.

2   The liability is accounted for as any other debt. As the amount repayable on redemption will normally exceed the amount allocated to the debt at the time of issue, a finance cost, additional to the coupon actually paid, will be accrued in each accounting period.

3   The amount of the proceeds which relates to the conversion rights is accounted for as a warrant. (See 2.2.8 below.)

4   In the event of conversion the liability is extinguished. The carrying amount of the liability is credited to called up share capital and share premium account.

The 'imputed interest' approach is similar in concept, but the accounting treatment is slightly different in its effect. It was originally proposed in TR 677, which suggested that 'an adjustment may need to be made to charge a fair interest cost in the profit and loss account and to treat the difference as a payment received for an option'.[18] In other words the proceeds of issue of the bond should be accounted for in the normal way, but thereafter the profit and loss account should be charged with a market rate of interest, with the excess charge over the actual coupon paid being credited to a capital reserve which is built up over the life of the bond to represent the equivalent of option proceeds, discussed at 2.2.8 below.

An example of these two approaches is shown below:

Example 15.1:   Split accounting and imputed interest

A company issues a bond for £50 million with an interest rate of 8% per annum, at a time when general interest rates indicate a rate of 12% per annum for straight borrowing. The bond is convertible into shares of the company after five years, and is otherwise redeemable at par. (Issue costs are ignored in this example.)

The 'split accounting' approach would analyse the proceeds of issue of the bond between two elements: one amount taken immediately to capital reserve to represent the value of the 'warrant' inherent in the bond, and the remainder shown as the liability under the straight borrowing element, in relation to which the coupon paid would represent a market rate of interest. The split would be made by discounting the interest payments of £4,000,000 per annum and the amount payable on redemption of £50,000,000 at 12%, to give a net present value of £42,790,000. The £7,210,000 difference between that and the proceeds of the issue is regarded as the amount attributable to the warrant and taken to reserves: in addition the £42,790,000 is built up to the redemption value of £50,000,000 by an additional finance cost charged in the profit and loss account. The mechanics would be as follows (all figures in £000s):

Year	Total finance cost	Interest paid	Amortisation of discount	Capital reserve
1	5,135	4,000	1,135	7,210
2	5,271	4,000	1,271	7,210
3	5,424	4,000	1,424	7,210
4	5,594	4,000	1,594	7,210
5	5,786	4,000	1,786	7,210
Total	27,210	20,000	7,210	

The 'imputed interest' method would calculate a finance cost of £6,000,000 per annum, being £50,000,000 at 12%. The £2,000,000 difference between that and the interest payment of

£4,000,000 is credited to capital reserve each year. The mechanics would be as follows (all figures in £000s):

Year	Total finance cost	Interest paid	'Warrant element'	Capital reserve
1	6,000	4,000	2,000	2,000
2	6,000	4,000	2,000	4,000
3	6,000	4,000	2,000	6,000
4	6,000	4,000	2,000	8,000
5	6,000	4,000	2,000	10,000
Total	30,000	20,000	10,000	

The essential difference between the two approaches is that split accounting accounts for the warrant element at the time of the issue of the bonds rather than building it up over their life, and takes account of the time value of money in making the split, in effect by discounting the value applied to the option element.

Such an analysis has obvious merit in reflecting the economic substance of the arrangement, but is regarded as rather too radical for the time being. FRS 4 rules out such an approach. It says that capital instruments should be accounted for separately only if they are capable of being transferred, cancelled or redeemed independently of each other.[19] Thus, for example, loan stock issued with detachable warrants would be accounted for as two instruments and the proceeds of the issue split between the two for accounting purposes, whereas convertible loan stock (which is very similar in substance) would be accounted for as one.

One problem with FRS 4's approach is that it continues to take hybrid instruments at face value, with the result that the finance cost is manipulable based on the terms of the instrument. In an extreme case, it could even be negative, as shown in this example:

Example 15.2:   Convertible bonds with negative finance cost

A company issues convertible debt for £1,000,000 which is repayable at £900,000. The debt carries no coupon; to compensate for this, the conversion terms are extremely favourable. However, FRS 4 does not permit conversion to be assumed, and says that the finance cost must be measured on the assumption that conversion will not take place. The finance cost is negative as a result and the company can therefore *credit* £100,000 to its profit and loss account over the life of the instrument. When the conversion option is exercised at the end of that period, the apparent consideration for the shares would be £900,000. (When shares are issued by conversion of debt, FRS 4 says that the consideration for the issue is the carrying amount of the debt immediately before conversion.)[20] However, it is obviously questionable whether this could be regarded as giving a true and fair view.

In substance, this is more like a warrant than a convertible debt, because the likelihood of redemption must be very small.[21] The example could be taken to a greater extreme by reducing the putative redemption amount yet further – even down to a negligible amount. FRS 4 would continue to imply that the whole of the difference between the amount subscribed and the amount available if the bond were not converted would be credited to the profit and loss account over the life of the instrument.

Clearly, a negative overall finance cost from such an arrangement would be regarded as too ridiculous to accept. However, a very low positive cost – perhaps even down to zero – might not. This is the essential weakness of accounting for hybrid instruments as if they were straight debt, which a split accounting approach would have gone some way to remedy.

Practice in this area is mixed. Granada shows a negative component of finance cost in relation to convertible preference shares which have a redemption option at a price below their issue price, as shown in this extract:

Extract 15.4: Granada Group PLC (1996)

	1996 £m	1995 £m
10 Dividends		
Equity shares:		
Interim Dividend of 4.235p (1995: 3.85p) per share, paid 2 October 1996	**34.9**	22.6
Proposed final dividend of 8.765p (1995: 7.9p) per share, payable 1 April 1997	**74.8**	46.2
	109.7	68.8
Non-equity shares:		
Dividend of 7.5p per share, paid in two instalments on 31 January and 31 July 1996	**13.1**	13.1
Finance credit (FRS 4)	**(1.2)**	(1.2)
	11.9	11.9
	121.6	80.7

In contrast, Williams Holdings has the same kind of instrument but has not taken credit for this negative component. This may reflect its view that redemption is unlikely to occur so that the potential profit on redemption will never materialise, or it may simply be on grounds of materiality (the total premium is about £8 million, to be spread over the term of the instrument).

Extract 15.5: Williams Holdings PLC (1996)

8 Dividends	1996 £m	1995 £m
Ordinary – interim paid 5.80p per share (1995 5.50p)	33.8	32.1
final proposed 9.25p per share (1995 8.75p)	53.8	50.8
Total equity	87.6	82.9
10¾% cumulative preference shares	0.2	0.2
8½% cumulative redeemable preference shares	2.1	2.1
8.0p cumulative convertible redeemable preference shares	21.6	21.6
Total non-equity	23.9	23.9
Total dividends	111.5	106.8

20 Share capital [extract]

Conversion and redemption details

(a) The 8.0p preference shares, which were issued at 103p, a premium over redemption value of 3p, are convertible to ordinary shares at the shareholders' option on the basis of 0.31746 ordinary shares for each 8.0p preference share, up to a maximum of 85.4m ordinary shares, in May of each year to 2008 inclusive. If not converted, the shares may be redeemed at the company's option within the period from 30th June 2008 to 30th December 2018. If not converted or redeemed by 30th December 2018, all outstanding shares will be redeemed at 100p on 31st December 2018.

2.2.3 The accounting treatment of debt instruments

Under FRS 4, debt should initially be recorded in the balance sheet at the fair value of the consideration received upon issue, less the amount of issue costs.[22] Usually, the consideration received is cash, and there is thus no difficulty in determining its value. Thereafter, the difference between that amount and the total payments required to be made under the debt (interest and repayment of principal together with any premium) represents the total finance cost,[23] which is accounted for over the term of the debt. Except to the extent that it may be capitalised (see Chapter 13), this finance cost should be charged to the profit and loss account over the term at a constant rate of interest on the outstanding amount of the debt.[24] The carrying value of the debt is increased annually by the amount of the finance cost relating to that period, and reduced by the amount of payments made.[25]

The measurement of the finance cost is discussed in more detail in 2.2.5 below, and the mechanics of the process are illustrated in the Examples shown in 4.1.

If debt is repurchased or settled before its maturity, the difference between the amount repaid and the carrying value should be recognised immediately in the profit and loss account.[26] The repurchase of debt is discussed further in 2.2.6 below.

2.2.4 *The accounting treatment of share capital*

With the exception of shares issued in a business combination which is accounted for as a merger, share issues should be recorded at the net proceeds received. These net proceeds are taken direct to shareholders' funds and reported in the reconciliation of movements in shareholders' funds.[27] As in the case of debt, 'net proceeds' is defined as the fair value of the consideration received less costs that are incurred directly in connection with the issue.[28]

In the majority of cases, shares are issued for cash and therefore the fair value of the consideration received will be easy to determine. In some circumstances, however (e.g. where shares are issued for property), the fair value of the consideration received may not be so easily determined and external valuations may be required. Although the standard focuses on the value of the consideration for the shares, sometimes it may be expedient to consider the market value of the shares issued, to provide indirect evidence of the fair value of non-cash consideration received for them.

The standard does not give guidance on how to allocate 'net proceeds' to the various elements of total shareholders' funds. However, this is dictated by company law; the amount at which share capital is recorded is determined by the nominal value of the shares issued. If the net proceeds from the issue exceed that amount, the excess is to be recorded as share premium.

Issue costs are regarded as inseparable from the consideration received, and are therefore taken straight to reserves; they should not be disclosed in either the statement of total recognised gains and losses or the profit and loss account. Provided the Companies Act conditions are satisfied, they may be set off against any share premium account.

The mechanics of a simple equity share issue are shown in the following example:

Example 15.3:   Equity share issue

A company issues 1 million £1 ordinary shares at par. Issue costs of £20,000 are incurred.

If there is a share premium account in existence, the share issue may be recorded by increasing share capital by £1,000,000 and setting off the issue costs against share premium account. In the analysis of total shareholders' funds, the equity interests will have increased by £980,000.

If there is no share premium account, share capital will be increased by £1,000,000 but the issue costs would be deducted from another reserve (usually profit and loss account reserve) subject to the provisions of the company's articles. Prior to FRS 4, companies in this situation had to charge the issue costs to the profit and loss account for the year.

The accounting for non-equity shares is slightly different, because finance costs are to be measured in the same way as for debt instruments,[29] except that they are shown as an appropriation in the profit and loss account rather than as an expense. The effect of this is that, for non-equity shares with a finite term, although issue costs are initially taken to reserves in the same way as for equity shares, they are subsequently recycled through the profit and loss account as an appropriation and charged in arriving at earnings per share.

Example 15.4:   Non-equity share issue

A company issues 1 million £1 redeemable preference shares at par. Issue costs of £20,000 are incurred. The shares carry a coupon of 7% and are redeemable at par in five years.

In the same way as for the equity share issue in Example 15.3 above, the non-equity interests will increase by £980,000 in the analysis of total shareholders' funds. However, thereafter the appropriation in the profit and loss account will include not only the £70,000 dividend but also an annual instalment to write off the issue costs. This has the effect of transferring £20,000 from equity shareholders' funds to non-equity shareholders' funds over the five year life of the preference shares, at the end of which the non-equity shareholders' funds will be stated at the redemption amount of £1 million.

However, where the non-equity share has no finite term, for example if it is an irredeemable preference share, it will not be appropriate to make this transfer and the issue costs will thus be dealt with in the same way as for equity shares.

2.2.5   The allocation of finance costs

As mentioned at 2.2.3 above, the standard requires that finance costs should be accounted for over the life of the instrument at a constant rate on the carrying amount – in other words, at the effective rate implicit in all the cash flows which are to be made.[30] This may sound complex, but it is in fact what happens automatically in the case of a simple loan on which the interest is paid over the term of the loan. However, the requirement also accommodates more complex forms of borrowing, such as where a premium is payable on redemption, or the interest is not paid evenly over the life of the loan.

Finance costs are defined by FRS 4 as 'the difference between the net proceeds of an instrument and the total amount of the payments (or other transfers of economic benefits) that the issuer may be required to make in respect of the instrument'.[31] When this definition refers to 'net proceeds', it means that the costs of issuing the instrument are to be deducted from the amount raised, with the result that such costs are to be spread over the life of the instrument as part of the finance cost. Issue costs are defined as 'the costs that are incurred directly in connection with the issue of a capital instrument, that is, those costs that would not have been incurred had the specific instrument in question not been issued'.[32] This definition is deliberately restrictive; it extends only to incremental costs, not to allocations of fixed costs, and they must be specific to the instrument in question.

It would be possible to interpret these words very narrowly indeed, by considering which of the costs would have been avoided on the hypothesis that an alternative instrument had been substituted for the actual instrument issued, and deciding that only these costs are specific to the actual instrument issued.

However, we doubt if such a narrow interpretation is intended. The costs of the actual issue will generally fall within the definition, even if they are not peculiar to the particular instrument chosen.

Examples of costs that qualify as issue costs include underwriting fees, or arrangement fees to cover the administrative work involved in assessing and setting up the loan. Examples of costs that would not qualify include:

(a)   costs of ascertaining the suitability or feasibility of particular instruments;

(b)   costs of researching different sources of finance;

(c)   allocations of internal costs that would have been incurred had the instrument not been issued (e.g. management remuneration);

(d)   costs of viability studies commissioned by the lender which are borne by the issuer;

(e)   costs of a financial restructuring or renegotiation (as they are incurred primarily to establish whether the whole exercise is worthwhile rather than related to the issue of replacement finance which occurs later).

The principles apply not only to debt but also to non-equity shares,[33] except that dividends and transfers to reserves are to be dealt with as appropriations of profit, whereas the costs of debt will be charged in arriving at profit before taxation. Where the instrument is classified as a minority interest, the finance cost will again be calculated in the same way, but included in minority interests in the profit and loss account.[34]

Under FRS 4, the term of a debt instrument has a direct impact on the calculation and allocation of the finance costs of the instrument. Oddly enough, it does not determine the classification of debt between short term and long term nor any other analysis of the maturity of debt. Separate rules apply here – see 2.2.7 below.

The term of an instrument is defined as follows:

'The period from the date of issue of the capital instrument to the date at which it will expire, be redeemed, or be cancelled. If either party has the option to require the instrument to be redeemed or cancelled and, under the terms of the instrument, it is uncertain whether such an option will be exercised, the term should be taken to end on the earliest date at which the instrument would be redeemed or cancelled on exercise of such an option. If either party has the right to extend the period of an instrument, the term should not include the period of the extension if there is a genuine commercial possibility that the period will not be extended.'[35]

This therefore means that the term is taken to be the minimum which either party could insist upon, and since this dictates the period over which issue costs have to be written off, the definition has a conservative bias. This cautious approach to evaluating options to reduce or extend the term of debt instruments disregards the actual intentions of the option holder. The effect of this is often to produce a shorter 'term' for accounting purposes than that which will materialise in practice. Where the borrower has the ability to repay the debt at any time, as will often be the case, a literal interpretation of the standard would suggest that the issue costs should be written off immediately, because the term of the debt (as defined) is zero.

Some instruments contain terms which allow the borrower to repay early, but at a price. A strict application of FRS 4 could produce some unexpected results:

Example 15.5:   Loan with issuer call option

A company issues a five year debt instrument carrying a fixed interest rate of 7%. The terms of the instrument include an 'issuer call option', permitting the company to redeem the debt early on payment of a premium.

On the face of it, the term of the instrument, as defined by FRS 4, is restricted to the period up to the first date at which the option could be exercised, as discussed in 2.2.5 above. This means that issue costs have to be written off over that period. It might also be thought to mean that the premium payable under the option would have to be accrued as part of the finance costs, whether or not the company intends to exercise the option. The effect of this would be that the company would be accounting for the repurchase of the instrument regardless of whether or not it actually intended to repurchase it.

In order to avoid this result, in 1994 the UITF issued an Abstract which made it clear that any payments required on the exercise of such options do not form part of the finance costs which have to be accounted for.[36] This is because they cannot be described as 'payments that the issuer may be required to make in respect of the instrument', since exercising the option, and therefore incurring the requirement to make the payment, is voluntary. However, the Abstract does not affect the determination of the term of the instrument, which remains governed by FRS 4. The result of this is that the issue costs still have to be written off over the period up to the date on which the call option could be exercised, even though it is otherwise being assumed that the option will not be exercised. The treatment of finance costs is therefore based on two mutually exclusive assumptions, which seems rather anomalous.

2.2.6   Repurchase of debt or shares

Where a company buys in its own debt (or repays it early) at a price which differs from the liability carried in the balance sheet, the difference between the two amounts is taken to the profit and loss account as an additional finance cost or credit.[37] This applies even if the debt is not cancelled. For example, a company which bought some of its own listed debentures in the market would be at liberty to sell them again at some time in the future, but would still record a gain or loss in the meantime; if it resold them, that would be treated as a new debt issue, recorded at the proceeds of that sale.

As explained at 2.1.5 above, this issue was originally addressed by UITF 8, which was replaced by FRS 4 soon after. The UITF had taken up the issue to resolve the question of whether or not companies which refinanced their fixed-rate debt should spread the resulting gain or loss over the life of the replacement debt, and it concluded that they should not, except in circumstances where either:

(a) the replacement borrowing gives the same effective economic result as the original borrowing and thus there has been no change of substance in the debt. For this to be the case, as a minimum the following conditions should be met:

- The replacement borrowing and the original borrowing are both fixed rate;

- The replacement borrowing is of a comparable amount to the original borrowing;

- The maturity of the replacement borrowing is not materially different from the remaining maturity of the original borrowing;

- The covenants of the replacement borrowing are not materially different from those of the original borrowing.

A refinancing may fall within this exception whether or not the lender of the replacement debt is the same as the lender of the original debt; or

(b) the overall finance costs of the replacement borrowing are significantly different from market rates.[38]

These exceptions were not repeated in FRS 4. Notwithstanding this, some companies clearly believe that they still apply. Tate and Lyle discloses this note in its 1996 accounts:

Extract 15.6: Tate & Lyle Public Limited Company (1996)

18 Borrowings [extract]

During the year the £190.5 million $5^3/_4$% Guaranteed Bonds were redeemed for £163.8 million and replaced by borrowings with substantially the same terms. The premium on redemption of £23.3 million is being amortised over the life of the replacement debt and is treated as a payment of interest in the statement of cash flows. The £163.8 million 7.863% unsecured borrowings due 2001, which replaces the Guaranteed Bonds, were fully drawn by a UK subsidiary undertaking and are guaranteed on a subordinated basis by Tate & Lyle PLC.

Although FRS 4 dictates how to account for the gain or loss on the repayment of debt, it does not address the equivalent issue when swaps are terminated, and some companies carry forward gains or losses that arise in these circumstances. Tesco is an example, as shown in this extract:

Extract 15.7 Tesco PLC (1997)

Note 16 Creditors falling due within one year [extract]

d) A gain of £45m, realised in a prior year, on terminated interest rate swaps is being spread over the life of replacement swaps entered into at the same time for similar periods. Accruals and deferred income include £5m (1996 – £5m) attributable to these realised gains with £23m (1996 – £28m) being included in creditors falling due after more than one year (note 17).

Sometimes, rather than repurchasing or repaying their debt, companies enter into arrangements which have a similar economic effect. For example, they might irrevocably deposit funds with a third party which are to be applied solely in settlement of the debt, and agree with the creditor that he can look only to those funds for repayment of the debt. Such arrangements are sometimes referred to as resulting in 'defeasance' (meaning extinguishment) of the debt. FRS 4 does not deal with this issue; it only addresses actual repayment. However the IASC discussion paper on financial instruments does offer some guidance. It says that such a transaction can be effective in removing both the deposit and the liability from the balance sheet provided the creditor accepts that he will look to the third party holding the funds for the settlement of the debt.[39] But otherwise the arrangement is described as only 'in-substance defeasance', and the IASC document says that the debt and the deposit should therefore remain on the balance sheet.[40] In the UK, the rules on offset in FRS 5[41] would lead to the same conclusion.

South West Water's accounts show that they have reduced the disclosed amount of lease payables by £150m because they have deposited this amount with the lessor's bank group, as shown in this extract:

Extract 15.8: South West Water Plc (1997)

25 Loans and other borrowings [extract]

Obligations under finance leases of £150.0m (1996 £150.0m) are not included above because cash of an equal amount has been deposited with the lessor's bank group (collateralization); South West Water Services Limited can insist this cash is utilised to meet the finance lease obligations as they fall due. Such cash deposits are likewise not shown on the balance sheet. South West Water Services Limited has no present plans to withdraw the cash deposits but, in the event that some, or all, of the deposits were withdrawn, an equivalent amount of finance lease obligations would require to be reinstated as a liability in the balance sheet.

It appears from the above description that South West Water is able to insist on a net settlement, even though the deposits are not with the lessor companies themselves but with other members of their group, and presumably this would still apply in the event of the insolvency of any of the parties, otherwise the FRS 5 offset conditions would not be satisfied.[42] However, it also seems that the deposits are not irrevocable; South West Water can still use the cash for other purposes. This would suggest that they have not met the more general FRS 5 test for derecognition of an asset, which would suggest that the amounts should continue to be shown gross.

Another kind of arrangement which has a similar economic effect to the repurchase of debt is illustrated in this extract from the 1994 accounts of Sears:

Extract 15.9: Sears plc (1994)

13. Debtors [extract]

Included within prepayments due after more than one year is a call option, which was purchased for £41.8 million on normal commercial terms and which gives the Company the right to acquire £50 million of Sears plc Bonds 1996. It is exercisable at certain dates up to January 1996 at an exercise price that is linked to the net present value of the remaining interest payable on the Bonds. Accordingly, the exercise price reduces during the period up to January 1996, resulting in an increase in the value of the call option. This increase in value is credited to interest receivable on an actuarial basis and is reflected in the carrying amount of the asset, which was £43.5 million at 31st January 1994.

£43.5 million equated to the present value of the principal of the debt (£50 million) if discounted at approximately 7.2%. From this it can be surmised that the exercise price under the option was little different from the present value of the outstanding interest payments. Subsequently, the 1996 accounts showed that the option had been sold for £50m on the same day as the debt was repaid. Interestingly, the purchase of the option was described in the 1994 accounts as 'Prepayment of 12½% bonds 1996' in the financing section of the cash flow statement, not as the purchase of an option in the investing section. It might therefore be argued that Sears had already repurchased its debt in substance, but in such a way that it did not have to write off the premium payable – instead, it was recognised over the remaining two years of the instrument as the difference between the interest payable on the debt, at 12½% and the accretion of interest on the prepayment, at 7.2%.

It is again debatable whether this should be regarded as the repurchase of debt or not. On the one hand, it achieves a similar result in economic terms, and therefore could be said to be a repurchase in substance. On the other, it would be possible to simulate a repurchase of debt in a variety of other ways, for example using derivatives without getting close to repurchasing the debt. Moreover, unless there is right of offset between the option and the debt, FRS 5 would again say that the two items should continue to be carried gross on opposite sides of the balance sheet.

The standard refers only fleetingly to the repurchase of *shares*. This subject is discussed at 3.3 below.

2.2.7 The disclosure of debt maturities

As discussed in 3.2 below, both the Companies Act and Stock Exchange rules require debt to be analysed in the accounts by reference to when the creditor is entitled to require repayment. The standard repeats that requirement.[43] However, in interpreting this rule, companies are to take account of committed facilities in existence at the year end that would permit short-term debt to be refinanced for a longer period, provided some exacting conditions are met. These conditions are as follows:

(a)   the debt and the facility are under a single agreement or course of dealing with the same lender or group of lenders;

(b)   the finance costs for the new debt are on a basis which is not significantly higher than that of the existing debt;

(c)   the obligations of the lender (or group of lenders) are firm: the lender is not able legally to refrain from providing funds except in circumstances the possibility of which can be demonstrated to be remote; and

(d)   the lender (or group of lenders) is expected to be able to fulfil its obligations under the facility.[44]

It is important to note that the borrower's own intentions and financial plans do not affect this reclassification; the rules require the position to be assessed only from the lenders' perspective.

An example of this classification is shown by Senior Engineering:

Extract 15.10: Senior Engineering Group plc (1996)

17 CREDITORS: Amounts falling due after more than one year [extract]

	Group		Company	
	1996	1995	1996	1995
	£000's	£000's	£000's	£000's
Loans comprise –				
Revolving credit facility	11,030	38,710	8,000	25,806
Other bank loans	15,368	18,683	–	–
Other loans	197	274	–	–
Less – Current portion	(106)	(109)	–	–
	26,489	57,588	8,000	25,806
8.57% Private placement loan – 2004	2,924	3,226	2,924	3,226
8.75% Private placement loan – 2007	14,620	16,129	14,620	16,129
11% Unsecured loan notes – 1999	60	80	60	80
Less –Current portion	(60)	(80)	(60)	(80)
	17,544	19,355	17,544	19,355
Total loans falling due after more than one year	44,033	76,913	25,544	45,161

Amounts drawn down under the revolving credit facility fall due for repayment in January 1997. However, the facility is committed for a period of five years ending in July 2000. Accordingly, under the terms of Financial Reporting Standard No. 4, the amounts drawn down have been classified as payable between two and five years (see Note 18).

18 ANALYSIS OF LOANS AND FINANCE LEASES [extract]

	Group 1996 £000's	Group 1995 £000's	Company 1996 £000's	Company 1995 £000's
Loans are payable as follows –				
Within one year				
Bank loans	2,324	1,559	–	–
Other	136	156	60	80
Between 1 and 2 years				
Bank loans	30	33	–	–
Other	75	152	–	–
Between 2 and 5 years				
Bank loans	26,148	57,088	8,000	25,806
Other	37	37	–	–
After 5 years				
Bank loans	190	239	–	–
Other	17,553	19,364	17,544	19,355
Total loans	46,493	78,628	25,604	45,241

Before FRS 4 was issued, many companies which issued commercial paper reported it as long term, by reference to back-up facilities. Commercial paper is generally a cheaper alternative to short-term direct bank borrowing for many large companies, and the maturity periods are very short – usually between 5 and 45 days. Most programmes are backed up by lines of credit from banks, but as the back-up facility is not provided by the lenders (i.e. the investors who buy the paper), condition (a) quoted above cannot be met, with the result that commercial paper borrowings will always be reported as short term.

Unusually, the relevant note in Redland's accounts shows its commercial paper initially as long term but then reclassifies it as short term for balance sheet purposes, although the amount involved seems immaterial in any case. This presentation is shown below:

Extract 15.11: Redland PLC (1996)

13   Loans and Bank Overdrafts [extract]

Repayment analysis as at 31st December 1996	Within 1 year £ million	Between 1 and 2 years £ million	Between 2 and 5 years £ million	Over 5 years £ million	Total £ million
Bank loans and overdrafts	29.6	2.8	21.1	9.6	63.1
Commercial paper	–	–	3.5	–	3.5
Other loans and finance leases	202.1	15.3	329.4	11.9	558.7
	231.7	18.1	354.0	21.5	625.3
Reclassification of commercial paper in accordance with FRS 4	3.5	–	(3.5)	–	–
As at 31st December 1996	235.2	18.1	350.5	21.5	625.3
As at 31st December 1995	263.1	221.6	208.5	151.1	844.3

Many companies also borrow on a short-term basis under multiple option funding facility agreements (MOFs). Short-term drawdowns under MOFs may be classified as long term by reference to the maturity date of the MOF provided all the four conditions above are met. Condition (a) will be satisfied even if it is not always the same banks who participate in individual financings under the MOF – they are regarded as being part of the same 'group of lenders' provided they are parties to the same agreement or course of dealing. Although the standard does not define the term 'course of dealing' which is used in condition (a), the choice of words suggests more latitude than the alternative – 'a single agreement'.

Condition (b) quoted above limits the choice of facilities even further. The drafting suggests that borrowings under the facility should be of the same type as those of the existing debt. So, for example, if the basis for determining the finance costs of the existing debt is a fixed margin over 1 month LIBOR, only facilities that allow borrowings that are priced on a similar basis should be considered. Hence it would not be possible to use a floating-rate medium-term facility to reclassify maturing fixed rate debt or vice versa.

In addition, the basis for determining the finance costs of borrowings under the facility should not be 'significantly higher'. The standard does not explain when one basis is significantly higher than another. However, in its discussion on the development of the FRS, the ASB implicitly provides an indication of how this condition should be interpreted. It discusses why commercial paper should be shown as short term notwithstanding the back-up facilities and explains that conditions (a) and (b) above are not usually met. The prices of commercial paper back-up facilities are thus considered to be 'significantly higher' than commercial paper rates.

Conditions (c) and (d) have a common goal. They seek to establish whether or not it is safe to rely on the borrowings under the facility. The conditions cover obvious escape routes that the provider of the facility (the lender) may have negotiated. Condition (d) is fairly straightforward; condition (c) focuses on the facility agreement and requires it to be both legally binding and genuinely committed. In this regard, the FRS requires that any circumstances specified in the facility agreement which permit the lender to refrain from providing new borrowings should be demonstrated to be remote, both at the balance sheet date and at the time the accounts are approved.

It will not be possible to confirm that the 'obligations of the lender are firm' if any of the circumstances in which the lender can refrain from providing new borrowings can only be interpreted subjectively. The example provided in the explanatory section of the FRS is that of a 'material adverse change' clause where that term has not been defined.[45] This is probably a stricter test than is applied for existing long-term borrowings, where the existence of a term which would entitle the lender to early repayment is disregarded provided it is reasonable to believe that the circumstances that would allow the term to be invoked will not arise.

If maturity of debt analysis has been compiled by reference to committed facilities in existence at the balance sheet date, the FRS also requires disclosure of the amounts of the debt involved, analysed by the earliest date on which the lender could demand repayment in the absence of the facilities.[46]

2.2.8 Warrants

A warrant is defined in FRS 4 as 'an instrument that requires the issuer to issue shares (whether contingently or not) and contains no obligation for the issuer to transfer economic benefits'.[47] When a warrant is issued, the standard requires the net proceeds to be credited direct to shareholders' funds;[48] the implication appears to be that it should be reported only in the reconciliation of shareholders' funds, not in the statement of total recognised gains and losses, presumably on the argument that it is a transaction with (potential) shareholders.

Thereafter the accounting depends on whether the warrant is exercised or is allowed to lapse. If it is exercised, the proceeds on the original issue of the warrant are included in the net proceeds of the shares issued;[49] if it lapses, they are included instead in the statement of total recognised gains and losses,[50] since the original issue has turned out not to have been a transaction with shareholders after all, but a gain.

These conclusions are questionable. Given that the warrant may lapse, in which case the proceeds will be shown never to have been a transaction with shareholders, there is a case for saying that it should be shown as deferred income until the outcome is known, not credited to shareholders' funds. However, the ASB's proposed definitions of the elements of financial statements (see Chapter 2) do not admit the possibility of deferred income, so presumably the Board felt that this was not a course open to them. Furthermore, if the warrant does lapse the proceeds will constitute a realised profit which arguably belongs in the profit and loss account, not the statement of total recognised gains and losses. The rule in FRS 4 seems to be based on the fact that the transaction has a 'capital' flavour.

2.2.9   Scrip dividends

Scrip dividends arise when shareholders are given the opportunity to receive further fully paid up shares in their company as an alternative to cash dividends. The standard deals with only some of the accounting issues which arise in relation to such transactions, and in a rather ambiguous way. It says that the value of the shares should be deemed to be the amount receivable under the cash alternative.[51] However, this is probably addressing only the initial recording of the dividend in the profit and loss account before the shareholders have chosen whether to take cash or shares, not the subsequent recording of the issue itself, in respect of which a later passage in the standard suggests that a different treatment might be appropriate.[52] The standard also says that the whole cash amount should be set up as a liability until the number of shareholders who will elect to receive the scrip dividend is known.[53] These various topics are discussed further at 4.6 below.

2.2.10 Disclosure requirements

A large number of disclosures are required by FRS 4. These are as follows:

(a)   The following analyses of balance sheet items:

   (i)   An analysis of shareholders' funds between equity and non-equity interests.[54] The non-equity interests should be further analysed into each class of non-equity shares and series of warrants for non-equity shares;[55]

   (ii)   An analysis of minority interests between equity and non-equity interests in subsidiaries;[56]

   (iii) An analysis of liabilities between amounts in respect of convertible debt and other amounts.[57]

   Where these analyses are given in the notes rather than on the face of the balance sheet, the balance sheet caption should indicate that non-equity interests or convertible debt is included in the amount shown.[58] The balance sheet should also disclose the amount of shareholders' funds in total.[59]

British Aerospace's balance sheet shows the following analysis:

Extract 15.12: British Aerospace Public Limited Company (1996)

BALANCE SHEETS [extract]

	Group		Company	
	1996	1995	**1996**	1995
Capital and reserves	**£m**	£m	**£m**	£m
Called up share capital	**110**	110	**110**	110
Share premium account	**38**	27	**38**	27
Statutory reserve	**202**	202	**202**	202
Revaluation reserve	**787**	222	**216**	217
Capital reserve	–	–	**24**	24
Profit and loss account	**556**	367	**745**	500
Shareholders' funds				
Equity: ordinary shares	**1,423**	658	**1,065**	810
Non-equity: preference shares	**270**	270	**270**	270
	1,693	928	**1,335**	1,080
Equity minority interests	**13**	11	–	–
Total capital employed	**1,706**	939	**1,335**	1,080

A number of companies have fallen foul of the requirement to analyse shareholders' funds between equity and non-equity categories and have had to restate their accounts after intervention by the Financial Reporting Review Panel. One was Ransomes, as shown in the following note:

Extract 15.13: Ransomes plc (1996)

22. Shareholders' Funds [extract]

After discussion with the Financial Reporting Review Panel, the analysis of shareholders' funds between equity and non-equity interests at 30th September 1995 has been restated to conform with Financial Reporting Standard 4. The restatement for the Group has resulted in a £47.9m decrease in equity interests and a £47.9m increase in non-equity interests. The change relates to the inclusion of the premium arising on the issue of the 8.25p preference shares in 1989. This amount had previously been regarded as having been set-off by the write off of goodwill of £47.9m. The restatement in the Company books is £15.1m and is lower as the goodwill set-off only related to the intangible assets purchased on the acquisition of the Cushman Group in 1989. The 8.25p cumulative convertible preference shares are not redeemable. Total shareholders' funds remain unchanged. The restated analysis of shareholders' funds as at 30th September 1995 is given in the table below:

Group

	1995 £'000	Restated 1995 £'000	Change £'000
Equity interests	6,793	(41,075)	(47,868)
Non-equity interests	9,307	57,175	47,868
Shareholders' funds	16,100	16,100	–

Company

	1995 £'000	Restated 1995 £'000	Change £'000
Equity interests	45,663	30,590	(15,073)
Non-equity interests	42,102	57,175	15,073
Shareholders' funds	87,765	87,765	–

Alexon has made a similar change, but has also changed its treatment of dividends on non-equity shares, as shown in this note:

Extract 15.14: Alexon plc (1996)

24 Non equity shareholders' funds

Group and Company

	1996	1995
	£000	£000
Non-equity shareholders' funds may be analysed as follows:		
Share capital	2,137	2,137
Share premium	18,219	18,220
Unamortised issue costs	(232)	(250)
Undeclared preference dividends	1,692	423
	21,816	20,530
Representing:		
6.25p (net) convertible cumulative redeemable preference shares of 10p each	21,698	20,416
5% (now 3.5% plus tax credit) cumulative preference shares of £1 each	105	101
Non-voting deferred shares of 10p each	13	13
	21,816	20,530

Following developments in the application of Financial Reporting Standard No. 4 (FRS 4) and an enquiry by the Financial Reporting Review Panel, the directors have reviewed the disclosure for equity and non-equity shareholders' funds and have restated the analysis at 28 January 1995 to accord with the method specified by FRS 4. The effect has been to reduce equity shareholders' funds by £17,970,000 and to increase non-equity shareholders' funds by the same amount, and to include the accrued preference dividends within non-equity shareholders' funds. This has resulted in an increase in total shareholders' funds by the amount of the accrued preference dividends, previously included within creditors.

As can be seen from this extract, Alexon has included the accrued dividends on its preference shares (which are in arrears) within shareholders' funds rather than showing them as a liability, even though they have also shown them as an appropriation in the profit and loss account as required by FRS 4. This means that the appropriation entry has been a circular one. The standard is not entirely clear about the balance sheet classification of accrued dividends; it can be read to require *all* proposed dividends (not simply those in arrears, or those relating to non-equity shares) to remain in shareholders' funds, because they do not become liabilities until they are declared, but this cannot have been intended by the ASB and it is certainly not an interpretation that is applied in practice other than in circumstances similar to Alexon (see 4.4.1 below).

The Rank Group gives this note to analyse its minority interests between equity and non-equity categories:

Extract 15.15: The Rank Group Plc (1996)

23 ANALYSIS OF MINORITY INTERESTS

	Equity £m	Non-equity £m	Total £m
Balances at 31st December 1995	–	25	25
Minority interest in the profit on ordinary activities after tax	1	2	3
Dividends payable to minority shareholders	–	(2)	(2)
Balances at 31st December 1996	1	25	26

(b)   A brief summary of the rights of each class of shares, including

　(i)　the rights to dividends;

　(ii)　the dates at which they are redeemable and the amounts payable in respect of redemption;

　(iii)　their priority and the amounts receivable on a winding up; and

　(iv)　their voting rights.

If the rights vary according to circumstances, the details should be explained. The summary of rights should also be sufficient to explain why the class of shares has been classified as equity or non-equity shares.[60] The same disclosure also has to be given in respect of any shares of a new class which may have to be issued because of any existing warrants or convertible debt.[61]

The description of rights specified above need not be given for routine equity shares with all of the following features:

　(i)　no rights to dividends other than those that may be recommended by the directors;

　(ii)　no redemption rights;

　(iii)　unlimited right to share in the surplus remaining on a winding up after all liabilities and participation rights of other classes of shares have been satisfied; and

　(iv)　one vote per share.[62]

BBA provides a good example of the disclosure of the rights of shares:

Extract 15.16: BBA Group plc (1996)

18 CAPITAL AND RESERVES [extract]

Rights of non-equity interests

5% Cumulative £1 preference shares

i.　entitle holders, in priority to holders of all other classes of shares, to a fixed cumulative preferential dividend at a rate of 3.5% per annum per share payable half yearly in equal amounts on 1 February and 1 August;

ii.　on a return of capital on a winding up, or otherwise, will carry the right to repayment of capital together with a premium of 12.5p per share and a sum equal to any arrears or deficiency of dividend; this right is in priority to the rights of the convertible preference and ordinary shareholders;

iii.　carry the right to attend and vote at a general meeting of the Company only if, at the date of the notice convening the meeting, payment of the dividend to which they are entitled is six months or more in arrears, or if a resolution is to be considered at the meeting for winding-up the company or reducing its share capital or sanctioning the sale of the undertaking of the Company or varying or abrogating any of the special rights attaching to them.

6.75% Cumulative redeemable convertible preference £1 shares

i.　entitle holders (subject to the prior rights of the 5% cumulative £1 preference shares) to a fixed cumulative preferential dividend at a rate of 6.75% per annum per share, payable half yearly in equal amounts on 31 May and 30 November;

ii.　carry the right to be converted into ordinary shares at the option of the holder on 31 May in any of the years 1997 to 2005 inclusive at the rate of 54.64 ordinary shares for every £100 nominal of convertible preference shares;

iii.　will be redeemed by the Company on 31 May 2006 at par (if not previously converted or redeemed) and any arrears of dividend will be paid;

iv.　on a return of capital on a winding up, or otherwise, will carry the right to repayment of capital and payment of accrued dividends in priority to ordinary shares but after the 5% cumulative £1 preference shares;

v.　carry the right to attend and vote at a general meeting of the Company only if, at the date of the notice convening the meeting, payment of the dividend to which they are entitled is six months or more in arrears, or if a resolution is to be considered at the meeting for winding-up the Company or for modifying or abrogating any special rights attaching to them.

(c)　In respect of non-equity minority interests, a description of any rights of the holders against other group companies.[63]

(d)　An analysis of the maturity of debt showing amounts falling due:

 (i)　in one year or less, or on demand;

 (ii)　between one and two years;

 (iii)　between two and five years; and

 (iv)　in five years or more.[64]

Where short-term debt has been reclassified as long term because the lender has granted a longer term facility, the amount of the debt which has been reclassified should be disclosed, analysed by its maturity before such reclassification.[65]

Pearson's accounts contain an example of this disclosure:

Extract 15.17: Pearson plc (1996)

17 Borrowings [extract]

	Group		Company	
	1996	1995	**1996**	1995
Borrowing summary (by maturity)	**£m**	£m	**£m**	£m
Short term				
Loans or instalments due within one year	**8.5**	12.1	**3.0**	7.3
Bank loans, overdrafts and commercial paper	**165.7**	248.9	**167.3**	282.0
Total due within one year	**174.2**	261.0	**170.3**	289.3
Medium and long term				
Loans or instalments thereof repayable:				
From one to two years	**7.8**	0.1	**–**	–
From two to five years	**6.3**	24.5	**4.8**	14.4
After five years not by instalments	**541.1**	449.8	**184.3**	224.8
Total due after more than one year	**555.2**	474.4	**189.1**	239.2
Total borrowing	**729.4**	735.4	**359.4**	528.5

In the absence of enforceable contracts from the relevant lenders to refinance current advances as they fall due, at the balance sheet date £84.3 of debt currently classified from two to five years and after five years would be repayable within one year.

(e)   For convertible debt:

(i)   the dates of redemption and the amounts payable on redemption;

(ii)   the number and class of shares into which the debt may be converted, and the dates at or periods within which conversion may take place; and

(iii) whether conversion is at the option of the issuer or the holder.[66]

Inchcape provides an example of this disclosure:

Extract 15.18: Inchcape plc (1996)

3 Treasury information [extract]

The £125m 6¼% Convertible Subordinated Bonds Due 2008 are convertible at the option of the holder, on or prior to 3 May 2008, into fully paid ordinary shares of 25p each of the Company at 689p per share. None of the bonds were converted during the year. If the conversion rights attaching to the bonds outstanding at 31 December 1996 were exercised, 18,142,235 ordinary shares of 25p each of the company would fall to be issued. The bonds may be redeemed at the option of the Company, in whole or in part, at any time after 30 May 1998 or earlier if certain conditions are met. Unless previously redeemed or converted, the bonds will be redeemed at par on 10 May 2008.

(f) For debt in general:

  (i) anything unusual about the legal nature of the debt, for example that it is subordinated or that the obligation to repay it is conditional; and

  (ii) the amount payable, or which could be claimed on a winding up, if it is significantly different from the carrying amount.

  These disclosures may be summarised and need not be given for each individual instrument.[67]

(g) Where the summary of the terms of an instrument (required by (b), (c), (e) and (f) above) cannot adequately convey its full commercial effect, that fact has to be stated and particulars given of where the relevant information can be obtained. The principal features of the instruments still have to be stated.[68]

(h) Any gain or loss arising on the repurchase or early settlement of debt.[69]

(i) The aggregate dividends for each class of shares, disclosing separately the total amounts in respect of the following:

  (i) dividends on equity shares;

  (ii) participating dividends on non-equity shares (those dividends which, under the memorandum and articles, are always equivalent to a fixed multiple of the dividend payable on an equity share);[70] and

  (iii) other dividends on non-equity shares.

  Any additional appropriations in respect of non-equity shares should also be disclosed.

  This information may be shown in the dividends note rather than on the face of the profit and loss account so long as the profit and loss account caption indicates that the distributions include amounts in respect of non-equity shares if that is the case.[71]

(j) An analysis of the amount of the minority interest charge in the profit and loss account between equity and non-equity interests.[72]

(k) For investment companies, the amount of any finance costs which have been allocated to capital rather than revenue (as a separately disclosed item in the statement of total recognised gains and losses), and the accounting policy on which this allocation has been based.[73]

One further disclosure was proposed in FRED 3 but did not survive as a requirement in the standard: this is the market value of the company's debt and non-equity shares.[74] However, the explanatory section of FRS 4 does suggest that this disclosure be considered where 'information on market values would assist users',[75] and it has now been proposed again in FRED 13 as part of the

ASB's project on financial instruments (see Chapter 9 at 3.2(h)). Disclosure of the fair values of financial instruments is also now required in the US (see 5.1.11 below).

The ASB has separately recommended that major companies should also give a narrative explanation of their financing arrangements in another part of the Annual Report. This comes from the Board's Statement on the 'Operating and Financial Review', published in July 1993. Among other things, this review should contain a section explaining 'the capital structure of the business, its treasury policy and the dynamics of its financial position – its sources of liquidity and their application, including the implications of the financing requirements arising from its capital expenditure plans.[76] As discussed in Chapter 9, FRED 13 proposes to require major companies to give detailed narrative disclosures about their financial strategies and objectives (see Chapter 9 at 3.1).

3   COMPANIES ACT REQUIREMENTS

3.1   Share capital

3.1.1   *Measurement*

Under the Companies Act, the amount at which share capital is recorded is dictated by the nominal value of the shares issued, and if the value of the consideration received for the issue of shares exceeds that amount, the excess is recorded in the share premium account.[77] The share premium account is regarded as permanent capital of the company and only certain expenses of a capital nature may be set off against it, namely:

(a)   the company's preliminary expenses;

(b)   the expenses of, or the commission paid or discount allowed on, any issue of shares or debentures of the company; or

(c)   the premium payable on redemption of debentures of the company.[78]

Under FRS 4, the costs of issuing debentures or non-equity shares have to be accounted for as a finance cost or an appropriation in the profit and loss account over the life of the instrument. The same is also true of any discounts on the issue of debentures and any premiums on their repayment. This treatment does not prevent such costs ultimately from being deducted from the share premium account, but they will have to get there by transfer from the profit and loss account reserve after having first been taken to the profit and loss account in accordance with the standard.

The Companies Act gives relief from the requirement to set up a share premium account in certain circumstances where shares are being issued in exchange for shares in another company, and to limit the amount of the share premium account when shares are being issued to effect a group reconstruction (see 2.1.2 of Chapter 6).[79] Correspondingly, the legislation allows the consideration received to be recorded at the nominal value of the shares issued. This may have been affected to some degree by FRS 4, which requires shares to be recorded on the basis of the fair value of the consideration received,[80] exempting only instances where merger *accounting* is applied,[81] not where merger relief is taken. However, it seems that this change, if indeed it was one, was inadvertent; accounting standards do not usually seek to withdraw reliefs specifically granted by legislation. The ASB subsequently made it clear in FRS 6 that its rules on acquisition accounting were not intended to have any effect on the parent company's own accounts and in particular to the availability of merger relief,[82] and we suggest that that interpretation be extended to FRS 4 as well.

The share capital of UK companies is generally denominated in sterling, but there is no requirement for this to be the case, except that a public company must have a minimum share capital of £50,000.[83] Neither FRS 4 nor SSAP 20 addresses the treatment of translation of share capital denominated in a currency other than the reporting currency. In theory two treatments are possible: the foreign currency share capital could be maintained at a fixed sterling amount by being translated at a historical rate of exchange, or it could be retranslated annually at the closing rate as if it were a monetary amount. In the latter case a second question would arise: whether to take the difference arising on translation to the profit and loss account or deal with it within reserves. The latter treatment is probably the most appropriate for forms of share capital which are closely akin to debt; however, it might be more appropriate to use a historical exchange rate where the shares which are denominated in a foreign currency are ordinary shares.

3.1.2 Disclosure

The main disclosure requirements in the Companies Act begin with the format in which the balance sheet is to be laid out. The formats require capital and reserves to be analysed as shown in the box.[84]

The Act also requires the following note disclosures in respect of share capital:

(a) the authorised share capital;

(b) where there is more than one class of shares, the number and aggregate nominal value of each class of share allotted;[85]

Capital and reserves

I   Called up share capital

II Share premium account

III Revaluation reserve

IV Other reserves
   1. Capital redemption reserve
   2. Reserve for own shares
   3. Reserves provided for by the articles of association
   4. Other reserves

V   Profit and loss account

(c)   these details about redeemable shares which have been allotted:

    (i)   their earliest and latest redemption dates;

    (ii)   whether redemption is automatic, or is at the option of either the company or the shareholder; and

    (iii)   the amount of any redemption premium;[86]

(d)   in relation to the allotment of shares during the year:

    (i)   the classes of shares allotted; and

    (ii)   the number allotted, their aggregate nominal value and the consideration received, in respect of each class of shares;[87]

(e)   in respect of contingent rights to the allotment of further shares (such as options to subscribe), the following information:

    (i)   the number, description and amount of the shares involved;

    (ii)   the period during which the right is exercisable; and

    (iii)   the price to be paid for the shares allotted;[88] and

(f)   the amount of any arrears of fixed cumulative dividends on any class of the company's shares, and the period for which they are in arrears.[89]

In respect of dividends, the Act requires that the total dividends paid and proposed in respect of the year are to be disclosed on the face of the profit and loss account, and the amount of proposed dividends has to be shown separately either on the face of the profit and loss account or in a note.[90] However, FRS 4 requires dividends on non-equity shares to be accounted for on an accruals basis if the entitlement to them is time-based,[91] and this may complicate the legal disclosure requirement if the accrued amount is not the same as that proposed for payment.

The Companies Act also contains various requirements for matters to be disclosed in the Directors' Report in respect of share capital. Those relating to directors' interests in shares are discussed in Chapter 28 at 3.1.1, while those in respect of the purchase by a company of its own shares are dealt with at 3.3 below. The Stock Exchange also requires listed companies to disclose details of holdings in the company's shares of 3% or more which have been notified to the company.[92]

3.2 Loan capital

In terms of the Companies Act, loan capital will fall under the general heading of creditors, which has to be analysed under the formats as shown here.[93]

Most UK companies follow Format 1 of the two formats available in the Act, and this means that they have to give two separate analyses under these headings, one for amounts falling due within one year and the other for amounts falling due after more than one year.

> Creditors
> 1. Debenture loans
> 2. Bank loans and overdrafts
> 3. Payments received on account
> 4. Trade creditors
> 5. Bills of exchange payable
> 6. Amounts owed to group undertakings
> 7. Amounts owed to undertakings in which the company has a participating interest
> 8. Other creditors including taxation and social security
> 9. Accruals and deferred income.

In distinguishing amounts between these two categories, the deciding factor is the earliest date at which the creditor could demand repayment.[94] As discussed in 2.2.7 above, FRS 4 interprets this restrictively.

In addition to the formats, the Act requires the following disclosures in respect of each item shown under creditors in the balance sheet:

(a) the amount that is not repayable within five years of the balance sheet date and the terms of repayment and interest for such items;[95] and

(b) the total amount in respect of which any security has been given, and an indication of the nature of the security.[96]

The Act also requires the following information to be given in relation to the issue of debentures:

(a) the classes of debentures issued; and

(b) the amount issued and the consideration received in respect of each class.[97]

Details must also be given of any debentures held by a nominee or a trustee for the company.[98]

A debenture is not defined in the Companies Act, except that it is said to *include* 'debenture stock, bonds and other securities of a company, whether constituting a charge on the assets of the company or not'.[99] In general legal use, it is a term applying to any document evidencing a loan, and in the context of company law it means a debt instrument issued by the company and usually giving some form of security or charge over its assets, although this is not an essential feature.

The Companies Act requires interest payable to be analysed into two categories:

(a) that relating to bank loans and overdrafts; and

(b)   interest on all other loans.[100]

3.3   The purchase of a company's own shares

At one time, UK companies were prohibited from purchasing their own shares and could redeem only preference shares. These restrictions were eased by the Companies Act 1981, and a new regime introduced which permitted both the purchase and redemption of shares on a wider basis, subject to various conditions and safeguards.[101] The most important of these are as follows:

(a)   the capital of the company must be maintained, either by freezing up an equivalent amount of distributable profits in a 'capital redemption reserve' or by making it good from the proceeds of a fresh issue of shares made for the purposes of the redemption. However, there is a relaxation of this principle for private companies, discussed below;

(b)   the shares which are redeemed or purchased must be cancelled and may not be reissued;

(c)   the transaction must be permitted under the company's articles, and in certain cases must also be authorised by shareholder resolution; and

(d)   a transaction may not be undertaken if its effect will be that no shares remain in issue, or that the only shares in issue will be redeemable shares.

Some examples of the accounting treatment of such transactions are shown below:

Example 15.6:   Redemption of own shares

A company has the following balance sheet:

	£
Cash	20,000
Ordinary £1 shares	8,000
Redeemable preference £1 shares	5,000
Profit and loss account	7,000
	20,000

It decides to redeem half of its preference shares at par. The entries to effect the redemption and to maintain the original capital are as follows:

		£	£
Dr.	Redeemable preference shares	2,500	
Cr.	Cash		2,500

To redeem the shares, and

		£	£
Dr.	Profit and loss account reserve	2,500	
Cr.	Capital redemption reserve		2,500

To maintain the capital at its original amount

As a result, the balance sheet will now be:

	£
Cash	17,500
Ordinary £1 shares	8,000
Redeemable preference £1 shares	2,500
Capital redemption reserve	2,500
Profit and loss account	4,500
	17,500

If there had been a fresh issue of shares, the second journal entry would not be needed except to the extent that the proceeds of the fresh issue fell short of £2,500.

If the redemption had been at a premium of (say) 20 pence per share, the entries and the balance sheet would have been as follows:

		£	£
Dr.	Redeemable preference shares	2,500	
Dr.	Profit and loss account reserve	500	
Cr.	Cash		3,000

To redeem the shares, and

		£	£
Dr.	Profit and loss account reserve	2,500	
Cr.	Capital redemption reserve		2,500

To maintain the capital at its original amount

As a result, the balance sheet will now be:

	£
Cash	17,000
Ordinary £1 shares	8,000
Redeemable preference £1 shares	2,500
Capital redemption reserve	2,500
Profit and loss account	4,000
	17,000

The redemption premium of £500 must be met out of distributable profits; it cannot be met out of the proceeds of a fresh issue.

If the redeemable shares had originally been issued at a premium, and there is a fresh issue for the purposes of the redemption, then the premium on redemption can be met out of the proceeds of the fresh issue up to the limit of the lesser of:

(a) the premium received by the company on the issue of the shares now being redeemed, or

(b) the current balance on the share premium account including any premium on issue of the new shares.[102]

This is shown in the following example:

Example 15.7:   *Redemption of own shares at a premium*

A company has the following balance sheet:	£
Cash	40,000
	_____
Ordinary £1 shares	20,000
Redeemable preference £1 shares	5,000
Share premium account	3,000
Profit and loss account	12,000
	_____
	40,000
	_____

The preference shares were originally issued at a premium of 10 pence per share. The company now decides to redeem all of its preference shares, which carry a redemption premium of 30 pence per share, and at the same time have a fresh issue of 2,000 ordinary shares at an issue price of £2 per share. The entries are as follows:

		£	£
Dr.	Cash	4,000	
Cr.	Ordinary £1 shares		2,000
Cr.	Share premium account		2,000

To record the proceeds of the new issue.

		£	£
Dr.	Redeemable preference shares	5,000	
Dr.	Share premium account	500	
Dr.	Profit and loss account reserve	1,000	
Cr.	Cash		6,500

To effect the redemption, and

		£	£
Dr.	Profit and loss account reserve	1,500	
Cr.	Capital redemption reserve		1,500

To make good the capital.

The amount initially credited to share premium account in respect of the preference shares (£500) is the limiting factor on what can be released to offset the premium payable on redemption of the shares – the rest has to be met from distributable profits. The capital has to be made good because the proceeds from the new issue (£4,000) less the amount already applied towards the redemption premium (£500) fell short of the nominal value of the shares redeemed (£5,000). The amount of £2,500 charged to the profit and loss account represents the difference between the redemption cost of £6,500 and the proceeds of the fresh issue of £4,000.

As a result, the balance sheet will now be:	£
Cash	37,500
	_____
Ordinary £1 shares	22,000
Redeemable preference £1 shares	–
Share premium account	4,500
Capital redemption reserve	1,500
Profit and loss account	9,500
	_____
	37,500
	_____

It can be seen that the aggregate of the share capital and undistributable reserves remains the same before and after the transaction, which is the objective of the rules which lie behind these journal entries.

	Before	After
	£	£
Ordinary £1 shares	20,000	22,000
Redeemable preference £1 shares	5,000	–
Share premium account	3,000	4,500
Capital redemption reserve	–	1,500
	28,000	28,000

As mentioned above, these capital maintenance rules are relaxed for private companies which are unable to meet the cost of redemption either out of their distributable profits or from the proceeds of a fresh issue.[103] In order to be permitted to do this, various procedures have to be followed which are designed to protect the creditors of the company from the consequences of eroding its capital base. In particular, the directors must make a statutory declaration that they are of the opinion that there will be no grounds on which the company could be found to be unable to pay its debts, both immediately following the transaction and for a year thereafter, and the auditors must confirm, after enquiry, that they are not aware of anything which would indicate that the directors' opinion was unreasonable. An example of the accounting treatment in such a case is set out below:

Example 15.8:   Redemption of own shares out of capital

A private company has the following balance sheet:

	£
Cash	20,000
Ordinary £1 shares	10,000
Redeemable preference £1 shares	5,000
Share premium account	3,000
Profit and loss account	2,000
	20,000

The directors decide that they wish to redeem all the preference shares at par. The distributable profits of the company are not adequate to allow this without reduction of its capital and accordingly the requirements of the Act must be followed to permit the transaction to proceed. When this has been done, the necessary entries will be as follows:

		£	£
Dr.	Redeemable preference shares	5,000	
Cr.	Cash		5,000

To effect the redemption, and

		£	£
Dr.	Profit and loss account reserve	2,000	
Cr.	Capital redemption reserve		2,000

To make good the capital so far as the company is able to do so from its distributable profits.

As a result, the balance sheet will now be:

	£
Cash	15,000
Ordinary £1 shares	10,000
Redeemable preference £1 shares	–
Share premium account	3,000
Capital redemption reserve	2,000
Profit and loss account	–
	15,000

This time, the aggregate of the share capital and undistributable reserves is not the same before and after the transaction, because of the shortfall. The amount of the shortfall (£3,000 in this example) is referred to in the Act as the 'permissible capital payment'.

	Before	After
	£	£
Ordinary £1 shares	10,000	10,000
Redeemable preference £1 shares	5,000	–
Share premium account	3,000	3,000
Capital redemption reserve	–	2,000
	18,000	15,000

The mechanics for accounting for purchases of shares are the same as those for redemptions as shown above. Where a company has purchased some of its shares, it has to make various disclosures in the directors' report. These include the number and nominal value of the shares purchased, together with the amount of the consideration paid and the reasons for the purchase, and the percentage of the called-up share capital which it represents. These and other similar disclosures are also required in other similar circumstances, such as where a company takes a lien or charge over its shares, or provides financial assistance for the purchase of its shares and has a beneficial interest in such shares.[104]

Guinness is an example of a company which has purchased its own shares. The relevant disclosures from its accounts are shown below:

Extract 15.19: Guinness PLC (1996)

Report of the Directors [extract]

Purchase and cancellation of Ordinary Shares

At the 1996 Annual General Meeting shareholders gave the Company renewed authority to purchase a maximum of 200 million shares of 25 pence each. During the year under review, the Company purchased 100 million Ordinary Shares of 25 pence each under the authority given at the 1995 Annual General Meeting. A further 44 million Ordinary Shares were purchased on 17 January 1997 under the 1996 authority.

The purchase by the Company of its own shares demonstrates the Company's continued commitment to ensuring that its balance sheet is managed in the long-term interests of its shareholders. The share re-purchases and the dividends paid since the beginning of 1996 bring the total cash returned to shareholders to £939 million.

A resolution seeking renewal of the authority will be put to the forthcoming Annual General Meeting.

Notes to the Group accounts

21. CALLED UP SHARE CAPITAL AND SHARE PREMIUM ACCOUNT

(B) Movement in called up share capital and share premium account [extract]

	Ordinary Shares £m	Share premium account £m	Total £m
At 1 January 1996	506	569	1,075
Issue of shares	2	21	23
Repurchase of shares	(25)	–	(25)
At 31 December 1996	**483**	**590**	**1,073**

On 22 March 1996 the Company repurchased and subsequently cancelled 100m Ordinary Shares, representing 4.9% of the called up share capital, at a price of 463p per share. The total cost of the repurchase, including expenses, was £466m and is charged against the profit and loss account reserve.

22. RESERVES AND GOODWILL

(A) Reserves [extract]

	Revaluation reserve £m	Capital redemption reserve £m	Merger reserve £m	Associated undertakings £m	Total other reserves £m	Profit and loss account £m
At 1 January 1996	169	49	1,781	70	2,069	2,440
Retained earnings	–	–	–	53	53	337
Repurchase of shares (Note 21(B))	–	25	–	–	25	(466)
Other	(6)	–	–	(1)	(7)	6
Exchange adjustments	(2)	–	–	3	1	(81)
At 31 December 1996	**161**	**74**	**1,781**	**125**	**2,141**	**2,236**

Listed companies have to give the following disclosure requirements in relation to the purchase of their own shares:

(a) any shareholders' authority which existed at the year end for the company to purchase its own shares;

(b)   the names of the sellers of any shares purchased or proposed to be purchased by the company during the year otherwise than through the market or by tender or partial offer to all shareholders; and

(c)   where purchases, or options or contracts to make such purchases, have been entered into since the year end, the number, nominal value and percentage of the called up shares of the class purchased, the consideration paid and the reasons for the purchase.[105]

4   ACCOUNTING FOR PARTICULAR TYPES OF INSTRUMENT

4.1   Bonds with no rights to conversion

4.1.1   *Fixed interest rate bonds*

This is the most straightforward kind of borrowing to account for and the only mild complication is that the issue costs have to be deducted from the amount borrowed so as to be spread over the life of the loan.

Example 15.9:   Fixed interest rate bonds

A company issues a £20 million bond for 5 years in respect of which the interest rate is 7%. The costs of the issue amount to £400,000.

FRS 4 requires the issue costs to be deducted from the proceeds of the borrowing to produce an initial net liability of £19.6 million. This is then accreted back up to the amount payable, in the following way (all figures in £000s):

Year	Total finance cost	Interest paid	Amortisation of issue costs	Balance sheet liability
0				19,600
1	1,469	1,400	69	19,669
2	1,474	1,400	74	19,743
3	1,480	1,400	80	19,823
4	1,485	1,400	85	19,908
5	1,492	1,400	92	20,000
Total	7,400	7,000	400	

The calculation of the total finance cost shown above is based on the rate inherent in all the cash flows (7.49% in this case), but in practice the amount of issue costs will usually not be material enough to require such rigour to be applied. Simplified methods of disposing of the issue costs, such as straight line amortisation or even immediate write-off will often be acceptable on materiality grounds.

4.1.2   *Variable interest rate bonds*

These are again simple borrowing arrangements, the only difference being that the interest cost varies in accordance with some external rate, such as LIBOR. FRS 4 does not require the finance cost to be 'equalised'; the interest is simply charged at whatever rate is in force for the period. The only mild complication is again created by any other components of finance cost (such as issue costs or premiums payable on redemption).

Example 15.10:   Variable interest rate bonds

A company issues a £20 million bond for 5 years in respect of which the interest rate is LIBOR plus 1%. The cost of the issue is again £400,000. LIBOR is 6% at the outset but changes to 8% after 2 years.

Initially, this example is identical to the previous one and if LIBOR did not change, the accounting result would be exactly the same. The only variation comes when LIBOR changes. At that time, FRS 4 strictly requires a fresh calculation of the interest rate implicit in the arrangement – in other words, what is the rate needed to discount the future payments of interest (now £1.8m per annum) and principal to a present value of £19,743,000 (the amount carried in the balance sheet at the end of year 2). In this example, the rate changes from 7.49% to 9.51% and produces the following result (all figures in £000s):

Year	Total finance cost	Interest paid	Amortisation of issue costs	Balance sheet liability
0				19,600
1	1,469	1,400	69	19,669
2	1,474	1,400	74	19,743
3	1,878	1,800	78	19,821
4	1,886	1,800	86	19,907
5	1,893	1,800	93	20,000
Total	8,600	8,200	400	

Clearly in this example, the change makes a negligible difference to the pattern of amortising the non-interest component of finance costs, and the calculation need not therefore be performed in the rigorous way required by the standard. However, in some cases (for example, where the instrument is a deep discounted bond with a long life), the effect might be sufficiently material to justify making the calculation.

4.1.3   Stepped bonds

Stepped bonds are borrowing instruments whose interest rate escalates over the life of the bond in a predetermined way. This is illustrated in the following example:

Example 15.11:   Stepped bonds

A company issues a £10 million bond for 10 years in respect of which the interest rate is 8% for the first three years, 10% for the next three and 13% for the final four. The annual interest payable therefore escalates from £800,000 to £1,300,000. (Issue costs are ignored in this example.)

If the company accounted for this on a cash basis it would record an artificially low finance cost in the early years and an artificially high cost towards the end of the life of the bond. FRS 4 requires that the total finance cost over the life of the bond should be calculated and charged to the profit and loss account at a constant rate on the outstanding amount rather than taking the cash payments at face value. This produces the following result (all figures in £000s):

Year	Finance cost	Interest paid	Difference	Accrued interest
1	1,006	800	206	206
2	1,027	800	227	433
3	1,050	800	250	683
4	1,075	1,000	75	758
5	1,082	1,000	82	840
6	1,091	1,000	91	931
7	1,100	1,300	(200)	731
8	1,080	1,300	(220)	511
9	1,057	1,300	(243)	268
10	1,032	1,300	(268)	0
Total	10,600	10,600		

The calculation of the interest charge shown above is again based on the rate inherent in all the cash flows, rather than simply the total interest charge (£10,600,000) divided by the period of the loan (10 years) which would give a flat annual charge of £1,060,000. Nevertheless in practice the straight line method is simpler and can often be used since it will seldom produce a material distortion.

4.1.4   Deep discounted bonds

A deep discounted bond is a bond which is issued at a discount to its par value and redemption value, and it is described as a deep discount because the proceeds on issue are considerably smaller than the par value. The instrument will normally pay either no interest (generally referred to as a zero coupon bond) or a very low annual rate of interest, so that the discount and any interest payable together represent a commercial rate of interest.

Under FRS 4, the discount forms part of the finance cost and is provided for through the profit and loss account over the life of the bond. The bond is therefore included as a liability at its issue price and thereafter accretes to the redemption value over its life, as shown in the example below:

Example 15.12:   Deep discounted bonds

A company issues a bond for £47 million which is redeemable at its par value of £100 million at the end of 10 years. The interest rate is 3% per annum, and the annual interest payable is thus £3 million. The costs of issuing the bond are £2 million. Spreading the discount and the issue costs over the life of the bond in addition to the interest charge produces the following result (all figures in £000s):

Year	Finance cost	Interest paid	Amortisation of discount and issue costs	Balance sheet liability
0				45,000
1	5,953	3,000	2,953	47,953
2	6,344	3,000	3,344	51,297
3	6,785	3,000	3,785	55,082
4	7,287	3,000	4,287	59,369
5	7,854	3,000	4,854	64,223
6	8,496	3,000	5,496	69,719
7	9,223	3,000	6,223	75,942
8	10,046	3,000	7,046	82,988
9	10,978	3,000	7,978	90,966
10	12,034	3,000	9,034	100,000
Total	85,000	30,000	55,000	

Once again, the calculation of the total finance charge shown above is based on the rate inherent in all the cash flows (in this case 13.23%), rather than simply the total charge (£85,000,000) divided by the period of the loan (10 years) which would give a flat annual charge of £8,500,000. In this case, the more rigorous calculation is materially different from that which would be produced by amortising the total discount on a straight line basis, and the latter is therefore unlikely to produce an acceptable answer.

Since the balance sheet figure in the final column of the table falls substantially short of the liability ultimately payable (by the amount of finance costs to be recognised in the future, other than interest), it is necessary to disclose the full liability by way of note.[106]

4.1.5   Index-linked bonds

FRS 4 requires that, where the payments to be made under a debt instrument are contingent on future events, these events should be taken into account in the calculation of finance cost only when they have occurred.[107] This applies to variable interest loans (discussed at 4.1.2 above) but also to those whose interest or redemption values vary in accordance with a price index, such as the RPI.

A bond which is index-linked is analogous to one which is denominated in a foreign currency, and the accounting follows a similar pattern. The effect on the principal of the movement in the index is treated similarly to a translation difference; in other words the whole amount of the movement in the period is dealt with in the profit and loss account, while the interest payable in the period continues to be charged at whatever amount results from applying the index adjustment to it.

Example 15.13:   Index-linked bonds

A company issues a £10 million bond for 5 years in respect of which the interest rate is 2%, but both interest and principal payments are linked to the RPI at the end of the year. Issue costs are ignored in this example. This will be accounted for in the following way (all figures in £000s):

Year	Index	Interest paid	Indexation adjustment	Total finance cost	Balance sheet liability
0	100				10,000
1	103	206	300	506	10,300
2	104	208	100	308	10,400
3	106	212	200	412	10,600
4	109	218	300	518	10,900
5	111	222	200	422	11,100
Total		1,066	1,100	2,166	

Sometimes, bonds that are linked to indexes which move in a predictable way may really only be stepped loans in disguise. These should be accounted for in accordance with their substance – by forecasting the total finance cost payable over the term of the instrument and allocating it so as to achieve a constant rate on the outstanding balance. Accordingly it is necessary to distinguish between arrangements with a genuine economic purpose and those which are contrived solely to have a particular accounting effect. Linking amounts payable under a loan to the RPI will have a commercial purpose; linking them to the age of the finance director's cat will not.

4.2   Convertible bonds

4.2.1   Traditional convertible bonds

A convertible bond is a hybrid instrument which initially has the character of a loan, bearing interest, but also entitles the bondholder to exchange the bond for shares in the company at some date in the future in accordance with specified conditions. Because of the conversion right, the coupon on the bond is set at a lower level than would be appropriate for straight borrowing. The effect from the equity shareholders' point of view is that they gain the benefits of cheap borrowing for a period but ultimately are likely to suffer a dilution in their holding in the company when the bonds are converted.

FRS 4 requires these to be accounted for as debt rather than equity and the finance cost to be measured on the assumption that the debt will never be converted. If conversion does take place, the carrying value of the instrument at that time is regarded as the consideration for the issue of the shares; no gain or loss is recorded on the conversion.[108]

4.2.2   Bonds with share warrants attached

In this case, a deep discount bond is issued together with a detachable warrant; such instruments are sometimes known as 'synthetic convertibles'. The warrant entitles the holder to obtain ordinary shares, and the further price that has to be paid for those shares on exercise of the warrant is paid out of the redemption of the bond at the end of its life.

In this case FRS 4 does take the view that the two elements should be accounted for separately, and the treatment required is therefore based on the example of 'split accounting' described at 2.2.2 above. It distinguishes the two cases on the basis that convertible debt is a single financial instrument whose various rights cannot be exercised independently, whereas bonds with warrants are really two separable instruments which should be accounted for individually. An example of this treatment can be found in the 1994 accounts of Pilkington, as shown below:

Extract 15.20: Pilkington plc (1994)

28. Called Up Share Capital [extract]

In April 1993 the company issued £80 million 7.5% bonds at an issue price of £95 million to finance the acquisition of the United Kingdom glass processing and merchanting business of Heywood Williams Group PLC. The bonds were issued with 78.2 million warrants, each warrant entitling the holder to procure up to 4 May 1998 the allotment of one share in Pilkington plc at a price of 120p.

The capital amount attributable to the warrants is £16.4 million and is included in other reserves.

4.2.3 Convertible bonds with premium puts or enhanced interest

A further elaboration on the convertible bond theme is to give the bondholder the option of putting his bond back to the company at a premium as an alternative to exercising his right to convert it into shares in the company. This raises a further question for the issuing company – whether to make provision for the premium over the life of the bond despite the fact that it may never become payable because the conversion option is exercised instead. A similar question arises when the interest rate on the bond is enhanced in later years if it remains unconverted; should the increased finance cost be accounted for from the outset, even though it may never be suffered?

FRS 4 requires that provision be made for such premiums or enhanced interest, and this is discussed in the Application Notes to the standard. This is consistent with an earlier ruling by the UITF[109] as well as the recommendation of TR 677. The standard requires that the finance cost on convertible debt should be calculated on the assumption that it will never be converted,[110] on the argument that this is the minimum return to which the holder is entitled, and is what he will be surrendering if he elects to convert. On the same argument, when conversion occurs, the consideration for the issue of the shares is the carrying amount of the debt, including the accrued premium.[111]

4.2.4 Convertible capital bonds

In the late 1980s, a number of groups issued convertible capital bonds, which are another form of hybrid instrument with features of both debt and equity. FRS 4 describes a typical example as being along the following lines: 'Convertible capital bonds are debt instruments on which interest is paid periodically, issued by a special purpose subsidiary incorporated outside the UK. Prior to maturity they may be exchanged for shares of the subsidiary which, at the option of the bondholder, are either immediately redeemed or immediately exchanged for ordinary shares of the parent. The bonds and payments in respect of the shares of the subsidiary are guaranteed by the parent. The parent has the right to issue convertible redeemable preference shares of its own in substitution for the bonds should it wish to do so.'[112]

A practice developed of showing such bonds at the end of the equity section of the balance sheet rather than within the liabilities section, on the argument that they were likely to form permanent capital of the company and that it was more realistic to include them with equity for such purposes as assessing the company's gearing. Because conversion into shares was mandatory except in a situation of default, it was argued that the liability to repay the debt was a remote contingency and could be disregarded. On this basis it was asserted that it was appropriate to treat the instrument as if it were a convertible preference share, the accounting for which is described at 4.4.2 below.

FRS 4 dismisses these arguments, because it does not permit conversion to be assumed under any circumstances. Accordingly, the relevant Application Note says that convertible capital bonds now have to be disclosed as debt in all cases.

4.2.5   Perpetual debt

Debt is sometimes issued on such terms that it is irredeemable, but that a coupon payment is to be made indefinitely. FRS 4 dismisses any suggestion that this means that no liability need be shown on the balance sheet, because the standard's guiding principle is to look at all the payments which the company is contractually bound to make, whether they are characterised as being capital or revenue. Where there is an obligation to pay a perpetual interest payment, the carrying value of the debt will by definition always be the original issue proceeds, because that is the figure derived from discounting the future payments at the rate implicit in the loan.

Sometimes a more artificial arrangement is devised, generally with a tax motive, whereby substantially all of the interest payments are made in the early part of the life of the debt, and the payments thereafter are negligible or even nil. The substance of such an arrangement is that the 'interest' payments are in reality a mixture of interest and capital repayments, and following the principles of FRS 4, this is how they should be accounted for. A variation on the same theme is to use very long-dated rather than perpetual debt. Often, any obligation to make payments of interest and capital beyond the initial term is transferred to another party for a small consideration, or another group company buys the right to receive such amounts from the original lender, with the result in either case that the group is left with only the liability for the significant payments during the initial term.

Examples of such instruments are disclosed in the accounts of Cadbury Schweppes:

Extract 15.21: Cadbury Schweppes p.l.c. (1996)

Notes on the Accounts

17 Borrowings [extract]

	Amounts due within one year £m	Amounts due after one year £m	Amounts due within one year £m	Amounts due after one year £m
	1996		**1995**	
Group				
Secured				
Bank overdrafts	1	–	2	–
Other loans	13	3	26	12
Unsecured				
5.875% Notes 1998 (US$200m)	–	118	–	129
8.5% Guaranteed Notes 1999 (A$75m)	–	35	–	36
6.25% Notes 1999 (US$300m)	–	177	–	193
8% Notes 2000 (£150m)	–	140	–	149
5.125% Guaranteed Notes 2001 (DM300m)	–	120	–	–
11.5% Senior Subordinated Discount Notes 2002 (US$39m)	23	–	185	23
Obligations under perpetual loan (FFr 894m)	8	93	9	117
Obligations under fixed rate notes	15	61	13	76
Commercial paper (A$124m and £161m)	219	–	93	–
Master notes (US$250m)	148	–	161	–
Bank loans in foreign currencies	39	13	39	29
Bank overdrafts	50	–	39	–
Other loans	43	3	27	60
Obligations under finance leases	9	34	11	40
Acceptance credits	28	–	4	–
	596	**797**	**609**	**864**

The obligations under the perpetual subordinated loan represent the present value of the future interest payments on the principal amount of FFr 1,600m which terminate in 2005; the interest rate is variable based on the Paris Inter-Bank Offered Rate. The obligations under the fixed rate notes represent the present value of future interest payments on £200 million of 12.55% Eurobonds up to 2001; the principal of the bonds and subsequent interest coupons have been acquired by a Group company.

4.3 Share options and warrants

As explained in 2.2.8, the standard requires the net proceeds of a warrant to be credited direct to shareholders' funds, and thereafter the accounting depends on whether the warrant is exercised or is allowed to lapse. If it is exercised, the proceeds on the original issue of the warrant are included in the net proceeds of the shares issued;[113] if it lapses, they are included instead in the statement of total recognised gains and losses.[114]

The question of what should be credited to share premium account is ultimately one of law.[115] It is not beyond legal doubt that warrant proceeds should be regarded subsequently as part of the consideration for the issue of shares if the warrant is exercised, which is the premise on which FRS 4's requirement is based. If this is the law, the same might be thought to apply to convertible instruments which are issued as an intermediate stage in a share issue, but this view does not always appear to be adopted in practice.

4.4   Preference shares

4.4.1   Redeemable preference shares

Redeemable preference shares can be regarded as quite similar in substance to fixed interest borrowings. There are, however, some important legal differences; for example, when they are redeemed, there is a requirement to make good the capital by a transfer to a capital redemption reserve; dividends can only be paid if there are sufficient distributable reserves; also, there are some significant differences between the treatment for both tax and accounting purposes of the dividends paid on shares compared to the interest paid on debt.

Dividends are regarded as a distribution of profits to the owners of the business rather than as an expense charged in measuring that profit. As such, prior to FRS 4 they were not generally accounted for on an accruals basis; this meant, for example, that when cumulative preference dividends were in arrears, they were not accrued in the accounts but simply noted as being in arrears. Similarly, if redeemable preference shares carried an escalating dividend rate, conventional accounting practice in the UK did not seek to 'equalise' the dividends in the way required for stepped bonds as discussed in 4.1.3 above. However, FRS 4 has changed this practice, so that appropriations are now made on an accruals basis, measured in the same way as for a debt instrument, unless ultimate payment is remote.[116] This is required even if the company currently has no distributable profits. The only apparent circumstances in which dividends should not be accrued are where they are non-cumulative, so that the holder permanently loses his right to a return on the shares for that period.

Where cumulative preference dividends which are in arrears are accrued under FRS 4, it has to be considered whether the credit entry should be shown as a liability or as an element of non-equity shareholders' funds. Since they have not been declared, they do not represent a liability of the company as defined in FRS 4 and there is therefore quite a persuasive argument that they should be shown in the shareholders' funds section; the only difficulty with this argument is that it applies to *all* accrued dividends which have not yet been declared, whereas conventional UK accounting practice is to show such dividends in the liabilities section. In the light of these conflicting arguments, we believe that either classification can be justified for preference dividends in arrears.

Signet Group shows its arrears of dividends within shareholders' funds rather than within liabilities, and describes the appropriation in the profit and loss account as an additional finance cost, not as a dividend, as shown below:

Extract 15.22: Signet Group plc (1997)

Consolidated profit and loss account

for the 52 weeks ended 1 February 1997 [extract]

	52 weeks ended 1 February 1997 £000	53 weeks ended 3 February 1996 £000
Profit for the financial period	**33,855**	17,517
Dividends	–	–
Additional finance costs of non-equity shares	**(26,398)**	(42,075)
Retained profit/(loss) attributable to equity shareholders	**7,457**	(24,558)

23 Non-equity shareholders' funds

On 20 January 1992 the directors announced that payment of dividends on all of the Company's various classes of preference shares would cease until further notice. No dividends have been paid since that date. Dividends on all classes of preference shares are cumulative and payment of arrears of preference dividends would be due to be made before payments of dividends on ordinary shares recommenced. Cumulative arrears of preference dividends as at 1 February 1997 amounted to £155,281,000 (1996: £128,517,000).

In addition to the dividend arrears above, £6,221,000 (1996: £6,587,000) of preference dividends were accumulated on a time basis at 1 February 1997, but not in arrears. The increase in unpaid preference dividends in the period is stated net of £5,012,000 exchange loss (1996: £3,867,000 loss). In accordance with FRS 4, the following analysis sets out net issue proceeds plus the cumulative amount of accrued finance costs in respect of each class of the Company's preference shares.

		1997		1996
	Net issue proceeds £000	Unpaid preference dividends £000	Total non-equity shareholders' funds £000	Total non-equity shareholders' funds £000
Analysis of non-equity shareholders' funds				
6.875p convertible preference shares of 20p each	33,841	13,093	46,934	44,565
Cumulative redeemable preference shares 1997 of £10 each	30,000	16,633	46,633	43,519
Variable term preference shares of US$1 each	149,537	87,832	237,369	222,956
Convertible preference shares of US$0.01 each	104,223	43,944	148,167	141,665
Total non-equity shareholders' funds	**317,601**	**161,502**	**479,103**	452,705

Equity shareholders' funds, representing the difference between total shareholders' funds and non-equity shareholders' funds, showed a deficit of £178,358,000 (1996: £181,378,000 deficit) for the Group. In the Company's balance sheet equity shareholders' funds at 1 February 1997 amounted to £117,437,000 (1996:£152,710,000).

FRS 4 requires the full finance cost of non-equity shares to be shown as appropriated from profits, even if the Company does not have sufficient distributable reserves to pay a dividend at that time. As it is not legally possible to show dividends payable if the Company has insufficient distributable reserves to support a dividend, the appropriation has been classified as an additional finance cost in respect of non-equity shares.

Upon the capital restructuring, which was approved by shareholders on 26 June 1997, becoming effective (expected to be on 21 July 1997), all of the preference shares will be converted into new ordinary shares and all arrears and accruals of preference dividends will be cancelled.

Preference shares are sometimes structured so that they have a variable dividend level which depends on prevailing interest rates, which may be set at auction; the investors who make the lowest bid each month hold the instrument. The cost of this form of finance is thus similar to that of commercial paper, and it might be regarded as in substance a debt issue, but under FRS 4 they are nonetheless classified as non-equity shares.

Cadbury Schweppes has issued some shares of this kind, whose terms are fully described in this extract from its financial statements:

Extract 15.23: Cadbury Schweppes p.l.c. (1996)

22 Capital and Reserves [extract]

(e) Cumulative Perpetual Preference shares

In 1990 the Company issued 350 US$ Auction Preference shares (Series 3 to 6) at a price of US$500,000. The dividend rate on each of these shares is reset at auctions normally held every 28 days. The rates of dividend paid during 1996 ranged between 4.19% and 4.87% and at 28 December 1996 the weighted average rate payable was 4.45%.

On 12 February 1997, the Company announced its intention to redeem the US$ Auction Preference Shares at their original issue price of $175m. Redemption will be completed on 25 March 1997.

4.4.2 *Convertible preference shares*

Such instruments are simply disclosed as a separate class of non-equity share capital, with details of their terms. Where the preference shares have been issued by the parent, the only available treatment is to show them as a component of shareholders' funds, but frequently such shares are issued by a subsidiary company for tax reasons. In this case they will either fall under the category of minority interest on consolidation or, if guaranteed by the parent or another group company, they will be shown as liabilities in the consolidated balance sheet.

Convertible preference share issues may be issued with a premium put, so that, in effect, if the redemption option is chosen, an enhanced dividend will be paid. As with convertible debt, FRS 4 requires this to be taken into account in measuring the finance cost of the instrument. This requires an additional annual appropriation of profits to be made, so that the total amount appropriated in respect of the shares is at a constant proportion to the total amount recognised for the shares in the balance sheet.[117]

4.5 Interest rate swaps

An interest rate swap is an agreement between two counterparties that they will exchange fixed rate interest for floating rate interest on a notional amount of principal. The principal is notional in the sense that it itself is not exchanged, only the amounts of interest determined by reference to it.

The objective of entering into an interest rate swap is effectively to convert existing finance from a fixed interest basis to a floating rate basis or vice versa. The treatment recommended by TR 677 was therefore to incorporate the terms of the swap into those of the existing finance; for example, if a company has a floating rate loan but enters into an interest rate swap because it prefers not to have exposure to floating rates, then the accounts would portray the loan as if it were at fixed rates. The Technical Release went on to say that 'there should be full disclosure of the arrangement in the notes to the financial statements, so that the true commercial effect on the whole transaction, including any possible risk of exposure in the event of the failure of the swap-party, is clearly explained'.[118] The subject of interest rate swaps or other similar hedges is not addressed in FRS 4, but is now being addressed in the ASB's project on financial instruments (see Chapter 9).

4.6 Scrip dividends

Scrip dividends arise when a company offers its shareholders the choice of receiving further fully paid up shares in the company as an alternative to receiving a cash dividend.

The FRS requires that a scrip dividend should initially be recorded at its cash amount as an appropriation in the profit and loss account. As it is unclear at that time how many shareholders will elect to receive shares, the whole amount of the dividend should be recorded as a liability in the balance sheet. This obviously applies to final dividends, since the take-up of the scrip will not be known until after the accounts have been prepared. However, where the interim dividend has taken the form of a scrip dividend during the year it will be possible to reflect exactly what has been paid in cash and what has been issued in the form of shares. We believe, however, that FRS 4 still intends that the dividend be shown as an appropriation in the profit and loss account at its full cash amount.[119]

Once shareholders have chosen to receive shares instead of cash, two possible approaches exist, described respectively as the reinvestment approach and the bonus share approach. As the name suggests, the former takes the view that a dividend has been paid, but then reinvested in shares; accordingly, the consideration for the issue of the shares is the amount of the dividend and is divided as appropriate between share capital (to the extent of their nominal value) and share premium account. The alternative view is that the shares are issued *instead* of a dividend; accordingly, no consideration has been received and the issue is a simple bonus issue, which results in the capitalisation of a suitable reserve to the extent of the nominal value of the shares issued.

FRS 4 is rather ambiguous about the choice between these approaches. On the one hand, paragraph 48 suggests that it favours the reinvestment approach, because it says that 'the value of such shares should be deemed to be the amount receivable if the alternative of cash had been chosen', but it may be that this is discussing only the initial treatment in the profit and loss account as mentioned above. Paragraph 99, on the other hand, says that if the 'scrip dividend takes the legal form of a bonus issue of shares, the appropriation should be written back as a reserve movement, and appropriate amounts transferred between reserves and share capital to reflect the capitalisation of reserves', which is the bonus share approach.

Lawyers tend to maintain that no choice is available between these two methods; the right method is dictated by the form of the transaction. They would say that the question of whether the shares are issued for consideration or not is one of legal fact, not of interpretation. Accordingly, where a shareholder signs a mandate form which says that he elects to receive an allotment of shares instead of the dividend (as is typically the case), he will thereafter receive a bonus issue, which should be accounted for as such. If one accepts this view, the normal accounting treatment would be as illustrated in this example:

Example 15.14:   Scrip dividend

A company declares a final dividend for the year ended 31 December 19X1 of 20 pence per share, but offers shareholders the alternative of accepting 1 share for every 10 held. The issued share capital of the company is 10 million £1 shares, and their current market price is £2 per share.

When it draws up its accounts for 19X1 it does not know how many shareholders will opt for the scrip dividend. Under FRS 4, it records £2 million (being the cash amount) as an appropriation in the profit and loss account and provides the same amount within creditors as 'dividends payable'.

Subsequently, the shareholders accept the cash dividend in respect of 8 million shares but opt for the further shares in respect of the remaining 2 million.

Assuming that the legal form of the scrip dividend was a bonus issue, the issue of shares to those who have opted for them is viewed as a bonus issue and accounted for at nominal value. Thus the further journal entries which have to be made are as follows:

		£000	£000
Dr.	Dividends payable	2,000	
Cr.	Cash		1,600
Cr.	Profit and loss account reserve		400

To reverse the previous entry to the extent of the scrip dividend and recognise the payment of the remainder, and

		£000	£000
Dr.	Reserves	200	
Cr.	Share capital		200

To record the bonus issue. The reserve to be used would depend on what was available, but could be, for example, a share premium account or a revaluation reserve as well as the profit and loss account reserve.

If, on the other hand, the scrip dividend did not take the legal form of a bonus issue, the share issue would have to be accounted for differently. This situation may arise if, under the mandate form, the shareholder elects to receive a cash dividend but irrevocably authorises the company to apply the cash on his behalf in subscribing for the appropriate number of new shares. As this is tantamount to an issue of shares for cash, FRS 4 would require the shares to be recorded by reference to the cash equivalent of the dividend foregone.

The guidance on scrip dividends in FRS 4 therefore remains rather ambiguous. It would seem likely that both the reinvestment approach and the bonus issue approach will continue to be used, subject to any legal advice which companies obtain as to the proper interpretation of the terms of the transaction and the particular requirements of the company's articles.

Examples of these approaches can be found in the following extracts – HSBC uses the bonus share approach while Hillsdown uses the reinvestment approach.

Extract 15.24: HSBC Holdings plc (1996)

8 Dividends

	1996		1995	
	Pence per share	**£m**	Pence per share	£m
First interim	**15.00**	**397**	9.25	243
Second interim	**26.00**	**693**	–	–
Final	–	–	22.75	600
	41.00	**1,090**	32.00	843

Of the first interim dividend for 1996, £89 million (1995: £53 million) was settled by the issue of shares. Of the final dividend for 1995, £101 million (1994: £120 million) was settled by the issue of shares in 1996.

32 Reserves [extract]

	Group £m	Company £m	Associated undertakings £m
Share premium account:			
At 1 January 1996	307	307	–
Shares issued under option schemes	7	7	–
Shares issued in lieu of dividends and associated issue costs	(15)	(15)	–
At 31 December 1996	**299**	**299**	–
Profit and loss account			
At 1 January 1996	**8,590**	**3,184**	**93**
Exchange and other movements	(676)	–	(3)
Retained profit (deficit) for the year	2,022	(283)	4
Goodwill written off on acquisition	(12)	–	–
Goodwill written back on part disposal of associated undertakings	9	–	–
Transfer of depreciation to revaluation reserve	34	–	–
Transfer of permanent diminution in value of land and buildings from revaluation reserve	(8)	–	–
Realisation on disposal of properties	2	–	–
Arising on shares issued in lieu of dividends	190	190	–
At 31 December 1996	**10,151**	**3,091**	**94**

As the above extract shows, HSBC has added back £190m to the profit and loss account within its reserves note, being the amount of dividends (£89m and £101m) taken in shares rather than cash. The £15m charged to share premium is the nominal value of the shares issued by way of the bonus issue.

Extract 15.25: Hillsdown Holdings plc (1996)

	1996 £m	1995 £m
7 Dividends		
Per 10p ordinary share		
Interim – 2.2p (1995: 2.2p)	**15.5**	15.3
Final – 7.8p (1995: 7.3p)	**55.7**	51.1
	71.2	66.4
Canadian C$1,000 preference shares	–	0.7
	71.2	67.1

18 Reserves [extract]

	Share premium £m	Revaluation reserve £m	Profit and loss account £m	Total reserves £m
Group				
At 1st January 1996	63.3	51.4	453.0	567.7
Movements in year				
Profit retained	–	–	24.2	24.2
Revaluation reserve realised	–	(9.6)	9.6	–
Revaluations	–	(3.1)	–	(3.1)
Issue of ordinary shares:				
Scrip dividend election	3.8	–	–	3.8
Share option schemes	8.5	–	–	8.5
Goodwill arising from acquisitions	–	–	(115.5)	(115.5)
Exchange adjustments	–	–	(6.2)	(6.2)
At 31st December 1996	**75.6**	**38.7**	**365.1**	**479.4**

This time there is a credit rather than a debit to share premium, because the new shares are regarded as having been issued in exchange for reinvested dividends, not as a bonus issue. There is no adjustment to the dividends that have been declared, nor any add-back to retained earnings.

4.7 Employee share schemes

FRS 4 does not address questions relating to transactions in the reporting entity's own shares for the purposes of employee share schemes. However, the Urgent Issues Task Force has issued two Abstracts dealing with different problems that have arisen in relation to such schemes. These are discussed below.

4.7.1 UITF 13 – Accounting for ESOP Trusts

The subject of employee share ownership plans ('ESOPs') came to the UITF as an off balance sheet finance question, requiring interpretation under FRS 5, although arguably the more important issue concerns the recognition and measurement of the cost of such arrangements, and it would have been better addressed from that perspective. Companies frequently establish share ownership schemes for their employees, whereby the employees are given the opportunity to buy shares in the company on favourable terms or to receive them free under a profit sharing scheme. Either new or existing shares may be used for this purpose; where existing shares are used, they are generally purchased by a trust or other third party, which is financed by a loan from either the company itself or from a bank. In the latter case, the bank loan will usually be guaranteed by the company. The accounting issue that arises under FRS 5 is how to deal with the trust in the employing company's accounts.

Arrangements of this sort are not discussed directly in FRS 5, but the UITF issued guidance on the matter by publishing its thirteenth Abstract in June 1995. This rules that certain assets and liabilities of the trust should be accounted for as those of the employer company itself where the company 'has de facto control of the shares held by the ESOP trust and bears their benefits or risks'.[120] More specifically, the Abstract goes on to say that:

(a) Until such time as the shares held by the ESOP trust vest unconditionally in employees, they should be recognised as assets of the sponsoring company. Where shares have been gifted unconditionally to specific employees, they should no longer be recognised as assets of the sponsoring company, even if they are still held by the ESOP trust.

(b) Where the shares are held for the continuing benefit of the sponsoring company's business they should be classified as 'own shares' within fixed assets; otherwise they should be classified as 'own shares' within current assets.

(c) Where the shares are classified as fixed assets, any permanent diminution in their value should be recognised immediately.

(d) Where shares are conditionally gifted or put under option to employees at below the book value determined in (c) above, (i.e. for fixed assets, after taking account of any permanent diminution in value), the difference between book value and residual value should be charged as an operating cost over the period of service of the employees in respect of which the gifts or options are granted.

(e) The sponsoring company should record as its own liability any borrowings of the ESOP trust that are guaranteed, formally or informally, by the sponsoring company.

(f) Finance costs and any administrative expenses should be charged as they accrue and not as funding payments are made to the ESOP trust.

(g) If dividend income is not waived, it should be included in arriving at profit before tax and in the earnings per share calculation, as should the shares held by the ESOP trust. However, where dividends are waived by the

ESOP trust the shares should be excluded from the basic earnings per share calculation.[121]

The general thrust of the above is that companies should account for the transactions of their ESOP trusts as if they had conducted them themselves; the trust is portrayed as merely an extension of the company. A possible alternative approach would have been to regard the trust as a quasi-subsidiary of the company which therefore had to be consolidated in it group accounts, but the Abstract goes further, by requiring the assets and liabilities of the trust to be treated as belonging directly to the employer company.

UITF 13 requires disclosure of sufficient information to enable readers of the accounts to understand the significance of the ESOP trust in the context of the sponsoring company, and in particular:

(a) a description of the main features of the ESOP trust including the arrangements for distributing shares to employees;

(b) the manner in which the costs are dealt with in the profit and loss account;

(c) the number and market value of shares held by the ESOP trust and whether dividends on those shares have been waived; and

(d) the extent to which these shares are under option to employees, or have been conditionally gifted to them.[122]

Appendix II to the Abstract gives a number of illustrative examples of the accounting treatment required under various scenarios.

The accounts of Enterprise Oil and BOC disclose the following information about the shares that are held in their ESOP trusts:

Extract 15.26: Enterprise Oil plc (1996)

13. Investments (held as fixed assets) [extract]

	At 1 January 1996	Additions	At 31 December 1996
Own shares held by employee share schemes	£m	£m	£m
– shares (at cost)	7.0	10.6	**17.6**
– amortisation	(0.9)	(1.9)	**(2.8)**
	6.1	8.7	**14.8**

iii) Own shares held by employee share schemes

Employee share schemes set up as trusts hold Enterprise Oil plc ordinary shares to meet potential obligations under the schemes.

Shares are held in trust until such time as they may be transferred to employees in accordance with the terms of the schemes, details of which are given on pages 35 to 37. Surplus shares may be held to satisfy future awards.

The group recognises the cost of the Enterprise Oil Long Term Performance Related Scheme through an annual amortisation charge based on management's estimate of the likely level of vesting of shares, apportioned over the period of service to which the award relates.

At 31 December 1996 the trusts held a total of 3,788,392 shares (1995: 1,846,186) with a market value at that date of £24.6 million (1995: £7.3 million). Dividends on these shares have been waived by the respective trustees.

9. Earnings per share [extract]

... The weighted average number of ordinary shares reflects adjustment ... for 3.8 million shares (1995: 1.8 million) held by employee share schemes on which no dividend is payable (see note 13 (iii)).

Extract 15.27: The BOC Group plc (1996)

9. Fixed assets – investments [extract]	Own shares
	at cost
a) Group	£million

At 1 October 1995	20.6
Acquisitions	3.3
Disposals	(1.3)
	——
At 30 September 1996	22.6
	——

ii) **Own shares**

For share-based incentive schemes which do not use new issue shares, options are satisfied by the transfer of shares held in trust for the purpose. At 30 September 1996, options over 4.5 million shares were outstanding under these schemes, for which 4.1 million shares in the Company were held pending exercise.

Loans for the purchase of shares in trust have been made either by the Company or its subsidiaries. If the value of the shares in trust is insufficient to cover the loans, the Company and subsidiaries will bear any loss. The Company also bears administrative costs on an accruals basis.

Based on the Company's share price on 30 September 1996 of 872p, the market value of the shares held in trust was £35.8 million. This compares with the acquisition cost shown above. During the year scrip dividends of 0.1 million shares were taken on 4.0 million shares.

Own shares are shown as fixed asset investments for accounting purposes, in accordance with FRS 5 and UITF Abstract 13. Information on share option schemes appears in the Report of the Management Resources Committee and notes 6 and 12.

In fact, these shares are carried only in BOC's group balance sheet, whereas those of Enterprise Oil appear in the balance sheets of both the group and parent company.

The economics of these arrangements are similar to those which arise under a defined benefits pension scheme. As in BOC's case, the employer generally has to meet any shortfall in value of the shares in the trust in the same way as it would have to meet the balance of cost necessary to provide final salary pensions, and it thus it has a direct economic interest in the fund even though the scheme is operated by independent trustees. However, FRS 5 does not require the assets and liabilities of pension funds to be brought on to the balance sheets of employers, saying that: 'As SSAP 24 contains the more specific provisions on accounting for pension obligations and does not require consolidation of pension funds, such funds should not be consolidated as quasi-subsidiaries.'[123]

An Appendix to the Abstract tries to reconcile its requirements with those applying to pension schemes, saying 'the substance of ESOP trusts is different from that of pension schemes ... in that pension schemes have a longer time-frame and are wider in scope with the result that the obligations imposed by trust law and statute have a much greater commercial effect in practice'.[124]

However it has to be said that this distinction is not entirely convincing and some ESOP trustees have even seen this comparison as impugning their integrity in a rather offensive way.

One awkward result of the Abstract's approach is that is not entirely clear what to do in the common situation where a number of operating subsidiaries each make contributions to the trust under a group scheme. Can it be said that each of them 'has de facto control of the shares held by the ESOP trust and bears their benefits or risks'? This wording rather assumes that the employer will be a single entity which both controls the trust and is exposed to the benefits or risks of the shares held; however, in a group situation the parent company is likely to be the only entity that can claim to exercise any control, whereas the exposure to benefits and risks lies with each of the operating companies in relation to their various employees. Clearly, the consolidated accounts will still follow the accounting treatment specified by the Abstract because these various elements are united at group level, but arguably the individual entities are not within its scope.

In fact, the whole approach to this issue – based as it is on FRS 5 and the recognition of assets and liabilities – has been both narrow and somewhat oblique. As noted above, a preferable approach might have been to view the question as one of expense recognition; coming at the issue from this direction might also have achieved a treatment that is more compatible with pension scheme accounting. This would have focused on the fact that benefits have been awarded to employees in the form of shares that entail a cost which must be systematically accounted for, and buying shares through an ESOP trust is only one of the possible ways of hedging that cost – as shown below, the 1996 accounts of Grand Met show that it is now hedging most of this exposure off balance sheet, through options on shares that were previously carried as assets:

Extract 15.28: Grand Metropolitan Public Limited Company (1996)

15 Fixed assets – investments [extract]

Other investments include £4m *(1995 – £217m)* in respect of 1,208,084 *(1995 – 53,428,489)* ordinary shares of 25p each in Grand Metropolitan Public Limited Company with an aggregate nominal value of £0.3m *(1995 – £13m)*. The shares are held for the sole purpose of satisfying obligations under employee share option schemes operated by the group. On 1st December 1995, 51,879,015 shares were sold to an independent third party, and employee share trusts simultaneously purchased options from the third party which gave them the right to obtain the shares, as required, at the same price as the employee share options.

4.7.2 UITF 17 – Employee share schemes

In April 1997, the UITF published its seventeenth Abstract, *Employee share schemes*.[125] This addresses the relatively narrow issue of how companies should recognise and measure the cost of new shares issued as part of an employee share scheme, and was designed to counter arrangements that had been contrived to charge the profit and loss account with only the nominal value of such shares. The Abstract does not apply to Inland Revenue approved Save-As-You-Earn schemes and similar arrangements.

UITF 17 says that the total amount charged to the profit and loss account in such circumstances should be the fair value of the shares at the time the right to the shares is granted to the employee (less any amount payable by him or her).[126] The shares are therefore regarded as issued at whatever the market value was at the date of grant, and this holds true even though the market value at the date of issue later turns out to be higher or lower. For the purposes of the rules on share premium account, however, the Task Force was advised that the consideration for the issue of the shares could normally be taken as being only the amount of cash subscribed for the shares, which means that the difference (the excess of the market value at the date of grant over the cash subscribed) can be credited to any other reserve, including profit and loss account reserve, on issue of the shares. The total credit entry will appear in the reconciliation of shareholders' funds, not in the statement of total recognised gains and losses.[127]

The accounting treatment described above assumes that the obligation to deliver shares to the employee is indeed eventually satisfied by a new issue of shares. In the event that existing shares are bought on the market by an ESOP instead, then the price paid (less the cash to be received from the employee) will become the cost instead of the market value at the date of grant.[128]

The cost is to be recognised in the profit and loss account over the period to which the employee's performance relates, usually on a straight line basis unless some other basis better matches the services received. This may be in one year, in the case of an annual bonus, or a longer period for a long-term incentive scheme.[129] The period will not normally extend to include any secondary 'loyalty' period (for which the employee must remain in employment after meeting the performance conditions) 'unless it is clear that the effect of the scheme is to reward services over the longer period'.[130] The amount charged to the profit and loss account will continue to be adjusted during this period as estimates of the total cost are refined – this will reflect changes in assumptions such as the likelihood of the performance conditions being met, the number of employees leaving the company before qualifying for the awards, and so on.[131]

The accounting treatment described above also applies to the grant of share options, with the result that any options granted at a discount to the then ruling market price of the shares will require the discount to be charged to the profit and loss account.[132] (This will rarely apply in relation to directors, because the Stock Exchange requires shareholder approval before listed companies can grant options to directors at a discount.)

An Appendix to the Abstract contains a number of illustrative examples that show the mechanics of the required accounting treatment.

The Abstract came into force for periods ending on or after 22 June 1997, with no transitional relief for costs of any schemes that arose in earlier periods,[133] and it could have a very material effect on the profit and loss account in some cases. An *Investors' Chronicle* article in January 1997 speculated about its possible effect on one company in these terms (based on the draft proposals at that time):

'... Profits at train operator Prism Rail may be hit by charges amounting to more than £10m as a result of a controversial share scheme set up to reward the company's founders and directors. ... Under incentive schemes at Prism ... , founders were handed free shares or paid a nominal sum for them, so gains have been huge. Prism directors were awarded 3.38m shares on flotation, when the 100p float price valued the package of shares at £3.38m. When the company issued shares to pay for its takeover of South Wales and West Railway and Cardiff Railway the directors converted about 1.2m deferred shares, with a nominal value of 5p each, into ordinaries. When the shares started trading they were valued at about 345p, giving a profit of more than £4m. Any shares issued to fund the West Anglia Great Northern Line franchise could yield another profit of more than £4m when they start trading later this month. If accounting rules lead to write-downs equivalent to directors' profits, ... Prism ... would be forced to record hefty losses. ... Prism said last week it was to discontinue its share scheme, after pressure was applied by institutional investors concerned at the magnitude of founders' profits'.[134]

The above article jumped to the not unnatural conclusion that the profit ultimately realised by the director would also be the cost charged in the profit and loss account, which is not in fact the case, but it nevertheless gave some idea of the scale of the sums involved. In the event, Prism's subsequent accounts were for the period to 31 March 1997, which was not governed by the requirements of UITF 17 and the profit and loss account accordingly bore no such charges. Since the Abstract has retrospective effect when first applied, however, it will be interesting to see whether it has an impact on the comparative figures when they are presented with the 1998 accounts. The share capital note in the 1997 accounts included the following information about shares issued in the year:

Extract 15.29: Prism Rail PLC (1997)

19 Share Capital [extract]

On 16 February 1996, 376,200 Ordinary Shares were allotted for a total consideration of £18,810.
...

On 22 and 23 April 1996, 103,848 Ordinary Shares were allotted for a total consideration of £540,000.

On 22 May 1996, 99,952 Ordinary Shares were allotted for a total consideration of £519,750 and 8,000,000 Ordinary Shares were allotted by way of a private placing at an issue price of £1 per share in connection with the acquisition of LTS Rail Limited for a total consideration of £8,000,000.

On 14 October 1996, 5,500,000 Ordinary Shares were allotted by way of rights at an issue price of £2.40 per share in connection with the acquisitions of South Wales & West Railway Limited and Cardiff Railway Company Limited for a total consideration of £13,200,000.

On 6 January 1997, 3,630,952 Ordinary Shares were allotted by way of rights at an issue price of £3.30 per share in connection with the acquisition of West Anglia Great Northern Railway Limited for a total consideration of £11,982,141.

Under an agreement dated 17 April 1996 between the Company and the Founder Shareholders, a total of 16,520,000 Deferred shares were allotted to the Founder Shareholders during the period for a total consideration of £826,000. A total of 3,102,157 of these Deferred Shares had been converted into Ordinary Shares on a one for one basis by 31 March 1997 and the balance of 13,417,843 are now unconvertible. The Deferred Shares do not carry any voting or dividend entitlements. ...

The Company's Ordinary Shares were priced at 357p at 31 March 1997. The Company's shares were first traded on 29 May 1996 and traded in the range 151p to 590p during the period.

---

5 COMPARISON WITH US AND IASC PRONOUNCEMENTS

5.1 US

5.1.1 *Share capital*

In the US, common stock issued by an enterprise is recorded at par value. Differences between the fair value of the proceeds of the issue and the par value are recorded as additional paid-in capital. When no-par-value stock is issued, the common stock account is credited with the entire proceeds of the issue.

The only exception to the general requirement to account for additional paid-in capital is when accounting for common stock issued to effect a business combination accounted for as a pooling.

For each class of shares, the following information is disclosed:

(a) the number and value of shares issued or outstanding;

(b) the title of the issue and number of shares authorised;

(c) the amount of any common shares subscribed but unissued. The amounts receivable should be presented as a deduction from stockholders' equity;

(d)   for each period for which an income statement is presented, the changes in the class of common shares;

(e)   the price at which preferred stock may be called or redeemed through sinking fund requirements or otherwise; and

(f)   the aggregate and per share amounts of cumulative preferred dividends in arrears.

Changes in stock and the number of shares outstanding for at least the most recent year are disclosed.

5.1.2   Redeemable shares

The initial carrying amount of redeemable preferred stock is its fair value at the date of issue. The difference between the fair value at the date of issue and the mandatory redemption amount should be accounted for by making periodical charges against retained earnings (not through the profit and loss account) so that the carrying amount will equal the redemption amount at the mandatory redemption date. These charges should be deducted from earnings for earnings per share purposes.

Preferred stocks which are subject to mandatory redemption requirements or whose redemption is outside the control (no matter how remote the event might be) of the issuer are included in an intermediate category between liabilities and stockholders' equity.

These disclosures are made for redeemable shares:

(a)   the title of each issue, the carrying amount and redemption amount;

(b)   the dollar amounts of any shares subscribed but unissued and the deduction of subscriptions receivable therefrom;

(c)   the accounting treatment of the difference between the carrying amount and the redemption amount;

(d)   the number of authorised shares and the number issued or outstanding;

(e)   in a separate note captioned 'Redeemable Preferred Stocks',

■   a general description of each issue including its redemption features;

■   the combined aggregate amount of redemption requirements for all issues each year for the five years following the date of the latest balance sheet; and

■   the changes in each issue for each period for which an income statement is presented.

5.1.3 Treasury stocks

In the US, an enterprise may acquire shares of its own capital stock for purposes other than retirement subject to state laws and the requirements of listing agreements. In such situations, the status of such shares is akin to that of authorised but unissued capital stock.

When treasury stock is acquired with the intention of retiring the stock, the excess of the price paid for the treasury stock over its par value may either:

(a) be charged entirely to retained earnings; or

(b) be allocated between additional paid-in capital arising from the same class of stock and retained earnings.

If the price paid is less than its par value, the difference is credited to additional paid-in capital. The original capital balances relating to the shares acquired are eliminated.

Treasury stock acquired for purposes other than retirement should be separately disclosed in the balance sheet as a deduction from stockholders' equity or alternatively accounted for as retired stock.

A gain on the sale of treasury stock should be credited to paid-in capital. Losses may be charged to paid-in capital but only to the extent of available net gains from previous sales or retirements of the same class of stock. Any excess should be charged against retained earnings. The dividends on treasury stock should not be credited to income.

5.1.4 Additional paid-in capital

Additional paid-in capital is broadly equivalent to a share premium account in the United Kingdom, but is not subject to the same restrictions on its use and distribution. Any of these events may result in an entry to additional paid-in capital:

(a) stock issued in excess of par or stated value or in a business combination;

(b) stock dividends;

(c) sale of treasury stock at a gain or loss;

(d) conversion of convertible preferred stock;

(e) issue and exercise of detachable stock warrants;

(f) donated assets from a related party (e.g. capital contributions);

(g) forgiveness of a debt from a stockholder; and

(h) expenses or liabilities paid by a principal stockholder.

Occasionally, common stock is issued below par or stated value. The holder of shares issued below par may nevertheless be required to pay the discount in the event of a liquidation where creditors will sustain a loss. The enterprise may either create a 'discount on stock' account or charge such amount to additional paid-in capital to the extent available from the same class of stock.

5.1.5 Dividends

In the US, dividends are a charge to retained earnings at the point in time at which they are formally declared by the board of directors. This contrasts with the position in the UK, where equity dividends are accounted for when they are proposed, even though they have not yet been formally declared, and time-based dividends are accrued.

Disclosure is made of the aggregate dividends and dividends per share for each class of stock,[135] and the same information is given for any arrears of cumulative preferred dividends.[136] Disclosure must also be made of restrictions which limit the payment of dividends by the company.[137]

5.1.6 Debt

A   Classification

Short-term obligations that are scheduled to mature within one year after the balance sheet date (or within the enterprise's operating cycle) are classified as current liabilities, except when:

(a)   the enterprise intends to refinance the obligation on a long-term basis; and

(b)   the enterprise's ability to consummate the refinancing is demonstrated by either a post balance sheet issue of a long-term obligation or equity securities, or the execution of a financing agreement which permits the refinancing of the short-term obligation on a long-term basis prior to the issuance of the financial statements.[138] If short-term obligations are excluded from current liabilities because they are expected to be refinanced, a general description is given of the financing agreement and the terms of any new obligation incurred or equity securities issued (or expected to be incurred/issued) as a result of a refinancing.[139]

A long-term obligation that becomes callable by the creditor because of a violation of the debt agreement which is not cured within any period of grace allowed is classified as a current liability.[140] If a violation exists but a waiver has been obtained for a stated period of time, the amount of the obligation and the period of the waiver are disclosed. Details of all breaches/defaults in debt agreements, sinking fund or redemption provisions at the date of the latest balance sheet are given in the notes.

B   Disclosure

Liabilities to the following are separately disclosed:[141]

- banks for borrowings;

- factors or other financial institutions for borrowings;

- holders of commercial paper;

- trade creditors; and

- related parties.

For long-term debt such as bonds, mortgages etc, the following disclosures are given for each issue or type of obligation:[142]

- the general character of each type of debt including rate of interest;

- the date of maturity or, if maturing serially, a brief indication of the serial maturities;

- if the payment of principal or interest is contingent, an indication of such contingency;

- a brief indication of priority (i.e. whether subordinated); and

- if convertible, the basis of conversion.

For each category of short-term borrowings, the following disclosures are given, in aggregate:[143]

- the balance at the end of the period;

- the maximum amount outstanding at any month-end during the period;

- the weighted average interest rate both during and at the end of the period; and

- the average amount outstanding during the period.

The amount and terms of unused lines of credit for short-term financing are also disclosed if significant.[144]

In relation to redeemable stock and other similar liabilities, the following are disclosed for each of the 5 years following the date of the latest balance sheet:[145]

- the combined aggregate amount of maturities and sinking fund requirements for all long-term borrowings; and

- the amount of redemption requirements for all issues of capital stock that are redeemable at fixed or determinable prices on fixed or determinable dates, separately by issue or in aggregate.

5.1.7 *Convertible debt and debt issued with warrants*

The entire proceeds of issue of convertible debt are credited to a liability account. It is not permitted to allocate part of the proceeds to the conversion option since the debt and the conversion option are inseparable.[146] This is in line with FRS 4. Conversely, where debt is issued with detachable stock purchase warrants then the proceeds of issue should be allocated between the two elements on the basis of their fair values; the portion attributed to the warrants should be accounted for as paid-in capital, and whatever discount or premium on the debt that results from the allocation should be amortised to the income statement as a component of finance cost.[147] Again, this is consistent with the UK standard. The distinction turns on the detachable nature of the warrants; if the warrants are not detachable, then the accounting is the same as for convertible debt. This therefore means that the interest cost recognised in respect of these instruments depends on whether the warrants can be separated from the debt, even though their economic substance is otherwise similar.

5.1.8   Convertible bonds with a 'premium put'

Where convertible bonds are issued with a 'premium put' (a redemption option entitling the bondholder to redeem the bonds at a specified date prior to maturity at a price above the issue price), US GAAP requires provision to be made for the premium over the life of the bond by a supplementary interest accrual. This applies regardless of how probable it is that the bondholder will convert rather than exercise the redemption option. This is consistent with the treatment required under FRS 4 (see 4.2.3 above).

Subsequently, if the redemption option expires without being exercised, the accounting treatment of the provision which has been built up depends on the relationship between the put price and the market value at that date of the underlying stock into which conversion can be made. If the market value exceeds the put price, the provision should be credited to additional paid-in capital; if the reverse is true, it is to be amortised to the profit and loss account over the remaining term of the debt as a reduction of interest expense.[148]

5.1.9   Extinguishment of debt

Extinguishment is the term used in US GAAP to describe the circumstance when debt ceases to be a liability that is recognised in the balance sheet. It is not to be confused with offsetting, which deals with how recognised assets and recognised liabilities should be presented in a balance sheet.

Under SFAS 125, debt is considered extinguished for financial reporting purposes when either of the following conditions is met:

(a)   the debtor pays the creditor and is relieved of its obligation for the liability. This may be done either by giving cash or other assets to the creditor or, if the debt takes the form of a security such as a bond, by reacquiring that security; or

(b)   the debtor is legally released as the primary obligor under the debt, either judicially or by the creditor.[149] The debtor can still derecognise the debt even if it remains secondarily liable under a guarantee, but must recognise the guarantee instead at its fair value, with a consequential reduction to any gain (or increase in any loss) arising on the extinguishment.

The previous standard, SFAS 76, also allowed debt to be derecognised in another circumstance, known as 'in-substance defeasance'. This occurred when the debtor irrevocably placed cash or certain other assets in a trust, solely for the purpose of satisfying the interest and principal payments of the debt, in such a way that the possibility that the debtor would be required to make further payments with respect to that debt was remote. The creditor was not a party to this arrangement, and indeed may well have been unaware that it had occurred. However, this is no longer possible under SFAS 125, and SFAS 76 has been withdrawn.

Gains and losses from all extinguishments of debt (including convertible debt) are recognised in income of the period of extinguishment and identified as a separate item. This is also true for repurchases of debt in the UK.

5.1.10 *Troubled debt restructuring*

A restructuring of a debt constitutes a 'troubled debt restructuring' if the borrower is experiencing financial difficulties and the lender, in an attempt to protect as much of its investment as possible, grants concessions that it would not otherwise consider. There are different ways in which a lender might grant such concessions to the borrower, which give rise to different accounting treatments:

(a)   Debt for equity swap

The borrower uses the fair value of the equity interest granted to the lender to account for the shares that are issued.[150] The difference between this and the carrying value of the debt which is thereby settled is recognised in the profit and loss account as an extraordinary item, if material.

(b)   Transfer of assets in full settlement

The borrower recognises a gain on restructuring payables where the carrying amount of the payable settled exceeds the fair value of the assets transferred.[151] Such gains are classified as extraordinary, if material. A difference between the fair value and carrying amounts of assets transferred to a creditor to settle a payable is recognised as a gain or loss on transfer of assets.[152]

(c)   Modification of debt agreement

Where the lender agrees to modify the debt agreement, the effects of the modification are generally accounted for prospectively from the time of the restructuring. If the carrying value of the debt at the time of the restructuring is lower than the total future cash payments due under the revised agreement (including contingent payments), a new effective rate of interest should be calculated and applied to determine the finance costs in the period to maturity. The concession granted by the lender is therefore spread over the term to maturity.[153]

If, however, the total future cash payments are less than the carrying value of the debt, the difference should be recognised as an extraordinary gain on restructuring. In subsequent periods, the cash payments made to the lender are applied to reduce the carrying value of the debt. No future interest cost arises under this approach.[154]

As mentioned in 2.1.4 above, the ASB at one stage intended to address the renegotiation of debt in FRS 4 but ultimately did not do so.

5.1.11 Financial instruments project

The FASB is currently engaged in a major project on the whole subject of financial instruments, which may eventually affect a number of the statements referred to above. One of the standards that has resulted from this project is SFAS 107 – *Disclosures about Fair Value of Financial Instruments* – issued in December 1991. It requires all entities to disclose the fair value of financial instruments where practicable, and this includes liabilities such as loans. Trade creditors whose fair value approximates to their carrying value are exempt, as are lease creditors and equity instruments issued by the company. Where disclosure of the fair value is impracticable, the reason for this has to be disclosed, together with information pertinent to estimating the fair value, such as the carrying amount, effective interest rate and maturity. In the UK, disclosure of the market value of loans has been encouraged but not required by FRS 4, as discussed in 2.2.10 above, and is now being proposed as a requirement under the ASB's financial instruments project.

As described more fully in Chapter 9 at 4.1.3, the FASB is currently developing a standard that addresses the recognition and measurement of financial instruments, with the primary focus on derivatives.

5.1.12 Employee shares

In October 1995, the FASB issued SFAS 123 – *Accounting for Stock-Based Compensation*. This had been one of the most fiercely-resisted pronouncements ever produced by the Board, and the final terms of the standard represent something of a compromise; the Board's preferred method of accounting is not mandatory, but if not adopted, the effect of not doing so has to be disclosed.

The standard applies to arrangements whereby employees are remunerated in the form of shares in the employer or in amounts that are determined by the price of such shares. The FASB's preferred method of accounting is to measure the cost of such remuneration at the fair value of the award at the date it is granted, and to expense that over the qualifying period of service. Where share options are granted to employees, for example, this requires the use of an option pricing model to value the award, and this takes account of the time value of the option as well as its intrinsic value. Under the alternative method, which was specified by the previous standard, APB 25 (which corresponds more closely to UITF 17), only the intrinsic value is recognised, i.e. any excess of the market price of the shares at the date of grant over the amount that the employee must pay to acquire the shares. The latter method would therefore record no cost unless the options were issued at a discount to their market value, whereas the former method seeks to value the option rather more scientifically by putting a value on the opportunity to buy the shares at some time in the future at a specified price.

5.2 IASC

As yet, there is no international accounting standard on capital instruments, but the IASC is conducting a project on financial instruments in partnership with the Canadian Institute of Chartered Accountants. This is a very ambitious project which deals with the appropriate accounting treatment in the accounts of both the issuer and the holder of the instruments. So far, two exposure drafts have been published – E40 in 1991 and E48 in 1994 – but neither was converted into a standard that dealt with the issue comprehensively; instead, a disclosure standard was published in 1995.[155] More recently, the Steering Group has published a further discussion paper which takes a very radical approach to the subject; as discussed in Chapter 9. The main proposals that are relevant to share and loan capital from the issuer's point of view are summarised below.

The most important definitions used in the draft are as follows.

A *financial liability* is any liability that is a contractual obligation:

(a)   to deliver cash or another financial asset to another enterprise; or

(b)   to exchange financial instruments with another enterprise under conditions that are potentially unfavourable.[156]

A *financial instrument* is any contract that gives rise to both a financial asset of one enterprise and a financial liability or equity instrument of another enterprise.[157]

An *equity instrument* is any contract that evidences a residual interest in the assets of an enterprise after deducting all of its liabilities.[158]

On this analysis, redeemable preference shares are regarded as liabilities rather than equity instruments.

The discussion paper espouses 'split accounting' (as described in 2.2.2 above) for hybrid instruments such as convertible bonds. In other words, the proceeds of issue of such a bond would be allocated between the amount that represents a straight financial liability and the element which represents an equity instrument.[159] This standard distinguishes between debt and equity depending on whether or not the issuer has a contractual obligation to deliver cash or another financial asset to the holder of the instrument (or to exchange another financial instrument with him on potential unfavourable terms), regardless of the legal form of the instrument.

Financial liabilities should be recognised when the entity becomes a party to the contractual provisions that create the liability.[160] They should be measured initially at the fair value of the consideration received (this precludes adjusting the carrying amount for gains and losses on any instruments that hedge the liability).[161] Thereafter, they should be remeasured at fair value at each balance sheet date and the difference included in the profit and loss account for the year.[162] The only exceptions are that the movement in fair value should be shown in 'other comprehensive income' rather than the profit and loss account if it arises on liabilities that hedge certain anticipated transactions or investments in foreign investments. This is the only concession made to hedge accounting; the proposals do not permit deferral of gains and losses on hedging instruments.

A financial liability should be removed from the balance sheet when it is extinguished (i.e. when the obligation has been discharged, cancelled or expires), or when the primary responsibility for it is transferred to another party.[163] The proposals envisage that this may apply to parts of liabilities as well as to the whole amount, in other words that liabilities may be subdivided into components for the purpose of determining questions of derecognition.

These proposals are controversial, and it remains to be seen whether they will be converted into an international standard. In the meantime, a disclosure standard – IAS 32 – is in place, which is summarised more fully in Chapter 9 at 4.2.2.[164]

6   CONCLUSION

FRS 4 has been useful in developing a framework of rules on capital instruments; the requirements of the Companies Act alone were no longer adequate to deal with innovative forms of finance. The standard has created much more consistency in the classification and disclosure of companies' share and loan capital than had been displayed in the years before it was issued. Although it does give rise to certain anomalies, it has proved to be one of the Board's most successful standards to date.

In developing FRS 4, the ASB was constrained to some degree by the balance sheet formats prescribed by the Companies Act, and was inhibited from adopting an approach which focused fully on the substance of the instrument in question. However, the use of the 'non-equity' classification and the detailed disclosure requirements as to the terms of complex instruments compensates for this drawback to a large degree.

In the longer term, however, more needs to be done on the measurement issues which complex instruments give rise to, and in particular ways of subdividing them into their component parts need to be explored. The scope of this study should include the 'split accounting' idea which the ASB has not yet pursued, but may also have a wider remit. It must not be forgotten that these issues have a profit and loss account dimension as well as a balance sheet one; for example, the use of split accounting in relation to convertible bonds seeks to charge earnings with a proper finance cost, which arguably is understated under the conventional accounting approach which FRS 4 endorses.

As discussed in Chapter 9, however, the real question is whether the ASB will abandon FRS 4's whole approach in favour of the mark-to-market model that it has espoused in its financial instruments project. This would be a very radical step and would again run into considerable legal difficulties. It is also far from certain that this is what the financial community wants, and as a result the proposal is likely to encounter significant resistance. Ultimately, much will depend on how the debate on financial instruments develops in North America and internationally over the next few years.

References

1 UITF Abstract 1, *Convertible bonds – Supplemental interest/premium*, UITF, July 1991.
2 ASB Discussion Paper, *Accounting for capital instruments*, ASB, December 1991.
3 FRED 3, *Accounting for Capital Instruments*, ASB, December 1992.
4 ASB Bulletin Issue No. 39, July 1993.
5 UITF 8, *Repurchase of own debt*, UITF, March 1993.
6 FRS 4, *Capital Instruments*, ASB, December 1993, para. 2.
7 *Ibid.*, para. 21.
8 *Ibid.*, para. 52.
9 The draft *Statement of Principles*, ASB, November 1995, para. 3.21.
10 FRS 4, para. 24.
11 CA 85, Sch. 4, para. 8.
12 FRS 4, para. 12.
13 *Ibid.*, para. 49.
14 *Ibid.*, para. 90.
15 *Ibid.*, para. 25.
16 E48, *Financial Instruments*, IASC, January 1994, para. 40.
17 ASB Discussion Paper, *Accounting for Capital Instruments*, Appendix 3.
18 TR 677, Appendix para. 5(a).
19 FRS 4, para. 22.
20 *Ibid.*, para. 26.
21 In fact, this would be the effective result under US GAAP. Where convertible debt is issued at a substantial premium over its face value, the premium is accounted for as additional paid-in capital. (APB 14, *Accounting for Convertible Debt and Debt Issued with Stock Purchase Warrants*, March 1969, para. 18.)
22 FRS 4, paras. 27 and 11.
23 *Ibid.*, para. 8.
24 *Ibid.*, para. 28.
25 *Ibid.*, para. 29.
26 *Ibid.*, para. 32.
27 *Ibid.*, para. 37.

28 *Ibid.*, para. 11.
29 *Ibid.*, para. 42.
30 *Ibid.*, para. 28.
31 *Ibid.*, para. 8.
32 *Ibid.*, para. 10.
33 *Ibid.*, para. 42.
34 *Ibid.*, para. 51.
35 *Ibid.*, para. 16.
36 UITF 11, *Accounting for Issuer Call Options*, UITF, September 1994.
37 FRS 4, para. 32.
38 UITF 8, para. 7.
39 *Accounting for Financial Assets and Financial Liabilities*, IASC, March 1997, Chapter 3, para. 4.7.
40 *Ibid.*, para. 4.8.
41 FRS 5, *Reporting the Substance of Transactions*, ASB, April 1994, para. 29.
42 *Ibid.* These rules also appear strictly to allow offset only if there are two parties involved, whereas there are at least three in this case, but we doubt if this was intended provided the offset conditions are otherwise satisfied.
43 FRS 4, para. 34.
44 *Ibid.*, para. 35.
45 *Ibid.*, para. 81.
46 *Ibid.*, para. 36.
47 *Ibid.*, para. 17.
48 *Ibid.*, para. 45.
49 *Ibid.*, para. 46.
50 *Ibid.*, para. 47.
51 *Ibid.*, para. 48.
52 *Ibid.*, para. 99.
53 *Ibid.*, para. 48.
54 *Ibid.*, para. 40.
55 *Ibid.*, para. 55.
56 *Ibid.*, para. 50.
57 *Ibid.*, para. 25.
58 *Ibid.*, para. 54.
59 *Ibid.*, para. 38.
60 *Ibid.*, para. 56.
61 *Ibid.*, para. 58.
62 *Ibid.*, para. 57.
63 *Ibid.*, para. 61.
64 *Ibid.*, para. 33.
65 *Ibid.*, para. 36.
66 *Ibid.*, para. 62.
67 *Ibid.*, para. 63.
68 *Ibid.*, para. 65.
69 *Ibid.*, para. 64.
70 *Ibid.*, para. 13.
71 *Ibid.*, para. 59.
72 *Ibid.*, para. 60.
73 *Ibid.*, para. 52.
74 FRED 3, para. 59.
75 FRS 4, para. 102.
76 *Operating and Financial Review*, ASB, July 1993, para. 23.
77 CA 85, s 130(1).
78 *Ibid.*, s 130(2).
79 *Ibid.*, ss. 131 and 132.
80 FRS 4, paras. 45 and 11.
81 *Ibid.*, para. 21c.
82 FRS 6, *Accounting for Business Combinations*, ASB, September 1994, Appendix I, para. 15.

83 CA 85, ss. 117 and 118.
84 *Ibid.*, Sch. 4, para. 8.
85 *Ibid.*, para. 38(1).
86 *Ibid.*, para. 38(2).
87 *Ibid.*, para. 39.
88 *Ibid.*, para. 40.
89 *Ibid.*, para. 49.
90 *Ibid.*, para. 3(7)(b) and (c).
91 FRS 4, para. 43.
92 *The Listing Rules*, London Stock Exchange, Chapter 12, para. 12.43(l).
93 CA 85, Sch. 4, para. 8.
94 *Ibid.*, para. 85.
95 *Ibid.*, para. 48(1) and (2).
96 *Ibid.*, para. 48(4).
97 *Ibid.*, para. 41(1).
98 *Ibid.*, para. 41(3).
99 *Ibid.*, s 744.
100 *Ibid.*, Sch. 4, para. 53(2).
101 CA 85, ss. 159–181.
102 *Ibid.*, s 170.
103 *Ibid.*, s 171 *et seq.*
104 *Ibid.*, Sch. 7, paras. 8 and 9.
105 *The Listing Rules*, London Stock Exchange, Chapter 12, para. 12.43(n).
106 FRS 4, para. 63.
107 *Ibid.*, para. 31.
108 *Ibid.*, para. 26.
109 UITF 1, para. 5.
110 FRS 4, para. 25.
111 *Ibid.*, para. 26.
112 *Ibid.* – Application Notes.
113 *Ibid.*, para. 46.
114 *Ibid.*, para. 47.
115 CA 85, s 130.
116 FRS 4, para. 43.
117 *Ibid.*, paras. 42 and 28.
118 TR 677, Appendix, para. 7.
119 FRS 4, para. 99.
120 UITF 13, *Accounting for ESOP Trusts*, UITF, June 1995, para. 8.
121 *Ibid.*
122 *Ibid.*, para. 9.
123 FRS 5, para. 44.
124 UITF 13, Appendix I.
125 UITF 17, *Employee share schemes*, UITF, April 1997.
126 *Ibid.*, para. 13(c).
127 *Ibid.*, para. 16.
128 *Ibid.*, para. 13(c).
129 *Ibid.*, para. 13(a).
130 *Ibid.*, para. 13(d).
131 *Ibid.*
132 *Ibid.*, para. 15.
133 *Ibid.*, para. 17.
134 Write-off threat to Prism profits, Andrew Yates, *Investors' Chronicle*, 31 January 1997, p. 13.
135 Statement S-X, SEC, para. 3-04.
136 APB 15, *Earnings per share*, para. 50, footnote 16.
137 SFAS 5, *Accounting for contingencies*, FASB, March 1975, para. 18.
138 SFAS 6, *Classification of Short-Term Obligations Expected To Be Refinanced*, FASB, May 1975, paras. 8–11.

139 *Ibid.*, para. 15.
140 SFAS 78, *Classification of Obligations That Are Callable by the Creditor*, FASB, December 1983, para. 5.
141 Statement S-X, SEC, para. 5-02.19–20.
142 *Ibid.*, para. 5-02.23.
143 *Ibid.*, para. 12-10.
144 *Ibid.*, para. 5-02.20.
145 SFAS 47, *Disclosure of Long-Term Obligations*, FASB, March 1981, para. 10.
146 APB 14, para. 12.
147 *Ibid.*, para. 16.
148 EITF Issue No. 85-29.
149 SFAS 125, *Accounting for Transfers and Servicing of Financial Assets and Extinguishment of Liabilities*, FASB, June 1996, para. 16.
150 SFAS 15, *Accounting by Debtors and Creditors for Troubled Debt Restructurings*, FASB, June 1977, para. 15.
151 *Ibid.*, para. 13.
152 *Ibid.*, para. 14.
153 *Ibid.*, para. 16.
154 *Ibid.*, para. 17.
155 IAS 32, *Financial Instruments: Disclosure and Presentation*, IASC, March 1995.
156 *Accounting for Financial Assets and Financial Liabilities*, IASC, March 1997, Chapter 2, para. 3.1.
157 *Ibid.*
158 *Ibid.*
159 *Ibid.*, Chapter 4, para. 4.7 *et seq.*
160 *Ibid.*, Chapter 3, para. 3.1.
161 *Ibid.*, Chapter 4, para. 2.1.
162 *Ibid.*, Chapter 5, para. 3.1, and Chapter 6, para. 5.1.
163 *Ibid.*, Chapter 3, para. 4.1.
164 IAS 32, *Financial Instruments: Disclosure and Presentation*, IASC, March 1995.

Chapter 16   Off balance sheet transactions

1   INTRODUCTION

1.1   Background

Off balance sheet finance can be difficult to define, and this poses the first problem in discussing the subject. The term implies that certain things belong on the balance sheet and that those which escape the net are deviations from this norm. But there are as yet no authoritative general principles which determine conclusively what should be on the balance sheet and when. As discussed in Chapter 2, the ASB is attempting to establish such principles in its *Statement of Principles* project and has used these as the basis of FRS 5 – *Reporting the substance of transactions* – which directly addresses the issue of off balance sheet finance.

The practical effect of off balance sheet transactions is that they do not result in full presentation of the underlying activity in the accounts of the reporting company. This is generally for one of two reasons. The items in question may be included in the balance sheet but presented 'net' rather than 'gross'; examples would include one-line presentation of an unconsolidated subsidiary rather than line by line consolidation, or netting off loans received against the assets they finance. Alternatively, the items might be excluded from the balance sheet altogether on the basis that they represent future commitments rather than present assets and liabilities; examples would include operating lease commitments, obligations under take-or-pay contracts or consignment stock agreements, contingent liabilities under options, and so on. The result in both cases will be that the balance sheet suggests less exposure to assets and liabilities than really exists, with a consequential flattering effect on certain ratios, such as gearing and return on capital employed.

There is usually also a profit and loss account dimension to be considered as well, perhaps because assets taken off balance sheet purport to have been sold (with a possible profit effect), and also more generally because the presentation of off balance sheet activity influences the timing or disclosure of associated revenue items. In particular, the presence or absence of items in the balance sheet usually affects whether the finance cost implicit in a transaction is reported as such or rolled up within another item of income or expense.

Depending on their roles, different people tend to react differently to the use of the term 'off balance sheet finance'. To an accounting standard setter, the expression carries the connotation of devious accounting, intended to mislead the reader of financial statements. Off balance sheet transactions are those which are designed to allow a company to avoid reflecting certain aspects of its activities in its accounts. The term is therefore a pejorative one, and the inference is that those who indulge in such transactions are up to no good and need to be stopped. From this perspective, FRS 5 is intended to be an anti-avoidance standard which seeks to prevent accounts being perverted by the effects of transactions whose primary motivation is cosmetic.

However, there is also room for a more honourable use of the term 'off balance sheet finance'. Companies may, for sound commercial reasons, wish to engage in transactions which share with other parties the risks and benefits associated with certain assets and liabilities. Increasingly sophisticated financial markets allow businesses to protect themselves from selected risks, or to take limited ownership interests which carry the entitlement to restricted rewards of particular assets. Also, off balance sheet transactions are often undertaken as an element of a company's tax planning strategy. Such transactions are not undertaken to mislead readers of their accounts, but because they are judged to be in the best commercial interests of the companies undertaking them.

Whatever the motivation behind these transactions, company accounts have to reflect them in such a way that a true and fair view is given. FRS 5 seeks to deal with transactions whose form is at variance with their economic substance. The thrust of the standard is to identify what the substance is in reality and represent the transactions in that light.

1.2   The forerunners of FRS 5

1.2.1   ICAEW Technical Release 603

In December 1985, the ICAEW issued Technical Release 603 – *Off-Balance Sheet Finance and Window Dressing* – as a preliminary document for discussion. It detailed certain points to be considered by preparers of financial statements in examining off balance sheet transactions:

'(1) In financial statements which are intended to give a true and fair view the economic substance of such transactions should be considered rather than their mere legal form when determining their true nature and thus the appropriate accounting treatment. Where items are included in the accounts on the basis of the substance of the transactions concerned and this is different from their legal form, the notes to the accounts should disclose the legal form of those transactions and the amounts of the items involved.

(2)   In the rare circumstances where accounting for a material transaction on the basis of its substance rather than its legal form would not comply with the requirements of the Companies Act, adequate disclosure should be made in order to provide a true and fair view, possibly by presenting separate pro-forma accounts prepared on the basis of the economic substance of the transactions.'[1]

The publication of this Technical Release stimulated a good deal of debate, both within the accounting profession and also with certain members of the legal profession. In particular, the Law Society stated that while agreeing with TR 603's basic objectives, they disagreed with its proposed solution. It was argued that a major purpose of financial statements was to provide comparability and consistency and this was best achieved by keeping subjectivity to a minimum. Further, the desired level of objectivity was said to be best achieved by reflecting the legal position relating to assets and liabilities in a set of financial statements. It was also pointed out that the 'true and fair override' could only be applied in narrowly limited circumstances and this did not permit widespread departure from the requirements of the Act to report the form of transactions in the course of a quest for their substance.

1.2.2   ED 42

As a result of the interest which this debate generated, the Accounting Standards Committee put the subject of off balance sheet transactions on its own agenda with a view to developing an accounting standard. In March 1988, it issued ED 42 – *Accounting for special purpose transactions*. A *special purpose transaction* was defined as one 'which combines or divides up the benefits and obligations flowing from it in such a way that they fall to be accounted for differently or in different periods depending on whether the elements are taken step by step or whether the transaction is viewed as a whole'.[2]

This exposure draft differed from most others produced by the ASC in that it addressed the issue from a conceptual angle rather than laying down a set of detailed rules. The essence of the argument it set out was as follows.

The concept of 'true and fair' demanded that transactions should be accounted for in accordance with their substance rather than their legal form; this was to be determined by examining all the aspects and implications of a transaction (or series of transactions, if they were linked), and concentrating on those which were likely to have commercial effect in practice.[3] The substance was to be determined by identifying whether the transaction had increased or decreased the assets or liabilities which were to be recognised in the financial statements of the enterprise.[4] When it was determined that assets and liabilities should be recognised in the financial statements, they were to be accounted for individually, rather than offset against each other: a right of set-off was to alter this principle only if the items were of the same type as each other.[5]

Much of the argument within the proposed standard rested on whether or not the transaction in question was regarded as giving rise to an asset or liability. These terms were described in the exposure draft in a broadly similar way to the definitions eventually incorporated in FRS 5.

There were specific rules to deal with 'controlled non-subsidiaries' (later termed 'quasi subsidiaries'). The exposure draft asserted that such a vehicle should be consolidated as if it were a subsidiary.[6]

The explanatory note of the exposure draft examined the application of the principles of the proposed standard to a number of common transactions and arrangements, but did not develop mandatory detailed rules in relation to these specific transactions.

1.2.3   ED 49

ED 42 received a fair measure of support from those people who responded to it. Nevertheless, it was two years before the ASC issued a further document on the subject. The delay was not due to inertia on the Committee's part; rather it was because a Companies Bill was in process in 1989 which had a very significant bearing on the subject, and it was necessary to see how that was finally enacted before the project could be progressed. Most significantly, the resultant Act changed the definition of a subsidiary which had to be consolidated from one based strictly on the form of the shareholding relationship between the companies to one which reflected the substance of the commercial relationship, and in particular focused on who exercised de facto control.

When the ASC did return to the subject, it decided that the climate had changed sufficiently to require it to issue a further exposure draft rather than an accounting standard. Accordingly, ED 49 – *Reflecting the substance of transactions in assets and liabilities* – was published in May 1990. The main changes from ED 42 were to refine the definitions of assets and liabilities and to give guidance on the criteria for their recognition in accounts, to add a new section on the identification of control (in the light of the Companies Act 1989) and to introduce detailed, mandatory Application Notes to prescribe the accounting treatment of some common forms of off balance sheet finance. The exposure draft no longer referred specifically to 'special purpose transactions' and indeed the title was changed to reflect this slightly different focus of attention.

As mentioned above, the definition of a 'subsidiary undertaking' introduced by the Companies Act 1989 allowed more straightforward recognition of de facto control than was possible under the previous legislation, and accordingly there was less need than before for an accounting standard to address this issue.

However, ED 49 took the view that even this new definition was not conclusive in determining what entities are to be included in consolidated accounts. It envisaged that there would be occasions where the need to give a true and fair view would require the inclusion of 'quasi subsidiaries' (defined in the same terms as ED 42 had used for 'controlled non-subsidiaries').

In publishing the exposure draft, the ASC set a relatively short period for comment, on the basis that the general principles of the proposed standard had not changed from ED 42, and that the main innovation requiring consultation was the Application Notes. Its hope was that a standard based on ED 49 could be brought into force relatively quickly, but in the event the ASB, which succeeded the ASC shortly afterwards, did not find it possible to do so.

1.2.4 FRED 4

The ASB published FRED 4 – *Reporting the substance of transactions* – nearly three years later, in February 1993 but with a consultation period running only to the end of April. Although the general thrust of the proposed standard was the same as that of ED 49, the new exposure draft was three times as long as its predecessor and much more complex. Among the innovations was a new proposition: the 'linked presentation', which was to allow liabilities to be shown on the balance sheet as a deduction from the assets which they financed, under certain closely defined circumstances. FRED 4 also borrowed much of its conceptual argument from the Board's draft *Statement of Principles* (see Chapter 2), including the definitions of assets and liabilities and rules for their recognition, and it also discussed offset and the treatment of options in greater detail than before.

The exposure draft attracted a good deal of further comment, not least because of its daunting size and complexity, but in the event it was converted into a standard a year later with relatively little alteration.

2 FRS 5

2.1 Scope and general requirements

FRS 5 – *Reporting the substance of transactions* – was published in April 1994, to take effect for accounting periods ending on or after 22 September 1994. Significantly, the standard gave no transitional relief to exempt transactions or arrangements which predated these periods, with the result that additional assets and liabilities often had to be recognised when the standard was applied for the first time.

The standard applies to all entities whose accounts are intended to give a true and fair view, but it excludes a number of transactions from its scope, unless they form part of a larger series of transactions that does fall within the scope of the standard. These exclusions are:

(a)   forward contracts and futures (such as those for foreign currencies or commodities);

(b)   foreign exchange and interest rate swaps;

(c)   contracts where a net amount will be paid or received based on the movement in a price or an index (sometimes referred to as 'contracts for differences');

(d)   expenditure commitments (such as purchase commitments) and orders placed, until the earlier of delivery or payment; and

(e)   employment contracts.[7]

The first three of these relate to financial derivatives and are presumably excluded in order that they may be addressed in the ASB's financial instruments project. However, the remaining two are more problematic. They seem to have been excluded only because the application of the recognition criteria in the standard would otherwise have some undesirable effects. Literal application of these criteria could require companies to include assets and liabilities in their accounts in respect of contracts for future performance; for example, the commitment to buy goods, or to employ staff, qualifies as a liability as the standard has defined it. Since including such liabilities in the balance sheet would be a radical and unwelcome result, the ASB has avoided the problem by scoping such transactions out of the standard altogether. This, however, seems a rather clumsy solution, when the real problem probably lies in the recognition rules themselves.

The interaction of FRS 5 with other standards and statutory requirements is also something which must be considered. Transactions which are directly addressed by other rules will sometimes also fall within the remit of FRS 5, and it is necessary to consider which set of rules takes precedence. The standard says that whichever rules are more specific should be applied.[8] A particular example quoted is the leasing standard, SSAP 21, which addresses a particular aspect of off balance sheet finance but in a more narrowly prescribed way. Straightforward leases which fall squarely within the terms of SSAP 21 should continue to be accounted for without reference to FRS 5, but where their terms are more complex, or the lease is only one element in a larger series of transactions, then FRS 5 comes into play. More generally, the standard says that its overall principle of substance over form should apply to the operation of other existing rules.[9]

FRS 5 deals with certain specific aspects of off balance sheet finance through the medium of detailed Application Notes. These cover the following topics:

■   Consignment stock

■   Sale and repurchase agreements

■ Factoring of debts

■ Securitised assets

■ Loan transfers.

These are intended to clarify and develop the methods of applying the standard to the particular transactions which they describe and to provide guidance on how to interpret it in relation to other similar transactions. They also contain specific disclosure requirements in relation to these transactions. The Application Notes are not exhaustive and they do not override the general principles of the standard itself, but they are regarded as part of the standard (i.e. they are authoritative) insofar as they assist in interpreting it. Each of these topics is discussed in 3 below.

As with the three earlier exposure drafts, the central premise of FRS 5 is that the substance and economic reality of an entity's transactions should be reported in its financial statements, and this substance should be identified by considering all the aspects and implications of a transaction, with the emphasis on those likely to have a commercial effect in practice. In determining the substance, it is necessary to consider whether the transaction has given rise to new assets and liabilities for the entity, and whether it has changed any of its existing assets and liabilities.[10]

Sometimes there will be a series of connected transactions to be evaluated, not just a single transaction. The overall substance of these transactions as a whole must be determined and accounted for, rather than accounting for each individual transaction. The standard quotes some examples of complex arrangements to which its provisions will be particularly relevant. These involve the following features:

(a) the separation of legal title to an item from rights or other access to the principal future economic benefits associated with it and exposure to the principal risks inherent in these benefits;

(b) the linking of a transaction with others in such a way that the commercial effect can be understood only by considering the series as a whole; and

(c) the inclusion of options or conditions on terms that make it highly likely that the option will be exercised or the condition fulfilled.[11]

Where transactions include options which may or may not be exercised or conditions which may or may not apply, it is necessary to form a view as to their likely outcome, by considering the motivations of all the parties to the transaction and the possible scenarios which they have contemplated in negotiating the terms of the deal. Only in this way can the commercial substance of the arrangement be identified.

2.2   Definition of assets and liabilities

For the purpose of the standard, assets and liabilities are defined as follows:

Assets are rights or other access to future economic benefits controlled by an entity as a result of past transactions or events.[12]

Liabilities are an entity's obligations to transfer economic benefits as a result of past transactions or events.[13]

These definitions are the same as those which the ASB has proposed in its draft *Statement of Principles,*[14] as discussed in Chapter 2.

2.3   Analysis of risks and rewards

The standard goes on to say that identifying the party that is exposed to variations in the benefits relating to an asset will generally indicate who has the asset itself.[15] It also says that if an entity is in certain circumstances unable to avoid an outflow of benefits, this will provide evidence that it has a liability.[16] The various risks and rewards relating to particular assets and liabilities are discussed in Application Notes which deal with different forms of off balance sheet finance.

In any consideration of where the risks and rewards lie as a result of a transaction, it is useful to remember that each of the risks and rewards relating to a particular asset or liability must lie *somewhere*. Although they may be partitioned and transferred as a result of the transactions, they cannot be increased or diminished in total. In addition, an analysis of the commercial effect of the deal can be expedited by looking at it from the point of view of each of the parties involved. By considering what risks and rewards they have acquired or disposed of, and their motivation for doing so, the substance of the transaction can be discerned more clearly than by considering the position of one of the parties alone.

2.4   Recognition

Once items which satisfy the definition of assets and liabilities have been identified, the next key question is whether they should be recognised in the balance sheet. This question, of course, is what the whole subject of off balance sheet finance is about. The standard says that 'where a transaction results in an item which meets the definition of an asset or liability, that item should be recognised in the balance sheet if:

(a)   there is sufficient evidence of the existence of the item (including, where appropriate, evidence that a future inflow or outflow of benefit will occur); and

(b)   the item can be measured at a monetary amount with sufficient reliability.'[17]

These principles are similar to those set out in the ASB's draft *Statement of Principles.*[18] They are rather abstract criteria, and are not particularly easy to understand in isolation; in particular, item (a) appears to add little but a reinforcement of the definition of an asset or liability. Critically, it does not really specify the defining event which dictates when to bring an item on to the balance sheet.

The difficulty is therefore in identifying exactly when an asset or liability is created in the terms in which they have been defined. Conventional accounting practice is to recognise most transactions only when they are performed, for example when goods are received under a purchase contract. However, an enthusiastic interpretation of the recognition criteria would say that merely entering into the contract has resulted in the creation of an asset (the right to the goods) and a liability (the amount due under the purchase contract). This is similar to the IASC's proposals on financial instruments, which says that 'An enterprise should recognise a financial asset or financial liability on its balance sheet when it becomes a party to the contractual provisions that comprise the financial instrument.'[19] However this would be a radical change of practice.

This idea that the creation, rather than the execution, of a contract should be the event which triggers the recognition of assets and liabilities has an obvious theoretical appeal. However, quite apart from the difficulty of capturing the relevant information in a company's accounting system, it is debatable whether this forms a sensible basis for the preparation of a balance sheet. The difficulty with it is that every commitment under contract would become a liability; examples might include all leasing commitments (not just those for finance leases, as at present),[20] long-term supply contracts for raw materials, and even future salary payments under employment contracts (at least for the required period of notice). There could also be some difficulty in defining and describing the nature of the corresponding asset in such cases. It is presumably to avoid this result that expenditure commitments and employment contracts have been scoped out of the standard, as discussed under 2.1 above, but this does not resolve the principle behind the recognition test.

2.5 Derecognition

2.5.1 General principles

As the word suggests, derecognition is the opposite of recognition. It concerns the question of when to remove from the balance sheet the assets and liabilities which have previously been recognised. FRS 5 addresses this issue only in relation to assets, not liabilities, and its rules are designed to determine one of three outcomes (together with a fourth possibility, the linked presentation, which is discussed at 2.6 below). These are summarised in the following diagram:

Summary of derecognition tests

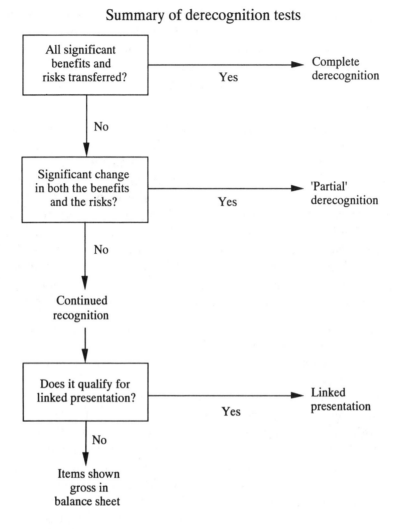

2.5.2   *Complete derecognition*

In the simplest case, where a transaction transfers to another party all the significant benefits and risks relating to an asset, the standard confirms that the entire asset should cease to be recognised.[21] In this context, the word 'significant' is explained further: it should not be judged in relation to all the conceivable benefits and risks that could exist, but only in relation to those which are likely to occur in practice.[22] This means that the importance of the risk retained must be assessed in the context of the total realistic risk which existed in the first place.

Thus, if a company sold an asset and agreed to compensate the buyer for any subsequent loss in its value up to a maximum of 2% of the selling price, the significance of that retention of risk depends on how realistic it is that a fall in value of more than 2% will occur. If the asset is a portfolio of high quality whatsoever of a claim on the entity being established other than against funds generated by that item (or the item itself); and

(b)   there is no provision whatsoever whereby the entity may either keep the item on repayment of the finance or reacquire it at any time.[30]

There are also some more specific conditions discussed below.

Part (b) above makes it clear that the non-recourse nature of the borrowing is not sufficient to justify the linked presentation; the entity must also relinquish its grip on the asset by dedicating it to repay the loan. The requirement to include both non-recourse finance and the related asset in a balance sheet illustrates an important feature of the standard's philosophy. Financiers tend to think of the isolation of risk as being the primary consideration in relation to questions of whether items should be included in the balance sheet or not. To them, the question as to which assets are available as security for which borrowings is of great significance and they would like the accounts to focus on this criterion. However, FRS 5 approaches the matter from a different angle: it wants to identify those assets and activities which are within the control of the reporting company and are a source of benefits and risks to it, because these are the things which are relevant to an assessment of the company's performance. In this context, the question of who has claims over which asset is of lesser importance, although perhaps it is one which lends itself to note disclosure.

The detailed qualifying criteria which have to be satisfied in order to justify a linked presentation are explained in the following terms:

(a)   the finance relates to a specific item (or portfolio of similar items) and, in the case of a loan, is secured on that item but not on any other asset of the entity;

(b)   the provider of the finance has no recourse whatsoever, either explicit or implicit, to the other assets of the entity for losses and the entity has no obligation whatsoever to repay the provider of finance;

(c)   the directors of the entity state explicitly in each set of financial statements where a linked presentation is used that the entity is not obliged to support any losses, nor does it intend to do so;

(d)   the provider of the finance has agreed in writing (in the finance documentation or otherwise) that it will seek repayment of the finance, as to both principal and interest, only to the extent that sufficient funds are generated by the specific item it has financed and that it will not seek recourse in any other form, and such agreement is noted in each set of financial statements where a linked presentation is used;

(e)   if the funds generated by the item are insufficient to pay off the provider of the finance, this does not constitute an event of default for the entity; and

(f)   there is no provision whatsoever, either in the financing arrangement or otherwise, whereby the entity has a right or an obligation either to keep the item upon repayment of the finance or (where title to the item has been transferred) to reacquire it at any time. Accordingly:

      (i)   where the item is one (such as a monetary receivable) that directly generates cash, the provider of finance will be repaid out of the resulting cash receipts (to the extent these are sufficient); or

      (ii)   where the item is one (such as a physical asset) that does not directly generate cash, there is a definite point at which either the item will be sold to a third party and the provider of the finance repaid from the proceeds (to the extent these are sufficient) or the item will be transferred to the provider of the finance in full and final settlement.[31]

The ASB has made it clear that these highly detailed criteria are indeed meant to be interpreted restrictively, and only a narrow category of assets is likely to qualify for linked presentation. The explanation section of FRS 5 enlarges on (a) above as follows: 'A linked presentation should not be used where the finance relates to two or more items that are not part of a portfolio, or to a portfolio containing items that would otherwise be shown under different balance sheet captions. Similarly, a linked presentation should not be used where the finance relates to any kind of business unit, or for items that generate the funds required to repay the finance only by being used in conjunction with other assets of the entity. The item must generate the funds required to repay the finance either by unwinding directly into cash (as in the case of a debt), or by its sale to a third party.'[32]

A number of the other conditions concern the need for the entity to be protected from losses in respect of the item transferred. Among the forms of recourse which could breach these conditions are the following:

■   an agreement to repurchase non-performing items or to substitute good items for bad ones;

■   a guarantee given to the provider of the finance or any other party (of performance, proceeds or other support);

■   a put option under which items can be transferred back to the entity;

■   a swap of some or all of the amounts generated by the item for a separately determined payment; or

■   a penalty on cancelling an ongoing arrangement such that the entity bears the cost of any items that turn out to be bad.[33]

Under the standard, the use of the linked presentation is expressed as being mandatory whenever all the conditions listed above are met. However, because compliance with some of the conditions is itself voluntary, the treatment is in reality optional. For example, both conditions (c) and (d) above mean that the

Extract 16.6: Lookers plc (1996)

12 STOCKS

	Group	
	1996	1995
	£000	£000
Goods for resale	**50,650**	40,626
Bulk deposit paid for vehicles on consignment	**938**	953
Interest bearing consignment vehicles	**3,857**	3,557
Motability buy-back vehicles	**13,123**	10,208
	68,568	55,344

Principal Accounting Policies
6. Stocks [extract]
Deposits paid for vehicles on consignment represent bulk deposits paid to manufacturers.
Interest bearing consignment vehicles and motability buy-back vehicles are included in stocks. The related liabilities are included in trade and other creditors respectively. Other creditors due after more than one year relate to motability buy-backs due to return between one and three years.

Henlys shows consignment stock within its stocks note, but distinguishes between those that it believes that it owns in substance and those that it does not, with the latter shown only in the footnote. The description of the former category seems to imply that the interest-bearing nature of the arrangement may have been a major deciding factor:

Extract 16.7: Henlys Group plc (1996)

13 Stocks

	Group 1996 £000	Group 1995 £000	**Company 1996 £000**	Company 1995 £000
Raw materials	**3,720**	3,321	**1,988**	2,354
Work in progress	**9,090**	9,339	**7,611**	7,728
Finished goods	**66,377**	58,589	**31,431**	28,758
Vehicle consignment stock	**9,730**	10,265	**4,855**	4,637
Motability buyback vehicles	**7,179**	8,207	**253**	984
	96,096	89,721	**46,138**	44,461

Interest bearing consignment vehicles have been recognised in stocks and the corresponding liability has been included in creditors.

The group also has vehicle consignment stock of £27,716,000 (1995 – £27,427,000), where the benefits and risks associated with the vehicles remain with the manufacturer until transfer of title and consequently this stock has not been recognised as an asset of the Group.

The Group has an obligation to repurchase vehicles under agreements with Motability Finance Limited, such repurchase is usually required after three years. The assets and corresponding liabilities have been recorded at the purchase price.

Where it is concluded that the dealer owns the stock in substance, it will appear on its balance sheet with a corresponding liability to the manufacturer (offset to the extent of any deposit). Where the liability escalates through time as a result of the application of interest, such interest will be charged to the profit and loss account as it accrues. Where it is concluded that the stock remains in the ownership of the manufacturer, the only item which the dealer will have to account for is any deposit paid, which will be shown as a debtor in its accounts. Whether or not the stock is on the balance sheet, the notes to the accounts should disclose the nature of the arrangement, the amount of consignment stock held and the main terms on which it is held, including the terms of any deposit.[47]

Signet, Cookson and Wolseley all disclose that they hold material amounts of consignment stock but that it remains off balance sheet, as shown in these extracts:

Extract 16.8: Signet Group plc (1997)

13 Stocks [extract]

Subsidiary undertakings held £30,523,000 of consignment stock as at 1 February 1997 (1996: £38,824,000) which is not recorded on the balance sheet. The principal terms of the consignment agreements, which can generally be terminated by either side, are such that the Group can return any or all of the stock to the relevant suppliers without financial or commercial penalties and the supplier can vary stock prices.

Extract 16.9: Cookson Group plc (1996)

12 Stocks [extract]

In addition to the stocks recorded in the balance sheet, the Group held precious metals on consignment terms with a total value at 31 December 1996 of **£125.5m** (1995: £159.6m).

The Group's precious metal fabrication operations utilise significant amounts of precious metals, primarily gold, held on consignment terms. The terms provide inter alia that the consignor retains title to the metal and both parties have the right of return over the metal without penalty. In the great majority of cases, when fabrication is complete the consignor sells or consigns the metal directly to the Group's customers, the Group charging customers solely for the fabrication process. In the other cases the Group purchases the metal and sells it concurrently to the customer. Under these arrangements the Group is neither liable to buy the metal nor is it at risk in relation to market fluctuations in metal prices. Accordingly the stocks are not recorded in the balance sheet. Consignment fees are charged by the consignors which totalled **£4.1m** in 1996 (1995: £3.0m).

The Group also holds precious metal on behalf of customers for processing, with a total value at 31 December 1996 of **£32.8m** (1995: £21.0m).

Extract 16.10: Wolseley Group plc (1996)

11. STOCKS [extract]

Certain subsidiary undertakings have consignment stock arrangements with suppliers in the ordinary course of business. Inventory drawn from consignment stock is generally invoiced to the companies concerned at the price ruling at the date of drawdown. The value of such stock, at cost, which has been excluded from the balance sheet in accordance with the application notes included in FRS 5, amounted to £8.5m (1995 £8.0m).

Application Note A does not discuss the appropriate treatment in the accounts of the manufacturer, but under general rules of revenue recognition (see Chapter 3) the manufacturer could not treat the stock as sold in most cases. It is therefore quite possible that the stock will end up being shown on the balance sheets of both parties. Bridon, however, discloses that it has classified stock made available to customers on consignment as debtors on the grounds that all risks and benefits of ownership have passed, but without recognising a profit until ultimate sale; on the face of it, this treatment seems slightly self-contradictory:

Extract 16.11: Bridon plc (1996)

Notes to the accounts

10. STOCKS [extract]

Stocks amounting to £2,797,000 (1995 £2,490,000) which have been supplied to customers on a consigned basis, which transfer all the risks and benefits of ownership, have been shown in trade debtors. No profit is taken on such stock until the stock is ultimately sold.

3.2 Sale and repurchase agreements

This type of arrangement is addressed by Application Note B of FRS 5. Transactions of this kind can take many forms, but the essential feature which unites them is that the company which purports to have sold the asset in question has not relinquished all the risks and rewards associated with the asset in the manner which would have been expected of a normal sale. If there is no significant change in the company's access to the benefits of the asset and exposures to its risks, FRS 5 requires that the sale should not be recorded and the asset in question should remain on the company's balance sheet. A straightforward illustration of the rules is given by this example:

Example 16.7:   Sale with contract to repurchase

A whisky blending company, W plc, has several years' worth of maturing whisky in stock. It contracts to sell a certain quantity of the whisky to a bank for £5 million, and agrees to buy it back one year later for £5.5 million. The whisky remains on its own premises.

Under FRS 5, this series of transactions would be accounted for as a financing deal. W has not transferred the risks and rewards of ownership of the whisky to the bank; instead, it has merely borrowed money on the security of the whisky. The accounts will continue to include the whisky stock in the balance sheet and show the £5 million received as the proceeds of a loan, extinguished one year later by the repayment of £5.5 million (which includes an interest charge of £0.5 million which would be accrued through the year).

This is a clear-cut arrangement with no uncertainty as to its outcome. However, it would not be difficult to imagine a more complex arrangement, such as this:

Example 16.8:   Sale with options to repurchase/resell

W plc sells the same quantity of whisky as before in Example 16.7 to X Limited (another whisky company) for £5 million. The whisky is stored in a third party warehouse and responsibility for the storage costs thus passes to X. W arranges put and call options with X to purchase the same quantity of the same or equivalent whisky in one year's time for £6 million. (The factor which makes the repurchase price higher in this case is that X has to bear the cost of storing the whisky for a year.)

If one assumes that the existence of both the put and the call options makes it inevitable that one or other party will exercise the option, then there seems little difference between this case and the previous one. Even though the precise identity of the whisky might be different when it gets it back, W seems to be disposing of its whisky stock only temporarily, and on that argument, FRS 5 requires it to remain on the balance sheet, with the £1 million differential in the price being accrued as warehouse rent and interest.

The example could be complicated further by removing the put option, so that W had the right to reacquire the whisky, but not the obligation to do so. Presumably, if it could buy the equivalent whisky cheaper from another source in a year's time it would do so (assuming it wanted the whisky back at all). Effectively, W would have retained the right to increases but disposed of the risks of decreases in value of the whisky. The appropriate accounting would depend on all the circumstances of the transaction; unless it was clear that the option was very likely to be exercised, then there would be a good argument that the sale should be taken at face value and the stock removed from the balance sheet; W's only remaining asset would be its option to purchase the whisky. However, this depends on all the terms of the arrangement, as discussed below.

The principal question to be answered in all such arrangements is whether the reporting company has made a sale in substance, or whether the deal is a financing one. In approaching this question, it is instructive to consider which of the parties involved will enjoy the benefits, and be exposed to the risks, of the property in question during the period between the sale and the repurchase transactions. In the most straightforward kind of arrangement, this will generally be indicated by the prices at which the two transactions are struck; for example, if they are both at the market values current at the date of each transaction, then the risks and rewards of ownership are passed to the purchaser for this period; however, if the second selling price is linked to the first by an interest element, then these risks and rewards remain with the original owner throughout the period and the purchaser has the position only of a lender in the deal.

Another key factor in evaluating such an arrangement is the part of the agreement which permits or requires the repurchase to take place. As already illustrated, this may take the form of a contractual commitment which is binding on both parties, but it may also take the form of a put option allowing the buyer to resell the asset to the vendor, a call option allowing the vendor to repurchase the asset from the buyer, or a combination of such options.

Where there is a binding commitment, it is clear that the asset will revert to the vendor and the only remaining factor which will determine the accounting treatment of the overall deal is the price at which the transactions are struck, as discussed above. The same is likely to be true where there is both a put and a call option in force on equivalent terms; unless the option is to be exercised at the then market price of the asset in question, it must be in the interests of one or other of the parties to exercise its option so as to secure a profit or avoid a loss, and therefore the likelihood of the asset remaining the property of the buyer rather than reverting to the vendor must be remote. However, the position is less clear where there is only a put option or a call option in force rather than a combination of the two.

Where there is only a put option, the effect will be (in the absence of other factors) that the vendor has disposed of the rewards of ownership to the buyer but retained the risks. This is because the buyer will only exercise its option to put the asset back to the vendor if its value at the time is less than the repurchase price payable under the option. This means that if the asset continues to rise in value the buyer will keep it and reap the benefits of that enhanced value; conversely if the value of the asset falls, the option will be exercised and the downside on the asset will be borne by the vendor.

This analysis does not of itself answer the question of whether the deal should be treated as a sale or as a financing transaction. The overall commercial effect will still have to be evaluated, by taking account of all the terms of the arrangement and by considering the motivations of both of the parties in agreeing to the various terms of the deal; in particular it will need to be considered why they have each agreed to have this one-sided option. It may be, for example, that the downside risks of the asset value compared to the option price can be seen to be negligible, in which case the fact that they remain with the vendor is not very important to the evaluation of the whole arrangement. However, in other cases the fact that the vendor retains these risks might be very significant, and sufficient to prevent the deal being treated as a sale; if the buyer has the right to put the asset back to the vendor, and if it appears reasonably likely that this option might be exercised, then it would be difficult for the vendor to say that it had made a sale, and realised any profit, on a transaction which the other party was at liberty to reverse. In other cases again, the transaction might qualify for partial derecognition as discussed at 2.5 above – for example, where a commercial vehicle manufacturer has sold a truck and given the customer an option to put it back at a guaranteed price in 5 years' time.

Where there is only a call option, the position will be reversed. In this case, the seller has disposed of the risks, but retained the rewards to be attained if the value of the asset exceeds the repurchase price specified in the option. Once again, the overall commercial effect of the arrangement has to be evaluated in deciding how to account for the deal. Emphasis has to be given to what is likely to happen in practice, and it is instructive to look at the arrangement from the point of view of both parties to see what their expectations are and what has induced them to accept the deal on the terms which have been agreed. It may be obvious from the overall terms of the arrangement that the call option will be exercised, in which case the deal will again be a financing arrangement and should be accounted for as such – for example, the seller may continue to use the asset, and it could be obvious that its commercial need for it would compel it to exercise the option. Similarly, the financial effects of *not* exercising the option (such as continued exposure to escalating costs) may sometimes make it obvious that the option will be exercised. But in other cases, it could be quite likely that the option will not be exercised and if this is the case the transaction could be treated as a sale. The seller need not include a liability in its balance sheet for the exercise price of the option if it is quite conceivable that it would not exercise it; correspondingly, the asset in its balance sheet would simply be the call option itself, not the underlying property that is the subject of the option.

Another example is shown below:

Example 16.9:   Sale at below market value with call option

A building company, B plc, sells part of its land bank to a property investment company, P plc, for £40 million at a time when its market value is £50 million. It has the right under the agreement to buy it back for the same price plus interest at any time in the next three years. Conversely, however, P has no corresponding put option to require B to buy it back.

The effect of this deal is that B is protected from a collapse in the value of the land below 80% of its former price, because it cannot be compelled to buy it back. It has therefore passed that risk to P (which has presumably charged for it accordingly in the interest rate implicit in the deal). But it has retained the rewards of ownership, because it can always benefit from an increase in value of the land by exercising its option. Moreover, at the time of entering into the deal, it must have expected that it would exercise the option – otherwise it would have sold the property for full value, not for £10 million less. FRS 5 would be likely to interpret this as a financing deal, rather than a sale.

Where the overall substance is that of a financing deal rather than a sale, neither a sale nor a profit will be recorded. Instead, the ostensible sales proceeds will be recorded as a loan, and any charges which are in substance interest on that loan will be accrued and disclosed as interest costs. (This means that they may qualify for capitalisation in appropriate circumstances – see Chapter 13.) A brief description of the arrangement and the status of the asset and the relationship between the asset and the liability should be disclosed in the notes to the financial statements.[48]

Where the seller has made a sale and has a new asset and/or liability (such as an option) it should recognise or disclose such residual items as appropriate. Any unconditional commitment to repurchase needs to be recognised in the balance sheet, not merely disclosed. Profits and losses should be recognised on a prudent basis. The notes to the accounts should disclose the main features of the arrangement including the status of the asset, the relationship between the asset and the liability and the terms of any provision for repurchase (including any options) and of any guarantees.[49]

Barratt's accounts include a note showing that they have kept on the balance sheet houses sold to BES companies subject to a guarantee:

Extract 16.12: Barratt Developments PLC (1996)

13. STOCKS

	1996 £m	1995 £m
Work in progress	331.7	290.5
Showhouse complexes and houses awaiting legal completion	132.9	113.0
Properties in Business Expansion Schemes	17.0	17.0
	481.6	420.5

In 1993 the group supported four Business Expansion Scheme companies to provide assured tenancy housing, all of which were fully subscribed at a total of £20.0m. A major portion of this amount was used to purchase properties at market value from various Barratt subsidiaries. The group has given a guarantee that there will be sufficient cash resources available for distribution from the four BES companies in 1998 and 1999 to provide the BES investors with a guaranteed return per share. As the guarantee is in place the sale of the properties has not been recognised in these accounts. The properties are held in the balance sheet at their original cost of £17.0m (1995 £17.0m). The sale proceeds of £18.9m (1995 £18.9m) are held in creditors and the profit attributable to the properties of £1.9m (1995 £1.9m) has not been recognised in these accounts.

Similarly, Gleeson discloses these notes in respect of properties sold to BES companies with an option to have them put back to it after five years:

Extract 16.13: M J Gleeson Group plc (1996)

1. Accounting policies [extract]

Stock and work in progress

iv) Properties sold to Cavendish Gleeson Guaranteed PLC, Cavendish Gleeson Second PLC and Cavendish Gleeson Cash Backed PLC are included in Stock and work in progress at their original cost and their sale proceeds are added to Deferred income.

6. Interest payable [extract]

The substance of the transactions with the three BES companies (further details of which are given in note 22) is that of secured loans and, in accordance with FRS 5, the cost of financing these debts (being the difference between the issue proceeds and the ultimate cost of exercising the options) is allocated over the periods of the loans at fixed rates.

22. Contingent liabilities [extract]

The Company has entered into commitments in the form of put and call options with three Business Expansion Scheme companies – Cavendish Gleeson Guaranteed PLC, Cavendish Gleeson Second PLC and Cavendish Gleeson Cash Backed PLC. The arrangement requires the Company, on exercise of the Options, to purchase residential properties from these companies at such prices as will enable the shareholders to receive respectively, £1.15, £1,15 and £1.20 for each £1 invested. The contingent liabilities at 30th June 1996 and option exercise dates are as follows:–

Cavendish Gleeson Guaranteed PLC	£5,750,000	19th February 1998
Cavendish Gleeson Second PLC	£2,854,000	15th March 1998
Cavendish Gleeson Cash Backed PLC	£6,000,000	31st December 1998

Although the information given in the last note is contained under the heading of contingent liabilities, and although the policy refers to the proceeds as deferred income, the outstanding amount is included within creditors in the balance sheet, which is where it belongs.

As discussed in Chapter 17 at 7.4.4, a number of companies have disclosed leases whose terms include options to purchase the leased assets that seem likely to be recognised.

3.3   Factoring of debts

Factoring is a long-established means of obtaining finance by selling trade debtors so as to accelerate the receipt of cash following a sale on credit. The essence of the question posed by FRS 5 (in Application Note C) is again whether the transaction is really a sale in substance or whether it is simply a borrowing transaction with the trade debtors being used as collateral. Once again, the overall terms of the arrangement have to be considered in aggregate, and there may be a number of different services that the factor provides which will feature in this evaluation. Since there is no likelihood of any upside benefit in relation to debtors (except perhaps through reduced finance cost as a result of early payment) the focus in this case is on the risks of ownership rather than the rewards.

Application Note C says there are three possible treatments: derecognition, a linked presentation and a separate presentation. It does not mention 'partial' derecognition, although this could also be appropriate in some circumstances. Derecognition will be appropriate if all the significant benefits and risks relating to the debts in question have been transferred to the factor. The standard indicates that this will normally be the case only if:

(a)   the transaction takes place at an arms' length price for an outright sale;

(b)   the transaction is for a fixed amount of consideration and there is no recourse whatsoever, either implicit or explicit, to the seller for losses from either slow payment or non-payment; and

(c)   the seller will not benefit or suffer in any way if the debts perform better or worse than expected.[50]

If the conditions for derecognition are met, the debtors transferred will be set against the proceeds received from the factor with the difference being taken to the profit and loss account. Insofar as this represents discount on the sale of the debts it would seem appropriate to treat this as a finance cost, while other factoring costs should be included in administrative expenses.

A linked presentation will be appropriate if the requirements of paragraphs 26 and 27 of FRS 5 are satisfied, as discussed in 2.6 above. In the context of debt factoring, this means that the trader may retain significant benefits and risks in relation to the factored debts, but there must be no arrangement permitting or requiring the trader to reacquire any of the debts and the trader must have limited its downside exposure to loss to a fixed monetary amount.[51]

Where a linked presentation is applied, the debtors will stay on the balance sheet but the amount of any non-returnable advance from the factor will be deducted from them rather than being shown as a separate liability. The factor's charges will be accrued, with the interest element being accounted for as interest expense, and other costs within administrative expenses, both of which are to be disclosed. The notes should also disclose the main terms of the arrangement and the gross amount of factored debts outstanding at the year end as well as the disclosures which are required by paragraph 27 of the FRS (see 2.6) whenever the linked presentation is used.[52]

If neither of these sets of conditions is satisfied, a separate presentation is required. This means that the debtors will remain on the trader's balance sheet and amounts advanced by the factor will be shown as a loan within current liabilities. As with the linked presentation, the factor's charges should be accrued and appropriately analysed between interest and administrative expenses, but in this case the standard does not require these to be separately disclosed. The only required disclosure is the amount of factored debts outstanding at the year end.[53]

The Application Note contains two examples which illustrate different scenarios which could lead to different accounting treatments. These are as follows:

Example 16.10: Debt factoring with recourse

A company (S) enters into a factoring arrangement with a factor (F) with the following principal terms:

- S will transfer all its trade debts to F, subject only to credit approval by F and a limit placed on the proportion of the total that may be due from any one debtor;

- F administers S's sales ledger and handles all aspects of collection of the debts in return for an administration charge at an annual rate of 1% payable monthly, based on the total debts factored at each month end;

- S may draw up to 70% of the gross amount of debts factored and outstanding at any time, such drawings being debited in the books of F to a factoring account operated by F for S;

- F credits collections from debtors to the factoring account, and debits the account monthly with interest calculated on the basis of the daily balances on the account using a rate of base rate plus 2%. Thus this interest charge varies with the amount of finance drawn by S under the finance facility from F, the speed of payment of the debtors and base rate;

- any debts not recovered after 90 days are resold to S for an immediate cash payment which is credited to the factoring account;

- F pays for all other debts, less any advances and interest charges made, 90 days after the date of their assignment to F, and debits the payment to the factoring account; and

- on termination of the agreement the balance on the factoring account is settled in cash.

FRS 5 concludes that in substance the effect of these terms is that the deal is a financing one rather than an outright sale of the debts, and a separate presentation should be adopted. S continues to bear both the slow payment risk (the interest charged by F varies with the speed of payment by the debtors) and the bad debt risk (it must pay F for any debts not recovered after 90 days), and its exposure to loss is therefore unlimited.

Example 16.11: Debt factoring without recourse

A company (S) sells debts to a factor (F) on the following terms:

■ S will transfer to F such trade debts as S shall determine, subject only to credit approval by F and a limit placed on the proportion of the total that may be due from any one debtor. F levies a charge of 0.15% of turnover, payable monthly, for this facility;

■ S continues to administer the sales ledger and handle all aspects of collection of the debts;

■ S may draw up to 80% of the gross amount of debts assigned at any time, such drawings being debited in the books of F to a factoring account operated by F for S;

■ weekly, S assigns and sends copy invoices to F as they are raised;

■ S is required to bank the gross amounts of all payments received from debts assigned to F direct into an account in the name of F. Credit transfers made by debtors direct into S's own bank account must immediately be paid to F;

■ F credits such collections from debtors to the factoring account, and debits the account monthly with interest calculated on the basis of the daily balances on the account using a rate of base rate plus 2.5%. Thus this interest charge varies with the amount of finance drawn by S under the finance facility from F, the speed of payment of the debtors and base rate;

■ F provides protection from bad debts. Any debts not recovered after 90 days are credited to the factoring account, and responsibility for their collection is passed to F. A charge of 1% of the gross value of all debts factored is levied by F for this service and debited to the factoring account;

■ F pays for the debts, less any advances, interest charges and credit protection charges, 90 days after the date of purchase, and debits the payment to the factoring account; and

■ on either party giving 90 days' notice to the other, the arrangement will be terminated. In such an event, S will transfer no further debts to F, and the balance remaining on the factoring account at the end of the notice period will be settled in cash in the normal way.

FRS 5 concludes that the effect of these terms is that S continues to bear the slow payment risk for 90 days (the interest charged by F varies with the speed of payment by the debtors) but thereafter all risks pass to F. Since it has not disposed of all significant risks, derecognition is not appropriate, but since its exposure is limited, a linked presentation is available. This allows the non-returnable proceeds from F to be shown on S's balance sheet as a deduction from the debts factored. The amount to be deducted will be the lower of the proceeds received and the gross amount of the debts less all charges to the factor in respect of them.

3.4   Securitised assets

Securitisation is a process whereby finance can be raised from external investors by enabling them to invest in parcels of specific financial assets. Domestic mortgage loans were the first main type of assets to be securitised in the United Kingdom, but in principle the technique can readily be extended to other assets, such as credit card receivables, other consumer loans, lease receivables and so on.

A typical securitisation transaction involving a portfolio of mortgage loans would operate as follows:

The company which has initially advanced the loans in question (the originator) will sell them to another company set up for the purpose (the issuer). The issuer may be a subsidiary or associate of the originator, or it may be owned by a charitable trust or some other party friendly to the originator; in either case, its equity share capital will be small. The issuer will finance its purchase of these loans by issuing loan notes on interest terms which will be related to the rate of interest receivable on the mortgages. The originator will continue to administer the loans as before, for which it will receive a service fee.

The structure will therefore be as shown in this diagram:

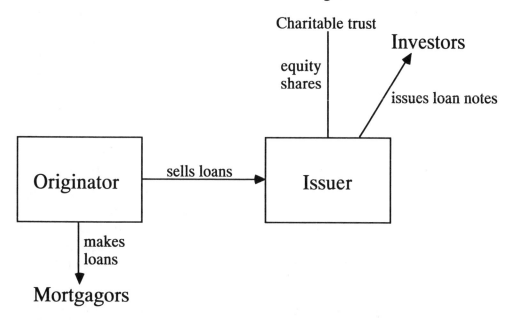

Potential investors in the mortgage-backed loan notes will want to be assured that their investment is relatively risk-free, and the issue will normally be supported by obtaining a high rating from a credit rating agency. This may be achieved by use of a range of credit enhancement techniques which will add to the security already inherent in the quality of the mortgage portfolio. Such techniques can include the following:

■   limited recourse to the originator in the event that the income from the mortgages falls short of the interest payable to the investors under the loan notes and other expenses. This may be made available in a number of ways; for example, by the provision of subordinated loan finance from the originator to the issuer; by the deferral of part of the consideration for the sale of the mortgages; or by the provision of a guarantee;

■ the provision of loan facilities from third parties to meet temporary shortfalls as a result of slow payments of mortgage interest; or

■ insurance against default on the mortgages.

The overall effect of the arrangement is that outside investors have been brought in to finance a particular portion of the originator's activities. These investors have first call on the income from the mortgages which back their investment, and earn a floating rate of interest which moves broadly in sympathy with the underlying rate paid on the mortgages. The originator is left with only the residual interest in the differential between the rates paid on the notes and earned on the mortgages, net of expenses; generally, this profit element is extracted by adjustments to the service fee or through the mechanism of interest rate swaps. He has thus limited his upside interest in the mortgages, while his remaining downside risk on the whole arrangement will depend on the extent to which he has assumed obligations under the credit enhancement measures.

The question of whether or not the mortgage loans and the loan notes should appear on the balance sheet of the originator can be subdivided into two main issues:

(a) has the sale of the mortgages succeeded in transferring the risks and rewards of ownership from the originator to the issuer? If it has not, then the mortgages will have to remain as an asset on the originator's balance sheet and the purported sales proceeds shown as a loan received; and

(b) is the issuer a subsidiary or quasi subsidiary of the originator? If it is, then the issuer's accounts will have to be consolidated with those of the originator, with the result that transactions between them will be eliminated on consolidation and the assets and liabilities which appear on the issuer's balance sheet will appear on the consolidated balance sheet of the originator.

When ED 49 addressed the overall question of whether to include securitised mortgages in the originator's balance sheet, it laid down a long list of qualifying conditions which were substantially based on those developed by the Bank of England for supervisory purposes in relation to loan transfers. However, a number of commentators pointed out that the criteria which might be appropriate for regulation of this kind, which focused on risk and capital adequacy, did not necessarily provide a sound basis for an accounting standard, which was designed to result in companies showing a true and fair view of their financial position and the results of their activities. They also criticised some of the detailed criteria as being inconsistent with the philosophy of the exposure draft itself.

The ASB made substantial modifications to the approach of the previous exposure draft in developing FRED 4. As a result, the previously straightforward on/off balance sheet decision became a three-way choice, and the qualifying conditions were also substantially changed. The possibilities became:

(a) separate presentation, whereby the gross securitised assets appear on the asset side of the balance sheet, with the proceeds of the issue within creditors;

(b) linked presentation, whereby the proceeds of the note issue are shown as a deduction from the securitised assets as a net figure within the assets section of the balance sheet; and

(c) derecognition, whereby the securitised assets are regarded as sold and therefore removed from the balance sheet.

This basic approach was carried through into FRS 5. Application Note D does not mention the possibility of 'partial' derecognition. This would only be appropriate if some of the significant benefits and some of the significant risks relating to the securitised assets were transferred to other parties as a result of the transaction while others were retained by the originator.

As with other forms of finance, FRS 5 says that derecognition is appropriate only if all the significant benefits and risks relating to the debts in question have been disposed of, which is likely to require that:

(a) the transaction takes place at an arms' length price for an outright sale;

(b) the transaction is for a fixed amount of consideration and there is no recourse whatsoever, either implicit or explicit, to the originator for losses from whatever cause. Normal warranties given in respect of the condition of the assets at the time of transfer would not breach this condition, but any warranties concerning their value or performance in the future would do so; and

(c) the originator will not benefit or suffer if the securitised assets perform better or worse than expected. This condition will not be satisfied where the originator has a right to further sums from the vehicle which vary according to the eventual value realised for the securitised assets.[54]

If all these conditions are met, the securitised assets are likely to be regarded as sold and will be removed from the balance sheet. They will be set against the proceeds received from the issue, with the difference being taken to the profit and loss account. If the conditions are not met, then either a linked presentation or a separate presentation is required.

A linked presentation will be appropriate if the requirements of paragraphs 26 and 27 of FRS 5 are satisfied, as discussed in 2.6 above. In the context of securitisation, this means that the originator may retain significant benefits and risks in relation to the securitised assets, but must have limited its downside exposure to loss to a fixed monetary amount.   There must also be no arrangement under which the originator can reacquire any of the securitised assets in the future. These conditions are discussed further in paragraphs D10 to D13 of the Application Note, which make it clear that they are to be applied restrictively.

Where a linked presentation is applied, the securitised assets remain on the balance sheet but the proceeds of the issue will be shown as deducted from them on the assets side of the balance sheet rather than as a liability. Extensive disclosure requirements are called for, namely:

(a)   a description of the assets securitised;

(b)   the amount of any income or expense recognised in the period, analysed as appropriate;

(c)   the terms of any options for the originator to repurchase assets or to transfer additional assets to the issuer;

(d)   the terms of any interest rate swap or interest rate cap agreements between the issuer and the originator that meet the conditions set out in paragraph D11 of the Application Note;

(e)   a description of the priority and amount of claims on the proceeds generated by the assets, including any rights of the originator to proceeds from the assets in addition to the non-recourse amounts already received;

(f)   the ownership of the issuer; and

(g)   the disclosures required by paragraph 27(c) and (d) of the standard.[55]

The standard also says that where there are several securitisation arrangements they may be shown in aggregate if they relate to a single type of asset, but should otherwise be presented separately. Similarly, the note disclosures should only deal with the arrangements in aggregate to the extent that they relate to the same type of asset and are on similar terms.[56]

Kingfisher has used the linked presentation in respect of securitised consumer receivables, as shown in this extract:

Extract 16.14: Kingfisher plc (1997)

Balance sheet [extract]

£ millions	1997	1997	1996	1996
Current assets				
Development work in progress		**32.9**		36.4
Stocks		**839.2**		836.9
Debtors due within one year		**308.9**		404.7
Debtors due after more than one year		**196.1**		108.7
Securitised consumer receivables	**181.2**		60.1	
Less: non-recourse secured notes	**(146.0)**	**35.2**	(49.6)	10.5
Investments		**208.2**		187.0
Cash at bank and in hand		**71.8**		119.8
		1,692.3		1,704.0

16 Securitised consumer receivables

In January 1996, the Group entered into an agreement to securitise consumer receivables (which derive principally from the provision of credit facilities by Time Retail Finance Ltd (TRF) to customers of the Group) through Time Finance Ltd (TFL). TRF sells the consumer receivables, with no impact on the profit and loss account, to TFL who issue Notes secured on those assets. The issue terms of the Notes include provisions that their holders have no recourse to TRF or any other member of the Group. Neither TRF nor any other Group company is obliged to support any losses, nor does it intend to. Principal and interest is repayable from, and secured solely on, the consumer receivables. At 1 February 1997 the amount of consumer receivables securitised was £181.2m (1996: £60.1m) raising funds of £146.0m (1996: £49.6m) and this is shown on the balance sheet using linked presentation.

If the conditions for derecognition or a linked presentation are not satisfied, a separate presentation is required, which means that the securitised assets will remain on balance sheet and the proceeds of the issue will be shown as a loan within creditors. The gross amount of assets securitised at the year end is to be disclosed.[57]

These considerations have been discussed above in relation to the originator's accounts, but the same factors apply to the issuer's accounts as well. However, in the latter case the answer is generally clear – a separate presentation is required.[58] A question which can then arise is whether the issuer has to be consolidated by the originator, and if so, how that will affect the presentation. Where the issuer is a quasi subsidiary of the originator, the standard allows the assets and liabilities of the issuer to be included in the originator's group accounts in a linked presentation (provided the qualifying conditions are met from the point of view of the group) even if a separate presentation is required in the accounts of the issuer itself.[59]

3.5 Loan transfers

Loan transfers is the collective term used to describe various methods by which banks and other lenders seek to transfer an advance to a different lender. Such transactions often involve a gain or loss because of movements in interest rates since the original loan was taken out, so they can have a profit and loss account dimension as well as giving rise to questions of balance sheet recognition and disclosure.

Since the original loan is a contract which is personal to the parties involved, its transfer is not straightforward. It is necessary to effect the transfer of benefits and risks less directly, by one of the three following arrangements:

(a)   Novation

This is where a new contract, with a new lender, is drawn up to replace the original one, which is cancelled. This therefore extinguishes the original loan altogether from the accounts of the lender as well as removing any residual obligations it had to the borrower (such as to make further advances under a committed facility). Unless there are any side agreements, no further questions of off balance sheet finance arise once this process has been completed.

(b)   Assignment

This involves the assignment of some or all of the original lender's rights (but not obligations) to another lender, and may be done on either a statutory or an equitable basis, which have different legal requirements and effects. They are both subject to equitable reliefs; in particular, the borrower's rights under its contract with the original lender are not to be prejudiced.

In accounting terms, the effect of an assignment is less clear cut than that of a novation, because the original lender may have some residual rights and obligations to the other parties involved.

(c)   Sub-participation

This does not involve the formal transfer of the legal rights and obligations involved in the loan, but the creation of a non-recourse back-to-back agreement with another lender (the sub-participant) whereby the sub-participant deposits with the original lender an amount in respect of the whole or part of the loan in exchange for the right to receive a share of the cash flows arising from the loan from the original lender. The accounting question that arises from such a transaction is whether the deposit and the loan can be offset to show only the net position.

The Application Note in ED 49 proposed detailed criteria for determining when a loan transfer could be treated as having transferred substantially all the risks associated with the loan so as to remove it from the balance sheet. These were derived from the Bank of England's paper of February 1989 on its supervisory policy on the treatment of loan transfers involving banks, which was also used as the basis for ED 49's proposals on securitised mortgages as discussed in 3.4 above. However, as with securitisation, this approach was not adopted by the ASB when it published FRED 4 and, subsequently, FRS 5.

FRS 5 discusses the possibilities in rather different terms. As for other forms of finance, the three options which Application Note E offers are derecognition, a linked presentation and a separate presentation. However, it also refers to the possibility of splitting a loan so that some of it is transferred while the rest is retained, which constitutes 'partial' derecognition.

Derecognition is appropriate when all the significant risks and rewards pertaining to the loans have been passed from the original lender to the transferee. In the absence of side agreements, this will generally be the case where the loan has been novated, but might also apply where there has been an assignment or a sub-participation.[60] The essential test is whether there are any circumstances in which the original lender retains the possibility of any benefit from the loans (or from the part transferred),[61] or might be called upon to repay the new lender so as to bear any losses or meet any obligations; if not, derecognition is appropriate and the loan is therefore taken off the balance sheet. The tests which generally have to be satisfied in order to achieve this are that:

(a)   the transaction takes place at an arms' length price for an outright sale;

(b)   the transaction is for a fixed amount of consideration and there is no recourse whatsoever, either implicit or explicit, to the lender for losses from whatever cause. Normal warranties given in respect of the condition of the loans at the time of transfer would not breach this condition, but any warranties concerning their condition or performance in the future would do so; and

(c)   the lender will not benefit or suffer in any way if the loans perform better or worse than expected. This condition will not be satisfied where the lender has a right to further sums which vary according to the future performance of the loans (i.e. according to whether, when or how much the borrowers pay).[62]

Derecognition also gives rise to a profit and loss account effect, because the loans are regarded as 'sold', and accordingly the difference between their carrying amount and the proceeds received is taken to the profit and loss account. Insofar as all the proceeds have been received in cash, this poses no difficulty, but otherwise the profit should be restricted to the amount realised if there is uncertainty as to its eventual amount. Losses should, however, be provided in full.[63]

As with the other examples discussed earlier in this chapter, a linked presentation is appropriate where some of the risks and rewards relating to the loans have been retained (thus rendering derecognition unavailable) but the original lender's downside risk is nonetheless definitely limited to a fixed monetary amount. This combination of circumstances is less likely to apply in the case of loan transfers; it is more likely that the risks and rewards will have been wholly disposed of or wholly retained. However, there are various possible transactions which involve a partial transfer of the loans and result in the original lender's maximum exposure being capped, and these may give rise to the use of the linked presentation.[64]

Where the conditions are met, the non-returnable proceeds received will be shown as a deduction from the loans to which they relate within the assets section of the balance sheet. Insofar as these proceeds exceed the amount of the loans, FRS 5 says that the difference should be taken to the profit and loss account, but the standard does not explicitly require the recognition of equivalent losses even if a loss is implicit in the transaction. We believe that it is appropriate to apply the same principle to both profits and losses.

Application Note E calls for the following disclosures when a linked presentation is used:

(a)   the main terms of the arrangement;

(b)   the gross amount of loans transferred and outstanding at the balance sheet date;

(c)   the profit or loss recognised in the period, analysed as appropriate; and

(d)   the disclosures required by paragraph 27(c) and (d) (see 2.6 above).[65]

Where the conditions for neither derecognition nor a linked presentation are satisfied, a separate presentation is required; in other words, the original loan stays on balance sheet as an asset and the amount received from the transferee appears on the other side of the balance sheet as a loan payable. The Application Note calls for disclosure of the amount of loans outstanding at the year end which are subject to loan transfer arrangements.[66]

3.6   Take-or-pay contracts and throughput agreements

Take-or-pay contracts and throughput agreements are unconditional commitments to buy goods or services from a supplier in the future, generally from a new operational facility created by the supplier. From the supplier's point of view, such contracts guarantee a certain level of sales which gives assurance that the facility will be viable, and expedite the financing; from the purchaser's point of view, it secures a medium or long-term source of supply, probably at favourable prices. Sometimes the supplier is set up by a consortium of customers who wish to share a particular facility, such as a pipeline to service the needs of a number of oil companies.

Take-or-pay contracts and throughput agreements are essentially the same in concept. The only distinction between the two terms (as defined in the US standard)[67] is that throughput agreements relate to the use of a supplier's transportation facility (such as a ship or a pipeline) or processing plant, whereas take-or-pay contracts relate to the supply of goods or other services.

Under these contracts, the purchaser is obliged to pay a certain minimum amount even if, in the event, it does not take delivery of the goods or make use of the services it has contracted for. The accounting question which therefore arises is whether the purchaser has to account for a liability (its commitment under the contract) together with a corresponding asset (its right to use the facilities it has contracted for).

FRS 5 does not address these transactions specifically. Under its general principles the rights and obligations under such contracts would seem to require to be recognised in the balance sheet, which would be a radical departure from present practice, and one which the FASB shied away from (see 4.1.4 below). Indeed, a literal application of the principles might require *all* purchase obligations to be recognised on the balance sheet whenever a purchase order is accepted, rather than when the contract is fulfilled, which would be an even more radical departure. However, the ASB has avoided this consequence by scoping all such transactions out of the standard; one of the exclusions from the scope of FRS 5 is 'expenditure commitments',[68] as a result of which it would appear that take-or-pay contracts are permitted to remain off balance sheet.

This, however, is not necessarily the end of the story. Such contracts might fall within the extended definition of a lease in SSAP 21, and therefore be bound by the terms of that standard. This definition says that 'the term "lease" as used in this statement also applies to other arrangements in which one party retains ownership of an asset but conveys the right to the use of the asset to another party for an agreed period of time in return for specified payments'.[69] Where this applies, it is necessary to consider whether the contract has the character of a finance lease, in which case the asset should be recognised in the balance sheet of the user. This will be the case where substantially all the risks and rewards of ownership of the asset are transferred to the user under the contract – typically where there is only ever going to be one user for the asset.

ICI discloses the existence of various take-or-pay contracts in its commitments note:

Extract 16.15: Imperial Chemical Industries PLC (1996)

38 Commitments and contingent liabilities [extract]

Significant take-or-pay contracts entered into by subsidiaries are as follows:

(i)   the purchase of electric power, which commenced April 1993, for 15 years. The present value of the remaining commitment is estimated at £704m.

(ii) the purchase of electric power, which will commence in the first quarter of 1998, for 15 years. The present value of this commitment is estimated at £167m.

(iii) the supply of ethane, which commenced May 1996, for 10 years. The present value of this commitment is estimated at £125m.

Scottish Power discloses this extensive range of commitments:

Extract 16.16: Scottish Power plc (1997)

30 Financial commitments [extract]

(b) Other contractual commitments

Under contractual commitments, the group has rights and obligations in relation to the undernoted contracts. The annual value of the purchases and income arising from these contracts is provided below:

	Notes	Commitment entered into	Commitment expires	Purchases/sales in year under group commitments 1997 £m	1996 £m
The purchase of electricity from Scottish Nuclear		1990	2005	**373.2**	442.2
The purchase of electricity from Hydro-Electric	(1)	1990	see below	**120.5**	121.4
The supply of electricity to Hydro-Electric		1990	2004	**15.7**	16.3
Revenue from the operation of the company's transmission system and access by Hydro-Electric to the Anglo-Scottish connector		1990	no fixed date of expiry	**24.7**	22.1
Purchase of coal from the Scottish Coal Company		1994	1998	**75.5**	75.6
Purchase of gas from various fields in the North Sea	(2)	see below	see below	**50.4**	19.3

(1) There are two agreements relating to the purchase of electricity from Hydro-Electric. These expire in 2012 and 2039.

(2) The group has entered into a number of contracts to purchase gas, primarily from various fields in the North Sea. Gas production from the fields commences on various dates between December 1994 and October 1997 and the duration of the production periods is likely to vary between three and fifteen years. The total expected purchase cost of the contracts entered into is £570 million and the output purchased is expected to be fully utilised by the group within the gas supply business and in the production of electricity by the power stations.

3.7   Transactions under the Private Finance Initiative

The Private Finance Initiative (PFI) is a fairly recent innovation, designed to provide a new mechanism for procuring public services. The basic idea is that, rather than having bodies in the public sector take on the whole responsibility for funding and building roads, bridges, railways, hospitals, prisons and other infrastructure assets, some of these should be contracted out to private sector operators from whom the public sector bodies would buy services. The overriding goal is to maximise value for money from the taxpayers' perspective by passing such risks to the private sector as that sector is best able to manage.

A typical PFI transaction, therefore, is a long term contract whereby a private sector entity agrees to provide services to a public sector entity in exchange for a stream of payments. The contract is likely to specify that these payments will vary according to complex formulae, involving such factors as the volume of services delivered, the level of adherence to defined quality standards, and so on.

The accounting challenge is to reflect the substance of these payments fairly in the accounts of both the contracting parties. It would be possible simply to take the contract at face value and account for the amounts paid and received as service payments; however, closer analysis may sometimes reveal that this is in reality a composite transaction whereby the public sector body is buying assets as well as services. In such a case, it will be appropriate to subdivide the contract into its components and account for the asset-related part as if it were a finance lease.

From the point of view of the public body, the main issue is whether or not to recognise an asset together with an associated borrowing, by treating some of the future contractual payments as being akin to finance lease rentals. From the private entity's point of view, a similar analysis applies in reverse, but the main concern is usually one of revenue recognition – does the substance of the contract mean that the new infrastructure asset has been sold to the public sector so that a construction profit can be recognised? A further complication in practice is that the private sector entity is often a joint venture made up of a construction company and a service provider, and has bought the asset from the construction company, so questions of associated company accounting can also apply (see Chapter 7 at 4.6).

The ASB is reported to be developing a further Application Note to FRS 5 to address the treatment of such transactions. In the meantime, however, it is necessary to apply the general principles of the standard (and also the requirements of SSAP 21, where it provides the more specific guidance for any particular transaction). What this requires in practice is a thorough analysis of the contract so as to determine its substance. In particular, this analysis should focus on the formula for varying the contractual payments in order to identify the reasons for these variations, and see whether they relate to risks associated with the ownership of the asset, or to the risks of operating it to deliver services. The purpose of this is to see whether the variations are more consistent with a hypothesis that the asset belongs in substance to the public sector body and not to its ostensible owner, the private sector entity. For example, if the variations relate largely to achievement of service quality standards but the public sector body is otherwise committed to pay much the same amount for the asset whether it uses it or not, then this will suggest that it is buying it in substance.

Needless to say, such an analysis may still not produce a clear-cut answer, not least because the contract may have been deliberately designed to produce an ambiguous accounting result. However, it is helpful to try to see it through the eyes of the contracting parties, and understand what has been in their minds in negotiating these particular terms. The main emphasis should be on those terms that are likely to be relevant in practice; those which would only come into effect under unrealistic scenarios should be given little weight. In other words, it is necessary to concentrate on what the parties believe to be most likely to occur in practice, and then see how much it could realistically vary from that result, and not to be diverted by outcomes that are improbable.

4   COMPARISON WITH US AND IASC PRONOUNCEMENTS

4.1   US

4.1.1   General

There is no one standard in the US which tries to address the whole spectrum of off balance sheet finance in a manner comparable to FRS 5. However, there are a large number of individual standards and Emerging Issues Task Force abstracts that deal with particular aspects of the subject, the chief of which are mentioned below. There is no equivalent to the idea of a linked presentation in US accounting practice.

4.1.2   Subsidiaries and quasi subsidiaries

In the US, the basic criterion which defines a subsidiary is the holding of a controlling financial interest, usually through ownership of over 50% of the outstanding voting shares. A subsidiary is described in APB 18 (which deals with equity accounting) as 'a corporation which is controlled, directly or indirectly, by another corporation. The usual condition for control is ownership of a majority (over 50%) of the outstanding voting stock. The power to control may also exist with a lesser degree of ownership, for example, by contract, lease, agreement with other stockholders or by court decree.' The US does not directly have the concept either of 'dominant influence' or of a quasi subsidiary, although the SEC has been known to require the consolidation of minority-owned investments that are subsidiaries in substance.

The FASB is currently undertaking a project which is concerned with consolidation policy and specific issues of consolidation techniques. It has been considering the implications of the 'economic unit concept' which is based primarily on control rather than the ownership of a majority voting interest, and issued an exposure draft on the subject in 1995 (see Chapter 5 at 6.1).

4.1.3 Sale of assets

SFAS 49 – *Accounting for Product Financing Arrangements* – produces results similar to those which follow from Application Note B of FRS 5. A product financing arrangement is a transaction in which an enterprise sells a product to another entity and in a related transaction agrees to repurchase the product (or a substantially identical product).[70] Where the arrangement is such that the product will be repurchased at a predetermined price, which is not subject to change except for fluctuations due to finance and holding costs,[71] then the original sale will not be treated as such but, rather, as a liability.[72] Such a treatment also applies where the enterprise has an option to repurchase the product and will be subject to a significant penalty if it fails to exercise the option or where the other party has an option whereby it can require the enterprise to purchase the product.[73]

4.1.4 Long-term obligations

In 1981, the FASB issued SFAS 47 – *Disclosure of Long-Term Obligations* – in response to requests to consider accounting for project financing arrangements. These are arrangements relating to the financing of a major capital project in which the lender looks principally to the cash flows and earnings of the project as the source of funds for repayment and to the assets of the project as collateral for the loan.[74] This says that 'the particular requests related to whether the unconditional purchase obligations and indirect guarantees of indebtedness of others typical of project financing arrangements result in participants acquiring ownership interests and obligations to make future cash payments that should be recognised as assets and liabilities on their balance sheets. The Board concluded … that the accounting questions could be answered better after further progress is made on the conceptual framework for financial accounting and reporting.' The statement is, therefore, an interim measure and only requires disclosures to be made about the obligations under such arrangements. However, although the FASB completed the relevant part of its conceptual framework in 1985, SFAS 47 has never been superseded. The scope exclusion for 'expenditure commitments' in FRS 5 similarly means that such obligations need not be included in the balance sheet in the UK.

4.1.5 Sales of real estate

This is covered by SFAS 66, a highly detailed standard which lays down rigid rules for the recognition of profit on property transactions, and has consequential effects on whether or not the property is removed from the balance sheet. The basic requirements are that profit should be recognised in full only when all the following criteria are met:

(a) the sale is consummated. This requires the following:

    (i) the parties are bound by the terms of the contract; and

(ii) all consideration has been exchanged (i.e. either all monies have been received, or all necessary contractual arrangements have been entered into for the ultimate payment of monies – such as notes supported by irrevocable letters of credit from an independent lending institution); and

(iii) any permanent financing for which the vendor is responsible has been arranged; and

(iv) all conditions precedent to closing the contract have been performed;[75]

(b) the purchaser's initial and continuing investments are adequate to demonstrate a commitment to pay for the property;

(c) the vendor's receivable is not subject to future subordination; and

(d) the vendor has transferred to the purchaser the usual risks and rewards of ownership in a transaction that is in substance a sale and does not have a substantial continuing involvement with the property.[76]

The following are some of the examples of the circumstances specified in the standard as falling foul of the last of these requirements:

■ The seller is obliged to repurchase the property, or has an option to do so.

■ The seller guarantees the return of the buyer's investment or a return on that investment for an extended period.

■ The seller has ongoing commitments to operate the property at his own risk.

■ The seller is contractually committed to develop the property in the future, to construct facilities on the land, or to provide off-site improvements or amenities.

■ The seller will participate in future profit from the property without risk of loss.

In each of these (and other) cases SFAS 66 indicates the further factors to be considered and discusses the appropriate accounting treatment. These rules appear to be more stringent than the equivalent requirements in FRS 5.

4.1.6 *Transfers of receivables*

The FASB issued SFAS 125 – *Accounting for Transfers and Servicing of Financial Assets and Extinguishments of Liabilities* – in 1996. This adopts a 'financial-components approach' – which permits partial derecognition because it allows assets and liabilities to be subdivided into components and accounted for separately – and it focuses on whether or not control over the items in question is maintained. It therefore takes quite a different approach from FRS 5 to questions such as debt factoring and securitisation transactions.

SFAS 125 says that transfers of financial assets (or components thereof) should be accounted for as a sale if the transferor surrenders control over the assets and in exchange receives consideration other than beneficial interests in the assets that have been transferred. To have surrendered control over the assets requires all of the following:

(a) the transferred assets have been isolated from the transferor so that they are beyond the reach of the transferor and its creditors, even in bankruptcy or receivership;

(b) the transferee obtains the right – free of conditions that constrain it from taking advantage of that right – to pledge or exchange the financial assets. (Where the transferee is a qualifying special purpose entity, these conditions apply to the holders of beneficial interests in that entity.); and

(c) the transferor does not maintain effective control over the transferred assets through (1) an agreement that both entitles and obligates the transferor to repurchase or redeem them before maturity or (2) an agreement that entitles the transferor to repurchase or redeem transferred assets that are not readily obtainable.[77]

These rules are more accommodating than those in FRS 5. For example, the retention of bad debt risk by the transferor does not prevent a sale being recorded; it simply requires a liability representing that risk to be recorded.

4.1.7 Offset

The FASB has interpreted the conditions for setting off assets against liabilities in terms similar to the offset rules in FRS 5, but with one extra criterion. This is that the reporting entity must actually intend to use the right of set off in settling the amounts in question. The ASB considered this criterion in developing FRS 5, but rejected it on the view that the intended manner of settlement is a matter of administrative convenience and does not affect the economic position of the parties.

4.2 IASC

The IASC has not issued any pronouncements dealing specifically with off balance sheet transactions. However, IAS 1 – *Disclosure of Accounting Policies* – states that three considerations should govern the selection and application of appropriate accounting policies. These are prudence, materiality and substance over form. The last of these is expressed as 'transactions and other events should be accounted for and presented in accordance with their substance and financial reality and not merely with their legal form'.[78]

The IASC's discussion paper on financial instruments puts forward recognition and derecognition tests for financial assets and liabilities. The recognition test states that 'an enterprise should recognise a financial asset or financial liability on its balance sheet when it becomes a party to the contractual provisions that comprise the financial instrument.'[79] This implies very early recognition of transactions, in advance of their execution, although some of the discussion in the paper suggests that they do not necessarily mean the rule to be interpreted in this way – for example, purchases of marketable securities are to be recognised only on settlement date, not on trade date, although the paper acknowledges that further consideration of this practice is needed.

The derecognition tests are slightly different as between assets and liabilities. The proposed rule for assets is that 'an enterprise should remove a financial asset (or a portion of a financial asset) from its balance sheet when the enterprise realises the rights to benefits specified in the contract, the rights expire, or the enterprise surrenders or otherwise loses control of the contractual rights that comprise the financial asset (or a portion thereof)'.[80] Like SFAS 125 in the US (see 4.1.6 above), this uses a 'financial-components' approach that allows assets to be subdivided, allowing a degree of partial derecognition. Unlike FRS 5, it allows factored debts to be taken off the balance sheet even if the transferor retains the bad debt risk; a financial liability in respect of that risk is recognised instead.

The proposed rule for liabilities is that 'an enterprise should remove a financial liability (or a portion of a financial liability) from its balance sheet when it is extinguished (that is when the obligation specified in the contract has been discharged, cancelled or expires), or when the primary responsibility for the liability (or a portion thereof) is transferred to another party'.[81]

5   CONCLUSION

FRS 5 has so far been fairly successful in curbing the wilder excesses of creative accountants. In particular, the requirement to consolidate quasi subsidiaries, together with the general injunction to account for the substance of transactions rather than being diverted by their narrow legal form, have provided useful ammunition against contrived schemes that rely on artificial structures or improbable interpretations of events. The five Application Notes have also been helpful in prescribing the accounting treatment of the transactions which they address.

Nonetheless, we believe that the standard requires substantial revision, because it is a large and impenetrable document and some of its key principles are questionable. Its recognition rules are difficult to understand and do not really underpin established practice. The derecognition rules are also insufficiently developed; in particular, the idea of partial derecognition appears in the standard as something of an afterthought and is not consistently applied even in the Application Notes. And the linked presentation is neither fish nor fowl, and would have been better strangled at birth. We hope that the ASB will take the opportunity to re-examine it before too long.

References

1   TR 603, para. 17.
2   ED 42, *Special purpose transactions*, ASC, March 1988, para. 56.
3   *Ibid.*, para. 57.
4   *Ibid.*, para. 58.
5   *Ibid.*, para. 62.
6   *Ibid.*, para. 65.
7   FRS 5, *Reporting the substance of transactions*, ASB, April 1994, para. 12.
8   *Ibid.*, para. 13.
9   *Ibid.*, para. 43.
10 *Ibid.*, para. 16.
11 *Ibid.*, para. 47.
12 *Ibid.*, para. 2.
13 *Ibid.*, para. 4.
14 Exposure Draft of *Statement of Principles for financial reporting*, ASB, November 1995, paras. 3.5 and 3.21.
15 FRS 5, para. 17.
16 *Ibid.*, para. 18.
17 *Ibid.*, para. 20.
18 Exposure Draft of *Statement of Principles for financial reporting*, para. 4.6.
19 Discussion Paper, *Accounting for financial assets and financial liabilities*, IASC, March 1997, Chapter 3, para. 3.1.
20 This, however, is a possible future development; see Chapter 17 at 1.6.
21 FRS 5, para. 22.
22 *Ibid.*, para. 25.
23 *Ibid.*, para. 21.
24 *Ibid.*, para. 72.
25 *Ibid.*, para. 73.
26 *Ibid.*, para. 24.
27 FRS 5, paras. 26 and 27.
28 The standard in fact appears to argue that the asset and liability *have* been derecognised and replaced by a new asset (i.e. the net amount) which is then grossed up again for presentation purposes. However, this tortuous argument appears to have been designed only to avoid breaching the general prohibition on offsetting assets and liabilities which would otherwise prevent the linked presentation being applied.
29 FRS 5, para. 81.
30 *Ibid.*, para. 26.
31 *Ibid.*, para. 27.
32 *Ibid.*, para. 82.
33 *Ibid.*, para. 83.
34 *Ibid.*, paras. 28 and 88.
35 CA 85, Sch. 4, para. 5.
36 FRS 5, para. 29.
37 *Ibid.*
38 FRS 5, para. 7.
39 *Ibid.*, para. 8.
40 *Ibid.*, para. 33.
41 CA 85, s 227(5) and (6).
42 FRS 5, para. 38.
43 *Ibid.*, para. 35.
44 *Ibid.*, para. 36.
45 *Ibid.*, para. 30.
46 *Ibid.*, para. 31.
47 *Ibid.*, Application Note A, paras. A11 and A12.
48 *Ibid.*, Application Note B, para. B19.

49   *Ibid.*, para. B21.
50   FRS 5, Application Note C, para. C12.
51   These conditions are discussed further in paras. C15 and C16 of the Application Note.
52   FRS 5, Application Note C, para. C19.
53   *Ibid.*, para. C20.
54   FRS 5, Application Note D, para. D8.
55   *Ibid.*, para. D22.
56   *Ibid.*, para. D23.
57   *Ibid.*, para. D24.
58   The reasons for this are explained in para. D16 of the Application Note.
59   FRS 5, Application Note D, para. D20.
60   This is explained more fully in para. E14 of Application Note E.
61   As discussed in para. 71 of FRS 5, where the proportionate share of benefits and risks of part of an asset has been transferred, that part can be treated as a separate asset.
62   FRS 5, Application Note E, para. E15.
63   *Ibid.*, para. E22.
64   *Ibid.*, paras. E19 and E20.
65   *Ibid.*, para. E23.
66   *Ibid.*, para. E24.
67   SFAS 47, *Disclosure of Long-Term Obligations*, FASB, March 1981, para. 23.
68   FRS 5, para. 12(d).
69   SSAP 21, *Accounting for leases and hire purchase contracts*, ASC, August 1984, para. 14.
70   SFAS 49, *Accounting for Product Financing Arrangements*, FASB, June 1981, para. 3.
71   *Ibid.*, para. 5.
72   *Ibid.*, para. 8.
73   *Ibid.*, para. 5.
74   SFAS 47, *Disclosure of Long-Term Obligations*, FASB, March 1981, para. 23(a).
75   SFAS 66, *Accounting for Sales of Real Estate*, FASB, October 1982, para. 6.
76   *Ibid.*, para. 5.
77   SFAS 125 – *Accounting for Transfers and Servicing of Financial Assets and Extinguishments of Liabilities*, FASB, June 1996, para. 9.
78   IAS 1, *Disclosure of Accounting Policies*, IASC, January 1975, para. 9(b).
79   *Accounting for financial assets and financial liabilities*, IASC, March 1997, Chapter 3, para. 3.1.
80   *Ibid.*, para. 4.1
81   *Ibid.*

Chapter 17   Leases and hire purchase contracts

1   INTRODUCTION

SSAP 21 broke new ground in UK financial reporting in two ways: first, it was the first accounting standard to apply the concept of substance over form. Through this, the requirement for companies to capitalise assets in their balance sheets (together with the corresponding obligations) in prescribed circumstances was introduced – irrespective of the fact that legal title to those assets vested in another party.

This approach is based on the view that a lease that transfers substantially all of the risks and benefits incident to the ownership of an asset to the lessee should be accounted for as the acquisition of an asset and the assumption of an obligation by the lessee and as a sale or financing by the lessor. Such leases were termed 'finance leases' and are equivalent to what are known as 'capital leases' in the US. In the case of leases which did not transfer substantially all the risks and rewards of ownership of an asset to the lessee, the accounting was relatively unchanged. These leases became known as 'operating leases' and do not require capitalisation in the balance sheet. Instead, operating lease rentals are charged to the profit and loss account of the lessee on a straight line basis over the lease term.

The second way in which SSAP 21 broke new ground is that it was the first standard to incorporate the present value basis of measurement within the historical cost model. This is because the 'asset' capitalised under a finance lease is the present value of the minimum lease payments under the lease and not the leased asset itself – although clearly the amount capitalised should approximate to the fair value of the asset acquired under the finance lease.

SSAP 21, together with its equivalent standards around the world, have been in place for many years. Consequently, the distinction between finance and operating leases and the related accounting consequences are now widely accepted internationally. At the same time, though, conventional accounting in this area is currently being challenged, and some major standard-setters around the world have strongly held views that the finance/operating distinction should be removed and that all rights and obligations arising under lease contracts should be recognised as assets and liabilities in the financial statements of lessees. This proposed new approach is discussed at 1.6 below.

1.1   What are leases and hire purchase contracts?

'A *lease* is a contract between a lessor and a lessee for the hire of a specific asset. The lessor retains ownership of the asset but conveys the right to the use of the asset to the lessee for an agreed period of time in return for the payment of specified rentals.'[1] The term 'lease' is also used to refer to any arrangement with a similar result.

'A *hire purchase contract* is a contract for the hire of an asset which contains a provision giving the hirer an option to acquire legal title to the asset upon the fulfilment of certain conditions stated in the contract';[2] usually, this merely involves the payment of a specified final rental.

1.2   The tax position

The tax position for both lessees and lessors can be briefly outlined as follows:

(a)   *lessees* – the total rentals payable are an allowable expense (with a restriction for cars costing more than £12,000)[3] whilst no capital allowances are received;

(b)   *lessors* – the total rentals receivable are taxable income and capital allowances are given on the cost of the leased assets.

Under Statement of Practice SP3/91, the Inland Revenue will normally allow tax relief to a lessee for amounts charged in the accounts in respect of finance costs if these are dealt with in accordance with SSAP 21. They will also allow a deduction for depreciation charged in respect of assets held under finance leases, as long as the charge is calculated on normal commercial accounting principles. In other situations the basis of allowance may have to be negotiated.

For hire purchase contracts or leases which include a realistic purchase option, however, any capital allowances are receivable by the hirer not the owner. As a result, the hirer can only claim the interest element of rentals payable as a tax deductible expense.

1.3   SSAP 21

SSAP 21 – *Accounting for leases and hire purchase contracts* – was issued in August 1984 after a lengthy and active exposure/discussion period. ED 29,[4] which led to SSAP 21, was issued in October 1981 after approximately five years of debate. It was argued that comparability between companies would require capitalisation of finance leases by lessees; in particular, the effects of non-capitalisation on companies' gearing and rates of return on assets were said to affect comparability. It was further argued that readers of financial statements could not determine the economic substance of asset financing transactions from the financial statements. One case highlighting this was that of Court Line Limited, a public company which collapsed in 1974. The group used leased aircraft to operate a package holiday business, and at 30th September 1973 had undisclosed leasing obligations relating to assets costing £40m.[5] The shareholders' funds shown in the group balance sheet at that date amounted to approximately £18m.[6] As the Inspectors stated, 'the amounts involved were material and should have been disclosed'.[7] Although this suggested that full disclosure might suffice (rather than new accounting treatments), it certainly highlighted the need for changes in financial statement presentation in order that readers could fully appreciate the financial position of a company involved in leasing.

At the time that it was issued, SSAP 21 was one of the most controversial accounting standards, as it effectively invoked a substance over form approach to give an accounting treatment possibly different from the legal ownership position. As discussed below, this is not done explicitly, however, as the lessee is required to capitalise the present value of minimum lease payments under a finance lease, not the leased asset itself. In practice, the fair value of the asset will approximate to the present value of minimum lease payments, and the inclusion of the latter as an asset achieves the accounting result of substance over form.

SSAP 21 essentially involves a decision as to whether or not a lease meets the given definition of a finance lease; if not, then an operating lease exists. Such decisions will be made independently by both the lessee and lessor to determine the appropriate accounting treatment and disclosures. Broad guidelines and requirements are given in SSAP 21, but many areas are not specifically covered or are discussed only in the Guidance Notes issued with it.[8]

Under SSAP 21, hire purchase contracts which are of a financing nature should be treated similarly to finance leases, whilst the others should be treated similarly to operating leases. The vast majority will be of a financing nature and were already, in fact, being accounted for similarly to the finance lease treatment required by SSAP 21. This is because it is usually intended that the hirer will obtain title to the asset concerned at the end of the hire period. All references in this Chapter to leases include hire purchase contracts of the appropriate type, unless the context requires otherwise.

SSAP 21 'does not apply to lease contracts concerning the rights to explore for or to exploit natural resources such as oil, gas, timber, metals and other minerals. Nor does it apply to licensing agreements for items such as motion picture films, video recordings, plays, manuscripts, patents and copyrights'.[9] This, however, does not preclude SSAP 21 from being referred to for general guidance where it is considered appropriate.

1.4   Accounting requirements of SSAP 21

Lessees should capitalise finance leases and recognise a corresponding obligation in creditors. The capitalised asset should then be depreciated over the shorter of the leased asset's useful life or the lease term (see 2.1.5 below); capitalised hire purchase contracts should be depreciated over the hired asset's useful life. The obligation will be reduced by the element of rental payments which is calculated to relate to such a repayment. Lessee accounting is discussed in detail at 3 below.

Lessors should treat finance leases to their customers as amounts receivable included in debtors, i.e. the assets which are so leased will not be included as fixed assets. The amount receivable will be reduced by the element of rental receipts which is calculated to relate to such a reduction. Lessor accounting is discussed in detail at 5 below.

SSAP 21 involves no special accounting treatment of operating leases unless the rentals are payable/receivable by the lessee/lessor other than on a straight-line basis. In such a case the rentals should be taken to profit and loss account on a straight-line basis unless a more systematic basis is more appropriate. This is discussed at 3.6 and 5.2 below for lessees and lessors respectively.

SSAP 21 specifies certain disclosures to be made by lessees and lessors in addition to the adoption of the required accounting treatments above. The disclosures are outlined and examples given at 4 (lessee) and 6 (lessor) below.

1.5   ICAEW review of SSAP 21

In the Autumn of 1991 the ASB requested the technical and research committees of the various CCAB bodies to review a number of existing SSAPs with a view to submitting a report on problems that are being encountered with them in practice. One of the SSAPs which the ICAEW was given to review was SSAP 21, and the resulting report was issued in March 1992 as a Technical Release of the Institute's Financial Reporting & Auditing Group, titled FRAG 9/92 – *Review, for major practical problems, of SSAP 21.*

FRAG 9/92 discusses a number of practical difficulties which have been experienced with SSAP 21, and in particular it focuses on the distinction between finance and operating leases, accounting for sale and leaseback transactions and accounting for residual values.

1.6   The potential impact of the conceptual frameworks on lease accounting

The development of conceptual frameworks for financial reporting by the ASB, the IASC and other standard setting bodies around the world could fundamentally change the way in which financial contracts such as leases are accounted for. Each of these conceptual frameworks identifies the elements of financial statements, including assets, liabilities, equity, gains and losses as the basic elements, and sets down recognition rules for their incorporation in financial statements. In the case of lease accounting, assets and liabilities are the most relevant elements, and the ASB's Draft *Statement of Principles* defines these particular elements as follows: assets are 'rights or other access to future economic benefits controlled by an entity as a result of past transactions or events',[10] whilst liabilities are 'obligations of an entity to transfer economic benefits as a result of past transactions or events'.[11]

Looking at these two definitions, it seems likely that most leases, including non-cancellable operating leases, will qualify for recognition as assets and liabilities. This is because, irrespective of whether the lease is finance or operating in nature, the lessee is likely to enjoy the future economic benefits embodied in the leased asset, and will have an unavoidable legal obligation to transfer economic benefits to the lessor.

This is the conclusion which was reached by a working group consisting of staff members of the standard-setting bodies of Australia, Canada, New Zealand, UK, the USA and the IASC (loosely known as the G4+1). In 1996 the working group published a paper entitled *Accounting for leases: a new approach*, which discusses the limitations of current lease accounting standards and sets out a new approach to lease accounting.[12] Although the paper has not been officially approved by the boards of the various standard-setters involved in its preparation, it is seen to be influential.

The working group claims that 'current lease accounting standards are now agreed by many observers to be unsatisfactory, at least with respect to accounting by lessees'.[13] It asserts that the 'most frequently noted concern relates to the fact that the standards do not require rights and obligations arising under operating leases to be recognised as assets and liabilities in the lessee's financial statements'.[14] According to the paper, the result has been that the standards have promoted the structuring of financial arrangements so as to meet the conditions for classification as an operating lease, thereby avoiding recognition in lessees' balance sheets of material assets and liabilities arising from operating lease contracts. Consequently, the paper advocates a new approach to accounting for lease contracts which is aimed at overcoming these perceived concerns about the effectiveness of current lease accounting.

The working group's new approach to accounting for lease contracts is based on the definitions of assets and liabilities contained in the various conceptual frameworks. Under the IASC's *Framework*, an asset is defined as 'a resource controlled by the enterprise as a result of past events and from which future economic benefits are expected to flow to the enterprise', whilst a liability is defined as 'a present obligation of the enterprise arising from past events, the settlement of which is expected to result in an outflow from the enterprise of resources embodying economic benefits'.[15] According to the working group, the clear implication of applying the IASC *Framework* to accounting for lease contracts 'is that it can be reasoned that all finance leases and most, if not all, operating leases qualify for recognition as assets and liabilities'.[16]

The working group's reasoning seems to be based on the belief that the rights and obligations established by operating leases would seem to be no different in nature to those established by finance leases. This conclusion is reached through the application of the asset and liability definitions of the IASC's *Framework*: under both finance and operating leases, the lessee acquires a contractual right to enjoy the future economic benefits embodied in the leased property and incurs a contractual obligation to compensate the lessor for the use of the leased property over the lease term.[17] However, the question which should be asked is whether the conclusion reached reflects a shortcoming in existing lease accounting or whether it exposes a flaw in the *Framework*.

Overall, the working group's paper is well written and thought provoking. On the other hand, though, whilst it raises a number of legitimate issues, it does not provide many solutions. For example, the paper is critical of the existing criteria laid down in accounting standards to distinguish between finance and operating leases (describing them as being 'arbitrary'), yet it does not resolve the problem of how to distinguish between cancellable and non-cancellable leases. In our view, it may be just as difficult to distinguish between leases on this basis as it is to distinguish between finance and operating leases.

Furthermore, the paper does not distinguish between non-cancellable leases and other commitments or executory contracts, such as electricity supply agreements, service contracts and contracted capital commitments. This is a major shortcoming of the paper and, in our view, it should not be progressed further until the uncertainty regarding the application of the paper's lease capitalisation principles to other executory contracts is resolved. In particular, existing disclosure requirements relating to executory contracts would seem currently to serve the needs of the capital markets adequately. However, the paper does not address the possibility of enhanced disclosures related to operating leases, and does not explain why – given the efficiency of the capital markets – the capitalisation of all non-cancellable leases is superior to such enhanced disclosure.

In any event, the IASC has announced that it will soon be carrying out a fundamental revision of lease accounting, and will consider requiring the capitalisation of all leases with a term of over one year. Moreover, from a UK perspective, it is worth noting that Sir David Tweedie is on record as having said that the ASB is likely to go down the route of requiring the capitalisation of all material non-cancellable operating leases. Nevertheless, whilst the ASB's Draft *Statement of Principles* remains in limbo, having been rejected by commentators, the conventional approach to lease accounting prevails.

2 DETERMINING THE LEASE TYPE

2.1 The 90% test

A finance lease is defined as 'a lease that transfers substantially all the risks and rewards of ownership of an asset to the lessee',[18] whilst an operating lease 'is a lease other than a finance lease'.[19]

SSAP 21 gives guidelines for deciding whether 'substantially all the risks and rewards' have passed to a lessee. It is stated that 'it should be presumed that such a transfer of risks and rewards occurs if at the inception of a lease the present value of the minimum lease payments, including any initial payment, amounts to substantially all (normally 90 per cent or more) of the fair value of the leased asset. The present value should be calculated by using the interest rate implicit in the lease ... . Notwithstanding the fact that a lease meets [these] conditions ... , the presumption that it should be classified as a finance lease may in exceptional circumstances be rebutted if it can be clearly demonstrated that the lease in question does not transfer substantially all the risks and rewards of ownership (other than legal title) to the lessee. Correspondingly, the presumption that a lease which fails to meet [these] conditions ... is not a finance lease may in exceptional circumstances be rebutted.'[20] The more important terms used in performing the 90% test in SSAP 21 are explained below.

2.1.1 The fair value

This 'is the price at which an asset could be exchanged in an arm's length transaction less, where applicable, any grants receivable towards the purchase or use of the asset'.[21] If this fair value cannot be determined for the purposes of the 90% test, then an estimate thereof should be used. This will not usually be required for lessors, but may be for lessees who are unaware of the cost of the leased asset.

2.1.2 The implicit interest rate

This 'is the discount rate that at the inception of a lease, when applied to the amounts which the lessor expects to receive and retain, produces an amount (the present value) equal to the fair value of the leased asset'.[22]

The amounts the lessor expects to receive and retain comprise the following:

(a) the minimum lease payments to the lessor (all elements (a) to (c) at 2.1.3 below); plus
(b) any unguaranteed residual value; less
(c) any part of (a) and (b) above for which the lessor will be accountable to the lessee.

If the implicit interest rate cannot be calculated due to inadequate information then an estimate may be used. This will not usually apply to the lessor as he is likely to have all relevant information available. However, a lessee may not have access to this information and may be unable to make estimates thereof. If the interest rate implicit in the lease is not determinable, it should be estimated by reference to the rate which a lessee would be expected to pay on a similar lease.

Nevertheless, it was pointed out by the ICAEW working party which reviewed SSAP 21 that situations may arise where the lessee might also not know the rate payable on a similar lease. The working party recommended that in these circumstances the lessee's incremental borrowing rate should be used.[23]

2.1.3   *The minimum lease payments*[24]

There are three possible elements of this:

(a)   the minimum payments over the remaining part of the lease term;

(b)   any residual amount guaranteed by the lessee or a party related to him; and

(c)   any residual amounts guaranteed by any other party.

The elements to be included depend on the intended use of the minimum lease payments calculation as follows:

(i)   all elements are used in the calculation of the implicit interest rate (for use in the 90% test);

(ii)   all elements are used in the 90% test performed by the lessor. The total of these elements plus any unguaranteed residual value will represent the lessor's gross investment in the lease (see 5.3 below);

(iii)   elements (a) and (b) are used in the 90% test performed by the lessee. The present value of this minimum lease payments figure will represent both the capitalised fixed asset and the initial finance lease obligation for the lessee (see 3.2 and 3.3 below respectively).

The minimum lease payments should not include any contingent rentals, e.g. those dependent on the level of use of the equipment. However if, for example, the lessee guaranteed to use the equipment to a certain level, then that level of rentals would be included.

2.1.4   *An unguaranteed residual value*

This is 'that portion of the residual value of the leased asset (estimated at the inception of the lease), the realisation of which by the lessor is not assured or is guaranteed solely by a party related to the lessor'.[25]

2.1.5   *The lease term*

This is 'the period for which the lessee has contracted to lease the asset and any further terms for which the lessee has the option to continue to lease the asset, with or without further payment, which option it is reasonably certain at the inception of the lease that the lessee will exercise'.[26] Usually a lease can be easily divided into the primary term during which the lessee is committed to make certain rental payments (with a termination rental payable upon termination before the end of the primary term) and a secondary term for which the lessee can extend the lease if desired. It is general practice that any secondary term is only included in the lease term for 90% test calculations if it is highly probable that the term will be so extended, i.e. the 'reasonably certain' criterion is generally strictly interpreted. If a peppercorn (nominal) rental is payable in the secondary lease term period, the lease term should normally include the secondary term although the rentals can probably be ignored on materiality grounds in performing the 90% test.

2.2 90% test example

The following example illustrates the application of the 90% test:

Example 17.1

Details of a non-cancellable lease are as follows:

(i)   Fair value (per 2.1.1 above) = £10,000

(ii)   Five annual rentals payable in advance of £2,000

(iii)   Total estimated residual value at end of five years = £3,000 of which £2,000 is guaranteed by the lessee.

The implicit interest rate in the lease (per 2.1.2 above) is that which gives a present value of £10,000 for the five rentals plus the total estimated residual value at the end of year 5. This rate can be calculated as 10.93%.

This rate is then used to calculate the present value of the minimum lease payments. As explained in 2.1.3 above, this example gives rise to identical minimum lease payments from both the lessee's and lessor's points of view. This is because there is no guarantee of any part of the residual by a party other than the lessee and the minimum lease payments will be the five annual rentals plus the residual guaranteed by the lessee of £2,000. The present value of these minimum lease payments is calculated as £9,405.

This present value figure is 94.05% of the asset's fair value and a finance lease is therefore indicated.

All of the above information will be known to the lessor as he will have used it in his pricing decision for the lease. However, the lessee may not know either the fair value or the unguaranteed residual value and, therefore, the implicit interest rate. If either of the first two of these is not known, the lessee is permitted by SSAP 21 to estimate what they are and so calculate the implicit interest rate. Alternatively, he may feel that such an estimation is better made of the implicit interest rate directly, rather than of a parameter which will then allow that rate to be calculated.

It is important to note that the 90% test can result in different answers being given for the lessor and lessee, e.g. it may indicate a finance lease from the lessor but an operating lease to the lessee. There are two possible reasons for this. First, and most commonly, the lessor may receive a guarantee of the estimated (significant) residual of the leased asset by a party other than the lessee and accordingly, using the 90% test, an operating lease may be indicated for the lessee whereas a finance lease is indicated for the lessor. Second, as shown above, the lessee may not have the full information available to the lessor and his estimates of fair value or residual value may be so different from the correct figures (known to the lessor) that his classification of the lease is incorrect.

2.3   Determining the lease type – other factors

In 1987 the ICAEW published TR 664 – *Implementation of SSAP 21 'Accounting for leases and hire purchase contracts'* – in an attempt to influence the practice of interpreting the 90% test as a firm rule. It stated that any evaluation of a lease agreement should involve an overall examination of substantial risks and rewards as follows: 'Lease agreements give rise to a set of rights, rewards, risks and obligations and can be complex. The package must be analysed with greater weight given to aspects of the agreement which are likely to have a commercial effect in practice. In this way the substance of the transaction can be identified and then reflected in the financial statements in order to give a true and fair view. ... [The 90% test] does not provide a strict mathematical definition of a finance lease. Such a narrow interpretation would be contrary to the spirit of SSAP 21 and SSAPs generally.'[27]

Consequently, although the 90% test outlined above is important, there are a number of other factors which need to be considered in deciding whether or not substantially all the risks and rewards of ownership have passed. The crucial question is whether the terms of the transaction, taken as a whole, are such that the lessor can expect to be fully compensated for his investment in the leased asset without having to enter into further transactions with other parties. Affirmative answers to the following questions would tend to indicate that a finance lease exists:

(a)   If the lessee can cancel the lease, will he bear any losses associated with the cancellation?

(b)   Will the lessee gain or lose from any fluctuations in the market value of the residual? (For example, he may receive a rental rebate equalling most of the sales proceeds at the end of the lease.)

(c)   Does the lessee have the ability to continue the lease for a secondary period at a nominal rental?

(d)   Is the expected lease term equal to substantially all of the asset's expected useful life?

(e)   Are the leased assets of a specialised nature such that only the lessee (or a limited number of other parties) can use them without major modifications being made?

One factor which is sometimes considered to be relevant in determining the lease type is whether or not the lessee is responsible for insurance, maintenance, etc. However, we do not believe that this should necessarily be a conclusive factor in determining the lease type. This is because, although under the lease

Example 17.2

A five year lease of an asset commences on 1 January 19X1. The rental is £2,600 p.a. payable in advance. The fair value of the asset at lease inception is £10,000 and it is expected to have a residual at the end of the lease of £2,372 (being its tax written down value at that time) which will be passed to the lessee as a refund of rentals. In addition, the lessee is responsible for all maintenance and insurance costs.

The minimum lease payments are 5 x £2,600 = £13,000 which gives finance charges of £13,000 – 10,000 = £3,000. The actuarial method attempts to calculate the finance charge in each period to give a constant periodic rate of charge on the remaining balance of the obligation for each period. This is done as follows:

Year	Capital sum at start of period £	Rental paid £	Capital sum during period £	Finance charge (15.15% per annum) £	Capital sum at end of period £
19X1	10,000	2,600	7,400	1,121	8,521
19X2	8,521	2,600	5,921	897	6,818
19X3	6,818	2,600	4,218	639	4,857
19X4	4,857	2,600	2,257	343	2,600
19X5	2,600	2,600	–	–	–
		13,000		3,000	

The finance charge of 15.15% is that which results in a capital sum at the end of 19X5 of zero and can be found by trial and error, using a financial calculator, computer program, mathematical formula or present value tables.

This lease involves fairly straightforward figures but it is still not easy to calculate manually. It is, therefore, possible to use the sum of the digits method to give an allocation of finance charge which is a close approximation to that given by the actuarial method.

The sum of the digits method calculations, for example, are as follows:

Year	number of rentals not yet due		total finance charge / sum of number of rentals		Finance charge per annum £
19X1	4	}			1,200
19X2	3	}			900
19X3	2	} x	£3,000 ÷ 10	=	600
19X4	1	}			300
19X5	–	}			–
	10	}			3,000

We can now compare the finance charges in each of the five years under the actuarial and sum of the digits methods:

| | Finance charge as % of total | | Finance charge | |
| | Actuarial | Sum of the digits | Actuarial | Sum of the digits |
Year	%	%	£	£
19X1	37	40	1,121	1,200
19X2	30	30	897	900
19X3	21	20	639	600
19X4	12	10	343	300
19X5	–	–	–	–
	100	100	3,000	3,000

In situations where the lease term is not very long (typically not more than seven years) and interest rates are not very high, the sum of the digits method gives an allocation of finance charges which is close enough to that under the actuarial method to allow the simpler approach to be used.

It should be noted that the expected residual of £2,372 (which will be paid to the lessee) does not affect any of the above calculations. This expected residual will merely influence the depreciation policy of the lessee as regards the capitalised asset. He will depreciate to an expected residual of £2,372 and any difference between this net book value figure and the amount received by the lessee will give rise to a gain or loss on disposal of the asset.

3.5   Carrying values

At any point during the lease term the depreciated book value of a capitalised leased fixed asset and the remaining finance lease obligation under that lease will not usually be equal. Normally, this is because the method of depreciation bears no relation to that for allocating finance charges to accounting periods, as can be seen in the following example:

Example 17.3

If the lessee in the previous example depreciates the asset to its residual value of £2,372 on a straight-line basis over its life of five years, then the net book value compared with the outstanding lease obligation (using the actuarial method) at the end of each year will be as follows:

| | | Outstanding |
| | Net book value | lease obligation |
Year	£	£
19X1	8,474	8,521
19X2	6,948	6,818
19X3	5,422	4,857
19X4	3,897	2,600
19X5	2,372	–

3.6 Operating leases

3.6.1 Lease rentals

SSAP 21 requires that operating lease rentals are charged to profit and loss account on a straight-line basis over the lease term irrespective of when payments are due.[35] This is logical as, for example, a large upfront payment made by the lessee should be allocated to the period over which a benefit is gained. Conversely, leases of land and buildings sometimes have a rent-free period in the early part of the lease, followed by a relatively higher rental over the remainder. Alternatively, leases are sometimes structured on the basis of stepped rentals, whereby lease rentals start at a below market rate, but are subject to pre-determined stepped increases, sometimes ending at above market rates to compensate for the lower rentals in the earlier years. In such cases, the rentals should again be charged to profit and loss account on a straight-line basis over the lease term. However, if a more systematic and rational basis is more appropriate, then that basis may be used; e.g. if the level of the use of the asset determines the level of rentals, then it would be appropriate to charge rentals when incurred.

3.6.2 Reverse premiums and similar incentives

An operating lease may include incentives for the lessee to enter into the lease. These incentives can take various forms, such as an up front cash payment to the lessee (a reverse premium), a rent-free period or a contribution to lessee costs. The question as to how such incentives should be accounted for in the accounts of lessees came to the fore following a decision of the Financial Reporting Review Panel in February 1994. The Panel was concerned about the adequacy of the information provided by Pentos plc in its 1992 accounts about the company's accounting treatment of reverse premiums received in respect of property leases. The relevant disclosures in Pentos' accounts were as follows:

Extract 17.1: Pentos plc (1992)

Accounting Policies

Reverse Premiums

Net income from reverse premiums is taken to profit over two accounting periods in order to match income received and start up costs incurred for new shops.

The amount taken to the profit and loss account in the year was included in 'Other Operating Expenses (Net)' and was not separately disclosed. The matter was resolved by the company agreeing to explain its accounting policy more fully in its 1993 accounts, and to disclose the amounts of reverse premiums received in 1993 and 1992. As a result, Pentos' 1993 accounts disclosed the following:

Extract 17.2: Pentos plc (1993)

Accounting Policies

Reverse Premia

Reverse premia arising in the period are matched with the costs of negotiating property leases and premia, and the costs of holding and maintaining unused property. The remaining balance of reverse premia is taken to profit over two accounting periods to match the initially low performance of new shops in the start up period.

Notes to the Accounts

3   Expenses [extract]

Included in other operating expenses are property costs which are reduced by gross reverse premia in the amount of £3.4m (1992 – £6.3m).

However, despite the findings of the Panel, it is not entirely clear as to exactly what it was that the Panel was querying. Perhaps Pentos' referral to the Panel was driven by the school of thought which says that lessees should account for incentive payments received on a straight line basis over the period of the lease (as is the requirement under US GAAP)[36] and should not therefore be taken to income over the first two years of the lease. Evidence for the fact that the Panel was pursuing more than a mere disclosure issue may be found in the following paragraph in the Press Notice which publicised the Panel's decision: 'The Panel noted that existing requirements in the law and accounting standards did not provide unequivocal guidance as to the correct accounting treatment of reverse premiums and is drawing this matter to the attention of the Accounting Standards Board.'

In any event, the issue ended up on the agenda of the UITF which, in December 1994, issued Abstract 12 dealing with the issue.[37] The UITF's consensus requires that all incentives, whatever form they take, should be spread by the lessee on a straight-line basis over the lease term or, if shorter than the full lease term, over the period to the review date on which the rent is first expected to be adjusted to the prevailing market rate. Where, exceptionally, the presumption can be rebutted that an incentive (however structured) is in substance part of the lessor's market return, another systematic and rational basis may be used, with the following disclosures:

(a)   an explanation of the specific circumstances that render the standard treatment specified by the Abstract misleading;

(b)   a description of the basis used and the amounts involved, and

(c)   a note of the effect on the results for the current and corresponding period of any departure from the standard treatment.[38]

If, in exceptional circumstances, another method of spreading is considered more accurately to adjust the rents paid to the prevailing market rate, UITF 12

Extract 17.4: Racal Electronics Plc (1997)

NOTES ON THE FINANCIAL STATEMENTS

20	OBLIGATIONS UNDER FINANCE LEASES	1997 £000	1996 £000
	Obligations under finance leases fall due as follows:		
(a)	between one and two years	16,280	13,001
(b)	between two and five years	39,294	40,472
(c)	in more than five years	41,469	46,121
		97,043	99,594
(d)	in one year or less	15,432	14,635
		112,475	114,229

As noted at 4.1(f) above, there is an alternative permitted method of disclosure of finance lease obligations. Rather than splitting the obligations by date of payment net of the future interest charges as illustrated in Extracts 17.3 and 17.4 above, some companies show the gross obligations with the future finance charges being deducted from the total. Cadbury Schweppes adopts this form of disclosure, as illustrated below:

Extract 17.5: Cadbury Schweppes plc (1996)

Notes on the Accounts

25 Leasing Commitments	The future minimum lease payments to which the Group was committed as at the year end under finance leases were as follows:	1996 £m	1995 £m
	Within one year	14	16
	Between one and five years	35	39
	After five years	13	19
		62	74
	Less: Finance charges allocated to future periods	(19)	(23)
		43	51

As noted at 4.1(g) above, the disclosure requirement which is somewhat deficient is that for payments committed to be made in the next year under non-cancellable operating leases. Far more useful disclosure would be that which is, for example, required under US GAAP – namely the future minimum rental payments payable over each of the next five years and in aggregate thereafter. In any event, though, there is an increasing trend amongst UK companies to provide this information on a voluntary basis. Included amongst these are British Airways, Reuters and, as illustrated below, BT:

Extract 17.6: British Telecommunications plc (1997)

NOTES TO THE FINANCIAL STATEMENTS

21. Financial commitments and contingent liabilities [extract]

	Group		Company	
	1997 **£m**	1996 £m	**1997** **£m**	1996 £m
Operating lease payments payable within one year of the balance sheet date were in respect of leases expiring:				
Within one year	**10**	7	**6**	3
Between one and five years	**32**	26	**19**	21
After five years	**131**	111	**92**	95
Total payable within one year	**173**	144	**117**	119

Future minimum operating lease payments for the group at 31 March 1997 were as follows:

Payable in the year ending 31 March:

	£m
1998	**173**
1999	**136**
2000	**127**
2001	**121**
2002	**118**
Thereafter	**1,325**
Total future minimum operating lease payments	**2,000**

Operating lease commitments were mainly in respect of leases of land and buildings.

As illustrated in the above extract, SSAP 21 applies to leases of land and buildings as for any other assets. However, where property companies act as lessees of long leasehold investment properties, the commitments for ground rents under these operating leases are not usually shown. In fact, MEPC states in its accounts that 'in the opinion of the directors, the disclosure requirements of SSAP 21 to show leasing commitments in respect of ground rents are not relevant to a property investment company'.[53] The reason for this view is unclear.

One element of the disclosure requirements of SSAP 21 which is rarely seen in practice is that in respect of finance lease and hire purchase contract commitments existing at the balance sheet date when at that date neither has the asset been brought into use nor have rentals started to accrue.[54] Presumably companies are aggregating these commitments (where they exist) with their general disclosure of capital commitments contracted but not provided for.

5   ACCOUNTING BY LESSORS

5.1   Introduction

Essentially, a lessor is required to show amounts due from lessees under finance leases as amounts receivable in debtors, and assets leased out under operating leases as tangible fixed assets. The mechanics of lessor accounting for finance leases are more complex than those for a lessee, although, of course, the criteria which determine the classification of leases as either finance or operating are identical for both lessors and lessees (see 2 above).

5.2   Operating leases

Rentals receivable under an operating lease should be recognised on a straight-line basis (irrespective of when rentals are actually receivable) unless another systematic and rational basis is more representative of the time pattern in which the benefit from the leased asset is receivable.[55] This requirement of SSAP 21 is an attempt to ensure a proper matching of revenues with associated costs. A non-straight-line basis may be appropriate where, for example, operating lease rentals are dependent on the level of use of the leased asset. In this case, rentals should be recognised in the periods they become receivable.

Examples of situations where a lessor should recognise operating lease rentals on a straight-line basis, even if they are not so received, are where there is a rent-free period at the beginning of a lease of land or buildings, or where a balloon payment is to be made at the beginning or end of the lease period.

5.3   Finance leases

Broadly, there are two stages in accounting for finance lease receivables; first, the calculation of the gross earnings (finance lease income) element of total lease rentals receivable and, second, the allocation of gross earnings to accounting periods over the lease term. Gross earnings represent:[56]

(a) the lessor's gross investment in the lease which is the total of the minimum lease payments and any unguaranteed residual value estimated as accruing to the lessor; *less*

(b) the cost of the leased asset less any grants receivable towards purchase or use of the asset.

Gross earnings should then be allocated to accounting periods to give a constant periodic rate of return on the lessor's net cash investment.[57] The net cash investment is the amount of funds invested in a lease by the lessor and comprises the cost of the asset plus or minus certain related payments or receipts.[58] Tax-free grants that are available to the lessor against the purchase price of assets acquired for leasing should be spread over the period of the lease and dealt with by treating the grant as non-taxable income.[59]

The allocation of gross earnings to accounting periods is detailed at 5.4 (finance leases) and 5.5 (hire purchase contracts) below.

Having calculated the allocation of gross earnings to accounting periods, the lessor must then consider the amount at which the receivable should be shown in its balance sheet. The finance lease receivable should equal the lessor's net investment in the lease. This net investment will initially equal the cost of the asset less any grants receivable (i.e. the fair value) and will then be reduced by a portion of total rentals received. This portion will be the element of rentals receivable in a period which is not taken as gross earnings in the calculations described above.

5.4   Allocation of gross earnings – finance leases

5.4.1   Introduction

Owing to differences in tax treatments (see 1.2 above), different methods are used to allocate gross earnings to accounting periods under finance leases and hire purchase contracts. The latter is dealt with at 5.5 below, and the justification for the different treatments of finance leases and hire purchase contracts is considered at 5.4.5 below.

For finance leases, the gross earnings allocation should be made to give a constant periodic rate of return on the lessor's net cash investment. This involves the use of an 'after tax' method of allocation; the two most common are the actuarial after tax method and the investment period method.[60]

5.4.2   Methodology

The actuarial after tax and investment period methods allocate gross earnings on a basis which takes the tax effect on cash flows into account. This approach is used because we are attempting to match the revenue recognised under the lease with the expenses incurred (which may be partly notional) in funding the lessor's investment in the lease.

At any time during the lease, the lessor's net cash investment will represent:

(a)   the original cost of the asset; less

(b)   cumulative cash flow receipts to date (rental income, grants received, tax relieved through both capital allowances and payment of interest, together with interest receivable during any period of negative net cash investment); plus

(c)   cumulative cash flow payments to date (interest payments and tax payable on both rental receipts and any interest receivable). This should also include an adjustment in respect of the profit the lessor takes out of the lease, because part of the rental receipts represents profit to the lessor over and above any interest he is estimated to be paying.

The interest payable/receivable is likely to be a notional figure using appropriate rates for the lessor as at lease inception to reflect an opportunity cost of funds raised or invested. Both interest payable/receivable and profit taken out should be calculated on the average net cash investment in any period. The profit taken out will be calculated at the percentage rate which results in a net cash investment of zero at the end of the lease term.

The actuarial after tax method and the investment period method differ in their use of the calculated net cash investment at each period end to allocate gross earnings. Under the actuarial after tax method, the estimated profit taken out in each period is grossed up for tax and estimated interest costs, to give a derived apportionment of gross earnings in each period.

In contrast, under the investment period method the estimated net cash investment at each period end is divided by the total of such figures over the lease term to give the fraction of total gross earnings allocated to each period. Whereas the actuarial after tax method is more accurate, the investment period method may be preferred (if resulting differences are immaterial) since it is arithmetically simpler.

The application of the actuarial after tax and investment period methods is illustrated in the following example:

Example 17.4

The terms of a lease are as in Example 17.2 above, i.e. a five year lease of an asset commences on 1 January 19X1. The rental is £2,600 p.a. payable in advance. The fair value of the asset at lease inception is £10,000 and it is expected to have a residual at the end of the lease of £2,372 (being its tax written down value at the time) which will be passed to the lessee. In addition, the lessee is responsible for all maintenance and insurance costs.

The lessor obtains writing down allowances on the leased asset at the rate of 25%. The rate of corporation tax is 35%. The lessor's accounting year-end is 31 December and he pays or recovers tax in the following year. Interest on funds borrowed is assumed to be 10% p.a., payable on 31 December.

The lessor's net cash investment in this lease can be analysed as follows:

	(a) Net cash investment at start of	(b) Cash flows in year	(c)	(d) Average net cash investment	(e) Interest	(f) Profit taken out of	(g) Net cash investment at end of
Year	year £	cost/tax £	rentals £	in year £	paid £	lease £	year £
19X1	—	(10,000)	2,600	(7,400)	(740)	(277)	(8,417)
19X2	(8,417)	224	2,600	(5,593)	(559)	(210)	(6,362)
19X3	(6,362)	(58)	2,600	(3,820)	(382)	(144)	(4,346)
19X4	(4,346)	(284)	2,600	(2,030)	(203)	(76)	(2,309)
19X5	(2,309)	(470)	2,600	(179)	(18)	(7)	(204)
19X6	(204)	204	–	–	–	–	–
		(10,000)	13,000		(1,902)	(714)	
		(384)					

Notes to table:

(a)   net cash investment at start of year: this is simply zero at the beginning of the lease and the previous year-end figure in later years;

(b)   cash flows in year – cost and tax: the £10,000 outflow in 19X1 is the purchase of the asset which is, for simplicity, assumed to take place on the day the lease commences. All other amounts relate to tax payable/repayable.

The basis of taxation of the lessor was detailed above and tax payable/repayable relates to the previous year's rentals receivable, interest paid and writing down allowance. The tax repayable in 19X6 relates to 19X5's rental receivable, interest paid, writing down allowance and the deduction relating to the passing of the asset's sales proceeds of £2,372 to the lessee. This deduction should actually enter the table in 19X7, as that is when the tax repayment would arise from the sale in 19X6, but is included in 19X6 for simplicity. The sales proceeds and payment to the lessee are not shown as their net effect on the cash flows is nil;

(c)   cash flows in year – rentals: the annual rentals received at the beginning of each year;

(d)   average net cash investment in year: this is the sum of columns (a) to (c). For the purposes of this example, all cash flows are assumed to arise on 1 January of each year;

(e)   interest paid: calculated at 10% of the average net cash investment in year shown in column (d);

(f)   profit taken out of lease: this represents the amount required by the lessor to give a return on the lease over and above tax and interest costs. It is the percentage of the average net cash investment in year shown in column (d) which results in a net cash investment at the end of the whole transaction of zero. It can be found by trial and error but computer programs are usually used to do this. In this example the annual rate is 3.75%;

(g)   net cash investment at end of year: this is the sum of columns (d) to (f). It can be seen that this is zero at the end of the whole transaction.

6 DISCLOSURE BY LESSORS

6.1 SSAP 21 requirements

The following lessor disclosures are required by SSAP 21:

(a) policies adopted for accounting for operating and finance leases and, in detail, the policy for accounting for finance lease income;[66]

(b) aggregate rentals receivable in respect of the relevant accounting period from (i) finance leases and (ii) operating leases;[67]

(c) if the provisions of SSAP 21 have not been applied retroactively to all leases existing at 1 July 1984, disclosure of the gross earnings from the finance leases and hire purchase contracts which have arisen under each of the methods used;[68]

(d) net investment in (i) finance leases and (ii) hire purchase contracts;[69]

(e) costs of assets acquired for the purpose of letting under finance leases and hire purchase contracts;[70]

(f) gross amount of fixed assets held for use under operating leases, together with the related accumulated depreciation.[71]

6.2 Related Companies Act requirements

It is suggested in the Guidance Notes on SSAP 21 that the net investment in finance leases and hire purchase contracts should be included in current assets under the heading of debtors.[72] Accordingly, lessors who have to comply with Schedule 4 of the Companies Act, will have to comply with the requirement that 'the amount falling due after more than one year shall be shown separately for each item included under debtors'.[73]

There are a number of other disclosures required by the Companies Act which may affect lessors, and these should also be considered; e.g. details of fixed assets.[74] (This is relevant to assets leased under operating leases.)

6.3   Disclosure in practice

The following are examples of disclosures given in practice by lessors:

Extract 17.7: RMC Group p.l.c. (1996)

Accounting Policies

FINANCE LEASE RECEIVABLES

Income from finance leasing contracts, being the excess of total rentals received over the cost of the net investment in finance leasing contracts, is taken to profit in accordance with the investment period method of accounting in direct relationship to the reducing capital invested during the primary leasing period.

Amounts written off the net investment in such leases are calculated to write off the cost over the primary periods of the contracts.

Extract 17.8: HSBC Holdings plc (1996)

2 Principal accounting policies

f   *Finance and operating leases*

   i   Assets leased to customers under agreements which transfer substantially all the risks and rewards associated with ownership, other than legal title, are classified as finance leases. Where the Group is a lessor under finance leases the amounts due under the leases, after deduction of unearned charges, are included in 'Loans and advances to customers' or 'Loans and advances to banks'. Finance charges receivable are recognised over the periods of the leases in proportion to the funds invested.

   ii   Where the Group is a lessee under finance leases, the leased assets are capitalised and included in 'Equipment, fixtures and fittings' and the corresponding liability to the lessor is included in 'Other liabilities'. Finance charges payable are recognised over the periods of the leases based on the interest rates implicit in the leases.

   iii All other leases are classified as operating leases and, where the Group is the lessor, are included in 'Tangible fixed assets'. Rentals payable and receivable under operating leases are accounted for on the straight line basis over the periods of the leases and are included in 'Administrative expenses' and 'Other operating income' respectively.

be wrong in this instance for the dealer to record a profit on the sale of the car and no finance income under the lease.

It is not appropriate to take a 'normal' level of selling profit if the gross earnings under the finance lease would then be lower than normally expected, because the selling profit is taken to the profit and loss account at the lease inception and, if it is partly offset by lower than normal gross earnings under the lease, prudence dictates that this be taken into account. The correct practice is, therefore, to calculate gross earnings under the finance lease at the normal level, with any remaining element of the overall profit being taken as selling profit at the lease inception.

How then should the appropriate level of gross earnings under the finance lease be estimated? This clearly depends on the estimated interest rate implicit in the lease. In some situations the M/D will have a normal implicit interest rate based on his other leasing activity. However, in other situations where the M/D does not conduct other leasing business, an estimate will have to be made of the implicit rate for such leasing activity.

7.7 Sub-leases and back-to-back leases

7.7.1 Introduction

Situations arise where there are more parties to a lease arrangement than simply one lessor and one lessee. The discussion below relates to situations involving an original lessor, an intermediate party and an ultimate lessee. The intermediate party may be acting either as both a lessee and lessor of the asset concerned or, alternatively, as an agent of the lessor in the transaction.

Both sub-leases and back-to-back leases involve the intermediate party acting as both lessor and lessee of the asset. The difference between the two arrangements is that, for a back-to-back lease, the terms of the two lease agreements match to a greater extent than would be the case for a sub-lease arrangement. This difference is really only one of degree, and the important decision to be made concerns whether the arrangement is one of agency or, rather, the intermediate party is acting as both lessee and lessor in two related but independent transactions.

7.7.2 The original lessor and the ultimate lessee

The accounting treatment adopted by these parties will not be affected by the existence of sub-leases or back-to-back leases. The original lessor has an agreement with the intermediate party which is not affected by any further leasing of the assets by the intermediate party unless the original lease agreement is thereby replaced.

Similarly, the ultimate lessee has a lease agreement with the intermediate party. He will have use of the asset under that agreement and must make a decision, in the usual way, as to whether the lease is of a finance or operating type per SSAP 21.

7.7.3   *The intermediate party*

The appropriate accounting treatment by the intermediate party depends on the substance of the series of transactions. This turns on whether the intermediate party is acting either as an agent/broker for the original lessor or as a principal in both transactions. In the latter case, the intermediate party will act as lessee to the original lessor and lessor to the ultimate lessee.

In determining the role of the intermediate party, the question of recourse is important. If the ultimate lessee defaults on his lease obligations (for whatever reason), does the original lessor have recourse against the intermediate party for the outstanding payments under the lease?

Another important factor in the decision of how the intermediate party should account for the transaction is what happens if the original lessor defaults, e.g. through his insolvency. If the intermediate party is merely a broker/agent, then he will suffer no loss upon such default, and the ultimate lessee would only have a claim against the original lessor.

If these factors indicate that the intermediate party is acting merely as a broker or agent for the original lessor, he should not include any asset or obligation relating to the leased asset in his balance sheet. The income received by such an intermediary should be taken to profit and loss account on a systematic and rational basis.[97]

If, on the other hand, the intermediate party is taken to be acting as both lessee and lessor in two independent although related transactions, he should recognise his assets and obligations under finance leases in the normal way.

The recognition of income as lessor will be affected by the lease from the original lessor. Clearly, if the intermediate party had purchased the asset concerned outright, then his income recognition as a lessor would be on the usual net cash investment basis explained in 5.3 above. However, as he has obtained use of the asset under a finance lease, his income recognition will be based on the net investment in the lease. This is because the intermediate party's investment in the leased asset will be shown as the present value of the minimum lease payments, as reduced throughout the lease by the capital portion of total rental payable to the original lessor. In other words, there are no major tax consequences of the lease from the original lessor. The net investment approach to income recognition used for hire purchase contracts will therefore be appropriate (see 5.5 above).

It should not be inferred from the above discussion that all situations encountered can be relatively easily allocated as one of either a broker/agent or lessee/lessor in nature. In practice this is unlikely to be the case, as the risks and rewards will probably be spread between the parties involved. This is especially likely where more than the three parties discussed above are involved. In all cases, it is a question of judgement as to whether substantially all the risks and rewards from an asset attach to any party under the leases.

B.S.G. International is an example of a company where part of its business involves back-to-back leases. As can be seen from the following extract, the company takes the net income arising on these leases to the profit and loss account on a straight-line basis. It is noteworthy that the outgoing rentals are not included in the future lease obligations note and only referred to as a future commitment in the contingent liabilities note, with the comment that they are secured by charges over the sub-rental agreements and exceeded by anticipated future income from customers.

Extract 17.14: B.S.G. International plc (1996)

Accounting Policies [extract]

Contract hire and leasing business

For the major part of its contract hire and leasing activity, the Group's leasing subsidiary undertakings enter into operating lease agreements with finance houses in respect of vehicles which are then sub-leased to customers. Other vehicles leased to customers are owned by the Group and recognised as fixed assets in the balance sheet. Depreciation on these vehicles is calculated by deducting the estimated residual value from original cost and allocating the resulting amount over the term of the lease.

Income from vehicle leasing and contract hire agreements is credited to the profit and loss account so as to allocate profits equally over the period of the lease.

Notes to the Financial Statements

23. Contingent liabilities and financial commitments [extract]

The Group has a financial commitment to pay future rentals to finance companies in connection with leasing agreements on vehicles which are sub-leased to customers and has guaranteed a minimum residual value on these vehicles. The sums payable to finance companies are secured by charges over the related sub-lease agreements and the anticipated future income from customers is in excess of the future rentals payable by the Group. The estimated realisable value of the vehicles exceeds the amounts guaranteed.

An illustration of the difficulties associated with transactions involving sub-leases can be found in the 1993 accounts of British Aerospace (BAe), which revealed for the first time the full extent of the seemingly significant financial risks that the group had been taking in order to sustain its civil aircraft manufacturing operations, including those associated with its participation in Airbus Industrie.

It has now become apparent that the bulk of BAe's commercial aircraft sales made in the 1980s were to banks and not airlines. It is understood that the banks then leased the aircraft back to BAe under 15 to 20 year agreements, and BAe leased the aircraft to airlines under sub-leases of between three and five years. The result was that the group was exposing itself to the risk of substantial losses if those sub-leases were not renewed. However, with the backdrop of a highly buoyant market in second-hand aircraft in the 1980s, this risk was presumably considered to be low, and deals of this nature were apparently common practice amongst commercial aircraft manufacturers. Furthermore, even when BAe did sell aircraft directly to airlines, the group often provided guarantees on leases which the airlines themselves entered into with banks.

Consequently, when the recession hit the travel industry following the Gulf War, the demand for second-hand commercial aircraft collapsed and the risks became a reality. The result was that BAe was faced with significant exposure to third party guarantees and other recourse obligations. Although the group's position has apparently improved since then, BAe's 1996 accounts still reveal significant financing commitments and contingent liabilities:

Extract 17.15: British Aerospace Public Limited Company (1996)

Notes to the Accounts

1 Accounting policies [extract]

Aircraft financing

The Group is exposed to actual and contingent liabilities arising from commercial aircraft financing, both from financing arranged directly by the Group and from that arranged by third parties where the Group has provided guarantees or has other recourse obligations. Provision for these risks is made on a systematic basis at the time of sale, having regard to the ability to re-lease or re-sell the underlying aircraft.

20 Commercial aircraft financing

Commercial aircraft are frequently sold for cash with the manufacturer retaining some financial exposure either by guaranteeing a minimum residual value of the aircraft at some date in the future or through the arrangement of lease finance on extended terms, which may include guarantees back to the manufacturer in the event of default by the lessee (the operator).

The following paragraphs summarise the actual and contingent liabilities of the Group in relation to Regional Jets, Turboprops and Airbus aircraft which arise from 1996 and prior year sales involving the types of financing arrangements described above.

Regional Jets and Turboprop aircraft

Aircraft financing commitments

Aircraft finance arranged by the Group may involve selling the aircraft to a third party lessor and leasing it back under an operating lease, the head lease. The aircraft are then leased under a sub-lease to an operator (the lessee) and it is not uncommon for an aircraft to be leased to several lessees during the period of the head lease. The commitment of the Group in respect of these head lease rental payments, which relate to sales in prior years, is set out below:

	1996 £m	1995 £m
Head lease commitments on operating leases		
At 1st January	**1,373**	1,543
New commitments entered into	**–**	10
Commitments paid off	**(147)**	(171)
Foreign exchange and interest movements	**–**	(9)
Reclassified aircraft	**(36)**	–
At 31st December	**1,190**	1,373
Payments due under head leases		
In one year or less	**143**	143
Between one and five years	**521**	517
In later years	**526**	713
	1,190	1,373

Aircraft contingent liabilities

Aircraft finance arranged by the Group may also involve selling the aircraft to third parties who lease the aircraft to operators; again this may be to several operators during the life of the aircraft. The risks and benefits associated with the operator lease payments and the residual values of the aircraft rest with the third parties. However, the Group may give guarantees in respect of certain head lease and finance payments to be made by those third parties. Sales are also made directly to operators and this may involve the Group guaranteeing certain head lease and finance payments on behalf of those operators.

In the event of the guarantees to third parties or operators described above being called, the Group's exposure would be offset by future sub-lease rentals and the residual values of the related aircraft.

Provision for financing commitments and contingent liabilities

The following table sets out the Group's exposure to the above head lease financing commitments and contingent liabilities. Provision for these risks has been made in the accounts on a net present value basis.

	1996 £m	1995 £m
Head lease commitments, as above	**1,190**	1,373
Finance leases on balance sheet	**20**	86
Aircraft contingent liabilities	**1,726**	1,766
	2,936	3,225
Contracted sub-lease income	**(1,051)**	(1,091)
Obligations less contracted income	**1,885**	2,134
Expected sub-lease income and residual aircraft values	**(1,203)**	(1,376)
Net risk	**682**	758
Adjustment to reduce to net present value	**(163)**	(173)
Recourse provision (note 19)	**519**	585

Head lease commitments (£1,190 million) arise from sale and operating leaseback transactions, which were entered into in prior years, and continue to reduce as existing obligations are paid off. As described above, these represent the amounts payable by the Group under head leases in future years.

Finance leases on balance sheet (£20 million) are the liability the Group has for aircraft held under finance leases. The decrease from 1995 arises from the restructuring of certain aircraft leases.

Aircraft contingent liabilities (£1,726 million) represent the exposure arising from transactions where the head lease obligations and finance payments of third parties have been guaranteed by the Group.

Contracted sub-lease income (£1,051 million) represents the outturn value of contracted lease income and takes into account the income due on these contracts to the first contractual right of an operator to return an aircraft. In many instances customers do not exercise such rights and will continue to lease aircraft to the full contractual term. Where anticipated, this additional income has been classified within expected sub-lease income.

Expected sub-lease income and residual aircraft values (£1,203 million) represent the amounts anticipated from extensions to existing contracted sub-leases and assumed future aircraft sub-leases on aircraft where the Group has a recourse exposure, and the anticipated market values of aircraft at the expiry of their head lease term based upon independent professional advice. The level of expected income has been calculated on a systematic basis, taking into account current and expected future market conditions, remarketing and other costs.

Given the long term nature of the liabilities, the Directors believe it is appropriate to state the recourse provision at its net present value. The *adjustment to reduce to net present value (£163 million)* reduces the expected liabilities described above from their outturn amounts to their anticipated net present value.

Residual value guarantees

In addition to the above, in some cases aircraft have been sold for cash with the transaction supported by a residual value guarantee. The majority of sales in 1996 were for cash with residual values guarantees given by the Group for values at specific dates in the future. At 31st December, 1996 the Group had given residual value guarantees for 52 aircraft totalling some £360 million (1995 20 aircraft, £160 million).

Based upon independent professional advice, the Directors believe that the Group's exposure to these guarantees is covered by the residual values of the related aircraft.

Airbus

The Group is involved in similar transactions through its participation in Airbus Industrie. Provision for the net exposure is included in the accounts of Airbus Industrie and included within the Group's share of the results of Airbus Industrie.

Although not yet part of UK GAAP, it is noteworthy that the measurement of the recourse provision at its net present value reflects the current thinking of both the ASB and IASC that the amount of a provision should be the present value of the expenditures required to settle the obligation.

8 COMPARISON WITH US AND IASC PRONOUNCEMENTS

8.1 US

In most situations there are not major differences between accounting for leases in the UK and the US. This is because SSAP 21 is based on the same principles as SFAS 13 – *Accounting for Leases* – which became effective for leases entered into on or after 1 January 1977.[98] There are, however, some differences in detail between the two standards.

As regards lease classification, SFAS 13 gives four classification criteria. If any of these criteria are met, then the lease is a capital lease (which is equivalent to a finance lease in the UK). A 90% test, similar to that in SSAP 21, forms one of these four criteria, which means that the 90% test is more accurately described and legalistically applied as a rule in the US. This is because if the 90% test indicates a capital lease under SFAS 13, then no other factors can change this classification. As has been discussed in this Chapter, the 90% test in SSAP 21 gives a rebuttable assumption of a particular lease classification (as finance or operating). The other three criteria are:

(a) the lease transfers ownership of the asset to the lessee at the end of the lease;

(b) the lease contains a bargain purchase option (i.e. a provision allowing the lessee, at his option, to purchase the asset at a price sufficiently lower than the fair value at the exercise date, such that it is reasonably assured that he will exercise the option); and

(c) the lease term is equal to 75% or more of the estimated remaining economic life of the asset. However, if the lease term begins within the last 25% of the total economic life of the asset, then this criterion should not be used for the purpose of classifying the lease.

Under US GAAP the position with regard to accounting for operating leases with rent-free periods and/or escalating rentals is clearly set out in two FASB Technical Bulletins.[99] Essentially, the effects of rental holidays and scheduled rent increases should be recognised on a straight-line basis over the lease term. The only exception to this rule is where scheduled rent increases are designed to accommodate the lessee's projected physical use of the property being leased. In this situation, Technical Bulletin No. 88-1 makes a distinction between agreements that give the lessee the right to control the use of the leased property at the beginning of the lease term and those that do not. Escalated rents under agreements that give the lessee the right to control the use of the entire leased property at the beginning of the lease term should be included in the minimum lease payments and recognised on a straight-line basis over the lease term. However, where the agreement provides that the lessee gains control over additional leased property during the course of the agreement, rental expense should be recognised on the basis of the relative fair value of the additional property leased and the period during which the lessee has the right to control the use of the additional property.[100]

Other requirements of SFAS 13 which are different from those of SSAP 21 include the following:

(a)   lessees with operating leases should disclose future minimum rental payments payable over each of the next five years and in aggregate thereafter;

(b)   specific rules are given for the classification of leases involving real estate although once this is done, accounting and disclosure are the same as for other leases;

(c)   lessor accounting for leveraged leases is based on additional specific rules, although the basic concept is the same as for other leases. Essentially, a leveraged lease is one that involves the lessor funding a large element of the purchase of the asset by non-recourse debt under a long-term credit arrangement; and

(d)   the net investment method is used by lessors to allocate gross earnings to accounting periods. SSAP 21 uses this only for hire purchase contracts, with the net cash investment method being used for finance leases.

8.2   IASC

IAS 17 was issued in September 1982 for accounting periods beginning on or after 1 January 1984.[101] Its basic requirements are similar to those of SSAP 21. A finance lease is defined as one that 'transfers substantially all the risks and rewards incident to ownership of an asset'.[102] Examples of situations where a lease would normally be classified as a finance lease are given, one of which is a 'present value test' which makes no reference to a specific percentage, such as the 90% mentioned in SSAP 21.

IAS 17 allows lessors accounting for finance leases to recognise finance income to reflect a constant periodic rate of return on either the net investment or net cash investment in the lease. The definitions of these terms are essentially the same as those in SSAP 21.

In January 1989 the IASC issued an exposure draft, E32 – *Comparability of Financial Statements* – which proposed to amend, inter alia, the requirements of IAS 17. The main changes proposed were as follows:

(a)   for finance leases other than leveraged leases, lessors were to recognise finance income to reflect a constant periodic rate of return on the net investment in the lease; the present option of using the net cash investment in the lease (which is that required by SSAP 21) would no longer be available;[103] and

(b) leveraged leases were to be distinguished from other finance leases, and lessors were to recognise finance income on leveraged leases to reflect a constant periodic rate of return on the net cash investment in the lease during periods in which the net cash investment is positive.[104]

However, in July 1990 the IASC published a Statement of Intent[105] which set out its decisions following its review of the comments received on E32. One of the issues on which the IASC deferred consideration pending further work related to IAS 17. At the time, the IASC stated that it 'believes that further study is required on the recognition of finance income on those leases on which the lessor's net investment outstandings is materially affected by income tax factors. It plans to develop an internationally acceptable definition of such a lease and delete the use of the term "leveraged lease".'[106]

The IASC eventually gave the subject its attention in 1997, when it published Exposure Draft E56 entitled *Leases*. E56 proposes a very limited review of IAS 17, focusing only on those issues that the International Organization of Securities Commissions (IOSCO) considers essential for the purpose of fulfilling the IASC/IOSCO plan to complete a comprehensive set of core accounting standards that will be acceptable to all major stock exchanges for cross-border listings.

The key proposals of E56 are as follows:

■ enhanced disclosures by lessees, such as disclosure of rental expenses, sub-lease rentals and a description of general leasing arrangements;[107]

■ enhanced disclosures by lessors, such as disclosure about future minimum rentals and amounts of contingent rentals included in income; and[108]

■ eliminating the current free choice of methods to recognise finance lease income by requiring the net investment method to be applied in all circumstances.[109]

The proposed disclosures are substantially similar to those required under US GAAP. Moreover, because leases are financial instruments, the relevant IAS 32 disclosures have been incorporated in E56, although these are not in the US lease disclosure standards.

Whilst the proposed enhanced disclosures are relatively uncontroversial, it is less than clear why it is that the IASC is proposing that the net cash investment method of recognising finance lease income should be eliminated. It is understood that IOSCO had asked the IASC to clarify the position as to when each of the two methods was appropriate – however this does not necessarily mean the elimination of one of the methods. What is clear is that in certain circumstances the net investment method is not appropriate (for example, when there are significant tax cash flows which affect the lessor) and that it does not make sense to require the net investment method to be applied in all circumstances. US GAAP requires the net investment method to be applied except in the case of leveraged leases as defined in SFAS 13, for which the net cash investment method is required. It would seem sensible for the IASC to adopt a similar approach.

However, whatever the outcome of E56, the IASC has announced that, after the completion of its current work programme, it will conduct a comprehensive review of lease accounting. This will include consideration of a fundamental reform – the capitalisation of all leases with a term of over one year (including leases currently classified as operating leases) along the lines proposed by the G4+1 as discussed at 1.6 above.

9   CONCLUSION

Although FRS 5 does not override SSAP 21, it does provide additional guidance on the factors to be considered in ensuring that leases are classified as finance or operating leases in accordance with their substance. This would seem to provide further evidence of the reduced significance of the 90% test in favour of an approach based on qualitative considerations.

However, this does not mean that the ASB's attention should be turned away from SSAP 21. The ICAEW's 1992 review of SSAP 21 highlighted a number of practical difficulties which were, and still are, being experienced with SSAP 21. Whilst FRS 5 has gone part of the way towards obviating some of these (such as sale and leasebacks involving options) a number of issues still remain to be resolved. Unfortunately, though, whilst we would strongly urge the ASB to give priority to the revision of SSAP 21, it is unlikely that its work programme will be able to accommodate such a project in the foreseeable future.

At the same time, though, it should be borne in mind that the ASB's on-going development of a *Statement of Principles* and its publication of FRS 5 have brought the UK one step closer to a fundamental change in the way that financial contracts are reflected in financial statements. It is only through specific exemptions contained in FRS 5 that transactions such as forward contracts, purchase commitments and, indeed, operating leases are not required to be recognised in the balance sheet. Consequently, it is quite feasible that the ASB is pursuing an altogether different agenda of removing the distinction between finance and operating leases through the introduction, via its *Statement of Principles*, of the requirement that certain financial contracts should be capitalised. It is also feasible that the ASB might see the G4+1 paper on lease accounting as providing it with a mandate to pursue such an agenda.

References

1 SSAP 21, *Accounting for leases and hire purchase contracts*, August 1984, para. 14.
2 *Ibid.*, para. 18.
3 Increased from £8,000 to £12,000 for contracts entered into after 10th March 1992.
4 ED 29, *Accounting for leases and hire purchase contracts*, October 1981.
5 Department of Trade, *Inspectors' Final Report on Court Line Limited*, p. 153.
6 *Ibid.*, Appendix J, p. 141.
7 *Ibid.*, p. 153.
8 ASC, *Guidance Notes on SSAP 21: Accounting for Leases and Hire Purchase Contracts*, August 1984.
9 SSAP 21, Introductory paragraph.
10 Exposure Draft, *Statement of Principles for Financial Reporting*, ASB, November 1995, para. 3.5.
11 *Ibid.*, para. 3.21.
12 Warren McGregor, *Accounting for leases: a new approach: Recognition by Lessees of Assets and Liabilities Arising under Lease Contracts*, FASB, 1996.
13 *Ibid.*, p. 3.
14 *Ibid.*
15 *Framework for the Preparation and Presentation of Financial Statements*, IASC, September 1989, paras. 49(a) and (b).
16 W McGregor, *op. cit.*, p. 16.
17 *Ibid.*, p. 17.
18 SSAP 21, para. 15.
19 *Ibid.*, para. 17.
20 *Ibid.*, paras. 15 and 16.
21 *Ibid.*, para. 25.
22 *Ibid.*, para. 24.
23 ICAEW, *Financial Reporting & Auditing Group, Technical Release FRAG 9/92*, March 1992, para. 33.
24 SSAP 21, para. 20.
25 *Ibid.*, para. 26.
26 *Ibid.*, para. 19.
27 ICAEW, Technical Release 664, *Implementation of SSAP 21 'Accounting for leases and hire purchase contracts'*, July 1987, paras. 4 and 5.
28 ICAEW, FRAG 9/92, para. 35.
29 *Ibid.*
30 *Ibid.*, para. 36.
31 FRS 5, *Reporting the Substance of Transactions*, ASB, 1994, para. 13.
32 *Ibid.*, para. 45.
33 SSAP 21, para. 35.
34 Guidance Notes on SSAP 21, para. 20.
35 SSAP 21, para. 37.
36 FASB Technical Bulletin No. 85-3, *Accounting for Operating Leases with Scheduled Rent Increases*, FASB, November 14, 1985.
37 UITF 12, *Lessee accounting for reverse premiums and similar incentives*, ASB, 5 December 1994.
38 *Ibid.*, para. 8.
39 *Ibid.*, para. 9.
40 *Ibid.*, para. 6.
41 SSAP 21, para. 57.
42 *Ibid.*, para. 55.
43 *Ibid.*, para. 53.
44 *Ibid.*, para. 50.
45 *Ibid.*
46 *Ibid.*, paras. 51 and 52.
47 *Ibid.*, para. 56.
48 *Ibid.*, para. 54.

49 CA 85, Sch. 4, para. 8.
50 *Ibid.*, para. 50(5).
51 *Ibid.*, paras. 42 to 44.
52 *Ibid.*, para. 48.
53 MEPC plc, 1996 Report and Financial Statements, Note 28, p. 40.
54 SSAP 21, para. 54.
55 *Ibid.*, para. 43.
56 *Ibid.*, para. 28.
57 *Ibid.*, para. 39.
58 *Ibid.*, para. 23.
59 *Ibid.*, para. 41.
60 Guidance Notes on SSAP 21, para. 92.
61 *Ibid.*, para. 121. See *Guidance Notes on ED 29: Accounting for Leases and Hire Purchase Contracts*, ASC, October 1981, paras. 81–86 for an illustration of the difference that can arise in such circumstances.
62 IAS 17, *Accounting for Leases*, IASC, September 1982, paras. 30 - 38.
63 IASC E56, *Leases*, IASC, April 1997, paras. 28 – 31.
64 SSAP 21, para. 39.
65 Guidance Notes on SSAP 21, para. 116.
66 SSAP 21, para. 60.
67 *Ibid.*
68 *Ibid.*, para. 61.
69 *Ibid.*, para. 58.
70 *Ibid.*, para. 61.
71 *Ibid.*, para. 59.
72 Guidance Notes on SSAP 21, para. 124.
73 CA 85, Sch. 4, para. 8.
74 *Ibid.*, paras. 42–44.
75 Guidance Notes on SSAP 21, para. 38.
76 SSAP 21, para. 34.
77 *Ibid.*, para. 48.
78 ICAEW, FRAG 9/92, para. 15.
79 *Ibid.*
80 *Ibid.*, para. 44.
81 SSAP 21, para. 46.
82 FRS 5, Application Note B, para. B20.
83 *Ibid.*, Application Note B, para. B6.
84 *Ibid.*, Application Note B, para. B11.
85 SSAP 21, para. 47.
86 Adapted from para. 122 of Guidance Notes on ED 29.
87 ICAEW, FRAG 9/92, para. 16.
88 *Ibid.*, para. 46.
89 SSAP 21, para. 30.
90 Guidance Notes on SSAP 21, para. 82.
91 ICAEW, FRAG 9/92, para. 47.
92 Guidance Notes on SSAP 21, para. 82.
93 ICAEW, FRAG 9/92, para. 48.
94 *Ibid.*, para. 49.
95 *Ibid.*, para. 58.
96 SSAP 21, para. 45.
97 Guidance Notes on SSAP 21, para. 165.
98 SFAS 13, *Accounting for Leases*, FASB, November 1976. See the detailed US requirements relating to leases in FASB, *Accounting Standards as of June 1, 1996, Current Text, Volume I, General Standards*, FASB, 1996, Section L10, pp. 29141–29259.
99 FASB Technical Bulletin No. 85-3, *Accounting for Operating Leases with Scheduled Rent Increases*, FASB, November 14, 1985; FASB Technical Bulletin No. 88-1, *Issues Relating to Accounting for Leases: Time Pattern of the Physical Use of the Property in an Operating Lease, Lease Incentives in*

an Operating Lease, Applicability of Leveraged Lease Accounting to Existing Assets of the Lessor, Money-Over-Money Lease Transactions, Wrap Lease Transactions, FASB, December 28, 1988.

100 FASB Technical Bulletin No. 88-1, para. 5.
101 IAS 17, *Accounting for Leases*, IASC, September 1982 (reformatted 1994).
102 *Ibid.*, para. 3.
103 E32, *Comparability of Financial Statements*, IASC, January 1989, para. 76.
104 *Ibid.*, para. 81.
105 Statement of Intent, *Comparability of Financial Statements*, IASC, July 1990.
106 *Ibid.*, Appendix 3.
107 IASC Exposure Draft E56, *Leases*, IASC, April 1997, paras. 21, 25 and 55.
108 *Ibid.*, paras. 37, 47 and 55.
109 *Ibid.*, paras., 28 – 31.

Chapter 18   Government grants

1   INTRODUCTION

Government grants are defined in SSAP 4, the relevant accounting standard on the subject, as 'assistance by government in the form of cash or transfers of assets to an enterprise in return for past or future compliance with certain conditions relating to the operating activities of the enterprise'.[1] Such assistance has been available to commercial enterprises for many years, although its form and extent have undergone various changes according to the shifting economic philosophies of the government of the day.

The accounting issue which arises is how to deal with the income which the grant represents. Before the original accounting standard on the subject was developed, the treatment adopted by different companies was diverse. At that time, the grants which were available were generally of a capital nature, intended to subsidise the purchase of fixed assets. Some companies adopted the policy of crediting the grant directly to income when received; some spread it over the life of the assets involved; some took it directly to reserves as a capital receipt so that it never featured in the profit and loss account at all. SSAP 4 – *The accounting treatment of government grants* – issued in 1974, elected for the second of these three options, adopting a matching approach as its guiding principle. This matching approach is still evident in the present version of SSAP 4, which was issued in July 1990, but the current standard offers more guidance on how to apply the principle to the many different kinds of government assistance which now exist.

2   THE DEVELOPMENT OF SSAP 4

2.1   The original SSAP 4

The original version of the standard was preceded by ED 9 – *The Accounting Treatment of Grants under the Industry Act 1972* – which was published in March 1973. As the title of the exposure draft suggests, it was introduced to deal with a very specific matter – the treatment of the Regional Development Grants introduced by that Act to provide a subsidy for capital expenditure.

SSAP 4 itself was issued in April 1974 and, although it had a less specific title, it was still relatively narrow in its scope. It extended to a mere ten paragraphs, eight of which comprised the explanatory note, and of the remaining two which stated the standard accounting practice to be adopted, the second merely gave the date from which the standard was to be applied. It concentrated solely on capital grants, stating that revenue grants 'do not produce accounting problems as they clearly should be credited to revenue in the same period in which the revenue expenditure to which they relate is charged'.[2]

2.2   ED 43

The general principle underlying SSAP 4, of matching the grant with the expenditure to which it relates, has never been seriously in question since the original standard was issued. However, it became increasingly evident over the years that the standard did not give adequate guidance on how to account for the widely varying forms of government assistance which later became available. Furthermore, the terms on which certain grants were by then being made did not precisely identify the expenditure to which they related; as a result, accountants were often faced with the problem of how to ascribe grants to specific expenditure. In addition, the ASC noted that various requirements of IAS 20 – *Accounting for Government Grants and Disclosure of Government Assistance* – which was issued in 1983 were not reflected in the UK standard, and that this should therefore be considered in a revision of it.

Consequently, the ASC issued a proposed revision to the standard, ED 43, in June 1988. A significant difference between the exposure draft and the original standard was the depth in which the subject was discussed; it followed the same basic approach, but ran to 45 paragraphs rather than SSAP 4's 10, and also had an Appendix illustrating the application of the rules to the particular forms of assistance available.

2.3   SSAP 4 (Revised)

The revised version of SSAP 4 was issued in July 1990 and closely followed the proposals in ED 43, although the Appendix showing how to apply the standard to current forms of assistance was dropped. The new standard became effective for accounting periods beginning on or after 1 July 1990. Subsequent references to SSAP 4 in this Chapter are to the revised version unless the original is specified.

3 THE REQUIREMENTS OF SSAP 4

3.1 Accounting

3.1.1 Treatment of capital grants

The single rule set out in the original version of SSAP 4 was that grants which related to fixed assets were to be credited to revenue over the expected useful life of the asset concerned.[3] This was to be accomplished either:

(a) by setting the grant directly against the cost of the asset in the balance sheet, so that depreciation was charged on the net figure; or

(b) by carrying the grant in the balance sheet as a deferred credit, and releasing it to income over the life of the related asset to offset the depreciation charge.[4]

ED 43 followed the same matching principle as SSAP 4, namely that grants of all kinds (both capital and revenue) should be recognised in income at the same time as the expenditure which they subsidise.[5] In respect of grants towards fixed assets, however, the exposure draft sought to eliminate option (a) above, requiring instead that the deferred credit approach be adopted. It advanced three reasons for this proposed change:

■ the netting approach might be in conflict with the Companies Act rules that fixed assets should be carried at their purchase price or production cost,[6] or that amounts representing assets should not be set off against amounts representing liabilities;[7]

■ the deferred credit approach allows the amount of grant credited to income to be disclosed (which was proposed as a new disclosure requirement in the exposure draft), whereas the netting approach loses this amount within the depreciation charge;

■ if grants become repayable, and the netting approach has been adopted, then there may need to be retrospective adjustments to the cost and depreciation of the asset concerned, which may be confusing to the user of the financial statements.

However, a large number of commentators questioned the need for this change, stressing that the netting approach was a convenient practical method, and expressing doubt that a conflict with company law necessarily existed.

The revised version of the standard left the option to use either form of balance sheet presentation, since the ASC considered that both treatments were acceptable and capable of giving a true and fair view. However the Committee went on to say that it had obtained Counsel's opinion that the 'netting' approach would be illegal for enterprises governed by Schedule 4 to the Companies Act 1985, since grant-aided assets would as a result not be stated at their purchase price or production cost.[8] The Companies Act requirement comes from the EC Fourth Directive, but it is interesting to note that it is not interpreted in this way in other countries governed by the Directive. In Germany, for example, it is normal to net capital grants off against the cost of fixed assets and this is not seen as a legal problem.

Under SSAP 4, therefore, enterprises not governed by Schedule 4 remain free to use either treatment, but the remainder should adopt the 'deferred credit' approach if they wish to avoid the risk of contravening the law. The great majority of companies now use the latter form of presentation.

Under the netting method, depreciation on fixed assets is charged net of government grants, thereby releasing the grant to income over the lives of the related assets in the form of a reduced depreciation charge. As discussed in 4.2 below, this form of presentation is also popular among companies which receive grants on assets that are not subject to depreciation.

The current version of SSAP 4 contains a number of other requirements on accounting for grants which had no equivalent in the original standard. These are set out below.

3.1.2   *Treatment of revenue-based grants*

The general rule, that grants should be recognised in the profit and loss account so as to match them with the expenditure towards which they are intended to contribute, applies equally to revenue-based grants as it does to capital grants. In some situations, the revenue costs towards which a grant is given may already have been incurred, in which case the grant would be included in the profit and loss account as soon as it is capable of being recognised under the rules discussed in 3.1.3 below. However, where a grant has been received, but not all of the revenue costs have been incurred, it will be necessary to defer a proportion of the grant so as to match it with those costs. The Weir Group is an example of a company whose accounting policy makes specific reference to revenue grants:

Extract 18.1: The Weir Group PLC (1996)

Accounting Policies [extract]

(d)   Government Grants

Grants related to expenditure on tangible assets are credited to profit at the same rate as the depreciation on the assets to which the grants relate. The amounts shown in the balance sheet in respect of grants consist of the total grants receivable to date, less the amounts so far credited to profit. Grants of a revenue nature are credited to income in the period to which they relate.

One of the difficulties which face companies is that grants are sometimes given to provide assistance for projects which involve both revenue and capital costs; the question then arises as to which costs the grant should be matched against. This is considered further in 4.1 below.

3.1.3 Accounting for receipt and repayment of grants

SSAP 4 requires that grants should not be recognised in the profit and loss account until the conditions for their receipt have been complied with and there is reasonable assurance that the grant will be received.[9] This rule sets the earliest limit for the recognition of the grant, but does not address the question of how it is to be matched against related expenditure; this is discussed at 3.1.4 below.

Grants are frequently received on terms which could result in their repayment if certain conditions are not met throughout a subsequent qualifying period. The revised version of the standard says that provision should be made for such repayment only to the extent that it is probable.[10] Again, the existence of these conditions does not directly enter into the question of when the grants should be recognised in income.

Where a grant does become repayable, the standard requires that the repayment should be accounted for by setting it off against any unamortised deferred credit relating to the grant, with any excess being charged to the profit and loss account.[11] This has the effect of minimising the impact on the profit and loss account; it means that any part of the grant which has not been retained will have been matched against depreciation of the earlier years of the asset's life (if a capital grant). An alternative approach would have been to recompute the release of grant to income as if the amount repaid had never been received, with the result that the reduced amount of the grant (if any) would be spread over the whole life of the asset involved, rather than allocated to the earlier years.

A literal interpretation of the above requirement could mean that, where the company uses the 'netting' method of presentation in the balance sheet (method (a) at 3.1.1 above), the whole amount of the repayment would have to be charged immediately to the profit and loss account because there is no deferred credit to absorb it. However, it is difficult to see the logic of this and we do not believe that such an interpretation was intended. We believe that the balance sheet treatment chosen should not influence the effect of a repayment on the profit and loss account, and that the reference to 'unamortised deferred credit' was intended to include the amount set off against the book value of the asset when the 'netting' approach is used.

3.1.4 Matching grants against related expenditure

In practice, this is the most significant accounting issue which arises in respect of government grants. The required approach is summarised by SSAP 4 as follows:

(a) provided the conditions for its receipt have been complied with and there is reasonable assurance that it will be received, a grant should be recognised in the profit and loss account so as to match it with the expenditure to which it is to contribute;

(b)   the grant should be assumed to contribute to whatever expenditure is the basis for its receipt, unless there is persuasive evidence to the contrary;

(c)   where the grant is a contribution to specific expenditure on fixed assets, it should be recognised over the expected useful economic lives of the related assets;

(d)   if the grant is made in order to give immediate financial support or assistance or to reimburse costs previously incurred, it should be recognised in the profit and loss account of the period in which it becomes receivable; and

(e)   if the grant is made to finance the general activities of an enterprise over a specific period or to compensate for a loss of current or future income it should be recognised in the profit and loss account of the period in which it is paid.[12]

The application of these rules still requires a significant amount of interpretation, and this is discussed in 4.1 below.

3.2   Disclosure

The original version of SSAP 4 contained only one explicit disclosure requirement: the amount of any deferred credit in respect of grants was to be shown separately if it was material, and was not to be included in shareholders' funds.[13] In terms of the Companies Act formats, this amount will normally be shown under the heading of 'Accruals and deferred income' in one of two optional positions in the balance sheet.[14]

ICI's accounts provide an example of this disclosure:

Extract 18.2: Imperial Chemical Industries PLC (1996)

BALANCE SHEETS

at 31 December 1996 [extract]

	Group		Company	
	1996	1995	**1996**	1995
	£m	£m	**£m**	£m
Creditors due after more than one year				
Loans	**1,174**	1,332	**200**	200
Other creditors	**72**	72	**688**	1,042
	1,246	1,404	**888**	1,242
Provisions for liabilities and charges	**757**	823	**56**	71
Deferred income: Grants not yet credited to profit	**20**	27	–	1

The revised version of the standard has not retained the original disclosure requirement in such specific terms. However, it requires that the effects of government grants on the financial position of the enterprise should be shown.[15]

The explanatory note to the standard makes it clear that this is to be done where the results of future periods are expected to be affected materially by the recognition in the profit and loss account of grants already received.[16] It would appear that the most straightforward way of doing this would simply be to disclose the amount of the deferred credit which is still to be released to income, so it may be taken that the previous disclosure requirement is unchanged despite the different manner in which it is expressed.

This extract from the accounts of J. Bibby & Sons shows the movement on the deferred credit and also explicitly discloses the amount to be released in the following period, which takes the requirement a stage further:

Extract 18.3: J. Bibby & Sons PLC (1996)

	£000's
14. Investment grants: consolidated	
Balance at 30th September 1995	1,033
Exchange fluctuation	(38)
Released to profit	(221)
Balance at 28th September 1996	**774**
of which to be released in 1997	221

Leeds Group has an even more elaborate disclosure, which is in effect a mirror image of its fixed assets note. It shows the following:

Extract 18.4: Leeds Group plc (1996)

21. Accruals and deferred income

Government Grants

	Group		
	Land and Buildings £000	Plant and machinery £000	Total £000
Received:			
At 1st October 1995	1,037	530	1,567
During the year	13	–	13
At 30th September 1996	1,050	530	1,580
Amortisation:			
At 1st October 1995	423	494	917
Credited for year	73	–	73
At 30th September 1996	496	494	990
Net amount:			
At 30th September 1995	554	36	590
At 30th September 1996	614	36	650

However, Bibby and Leeds Group are very much the exceptions; few companies give such detailed analysis of the deferred credit.

The revised SSAP 4 introduced these additional disclosure requirements:

(a)   the accounting policy adopted for government grants[17] (this is in any case required in general terms by SSAP 2);

An example is shown in Extract 18.1 above.

(b)   the effect of government grants on the results of the period;[18]

Such a disclosure can be found in the accounts of Adwest Group.

Extract 18.5: Adwest Group p.l.c. (1996)

4 Operating Profit [extract]

	1996 £000	1995 £000
Operating profit is after crediting:		
Rents receivable	**2,437**	2,336
Pension credit	**876**	1,015
Industrial development government grant	**80**	185

(c)   any potential liability to repay grants in specified circumstances which needs to be disclosed, if necessary, in accordance with paragraph 16 of SSAP 18[19] (which means that no disclosure is necessary if the possibility is remote, although consideration would have to be given to the requirements of the Companies Act).[20] Once again, this disclosure is clearly already required in terms of SSAP 18 (and the Companies Act);

(d) where the results of the period are affected materially by the receipt of government assistance in a form other than grants, the nature of that assistance and an estimate of its effects on the financial statements, to the extent that these effects can be measured.[21]

In the explanatory note section of the standard, a further disclosure requirement is suggested. This is that the period or periods over which grants are released to the profit and loss account should be disclosed, insofar as it is practicable given the number and variety of grants that are being received; it is suggested that normally a broad indication of the future periods in which grants already received will be recognised in the profit and loss account will be sufficient.[22] However, this apparent requirement does not appear in the standard section of SSAP 4, so its status is unclear, and it is virtually never seen in practice. It would seem likely that most companies will regard the disclosure of fixed asset lives which they will be giving as part of their depreciation policy note as a sufficient provision of this information, assuming that the grant relates to capital expenditure. However, there may be exceptional cases where a more explicit disclosure would be helpful to an understanding of the accounts.

4 PROBLEM AREAS

4.1 Achieving the most appropriate matching

Most problems of accounting for grants fall into a single category: that of interpreting the requirement to match the grant against the expenditure towards which they are expected to contribute. This apparently simple principle can be extremely difficult to apply, because it is sometimes far from clear what the essence of the grant was, and in practice grants are sometimes given for a particular kind of expenditure which forms an element of a larger project, making the allocation a highly subjective matter. For example, government assistance which is in the form of a training grant might be:

(a) matched against direct training costs; or

(b) taken over a period of time against the salary costs of the employees being trained, for example over the estimated duration of the project; or

(c) taken over the estimated period for which the company or the employees are expected to benefit from the training; or

(d) not distinguished from other project grants received and therefore matched against total project costs; or

(e)   taken to income systematically over the life of the project, for example the total grant receivable may be allocated to revenue on a straight-line basis; or

(f)   as in (d) or (e) above, but using, instead of project life, the period over which the grant is paid; or

(g)   taken to income when received in cash.

Depending on the circumstances, any of these approaches might produce an acceptable result. However, we would comment on them individually as follows:

Under method (a), the grant could be recognised as income considerably in advance of its receipt, since often the major part of the direct training costs will be incurred at the beginning of a project and payment is usually made retrospectively. As the total grant receivable may be subject to adjustment, this may not be prudent or may lead to mismatching.

Methods (b) to (e) all rely on different interpretations of the expenditure to which the grant is expected to contribute, and could all represent an appropriate form of matching.

Method (f) has less to commend it, but the period of payment of the grant might in fact give an indication (in the absence of better evidence) of the duration of the project for which the expenditure is to be subsidised.

Similarly, method (g) is unlikely to be the most appropriate method per se, but may approximate to one of the other methods, or may, in the absence of any conclusive indication as to the expenditure intended to be subsidised by the grant, be the only practicable method which can be adopted.

Many grants are taxed as income on receipt; consequently, this is often the argument advanced for taking grants to income when received in cash. However, SSAP 4 specifically states that 'the treatment of an item for tax purposes does not necessarily determine its treatment for accounting purposes, and immediate recognition in the profit and loss account may result in an unacceptable departure from the principle that government grants should be matched with the expenditure towards which they are intended to contribute'.[23] Consequently, the recognition of a grant in the profit and loss account in a period different to that when it is taxed gives rise to a timing difference, and should be accounted for in accordance with SSAP 15 – *Accounting for deferred tax*.

In the face of the problems (described above) of attributing a grant to related expenditure, it is difficult to offer definitive guidance; companies will have to make their own judgements as to how the matching principle is to be applied. The only overriding considerations are that the method should be systematically and consistently applied, and that the policy adopted (in respect of both capital and revenue grants, if material) should be adequately disclosed. However, it is possible to offer the following points for consideration:

4.1.1   Should the grant be split into its elements?

The grant received may be part of a package, the elements of which have different costs/conditions. It may be appropriate to treat these different elements on different bases rather than accounting for the entire grant in one way.

4.1.2   What was the purpose of the grant?

As discussed in 3.1.4 above, SSAP 4 says that in the absence of persuasive evidence to the contrary, government grants should be assumed to contribute towards the expenditure which is the basis for their payment.[24] However, the method by which the amount of grant receivable is calculated does not conclusively determine its accounting treatment. For example, the amount of the grant may be based on the creation of jobs but it may be intended to contribute towards capital expenditure or other costs as well. It will be necessary to examine the full circumstances of the grant in order to determine its purpose.

4.1.3   What is the period to be benefited by the grant?

The qualifying conditions which have to be satisfied are not necessarily conclusive evidence of the period to be benefited by the grant. For example, certain grants may become repayable if assets cease to be used for a qualifying purpose within a certain period; notwithstanding this condition, the grant should be recognised over the whole life of the asset, not over the qualifying period. The same may apply to the period during which new jobs have to be maintained (although the contrary suggestion is made in the explanatory note to SSAP 4).[25]

4.1.4   Is a grant capital or revenue?

In general, we recommend that grants should be regarded as linked to capital expenditure where this is a possible interpretation and there is no clear indication to the contrary, particularly where the payment of the grant is based on capital expenditure. However, we believe that the most important consideration where there are significant questions over how the grant is to be recognised, and where the effect is material, is that the accounts should explicitly state what treatment has been chosen and what is the financial effect of adopting that treatment.

4.2   Capital grants on non-depreciating assets

Grants are sometimes given as a contribution to assets which are not depreciated on the grounds that they do not have a finite life. In these circumstances, following the basic rule of SSAP 4, the release of the grant to the profit and loss account is also indefinitely postponed. The question which then arises is whether it makes sense to show the amount received as deferred income, given that it is likely to be there permanently.

Public utility companies, such as those in the water or electricity industries, frequently face this issue. They often receive contributions to the costs of their infrastructure assets, which are not regarded as depreciating assets because of their obligation to maintain them indefinitely; their usual response to the problem is to revert to the 'netting' approach, crediting the contributions against the cost of the asset concerned. An example of this approach is to be found in the accounts of Severn Trent:

Extract 18.6: Severn Trent Plc (1997)

Accounting policies [extract]

g) Grants and contributions

Grants and contributions received in respect of non infrastructure assets are treated as deferred income and are transferred to the profit and loss account in accordance with the asset lives of those assets.

Grants and contributions received relating to infrastructure assets have been deducted from the cost of fixed assets. This is not in accordance with Schedule 4 to the Act, which requires assets to be shown at their purchase price or production cost and hence grants and contributions to be presented as deferred income. This departure from the requirements of the Act is, in the opinion of the Directors, necessary to give a true and fair view as no provision is made for depreciation and any grants and contributions relating to such assets would not be taken to the profit and loss account. The effect of this departure is that the net book value of fixed assets is £134.4 million lower than it would otherwise have been (1996: £120.1 million).

The last three sentences of this note give the information required by UITF 7 when the 'true and fair override' is used to depart from the detailed requirements of the Companies Act.[26] However, many companies that use this approach do not agree that it is a departure from the Act, and thus do not make the disclosure.

5   COMPARISON WITH THE IASC PRONOUNCEMENT

IAS 20 – *Accounting for Government Grants and Disclosure of Government Assistance* – was issued in April 1983. It follows the same basic approach that is adopted in the UK, and also permits grants related to assets to be presented in the balance sheet either by setting up the grant as deferred income or by deducting the grant in arriving at the carrying amount of the asset. Inevitably, because of the international context in which it is written, it does not address specific questions which relate to particular types of grant that are available in individual countries.

References

1   SSAP 4, *Accounting for government grants*, ASC, Revised July 1990, para. 22.
2   SSAP 4 (Original), *The accounting treatment of government grants*, April 1974, para. 2.
3   *Ibid.*, para. 9.
4   *Ibid.*
5   ED 43, para. 27.
6   CA 85, Sch. 4, para. 17.
7   *Ibid.*, para. 5.
8   SSAP 4, para. 15.
9   *Ibid.*, para. 24.
10 *Ibid.*, para. 27.
11 *Ibid.*
12 *Ibid.*, para. 23.
13 SSAP 4 (Original), para. 9.
14 CA 85, Sch. 4, para. 8.
15 SSAP 4, para. 28(b).
16 *Ibid.*, para. 18.
17 *Ibid.*, para. 28(a).
18 *Ibid.*, para. 28(b).
19 *Ibid.*, para. 29.
20 CA 85, Sch. 4, para. 50(2).
21 SSAP 4, para. 28(c).
22 *Ibid.*, para. 17.
23 *Ibid.*, para. 7.
24 *Ibid.*, para. 23.
25 *Ibid.*, para. 9.
26 UITF 7, *True and fair view override disclosures*, UITF, December 1992, para. 4.

Chapter 19   Segmental reporting

1   INTRODUCTION

1.1   Historical background

Segmental reporting involves the reporting of disaggregated financial information, such as turnover, profits and assets, about a business entity. This information is generally analysed in two ways:

(a) by industry segment. Industry segments are the distinguishable components of an entity each engaged in providing a different product or service, or a different group of related products or services, primarily to customers outside the entity;[1] and

(b) by geographical segment. Geographical segments are the distinguishable components of an entity engaged in operations in individual countries or groups of countries within particular geographical areas.[2]

Segmental reporting has been debated since the early 1960s, that period being significant for the rapid emergence and growth, especially in the US, of the multinational conglomerate business entity.

As enterprises became involved in a large number of distinct products and markets, even industries, the readers of their accounts found it increasingly difficult to analyse the effect of different segments' results on past performance and the likely effect on future performance. Clearly, there could be a wide range of levels of profitability, levels of growth and risk factors concealed within the consolidated accounts of a diversified multinational business enterprise. Pressures grew, mainly from the investment analyst community, for disclosure of the results and resources of the different segments which comprised the whole business. As Mautz noted, 'The progress and success of a diversified company are composites of the progress and success of its several parts. The analyst must have some knowledge about each of these parts to have a basis for forecasting the future of the company. By definition the diversified company is subject to internally varying rates of profit, degrees of risk and potential for profit.'[3]

Since the early 1960s, most major industrialised countries have introduced segmental reporting requirements to varying degrees; by legislation, accounting standard and Stock Exchange pronouncement.

Despite the emergence of some more recent trends towards demerger, the growth of the diversified, multinational business entity has continued to the present day; it is a predominant feature of modern business and there is no evidence that this will change in the future. Recurring periods of merger and acquisition activity merely confirm that the justification for segmental reporting is as strong as ever.

1.2   The objectives of segmental reporting

1.2.1   Introduction

The objectives of segmental reporting derive from the fact that users need a greater level of detail of information about the results and resources of a business entity than is provided by its profit and loss account and balance sheet in order to make more informed economic decisions. There is, obviously, a vast amount of detail that could be given about a large business entity's financial activities. Nevertheless, it is presumably as a result of pressure from interested parties that this additional feature of financial reporting has developed and that there is a need, or a perceived need, for such information.

To understand the objectives of segmental reporting it is useful to discuss these in the context of a number of the user groups identified in Chapter 2. The groups most likely to benefit from segmental information are:

1.2.2   The shareholder group

Shareholders are interested in assessing the potential profits and cash flows of the company. If they are provided with disaggregated data, it is presumed that they will be able to make more informed decisions. Research undertaken, both in the US and the UK, has indicated that segmental information does improve the ability of shareholders to predict an entity's future profits.

Shareholders will also be interested in the stewardship of their funds in the past. Therefore they may regard relatively poor performance in one segment as an indication that their company has failed to use its resources in the most efficient manner.

1.2.3   The investment analyst group

The objectives of the investment analyst group are broadly similar to those of the individual shareholder. However, because they are more expert in the techniques of financial analysis, segmental information is, perhaps, even more useful to this group. This is reflected in the fact that much of the early pressure for segmental reporting came from investment analysts.

It would be likely that investment analysts would be supplied with more segmental information, if it were not for the fact that reporting entities have to bear both the costs of producing the information and the possible risk that some advantage may accrue to competitors having more detailed knowledge of their activities. Therefore, opposing pressures are likely to lead to a compromise position, although the compromise position may change over time.

1.2.4 *The lender/creditor group*

To the extent that segmental information improves the ability to predict future profits and cash flow, lenders and creditors will be similarly interested in having such information available. Improved ability to predict cash flows will assist lenders and creditors to make decisions regarding short-term liquidity and long-term solvency.

1.2.5 *Government*

Governments could be interested in segmental information for a number of reasons. It is likely that segmental information assists governmental bodies to collate statistics on macro-economic performance; for example, the investment in and the performance of various industries and products.

Geographical analysis of results and resources may be of significant interest to foreign Governments. They will be better able to assess the activities of the reporting company within their borders. This assessment may lead to a change in level of regulation, revision of tax status, adjustment to the amount of financial assistance and so on.

Government may also take the view that more detailed information will act as an aid to competition, thus resulting in benefits to the general economy.

2 THE UK POSITION

2.1 Legislative requirements

The Companies Act 1967 introduced the requirement that where a company carried on business of two or more classes which 'in the opinion of the directors, differ substantially from each other', turnover and profit before tax split into those classes should be disclosed. This disclosure was to be made in the directors' report.[4]

The 1967 Act also required the directors' report to include a statement of the value of goods exported from the UK (unless turnover did not exceed £50,000). If the directors were able to satisfy the Board of Trade that it was not in the national interest to disclose this export information the requirement could be waived.[5]

These requirements were extended by the Companies Act 1981. Firstly, the requirement to state the value of goods exported from the UK was replaced by a requirement to disclose turnover by export market.[6] Secondly, this disclosure and the disclosure of turnover and profit before tax split by class of business required by the 1967 Act were to be made in the notes to the accounts rather than in the directors' report.

The exemption from the requirement to disclose this information was also extended by the 1981 Act. Exemption was permitted 'where in the opinion of the directors, the disclosure ... would be seriously prejudicial to the interests of the company'. However, the fact that the information had not been disclosed was required to be stated.[7]

These legislative requirements were consolidated into the Companies Act 1985,[8] although the requirement to disclose pre-tax profit by class of business has since been deleted.[9]

2.2   SSAP 25

2.2.1   *The development of the standard*

The exposure draft which preceded the standard was ED 45, which was issued in November 1988 with an exposure period to April 1989.[10] The eventual accounting standard was issued in June 1990 and took effect for accounting periods beginning on or after 1 July 1990.[11] In developing SSAP 25, the ASC made relatively few changes to the proposals in the exposure draft, although one notable omission was a suggested requirement to disclose the basis of inter-segment pricing, which had attracted a good deal of adverse comment in the exposure period and was not retained.[12]

The standard has continued without amendment until the present day. However, the ASB is now considering possible revisions to the standard in the light of the new standards that have been developed by the FASB in the US and by the IASC (see 4.1 and 4.2 below). In May 1996 it published a discussion paper[13] explaining what was being proposed internationally and seeking comment. At the time, the responses showed little enthusiasm for change, but now that these two standards have been finalised it is likely that the Board will soon seek to replace SSAP 25 with an FRS along the lines of the IASC model.

2.2.2   *General approach*

SSAP 25 is based on the principle that, unless the financial statements of an entity contain segmental information, they do not enable the reader to make judgements about the nature of the different activities or of their contribution to its overall financial result.[14]

It aims to contribute to improved segmental reporting in two ways: first, by providing guidance as to how the reportable segments should be determined and, second, by specifying the information to be disclosed.

2.2.3 Scope

The standard contains two levels of disclosure requirements: those relating to the statutory requirements contained in the UK companies legislation apply to all companies (and to other entities to whom the standard applies),[15] and a number of additional provisions relating to segmental disclosures which are not required by companies legislation. These additional provisions only apply to:[16]

(a) public limited companies (as defined in section 1 of the Companies Act 1985) or holding companies that have one or more public companies as a subsidiary;

(b) banking and insurance companies or groups as defined in section 744 of the Companies Act, and preparing accounts in accordance with Schedules 9 or 9A thereto; and

(c) private companies (and other entities) which exceed the criteria, multiplied in each case by ten, for defining a medium-sized company under section 247 of the Companies Act.

At present, this means that entities with any two of the following will have to give the extra information:

(i) turnover exceeding £112m,

(ii) total assets exceeding £56m, and

(iii) average number of employees exceeding 2,500.

The additional provisions which apply to the entities referred to above are dealt with in 2.2.5 below.

Where both parent entity and consolidated accounts are presented, segmental information is to be presented on the basis of the consolidated accounts.[17] Comparative figures for the previous accounting period are to be given.

The exemption remains that where, in the opinion of the directors, the disclosure of any information required would be seriously prejudicial to the interests of the company that information need not be disclosed, but the fact that any such information has not been disclosed must be stated.[18] In practice few companies choose to take advantage of this exemption. One which does is Yorkshire Group, as shown in this extract:

Extract 19.1: Yorkshire Group Plc (1996)

2. TURNOVER [extract]

Yorkshire Group Plc competes internationally with specialist divisions of the world's chemical majors. Because detailed information relating to this competitor activity is not published, the directors are of the opinion that to comply fully with the requirements of SSAP 25 'Segmental Reporting' would be seriously prejudicial to the interests of the group.

Arjo Wiggins Appleton also uses the exemption to a minor extent. It gives extensive analysis of its activities, but includes the following footnote:

Extract 19.2: Arjo Wiggins Appleton p.l.c. (1996)

SEGMENTAL INFORMATION [extract]
European manufacturing consists of the business operations of Carbonless and Thermal Papers, Coated Papers, Fine Papers and Speciality Papers. In the opinion of the directors, the disclosure of separate segmental information for these divisions would be prejudicial to the interests of the Group.

2.2.4 *What is a reportable segment?*

Information can be segmented in two main ways – by class of business and geographically. SSAP 25 supports the provisions of the Companies Act 1985 which state that it is the directors' responsibility to determine the analysis of the segments.[19] The standard does not seek to override these provisions; instead it aims to provide guidance on factors which should influence the definition of segments.

The basic guidance of the standard is that directors should have regard to the overall purpose of presenting segmental information and the need for the readers of the financial statements to be informed if a company carries on operations in different classes of business or in different geographical areas that:

(a) earn returns on investment that are out of line with the remainder of the business; or

(b) are subject to different degrees of risk; or

(c) have experienced different rates of growth; or

(d) have different potentials for future development.[20]

In establishing segments for both classes of business and geographical areas, there is no single set of factors which is universally applicable, nor is any single factor predominant in all cases. However, the standard suggests that in order to determine whether or not a company operates in different classes of business the directors should take into account the following:

(a) the nature of the products or services;

(b) the nature of the production processes;

(c) the markets in which the products or services are sold;

(d) the distribution channels for the products;

(e) the manner in which the entity's activities are organised; and

(f) any separate legislative framework relating to part of the business.[21]

Similarly, in determining whether or not a company operates in different geographical segments the directors should take into account the following:

(a) expansionist or restrictive economic climates;

(b) stable or unstable political regimes;

(c) exchange control regulations; and

(d) exchange rate fluctuations.[22]

Particularly in some parts of the world, adjacent countries may not share similar characteristics of these kinds and it may be appropriate to analyse them separately. The standard emphasises that 'although geographical proximity may indicate similar economic trends and risks, this will not always be the case'.[23]

Having established that a segment is distinguishable on the basis of features such as these, it is also necessary to consider whether it is significant enough to warrant separate disclosure. A segment will normally be regarded as significant if:

(a) its third party turnover is 10% or more of the total third party turnover of the entity; or

(b) its segment result, whether profit or loss, is 10% or more of the combined result of all segments in profit or of all segments in loss, whichever combined result is the greater; or

(c) its net assets are 10% or more of the total net assets of the entity.[24]

It should be noted that the segment need satisfy only one of these three criteria in order to be regarded as significant. The criteria above are similar to those set out in the US accounting standards SFAS 14 and SFAS 131 (see 4.1 below) to determine a reportable industry segment.[25]

2.2.5 What is to be reported?

The company should define each of its reported classes of business and geographical segments.[26] For each separate class of business and geographical segment, those companies which are subject to the full requirements of the standard (broadly all public and large private companies, and those involved in banking or insurance – see 2.2.3 above) are required to disclose:

(a) turnover;

(b) results; and

(c) net assets.[27]

The discussion which follows is of the full requirements. The exemptions for smaller private companies are shown at the end of this section.

Turnover should be analysed between sales to external customers and sales between segments.[28]

The geographical analysis of turnover is to be given, in the first instance, with reference to its source (i.e. the geographical location from which products or services are supplied). This is consistent with the most likely basis for disclosure of geographical analyses of results and net assets. However, it is recognised that it would also be useful to readers of accounts to be provided with information on the markets which the company serves, which is the basis of the Companies Act requirement. There is, therefore, the additional requirement that turnover (but not results or net assets) be analysed between geographical segments with reference to its destination (i.e. the geographical area to which products or services are supplied). Where this amount is not materially different from turnover to third parties with reference to its source, disclosure is not required but a statement that this is the case should be made.[29]

The standard says that entities that are not required by statute to disclose turnover are not required to analyse such turnover segmentally, but this fact should be stated.[30] This referred at the time to banks, but the subsequently revised Schedule 9 to the Companies Act makes this exemption largely irrelevant. The schedule contains various segmental disclosure requirements,[31] and the banks have also published their own SORP on the subject.[32] However, the rules for specialised industries are beyond the scope of this book.

'Results' means the profit or loss before tax, minority interests and extraordinary items.[33] Profit or loss is normally taken before accounting for interest also. However, the profit or loss after interest is likely to be used in those companies where the earning of interest income or the incurring of interest expense is fundamental to the nature of the business; for example, companies in the financial sector.[34] In giving the geographical analysis of results it is considered that it will be more appropriate if it is based on the areas from which goods or services are supplied.[35] To gather the information based on destination would usually be very difficult in any event.

'Net assets' is not defined in the standard. Generally it is taken as non-interest bearing operating assets less non-interest bearing operating liabilities. However, where interest income/expense has been included in arriving at the segmental results the related interest bearing assets/liabilities should be taken into account in determining the net assets.[36] The aim should be to relate the definition of net assets to the definition of results so that a 'return on investment' type calculation can be performed. Operating assets and liabilities which are shared by more than one segment are to be allocated, as appropriate, to those segments.[37]

Because of the wide differences in their circumstances, it is inevitable that companies interpret net assets in various ways. The best that can be achieved is for companies to settle on one definition of net assets that is meaningful for themselves, and apply it consistently. This means that the value of comparison between companies of returns on assets employed may be limited, even apart from the effects of other differences of accounting policy.

The total of the information disclosed by segmental analysis should agree with the related totals in the financial statements. If they do not agree, a reconciliation between the two figures is required, with reconciling items properly identified and explained.[38]

As indicated in 2.2.3 above, certain of the disclosure requirements of SSAP 25 only apply to public companies (and groups with a public company as subsidiary), banking and insurance companies or groups and very large private companies (and other entities). Companies which are not within these categories need not disclose the following (although disclosure is still encouraged):[39]

(a) split of turnover between external customers and other segments;

(b) segmental analysis of results;

(c) net assets;

(d) share of results and net assets of significant associated undertakings; and

(e) geographical analysis of turnover by reference to its source (analysis by destination is still required by the Companies Act).

2.2.6   Associated undertakings

The standard requires groups to give segmental disclosure, in their consolidated accounts, of the following information in respect of their associated undertakings:

(a) their share of the profits or losses of associated undertakings before accounting for taxation, minority interests and extraordinary items; and

(b) their share of the net assets of associated undertakings (including goodwill to the extent it has not been written off) stated, where possible, after attributing fair values to the net assets at the date of the acquisition of the interest in each associated undertaking.

This disclosure should be of the aggregate information for all associated undertakings and should be shown separately in the segmental report.[40]

The disclosure is only required if the results or assets of associated undertakings form a material part of the group's results or assets. For this purpose, associated undertakings form a material part of the reporting company's results if, in total, they account for at least 20% of the total results or at least 20% of the total net assets of the reporting group (including the group's share of the results and net assets of the associated undertakings).[41]

An example of such disclosure can be seen in the following extract from the financial statements of Chrysalis Group. The results and net assets figures thus analysed had already been included in a similar analysis in respect of the group; it would have been more usual to show the group figures excluding associates. As well as giving details of the associates' results and net assets, Chrysalis analyses its share of their turnover:

Extract 19.3: Chrysalis Group PLC (1996)

3. ANALYSIS OF ASSOCIATED UNDERTAKINGS' TURNOVER, PROFIT/(LOSS) BEFORE TAX AND NET ASSETS/(LIABILITIES)

	Third party turnover		Share of result before taxation		Share of total net assets/ (liabilities)	
	1996	1995	**1996**	1995	**1996**	1995
	£'000	£'000	**£'000**	£'000	**£'000**	£'000
a ANALYSIS BY CLASS OF BUSINESS						
Music	**1,463**	1,204	**48**	73	**155**	114
Export	**1,655**	383	**176**	17	**124**	15
Visual entertainment	**14,780**	10,803	**1,010**	802	**857**	672
Radio and other businesses	**1,059**	977	**5**	(4,278)	**2,895**	(5,634)
	18,957	13,367	**1,239**	(3,386)	**4,031**	(4,833)
Discontinued activity	**–**	11	**(92)**	(11)	**(100)**	(48)
	18,957	13,378	**1,147**	(3,397)	**3,931**	(4,881)
Net interest	**–**	–	**6**	(449)	**–**	–
Total	**18,957**	13,378	**1,153**	(3,846)	**3,931**	(4,881)
b ANALYSIS BY GEOGRAPHICAL LOCATION						
United Kingdom	**4,605**	6,506	**(47)**	(4,652)	**2,637**	(5,747)
Europe	**14,352**	6,872	**1,200**	806	**1,294**	866
Total	**18,957**	13,378	**1,153**	(3,846)	**3,931**	(4,881)

Another good example is to be found in the accounts of Pearson:

Extract 19.4: Pearson plc (1996)

11 Partnerships and associated undertakings [extract]

	Profit		Net Assets	
	1996	1995	**1996**	1995
Analysis of partnerships and associated undertakings	**£m**	£m	**£m**	£m
Business sectors				
Information	**10.9**	10.9	**(7.1)**	(13.8)
Education	**3.0**	4.2	**5.1**	6.4
Entertainment	**(1.6)**	(11.7)	**70.7**	52.6
Investment Banking	**40.8**	39.9	**113.9**	122.1
	53.1	43.3	**182.6**	167.3
Geographical markets supplied and location of net assets				
UK	**20.6**	18.6	**103.9**	85.1
Continental Europe	**12.9**	7.1	**38.1**	35.7
North America	**17.2**	14.0	**36.7**	42.0
Rest of World	**2.4**	3.6	**3.9**	4.5
	53.1	43.3	**182.6**	167.3

Associated undertakings themselves often do not come within the scope of the standard and therefore do not disclose segmental information in their own accounts. Where this is the case the investing company may be unable to obtain the necessary information to meet the requirement of the standard as it does not control the associated undertaking. Similarly, publication of the information may be thought to be prejudicial to the business of the associate where, for example, its competitors are not owned by an entity to which all of the provisions of SSAP 25 apply. SSAP 25 recognises these problems by providing an exemption to the effect that the segmental information requirements do not apply where the company is unable to obtain the information or where publication of the information would be prejudicial to the business of the associate. However, in these circumstances, the reason for the non-disclosure should be stated by way of note, together with a brief description of the omitted business or businesses.[42]

The standard makes no specific reference to disclosure of the segmental results of joint ventures which are accounted for by proportional consolidation, but it would obviously be desirable to include this analysis where it is material to an understanding of the group's activities.

2.2.7 Common costs

Common costs are costs relating to more than one segment.[43] The standard merely requires that they are treated in the way that the directors deem most appropriate with regard to the objectives of segmental reporting. If the apportionment of common costs would be misleading, then they should not be apportioned but the total should be deducted from the total of the segment results.[44]

2.2.8 Disclosure in practice

Most companies present their segmental information in a separate note to the accounts while a few show it in a separate statement alongside the primary statements. Some good examples of segmental disclosures are set out below:

Extract 19.5: Imperial Chemical Industries PLC (1996)

5   SEGMENT INFORMATION

Classes of business

	Turnover		Trading profit before exceptional items		Profit before interest and taxation after exceptional items	
	1996	1995	**1996**	1995	**1996**	1995
	£m	£m	**£m**	£m	**£m**	£m
Paints	**2,437**	2,003	**171**	107	**127**	38
Materials	**1,991**	2,067	**206**	195	**178**	237
Explosives	**808**	778	**40**	49	**(25)**	12
Industrial Chemicals	**4,045**	4,250	**109**	496	**124**	552
Regional Businesses	**1,682**	1,604	**139**	146	**156**	130
Inter-class eliminations	**(443)**	(433)	**–**	1	**–**	1
Share of profits less losses of associated undertakings					**27**	18
	10,520	10,269	**665**	994	**587**	988

The Group's policy is to transfer products internally at external market prices. Inter-class turnover affected several businesses the largest being sales from Industrial Chemicals to Materials of £157m (1995 £181m).

	Depreciation		Capital expenditure		Total assets less current liabilities	
	1996	1995	**1996**	1995	**1996**	1995
	£m	£m	**£m**	£m	**£m**	£m
Paints	**49**	47	**94**	69	**1,018**	804
Materials	**100**	101	**247**	108	**1,197**	1,293
Explosives	**49**	45	**77**	58	**377**	385
Industrial Chemicals	**154**	153	**419**	297	**2,275**	2,306
Regional Businesses	**64**	66	**189**	125	**1,001**	875
Net operating assets					**5,868**	5,663
Net non-operating assets					**231**	936
	416	412	**1,026**	657	**6,099**	6,599

	1996 £m	1995 £m
Net non-operating assets comprise		
Fixed asset investments	172	172
Non-operating debtors	70	68
Investments and short-term deposits	560	1,337
Cash	341	336
Short-term borrowings	(186)	(179)
Current instalments of loans	(243)	(251)
Non-operating creditors	(483)	(547)
	231	936

	Employees	
	1996	1995
Average number of people employed by the Group		
Paints	19,600	17,300
Materials	7,000	7,400
Explosives	10,700	12,600
Industrial Chemicals	15,000	16,100
Regional Businesses	10,000	9,800
Corporate		
Board support	200	200
Group technical resources and other shared services	1,500	1,400
Total employees	64,000	64,800

Geographic areas

The information [opposite] is re-analysed in the table below by geographic area. The figures for each geographic area show the turnover and profits made by, and the net operating assets owned by, companies located in that area; export sales and related profits are included in the areas from which those sales were made.

	Turnover		Trading profit before exceptional items		Profit before interest and taxation after exceptional items	
	1996 £m	1995 £m	1996 £m	1995 £m	1996 £m	1995 £m
United Kingdom						
Sales in the UK	2,249	2,125				
Sales overseas	1,823	2,017				
	4,072	4,142	145	356	128	384
Continental Europe	1,435	1,476	39	91	33	70
The Americas	3,133	2,849	234	220	162	179
Asia Pacific	2,556	2,431	190	269	180	274
Other countries	458	462	57	59	57	64
	11,654	11,360	665	995	560	971
Inter-area eliminations	(1,134)	(1,091)	–	(1)	–	(1)
Share of profits less losses of associated undertakings					27	18
	10,520	10,269	665	994	587	988

Inter-area turnover shown above includes sales of £650m (1995 £721m) from the United Kingdom to overseas subsidiaries.

	Turnover by customer location		Net operating assets	
	1996	1995	**1996**	1995
Continuing operations	**£m**	£m	**£m**	£m
United Kingdom	**2,169**	2,152	**1,722**	1,704
Continental Europe	**1,977**	2,117	**630**	696
The Americas	**3,093**	2,775	**1,392**	1,447
Asia Pacific	**2,629**	2,542	**1,801**	1,628
Other countries	**652**	683	**323**	188
	10,520	10,269	**5,868**	5,663

	Employees	
	1996	1995
Average number of people employed by the Group		
United Kingdom	**17,700**	18,900
Continental Europe	**6,100**	6,100
The Americas	**16,600**	15,600
Asia Pacific	**14,200**	13,400
Other countries	**9,400**	10,800
Total employees	**64,000**	64,800

The number of people employed by the Group at the end of 1996 was 63,300 (1995 63,800).

Extract 19.6: Coats Viyella Plc (1996)

	Turnover		Operating profit		Net Assets	
	1996	1995	**1996**	1995	**1996**	1995
2 Analysis of turnover, operating profit and net assets	**£m**	£m	**£m**	Restated £m	**£m**	£m
Product category:						
Crafts	**445.7**	434.0	**36.3**	45.3	**215.0**	249.7
Industrial	**659.9**	638.5	**54.0**	55.5	**384.0**	409.5
Thread	**1,105.6**	1,072.5	**90.3**	100.8	**599.0**	659.2
Clothing	**586.3**	564.5	**19.1**	21.8	**142.4**	142.6
Home Furnishings	**174.5**	163.5	**12.5**	8.8	**70.7**	69.6
Fashion Retail	**170.6**	161.9	**13.1**	11.7	**72.7**	73.9
Precision Engineering	**325.7**	277.0	**37.6**	40.1	**93.5**	102.6
Other textiles	**92.4**	99.8	**7.8**	7.1	**49.4**	55.2
Corporate	–	–	**(6.1)**	(3.2)	**39.2**	10.6
Continuing operations	**2,455.1**	2,339.2	**174.3**	187.1	**1,066.9**	1,113.7
Discontinued operations	–	120.4	–	0.3	–	–
	2,455.1	2,459.6	**174.3**	187.4	**1,066.9**	1,113.7
Reorganisation costs			**(54.9)**	(10.3)		
			119.4	177.1		
Less: 1994 provision			–	(0.9)		
Operating profit			**119.4**	176.2		
Other items			**11.1**	20.8		
Profit before interest			**130.5**	197.0		
Acquisitions in the year have been included in the following segments						
Thread	**16.5**		**2.1**		**10.4**	
Home furnishings	**3.0**		**0.2**		**1.2**	
	19.5		**2.3**		**11.6**	

	Turnover		Operating profit		Net Assets	
	1996	1995	**1996**	1995	**1996**	1995
				Restated		
	£m	£m	**£m**	£m	**£m**	£m
Geographical analysis by location:						
United Kingdom	**868.4**	824.4	**37.8**	36.3	**337.0**	313.3
Rest of Europe	**508.5**	505.0	**31.7**	43.7	**180.7**	206.5
North America	**567.3**	507.6	**65.7**	60.6	**230.7**	261.7
South America	**157.6**	154.7	**7.7**	12.2	**105.0**	105.3
Africa, Asia, Australasia	**353.3**	347.5	**31.4**	34.3	**213.5**	226.9
Continuing operations	**2,455.1**	2,339.2	**174.3**	187.1	**1,066.9**	1,113.7
Discontinued operations	–	120.4	–	0.3	–	–
	2,455.1	2,459.6	**174.3**	187.4	**1,066.9**	1,113.7
Reorganisation costs			**(54.9)**	(10.3)		
			119.4	177.1		
Less: 1994 provision			–	(0.9)		
Operating profit			**119.4**	176.2		
Other items			**11.1**	20.8		
Profit before interest			**130.5**	197.0		
Associated companies					**1.8**	2.0
					1,068.7	1,115.7
Net debt					**(294.5)**	(293.8)
Other fixed and current asset investments					**26.8**	31.7
Net assets per consolidated balance sheet					**801.0**	853.6
Acquisitions in the year have been included in the following segments						
Europe	**7.8**		**(0.1)**		**2.5**	
North America	**3.8**		**0.6**		**0.7**	
South America	**7.9**		**1.8**		**8.4**	
	19.5		**2.3**		**11.6**	

Note　Operating profits for 1995 have been restated to show reorganisation costs separately.

The geographical analysis of discontinued operations by location was						
United Kingdom	–	81.4	–	(0.5)	–	–
Rest of Europe	–	32.1	–	0.5	–	–
North America	–	3.8	–	0.2	–	–
Africa, Asia, Australasia	–	3.1	–	0.1	–	–
	–	120.4	–	0.3	–	–

Geographical analysis of sales by destination:

	1996 £m	1995 £m
United Kingdom	824.5	836.9
Rest of Europe	548.1	592.4
North America	581.3	518.8
South America	158.2	156.3
Africa, Asia, Australasia	343.0	355.2
	2,455.1	2,459.6

Note
Associated companies are principally Thread businesses based in Asia.

Guidance on the form of presentation which may be followed in disclosing all of the information required by the standard is provided in the appendix to SSAP 25. During the development of the standard it was, at one point, suggested that a matrix format be encouraged. This gives additional information, because it means that each geographical segment is also analysed by activity and vice versa. However, while many commentators felt that a matrix approach had some merit, others contended that a complex matrix of segmental information may confuse readers as well as giving competitors valuable commercial advantage.

One company which does in fact present its segmental information for turnover in matrix form is BOC, as illustrated in the following extract:

Extract 19.7: The BOC Group plc (1996)

1 Segmental information [extract]

a) Turnover analysis

1996	Gases and Related Products £ million	Health Care £ million	Vacuum Technology £ million	Distribution Services £ million	Total by origin £ million	Total by destination £ million
Europe[1]	**642.9**	**181.0**	**122.9**	**282.5**	**1229.3**	**1150.3**
Africa	**354.4**	–	–	–	**354.4**	**360.5**
Americas[2]	**754.7**	**259.5**	**211.1**	–	**1225.3**	**1217.7**
Asia/Pacific	**1062.2**	**65.4**	**82.9**	–	**1210.5**	**1291.0**
Turnover[3]	**2814.2**	**505.9**	**416.9**	**282.5**	**4019.5**	**4019.5**
1995						
Europe[1]	589.5	180.6	96.7	263.2	1130.0	1083.7
Africa	337.0	–	–	–	337.0	341.4
Americas[2]	696.5	278.5	170.9	–	1145.9	1113.0
Asia/Pacific	1009.1	68.2	61.7	–	1139.0	1213.8
Turnover[3]	2632.1	527.3	329.3	263.2	3751.9	3751.9

1 Segmental information for the UK is: turnover, £898.0 million (1995: £826.4 million); operating profit, £175.4 million (1995: £156.4 million); capital employed, £933.0 million (1995: £903.5 million) and capital expenditure, £130.0 million (1995: £124.8 million).

2 Segmental information for the US is: turnover, £1117.5 million (1995: £1059.7 million); operating profit, £79.7 million (1995: £87.7 million); capital employed, £926.2 million (1995: £736.1 million) and capital expenditure, £229.7 million (1995: £134.0 million).

3 Gases and Related Products includes Group share of related undertakings' turnover of £267.4 million (1995: £208.0 million) and Group share of profit of related undertakings of £57.5 million (1995: £45.4 million).

Such a presentation is fairly rare, but it does provide a great deal of information; not only is the user given the level of turnover attributable to, say, health care (£505.9 million) and the level of turnover attributable to Europe (£1,229.3 million), but also the amount of turnover attributable to health care in Europe (£181 million). BOC does not, however, use a matrix approach in giving its segmental analyses of operating profit, capital employed and capital expenditure.

2.3   Voluntary segmental disclosures

A number of companies give segmental information which goes beyond present requirements. As shown in Extract 19.5 above, ICI gives segmental analyses of its depreciation charge, capital expenditure and employees. Some other examples of voluntary segmental disclosures are illustrated in the following extracts.

British Petroleum analyses its fixed assets by business segments:

Extract 19.8: The British Petroleum Company p.l.c. (1996)

15 Tangible assets – property, plant and equipment [extract]   **£ million**

	Exploration and Production	Refining and Marketing	Chemicals	Other businesses and corporate	Total	of which Assets under construction
Cost						
At 1 January 1996	27,773	10,268	3,095	507	41,643	2,286
Exchange adjustments	(1,382)	(954)	(127)	(9)	(2,472)	(92)
Additions	1,776	716	210	20	2,722	1,750
Transfers	111	(21)	(4)	36	122	(1,424)
Deletions	(1,014)	(594)	(286)	(267)	(2,161)	(160)
At 31 December 1996	**27,264**	**9,415**	**2,888**	**287**	**39,854**	**2,360**
Depreciation						
At 1 January 1996	14,572	5,540	1,763	230	22,105	
Exchange adjustments	(793)	(541)	(90)	(4)	(1,428)	
Charge for the year	1,441	429	113	20	2,003	
Transfers	(3)	(6)	–	9	–	
Deletions	(820)	(508)	(196)	(107)	(1,631)	
At 31 December 1996	**14,397**	**4,914**	**1,590**	**148**	**21,049**	
Net book amount						
At 31 December 1996	**12,867**	**4,501**	**1,298**	**139**	**18,805**	**2,360**
At 31 December 1995	13,201	4,728	1,332	277	19,538	2,286

RTZ-CRA is one of a number of groups which gives segmental analysis of its employees, and does so both by activity and geographical location:

Extract 19.9: The RTZ Corporation PLC – CRA Limited (1996)

24 EMPLOYEES [extract]

	Subsidiaries		Associated companies		Group total	
	1996	1995	1996	1995	1996	1995
The average number of employees within each category was:						
Metals and coal	**21,956**	22,191	**14,473**	13,901	**36,429**	36,092
Industrial minerals	**4,816**	5,727	**1,777**	1,874	**6,593**	7,601
Other including administration, exploration and research	**5,104**	5,395	**2,569**	2,404	**7,673**	7,799
Continuing operations	**31,876**	33,313	**18,819**	18,179	**50,695**	51,492
Discontinued operations	**–**	1,450	**–**	–	**–**	1,450
Total	**31,876**	34,763	**18,819**	18,179	**50,695**	52,942
The principal locations of employment were:						
North America	**7,176**	7,902	**38**	100	**7,214**	8,002
Australia and New Zealand	**12,444**	13,161	**1,128**	1,286	**13,572**	14,447
Africa	**6,624**	6,993	**2,168**	2,277	**8,792**	9,270
Europe	**2,686**	2,610	**2,722**	2,819	**5,408**	5,429
South America	**1,444**	1,517	**4,524**	4,242	**5,968**	5,759
Other countries	**1,502**	1,130	**8,239**	7,455	**9,741**	8,585
Continuing operations	**31,876**	33,313	**18,819**	18,179	**50,695**	51,492
Discontinued operations	**–**	1,450	**–**	–	**–**	1,450
Total	**31,876**	34,763	**18,819**	18,179	**50,695**	52,942

J. Bibby analyses its stocks by segment as well as under the SSAP 9 rules:[45]

Extract 19.10: J. Bibby & Sons PLC (1996)

	1996 £000's	1995 £000's
8 Stocks [extract]		
Industrial	**41,079**	40,157
Materials Handling	**29,751**	31,900
Capital Equipment	**58,870**	58,948
	129,700	131,005

3 PROBLEM AREAS

3.1 How to define the segments

SSAP 25 specifies that the definition of segments should be made by the management of the reporting company. Guidance on how such segments are defined can be given but only in very general terms (see 2.2.4 above).

Use of the Standard Industrial Classification system has been advocated as a consistent method of grouping products and services. In the US, however, SFAS 14 notes that the FASB 'has examined several systems that have been developed for classifying business activities, such as the Standard Industrial Classification and the Enterprise Standard Industrial Classification systems and has judged that none is, by itself, suitable to determine industry segments. Nonetheless, those systems may provide guidance for the exercise of the judgement required to group an enterprise's products and services by industry lines.'[46]

Similarly SSAP 25 concludes that 'determination of an entity's classes of business must depend on the judgement of the directors'.[47]

The factors which provide guidance in determining an industry segment are often the factors which lead a company's management to organise its enterprise into divisions, branches or subsidiaries. In turn, this means that the company's own management accounts may well be prepared in this form and the information required for segmental reporting will be more readily available.

EMAP provides an unusual example because it analyses its turnover into segments of two different kinds, as shown in the following extract:

Extract 19.11: EMAP plc (1997)

GROUP ACTIVITY ANALYSIS [extract]

for the financial year ended 31 March 1997

	Continuing operations 1997 £m	Discontinued operations 1997 £m	Total 1997 £m	%	Total 1996 £m	%
Turnover by category						
Advertising	292.8	19.5	312.3	41	325.4	46
Circulation	347.6	2.8	350.4	46	280.9	40
Exhibitions	46.7	–	46.7	6	36.8	5
Other	54.5	0.7	55.2	7	47.8	7
Newspaper Printing	–	3.6	3.6	–	14.1	2
	741.6	26.6	768.2	100	705.0	100
Turnover by division						
Consumer Magazines UK	235.0	–	235.0	31	211.7	30
Consumer Magazines France	252.1	–	252.1	33	175.1	26
Business Communications	189.4	–	189.4	25	170.8	24
Radio	65.1	–	65.1	8	46.6	6
Newspapers and Newspaper Printing	–	26.6	26.6	3	100.8	14
	741.6	26.6	768.2	100	705.0	100

The standard recommends that the directors should review their definitions annually and redefine them when appropriate.[48] Where this is done, the comparative figures should be restated to reflect the change; disclosure of the nature of, the reasons for, and the effect of the change should also be made.[49] Such a change is evident in the accounts of First Leisure:

Extract 19.12: First Leisure Corporation PLC (1996)

1 Turnover, profit before taxation and net assets

The divisional analysis of turnover, profit on ordinary activities before taxation and net assets is stated after an internal reorganisation of certain trading units between divisions. This reorganisation consolidates all stand-alone Bar operations into a single organisational unit with a dedicated management team. The results of the Bars are reported within the Dancing division which has been renamed the Nightclubs & Bars division. Previously, several of the Bars were included in the Resorts division. Additionally, the small Superbowl operated by the Resorts division in Blackpool has been transferred to the Sports division. The comparatives have been restated to reflect the reorganisation.

	1996 £m	1995 £m
Turnover		
Nightclubs & Bars	68.5	60.7
Sports	46.7	42.1
Bingo	25.1	15.5
Resorts	42.6	40.4
	182.9	158.7

Under the previous organisation structure, turnover would have been reported for Dancing as £62.0m (1995 £57.1m), Sports £46.1m (1995 £41.5m) and Resorts £49.7m (1995 £44.6m).

Profit on ordinary activities before taxation		
Nightclubs & Bars	21.8	18.8
Sports	13.0	11.3
Bingo	0.2	1.9
Resorts	10.7	9.3
Theatres	0.1	0.6
Operating profit	45.8	41.9
Profit on fixed asset disposals	1.6	1.1
Net interest payable	(3.7)	(2.9)
	43.7	40.1

Under the previous organisation structure, operating profit would have been reported for Dancing as £19.6m (1995 £17.8m), Sports £12.9m (1995 £11.2m) and Resorts £13.0m (1995 £10.4m).

Net assets		
Nightclubs & Bars	105.3	98.6
Sports	110.7	98.3
Bingo	47.5	37.0
Resorts	92.9	88.5
Theatres	7.4	7.4
	363.8	329.8
Tax and dividends	(23.4)	(20.7)
Group borrowings, bank balances and cash in hand	(54.0)	(47.8)
	286.4	261.3

Under the previous organisation structure, net assets would have been reported for Dancing as £95.5m (1995 £90.7m), Sports £109.5m (1995 £97.1m) and Resorts £103.9m (1995 £97.6m).

Companies who operate in global markets can have particular difficulty in analysing their operations geographically. The following extracts show the approaches of British Airways, Barclays and Reuters to this problem:

Extract 19.13: British Airways Plc (1997)

ACCOUNTING POLICIES

SEGMENTAL REPORTING

b *GEOGRAPHICAL SEGMENTS*

i) *Turnover by Destination*

The analysis of turnover by destination is based on the following criteria:

Scheduled and non scheduled services Turnover from domestic services within the United Kingdom is attributed to the United Kingdom. Turnover from inbound and outbound services between the United Kingdom and overseas points is attributed to the geographical area in which the relevant overseas point lies.

Other revenue Revenue from the sale of package holidays is attributed to the geographical area in which the holiday is taken, while revenue from aircraft maintenance and other miscellaneous services is attributed on the basis of where the customer resides.

ii) *Turnover by origin*

The analysis of turnover by origin is derived by allocating revenue to the area in which the sale was made. Operating profit resulting from turnover generated in each geographical area according to origin of sale is not disclosed as it is neither practical nor meaningful to allocate the Group's operating expenditure on this basis.

iii) *Geographical analysis of Net Assets*

The major revenue-earning assets of the Group are comprised of the aircraft fleets, the majority of which are registered in the United Kingdom. Since the Group's aircraft fleets are employed flexibly across its worldwide route network, there is no suitable basis of allocating such assets and related liabilities to geographical segments.

Extract 19.14: Barclays PLC (1996)

Accounting policies [extract]

Analyses by geographical segments and classes of business

The analyses by geographical segment are generally based on the location of the office recording the transaction.

In note 59, the global swaps business is included within the United Kingdom segment. Foreign UK-based comprises activities in the United Kingdom with overseas customers, including sovereign lendings, and the main foreign exchange trading business arising in the United Kingdom. Of the £9bn of assets reported under this heading in 1996, it is estimated that £4bn relates to customers domiciled in Other European Union countries and £1bn relates to customers domiciled in the United States.

United States includes business conducted through the Bahamas and the Cayman Islands.

The world-wide activities of Barclays are highly integrated and, accordingly, it is not possible to present geographical segment information without making internal allocations, some of which are necessarily subjective. Where appropriate, amounts for each geographical segment and class of business reflect the benefit of earnings on a proportion of shareholders' funds, allocated generally by reference to weighted risk assets. ...

Extract 19.15: Reuters Holdings PLC (1996)

1. SEGMENTAL ANALYSIS

The table below is a segmental analysis of revenue, costs and contribution. Central costs comprise the costs of corporate administration and the centrally controlled elements of development, marketing and technical operations. The table does not purport to show geographical profitability but reflects how Reuters controls costs and monitors contribution including the worldwide activities of Instinet and TIBCO which are managed separately. Because of the interactive nature of the worldwide operations of Reuters, Instinet and TIBCO costs incurred in one location often relate to revenues earned in other locations.

	1996 £M	% CHANGE	1995 £M	% CHANGE	1994 £M
Revenue					
Europe, Middle East and Africa	1,564	6	1,475	18	1,250
Asia/Pacific	504	3	491	9	449
The Americas	440	6	417	8	388
	2,508	5	2,383	14	2,087
Instinet	346	97	243	31	186
TIBCO (see note below)	60	(23)	77	–	36
	2,914	8	2,703	17	2,309
Operating costs where incurred					
Europe, Middle East and Africa	(981)	2	(967)	16	(837)
Asia/Pacific	(312)	5	(299)	9	(274)
The Americas	(423)	8	(392)	12	(350)
	(1,716)	4	(1,658)	13	(1,461)
Instinet	(211)	24	(170)	28	(133)
TIBCO	(48)	7	(44)	–	(30)
	(1,975)	5	(1,872)	15	(1,624)
Contribution					
Europe, Middle East and Africa	583	15	508	23	413
Asia/Pacific	192	–	192	10	175
The Americas	17	(31)	25	(34)	38
	792	9	725	16	626
Instinet	135	87	73	38	53
TIBCO	12	(64)	33	–	6
	939	13	831	21	685
Central costs	(309)	29	(240)	21	(199)
Net currency gain/(loss)	11	–	(40)	–	(25)
Operating profit	641	16	551	20	461
Income from fixed asset investments	6	–	–	–	–
Net interest receivable	61	2	60	16	51
Loss from associated undertakings	(7)	–	(12)	–	(2)
Profit on ordinary activities before taxation	701	17	599	17	510

United Kingdom and Ireland revenue was £477 million (1995 – £435 million, 1994 – £366 million). Instinet's and TIBCO's operations are predominantly based in the Americas. The above figures for TIBCO only include the period since acquisition in March 1994 and, therefore, percentage growth figures are not given for 1995.

Revenue is generally invoiced by Reuters in the same geographical area in which the customer is located. Revenue earned, therefore, generally represents revenue both by origin and by destination. The main exception is TIBCO, where a substantial proportion of revenue billed by the Americas is from customers located elsewhere. In 1996, 42% (1995 – 38%, 1994 – 46%) of TIBCO's revenue was generated from customers in the Americas, 39% (1995 – 42%, 1994 – 35%) from customers located in Europe, Middle East and Africa and 19% (1995 – 20%, 1994 – 19%) from customers in Asia/Pacific.

Revenue by product category	1996 £M	% CHANGE	1995 £M	% CHANGE	1994 £M
Information products					
Europe, Middle East and Africa	**1,145**	**5**	1,090	16	944
Asia/Pacific	**365**	**1**	361	7	337
The Americas	**322**	**3**	313	4	300
TIBCO	**60**	**(23)**	77	–	36
	1,892	**3**	1,841	14	1,617
Transaction products					
Europe, Middle East and Africa	**286**	**9**	263	28	206
Asia/Pacific	**108**	**7**	101	17	86
The Americas	**73**	**14**	64	31	49
Instinet	**346**	**42**	243	31	186
	813	**21**	671	27	527
Media and professional products					
Europe, Middle East and Africa	**133**	**9**	122	21	101
Asia/Pacific	**31**	**8**	29	12	26
The Americas	**45**	**11**	40	5	38
	209	**9**	191	16	165
	2,914	**8**	2,703	17	2,309

Reuters operates in a single class of business: the provision of news and financial information and related services. With the exception of Instinet and TIBCO, Reuters products are delivered and sold through a common network and geographical infrastructure.

Revenue by type	1996 £M	% CHANGE	1995 £M	% CHANGE	1994 £M
Recurring	**2,232**	**5**	2,128	12	1,898
Usage	**478**	**34**	358	38	259
Outright sales	**204**	**(6)**	217	43	152
	2,914	**8**	2,703	17	2,309

Recurring revenue is derived from the sale of subscription services, including maintenance contracts. Usage revenue is based on volume and primarily relates to transaction products, including Instinet and certain activities of Reuters Television. Outright sales mainly represents once-off sales of information management systems.

Notes on the Consolidated Balance Sheet

14. SEGMENTAL ANALYSIS

The tables below show net assets and total assets by location on a basis consistent with the segmental analysis of profit in note 1. For the reasons discussed in that note, the net assets in any location are not matched with the revenue earned in that location.

Location of net assets	**1996 £M**	1995 £M	1994 £M
Non-interest bearing assets/(liabilities)			
Europe, Middle East and Africa	**295**	267	276
Asia/Pacific	**98**	105	102
The Americas	**80**	46	4
Instinet	**37**	43	36
TIBCO	**4**	(3)	(11)
Central	**(296)**	(270)	(176)
Non-interest bearing net assets	**218**	188	231
Interest bearing net assets	**1,043**	760	509
	1,261	948	740

Central non-interest bearing liabilities consist principally of dividend and taxation liabilities. Interest bearing net assets include items discounted for accounting purposes.

Location of total assets	**1996 £M**	1995 £M	1994 £M
Europe, Middle East and Africa	**584**	583	545
Asia/Pacific	**206**	205	246
The Americas	**195**	189	169
Instinet	**316**	235	152
TIBCO	**33**	33	21
Central	**1,004**	860	515
	2,338	2,105	1,648
Fixed assets	**828**	735	687
Current assets	**1,510**	1,370	961
	2,338	2,105	1,648

Central assets consist principally of short-term investments and cash.

One or two companies assert that they have only one business operation, but then go on to give some further analysis of it. Since they do not regard the sub-units as separate segments, they avoid having to give the full range of disclosures required by SSAP 25. Safeway is an example:

Extract 19.16: Safeway plc (1997)

1.0 Sales and profit

The group's sole trading activity is grocery retailing which is carried out almost entirely in the United Kingdom. In order to provide shareholders with additional information, the group's sales and operating profit have been analysed between its two retail brands, as set out below:

	1997	1996
	£m	£m
Sales		
Safeway	**6,627.8**	6,031.1
Presto	**438.6**	468.9
	7,066.4	6,500.0
Turnover, excluding VAT		
Safeway	**6,178.5**	5,630.1
Presto	**411.2**	439.3
	6,589.7	6,069.4
Operating profit		
Safeway	**430.2**	386.4
Presto	**31.6**	31.1
	461.8	417.5
% margin – VAT excl.	**7.0%**	6.9%
Investment income	**–**	3.7
Net interest payable excluding effect of share capital buyback	**(20.9)**	(20.0)
Profit after interest (before share capital buyback)	**440.9**	401.2
Net interest payable due to share capital buyback	**(10.8)**	–
Profit after interest (after share capital buyback)	**430.1**	401.2
Net property losses	**(9.5)**	(9.5)
Profit before taxation and disposal of investments	**420.6**	391.7

3.2   Inter-segment sales

The standard requires that the turnover disclosed for each segment be split between sales to external customers and sales to other segments. Prior to the introduction of SSAP 25 few companies disclosed all such information; they either disclosed the total turnover for each segment and deducted one figure for inter-segment sales or disclosed sales to external customers only.

While ED 45 proposed the disclosure of the basis of transfer pricing, this proposal was not reflected in SSAP 25 as many commentators felt that companies would either argue that disclosure would be prejudicial or would provide a suitably vague and unhelpful general statement. Conscious of the effect on the credibility of the standard as a whole if there was widespread avoidance of this requirement, the ASC omitted it from the eventual standard. The absence of such information can, however, limit the usefulness of the disclosure of segmental results.

Some companies do however state the basis on which inter-segment sales are conducted. One example is ICI, as shown in Extract 19.5 above. Another is Unilever, which gives this description in its accounting policies, as shown below:

Extract 19.17: Unilever PLC (1996)

Accounting policies [extract]

Transfer pricing

The preferred method for determining transfer prices for own manufactured goods is to take the market price. Where there is no market price, the companies concerned follow established transfer pricing guidelines, where available, or else engage in arm's length negotiations.

Trade marks owned by the parent companies and used by the operating companies are, where appropriate, licensed in return for royalties or a fee.

General services provided by central advisory departments and research laboratories are charged to group companies on the basis of fees.

3.3   Common costs

Common costs will normally take the form of central administration overheads, but in practice there could be a wide range of categories of common costs. However, the standard emphasises that 'costs that are directly attributable to individual reportable segments are not common costs for the purposes of this accounting standard and therefore should be allocated to those segments, irrespective of the fact that they may have been borne by a different segment or by Head Office'.[50]

SSAP 25 allows common costs to be allocated to different segments on what the company's management believes is a reasonable basis (see 2.2.7 above) but where the apportionment of common costs would be misleading, the standard requires that they should not be apportioned but the total should be deducted from the total of the segment results. Notwithstanding this, one or two companies disclose that they have apportioned such costs, as shown in these extracts:

Extract 19.18: Cookson Group plc (1996)

2 Segmental analyses of results of operations/Group employee information [extract]

In each of the following analyses, head office and service costs have been allocated according to the relative contribution of each segment to the total. In addition, as a consequence of the Group's borrowing requirements being centrally managed, it is not considered appropriate or meaningful to allocate the Group's net interest charge across segments in order to give a segmental analysis of Group profit before taxation. ...

Extract 19.19: Standard Chartered PLC (1996)

38   Segmental information [extract]

... Group central expenses have been distributed between segments in proportion to their direct costs. Group capital (representing net assets employed), assets held at the centre and the benefit of the Group's capital have been distributed to segments in proportion to their risk weighted assets.

Such a practice is consistent with the ASB's proposals for the assessment of impairment of assets, whereby central assets such as head offices have to be apportioned across income-generating units for the purposes of the test (see Chapter 10 at 4.4). Nevertheless, we do not believe this to be a helpful approach, because it implies a relationship where none exists and is unlikely to add to the usefulness of the segmental information disclosed.

3.4   Allocation of interest income and interest expense

SSAP 25 suggests that in the majority of companies the individual segments will be financed by interest-bearing debt and equity in varying proportions. The interest earned or incurred by the individual segments is, therefore, a result of the holding company's overall policy rather than a proper reflection of the results of the various segments. For this reason, the standard requires that in these circumstances the results should exclude interest as 'comparisons of profit between segments or between different years for the same segment are likely to be meaningless if interest is included in arriving at the result'.[51]

However, where interest is fundamental to the nature of the business, the standard suggests that interest should be included in arriving at the segment result. Such an approach would be relevant to those companies involved in the financial sector, but it can also apply to diverse groups where some divisions are cash-generative and finance the others.

Whitbread has allocated interest payable to its 'beer and other drinks' segment to the extent that it reflects the net cost of financing trade loans to customers in that segment:

Extract 19.20: Whitbread PLC (1997)

2. Segmental analysis of turnover, profit and net assets [extract]

By business segment	1996/7 Turnover £m	1996/7 Profit £m	1996/7 Net assets £m	1995/6 Turnover £m	1995/6 Profit £m	1995/6 Net assets £m
Beer	1,009.7	49.9	305.8	943.9	44.9	282.0
Pub Partnerships	160.2	57.6	429.4	167.5	59.2	451.6
Inns	729.9	146.8	1,072.2	660.5	128.9	937.1
Restaurants and Leisure	1,451.8	121.9	1,358.5	1,290.6	88.3	1,202.3
	3,351.6	376.2	3,165.9	3,062.5	321.3	2,873.0
Income from investments and property development	0.2	8.8	32.8	1.1	9.5	28.7
	3,351.8	385.0	3,198.7	3,063.6	330.8	2,901.7
Deduct:						
Inter-segment turnover	(324.6)			(313.7)		
Central services		(29.8)	(185.2)		(26.8)	(194.8)
Allocation to Whitbread Share Ownership Scheme		(5.0)			(5.5)	
Interest (see note below)		(33.7)	(749.0)		(15.4)	(449.7)
	3,027.2	316.5	2,264.5	2,749.9	283.1	2,257.2

... In the business segmental analysis a charge for interest has been made to Beer to reflect the cost of financing trade loans made to customers. Interest stated above has therefore been adjusted by a charge to Beer of £3.6m (1995/6 – £4.6m), and the funding of such loans, amounting to £44.9m (1996 – £52.2m) has been allocated to Beer in the net assets column. ...

3.5   Exceptional items

The results which are to be analysed in terms of SSAP 25 are those 'before accounting for taxation, minority interests and extraordinary items', and usually also before interest.[52] The standard predated FRS 3 (see Chapter 22), which has virtually abolished extraordinary items but expanded the categories of exceptional items to be disclosed instead, and it is necessary to consider how these should be dealt with for segmental reporting purposes.

Exceptional items are not specifically addressed in SSAP 25, and by implication are to be included in the analysed results. In practice, some companies analyse their results before exceptional items, and do not always fully disclose to which segments the exceptional items belong.

In its 1993 accounts, BET excluded exceptional items from its operating profit and also its segmental analysis, but after the intervention of the Financial Reporting Review Panel, it restated the figures in its 1994 accounts, as shown below:

Extract 19.21: BET Public Limited Company (1994)

Accounting policies [extract]

The 1993 comparatives have been restated to show operating exceptional items of £76.0 million within the statutory format headings to which they relate (£60.2 million in cost of sales and £15.8 million in administrative expenses) in recognition of developing practice in the application of FRS 3 and after a recent discussion with the Financial Reporting Review Panel. The restatement of the previously disclosed operating exceptional items is highlighted in Note 1(c) on page 39.

Notes to the consolidated accounts

Note 1   Analysis of profit and loss account [extract]

(c) Adjustment to 1993 comparatives

	1993 Published £m	Adjustment £m	1993 Restated £m
BY BUSINESS SECTOR			
Business services	25.6	(11.5)	14.1
Distribution services	20.8	(11.5)	9.3
Plant services	26.5	(10.7)	15.8
Textile services	28.1	(22.5)	5.6
Trading activities	101.0	(56.2)	44.8
Associated undertakings	7.3	–	7.3
Corporate and other	(24.6)	(10.7)	(35.3)
Loss on disposal of property	(4.0)	–	(4.0)
Continuing operations	79.7	(66.9)	12.8
Discontinued operations	(5.5)	(9.1)	(14.6)
	74.2	(76.0)	(1.8)
Costs previously disclosed as operating exceptional items	(76.0)	76.0	–
Operating loss	(1.8)	–	(1.8)
BY GEOGRAPHICAL LOCATION			
Europe – UK	33.3	(51.7)	(18.4)
– Continent	20.3	(14.3)	6.0
North America	13.5	(9.4)	4.1
Rest of the World	7.1	(0.6)	6.5
	74.2	(76.0)	(1.8)
Costs previously disclosed as operating exceptional items	(76.0)	76.0	–
Operating loss	(1.8)	–	(1.8)

In our view the best approach is to analyse the profit after exceptional items, while also making it clear how much each segment has been affected by such items.

3.6   Changes in composition of the group

FRS 3 requires that 'where an acquisition, or a sale or termination, has a material impact on a major business segment this should be disclosed and explained'.[53]

Coats Viyella (Extract 19.6 above) gives a comprehensive segmental analysis of its acquisitions, by both class of business and geographical region. However, this disclosure is relatively uncommon, perhaps because most companies make fewer acquisitions in any one year, and it is often self-evident from their description which segments are affected.

Some of the companies shown earlier in this chapter have shown discontinued operations separately in their segmental analyses, including Coats Viyella (Extract 19.6) and BET (Extract 19.21). The most common form of disclosure is simply to show discontinued operations as a residual category, analysing only the continuing operations into segments (which is not strictly what FRS 3 requires). Again, however, it is often evident from the discussion elsewhere in the accounts what the discontinued businesses related to.

The requirement in FRS 3 is a rather glib one, and deserves reconsideration when the standard comes up for review. In fact, a more rewarding approach might be to readdress the issue in any future revision of SSAP 25, because it would be more natural to incorporate such requirements into the framework of existing segmental disclosures. Indeed, the whole topic of disclosing the effects of acquisitions and discontinuances arguably fits more comfortably in the context of segmental reporting than in a general standard on the format of the profit and loss account.

3.7   How to define net assets

Net assets are not defined in the standard although it does indicate that, in most cases, these will be the non-interest bearing operating assets less the non-interest bearing operating liabilities. Where, and to the extent that, the segment result is calculated after accounting for interest, for example by companies in the financial sector, then the corresponding interest bearing assets and liabilities should be included in the calculation of net assets.[54]

Operating assets of a segment should not normally include loans or advances to, or investments in, another segment unless interest therefrom has been included in arriving at the segment result.[55]

Operating liabilities will normally include creditors which are included in working capital but will exclude liabilities in respect of proposed dividends and corporation tax as well as interest bearing liabilities such as loans, overdrafts and debentures. In the case of a consolidated balance sheet with a minority interest, the calculation of net assets should not involve the deduction of that interest.

Non-operating assets and liabilities, as well as unallocated assets and liabilities, should therefore be shown in the segmental analysis as reconciling items between the total of the individual segments' net assets and the figure for net assets appearing in the balance sheet.

As shown in Extract 19.5 above, ICI has shown a total of net non-operating assets which reconciles the segmentally analysed net assets to the balance sheet, and has listed the items included therein. There are a number of other ways of giving this information; British Petroleum has a reconciliation to tie up the segmental figures with the balance sheet:

Extract 19.22: The British Petroleum Company p.l.c. (1996)

30 Group balance sheet analysis £ million

By business	Capital expenditure and acquisitions		Operating capital employed	
	1996	1995	**1996**	1995
Exploration and Production	**2,415**	1,910	**12,187**	11,940
Refining and Marketing	**761**	683	**5,137**	4,637
Chemicals	**239**	247	**2,221**	2,439
Other business and corporate	**27**	15	**(712)**	(483)
Total	**3,422**	2,855	**18,833**	18,533
By geographical area				
UK [a]	**1,321**	989	**6,559**	6,127
Rest of Europe	**378**	318	**2,144**	2,325
USA	**822**	749	**5,127**	5,275
Rest of World	**921**	799	**5,003**	4,806
Total	**3,442**	2,855	**18,833**	18,533

[a] UK area includes the UK-based international activities of BP Oil

	1996	1995
Operating capital employed	18,833	18,533
Liabilities for current and deferred taxation	(1,397)	(1,113)
Capital employed	17,436	17,420
Financed by:		
Finance debt	4,532	5,498
Minority shareholders' interest	109	108
BP shareholders' interest	12,795	11,814
	17,436	17,420

Firth Rixson analyses the excluded items more fully, as shown below:

Extract 19.23: Firth Rixson plc (1996)

18 Segmental analysis of net assets

	United Kingdom 1996 £'000	1995 £'000	United States 1996 £'000	1995 £'000	Total 1996 £'000	Total 1995 £'000
Net operating assets	**46,636**	50,312	**19,374**	16,308	**66,010**	66,620
Cash and short term deposits	**4,506**	5,064	**1,430**	862	**5,936**	5,926
Bank overdrafts	**(2,673)**	(3,092)	–	–	**(2,673)**	(3,092)
Taxation recoverable	–	47	–	–	–	47
Taxation payable	**(1,565)**	(1,490)	**(32)**	–	**(1,597)**	(1,490)
Dividends payable	**(1,414)**	(987)	–	–	**(1,414)**	(987)
Loans	**(13,608)**	(13,194)	**(4,386)**	(5,414)	**(17,994)**	(18,608)
Deferred taxation	**(100)**	(183)	–	–	**(100)**	(183)
Net assets	**31,782**	36,477	**16,386**	11,756	**48,168**	48,233

The standard does not explicitly say that the net assets figure disclosed is to be based on the year end position, although this is the normal interpretation used. However, BTR has adopted a different view and based it on the average position during the year, which is more appropriate to an assessment of the return on capital employed when the year end is not representative of the average position. The relevant extract from the accounts is shown below:

Extract 19.24: BTR plc (1996)

1 Analysis of sales, profit before tax and operating net assets [extract]

Average operating net assets represent, in the opinion of the directors, the best estimate of net asset utilisation by the Business Groups and exclude taxation, dividends, net debt and provisions for liabilities and charges.

4 COMPARISON WITH US AND IASC PRONOUNCEMENTS

4.1 US

4.1.1 Introduction

In 1969 the SEC issued requirements for reporting line-of-business information in registration statements. In 1970, those requirements were extended to annual reports filed with the SEC on Form 10-K and in 1974 they were extended to the annual report to security holders of companies filing with the SEC. The FASB responded with the issue of SFAS 14 – *Financial Reporting for Segments of a Business Enterprise* – which was issued in 1976 and until recently has formed the main basis for segmental reporting in the US.[56] In June 1997, however, the FASB issued SFAS 131 – *Disclosures about Segments of an Enterprise and*

Related Information – and this standard becomes effective for periods beginning after 15 December 1997.

4.1.2 SFAS 14

The requirements of SFAS 14 (as amended) are essentially the same as those of SSAP 25 in that disclosure of turnover, profits and assets analysed by industry and geographical segments is required. The major differences are as follows:

A   Scope

SFAS 14 applies to all enterprises (a) whose debt or equity securities trade in a public market on a foreign or domestic stock exchange or in the OTC market, or (b) which are required to file financial statements with the SEC.[57] SSAP 25 applies to all companies to the extent that its requirements are equivalent to those contained within Schedule 4 to the Companies Act 1985 and, generally, to public companies (whether their securities are publicly traded or not), to banking and insurance companies or groups and to large private companies (and other entities). There is no exemption in SFAS 14 to allow companies not to disclose segmental information on the grounds that disclosure would be prejudicial to their interests.

B   Turnover

As with SSAP 25, SFAS 14 requires sales to third parties and other segments to be separately disclosed in the segmental analysis. However, unlike SSAP 25, SFAS 14 requires the basis of inter-segment pricing to be disclosed. Where the basis is changed, disclosure is required of the nature of the change and its effect on the segments' profit or loss in the period of change. Furthermore, for the purposes of SFAS 14, sales to other segments are required to be accounted for, on the same basis used by the enterprise to price its inter-segment sales or transfers.[58]

C   Profits

SFAS 14 requires the operating profit or loss of each reportable industry segment to be disclosed.[59] This will generally be the same as the results that are required to be analysed by SSAP 25. SFAS 14 also requires that a company's share of profits or losses of associated companies are to be excluded whereas SSAP 25 requires segmental disclosure of the aggregate of the reporting entity's share of the associated undertakings' results and net assets where associated undertakings form a significant part of the reporting entity's results or net assets.

SFAS 14 also requires that where any unusual or infrequently occurring items have been added or deducted in computing operating profit or loss, the nature and amount shall be explained.[60]

D   Assets or net assets?

SSAP 25 requires segmental analysis of net assets, i.e. operating assets less operating liabilities. SFAS 14, on the other hand, requires the aggregate carrying amount of identifiable assets to be presented for each reportable segment.[61] Identifiable assets of an industry segment are defined as those tangible and intangible assets (i.e. without deduction of operating liabilities) used exclusively by that segment and an allocated portion of assets used jointly by that industry segment and one or more other industry segments. Allocations should be made on a reasonable basis.[62]

E   Reportable industry segments

SFAS 14 takes a similar approach to SSAP 25 in leaving the determination of the different industry segments of an enterprise to the management of the reporting entity and requiring that each industry segment which is significant to an entity as a whole should be identified.[63] For this purpose, significance is determined by applying a set of criteria which are very similar to those set out in SSAP 25 for determining whether a class of business or geographical segment is significant (see 2.2.4 above).[64]

Disclosure of the types of products and services supplied by each reportable segment is required.[65]

A further test is applied once the reportable segments are identified, in order to determine 'whether a substantial portion of an enterprise's operations is explained by its segment information'.[66] The total revenue from sales to unaffiliated customers of all *reportable* segments must constitute at least 75% of total revenue from sales to unaffiliated customers of all *industry* segments. If the 75% criterion is not met, additional industry segments must be identified as reportable until the 75% test is met. Though a limit is not set, ten reportable segments is given as an indication of a practical maximum.[67]

In circumstances where an enterprise has one industry segment or a dominant segment (i.e. revenue, operating profit or loss and identifiable assets each constitute more than 90% of the totals for all industry segments), disclosures required for reportable segments do not need to be made except that the industry must be identified.[68]

F   Reportable geographical segments

Again SFAS 14 takes a similar approach to SSAP 25 in leaving the determination of the different geographical segments of an enterprise to the management of the reporting company.

However, information is only required if either of the following conditions is met:

(a)   sales revenue generated by the enterprise's foreign operations is at least 10% of consolidated revenue as reported in the enterprise's income statement; or

(b)   identifiable assets of the enterprise's foreign operations are at least 10% of consolidated total assets as reported in the enterprise's balance sheet.[69]

Foreign operations are defined as those revenue producing operations that:

(a)   are located outside the enterprise's home country; and

(b)   are generating revenue either from sales to unaffiliated customers or from intra-enterprise sales or transfers between geographic areas.[70]

If information is required and the enterprise conducts its foreign operations in two or more geographic areas, then that information is to be presented for each significant foreign geographic area and in aggregate for all foreign geographic areas not deemed significant. A foreign geographic area is deemed to be significant if its sales revenue to unaffiliated customers or its identifiable assets are at least 10% of related consolidated amounts.[71]

Foreign geographic areas are individual countries or group of countries as may be determined to be appropriate in an enterprise's particular circumstances.

G   Export sales

SFAS 14 does not require a geographical analysis of turnover by destination except for export sales to unaffiliated customers made by an enterprise's *domestic* operations. Where the amount of export sales revenue is at least 10% of total sales revenue to unaffiliated customers that amount shall be reported, in aggregate, and by such geographic areas as are considered appropriate in the circumstances.[72]

H   Other related disclosures

SFAS 14 requires disclosure of information which is additional to that required by SSAP 25 as follows:

(a)   for each reportable industry segment, disclosure shall be made of:

    (i)   the aggregate amount of depreciation, depletion and amortisation,

    (ii)   the amount of capital expenditure, and

    (iii)   the enterprise's equity in the net income from and investment in the net assets of the unconsolidated subsidiaries and other equity method investees whose operations are vertically integrated with the operations of that segment;[73]

(b)   if an enterprise's sales to one customer (or a group of entities under common control) are 10% or more of its total revenue, that fact and the amount of revenue from each customer must be disclosed. The identity of the customer does not need to be disclosed but the industry segment making the sales must be disclosed.[74]

4.1.3 SFAS 131

SFAS 131 differs from SFAS 14 by adopting a 'management approach' to defining what segmental information is to be reported. This reflects the way in which the management of the business organises its operating segments for decision-making purposes. The guiding principle is that the manner in which segmental information is presented to the chief executive officer should also determine how it is reported externally; this is thought both to be the most relevant information (since it presents the business as the management itself sees it) and the easiest to produce. However the application of this principle means that the information presented may be less easy to compare with that of other enterprises; it may even be produced using different accounting policies from those used in the accounts as a whole. SFAS 131 requires any such measurement differences to be explained,[75] and also requires segmental information to be reconciled to the totals shown in the consolidated accounts.[76]

A   Scope

Like SFAS 14, SFAS 131 applies to public business enterprises, which are defined as those (a) whose debt or equity securities trade in a public market on a foreign or domestic stock exchange or in the OTC market, or (b) which are required to file financial statements with the SEC.[77]

B   Definition of segments

An operating segment is defined as a component of an enterprise:

(a)   that engages in business activities from which it may earn revenues and incur expenses (including revenues and expenses relating to transactions with other components of the same enterprise),

(b)   whose operating results are regularly reviewed by the enterprise's chief operating decision-maker to make decisions about resources to be allocated to the segment and assess its performance, and

(c)   for which discrete information is available.[78]

Similar segments may be reported in aggregate rather than separately if they are similar in all the following respects:

(a)   the nature of the products and services;

(b)   the nature of the production processes;

(c)   the type or class of customer for their products and services;

(d)   the methods used to distribute their products or provide for their services; and

(e)   if applicable, the nature of the regulatory environment, for example, banking, insurance, or public utilities.[79]

Separate information should be given where a segment contributes 10% or more of the enterprise's revenues, assets, profits or losses.[80] Profits and losses are to be assessed for this purpose by comparing the segment's profit with all other profitable segments or its loss with all other loss-making segments. As with SFAS 14, the separately reported segments must account for at least 75% of the enterprise's revenue – in other words, no more than 25% of the total can be classified as 'other'.[81] Disclosure has to be made of the factors that have been used to identify the segments, and the types of products or services from which they derive their revenues.

C   *Information to be disclosed*

SFAS 131 requires the results and total assets of each segment to be disclosed, but whether more detail is given depends on whether it is reviewed by the chief executive officer. The following profit and loss account items should be disclosed if they meet that test:

■   External sales

■   Inter-segment sales

■   Interest receivable

■   Interest payable

■   Depreciation and amortisation, and other significant non-cash items

■   Unusual items and extraordinary items

■   Share of associates' results

■   Tax.[82]

Similarly, this information has to be given about assets if it is reviewed by the chief executive officer:

■   Investments in associates

■   Capital expenditure

■   Long-term customer relationships of a financial institution

■   Mortgage and other servicing rights

■   Deferred policy acquisition costs

■   Deferred tax assets.[83]

As a minimum, SFAS 131 requires segmental disclosure of external sales by product or service, and also geographical analysis of external sales and fixed assets. If the above 'management approach' has not delivered that disclosure, it has to be given in addition, this time using the same policies and bases as are used in the consolidated accounts.[84]

As with SFAS 14, if sales to one customer (or a group of entities under common control) are 10% or more of the total revenue, that fact and the amount of revenue from each customer must be disclosed. The segment making the sales must be named, but not that of the customer.[85]

4.2   IASC

The international standard on the issue of segmental reporting is IAS 14 – *Segment Reporting*. The original version was published by the IASC in August 1981[86] and reformatted in 1994, but has been revised again in 1997. The latest version becomes effective for periods beginning on or after 1 January 1998. The original IAS 14 was similar to SSAP 25 in that the definition of reportable segments is left to the management of the reporting company and that disclosure of turnover, profits and assets analysed by industry and geographical segments is required, but the revised version contains a little more of the flavour of SFAS 131. The main features of both the old and the new versions, and how they compare with SSAP 25, are set out below:

4.2.1   Scope

IAS 14 now applies to all enterprises whose equity or debt securities are publicly traded (or are about to be). The original version also applied to other 'economically significant entities', including subsidiaries. SSAP 25 applies to all companies to the extent that its requirements are equivalent to those contained within Schedule 4 to the Companies Act 1985 and, generally, to public companies (whether their securities are publicly traded or not), to banking and insurance companies or groups and to large private companies (and other entities). There is no exemption in IAS 14 to allow companies not to disclose segmental information on the grounds that disclosure would be seriously prejudicial to the interests of the company. SSAP 25 acknowledges that, in this respect, compliance with SSAP 25 will not ensure compliance with IAS 14.

4.2.2   Identification of segments

IAS 14 requires information to be reported for both business segments and geographical segments, but one of these is to be regarded as the primary basis and the other as the secondary basis (requiring less information to be disclosed), depending on which is regarded as providing the more meaningful analysis of the predominant source and nature of risks and returns. The segments are to be identified on the basis of the internal organisational structure and reporting systems, because they are presumed to be aligned to the same objectives. However, if the systems place equal emphasis on these two dimensions, the business segmentation is to be regarded as the primary basis for analysis and the geographical segmentation as the secondary one.

In contrast, SSAP 25 gives equal prominence to business and geographical segmental information. More generally, IAS 14's emphasis on the use of internal reporting systems as the key to identification of segments owes more to the US standard than to SSAP 25 (and the original version of IAS 14; however, it may well be that there is no substantial difference in practice, and that the same segments would often be identified under all these standards.

4.2.3   Information to be disclosed

In respect of the primary segmental analysis, IAS 14 requires the following to be disclosed:

■   Segment revenue (both external and intra-segment)

■   Segment result

■   Total segment assets

■   Segment liabilities

■   Capital expenditure

■   Depreciation

■   Other significant non-cash expense

■   Share of results of associates and joint ventures, and aggregate investment in these entities

All these amounts should be reconciled to the totals in the accounts of the reporting enterprise. These go some way beyond the equivalent requirements in the UK; in particular, SSAP 25 does not require disclosure of capital expenditure, depreciation and other non-cash expense, or details about associates, and it does not require segmental net assets to be grossed up to show total assets and liabilities by segment.

For the secondary analysis, the main items to be reported are the segment result, total assets and capital expenditure.

4.2.4   Basis of inter-segment pricing

IAS 14 requires the basis of inter-segment pricing to be disclosed. Although this was proposed by ED 45, it was not carried through to SSAP 25 because it was felt that the quality of compliance with this requirement was likely to be poor and could adversely affect the credibility of the standard as a whole. Again, to this extent, compliance with SSAP 25 will not ensure compliance with IAS 14.

5   CONCLUSION

It is clear that the general standard of segmental reporting in the UK has significantly improved in the years since SSAP 25 was introduced. As shown by some of the extracts reproduced in this chapter, large companies typically now devote a substantial amount of space in their annual reports to the description and analysis of their divisional activities. Provided it is applied constructively and with common sense, the present reporting framework gives companies the opportunity to present a good deal of useful information for the readers of accounts.

The recent revisions of the US and international standards, however, suggest that a revision of SSAP 25 is on the cards. This is not to respond to the 'management approach' relied upon by SFAS 131 and, to some extent, IAS 14; if this rather curious approach of using internal information really had merit, it would be appropriate to extend the principle to all aspects of financial reporting, not just for segmental reporting, which would substantially reduce the need for accounting standards. Rather it is to recognise that the extent of segmentally reported information has expanded substantially and SSAP 25's requirements now look rather flimsy against these international yardsticks.   We might therefore expect to see proposals for a new UK standard on the subject before too long.

References

1   IAS 14, *Reporting Financial Information by Segment*, IASC, August 1981, para. 5.
2   *Ibid.*
3   R. K. Mautz, *Financial Reporting by Diversified Companies*, Financial Executives Research Foundation, 1968, p. 94.
4   CA 67, s 17.
5   *Ibid.*, s 20.
6   CA 81, Sch. 1, para. 55(2).
7   *Ibid.*, para. 55(5).
8   CA 85, Sch. 4, para. 55.
9   By the Companies Act 1985 (Miscellaneous Accounting Amendments) Regulations 1996 (SI96/189).
10   ED 45, *Segmental reporting*, November 1988.
11   SSAP 25, *Segmental reporting*, June 1990.
12   ED 45, para. 37(a).
13   Discussion Paper – *Segmental Reporting*, ASB, May 1996.
14   SSAP 25, para. 1.
15   *Ibid.*, paras. 3 and 40.
16   *Ibid.*, paras. 4 and 41.
17   *Ibid.*, para. 35.
18   *Ibid.*, para. 43.
19   *Ibid.*, paras. 7 and 8.
20   *Ibid.*, para. 8.
21   *Ibid.*, para. 12.

22 *Ibid.*, para. 15.
23 *Ibid.*, para. 16.
24 *Ibid.*, para. 9.
25 SFAS 14, *Financial Reporting for Segments of a Business Enterprise*, FASB, December 1976, para. 15, and SFAS 131, *Disclosure about Segments of a Business and Related Information*, FASB, June 1997, para. 18.
26 SSAP 25, para. 34.
27 *Ibid.*
28 *Ibid.*, para. 34(a).
29 *Ibid.*, para. 34.
30 *Ibid.*, para. 44.
31 See CA 85, Sch. 9, Part I, para. 76.
32 *Segmental Reporting*, British Bankers' Association and Irish Bankers' Federation, January 1993.
33 SSAP 25, para. 34.
34 *Ibid.*, para. 22.
35 *Ibid.*, para. 21.
36 *Ibid.*, para. 24.
37 *Ibid.*, para. 25.
38 *Ibid.*, para. 37.
39 *Ibid.*, paras. 4 and 41.
40 *Ibid.*, para. 36.
41 *Ibid.*
42 *Ibid.*
43 *Ibid.*, para. 23.
44 *Ibid.*
45 SSAP 9 para. 27, which in turn refers to the statutory formats in CA 85, Sch. 4.
46 SFAS 14, para. 91.
47 *Ibid.*, para. 13.
48 *Ibid.*, para. 10.
49 *Ibid.*, para. 39.
50 SSAP 25, para. 23.
51 SSAP 25, para. 22.
52 *Ibid.*, para. 34.
53 FRS 3, *Reporting Financial Performance*, ASB, December 1992, para. 15.
54 SSAP 25, para. 24.
55 *Ibid.*, para. 25.
56 There were also a number of subsequent US standards that amended SFAS 14, namely: SFAS 18, *Financial Reporting for Segments of a Business Enterprise — Interim Financial Statements*; SFAS 21, *Suspension of the Reporting of Earnings per Share and Segment Information by Nonpublic Enterprises*; SFAS 24, *Reporting Segment Information in Financial Statements That Are Presented in Another Enterprise's Financial Report*; and SFAS 30, *Disclosure of Information about Major Customers*.
57 SFAS 21, *Segment Information by Nonpublic Enterprises*, FASB, April 1978, paras. 12 and 13.
58 SFAS 14, para. 23.
59 *Ibid.*, para. 24.
60 *Ibid.*
61 *Ibid.*, para. 26.
62 *Ibid.*, para. 10(e).
63 *Ibid.*, para. 15.
64 *Ibid.*
65 *Ibid.*, para. 22.
66 *Ibid.*, para. 17.
67 *Ibid.*, paras. 17–19.
68 *Ibid.*, para. 20.
69 *Ibid.*, para. 32.
70 *Ibid.*, para. 31.
71 *Ibid.*, para. 33.

72 *Ibid.*, para. 36.
73 *Ibid.*, para. 27.
74 SFAS 30, *Disclosure of Information about Major Customers*, FASB, August 1979, para. 6.
75 SFAS 131, para. 31.
76 *Ibid.*, para. 32.
77 *Ibid.*, para. 9.
78 *Ibid.*, para. 10.
79 *Ibid.*, para. 17.
80 *Ibid.*, para. 18.
81 *Ibid.*, para. 20.
82 *Ibid.*, para. 27.
83 *Ibid.*, para. 28.
84 *Ibid.*, paras. 37 & 38.
85 *Ibid.*, para. 39.
86 IAS 14 (original), *Reporting Financial Information by Segment*, IASC, 1981.

Chapter 20   Pension costs

1 INTRODUCTION

1.1 Background

Accounting for the costs of pensions and similar benefits in the accounts of employer companies presents one of the most difficult challenges in the whole field of financial reporting. The amounts involved are large, the timescale is long, the estimation process is complex and involves many areas of uncertainty which have to be made the subject of assumptions; in addition the actuarial mechanisms used for matching the costs to years of employment are complicated and their selection open to debate.

Before the introduction of SSAP 24, generally accepted practice in the UK had been to charge pension costs in the profit and loss account on the basis of funding payments made to the pension scheme, which obviously meant that the reported profit of the employer company was susceptible to fluctuations because of changes in the contributions made. In addition, most companies gave only very limited information in their accounts about the obligations to pay the pensions to which they were committed, and the assets which had been built up in their pension funds to meet these obligations.

The effect of SSAP 24 has been to look through the veil that lies between the employer company and its pension fund. The measure of pension cost is no longer simply the amount of contributions paid to the fund; instead it is necessary to examine the condition of the fund itself to see what the long-term cost of providing pensions really is. Thus, pension expense is derived directly from actuarial valuations of the scheme, although the standard requires that changes in these valuations are to be recognised only gradually, by amortising them over a number of years, so as to reduce the volatility which would otherwise result.

The philosophy of the standard therefore rests on the premise that the pension fund is in substance a vehicle of the employer company and that any surplus held by the fund should be regarded as a company asset, even if it is not directly shown as such on the company's balance sheet. This follows from the argument that, in a final salary scheme, the employer has to bear whatever cost is needed to provide the pensions promised to the workforce after taking account of their own (fixed) contributions; any excess of assets which emerges in the form of a pension scheme surplus therefore belongs to the employer. However, this stance is not free from controversy. Employees and their representatives frequently assert that a pension fund surplus morally belongs to the members, and the legal position will depend on the precise terms of the scheme and the trust deed under which the fund is administered. Some recent decisions by the Pensions Ombudsman, supported by the courts, have given strength to this view.

Certainly, if a pension scheme surplus is an asset, it is not one which the company can easily get its hands on. Although there are circumstances whereby the company may take refunds from an over-funded scheme, it can only do so under penalty of tax at a rate of 40% and provided certain conditions are satisfied. However, the surplus gives the company the opportunity to reduce its future contributions to the fund below what they would otherwise be, and in these terms it may be appropriate to think of it as an asset; this is probably the main rationale for the approach adopted by the standard.

The meaning and treatment of the balance sheet figure has become the main area of controversy in the application of SSAP 24. The ASB is considering revisions to the standard and, influenced both by its draft *Statement of Principles* and by international developments, is likely to focus much more on the balance sheet than the profit and loss account in any replacement standard. Whether such a change of emphasis is really appropriate, however, given the long-term nature of pension provision, is a matter for debate.

1.2   The development of an accounting standard in the UK

1.2.1   Napier interim report

The first document on the subject to be published by the ASC comprised an assessment of the issues to be addressed, set out in an interim report by Christopher Napier of the London School of Economics in 1982.[1] Napier's interim report was a by-product of a research study commissioned by the Institute of Chartered Accountants in England and Wales in 1981, and his full report was finally published by the Institute in 1983.[2]   This comprises a comprehensive and lucid exposition of the issues involved in accounting for pension costs, and is of particular value in explaining the mechanics of the actuarial valuation process and how they may be adapted to accounting use.

This paper identified certain key characteristics of pension schemes which subsequently formed the foundation of the ASC's thinking on the subject. These were that pensions should be seen simply as a form of deferred remuneration; that the application of the accruals concept would require that their cost should be matched against the benefits of the employees' services over their working lives; and that although the objective of funding the pension scheme was also to provide for the ultimate cost of the pensions, the pattern of funding payments depended on management decisions which were not necessarily a good basis for measuring the annual cost for accounting purposes.

The paper also drew a distinction between 'normal' costs of providing for pensions, and 'abnormal' or 'special' costs. Normal costs were described as those which would arise if (a) no credit was given by the pension scheme for service prior to the scheme's introduction, and (b) the assumptions of the actuary as to mortality, employee turnover, salary progression, investment returns etc. were borne out by subsequent events. Abnormal or special costs were therefore those costs which arose because of variations in the assumptions in (a) and (b) above. This distinction subsequently formed the basis for that used in SSAP 24 between the regular ongoing cost and the effects of variations, which are discussed in 2.5.1 and 2.5.2 below.

Napier also briefly touched on the need for disclosure of information about pension arrangements in company accounts, and listed several possible disclosures for consideration.

1.2.2 ED 32

At the time of publishing Napier's interim report, the ASC was already working on the subject of pension costs, and in 1983 they published the exposure draft of a standard on the subject, ED 32 – *The disclosure of pension information in company accounts*.[3] As the title reveals, the Committee had decided as a first stage to limit its strategy to one of ensuring better disclosure in accounts about the details of company pension schemes, before proceeding towards the more difficult question of measurement in the profit and loss account. The main thrust of the proposals of the exposure draft was contained in a single, lengthy, paragraph, which read as follows:

'Disclosure should be made in financial statements of sufficient information concerning pension arrangements to enable users of the statements to gain a broad understanding of the significance of pension costs in the accounting period and of actual and contingent liabilities and commitments at the balance sheet date. Towards this general objective, the disclosures should include at least the following, subject to any necessary modifications in the case of employees paid abroad and to summarising to a reasonable extent in the case of individual companies or groups with a number of different pension schemes:

(a) the nature of the pension schemes (e.g. defined benefit or defined contribution), whether they are externally funded or internally financed and any legal obligations of the company (e.g. undertakings to meet the balance of cost);

(b) the accounting policy, and the funding policy if different from the accounting policy, indicating the basis used for allocating pension costs to accounting periods;

(c)   whether the pension costs and liabilities are assessed in accordance with the advice of a professionally qualified actuary and, if so, the date of the most recent actuarial valuation;

(d)   the amount charged in the profit and loss account for pension costs, distinguishing between normal charges related to employees' pay and service in the accounting period and other charges or credits (e.g. additional charges to cover the cost of post-retirement awards not covered by the normal charge, or reductions in the normal charge to take account of contribution holidays or a temporarily reduced contribution rate resulting from overfunding), with explanations of such charges or credits;

(e)   any commitments to change the rate of contributions or to make special contributions;

(f)   any provisions or prepayments in the balance sheet, resulting from a difference between the accounting policy and the funding policy;

(g)   the amount of any deficiency on a discontinuance basis actuarial valuation or on the requirements of the Occupational Pensions Board, indicating the action, if any, being taken to deal with it in future financial statements;

(h)   the amount of any material self-investment (i.e. investment by the pension fund in the employer company itself);

(i)   in the case of internally financed schemes, the amount of the provision at the balance sheet date and of any identifiable fund of assets representing the provision; and

(j)   expected significant effects on future financial statements of any changes which have occurred in the above, including the effects of any material improvements in benefits.'[4]

This list picked up a number of the requirements which Napier had suggested, but also introduced a number of new ones. The exposure draft drew attention to the Companies Act requirements to disclose pension costs and commitments (described in 5 below), but said that compliance with the ED would not necessarily ensure compliance with the legal requirements.

1.2.3   Statement of Intent

In 1984, the ASC published a further document on the subject; this time it was a consultative Statement of Intent.[5] This revealed that the Committee had altered its strategy and was now ready to address the measurement of pension costs, rather than merely proposing disclosure requirements about pension arrangements. The broad principles which it outlined were consistent with those recommended by Napier, but were discussed in rather more detail than in Napier's interim report.

1.2.4   ED 39

Having received and considered the reaction to its statement of intent, the ASC proceeded to formulate an exposure draft based on the principles which the statement had outlined, and in May 1986 it published ED 39 – *Accounting for pension costs*.[6] The exposure draft dealt both with the measurement of pension cost for profit and loss account purposes and with fairly extensive disclosure requirements. Its main proposals were as follows:

(a)   pension costs should be recognised on a systematic basis over the expected service lives of employees;

(b)   total pension cost charged in the profit and loss account should be equal to regular cost plus variations arising from experience deficiencies and surpluses, changes in assumptions, etc. This broadly corresponded to the analysis made by Napier of 'normal' and 'abnormal' costs;

(c)   for a defined benefit scheme, the regular pension cost should be a substantially level percentage of pensionable payroll. (For defined contribution schemes, the cost is simply the contribution payable, since that is the extent of the employer's commitment.);

(d)   variations from regular cost should generally be allocated over expected average remaining service lives of employees. The only exceptions would be if prudence dictated that a deficiency should be recognised over a shorter period, or if the variation were linked to an extraordinary item, in which case it would be recognised immediately as part of that item;

(e)   a liability should be provided for if the cumulative pension cost charged against profits has not been completely discharged by contributions or directly paid pensions; and

(f)   various proposals were made on how to account for the pension arrangements of an acquired company.

The exposure draft also proposed a fairly comprehensive list of disclosure requirements.

1.2.5   SSAP 24

In May 1988, the ASC finally issued SSAP 24[7] which was modelled on ED 39. The main amendments which were made from the exposure draft were to incorporate some exceptions to the basic rule that variations from regular cost should be spread over the average future working lives of the employees, to add transitional provisions, to soften the requirement to take account of expected discretionary pension increases, and to modify certain aspects of the disclosure requirements. In addition, the proposals concerned with accounting for the pension costs of an acquired company were deleted, since the subject was instead being addressed by the ASC under its project on accounting for fair values in the context of an acquisition. The standard became effective for periods beginning on or after 1 July 1988.

1.2.6 Subsequent developments

Two further relevant pronouncements have been issued since SSAP 24 came into force. In 1992, the Urgent Issues Task Force issued an Abstract that extended the principles of the standard to health care and other similar post-retirement benefits; this is dealt with in 4.8 below. Later, in 1994, the ASB addressed the question of accounting for the pension arrangements of acquired companies in FRS 7. This necessarily adopted a balance sheet focus, and it introduced a new angle that is absent from SSAP 24: the recoverability of the pension asset in the balance sheet (see Chapter 6 at 2.4.3 D).

More recently the ASB has been considering a wholesale revision of the standard, and in June 1995 it published a Discussion Paper – *Pension Costs in the Employer's Financial Statements*. This set out two possible approaches to accounting for defined benefit schemes. The approach preferred by the majority of the board was to retain SSAP 24's overall philosophy, but to limit some of the options available to preparers when applying the standard and improve the disclosure requirements. However, a minority favoured an alternative approach which required the 'market value' of the scheme to be recognised on the balance sheet each year. This is an estimate of the amount that a hypothetical third party would pay or receive in exchange for taking the future pension obligation away from the reporting entity. However, since the pension ultimately paid will be based on a future, as yet undetermined, salary, such a value is not readily available, and a calculation to approximate to this value was proposed. To limit the annual volatility to the profit and loss account it was also proposed that some movements would be taken to the statement of total recognised gains and losses.

Respondents to this Discussion Paper strongly favoured the majority view and were dismissive of the alternative. Since then, however, the IASC has been developing its own revised standard and its proposals are much more in line with the approach favoured by the minority on the ASB. It therefore remains possible that SSAP 24 will eventually be replaced by a standard that seeks to incorporate an annual valuation of the pension fund in the employer's balance sheet.

2 REQUIREMENTS OF SSAP 24

2.1 Scope

SSAP 24 is very broad in its scope. It applies to all pension arrangements, whether they arise from an explicit contractual commitment, or from custom and practice, or even if they are of an ex gratia nature; it applies to both funded and unfunded schemes; it applies to defined benefit schemes, defined contribution schemes and to those which are a hybrid mixture of the two; it applies to all schemes, whether insured or self-administered; it applies both to UK schemes and to foreign schemes (although when it is difficult to apply it to the latter, there is a hint of de facto relaxation of the requirements in the standard); and it applies to schemes of all sizes. The only specific exclusions from the scope of the standard are in respect of state social security contributions and redundancy payments.

The application of the standard to other post-retirement benefits, such as private health care, was an area of some confusion. The standard itself says that its principles may be applicable to such benefits,[8] but the ASC subsequently indicated that this was not intended to be mandatory.[9] However, in November 1992 the UITF published an Abstract requiring SSAP 24 principles to be applied to all such benefits, although with an extended period for implementation.[10] This is discussed in more detail in 4.8 below.

2.2 Accounting objective

The basic accounting objective which the standard sets is that the employer should recognise the cost of providing pensions on a systematic and rational basis over the period during which he receives benefit from the employees' services.[11] The standard explicitly distinguishes this from the funding objective, which is described as being to build up assets in a prudent and controlled manner in advance of the retirement of the members of the scheme, in order that the obligations of the scheme may be met without undue distortion of the employer's cash flow.[12] It is emphasised that the funding plan will not necessarily provide a satisfactory basis for the allocation of pension cost to accounting periods.

The standard is expressed in terms of the profit and loss account, and no explicit objective is set in relation to the balance sheet. However, it can be demonstrated that the balance sheet will reflect the underlying surplus or deficit in the pension scheme, although this figure will be combined with the amount of variations in pension cost which are being carried forward for recognition in the profit and loss account of future years. The balance sheet dimension of SSAP 24 is explored further in 2.5.4 below.

2.3 Definition of terms

There are several technical terms relating to pensions which have specific meanings laid down by the standard. These are shown below.

Accrued benefits are the benefits for service up to a given point in time, whether the rights to the benefits are vested or not. They may be calculated in relation to current earnings or projected final earnings.

An *accrued benefits method* of actuarial valuation is a valuation method in which the actuarial value of liabilities relates at a given date to:

(a)   the benefits, including future increases promised by the rules, for the current and deferred pensioners and their dependants; and

(b)   the benefits which the members assumed to be in service on the given date will receive for service up to that date only.

Allowance may be made for expected increases in earnings after the given date, and/or for additional pension increases not promised by the rules. The given date may be a current or future date. The further into the future the adopted date lies, the closer the results will be to those of a prospective benefits valuation method (which is defined below).

The *average remaining service life* is a weighted average of the expected future service of the current members of the scheme up to their normal retirement dates or expected dates of earlier withdrawal or death in service. The weightings can have regard to periods of service, salary levels of scheme members and future anticipated salary growth in a manner which the actuary considers appropriate having regard to the actuarial method and assumptions used.

A *current funding level valuation* considers whether the assets would have been sufficient at the valuation date to cover liabilities arising in respect of pensions in payment, preserved benefits for members whose pensionable service has ceased and accrued benefits for members in pensionable service, based on pensionable service to and pensionable earnings at, the date of valuation including revaluation on the statutory basis or such higher basis as has been promised. (This is sometimes called a 'discontinuance' basis, because it evaluates the scheme's ability to meet its obligations if it were to be discontinued.)

A *discretionary or ex gratia increase* in a pension or an *ex gratia pension* is one which the employer has no legal, contractual or implied commitment to provide.

A *defined benefit scheme* is a pension scheme in which the rules specify the benefits to be paid and the scheme is financed accordingly. (These are commonly referred to as 'final salary' schemes. This means that the employer promises to pay the member a pension which is related to (usually) his final salary at or near the date of retirement; a typical example might give the employee a pension which was calculated at one sixtieth of his final salary for each year in which he was an employee and a member of the scheme. Because various factors, notably the amount of the final salary, will not be known until many years have elapsed, the eventual cost of providing the pension will have to be estimated.)

A *defined contribution scheme* is a pension scheme in which the benefits are directly determined by the value of contributions paid in respect of each member. Normally the rate of contribution is specified in the rules of the scheme. (These are commonly referred to as 'money purchase' schemes. In contrast to defined benefit (final salary) schemes, the employer has no obligation to provide a pension beyond that which is earned by the contributions which are payable under the scheme, so the cost of providing the pension is fixed and known from the outset.)

An *experience surplus or deficiency* is that part of the excess or deficiency of the actuarial value of assets over the actuarial value of liabilities, on the basis of the valuation method used, which arises because events have not coincided with the actuarial assumptions made for the last valuation.

A *funding plan* is the timing of payments in an orderly fashion to meet the future cost of a given set of benefits.

A *funded scheme* is a pension scheme where the future liabilities for benefits are provided for by the accumulation of assets held externally to the employing company's business.

The *level of funding* is the proportion at a given date of the actuarial value of liabilities for pensioners' and deferred pensioners' benefits and for members' accrued benefits that is covered by the actuarial value of assets. For this purpose, the actuarial value of future contributions is excluded from the value of assets.

An *ongoing actuarial valuation* is a valuation in which it is assumed that the pension scheme will continue in existence and (where appropriate) that new members will be admitted. The liabilities allow for expected increases in earnings.

Past service is used in SSAP 24 to denote service before a given date. It is often used, however, to denote service before entry into the pension scheme.

Pensionable payroll/earnings are the earnings on which benefits and/or contributions are calculated. One or more elements of earnings (e.g. overtime) may be excluded, and/or there may be a reduction to take account of all or part of the state scheme benefits which the member is deemed to receive.

A *pension scheme* is an arrangement (other than accident insurance) to provide pension and/or other benefits for members on leaving service or retiring and, after a member's death, for his/her dependants.

A *prospective benefits method* of valuation is a valuation method in which the actuarial value of liabilities relates to:

(a) the benefits for current and deferred pensioners and their dependants, allowing where appropriate for future pension increases; and

(b) the benefits which active members will receive in respect of both past and future service, allowing for future increases in earnings up to their assumed exit dates, and where appropriate for pension increases thereafter.

Regular cost is the consistent ongoing cost recognised under the actuarial method used.

2.4 Defined contribution schemes

2.4.1 *Accounting*

Accounting for defined contribution ('money purchase') schemes remains straightforward under SSAP 24. Since the employer has no obligation beyond payment of the contributions which he has agreed to make, there is no difficulty in measuring the cost of providing pensions; it is simply the amount of those contributions payable in respect of the accounting period.[13] If the amount actually paid in the period is more or less than the amount payable, a prepayment or accrual will appear in the balance sheet in accordance with normal accounting practice, but otherwise the payments made will simply be charged in the profit and loss account when made.

2.4.2 *Disclosure*

A Requirements

The disclosure requirements of the standard for defined contribution schemes are also very simple, and add little to the requirements of SSAP 2 and the Companies Act. They are:

(a) the nature of the scheme (i.e. the fact that it is a defined contribution scheme);

(b) the accounting policy (arguably required already by SSAP 2);

(c) the pension cost charge for the period (already required by the Companies Act – see 5.2 below);

(d) any outstanding or prepaid contributions at the balance sheet date.[14]

All these details could be given in a single note, but it is more common to deal with the different elements of the disclosure in different places. The policy and the nature of the scheme can be dealt with together as part of the statement of accounting policies, the expense for the year will be included in the statutory staff costs note, and any prepayment or accrual can readily be shown on the balance sheet or in a note analysing the relevant balance sheet figure. An example of a company which operates a defined contribution scheme is Microvitec, and it gives all the information in a single note, as shown below:

Extract 20.1: Microvitec PLC (1996)

25 PENSIONS

During the year the group continued to operate money purchase pension schemes with defined contribution levels covering the majority of its employees, including directors. Contributions to the schemes are independently administered by insurance companies.

The pension cost charge represents contributions payable by the group to the schemes and amounted to £397,000 (1995: £359,000). Contributions of £Nil (1995: £17,000) were payable to the schemes at the year end.

2.5 Defined benefit schemes

The accounting requirements for defined benefit ('final salary') schemes are very much more complicated. In this case the employer's commitment is open-ended, and in order to achieve the accounting objective mentioned at 2.2 above it is necessary to apply actuarial valuation techniques and use a large number of assumptions. The standard seeks to achieve this by drawing a distinction between regular (ongoing) pension cost and variations from that cost. The essence of the standard's measurement rules is that the basic charge for pension cost in the profit and loss account should be the regular cost, but with adjustments for the effects of the variations from that cost which arise from time to time. In addition, there is a third element of pension cost to be recognised, although regrettably SSAP 24 does not make this sufficiently clear. This is interest on the balance sheet figure,[15] and is discussed in more detail in 4.1 below.

2.5.1 Regular pension cost

As can be seen from the list of definitions in 2.3 above, regular cost is the consistent ongoing cost recognised under the actuarial method used. The standard goes on to say that 'where a stable contribution rate for regular contributions, expressed as a percentage of pensionable earnings, has been determined, that rate will provide an acceptable basis for calculating the regular cost under the stated accounting objective so long as it makes full provision for the expected benefits over the anticipated service lives of employees'.[16] The actuary will be able to inform the company of the amount of the total cost which is to be regarded as the regular cost component.

Essentially, the regular cost is that amount which the actuary would regard as a sufficient contribution to the scheme to provide the eventual pensions to be paid in respect of future service, provided present actuarial assumptions about the future were borne out in practice and there were no future changes to the terms of the scheme. Even then, this amount will depend on the particular method which the actuary is using to attribute cost to individual years. (The standard does not stipulate that a particular actuarial method be used, provided that it meets the accounting objective of recognising the cost of pensions on a systematic and rational basis over the employees' working lives. However, the

ASB's Discussion Paper proposes that a future standard will require the use of the projected unit method.[17])

2.5.2 Variations from regular cost

A Examples of variations

The standard identifies four categories of variations from regular cost.[18] The first two are to do with the actuarial process and the methods and assumptions which it entails, while the second two are to do with changes in the scope or the terms of the scheme itself. The four categories are:

(a) experience surpluses or deficiencies. These are surpluses or deficiencies which are identified in the course of an actuarial valuation of the scheme which have arisen because the assumptions which were made at the time of the previous valuation have not been fully borne out by subsequent experience. For example, an assumption will have been made as to the rate of return to be earned on the scheme's investments. If this rate was in fact exceeded in practice, this will give rise to a surplus at the time of the next valuation, and this will be an experience surplus as the term is used in the standard. Similar variations may arise in relation to all the other main assumptions, such as those relating to salary inflation, the pattern of people joining and leaving the scheme, and so on;

(b) the effects on the actuarial value of accrued benefits of changes in assumptions or method. Insofar as they relate to assumptions, these are similar to the previous category, except that they relate to the period beyond the date of the present valuation, rather than to the period since the previous valuation. Thus, a change in the assumption to increase the rate of predicted salary inflation in a final salary scheme would have the effect of increasing the total pension cost to be recognised and give rise to a variation. A change in actuarial method will have similar effects, in that it will give rise to a different present valuation of the scheme because of the particular way of attributing cost to particular years of service.

The wording of the standard is perhaps deficient in referring only to the effects on the value of the accrued *benefits*, which might be regarded, by implication, as excluding effects on the valuation of assets available to meet these benefits. We do not believe that any such distinction was intended, and we believe that the proper way to apply the standard is to regard changes affecting any part of the actuarial valuation of the scheme as variations and account for them as such;

(c) retroactive changes in benefits or in conditions for membership. These might arise, for example, when the scope of a scheme is changed to include a class of employee which was previously excluded, and some credit is given for their past service with the company; alternatively, it might be an enhancement of the rights of existing members, say to give them an improvement in the terms of the formula under which their eventual pension will be calculated. These will generally entail an increase in the overall cost of pensions to the employer, and the past service element will give rise to a variation from regular cost; and

(d)   increases to pensions in payment or to deferred pensions for which provision has not previously been made. The standard takes the position that all such increases, including those of a discretionary or an ex gratia nature, should preferably be embraced within the scope of the actuarial assumptions. Where this has been the position, but the actual increases granted are not in line with those previously assumed, the difference will give rise to a variation. However, where the increases are of a discretionary or ex gratia nature and no allowance has previously been made for them in the actuarial assumptions, then they fall outside the scope of the valuation of the scheme; they are not treated as variations under the standard but are dealt with separately (see 2.5.3 below).

B   Normally allocated over the remaining service lives of current employees

The basic rule set by the standard for all such variations from regular cost is that they should not be recognised immediately, but rather spread forward over the expected remaining service lives of employees in the scheme. There are, however, a number of exceptions to this basic rule, some of which in our view detract from the conceptual cohesion of the standard. These are discussed at C to F below.

The rationale for this basic rule merits some discussion. First of all it has to be looked at in the context of the standard's overall approach, which is directed towards achieving a steady charge in the profit and loss account rather than valuing the fund in the balance sheet. If actuarial surpluses and deficiencies were included directly in the balance sheet as soon as they were recognised, there would be enormous volatility in the amounts reported and, assuming the differences between the balance sheet figures were charged or credited directly in the profit and loss account, there could be a very significant effect on earnings in the years of actuarial valuation. The standard has instead opted for a smoothing approach, so that these effects are recognised in the profit and loss account gradually rather than immediately following a valuation.

Insofar as these variations arise from changes to do with the actuarial process (categories (a) and (b) above), this treatment can be justified because of the high degree of uncertainty and subjectivity inherent in actuarial valuations; it would be wholly inappropriate to give immediate recognition to such changes, which are of a very long-term nature and may easily be reversed at the time of the next valuation. However, at first sight it may seem more justifiable to give immediate recognition to the other broad class of variations – those reflecting changes in the scheme itself, described above under headings (c) and (d).

Broadly, the reason for not doing so is that such changes, even if they are expressed in terms which give credit for periods relating to the past, are made with a view to providing benefits for the future, not to meet any latent obligation which already exists. An improvement to the pension terms of an employee is only one of a range of possible improvements to his remuneration package; it may be decided on, for example, as an alternative to (or in conjunction with) a future salary increase. Accordingly, it is thought appropriate to spread such increases forward over the employee's working life.

In its 1995 Discussion Paper, the ASB recommended that experience differences should continue to be spread over the working lives of employees. However, improvements in benefits for former employees should be written off immediately, on the basis that they would render no further service and thus there was no future benefit to be matched with the cost.[19]

SSAP 24 does not specify exactly how variations are to be amortised, and there are various possible ways of doing so. This is discussed in more detail at 4.2.2. Although factors such as interest and salary inflation should be built into the amortisation pattern in practice, these have been excluded from some of the worked examples shown in the remainder of this chapter for the purposes of simplicity. These examples also use an average period to represent the working lives of members in the scheme.

SSAP 24 does not provide any worked examples of the spreading treatment, but the forerunner of the standard, ED 39, contained two such examples, the second of which[20] is reproduced below to illustrate the mechanics of the accounting process:

Example 20.1:   Spreading variations from regular cost

The actuarial valuation at 31 December 19X0 of the pension scheme of company B showed a surplus of £260m. The actuary recommended that B eliminate the surplus by taking a contribution holiday in 19X1 and 19X2 and then paying contributions of £30m p.a. for 8 years. After that the standard contribution would be £50m p.a. The average remaining service life of employees in the scheme at 31 December 19X0 was 10 years. B's year end is 31 December.

Assuming no change in circumstances, the annual charge in the profit and loss account for the years 19X1 to 19Y0 will be:

$$\text{Regular cost} - \frac{\text{surplus}}{\text{average remaining service life}} = £50\text{m} - \frac{£260\text{m}}{10} = £24\text{m}$$

The funding in these periods will be:

19X1–X2	Nil
19X3–Y0	£30m p.a.

The difference between the amounts funded and the amounts charged in the profit and loss account will be recognised as a provision, as follows:

Year	Funded £m	Charged £m	(Provision) £m
19X1	–	24	(24)
19X2	–	24	(48)
19X3	30	24	(42)
19X4	30	24	(36)
19X5	30	24	(30)
19X6	30	24	(24)
19X7	30	24	(18)
19X8	30	24	(12)
19X9	30	24	(6)
19Y0	30	24	–

The effect can be shown in graphical form, as follows:

Spreading variations from regular cost

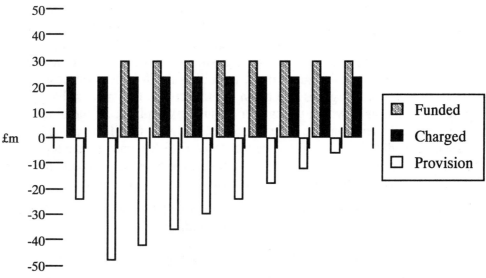

19X1 19X2 19X3 19X4 19X5 19X6 19X7 19X8 19X9 19Y0

The example notes that in practice further actuarial valuations will occur, usually triennially, during the 10 year amortisation period and that these may reveal a surplus or deficiency which will require an adjustment to the charge and prepayment/provision in succeeding periods. However, it does not specify how this might be calculated. This point is considered below at 4.2.5.

C   *Reductions in employees relating to the sale or termination of an operation*

The original version of the standard said that where the variation was associated with an event which gave rise to an extraordinary item, such as the closure of a business segment, the spreading rule was overridden by the requirements of SSAP 6.[21] When FRS 3 replaced SSAP 6, extraordinary items were defined almost out of existence, and consequential amendments were made to SSAP 24. As a result, the relevant paragraph of SSAP 24 now says that where a 'significant reduction in the number of employees is related to the sale or termination of an operation, the associated pension cost or credit should be recognised immediately to the extent necessary to comply with paragraph 18 of FRS 3'.[22] It is explained that 'this is because FRS 3 requires provisions consequent on the sale or termination of an operation to be made after taking account of future profits of the operation or the disposal of its assets'.[23]

The drafting of these paragraphs is unfortunate. They link the rule to paragraph 18 of FRS 3, which deals with provisions made in anticipation of a sale or termination rather than with the sale or termination itself. The literal result is that any pension credit arising on the sale or termination should be recognised immediately only to the extent that it offsets a provision for other aspects of the sale or termination, and that any excess credit therefore falls instead into exception D, as discussed below. However, we doubt if this was intended and we do not think it produces a sensible result. We believe that a company which closes or sells a segment of its business should account for all the financial effects of that event at the same time, including the full pension cost or credit that results. Where this gives rise to an overall credit, this means that it will be reported in the year in which the sale or closure takes place; on the other hand, if it is a net debit there may be circumstances in which it will be provided for in advance, provided the rules of paragraph 18 of FRS 3 regarding such provisions are satisfied. In neither case, however, does it make sense to dislocate any part of the pension effect from the other consequences of the sale or closure.

The operation of this exception can be illustrated by the following example, which is based on the figures used in Example 20.1:

Example 20.2:   Variations arising from the sale or closure of an operation

The actuary advises that £50m out of the £260m surplus is attributable to the redundancy programme associated with the closure of a business segment in 19X1. The accounting treatment in this instance will be to deal with this variation from regular cost immediately, as a credit to the cost of the closure, and to deal with the remaining £210m by amortising it over the working lives of the employees in the scheme.

The effect of this amortisation on the amount charged will be as follows:

$$\text{Regular cost} - \frac{\text{surplus}}{\text{average remaining service life}} = £50m - \frac{£210m}{10} = £29m$$

The effect on the accounts will therefore be:

Year		Funded £m	Charged (Credited) £m	Prepayment (Provision) £m
19X1	ordinary charge	–	29	
	exceptional credit		(50)	
			(21)	21
19X2		–	29	(8)
19X3		30	29	(7)
19X4		30	29	(6)
19X5		30	29	(5)
19X6		30	29	(4)
19X7		30	29	(3)
19X8		30	29	(2)
19X9		30	29	(1)
19Y0		30	29	–

D   Other significant reductions in the number of employees

The next exception from the general 'spreading' rule occurs where there is a significant change in the normal level of contributions in order to eliminate a surplus or a deficiency which results from a significant reduction in the number of employees in the scheme that does not arise from the sale or termination of an operation. The standard says that where these circumstances apply, the effect of the variation in cost should not be spread over the average working lives of the remaining employees, but rather recognised when the reduction in contributions occurs.[24] An example of this rule being invoked is to be found in the following extract from the 1991 accounts of ECC Group:

Extract 20.2: ECC Group plc (1991)

3 EXCEPTIONAL ITEMS

In the fifteen months to 31st December 1990, the programme of reorganisation and cost reduction resulted in a provision of £32.0M being made which was shown as an exceptional item. As a result of this restructuring the Actuary has advised that at least £5M of the surplus within the Group's UK pension schemes is attributable to the reduction in manpower. Accordingly, the Group has reduced its contributions by £2.2M in 1991 (also shown as an exceptional item) and will take credit for a similar amount in 1992.

The rationale for this exception is probably that it makes little sense to spread this effect over the working lives of those who remain, when it arises from those who have left. An illustration of the effect of the exception is set out below, again using the same figures as for Example 20.1 above:

Example 20.3: Variations arising from a significant reduction in employees

The actuary advises that £50m out of the £260m surplus is attributable to a major redundancy programme occurring since the date of the last valuation. Accordingly the accounting treatment will be to deal with this variation from regular cost in line with the adjustments made to the funding programme, and deal with the remaining £210m by amortising it over the working lives of the employees in the scheme.

The effect of this amortisation on the amount charged will again be as follows:

$$\text{Regular cost} - \frac{\text{surplus}}{\text{average remaining service life}} = £50m - \frac{£210m}{10} = £29m$$

However it is still necessary to decide when to recognise the effect of the £50m which is attributable to the reduction of employees, because in reality the contributions have been adjusted to eliminate the whole of the £260m surplus, not just the £50m. If the whole of the contribution holiday in the first year were designated as intended to deal with this part of the surplus, the effect would be as follows:

Year	Funded £m	Charged (Credited) £m	Prepayment (Provision) £m
19X1	–	(21)	21
19X2	–	29	(8)
19X3	30	29	(7)
19X4	30	29	(6)
19X5	30	29	(5)
19X6	30	29	(4)
19X7	30	29	(3)
19X8	30	29	(2)
19X9	30	29	(1)
19Y0	30	29	–

The credit in 19X1 is calculated in the same way as in Example 20.2, although the whole effect is shown as part of the ordinary pension cost in this case. In fact, the result is the same as in that example only because the contribution holiday in 19X1 is large enough to deal with the whole amount of the surplus arising from withdrawals.

Clearly, this produces a rather extreme and, some may say, unfair result. It would be possible to arrive at different results by attributing the changes in the contribution rates to their underlying reasons in a different way. For example if the allocation were made in proportion to the changes in the contribution rate, the effect would be as follows:

Year	Funded £m	Charged £m	(Provision) £m
19X1	–	19.2	(19.2)
19X2	–	19.2	(38.4)
19X3	30	25.2	(33.6)
19X4	30	25.2	(28.8)
19X5	30	25.2	(24.0)
19X6	30	25.2	(19.2)
19X7	30	25.2	(14.4)
19X8	30	25.2	(9.6)
19X9	30	25.2	(4.8)
19Y0	30	25.2	–

(The effect on the funding rate has been to reduce it by £50m in each of the first two years and by £20m in the remaining eight. Accordingly, the total surplus of £50m attributable to the redundancy programme has been apportioned over that period in the same way, to reduce the £29m charge (calculated as shown above) by £9.8m in the first two years and by £3.8m in the remaining eight years.)

This appears to produce a more sensible and consistent charge, and may be regarded as preferable for that reason. Nevertheless either allocation, or indeed any other reasoned allocation, would appear to be acceptable under the terms of the standard. After the first year, the difference between the two approaches is not very significant in terms of the profit and loss account, but the effect on the balance sheet remains quite different for some time.

Overall, we do not believe that this exception to the general spreading rule stands up very well to closer examination. The standard requires that recognition be given to the effects of significant reductions in the number of employees in line with the consequential change in contributions, which is an uneasy compromise between the basic spreading rule described at B above and the immediate recognition required in the circumstances of C. Moreover, this leaves the timing of recognition to the whim of management, who may take it in the form of a contribution holiday, by a longer term reduction of the contribution rate, or they may even decide to make no change in the contribution rate at all. As illustrated above, even when they have amended the contribution rate they will still have to decide how to allocate the change in rate against the various factors which have given rise to it. As a result, we do not believe that this exception improves comparability and consistency in financial reporting.

In any event, the general thrust of the standard is to treat variations of all kinds in the same manner, and to look at the workforce as a whole, rather than to focus attention on particular groups of employees. We therefore think it odd to make an exception for these particular circumstances.

E   *Refunds subject to tax may be taken in the period the refund occurs*

Another exception to the normal spreading rule which is allowed by the standard is where the company receives a refund from the scheme, subject to the deduction of tax. This is governed by rules in tax legislation,[25] which are designed to prevent companies from making excessive funding payments (which are tax-deductible) to their pension schemes and, if necessary (and if permitted by the trust deed), to remedy the situation by obtaining a refund from the scheme after deduction of tax at a rate of 40%.

The standard provides that, where such refunds are taken, the company is allowed (but not required) to credit the refund to income in the year of receipt, rather than spreading the effects of the variations which have given rise to the surplus forward.[26] In other words, it allows a cash basis to be used for this transaction if desired. It is very difficult to see any conceptual merit in this exception to the basic spreading rule. The only concession to comparability made by the standard is to require full disclosure of the treatment where a refund is taken.

As is discussed at 2.5.4 below, it can be shown that the surplus or deficit in the fund is represented in the balance sheet figure, although it will usually be combined with an amount which represents deferred variations which are being released to the profit and loss account. For this reason, it seems clear that the appropriate accounting treatment should be to credit the amount of any refund to the balance sheet figure and not to the profit and loss account, otherwise a double counting effect could result. This is most obvious in the case of a company which had a surplus in its scheme at the time of first implementing SSAP 24 and chose to incorporate the surplus in its balance sheet as a pension prepayment; if it subsequently took a refund from the scheme and accounted for it in the profit and loss account, the asset would remain intact in the balance sheet even though it had been converted into cash to the extent of the refund. But arguably the same is true even if the company did not incorporate the surplus in its balance sheet on transition, because as demonstrated in 2.5.4, the surplus is still indirectly represented in the balance sheet figure and this is where the credit should go; at the very least, if the refund is taken to the profit and loss account, the subsequent release of variations to the profit and loss account must be reduced by an equivalent amount.

We regret that the option to credit refunds direct to the profit and loss account is available, because we believe that there is no logical case for it within the framework of SSAP 24. We hope that it will be removed when the standard is revised, and are glad that the ASB has indicated its intention to do so.[27]

RTZ-CRA provides an example of a group which has received a refund from its pension scheme but has deducted it from the balance sheet figure rather than crediting it to the profit and loss account:

Extract 20.3: The RTZ Corporation PLC – CRA Limited (1996)

33 POST RETIREMENT BENEFITS [extract]

Due to the high level of cover, the Trustees of the UK schemes and the Company agreed to combine the schemes into one fund, improve the benefits and refund to the Company the excess surplus as defined by the Inland Revenue. The refund occurred in September 1996. The payment to the Company, net of tax, was £59 million.

12 ACCOUNTS RECEIVABLE AND PREPAYMENTS [extract]

1996 A$m	1995 A$m	1996 £m	1995 £m		1996 US$m	1995 US$m
667	716	**310**	343	Pension prepayments*	**530**	533

* A refund of US$92 million of the surplus in the UK pension fund was received during the year and deducted from the pension prepayment

F   *In certain circumstances material deficits may be recognised over a shorter period*

The standard provides that, in very limited circumstances, prudence may require that recognition should be given to the costs of making good a material deficit over a period shorter than the normal amortisation period. This exception applies only where significant additional contributions have been required, and where the deficiency has been occasioned by a major event or transaction which has not been allowed for in the actuarial assumptions and is outside their normal scope.[28] An example which is quoted in the standard is that of a major mismanagement of the scheme's assets (presumably resulting in their loss for reasons other than the normal risks of investment). Although this may be a justifiable exception in certain cases, it is expected to be only very rarely applicable; however, it was applied by Mirror Group Newspapers in 1991 following the misappropriation of a large part of its pension fund.

G   *Transitional provisions*

The standard offered a choice between two methods of implementation in the year of adoption. Companies could look upon the actuarial surplus or deficiency in the scheme as equivalent to an experience surplus or deficiency which gave rise to a variation from regular pension cost, and accordingly spread it forward over the working lives of the members in the scheme. Alternatively, they could incorporate the surplus or deficiency in the balance sheet by means of a prior year adjustment, as a pension prepayment or accrual, which meant that the pension charge until the next valuation of the scheme would be solely the regular cost.[29] Where the company had a surplus in its fund, it could therefore apply it either to subsidise its future earnings, by reducing the future pension costs to be charged, or to increase its assets and reserves immediately.

In practice, the great majority of companies chose the first of these options, and indeed none of the top 100 UK companies followed the prior year adjustment route.[30]

2.5.3 *Discretionary and ex gratia pension increases and ex gratia pensions*

As mentioned in 2.5.2 A (d) above, the standard suggests that allowance should be made in the actuarial assumptions for pension increases of all kinds, even where these are not the result of any contractual obligation. Where this applies, any increases in pensions which are different from those previously assumed will be dealt with as giving rise to variations, to be treated as discussed in the previous section.

However, where no allowance has been made for such increases, different rules apply. The standard requires that the full capitalised value of these is provided for in the year in which they are made, except to the extent that they are covered by an existing surplus. This would appear to mean that if there is a surplus in the scheme at the time the increases are granted then the cost can, in effect, be spread forward (as a reduction of a variation which would otherwise have reduced future pension cost), but if there is no such surplus, or an insufficient surplus, then the cost must be charged against current profits.

It is not clear whether this applies only where it is possible in fact to use the surplus in the fund to meet this expense. This may be impossible if the provisions of the scheme do not permit the trustees to apply the funds for this purpose. It is arguable that even then the treatment may still be justifiable because the unrecognised gain in the fund provides sufficient reason to justify non-recognition of the unfunded liability for the discretionary or ex gratia award. However, we believe that the standard intended the narrower interpretation, that the offset can be applied only when the surplus in the scheme is in fact applied to meet the cost of the new award. Furthermore, we assume that the treatment is only available to the extent that the surplus has not already been recognised in the balance sheet; in other words the offset is permitted only against an *unrecognised* surplus, and even then it will be necessary to reduce the future variations being released to the profit and loss account by an equivalent amount.

The accounting policy of Wolseley makes specific reference to ex gratia payments:

Extract 20.4: Wolseley plc (1996)

Accounting policies
Pensions [extract]
... The cost of ex gratia pensions is provided in full in the year in which they are awarded.

2.5.4 Balance sheet

As explained earlier, the standard is expressed mainly in terms of the profit and loss account, and the asset or liability which appears in the balance sheet is literally the balancing figure. It is the cumulative difference between the amount which has been charged in the profit and loss account and the amount which has been paid in the form of contributions, and under SSAP 24 it is to be shown as a prepayment or an accrual, representing the extent to which contributions have been paid either ahead of or behind the recognition of cost. Since companies will generally continue to have contributions allowed for tax when they are paid, this figure will also represent the cumulative timing difference which has to be taken into account for the purposes of deferred tax.

It might be thought that this balance has no definable meaning, particularly as there are circumstances where it appears to 'go the wrong way'. For example, as is shown above in Example 20.1, a company which takes a contribution holiday because there is an underlying surplus in the fund may end up showing a liability in its accounts, which may seem incongruous. However, in reality the balance can be explained as being the combination of two figures; the most recently reported actuarial surplus or deficiency in the fund (as adjusted for subsequent contributions and regular costs), combined with the cumulative amount of unamortised variations awaiting recognition in the profit and loss account. This can be illustrated by reference to the figures shown in that example. The analysis of the balance is shown in this chart, and explained below:

Analysis of balance sheet figure

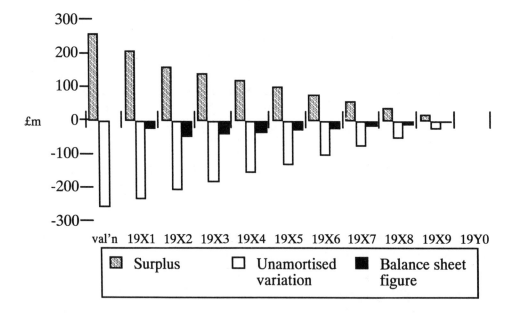

Example 20.4:   *Explanation of balance sheet figure*

	Fund			Financial statements	
	1	2	3	4	5
Year	Contribution £m	Regular cost £m	Surplus £m	Unamortised variation £m	Balance £m
Actuarial surplus/ variation			260	(260)	–
19X1	–	50	210	(234)	(24)
19X2	–	50	160	(208)	(48)
19X3	30	50	140	(182)	(42)
19X4	30	50	120	(156)	(36)
19X5	30	50	100	(130)	(30)
19X6	30	50	80	(104)	(24)
19X7	30	50	60	(78)	(18)
19X8	30	50	40	(52)	(12)
19X9	30	50	20	(26)	(6)
19Y0	30	50	–	–	–

Columns 1 to 3 show the theoretical movements in the fund after the valuation resulting from the effects of contributions and regular costs; for the sake of simplicity the effects of interest and the time value of money have been ignored. Column 4 is the amount of the unrecognised variation, being the variation identified in the 19X0 valuation, successively reduced by annual amortisation of £26m p.a. to reduce the pension cost charged in the profit and loss account. Column 5 is the net of columns 3 and 4 and is the amount shown as a provision in the balance sheet. Although it may seem odd that a liability is shown when an underlying surplus exists, it simply reflects the fact that the effects of the surplus have been recognised more quickly in cash terms (by the contribution holiday) than for accounting purposes.

When the prepayment or accrual is explained in this way, it can be seen that the standard is more balance sheet orientated than is often recognised. In effect, it is possible to regard SSAP 24 as requiring companies to adopt a half-hearted form of equity accounting for their pension funds, particularly if they adopted the 'prior year adjustment' method of implementing the standard and recognise interest on the surplus (as discussed at 4.1 below). The treatment is 'half-hearted' in the sense that the effect of variations is recognised gradually rather than immediately, and because there is no requirement to undertake an annual actuarial valuation of the pension fund to be reflected in the accounts.

This perception of the standard has a bearing on a number of other questions of interpretation which arise, such as the treatment of interest and its relationship with the amortisation of variations, and whether it is legitimate to recognise a negative pension cost (where regular cost is outweighed by variations or interest credited to the profit and loss account). These matters are discussed at 4.1 and 4.3 below.

As mentioned above, the standard requires any excess of contributions paid over the amount of cumulative pension cost charged to be shown as a prepayment (or provision if it is a shortfall) in the balance sheet. When the balance is described in these terms, its classification as a current asset or liability seems entirely reasonable; however, when its underlying nature is examined under the analysis set out above, it can be seen that it is really a composite figure made up of two long-term items: the surplus in the fund and the amount of unamortised variations. The first of these is itself a net figure, being the excess of the investments held by the pension scheme over its obligations to pay pensions (both long-term items), while the second is a deferred credit awaiting transfer to the profit and loss account over a number of years.

To include this composite figure as a prepayment has a major effect on some conventional balance sheet ratios. Initially, the position was accentuated for the minority of companies who originally chose to implement the standard by incorporating the surplus in the balance sheet, rather than by spreading it forward to reduce pension cost over the service lives of the members, because in these circumstances there would have been no offsetting deferred credit to reduce the composite figure to manageable proportions. But even companies who did not do so have often found that a material figure can quickly build up, since the balance sheet figure will always tend towards the amount of the surplus or deficit in the scheme as the deferred element is gradually released (although, of course, new valuations will create further variations to be deferred and released in this way). As shown in this extract, the prepayment in British Petroleum's accounts at the end of 1996 stood at £930 million:

Extract 20.5: The British Petroleum Company p.l.c. (1996)

18 Debtors

	1996 Within 1 year	1996 After 1 year	Group 1995 Within 1 year	1995 After 1 year
Trade	4,948	–	4,209	–
Associated undertakings	68	2	54	2
Prepayments and accrued income	483	90	382	90
Taxation recoverable	33	191	70	299
Pension prepayment	–	930	–	830
Other	744	101	521	77
	6,276	1,314	5,236	1,298

There is no easy solution to this problem. One approach would be to 'explode' the balance into its underlying components, so as to show the surplus within fixed asset investments and the unamortised variations within deferred income (preferably outside the current liabilities total). Alternatively, the prepayment classification could be maintained, but backed up by a note which 'explodes' it in the same way. In effect, this would provide a reconciliation between the balance sheet figure and the funded status of the scheme, which is a requirement of SFAS 87, the equivalent standard in the USA, and has been proposed in the ASB's Discussion Paper.[31] Whatever approach is adopted, however, it would appear to be incumbent on the directors to provide a sufficient explanation of the balance to avoid giving a misleading impression of the liquidity of the company. As shown above, British Petroleum has correctly identified it as an amount not receivable within one year and many other companies do the same.

W H Smith has shown it after a subtotal of other current assets in its balance sheet (but still within net current assets) which involves using the alternative position for prepayments specified in the balance sheet formats in the Companies Act:

Extract 20.6: W H Smith Group PLC (1996)

BALANCE SHEET [extract]

	Note	Group 1996 £m	Group 1995 £m
Current assets			
Stocks		273.5	333.8
Debtors		163.0	130.7
Cash at bank and in hand		74.1	70.3
		510.6	534.8
Pension prepayment	24	72.6	69.3
Creditors – amounts falling due within one year		(457.5)	(494.2)
Net current assets		125.7	109.9

24 Pensions [extract]

	£m
Pension prepayment	
Group	
At 4 June 1995	69.3
Cash contributions to pension funds	–
Regular cost	(20.3)
Variation from regular cost	22.1
Variation from regular cost attributable to sale of operations	1.5
At 1 June 1996	72.6

In July 1992, the UITF published an Abstract dealing with the general question of long-term debtors in current assets, mentioning pension assets as a possible example of such an item. This ruled that where amounts due after more than one year are very material, they should be shown separately on the face of the balance sheet (but still within current assets).[32] Hepworth provides an example of such a disclosure, which goes on to give alternative totals for net current assets that include and exclude the pension prepayment, which goes beyond the requirements of UITF 4:

Extract 20.7: Hepworth PLC (1996)

Balance sheets [extract]

	Group		Company	
	1996	1995	**1996**	1995
At 31st December 1996	**£m**	£m	**£m**	£m
Current assets				
Stocks	**122.5**	129.8	–	–
Debtors	**176.4**	195.7	**100.5**	179.1
Pension scheme (due after one year)	**11.7**	17.4	–	–
Cash at bank and in hand	**25.7**	39.8	–	–
	336.3	382.7	**100.5**	179.1
Creditors (due within one year)				
Finance debt	**26.6**	29.8	**14.9**	14.9
Other creditors	**224.6**	245.9	**25.7**	27.0
	251.2	275.7	**40.6**	41.9
Net current assets **due within one year**	**73.4**	89.6	**59.9**	137.2
due after one year	**11.7**	17.4	–	–
total	**85.1**	107.0	**59.9**	137.2

2.5.5 Disclosure

A   Requirements

Although the standard does deal with the calculation of pension cost, there is still a large degree of flexibility as to the measurement of the amounts to be recognised, partly because of the exceptions to the basic spreading rule mentioned above but also because there is a large degree of subjectivity inherent in the actuarial process, and because no single actuarial method has been specified. In this light, it is still possible to characterise the standard as being primarily a disclosure standard, because the disclosure requirements which it introduced are very extensive. These are as follows:[33]

(a)   the nature of the scheme (i.e. the fact that it is a defined benefit scheme);

(b)   whether it is funded or unfunded;

(c)   the accounting policy and, if different, the funding policy;

(d)   whether the pension cost and provision (or asset) are assessed in accordance with the advice of a professionally qualified actuary and, if so, the date of the most recent formal actuarial valuation or later formal review used for this purpose. If the actuary is an employee or officer of the reporting company, this fact should be disclosed;

(e) the pension cost charge for the period together with explanations of significant changes in the charge compared to that in the previous accounting period;

(f) any provisions or prepayments in the balance sheet resulting from a difference between the amounts recognised as cost and the amounts funded or paid directly;

(g) the amount of any deficiency on a current funding level basis (a 'discontinuance' basis) indicating the action, if any, being taken to deal with it in the current and future accounting periods. Where there is more than one pension scheme, the standard emphasises that it is not permitted to set off a surplus of this type arising on one scheme against a deficiency on another;

(h) an outline of the results of the most recent formal actuarial valuation or later formal review of the scheme on an ongoing basis. This should include disclosure of:

   (i) the actuarial method used and a brief description of the main assumptions (for SSAP 24 purposes, not for funding purposes, where the two are different).[34] This should include the assumption made regarding new entrants unless it is apparent from the description of the method used.[35] If there has been a change in the method, this fact should be disclosed and the effect quantified;[36]

   (ii) the market value of scheme assets at the date of their valuation or review. (Note that this means the actual market value of the assets, which will not generally be the same as the value on the basis used by the actuary for valuing the scheme – see 3.1.5 below);

   (iii) the level of funding expressed in percentage terms.[37] (This, taken with the previous requirement, will allow a reasonable estimate of the actuarial surplus or deficiency to be derived. It will be only an estimate because the previous requirement calls for the market value of the assets to be shown, rather than the value put on them for the purposes of the actuarial valuation);

   (iv) comments on any material actuarial surplus or deficiency indicated by (iii) above;[38] and

   (v) the effects of any significant post-valuation events;[39]

(i) any commitment to make additional payments over a limited number of years;

(j) the accounting treatment adopted in respect of a refund made under deduction of tax (see 2.5.2 E above), where a credit appears in the financial statements in relation to it. (We presume that this means a credit in the profit and loss account rather than in the balance sheet, otherwise the last few words of the previous sentence add nothing to the requirement);

(k)   details of the expected effects on future costs of any material changes in the company's pension arrangements; and

(l)   in the first year of implementing the standard, the way in which the transitional provisions have been applied.[40]

Many of these requirements are similar to those contained in the ASC's original proposals on the disclosure of pension cost information (ED 32),[41] but SSAP 24 goes further in its requirements relating to actuarial information. Conversely, the standard does not contain the requirement to disclose any material self-investment (i.e. investment by the pension fund in the employer company itself), which was one of ED 32's suggestions.

B   *Extracts illustrating disclosure requirements*

Examples of comprehensive notes, taken from the accounts of Smiths Industries, BOC and SmithKline Beecham are set out below:

Extract 20.8: Smiths Industries plc (1996)

11   Post-Retirement Benefits

Smiths Industries operates a number of pension schemes throughout the world. The major schemes are of the defined benefit type with assets held in separate trust administered accounts.

Contributions to pension schemes are made on the advice of independent qualified actuaries, using, in the United Kingdom, the Projected Unit method and in the USA a type of Aggregate Method. The aim is for the benefits to be fully funded during the scheme members' working lives. In both countries the regular pension cost is assessed under the Projected Unit method. The latest actuarial assessments were as at 31 March 1995 in the UK and 31 July 1996 overseas. The most significant assumptions were:

Investment Return	9% per annum
Salary Inflation	7% per annum
Dividend Growth	4.5% per annum
Pension Increases	4.5% per annum

The variation from regular cost, which recognises the excess of assets over liabilities in the pension schemes, including that existing at the time of initially adopting the present accounting policy, has been spread over approximately 10 years, being the average remaining working life.

The company's defined benefit schemes had assets with a market value of £515m. The actuarial value of the scheme assets represented 111% of the liabilities for benefits that had accrued to members, after allowing for expected future increases in salaries.

A prepayment of £28.1m is included in debtors, this being the excess of the amount funded over the accumulated pension cost.

Smiths Industries operates post retirement healthcare benefit plans, principally at Grand Rapids in the United States. These costs are accounted for on a basis similar to pensions. The liabilities in respect of the benefits are assessed by qualified independent actuaries and are fully accrued. The major assumptions are interest rate 7% p.a., and medical inflation 7% p.a.

Extract 20.9: The BOC Group plc (1996)

6. Employees

e) Retirement benefits

i) Pensions

The Group operates a number of pension schemes throughout the world. The majority of the schemes are self-administered and the schemes' assets are held independently of the Group's finances. Pension costs are assessed in accordance with the advice of independent professionally qualified actuaries. The cost for the year was:

	1996 £ million	1995 £ million
Principal schemes		
Regular pension cost	34.8	33.1
Variations from regular cost	(34.5)	(29.4)
Interest	(1.5)	(1.3)
Other schemes	12.6	13.0
Net pension cost	11.4	15.4

ii) Principal schemes

The principal schemes are of the defined benefit type. In the UK and Australia they are based on final salary and in the US on annual salary. On the advice of respective actuaries, Group funding is suspended and is unlikely to be required during the next financial year. The results of the most recent valuations of the principal schemes were:

	UK	US	Australia
Valuation data			
Date of latest valuation or review	31 March 1993 [1]	1 January 1995	31 December 1994
Market value of investments (£ million)	653	264	100
Level of funding[2]	119%	129%	141%
Method used	Projected Unit	Projected Unit	Projected Unit
Main assumptions for accounting purposes			
Rate of price inflation	5.0%	6.0%	6.0%
Return on investments[3]	4.5%	3.0%	3.5%
Increase in earnings[3]	2.0%	0.8%	1.5%

iii) Other retirement costs

In the US, the Group provides post-retirement benefits to former employees. These costs are accounted for on a basis similar to pensions. The cost for the year was:

	1996 £ million	1995 £ million
Regular cost	1.4	1.5
Variations from regular cost	(1.0)	(0.9)
Interest	2.3	2.5
Curtailment gain	–	(2.4)
	2.7	0.7

1 The disclosures for the UK schemes are based on the last triennial funding valuation. For the purposes of determining the pension cost in e(i), interim valuation figures as at 31 March 1996 have been used based on the accounting assumptions above.

2 The actuarial value of assets expressed as a percentage of the accrued service liabilities.

3 Above price inflation

Since footnote 1 shows that the cost has been calculated based on a 1996 valuation, it is not clear why the other UK information disclosed is based on an earlier funding valuation. As the above example also shows, in 1996 BOC experienced a negative pension cost in relation to its main schemes, although the overall effect of all its schemes still produced a net charge to the profit and loss account. The question of negative pension cost is discussed further at 4.3 below.

Extract 20.10: SmithKline Beecham plc (1996)

28   RETIREMENT BENEFITS

The Group operates plans throughout the world covering the majority of employees. These plans are devised in accordance with local conditions and practices in the countries concerned and include defined contribution and benefit schemes. The assets of the plans are generally held in separately administered trusts or are insured, although in Germany the plans are not externally funded. Pension plan assets are managed by independent professional investment managers. It is the Group's policy that none of the assets of the funds are invested directly or indirectly in any Group company. The contributions to the plans are assessed in accordance with independent actuarial advice mainly using the projected unit credit method.

The total pension cost was £89 million (1995 – £76 million; 1994 – £79 million) of which £59 million (1995 – £45 million; 1994 – £41 million) relates to defined benefit plans in the UK, US and Germany which cover some 55% of total employees, and for which further disclosures are set out below.

	UK	US	Germany
Main assumptions:			
Investment return	10%	10%	7%
Salary increases p.a.	7%	5.5%	4.5%
Pension increases p.a.	3.5%	–	3%
Last valuation date	31.12.95	1.1.96	1.1.96
Level of funding, being the actuarial value of assets expressed as percentage of the accrued service liabilities	102%	81%	n/a
	£m	£m	£m
Market valuation of investment at last valuation date	639	682	n/a
Regular pension cost	14	25	2
Variations from regular cost	–	14	4
Total pension costs for 1996	14	39	6

Variations from regular cost are spread over the remaining service lives of current employees in the plans. A provision of £165 million (1995 – £150 million) is included in provisions for liabilities and charges, representing the excess of the accumulated pension cost over the amount funded (see note 16) including £48 million (1995 – £56 million) relating to Germany.

In addition to pension benefits, approximately 20,000 of SB's employees in the US become eligible for certain healthcare and life insurance benefits upon retirement. The amount charged to the profit and loss account in the year for these items was £22 million (1995 – £29 million; 1994 – £34 million). The main assumptions used in determining the required provision are an investment return of 10% and medical cost inflation of 7.75% reducing to 5% by the year 2003. The last valuation date was 1 January 1996.

Some of the most varied forms of disclosure have been those relating to the actuarial assumptions used. In addition to the extracts shown above, some further examples of such disclosures from accounts are set out below. A straightforward form of this disclosure is given by Cadbury Schweppes:

Extract 20.11   Cadbury Schweppes p.l.c. (1996)

29   Pension arrangements [extract]

The major scheme is the Cadbury Schweppes Pension Fund in the UK for which the last full valuation was made as at 5 April 1996 on the projected unit method when the market value of the assets was £990m. The level of funding on the assumptions shown below was 110%.

The principal long term assumptions used for the purposes of the actuarial valuation were as follows:

Rate of return on new investments	8.5%
Earnings increases	6.0%
Pensions increases	4.0%
Growth of dividends	4.0%

Another approach to disclosing aggregated information about a large number of different schemes is illustrated by the accounts of ICI. The company has disclosed the main assumptions by means of weighted averages, rather than simply giving ranges of assumptions used:

Extract 20.12: Imperial Chemical Industries PLC (1996)

36 PENSION COSTS

Group

The Company and most of its subsidiaries operate retirement plans which cover the majority of employees (including directors) in the Group. These plans are generally of the defined benefit type under which benefits are based on employees' years of service and average final remuneration and are funded through separate trustee-administered funds. Formal independent actuarial valuations of the group's main plans are undertaken regularly, normally at least triennially and adopting the projected unit method.

The actuarial assumptions used to calculate the projected benefit obligation of the Group's pension plans vary according to the economic conditions of the country in which they are situated. The weighted average discount rate used in determining the actuarial present values of the benefit obligations was 8.8% (1995 8.8%). The weighted average expected long-term rate of return on investments was 8.9% (1995 8.9%). The weighted average rate of increase of future earnings was 6.0% (1995 5.8%).

The actuarial value of the fund assets of these plans was sufficient to cover 94% (1995 9.2%) of the benefits that had accrued to members after allowing for expected future increases in earnings; their market value was £6,281m (1995 £5,558m).

The total pension cost for the Group for 1996 was £141m (1995 £164m). Accrued pension costs amounted to £17m (1995 £24m) and are included in other creditors; provisions for the benefit obligation of a small number of unfunded plans amounted to £155m (1995 £139m) and are included in provisions for employee benefits. Prepaid pension costs amounting to £183m (1995 £110m) are included in debtors.

ICI Pension Fund

The ICI Pension Fund accounts for approximately 83% of the Group's plans in asset valuation and projected benefit terms.

From the date of the actuarial valuation of the ICI Pension Fund as at 31 March 1994 the Company has been making payments into the fund to reflect the extra liabilities arising from early retirement as retirements occur. In addition, the Company agreed to make accelerated contributions to the Fund over the subsequent six years. A Funding Review as at 31 March 1996 disclosed a solvency ratio on a current funding level basis, which assumes a cessation of operation, of 99%. The deficit of £64m in market value terms is planned to be eliminated by 1997. The solvency ratio, on an ongoing basis, is 94% and this deficit, together with the prepayment, is taken into account in arriving at the employers' pension cost by being amortised as a percentage of pensionable emoluments over the expected working lives of existing members.

Sometimes, companies are less forthcoming about the absolute amounts of the assumptions used, perhaps because they believe that the disclosure of the salary assumption might compromise their negotiating position with the unions, although this information is in any event generally given in the actuarial statement which accompanies the fund accounts. One form of disclosure which is sometimes used is to give the information by reference to an (undisclosed) inflation assumption:

> *Extract 20.13: BICC plc (1996)*
>
> **22   Pensions** [extract]
>
> At the date of the latest valuations of the principal defined benefit schemes the market value of the assets of those schemes amounted to £1,452m. The actuarial value of those assets exceeded the benefits which had accrued to members after allowing for expected future increases in earnings. The latest actuarial valuation of the main UK scheme was carried out by independent actuaries at 5 April 1996 using the projected unit method and disclosed a surplus of assets over past service liabilities of 16%, which is being used to improve benefits for members and to reduce company contributions over a period of 10 years. The principal actuarial assumptions of the main UK scheme are for new investment returns to exceed inflation by 4.5% and for dividends to grow at the rate of inflation.

Although in principle this might be a permissible way of complying with the standard, BICC does not seem to have disclosed the salary inflation assumption at all, which is important information for an assessment of the strength of the actuarial valuation.

Another way of disclosing these assumptions which is often seen in practice is simply to give their relationship to each other, without actually disclosing the absolute figures. One company which has adopted this approach is Glynwed International:

> *Extract 20.14: Glynwed International plc (1996)*
>
> **5   EMPLOYEE INFORMATION** [extract]
>
> The latest valuations of the main schemes were carried out by Watson Wyatt Partners, consulting actuaries, as at 31st March 1995 using the projected unit credit method. The principal assumptions on which these valuations were based were that the investment return would be 3.0% greater than general salary increases and 4.5% greater than increases in future pension payments. The results of these valuations showed that together the schemes had a market value of £422.7m and were 127% funded. The valuations have been used in assessing the expected cost of providing pensions for 1996 and future years and the surplus has been spread over the expected future service of employees as a level percentage of wages and salaries.

It is true that the relationship between the figures is generally more significant than the figures themselves, particularly the gap between the assumed investment return and the salary inflation assumption. Nevertheless the presentation of the absolute figures, as has been done in most of the extracts illustrated here, would provide the reader with this information in a more straightforward and understandable way.

General Accident is an example of a company which changed its actuarial valuation method in its 1993 accounts. The effect of the change is disclosed, as shown in the following extract:

Extract 20.15: General Accident plc (1993)

5 Pension and Other Post Retirement Benefits

(a) Staff Pension Costs

The principal pension schemes operate in the UK and North America. These schemes are of the defined benefit type and their assets are held in separate trustee administered funds. Each of the schemes has been subject to actuarial valuation or review in the last twelve months using the 'Projected Unit Credit' method. In previous years the 'Entry Age' method of actuarial valuation was applied in respect of the UK schemes. The effect of this change in method has been to reduce the annual pension cost by approximately £3.6 million. The actuarial valuation of the defined benefit scheme was carried out by a qualified actuary who is an employee of the Group.

---

3 THE ACTUARIAL ASPECTS OF SSAP 24

3.1 Actuarial valuation methods

3.1.1 Background

Actuarial methods have been developed, not with the objective of generating figures for the measurement of pension cost for accounting purposes, but with a view to valuing the fund and determining appropriate contribution rates. The focus of funding recommendations is to ensure that assets are set aside in a prudent and orderly way so as to meet the obligations of the scheme when they become due for payment; it is to do with cash flows, not with profit measurement.

Nevertheless, although the methods have been developed for funding purposes, they can provide a good basis for attributing cost to the years in which the employees render their services to the employer company. The difficulty is that, even if the actual amount of pensions which would eventually be paid to existing employees were known with precision, there is no particular method of attributing the cost of that pension to individual years of employment which is unarguably the best way of applying the matching concept. Different actuarial methods would approach this task in different ways.

To explain such differences it is helpful to draw the distinction between the two main families of methods used by actuaries – 'accrued benefits methods' and 'projected benefits methods' (or 'level contribution methods' as they are sometimes called). These terms are defined in the standard as shown in 2.3 above, but the essential difference between the two can be explained, slightly simplistically, as follows:

- the accrued benefits approach measures the cost of providing the pension by putting a value directly on each incremental year's service so that it builds up towards the final liability which will arise on retirement;

■   the projected benefits approach looks directly at the expected eventual
    liability and seeks to provide for it evenly over the whole period of
    service.

The first method will tend to show a rising trend of cost over the employee's
working life, while the second will tend to show a flatter charge. The methods,
and some of their different versions, are described more fully in 3.1.3 and 3.1.4
below.

There are different possible accounting arguments as to why either of these
might be the more desirable way of matching cost and benefits. For example, the
accrued benefits method could be portrayed as an approach which tries more
precisely to measure the cost of the pension which has accrued in any specific
year, and therefore is a more faithful application of the matching concept than
the projected benefits method, which seems to adopt more of a 'smoothing'
approach. Conversely, it may be argued that the benefits from employees'
services accrue over their whole working lives and that the total cost of their
pensions should be recognised evenly over those lives, as is achieved by the
projected benefits approach, rather than weighting it towards the later years of
their employment, as happens under the accrued benefits approach. A variety of
further arguments could be summoned to support either side of the debate; but
suffice it to say that there is no unanswerable point which seems to make either
method conclusively the best.

The distinctions between the methods are in practice blurred when one moves
from considering the cost of the pension of an individual employee to looking at
the cost of a scheme comprising many employees, with a range of ages. For
mature schemes where the age profile of the scheme remains steady through
time, there will be comparatively little difference between the total cost
calculated under either approach.

3.1.2   *The approach taken by the standard*

As has been explained already, SSAP 24 does not prescribe a particular
valuation method, and leaves it to the employer, with the benefit of actuarial
advice, to ensure that the method chosen can fulfil the accounting objective set
out in the standard, that the cost should be recognised on a systematic and
rational basis over the working lives of the employees in the scheme. Both of the
broad categories of actuarial method described above could generally be said to
meet that objective, although some of their variants may not, as discussed in the
two sections which follow.

The standard says comparatively little about particular actuarial methods, but
discusses them briefly in the following terms: 'In practice, it is common for
actuaries to aim at a level contribution rate, as a proportion of pensionable pay in
respect of current service. The contribution rate thus determined depends on the
particular actuarial method used and the assumptions made regarding new

entrants to the scheme. In broad terms, in projecting a stable contribution rate, accrued benefits methods rely on the assumption that the flow of new entrants will be such as to preserve the existing average age of the workforce; prospective benefits methods, on the other hand, normally look only to the existing workforce and seek a contribution rate that will remain stable for that group despite its increasing age profile until the last member retires or leaves. In a mature scheme both types of method may in practice achieve stable contribution rates, but the size of the fund under a prospective benefits method will tend to be larger than under an accrued benefits method because it is intended to cover the ageing of the existing workforce.'[42]

A group of companies will often have a number of different pension schemes in operation for different subsidiaries and the question often arises as to whether they must be valued using the same actuarial methods and assumptions. On the basis that the various methods attribute pension costs to years of service in a different way, there is an argument that a single method should be used throughout the group, just as it would be desirable to use the same depreciation method consistently throughout the group. However, provided the methods chosen all achieve the standard's aim of charging pension cost as a relatively consistent percentage of payroll, then it is acceptable to use different methods. It can be seen from Extract 20.8 that uniform valuation methods are not necessarily used in practice.

It can also be seen from several of the extracts quoted in this chapter that different actuarial assumptions are commonly used for different schemes. Again this is quite legitimate provided the assumptions are appropriate for the schemes to which they are applied, and since the schemes themselves will not be uniform, there is no reason why the assumptions should be. In particular the economic assumptions used for the schemes of an international group will need to reflect the circumstances of each country, although a greater degree of consistency would be expected between schemes within the same country.

3.1.3   *Possible actuarial methods – accrued benefits methods*

As mentioned above, the accrued benefit approach focuses directly on the incremental liability which builds up year by year as pensionable service is recorded by the employee. It sees each year as giving rise to a further unit of pension entitlement, and values each unit separately to build up the total accrued liability.

Although the emphasis is on the benefits that have been earned to date, this does not mean that the method is incapable of looking to the future, and in particular it is not necessarily the case that it does not anticipate future pay rate inflation (which is a vital factor in a final salary scheme). Admittedly some variants of the accrued benefits approach do not take such factors into account, but the most significant version, the projected unit method, is based on estimates of final salary rather than on present rates of pay. (Confusingly, the projected unit method is in the 'accrued benefit' family of valuations, not the 'projected benefit' family.) This method is discussed below.

A   *Projected unit method*

A description of the main features of this method runs as follows:

'Under the projected unit method, a standard contribution rate expressed as a percentage of earnings is obtained by dividing the present value of all benefits which will accrue in the year following the valuation date (by reference to service in that year and projected final earnings) by the present value of members' earnings in that year. An actuarial liability is calculated by summing the present value of all benefits accrued at the valuation date (based on projected final earnings for members in service). The recommended contribution rate expressed as a percentage of earnings is obtained by modifying the standard contribution rate to reflect the difference between the value placed on the scheme assets for valuation purposes and this actuarial liability.'[43]

A diagrammatic representation of the valuation of the fund using the projected unit method could appear as follows:

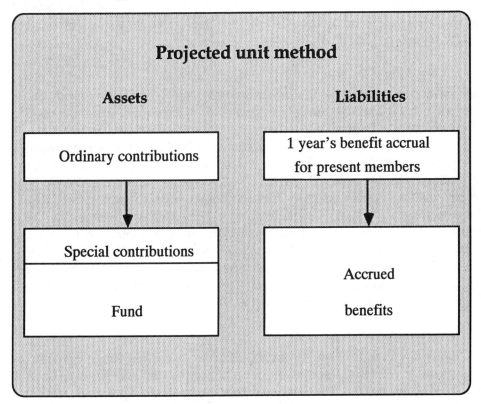

The 'special contributions' shown in the diagram are those that are needed to take account of a deficiency in the fund which may have arisen due to factors such as experience differences or benefit improvements. It is equally possible that a surplus might emerge, so that reduced contributions become an available option. In terms of SSAP 24, therefore, the 'special contributions' shown in the diagram is equivalent to variations, while the amount shown as 'ordinary contributions' represents the regular cost.

This method can result in a stable level of contributions provided the age profile of the workforce remains steady. In these circumstances it will generally form a suitable basis for the measurement of cost under SSAP 24. However, its use might have to be more critically considered if the characteristics of the scheme are likely to result in a more volatile contribution rate, and actuarial advice on this point may be necessary. Guidance Note 17 (GN 17) issued by the actuarial profession comments that the method 'is unlikely to be satisfactory if it is evident from the circumstances that the standard contribution rate is likely to change in future years. A change might for example be foreseeable because (a) the scheme is or will be closed to new entrants, or (b) new entrants are admitted on a pension scale which is materially different in cost from the scale applicable to current members.'[44]

This method has emerged as the one which commands majority support among large companies; 82% of the companies in the FT-SE 100 index now use it.[45] It has also been suggested by the ASB that the method may be made mandatory in a future revision of SSAP 24.[46]

B　Current unit method

This method is essentially similar to the projected unit method, with the vital distinction that it looks at current, rather than projected pay rates. As a result, the effects of salary inflation have to be picked up in future years in an accelerating pattern, which means that the cost is likely to be heavily skewed towards the later years of employment. For this reason such a method does not meet the accounting objective of SSAP 24. GN 17 comes to a similar conclusion, saying that the method 'is unsatisfactory if used without a control period [see below] of adequate length, or if it is evident from the circumstances that the standard contribution rate is likely to change materially in future years. A change might for example be foreseeable (a) if the scheme is or will be closed to new entrants or if new entrants are admitted on a pension scale which is materially different in cost from the scale applicable to current members, or (b) as an effect of future pay increases upon accrued pension rights.'[47]

C　Discontinuance method

This method, which is described in SSAP 24 as a 'current funding level' basis, is, as its name suggests, founded on the premise that the scheme is to be wound up immediately and the assets applied to meet the existing entitlements of the members. It therefore does not form an appropriate method for valuing the scheme on a forward-looking, going concern basis. Because of the objectives of the method, contribution rates are not calculated, and for all these reasons the use of a discontinuance approach could not provide an appropriate measure of cost under SSAP 24.

A variant of the discontinuance method, which is sometimes referred to as the 'discontinuance target method', is occasionally used to determine funding rates, and is quite commonly used by insurance companies. This involves funding for the discontinuance liability which would arise if the scheme were to be wound up at some specified time, say 20 years, in the future. The period chosen is referred to as the 'control period' in actuarial parlance. In principle this method would still not follow the accounting objective of SSAP 24, because it does not look through to the final salaries on which the pensions are expected to be paid. However, the greater the length of the control period, the nearer the method will become to one which is acceptable under the standard. Where the method is used, it will be necessary to obtain actuarial advice on whether it produces results which are materially different from one which is based on projected final salaries.

GN 17 says that 'a control period can be regarded as of adequate length if (a) the resulting standard contribution rate, which is to be used as the regular cost, is not altered materially by extending the control period and (b) the calculation of the pension cost makes specific provision for future increases in earnings not materially different from a full provision for all future increases in earnings, including merit increases, and not solely those occurring up to the end of the control period'.[48]

3.1.4 *Possible actuarial methods – projected benefits methods*

As discussed previously, these methods try to look at the eventual amount of pensions which are expected to be paid, and establish contribution rates which are designed to remain stable over the period of the employees' service. Usually, this means that they are designed to represent a level percentage of payroll costs, not a level figure in pounds, but the latter is also theoretically possible (although not an appropriate method for SSAP 24 purposes).

A *Aggregate method*

The actuaries' description of this method reads as follows:

'Under the aggregate method, a recommended contribution rate expressed as a percentage of earnings is obtained by dividing the excess of the present value of all benefits which have accrued and will accrue (based on total service and projected final earnings for members in service) over the value placed on the scheme assets for valuation purposes by the present value of total projected earnings for all members throughout their expected future membership.'[49]

A diagrammatic view of this method would show:

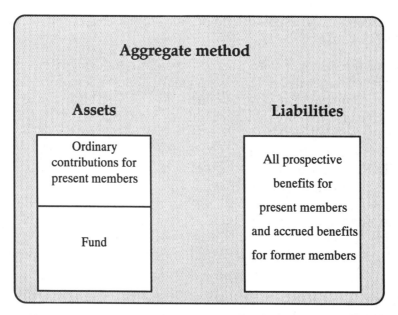

The 'Ordinary contributions' box represents the balancing figure in the valuation, and the method does not in fact identify either the surplus or deficit on the fund or the element of contributions which relates to variations from regular cost. As a result it does not provide the analysis which the standard requires and is seldom likely to be a usable method without modification. It is regarded by some as rather a simplistic method of valuation, and while it has been quite extensively used in the past in the UK, it is now much less common.

GN 17 takes a similar view, but notes that it may be seen as a variant of the Attained Age Method or the Entry Age Method (both described below). It comments that it may be suitable where the scheme is closed to new entrants, but that otherwise one of these other two methods should be used so as to distinguish regular cost from variations.[50]

B   Attained age method

This method is described by the actuaries thus:

'Under the attained age method, a standard contribution rate expressed as a percentage of earnings is obtained by dividing the present value of all benefits which will accrue to present members after the valuation date (by reference to service after the valuation date and projected final earnings) by the present value of total projected earnings for all members throughout their expected future membership. An actuarial liability is calculated by summing the present value of all benefits accrued at the valuation date (based on projected final earnings for members in service). The recommended contribution rate expressed as a percentage of earnings is obtained by modifying the standard contribution rate to reflect the difference between the value placed on the scheme assets for valuation purposes and the accrued actuarial liability.'[51]

On a diagram, a valuation under this method looks like this:

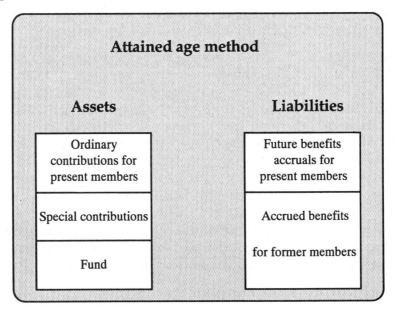

In concept, this is not dissimilar to the aggregate method, and if the 'special contributions' are paid as well as the ordinary contributions they will produce the same total contribution as under that method. The main difference is that the liabilities are split between those benefits which have already accrued and those which are projected to accrue in the future for existing members. By splitting it in this way, the amount of 'special contributions' can be identified which represents the amount needed to redress the deficit between the value of the fund and the accrued benefits. Again, this could be a negative figure if the scheme were in surplus.

For SSAP 24 purposes, the 'ordinary contributions' shown in the diagram again equate to regular cost, and the 'special contributions' to variations from that regular cost.

GN 17 comments that the method is unlikely to be satisfactory '(a) where a scheme has a regular and significant flow of new entrants and if the payment of the standard contribution rate in respect of the new entrants is expected to create material surpluses or deficits, or (b) where a scheme is or will be closed to new entrants and the standard contribution rate is expected to increase materially at each succeeding valuation. (However the method can be satisfactory for a closed scheme where the regular cost is based throughout upon the standard contribution rate calculated in respect of the membership present at the time when the scheme was closed.)'[52]

C   *Entry age method*

This method is comparatively rare in the UK, but has been more commonly used in North America. It is described as follows:

'Under the entry age method, a normal entry age is chosen which may be estimated from the actual membership records. A standard contribution rate expressed as a percentage of earnings is obtained by dividing the present value of all future benefits by reference to projected final earnings for a member entering at the normal entry age by the present value of total projected earnings throughout his expected future membership. An actuarial liability is calculated by deducting from the present value of total benefits (based on projected final earnings for members in service) the value of the standard contribution rate multiplied by the present value of total projected earnings for all members throughout their expected future membership. The recommended contribution rate expressed as a percentage of earnings is obtained by modifying the standard contribution rate to reflect the difference between the value placed on the scheme assets for valuation purposes and this actuarial liability.'[53]

In diagrammatic form, such a valuation appears as follows:

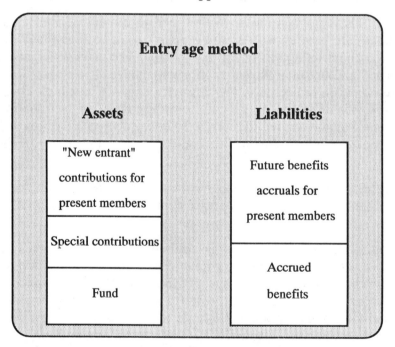

In this case the calculation of the liabilities is the same, but the amount of 'special contributions', which is the balancing figure (and could again be negative), is determined after calculating the ordinary contributions in a different way; rather than basing it on the actual contributions to be made by the existing members, it is calculated on the basis that existing members are at the age of the typical new entrant to the scheme. This creates a difficulty in theory at least,

Where the company has chosen to implement SSAP 24 by incorporating the surplus directly in the balance sheet (rather than spreading it forward as a quasi-variation), columns 1 and 2 show the figures that will appear in its balance sheet and profit and loss account, provided that it recognises interest on the balance sheet figure. On implementing the standard, the company will set up the £1.4 million asset in its balance sheet, and in the profit and loss account for year 1 it will show a pension cost of £251,000, which represents the regular cost of £360,000 less interest of £109,000 (9% of (£1,400,000 + £173,000 - £360,000) – to simplify the calculation it is assumed that all movements in the fund are reflected at the beginning of the year) deemed to be earned on the balance sheet figure. The excess of this cost over the contributions paid of £173,000 will be applied to reduce the balance sheet figure by £78,000 to leave the closing balance sheet with an asset of £1,322,000. The same process is repeated in each year, and it can be seen that the balance sheet figure tracks the amount of the surplus in the fund throughout the period.

It is worth considering what would happen if interest on the balance sheet figure were not recognised. In this case the profit and loss account charge would simply be the regular cost of £360,000, and the balance sheet asset would be reduced by £187,000 (the difference between the profit and loss account charge and the £173,000 contribution). By the end of the eight year period this would result in the balance sheet showing a liability of £515,000, which would have no equivalent in the fund; it would simply be the amount of the interest earned in the fund over that period which the accounts had failed to recognise. Any new actuarial valuation carried out during the period would show an apparent variation (being the amount of unrecognised interest) which, in terms of SSAP 24, would be recognised prospectively, as an offset to the pension cost of the next 8 years. It would seem much more sensible to recognise this interest in the years in which it accrues rather than over a protracted future period.

Columns 3 and 4 show the figures which would appear in the balance sheet and the profit and loss account if the company adopted the other possible way of implementing the standard – treating the surplus as a quasi-variation and spreading it forward over the remaining service lives of the employees. The calculation of the pension cost is based on the regular cost of £360,000 less the release of an instalment of the £1.4 million quasi-variation which is spread in this example using the 'straight line method', and plus interest on the opening balance sheet figure in each year. There are two interest elements in this calculation. As well as the interest added on the balance sheet figure, the amortisation of the quasi-variation is done by releasing amounts which include interest so that their *present value* totals £1.4 million (see 4.2.2 below for a more detailed discussion of spreading methods). The balance sheet figure is simply the cumulative difference between the profit and loss account charge and the contributions paid.

It can be seen that, over the eight years, the total charge to the profit and loss account under the 'prospective' method (column 4) is £1.4 million less than that under the 'PYA' method (column 2). This simply reflects the fact that the surplus is being channelled through the profit and loss account under the former method but taken straight to reserves under the latter. Column 5 shows how this total difference is allocated to each of the years involved; in this example it is a level amount of one-eighth of the total surplus, because the straight line method of amortisation was used. Column 6 shows the amount of the surplus remaining to be recognised at the end of each year, in other words the amount of the initial surplus successively reduced by the figures in column 5. Column 6 also represents the difference between the balance sheet figures under each of the two methods at the end of each year. (As explained at 2.5.4 above, the balance sheet figure under SSAP 24 can be defined as the net of the surplus or deficit in the fund and the amount of unamortised variations awaiting recognition in the profit and loss account.)

		1	2	3	4	5	6
		PYA method		Prospective method			
Year	Movements in pension fund	Balance sheet	P&L account	Balance sheet	P&L account	Difference	Unamortised variations
		£000	£000	£000	£000	£000	£000
1	Surplus	1,400					
	Contribution	173					
	Regular cost	(360)					
	Interest	109					
	P&L charge		251		76	175	
2	Balance	1,322		97			1,225
	Contribution	186					
	Regular cost	(385)					
	Interest	101					
	P&L charge		284		109	175	
3	Balance	1,224		174			1,050
	Contribution	198					
	Regular cost	(412)					
	Interest	91					
	P&L charge		321		146	175	
4	Balance	1,101		226			875
	Contribution	212					
	Regular cost	(441)					
	Interest	79					
	P&L charge		362		187	175	
5	Balance	951		251			700
	Contribution	227					
	Regular cost	(472)					
	Interest	64					
	P&L charge		408		233	175	
6	Balance	770		245			525
	Contribution	243					
	Regular cost	(505)					
	Interest	46					
	P&L charge		459		284	175	
7	Balance	554		204			350
	Contribution	260					
	Regular cost	(540)					
	Interest	25					
	P&L charge		515		340	175	
8	Balance	299		124			175
	Contribution	279					
	Regular cost	(578)					
	Interest	0					
	P&L charge		578		403	175	
9	Balance	0		0			0
	Totals		3,178		1,778	1,400	

To illustrate the application of the calculations further, another example is shown in the table on the next page which assumes the same basic facts, except that the company has chosen to eliminate the surplus more quickly by taking a contribution holiday rather than reducing its rate of contribution over a longer period.

Example 20.6   Application of interest to balance sheet figure

This example alters the facts in Example 20.5 slightly, and shows the figures which would arise if the company eliminated the surplus by taking a contribution holiday for nearly four years rather than by reducing its contributions for eight years. Once again, column 1 in the table on the next page shows the movements in the fund itself; the surplus is run off over four years as a result of the contribution holiday, and thereafter the fund is kept in equilibrium because the contributions are restored to an amount equal to the regular cost.

As before, columns 1 and 2 show the figures that will appear in the company's balance sheet and profit and loss account, provided that interest is recognised on the balance sheet figure. In this case the pension cost will be higher than in the previous example because the surplus in the fund is being reduced more sharply and as a result is earning less interest. From year 5 on, there is no surplus in the fund and the charge in the profit and loss account is simply the regular cost. Once again, the balance sheet figure tracks the amount of the surplus in the fund throughout the period, provided interest is recognised on the balance sheet figure.

Columns 3 and 4 again show the figures which appear in the balance sheet and the profit and loss account under the prospective approach. It can again be demonstrated that, over the eight years, the total charge to the profit and loss account under the prospective method is £1.4 million less than that under the PYA method.

Having given these illustrations, it is now possible to consider why the figures work out in the way that they do. Where the balance sheet figure simply represents the surplus in the fund (as it will to begin with under the PYA approach) then it is easy to see that it is necessary to recognise the interest which the fund is earning in the company accounts in order to preserve that relationship. However, where the prospective method is applied, it is harder to understand why interest should be applied to the balance sheet figure, and indeed, as in Example 20.6, it may be difficult to explain why an extra interest *charge* should be made on a balance sheet liability when the fund is still *earning* interest on a surplus.

To explain this, it is necessary to see the balance sheet figure in the light that has been discussed in 2.5.4 above, as a composite figure which is the net of the surplus in the fund and the amount of unamortised variations awaiting recognition in the profit and loss account. Thus, the liability of £91,000 at the end of year 1 under the prospective method (column 3 in Example 20.6) is the net of the surplus in the fund of £1,134,000 and the unamortised variations of £1,225,000 (columns 1 and 6). Applying interest to the £91,000 can similarly be interpreted as a credit for interest on the surplus in the fund which is more than offset by a charge on the amount of the unamortised variations.

Year	Movements in pension fund	1 PYA method Balance sheet	2 PYA method P&L account	3 Prospective method Balance sheet	4 Prospective method P&L account	5 Difference	6 Unamortised variations
		£000	£000	£000	£000	£000	£000
1	Surplus	1,400					
	Contribution	0					
	Regular cost	(360)					
	Interest	94					
	P&L charge		266		91	175	
2	Balance	1,134		(91)			1,225
	Contribution	0					
	Regular cost	(385)					
	Interest	67					
	P&L charge		318		143	175	
3	Balance	816		(234)			1,050
	Contribution	0					
	Regular cost	(412)					
	Interest	36					
	P&L charge		376		201	175	
4	Balance	440		(435)			875
	Contribution	1					
	Regular cost	(441)					
	Interest	0					
	P&L charge		441		266	175	
5	Balance	0		(700)			700
	Contribution	472					
	Regular cost	(472)					
	Interest	0					
	P&L charge		472		297	175	
6	Balance	0		(525)			525
	Contribution	505					
	Regular cost	(505)					
	Interest	0					
	P&L charge		505		330	175	
7	Balance	0		(350)			350
	Contribution	540					
	Regular cost	(540)					
	Interest	0					
	P&L charge		540		365	175	
8	Balance	0		(175)			175
	Contribution	578					
	Regular cost	(578)					
	Interest	0					
	P&L charge		578		403	175	
9	Balance	0		0			0
	Totals		3,496		2,096	1,400	

This analysis offers a different way of looking at the make-up of the pension cost charge, which may be more readily understood. The total pension cost can be explained as being made up of the regular cost less the interest on the surplus (even though it is not included in the balance sheet) and less the release of the quasi-variation into the profit and loss account. This can be illustrated as follows using the figures from Example 20.5:

Year	Regular cost	Interest in fund	Release of variations	Total
	£000	£000	£000	£000
1	360	109	175	76
2	385	101	175	109
3	412	91	175	146
4	441	79	175	187
5	472	64	175	233
6	505	46	175	284
7	540	25	175	340
8	578	0	175	403
	3,693	515	1,400	1,778

The method shown in Example 20.5 differs from this in two ways, which cancel each other out:

(a) interest is applied to the whole balance sheet figure, not just the surplus (i.e. it is also applied to the component which represents the deferred variations awaiting recognition in the profit and loss account);

(b) the variations are taken into the profit and loss account at amounts whose *net present value* adds up to £1.4m, not their absolute amount.

This analysis may be easier to understand in concept, but that which is given in Example 20.5 may be easier to apply in practice because it simply involves applying interest to the balance sheet figure, whatever it may be, rather than looking through it to see what the actual surplus in the fund is.

When interest is recognised in the profit and loss account, it is necessary to consider whether to include it as a component of pension cost, or as an amount of interest payable or receivable within the general classification of finance costs. Respectable arguments can be mounted for either treatment where the interest is simply that which is being earned in the fund itself (where the balance sheet figure directly represents the balance in the fund). However, where the interest is charged on a composite figure which includes an amount of unamortised variations, the interest charge or credit has no real significance by itself because it is inseparably linked to the release of these variations. For this reason, it is suggested that the preferable treatment in all cases is to include the interest as a component of pension cost. This is the tentative conclusion of the

ASB in its Discussion Paper,[59] although the contrary suggestion has been made in the Board's more recent paper on Discounting.[60]

In conclusion, it can be seen from the illustrations given above that interest considerations pervade the calculations which underlie pension accounting, and that unless they are consistently accounted for, the accounts will not allocate them to the periods to which they belong. Despite the apparent complexity of these examples, the rules to be applied are relatively straightforward; companies should both account for imputed interest on the balance sheet figure and also spread any variations into the profit and loss account on a basis which includes the effects of interest. If they do not do so, apparent variations will arise in subsequent actuarial valuations which are simply the result of the company's failure to recognise interest in the periods in which it has accrued.

4.2   Variations from regular cost

4.2.1   *Calculation of remaining service lives*

The standard says that variations should normally be spread over the remaining service lives of employees currently in the scheme after making suitable allowances for future withdrawals, and that it is possible to apply this principle by using an average period relevant to the current membership if desired.[61] This issue is discussed at 2.5.2 B above. Where the average approach is taken, this will be determined by the actuary on the basis of the age profile of the workforce and the assumptions made about mortality, retirements and withdrawals. The period is usually likely to be shorter than might intuitively be assumed, and a range of 10 to 15 years might be typical.

SSAP 24 does not require the period of amortisation to be disclosed, but in practice a number of companies do so and we regard this as a helpful disclosure. Two examples are shown in Extracts 20.16 and 20.17 below.

4.2.2   *How should variations be amortised?*

As mentioned in 2.5.2 B and at 4.2.1 above, the standard does not specify the particular method by which variations should be amortised, saying only that they should be amortised over the expected remaining service lives of the employees in the scheme, and that an average period may be used if desired.[62] Three main methods have emerged in practice, although others may also be permissible if they meet the objective described above. These three are known as (a) the straight line method (b) the mortgage method and (c) the percentage of pay method, and they are illustrated in the following three extracts:

Extract 20.16: The RTZ Corporation PLC – CRA Limited (1996)

PRINCIPAL ACCOUNTING POLICIES

1 Post retirement benefits

The expected costs of post retirement benefits under defined benefit arrangements are charged to the profit and loss account so as to spread the costs over the service lives of employees entitled to those benefits. Variations from the regular cost are spread on a straight line basis over the expected average remaining service lives of relevant current employees. Costs are assessed in accordance with the advice of qualified actuaries.

NOTES TO THE 1996 ACCOUNTS

33 POST RETIREMENT BENEFITS

... The expected average remaining service life in the major schemes ranges from 12 to 21 years with an overall average of 14 years. ...

Extract 20.17: Reed Elsevier plc (1996)

4 Pension schemes [extract]

... The actuarial surplus is being spread as a level amount over the average remaining service lives of current employees, which has been assessed as eight years. ...

Extract 20.18: Whitbread PLC (1997)

Accounting policies

I. Pension funding

Pension costs are charged to the profit and loss account over the average expected service life of current employees. Actuarial surpluses are amortised over the expected service lives of current employees, using the percentage of pensionable salaries method. Differences between the amount charged in the profit and loss account and payments made to the schemes are treated as assets or liabilities in the balance sheet.

There is no explicit requirement in SSAP 24 to disclose the method used, and most companies do not do so. However, the different methods can produce answers which are materially different, and we strongly encourage disclosure of the method chosen: this has also been recommended by the ICAEW.[63] The majority of those companies who do make this disclosure use the percentage of pay method.

The mechanics of the three methods are illustrated by the following example, which is based on the same situation as described in Example 20.5:

Example 20.7:   Methods of amortisation of variations

An actuarial valuation of a company's pension scheme identifies a variation of £1,400,000 to be spread over the working lives of the employees, which is assessed to be 8 years. The company's payroll cost is expected to increase at a rate of 7% per annum and the return earned on the fund's investments will be 9%. The figures derived from the three most common methods of spreading the variation are set out below.

Year	Straight line method £000	Mortgage method £000	Percentage of pay method £000
1	277	232	186
2	262	232	200
3	247	232	213
4	233	232	229
5	218	232	244
6	204	232	262
7	189	232	280
8	175	232	300
Total	1,805	1,856	1,914

The straight line method is computed by dividing the amount to be spread (£1,400,000) by the number of years (8) to achieve a level capital amount of £175,000. Interest is added to the balance which remains unamortised in each year to give the total charge.

The mortgage method involves calculating the annuity for 8 years which equates, at an interest rate of 9%, to a capital value of £1,400,000. The resulting annual figure can be regarded, as with the repayments under a mortgage, as comprising a relatively small capital element and a large interest element at the outset with the proportions reversing in later years.

The percentage of pay method is calculated by determining the stream of payments, escalating at the rate of annual payroll inflation (7% in this example) which has a present value of the amount to be amortised (£1,400,000).

It can be seen that each of these methods results in the amortisation of a total figure which exceeds the apparent amount (£1,400,000 in this example) which was to be amortised. This is because an actuarial surplus is not an absolute amount, but rather a discounted figure because of the calculations implicit in the valuation method. It is therefore necessary to include an interest element in the amortisation calculation, as is described in each of these methods. As has been shown under 4.1 above, it is also necessary to charge or credit interest on the balance sheet figure in order to reflect fully the time value of money which is inherent in the calculation.

The three methods produce quite different profiles. The mortgage method produces a level amount, the straight line method results in a declining amount, while the percentage of pay method has the reverse effect. The effect of using these methods in the calculation of pension costs in the circumstances of Example 20.5 will be as shown in this graph:

members of the scheme it may in theory be possible to allocate the cost to the companies for whom they work; however, where the variation relates to the performance of the fund, no such specific allocation would be possible, and in practice some simpler form of apportionment will have to be applied such as the uniform percentage of payroll referred to in the previous paragraph.

However, the starting point for allocating both the regular cost and variations is to consider how the group intends to recover the cost from the individual subsidiary companies. The accounting in each company should then follow whatever commercial decision is made as to the allocation of the charge. For example, some groups may prefer to deal with all variations at holding company level, and therefore charge individual companies with the regular cost, in which case the accounting should reflect that decision. Whatever the basis used, it is important that the notes to the accounts of the subsidiaries should indicate that the company is a member of a group scheme and explain the basis of the charge made.

4.10 Multi-employer schemes

Where a company participates in a scheme which has been established for a number of employers (perhaps a whole industry) it is necessary to adapt the measurement and disclosure rules of the standard appropriately. Sometimes the nature of the arrangement is such that, in essence, it constitutes a defined contribution scheme and should be accounted for as such. However, where it is in the nature of a defined benefit scheme it will be necessary to determine what portion of the total fund is attributable to the reporting company.

Lookers provides an example of such an arrangement, as shown in the following extract:

Extract 20.25: Lookers plc (1996)

Principal Accounting Policies

9. Pension costs [extract]

The Group participates in the Retail Motor Industry Pension Plan which is a defined benefit scheme providing benefits based on final pensionable salary. The scheme has been registered with the Registrar of Pensions.

The assets of the scheme are held separately from those of the Group, being held in separate funds by the Trustees of the RMI plan.

Contributions to the scheme are charged to the profit and loss account so as to spread the cost of pensions over employees' working lives with the Group. The contribution rate is recommended by a qualified actuary on the basis of triennial valuations, using the projected unit method.

NOTES TO THE FINANCIAL STATEMENTS

9. INFORMATION REGARDING DIRECTORS AND EMPLOYEES [extract]

The Group participates in the Retail Motor Industry Pension Plan and the most recent valuation was at 6th April 1996 using the Projected Unit Method. The assumptions which have the most significant effect on the results of the valuation are those relating to the rate of return on investments and the rate of increase in salaries. It was assumed that the investment return would be 2% p.a. higher than the increase in salaries in the period up to retirement. No allowance was made for any future discretionary increases in benefits.

The latest available actuarial valuation showed that the market value of the scheme's assets attributable to the Lookers Group was £25,940,000 and that the actuarial value of the assets represented 119% of the liabilities at the valuation date, after allowing for expected future increases in earnings. The employer's future service contribution rate has been adjusted to take into account the surplus disclosed by the valuation, spread over the average remaining service lives of the members of the scheme. By 30th September 1996, the employees of Charles Hurst had been transferred into the Lookers scheme.

---

5   RELATED COMPANIES ACT REQUIREMENTS

5.1   Pension commitments

The Companies Act 1985 requires that particulars should be disclosed of:

(a)   any pension commitments included under any provision shown in the company's balance sheet; and

(b)   any such commitments for which no such provision has been made.[75]

The requirement goes on to say that separate disclosure should be given to any part of these commitments which relate to pensions payable to former directors of the company.

The Act offers no further interpretation of what constitutes a pension commitment for the purposes of this disclosure requirement. It could be interpreted very broadly, so that disclosure of the commitment would require a full description of the obligation which the company had accepted in making pension promises to its employees; this would involve giving details of the terms of the pension scheme, together with a description of the arrangements which had been made to meet that obligation. This broad interpretation is supported by ED 32, which proposed quite extensive disclosure requirements, and went on to say that 'the disclosures required by this proposed standard have been framed having regard to the requirements in company legislation for the disclosure of pension information. Compliance with these proposals, however, will not necessarily ensure compliance with these legal requirements which must be considered in the light of each company's individual pension arrangements.'[76]

In practice, however, the general interpretation of the requirement has been much narrower. Many companies appear to have taken the view that as long as the pension scheme is adequately funded, there is no further commitment on the part of the company itself which has to be disclosed. Companies have generally confined their disclosure to a relatively brief description of the pension arrangements in force and the fact that the schemes were fully funded. Since the introduction of SSAP 24, the disclosures given by employer companies have been much more extensive (see 2.4.2 and 2.5.5 above), and we believe that this satisfies the Companies Act requirement to disclose pension commitments.

5.2 Pension costs

The Act also requires disclosure of pension costs charged in the profit and loss account. This is one of three elements of staff costs which have to be disclosed, the other two being wages and salaries and social security costs.[77] The Act goes on to say that for this purpose pension costs 'includes any costs incurred by the company in respect of any pension scheme established for the purpose of providing pensions for persons currently or formerly employed by the company, any sums set aside for the future payment of pensions directly by the company to current or former employees and any pensions paid directly to such persons without having first been set aside'.[78]

5.3 Directors' emoluments

There are detailed requirements in the Companies Act for the disclosure of directors' emoluments, including pensions. These are discussed in detail in Chapter 30.

6 COMPARISON WITH US AND IASC PRONOUNCEMENTS

6.1 US

6.1.1 Background

There have been professional pronouncements in the US dealing with accounting for pension costs for many years. The subject was dealt with briefly in the compendium Accounting Research Bulletin (ARB) 43 which was issued in 1953 and subsequently in ARB 47 in 1956, but was given much more comprehensive treatment in Accounting Principles Board (APB) Opinion No. 8

– *Accounting for the Cost of Pension Plans*, issued in November 1966. The FASB first got involved with disclosure issues, publishing SFAS 36 – *Disclosure of Pension Information*, in May 1980, and later dealt with related topics in SFAS 74 – *Accounting for Special Termination Benefits Paid to Employees* – and SFAS 81 – *Disclosure of Postretirement Health Care and Life Insurance Benefits*.

The FASB's current pronouncements on pension costs are the two statements published in December 1985, SFAS 87 – *Employers' Accounting for Pensions*, and SFAS 88 – *Employers' Accounting for Settlements and Curtailments of Defined Benefit Pension Plans and for Termination Benefits*. These last two statements have superseded all the earlier pronouncements on the subject. In December 1990, the Board issued SFAS 106 – *Employers' Accounting for Postretirement Benefits Other Than Pensions*, and this superseded SFAS 81.

6.1.2   SFAS 87

SFAS 87 requires a particular actuarial approach to be used for measuring cost, and in general prescribes tightly drawn rules as to the computation and disclosure of pension figures in the accounts. It also breaks down the cost to be charged into six components, and has detailed provisions dealing with how these are to be calculated.

Under the standard, the pension cost to be attributed to a period is that which accrues in respect of the period under the terms of the pension scheme. That is to say, it applies an accrued benefit approach to the allocation of cost to periods (as discussed in 3.1 above). This means that for final salary schemes, the statement requires that the cost be calculated using the projected unit method (as we would call it in the UK – in the US it would be described as the projected unit *credit* method).

For defined benefit schemes, the cost must be analysed into the following components:

■   service cost;

■   interest cost;

■   actual return on plan assets, if any;

■   amortisation of unrecognised prior service cost, if any;

■   gain or loss (including the effects of changes in assumptions) to the extent recognised; and

■   amortisation of the unrecognised net obligation (and loss or cost) or unrecognised net asset (and gain) existing at the date of initial application of the statement.

Each of these terms is further defined and the required accounting specified.

22 *Ibid.,* (as revised by FRS 3, para. 33(m)).
23 *Ibid.,* para. 26 (as revised by FRS 3, para. 33(k)).
24 *Ibid.,* para. 81.
25 ICTA 1988 ss. 601–603 and Sch. 22.
26 SSAP 24, para. 83.
27 *Pension Costs in the Employer's Financial Statements,* para. 5.7.3.
28 SSAP 24, para. 82.
29 *Ibid.,* para. 92.
30 As reported in the survey published in Spring 1992 by William M. Mercer Fraser Limited, entitled *SSAP 24 — Survey of company pension disclosures 1991.*
31 *Pension Costs in the Employer's Financial Statements,* para. 6.2.13.
32 UITF Abstract 4, *Presentation of long-term debtors in current assets,* July 1992.
33 SSAP 24, para. 88.
34 GN 17: *Accounting for pension costs under SSAP 24,* Institute and Faculty of Actuaries, April 1991, para. 28.
35 SSAP 24, para. 48. Arguably, this requirement, and those referred to in footnotes 36 and 39 below, are not mandatory because they appear only in the Explanatory Note of SSAP 24, and not in the Standard section itself. However, they should nonetheless be disclosed if it is sufficiently important to an understanding of the overall position.
36 *Ibid.,* para. 18.
37 The guidance issued by the actuarial profession indicates that this should be calculated using the Projected Accrued Benefit Method (GN 17, para. 30).
38 GN 17, para. 31 explains that part of this surplus or deficiency will be attributable to the use of the Projected Accrued Benefit Method for the previous disclosure unless the method used for funding is the Projected Unit method or the Attained Age method, and this fact should be explained.
39 SSAP 24, para. 49.
40 *Ibid.,* para. 92.
41 ED 32, *The disclosure of pension information in company accounts,* ASC, May 1983.
42 SSAP 24, para. 14.
43 Pension Fund Terminology — Specimen descriptions of commonly used valuation methods, The Institute of Actuaries and The Faculty of Actuaries, May 1986.
44 GN 17, para. 17.
45 As reported in the 1996 survey of SSAP 24 practices published by Lane Clark & Peacock.
46 Discussion Paper, *Pension Costs in the Employer's Financial Statements,* ASB, June 1995, para. 3.3.
47 GN 17, para. 18.
48 *Ibid.,* para. 20.
49 Pension Fund Terminology — Specimen descriptions of commonly used valuation methods.
50 GN 17, para. 19.
51 Pension Fund Terminology — Specimen descriptions of commonly used valuation methods.
52 GN 17, para. 16.
53 Pension Fund Terminology — Specimen descriptions of commonly used valuation methods.
54 GN 17, para. 15.
55 SSAP 24, para. 79.
56 GN 17, para. 24
57 Auditing Practices Committee, August 1987.
58 It is, however, explicitly recognised as being the third component of cost in GN 17, para. 12. and by the ICAEW in FRAG 10/92, *Review, for major practical problems, of SSAP 24,* paras. 26 *et seq.*
59 *Pension Costs in the Employer's Financial Statements,* para. 5.3.4.
60 *Discounting in Financial Reporting,* ASB, April 1997, para. 7.3.
61 SSAP 24, para. 23.
62 *Ibid.,* para. 80.
63 FRAG 10/92, para. 42.
64 *Pension Costs in the Employer's Financial Statements,* para. 5.2.10
65 *Ibid.,* para. 5.6.
66 *Ibid.,* para. 5.5.
67 SSAP 24, para. 91.
68 SSAP 15, *Accounting for deferred tax,* Revised 1985, paras. 24–36.

69 *Ibid.*, para. 32A, as inserted by *Amendment to SSAP 15 'Accounting for Deferred Tax'* — December 1992, ASB, para. 1.
70 UITF 6, *Accounting for post-retirement benefits other than pensions*, UITF, November 1992.
71 *Ibid.*, para. 8.
72 *Ibid.*, para. 7.
73 *Ibid.*
74 *Ibid.*, para. 9.
75 CA 85, Sch. 4, para. 50(4).
76 ED 32, para. 40.
77 CA 85, Sch. 4, para. 56(4).
78 *Ibid.*, para. 94(2).
79 IAS 19, *Retirement Benefit Costs*, IASC, Revised November 1993, paras. 42 and 44.
80 *Ibid.*, para. 46.
81 *Ibid.*, para. 28.
82 *Ibid.*, para. 32.
83 *Ibid.*, para. 38.
84 *Ibid.*, para. 33.
85 E54, *Employee Benefits*, IASC, October 1996.
86 *Ibid.*, para. 51.
87 *Ibid.*, paras. 60, 96 and 97.
88 *Ibid.*, para. 87.

Chapter 21   Taxation

1   INTRODUCTION

The two accounting standards that govern tax in the UK are relatively long-established. SSAP 8 was issued in 1974 and SSAP 15 in 1978, and although there have been various amendments since then, the basic rules for accounting for tax have not changed significantly since their original publication. In 1995, however, the ASB published a Discussion Paper[1] which reviewed the subject from first principles and concluded that major change was needed. There have also been significant amendments to the equivalent standards of other countries and of the IASC in recent years, and it seems likely that the Board will bring forward proposals for a new regime for tax accounting before long.

1.1   The nature of taxation

A discussion of how to deal with taxation in accounts must begin with some consideration of what it is that is to be accounted for. Although it might be supposed that this is a simple question, and that taxation is a business expense to be dealt with in the same manner as any other cost, it has certain characteristics which set it apart from other costs and which might justify a different treatment. These characteristics include the fact that tax payments are not made in exchange for any goods or services and the fact that the business has no say in whether or not the payments are to be made. It is held by some that these elements mean that taxation is more in the nature of a distribution than an expense; in essence that the government is a stakeholder in the success of the business and participates in its results (generally in priority to other stakeholders).

The validity of this suggestion rather depends on what view is taken as to the purpose of accounts and the nature of the reporting entity. It is consistent with a perspective which is sometimes adopted that business entities have an existence which is independent from that of their shareholders, and should account not simply to their legal owners but to all those with an economic interest in their activities.

Adoption of the 'distribution' view of taxation would render irrelevant most of the accounting questions which follow; these are generally to do with how to allocate taxation expense to accounting periods. If taxation were regarded as a distribution, however, the question of allocation would not arise, since distributions are generally not allocated to accounting periods in the same way as is done for items of expense.

It is fair to say, however, that the 'distribution' view of taxation is not adopted in practice, although some of the accounting approaches that are sometimes proposed to deal with certain issues have their roots within it. For all practical purposes, taxation is dealt with as an expense of the business, and the accounting rules which have been developed are based on that premise.

1.2   Allocation between periods

1.2.1   Background

The most significant accounting question which arises in relation to taxation is how to allocate the tax expense between accounting periods. The recognition of trading transactions in the accounts relating to a particular year is governed primarily by the application of generally accepted accounting practice, and to a certain extent by the impact of company law. However, the timing of recognition of transactions for the purposes of measuring the taxable profit is governed by the application of tax law, which in some cases follows different rules from those under which the accounts are drawn up. It is necessary to seek some reconciliation between these different sets of rules in order to apply a matching approach to the allocation of tax expense to accounting periods, and this is where the concept of deferred taxation is brought into use.

As an aside, a recent trend in tax legislation in the UK has been to bring the tax rules more into line with accounting standards, in areas such as leasing, foreign currencies and financial instruments. This may have the benefit of removing some of the differences that cause tax accounting problems, but the trend is not entirely welcome in other ways: in fact it is likely to put a greater strain than before on some of the accounting rules, which were not designed to provide a robust basis for the measurement of tax, and may not withstand the attentions of imaginative tax planners.

The differences between the profit as calculated for accounting and for taxation purposes are traditionally analysed into two categories, 'permanent differences' and 'timing differences'.[2] The former comprises those items of income which are not taxable, or items of expense which are not deductible against tax, and which therefore do not appear in the tax computation of any period; the latter represent items of income or expenditure which *are* taxable or deductible, but in periods different from those in which they are dealt with in the accounts. Timing differences therefore arise when items of income and expenditure enter into the measurement of profit for both accounting and taxation purposes, but in different accounting periods. They are said to 'originate' in the first of these periods and 'reverse' in one or more subsequent periods; examples of these are given in 1.2.3 below. Deferred taxation is the taxation which relates to timing differences.

Consistent with their conceptual frameworks, both the US and the international standards now seek to apply a balance sheet perspective rather than focusing on the allocation of tax expense between periods, and they have dropped the concept of timing differences in favour of 'temporary differences'. These are defined in the IASC standard as 'differences between the carrying amount of an asset or liability in the balance sheet and its tax base'.[3] As discussed in 5 below, this is an unhelpful change, because it inadvertently brings certain permanent differences into the scope of deferred tax. It remains to be seen whether the ASB will feel impelled to adopt similar terminology.

1.2.2 Permanent differences

A permanent difference can arise in two main ways under the UK tax system:

(a) where non-taxable income is included in the accounting profit, for example if certain government grant income is received; and

(b) where certain types of expenditure are charged against accounting profit but not allowed as an expense against taxable profit, for example if c. ___ charitable donations are made, or if depreciation is charged against fixed assets for which there is no corresponding tax deduction.

It is generally accepted that there is no need to adjust the accounts for permanent differences. The transaction giving rise to the permanent difference has no tax effect. Although the tax charge for the year in which the item is reported in the accounts will deviate from the charge which would have been expected if the normal tax rate had been applied to the reported profits, this is not a distortion of the charge that needs to be corrected in any way; indeed, any 'correction' would introduce such a distortion.

1.2.3 Timing differences

A timing difference can arise in a number of ways:

(a) income is included in the accounts but recognised in taxable profit in later years; for example, a foreign dividend receivable might be accrued in the accounts but only taxed in the period in which it was due and payable;

(b) income may be included in taxable profit in a year earlier than it is recognised in the accounts;

(c) expenditure or losses in the accounts might not be deductible in arriving at taxable profit until a later period; for example, a general bad debt provision could be charged in the accounts, but a tax deduction given only when the specific bad debt charge was known; or

(d)   expenditure or losses might be deducted from taxable income prior to their being charged against accounting profit; for example, research and development expenditure might be allowed as an immediate deduction against tax, but capitalised in the accounts and amortised over its useful life.

The common characteristic of all timing differences is the fact that the period in which the accounting effect of the transaction is recognised is different to the period in which the transaction falls to be taxed or deducted against taxable profit. The tax benefit or cost associated with such differences always reverses in future periods.

Timing differences are sometimes split into two categories, short-term and other.[4] A short-term timing difference is one which arises because an item is treated on a cash basis for tax purposes whereas the accruals concept is used in the accounts. When the term was first coined, it mainly involved such things as interest accruals, which usually reversed within a year of their origination (hence the name). More recently, however, the major timing differences of this sort have arisen on items such as pension costs, which are allowed for tax on the basis of cash contributions but accounted for on an accruals basis. Such timing differences are anything but short term, particularly for unfunded schemes, and this has shown that the category is not a very meaningful one.

The most common form of 'other' (i.e. other than 'short-term') timing difference is created by the effect of capital allowances and the charge for depreciation. Capital allowances are the amounts by which fixed assets may be written down to arrive at taxable profit, and are therefore the tax equivalent of the charge for depreciation in the accounts. Since they are deducted from profit to arrive at the taxable profit, the amount charged in the accounts for depreciation is always disallowed in the tax computation. Usually, because capital allowances might be given to provide some economic incentive for businesses to invest, the tax allowance will be given at a faster rate than the rate at which depreciation is charged in the accounts, and the timing differences created are thus sometimes referred to as '*accelerated* capital allowances'.

A timing difference arises since both the charge for depreciation and the capital allowance (after an adjustment for a balancing charge or allowance) will reduce the cost of the asset to its recoverable amount at the end of its useful life, but the sums charged against accounting profit and against taxable profit, although the same in total, are likely to differ in each year. An example will illustrate the impact:

Example 21.1:   Illustration of timing differences

An item of plant and machinery is purchased in 19X1 for £48,000 and is estimated to have a seven year useful life, at the end of which it is estimated that it will be sold for £6,000. The depreciation charge will therefore be £6,000 p.a. (£48,000 – £6,000 over seven years).

For the purpose of this example, the rate of capital allowance for plant and machinery is assumed to be 25% p.a. on a reducing balance basis.

The timing differences will arise as follows (all figures in £000s):

	19X1	19X2	19X3	19X4	19X5	19X6	19X7
Accounts							
Carrying value of asset	48	42	36	30	24	18	12
Depreciation charge	6	6	6	6	6	6	6
Written down value	42	36	30	24	18	12	6
Tax computation							
Carrying value of asset	48	36	27	20	15	11	8
Capital allowance	12	9	7	5	4	3	2
Tax written down value	36	27	20	15	11	8	6
Timing difference arising							
Charge in accounts	6	6	6	6	6	6	6
Allowed in tax computation	12	9	7	5	4	3	2
Originating/(reversing)	6	3	1	(1)	(2)	(3)	(4)

The table shows that there is an originating difference of £6,000 p.a. in the first year, but this progressively diminishes and eventually reverses in subsequent years. For each of the first three years of the asset's life, the tax currently assessed (and hence the amount provided in the accounts as the current year tax charge for those years) is lower than the tax that will eventually fall to be paid on the profit reported in the accounts. The difference reverses from year four onwards, when the tax allowances have fallen below the level of the depreciation charge. The tax assessed (and hence the amount provided in the accounts as the current year tax charge for those years) will be higher than the sum due on the profit reported in the accounts.

The timing differences may be looked at either in terms of the profit and loss account or the balance sheet, and correspondingly computed in either of two ways. The timing difference arising in any year may be determined by comparing the depreciation provided in the accounts with the capital allowance given in the tax computation:

Computation of the timing difference	19X1 £'000	19X2 £'000
Depreciation per accounts	6	6
Capital allowances	12	9
Originating timing difference	6	3

Or the cumulative timing difference may be computed by comparing the written down value of the asset in the accounts with its written down value in the capital allowance computation:

Computation of the cumulative timing difference	19X1 £'000	19X2 £'000
Written down value per accounts	42	36
Written down value per tax computation	36	27
Cumulative timing difference	6	9

The computation of the total timing differences in existence at any point in time is essentially a mathematical exercise. It is after this point that the picture becomes less clear, and different points of view arise as to:

(a)   what rate of tax the timing difference should be provided at; and

(b)   whether a company should account for deferred tax that it does not expect to pay, because it can foresee that timing differences will not reverse in the future.

These questions lead us initially into the consideration of various methods of providing for deferred tax, and then into the area of the 'partial provision' approach to deferred tax.

1.2.4   The deferral method

The deferral method was for many years the required method in North America. It is an approach which places emphasis on the profit and loss account, and seeks to quantify the extent to which it has been affected by tax deferrals arising through the incidence of timing differences. When timing differences reverse, the deferral method takes the view that it is the former tax deferral which has become payable, and accordingly the deferred tax account is maintained in terms of the rates of tax which were in force when the various timing differences originated. On reversal, the amount taken out of the deferred tax account will be the amount that was accrued there when the timing difference was provided for. The profit and loss account is therefore charged with a reversal which is unaffected by changes in the rates of tax in the years between origination and reversal.

By contrast, the method does not seek, as its primary purpose, to generate deferred tax figures in the balance sheet which represent accurate measurements of assets and liabilities. Where tax rates change, the balance on the deferred tax account will no longer be the amount that the company will pay or receive in future years when the timing differences reverse, because the reversal will be taxed at the rate ruling at the time of the reversal, and the rate ruling at the time that the difference originated will be of no relevance to the amount of tax paid.

Deferred tax balances under this method might be more properly thought of as deferred income and deferred expenditure, which could be said to represent the tax benefit or cost derived from the effect of timing differences quantified by reference to the rate of tax ruling at the date that the timing difference originated. This is seen as the deferral of a cost which otherwise would have arisen that year and accordingly the rate of tax applicable to that year is the one most appropriate to use in quantifying the benefit derived. On reversal the cost arising is seen as merely the amount of the earlier benefit which has now been withdrawn.

Some would argue that this method is the most conceptually pure, because the fundamental purpose of deferred tax accounting is the inter-period allocation of tax expense with taxable profits; in other words it is an application of the matching concept, which is profit and loss account driven. From this perspective, the balance sheet figures are merely the by-product of whatever amounts are passed through the profit and loss account, and it is therefore of little concern that they might not reflect current tax rates if they have changed since the timing differences originated. The liability appearing in the balance sheet is not a 'real' liability in the sense that it is not an obligation which is due to anyone; so far as tax is concerned, the only 'real' liability is that shown by the tax computation. Indeed, it can be argued that this liability is not actually *paid* in future years, it is simply released back to the profit and loss account to ensure that the reported profits are matched with an appropriate amount of tax expense. This can be shown by using the figures used in Example 21.1 above:

Example 21.2:   Illustration of timing differences

A company makes annual profits before tax of £80,000 and is taxed at 25%. It experiences the following timing differences (all figures in £s):

	19X1	19X2	19X3	19X4	19X5	19X6	19X7
Originating/(reversing)	6,000	3,000	1,000	(1,000)	(2,000)	(3,000)	(4,000)

Its tax computations for each year therefore show the following:

	19X1	19X2	19X3	19X4	19X5	19X6	19X7
Accounting profit	80,000	80,000	80,000	80,000	80,000	80,000	80,000
Timing differences	(6,000)	(3,000)	(1,000)	1,000	2,000	3,000	4,000
Taxable profit	74,000	77,000	79,000	81,000	82,000	83,000	84,000
Tax payable @ 25%	18,500	19,250	19,750	20,250	20,500	20,750	21,000

Its accounts will show the following:

	19X1	19X2	19X3	19X4	19X5	19X6	19X7
Profit before tax	80,000	80,000	80,000	80,000	80,000	80,000	80,000
Tax payable @ 25%	18,500	19,250	19,750	20,250	20,500	20,750	21,000
Deferred tax	1,500	750	250	(250)	(500)	(750)	(1,000)
Profit after tax	60,000	60,000	60,000	60,000	60,000	60,000	60,000

The amount shown for deferred tax in the balance sheet will be:

1,500	2,250	2,500	2,250	1,750	1,000	0

This approach looks upon deferred tax accounting in terms which might be described as 'tax equalisation' accounting. The purpose is more to do with preserving appropriate relationships for financial reporting purposes between pre- and post-tax figures, than with quantifying a liability which will have eventual cash flow consequences.

However, others will argue that the balance sheet figure should be seen as an important figure in its own right and that the deferral method is deficient because it can produce meaningless balance sheet amounts when tax rates change. Adherents to this view would favour one of the variants of the liability method of accounting for deferred tax, which are described in the next two sections.

1.2.5   The liability method (with full provision/comprehensive allocation)

In contrast to the deferral method, the liability method places emphasis on the balance sheet rather than the profit and loss account, and focuses on the future rather than on the past.[5] It treats the tax effects of timing differences as liabilities for taxes payable in the future (or as assets recoverable in the future), and the practical effect of this is that it responds to changes of tax rate by recalculating the asset or liability in the balance sheet on the basis of the new rate. This means that the charge for deferred tax in the profit and loss account will include the effects of any such change in rate which is applied to the opening balance of cumulative timing differences.

The principal objective of the liability method is to quantify the amount of tax that will become payable or receivable in the future. It follows, therefore, that the deferred tax balance is maintained at the current rate of tax since this rate is the best estimate of the rate that is likely to apply in the future when the timing differences reverse. Of course if the future rates of tax are already set, it is necessary to examine the periods in which the timing differences will reverse, and then provide the amount of tax that is foreseen to arise as each year's reversal occurs.

The difference between the deferral method and the liability method can be illustrated as follows:

Example 21.3:   Illustration of the difference between the deferral and liability methods

A company invests £48,000 in a fixed asset at the beginning of 19X1, and depreciates it at £6,000 p.a. The asset attracts capital allowances of £12,000 in 19X1 and £9,000 in 19X2. In 19X1, the tax rate is 50% and in 19X2 it falls to 30%.

Under the deferral method, the calculation would be made by reference to the timing differences arising in each year in the profit and loss account, thus:

Computation of the timing difference	19X1	19X2
	£	£
Depreciation per accounts	6,000	6,000
Capital allowances	12,000	9,000
Originating timing difference	6,000	3,000
Deferred tax provided, at 50%/30%	3,000	900
Deferred tax balance carried forward	3,000	3,900

(Under the deferral method, it is a matter of no concern that the balance carried forward, of £3,900, has no meaning in terms of the cumulative timing difference of £9,000 and the present tax rate of 30%.)

Under the liability method, the deferred tax account would be calculated by reference to the cumulative timing difference (computed by comparing the net book value of the asset in the accounts with its written down value in the capital allowance computation, thus):

Computation of the cumulative timing difference	19X1	19X2
	£	£
Net book value per accounts	42,000	36,000
Written down value per tax computation	36,000	27,000
Cumulative timing difference	6,000	9,000
Deferred tax balance, at 50%/30%	3,000	2,700
Deferred tax provided/(released)	3,000	(300)

The amount of deferred tax in the profit and loss account is simply the movement between the two balance sheet figures. In this example the £300 release in 19X2 is reconciled thus:

	£
Originating timing difference in 19X2 – £3,000 @ 30%	900
Effect of change in rate on opening balance of cumulative timing differences – £6,000 x (50% - 30%)	(1,200)
	(300)

Where the whole amount of the cumulative timing difference is reflected in the amount provided in the balance sheet, the approach can be described as 'full provision', or 'comprehensive allocation'. This is to distinguish the method from a variant of the liability approach, 'partial provision', which is described below. The liability method with full provision has gained ascendancy internationally, although there are still a number of different variants of it.

In its 1995 Discussion Paper, the ASB tentatively concluded that the UK should move to the full provision method,[6] partly because of this growing international consensus and partly because it saw the method as the most consistent with its draft *Statement of Principles* – the amounts arising being derived from past transactions or events and taking no account of future transactions or events. However, members of the Board have different interpretations of what the deferred tax balance signified. Some saw it straightforwardly as an asset or liability, because the incidence of timing differences had a direct incremental effect on future tax liabilities, but others saw it more as representing valuation adjustments to other assets and liabilities in the balance sheet.

1.2.6   The liability method (with partial provision)

Partial provision is the required UK method of accounting for deferred tax under the present standard, SSAP 15. Under this approach, the full amount of the deferred tax liability is calculated, but only a portion of that full liability might actually be provided in the accounts. The amount provided is based on an estimate of the liability that is expected to arise in the future, based on a projection of the extent to which the cumulative timing differences are expected to reverse in net terms. A proportion of the timing differences can be viewed as non-reversing and thus equivalent to permanent differences (on which deferred tax is not provided).

Individual timing differences (by definition) will always reverse. However, the partial provision approach permits these reversals to be offset by such new originating timing differences as can be predicted with sufficient certainty to arise in the future. This can be illustrated by an example:

Example 21.4:   Illustration of partial provision

Consider a company which commenced trade in 19X1 by purchasing fixed assets for £1,000,000. It has an annual capital expenditure budget for the next four years of £400,000, £500,000, £600,000 and £700,000 respectively. Assets are depreciated over their useful lives of ten years and are expected to have a nil recoverable amount at that time. Capital allowances are 25% p.a. on a reducing balance basis, and tax is charged at a rate of 31%.

Fixed assets in accounts	19X1	19X2	19X3	19X4	19X5
	£'000	£'000	£'000	£'000	£'000
Opening balance	–	900	1,160	1,470	1,820
Additions	1,000	400	500	600	700
Depreciation	(100)	(140)	(190)	(250)	(320)
Closing balance	900	1,160	1,470	1,820	2,200

Tax computation	19X1	19X2	19X3	19X4	19X5
	£'000	£'000	£'000	£'000	£'000
Opening balance	–	750	862	1,022	1,216
Additions	1,000	400	500	600	700
Writing down allowance	(250)	(288)	(340)	(406)	(479)
Closing balance	750	862	1,022	1,216	1,437
Timing difference	150	298	448	604	763
Increase therein		148	150	156	159

This can be shown in the form of a graph, thus:

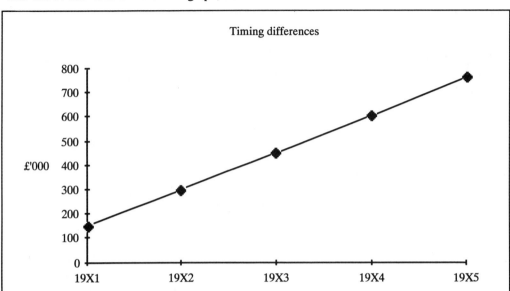

Under the full provision approach, the company would provide deferred tax at the end of 19X1 of £46,500, being 31% of the timing difference of £150,000 at that time. However, the partial provision approach would consider whether any net reversal of the timing difference could be foreseen to arise in the future, and since the cumulative amount of timing differences is expected to rise, would make no provision at all in this case.

If timing differences were in fact expected to decline below the present level in the future, then provision would be made for the extent to which the timing differences were expected to reverse. Thus if the figures were the same as those above, except that the cumulative timing differences at the end of 19X1 amounted to £400,000 rather than £150,000, then provision would be made for the net reversal which could be foreseen to arise when they fell to £298,000. The amount provided would be £31,620 ((£400,000 - £298,000) @ 31%). This pattern is shown in the following graph:

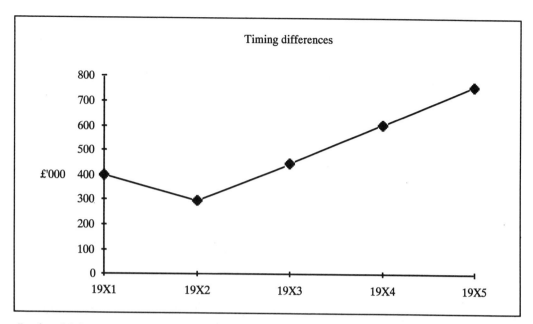

It should be noted that provision has to be made for this reversal, even though the reversal itself is expected to be temporary (in the sense that the timing differences expected to arise beyond 19X2 will again lift the cumulative level above the present level). The basic rule is that provision should be made for tax on the excess of the present level of timing differences over the lowest level to which it is expected to fall at any year end in the future.

Where a converse pattern is foreseen (as shown in the next graph), the same basic rule still applies; in the following example, therefore, no provision would be needed because, although net reversals can be foreseen in years 19X4 and 19X5, they do not bring the cumulative level at the end of that period below its present level. However, if it were expected that this declining pattern would continue beyond 19X5, it would be necessary to see to what level the timing differences could be expected to fall in the longer term, and if at any time it was expected that they would be less than the present level of £400,000, then provision would have to be made for the effect of that net reversal.

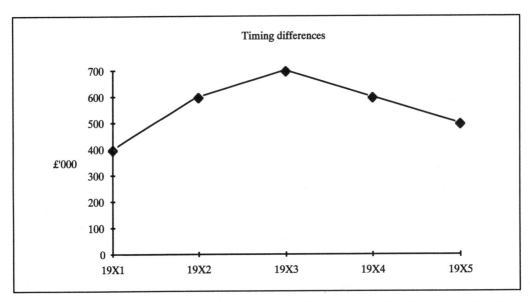

Because timing differences can be either positive or negative (representing the deferment or acceleration of tax), it is possible that the projection of future timing differences will show that they will cross the zero axis, as shown on this graph:

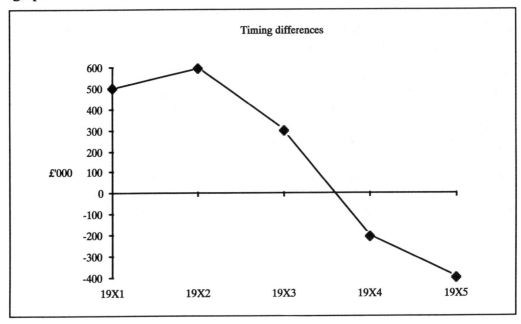

In these circumstances, the whole amount of the potential liability would be provided (£155,000 in the example – £500,000 @ 31%), but no provision would be made for the further effect of the future timing differences which went beyond the axis. The partial provision basis does not involve accounting for timing differences based on their future level; it simply seeks to identify whether a 'hard core' of timing differences exists, and if so, to avoid making provision for that amount because in substance it represents a permanent deferment of tax.

The partial provision approach arouses strong passions, both from those who support it and from those who condemn it. Most of the arguments in favour are in fact criticisms of the full provision approach on the grounds that it can lead to the provision of large sums for deferred tax which have only a remote likelihood of becoming payable. To provide for deferred tax on timing differences which are unlikely on reversal to give rise to a tax liability is said by advocates of the partial provision method to be pursuing form rather than substance and to mislead the users of accounts through the understatement of profit and capital employed. It can thereby portray companies as being more highly geared than they are in reality and give a false impression of poor creditworthiness. Further, it could affect a company's borrowing powers if they were computed by reference to reserves, because those reserves were understated because of a provision for deferred tax which might be regarded as unnecessary. In contrast, partial provision gives rise to liabilities that can be regarded as more realistic. Perhaps more importantly, the method produces an effective tax rate in the profit and loss account that reflects the company's tax planning strategies, whereas full provision simply reports a statutory tax rate which is impervious to its degree of success in managing its tax affairs more efficiently.

Those people who criticise the partial provision approach generally say that the failure to provide for an expected reversal on the grounds that replacement will take place wrongly anticipates a future event (such as that a certain level of capital expenditure will take place). This is thought to be inappropriate partly because it may be at variance with the prudence concept, but partly also because it departs from normal accounting rules which account for the effects of transactions individually, rather than in combination with the effects of transactions which have not yet occurred. It is also argued that the method brings volatility and distortion into the profit and loss account, because earnings are affected by the incidence of transactions unrelated to trading performance, such as the acquisition of fixed assets which attract allowances for which no deferred tax provision is made.

The conceptual weakness of the partial provision approach was highlighted in 1992 when the UITF issued its sixth Abstract, relating to post-retirement health care costs (see Chapter 20 at 4.8). This requires a company to charge such costs in its profit and loss account over the working lives of its employees and set up the corresponding liability in the balance sheet; however, it will not receive any tax deduction in respect of the health care costs until the payments are eventually made. Under a comprehensive allocation approach, this would give rise to a deferred tax asset, but because such an asset will continue to grow indefinitely (because the provision for health care costs will be doing so) the partial provision approach would require that no recognition be given to the asset. This highlighted the main conceptual inconsistency between SSAP 15 and accounting practice in all other areas; partial provision applies a principle which has no parallel in other areas of accounting, namely that assets and liabilities should not be recognised when they are expected to be replaced by equivalents in the future. If the same principle were applied to the health care costs themselves, then no provision would have to be set up so long as the existing workforce continued to earn entitlement to health care as fast as their predecessors became eligible to receive them; a 'pay-as-you-go' basis would be applied, which would not be permitted under UITF 6. Critics pointed out that the deferred tax asset was as real an asset as the pension provision was a liability.

As a result of this, in December 1992 the ASB amended SSAP 15 so as to allow (but not require) deferred tax relating to all post-retirement costs (including pensions themselves) to be accounted for on a comprehensive allocation basis, despite the fact that all other timing differences remained on a partial provision basis.[7] Mirror Group adopts this approach, as shown in the following extract:

Extract 21.1: Mirror Group plc (1996)

19 Provisions for liabilities and charges [extract]

The amounts provided for deferred tax liabilities and the full potential liability for deferred taxation and taxes that could arise if property and publishing rights and titles were to be disposed of at their revalued amounts are as follows:

	Provision made		Full potential liability	
	29 December 1996	31 December 1995	**29 December 1996**	31 December 1995
	£m	£m	**£m**	£m
Accelerated capital allowances	**18.0**	14.9	**55.8**	46.6
Other timing differences	**(1.2)**	(9.0)	**15.5**	11.0
Newspaper titles	–	–	**141.8**	143.6
	16.8	5.9	**213.1**	201.2

In addition, the Group has recorded a deferred tax asset in respect of the provision for the pension fund deficiency (note 14).

14 Deferred tax asset

The deferred tax asset of £4.2 million (1995: £4.2 million) is in respect of the provision for the actuarially estimated deficit of certain of the group's pension schemes, which are described in note 22. The majority of this asset will be recovered after more than one year.

This amendment to SSAP 15 has really only compounded the inconsistencies inherent in the standard. The problem was not unique to post-retirement costs, but related to all timing differences which arise from the use of the matching concept in accounts when a different basis is used in the tax computation.

It is worth remembering that the partial provision method was introduced at a time when very substantial tax deductions were available in the form of stock appreciation relief and 100% first year allowances for capital investment, and it was much more appropriate in that context than it is now that these features have been removed from the tax system. Given that the international consensus has now moved distinctly in favour of full provision, it seems likely that SSAP 15 will be amended before long.

This was the ASB's tentative conclusion in its 1995 Discussion Paper.[8] It also criticised the partial provision approach on several conceptual grounds by reference to its own proposed framework: it used criteria for recognition that were not found elsewhere in GAAP; it inappropriately recognised the effects of future transactions; it relied on management intent; and it was internally inconsistent. The Board therefore suggested that the method should be abandoned in favour of full provision.

1.2.7 The hybrid method

This method seeks to combine features of the two principal methods of accounting for deferred tax (i.e. the deferral method and the liability method), by selecting the most appropriate method for the particular type of timing difference which has arisen, such that the deferred tax balance consists of elements derived under the deferral method and other elements derived under the liability method.

As discussed at 1.2.3 above, there are four basic classes of timing differences:

(a) income can be recognised in the accounts before being taxed;

(b) income can be taxed before being recognised in the accounts;

(c) expenditure can be recognised in the accounts before being allowed for tax;

(d) expenditure can be allowed for tax before being recognised in the accounts.

The hybrid method draws a distinction between those where the first leg of the timing difference passes through the accounts ('book before tax' – (a) and (c) above) and those where it passes through the tax computation ('tax before book' – (b) and (d) above).

When items of income or expenditure have been recognised in the accounts but not recognised for tax purposes, the deferred tax liability cannot be quantified with absolute certainty. It is not possible to determine the tax consequences of these transactions as they will only be apparent in the future, and the ultimate liability will be determined by the rate of tax in effect at the time of the reversal. Accordingly the best estimate of the future liability is made and tax is provided at the latest known rate. Thus deferred tax on these types of timing differences is provided using the liability method.

However, when items of income or expenditure pass through the tax computation before they are recognised in the accounts, the tax effect of those transactions is known, and the tax expense or benefit is fixed. Accordingly, deferred tax on these types of timing differences is provided using the deferral method.

If the hybrid method is used the effect of a change in the rate of tax will affect only that part of the balance computed using the principles of the liability method. That part of the deferred tax balance computed using the deferral method is not adjusted since the tax effects of these timing differences is already known.

Although there is a degree of theoretical merit in this approach, it is not adopted as standard accounting practice in any of the major developed countries of the world. This may be because it is more complicated to apply, rather than being a reflection of any lack of theoretical soundness to the approach. It is not considered further in this chapter.

1.2.8 Discounting the liability

Another suggestion which is sometimes made is that deferred tax should be provided on a discounted basis. This has obvious theoretical merit, because by definition deferred tax involves the postponement of the tax liability, and it is possible therefore to regard the deferred liability as equivalent to an interest-free loan from the tax authorities. An appropriate way to reflect the benefit of this postponement could be to discount the liability by reference to the period of the deferment, and accordingly to record a lower tax charge by reason of that discount. The discount would then be amortised over the period of the deferment.

Such an approach was advocated by some respondents to ASC exposure drafts on deferred tax, as well as by the ICAEW Technical Committee in a general paper on discounting.[9] It is not specifically precluded by SSAP 15, but it has seldom been adopted in practice in the UK; it is explicitly prohibited in the US and IASC standards. It raises general questions about how to account for the time value of money, which are relevant to a number of accounting issues; but UK practice in this regard could be described as relatively unsophisticated other than in relation to a few specific issues, such as pension costs, leasing contracts and certain financial instruments.

Discounting was considered in some detail by the ASB in its 1995 Discussion Paper, and the Board tentatively concluded that it should be adopted in conjunction with the full provision method.[10] However, the paper did show that some quite complicated issues were involved. In particular, it is necessary to identify when the tax cash flow that is to be discounted is to be assumed to arise, and a choice immediately emerges which is the parallel of the basic dilemma between full provision and partial provision: are the effects of future offsetting timing differences to be assumed or not? The paper concludes that no such offsetting effect should be taken into account. The hybrid approach is also discussed, with the argument that only 'book before tax' timing differences should be discounted, since only they have a future tax cash flow effect, but this view is rejected. Even with these simplifications, however, it is clear that discounting would add substantial complexity to the method and responses to the whole idea have been unenthusiastic.

1.2.9   The net of tax method

The net of tax approach is not a discrete method of measuring the tax effects of timing differences, but is concerned with the manner of its presentation in the accounts. The method recognises the tax effects of timing differences as an integral part of the asset or liability that caused the timing difference to arise. Before applying the net of tax approach the deferred tax liability is computed via the deferral method or the liability method (or conceivably the hybrid method), but then included in the carrying value of the item to which the difference relates. Thus, a deferred tax liability arising from accelerated capital allowances would be deducted from the balance sheet carrying value of the asset concerned, or the amount of a disallowable provision (such as a general bad debt provision) would be stated net of the tax effect which would arise when the provision was utilised and became tax deductible.

This method has seldom been used in practice, although there are occasions, particularly in relation to net-of-tax provisions as described above, where it has been applied. SSAP 15 dismisses it by saying that 'it fails to distinguish between a transaction and its tax consequences and therefore should not be used in financial statements'.[11] The ASB's Discussion Paper mentioned it in the context of full provision (since some Board members apparently think of deferred tax as a valuation adjustment to other items) but did not support this form of presentation. More recently, the ASB has published an exposure draft on impairment of assets which requires the recoverability of assets to be measured on an after tax basis, but then to be grossed up for presentation purposes.[12]

1.2.10   The flow-through method

This theoretical approach is not really a method of accounting for deferred tax at all, but rather a justification for not accounting for it. Under the flow-through method, the tax charge is simply the amount payable based on the profits of that year, with no attempt to reallocate it between periods by reference to timing differences. The method therefore deals with tax as if it were either a period cost or a distribution (see 1.1 above). However, although it sometimes advocated, it is not presently regarded as an acceptable approach.

The ASB's Discussion Paper considered the method at some length, but ended up rejecting it,[13] partly because it is not used internationally, and partly because the Board did not consider it appropriate within its conceptual framework.

1.3   Allocation within periods

As well as allocating tax to particular accounting periods, it is also sometimes necessary to allocate it within an accounting period for presentation purposes. Normally, it will be shown in the profit and loss account under the caption of tax on profit on ordinary activities, but it may have to be allocated to other components of the movements in shareholders' equity, such as extraordinary items, any taxable exchange differences on loans taken to reserves under the cover method, prior year adjustments or revaluation reserve. This issue is discussed in Chapter 22 at 2.10; in general the principle is that the tax effect should follow the item that gives rise to it. This principle was supported by the ASB's 1995 Discussion Paper.[14]

The windfall tax levied on privatised utilities in the July 1997 Budget has given rise to some debate as to how it should be presented. Because it is based on a formula which relies on the capitalised value of profits over a period of up to four years, it is arguably inappropriate to include it in the normal tax line in the profit and loss account, which under the Companies Act formats is captioned 'tax on profit or loss on ordinary activities'. A more appropriate alternative under these formats might be the penultimate line, 'Other taxes not shown under the above items'. In practice, however, the latter caption is rarely, if ever, used, even though it might be equally appropriate for certain other amounts of tax expense that are not strictly based on ordinary profits; irrecoverable ACT written off would be another example. It would therefore seem perfectly acceptable to show the windfall tax as an exceptional charge within the normal tax line.

2   THE DEVELOPMENT OF ACCOUNTING FOR TAXATION IN THE UK

2.1   Accounting for tax payable

2.1.1   ED 12

The introduction of the imputation system of taxation in the Finance Act 1972, which took effect from April 1973, meant that the earlier guidance on the treatment of tax in the accounts of companies, contained in the ICAEW statement N27, needed amendment. An exposure draft[15] was issued by the ASC in May 1973, entitled 'The treatment of taxation under the imputation system in the accounts of companies'. Its principal requirements were as follows:

(a) the particulars in the profit and loss account of the charge for corporation tax should show, where material, the relief for recoverable ACT and the amount of any irrecoverable ACT;

(b) appropriations for dividends payable should not include either the related ACT or the attributable tax credit;

(c) proposed dividends should be included in current liabilities without the addition of attributable ACT: the ACT on proposed dividends, whether or not recoverable, should be included as a current tax liability. Recoverable ACT on proposed dividends should be deducted from the deferred tax account if available, or otherwise shown as a deferred asset; and

(d) dividends receivable from UK resident companies could be shown either inclusive or exclusive of the related tax credit (so long as the policy was applied consistently).

2.1.2 SSAP 8

The exposure draft was converted into a Statement of Standard Accounting Practice in the following year, with comparatively little change; however, it removed the option mentioned at 2.1.1 (d) above, by requiring that dividends receivable should be included at an amount which included the associated tax credit. The requirements of SSAP 8 are dealt with in 3.1 below.

2.2 Accounting for deferred tax

2.2.1 ED 11

The first exposure draft on deferred tax in the UK was published in May 1973.[16] Until that time, most companies had accounted for deferred tax, but it was not mandatory to do so and a variety of practices were followed. The exposure draft was controversial in that it proposed that the deferral method should be used, whereas most UK companies had up to that time been using the liability method. It also specified that revaluations of assets should be regarded as giving rise to timing differences, for which deferred tax should therefore be provided; not all companies had been taking that view.

2.2.2 SSAP 11

The exposure draft was converted into an accounting standard in 1975, to be effective for periods beginning on or after 1 January 1976.[17] However, the standard was different from the exposure draft in one fundamental respect. The requirement to use the deferral method had been relaxed, and companies were now offered the option of using the liability method as an alternative.

SSAP 11 was short lived. In many ways it was issued at precisely the wrong time. The UK was in its highest period of inflation for very many years. Capital allowances were at their most accelerated, and there was a system of 'stock appreciation relief' in force which gave businesses a tax deduction for the increase in the balance sheet value of stocks held by them. The net result was that, even though there were comparatively high nominal rates of tax in force (50–52%), a large number of companies were paying no corporation tax at all, other than ACT.

As a result of these factors many companies began to build up large deferred tax provisions in their balance sheets, when in reality they could not see that the liability was ever likely to be paid. A campaign began to gather momentum to have the subject re-examined. In the meantime, the ASC was formulating a statement on current cost accounting, which dealt with a wide range of accounting issues, and the exposure draft which was published on this subject contained the radical proposal that deferred tax should be calculated on the basis of only those timing differences which were expected to reverse without being replaced – the partial provision approach.[18] In the light of this, in October 1976 the Committee suspended indefinitely the implementation date of SSAP 11 (effectively before it came into force).

2.2.3   ED 19

A further exposure draft was issued in 1977 which was based on the approach which had been set out in ED 18.[19] This proposed that deferred tax should be provided in full, using the liability method, unless it could be demonstrated with reasonable probability that the tax reduction would continue for the foreseeable future. It also proposed that disclosure should be required of the full potential liability to deferred tax by way of note, analysed into categories of timing difference and showing how much had been provided in respect of each category.

The exposure draft differentiated short-term timing differences from others, saying that it was generally accepted that provision should be made in full for short-term differences, but that the remaining timing differences should be considered jointly to see whether it could be established that some part of the potential liability need not be provided. The reason for this distinction was not more fully explained.

2.2.4   SSAP 15

In October 1978, the ASC finally withdrew SSAP 11 and issued SSAP 15, which was based on ED 19.[20] However, there were a number of significant changes from the exposure draft, as summarised below:

(a)   the liability method was no longer mandated, and indeed the standard did not make any mention of either the liability method or the deferral method. Implicitly, therefore, the deferral method was allowed even though it did not fit naturally with the forward-looking orientation of the partial provision approach;

(b) more specific criteria were laid down which had to be satisfied in order to justify the non-provision of deferred tax. These were that the company had to be a going concern, and that the directors had to be able to foresee, on reasonable evidence, that no liability was likely to arise as a result of reversal of timing differences for some considerable period (at least three years) ahead, and that there was no indication after that period that the situation was likely to change so as to crystallise the liabilities;

(c) it was even more clearly stipulated that full provision was required on short-term timing differences;

(d) a disclosure requirement was added in relation to the effect of unprovided deferred tax on the tax charge in the profit and loss account; and

(e) the standard changed the approach to deferred tax in relation to revalued fixed assets, by stating that provision need be made in respect of a timing difference arising from a revaluation only if it had been decided in principle to dispose of the asset in question and if no rollover relief was available.

The standard took effect for accounting periods commencing on or after 1 January 1979.

2.2.5 ED 33

The ASC set up a working party to review SSAP 15 in 1982, for two principal reasons:

(a) to incorporate the new legal requirements of the Companies Act 1981 into the standard; and

(b) to take account of the change in the basis of stock relief in the Finance Act 1981.

The revision was also intended to take into account comments arising out of the experience gained from applying SSAP 15 in practice. On the basis of this review, a further exposure draft was issued in 1983.[21] This proposed the following main changes:

(a) the exposure draft described the liability method as the appropriate approach to use, because the deferral method was not compatible with the partial provision concept. However, this was not stated explicitly as a requirement;

(b) the previous requirement to set up deferred tax unless it could be demonstrated that it would not be required was expressed more neutrally, by saying that deferred tax should be provided to the extent that it was probable that a liability would crystallise and not set up to the extent that it would not;

(c)   there was no longer a specific reference to a period (mentioned in SSAP 15 as at least three years) for which positive evidence should be sought as to the likelihood of the liability crystallising;

(d)   the distinction between short-term and other timing differences was discontinued; all timing differences were to be considered jointly when considering the need to make provision for deferred tax;

(e)   more guidance was added on the criteria to be considered in deciding whether debit balances in respect of deferred tax could be regarded as recoverable. It was stated that they could be carried forward only where their recovery without replacement by equivalent debit balances was assured beyond reasonable doubt;

(f)   the requirement to analyse the deferred tax which was provided into its principal categories was to be replaced by one which required disclosure of the period or periods of time in which the liability was expected to crystallise;

(g)   the requirement to show the full potential liability to deferred tax, analysed into its components, was replaced by a requirement to show a similar analysis of only the unprovided amount; and

(h)   a requirement was proposed that, where deferred tax was not provided in respect of overseas earnings of a subsidiary on the grounds that there was no intention to remit them to the UK, that the intention not to remit them should be disclosed.

2.2.6   *SSAP 15 (Revised)*

A revised version of SSAP 15[22] was issued in 1985, which was very similar to ED 33, but which included the following further changes:

(a)   it was now explicitly stated that the liability method was the required method of provision for deferred tax;

(b)   the proposal to require disclosure of the period or periods of time in which the liability was expected to crystallise was dropped; and

(c)   the proposed requirement to state that overseas earnings were not planned to be remitted to the UK (where applicable) was replaced with one to state simply that no deferred tax had been provided in respect of these earnings.

The requirements of SSAP 15 (Revised) are set out in more detail in 3.2 below. For the remainder of this chapter, all references to SSAP 15 are to this revised version.

2.2.7   *Amendment to SSAP 15 following UITF 6*

As mentioned in 1.2.6 above, the ASB made a further minor amendment to SSAP 15 in December 1992. The effect of the change was to allow deferred tax relating to all post-retirement costs such as pensions and health care to be accounted for in full even though all other timing differences remained on a partial provision basis.[23]

2.2.8   *The ASB's Discussion Paper*

In March 1995, the ASB published a comprehensive Discussion Paper – *Accounting for tax* – which addressed the subject from first principles and put forward some tentative proposals as to how SSAP 15 might be amended. It concluded that allowing SSAP 15 to remain in force was untenable and that it should be replaced with a standard requiring some variant of full provision on a discounted basis, although the Board was divided as to whether this should cover fair value adjustments following an acquisition and revaluation adjustments. The Board also recommended expanded disclosures, notably a reconciliation between the actual and the expected tax charge.

This discussion paper received a rather cool reception from respondents, and the project has not so far been progressed further.

2.3   Other pronouncements

2.3.1   *SSAP 5*

As well as dealing with the accounting treatment of tax on profits as described above, the ASC published a statement on accounting for value added tax in 1974,[24] based on an exposure draft which had been published in the previous year.[25] The statement is a very brief one, simply requiring that:

(a)   turnover should be shown net of VAT on taxable outputs (or shown as a deduction if the gross amount is also shown);[26] and

(b)   irrecoverable VAT should be included in the cost of fixed assets and any other disclosed items in the financial statements to which it relates, where it is practicable to do so and material.[27]

2.3.2   *ED 28*

In 1981, the ASC issued an exposure draft of a statement on Accounting for Petroleum Revenue Tax.[28] The subject was not proceeded with and the exposure draft was subsequently withdrawn. The Oil Industry Accounting Committee also studied the topic with the aim of producing a SORP, but has not continued the project. The tax is a highly complex one which presents difficult accounting problems, but its specialised nature places it beyond the scope of this chapter.

2.3.3   UITF 16

In February 1997, the UITF issued an Abstract dealing with *Income and expenses subject to non-standard rates of tax*. The issue was solely one of presentation; it addressed the practice that had developed, particularly in the financial services sector, of grossing-up the post-tax results of certain transactions in the profit and loss account so as to show a standardised tax charge and pre-tax result whereas the actual economics of the transaction depended on non-standard tax effects for their profitability. The UITF's consensus was that this practice was inappropriate, and that the profit and loss account should show the actual pre-tax and tax numbers without any such adjustment.[29] The Abstract became effective for periods ending on or after 22 June 1997.

Lloyds TSB's accounts show the effect of this change:

Extract 21.2: Lloyds TSB Group plc (1996)

NOTES TO THE ACCOUNTS

2   Accounting policies

Accounting policies are unchanged from 1995. Abstract 16 issued by the Urgent Issues Task Force of the Accounting Standards Board, requires the gross-up calculations on certain transactions, the overall profitability of which is determined on a post-tax basis, to be made at the underlying rate of tax. In previous years, for the purposes of presentation in the profit and loss account, the income from these transactions has been grossed-up using the standard rate of tax. The 1996 accounts have been adjusted to take account of the new requirement, which has the effect of reducing total income and profit before tax by £22 million (net interest income by £12 million and other income by £10 million). The tax charge is also reduced by the same amount, so the resulting after tax figure is unaffected. No adjustment has been made to the comparative 1995 figures on the grounds of immateriality.

---

3   THE REQUIREMENTS OF THE RELEVANT ACCOUNTING STANDARDS AND COMPANY LAW

3.1   SSAP 8

3.1.1   *Outgoing dividends and the related ACT*

The standard considers whether ACT on outgoing dividends should be treated as part of the cost of the dividend or whether it should be treated as part of the tax on the company's profits. The amount declared as a dividend (as a sum payable per share or as a percentage) is the amount that will be received by the members. The fact that the dividend will carry a tax credit is considered to be a matter which affects the member as a recipient, rather than a matter which affects the company and the way in which it should be accounted for. It is therefore considered appropriate that outgoing dividends should be shown in the profit and loss account at the amount paid or payable to the shareholders.[30]

In the UK, outgoing dividends are accounted for in the period to which they relate, which contrasts with the treatment in the United States where they are accounted for in the period in which they are declared. Accordingly, if the final dividend is expected to be declared after the year end then, even though it is subject to shareholder approval, it should be provided for in the accounts for the year just completed.

The ACT payable in respect of dividends proposed but not paid at the year end will fall due for payment to the Inland Revenue within a period of between two weeks to three and a half months after the dividend has been paid, depending on whether the date the dividend is due and payable falls at the end or the beginning, respectively, of a return period. The ACT due on the dividend will therefore in most cases be a current liability. It will generally rank for set off against mainstream corporation tax payable 21 months after the year end (relating to the following period), because ACT paid must initially be set off against the mainstream liability of the period in which the ACT is due and payable. ACT on proposed dividends therefore cannot normally be offset against the tax due on profits for the year to which the dividend relates.

3.1.2   Recoverable ACT

Recoverable ACT is defined in SSAP 8 as that amount of the ACT paid or payable on outgoing dividends paid and proposed which can be:

(a)   set off against a corporation tax liability on the profits of the period under review or of previous periods; or

(b)   properly set off against a credit balance on deferred tax account; or

(c)   expected to be recoverable taking into account expected profits and dividends – normally those of the next accounting period only.

Irrecoverable ACT is defined as ACT paid or payable on outgoing dividends paid and proposed other than recoverable ACT.[31]

The amount of ACT available under (a) above is therefore the ACT paid in respect of dividends due and payable in the accounting period together with any ACT previously paid and not yet set off.

Under (b), the ACT is set against deferred tax because it would be available to relieve tax arising from the expected reversal of timing differences at some point in the future. This is considered more fully in 4.5 below.

The amount of ACT to be carried forward under (c) is ostensibly restricted by the standard to that amount which is likely to be relieved out of the taxable profits of the next accounting period, although the inclusion of the word 'normally' leaves some apparent room for manoeuvre. In certain cases, there may be a reasonable argument for carrying the ACT forward if the company foresees with reasonable certainty that its expected profits and planned dividends will allow the ACT to be relieved outside the strict one year timescale laid down by the standard. The question of carrying forward ACT as an asset is also dealt with in SSAP 15, as discussed in 3.2.3 below.

ACT which is carried forward on the grounds that it will be recovered against future taxable profit, when not shown as a reduction of the deferred tax account, should be shown as a deferred asset, and would generally be shown under the caption of 'prepayments and accrued income'.

The availability for set off of ACT is perhaps best illustrated by an example.

Example 21.5:   Set off of ACT

A company has a financial year end of 31 March 19X2, in which it made a taxable profit of £500,000. An interim dividend of £50,000 was paid on 26 June 19X1 and the directors recommend a final dividend of £100,000, to be paid on 15 May 19X2. Last year's final dividend was £150,000, and was paid on 15 May 19X1.

The corporation tax provided on the taxable profits for the year would be £155,000 (31% of £500,000). The company will have submitted a return of franked payments for the quarter ended 30 June 19X1, because of the interim dividend paid on 26 June, together with the final dividend paid on 15 May. The ACT paid amounted to 20/80ths of £200,000, or £50,000. The sum due would have been paid by 14 July 19X1 (14 days after the end of the quarter).

When the final dividend is paid on 15 May 19X2, the company will make a second return of franked payments in respect of the quarter ending 30 June 19X2. ACT of 20/80ths of £100,000, or £25,000, is therefore provided. Both the dividend and the ACT are included in the accounts for the year ended 31 March 19X2. The ACT due on the final dividend will be paid by 14 July 19X2.

This will be due nine months after the year end , i.e. on 31 December 19X2. The mainstream liability arising in respect of the accounting period to 31 March 19X2 can be reduced only by the amount of ACT relating to dividends paid in that accounting period.

First, the maximum amount of ACT which can be offset is calculated: this is the amount of ACT which together with the related dividend absorbs the whole of the company's taxable income for the accounting period. The taxable income for the year is £500,000, so the maximum ACT which may be set off is 20% of £500,000, or £100,000.

Then the amount of ACT paid in the year is calculated:

Dividend paid on 15 May 19X1	£37,500	(20/80ths of £150,000)
Dividend paid on 26 June 19X1	12,500	(20/80ths of £50,000)
	£50,000	

This is within the maximum set off allowed. Accordingly the ACT paid in respect of the interim dividend can be offset against the mainstream liability. The ACT on the final dividend cannot be offset (because the dividend is not paid until 15 May 19X2, which is after the end of the accounting period). The mainstream liability is therefore £155,000 – £50,000, or £105,000, which is a current liability at the March 19X2 year end.

The ACT relating to the final dividend is carried forward (since it cannot be netted off against the liability) either as a deduction from the deferred tax account (subject to certain limitations), or if this account is insufficient, as a deferred asset. Unless it can be relieved in any other way, the earliest date that it may be used is 31 December 19X3, being the date that a mainstream liability would be due if taxable profits are made in the year ending 31 March 19X3.

3.1.3   Incoming dividends

SSAP 8 discusses two possible ways of dealing with franked investment income in the accounts:

(a)   to bring into the profit and loss account the cash received or receivable; or

(b)   to bring in the full amount of the franked investment income, i.e. including the tax credit, with an equivalent amount treated as part of the tax charge.[32]

The standard requires the second option to be adopted on the basis that it allows recognition of the income at both the pre-tax and the post-tax stage in a way which is consistent with every other item of income and expenditure. Accordingly, incoming dividends from United Kingdom resident companies are included in the profit and loss account at the amount of cash received plus the related tax credit.[33]

It is questionable whether this treatment still makes sense. SSAP 8 was written at the time of the introduction of the imputation system, but the tax rules have changed substantially since then. Most significantly, as a result of the July 1997 Budget, pension funds and UK companies can no longer claim a repayment of the tax credit, and indeed banks are taxed on the (net) dividend income they receive in respect of investments that are held as trading assets. In these circumstances, it is questionable whether showing a grossed-up amount of income nowadays reflects the reality of the position, and accordingly SSAP 8 may need to be revised.

SSAP 8 does not address the equivalent treatment of Foreign Income Dividends. However, they were mentioned in passing by the UITF in its sixteenth Abstract, to the effect that: 'in the case of Foreign Income Dividends, there is no tax credit and no adjustment to the amount of the dividend received is to be made'.[34]

3.1.4   Disclosure of the tax charge in the profit and loss account

SSAP 8 requires that the following items be included in the tax charge in the profit and loss account and, where material, should be separately disclosed:

(a)   the amount of the United Kingdom corporation tax specifying:

   (i)   the charge for corporation tax on the income of the year (where such corporation tax includes transfers between the deferred tax account and the profit and loss account these should also be separately disclosed where material),

   (ii)   tax attributable to franked investment income,

   (iii) irrecoverable ACT,

(iv) the relief for overseas taxation; and

(b)   the total overseas taxation, relieved and unrelieved.[35]

As general guidance, Appendix 1 to the standard gives one method of showing (by way of note) the required information, whilst acknowledging that in simple cases the information may be given entirely within the profit and loss account. Appendix 1 is as follows:

	£'000
Corporation tax on income at x per cent (including £b transferred to/from deferred taxation account)	a
Less relief for overseas taxation	c
	d
Overseas taxation	e
Tax credit on UK dividends received	f
Irrecoverable advance corporation tax	g
	H

In practice, most companies show corporation tax and deferred tax as separate items rather than in the above format. See, for example, Extract 21.3 at 3.2.4 below.

A   Tax rate

If the rate of corporation tax is not known for the whole or part of the period covered by the accounts, the latest known rate should be used and disclosed.[36]

If the company's accounting period is other than a year ending 31 March in a period of changing rates of corporation tax, the rate applied to the profits will need to be apportioned and the effective rate of tax disclosed. For example, for a company with an accounting period ending on 31 December 1997, the first three months of the company's profit fall to be taxed at 33%, being the rate applicable up to 31 March 1997, and the remainder at the rate of 31% which applies for the following year. The following calculation gives the effective rate of tax to be disclosed in the accounts:

		%
The period January to March 1997	3/12 @ 33% =	8.25
The period April to December 1997	9/12 @ 31% =	23.25
Effective rate of corporation tax		31.50

B   Irrecoverable ACT

As noted above, the standard requires that the amount of irrecoverable ACT should be separately disclosed if material. This is required because although the most appropriate treatment is to regard the irrecoverable amount as a charge to tax on the company's profits (the alternative view being that it is part of an appropriation), some readers or analysts may wish to regard ACT 'in some other manner',[37] and separate disclosure enables them to make any adjustment they deem necessary.

C Unrelieved overseas tax

Appendix 2 to the standard considers the case of unrelieved overseas tax. If the rate of overseas tax on the company's overseas income exceeds the rate of UK tax, then the excess element of the overseas tax will be unrelieved.

3.2 SSAP 15

3.2.1 General approach

The standard indicates that it is concerned with accounting for tax on profits and surpluses which are recognised in the accounts in one period but assessed in another. It thus relates primarily to deferred corporation tax and income tax in the United Kingdom and in the Republic of Ireland and, insofar as the principles are similar, to overseas taxes on profits payable by UK and Irish enterprises or their subsidiaries.[38]

Interestingly, the standard considers other taxes also, by providing that 'a number of other taxes, including value added tax, petroleum revenue tax and some overseas taxes, are not assessed directly on profits for an accounting period and are therefore not addressed specifically in this statement. For such taxes, enterprises should generally follow the principle underlying this statement, that deferred tax should be provided to the extent that it is probable that a liability or asset will crystallise but not to the extent that it is probable that a liability or asset will not crystallise.'[39]

The standard chooses the partial provision method as its general approach, and summarises it as follows:

'Deferred tax should be accounted for in respect of the net amount by which it is probable that any payment of tax will be temporarily deferred or accelerated by the operation of timing differences which will reverse in the foreseeable future without being replaced. Partial provision recognises that, if an enterprise is not expected to reduce the scale of its operations significantly, it will often have what amounts to a hard core of timing differences so that the payment of some tax will be permanently deferred. On this basis, deferred tax has to be provided only where it is probable that tax will become payable as a result of the reversal of timing differences.'[40]

The standard considers that there are two main methods of computation, the liability method and the deferral method. It then points out that the liability method is the method consistent with the aim of partial provision, which is to provide the deferred tax which it is probable will be payable or recoverable.[41]

3.2.2 Definitions

Part 2 of the standard contains the definitions of the terms that are used throughout its text.

Deferred tax is the tax attributable to timing differences.[42]

Timing differences are differences between profits or losses as computed for tax purposes and results as stated in financial statements, which arise from the inclusion of items of income and expenditure in tax computations in periods different from those in which they are included in financial statements. Timing differences originate in one period and are capable of reversal in one or more subsequent periods.[43]

The following definitions are given for specific timing differences:

(a)   a loss for tax purposes which is available to relieve future profits from tax constitutes a timing difference;[44]

(b)   the revaluation of an asset (including an investment in an associated or subsidiary company) will create a timing difference when it is incorporated into the balance sheet, insofar as the profit or loss that would result from realisation at the revalued amount is taxable, unless disposal of the revalued asset and of any subsequent replacement assets would not result in a tax liability, after taking account of any expected rollover relief;[45]

(c)   the retention of earnings overseas will create a timing difference only if:

(i)   there is an intention or obligation to remit them; and

(ii)   remittance would result in a tax liability after taking account of any related double tax relief.[46]

The *liability method* is a method of computing deferred tax whereby it is calculated at the rate of tax that it is estimated will be applicable when the timing differences reverse. Under the liability method deferred tax not provided is calculated at the expected long-term tax rate.[47]

3.2.3 Detailed accounting requirements

A   Method of computation

Deferred tax should be computed under the liability method. Tax deferred or accelerated by the effect of timing differences should be accounted for to the extent that it is probable that a liability or asset will crystallise. Tax deferred or accelerated by the effect of timing differences should not be accounted for to the extent that it is probable that a liability or asset will not crystallise.[48] For this purpose, the combined effect of all timing differences should be considered rather than looking at individual categories in isolation,[49] except that timing differences relating to post-retirement benefits may be considered separately and provided for in full as a result of the amendment to SSAP 15 referred to in 2.2.7 above.

B   Future projections

The assessment of whether deferred tax liabilities or assets will or will not crystallise should be based upon reasonable assumptions. The assumptions should take into account all relevant information available up to the date on which the accounts are approved by the board of directors, and also the intentions of management. Ideally this information will include financial plans or projections covering a period of years sufficient to enable an assessment to be made of the likely pattern of future tax liabilities. A prudent view should be taken in the assessment of whether a tax liability will crystallise, particularly where the financial plans or projections are susceptible to a high degree of uncertainty or are not fully developed for the appropriate period.[50]

Under the original SSAP 15, it was easy for an enterprise to ignore the partial provision approach and to remain fully provided, simply by failing to produce, or pleading an inability to produce, future plans or projections. Under the revised requirements, it is theoretically not permissible to do this, as there are two separate requirements, to provide for the tax that is expected to crystallise, and not to provide for tax that is not expected to crystallise; however, an inability to foresee the future with enough clarity may still lead to full provision in practice.

There is no longer a minimum time period which should be covered by the projections, which is a change from SSAP 15 in its original form, where 'normally three years' was quoted, although the Appendix to the standard now mentions a period of three to five years as an example of a relatively short period which might be appropriate where the pattern of timing differences is expected to be regular.[51] In practice the projection will obviously become less reliable the further into the future it goes, and the period which may be forecast with a reasonable degree of accuracy is perhaps no more than two years. Much depends on whether a pattern of originating or reversing timing differences can be discerned, which will depend on such factors as whether expansion is envisaged, and whether capital expenditure has a cyclical nature.

Each year the pattern of expected timing differences should be compared against the reversal of timing differences experienced in the past. Plans and projections require regular review; they can be influenced by many indirectly related factors, for example the reassessment of asset lives, a decision to close part of the business which renders certain assets no longer needed, or the provision of a sum in respect of the permanent diminution of an asset.

It is important that the plans and projections are based on reasonable and realistic assumptions. In particular, a planned expansion programme may allow timing differences to be projected as continuing to originate well into the future, but the working capital resources to finance the expansion need to be available to the enterprise for that expansion programme to take place.

C   *Debit balances*

(a)   General

The provision for deferred tax liabilities should be reduced by any deferred tax debit balances arising from separate categories of timing differences and any advance corporation tax which is available for offset against those liabilities.[52] This provides for the situation where there is advance corporation tax recoverable (in excess of the mainstream tax liability), which will effectively rank as a payment on account for the tax due on the future reversal of any timing differences. Further, it allows unrelieved tax losses to be netted off against deferred tax liabilities.

Deferred tax net debit balances should not be carried forward as assets, except to the extent that they are expected to be recoverable without replacement by equivalent debit balances.[53] This is simply the obverse of the same rule for liabilities. Under SSAP 15, a liability is not provided where there is a 'hard core' of timing differences which represent a perpetual postponement of tax; correspondingly, a hard core of timing differences which represents a permanent acceleration of the tax liability should not be regarded as an asset.

(b)   Tax losses

Particular guidance is given in the Appendix to the standard on when it is permitted to regard tax losses as recoverable assets (which is distinguishable from when they may be set off against deferred tax liabilities). The conditions to be satisfied are as follows:

(i)   the loss has resulted from an identifiable and non-recurring cause; and

(ii)   the enterprise, or predecessor enterprise, has been consistently profitable over a considerable period, with any past losses being more than offset by income in subsequent periods; and

(iii)   it is assured beyond reasonable doubt that future taxable profits will be sufficient to offset the current loss during the carry-forward period prescribed by tax legislation.[54]

There are corresponding rules relating to capital losses, which prescribe the following conditions:

(i)   a potential chargeable gain not expected to be covered by rollover relief is present in assets which have not been revalued in the financial statements to reflect that gain and which are not essential to the future operations of the enterprise; and

(ii)   the enterprise has decided to dispose of these assets and thus realise the potential chargeable gain; and

(iii) the unrealised chargeable gain (after allowing for any possible loss in value before disposal) is sufficient to offset the loss in question, such that it is assured beyond reasonable doubt that a tax liability on the relevant portion of the chargeable gain will not crystallise.[55]

(c)   ACT

Debit balances arising in respect of advance corporation tax on dividends payable or proposed at the balance sheet date should be carried forward to the extent that it is foreseen that sufficient corporation tax will be assessed on the profits or income of the succeeding accounting period, against which the advance corporation tax is available for offset.[56] The advance corporation tax on an unpaid dividend cannot be offset against the mainstream liability for the period, since this can only be reduced by ACT on dividends actually paid in the period. Accordingly, ACT on a proposed dividend is normally recorded as a current liability (representing the payment that will be made to the Inland Revenue when the dividend is remitted to shareholders), and as a deferred asset or a deduction from a deferred tax liability (representing the recoverability of the amount paid to the Inland Revenue against a future mainstream tax liability).

The standard requires that debit balances arising in respect of ACT other than on dividends payable or proposed at the balance sheet date should be written off unless their recovery is assured beyond reasonable doubt. It further provides that such recovery will normally be assured only where the debit balances are recoverable out of corporation tax arising on profits or income of the succeeding accounting period, without replacement by equivalent debit balances.[57]

3.2.4   Disclosure

The standard requires disclosure of the following:

(a)   The amount of deferred tax charged or credited in the profit and loss account for the period, split between that relating to ordinary activities and that relating to any extraordinary items.[58]

There is also a requirement within FRS 3 to disclose the amount of taxation (i.e. not just deferred taxation) attributable to extraordinary items, as well as that relating to certain exceptional items.[59]

(b)   The amount of any unprovided deferred tax in respect of the period, analysed into its major components.[60]

The following extract shows this disclosure:

Extract 21.3: John Lewis Partnership plc (1997)

6 Tax on profit on ordinary activities

	1997	1996
	£m	£m
Corporation tax based on the profit for the year	**41.1**	26.3
Corporation tax – previous years	**(0.2)**	0.1
Deferred tax	**4.3**	2.2
	45.2	28.6

The tax charge is based on a corporation tax rate of 33% (33%) and has been reduced by £2.4m (£3.0m) as a result of capital allowances in excess of depreciation.

Total taxation deferred and unprovided in respect of all capital allowances in excess of depreciation amounts to £89.6m (£84.7m) based on corporation tax at 33% (33%).

No provision has been made in these accounts for the liability to taxation of £16.6m (£15.9m) on capital gains, which would arise if properties were to be sold at the amounts at which they have been revalued and included in these accounts.

The wording of the requirement in the standard presupposes that the effect to be disclosed is of new originating differences for which no provision is made. However, sometimes companies have to disclose the opposite effect – that the tax charge for the year has been increased by unanticipated reversals.

(c)   Any adjustments to deferred tax passing through the profit and loss account which relate to changes in tax rates or in tax allowances. The effect of any fundamental change in the tax system should be separately disclosed within the tax charge on the face of the profit and loss account.[61] Before FRS 3 was issued, the effect of such a change was treated as an extraordinary item if it was sufficiently material,[62] but this is no longer possible.

(d)   The deferred tax balance, analysed into its major components, and the amount of unprovided deferred tax, similarly analysed.[63] Where no information on unprovided deferred tax in respect of a revalued asset is given on the grounds that it is argued not to be a timing difference (because it will never crystallise), the fact that the potential liability has not been quantified should be stated.[64]

An example of this disclosure appears in the accounts of Rank in relation to its investments:

Extract 21.4: The Rank Group Plc (1996)

19 DEFERRED TAXATION [extract]

	Provided Group		Not provided (recognised) Group	
	1996	1995	**1996**	1995
	£m	£m	**£m**	£m
Capital allowances	**15**	19	**(2)**	51
Other timing differences	**(6)**	4	**–**	4
	9	23	**(2)**	55
Advance Corporation Tax	**–**	(13)	**(17)**	(41)
	9	10	**(19)**	14

The above figures exclude: ...

(b) taxation payable on capital gains which might arise from the sale of certain investments at the values at which they are stated in the Group's balance sheet ...

The absence of a provision, or at least disclosure of the potential liability, seems rather odd, however, because Rank's main investment is in Rank Xerox; as disclosed in Extract 7.2 of Chapter 7, this is no longer held for the long term and the holding has been revalued upwards by almost £500 million. Under these circumstances, one would have thought that the tax consequences of its possible disposal would have been highly relevant.

Brunel's accounts contain the following example of this analysis:

Extract 21.5: Brunel Holdings plc (1996)

20. **Provisions for liabilities and charges** [extract]

The amounts of deferred taxation provided and unprovided in the financial statements are:

	Provided		Unprovided	
	1996	1995	**1996**	1995
	£000	£000	**£000**	£000
Capital allowances in excess of depreciation	**1,914**	2,434	**(120)**	(46)
Other timing differences	**554**	940	**(278**	(189)
Losses available for offset	**(1,782)**	(2,477)	**(11,365)**	(15,509)
Pension prepayment	**6,241**	6,289	**–**	**–**
ACT not immediately recoverable	**(6,118)**	(6,340)	**–**	**–**
	809	846	**(11,763)**	(15,744)

No tax liability is expected to arise in the foreseeable future on realisation of properties, and accordingly this is not provided or quantified.

Rather than analysing the *unprovided* amount as required by the standard, a number of companies continue to follow the requirement of the original SSAP 15 (before it was amended in 1985), which involved showing the full potential liability and the amount which has been provided, analysed by category.[65] Of course, this information allows the reader to derive the analysis of the unprovided amount, by a simple process of subtraction. An example of this form of disclosure is to be found in the accounts of The Davis Service Group:

Extract 21.6: The Davis Service Group Plc (1996)

	Group		Company	
	1996	1995	**1996**	1995
20 PROVISIONS FOR LIABILITIES AND CHARGES	**£'000**	£'000	**£'000**	£'000
a) The provisions for liabilities and charges comprise deferred taxation which is attributable to				
Excess of tax allowances over depreciation	**5,603**	4,101	–	–
Other timing differences	**(58)**	(148)	**(32)**	(121)
	5,545	3,953	**(32)**	(121)
The movement during the year in the provision for deferred tax was:				
Beginning of the year	**3,953**	4,929	**(121)**	(138)
Acquisition of subsidiary	**1,164**	–	–	–
Currency translation differences	**(14)**	–	–	–
Movement in respect of current and prior years	**442**	(976)	**89**	17
End of year	**5,545**	3,953	**(32)**	(121)
b) The full potential amount of deferred taxation on all timing differences is as follows				
Excess of tax allowances over depreciation	**7,478**	7,096	**(59)**	(54)
Other timing differences	**(1,735)**	(2,084)	**(162)**	(223)
Attributable to trading activities	**5,743**	5,012	**(221)**	(277)
Corporation tax on capital gains arising on the disposal of property that have been deferred under the roll-over provisions	**1,650**	2,082	–	–
Taxes that would arise if properties were to be disposed of at their revalued amounts	**1,435**	1,899	–	–

It is in fact arguable that the analysis of the full potential liability gives more meaningful information than can be obtained by analysing the amount which has been provided or the amount which has not been provided. Since SSAP 15 specifies that all categories of timing difference are to be considered in aggregate rather than individually for the purposes of deciding the overall net reversal which is to be provided for, it often makes little sense to try to say which particular category has been included in the provision and which has not.

Unusually, Arjo Wiggins Appleton grosses up its net deferred tax provision to show deferred tax assets separately from deferred tax liabilities, as shown below. The basis of the split, however, is not made clear:

Extract 21.7: Arjo Wiggins Appleton p.l.c. (1996)

15. Provisions for liabilities and charges [extract]

Group

	Deferred taxation £m
At 31 December 1995	20.6
Deferred taxation asset included in debtors (see note 12)	(14.7)
Net deferred taxation balance at 31 December 1995	5.9
Currency retranslation	(1.2)
Adjustment to the fair value of net assets acquired in 1995	0.8
Charged/(released) to profit and loss account	(1.8)
Increase in ACT set-off	(0.3)
Net deferred taxation balance at 31 December 1996	3.4
Deferred taxation asset included in debtors (see note 12)	8.1
At 31 December 1996	11.5

(e)   Transfers to and from the deferred tax balance.[66]

A good example of the disclosure of movements on the deferred tax balance during the year is contained in the accounts of Laporte:

Extract 21.8: Laporte plc (1996)

17 Provisions for liabilities and charges [extract]

	Deferred tax £m
Balance at start of year	44.6
Profit and loss account	
Before exceptional items	1.4
Disposal of subsidiary undertakings	(3.6)
Advance corporation tax	0.2
Overseas advance taxes	0.6
Currency translation differences	(4.4)
Balance at end of year	38.8

(f)   Movements in reserves which relate to deferred tax.[67]

(g)   Where the value of an asset is disclosed by way of note and differs from its book value, the tax effect of disposing of it at that value.[68]

(h)   Any assumptions regarding the availability of group relief and the payment therefor which are relevant to an understanding of the company's deferred tax position.[69]

(i)   The fact (if applicable) that provision has not been made for tax which would become payable if retained earnings of foreign subsidiaries were remitted to the UK.[70]

EMI includes the following footnote in its accounts to explain this point:

Extract 21.9: EMI Group plc (1997)

22. DEFERRED TAXATION [extract]

No provision has been made for further taxes which could arise if subsidiary or associated undertakings are disposed of or if overseas companies were to remit dividends to the UK in excess of those anticipated in these accounts: it is considered impracticable to estimate the amount of such taxes.

Cable and Wireless similarly makes no provision, but quantifies the unprovided amount:

Extract 21.10: Cable and Wireless plc (1997)

23. DEFERRED TAXATION [extract]

The potential deferred tax liability does not include an amount of £616m (1996 – £521m) of contingent tax liability arising on the reserves of overseas subsidiary and associated undertakings which the Group does not expect to remit to the United Kingdom.

Companies sometimes do make provision for this liability. Taylor Woodrow discloses the following policy:

Extract 21.11: Taylor Woodrow plc (1996)

Accounting Definitions and Policies

Deferred taxation [extract]

Deferred taxation is provided on the profits of overseas subsidiary and associated undertakings where the local tax charge is at a low rate.

In July 1992, the ASB published FRS 2 and added a further layer of complication to the rules on this subject, by requiring disclosure of:

■   the extent to which deferred tax has been accounted for in respect of future remittances of the accumulated reserves of overseas subsidiary undertakings; and, unless provision has been made in full,

■   the reason for not making full provision.[71]

The first of these seems redundant, because it is already required to analyse the deferred tax balance into its main components. Moreover, the second appears to be based on the premise that full remittance of profits is the norm from which deviations must be explained, and also that there would not usually be any offsetting effects which would limit the tax payable in such an eventuality. This does not seem to be a realistic foundation on which to base the rule, and it does not seem to have resulted in the provision of much useful information.

3.3   Companies Act 1985

The Companies Act also imposes various disclosure requirements in relation to taxation. These can be summarised as follows:

(a)   any special circumstances affecting the liability to tax on profits, income or capital gains for the current or future years.[72] (There is a similar requirement in FRS 3, which also requires the individual effects to be quantified.)[73]

An example of a note containing such a disclosure can be found in the accounts of Sedgwick:

Extract 21.12: Sedgwick Group plc (1996)

9   Taxation on profit on ordinary activities [extract]

Current overseas taxation is reduced by £5.7m (1995 £4.2m) by reason of overseas taxation relief in respect of the amortisation of intangible assets recognised in the accounts of certain of the group's overseas subsidiaries. In accordance with the group's accounting policies, these assets were written off to reserves on consolidation. Further such overseas taxation relief amounting to £26.9m is expected to be available over the period to 2012.

Cookson and Glaxo Wellcome give more detailed reconciliations, to explain the difference between the actual tax charge and that which would have been derived from applying the statutory tax rate to the reported profit for the year:

Extract 21.13: Cookson Group plc (1996)

7 Taxation on profit from ordinary activities [extract]

The group taxation charge, as a percentage of profit before taxation, differs from the rate of UK corporation tax (33.0%) as follows:

	1996 £m	1995 £m
Taxation charge calculated at 33.0%	14.7	55.5
Exceptional items	26.4	10.2
Tax losses utilised	(2.3)	(3.1)
Tax losses not utilised	4.8	4.1
Excess of capital allowances	(3.6)	(3.2)
Other timing differences	(1.1)	(2.4)
Effect of overseas tax rates	(0.3)	2.2
Advance Corporation Tax written back	(0.5)	–
Other items	(2.6)	(2.3)
Taxation charge as reported –1996: 79.6% (1995: 36.2%)	35.5	61.0

Extract 21.14: Glaxo Wellcome plc (1996)

9. TAXATION [extract]

	12 months to 31.12.96	18 months to 31.12.95	12 months to 30.6.94 (restated)
	£m	£m	£m
Reconciliation of the tax charge:			
Profit on ordinary activities before taxation at the UK statutory rate of 33%	978	788	606
Deferred taxation not provided on fixed assets	(6)	(48)	(58)
Effect of special taxation status in Singapore	(109)	(112)	(46)
Net cost of different rates of taxation in overseas undertakings	29	34	32
Taxation effect of disallowed integration costs	–	134	–
Advance corporation tax written off	–	37	–
Other differences	41	34	(10)
Taxation charge in the accounts	933	867	524

Included in the taxation charge for the 18 months to 31st December 1995 is a credit of £230 million in respect of integration.

Profits arising from manufacturing operations in Singapore are taxed at a reduced rate until 30th June 2002. The effect of this reduction in the taxation charge increased earnings per share by 3.1p in the year to 31st December 1996, by 3.4p in the 18 months to 31st December 1995 and by 1.5p in the year to 30th June 1994.

(b) the amount of the tax charge on ordinary activities and on extraordinary items, respectively analysed into:

   (i)   UK corporation tax, and the amount by which it has been reduced by the application of double tax relief,

   (ii) UK income tax,

   (iii) overseas tax;[74]

(c) the amount of the taxation creditor balance.[75] Where there is an amount receivable in respect of tax, the Schedule 4 formats do not specify that it should be shown separately, although it is likely that it will be disclosed if material as a separate item within debtors;

(d) movements during the year on any provision in respect of tax;[76] and

(e) the amount of any provision for deferred taxation, shown separately from any other taxation provision.[77]

As can be seen from the above, there is substantial overlap between the disclosure requirements of accounting standards and those of the Companies Act. Illustrations of most of these disclosures have already been given.

Extract 21.21: Sears plc (1997)

12. Debtors [extract]

	Group		Company	
	1997	1996	**1997**	1996
	£m	£m	**£m**	£m
Due in less than one year:				
Trade debtors	**358.0**	330.8	–	–
Group undertakings	–	–	**246.9**	286.9
Other debtors	**91.8**	46.6	–	–
Corporation tax recoverable	–	–	**44.9**	0.8
Prepayments and accrued income	**39.8**	52.5	–	0.4
	489.6	429.9	**291.8**	288.1
Due after more than one year:				
Group undertakings	–	–	**441.9**	176.7
Other debtors	**3.0**	3.0	–	–
Prepayments	**9.7**	–	–	–
Advance corporation tax	**11.1**	11.0	**11.1**	11.0
	513.4	443.9	**744.8**	475.8

16. Provisions for liabilities and charges [extract]

Details of the full potential liability for deferred taxation and the extent to which provision has been made in these accounts are set out below:

	Full potential liability		Provision made	
	1997	1996	**1997**	1996
	£m	£m	**£m**	£m
Capital allowances	**17.8**	17.6	**1.4**	0.9
Short term and other timing differences	**19.2**	15.3	**19.2**	15.3
	37.0	32.9	**20.6**	16.2

Provided the ACT can be regarded as recoverable, all the above possibilities are simply matters of classification in the balance sheet, and any of the treatments is probably, therefore, acceptable. In its 1995 Discussion Paper, the ASB favoured the treatment used by Argos – dividing the recoverable ACT between the amount that can be set off against the deferred tax balance and the excess that is carried as an asset.[88]

SSAP 8 also states that to the extent to which the deferred taxation account represents deferred chargeable gains, it is not available for offsetting ACT.[89]

This is no longer the case; as a result of subsequent changes in the tax legislation, it is now possible to offset ACT against tax payable in respect of chargeable gains.

Where the holding company has no trade of its own to give rise to a deferred tax liability, it will generally recover its ACT by surrendering it to its subsidiaries to be offset against their tax or deferred tax liabilities. In these circumstances, it will be appropriate for it to carry forward such ACT as it expects to recover as an asset in its own balance sheet.

4.6 Changes in tax rates

4.6.1 Corporation tax

In providing for the amount of current corporation tax that should be accrued in the accounts the best estimate of the amount payable is made. This involves a number of estimates, including the extent of disallowable expenditure (for items such as entertaining, legal fees, etc.), the amount of expenditure that will qualify for capital allowances (particularly expenditure on certain types of plant and machinery), and the standard rate of corporation tax that will apply to the taxable profits. Companies which qualify for the small companies rate or for marginal relief should make the provision in their accounts on the basis of these concessions if they estimate that the taxable profits are at the appropriate level.

In contrast with the US, where tax rate changes cannot be recognised until they have been enacted, UK changes in rate are recognised for accounting purposes as soon as they are announced by the Chancellor of the Exchequer in the budget. There is, of course, a possibility that the budget proposals, in the form of the Finance Bill, are not successful in their passage through Parliament, and the rate suffered may therefore eventually be different to the rate used by companies in the preparation of their accounts. If this is so, then the under or over accrual flows through the company's profit and loss account as (a separately disclosed) part of the following year's tax charge. (Similarly if companies provided tax in their accounts using the small companies rate or marginal relief concessions, and the final agreed profits fell to be taxed at the standard rate, then a charge will arise in the following year's profit and loss account representing the under accrual.)

4.6.2 Deferred tax

At each year end a company will provide for the appropriate level of deferred tax and will use the best estimate of the rate that will be payable on the taxable profits when the timing differences reverse. This is the fundamental approach of the liability method.

Timing differences by their very nature will reverse over many years and the rate of tax will not normally be known in advance for these years. Of course, if rates were set some years in advance then those rates would be applied to the element of timing differences expected to reverse in each of the future years, and the liability computed accordingly.

Generally, the best estimate of the rate of tax that will be applied to reversing differences is the standard rate of tax currently in force, and accordingly deferred tax provisions are made on this basis. Any under or over accrual arising from a rate change will pass through the company's profit and loss account as (a separately disclosed) part of the deferred tax charge for the year, in the year in which the rate changes, or the change is announced, whichever is the earlier. Indeed, if the change of rate is announced after the year end but before the accounts are prepared, the effect will be reflected in the year which has already ended; this is given in the Appendix to SSAP 17 as an example of an adjusting event.[90] This is computed by taking the net timing differences on which deferred tax was provided in the preceding year's balance sheet and applying the difference between the old rate and the new rate.

There are exceptions to the above for those companies which qualify for the small companies rate or for marginal relief. Those companies which suffer tax at the small companies rate should generally provide for deferred tax at that rate unless they foresee that the taxable profits in the forthcoming years will rise above the small company threshold. Such taxable profits are not just the timing differences that are expected to reverse in a particular year, but must include an estimate of the taxable trading profit that will arise, since this will form part of the total taxable profits of the company. A similar estimate should be made to determine if the marginal relief provisions will apply to any of the forthcoming years, but this can be even more difficult to assess. It may in certain circumstances be impossible to determine if the marginal reliefs will apply, and in such cases the prudent view should prevail and the standard rate of tax should be used to calculate the provision.

4.7 Revaluations of fixed assets

SSAP 15 discusses the revaluation of fixed assets in relation to the tax consequences which would arise if they were disposed of at their revalued amounts. However, it contains no discussion of the effects of revaluation on the calculation of deferred tax relating to timing differences between the amounts of depreciation charged in the accounts and of capital allowances in the tax computation. Furthermore, the standard does not contain a clear statement of the concept on which it is based, from which it might be possible to infer what the treatment should be. Indeed, a large part of the problem is that the conceptual reasons for including revaluations in historical cost accounts are themselves elusive. The rules on this issue are therefore obscure; the two main possibilities are described below.

For the purposes of this discussion, it is assumed that the assets in question are depreciated and attract capital allowances, so that they will be written off over a period for both accounting and tax purposes.

The first way of looking at the revaluation of a depreciable asset is that it creates a further timing difference, because in effect it is an adjustment of depreciation, which is itself an element of a timing difference. Where, for example, an asset is purchased for £10,000, subsequently depreciated to £6,000 and then revalued to £9,000, the £3,000 revaluation surplus could be regarded as reinstating the depreciation which was previously charged, and therefore reversing the deferred tax effect of charging that depreciation. On this basis, the £9,000 would be compared with the tax written down value of the asset in order to determine the amount of the timing difference which gives a potential liability to deferred tax. This is the view taken by the Accountants Digest on SSAP 15.[91]

The alternative viewpoint sees the revaluation as giving rise to a permanent difference. This is on the basis that the revaluation, and its subsequent reversal through depreciation, has no equivalent within the tax computation and hence does not give rise to a timing difference. The revaluation is not a reversal of previous depreciation, which properly reflected the consumption of part of the asset based on its then carrying value; it simply means that the remaining part of the asset has a different value and its consumption will be measured at a different amount. The future depreciation charge will have two components; the original charge based on cost, and the further amount based on the revaluation surplus. That further amount has no tax equivalent and it would be wrong to make any tax adjustment in respect of it.

We believe that both of these arguments are coherent, and in the absence of more definitive guidance from the standard itself, we consider that they are both acceptable, so long as the approach taken is consistently applied.

Where the revaluation takes the value of the asset above its original cost, it takes the matter out of the realm of accelerated capital allowances and into that of chargeable gains. As mentioned above, SSAP 15 does deal with this issue and says that a timing difference will be created 'insofar as the profit or loss that would result from realisation at the revalued amount is taxable, unless disposal of the revalued asset and of any subsequent replacement assets would not result in a tax liability, after taking account of any expected rollover relief'.[92] Provision for this should then be considered if it is intended to dispose of the asset, unless the tax effect would be mitigated by the effects of other originating timing differences.

The reference to rollover relief in the passage quoted above adds a further element of confusion to an already confused topic. Since the effect of rollover relief is to postpone the crystallisation of a tax liability rather than to cancel it altogether, it is difficult to see whether its availability has a bearing on whether or not a timing difference has been created, although it does of course have a bearing on whether provision has to be made in respect of it. No change to a company's tax exposure is made by rolling a gain on to a replacement asset rather than keeping the old asset, and it is therefore hard to see why this should be thought to reduce any timing difference considered to have arisen as a result of the revaluation.

Rollover relief is not only relevant in the context of revalued assets. Where an asset has been sold at a profit, and tax has been deferred by the operation of rollover relief, a latent tax liability will exist quite independently of whether or not the old asset had been revalued, and arguably this should be disclosed as a potential liability. The Appendix to SSAP 15 mentions this, but in an unsatisfactory way; it says: 'Where rollover relief has been obtained on the sale of an asset, with the "base cost" of the replacement asset for tax purposes thereby being reduced, and the potential tax liability has not been disclosed, the standard requires disclosure of the fact that the revaluation does not constitute a timing difference and that tax has therefore not been quantified, as it will not otherwise be evident from the accounts.'[93] However, this mixes up two unrelated matters; as mentioned above, the tax exposure can arise without any revaluation ever having occurred, and we recommend that it should be disclosed as a potential liability.

4.8   Overseas earnings

When a UK group incorporates the earnings of a foreign subsidiary or associate in its consolidated accounts, a timing difference will arise if the earnings are to be remitted to the UK in a later period and will give rise to incremental tax payments when they are remitted. SSAP 15 requires that these timing differences should be taken into account in the calculation of deferred tax unless it is intended to retain the earnings in the foreign country indefinitely so that no further tax liability will arise. Scholl provides an example of a company which makes such provision:

Extract 21.22: Scholl PLC (1996)

18. Provisions for liabilities and charges

Deferred taxation [extract]

Deferred tax has been provided as follows:

	Group		Company	
	1996	1995	**1996**	1995
	£000	£000	**£000**	£000
Excess of tax allowances over book depreciation of fixed assets	**569**	494	**5**	57
Other timing differences related to:				
– UK tax remittances from overseas subsidiary undertakings	**564**	1,215	**–**	651
– capital gains	**688**	690	**–**	–
– pensions	**408**	246	**104**	106
– current assets and liabilities	**708**	438	**–**	106
– restructuring costs	**(4,417)**	(629)	**(182)**	(38)
– ACT recoverable	**–**	(462)	**–**	(462)
	(1,480)	1,992	**(73)**	420

In practice it can be extremely difficult to determine how much to provide, since this will be subject to many uncertainties; the amount of any liability will depend on factors such as the relative tax rates of the UK and the foreign country concerned, the provisions of any tax treaty between the countries, and the level of UK taxable profits at the time of the remittance. Furthermore, groups may find methods of restructuring their groups so as to minimise their tax liabilities if a major repatriation of dividends becomes necessary. Nonetheless it is necessary that companies which expect that a liability will emerge should make the best estimate that they can in the circumstances.

As indicated in 3.2.4 above, it is necessary to disclose both the fact that provision has not been made, where this is the case,[94] and also now the reason for not making *full* provision.[95] However, the reasoning behind these rules is somewhat confused. The first of the two requirements was added in substitution for the proposed requirement in ED 33 to state that there were no plans to remit overseas earnings, where this applied,[96] but the two cannot be regarded as equivalent to one another. Even where earnings *will* be remitted, and where tax *will* become payable as a result, it might be concluded that no provision is needed because other originating timing differences are forecast to arise in the year of remittance. Accordingly, it is not really possible to read very much into this disclosure when it is made. Furthermore, since it will only be in rare cases that full provision will be appropriate, the thrust of the second requirement also seems rather misguided.

5 COMPARISON WITH US AND IASC PRONOUNCEMENTS

5.1 US

5.1.1 APB 11

For over 20 years, accounting for taxation in the USA was governed by an Opinion of the Accounting Principles Board issued in 1967 – APB 11.[97] This required full provision for deferred tax using the deferral method. Its objective was to match initial tax effects of timing differences with related income and expense recognised in pre-tax profits. Such an approach focused on obtaining matching in the profit and loss account, rather than on the measurement of deferred tax assets and liabilities in the balance sheet.

The computation of deferred tax on originating timing differences was conducted using the 'with-and-without' approach (i.e. with and without the inclusion of the transaction representing the timing difference). Reversals of timing differences were calculated using either the 'net change' method (i.e. at current tax rates) or the 'gross change' method (i.e. the rates at which the originating timing difference was recorded).

The tax benefit of losses carried forward could be recognised as an asset if its realisation were assured beyond reasonable doubt. In the year of realisation (if later than the year of the loss) the benefit of the loss on the tax charge would be reported as an extraordinary item.

The deferred tax account was analysed and disclosed as either current or non-current in the balance sheet, depending on the classification of the asset to which it related.

5.1.2 SFAS 96

In 1987, the FASB issued SFAS 96 – *Accounting for Income Taxes*.[98] This Statement was originally intended to become effective for accounting periods beginning on or after 15 December 1988, superseding APB 11 and other related pronouncements. However, because of the complexity and perceived artificiality of the standard, its implementation date was continually postponed to allow the FASB to give further consideration to certain aspects of the statement. They subsequently withdrew it and issued a different standard instead, SFAS 109, which is described below.

5.1.3 SFAS 109

In 1992 the FASB issued a new accounting standard on deferred tax – Statement No. 109,[99] superseding APB 11 and SFAS 96. This standard became effective for years beginning after 15 December 1992.

In contrast to the deferral method required by APB 11, SFAS 109 uses a liability method, placing emphasis on the balance sheet rather than the profit and loss account. The principal objective is to quantify the amount of tax that will become payable or receivable in the future due to temporary differences and tax loss carryforwards existing at the balance sheet date.[100] Changes in the amounts recognised in the balance sheet during the year represent the charge or benefit in the profit and loss account.

This fundamental change of approach to accounting for taxation was due to several reasons, but one of the most significant was that the balance sheet figures created by the deferral approach which APB 11 required had increasingly been regarded as having very little meaning. In particular, they did not conform to the definitions of assets and liabilities which the FASB had adopted in its conceptual framework study.[101]

SFAS 109 uses the concept of 'temporary differences'; differences between the tax bases of assets or liabilities and their book values that will result in taxable or tax deductible amounts in future years. They are created mainly due to timing differences (as defined in SSAP 15) but can arise for other reasons including the case where the fair values assigned to acquired assets and liabilities differ from their tax bases on an acquisition. Temporary differences that result in taxable amounts in future years are known as taxable temporary differences whilst those that will result in tax deductible differences in future years are referred to as deductible temporary differences.[102]

The rules require deferred tax liabilities to be recognised for all taxable temporary differences, and deferred tax assets for deductible temporary differences and tax loss carryforwards if they are expected to be realised. The tax effects of temporary differences and tax loss carryforwards are calculated using enacted tax rates expected to apply to taxable income in future years.[103] The rules are to be applied separately to each entity (or group of entities in cases where a consolidated tax return is submitted) in each tax jurisdiction.

Under SFAS 109, deferred tax assets should be recognised in full unless it is 'more likely than not' that some portion or all of the deferred tax assets will not be realised. A provision (or 'valuation allowance') should be made to reduce the tax asset to an amount that is 'more likely than not' to be realised.[104] 'More likely than not' means a level of likelihood that is greater than 50 per cent. It is not as prohibitive as the 'assured beyond a reasonable doubt' criterion contained in APB 11 and SSAP 15 and requires considerable judgement. In practice, companies that can demonstrate that they are likely to generate sufficient future taxable income will be able to recognise deferred tax assets in full. Evidence about such future taxable income can be obtained by considering both reversals of existing taxable temporary differences and also the results of future trading.

If consideration of taxable temporary differences and the results of future trading is not sufficient to justify full recognition of deferred tax assets (i.e. if a valuation allowance is still felt to be necessary), management is required to consider tax-planning strategies in determining the amount of the provision to be

29 UITF 16, *Income and expenses subject to non-standard rates of tax*, UITF, February 1997, para. 11.

30 SSAP 8, *The treatment of taxation under the imputation system in the accounts of companies*, August 1974, ASC, para. 24.

31 *Ibid.*, para. 20.

32 *Ibid.*, para. 13.

33 *Ibid.*, para. 25.

34 UITF 16, para. 7.

35 SSAP 8, para. 22. It should be noted that changes in tax legislation since SSAP 8 was issued have meant that unrelieved overseas taxation will not arise from the payment or proposed payment of dividends. Consequently, SSAP 8's requirement for the separate disclosure of such amounts is now redundant.

36 *Ibid.*, para. 23.

37 *Ibid.*, para. 9.

38 SSAP 15, para. 1.

39 *Ibid.*, para. 2.

40 *Ibid.*, para. 12.

41 *Ibid.*, para. 14.

42 *Ibid.*, para. 17.

43 *Ibid.*, para. 18.

44 *Ibid.*, para. 19.

45 *Ibid.*, para. 20.

46 *Ibid.*, para. 21.

47 *Ibid.*, para. 23.

48 *Ibid.*, paras. 24–26.

49 *Ibid.*, Appendix, para. 4.

50 *Ibid.*, paras. 27 and 28.

51 *Ibid.*, Appendix, para. 4.

52 *Ibid.*, para. 29.

53 *Ibid.*, para. 30.

54 *Ibid.*, Appendix, para. 14.

55 *Ibid.*, Appendix, para. 15.

56 *Ibid.*, para. 31.

57 *Ibid.*, para. 32.

58 *Ibid.*, paras. 33 and 34.

59 FRS 3, paras. 22 and 20.

60 SSAP 15, para. 35.

61 FRS 3, para. 23.

62 SSAP 15, para. 36.

63 *Ibid.*, paras. 37 and 40.

64 *Ibid.*, para. 41.

65 Original SSAP 15, para. 33.

66 SSAP 15, para. 38.

67 *Ibid.*, para. 39.

68 *Ibid.*, para. 42.

69 *Ibid.*, para. 43.

70 *Ibid.*, para. 44.

71 FRS 2, *Accounting for subsidiary undertakings*, ASB, July 1992, para. 54.

72 CA 85, Sch. 4, para. 54(2).

73 FRS 3, para. 23.

74 CA 85, Sch. 4, para. 8 Profit and loss account formats and para. 54(3).

75 *Ibid.*, para. 8 Balance sheet formats.

76 *Ibid.*, para. 46.

77 *Ibid.*, para. 47.

78 SSAP 15, Appendix, para. 4.

79 Accountants Digest No. 174, ICAEW, *A Guide to Accounting Standards — Deferred Tax*, Summer 1985.

80 SSAP 15, Appendix, para. 14.

81 CA 85, Sch. 4, para. 54(2) and FRS 3, para. 23.
82 SSAP 15, para. 43.
83 SSAP 8, para. 20(c).
84 SSAP 15, para. 31.
85 *Ibid.*, para. 32.
86 SSAP 8, para. 7.
87 SSAP 15, Appendix, para. 17.
88 *Accounting for Tax*, para. 10.5.4.
89 SSAP 8, para. 7.
90 SSAP 17, *Accounting for post balance sheet events*, August 1980, Appendix, item (g) of examples of adjusting events.
91 Accountants Digest No. 174, p. 12.
92 SSAP 15, para. 20.
93 *Ibid.*, Appendix, para. 11.
94 *Ibid.*, para. 44.
95 FRS 2, para. 54.
96 ED 33, para. 35.
97 APB 11, *Accounting for Income Taxes*, AICPA, December 1967.
98 SFAS 96, *Accounting for Income Taxes*, FASB, December, 1987.
99 SFAS 109, *Accounting for Income Taxes.*
100 *Ibid.*, paras. 6–9.
101 SFAC No. 6, *Elements of Financial Statements*, FASB, December 1985, paras. 25 and 35.
102 SFAS 109, para. 13.
103 *Ibid.*, para. 18.
104 *Ibid.*, para. 17.
105 *Ibid.*, para. 22.
106 *Ibid.*, para. 41.
107 APB 16, Business Combinations, Accounting Principles Board, August 1970, para. 89.
108 E33, *Accounting for Taxes on Income*, IASC, January 1989.
109 E49, *Income Taxes*, IASC, October 1994.

Chapter 22   Reporting financial performance

1   THE NEED FOR A STANDARD

1.1   Income measurement

Chapter 2 discusses the concept of income and outlines the emphasis placed on the transactions approach to income measurement in the development of historical cost accounting theory. In summary, financial accounting under the historical cost system essentially involves allocating the effects of transactions between reporting periods, with the result that the balance sheet consists of the residuals of the income measurement process. Despite the conflict between the asset and liability vs. the revenue and expense viewpoints discussed in Chapter 2, the importance attributed to income measurement is highlighted by the FASB's Concepts Statement No. 1, which states that 'the primary focus of financial reporting is information about an enterprise's performance provided by measures of earnings and its components. Investors, creditors, and others who are concerned with assessing the prospects for enterprise net cash inflows are especially interested in that information.'[1] In addition, the emphasis that analysts place on companies' reported earnings as a measure of performance further illustrates the importance of income measurement.

Although the term 'income' is used to describe a concept, rather than something which is specific or precise, specific rules and procedures have been developed by accountants to measure income. These rules have been based on the concept of financial capital maintenance, which has been subscribed to by the FASB in SFAC No. 6 in terms of 'comprehensive income'. Comprehensive income is defined as 'the change in equity of a business enterprise during a period from transactions and other events and circumstances from nonowner sources'.[2] Therefore, the comprehensive income of a business enterprise over its entire lifetime will be the net of its cash receipts and cash outlays.[3] In June 1997 the FASB issued SFAS 130 – *Reporting Comprehensive Income* – with the aim of establishing standards for the reporting and display (but not recognition and measurement) of comprehensive income and its components in a full set of general purpose financial statements.[4] SFAS 130 is discussed at 4.1.4 below. However, it is perhaps worth noting here that it is an uncharacteristically tentative standard which, despite using SFAC Nos. 5 and 6 as its *raison d'être*, does not sit very well with the FASB's conceptual framework.

In any event, the need for businesses to measure their income over shorter periods for financial reporting purposes than over their entire lifetimes highlighted two major accounting issues. First, there was the issue of how to allocate the effects of transactions between accounting periods for reporting purposes, instead of merely allowing them to fall in the periods in which the transactions took place. This issue is dealt with through the development of allocation rules based on the fundamental accounting concepts of matching and prudence. The second issue which arose was whether or not all recorded transactions should be included in the calculation of the figure for 'net profit/loss for the period'. Some accountants have held the view that net profit/loss should reflect the effects of all recorded transactions, whilst others have contended that net profit/loss should not be distorted by abnormal, unusual and non-recurring events and transactions. These differing viewpoints have led to two basic concepts of income: the all-inclusive concept and the current operating performance concept.[5]

1.1.1   The all-inclusive (comprehensive income) concept

Under this concept, net profit/loss would include all transactions (except dividends and capital transactions) which affect the net change in equity. Proponents of the all-inclusive concept put forward the following arguments in favour of this basis of income measurement:

(a)   the annual reported net profits/losses, when aggregated over the life of the business enterprise, should be equal to the comprehensive income of the enterprise. Therefore, since charges and credits arising from extraordinary events and from corrections of prior periods are part of an enterprise's earnings history, the omission of such items from periodic income statements will result in the misstatement of the net profit/loss for a series of years;

(b)   the omission of certain charges and credits from the computation of the net profit/loss for a period opens the door to possible manipulation or smoothing of results over a period;

(c)   a profit and loss account which includes the effects of all transactions is more easily understood and less subject to variations resulting from the application of subjective judgements; and

(d)   full disclosure in the profit and loss account of the nature of all transactions will enable users to make their own assessments of the importance of the items and derive an appropriate measurement of income based on their own specific needs.

Group profit and loss account

FOR THE YEAR ENDED DECEMBER 31, 1996

	Notes	Continuing operations Ongoing £m	To be discontinued £m	1996 £m	1995 £m
Turnover	2	**4,045**	**246**	**4,291**	3,597
Cost of sales		**(3,355)**	**(344)**	**(3,699)**	(2,994)
Gross profit/(loss)		**690**	**(98)**	**592**	603
Commercial, marketing and product support costs		**(141)**	**(2)**	**(143)**	(139)
General and administrative costs		**(119)**	**(13)**	**(132)**	(112)
Research and development (net)		**(196)**	**(3)**	**(199)**	(206)
Share of profits of associated undertakings		**8**	**–**	**8**	9
Operating profit/(loss)		**242**	**(116)**	**126**	155
(Loss)/profit on sale/termination of businesses	3	**–**	**(147)**	**(147)**	23
Profit on sale of property		**–**	**–**	**–**	9
(Loss)/profit on ordinary activities before interest	2	**242**	**(263)**[1]	**(21)**	187
Net interest payable	4			**(7)**	(12)
(Loss)/profit on ordinary activities before taxation	3			**(28)**	175
Taxation	5			**(16)**	(31)
(Loss)/profit on ordinary activities after taxation				**(44)**	144
Equity minority interests in subsidiary undertakings				**(3)**	(2)
(Loss)/profit attributable to ordinary shareholders				**(47)**	142
Dividends	6			**(78)**	(73)
Transferred (from)/to reserves	22			**(125)**	69
(Loss)/earnings per ordinary share	7				
Net basis				**(3.19)p**	10.25p
Net basis before exceptional and non-operating items				**12.70p**	7.94p
Nil distribution basis				**(3.19)p**	11.40p

There have been no material acquisitions or discontinued operations.

As permitted by the Companies Act 1985, a separate profit and loss account for the Company has not been included in these financial statements. Of the Group '(Loss)/profit attributable to ordinary shareholders', a profit of **£119m** (1995 £108m) has been dealt with in the profit and loss account of the Company.

[1] Includes an exceptional loss of **£248m** (see note 3).

Interestingly enough, the particular disclosure route which Rolls-Royce has chosen to go down reflects what seems to be the IASC's current thinking on the issue of discontinuing operations. At its July 1997 meeting, the IASC Board approved for issue an Exposure Draft on the subject of Discontinuing Operations. It seems that the Exposure Draft will only deal with matters of presentation and disclosure, since the IASC Board decided that there was no need for any specific recognition and measurement requirements for discontinuing operations as the requirements of other draft standards (such as Impairment and Provisions and Contingencies) should apply. In approving the

Exposure Draft for issue, the IASC Board agreed that financial information about a discontinuing operation should initially be disclosed where there is a board decision and a public announcement of the proposed discontinuance. The Exposure Draft will further propose that when an enterprise is committed to a disposal without a realistic possibility of withdrawal, the assets, liabilities, income, expenses and cash flows of a discontinuing operation should be segregated from those of continuing operations.

Consequently, there is a fairly significant difference in philosophy between the ASB's approach on discontinued operations and that of the IASC on discontinuing operations. Whilst FRS 3 focuses in on operations which have ceased permanently in the current financial year, the IASC calls for disclosure at an earlier point in time, namely, as soon as there is a board decision and public announcement. Relating this to the situation of Rolls-Royce as illustrated in the above extract, the proposed discontinuances do not qualify as discontinued operations under FRS 3, yet it appears that they would be classified as discontinuing operations under the IASC's forthcoming proposals.

A question which sometimes arises is whether the partial disposal of a business (for example, the sale of a 70% interest in a previously wholly-owned subsidiary) meets FRS 3's definition of a discontinued operation. There is a school of thought that argues that a subsidiary becoming an associated undertaking is, ipso facto, a discontinuance. However, we see no grounds for this argument: it is quite clear that for a sale to be classified as a discontinued operation it must still satisfy all the necessary conditions contained in paragraph 4 of FRS 3.

It is perhaps noteworthy that this situation has been addressed in the US in a SEC Staff Accounting Bulletin. The situation considered by the SEC staff was that of a company which disposes of a controlling interest in a business segment and either retains a minority voting interest directly in the segment or holds a minority voting interest in the buyer of the segment. This minority interest enables the company to exert significant influence over the operating and financial policies of the segment thereby requiring it to account for its residual investment using the equity method. In the view of the SEC staff, the retention of an interest sufficient to enable the company to exert significant influence was inconsistent with a discontinued operations classification.[43]

2.4 Accounting for the consequences of a decision to sell or terminate an operation

Although FRS 3 is primarily a disclosure standard, it also deals with some recognition and measurement issues. Perhaps the most controversial amongst these relates to the principle underlying the establishment of provisions as a consequence of a decision to sell or terminate an operation. This is because the principle used in the standard stems from the definition of a liability in the ASB's Draft *Statement of Principles* – namely, that a provision is only raised when an obligation to transfer economic benefits arises. As explained below, this approach is somewhat controversial as it seems to fly in the face of SSAP 2's fundamental accounting concept of prudence.

The standard requires that if a decision has been made to sell or terminate an operation, any consequential provisions should reflect the extent to which obligations have been incurred that are not expected to be covered by the future profits of the operation or the disposal of its assets.[44] Further, the FRS requires that a provision is not set up until the reporting entity is demonstrably committed to the sale or termination, arguing that it is only at this point that the obligation arises. This should be evidenced, in the case of a sale, by a binding sale agreement and, in the case of a termination, by a detailed formal plan for termination from which the reporting entity cannot realistically withdraw. In the explanation section of the standard the ASB states that evidence of such a commitment might be the public announcement of specific plans, the commencement of implementation, or other circumstances effectively obliging the reporting entity to complete the sale or termination. A binding contract entered into after the balance sheet date may provide additional evidence of asset values and commitments at the balance sheet date. In the case of an intended sale for which no legally binding sale agreement exists, no obligation has been entered into by the reporting entity and accordingly no provision for the direct costs of the decision to sell and for the future operating losses should be made. However, in accordance with normal practice, any permanent diminution in asset values should be recognised in the financial statements.[45]

The provision should cover only:

i)   the direct costs of the sale or termination; and

ii)   any operating losses up to the date of the sale or termination.

In both cases, the provision should be calculated after taking into account the aggregate profit, if any, to be recognised in the profit and loss account from the future profits of the operation or disposal of its assets.

Where the operation is classified as continuing in the period under review the write down of assets and the provision for operating losses and for the loss on sale or termination will be included in the continuing operations category. In the subsequent period the provisions will be used to offset the results of the operations. The related disclosure in that subsequent period will be to show the trading results of the operation under each of the statutory format headings with the utilisation of the provisions being separately highlighted on the face of the profit and loss account under the operating loss and, if appropriate, the loss on sale or termination of the operation. The results will be included in whichever category is appropriate, either discontinued or still under continuing. The following extract from one of FRS 3's profit and loss account examples illustrates the presentation:

	1993	1993	1992 as restated
	£ million	£ million	£ million
Operating profit			
Continuing operations		50	40
Acquisitions		6	
		56	
Discontinued operations		(15)	12
Less 1992 provision		10	
		51	52
Profit on sale of properties in continuing operations		9	6
Provision for loss on operations to be discontinued			(30)
Loss on disposal of discontinued operations	(17)		
Less 1992 provision	20		
		3	
Profit on ordinary activities before interest		63	28

FRS 3's rules on the establishment of provisions as a consequence of a decision to sell or terminate an operation reflect the ASB's underlying philosophy that costs and losses should be charged in the profit and loss accounting in the periods to which they relate and that future income should not be enhanced by 'buckets' of provisions being established in the current year. This was a practice which had grown from SSAP 6's somewhat liberal approach to accounting for terminated activities. Under SSAP 6, as soon as a decision had been made to discontinue a business segment, provision would be made for all anticipated future costs and losses which were expected to arise in connection with the discontinuance – even if the discontinuance was expected to take several years to complete. Since these provisions were generally charged as extraordinary items, the current and future earnings per share were protected against loss-making operations which were in the process of termination.

FRS 3 clearly takes a much stricter line on the way in which discontinuing operations are accounted for and disclosed. Not only must the sale or termination be completed in the period to qualify for a discontinued classification in the profit and loss account, but there is now much less facility for exuberant provisioning. This is because there needs to be more than just a decision to sell or terminate: in the case of a sale, there needs to be a binding sale agreement and, in the case of a termination, a detailed formal plan for termination from which the reporting entity cannot realistically withdraw.

However, this does raise the issue of the possible conflict between SSAP 2 and FRS 3. Under the concept of prudence, provision is made for all known liabilities (expenses and losses) whether the amount of these is known with certainty or is a best estimate in the light of the information available.[46] On the other hand, FRS 3 will only permit a provision to be established for known

---

Extract 22.7: Hanson PLC (1996)

CONSOLIDATED PROFIT AND LOSS ACCOUNT

For the year ended October 1, 1996 [extract]

Note		1996 Before exceptional items £ million	1996 Exceptional items £ million	1996 Total £ million	1995 Before exceptional items £ million	1995 Exceptional items £ million	1995 Total £ million
5	**Exceptional items before interest and taxation**						
	Profit (loss) on disposal of fixed assets						
	continuing operations	—	12	12	—	(6)	(6)
	discontinued operations	—	—	—	—	(15)	(15)
	Profit (loss) on disposal of operations						
	continuing operations	—	—	—	—	(34)	(34)
	discontinued operations	—	633	633	—	4	4
	Release of environmental provisions						
	discontinued operations	—	193	193	—	—	—
	Reorganisation costs						
	continuing operations	—	(31)	(31)	—	(29)	(29)
	discontinued operations	—	(120)	(120)	—	(18)	(18)
		—	687	687	—	(98)	(98)

2.6.4 Disclosure of exceptional items in practice

Perhaps not unexpectedly, the disclosures in practice of exceptional items have become somewhat varied as between companies. For example, one company might show abortive acquisition costs as a non-operating exceptional item, whilst another might choose to show the same costs as an exceptional item under the format heading 'Administrative expenses'. This is perhaps not surprising, given that operating profit is not defined in FRS 3, with the result that directors are required to select a definition which is most appropriate to the circumstances of their business. Consequently, the profit and loss account positioning of individual exceptional items will depend on the nature of the item, the nature of the entity's operations and the judgement of the directors.

This has become necessary largely as a result of an ill-conceived rule in FRS 3 which is based on the premise that the statutory format headings cater for all eventualities and that the objectives of FRS 3 can be achieved within the strait-jacket of the Companies Act formats. Not only do the various formats contain different headings, but a company which had adopted either Format 3 or 4 would find it is virtually impossible to comply with FRS 3. Furthermore, because FRS 3 contains no additional guidance or explanation as to the criteria which differentiate 'fundamental' reorganisations and restructuring from other (non-fundamental) ones, it is difficult to see any pattern of consistency in the presentation of these items.

2.6.5 *The impact of the effective abolition of extraordinary items*

We agree that it was appropriate for the ASB to limit the use of extraordinary items to very rare circumstances, but we consider that the standard should explain exactly what these circumstances are, and give examples. On the other hand, if FRS 3's abstruse drafting in this area reflected the ASB's intention to ensure that companies do not report extraordinary items under any circumstances, it seems to have succeeded.

However, since most items which were once shown as extraordinary are now shown as exceptional, we are concerned about the growing perception that the 'important' figure to look at in the profit and loss account is the profit from continuing operations before exceptional items, particularly as FRS 3 requires prominence to be given to certain exceptional items as a separate category on the face of the profit and loss account. Such a presentation will encourage the same misconception which was previously applied to extraordinary items under SSAP 6 – namely, that these items are something apart from the trading operations of the business and may be set on one side in any consideration of its performance. At the same time, FRS 3's definition of exceptional items is weaker even than SSAP 6's definition of extraordinary items, which can make it very easy to 'manage' the pre-exceptional figure. Apart from the three non-operating exceptional items discussed above, the exceptional item classification may now include:

- highly unusual items which would previously have been classified as extraordinary;

- items which quite often arise, but not in every year, which might previously have been classified as exceptional; and

- items which arise annually, but happen to be unusually large in the current year.

In the last of these three items, the exceptional effect on the results is not the whole amount of the item, but only the excess over a 'normal' amount. Similarly, it could be misleading to show the whole amount of a charge for bad and doubtful debts as exceptional. In any event, we think it is unnecessary that exceptional items be overemphasised on the face of the profit and loss account. We would have preferred FRS 3 to have given emphasis to the overall result for the year and to have regarded the analysis of it as a secondary disclosure. As demonstrated by the current fixation on earnings per share, simplistic classifications on the face of the primary statements merely tend to encourage superficial analysis.

Cookson is an example of a company that has highlighted its results and earnings per share before exceptional items. This is well illustrated by the following extract from its 1996 accounts:

Extract 22.8: Cookson Group plc (1996)

Group profit and loss account

for the year ended 31 December 1996

	Note	1996 Before exceptional items £ m	1996 Exceptional items £ m	1996 Total £ m	1995 Before exceptional items £ m	1995 Exceptional items £ m	1995 Total £ m
Turnover	2	**1,878.4**	—	**1,878.4**	1,800.1	—	1,800.1
Share of turnover of associated companies		**(249.2)**	—	**(249.2)**	(239.9)	—	(239.9)
Turnover of Group subsidiary companies		**1,629.2**	—	**1,629.2**	1,560.2	—	1,560.2
Operating profit	2,3	**188.6**	**(25.9)**	**162.7**	200.3	—	200.3
Net loss on sale or termination of operations	4	—	**(86.3)**	**(86.3)**	—	(11.8)	(11.8)
Net loss on disposal of fixed assets	5	—	**(9.2)**	**(9.2)**	—	(1.1)	(1.1)
Profit on ordinary activities before interest		**188.6**	**(121.4)**	**67.2**	200.3	(12.9)	187.4
Interest	6	**(22.6)**	—	**(22.6)**	(19.1)	—	(19.1)
Profit on ordinary activities before taxation		**166.0**	**(121.4)**	**44.6**	181.2	(12.9)	168.3
Taxation on profit on ordinary activities	7	**(49.1)**	**13.6**	**(35.5)**	(55.1)	(5.9)	(61.0)
Profit on ordinary activities after taxation		**116.9**	**(107.8)**	**9.1**	126.1	(18.8)	107.3
Minority interests	24	**(2.4)**	—	**(2.4)**	(2.5)	—	(2.5)
Profit for the financial year		**114.5**	**(107.8)**	**6.7**	123.6	(18.8)	104.8
Dividends	8			**(58.4)**			(54.0)
Net (loss)/profit transferred to reserves	23			**(51.7)**			50.8
Earnings per share	9	**17.0p**	**(16.0)p**	**1.0p**	18.9p	(2.9)p	16.0p

Notes to the accounts

9   Earnings per share

Earnings per share are calculated using an average of **675.3m** (1995: 653.3m) ordinary shares in issue during the year. The fully diluted earnings per share is not materially different to earnings per share as reported.

On the face of the Group profit and loss account, earnings per share are shown both before and after exceptional items. In 1996, rationalisation costs of £25.9 million are reported as exceptional items within operating profit. There were no such costs in 1995. In prior years, exceptional items included within operating profit did not have as significant an effect on operating profit as in 1996 and therefore were not excluded from the calculation of earnings per share. Consequently, the Directors believe that for 1996, the calculation for earnings per share excluding all exceptional items together with the associated tax charge or credit gives the most appropriate measure of the underlying earning capacity of the Group.

Clearly, the directors of Cookson want to focus the readers' attention on the first column in the Group's profit and loss account, which reflects a profit for the financial year before exceptional items of £114.5m and an earnings per share of 17.0p, as opposed to the year's actual profit of £6.7m and an earnings per share of 1.0p. It is a moot point as to whether or not pre-exceptional profit is 'the most appropriate measure of the underlying earning capacity of the Group'. In any event though, in order for the shareholders of the group to assess management performance and stewardship, they need to look at the group's *total* performance.

2.7   Profit or loss on the disposal of an asset

Prior to FRS 3, when an entity disposed of an asset carried at valuation, the directors had the choice of calculating the profit or loss on disposal by reference either to the depreciated historical cost or to the amount at which the asset was carried in the balance sheet. If the latter option was selected, that portion of the revaluation reserve which related to the asset would usually be transferred, as a reserve movement, to realised reserves.

FRS 3 removed this choice, requiring that the profit or loss on the disposal of an asset must be calculated as the difference between the net sale proceeds and the net carrying amount, whether carried at historical cost (less any provisions made) or at valuation.[59] A subsequent amendment to FRS 3 has allowed insurance businesses limited relief from this particular requirement as it applies to the gains and losses arising on the disposal of investments. The amendment applies to insurance companies and insurance groups, both in relation to their own accounts and where these are incorporated in the consolidated accounts of a group whose main business is not insurance. These entities are thus granted an exemption from the requirement to calculate gains and losses on disposal of investments by reference to their carrying amount rather than original cost.[60]

The reason for this revised approach to determining the profit or loss on the disposal of an asset lies in the ASB's balance sheet approach to the recognition of gains and losses (see section 4.1 of Chapter 3 of this book). Under its Draft *Statement of Principles*, the ASB defines gains and losses as being increases and decreases in ownership interest, other than those relating to contributions from and distributions to owners. Recognition is triggered where a past event indicates that there has been a measurable change in the assets and liabilities of the entity. Thus, where a change in assets is not offset by an equal change in liabilities, a gain or a loss will result (unless the change relates to a transaction with the entity's owners, in which case a contribution from owners or distribution to owners will be recognised). Consequently, once an asset has been revalued in an entity's balance sheet, any subsequent transactions must be based on the balance sheet carrying amount of that asset.

It is therefore clear why the ASB has removed the option of calculating the profit or loss on disposal of a revalued asset by reference to the asset's historical cost. Nevertheless, it did receive a rather mixed reaction from the business community, including the following amusing comment from the chairman of Ilex Limited, a property investment company:

> *Extract 22.9: Ilex Limited (1993)*
>
> **CHAIRMAN'S STATEMENT**
>
> Profits after tax have risen from £564,000 to £1,698,000. These figures have been drawn up in accordance with the latest Accounting Standards and last year's figure is adjusted to make it comparable. The main change is to the manner in which capital items are taken through the Profit and Loss Account with a resulting volatility in earnings per share. We consider this a mistaken method for property investment companies which will only serve to confuse shareholders. Since it is mandatory, we accept it somewhat grumpily: the accounting profession seems to have an endemic tendency towards committees recommending changes which add to its workload and its clients' fees.

Some might argue that, so long as UK accounting is underpinned by a system of company law which recognises capital maintenance and distributable profits on an historical cost basis, companies should be able to report profits in the profit and loss account on an historical cost basis. However, there is the alternative view that income statements should be primarily concerned with the measurement of performance, and that when reported figures are not related to current values there may be over- or understatement of performance as measured by profits and return on assets. Consequently, the ASB has taken the view that, in the light of the present modified historical cost system and all its associated problems, companies which revalue assets should be required to measure future transactions by reference to the revalued amount.

2.8 Note of historical cost profits and losses

Because the profit or loss on the disposal of an asset is now to be calculated by reference to the asset's balance sheet carrying amount, FRS 3 introduced the requirement that, where there is a material difference between the result as disclosed in the profit and loss account and the result on an unmodified historical cost basis, a note of the historical cost profit or loss for the period should be presented.[61] This is a memorandum item that is an abbreviated restatement of the profit and loss account, adjusting the reported profit or loss so as to show it as if no asset revaluations had been made. Where full historical cost information is unavailable or cannot be obtained without unreasonable expense or delay, the earliest available values should be used. The note should include a reconciliation of the reported profit on ordinary activities before taxation to the equivalent historical cost amount and should also show the retained profit for the financial year reported on the historical cost basis.

Essentially, the note will incorporate adjustments for (i) the difference between the profit on the disposal of an asset calculated on depreciated historical cost and that calculated on a revalued amount, and (ii) the difference between an historical cost depreciation charge and the depreciation charge calculated on the revalued amount included in the profit and loss account of the period. The following extract from the example contained in the Appendix to FRS 3 illustrates the presentation of the note:

Note of historical cost profits and losses

	1993	1992 as restated
	£ million	£ million
Reported profit on ordinary activities before taxation	45	13
Realisation of property revaluation gains of previous years	9	10
Difference between a historical cost depreciation charge and the actual depreciation charge of the year calculated on the revalued amount	5	4
Historical cost profit on ordinary activities before taxation	59	27
Historical cost profit for the year retained after taxation, minority interests, extraordinary items and dividends	35	20

The note should be presented immediately following the profit and loss account or the statement of total recognised gains and losses. In consolidated financial statements, the profit and loss account figure for minority interests should be amended for the purposes of this note to reflect the adjustments made where they affect subsidiary companies with a minority interest.

The standard does not contain a definition of an unmodified historical cost basis. However, it is stated in the explanation section of the standard that the following are not deemed to be departures from the historical cost convention: (a) adjustments necessarily made to cope with the impact of hyper-inflation on foreign operations and (b) the practice of market makers and other dealers in investments of marking to market where this is an established industry practice.[62]

This still leaves open the position of entities marking to market where it is not industry practice. The implication from the FRS is that these other entities are deemed to have departed from the unmodified historical cost basis. However, there is an alternative view, which we support, that marking to market is not a departure from the historical cost convention, but is a method to ensure appropriate revenue recognition and as such it applies irrespective of the industry in which the entity operates. We would not therefore expect any adjustments to be included in the note of historical cost profits and losses in respect of marking current asset investments to market.

2.9 Statement of total recognised gains and losses

2.9.1 *Primary financial statement*

FRS 3 introduced into UK GAAP a fourth primary financial statement: the statement of total recognised gains and losses. The statement has to be presented with the same prominence as the other primary statements and must show the components as well as the total of recognised gains and losses. Although there is not necessarily general agreement on the point, the statement is regarded by the ASB at least as being a statement of performance or 'comprehensive income'. It represents the ASB's first step towards requiring the reporting of changes in wealth as opposed to traditional historical cost profit and loss. The ethos of the statement lies in the ASB's Draft *Statement of Principles* and, in particular, in its balance sheet approach to the recognition of assets, liabilities, gains and losses.

According to the Draft *Statement of Principles*, recognition is triggered where a past event indicates that there has been a measurable change in the assets and liabilities of an entity, and where a change in assets is not offset by an equal change in liabilities a gain or loss will result (unless the change relates to a transaction with the entity's owners, in which case a contribution from owners or distribution to owners will be recognised). Gains or losses should be recognised either in the profit and loss account or in the statement of total recognised gains and losses.

Because of the company law framework which underpins UK financial reporting, it might be logical to assume that gains which are earned and realised are recognised in the profit and loss account, whilst gains which are earned (but not realised) are recognised in the statement of total recognised gains and losses – and this is more or less how things work at the moment. However, it is evident from the ASB's Draft *Statement of Principles* that it is seeking to change this approach. The ASB has stated in the *Statement of Principles* that 'a more useful analysis of the quality of profits than that into realised and unrealised profits is an analysis into those gains and losses that derive from operating activities and those that result from changes in the value of those assets and liabilities that are held on a continuing basis for use in the entity's business.'[63] It follows from this perspective that the same gains and losses should not be recognised twice; for example, a holding gain recognised when a fixed asset is revalued should not be recognised a second time when the revalued asset is sold. Although the ASB has not always faithfully followed the principles outlined above in respect of the statement of total recognised gains and losses, this does explain the logic behind FRS 3's requirement that the profit or loss on the disposal of an asset must be calculated as the difference between the net sale proceeds and the net carrying amount, whether carried at historical cost (less any provisions made) or at valuation (see 2.7 above).

The following extract from the example contained in the Appendix to FRS 3 illustrates the presentation of the statement:

Statement of total recognised gains and losses

	1993	1992 as restated
	£ million	£ million
Profit for the financial year	29	7
Unrealised surplus on revaluation of properties	4	6
Unrealised (loss)/gain on trade investment	(3)	7
	30	20
Currency translation differences on foreign currency net investments	(2)	5
Total recognised gains and losses relating to the year	28	25
Prior year adjustment (as explained in note x)	(10)	
Total gains and losses recognised since last annual report	18	

The £18 million net total gains represents the increase in net assets which occurred between the opening and closing balance sheet dates, and which were brought about by all transactions that the entity had entered into, other than those involving shareholders. Since the statement comprises total realised and unrealised gains and losses, the realised profit for the financial year (before dividends) is brought in as the first line of the statement. This means that the profit and loss account now provides the detailed analysis of the single line in the statement of total recognised gains and losses, whilst the unrealised gains and losses are itemised in the statement (see Chapter 2 at 5.7 for an illustration of the relationship between the balance sheet, the profit and loss account and the statement of total recognised gains and losses).

Where a reporting entity has no recognised gains or losses other than the profit or loss for the period, a statement to this effect immediately below the profit and loss account will suffice.

2.9.2   Goodwill

The ASB explained in UITF 3 *Treatment of goodwill on disposal of a business* that neither purchased goodwill eliminated against reserves on acquisition nor any subsequent reinstatement of that goodwill on disposal represents a recognised loss or gain and thus should not be included in the statement of total recognised gains and losses.

UITF 3 requires that in the year that a previously acquired business, subsidiary or associated undertaking is either sold or closed the goodwill written off against reserves in the year of acquisition should be reinstated and included in the calculation of profit or loss on sale or closure that is recognised in the profit and

provisions of FRS 3, or they could spread it forward over the expected remaining service lives of current employees.[83]

2.14.4 Correction of fundamental errors

The standard stresses that a fundamental error is only likely to occur in exceptional circumstances. The term 'fundamental' is implicitly defined as being of such significance as to destroy the presentation of a true and fair view and hence the validity of those financial statements.[84] The corrections of such fundamental errors and the cumulative adjustments applicable to prior periods have no bearing on the results of the current period and they are therefore not included in arriving at the profit or loss for the current period.

However, it is worth noting that when SSAP 6 was introduced there was no available procedure which allowed companies to correct and reissue accounts which are considered to be defective. Such provisions now exist in the law,[85] which means that the facility to correct fundamental errors by means of a prior year adjustment must be of less significance as a result; if the directors consider their accounts to be defective then they should avail themselves of the provisions under the Companies Act which enable them to revise the accounts; they do not have to wait to make the amendment in the accounts of the following year by means of a prior year adjustment. Nevertheless, circumstances will arise where a fundamental error is either discovered shortly before the following year's accounts are due to be issued or does not, in the opinion of the directors, warrant the preparation of revised accounts. In both instances, therefore, it would be appropriate to follow FRS 3's procedures for the correction of the error.

It is tempting to think of any adjustment which relates to an event or circumstance which arose in a prior year as a prior year item; however, if the adjustment derives from new information about that event, then it simply represents a change in the estimate of the effect of that event and is therefore a current period item. For example, if a company has to write off a debt which it previously considered to be recoverable, then the charge should be reflected in the current year's profit or loss and not accounted for by way of prior year adjustment. It is therefore appropriate to consider whether the information which indicates that a fundamental error has arisen was actually available at the time that the financial statements for the prior period were approved.

2.14.5 Accounting treatment

FRS 3 requires that prior period adjustments be accounted for by restating the comparative figures for the preceding period in the primary statements and notes and adjusting the opening balance of reserves for the cumulative effect. The cumulative effect of the adjustments should also be noted at the foot of the statement of total recognised gains and losses of the current period.[86]

This means that in the case of a change in accounting policy, the amounts for the current and corresponding periods should be restated on the basis of the new policy. The cumulative adjustments should also be noted at the foot of the statement of total recognised gains and losses of the current period and included in the reconciliation of movements in shareholders' funds of the corresponding period in order to highlight for users the effect of the adjustments. The following example illustrates the mechanics of such a process:

Example 22.1:   Illustration of a change in accounting policy

Up until 31 December 19X5, a company has adopted a policy of writing off its development expenditure in the year in which it was incurred. The company's financial statements for the year ended 31 December 19X5 disclosed the following:

Profit and loss account	19X5	19X4
	£'000	£'000
Profit on ordinary activities before taxation	4,200	3,800
Taxation	(1,575)	(1,400)
Profit on ordinary activities after taxation	2,625	2,400
Dividends	(600)	(500)
Retained profit for year	2,025	1,900

Balance sheet		
Tangible fixed assets	8,000	7,100
Net current assets	2,025	800
	10,025	7,900
Deferred taxation	(1,000)	(900)
	9,025	7,000
Share capital	1,000	1,000
Profit and loss account	8,025	6,000
	9,025	7,000

In preparing its financial statements for the year ended 31 December 19X6 it considers that a policy of capitalising the development expenditure and amortising it over a period of four years from the date of commencing production would give a fairer presentation of the results and financial position of the company. Accordingly, it will be necessary to restate the figures for 19X5 on the basis of the new policy. This initially involves computing:

(i)   the net book value of the development expenditure at 31 December 19X5;

(ii)   the amortisation charge for the year ended 31 December 19X5; and

(iii)   the net book value of the development expenditure at 31 December 19X4.

The development expenditure incurred in each of the five years ended 31 December 19X5 and the calculation of the above figures are as follows (for the purposes of this example the date of commencing production is taken to be 1 January following the year in which the development expenditure was incurred):

Year	Development expenditure incurred £'000	(i) £'000	(ii) £'000	(iii) £'000
19X1	260	–	65	65
19X2	100	25	25	50
19X3	240	120	60	180
19X4	400	300	100	400
19X5	40	40	–	–
		485	250	695

Development expenditure in 19X6 amounted to £800,000.

The adjustment to the pre-tax profit for 19X5 will, therefore, be a reduction of £210,000 being the amortisation of £250,000 less the development expenditure of £40,000 previously charged to the profit and loss account.

Having computed these figures it is then necessary to ascertain whether any other figures in the financial statements will be affected by the change in policy; in particular, deferred taxation and stocks. For the purposes of this example the only other figures, apart from retained profits, affected by the change in policy are those relating to deferred taxation. Assuming that the development expenditure has been fully allowed as a deductible expense in arriving at the corporation tax payable in respect of the year in which it was incurred, then the new policy will give rise to timing differences for which deferred tax may have to be provided. The company considers that full provision has to be made for deferred tax and accordingly the provision at 31 December 19X5, the charge for the year then ended, and the provision at 31 December 19X4 have to be adjusted as follows:

	Gross timing difference £'000	Provision at 35% £'000
31 December 19X5	485	170
31 December 19X4	695	243
Tax charge for year		(73)

As a result of these calculations the financial statements for the year ended 31 December 19X6 will therefore show the following figures in the profit and loss account, the statement of total recognised gains and losses, the balance sheet and reconciliation of movements in shareholders' funds (the 19X6 figures having been prepared on the basis of the new accounting policy):

Profit and loss account

	19X6 £'000	Restated 19X5 £'000
Profit on ordinary activities before taxation	5,000	3,990
Taxation	(1,820)	(1,502)
Profit on ordinary activities after taxation	3,180	2,488
Dividends	(700)	(600)
Retained profit for year	2,480	1,888

Statement of total recognised gains and losses

	19X6 £'000	Restated 19X5 £'000
Profit for the financial year	3,180	2,488
Total recognised gains and losses relating to the year	3,180	2,488
Prior year adjustment	315	
Total gains and losses recognised since last annual report	3,495	

Balance sheet

	19X6 £'000	Restated 19X5 £'000
Fixed assets		
Intangible	1,090	485
Tangible fixed assets	10,000	8,000
	11,090	8,485
Net current assets	2,212	2,025
	13,302	10,510
Deferred taxation	(1,482)	(1,170)
	11,820	9,340
Share capital	1,000	1,000
Profit and loss account	10,820	8,340
	11,820	9,340

Reconciliation of movements in shareholders' funds

	Restated 19X6 £'000	19X5 £'000
Profit for the financial year	3,180	2,488
Dividends	(700)	(600)
Net addition to shareholders' funds	2,480	1,888
Opening shareholders' funds (originally £9,025,000 before adding prior year adjustment of £315,000)	9,340	7,452
Closing shareholders' funds	11,820	9,340

Reserves note

	Profit and loss account £'000
At 1 January 19X6	
— as previously reported	8,025
Prior year adjustment	315
— as restated	8,340
Retained profit for the year	2,480
At 31 December 19X6	10,820

Where prior year figures are restated it will generally be necessary (unless the effect would be immaterial) to restate the balance sheet and profit and loss account, but it should be unnecessary to amend the cash flow statement because, of course, the cash flows have not changed. However, some of the reconciling notes to the cash flow statement may be affected, particularly the calculation of operating cash flow where the indirect method has been used to generate this figure. Care should also be taken to ensure that all figures in the accounts which are affected by the change in policy are adjusted, in particular, deferred taxation.

2.14.6 *Disclosing the effect of a change in accounting policy*

One further requirement of FRS 3 in respect of prior period adjustments is that 'the effect of prior period adjustments on the results for the preceding period should be disclosed where practicable'.[87] This overlaps with the Companies Act disclosures which are required when there is a departure from the fundamental accounting principles laid down in the Act.[88] In the case of a change in accounting policy, it will be necessary for the directors to depart from the fundamental principle of consistency, in which case they are required to disclose in a note to the accounts the particulars of and reasons for the departure 'and its effect'.[89]

This gave rise to an issue of interpretation as to whether the Companies Act requirement to disclose 'its effect' related to the current period, the prior period or both. In tracing the requirement back to the EC Fourth Directive, it seems clear that the intention of the legislation was for companies to disclose the effect of the departure on the current year's financial statements as a whole, and not just on the results. The wording of the relevant Article in the Fourth Directive is as follows: 'Any such departures must be disclosed in the notes on the accounts and the reasons for them given together with an assessment of their effect on the assets, liabilities, financial position and profit or loss.'[90]

However, irrespective of what might have been the original intention of the legislation, the practice which had developed was to provide only details of the effect on the prior period's results (i.e. the information which is required by FRS 3). Apart from anything else, the principal reason for this was that it is often impracticable to provide the information in respect of the current period. For example, a company preparing its first set of accounts in compliance with FRS 4 and FRS 5 would, in order to illustrate fully the effect of the relevant changes, effectively have to present alongside the current year's accounts, a second set of accounts prepared under the old rules. Not only is this impracticable, but it is of little value to the user.

Nevertheless, this is an issue which was referred to the UITF – apparently at the insistence of the Review Panel. The UITF's deliberations resulted in UITF Abstract 14 – *Disclosure of changes in accounting policy* – which was issued in November 1995. The consensus reached by the UITF was that the disclosures necessary when a change of accounting policy is made should include, in addition to the disclosure of the effect required by FRS 3, an indication of the effect on the current year's results. In those cases where the effect on the current year was either immaterial or similar to the quantified effect on the prior year 'a simple statement saying this would suffice'. The Abstract provides further that where it is not practicable to give the effect on the current year, that fact, together with the reasons, should be stated.[91] As stated above, we believe that these are sometimes meaningless and impracticable disclosures, and companies will in such cases make use of UITF 14's get-out to avoid having to provide them.

2.15   Comparative figures

Comparative figures are required both for the figures in the primary statements and such notes thereto as are required by the standard. The comparatives in respect of the profit and loss account have to be analysed into continuing, acquisitions and discontinued to the same level as the current year's results. However, the analysis of the comparatives does not have to be on the face of the profit and loss account, but can be given in the notes.

The comparative figures will, in total, be the same as the figures reported in the previous year's profit and loss account. However, the analysis will be different;

the continuing category in the comparatives should only include results of activities that are classified as continuing in the current year. Consequently the discontinued column in the comparatives will include the results of the activities that were discontinued in both the current and the previous year. The results of the operations that were classified as acquisitions in the previous year's profit and loss account will not be presented as acquisitions in the comparative figures for the current period; they will be included in continuing activities. This is because the analysis of the comparative figures must be based on the status of an operation in the current year's profit and loss account. The only time that there will be an acquisitions category in the comparatives is when an acquisition of the current period has been accounted for as a merger; in this case the comparatives will be restated as if the companies had been combined throughout the previous period and so there will be an element in the comparatives relating to operations classified as acquisitions in the current period.

The standard provides that in some circumstances it may also be useful to disclose the results of acquisitions for the first full financial year for which they are a part of the reporting entity's activities. In this case the FRS suggests that it may be helpful also to provide the comparative figures for the acquisitions.

3   HISTORICAL SUMMARIES, HALF-YEARLY REPORTS AND PRELIMINARY PROFIT STATEMENTS

Although the London Stock Exchange published a major revision of its Listing Rules in 1993, the revised Rules take no account of the substantial changes made to the profit and loss account by FRS 3. This means that although extraordinary items remain only a theoretical possibility, the Rules specifically require that such items be disclosed in all half-yearly reports and preliminary profits statements of listed companies;[92] on the other hand, the various new components of performance which the ASB has identified as being important – notably those relating to exceptional items and discontinued operations – are not required to be identified.

Unlike SSAP 6, FRS 3 does not refer to historical summaries, half-yearly reports and preliminary profit statements. Nevertheless, there is a growing trend for companies to include comprehensive profit and loss accounts and statements of total recognised gains and losses in accordance with FRS 3 in their half-yearly reports.

Although there are no rules governing historical summaries, it is our view that they should normally be restated retrospectively for prior year adjustments. However, if this is not practicable, the part of the summary which has not been restated should be identified and the reason for not restating it explained.

4 COMPARISON WITH US AND IASC PRONOUNCEMENTS

4.1 US

There are a number of US pronouncements which have been issued relating to this area of accounting. The main ones which are still relevant today are as follows: APB Opinion No. 20 – *Accounting Changes*; APB Opinion No. 30 – *Reporting the Results of Operations–Reporting the Effects of Disposal of a Segment of a Business, and Extraordinary, Unusual and Infrequently Occurring Events and Transactions*; AIN-APB 30 – *Reporting the Results of Operations: Accounting Interpretations of APB Opinion No. 30*; and SFAS 16 – *Prior Period Adjustments*. In addition, EITF Abstract 94–3 dealing with restructuring charges and SEC Staff Accounting Bulletin SAB No. 93 regarding discontinued operations are also relevant. More significantly, though, in June 1997 the FASB issued SFAS 130 – *Reporting Comprehensive Income*. This is discussed at 4.1.4 below.

4.1.1 Extraordinary items

Prior to FRS 3, extraordinary items were much more of a rare phenomenon in the US than in the UK. In fact, very few of the items which were being disclosed as extraordinary in financial statements in the UK would have remained so under US GAAP. However, given FRS 3's effective ban on extraordinary items, the situation has been turned on its head. Although extraordinary items are rarely found in US GAAP accounts, at least it is recognised that they can arise under certain circumstances.

The US position on extraordinary items is primarily contained within APB 30. The key issues addressed relate to the definition of an extraordinary item; the treatment of the results of discontinued activities; and the definition of a business segment. The definition of extraordinary is broadly similar to that used in FRS 3, in that it incorporates the two key elements that the event must be of an unusual nature (and possess a high degree of abnormality) and that the event would not reasonably be expected to recur in the foreseeable future.[93] However, differences in interpretation arise for two principal reasons: first, APB 30 gives a detailed interpretation of the definition of extraordinary by discussing the two key terms 'unusual nature' and 'infrequency of occurrence'.[94] Second, it lists a number of items which should not be reported as extraordinary;[95] this is complemented by AIN-APB 30 which gives specific examples of items which would be regarded as extraordinary and those which would not.[96] In contrast, FRS 3's definition of ordinary activities effectively eliminates the possibility of any item being regarded as extraordinary.

Nevertheless, APB 30's detailed discussion of the definition of extraordinary also results in a very narrow interpretation of the term. For example, it comments that an unusual event should possess a high degree of abnormality and be of a type clearly unrelated to the ordinary and typical activities of the company.[97] Furthermore, in discussing 'infrequency of occurrence' APB 30 comments that the event or transaction should be of such a type that would not be expected to occur again in the foreseeable future.[98]

The examples of items listed in APB 30 which should not be reported as extraordinary items because they are usual in nature or may be expected to recur as a consequence of customary and continuing business activities include, inter alia, the write-down or write-off of assets, e.g. debtors and stocks, and gains or losses from sale or abandonment of property, plant and equipment. Whilst such items were frequently treated as extraordinary in the financial statements of UK companies prior to FRS 3, they would now not under any circumstances be regarded as extraordinary. On the other hand, APB 30 recognises that there may be occasions when such items can be properly treated as extraordinary items, but emphasises that these will be rare; for example, as result of an earthquake or expropriation.[99] It also specifically states that gains or losses on disposal of a segment of a business should not be treated as an extraordinary item (see 4.1.2 below).

One of the examples given in AIN-APB 30 which illustrates the differences in interpretation is that of a disposal of an investment in another company held for investment purposes. If the company has never owned another investment, then clearly the disposal is of an unusual nature and could not in current circumstances ever recur and therefore the gain or loss can be regarded as extraordinary. However, if the company holds a portfolio of investments, even if their disposal is infrequent, the disposal cannot be regarded either as unusual or unlikely to recur.[100] Under FRS 3, neither disposal would give rise to an extraordinary item.

One other particular requirement which is worthy of note is provided by SFAS 4,[101] which expressly requires the disclosure of gains or losses arising from early extinguishment of debt to be disclosed as extraordinary.

4.1.2 *Discontinued operations*

APB 30 deals with discontinued operations very differently to FRS 3. Whilst FRS 3 lays down four strict criteria which must be satisfied for an operation to be classified as discontinued (see 2.3.1 above), APB 30 uses the term 'segment of a business' in order to determine whether the effect of certain activities being discontinued merits separate accounting treatment.[102]

Consequently, the term discontinued operations refers to the operations of a segment of a business that has been sold, abandoned, spun off, or otherwise disposed of or, although still operating, is subject to a formal plan for disposal. In the usual circumstance, it would be expected that the plan of disposal would be carried out within a period of one year from the 'measurement date' (see below).

'Segment of a business' refers to a component of an entity whose activities represent a separate major line of business or class of customer. A segment may be in the form of a subsidiary, a division or a department and in some cases a joint venture, provided that its assets, results of operations, and activities can be clearly distinguished, physically and operationally and for financial reporting purposes, from the other assets, results of operations, and activities of the entity. The inability to identify the results of operations of the part of the business being disposed of would clearly suggest that the definition of a segment has not been met.

The SEC staff believe that there is a rebuttable presumption that the above definition of segment of a business cannot be satisfied unless the operations in question were previously disclosed as a business segment in accordance with SFAS 14, or as a separate line of business or class of customer in the segment information contained in management's discussion and analysis of financial condition and results of operations.

Furthermore, although the definition of a business segment contained in APB 30 is fairly wide, AIN–APB 30 provides illustrative examples of the application of APB 30 which assist in preventing too wide an interpretation being placed on the definition. In particular, AIN–APB 30 provides detailed guidance with regard to the interpretation of what comprises a separate major line of business as distinct from a product line.

APB 30 requires that the income statement be completely reclassified so that the results of discontinued operations up to the measurement date are disclosed separately after the results of continuing operations.

The standard defines the measurement date as the date on which the management having authority to approve the action commits itself to a formal plan to dispose of a segment of the business. The plan of disposal should include as a minimum:

- identification of the major assets to be disposed of;
- the expected method of disposal;
- the period expected to be required for completion of the disposal;
- an active programme to find a buyer if disposal is to be by sale;
- the estimated results of operations of the segment from the measurement date to the disposal date; and
- the estimated proceeds or salvage to be realised by disposal.

The computation of the estimated gain or loss on disposal should take into account the estimated results from the discontinued operation between the measurement date and the expected disposal date. If a loss is expected from the discontinuance of a business segment, the estimated loss shall be provided for as of the measurement date. If a gain is expected, it should be recognised when realised, which ordinarily is the disposal date.

If a company expects to realise a net gain consisting of an estimated gain on disposal of the segment that will be reduced by estimated operating losses during the period between the measurement date and the expected disposal date, the estimated operating losses should be deferred until the disposal date.

The gain or loss on disposal should include such adjustments, costs, and expenses which are clearly a direct result of the decision to dispose of the segment and are clearly not the adjustments of carrying amounts or costs, or expenses that should have been recognised on a going concern basis prior to the measurement date. Results of operations after the measurement date should be included in the gain or loss on disposal.

If a large segment, a separable group of assets of an acquired company or the entire acquired company is sold, all or a portion of the unamortised cost of the goodwill recognised in the acquisition should be included in the cost of the assets sold.

The notes to the financial statements should also disclose:

- the identity of the segment;
- the expected disposal date;
- the expected manner of disposal;
- a description of the remaining assets and liabilities of the segment at the balance sheet date; and
- the income or loss from operations and any proceeds from disposal of the segment during the period from the measurement date to the date of the balance sheet.

The above should be disclosed for periods subsequent to the measurement date and including the period of disposal. In the case of the last item above, a comparison with prior estimates should also be given.

4.1.3 Prior year adjustments

US accounting practice on changes in accounting policy and prior year adjustments is prescribed by APB 20 and SFAS 16 respectively.

The major difference between US GAAP and FRS 3 relates to the accounting treatment of a change in accounting policy or principle. Under US GAAP, the general rule is that where a company voluntarily changes an accounting policy, the cumulative effect of the change, i.e. the difference between retained profits at the beginning of the year as previously reported and the figure that would have been reported if the new policy had been applied retroactively for all prior periods, should be disclosed in the profit and loss account, albeit after the profit or loss on extraordinary items.[103] Consequently, comparative figures are not restated although pro forma comparatives should be disclosed for the profit or loss before extraordinary items and the net profit or loss for the year.[104] Comparatives are not adjusted, as a strict interpretation of the 'all-inclusive concept' results in the conclusion that the effect of the changes should be included in computing the net profit or loss for the period. APB 20 also comments that there could potentially be a dilution of public confidence in financial statements if prior periods were restated.[105]

However, there are certain specific exceptions, where the effect of a change in accounting policy must be accounted for retroactively as a prior period adjustment. The principal exceptions are as follows:[106]

(a)   a change from the LIFO method of stock valuation;

(b)   a change in the method of accounting for long-term construction-type contracts;

(c)   a change from the 'full cost' method in the oil and gas and similar extractive industries.

In addition, prior period adjustments are also required for correction of an error in prior periods.[107]

4.1.4   *Reporting Comprehensive Income*

The term 'comprehensive income' was first introduced in the official US literature via the FASB's conceptual framework. SFAC No. 5 concluded that comprehensive income and its components should be reported as part of a full set of financial statements. This has now come to pass through the publication of SFAS 130 – *Reporting Comprehensive Income* – which was issued by the FASB in June 1997.[108] However, a close examination of the statement soon reveals that it resembles in name only what was envisaged by the conceptual framework. This perhaps accounts for the fact that the statement was passed with two of the seven FASB members dissenting.

Some of the proposals contained in the Exposure Draft which preceded SFAS 130 met with quite strong resistance both in comment letters and at a public hearing. For example, the exposure draft proposed that comprehensive income should be seen as a performance measure and that entities should be required to disclose a per-share amount for comprehensive income. As a result of the not inconsiderable opposition to many of its proposals, the FASB decided to limit the project's scope to issues or presentation and disclosure 'so that it could complete the project in a timely manner'.[109] As a result, the statement does not address issues of recognition or measurement of comprehensive income and its components.

Consequently, the statement is unusually tentative for the FASB. It uses the SFAC No. 6 definition of comprehensive income, namely the change in equity of a business enterprise during a period from transactions and other events and circumstances from non-owner sources. It includes all changes in equity during a period except those resulting from investments by owners and distributions to owners. The statement uses the term 'comprehensive income' to describe the total of all components of comprehensive income, including net income. It then uses the term 'other comprehensive income' to refer to revenue, expenses, gains and losses that are included in comprehensive income but excluded from net income.

However, having set down these basic concepts, the statement then, in effect, gives preparers *carte blanche* to report comprehensive income in virtually whatever manner they choose, provided that all components of comprehensive income are reported in the financial statements in the period in which they are recognised, and the total amount of comprehensive income is disclosed in the financial statement where the components of other comprehensive income are reported.[110]

Appendix B to SFAS 130 contains four different formats for reporting comprehensive income. These comprise a single statement approach, a two statement approach, and two alternative ways of displaying comprehensive income as part of the statement of changes in equity. But even then, other formats are possible: the statement states that 'other formats or levels of detail may be appropriate for certain circumstances'.[111] An observer may be forgiven for thinking that this seems to be a bit of a free-for-all. In fact, this was the root of the concern of the two FASB members who voted against the statement. In their dissenting opinion, they expressed the concern that 'it is likely that most enterprises will meet the requirements of this Statement by providing the required information in a statement of changes in equity, and that displaying items of other comprehensive income solely in that statement as opposed to reporting them in a statement of financial performance will do little to enhance their visibility and will diminish their perceived importance'.[112]

Perhaps the most interesting aspect of the statement is that it contains requirements relating to 'reclassification adjustments' (otherwise known as recycling). The statement states that these adjustments need to be made in order to avoid double counting in comprehensive income items that are displayed as part of net income for a period that also had been displayed as part of other comprehensive income in that period or earlier periods.[113] This is where SFAS 130 is fundamentally different to FRS 3. Under FRS 3, once an item has been reported in either the profit and loss account or the statement of total recognised gains and losses, it is not reported again in either of the statements. So for example, if an investment is revalued, the revaluation is reported in the statement of total recognised gains and losses, and if it is later sold for its revalued amount, no further amount is reported in either statement. Not so with SFAS 130. In this example, the gain would again be reported, this time in the income statement and, so as to avoid double counting, a deduction would be made at the same time through other comprehensive income for the period. This requirement to record reclassification adjustments does, indeed, mean that the statement of comprehensive income is not a measure of performance. Consequently, the term 'comprehensive income' is somewhat of a misnomer.

4.2   IASC

The international position is set out in IAS 8 – *Net Profit or Loss for the Period, Fundamental Errors and Changes in Accounting Policies* – which was issued in revised form in December 1993 as part of the IASC's comparability/ improvements project. Its main features are as follows:

- All items of income or expense recognised in the income statement should be included in the determination of profit or loss unless an IAS permits or requires otherwise.[114]

- The profit or loss for the period is to be split between (a) the profit and loss from ordinary activities and (b) extraordinary items, both of which are to be disclosed on the face of the income statement,[115] with the nature and amount of each extraordinary item disclosed in a note.[116] The definitions of extraordinary items and ordinary activities are less rigorous than the equivalent FRS 3 definitions, although IAS 8 states that 'only on rare occasions does an event or transaction give rise to an extraordinary item'.[117]

- Amounts which are of such size, nature or incidence as to be relevant to an explanation of the performance for the period are to be disclosed (the term 'exceptional items' is not used).[118]

- The standard defines a discontinued operation rather loosely as something which results from the sale or abandonment of an operation that represents a separate, major line of business of an enterprise and of which the assets, net profit or loss and activities can be distinguished physically, operationally and for financial reporting purposes.[119]   Although it is not difficult to detect the influences of US GAAP on this definition, the related accounting requirements are less rigorous.   Not only does the standard allow considerable flexibility in determining whether or not a disposal constitutes a discontinued operation, but it also permits the results of discontinued operations to be classified under both ordinary and extraordinary activities.[120]

  However, the standard does require a number of disclosures to be given for each discontinued operation.   These are the nature of the discontinued operation, the manner and effective date of the discontinuance, the gain or loss on discontinuance, and the discontinued operation's revenue and profit or loss from ordinary activities for the period and the comparative period.[121]

- The effect of a change in an accounting estimate should be included in the determination of net profit or loss in the period of the change (if the change affects the period only), or in the period of the change and future periods (if the change affects both).[122] The effect of a change in an accounting estimate should be included in the same income statement classification as was used previously for the estimate.[123]

■   Fundamental errors and changes in accounting policy are to be dealt with either as a prior year adjustment (the 'benchmark treatment') or as a separate item in the current year's profit or loss (the 'allowed alternative treatment').[124]

In July 1996, the IASC issued Exposure Draft E53 – *Presentation of Financial Statements* – which was aimed at consolidating and replacing IAS 1 – *Disclosure of Accounting Policies*, IAS 5 – *Information to be Disclosed in Financial Statements*, and IAS 13 – *Presentation of Current Assets and Current Liabilities*. The proposals could best be described as the IASC's version of the EC Fourth Directive. E53 dealt with such matters as fair presentation, fundamental accounting concepts, disclosure of accounting policies and balance sheet classification. The proposals were only really controversial in two respects: (1) E53 proposed that there should be the facility in IAS standards to apply a fair presentation override, and (2) it proposed that some sort of statement of comprehensive income should be added as a fourth primary financial statement.

E53 was approved as a standard at the July 1997 meeting of the IASC Board. It will be issued as IAS 1 (Revised) and will supersede IASs 1, 5 and 13. It will apply to accounting periods beginning on or after 1 July 1998.

In approving the Standard, the IASC Board agreed that, in extremely rare circumstances, enterprises may depart from a requirement if to do so is necessary in order to achieve fair presentation. On the matter of the statement of comprehensive income, the Board agreed that financial statements should include, as a separate component, a statement showing:

■   the net profit or loss for the period;

■   each item of income and expense which, as required by other Standards, is recognised directly in equity, and the total of these items; and

■   the cumulative effect of changes in accounting policy, and correction of fundamental errors, dealt with under the Benchmark treatment in IAS 8.

The Board also agreed that an enterprise should also present, either within this statement or in the notes:

■   capital transactions with owners and distributions to owners;

■   the balance of accumulated profit or loss at the beginning of the period and at the balance sheet date, and the movements for the period; and

■   a reconciliation between the carrying amount of each class of equity capital, share premium and of each reserve, at the beginning and the end of the period, separately disclosing each movement.

This is, of course, a compromise solution which is aimed at satisfying a number of different constituencies. For example, from a UK perspective the first three parts correspond to FRS 3's statement of total recognised gains and losses, with the result that the remaining three items can be disclosed in the notes thereby leaving the statement of total recognised gains and losses intact. The proposals are also compatible with SFAS 130 as a result of the flexibility on both sides. The IASC does not view the statement as a statement of performance, but it can be made into one if people so desire. Moreover, it provides a framework within which other IASC projects such as financial instruments and employee benefits can work.

5   CONCLUSION

FRS 3 represented a radical new approach to the reporting of financial performance. Contrary to first appearances, it was much more than a mere exercise in the reformatting of the profit and loss account and introduction of additional analyses of reserve movements; it significantly changed the rules of recognition and measurement in respect of many aspects of a company's performance, including discontinued operations, extraordinary and exceptional items and provisions.

More importantly, though, FRS 3 was the first manifestation of the ASB's balance sheet approach to income recognition as outlined in the Board's Draft *Statement of Principles*. This was highlighted through the introduction into UK GAAP of an additional primary statement of financial performance – the statement of total recognised gains and losses – which focuses on changes in wealth as the means of performance measurement, rather than traditional historical cost profit and loss. As shown above, this approach is now being embraced by other standard-setters, albeit more cautiously. What concerns us about this is the fact that the ASB has entrenched into an accounting standard a conceptual approach which has not been the subject of due process, has no general agreement and which is still only at an early stage of development and discussion.

Nevertheless, we support the general principles of FRS 3 which require companies to analyse the relevant components of their results, both good and bad, so that readers can better understand the performance for the period. The reader should be able to identify items which are unlikely to recur at a similar level and thereby make more accurate assessments of likely future performance by attaching appropriate weight to the different components of reported profit. On the other hand, directors should not be able to use the manner in which these

Chapter 23 Earnings per share

1 INTRODUCTION

Earnings per share (EPS) is one of the most widely quoted statistics in financial analysis. It came into great prominence in the US during the late 1950s and early 1960s due to the widespread use of the price earnings ratio (PE) as a yardstick for investment decisions. By the late 1960s, its popularity had switched across the Atlantic and for the purposes of consistency and comparability, it became important that an agreed method of computed EPS was established.

In March 1971, the Accounting Standards Steering Committee issued an exposure draft, ED 4 – *Earnings per share*. The exposure draft represented a departure by UK accounting bodies into the area of financial ratios and financial analysis. ED 4 was, in general, favourably received and in February 1972, SSAP 3 – *Earnings per share* – was issued with the objective of providing a minimum standard for disclosure of EPS in financial statements and the basis of its calculation.

It would appear that reported and forecast EPS can, through the PE ratio, significantly affect a company's share price. This is evident whenever events occur that alter market expectations of future EPS. For example, on June 25, 1987, there was a significant decline in share prices in the stores sector; the following day, the *Financial Times* explained the drop as follows:

> 'Shares across the stores sector tumbled yesterday on fears of an onset of conservative accounting. The widespread decline was triggered by the Argyll group's decision to treat the £90m cost of reorganising its Presto stores as an "exceptional" item rather than an "extraordinary" one.
>
> 'The move, following the company's £681m acquisition of Safeway in January, will reduce the company's pre-tax profits and earnings per share over the next four years.
>
> 'Worries that acquisitive companies would have to reduce their profits in a similar way affected the sector overall. Burton fell 14p to close 311p, Dee went down 15p to 228p, Woolworths lost 22p to

finish at 400p and Ward White dropped 14p to 394p. Even Marks and Spencer, a company not prone to takeover activity, ended 9p off at 243p.'[1]

Despite the apparent absurdity that a mere profit and loss account classification (which has no cash flow implication) can affect the intrinsic value of securities, the above article nonetheless illustrates the ostensible market sensitivity to EPS. It seems, therefore, that companies are perhaps more concerned with reporting a level of earnings in line with market expectations, rather than the manner by which they have been achieved. Consequently, a somewhat disproportionate level of importance is placed on published EPS data.

EPS has also served as a means of assessing the stewardship and management role performed by company directors and managers; by linking remuneration packages to EPS growth performance, some companies deliberately increase the pressure on management to improve EPS. Not surprisingly, such powerful factors and incentives have all contributed to the growth of attempts to distort EPS.

The ASB has stated its belief that undue emphasis is placed on EPS numbers and that this leads to simplistic interpretations of financial performance. As a result in October 1992 when it issued FRS 3 – *Reporting of financial performance* – the ASB attempted to de-emphasise EPS by requiring it to be calculated *after* extraordinary items. In view of this change and the other requirements of FRS 3 (see Chapter 22) the EPS number which companies are required to disclose has become much more volatile and is now really only a starting point for further analysis. The ASB recognised that companies would therefore be likely to provide additional EPS numbers prepared on what they saw as a more meaningful basis and therefore introduced rules dealing with such additional numbers. This is discussed further at 5.7 below.

In May 1996 the ASB issued a Discussion Paper – *Earnings Per Share*. This did not contain any proposals to change the requirements in the UK, but was merely soliciting comments on proposals put forward by the IASC in its exposure draft (E52) on the topic.[2] The FASB had also issued a similar exposure draft to E52.[3] Both of these bodies have since published new standards based on these proposals (see 8 below). In the interests of international harmonisation the ASB therefore issued FRED 16[4] in June 1997 containing proposals for a revised standard which, with minimal exceptions, follows the international standard, IAS 33. The proposals contained in FRED 16 are discussed further at 7 below.

2   SCOPE OF SSAP 3

SSAP 3 applies to all companies with an equity listing on the Stock Exchange. Companies whose shares are traded on the Alternative Investment Market are

---

Extract 23.22: Tate & Lyle Public Limited Company (1996)

8   Earnings per Share [extract]

The fully diluted earnings per share are calculated on the basis of the following assumptions:

(a)   that the outstanding options over 8,935,382 shares had been exercised and that the funds so generated would give rise to net earnings of £1.8 million;

(b)   that the issued share capital had been increased by 30,350,130 ordinary shares on conversion of the convertible cumulative redeemable preference shares.

Another example is shown in Extract 23.6 at 4.2 above.

The standard states that the fully diluted EPS for the corresponding period should not be shown unless the assumptions on which it was based still apply.[33] Unfortunately, the standard does not give examples of such 'assumptions' but typically, these include the terms of the conversion rights of convertible stockholders, conditions determining the number of equity shares to be issued at a future date pursuant to a deferred consideration agreement etc. The justification provided for this position is that investors are primarily concerned with future dilution based on current facts and comparatives for corresponding periods become meaningless unless the assumptions inherent in the fully diluted calculation remain unchanged. However, a strict literal interpretation of the recommendation conflicts with the purpose of including comparatives in financial statements. It is our view that disclosure of comparative fully diluted EPS figures should be made notwithstanding changes in assumptions inherent in their calculation in subsequent years.

6.3   Calculation of fully diluted EPS

Fully diluted EPS should be calculated on the assumption that the conversion rights or options to subscribe had been exercised in full on the first day of the accounting period[34] or the date of issue of the securities giving rise to the rights or options if later, in which case a weighted average calculation should be performed.

6.3.1   *Equity shares with future dividend entitlement*

If there is a class of equity capital not yet ranking for dividend but which will do so in the future, the number of shares used in the basic EPS calculation will be increased at some future date. However, since there will be no inflow of funds to the company accompanying the change in dividend rights, aggregate earnings would not be affected. Fully diluted EPS is therefore calculated using the same earnings figure but on the assumption that the shares ranked for dividend from the beginning of the period or date of their issue if later.[35]

Example 23.6: Simple fully diluted EPS calculation

Capital structure

Issued share capital as at 31 December 19X1:
£200,000 'A' ordinary shares of 50 pence each.

On 1 July 19X2 the company issued 80,000 'B' ordinary shares which will not rank for dividend until 19X5 whence they will have the same dividend rights as the 'A' ordinary shares.

Trading results

Profit for equity shareholders after taxation:

	£
Year ending 31 December 19X1	55,000
Year ending 31 December 19X2	74,000

Calculation of basic EPS

		19X2	19X1
Earnings		74,000	55,000
Number of equity shares ranking for dividend		400,000	400,000
Basic EPS	=	18.5p	13.75p

Calculation of fully diluted EPS

	19X2	19X1
Number of shares		
'A' ordinary	400,000	400,000
New issue 80,000 'B' ordinary x 6/12	40,000	–
	440,000	400,000

	19X2	19X1
Fully diluted EPS	74,000 / 440,000	Same as basic EPS
	= 16.82p	

The fully diluted EPS indicates a dilution of 9.08% of the basic EPS which would be 'material'. No comparative would be required in this case because the company did not have any obligations which would have diluted the EPS.

6.3.2 Convertible securities

In order to secure a lower rate of interest, companies sometimes attach benefits to loan stock or debentures in the form of conversion rights. These permit the stockholder to convert his holdings in whole or part into equity capital. The right is normally exercisable between specified dates. The ultimate conversion of the loan stock will have the following effects:

(a)   there will be an increase in earnings by the amount of the loan stock interest no longer payable. Because this interest is allowable for corporation tax purposes, the effect on earnings will be net of corporation tax relief; and

(b)   the number of shares ranking for dividend will increase. The fully diluted
       EPS should be calculated assuming that the loan stock is converted into the
       maximum possible number of shares.

Example 23.7:   Treatment of convertible loan stock in fully diluted EPS calculations

Assuming no conversion occurs during the year:

Capital structure

Issued share capital at 31 December 19X1:
1,000,000 ordinary shares of £1 each

Since 1 January 19X0, there has been £200,000 of 10% convertible loan stock in issue.
The terms of conversion are, for every 100 nominal value of loan stock:

On	31 March 19X1	115 ordinary shares
	31 March 19X2	120 ordinary shares
	31 March 19X3	125 ordinary shares
	31 March 19X4	130 ordinary shares

Trading results

	19X1 £	19X0 £
Profit for equity shareholders after taxation	250,000	175,000

Corporation tax for both periods is 35%
Income tax is 25%.

The company has surplus ACT carried forward as at 31 December 19X1 which has been written
off as irrecoverable.

Calculation of basic EPS

	19X1	19X0
Earnings	250,000	175,000
Number of equity shares ranking for dividend	1,000,000	1,000,000
Basic EPS =	25p	17.5p

Calculation of fully diluted EPS

Impact on earnings:

	19X1 £	19X0 £
Profit for basic EPS	250,000	175,000
Add: Interest saved	20,000	20,000
Less: Corporation tax relief*	(2,000)	(2,000)
Adjusted earnings for equity	268,000	193,000

* Corporation tax relief is after writing back irrecoverable ACT (the maximum set-off of ACT
against corporation tax for any year is the amount of ACT that would have been payable in
respect of a dividend equal to the taxable profits for that year).

Number of equity shares if loan stock was converted:

	19X1	19X0
Number of equity shares for basic EPS	1,000,000	1,000,000
On conversion 200,000 x $\dfrac{120}{100}$	240,000	230,000*
Adjusted capital	1,240,000	1,230,000

* At 31 December 19X0 the conversion terms were 115 shares for every £100 of loan stock.

It should be noted that even though it is assumed that the shares have been in issue throughout the year any conversion terms during the year are not relevant if the stockholders did not take advantage of the opportunity to convert. The maximum number of shares that could be issued in the future as determined at the balance sheet date should be used in the fully diluted EPS calculation irrespective of whether, by the time the financial statements are finalised, the amount of loan stock actually converted at the next conversion date is known.

Fully diluted EPS	$\dfrac{268,000}{1,240,000}$	$\dfrac{193,000}{1,230,000}$
=	21.61p	15.69p

Note that the fully diluted EPS comparative has been disclosed even though the assumptions (namely the conversion terms) on which last year's computation was based no longer apply.

Partial conversion during the year:

Where part of the loan stock is converted during the current accounting period, provided the new shares rank for dividend, the weighted average of shares in issue during the year should be used in the calculation of the basic EPS.

When calculating the fully diluted EPS, the maximum number of shares in issue and issuable at the end of the accounting period must take into account the stock still to be converted.

Final conversion during the year:

Similar considerations to those outlined above for a partial conversion will apply on final conversion. However, unless the conversion takes place on the first day of the current year in which case the shares issued would therefore have ranked for dividend for *the full year*, the fully diluted EPS should be shown for the current year, if material.[36]

This recommendation is consistent with the objective of the fully diluted EPS calculation, namely to disclose any material dilution in future earnings per share. The fully diluted EPS figure calculated in this instance will give an indication of next year's basic EPS, assuming no earnings growth and no changes in equity share capital.

The rules for convertible preference shares are very similar to those detailed above in the case of loan stock, i.e. the dividend is added back to earnings and the maximum number of ordinary shares that could be issued on conversion should be used in the calculation. Irrecoverable ACT which has been written off as part of the tax charge for the year and relates to preference share dividends would have to be added back to earnings when calculating the fully diluted EPS.

6.3.3 *Options or warrants to subscribe for equity shares*

Companies may grant options to directors and senior executives or issue warrants which give holders (not usually employees) the right to subscribe for shares at fixed prices on specified future dates. If the options or warrants are exercised then:

(a) the shares ranking for dividend will be increased; and

(b) funds will flow into the company and these will produce income.

As it is not possible to estimate the earnings which these proceeds will generate, SSAP 3 requires that it is to be assumed that the new funds are invested on the first day of the accounting period in $2^{1}/_{2}\%$ Consolidated Stock.[37] This notional income (net of corporation tax) is then used to compute adjusted earnings for the fully diluted EPS calculation. The price of $2^{1}/_{2}\%$ Consolidated Stock can be found in the *Financial Times*; if the price is £25, this indicates a yield of 10%.

As in the case of convertible stocks, it should be assumed that the maximum number of new shares had been issued under the terms of the options or warrants and that these had been exercised on the first day of the period or the date of issue if later.[38] Similar considerations to those described in 6.3.2 above apply on final subscriptions in the case of options or warrants to subscribe.

Example 23.8: Treatment of share options in fully diluted EPS calculations

Capital structure

Issued share capital for both years ending 31 December 19X1 and 19X2:
400,000 ordinary shares of 25p each.

Options have been granted to the directors and certain senior executives giving them the right to subscribe for ordinary shares between 19X6 and 19X8 at 90 pence per share.

| Options outstanding at | 31 December 19X1 | 40,000 |
| | 31 December 19X2 | 50,000 |

(The additional 10,000 options were granted on 1 January 19X2.)

| The price of $2^{1}/_{2}\%$ Consols | 31 December 19X0 | £25.00 |
| | 31 December 19X1 | £20.83 |

Trading results

Profit for equity shareholders after taxation:

| Year ending 31 December 19X1 | £60,000 |
| Year ending 31 December 19X2 | £70,000 |

Assume corporation tax at 35%.

Calculation of basic EPS

	19X2	19X1
Earnings	70,000	60,000
=		
Number of equity shares ranking for dividend	400,000	400,000
=	17.5p	15p

Calculation of fully diluted EPS

Impact of conversion on earnings:

	19X2 £	19X1 £
Profit for basic EPS	70,000	60,000
Notional income on proceeds of options issuable		
(50,000 @ 90p) x 12%*	5,400	–
(40,000 @ 90p) x 10%	–	3,600
Less taxation thereon (35%)	(1,890)	(1,260)
Adjusted earnings for equity	73,510	62,340

$$\text{* The market yield on the } 2\tfrac{1}{2}\% \text{ Consols} = \frac{2.5}{20.83} \text{ x } 100 = 12\%$$

Number of equity shares after exercise of options:

	19X2 No	19X1 No
Number of equity shares for basic EPS	400,000	400,000
Maximum issuable	50,000	40,000
Adjusted capital	450,000	440,000

Fully diluted EPS	19X2	19X1
=	73,510	62,340
	450,000	440,000
=	16.34p	14.17p

In the above example, the dilution in 19X2 is sufficiently material (6.63%) to require disclosure of fully diluted EPS. In our view the comparative figure of 14.17p should also be disclosed even though the assumptions on which it was based no longer apply (i.e. the yield on the $2\tfrac{1}{2}\%$ consols is no longer 10%).

6.3.4   *Fully diluted EPS calculations involving more than one type of potentially dilutive security*

Companies may have more than one type of convertible debenture or loan stock (or preference shares) in issue with differing conversion rights, or may also have issued shares to rank for dividend in a future period or have granted warrants or options to subscribe. In these situations, the fully diluted EPS should take into

77   *Ibid.*
78   *Ibid.*, para. 37.
79   *Ibid.*, paras. 20-25 and 29.
80   *Ibid.*, paras. 31-34
81   *Ibid.*, Appendix C, Illustrations 6-8.

Chapter 24   Post balance sheet events

1   THE DEVELOPMENT OF ACCOUNTING FOR POST BALANCE SHEET EVENTS

1.1   Introduction

A 'post balance sheet event' is defined by SSAP 17 – *Accounting for post balance sheet events* – as 'those events, both favourable and unfavourable, which occur between the balance sheet date and the date on which the financial statements are approved by the board of directors'.[1] This definition, therefore, incorporates all events occurring between those dates – irrespective of whether or not they relate to conditions which existed at the balance sheet date. Consequently, the principal issue to be resolved is which post balance sheet events should be reflected in the financial statements?

Since the financial statements of an entity purport to present, inter alia, its financial position at the balance sheet date, it is clear that the statements should be adjusted for all post balance sheet events which offer greater clarity of conditions that existed at the balance sheet date. However, the application of the prudence concept might take this further and suggest that *all* post balance sheet events which adversely affect the value of assets and liabilities should be reflected in financial statements – even if they relate to conditions which arise subsequent to the balance sheet date. Indeed, this argument could be taken even further to suggest that provisions may be required to take account of events which could not have been foreseen at the balance sheet date.

It is as a result of the conflict between matching and prudence and the variation of positions taken by different businesses, that the accounting treatment of post balance sheet events and their presentation in financial statements, has varied considerably.

In addition to the above, there has sometimes been a practice of manipulating the balance sheet by going outside the normal trading pattern of the business on a short-term basis in order to display a more favourable financial position. This has been done by either delaying or bringing forward specific transactions or by entering into transactions which are reversed shortly after the balance sheet date. The term used to cover such practices is 'window dressing'.

1.2 ICAEW Recommendation N17

In October 1957, the ICAEW issued Recommendation N17 'Events occurring after the balance sheet date'. This discussed the treatment of post balance sheet events and gave examples of how specific items should be treated.

N17 stated that events which are known to have occurred after the balance sheet date should not be reflected in the financial statements unless either:

(a) they assist in forming an opinion as to the amount properly attributable, in the conditions on the balance sheet date, to any item the amount of which was subject to uncertainty on that date; or

(b) they arise from legislation affecting items in the accounts, for example changes in taxation, or are required by law to be shown in the accounts, for example appropriations and proposed appropriations of profit.[2]

The Recommendation[3] discussed the realisation of certain assets and liabilities subsequent to the balance sheet and how consideration should be given to additional evidence received upon realisation of those assets and liabilities.

It also stated that there may be events occurring after the balance sheet date which should be excluded from the financial statements but may be of such importance to shareholders that they would need to be disclosed in some other way. Examples given of such events were the disposal of a significant part of a business or a profit or loss, either capital or revenue, which would have a considerable influence on 'the financial resources of the business'.[4]

1.3 ED 22

Despite the recommendations in N17, a variety of disclosures continued to be adopted by businesses and some confusion remained as to what represented events that required disclosure to shareholders and how events that had a significant effect on a business's continuing existence should be reflected. This led to the ASC issuing ED 22 – *Accounting for post balance sheet events* – in February 1978.

ED 22 differentiated between 'adjusting events' and 'non-adjusting events' and gave examples of each.[5] It explained that no separate disclosure was required for adjusting events as they merely gave additional evidence in support of items in financial statements, but non-adjusting events needed to be disclosed where their materiality would mean that not to do so would result in the financial statements presenting a misleading financial position. ED 22 stated that disclosure should be made of non-adjusting events which:

'(a) do not affect the condition of assets or liabilities at the balance sheet date, but do represent abnormal changes to them since that date; or

(b) do not relate to the financial position at the balance sheet date, but are of such importance that their non-disclosure would affect the ability of the users of the financial statements to make proper evaluations.'[6]

ED 22 clarified the date up to which post balance sheet events should be taken into account for inclusion in the financial statements.[7]

1.4 SSAP 17

In general the contents of ED 22 were supported by those who commented on it. However, concern was expressed that no guidance was given on what to do when the going concern concept was questioned by a post balance sheet event, which was defined as a non-adjusting event in the ED. In addition, the ASC was forced to react to increasing adverse opinion about the practice of window dressing, including pressure from the government of the day.

These problems were therefore dealt with when SSAP 17 – *Accounting for post balance sheet events* – was issued in August 1980.The detailed provisions of the standard are discussed at 2 below.

2 REQUIREMENTS OF SSAP 17

2.1 Definitions

As stated in 1.1 above, SSAP 17 defines post balance sheet events as 'those events, both favourable and unfavourable, which occur between the balance sheet date and the date on which the financial statements are approved by the board of directors'.[8]

This therefore includes events that provide additional evidence as to conditions which existed at the balance sheet date and those that do not.

Adjusting events are 'post balance sheet events which provide additional evidence of conditions existing at the balance sheet date. They include events which because of statutory or conventional requirements are reflected in the financial statements.'[9]

Examples given of events normally classified as adjusting are as follows:[10]

(a) the subsequent determination of the purchase price or the sales proceeds of fixed assets purchased or sold before the year end;

(b) a valuation of property which indicates a permanent diminution in value of the asset at the balance sheet date;

(c)   the receipt of information, such as financial statements of an unlisted company, which provides evidence of a permanent diminution in value of a long-term investment;

(d)   the sale of stock after the balance sheet date showing that the estimate of net realisable value was incorrect;

(e)   the discovery of evidence showing that estimates of accrued profit on a long-term contract were inaccurate;

(f)   a trade debtor going into liquidation or receivership;

(g)   the declaration of dividends by subsidiaries and associated companies for periods prior to the balance sheet date;

(h)   a change in taxation rates applicable to periods before the balance sheet date;

(i)   the receipt of insurance claims which were in the process of negotiation at the balance sheet date; and

(j)   the discovery of significant errors or frauds which show that the financial statements were misstated.

The standard states that non-adjusting events are 'post balance sheet events which concern conditions which did not exist at the balance sheet date'.[11]

The appendix to the standard gives examples of items which would usually be classified as non-adjusting events.[12] These include:

(a)   mergers and acquisitions;

(b)   reconstructions and proposed reconstructions;

(c)   the issue of shares and debentures;

(d)   the purchase or disposal of fixed assets and investments;

(e)   the loss of fixed assets or stocks due to a catastrophe such as a fire or a flood;

(f)   the opening of new trading activities or extension of existing trading activities;

(g)   the closing of a significant part of trading activities if this was not foreseen at the balance sheet date;

(h)   a decrease in the value of property and investments held as fixed assets, if it can be shown that the decline took place subsequent to the balance sheet date;

(i)   changes in foreign currency exchange rates;

(j)   government action, such as nationalisation;

(k)   strikes and other labour disputes; and

(l)   the augmentation of pension benefits.

2.2   Events requiring adjustment

SSAP 17 requires that the financial statements be adjusted to take account of:

(a)   an adjusting event; or

(b)   a post balance sheet event which indicates that the application of the going concern concept to the whole or a material part of the company is no longer appropriate.[13]   This could include a deterioration of trading results and the financial position, or the refusal of the bank to continue overdraft facilities.

2.3   Events not requiring adjustment but requiring disclosure

The standard states that an event of this type should be disclosed where:

'(a)   it is a non-adjusting event of such materiality that its non-disclosure would affect the ability of the users of financial statements to reach a proper understanding of the financial position; or

(b)   it is the reversal or maturity after the year end of a transaction entered into before the year end, the substance of which was primarily to alter the appearance of the company's balance sheet.'[14]   Such alterations include those commonly known as 'window dressing' (see 3.5 below).

The ambiguity which renders SSAP 17 relatively meaningless in the case of (a) above is the *date* as at which the financial position is to be understood by the users. If it is the balance sheet date (which is what the law requires), then non-adjusting events need never be disclosed, since it is difficult to see how the financial statements could ever fail to give a true and fair view of the year end position because of the absence of such disclosure. What the standard's requirements in this area boil down to, therefore, is to highlight those major non-adjusting post balance sheet events which have resulted in the financial position at the date of approval being significantly different from that portrayed by the balance sheet.

The non-adjusting events which appear most regularly in financial statements are possibly the acquisition/disposal of a fixed asset, normally an investment, or a merger subsequent to the balance sheet date. We consider the following extracts to be good examples of disclosure in such situations:

Extract 24.1: Amersham International plc (1997)

34   Post balance sheet event

Merger of Amersham Life Science and Pharmacia Biotech Subsequent to the balance sheet date, Amersham has entered into a conditional agreement with Pharmacia & Upjohn Inc. ('P&U') to merge Amersham Life Science with Pharmacia Biotech, the biotechnology supply business of P&U, forming a new Company, proposed to be named Amersham Pharmacia Biotech Limited ('Amersham Pharmacia Biotech').

Under the terms of the merger, Amersham and P&U will transfer their respective life science businesses to Amersham Pharmacia Biotech, of which Amersham will own 56% of the issued ordinary share capital and P&U will hold the remaining 45%. In addition, Amersham and P&U will receive US$61m (£37m) and US$50m (£31m) respectively of preference shares. Amersham and P&U will also, in effect, contribute US$89m (£55m) and US$52m (£32m) respectively of debt to the combined entity.

The merger of the two businesses, will for accounting purposes, be treated by Amersham as a disposal of a 45% minority interest in Amersham Life Science and an acquisition of a 55% controlling interest in Pharmacia Biotech.

The following unaudited *pro forma* statement of net assets of the enlarged Amersham Group is provided for illustrative purposes only. Its purpose is to illustrate the effect on the net assets and equity shareholders' funds of the Amersham Group of the merger of the two life science businesses.

	Amersham Group as at 31 March 1997 (audited) £m	Pharmacia Biotech as at 31 December 1996 (unaudited) £m	Adjustments £m	Pro forma £m
Fixed assets				
Intangible assets	1.3	–	–	1.3
Tangible assets	120.9	84.6	–	205.5
Investments	34.5	1.1	–	35.6
	156.7	85.7	–	242.4
Current assets				
Stocks	41.3	48.8	–	90.1
Debtors	100.5	75.3	–	175.8
Short term deposits and interest bearing investments	16.8	–	–	16.8
Cash at bank and in hand	9.5	12.4	(12.4)	9.5
	168.1	136.5	(12.4)	292.2
Creditors: amounts due within one year				
Loans	(16.4)	(61.7)	61.7	(16.4)
Other creditors	(83.5)	(86.8)	27.9	(142.4)
	(99.9)	(148.5)	89.6	(158.8)
Net current assets/(liabilities)	68.2	(12.0)	77.2	133.4
Total assets less current liabilities	224.9	73.7	77.2	375.8

Creditors: amounts falling due after more than one year				
Loans	(73.6)	(7.3)	(30.9)	(111.8)
Other creditors	(3.7)	(1.0)	–	(4.7)
	(77.3)	(8.3)	(30.9)	(116.5)
Provisions for liabilities and charges	(38.3)	(32.2)	–	(70.5)
Accruals and deferred income				
Investment grants	(4.8)	–	–	(4.8)
Total net assets	104.5	33.2	46.3	184.0
Minority interest	(1.8)	–	(42.6)	(44.4)
Equity shareholders' funds	102.7	33.2	3.7	139.6

Notes

1 The Pharmacia Biotech figures have been extracted from unaudited financial information for the year ended 31 December 1996 adjusted for UK GAAP and are stated before any fair value adjustments.

2 The adjustments represent certain assets and liabilities of Pharmacia Biotech retained by P&U, additional debt injected into Pharmacia Biotech prior to completion and the increase in minority interest.

3 Pharmacia Biotech's financial information has been translated into sterling at a rate of £1:SEK11.685, being the rate of exchange as at the close of business on 31 December 1996.

4 The *pro forma* balance sheet excludes any trading results or cash flows by Pharmacia Biotech after 31 December 1996 and Amersham Group after 31 March 1997 and is stated before transaction costs.

Extract 24.2: Ferguson International Holdings PLC (1996)

34   Post Balance Sheet Events

Disposal of the Hangers division, excluding Morplan

On 9 May 1996 the Company disposed of the Hangers division, excluding Morplan for a net consideration, after expenses, of £16.8 million. This included net borrowings of £6.3 million. In addition, the consideration may be increased or reduced by up to £1.5 million dependent on the profitability of Red Wing Products Inc during the year ending 28 February 1997.

A provision of £6.5 million has been made at 29 February 1996 in relation to the excess of the net asset value of the disposed business at 29 February 1996 over the net proceeds arising from the disposal.

Disposal of the Communications Components division

On 9 May 1996 the Company disposed of the Communications Components division for a net cash consideration, after expenses, of £18.8 million. The excess of the net sale proceeds over the net asset value of the division at 29 February 1996 amounted to £9.9 million which will be recognised in the accounts for the year ending 28 February 1997. A provision of £2.7 million in respect of diminution in the value of goodwill has been made in these accounts (see note 4)

In view of the significance of these two transactions on the group balance sheet an unaudited pro-forma balance sheet has been shown on page 38 which reflects the disposal of the two businesses. This pro-forma balance sheet does not form part of the audited financial statements.

Purchase of Label Image

On 9 May 1996 the whole of the issued share capital of Label Image Holdings Limited was acquired for a consideration of £5.25 million of which £3.0 million was paid in cash on completion and £2.25 million is payable by way of non-interest bearing loan notes. In addition the Company assumed the net borrowings of Label Image amounting to approximately £3.2 million.

Unaudited pro-forma consolidated balance sheet
as at 29 February 1996

	Group 1996 £000	Sale of Hangers £000	Sale of TVC £000	Pro-forma £000
Fixed assets				
Tangible assets	43,129	(14,358)	(741)	28,030
Current assets				
Stock	24,350	(5,993)	(5,604)	12,753
Debtors	37,719	(7,528)	(6,978)	23,213
Cash at bank and in hand	4,300	9,222	16,742	30,264
	66,369	(4,299)	4,160	66,230
Creditors: amounts falling due within one year				
Loans and overdrafts	(18,731)	5,379	10	(13,342)
Other creditors	(40,479)	6,380	6,469	(27,630)
	(59,210)	11,759	6,479	(40,972)
Net current assets	7,159	7,460	10,639	25,258
Total assets less current liabilities	50,288	(6,898)	9,898	53,288

Creditors: amounts falling due after more than one year				
Loans and overdrafts	(11,503)	1,233	11	(9,809)
Other creditors	(783)	771	–	(12)
	(11,836)	2,004	11	(9,821)
Provisions for liabilities and charges	(8,926)	4,894	–	(4,032)
Net assets	29,526	–	9,909	39,435
Capital and reserves				
Called up equity share capital	10,109	–	–	10,109
Share premium account	16,993	–	–	16,993
Revaluation reserve	69	–	–	69
Other reserves	(28,124)	–	9,909	(18,215)
Profit and loss account	30,479	–	–	30,479
Shareholders' funds	29,526	–	9,909	39,435

Notes

1. The unaudited pro-forma balance sheet above is for illustrative purposes only and does not give a complete picture of the Group's financial position. The only accounting entries dealt with in the above balance sheet are those resulting from the disposals of Hangers and Communications Components which were both completed on 9 May 1996. The acquisition of Label Image has not been reflected.

2. The figures for both disposals assume that the costs associated with the disposals have been paid and any deferred proceeds have been received.

Extract 24.3: Cadbury Schweppes p.l.c. (1996)

31 Post balance sheet events

(a) Details of the disposal of the Group's interest in Coca-Cola & Schweppes Beverages Ltd are provided in Note 2.

(b) Details of the announced redemption of the US$ Auction Preference Shares are provided in Note 22(e).

(c) On 12 February 1997 the Group purchased the Food Industries Development Co. (Bim Bim) an Egyptian confectionery company with a net tangible asset value of £35m.

2 Disposal of Coca-Cola & Schweppes Beverages Ltd

On 10 February 1997, the Group concluded the disposal of its 51% share in Amalgamated Beverages Great Britain Ltd, the parent company of Coca-Cola & Schweppes Beverages Ltd ("CCSB") for £623m, including £458m of loan notes at 5.75% due January 1998 and dividend payments of £140m. Tax arising on the disposal is not expected to be payable until 1999. The net gain on disposal is not expected to be less than £300m. The operating results of CCSB have been separately reported as discontinued operations in the profit and loss account for 1996 and 1995.

The assets and liabilities of CCSB which were consolidated in the Group Balance Sheet at 28 December 1996 were as follows:

	£m
Fixed assets	197
Other assets and liabilities	6
Net borrowings	(23)
Minority interests	(88)
Group share	92

The cash flows resulting from CCSB's 1996 operations included in the Group Cash Flow Statement are as follows:

Cash flow from operating activities	£m
Operating profit	124
Depreciation	36
Other non-cash items and changes in working capital	16
	176
Returns on investments and servicing of finance	
Net interest paid	(7)
Minority dividend paid	(33)
	(40)
Taxation	(70)
Capital expenditure	(41)
Cash inflow before use of liquid resources and financing	25

Extract 25.5: B.A.T Industries p.l.c. (1996)

40 Contingent liabilities and financial commitments [extract]

There are contingent liabilities in respect of litigation, overseas taxes and guarantees in various countries.

Group companies, notably Brown & Williamson Tobacco Corporation ("B&W") and The American Tobacco Company ("ATCo"), which was acquired in December 1994 and subsequently merged into B&W as well as other leading cigarette manufacturers, are defendants, principally in the United States in a number of product liability cases, including a substantial number of new cases filed in 1996. Significant compensatory and punitive damages are being sought by the plaintiffs.

The total number of US cases pending at year end involving Group companies was 253 cases (as at 31 December 1995, there were 164 cases on a comparable basis). The cases fall into three broad categories, as follows:

First, the Attorneys General of 30 states and certain counties and others have filed separate actions against B&W and ATCo, and other tobacco manufacturers, seeking to recover the amounts spent on health care costs resulting from diseases allegedly caused by smoking. Three suits are scheduled to be tried in 1997, in Mississippi, Florida and Texas.

Secondly, B&W or ATCo are named as defendants in 18 separate actions in which plaintiffs are attempting to assert claims on behalf of a class of persons allegedly injured by smoking. Courts in most of these cases have not yet decided whether to certify classes, but courts in two Florida cases have certified classes.

In one case *(Engle)*, the class is limited to Florida citizens claiming addiction to cigarettes and an alleged ensuing medical condition. In the second *(Broin)*, the class is nationwide and composed of flight attendants of US based airlines who allegedly have been injured by environmental tobacco smoke in airline cabins. Both these cases are set for trial in 1997.

A third case *(Castano)*, was certified as a nationwide (federal) class by the trial court, but certification was overturned on appeal. The plaintiffs' attorneys who had brought the *Castano* action have since filed statewide class actions in 9 states, the District of Columbia and Puerto Rico asserting statewide class actions on behalf of people who are allegedly addicted to cigarettes.

One of these cases *(Arch,* Pennsylvania) is set for trial in 1997. Even if the classes remain certified and the possibility of class-based liability is eventually established, it is likely that individual trials will still be necessary to resolve any actual claims. If this happens, the defences that have contributed to more than 500 individual cases being successfully disposed of by the industry without, ultimately, monetary loss over the years will be available to the industry.

The third category consists of all other litigation involving or relating to smoking and health allegations, including suits filed in various jurisdictions by individuals, or their estates if deceased individuals, in which it is contended that diseases or deaths have been caused by cigarette smoking or by exposure to cigarette smoke in the air.

Two such cases were tried in 1996. In the *Carter* case, which is under appeal, a Florida state court jury awarded US$750,000 in damages against B&W to a long term smoker. B&W is appealing this case. In the *Rogers* case, an Indiana state court jury returned a verdict in favour of the cigarette manufacturers, including ATCo. Several cases brought on behalf of individual smokers are expected to be tried in 1997.

In addition to litigation, B&W has been subjected to US Grand Jury and other investigations on various topics, some of which have been discontinued without further action. Furthermore, the United States Food and Drug Administration has announced additional regulation of the tobacco industry, which is scheduled to go into effect during 1997 and which is being vigorously challenged by the industry.

In Australia, the trial of a broadly-based claim by an individual against all the tobacco companies in that market is scheduled for trial in 1997.

In some 34 cases B.A.T Industries and/or its UK tobacco subsidiaries is a named co-defendant. In the only three cases (one Medicaid reimbursement case, one class action and one individual case) to date that have decided the point, B.A.T Industries has been found not to be subject to the court's jurisdiction. B.A.T Industries has been dropped from 26 further cases so far by agreement and will bring forward motions that it should not be subject to the courts' jurisdiction, in due course, in other cases.

It is not possible to predict the commencement of new cases nor, with certainty, the eventual outcome of current product related litigation, investigations and regulatory proceedings or provide a meaningful estimate of any loss that could result from them. All the actions are being defended vigorously and are, in any event, likely to be the subject of extended appeal, whichever party may prevail at trial. It is not considered that the ultimate outcome of all this litigation will have a material adverse impact on the financial condition of the Group.

Extract 25.6: Charter plc (1996)

21 COMMITMENTS AND CONTINGENCIES [extract]

Charter, together with certain of its wholly-owned subsidiaries, has been named as defendant in a number of asbestos-related actions in the United States on the basis that it is allegedly liable for the acts of a former subsidiary Cape PLC. Charter contests the existence of any such liability. The issue went to trial in three cases involving the Company's principal subsidiary, Charter Consolidated P.L.C., and other wholly-owned subsidiaries, between 1985 and 1987. In the first of these cases, tried in Pennsylvania, after an adverse lower court decision the appeal court gave judgement in the Charter defendants' favour. In the second case, in New Jersey, judgement was also given for the Charter defendants. The third case in South Carolina, was dismissed for lack of subject matter jurisdiction, without a decision having been rendered on the issue. Recently, Charter and/or certain of its subsidiaries have been served in a number of cases in Mississippi and a few other states. Charter is seeking dismissals in these pending cases. Upon advice of counsel, Charter has settled the majority of the cases brought in Mississippi. Charter will continue to pursue dismissals in the remaining cases. The directors have received legal advice that Charter and its wholly-owned subsidiaries should be able to continue to defend successfully the actions brought against them, but that uncertainty must exist as to the eventual outcome of the trial of any particular action. It is not practicable to estimate in any particular case the amount of damages which might ensue if liability were imposed on Charter or any of its wholly-owned subsidiaries. The litigation is reviewed each year and, based on that review and legal advice, the directors believe that the aggregate of any such liability is unlikely to have a material effect on Charter's financial position. In these circumstances, the directors have concluded that it is not appropriate to make any provision in respect of such actions.

One company that adopted this approach was GKN, which in its 1995 accounts disclosed the following:

Extract 25.7: GKN plc (1995)

26 COMMITMENTS AND CONTINGENT LIABILITIES [extract]

Meineke Discount Muffler Shops, Inc has recently received a claim for damages in relation to the operation of its franchise business. No provision has been made in the accounts since the matter is at an early stage and, based on legal advice that the company has strong defences, the directors will firmly resist the claim. In their opinion the outcome will not have a material effect on the Group.

However, in its 1996 accounts, following an adverse judgement in the courts, it has now made a provision of £270m in respect of the claim, as disclosed below:

Extract 25.8: GKN plc (1996)

27   POST BALANCE SHEET EVENT [extract]

On 6th March 1997 the US District Court, Charlotte, North Carolina issued judgement in the class action brought by certain of its franchisees against Meineke Discount Muffler Shops Inc ('Meineke') together with its subsidiary New Horizons Inc, its immediate parent company GKN Parts Industries Corporation and GKN plc alleging breach of contract and fiduciary duty in relation to an advertising fund operated by Meineke. The value of the judgement was US$591 million plus interest of US$10 million accruing since the jury verdict issued on 18th December 1996. This will be reduced by not less than 34% being the value of releases of their claims given by certain members of the plaintiff class, the validity of which has been confirmed by the court.

As part of the post judgement procedures further submissions will be made on legal issues which are expected to be resolved by the end of April 1997. At that point the way will be clear to take the case to the US Court of Appeals. Given that GKN is advised that it has very strong substantive and procedural grounds for doing so, it will appeal as soon as possible. It is expected that the appeal will take about 18 months to resolve.

Notwithstanding the intention to appeal, in the interests of prudence, a provision of £270 million, based on the judgement less the effect of the releases, has been made as an exceptional charge within operating profit in the 1996 accounts. This figure includes interest and legal costs likely to accrue pending the outcome of the appeal but, at this stage, no tax relief has been assumed.

Having made this provision, the Directors are of the opinion that the outcome of the case will not have a material adverse impact on the Group.

It may be that companies are unable to disclose the potential amount of the loss because a claim is made for unspecified damages, as shown in the following extract from the 1993 accounts of Reuters:

Extract 25.9: Reuters Holdings PLC (1993)

32.   Contingent liabilities

US class actions In late 1990 and early 1991, two American Depository Share holders commenced purported class actions against Reuters, a subsidiary and certain directors and officers of one or both. These actions alleged that certain false and misleading statements had been made in public filings and otherwise concerning the development, testing and introduction of and expected revenue and earnings from the second phase of Dealing 2000. The purported class actions subsequently were consolidated into one action. The complaint, which seeks unspecified damages, asserts claims under sections 10(b) and 20(a) of the United States Securities Exchange Act of 1934, and for common law fraud and negligent misrepresentation. A motion to dismiss the action filed by Reuters has been denied and discovery has commenced. In October 1993, the court certified the action as a class action on behalf of all persons who purchased Reuter ADSs between 1 December 1988 and 4 December 1990. The consolidated action continues to be defended strenuously.

Some companies only quantify the potential amount in respect of certain of the claims made against them, as illustrated below:

Extract 25.10: First Choice Holidays PLC (1996)

26   CONTINGENT LIABILITIES

Under the terms of guarantees given to the Civil Aviation Authority and the Minister of Tourism of the Republic of Ireland by the Company in respect of certain subsidiaries, in the event of default, the Company could be held liable to the extent of the subsidiaries' net liabilities at the time of default (see note 15.)

Two subsidiaries of the Group, Olympic Holidays Limited and First Choice Holidays & Flights Limited are defending an action for compensation for termination of an agency agreement. The amount claimed is £0.8 million. The Group is advised that there is a good prospect of successfully defending the action and has accordingly not provided for the amount of the claim.

The Company is defending an action for damages for an amount or consideration which it is alleged is payable for shares in a subsidiary sold to the Company by the plaintiff. Due to the nature of the claim it is not practicable to make an estimate of the value of the claim. The Company is advised that it has a reasonable prospect of defending the action and has accordingly not made provision for any potential sum payable under the claim.

A subsidiary of the Group, First Choice Holidays & Flights Limited is defending various actions for personal injury or loss of enjoyment, for which provision for the likely settlement has been made in the Accounts.

The Group has a number of empty leasehold properties for which the leases expire between one and eighteen years. An empty property provision has been made, based on the opinion of the Directors, for the anticipated future net rental costs which will be met by the Group. A contingent liability exists for the remainder of the costs associated with the properties of £9.1 million.

As indicated above, where an estimate of the financial effect cannot be made, SSAP 18 requires a statement that it is not practicable to do so. Two companies which have made such disclosure are Mirror Group and Arjo Wiggins Appleton, as illustrated below:

Extract 25.11: Mirror Group plc (1996)

23   Contingent liabilities [extract]

Investigation under Sections 432 and 442 of the Companies Act 1985

On 8 June 1992 the President of the Board of Trade appointed inspectors under Sections 432 and 442 of the Companies Act 1985 to examine the affairs of the Group, particularly the circumstances surrounding its flotation in April 1991. The directors have been advised that it is possible that the circumstances surrounding the flotation, and the conduct of its affairs between its flotation in April 1991 and December 1991, may give rise to claims against the Company. However, it is not at this stage possible to identify specific claims against the Company nor to quantify either the prospect of success of such claims or the magnitude of any potential liability. Moreover, if such claims were successfully established the Company might have claims against certain of its professional advisers who acted at that time. After discussing all circumstances known to the Company with its legal advisers, no provision has been made in the financial statements for any such claims.

Unusual receipts and payments during 1991

During 1991 the Group recorded substantial payments to and receipts from financial institutions and payments from Maxwell controlled companies outside the ordinary course of business. The directors are unaware of any unprovided claims against the Group arising from these transactions and, other than where the receipt of cash is certain, no benefit has been taken for potential recoveries.

Extract 25.12: Arjo Wiggins Appleton p.l.c. (1996)

28. Contingent liabilities [extract]

As reported previously, Appleton Papers Inc. (API) is engaged in litigation with Minnesota Mining and Manufacturing Company (3M) in relation to a patent dispute, the outcome of which is not, in itself, material in the context of API's business. However, 3M also alleges breaches of US antitrust legislation by API in relation to its sale of carbonless papers, of which it is the largest producer in the US. These allegations are strenuously denied. The directors of the Company are of the opinion that, although the outcome of the case cannot be predicted with certainty, any ultimate liability arising from it should not have a material adverse effect on the Group's balance sheet and, therefore, no provision has been made.

API was notified, in January 1997, by the US Fish and Wildlife Service that, together with NCR Corporation (NCR) and five other paper companies, it is to be sued in connection with alleged contamination of the Fox River and related waterways. The damage is alleged to have arisen in part, as a result of carbonless paper manufacturing carried on at the Appleton and Combined Locks facilities prior to their acquisition by API from NCR in 1978. Together with the other companies, API has agreed, without admission of liability, to contribute to the cost of studies to determine the extent of the alleged contamination and to evaluate potential remedies. Neither the source, nor magnitude, of the contamination is known, nor is it known whether, or what, remedial action needs to be taken. Consequently, API's share, if any, of any remedial costs and damages cannot be predicted at this time. However. API believes that it will be entitled to indemnification from NCR for any liability that may be attributed to it. NCR disputes this. Again, no provision has been made in the Group's balance sheet, other than for API's share of the estimated costs of the studies referred to above.

There are other contingent liabilities, arising in the ordinary course of business, in respect of litigation and guarantees in various countries, which the directors believe will not have a significant effect on the financial position of the Company and its subsidiary undertakings.

As noted at 2.6 above, the amount of the contingency to be disclosed should be reduced by any amounts that have been accrued. An example of this is shown in Extract 25.2 above.

3.4 Litigation and disclosure of potentially prejudicial information

One of the reasons why companies adopt such an approach may be that they consider that disclosing the full potential liability under such claims could prejudice their position in settling the claims.

The arrival of SSAP 18 was not welcomed in many quarters because it did not grant exemption from the disclosure of sensitive information which could prejudice a company's position. This was particularly important in the area of litigation where it was believed that an assessment of the estimated likely outcome of a pending legal claim could compromise the amount of any settlement.

Possibly the most difficult sort of contingency to assess is litigation. This is due to the inherent uncertainty in the judicial process itself and to the occasional reluctance of the legal profession to express an opinion on the potential outcome of litigation.

Appendix A to SFAS 5 lists the following three factors which should be considered in determining whether accrual and/or disclosure is required with respect to pending or threatened litigation:

(a)   the period in which the underlying cause for action of the pending or threatened litigation occurred;

(b)   the degree of probability of an unfavourable outcome; and

(c)   the ability to make a reasonable estimate of the amount of loss.[29]

However, the overriding consideration is that it is desirable that a company should disclose all relevant information necessary for the users of the financial statements to gain a proper understanding of that company's financial position.

Other examples where a company may be unwilling or unable to give quantified disclosure include the following:

(a)   Inland Revenue investigations and additional claims over and above the company's tax computation; and

(b)   breach of copyright or infringement of patent rights, where to disclose the contingency would advertise the breach.

Examples of disclosure of a contingent liability in respect of a disputed tax position are shown below:

Extract 25.13: Berisford plc (1996)

26   Contingencies [extract]

b)   Taxation:

Taxation has been provided on the disposal in 1991 of the Group's investment in British Sugar plc to the extent it is believed amounts will be ultimately payable. In the event that losses believed to be available to offset the gain on the disposal ultimately prove not to be available, an additional sum which should not exceed £43.7m would become payable.

Extract 25.14: BG plc (1996)

21   Commitments and contingencies [extract]

i)   Tax

The Inland Revenue has contended that, for certain past periods, the transfer price for PRT and royalty purposes of gas sold from the South Morecambe gas field by British Gas Exploration and Production Limited, and subsequently Hydrocarbon Resources Limited, to British Gas plc, and subsequently to British Gas Trading Limited, should have been higher. The British Gas Group has been advised by counsel that it has a good case in resisting this contention.

3.5 Disclosure of remote contingencies

SSAP 18 states that where the possibility of a contingent loss being confirmed is remote disclosure is not required.[30] The Accountants Digest which deals with accounting for contingencies states that 'the application of this concession is, however, limited by the over-riding requirements of the 1948 and 1967 Companies Acts which require disclosure of the "general nature of any contingent liabilities not provided for and, where practicable, the aggregate amount or estimated amount of those liabilities, if it is material".'[31]

Since the publication of the Accountants Digest, the Companies Act provisions have been amended to require disclosure of the following information in respect of any material contingent liability not provided for:

(a)   the amount or estimated amount of the liability;

(b)   its legal nature; and

(c)   whether any valuable security has been provided by the company in connection with that liability and if so, what.[32]

Consequently, because of this apparent overriding Companies Act requirement to disclose *all* material contingent liabilities not provided for, it would appear that in practice companies sometimes include information in their financial statements on contingencies which could be considered to be remote. Examples of such disclosures often given include:

(a)   guarantees of subsidiary company liabilities;

(b)   bills discounted with recourse;

(c)   membership of VAT groups; and

(d)   performance bonds.

The following extract illustrates the disclosure of contingencies which might be considered to be remote, but are presumably disclosed in compliance with the Companies Act requirement:

Extract 25.15: Marley plc (1996)

29   Contingent liabilities

	1996	1995
	£m	£m
Consolidated		
Guarantees, performance bonds and other similar obligations		
Trade related	**3.4**	2.6
Borrowing related	**4.3**	0.3
	7.7	2.9
Parent		
Guarantees of subsidiaries' obligations included in the consolidated accounts		
Trade related	**0.6**	0.4
Borrowings related	**60.6**	86.8
	61.2	87.2

Borrowing related contingent liabilities of the parent include guarantees in respect of the US $41.7 million unsecured Loan Notes 9.79% 1997/2001 and the US $40 million unsecured Loan Notes 7.75% 1997/2002.

In addition to the above there are contingent liabilities in respect of certain claims and litigation. In the opinion of the directors these are not expected to give rise to any significant liability.

A number of questions often arise as to what should be disclosed in respect of the situations listed above and these are considered in 3.6 below.

3.6   Other problem areas

3.6.1   Guarantees – year end or maximum liability

Where companies are disclosing the fact that they have guaranteed the liabilities of another party, consideration has to be given as to what amount should be disclosed in respect of the guarantee. The disclosure given is often merely the year end liability guaranteed, whilst in other cases it is not stated whether the amount given is the year end liability or the maximum liability guaranteed. It could be argued that both amounts require disclosure as the maximum amount is part of the 'nature' of the guarantee and the year end amount is the 'estimate' of the financial effect. We therefore believe that best practice is to disclose both the year end liability and the maximum amount guaranteed, as shown in the following extracts:

Extract 25.16: Inchcape plc (1996)

11   Contingent liabilities [extract]

The company has given guarantees in respect of various subsidiaries' bank facilities totalling £354.2m at 31 December 1996 (1995 - £326.0m). £17.5m (1995 - £nil) has been drawn against these facilities.

Extract 25.17: T&N plc (1996)

28   Commitments and contingent liabilities [extract]

At 31 December 1996 the Company and its UK subsidiaries had contingent liabilities of £64.3m (1995 £61.2m) in connection with guarantees relating to bank borrowings of certain overseas subsidiaries. The maximum potential liability under those guarantees is £121.4m (1995 £108.2m).

Extract 25.18: B.A.T Industries p.l.c. (1996)

40   Contingent liabilities and financial commitments [extract]

B.A.T Industries has guaranteed borrowings by subsidiary undertakings of **£2,594 million** 1995 £2,766 million and borrowing facilities of **£4,489 million** 1995 £4,910 million which were not utilised at the balance sheet date.

One company which discloses only the year end liability is Silentnight Holdings, as shown below:

Extract 25.19: Silentnight Holdings Plc (1997)

28   Contingent Liabilities [extract]

Bank Guarantees

The Company has provided cross guarantees in respect of certain bank loans and overdrafts of subsidiary undertakings, the amount outstanding at 1 February 1997 being £3,151,000 (1996; £4,648,000).

Where the amount of the liability at the year end varies significantly with the amount at the date on which the financial statements are approved by the board of directors, consideration should be given to disclosing both amounts.

On the other hand some companies do not disclose any amounts in respect of the guarantees but just disclose the fact that they have given guarantees. For example:

Extract 25.20: More Group Plc (1996)

23   CONTINGENT LIABILITIES

The Company has granted in respect of the financial year ended 31st December 1996, irrevocable guarantees of the liabilities of More Group Ireland Limited and More O'Ferrall Ireland Limited, which companies have availed themselves of the exemption provided by Section 17 of the Companies (Amendment) Act, 1986.

3.6.2   *Discounted bills of exchange*

Clearly, where a company discounts bills without recourse in the event of the bills being dishonoured on maturity, no contingent liability exists and, therefore, no disclosure is required. Also under FRS 5, where bills have been discounted with recourse, it will in most circumstances be necessary to account for such liabilities on the balance sheet, not simply as a disclosed contingency – see Chapter 16.

However, where bills are discounted with recourse and a liability does not need to be recognised under FRS 5, the question arises as to what amount should be disclosed in the financial statements as the contingent liability. Is it the amount which relates to all such bills discounted at the balance sheet date, or is it the amount which relates to those bills which have yet to mature at the date of approval of the financial statements? It could be argued that it is the latter and, therefore, if all the bills have matured by that date no disclosure is required. However, if the company is continually discounting bills of exchange then at the date of approval the company will have a contingent liability in respect of bills discounted since the year end. Consequently, we believe that in order to provide information relevant to the financial position of the company, the amount of bills outstanding at the balance sheet date should be disclosed.

Examples of companies which disclose contingent liabilities in respect of discounted bills of exchange are Caradon and UniChem, as shown in the following extracts:

Extract 25.21: Caradon plc (1996)

20   Contingent liabilities [extract]

	1996 Group **£m**	1995 Group £m
Trade bills discounted	**3.0**	4.1

Extract 25.22: UniChem PLC (1996)

(28) Contingent liabilities [extract]

UniChem Farmaceutica has discounted bills receivable of £5.9m (1995 £5.0m) with banks who have recourse should the bill not be honoured by the customer.

3.6.3   VAT groups

Companies may be part of a VAT group and as such have joint and several liability for the whole of the group VAT liability. Again, similar considerations apply as to the amount to be disclosed as were discussed at 3.6.2 above in relation to discounted bills. Consequently, we believe that the amount of this contingent liability at the balance sheet date should be disclosed in each group member's financial statements. For example:

Extract 25.23: British Polythene Industries plc (1996)

26. Contingent Liabilities [extract]

The company also has an obligation under the Group VAT registration amounting at 31 December 1996 to £4,795,000 (1995 – £3,271,000).

3.6.4 Performance bonds

It is common practice in many industries for companies to arrange a guarantee to customers that goods will be delivered to a specific standard. The question then arises as to whether the existence of such a performance bond means that the company has a contingent liability which has to be disclosed. The granting of the performance bond does not normally impose any greater liability on the company than does the contract itself. If a company regularly produces goods either on time or up to the required standard and there is nothing to suggest that there are any unusual circumstances which might affect this, then there is justification in deciding that there is no contingency which needs to be disclosed.

In addition to performance bonds, companies may also arrange tender bonds (i.e. a guarantee against the company withdrawing from the contract after having submitted a tender for the contract which has been accepted) and advance payment bonds (i.e. a guarantee to reimburse advance payments made by the customer if the company cannot fulfil the contract).

In most cases the above bonds or guarantees will be given by the company's bankers and the company will indemnify the bank. Again, this does not normally impose any greater liability on the company than that under the contract with the customer.

Although it could be argued that in most cases above no contingent liability arises and therefore no disclosure is necessary, it would appear that many companies do give some disclosure in respect of such bonds. In practice, many companies merely note the existence of such bonds. For example:

Extract 25.24: BICC plc (1996)

24 Contingent liabilities [extract]

BICC plc and certain subsidiary undertakings have, in the normal course of business, given guarantees and entered into counter indemnities in respect of bonds relating to the Group's own contracts and given guarantees in respect of the Group's share of certain contractual obligations of associated undertakings.

Other companies do, however, quantify the amount of the bonds or guarantees. For example:

Extract 25.25: *Trinity Holdings PLC (1997)*

20.   CONTINGENT LIABILITIES [extract]

	1997	1996
	£'000	£'000
The group has given, in the normal course of business, the following guarantees in respect of:		
Acceptances and guarantees given by banks	**422**	1,387
Performance bonds	**2,501**	1,660
Advance payment bonds	**456**	1,160

In our view, given the fact that the company in most cases will incur no extra liability as a result of the performance bond, it is sufficient just to disclose the existence of the bonds without quantification. Where, however, a parent company or other group company guarantees or counter-indemnifies a bank for the performance of another group company then it would be preferable if the amount were quantified as this would be consistent with the approach generally taken in respect of guarantees of group borrowings.

4   FRED 14

As indicated earlier, FRED 14 has been expanded to embrace contingencies and it is intended to supersede SSAP 18.

FRED 14 defines a contingency in similar terms to that contained in SSAP 18. However, the recognition, measurement and disclosure rules in respect of contingencies are to be aligned with those proposed for provisions generally. Accordingly, a contingent loss is to be recognised, i.e. charged to the profit and loss account, 'when and only when there is sufficient evidence to indicate that there is an obligation to transfer economic benefits as a result of past events and a reasonable estimate of the contingent loss can be made. Sufficient evidence exists when it is more likely than not that a transfer of economic benefits will result from past events.'[33] The amount of the loss to be recognised should be a realistic and prudent estimate of the expenditure required to settle the obligation, discounted where the effect is material.[34] The proposed recognition, measurement and disclosure requirements in respect of provisions are discussed further in Chapter 26 at 2.2.

One particular aspect of FRED 14 relating to disclosure which may be relevant to provisions in respect of contingencies, particularly in respect of litigation, is the proposed exemption from disclosure on grounds that it may seriously prejudice the position of the entity in its negotiations with other parties. In such cases the detailed disclosures need not be made, but the general nature of the provision and the fact and reason why the information has not been disclosed is to be stated. The ASB envisages that such an exemption should only apply in extremely rare cases, for example where only one material provision exists.[35]

Where a contingent loss has to be recognised, the amount is not to be reduced by any related claim against a third party but any anticipated recovery should be treated as a separate asset. A counterclaim is similarly to be treated as a separate asset, unless it is eligible for offset under FRS 5 (see Chapter 16 at 2.7).[36]

Unless it is reducing a recognised contingent loss as discussed above, a contingent gain is not be recognised until it is virtually certain.[37] It is unclear whether this is intended to be a higher threshold than the 'reasonably certain' one used in SSAP 18. The main impact of FRED 14 in respect of contingent gains will be on disclosure, as discussed below.

For all unrecognised contingencies, whether they are contingent gains or losses, FRED 14 proposes similar information to be disclosed as that presently required by paragraph 18 of SSAP 18, i.e:

(a)   a brief description of the nature of the contingency;

(b)   the uncertainties that are expected to affect the ultimate outcome of the contingency; and

(c)   an estimate of the potential financial effect, made at the date on which the accounts are approved by the directors; or a statement that it is not practicable to make such an estimate.

However, the potential financial effect is to be measured using the same measurement rules as for provisions.[38] It is unclear how this is intended to apply to contingent gains. The requirement to disclose the tax implications appears to have been dropped.

Where the possibility of a receipt or transfer of future economic benefits is remote, disclosures need not be made.[39]

5   COMPARISON WITH US AND IASC PRONOUNCEMENTS

5.1   US

In March 1975, the FASB published SFAS 5 – *Accounting for Contingencies* – which superseded ARB No. 50 – *Contingencies*. The requirements within the statement are broadly similar to those adopted by SSAP 18, although the level of disclosure is more extensive.

A contingency is defined in SFAS 5 as 'an existing condition, situation, or set of circumstances involving uncertainty as to possible gain ... or loss ... to an enterprise that will ultimately be resolved when one or more future events occur or fail to occur'.[40]   The statement requires that the estimated loss from a loss contingency should be accrued if both the following conditions are met:

'a. Information available prior to issuance of the financial statements indicates that it is probable that an asset had been impaired or a liability had been incurred at the date of the financial statements. It is implicit in this condition that it must be probable that one or more future events will occur confirming the fact of the loss.

b. The amount of loss can be reasonably estimated.'[41]

The principal difference is that SFAS 5 requires disclosure of certain loss contingencies even though the possibility of loss may be remote. The standard states that the common characteristic of such a contingency is a 'guarantee'. Examples given include:

(a) guarantees of indebtedness to others;

(b) guarantees to repurchase receivables that have been sold in certain situations;

(c) obligations of banks under 'standby letters of credit'.[42]

However, it should be noted that although SSAP 18 does not require the disclosure of a contingency where the possibility of loss is remote, disclosure may still be required in the UK in terms of the requirements of the Companies Act 1985 (see 3.5 above).

In September 1976, the FASB published FASB Interpretation No. 14 – *Reasonable Estimation of the Amount of a Loss* – to give guidance on the treatment to be adopted where a loss is probable, and the amount lies within a range of figures (see 3.2 above).

5.2   IASC

IAS 10 – *Contingencies and Events Occurring After the Balance Sheet Date* – includes requirements which are in essence the same as those of SSAP 18. IAS 10's disclosure requirements in respect of the estimated financial effect of a contingent loss are less detailed that those of SSAP 18, in that IAS 10 does not require disclosure of the taxation implications of a contingency crystallising.[43] Consequently, by complying with SSAP 18, compliance with IAS 10 is assured.

In November 1996, the IASC issued a Draft Statement of Principles – *Provisions and Contingencies*. In order that it was consistent with its proposals in respect of provisions (see Chapter 26 at 4.2) this proposed to amend IAS 10 such that contingencies should be recognised and measured in the same way as provisions.[44] In July 1997, the IASC approved an exposure draft on this basis, with little change, and hopes to finalise a standard on the subject early in 1998.

References

1 SSAP 18, *Accounting for contingencies*, ASC, August 1980, para. 14.
2 CA 48, Sch. 8, para. 11(5).
3 *Ibid.*, para. 11(4).
4 CA 67, Sch. 2, paras. 11(4) and (5).
5 N17, *Events occurring after the balance sheet date*, ICAEW, October 1957, para. 3.
6 N18, *Presentation of balance sheet and profit and loss account*, ICAEW, October 1958, para. 25.
7 CA 85, Sch. 4, para. 50(2).
8 ASB Discussion Paper, *Provisions*, ASB, November 1995.
9 FRED 14, *Provisions and contingencies*, ASB, June 1997.
10 SSAP 18, para. 14.
11 *Ibid.*
12 *Ibid.*, para. 17.
13 *Ibid.*, para. 4.
14 *Ibid.*, para. 14.
15 *Ibid.*, para. 15.
16 *Ibid.*, para. 6.
17 *Ibid.*, para. 21.
18 *Ibid.*, para. 18.
19 *Ibid.*, para. 19.
20 *Ibid.*, para. 20.
21 SFAS 5, *Accounting for Contingencies*, FASB, March 1975, para. 3.
22 G. R. Chesney and H. A. Weir, 'The challenge of contingencies: Adding precision to probability', *CA Magazine*, April 1985, pp. 38–41.
23 SSAP 18, para. 15.
24 FASB Interpretation No. 14, *Reasonable Estimation of the Amount of a Loss*, FASB, September 1976, para. 3.
25 IAS 10, *Contingencies and Events Occurring After the Balance Sheet Date*, IASC, Reformatted 1994, para. 11.
26 SSAP 2, para. 14.
27 Draft Statement of Principles, *Provisions and Contingencies*, IASC, November 1996, paras. 92 and 93.
28 SSAP 18, para. 18.
29 SFAS 5, Appendix A, para. 33.
30 SSAP 18, para. 16.
31 Accountants Digest No. 113, *Accountants Digest Guide to Accounting Standards – Accounting for Contingencies*, Winter 1981/82, p. 5.
32 CA 85, Sch. 4, para. 50(2).
33 FRED 14, para. 24.
34 *Ibid.*, paras. 7, 9 and 24.
35 *Ibid.*, paras. 20 and 66.
36 *Ibid.*, para. 25.
37 *Ibid.*, para. 26.
38 *Ibid.*, para. 27.
39 *Ibid.*, para. 28.
40 SFAS 5, para. 1.
41 *Ibid.*, para. 8.
42 *Ibid.*, para. 12.
43 SSAP 18, para. 20.
44 Draft Statement of Principles, *Provisions and Contingencies*, IASC, November 1996, paras. 89 - 95.

Chapter 26   Provisions

1   INTRODUCTION

A provision is defined in the Companies Act as 'any amount retained as reasonably necessary for the purposes of providing for any liability or loss which is either likely to be incurred, or certain to be incurred but uncertain as to amount or as to the date on which it will arise.'[1] This definition applies only to 'provisions for liabilities or charges', in other words those that appear in the liabilities section of the balance sheet, and not to provisions for depreciation or diminution in value of assets, which are separately defined in the Act.[2] Similarly, this chapter focuses only on provisions that are shown as liabilities, and does not deal with amounts written off against assets.

The ASB proposes a slimmed-down variant of the Act's definition: 'Liabilities in respect of which the amount or timing of the expenditure that will be undertaken is uncertain'.[3] The Board says that the two definitions are not inconsistent,[4] but it is clear that its own wording has deliberately excluded some aspects of the Act's version that it has found troublesome. In particular, the reference in the Act to *retaining* amounts carries connotations of appropriations, and sounds altogether too discretionary for the Board's taste. Consistent with its proposed *Statement of Principles*, the Board is anxious to ensure that only those amounts that meet its definition of liabilities end up being reported as such in the balance sheet.

The Act's reference to 'providing for any ... loss that is ... likely to be incurred' also opens up a possibility that the ASB wishes to close down; the Board is anxious to prevent companies from providing for future operating losses, because they properly belong in the future. However, as discussed later in this chapter, this distinction is sometimes less easy to make than it might seem.

There is clearly an area of overlap between provisions and contingent liabilities, and indeed the ASB has chosen to address them in a single standard. Contingent liabilities are, by definition, not certain to be incurred, but provision may nonetheless be required for them if they are sufficiently likely to arise. However, the topic of contingencies extends to both assets and liabilities and it is not considered further in this chapter but rather dealt with in Chapter 25.

A further demarcation line has to be drawn between provisions and other liabilities, such as trade creditors and accruals. The ASB differentiates them by saying that 'the distinguishing feature of provisions is uncertainty over either the timing or amount of the future expenditure. By contrast:

- trade creditors are liabilities to pay for goods or services that have been received or supplied and have been invoiced or formally agreed with the supplier

- accruals are liabilities to pay for goods or services that have been received or supplied but have not been invoiced or formally agreed with the supplier. Although it is sometimes necessary to estimate the amount or timing of accruals, the uncertainty is generally much less than is the case for provisions. Accruals would normally be reported as part of trade and other creditors whereas provisions would be separately reported.'[5]

This is true, but by concentrating on trade creditors and their associated accruals the Board has cited only the most straightforward case. In practice the difference between provisions and liabilities is often far from clear-cut, and reclassification from one category to the other is not uncommon. Courtaulds Textiles provides an example:

Extract 26.1: Courtaulds Textiles plc (1996)

STATEMENT OF ACCOUNTING POLICIES

Basis of accounting [extract]

... Within creditors, the comparative figures have been restated for restructuring provisions which have been reclassified from creditors to provisions for liabilities and charges.

One reason why this distinction matters is that provisions are subject to disclosure requirements which do not apply to other creditors. The Companies Act requires disclosure of the amount of provisions at the beginning and the end of the year and movements during the year saying where they have come from and gone to, except for those amounts which have been applied for the purpose for which the provision was established.[6] A typical note that shows this analysis can be found in the accounts of Harrisons & Crosfield:

Extract 26.2: Harrisons & Crosfield plc (1996)

20 Provisions for liabilities and charges [extract]

	Deferred tax £m	ACT recoverable £m	Post-retirement benefits £m	Acquisition provisions £m	Other provisions £m	Total £m
At 1st January 1996 (restated)	8.4	(4.3)	27.5	9.2	24.9	65.7
Utilised during the year	0.3	1.6	(14.1)	(1.5)	(13.3)	(27.0)
Acquisition of businesses	(0.4)	–	–	–	1.0	0.6
Disposal of business	(0.6)	–	–	–	–	(0.6)
Reclassification	–	–	–	(7.1)	7.1	–
Charge/(credit) to profit and loss account	(2.0)	–	11.1	0.4	11.3	20.8
Currency translation differences	(0.1)	–	(1.2)	(0.8)	(1.3)	(3.4)
At 31st December 1996	5.6	(2.7)	23.3	0.2	29.7	56.1

Even such a detailed note is not entirely transparent, because a frequent difficulty with provisions is that their individual components are not well differentiated and explained. Quite often the biggest disclosed balance is simply 'other provisions', as indeed is the case in this example. However, in the previous year's accounts, no information on the 'other provisions' was disclosed at all, because its components had simply been included in 'other creditors' with no identification of their nature, either individually or collectively. Harrisons & Crosfield is therefore another example of a company that has reclassified these amounts, as shown in this extract from the same accounts:

Extract 26.3: Harrisons & Crosfield plc (1996)

1 Accounting policies [extract]

... Balance sheet comparatives have been restated such that all amounts accrued for potential environmental obligations, self insurance and rationalisation costs have been reclassified as other provisions.

In fact, although questions of recognition and measurement are important, transparency of disclosure is perhaps the most significant issue in the whole subject of accounting for provisions. The problem is that, once a provision has been established, expenditure that is charged to it bypasses the profit and loss account and therefore disappears from view. The original charge may well have been dealt with as an exceptional item and glossed over by management in any discussion of their performance, and the subsequent application of the provision has no further impact on earnings – giving rise to a kind of 'off profit and loss account' treatment. And in recent years, some of the provisions that have been set up have been extremely large and wide-ranging. An example is to be found in the 1993 accounts of what was then British Gas:

Extract 26.4: British Gas plc (1993)

Review of operating results

Operating costs [extract]

The results for 1993 include an exceptional charge of £1,650 million for the major restructuring of the UK Gas Business. This restructuring into five separate business streams will ensure that the Company's UK Gas Business will be leaner, more competitive and more commercially focused at a time when the gas market in Great Britain is undergoing radical change. The exceptional charge comprises severance and pension costs associated with the reduction in approximately 25,000 people and the related costs of restructuring the integrated UK Gas Business. The cash effect of this restructuring will be borne largely over the next three years.

The corresponding note to the profit and loss account contained substantially the same information but added that the amount also included 'other incremental costs that will be required to implement the restructuring, such as training, property related costs and information technology costs'. The effect of this charge was to convert a pre-tax profit of approximately £1 billion into a loss of £613 million.

The need to restrict the creation of such 'big bath' provisions has provided much of the impetus for the ASB's project on provisions, although the Board has introduced some other important issues as well, notably on how provisions should be measured. Progress towards an accounting standard is discussed in the next section.

2   THE DEVELOPMENT OF AN ACCOUNTING STANDARD

2.1   The ASB Discussion Paper

The ASB first published a Discussion Paper – *Provisions* – in November 1995. This proposed the general principles that should govern the recognition, measurement and disclosure of provisions; these were derived from the Board's *Statement of Principles*, which was published in draft on the same day. It is interesting to note, however, that whereas the latter draft did not command acceptance and is to be revised, the provisions project that relies on it is proceeding without any hesitation on the part of the Board.

The Discussion Paper devoted much of its content to the consideration of three particular kinds of provision: those for future operating losses, reorganisation costs and environmental liabilities. As we shall see, these topics have continued to feature prominently in the project as it progresses towards an accounting standard.

2.2   FRED 14

The ASB published FRED 14 in June 1997. Its main objective is to ensure that provisions are recognised and measured on a consistent basis and that sufficient information is disclosed in the notes to the financial statements to enable users to understand their nature, timing and amount.[7]

The exposure draft closely follows the philosophy of the Discussion Paper, but it has been expanded to embrace contingencies as well as provisions and accordingly is intended to supersede SSAP 18. (The aspects that relate to contingencies are discussed in Chapter 25.)

2.2.1 Scope

The proposed standard is to apply to all entities and its only explicit exemption is for provisions relating to insurance contracts that are made in the accounts of insurance companies (which are also beyond the scope of this book). However, the standard also says that provisions whose accounting treatment is laid down more specifically by another accounting standard should be governed by that standard rather than the eventual provisions standard where there is any conflict between the two.[8] This would apply in relation to topics such as deferred tax or pension cost accounting. The wording of this is not entirely clear; it could be read as implying, for example, that the disclosure requirements of FRED 14 should be extended to these other topics because they cannot be said to be in conflict with the existing standards. We hope that this is clarified in the eventual standard.

2.2.2 Recognition

The exposure draft draws its inspiration from the ASB's draft *Statement of Principles*, and concludes that provisions are a subset of liabilities and not a separate element of financial statements.[9] It says that provisions should be recognised when, and only when, the reporting entity has a legal or constructive obligation to transfer economic benefits as a result of past events,[10] and provided it is possible to make a reasonable estimate of the obligation, at least within a reasonable range of possible outcomes.[11] This proviso is intended to allow a provision to escape recognition only in extremely rare cases.[12] Provisions may only be used for the purposes for which they have been established.[13]

It is not necessary to know the identity of the party or parties to whom the obligation is owed before making a provision, but in principle there must be another party.[14] FRED 14 argues that the mere intention or even necessity to incur expenditure is not enough to create an obligation.[15]

These recognition principles are supplemented by more explicit rules for three specific cases: future operating losses, reorganisations and environmental liabilities. They are respectively discussed in 3.1, 3.2 and 3.3 below.

The need to provide for legal obligations is obvious, although there is an important issue of timing, which is to do with identifying the past event that triggers recognition. The less straightforward matter concerns the broader concept of a constructive obligation. This is not formally defined in the draft, but is described as follows:

'Sometimes the actions or representations of the entity's management or changes in the economic environment directly influence the reasonable expectations of those outside the entity and, although they have no legal entitlement, they have other sanctions that leave the entity with no realistic alternative to certain expenditures. Such obligations are sometimes called "constructive obligations". ... In cases where the entity retains discretion to avoid expenditure, a liability does not exist and no provision should be recognised. It follows that a board decision, of itself, is not sufficient for the recognition of a provision.'[16] Examples offered by the exposure draft are where a retailer has a constructive obligation to give refunds to dissatisfied customers to preserve its reputation, and where a manufacturer has a constructive obligation to clean up environmental damage because of its published policies, past actions, and its relationship with the community.[17]

The essence of the rule is therefore that the entity may be irretrievably committed to certain expenditure because any alternative would be too unattractive to contemplate, in which case it should make a provision. We find this a rather hazy concept, as is demonstrated by the discussion of some of the examples in 3 below. That is not to say that we believe that only legal obligations deserve to be in the balance sheet, but we doubt if this particular formulation is the best way of determining which additional items deserve to be there. As with other aspects of the ASB's framework and its recognition criteria in particular, we think that the question is in reality one of expense recognition – in what period should the cost be charged to the profit and loss account – not liability recognition at all.

2.2.3 Measurement

FRED 14 says that the amount provided should be a realistic and prudent estimate of the expenditure required to settle the obligation that existed at the balance sheet date;[18] however, it counsels against excessive prudence.[19] The draft equates this estimate with 'the amount that represents as closely as possible what the entity would rationally pay to settle the obligation immediately or to persuade a third party to assume it'.[20] It is interesting that this hypothetical transaction should be proposed as the conceptual basis of the measurement required, rather than putting the main emphasis upon the actual expenditure that is expected to be incurred in the future. The proposed basis represents 'relief value' as it is described in the ASB's draft *Statement of Principles*,[21] and belongs in a current value system rather than one founded on historical cost.

The draft acknowledges that there may be no opportunity to settle the obligation or transfer it to a third party and that alternative methods of measurement may be necessary. It next advances the use of 'expected value', which is a mathematical computation which weights the cost of all the various possible outcomes according to their probabilities, and notes that this would be an appropriate method for large populations of similar items, such as warranty obligations.[22] In principle, the Board seems to favour the method for single items as well (although this could only be defended in a current value context, because it would not represent any actually expected outcome), but says that 'there may be insufficient evidence of the various possible outcomes and their probabilities to permit an explicit valuation of expected values. In these situations, other methods of estimation may be more appropriate. Where there is an equal chance that the outcome will be greater or less than the most likely outcome, the most likely outcome should be used. Where there is a continuous range of possible outcomes, and each point in the range is as likely as any other point, the mid-point of the range should be used.'[23] (It is, however, not obvious that this equates with the requirement to use a reasonable *and prudent* estimate.)

FRED 14 also says that the provision should be discounted to its present value where this has a material effect,[24] and the subsequent unwinding of the discount is to be charged as a separately disclosed element of interest expense.[25] The exposure draft proposes that a risk-free rate should be used, on the basis that a prudent estimate of cash flows will already have reflected risk, and suggests in particular that a government bond rate should be used that reflects the term and currency appropriate to the liability.[26] This seems counter-intuitive, particularly if the intention is to simulate the amount at which a third party might take on the liability. The use of a prudent estimate of cash flows and the use of a risk free discount rate both have the effect of increasing the amount provided, whereas the Board's rationale given above seems to imply that these effects are meant offset each other.

Equally controversially, however, it says that the rate should be a post-tax rate and that the provision itself should be calculated net of tax and then grossed up presentationally to show the tax separately as part of deferred tax.[27] The mechanics of this are not very clearly explained, but in any case the whole approach seems rather inconsistent with established practice in accounting for deferred tax. The draft also says that companies may either use current prices discounted by a real interest rate or future prices (including assumed inflation) discounted by a nominal rate.[28] In the former case, changes in the provision as a result of inflation are to be charged in the profit and loss account along with the amortisation of the discount.[29]

More generally, it is proposed that provisions should be revised annually to reflect any material changes in the assumptions underlying the estimates.[30] This seems uncontroversial, except perhaps for the discounting dimension: while the draft is not explicit on the subject, it seems that this will also require discounted provisions to be revised annually to reflect any general movements in interest rates. As with the equivalent proposals in relation to financial instruments and impaired assets (see Chapters 9 and 10 respectively) this implicitly introduces a new capital maintenance concept into accounting, based on the ability of the entity to earn a current market rate of return.

2.2.4   Offset

The exposure draft adopts the same strict rules on offsetting that are contained in FRS 5. It says that 'where some or all of the expenditure required to settle a provision is expected to be recovered from a third party, the liability and anticipated recovery should be offset where and only where the reporting entity no longer has an obligation for the part of the expenditure to be met by the third party'.[31]

We are not convinced that this is appropriate. Again, it is a consequence of approaching the subject from a balance sheet perspective rather than as an expense recognition issue. Furthermore, it is inconsistent with existing practice under a number of other standards and proposals. For example, under FRS 3, provisions for the sale or termination of an operation have to be calculated 'after taking into account the aggregate profit ... from the future profits of the operation or disposal of its assets'.[32] Under SSAP 9 provision has to be made for long-term contracts which are projected to make a loss, but there is no suggestion that the remaining revenue and costs would have to be recorded in the balance sheet in full even though the contract had not been completed.[33] And even the ASB's earlier Discussion Paper said that provisions for vacant leasehold properties should be net of expected recoveries from subletting the property, and did not suggest that all future rental income and expenditure should be brought on to the balance sheet.[34]

In an attempt to rationalise the inconsistency, FRED 14 acknowledges the FRS 3 case cited above but says that 'the Board is of the view that it is appropriate to calculate closure provisions on a net basis because a unit that is not a going concern is most usefully represented to users in one line, separately from continuing operations'.[35] This does nothing to justify the inconsistency, but it does at least open up a new possibility: perhaps it would be equally 'useful' simply to abandon the supposed sanctity of the offsetting rule in relation to provisions of other kinds as well.

2.2.5   Disclosures

FRED 14 proposes that the following information should be required to be disclosed in relation to provisions:

(a)   For each material class of provision

    (i)   a brief indication of the nature of the obligation including an indication of the timing of payment and, where there is significant uncertainty over the amount or timing of the future expenditure, the factors that are relevant to determining them;

(ii) the amount provided for and, if estimated, the basis on which the estimate has been made; and

(iii) where the amount provided for is discounted, the discount rate.[36]

(b) The movements in the year on each material class of provision, showing separately:

(i) additional provisions made in the year and adjustments to existing provisions;

(ii) amounts used (i.e. incurred and charged against the provision);

(iii) amounts released unused;

(iv) where the provision is discounted, the amortisation of the discount; and

(v) exchange differences.[37]

Depending on materiality, it may also be appropriate to break down 'classes' of provisions into smaller categories.[38]

The items in (b) above build on the requirements of the Companies Act to show movements in provisions. One of the important disclosures that it reinforces is the release of provisions that have been found to be unnecessary. The accounts of Mirror Group show the release to the profit and loss account of £10.7 million of provision for 'unusual contingencies' that was no longer required:

Extract 26.5: Mirror Group plc (1996)

4 Other exceptional items [extract]	**1996**
	£m
Unusual contingencies	12.8

During the year the Group completed the purchase and sale of a property at Great Dover Street giving rise to a net cash outflow of £3.9 million. The provision held at 31 December 1995 was £6.0 million, resulting in a net credit of £2.1 million. The remaining £10.7 million relates to the release of other provisions no longer required in respect of Maxwell related items.

The exposure draft offers some exemption from the various disclosures set out above 'in extremely rare cases' to the extent that it might seriously prejudice the entity's position in negotiations with other parties in respect of the matter provided for – an example might be where the provision was made in respect of a legal dispute. As FRED 14 notes, this is likely to apply only where there is a single material dispute, because if there are several similar matters being provided for their aggregated disclosure is unlikely to be interpretable by any individual litigious party in such a way as to be prejudicial.[39] If advantage is taken of the exemption, it will be necessary to disclose the general nature of the provision, the fact that information has not been disclosed and the reason for non-disclosure.[40]

Where a provision has not been recognised because a reasonable estimate of the amount to be provided cannot be made, the accounts should give a brief description of the nature of the obligation and the factors that are relevant to determining the amount and timing of the future expenditure.[41]

There are also some specific disclosure requirements proposed for reorganisation provisions (see 3.2 below).

3   EXAMPLES OF PROVISIONS IN PRACTICE

3.1   Onerous contracts and operating losses

One of FRED 14's explicit rules on recognition is that no provision should be made for future operating losses, although it does say that a net loss should be recognised when a contract becomes onerous.[42] For this purpose, an onerous contract is defined as 'a contract entered into with another party under which the unavoidable costs of fulfilling the terms of the contract exceed any revenues expected to be received from the goods or services supplied or purchased directly or indirectly under the contract and where the entity would have to compensate the other party if it did not fulfil the terms of the contract'.[43]

This seems to require that the contract be onerous to the point of being directly loss-making, not simply uneconomic by reference to current market prices. In this respect the definition seems narrower than might be applied in the context of acquisition accounting, where the task is to put a fair value on identifiable assets and liabilities. The definition also appears to be worded to address only contracts with suppliers, not those with customers, although we would have thought the same principle should apply in each case.

Allied Domecq discloses this provision in respect of an uneconomic contract:

Extract 26.6: Allied Domecq PLC (1996)

7. SALE OR TERMINATION OF BUSINESSES [extract]

The brewing operation sold in the year to 31 August 1996 was Carlsberg-Tetley and a provision of £63m was set up to cover the uneconomic supply of beer to Allied Domecq Retailing from the date of disposal in August 1996 until the end of the supply agreement with Carlsberg-Tetley in December 1997.

We concur with FRED 14's basic proposition that future operating losses should be left to be reported in the future in the same way as future profits are. However, we think that this only scratches at the surface of a difficult subject, because there are some circumstances under which operating losses are in effect anticipated, for example:

- under SSAPs 9 and 12, both stocks and fixed assets are written down to the extent that they will not be recovered from future revenues, rather than leaving the non-recovery to show up as future operating losses. Indeed, if FRED 15 becomes a standard and requires fixed asset impairment to be measured on the basis of the present value of future operating cash flows (see Chapter 10 at 4.4), then provision will be made not simply for future operating losses but for sub-standard operating profits as well;

- provision is made for future operating losses of operations that are committed to be sold or terminated under FRS 3 (see Chapter 22 at 2.4);

- provision is made for losses expected on long-term construction contracts under SSAP 9 (see Chapter 14). Indeed, this sometimes extends even to provision for future administration costs where existing unprofitable contracts will absorb a large part of the company's future capacity.[44]

This is therefore a rather more complex issue than it might appear. As operating losses arise because expenses exceed revenues, perhaps a more effective approach of tackling the problem would be to define when 'costs' should be recognised in accounts and then whether there should be any exceptions to the general rule. We believe that this should be addressed at the level of general concepts, perhaps in a future version of the *Statement of Principles*.

One particular example of an onerous contract mentioned by FRED 14 relates to leasehold property.[45] From time to time entities may hold vacant leasehold property (including property which is only partly occupied) which they have substantially ceased to use for the purpose of their business and where reoccupation is unlikely. The question arises as to how to account for the rent payable and other expenses on such property.

This matter was previously considered by the UITF. In 1993 it issued a Draft Abstract – *Accounting for rent payable and other expenses of vacant leasehold property* – proposing that where reoccupation or assignment without loss of vacant leasehold property is unlikely, then to the extent that the recoverable amount through sale or rental is expected to be insufficient to cover the future obligations related to the lease (taking account also of any amount recognised as an asset), a loss has arisen which should be recognised as soon as the shortfall is identified.

The specific proposals contained in the UITF's Draft Abstract were as follows:

- when a property substantially ceases to be used for the purposes of the business or a commitment is entered into which would cause this to occur, provision should be made to the extent that the recoverable amount of the interest in the property is expected to be insufficient to cover the future obligations relating to the lease (taking account also of any amount recognised as an asset);

- any provision necessary should be based on market conditions at the balance sheet date, taking account of what is likely to happen in practice regarding the disposal or sub-letting of the leasehold interest and the settlement of related obligations;

■   the provision should also take account of other on-going expenses (such as rates and costs of security) together with any costs associated with vacating the property (including moving costs); and

■   to be consistent with the Companies Act 1985 requirement in paragraph 14 of Schedule 4, leases should be considered separately and not on a portfolio basis (other than where more than one lease relates to the same property).

However, the business community showed considerable interest in the Draft Abstract, and the UITF received a number of letters commenting on the proposals. In the light of these comments and following further discussion, the UITF concluded that existing accounting standards and principles do not yet provide 'a sufficient basis for it to develop a ruling in general terms that would ensure appropriate treatment for all the diverse circumstances that existed in practice'.[46] It thus shifted the responsibility for the matter to the ASB, with the result that it may now be resolved by the standard that follows from FRED 14.

In explaining its decision not to proceed with the subject, the UITF did not retreat completely from the position taken in the draft abstract. The Task Force made it clear that 'it was in no way discouraging the use of the accounting treatment in the draft Abstract by any company that found it to be appropriate for its particular circumstances'. It suggested three possible treatments for dealing with the costs of vacant leasehold property depending upon the circumstances of the case. These were:

■   full provision in line with the draft abstract;

■   disclosure of the full commitment or, where quantifiable, the net costs up to disposal; or

■   no special action on the grounds that the property could not be viewed in isolation from the continuing activities of the enterprise.

Although the issue is no longer on its agenda, the UITF at the time said that it would keep the situation under review and would consider issuing an abstract if abuses arose in particular areas. In the meantime, in those cases where the accounting treatment materially affects results, the UITF encourages disclosure of the accounting policies followed for vacant leasehold property (including property which is only partly occupied) which has ceased to be used for the purposes of the business and where reoccupation is unlikely.[47] Three examples follow.

Cordiant discloses this policy on the provision for leasehold costs:

Extract 26.7: Cordiant plc (1996)

Principal accounting policies

Long term property provisions

Provision is made for the future rent expense and related costs of leasehold property: where it is vacant; the leasehold property is sublet at a loss; or the sublease is not coterminous with the Group's lease commitment.

Rank, on the other hand, discloses that its policy is not to provide for such costs:

Extract 26.8: The Rank Group Plc (1996)

Accounting policies

VIII LEASED ASSETS [extract]

… Operating lease payments are charged to the profit and loss account as incurred. No provision is made for future costs on vacant leasehold properties. Such costs are expensed as incurred.

Graseby discloses this note on the subject:

Extract 26.9: Graseby plc (1996)

27 Commitments under leases [extract]

Of the group commitments £202,000 relates to properties formerly occupied by group operations but which were either vacant or let at an under-rent at 31st December 1996 and for which the outstanding periods of the leases range from 3 to 15 years. The rents for these properties are charged to the profit and loss account as incurred to the extent that they exceed the provision established at the time of the vacation for the then expected period of time to disposal of the lease.

This last example, however, seems something of a hybrid. One would have expected that the provision, once established, would have been reassessed annually rather than simply expensing unprovided amounts as they fall due for payment.

3.2 Reorganisation provisions

FRED 14 defines a reorganisation as:

A programme that is planned and controlled by management and has a material effect on:

(a) the nature and focus of the reporting entity's operations; or

(b) the scope of a business undertaken by the reporting entity in terms of the products or services it provides or where they are provided, whilst not materially affecting the nature and focus of its operations; or

(c) how a business undertaken by the reporting entity is conducted.[48]

This is said to include:

(a)   terminating a line of business (which may or may not be a geographical segment or class of business for the purposes of segmental reporting);

(b)   the closure of locations where business is carried on, and the relocation of business activities from one location to another;

(c)   changes in management structure, for example eliminating a layer of management; and

(d)   major cost-reduction programmes.[49]

The kind of expenditure covered by such programmes includes redundancy costs, lease termination payments, the costs of breaking contracts and other direct costs of effecting the reorganisation.[50] FRED 14 also emphasises that such costs may not be capitalised as an asset.[51]

As exemplified by the British Gas provision shown at Extract 26.4 above, some of the biggest provisions made in company accounts in recent years have been for reorganisation or restructuring costs, and regulating this practice is one of the main targets of FRED 14. The exposure draft says that 'provisions for reorganisations should be recognised when and only when the entity is demonstrably committed to the reorganisation. An entity is demonstrably committed when it has a detailed plan for, and cannot realistically withdraw from, the reorganisation.'[52] This means that 'specific actions must have been taken so that others can be expected to act on the basis that the reorganisation will proceed and, in so doing, leave the entity without realistic possibility of withdrawal. Evidence of the commitment might be the public announcement of the detailed plan, the commencement of implementation or other circumstances constructively obliging the entity to complete the reorganisation.'[53]

The exposure draft goes on to say that 'the detailed plan would normally, as a minimum, identify:

(a)   the business or part of a business concerned;

(b)   the principal locations affected;

(c)   the location, function and approximate number of employees whose services are to be terminated or duties changed;

(d)   the expenditures that will be undertaken; and

(e)   the time at which the plan will be implemented. Implementation should begin as soon as possible and the period of time to complete implementation should be such that significant changes to the plan are not likely.'[54]

FRED 14 emphasises that neither the existence of a detailed plan nor a public announcement are by themselves enough to create an obligation: the important thing is that they must commit the management to action from which it can no longer withdraw.[55] It also says that any extended period before commencement of implementation will suggest that a provision is premature, because management is still likely to have a chance of withdrawing from the plan. Examples of commencement include dismantling plant, selling assets, notifying employees, customers and suppliers, and so on.[56]

These conditions therefore require the plan to be detailed and specific, to have gone beyond the directors' powers of recall and to be put into operation without delay or significant alteration. It seems unlikely that British Gas's plan to spend £1,650,000,000 'largely over the next three years' would have met these tests had they been in force in 1993.

Although the time scale was much shorter, Arjo Wiggins Appleton's 1995 restructuring plan may also not have been specific enough to meet FRED 14's exacting conditions. The 1995 accounts disclosed the following:

Extract 26.10: Arjo Wiggins Appleton p.l.c. (1995)

Chairman's statement

Restructuring of European manufacturing

In November 1995, we announced a substantial programme of investment in rationalisation and cost reduction throughout our European manufacturing operations.

The costs of this restructuring, for which full provision has been made as an exceptional charge against operating profit for 1995, are expected to be £120.6 million, comprising £65.6 million in respect of cash expenditure on redundancies, closures and related matters, and £55.0 million, primarily relating to writedowns of equipment that will be decommissioned but also reflecting a permanent diminution in the value of tangible fixed assets of certain businesses. Details are given in the Chief Executive's operating and financial review.

Chief Executive's operating and financial review.

Restructuring

The European manufacturing operations have been subjected to major rationalisation since the merger of Wiggins Teape Appleton and Arjomari in 1990; two paper machines have been decommissioned, one mill sold and the workforce reduced by some 800 people. By 1995 it had become clear that a further substantial programme of rationalisation and cost reduction was now required, as part of the continuous process of improvement; in particular, as noted in the Interim Report, the returns from the carbonless business remained unsatisfactory in relation to the capital invested.

The board's commitment to this programme to enhance the European manufacturing base was announced in November 1995, followed in January 1996 by details of the units affected. The impact of the restructuring across the European manufacturing businesses is further analysed later. As outlined in the Chairman's statement, an exceptional restructuring charge of £120.6 million has been made against operating profit in the 1995 accounts.

The programme is being implemented progressively during 1996 and the first half of 1997 and is expected to produce a major improvement in this segment's profitability, consolidating leadership in its markets and allowing better service to its customers.

2. Exceptional items [extract]

An exceptional charge before tax of £120.6 million has been made in 1995 to reflect the cost of restructuring the Group's European manufacturing operations. This charge comprises £65.6 million in respect of redundancy, closure and other costs involving a cash outlay, £1.0 million for writing down working capital, £49.6 million for writing down the book value of tangible fixed assets and £4.4 million in relation to the elimination, through the profit and loss account, of goodwill associated with the sale or closure of businesses (such goodwill having been previously written off direct to reserves at the time the businesses were acquired). The tax effect of these charges is shown in note 5.

By the end of the following year some modifications to the provision were necessary, to write back excessive provisions against assets and to provide for further redundancy costs:

Extract 26.11: Arjo Wiggins Appleton p.l.c. (1996)

2. Exceptional items [extract]

An exceptional charge before tax of £120.6 million was made in 1995 to reflect the cost of restructuring the Group's European manufacturing operations. This charge comprised £65.6 million in respect of redundancy, closure and other costs involving a cash outlay, £1.0 million for writing down working capital, £49.6 million as a provision for the permanent diminution in value of tangible fixed assets and £4.4 million in relation to the elimination of goodwill associated with the sale or closure of businesses.

During 1996, a further £5.6 million was charged to the profit and loss account in respect of these restructuring plans. This comprised additional redundancy and other costs involving a cash outlay of £19.5 million, of which £0.5 million was spent in 1996, partially offset by a net £14.1 million write-back in the provision for the permanent diminution in value of tangible fixed assets.

The recognition tests for reorganisation costs that FRED 14 has established and that are set out above are designed to establish whether or not there is a liability at the balance sheet date, which is consistent with the conceptual approach of the draft standard and indeed with the ASB's draft *Statement of Principles*. It is therefore rather surprising to find an additional paragraph in the exposure draft that further limits the costs that can be provided for and which is founded on quite a different conceptual approach. This says that 'provisions for reorganisations should include only those expenditures that are both (a) necessarily entailed by a reorganisation to which the entity is demonstrably committed; and (b) not associated with ongoing or new activities of the entity'.[57] While (a) is perhaps a further elaboration of the rules for defining the extent of the company's obligations, (b) is nothing of the sort; indeed it might directly contradict the basic recognition rule, to the extent that certain amounts which pass all the tests for recognition as a liability must nonetheless not be recognised.

The rationale for this change of tune comes in the explanation section of the exposure draft. It says that 'these expenditures relate to and will benefit the ongoing business and should be accounted for as such – ie recognised at the same time and using the same description as would be used under normal accounting practice in the absence of a reorganisation'.[58] This is therefore an approach based on expense recognition, a concept not acknowledged by the ASB's draft *Statement of Principles*, but one which the Board seems unable to do without.

Medeva discloses a restructuring provision in its 1996 accounts, and describes it in the following terms:

Extract 26.12: Medeva plc (1996)

Financial Review

RESTRUCTURING

As announced at the time of the RPR acquisitions, we have taken a restructuring charge in respect of the US operations of £65m before tax, the bulk of which has been included within cost of sales (£60m). The largest element of the provision is to establish and sustain a high quality facility at Rochester suitable for manufacturing a wide range of Medeva's existing US products and others it may develop or acquire in the future. The total revenue cost of upgrading the Rochester site will be £28m of which £8m was spent in 1996; the majority of the remaining expenditure will occur in 1997 with the balance in 1998/99 reflecting the time needed to obtain appropriate FDA manufacturing licences. Another key element of the restructuring plan is the integration and rationalisation of the existing US manufacturing and administrative operations which previously operated from seven sites. The total cost of integration is £37m of which £18m is to write off fixed assets, principally at IMS. A £5m cash outflow, mainly relating to the relocation of administrative functions to Rochester, was incurred in 1996, with the balance to come over the next two years.

18. PROVISIONS FOR LIABILITIES AND CHARGES [extract]

	Restructuring provision £m
Provided in the year	65.2
Utilised in the year	
Cash spend	(12.8)
Transferred to creditors less than one year	(16.0)
Fixed asset write-down	(11.1)
At 31st December 1996	**25.3**

As the description of these costs shows, a significant part of the expenditure appears to be associated with ongoing activities, which means that it would not be permitted to be provided for in advance if FRED 14 became a standard. (Presumably for the same reason, £17.8 million of the profit and loss account charge has been added back for US GAAP purposes in Medeva's reconciliation between UK and US accounting principles; see 4.1.1 below.)

In fact, we think this expense recognition approach is much more relevant than a tortuous attempt to define constructive liabilities which is principally designed to try to remove management's discretion. If the definition of the costs that may be provided for can be narrowed in this way, the issue of *when* the provision can be made is defused.

If anything, we think FRED 14 compounds the restructuring costs problem by proposing a very wide definition of a reorganisation, which extends to anything that has 'a material effect on ... how a business undertaken by the reporting entity is conducted'. This presents a golden opportunity to management to classify all kinds of operating costs as reorganisation costs, and thereby invite the reader to perceive them in a different light. Even though FRED 14 might then intervene to prevent such costs being expensed too early, and FRS 3 might stop them being charged outside the operating profit section of the profit and loss account, their separate disclosure as reorganisation costs may nonetheless cause users of accounts to misinterpret the business's performance. A more effective approach could be to follow the US lead (discussed at 4.1.1 below) by considering the individual costs which are typically reported within reorganisation charges and developing guidance for accounting for those items rather than trying to define a reorganisation.

We also disagree with FRED 14's dismissal of the significance of board decisions. We believe that it is wrong to try to exclude the effect of management intentions in portraying the financial performance and position of an entity, as this can often be highly relevant to an understanding of the entity's affairs. Although board decisions are capable of being reversed, this does not happen as a general rule. We believe that board decisions are a legitimate trigger point for recognition as they commit organisations to specific courses of action (particularly if supported by subsequent events occurring prior to the approval of the accounts). Discarding them results in overly restrictive recognition criteria and omission of the financial consequences of potentially significant management decisions taken in the accounting period. In turn, this will not only make accounts less relevant to the decision-making needs of users but will introduce unjustifiable inconsistencies.

Take the fairly common situation of a reorganisation which is announced shortly after the balance sheet date and involves closure of plants/sites and large scale redundancies. Under the proposals contained in the exposure draft, the reporting entity would be precluded from recognising the direct costs of such a reorganisation in the accounts for the financial year just ended (notwithstanding that such costs will not yield future benefits) as the entity 'will not be demonstrably committed ... if the only relevant event prior to the balance sheet date is a board decision'. However, despite this, the entity may simultaneously be obliged to record impairment in the carrying values of plant and other assets at the affected sites (see Chapter 10 at 4). Hence, board decisions would appear to be relevant when assessing impairment of assets but not when determining the reporting entity's liabilities as at the balance sheet date. We see no merit in dealing with these effects at different times if they flow from the same decision.

In any event, the apparently robust tests of a constructive obligation proposed by FRED 14 are actually weaker than they seem. Concepts such as 'demonstrably committed', 'cannot realistically withdraw', 'no realistic alternative' and 'others can be expected to act on the assumption that the reorganisation will proceed' do not reliably identify an event that triggers the recognition of liabilities.

Furthermore, they are at least as manipulable as board decisions. Companies anxious to accelerate or postpone recognition of a liability could readily do so by advancing or deferring the event that signals such a commitment, such as a public announcement, without any change to the substance of their position.

Overall, we think that genuine board decisions should act as a trigger, and if only those costs that are not associated with the pursuit of future revenue can be provided for, there is no significant possibility of big bath provisions. Of course, the question of what is a 'genuine' decision then arises. We agree that some of the criteria in FRED 14 might be used to exclude those plans that are not sufficiently specific or imminent to warrant provision. We also do not think that any concept of 'demonstrable commitment' *at the balance sheet date* is needed to justify setting up a provision, although we would expect to see similar considerations being applied to circumstances at the time of approval of the accounts, so as to confirm that the decision was indeed a meaningful one.

Although it focuses heavily on recognition issues, FRED 14 also contains some specific disclosure provisions for reorganisation provisions. These are as follows:

(a) For all reorganisations: in each year until the reorganisation is completed the nature of the costs included in the balance sheet provision should be disclosed and an indication given of the likely timing of the expenditure;

(b) For reorganisations that meet the definition of an exceptional item in FRS 3 'Reporting Financial Performance': the amount of costs included in each profit and loss account heading should be separately disclosed and the business or part of the business to which they relate should be stated; and

(c) For fundamental reorganisations: an explanation should be given of the reason the reorganisation qualifies as 'fundamental' and a numerical analysis should be provided in the notes to the accounts showing the nature of the costs (for example, employee costs, costs of sales, costs of termination of contracts with customers).[59]

The exposure draft also requires that cash flows relating to a reorganisation previously disclosed as an exceptional item in the profit and loss account be disclosed when the provision is subsequently used, and that this information should be given separately for each reorganisation that was treated as a fundamental reorganisation.[60]

The above disclosures are in addition to the general disclosure requirements discussed at 2.2.5 above. These proposals seem rather complex; in particular it is questionable whether the extent of disclosure should really depend to such an extent on the categorisation of the provision in the profit and loss account, since the distinctions made between 'fundamental' and other reorganisations are not particularly meaningful in practice.

The explanation section of FRED 14 contains one further non-mandatory suggestion for disclosure. It notes that, because of the other rules proposed in the exposure draft, provisions that were previously accounted for as one amount may be charged in different accounting periods and under different profit and loss account headings, and suggests that readers of the accounts may find it useful for the totality of the costs to be disclosed, together with any related capital expenditure. It therefore encourages disclosure of such information.[61]

3.3   Environmental and decommissioning provisions

FRED 14 contains this specific recognition rule in relation to environmental liabilities:

'Provisions for environmental liabilities should be recognised at the time and to the extent that the entity becomes obliged, legally or constructively, to rectify environmental damage or to perform restorative work on the environment.'[62] The further discussion in the draft focuses on the idea of 'constructive obligations', making it clear that provision is possible only if the company has no real option but to carry out the remedial work.[63]

ICI and British Petroleum disclose these respective policies on environmental liabilities:

Extract 26.13: Imperial Chemical Industries PLC (1996)

Accounting policies

Environmental liabilities

The Group is exposed to environmental liabilities relating to its past operations, principally in respect of soil and groundwater remediation costs. Provisions for these costs are made when expenditure on remedial work is probable and the cost can be estimated within a reasonable range of possible outcomes.

Extract 26.14: The British Petroleum Company p.l.c. (1996)

Accounting policies

Environmental liabilities

Environmental expenditures that relate to current or future revenues are expensed or capitalised as appropriate. Expenditures that relate to an existing condition caused by past operations and that do not contribute to current or future earnings are expensed.

Liabilities for environmental costs are recognised when environmental assessments or clean-ups are probable and the associated costs can be reasonably estimated. Generally, the timing of these provisions coincides with the commitment to a formal plan of action or, if earlier, on divestment or on closure of inactive sites.

FRED 14 is not particularly controversial on these matters and seems to correspond to prevailing practice as shown in these policies. The more revolutionary issue concerns decommissioning costs, which arise, for example, when an oil rig or nuclear power station has to be dismantled at the end of its life. British Petroleum deals with decommissioning in this separate policy note:

Extract 26.15: The British Petroleum Company p.l.c. (1996)

Accounting policies

Decommissioning

Provision is made for the decommissioning of production facilities in accordance with local conditions and requirements on the basis of costs estimated as at the balance sheet date. The provision is allocated over accounting periods using a unit-of-production method based on estimated proved reserves.

The scale of its obligations for both decommissioning and environmental costs is evident from its provisions note:

Extract 26.16: The British Petroleum Company p.l.c. (1996)

23 Other provisions [extract]   **£ million**

	Decommissioning	Environmental
At 1 January 1996	1,576	722
Exchange adjustments	(79)	(53)
Charged to income	65	21
Utilised/deleted	(77)	(56)
At 31 December 1996	**1,485**	**634**

BNFL has possibly the largest and longest-term decommissioning obligations of any British company. It discloses the position in the following notes, which show that at 31 March 1996 it foresaw eventual expenditure of over £17 billion being required, even without allowing for future inflation:

Extract 26.17: British Nuclear Fuels Limited (1996)

Accounting policies

4.   Provisions and long-term commitments

In the majority of cases, the Company's contracts provide for the recovery of future costs associated with each particular contract.

a.   To the extent that all costs are not considered to be recoverable from customers by way of a specific charge:

i.   Provision for decommissioning the Group's radioactive facilities is made over their useful life and covers complete demolition within 100 years of being taken out of service, together with disposal of the associated waste.

ii.   Provision is made for the defuelling, reprocessing and waste management of the final cores of the Group's reactors.

iii.   The costs associated with the arisings of waste products for which an authorised disposal route is already in use, principally low-level waste at present, are written off in the year in which they occur. Provision is made for the treatment, handling and disposal of the Group's remaining waste products.

iv.   Provision is made for future reprocessing costs which are expected to arise on fixed price contracts entered into at the balance sheet date, whether or not work on these contracts has commenced.

These provisions, which are expressed at current price levels, are based on the latest technical assessments of the processes and methods likely to be used in the future and represent estimates derived from a combination of the latest technical knowledge available, existing legislation and regulations and commercial agreements.

b.   These liabilities will not crystallise until reasonably distant dates and, in accordance with practice in other sections of the industry, the provisions for them are discounted at an appropriate real rate of return to take account of the delay in meeting the expenditure. These estimates are reviewed annually and any consequential changes to the provision that are required, including price level changes, are taken up in the accounts for the year in which they arise, together with the recognition of a real rate of return on past provisions.

17. Provisions for liabilities and charges [extract]

A summary of the provisions for liabilities and charges is as follows:

	Decommissioning (note a)	Final reactor core costs (note a)	Waste products (note a)	Future reprocessing costs on fixed price contracts (note a)	Deferred tax (note b)	Other provisions (note c)	Total
Group	£M	£M	£M	£M	£M	£M	£M
Balance at 1 April 1995	322	31	517	144	1	411	1426
Adjustment arising from changes in price levels and interest credited	16	2	22	1	–	3	44
Charge in the year	62	(5)	1	(1)	356	130	543
Expenditure in the year	(1)	–	(15)	(6)	–	(74)	(96)
Recoverable advance corporation tax	–	–	–	–	(17)	–	(17)
Reclassifications	13	1	16	–	–	(14)	16
Balance at 31 March 1996	**412**	**29**	**541**	**138**	**340**	**456**	**1916**

a.   These provisions have been discounted. The table below analyses total costs still to be incurred at the Company's sites (both undiscounted at current prices and discounted to the balance sheet date), BNFL's share of these costs and the amounts provided to date:

	Total costs Undiscounted £M	Discounted £M	BNFL share Undiscounted £M	Discounted £M	Provided to date £M
Decommissioning	6310	3040	1571	798	412
Waste management and other costs	11007	7885	1044	777	708
At 31 March 1996	**17317**	**10925**	**2615**	**1575**	**1120**
At 31 March 1995	16871	10657	2253	1402	1014

The difference between total discounted costs of £10925M and £1120M provided to date represents costs of £9350M which are to the charge of customers and costs of £455M which will be provided over remaining plant lives in accordance with the Group's accounting policy.

The impact of FRED 14 on decommissioning policies is much more profound. Whereas present practice is to build up the required provision over the life of the facility by appropriate charges against revenues, FRED 14 adopts a balance sheet focus to the liability that requires it to be established as soon as the obligation exists, which may well be at the commencement of operations. The amount provided can anticipate the effects of future technology and legislation, but only to the extent that there is enough objective evidence that these changes will take place.[64] The draft then says 'provisions should be capitalised as assets when, and only when, the expenditure provides access to future economic benefits; otherwise the provision should be charged immediately to the profit and loss account'.[65] What this means is that the balance sheet will be grossed up so as to show the eventual decommissioning expenditure as an asset from the outset, which is then written off over the life of the facility.

This form of presentation was considered but rejected by the Oil Industry Accounting Committee when it produced its SORP on the subject. Although acknowledging the conceptual arguments that now lie behind FRED 14, it said that 'the OIAC has no doubt that the gradual build-up of the provision is the appropriate method of recognising this obligation because of the fact that changes in the scope of work, technology and prices are likely to result in great subsequent changes, downwards as well as upwards, in the amounts originally recognised. Whilst changes in estimates of liabilities are an unavoidable and therefore accepted feature of historical cost accounting, these changes would also affect the recorded amounts of assets. The OIAC believes that the resulting changes to the structure of oil company balance sheets would be unlikely to enhance their usefulness.'[66] Although this point was made specifically in relation to the oil industry, it must clearly apply even more forcibly to the nuclear industry, where the time scale is even greater and the future costs that will eventually be expended even more uncertain.

Although we understand why the Board's conceptual framework pushes it towards recognition of the full liability, it seems that this can only be achieved by including a spurious asset on the other side of the balance sheet. In any case, if the principle that a liability should be recognised once costs have become unavoidable were really to be applied on a consistent basis, various other commitments (for example, expenditure commitments under licence agreements) would also be caught and there would be considerable grossing up of balance sheets. We therefore question whether this proposed change has much merit.

FRED 14 is not entirely clear on how it means changes in the capitalised assets to be dealt with. It says that 'where a provision ... subsequently changes, the carrying amount (net of accumulated depreciation) should be recalculated based on current knowledge and the balance of the change in the provision should be recognised in the profit and loss account'.[67] (Although this passage refers twice to provisions, and indeed is headed 'Change in provisions', we presume from the reference to capitalisation and depreciation that it is in fact talking about the corresponding asset.) This seems to imply that the provision and the corresponding asset should be recalculated ab initio in each year and all differences dealt with as a catch-up adjustment through the profit and loss account, whereas present practice for oil companies is to deal with changes in estimate prospectively by adjusting the amount charged to the profit and loss account over the remaining life of the facility.[68] However, the above extract is far from clear and may not reflect what the ASB intends.

The more significant change for most companies, however, will involve the use of discounting for the measurement of the liability. Although this is done by BNFL, it is not consistent with present accounting practice for oil companies. The effect on the profit and loss account will be to split the cost of the eventual decommissioning into two components: an operating cost based on the discounted amount of the provision; and an interest element representing the unwinding of the discount. The overall effect will be to produce a rising pattern of cost over the life of the facility. In contrast, present practice for oil companies is to show the whole amount in arriving at their operating results, and to aim to charge a level amount for each barrel of oil extracted, although the effects of changing estimates of costs, particularly inflation (which is not factored into the original estimates made), is likely to mean that this will not be achieved.

We are not convinced that this proposal in FRED 14 represents an improvement on the practices that have been codified by the OIAC SORP. At the moment, both exploration and development costs (including the cost of constructing production facilities such as platforms) and estimated decommissioning costs are charged against revenues in the same way, on a unit-of-production basis. Introducing an interest component in relation to the latter but not the former only introduces a fresh inconsistency; it seems odd to account for the time value of money in relation to cash flows occurring at the end of the life of the field but not those occurring at the beginning, when both these costs are being recovered from revenues generated throughout the field's life. We also question the wisdom of showing part of the cost of decommissioning as a finance cost rather than as an operating cost. We see no need to change established oil industry practice in this area.

3.4 Cyclical repairs

Some companies account for the costs of major periodic repair to large assets by making regular provisions against which the repairs are then charged when incurred. Examples are to be found in the accounts of St Ives, Pilkington and Rugby Group:

Extract 26.18: St Ives plc (1996)

1. Accounting policies

(h) Provisions for repairs

Provision is made for repairs to major items of plant and machinery and freehold and leasehold premises based on estimates of expenditure required to sustain the operating capacity of the assets at present levels over their estimated useful lives.

17. Provisions for liabilities and charges [extract]

	The Group Provision for repairs £'000	The Company Provision for repairs £'000
Balance at 28 July 1995	2,411	250
Charged to profit and loss account	1,594	50
On acquisition of subsidiary undertaking	285	–
Applied	(513)	–
Exchange differences	8	–
	3,785	300

Extract 26.19: Pilkington plc (1997)

Accounting policies

8 Glass tank repairs

A charge is made annually against profits to provide for the accrued proportion of the estimated revenue cost of major glass tank repairs which are carried out periodically.

The actual revenue cost of such repairs, when incurred, is charged against the provision.

Notes on the financial statements

27 Provisions for liabilities and charges [extract]

For the year ended 31st March 1997	Other provisions £m
Group	
At beginning of year	196
Exchange rate adjustments	(16)
Provided during year	37
Utilised during year	(43)
Changes in composition of the Group	3
At end of year	177

Other provisions at 31st March 1997 include £17 million (1996 £16 million) for tank repairs …

Extract 26.20: The Rugby Group plc (1996)

1. Accounting policies

DEFERRED REPAIRS

Provision is made for future repairs to major items of plant by spreading the expected cost over the appropriate period of production.

Notes on the accounts

16 PROVISIONS FOR LIABILITIES AND CHARGES [extract]

	Other £ million
Group	
At 1st January 1996	13.8
Purchase of businesses	0.3
Sale of businesses	(0.3)
Impact of exchange rate changes	(0.5)
Utilised	(4.7)
Charge to profit and loss account	6.2
At 31st December 1996	14.8

Other provisions includes provisions for repairs of **£8.5 million** (1995: £9.0 million) ...

This is discussed in an Application Note to FRED 14, which concludes that the practice is inappropriate because there is no obligation that qualifies to be recognised as a liability. Instead, the exposure draft proposes that such expenditure should be capitalised when incurred and written off over a future period.

Similar policies are also followed by water companies in relation to the maintenance of their infrastructure assets. In this case there are slightly different arguments because external regulation on both pricing structures and service standards have a bearing on the maintenance required. South West Water provides an example of a typical policy:

Extract 26.21: South West Water Plc (1997)

1. Accounting policies

d Tangible fixed assets and depreciation

i Infrastructure assets [extract]

Expenditure on maintaining the operating capability of the network is charged as an operating cost. Expenditure on the maintenance of infrastructure assets may vary significantly from the long term normal annual level. In such instances, the charge against profits is equalised by way of accruals or deferrals as appropriate to reflect the long term normal level of charges, in accordance with defined standards of service.

21 Provisions for liabilities and charges [extract]

	At 1 April 1996 £m	Charged against profits £m	Utilised during year £m	**At 31 March 1997 £m**
Infrastructure renewals	2.1	6.8	(6.5)	**2.4**

This case is not specifically addressed in the Application Note, which only talks about large individual assets that need to be repaired every few years. It is not clear whether the ASB would regard the presence of an external regulator, or indeed the expectations of the public, as sufficient grounds for concluding that a constructive obligation exists – on the basis of concepts such as 'the company has no discretion to avoid the expenditure'. Of course this absence of discretion can equally be said to apply to, say, an airline because it cannot opt to avoid maintaining its planes, and indeed is subject to regulation on this matter. This rather demonstrates the nebulous nature of the 'constructive obligation' test on which much of FRED 14 is founded. As with other similar areas of accounting, we think the real issue is one of expense recognition, not liability recognition; we see no real problem with a well-considered and systematic policy of providing for major repairs and we see it as at an equally effective way of matching costs with revenues as the depreciation approach that the ASB prefers.

3.5   Year 2000 costs

A particular form of 'repair' cost that is currently preoccupying the management of many companies is the need to rectify inadequate computer systems for their inability to cope with the change of dates entailed by the new millennium; many computers have been programmed to record only the last two digits of the year, and will be unable to cope with the implications of a change in the first two.

The UITF briefly considered the issue of how to account for the costs of such rectification but decided not to develop an Abstract on the subject. However, it mentioned its discussion in an Information Sheet and said that in its view such costs should be written off as incurred.[69] It might be inferred from that that the Task Force did not believe that provisions should be established in respect of the Year 2000 costs, but in fact the issue that had been discussed was simply one of whether such costs could be capitalised, not whether they may be anticipated in a provision, to which there is no obstacle under present accounting practice. It is possible, however, that the Task Force will return to this issue.

3.6 Warranty provisions

Warranty provisions are not specifically addressed in the body of FRED 14, but are discussed briefly in an Application Note appended to it, which concludes that such provisions are appropriate. We concur with this view, although in practice considerations of materiality may permit it to be treated on a pay-as-you-go basis. Thorn is an example of a company that discloses a policy of provision:

Extract 26.22: Thorn plc (1997)

Warranty provisions

Some products carry formal guarantees of satisfactory performance of varying periods following their purchase by customers. Provision is made for the estimated cost of honouring unexpired warranties.

On the other hand, Rentokil (as it was then called) disclosed this pay-as-you-go policy in its 1995 accounts (the 1996 accounts are silent on the matter, although no change of policy appears to have been made):

Extract 26.23: Rentokil Group PLC (1995)

Accounting policies

WARRANTIES

Some service work is carried out under warranty. The cost of claims under warranty is charged against the profit and loss account of the year in which the claims are settled.

3.7 Self insurance

An Application Note to FRED 14 deals with the practice of self insurance, which arises when an entity decides not to take out external insurance in respect of a certain category of risk because it would be uneconomic to do so. This concludes that the entity should recognise the reality of the situation – that it is uninsured – and report losses based on their actual incidence, rather than smoothing them from period to period by reference to a simulated insurance premium that it has not in fact paid. As a result, any provisions that appear in the balance sheet should reflect only the amounts expected to be paid in respect of those losses that have occurred by the balance sheet date.

Few companies disclose policies in relation to this issue, although some show evidence of self insurance provisions. As shown in Extract 26.3 above, Harrisons & Crosfield includes such provisions within its 'other provisions' category.

4   COMPARISON WITH US AND IASC PRONOUNCEMENTS

4.1   US

The US does not have an accounting standard on the general issue of provisions, but does have detailed rules in relation to some of the specific issues covered by FRED 14, as set out below.

4.1.1   Restructuring costs

In January 1995, the Emerging Issues Task Force of the FASB issued Abstract 94-3 which was the forerunner of FRED 14's proposals on reorganisation costs.[70] This considered, but did not adopt, the approach of trying to define restructuring costs and instead simply laid down rules for certain kinds of costs that typically arise in a restructuring.

The conditions set for the recognition of redundancy costs were these:

(a)   Prior to the date of the financial statements, management having the appropriate level of authority to involuntarily terminate employees approves and commits the enterprise to the plan of termination and establishes the benefits that current employees will receive upon termination.

(b)   Prior to the date of the financial statements, the benefit arrangement is communicated to employees. The communication of the benefit arrangement includes sufficient detail to enable employees to determine the type and amount of benefits they will receive if they are terminated.

(c)   The plan of termination specifically identifies the number of employees to be terminated, their job classifications or functions, and their locations.

(d)   The period of time to complete the plan of termination indicated that significant changes to the plan of termination are not likely.

In relation to other costs to exit an activity, the EITF decided that liabilities for such costs could be recognised if they met the following conditions:

(a)   Prior to the date of the financial statements, management having the appropriate level of authority approves and commits the enterprise to an exit plan.

(b)   The exit plan specifically identifies all significant actions to be taken to complete the exit plan, activities that will not be continued, including the method of disposition and location of these activities, and the expected date of completion.

(c)   Actions required by the exit plan will begin as soon as possible after the commitment date, and the period of time to complete the exit plan indicates that significant changes to the exit plan are not likely.

The only costs that qualify to be accrued even if they meet the above conditions are those that are not associated with or do not benefit activities that will be continued, and that meet either criterion (a) or (b) below:

(a)   The cost is incremental to other costs incurred by the enterprise in the conduct of its activities prior to the commitment date and will be incurred as a direct result of the exit plan. The notion of incremental does not contemplate a diminished future economic benefit to be derived from the cost but rather the absence of the cost in the enterprise's activities immediately prior to the commitment date.

(b)   The cost represents amounts to be incurred by the enterprise under a contractual obligation that existed prior to the commitment date and will either continue after the exit plan is completed with no economic benefit to the enterprise or be a penalty incurred by the enterprise to cancel the contractual obligation.

These conditions are rather more detailed than those in FRED 14, but are similar in their general approach. However, it is noteworthy that the EITF's rules permit a liability to be set up on the basis of a management commitment, even if they have not yet put the decision beyond their powers of recall.

4.1.2   Environmental costs

In October 1996, the Accounting Standards Executive Committee of the AICPA issued Statement of Position (SOP) 96-1 – _Environmental Remediation Liabilities_. This interprets SFAS 5 – _Accounting for Contingencies_ – which requires provision for environmental liabilities if it is probable that a liability has been incurred and the amount of the loss can be reasonably estimated. It says that the 'probable liability' test is met for environmental liabilities if, by the time the accounts are issued:

(a)   Litigation, a claim, or an assessment can be asserted, or is probable of being asserted; and

(b)   It is probable that the outcome of such litigation, claim, or assessment will be unfavourable.[71]

Given the US climate on environmental litigation, there is a presumption that (b) will be established if the reporting entity is associated with a contaminated site in respect of which litigation has commenced or a claim or assessment has been asserted (or if such actions are probable).[72]

Measurement of the liability will often be difficult, but at least the minimum amount in the range of possible loss should be accrued. This should be based on both the direct incremental costs of the remediation effort and the payroll cost of those employees who are expected to spend a significant amount of time on it.[73] Where the entity is one of a number of parties against whom the claim is made, it should accrue its share of the costs after taking account of the possible effect of other responsible parties failing to meet their share.[74] The costs accrued should be based on present legislation and technology,[75] and may be discounted only if the amount and timing of the expenditure that is provided for are reasonably estimable.[76]

4.1.3   Decommissioning costs

Present accounting practice in the US is similar to that used by oil companies in the UK under the OIAC SORP described at 3.3 above. However, the FASB is presently developing an accounting standard which seeks to change it in a similar way to FRED 14. An exposure draft was issued in February 1996 – *Accounting for Certain Liabilities Related to Closure or Removal of Long-Lived Assets* – proposing that such obligations should be recognised as a liability when the obligation is incurred, with a corresponding increase in the cost of the related asset. The liability is to be discounted at a risk-free rate of interest. Changes in the estimated cost are to be recognised as an adjustment to the cost of the asset, and depreciation revised prospectively. The last point may be different from FRED 14, which can be read to require retrospective adjustment but, as explained in 3.3 above, FRED 14 is far from clear on this issue.

4.1.4   Vacant leasehold property

In 1988 the EITF considered the question of how to deal with the remaining rental payments on leased property when the entity moved to a replacement property. It concluded that if the leased property had no substantive future use of benefit to the entity these rentals, together with any other associated costs, should be expensed, net of any actual or probable sublease income. The amount provided could be measured on either a discounted or an undiscounted basis.[77]

4.1.5   Year 2000 costs

The EITF issued an Abstract on this subject in 1996.[78] The consensus of the Task Force was that external and internal costs specifically associated with modifying internal-use software for the year 2000 should be charged to expense as incurred.

4.2   IASC

The IASC is developing a standard on Provisions and Contingencies which is very similar to FRED 14; indeed members of the ASB have been prominent in its development. In November 1996 the Committee published a Draft Statement of Principles on the subject, of which the main difference from FRED 14 is that the international version expresses even more enthusiasm for the use of expected values. In July 1997, the IASC voted to convert this into an exposure draft with little change, and hopes to finalise a standard on the subject early in 1998. Since the IASC approach to the subject mirrors that of the ASB in all material respects, a detailed understanding of what the IASC is proposing can be gained from the above summary of FRED 14.

5   CONCLUSION

The subject of provisions is a wide ranging one, but at its heart lie fundamental questions concerning the recognition and measurement of items in the accounts. The ASB sees these issues straightforwardly in terms of liability recognition, and seeks to apply its draft *Statement of Principles* as a means of resolving them, but in some cases we think this does not work well and that it is more fruitful to address the question from the point of view of expense recognition. In particular, we think the concept of the 'constructive obligation' is rather more nebulous than it is represented to be, and not always useful in identifying reliably when to include certain items in the accounts. We would not be as dismissive about the relevance of management intent, since accounts necessarily represent the report of management and it is futile to try to divorce them from that context. We are also concerned that the Board's approach means that the balance sheet will be inappropriately grossed up in some cases so as to include dubious assets.

The measurement proposals also have their difficulties. We are concerned that they seem to be seeking to derive some form of theoretical market value for the obligations reported whereas we would prefer to focus more directly on the actual expenditure that the company is likely to make. We also think that the proposals on discounting, particularly on an after-tax basis, deserve much deeper consideration.

We therefore hope that the Board does not rush ahead with this project. It depends very heavily on the draft *Statement of Principles* for its arguments, and it does not seem appropriate to finalise a standard on the subject until the ASB has secured some measure of acceptance for its framework as a whole.

References

1   CA 85, Sch. 4, para. 89.
2   *Ibid.*, para. 88.
3   FRED 14, *Provisions and Contingencies*, ASB, June 1997, para. 2.
4   *Ibid.*, Appendix 1, para. 5.
5   *Ibid.*, para. 32.
6   CA 85, Sch. 4, para. 46(1) and (2).
7   FRED 14, para 1.
8   *Ibid.*, para. 4.
9   *Ibid.*, para. 31.
10 *Ibid.*, para. 5.
11 *Ibid.*, para. 6.
12 *Ibid.*, para. 49.
13 *Ibid.*, para. 17.
14 *Ibid.*, para. 36.
15 *Ibid.*, para. 40.

16 *Ibid.*, paras. 37 and 39.
17 *Ibid.*, para. 38.
18 *Ibid.*, para. 7.
19 *Ibid.*, paras 53–55.
20 *Ibid.*, para. 50.
21 Exposure draft of *Statement of Principles*, ASB, November 1995, para. 5.27.
22 FRED 14, para. 51. (However, the example showing the computation of expected value in this paragraph is incorrect.)
23 *Ibid.*, para. 52.
24 *Ibid.*, para. 9.
25 *Ibid.*, para. 11
26 *Ibid.*, para. 9.
27 *Ibid.*, para. 10 and 60.
28 *Ibid.*, para. 10(a).
29 *Ibid.*, para. 15.
30 *Ibid.*, para. 7.
31 *Ibid.*, para. 16.
32 FRS 3, *Reporting financial performance*, ASB, October 1992, para. 18.
33 SSAP 9, *Stocks and long-term contracts*, ASC, revised September 1988, para. 11.
34 Discussion Paper – *Provisions*, ASB, November 1995, para. 2.6.
35 FRED 14, Appendix III, para. 21.
36 FRED 14, para. 18.
37 *Ibid.*, para. 19.
38 *Ibid.*, para. 64.
39 *Ibid.*, paras. 20 and 66.
40 *Ibid.*, para. 20.
41 *Ibid.*, para. 23.
42 *Ibid.*, para. 5.
43 *Ibid.*, para. 2.
44 SSAP 9, para. 11.
45 FRED 14, para. 41.
46 UITF, Information Sheet No. 9, 21 July 1993, *Accounting for rent payable and other expenses of vacant leasehold property.*
47 *Ibid.*
48 FRED 14, para. 2.
49 *Ibid.*, para. 33.
50 *Ibid.*, para. 61
51 *Ibid.*, para. 63.
52 *Ibid.*, para. 5(b).
53 *Ibid.*, para. 42.
54 *Ibid.*, para. 43.
55 *Ibid.*, paras. 44 and 45.
56 *Ibid.*, paras. 46 and 47.
57 *Ibid.*, para. 12.
58 *Ibid.*, para. 62.
59 *Ibid.*, para. 21.
60 *Ibid.*, para. 22.
61 *Ibid.*, para. 67.
62 *Ibid.*, para. 5(c).
63 *Ibid.*, para. 48.
64 *Ibid.*, paras. 8 and 57–59.
65 *Ibid.*, para. 13.
66 *Accounting for abandonment costs*, OIAC, June 1988, para. 10.
67 FRED 14, para. 14.
68 *Accounting for abandonment costs*, para. 36.
69 Information Sheet No 19, UITF, 7 November 1996.

70   EITF 94-3, *Liability Recognition for Certain Employee Termination Benefits and Other Costs to Exit an Activity (including Certain Costs Incurred in a Restructuring)*, EITF, January 1995.

71   SOP 96-1, *Environmental Remediation Liabilities*, AICPA, October 1996.

72   *Ibid.*, para. 5.6.

73   *Ibid.*, para. 6.5.

74   *Ibid.*, para. 6.14.

75   *Ibid.*, paras. 6.10 and 6.11.

76   *Ibid.*, para. 6.13.

77   EITF 88-10, *Costs Associated with Lease Modification or Termination*, EITF, April 1988.

78   EITF 96-14, *Accounting for the Costs Associated with Modifying Computer Software for the Year 2000*, EITF, July 1996.

Chapter 27   Cash flow statements

1   EVOLUTION OF THE CASH FLOW STATEMENT

1.1   Statements of source and application of funds

The inclusion of statements of source and application of funds in annual reports can probably be attributed to a desire to provide users with a more complete picture of resource flows than that provided by the profit and loss account.[1] The latter is concerned with resource flows that are part of the earnings activity and does not report changes resulting from the business's investing or financing activities nor does it distinguish between the different types of resources consumed in the earnings activity.[2]

By the 1950s there was widespread experimentation by US companies with the inclusion of various forms of 'funds statement'[3] in annual reports.[4] This became a source of concern for the AICPA which commissioned a research study on cash flow analysis and the funds statement.[5] It is clear from the director's preface that the AICPA saw 'the increased use of the statement of source and application of funds and the recent emergence of an amorphous concept known as "cash flow" ' as a threat to the perfection of the accrual basis of accounting.[6]

In 1963, following the publication of the study, the Accounting Principles Board issued Opinion No. 3 – *The Statement of Source and Application of Funds* – which encouraged (but did not require) the presentation of a funds statement. This was the first official pronouncement on funds statements to be issued by a major accounting body. It received wide support from the principal stock exchanges and the business community in the US and resulted in a significant increase in the inclusion of such statements in US company annual reports. In 1970 the SEC made the funds statement an obligatory element of financial statement filing.

In 1971 APB Opinion No. 3 was superseded by APB Opinion No. 19, which required a 'statement summarizing changes in financial position [to] be presented as a basic financial statement for each period for which an income statement is presented'.[7]

In contrast to the US, there was a much slower acceptance in the UK of the view that the funds statement should be a complementary statement to the balance sheet and profit and loss account. Prior to the 1970s, few British companies published funds statements. Whereas in the US and Canada the emphasis was on achieving the most useful form and content of the funds statement, UK companies were still trying to decide whether the statement should be included in their annual reports at all. It was not until ED 13[8] was issued in April 1974 that the ASC offered any guidance on the subject. ED 13 led ultimately to the publication in July 1975 of SSAP 10,[9] which had the objective of establishing 'the practice of providing source and application of funds statements as a part of audited accounts and to lay down a minimum standard of disclosure in such statements'.[10]

1.2   The SSAP 10 funds statement

The form and content of the SSAP 10 funds statements were governed by two principal factors: the objective of the statement and the interpretation of the concept of 'funds'. However, there was widespread dissatisfaction with SSAP 10 in that it failed either to establish the objective of the funds statement or to define 'funds' adequately. Furthermore, the standard did not prescribe a specific format designed to provide useful and meaningful information in a consistent manner. A common criticism of the funds statement was that it was a repetitive and unnecessary rearrangement of figures already appearing in the financial statements. In fact, paragraph 4 of SSAP 10 bears out this charge, confirming that the funds statement was effectively a reconciliation of the information already provided in the accounts, providing the user with virtually no new information:

> 'The funds statement will provide a link between the balance sheet at the beginning of the period, the profit and loss account for the period and the balance sheet at the end of the period. ... The figures from which a funds statement is constructed should generally be identifiable in the profit and loss account, balance sheet and related notes.'

This contrasted significantly with the purpose of the funds statement as set out in a study on the subject by the Accountants International Study Group:

> 'The objective of the funds statement is to provide information as to how the activities of the enterprise have been financed and how its financial resources have been used during the period covered by the statement. It is not intended to, nor can it, supplant the balance sheet, income statement and retained earnings statement; neither is it a supporting schedule to these statements. The funds statement is, rather, a complementary statement which is important in its own right and which is designed to present information that the other financial statements either do not provide or provide only indirectly.'[11]

It is indeed difficult to determine precisely what the drafters of SSAP 10 saw as the objective of the funds statement.[12] The following extracts from the standard illustrate conflicting views (emphases added):

'The objective of such a statement is to show the manner in which the operations of a company have been financed and in which its *financial resources* have been used and the format selected should be designed to achieve this objective.'[13]

'... it is necessary also to identify the movements in net assets, liabilities and capital which have taken place during the year and the resultant effect on *net liquid funds.*'[14]

'It should show clearly the funds generated or absorbed by the operations of the business and the manner in which any resulting surplus of *liquid assets* has been applied or any deficiency of such assets has been financed, distinguishing the long term from the short term.'[15]

'The statement should distinguish the use of funds for the purchase of new fixed assets from funds used in increasing the *working capital* of the company.'[16]

It was not surprising that a statement purporting to accommodate all of the above turned out to be largely meaningless. SSAP 10 certainly did not promote uniformity in reporting practice, evidenced by the varying ways in which it was interpreted by companies in practice. The principal shortcoming was the focus on balance sheet classifications. The statement analysed the sources and applications of funds (however defined) in terms of movements within individual categories and groupings of assets and equities, rather than in terms of how the various activities of the business had either generated or absorbed funds. A funds statement prepared under SSAP 10 was largely a reconciliation of balance sheet changes, rather than a statement which provided additional information useful to the user.

Meanwhile, US companies were also encountering difficulties with the form and content of the funds statement presented under APB Opinion No. 19. The FASB had identified certain practical problems, 'including the ambiguity of terms such as *funds*, lack of comparability arising from diversity in the focus of the statement (cash, cash and short-term investments, quick assets, or working capital) and the resulting differences in definitions of funds flows from operating activities (cash or working capital), differences in the format of the statement (sources and uses format or activity format), variations in classifications of specific items in an activity format, and the reporting of net changes in amounts of assets and liabilities rather than gross inflows and outflows'.[17] This diversity in reporting practice was seen to be caused mainly by the lack of clear objectives for the funds statement.[18]

1.3   The move towards cash flow information

There was an increasing acknowledgement through the 1980s of the critical role played by cash in the operation of any economic entity. Hendriksen states that 'in the final analysis, cash flows into and out of a business enterprise are the most fundamental events upon which accounting measurements are based and upon which investors and creditors are assumed to base their decisions'.[19]

The importance of providing cash flow information was reinforced by the FASB through its concepts statements. SFAC No. 1 states that 'financial reporting should provide information to help present and potential investors and creditors and other users in assessing the amounts, timing, and uncertainty of prospective cash receipts from dividends or interest and the proceeds from the sale, redemption, or maturity of securities or loans. The prospects for those cash receipts are affected by an enterprise's ability to generate enough cash to meet its obligations when due and its other cash operating needs, to reinvest in operations, and to pay cash dividends ... . Thus, financial reporting should provide information to help investors, creditors, and others assess the amounts, timing, and uncertainty of prospective net inflows to the related enterprise.'[20]

Further recognition of the need for business enterprises to provide cash flow information in their external reporting was given by SFAC No. 5, which states that 'a full set of financial statements for a period should show: ... cash flows during the period'.[21]   It then goes on to say that 'a statement of cash flows directly or indirectly reflects an entity's cash receipts classified by major sources and its cash payments classified by major uses during a period. It provides useful information about an entity's activities in generating cash through operations to repay debt, distribute dividends, or reinvest to maintain or expand operating capacity; about its financing activities, both debt and equity; and about its investing or spending of cash. Important uses of information about an entity's current cash receipts and payments include helping to assess factors such as the entity's liquidity, financial flexibility, profitability, and risk.'[22]

Liquidity reflects an asset's or liability's nearness to cash; whilst financial flexibility is the ability of an entity to raise cash at short notice so that it can meet unforeseen contingencies or take advantage of favourable opportunities that may arise. Although the balance sheet includes information that is often used in assessing an entity's liquidity and financial flexibility, it only provides an incomplete picture of these factors, unless it is used in conjunction with at least a cash flow statement.[23]

As a result of the increasing recognition of the significance of cash flow information, coupled with the diversity in the formats caused by the lack of a clear objective for the funds statement, the FASB issued SFAS 95 – *Statement of Cash Flows* – in November 1987. This superseded APB Opinion No. 19 and requires that 'a business enterprise that provides a set of financial statements that reports both financial position and results of operations shall also provide a statement of cash flows for each period for which results of operations are provided'.[24]

The US requirement to present a statement of cash flows started a worldwide trend in financial reporting, with several standard-setting bodies re-examining the nature and objectives of the funds statement, and concluding that the statement should focus on flows of cash rather than flows of working capital, or some other concept of funds.[25] In September 1991, the ASB published FRS 1 – *Cash flow statements* – which superseded SSAP 10 and required reporting entities to prepare a modified US-style cash flow statement instead of a SSAP 10 funds statement. In 1992, the IASC revised IAS 7, which now requires enterprises to prepare a cash flow statement instead of a statement of changes in financial position.

1.4   The distinction between 'funds flow' and 'cash flow'

Although the examples given in the Appendix to SSAP 10 seemed to emphasise a 'working capital' interpretation of funds, the funds statement was required to include all movements in financial resources. The 'all financial resources' concept, which originated from APB Opinion No. 3, sought to include in the funds statement all additions to, distributions of, and changes in composition of the financial resources of the entity. Accordingly, transactions such as the issue of shares for non-cash consideration or the conversion of loans to share capital were reflected in the funds statement, even though they did not affect working capital.

In contrast to the funds statement, a cash flow statement reflects only those transactions which result in an increase or decrease in cash. Thus, the initial purchase of a fixed asset under a finance lease will not appear in the cash flow statement (except to the extent that lease premiums are paid in cash), whereas the gross amount capitalised as an asset would have been shown as an application of funds and the assumption of the lease obligation as a source of funds in the funds statement. Similarly, neither the conversion of debt to equity nor the acquisition of a subsidiary settled by issue of shares will feature in a cash flow statement.

The publication of FRS 1 also had the effect of dispelling the frequently held notion that profit after tax plus depreciation equated to operating cash flow. This misconception was, to a certain extent, reinforced by the accounts of some major companies. For example, the 1990 group flow of funds statement of Reckitt & Colman described funds from ordinary operations after tax as being 'net cash generation', as shown in the following extract:

Extract 27.1: Reckitt & Colman plc (1990)

Group flow of funds statement
for the financial year ended 29 December 1990 [extract]

	1990 £m	1989 £m
Generation of funds from ordinary operations:		
Profit before tax	**235·17**	217·40
Depreciation	**47·08**	40·15
Disposal of fixed assets	**16·04**	10·67
	298·29	268·22
Tax paid	**(56·33)**	(54·06)
Net cash generation	**241·96**	214·16

In 1991, Reckitt & Colman opted for early implementation of FRS 1 and presented a cash flow statement which showed the following:

Extract 27.2: Reckitt & Colman plc (1991)

Group cash flow statement
for the fifty-three weeks ended 4 January 1992 [extract]

	£m	1991 £m	£m	1990 £m
Net cash inflow from trading activities		**329·97**		276·07
Returns on investments and servicing of finance				
Interest received	**20·57**		39·44	
Interest paid	**(63·02)**		(55·40)	
Coupon on convertible capital bonds	**(19·08)**		(2·04)	
Dividends paid (including minorities)	**(50·57)**		(43·25)	
Net cash outflow from returns on investments and servicing of finance		**(112·10)**		(61·25)
Taxation		**(50·25)**		(56·33)
Net cash inflow before investing and financing		**167·62**		158·49

It is interesting to contrast the 'net cash generation' of £241.96m for 1990 shown in the funds statement with the pre-dividend net cash inflow before investing and financing of £201.74m (i.e. £158.49m + £43.25m) for 1990 shown in the cash flow statement. Clearly, FRS 1 enabled Reckitt & Colman to define its operating cash flows more precisely than it was able to under the SSAP 10 funds statement. At the same time, the above two extracts illustrate one of the fundamental differences between funds flow and cash flow.

Since the Companies Act distribution rules allow the payment of dividends on the strength of net profit after tax and extraordinary items, a company is permitted to pay cash dividends on accrual based profits, even though it may not have generated sufficient cash flow from operations to cover such dividends. Whilst it was not always easy to determine from the funds statement whether the company had generated sufficient cash to cover its dividend payment, this will be evident from the cash flow statement. The importance of this information has been highlighted by corporate failures where the companies concerned had been unable to convert profits into cash and yet had maintained or even increased the payment of cash dividends.

1.5   The original FRS 1

FRS 1 was loosely based on ED 54 – *Cash flow statements* – the second to last exposure draft issued by the ASC before it was disbanded in July 1990. In fact, what ED 54 proposed was essentially a reformatted source and application of funds statement which used the 'cash and cash equivalents' definition of funds. Consequently, although ED 54 served as the catalyst in introducing the cash flow statement as the third primary financial statement, the requirements of FRS 1 were substantially different to those proposed in ED 54.

The statement required by FRS 1 was in many respects a modified US-style cash flow statement. Cash flows (defined as increases or decreases in 'cash and cash equivalents') were to be analysed under five standard headings:

- operating activities;

- returns on investments and servicing of finance;

- taxation;

- investing activities; and

- financing.

Presentation was required to follow the above sequence with a total being shown for the net cash flow for each standard heading.[26] In addition, the total net cash inflow or outflow before financing was required to be disclosed. This was intended to focus the statement on the effect of cash flows on the debt financing needs of the reporting entity, rather than on the balances held in cash and cash equivalents (these often being insignificant in size in relation to the level of debt).

Cash and cash equivalents were defined in FRS 1 as follows:[27]

Cash – Cash in hand and deposits repayable on demand with any bank or other financial institution. Cash includes cash in hand and deposits denominated in foreign currencies.

Cash equivalents – Short-term, highly liquid investments which are readily convertible into known amounts of cash without notice and which were within three months of maturity when acquired; less advances from banks repayable within three months from the date of the advance. Cash equivalents include investments and advances denominated in foreign currencies provided that they fulfil the above criteria.

Although the focus of the statement was on cash rather than on funds, restricting the definition to cash in hand or at the bank would not have reflected the reality of the cash management policies employed by reporting entities. Cash in excess of immediate needs is often invested in short-term investments. So long as these investments are highly liquid, are convertible into known amounts of cash without notice and are not subject to any significant changes in value because of changes in interest rates, they are virtually equivalent to cash. The statement therefore focused not just on flows of cash, but on flows of cash and cash equivalents.

Highly liquid investments realisable at any point for a known amount of cash did not qualify as cash equivalents where the term to maturity was long, for example Treasury Stock 9% 2008. This was because a change in interest rates would significantly affect the value of the stock. For this reason, the FRS restricted the definition of cash equivalents to those investments having a maturity of three months or less at date of acquisition.

Negative balances had to be set off against the positive balances in computing the net holding of, and movement in, cash and cash equivalents. The FRS required short term advances to be treated as negative cash equivalents. However, only overdrafts and short-term bank advances were to be treated in this manner. Other short-term advances and loans constituted financing flows. In deciding whether a short-term bank loan could be included within cash and cash equivalents, a cut-off period of three months was adopted, consistent with the approach for short-term investments.

1.6   The need for revision

Without doubt the publication of FRS 1 was a quantum leap in the ASB's financial reporting reform process. It generally worked well in practice and enhanced the quality of financial reporting considerably. Nevertheless, the decision by the ASB to call for comments on the functioning of the standard in March 1994 (as part of the Board's policy for reviewing the effectiveness of major new standards) was well received. It was felt that the standard fell short in a number of respects from what could be achieved.[28]

The most common complaint concerned the definition of cash equivalents. In practice, companies' treasury operations did not draw the distinction between investment and cash management in the way that the original standard seemed to imply, since the three month cut-off for cash equivalents bore little relationship to companies' treasury maturity horizons. Normal treasury management meant investing in instruments which, as far as the company was concerned, were cash equivalents, but which were not regarded as such for FRS 1 purposes. Cash flows related to these instruments had to be included under the investing activities heading. This resulted in a meaningless sub-total (struck after the investing activities heading) which purported to show the cash inflow or outflow before financing.

Dawson International dealt with this problem by splitting the investing activities section into two parts (long-term and other), thereby focusing attention on a sub-total showing the net cash flow before financing and deposits over three months maturity:

Extract 27.3: Dawson International PLC (1996)

CONSOLIDATED CASH FLOW STATEMENT
for the financial year ended 30 March 1996 [extract]

	1995/96 **£million**	1994/95 £million
Investing activities		
Investment in associated undertakings	(3.0)	(0.8)
Payment of deferred consideration for investment in subsidiary company	(0.3)	(0.3)
Acquisition of business	(0.1)	–
Disposals of businesses and subsidiary companies	27.6	–
Purchase of tangible fixed assets	(12.6)	(14.8)
Sale of tangible fixed assets	6.2	2.3
Net cash inflow/(outflow) from long term investing activities	17.8	(13.6)
Net cash inflow/(outflow) before financing and deposits over three months maturity	4.9	(14.5)
Decrease in deposits of over three months maturity	9.5	20.4
Net cash inflow from investing activities	27.3	6.8

The following extract from Marks and Spencer illustrates a different approach to solving essentially the same problem. Instead of showing non-cash equivalent deposits and short-term investments under investing activities, the company changed the next section to 'Financing and treasury activities' which allowed their inclusion under that heading. The sub-total showing the cash inflow before financing required by FRS 1 was accordingly changed to 'net cash (outflow)/inflow before financing and treasury activities'. It was therefore possible to exclude the movement in short-term funds (£109.1m in 1996 and £140.6m in 1995) from the sub-total required by FRS 1:

Extract 27.4: Marks and Spencer p.l.c. (1996)

Consolidated cash flow statement

FOR THE YEAR ENDED 31 MARCH 1996 [extract]

	1996	1995
	£m	£m
NET CASH (OUTFLOW)/INFLOW BEFORE FINANCING AND TREASURY ACTIVITIES	(29.0)	19.7
FINANCING AND TREASURY ACTIVITIES		
Shares issued under employees' share schemes	36.2	32.0
Redemption of cumulative preference shares	–	(1.4)
Repayment of long-term borrowing	–	(15.0)
Increase in non-cash equivalent bank loans and overdrafts	96.2	16.8
Increase in non-cash equivalent deposits and short-term investments	(109.1)	(140.6)
Net cash inflow/(outflow) from financing and treasury activities	23.3	(108.2)

Not surprisingly, dissatisfaction with the arbitrary cut-off in the definition of 'cash equivalents' featured prominently in the replies to the ASB's call for comments on FRS 1. Other matters raised by respondents included the exemptions from the scope of the standard; when net presentation of cash flows was appropriate; the implications of the changes to the profit and loss account brought about by FRS 3 and the need generally for further guidance on the classification of cash flows under the standard headings; the treatment of intragroup cash flows involving foreign currency; the presentation of cash flows resulting from hedging transactions and the treatment of cash subject to restriction.[29]

1.7   FRS 1 (Revised 1996)

The revised version of FRS 1 was published in October 1996, more than two years after the ASB's call for comments on the functioning of the existing standard. The ASB had warned that any changes were unlikely to come into effect before 1995. In the event, the process took longer than envisaged and FRED 10, the exposure draft of the revised standard, was published only in December 1995. The revised standard became mandatory for accounting periods ending on or after 23 March 1997. Earlier adoption was encouraged and this chapter contains several extracts from companies who elected to implement the new standard in their 1996 accounts.

2 THE REQUIREMENTS OF FRS 1 (REVISED 1996)

2.1 Scope and exemptions

Like its predecessor, the revised FRS 1 applies to accounts intended to give a true and fair view of the reporting entity's financial position and profit or loss (or income and expenditure). Although the relevance of a statement of cash flows to the truth and fairness of the financial position or the profit or loss for the period has never been entirely clear, the press release which accompanied the original FRS 1 stressed that the cash flow statement formed 'an essential element of the information required for accounts to give a true and fair view of the state of affairs of [large] companies at the end of the financial year, and of the profit or loss for the year. Accordingly, non-compliance with the standard may be a matter to be taken into account by the Financial Reporting Review Panel or the court in any consideration of whether or not accounts comply with the Companies Act.'[30] The Auditing Practices Board seems to have adopted a similar line of reasoning because their example of a qualified audit report in circumstances where a cash flow statement has been omitted explains that 'information about the company's cash flows is necessary for a proper understanding of the company's state of affairs and profit [loss].'[31]

The importance of cash flow information to the truth and fairness of the accounts aside, the revised standard exempts certain entities from the requirement to prepare a cash flow statement:[32]

(a) *Subsidiary undertakings where 90% or more of the voting rights are controlled within the group, provided that group accounts which include the subsidiary are publicly available*

This represents a significant relaxation of the tightly drawn exemption in the original standard. The latter was effectively confined to wholly owned subsidiaries of UK parents. The new exemption applies regardless of the country of incorporation of the parent or whether that entity prepares a group cash flow statement. The choice of a 90% threshold would seem to be a pragmatic compromise designed to deal with subsidiaries with small amounts of voting preference shares, or small numbers of shares held by employees.

The exemption would appear to be based on a similar one in FRS 8 (see chapter 28, section 2.3.5 C). Neither FRS gives any guidance as to what is meant by 'publicly available'. The rationale behind this stipulation is a little puzzling since there is no requirement for the publicly available group accounts to contain a cash flow statement, or for that matter to be in English.

The reason given by the ASB for exempting subsidiaries where 90% of the votes are held by the group is that the solvency, liquidity and financial adaptability of these entities will essentially depend on the group rather than their own cash flows.[33]

Because the exemption applies to subsidiaries where 90% or more of the votes are *held by the group*, the effective interest held by the parent company is irrelevant, as illustrated below:

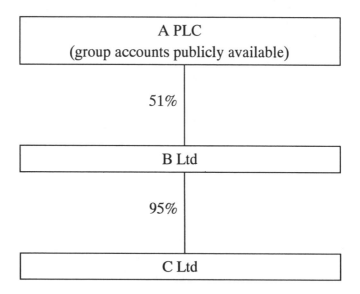

C Ltd is entitled to the exemption regardless of whether B Ltd prepares group accounts because more than 90% of C Ltd's voting rights are controlled within the group (comprising itself, B Ltd and A PLC).

(b)   *Mutual life assurance companies*

The ASB is of the view that insurance companies should include the cash flows of their long-term business only to the extent of cash transferred and available to meet the obligations of the company or group as a whole.[34] This is because the shareholders of an insurance company generally have restricted rights to the profits and associated cash surpluses made by their long-term business. Mutual life assurance companies, which are owned by policy holders, are accordingly exempt from the requirements of the FRS.

(c)   *Pension funds*

The original FRS 1 did not contain an exemption for pension funds. The revised standard formally ratifies the practice of not preparing cash flow statements on the basis that they add little information to that already available from the rest of the accounts.

(d) *Open-ended investment funds substantially all of whose investments are highly liquid and carried at market value, on condition that a statement of changes in net assets is provided*

This is a new exemption, similar to that for pension funds, which recognises that a cash flow statement would be of limited additional use. The definition of an 'investment fund' in the standard is based on that used in companies legislation, but with the notable exception that there is no restriction on the distribution of capital profits.[35]

(e) *Building societies that prepare a statement of source and application of funds in a prescribed format as required by law*

The revised standard retains the existing exemption for building societies despite the ASB's belief that the similarity and competition between banks and building societies is such that both should prepare cash flow statements.[36] The exemption for building societies will end should there be a change in the legislation which requires source and application of funds statements to be prepared. The exemption will not be available in any case after two years from the effective date of the revised FRS. By then, the ASB hopes to have developed a consensus on cash flow statements and related aspects of financial reporting for banks and building societies.[37]

(f) *Small (but not medium-sized) companies entitled to the filing exemptions under sections 246 and 247 of the Companies Act 1985*

As at July 1997, these are, broadly speaking, companies which satisfy two of the following criteria:

- turnover not more than £2.8 million;
- balance sheet total not more than £1.4 million; and
- not more than 50 employees.

PLCs, banks, insurance companies and companies authorised under the Financial Services Act 1986 do not qualify for the exemption, nor do members of a group which contains any of these entities.

The revised standard is silent on the reasons for this exemption It says simply that the exemption will be re-examined as part of the wider examination of the reporting requirements for small entities which is currently in progress.[38]

(g) *Small entities which would have qualified under the previous category had they been companies*

This exemption is a natural consequence of the exemption for small companies.

2.2   The definition of cash

Since the objective of a cash flow statement is to provide an analysis of the reporting entity's inflows and outflows of cash, the definition of cash is crucial to its presentation. The revised standard contains the following definition of 'cash':[39]

Cash – Cash in hand and deposits repayable on demand with any qualifying financial institution, less overdrafts from any qualifying financial institution repayable on demand. Deposits are repayable on demand if they can be withdrawn at any time without notice and without penalty or if a maturity or period of notice of not more than 24 hours or one working day has been agreed. Cash includes cash in hand and deposits denominated in foreign currencies.

Overdrafts ('a borrowing facility repayable on demand that is used by drawing on a current account with a qualifying financial institution')[40] are often a source of finance that extends for a significant period of time. Nevertheless, the revised standard is clear that they should be treated as negative cash balances. Pragmatically, this is the only possible treatment, since otherwise all cheques written on an overdrawn account would have to be shown under the financing heading of the cash flow statement as new borrowings and all payments in to the account would have to be separately shown as repayments of borrowings.

It has been argued that certain deposits with notice or maturity periods in excess of 24 hours should be treated as cash. This is because these funds will often be available on demand albeit that interest is then recalculated as if the deposit were a current account. The revised standard makes it clear that deposits qualify as cash only if the money is available within 24 hours *without penalty*.

The more restrictive definition of cash is the most important change made to the original standard, where the focus was on inflows and outflows of cash and cash equivalents. The adoption of a pure cash approach avoids an arbitrary cut-off point in the definition of cash equivalents and provides information about an entity's treasury activities that was previously unavailable.

It is evident from the new definition of cash that the amount shown alongside 'cash at bank and in hand' in the balance sheet will rarely be a reliable guide to 'cash' for FRS 1 purposes. Apart from the need to include overdrafts for cash flow purposes, the balance sheet caption will often include bank deposits with notice or maturity periods in excess of 24 hours. Because the standard requires the amount of cash and other components of net debt to be traced back to the equivalent captions in the balance sheet,[41] any difference between 'cash' for FRS 1 purposes and 'cash' for balance sheet purposes will be evident from this note, as illustrated in the following extract:

Extract 27.5: The Burton Group plc (1996)

Notes to the accounts

---

25 Cash flow [extract]

	Cash at bank and in hand £m	Funding debt due within one year £m	Funding debt due after one year £m	Net debt £m
b Analysis of net debt				
At 3rd September 1995	249.1	(21.1)	(245.1)	(17.1)
Increase/(decrease) in cash	35.7	(31.0)	–	4.7
Decrease/(increase) in debt	–	12.5	(9.9)	2.6
Movement in short term cash deposits with banks	(85.1)	–	–	(85.1)
Finance leases of Innovations Group	–	(0.1)	(0.6)	(0.7)
Non-cash movements in net debt	–	–	(11.1)	(11.1)
Change in maturity of prior year debt	–	(102.2)	102.2	–
At 31st August 1996	**199.7**	**(141.9)**	**(164.5)**	**(106.7)**

Although cash at bank and in hand per the balance sheet declined from £249.1m to £199.7m during the year, £85.1m of this movement was attributable to short-term deposits. The increase in cash for FRS 1 purposes was therefore £35.7m (before including the increase in bank overdrafts of £31.0m). The apparent anomaly between cash for balance sheet purposes ('cash at bank and in hand') and cash for FRS 1 purposes was explained in a separate note to the 1996 accounts as follows:

Extract 27.6: The Burton Group plc (1996)

Notes to the accounts

---

13 Cash at bank and in hand [extract]
Cash at bank and in hand includes short term cash deposits with banks. Of the Group's cash, these amounted to £138.4 million (1995 – £223.5 million).

The tight definition of cash in the revised standard produces greater visibility of cash flows previously shown net as part of the overall movement in cash and cash equivalents. For example, borrowing on an overdraft to purchase an investment defined as a cash equivalent which is later realised for cash would previously not have been reflected in the cash flow statement. Under the revised standard, however, movements in term deposits and other highly liquid investments which were within three months of maturity when acquired are now required to appear under the management of liquid resources heading (see section 2.4.8 below). Advances from banks (other than overdrafts) repayable within three months from the date of the advance are moved to the financing heading.

2.3　Format of the cash flow statement

The format of the cash flow statement continues to be tightly prescribed. Cash flows are required to be presented under a series of standard headings:[42]

- operating activities;

- returns on investments and servicing of finance;

- taxation;

- capital expenditure and financial investment;

- acquisitions and disposals;

- equity dividends paid;

- management of liquid resources; and

- financing.

The first six headings (but not necessarily the last two – see Extract 27.7 below) should follow the sequence shown above.[43]　Cash flows relating to the management of liquid resources and financing can be combined under a single heading provided that the cash flows relating to each are shown separately and that separate sub-totals are given.[44]

The dispensation in the original standard, to devise an appropriate alternative in the 'extremely rare circumstances' where the standard headings would not fairly portray the activities of the reporting entity, has been deleted.

The following extract, taken from the 1996 accounts of BP, illustrates the new format. Of particular interest is that the statement does not focus on the net decrease or increase in cash. Instead, the last three headings have been combined to produce a sub-total which equates to the 'net cash inflow' for the year. In amending the standard, the ASB considered prescribing a format that results in the increase or decrease in cash being shown as the residual amount. This approach had a number of supporters but they did not want it to be mandatory. Preparers have accordingly been allowed to choose the format of their cash flow statements 'provided that these comply with the requirements for classification and order'.[45]

Extract 27.7: The British Petroleum Company p.l.c. (1996)

Group cash flow statement [extract]

	£ million	
For the year ended 31 December	**1996**	1995
Net cash inflow from operating activities	**4,992**	5,095
Servicing of finance and returns on investments		
Interest received	**91**	94
Interest paid	**(477)**	(495)
Dividends received	**15**	16
Net cash outflow from servicing of finance and returns on investments	**(371)**	(385)
Taxation		
UK corporation tax	**(278)**	(198)
Overseas tax	**(671)**	(116)
Tax paid	**(949)**	(314)
Capital expenditure		
Payments for fixed assets	**(3,114)**	(2,646)
Proceeds from the sale of fixed assets	**319**	202
Net cash outflow for capital expenditure	**(2,795)**	(2,444)
Acquisitions and disposals		
Investments in associated undertakings	**(126)**	(171)
Proceeds from the sale of businesses	**283**	215
Net cash inflow for acquisitions and disposals	**157**	44
Equity dividends paid	**(720)**	(525)
Net cash inflow	**314**	1,471
Financing	**557**	1,264
Management of liquid resources	**(45)**	43
(Decrease) increase in cash	**(198)**	164
	314	1,471

Within each standard heading, the FRS identifies certain individual categories of cash inflows and outflows which are to be separately identified, where they are material. This can be done either on the face of the statement or in a note.[46] In the above extract, the former option has been used for the returns on investments and servicing of finance, taxation, capital expenditure and acquisitions and disposals headings. The individual cash flows under the financing and management of liquid resources headings appear in a separate note to the accounts:

Extract 27.8: The British Petroleum Company p.l.c. (1996)

33 Group cash flow statement analysis [extract]

	£ million	
(c) **Financing**	**1996**	1995
Long-term borrowing	**(23)**	(27)
Repayments of long-term borrowing	**1,278**	906
Short-term borrowing	**(846)**	(189)
Repayments of short-term borrowing	**182**	616
	591	1,306
Issue of ordinary share capital	**(34)**	(42)
Net cash outflow	**557**	1,264

	£ million	
(d) **Management of liquid resources**	**1996**	1995
Purchases	**209**	178
Sales	**(254)**	(135)
Net cash (inflow) outflow	**(45)**	43

Regardless of whether the individual categories of inflows and outflows under the standard headings are shown on the face of the statement or in a note, they must be shown gross. This rule does not apply to cash flows relating to operating activities and certain cash flows under the management of liquid resources and financing headings.[47]   To qualify for net presentation, the cash flows within management of liquid resources and financing must *either*:

- be related in substance to a single financing transaction as defined by FRS 4 (one where the debt and the facility are under a single agreement with the same lender, the finance costs for the new debt are not significantly higher than the existing debt, the obligations of the lender are firm and the lender is expected to be able to fulfil its obligations);[48] *or*

- be due to short maturities and high turnover occurring from rollover or reissue.[49]

The following extract is an example of net presentation of cash inflows and outflows using the second dispensation described above:

Extract 27.9: The British Petroleum Company p.l.c. (1996)

33 Group cash flow statement analysis [extract]

(e) Commercial paper
Net movements in commercial paper are included within short-term borrowings or repayment of short-term borrowings as appropriate.

The cash flows arising under a commercial paper programme do not qualify as a single financing transaction as defined in FRS 4. This is because the debt and the back-up facility are not under a single agreement with the same lender. Under the old FRS 1, the related cash flows were strictly required to be shown gross under the financing heading. The revised standard effectively sanctions the widespread practice of showing only the net inflow or outflow during the period on the basis that the cash flows 'are due to short maturities and high turnover arising from rollover or reissue'.[50]

By contrast, many cash flows under the management of liquid resources heading will not automatically qualify to be shown net. The placing of surplus cash on short-term deposit from time to time followed by the subsequent withdrawal of these funds gives rise to two gross cash flows, one out and the other in. These cash flows do not qualify for net presentation because there is no rollover or reissue. As illustrated in Extract 27.8 above, BP shows both the purchase and sale of liquid resources under the management of liquid resources heading. This presentation can be contrasted with the following extract taken from the 1996 accounts of The Burton Group:

Extract 27.10: The Burton Group plc (1996)

Cash flow statement [extract]

	1996	1995
FOR THE FINANCIAL YEAR ENDED 31ST AUGUST 1996	**£m**	£m
Management of liquid resources		
Movement in short term deposits with banks	**85.1**	(58.8)

Extract 27.6 above reveals that short-term deposits included in the cash at bank and in hand total in Burton's balance sheet declined from £223.5m to £138.4m during 1996. Readers of Burton's accounts might conclude from the presentation in the cash flow statement that no new funds were placed on deposit during 1996 or (probably more realistically) that disclosure of the gross outflows and inflows arising from the investment and withdrawal of surplus cash would not have provided any useful additional information. In many instances it will not be possible to extract this information from the books and records without expending considerable time and effort.

2.4   Classification of cash flows by standard heading

2.4.1   *General principle*

The revised standard requires each cash flow to be classified according to the substance of the transaction or event giving rise to it.[51]   Because the other primary statements are based on accounting standards which, in theory, use the same substance principle, the end result should be consistent treatment across all the primary statements. In essence, this means that capitalised development costs should appear under capital expenditure and financial investment. Finance lease rentals should be split into their interest and capital elements, with the former appearing under returns on investments and servicing of finance and the latter under financing. Operating lease rentals should appear under operating activities. Classification in the cash flow statement effectively becomes a function of the accounting policies adopted by the reporting entity. Some might regard this as counterintuitive, but it is designed to achieve the ASB's objective of consistent treatment in all the primary statements.

Whether consistent treatment is achievable in practice, however, remains to be seen. The following extract highlights a potential problem with the 'substance principle':

Extract 27.11: Anglian Water Plc (1997)

Group Cash Flow Statement
For the year ended 31 March [extract]

	1997 £m	1996 £m
Capital expenditure and financial investment		
Purchase of tangible fixed assets	(322.3)	(246.3)
Investment in infrastructure renewals	(32.4)	(20.9)
Grants and contributions received	21.8	22.8
Disposal of tangible fixed assets	3.3	4.5
Purchase of own shares for Long Term Incentive Plan	(0.4)	–
	(330.0)	(239.9)

Anglian Water's 1997 profit and loss account includes a charge of £17.7m for infrastructure renewals, shown as part of operating costs for the year. This amount is added back in arriving at the cash inflow from operating activities with the related cash outflow of £32.4m being shown under capital expenditure and financial investment (see above). Although treatment of this item as an operating cost in the profit and loss account would suggest that the underlying transaction was of an operating nature, the company presumably felt that its substance was of an investing nature (which justified its inclusion under capital expenditure and financial investment). By contrast, several other water companies appear to have arrived at a different conclusion since their cash outflows related to infrastructure renewals would seem to be included under operating activities.[52]

2.4.2 *Operating activities*

Somewhat tentatively, the revised standard explains that cash flows from operating activities are *in general* those related to operating or trading activities, *normally* shown in the profit and loss account in arriving at operating profit.[53]

'Operating or trading activities' are not defined which leaves the definition dangerously close to being circular: operating cash flows are operating cash flows. However, the revised standard does contain some examples of operating or trading activities (receipts from customers, payments to suppliers and payments to employees, including redundancy) which should mitigate the problem.[54]

A particular issue concerns the presentation of cash flows related to the (sometimes fundamental) reorganisation and restructuring of businesses, both existing and acquired. Inclusion of these cash flows under operating activities is illustrated below:

Extract 27.12: The Greenalls Group plc (1996)

Consolidated Cash Flow Statement
for the year ended 27th September 1996 [extract]

	1996	1995
	£000	£000
NET CASH INFLOW FROM OPERATING ACTIVITIES	**227,761**	156,569
Net cash outflow in respect of reorganisation and restructuring costs:		
Boddington	**(22,195)**	–
Other	**(2,887)**	(1,803)
	202,679	154,766

In contrast to the presentation shown above, it was not uncommon to find cash flows related to certain reorganisation costs under investing activities. In an attempt to standardise practice in this area, the revised standard states that 'operating item cash outflows relating to provisions' should appear under operating activities *regardless* of whether the provision was deducted in arriving at operating profit.[55] As examples of such cash flows, the standard[56] cites operating item cash flows provided for on an acquisition and redundancy payments provided for on the termination of an operation or for a fundamental reorganisation or restructuring, the last two under paragraphs 20a and 20b of FRS 3.[57]

Whether the cash flows related to these provisions appear under operating activities as envisaged by the ASB will depend on a consistent interpretation of 'operating or trading activities'. FRED 10 boldly asserted that reorganisation costs were 'essentially operating in nature' but this has not been repeated in the revised standard.[58]

In Cadbury Schweppes' profit and loss accounts for 1995 and 1996, the cost of restructuring acquired subsidiaries is charged in arriving at operating profit. However, in preparing the 1996 cash flow statement under the revised standard, the company was presumably of the view that the related cash outflows were not related to operating items:

Extract 27.13: Cadbury Schweppes p.l.c. (1996)

Group Cash Flow Statement
for the 52 weeks ended 28 December 1996 [extract]

	1996 £m	1995 £m
Acquisitions and disposals		
Acquisition of businesses	(135)	(1,173)
Expenditure on post-acquisition restructuring	(18)	(26)
Proceeds from sale of investments in subsidiary undertakings	–	26

The revised standard continues to allow a choice between the direct and indirect methods of presenting operating cash flows. The direct method is essentially based on an analysis of the cash book. It shows operating cash receipts and payments, including cash receipts from customers, cash payments to suppliers and cash payments to and on behalf of employees which, when added to the other operating cash payments, aggregate to the net cash flow from operating activities.

A   *The indirect method*

The indirect method arrives at the same net cash flow from operating activities, but does so by working back from operating profit in the form of a reconciliation.

To obtain the cash flow information, the balance sheet figures have to be analysed according to the various standard headings in the cash flow statement. Thus the reconciliation of operating profit to cash flow from operating activities will include, not the increase or decrease in all debtors or creditors, but only those elements which relate to operating activities. Accordingly, accrued interest or amounts payable in respect of the acquisition of fixed assets or investments will be excluded from the movement in creditors included in this reconciliation. Although this may not present practical difficulties in the preparation of single company cash flow statements, it is necessary to ensure that sufficient information is collected from subsidiaries for purposes of preparing the group cash flow statement. Where a group has made an acquisition of a subsidiary during the year, the change in working capital has to be split between the increase due to the acquisition (which will be shown under acquisitions and disposals to the extent that the purchase consideration is settled in cash) and the element related to operating activities which will appear in the operating profit reconciliation. An example of the reconciliation which forms the basis of the indirect method is contained in the following extract:

Extract 27.14: United News & Media plc (1996)

26. Reconciliation of operating profit to cash inflow from operating activities [extract]

	Continuing 1996 £m	Discontinued 1996 £m	Total 1996 £m
Operating profit	118.0	11.1	129.1
Depreciation charges	54.7	1.7	56.4
Share of associated losses less dividends	44.9	–	44.9
Profit on sale of tangible fixed assets	(2.5)	–	(2.5)
Payments against provisions	(9.9)	–	(9.9)
Decrease in stocks	1.2	1.0	2.2
(Increase) in debtors	(13.0)	(1.8)	(14.8)
(Decrease) increase in creditors	(26.5)	7.2	(19.3)
Increase in Wagon loan portfolio	–	(34.7)	(34.7)
Other non-cash items including movements on provisions	88.9	–	88.9
Cash inflow (outflow) from operating activities	**255.8**	**(15.5)**	**240.3**

United News & Media has analysed the cash inflow from operating activities between continuing and discontinued operations. Reporting entities are encouraged, but not required, to disclose additional information like this.[59] Other suggestions put forward by the ASB include the provision of segmental information[60] and the division of cash flows in a way that highlights different degrees of access to the underlying cash balances which might be of special relevance to regulated industries like insurance.[61]

The reconciliation of operating profit to cash inflow from operating activities in the extract above also illustrates the requirement to disclose separately the movements in stocks, debtors and creditors related to operating activities and other differences between cash flows and profits.[62] The reconciliation also includes an adjustment for the difference between the share of associates' losses and dividends received. This is a new requirement which stems from the rule that dividends received from associates should be included as part of the cash inflow from operating activities where the group's share of their profits or losses is included as part of operating profit.[63] The resulting adjustment to operating profit should also be shown separately in the reconciliation.[64]

The revised standard allows the reconciliation of operating profit to cash inflow from operating activities either to adjoin the cash flow statement itself (provided it is clearly labelled), or to appear in a note.[65]   Two of the four illustrative examples in Appendix I to the standard show the cash flow statement wedged in between two reconciliations – one to operating profit and the other to net debt (or its equivalent). To comply with the labelling requirement, the heading 'Cash Flow Statement' has to be duplicated – an untidy outcome.

B   The direct method

The ASB encourages disclosure of the information provided by the direct method where it is not too costly to obtain.[66]   However, the information provided by the indirect method is required even where the direct method has been adopted[67] so there is little incentive to adopt the direct method. This, coupled with the additional clerical burden involved in collecting and analysing the underlying cash transactions, means that it is rarely used in practice. It is, however, not uncommon to find the direct method used by property companies, possibly because the nature of their business is such that the information systems collect the information in any event:

Extract 27.15: Greycoat PLC (1997)

22. Notes to the cash flow statement [extract]
Analysis of cash flows for headings netted in the cash flow statement

	1997 £m	1996 £m
Operating activities		
Net rental income	**28.3**	33.7
Fee income	**0.4**	0.3
Administration and other expenses including reorganisation costs	**(3.1)**	(3.6)
Exceptional items	**(0.5)**	–
Cash flow from operating activities	**25.1**	30.4

Reconciliation of operating profit to net inflow from operating activities

	1997 £m	1996 £m
Operating profit	**29.1**	31.9
Associated undertakings' profits	**(0.8)**	(0.5)
Depreciation charge	**0.1**	0.1
Increase in debtors	**(1.5)**	(0.3)
Decrease in creditors	**(1.8)**	(0.8)
Net cash inflow from operating activities	**25.1**	30.4

There are similar provisions in the US regarding the use of the direct and indirect methods of reporting the cash flow from operating activities. However, as in the UK, the reconciliation between operating profit and the cash flow from operating activities must be provided when the direct method is used.

2.4.3 Returns on investments and servicing of finance

Returns on investments and servicing of finance are receipts resulting from the ownership of an investment and payments to providers of finance, non-equity shareholders and minority interests, excluding those items which are specifically required by the standard to be classified under another heading.[68] The extract below illustrates many of the items which are required to be separately disclosed under this heading.[69] In addition, dividends paid on preference and other non-equity shares should also be separately disclosed under this heading. However, dividends relating to equity shares (as defined in FRS 4) are required to appear under their own heading lower down the statement (see section 2.4.7 below).

As noted at 2.4.2 above, dividends received from associates will form part of operating activities if the equity accounted results are included as part of operating profit. In the profit and loss account of the Daily Mail and General Trust, the share of associates' profits and losses is disclosed after operating profit and the related dividends received are therefore included as part of returns on investments and servicing of finance:

Extract 27.16: Daily Mail and General Trust plc (1996)

Group Cash Flow Statement [extract]
for the year ended 29th September, 1996

	1996 £m	1995 £m
Returns on investments and servicing of finance		
Interest received	**7.7**	7.3
Interest paid	**(23.9)**	(18.7)
Interest element of finance lease rental payments	**(1.5)**	(1.3)
Issue costs of Eurobond	**(1.3)**	(0.8)
Dividends received from associated undertakings	**7.2**	4.7
Dividends received from other investments	**5.4**	3.1
Dividends paid to minority shareholders	**(3.8)**	(3.7)
	(10.2)	(9.4)

Because the revised standard requires cash flows that are treated as finance costs under FRS 4 to be shown under returns on investments and servicing of finance,[70] debt and non-equity share issue costs will now appear under this heading, as shown in the above extract. The gross proceeds received by the Daily Mail and General Trust on the issue of the Eurobonds is shown under financing. Under the old standard, the net proceeds received (after deducting issue costs) would have appeared under financing. The new rule also has implications for the redemption of deep discount bonds. Under the original standard, the amount paid on redemption was usually shown under financing. It will now be necessary to separate interest and principal, with the former being shown under returns on investments and servicing of finance and the latter under financing.

Although the cash flows to be included under the returns on investments and servicing of finance heading are essentially interest and dividends received and paid, there are some complications in the identification of the relevant amounts. With respect to interest, deduction of tax at source means that amounts received may be net of tax. The amount of cash actually received should be shown as a cash inflow but if any tax withheld is subsequently recovered, this should also be included as part of interest received. Similarly, where tax is withheld when interest is paid, the interest actually paid should be included as a cash outflow together with the tax paid to the relevant tax authority.

Dividends received should be disclosed net of any associated tax credit, i.e. the amount of cash actually received. Utilisation of the tax credit in a reduction of the ACT to be paid over to the tax authorities, however, is not treated as an inflow under this heading. This might be regarded as inconsistent with the treatment of tax associated with interest received, but reflects the differing ways in which the tax credit is recovered. Dividends paid are to be shown at the net amount of the cash paid, i.e. excluding any tax credit.

In a departure from the general principle outlined under 2.4.1 above, the revised standard requires all interest paid (even if capitalised) to appear under this heading. This is because the Board wants the cash flow statement to 'give a complete picture' of the interest cash flows.[71] This is a difference in treatment between SFAS 95 and FRS 1. Under SFAS 95 the payment of capitalised interest is reported as part of the cost of the asset, and therefore as part of investing activities. The approach adopted by SFAS 95 presumably reflects the philosophy that interest is an intrinsic part of the historical cost of an asset.

2.4.4   Taxation

Cash flows included under the taxation heading are those to or from taxation authorities in respect of the reporting entity's revenue and capital profits.[72] This approach is different to the treatment adopted in the US under SFAS 95, where taxation cash flows are included as part of the cash flows from operating activities.

Cash flows in respect of VAT, other sales taxes, property taxes and any other taxes not assessed on the profits of the reporting entity should not be included here. Payments of ACT and purchases of certificates of tax deposit, however, are appropriately included under this heading since they relate to tax on profits rather than to other taxes.

Cash flows associated with VAT and other sales taxes should normally be dealt with as a single net cash flow in the operating activities section of the statement. Thus, all cash flows should be shown net of any attributable VAT or other sales tax. Although the actual cash flows will include VAT where appropriate, the taxation element has only a short-term effect on the entity's overall cash position.

Although the practice of collapsing sales tax flows into a net payment to or from the tax authorities is the one which should usually be adopted, a different treatment may be applied if it is more appropriate. In particular, where VAT or other sales tax paid by a business is irrecoverable, cash flows should include the associated tax. If this is impracticable, the irrecoverable tax should be included under the most appropriate standard heading. This will be the case for businesses which are exempt or partially exempt, for example charities.

The extract below illustrates the items which will commonly be disclosed under the taxation heading:

Extract 27.17: United News & Media plc (1996)

Group cash flow statement
for the year ended 31 December 1996 [extract]

	1996 £m	1995 £m
Tax		
UK corporation tax paid (including ACT)	**(40.9)**	(43.8)
Overseas tax paid	**(47.3)**	(33.8)
Tax paid	**(88.2)**	(77.6)

The revised standard includes guidance on cash flows relating to group relief. These should be included under 'taxation' even though they are not paid to a taxation authority.

2.4.5 Capital expenditure and financial investment

The revised FRS 1 splits the former investing activities heading into two new captions: 'capital expenditure and financial investment' and 'acquisitions and disposals'. At first glance, this would seem to be little more than tinkering since it adds no new information nor does it result in a meaningful sub-total being given. The change has its origin in what might be described as the ASB's pursuit of the 'free cash flow' Holy Grail. When the new eight-heading format for the cash flow statement was first introduced, FRED 10 raised the possibility of striking a sub-total after capital expenditure but before acquisitions and disposals.[73] Responses to the exposure draft persuaded the ASB to abandon this proposal. The explanation given in Appendix III to the new FRS was that 'there were several interpretations of the exact composition of "free cash flows" – indeed the commentators themselves suggested several different definitions – but a key issue was to distinguish cash flows for investing to maintain the business from cash flows for investing to expand the business'.[74] One company that regularly makes such a distinction is Whitbread, as revealed in the following extract:

Extract 27.18: Whitbread PLC (1997)

Operating and Finance Review

Cash flow [extract]

The planned expansion programme resulted in a net cash outflow before use of liquid resources and financing of £286 million.

In order to assess the underlying cash flow of the group, it is necessary to adjust this figure for the acquisition and disposal of businesses and non-trade investments (outflow of £183 million) and the investment in new retail outlets (outflow of £221 million included within 'property and plant purchased'). These adjustments reveal an underlying cash inflow of £118 million.

Although Whitbread has identified £221m of the cash outflow for property and plant purchased as being in respect of investment to expand the business, the ASB felt it was not feasible for an accounting standard 'to set out how to distinguish expenditure for expansion from expenditure for maintenance'.[75] This was the same conclusion the Board reached in 1991 when it commented that 'criteria for distinguishing expenditure to expand the level of operations would vary from reporting entity to reporting entity and would distort the comparability provided by the standard headings. Similar problems arise in analysing changes in working capital'.[76]

Despite having reverted to its 1991 position, the Board nevertheless decided that cash flows relating to capital expenditure should be shown separately from acquisitions and disposals. The reason for this is hard to fathom, given the Board's warning that 'this distinction should not be interpreted as reflecting on the one hand maintenance expenditure and on the other expenditure for expansion because these may both fall under either heading depending on the circumstances'.[77]

Although the sub-total (after capital expenditure and financial investment) proposed in FRED 10 was not incorporated into the revised standard, there is nothing to prevent companies from including it (or indeed any other sub-total) in their cash flow statements as illustrated in the following extract taken from the 1996 accounts of Guinness:

Extract 27.19: Guinness PLC (1996)

Group cash flow statement

For the year ended 31 December 1996 [extract]	1996 £m	1995 £m
Cash flow from operating activities	**1,020**	989
Interest received	25	33
Interest paid	(178)	(153)
Dividends paid to minority shareholders in subsidiary undertakings	(34)	(22)
Returns on investments and servicing of finance	**(187)**	**(142)**
United Kingdom corporation tax paid	(194)	(127)
Overseas tax paid	(61)	(81)
Taxation	**(255)**	**(208)**
Purchase of tangible fixed assets:		
Spirits	(58)	(56)
Brewing	(134)	(123)
Sale of tangible fixed assets	22	24
Capital expenditure and financial investment	**(170)**	**(155)**
Free cash flow before dividends	**408**	484

Under the revised standard, cash flows required to be included under capital expenditure and financial investment are those related to the acquisition or disposal of fixed assets (including investments).[78] In addition, any current asset investments that do not qualify as 'liquid resources' (see 2.4.8 below) will effectively default to this section. Cash flows related to the acquisition or disposal of investments in associates and joint ventures should be excluded because they are required to be shown under acquisitions and disposals.[79]

Capital expenditure and financial investment will usually include the following cash flows, which should be separately disclosed:

(a) receipts from sales of, and payments made to acquire, property, plant and equipment;

(b) receipts from the repayment of, and loans made to, other entities (other than payments forming part of an acquisition or disposal or a movement in liquid resources – see 2.4.6 and 2.4.8 below); and

(c) receipts from the sale of, and payments to acquire, debt instruments of other entities (other than payments forming part of an acquisition or disposal or a movement in liquid resources – see 2.4.6 and 2.4.8 below).

Where there are no cash flows relating to financial investment (i.e. those under (b) and (c) above), the heading of this section may be reduced to capital expenditure.[80]

The treatment of loans to associates (and the repayment thereof) is not entirely clear and has given rise to some inconsistency in practice, as illustrated in the following two extracts:

Extract 27.20: Blue Circle Industries PLC (1996)

Group Cash Flow Statement
Year ended 31 December 1996 [extract]

	1996 £m	1995 £m
Capital expenditure and financial investment		
Purchase of tangible fixed assets	**(153.0)**	(124.1)
Disposal of tangible fixed assets	**22.4**	20.8
Loan to related company	**(23.1)**	–
Loan repayments from related company	**0.7**	–
Net cash outflow from capital expenditure and financial investment	**(153.0)**	(103.3)

In 1996, a subsidiary of Blue Circle, Malayan Cement Berhad, provided a shareholder loan of £23.1m to its related company, Associated Pan Malaysia Cement Snd Bhd (50% owned).[81] As shown above this cash outflow was included under capital expenditure and financial investment in the group cash flow statement.

By contrast, United News & Media has included all investment in associates (both the acquisition of shares and the making of loans) under the acquisitions and disposals heading:

Extract 27.21: United News & Media plc (1996)

Group cash flow statement
for the year ended 31 December 1996 [extract]

	1996 £m	1995 £m
Acquisitions and disposals		
Payments to acquire subsidiary undertakings	**(554.2)**	(105.4)
(Investments) sales in associated undertakings	**(19.6)**	1.3
Receipts from sales of subsidiary undertakings	**252.3**	9.4
Net cash outflow from acquisitions and disposals	**(321.5)**	(94.7)

Uncertainty about the treatment of loans to associates stems from whether they constitute an 'investment in' the associate concerned or whether they are simply loans made to another entity. The latter clearly belong under the capital expenditure and financial investment heading.

The outflow shown in the cash flow statement in respect of the acquisition of property, plant or equipment is unlikely to be the same as 'additions' as reported in the fixed assets note. Whilst this is usually a function of movements in creditors relating to fixed assets and the inception of finance leases, it may also be due to exchange rate differences on foreign currency liabilities incurred on the purchase of fixed assets. The amount paid might be different to that used to record the increase in fixed assets, with the difference taken to the profit and loss account as an exchange gain or loss.

The purchase of fixed assets on credit is a complicated area because the associated cash flows may sometimes not be capital expenditure. In the US, SFAS 95 takes the line that only advance payments, the down payment or other amounts paid at or near to the time of purchase of fixed assets are investing cash flows.[82] This treatment also appears to be implicit in FRS 1. The most common example of this (although the payments are strictly not made to purchase the asset) is where a reporting entity makes payments in respect of assets obtained under a finance lease. In this case, the payments of principal are classified as financing rather than capital expenditure. The interest element of the lease payments would be shown under returns on investments and servicing of finance. The acquisition of assets under hire purchase contracts would be dealt with in a similar way. On the other hand, short-term differences between acquisition and payment should not be interpreted as changing the nature of the cash flow from capital expenditure to financing.

2.4.6 Acquisitions and disposals

Included under this heading are cash flows related to the acquisition or disposal of any trade or business, or of an investment in an entity that is or, as a result of the transaction, becomes or ceases to be either an associate, a joint venture or a subsidiary.[83]

The following extract is an example of the cash flows commonly found under this heading:

Extract 27.22: Carlton Communications Plc (1996)

Consolidated statement of cash flows
For the year ended 30 September 1996 [extract]

	1996 £m	1995 £m
Acquisitions and disposals		
Purchase of subsidiary undertakings	(63.7)	–
Cash less overdrafts acquired with subsidiaries	(1.8)	–
Sale of businesses	15.4	54.7
Investment in associates	(4.9)	(1.2)
	(55.0)	53.5

In addition to the payments made on the purchase of subsidiaries, the revised standard requires any balances of cash and overdrafts acquired to be shown separately.[84]   The same rule applies to any balances of cash and overdrafts transferred as part of the sale of subsidiaries.[85]

It is not entirely clear whether the separate disclosure of cash balances and overdrafts should be on the face of the cash flow statement or whether it could be relegated to a note. The illustrative example in the Appendix to the standard shows the net overdraft acquired as a separate line under the acquisitions and disposals heading.[86]   In the extract above, Carlton Communications adopted a similar approach by disclosing cash less overdrafts acquired on the face of the cash flow statement. Surprisingly, however, the company showed cash less overdrafts transferred as part of the sale of subsidiaries (and undisclosed transaction costs) not on the face of the statement but in note 29 to the accounts, as illustrated in the following extract:

Extract 27.23: Carlton Communications Plc (1996)

29. Sale of businesses [extract]

During the year the Group sold 16% of Independent Television News Limited and all of GIB Music and Distribution GmbH, Carlton Home Entertainment Sverige AB and the net trading assets of Carlton Home Entertainment Ireland Limited.

	1996 £m	1995 £m
Net assets disposed of		
Intangible and tangible fixed assets	1.3	12.8
Investment in associate	6.9	–
Net current assets	1.2	26.1
Deferred tax	–	(0.1)
Goodwill previously written off to reserves	6.6	22.9
	16.0	61.7
Loss on sale of businesses	(0.6)	(7.0)
	15.4	54.7
Satisfied by		
Cash consideration	16.9	56.8
Cash less overdrafts sold and transaction costs	(1.5)	(2.1)
	15.4	54.7

The treatment of the proceeds on disposal of an associated company (Independent Television News Limited in the above extract) should be contrasted with the sale of a trade investment. The latter should appear under capital expenditure and financial investment, as shown in the illustrative example in Appendix I to the revised standard.[87]

The repayment of loans previously made by the vendor of a newly acquired subsidiary is not specifically addressed in the revised standard. However, as the vendor will usually require repayment of these loans as a condition of the sale, the resulting cash outflow can probably be regarded as 'related to' the acquisition, thereby justifying its inclusion under acquisitions and disposals. By contrast, the post acquisition repayment of external debt acquired with the new subsidiary would fall to be included under the financing heading.

A similarly fine distinction might apply on the demerger of subsidiaries. These transactions often involve the repayment of substantial amounts of intra-group indebtedness out of external finance raised by the demerged subsidiary. If the money is raised immediately prior to the demerger, it is strictly a financing inflow in the parent company's consolidated cash flow statement. If raised and repaid after the demerger, there would be an argument for showing it under capital expenditure and financial investment, being the repayment of a loan to another entity. Alternatively, it could conceivably be shown under acquisitions and disposals, being a cash inflow 'related to' to an entity that has ceased to be a subsidiary undertaking. In ICI's eight year financial record, 'Zeneca debt repayment' (being a cash inflow of £1,364m in 1993 and £568m in 1994 related to the former subsidiary demerged in 1993) is highlighted as a separate item after 'Capital expenditure, acquisitions and disposals'.[88]

The principle discussed at 2.4.5 above regarding the acquisition of fixed assets on credit also applies to deferred consideration on the acquisition of a subsidiary. No cash flows arise at the time that the liability is set up. When the deferred consideration is ultimately paid, the resulting cash flow should arguably be shown under financing. However, practice under the old standard has been to include these payments under investing rather than financing.[89] The revised standard is silent on this point and they will probably now appear under acquisitions and disposals.

2.4.7 Equity dividends paid

Included under this heading are dividends paid on the reporting entity's equity shares (as defined in FRS 4).[90] As noted at 2.4.3 above, the amount shown should exclude any related tax credit.

The ASB originally intended to include all dividends, including those paid to preference and minority shareholders, under this heading.[91] However, the proposal in FRED 10 was amended in response to comments that non-equity dividends and those paid to minority shareholders should appear alongside interest paid.

2.4.8 Management of liquid resources

The introduction of this heading is an effective solution to the most common complaint about the usefulness of the old FRS 1: the three month cut-off in the definition of cash equivalents. In many instances, normal treasury management meant investing in instruments which, as far as the company was concerned, were cash equivalents, but which were not considered to be so for FRS 1 purposes. Cash flows related to these instruments were required to be included under the investing activities heading. By creating a new format heading, the ASB has effectively separated treasury management cash flows from the purchase and sale of fixed assets and new businesses. Although it might have been possible to solve the problem by adopting a more flexible definition for cash equivalents (similar to those in IAS 7 and SFAS 95 which are arguably more likely to include the instruments used by a typical treasury department) this would not have provided additional information about treasury activities.

Cash flows required to be classified under the management of liquid resources heading are those related to 'current asset investments held as readily disposable stores of value'.[92] The key to this definition is 'readily disposable', by which is meant that the investment 'is disposable by the reporting entity without curtailing or disrupting its business; and is *either*:

■ readily convertible into known amounts of cash at or close to its carrying amount, *or*

■ traded in an active market'.[93]

In the ASB's view, the first bullet point above would tend to exclude short-term deposits with a maturity of more than one year, measured from the date the deposit was made.[94] That aside, the definition deliberately allows the inclusion of a wide range of investments in order to recognise the different ways in which reporting entities manage their resources to ensure the availability of cash to carry on or expand the business. Reporting entities must explain their policy for determining liquid resources and any changes to it.[95]

Cash inflows from the management of liquid resources will include the following, which should be separately disclosed:

(a) withdrawals from short-term deposits not qualifying as cash; and

(b) inflows from the disposal or redemption of any other investments (such as government securities, loan stock, equities and derivatives) held as liquid resources.[96]

Cash outflows will include the following separately disclosable items:

(a) payments into short-term deposits not qualifying as cash; and

(b) outflows to acquire any other investments (such as government securities, loan stock, equities and derivatives) held as liquid resources.[97]

The following extract is an example of the cash flows required to be shown under this heading. It includes unlisted securities (which may not be readily convertible into known amounts of cash) which is a little unusual although the amounts involved are possibly not material:

> *Extract 27.24: Reuters Holdings PLC (1996)*
>
> **10. ANALYSIS OF CASH FLOWS FOR HEADINGS NETTED IN THE CASH FLOW STATEMENT**
> [extract]
>
> | | **1996** | 1995 | 1994 |
> |---|---|---|---|
> | **Management of liquid resources** | **£M** | £M | £M |
> | Increase in term deposits | **(6,110)** | (3,495) | (3,205) |
> | Decrease in term deposits | **5,982** | 3,304 | 3,329 |
> | Purchase of certificates of deposit | **(433)** | (380) | (197) |
> | Sale of certificates of deposit | **432** | 240 | 124 |
> | Purchase of listed/unlisted securities | **(74)** | (89) | (76) |
> | Sale of listed/unlisted securities | **31** | 68 | 54 |
> | | **(172)** | (352) | 29 |

As discussed in section 2.3 above, net presentation is allowed under this heading where the cash inflows and outflows are due to short maturities and high turnover occurring from rollover or reissue. However, the placing of surplus cash on term deposit followed by the subsequent withdrawal of these funds gives rise to two cash flows, one out and the other in. These gross cash flows do not qualify for net presentation because there is no rollover or reissue, as illustrated in the above extract. Term deposits shown in the consolidated balance sheet of Reuters Holdings increased from £517m to £633m during 1996.[98]

2.4.9 Financing

Financing cash flows are receipts from, and repayments to, external providers of finance.[99] However, as discussed at 2.4.3 above, only cash flows relating to *principal* amounts of finance are dealt with here, since cash flows relating to the servicing of finance are dealt with under returns on investments and servicing of finance.

Financing cash flows include the following separately disclosable items:

(a) receipts from the issue of shares and other equity instruments;

(b) receipts from the issue of debentures, loans, notes and bonds and from other long-term and short-term borrowing (other than overdrafts);

(c) repayments of amounts borrowed (other than overdrafts);

(d) the capital element of finance lease rental repayments;

(e) payments to reacquire or redeem the entity's shares; and

(f) payments of expenses or commissions on any issue of equity shares.[100]

In addition, any financing cash flows received from or paid to equity accounted entities should be disclosed separately.[101]

The following extract illustrates the items likely to be found under this heading:

Extract 27.25: Cable and Wireless plc (1997)

Consolidated cash flow statement

for the year ended 31 March [extract]	1997 £m	1996 £m
Financing		
Issue of ordinary share capital – parent	**49**	37
– subsidiary	**7**	53
Issue of Eurobonds	**–**	200
Capital element of finance lease rental repayments	**(12)**	(19)
Other long term debt issued	**755**	439
Long term debt repaid	**(473)**	(167)
	326	543

In accordance with the revised standard, Cable and Wireless has reclassified the issue costs of the Eurobonds under returns on investments and servicing of finance. In the 1996 cash flow statement, the Eurobonds were shown at the net proceeds received (£197m).[102]

Another change brought about by the revised standard is that cash flows related to borrowings (other than overdrafts) which previously qualified as 'cash equivalents' will now appear under financing.

2.4.10 *Exceptional and extraordinary items*

The revised standard contains significantly better guidance than its predecessor on the presentation of cash flows related to items shown as exceptional or extraordinary in the profit and loss account. It also recognises the possibility that cash flows might be exceptional of themselves, by virtue of their size or incidence.

To allow users to understand the effect on cash flows of items shown as exceptional or extraordinary in the profit and loss account, there is a requirement to identify the related cash flows and to explain their relationship with the originating item in profit and loss account.[103] This is illustrated in the following extract:

Extract 27.26: Imperial Chemical Industries PLC (1996)

25 Net cash inflow from operating activities

	1996 £m	1995 £m
Trading profit	**528**	900
Exceptional charges within trading profit	**137**	94
Trading profit before exceptional items	**665**	994
Depreciation	**402**	391
Stocks decrease (increase)	**62**	(203)
Debtors increase	**(86)**	(97)
Creditors increase	**93**	105
Other movements, including exchange	**(7)**	87
	1,129	1,277
Outflow related to exceptional items	**(123)**	(86)
	1,006	1,191

Outflow related to exceptional items includes expenditure charged to exceptional provisions relating to business rationalisation and restructuring and for sale or closure of operations, including severance and other employee costs, plant demolition and site clearance. The major part of the 1996 expenditure relates to provisions raised in 1995 and prior years.

Cash flows related to exceptional items should appear under the format heading which best reflects the nature of the item.[104] Of course, many exceptional items will not entail any cash flow. Provisions for permanent impairment in the carrying values of fixed assets and exceptional stock provisions clearly have no consequences for the cash flow statement. For other exceptional items like the profit or loss on disposal of fixed assets, the inclusion of the cash proceeds from the sale under capital expenditure and financial investment is uncontroversial and hardly needs to be spelt out as exceptional.

In recognising that some cash flows might be exceptional of themselves, the revised standard is addressing the possibility that the operating activities section might include significant non-recurring cash flows – such as the advance payment of utility bills which the electricity companies received in 1994. Users would undoubtedly like exceptional cash flows to be highlighted but drafting guidance for preparers of accounts is far from straightforward. The revised standard is not very forthcoming on this point, but says simply that 'for a cash flow to be exceptional on the grounds of its size alone, it must be exceptional in relation to cash flows of a similar nature'. The only example provided by the ASB is a large prepayment against a pension liability.[105]

Ever since the publication of FRS 3, which effectively outlawed extraordinary items, the disclosure of extraordinary cash flows has been a non-issue.

2.5 Reconciliations

In addition to the reconciliation to operating profit discussed at 2.4.2 above, the revised FRS 1 requires two additional reconciliations to be given.

The first is a requirement to link the increase or decrease in cash with the movement in net debt in the period.[106] The revised standard explains that movements in net debt are widely used as indicators of changes in liquidity and in assessing the financial strength of the reporting entity. The reconciliation to net debt is accordingly intended to provide information that assists in the assessment of liquidity, solvency and financial adaptability,[107] a key objective of the standard.[108]

'Net debt' is defined as borrowings (being capital instruments that are classified as liabilities under FRS 4) together with related derivatives and obligations under finance leases, less cash and liquid resources.[109] As explained at 2.4.8 above, liquid resources are essentially current asset investments held as readily disposable stores of value. The reference to FRS 4 means that redeemable preference shares issued by the reporting entity are excluded from net debt whereas the same shares issued by a subsidiary, but guaranteed by the parent, would be included. Where cash and liquid resources exceed debt, the resulting figure should be described as 'net funds'.[110]

To reconcile the movement of cash in the period to the movement in net debt, it is necessary first to adjust the change in cash shown at the foot of the cash flow statement to arrive at the change in net debt resulting from cash flows. This entails adding back the cash flows related to borrowings and finance leases shown under financing as well as the cash flows shown under management of liquid resources. The second stage is to include the changes in net debt which have been excluded from the cash flow statement because they do not involve cash flows, such as:

■ liquid resources and borrowings in entities acquired or disposed of during the period;

■ debt instruments issued as consideration for acquisitions;

■ new finance leases;

■ the conversion of debt into equity;

■ exchange adjustments to cash, borrowings and liquid resources; and

■ other adjustments such as the amortisation of debt issue costs, the accretion of redemption premiums, changes in market value and the profit or loss on the sale of current asset investments qualifying as liquid resources.

The first five items listed above are included in the following example of a reconciliation of net cash flow to movement in net debt:

Extract 27.27: J Sainsbury plc (1997)

Reconciliation of Net Cash Flow to Movement in Net Debt [extract]

	1997	1996
	£m	£m
Increase/(decrease) in cash in the period	149	(29)
Cash inflow from increase in debt and lease financing	(381)	(470)
Cash inflow from change in liquid resources	–	–
Change in net debt resulting from cash flows	(232)	(499)
Loans and finance leases acquired with Subsidiary	–	(20)
New finance leases	(13)	(18)
Currency translation difference	26	(15)
Debt converted into share capital	–	44
Loan note issued as settlement for acquisition	–	(18)
Movement in net debt in the period	(219)	(526)
Net debt at the beginning of the period	(1,217)	(691)
Net debt at the end of the period	(1,436)	(1,217)

The reconciliation to net debt should be given either adjoining the cash flow statement or in a note.[111] It replaces the old requirement to reconcile the cash flows shown under financing to the opening and closing balance sheets.

'Net debt' will not be readily apparent from the accounts so the revised standard requires a second reconciliation whereby the component parts are traced back to the equivalent captions in the opening and closing balance sheets:

Extract 27.28: J Sainsbury plc (1997)

26 Analysis of Net Debt [extract]

	At 10th March 1996 £m	Cash flow £m	Other non-cash movements £m	Exchange movements £m	At 8th March 1997 £m
Cash in hand, at bank	209	35		(3)	241
Overdrafts	(240)	114		4	(122)
		149			
Debt due within 1 year	(561)	(124)	(143)	18	(810)
Debt due after 1 year	(516)	(260)	143	3	(630)
Finance leases	(109)	3	(13)	4	(115)
		(381)			
	(1,217)	(232)	(13)	26	(1,436)

The revised standard requires the note illustrated above to show the changes in the component parts of net debt, analysed between:

(a)   the cash flows of the entity;

(b)   the acquisition or disposal of subsidiaries;

(c)   other non-cash changes; and

(d)   the recognition of changes in market value and exchange rate movements.[112]

A number of companies have elected to combine the reconciliations illustrated in Extracts 27.27 and 27.28 above into one enlarged note. In doing this, it should be borne in mind that comparative figures are required for the former but not the latter.[113] Combining the two therefore has the disadvantage of having to present comparative figures for the changes in the component parts of net debt.

2.6   Comparative figures

Comparative figures are required for all items in the cash flow statement and the related notes. The only exceptions are the note analysing changes in the balance sheet amounts making up net debt (see Extract 27.28 above) and the note showing the material effects of acquisitions and disposals on the standard headings (see 2.7.1 below).[114]

2.7   Groups

The cash flow statement presented with group accounts should reflect the external cash flows of the group. Cash flows that are internal to the group (such as payments and receipts for intra-group sales, management charges, dividends, interest and financing arrangements) should be eliminated.[115]   However, dividends paid to minority shareholders in subsidiaries represent an outflow of cash from the perspective of the shareholders in the parent company. They should accordingly be included under returns on investments and servicing of finance.[116]

2.7.1 Acquisition and disposal of subsidiaries

Where a subsidiary joins or leaves the group, it should be included in the group cash flow statement for the same period as its results are reported in the group profit and loss account.[117]

As noted under section 2.4.6 above, the consideration shown under acquisitions and disposals should be the cash paid or received, together with any cash balances (including overdrafts) obtained or surrendered as part of the purchase or sale.

Although the impact of on the cash flow statement itself might be limited, a note is required of the effects of the acquisition or disposal, indicating how much of the consideration comprised cash:[118]

Extract 27.29: Williams Holdings plc (1996)

25 Acquisition and disposal of subsidiary and associated companies

	Acquisitions		Disposals
	1996	1995	1996
	£m	£m	£m
Fixed assets	(35.2)	(20.0)	96.2
Investments	(9.6)	–	0.7
Stocks	(23.3)	(10.7)	46.3
Debtors	(54.8)	(12.9)	87.0
Cash	(16.3)	(0.3)	23.4
Bank overdrafts	0.1	1.5	–
Loans and finance leases	4.6	10.8	(2.8)
Creditors	71.2	8.9	(80.4)
Deferred tax	(7.9)	(3.0)	(12.9)
Provisions for liabilities and charges	37.2	2.0	7.6
	(34.0)	(23.7)	165.1
Profit on disposal before tax	–	–	97.1
Goodwill	(270.2)	(37.5)	165.3
	(304.2)	(61.2)	427.5
Deferred consideration	6.7	–	–
Cash consideration	(297.5)	(61.2)	427.5
Cash acquired (sold)	16.3	0.3	(23.4)
Bank overdrafts acquired	(0.1)	(1.5)	–
	(281.3)	(62.4)	404.1

Acquisitions in the year are shown in note 22. Disposals are shown before the costs of reinvestment in Saia Burgess Holdings (Jersey) Ltd of £7.0m and Newmond PLC of £58.4m. The deferred consideration relates primarily to the acquisition of Corni Serrature srl, which is conditional upon approval from the Italian courts.

The companies acquired in the year contributed £15.2m to the group's net cash flow from operating activities, and paid £11.6m in respect of tax and £3.6m in respect of capital expenditure and financial investment. The disposals in the year contributed £42.1m to the group's net cash flow from operating activities, and paid £5.2m in respect of tax and £13.6m in respect of capital expenditure and financial investment.

Williams has followed the illustrative example in the FRS and provided a full breakdown of the assets and liabilities acquired and disposed of, together with an analysis of the consideration paid and received. Comparative figures have been given where appropriate (there were no disposals in 1995). It is not entirely clear whether 'a summary of the effects of acquisitions and disposals of subsidiary undertakings indicating how much of the consideration comprised cash'[119] requires this extent of detail. Some companies have read FRS 1 as requiring disclosure of the more limited information about the cash consideration paid and any cash balances acquired.[120]

Extract 27.29 above also contains details of the effect (where material) on the standard headings in the cash flow statement of the cash flows of subsidiaries acquired or disposed of in the period. This is another, separate, disclosure required by FRS 1 (where practicable).[121]   Comparative figures are not required.[122]

2.7.2   Preparation of the group cash flow statement

In principle, the group cash flow statement should be built up from the cash flow statements prepared by individual subsidiaries with intra-group cash flows being eliminated as part of the aggregation process.

In practice, however, it may be possible to work at a more consolidated level, using the adjustments performed as part of the accounts consolidation process together with external cash flow information provided by individual subsidiaries. Thus, the group's cash flow from operating activities could be calculated using the indirect method based on operating profit in the consolidated profit and loss account. The cash flows under the other standard headings could similarly be derived from a reconciliation of profit and loss account entries to balance sheet movements. In all cases, however, subsidiaries would have to provide supplementary information to prevent gross cash flows from being netted off and to ensure that the cash flows are shown under the correct headings. In particular, detailed information about debtors and creditors is essential to ensure that the movements included in the reconciliation of operating profit to cash inflow from operating activities relate only to operating debtors and creditors.

The 'consolidated level' approach described above becomes unduly complicated when there are overseas subsidiaries accounted for under the closing rate/net investment method. The movement in stocks, debtors and creditors between the opening and closing group balance sheets will include the effect of changes in exchange rates. For example, an increase in stocks held by a German subsidiary from DM240 to DM270 during the year will be reported as a decrease from £100 to £90 in the group balance sheet if the opening exchange rate of £1=DM2.40 becomes £1=DM3.00 by the year-end. In these circumstances it is usually easier to use the financial statements of the foreign subsidiary as the starting point. The DM30 increase in stocks can then be translated into sterling using either the closing or average exchange rate, as further discussed at 2.8.2 below.

2.7.3 Associates and joint ventures

The cash flow statements of associates and joint ventures accounted for under the equity method have a limited impact on the group cash flow statement, which will reflect only the cash actually transferred between the group and the associate or joint venture. Examples include cash dividends received and loans made or repaid. The amounts of any financing cash flows received from, or paid to, equity accounted entities should be disclosed separately, as should any cash dividends received.

In contrast to the limited impact of the equity method of accounting, the consequences of proportional consolidation are considerable. In these circumstances, the group's share of the joint venture's cash flows should be included in the consolidated cash flow statement on a line by line basis. Adjustments may have to be made to eliminate cash movements between the group and the joint venture.

2.8 Foreign currency

2.8.1 Individual entities

When an entity enters into a transaction denominated in a foreign currency, there are no consequences for the cash flow statement until payments are received or made. The receipts and payments will be recorded in the accounts at the exchange rate ruling at the date of payment (or at the contracted rate if applicable) and these amounts should be reflected in the cash flow statement.

Exchange differences will appear in the profit and loss account when the settled amount differs from the amount recorded at the date of the transaction. Alternatively, if the transaction remains unsettled, exchange differences will also be taken to the profit and loss account on the retranslation of the unsettled monetary balances at year-end rates.

Where the exchange differences relate to operating items such as sales or purchases of stock, no further adjustments need be made when the indirect method of calculating the cash flow from operating activities is used. Thus, if a sale transaction and settlement take place in the same period, the operating profit will include both the amount of the sale and the amount of the exchange difference, the combined effect being the amount of the cash flow. No reconciling item would therefore be needed in the reconciliation of operating profit to cash flow from operating activities. Similarly, where an exchange difference has been recognised on an unsettled balance no reconciling item is needed. This is because the movement in the related debtor or creditor included in the reconciliation to operating profit will incorporate the exchange gain or loss, effectively reversing the amount taken to the profit and loss account.

However, where an exchange difference on a non-operating item such as the purchase of plant has been accounted for in arriving at operating profit, this should appear as a reconciling item between operating profit and the cash flow from operating activities. The difference needs to be taken into account in calculating the cash flow to be shown under the relevant standard heading, in this case capital expenditure and financial investment, which would otherwise be recorded at the amount shown in the fixed assets note.

Exchange differences arising on foreign currency denominated cash balances, borrowings and liquid resources which have been taken to the profit and loss account should be extracted and shown as part of the reconciliation to net debt. These exchange differences do not represent cash flows and have no place in the cash flow statement.

2.8.2 Groups

Where the temporal method is used to account for an overseas operation, the issues that arise are no different to those for foreign currency denominated transactions discussed at 2.8.1 above. Use of the closing rate/net investment method, by contrast, requires the application of very different principles which are discussed below.

Like its predecessor, the revised standard requires the cash flow statements of foreign subsidiaries to be translated into sterling at the same exchange rate used for their profit and loss accounts (which under the closing rate method will be either the year-end exchange rate or an average for the reporting period). This rate must be applied to *all* the foreign entity's cash flows, not just those from operating activities. Thus, an external loan raised on the first day of the financial period would be translated into sterling at the closing rate rather than the rate prevailing at the date of the transaction.

When the indirect method is used to calculate the cash inflow from operating activities, the movement in stocks, debtors and creditors shown in the reconciliation to operating profit should be arrived at by converting the foreign currency movement into sterling at the same exchange rate used for the profit and loss account.[123] For example, an increase in stocks held by a German subsidiary from DM240 to DM270 during the year will be translated into sterling at either the year-end exchange rate or the average for the period, depending on which rate is used to translate the German subsidiary's operating profit. The reconciliation of operating profit to operating cash inflow should show an increase in stocks regardless of the direction of the movement in the sterling balance sheet. The latter may, for example, show a decrease from £100 to £90 if the opening exchange rate of £1=DM2.40 becomes £1=DM3.00 by the year-end. Using the same exchange rate to translate operating profit and the movement in stocks, debtors and creditors ensures that the cash inflow from operating activities under the indirect method is the same as the sterling equivalent of subsidiary's cash inflow from operating activities as calculated under the direct method.

The anomaly highlighted in the previous paragraph of an increase in stocks for FRS 1 purposes when the balance sheet shows a decrease, could apply equally to the balance sheet items making up net debt. In the latter case, the impact needs to be quantified and disclosed in the reconciliation to net debt. Using the figures in the previous example, the change in cash reported in the cash flow statement would be the sterling equivalent of the increase from DM240 to DM270. This should be reconciled to the balance sheet movement in net funds, being a decrease from £100 to £90. Where the closing rate is used to translate the increase of DM30 into £10, the only exchange difference will be that arising on the retranslation of the opening components of net funds from opening rate to closing rate (a loss of £20). When the average rate is used, two elements have to be recorded. These are the retranslation of the opening balances from opening rate to closing rate and the difference arising on the translation of the cash flows in the period from average rate to closing rate.

A particular problem with translating a foreign subsidiary's cash flows into sterling at the same exchange rate used for the profit and loss account concerns the treatment of intra-group cash flows. There will invariably be a residual exchange difference, as illustrated in the following simplified example:

Example 27.1:   Non-elimination of intra-group cash flows

A UK holding company takes out a 5-year loan of £10m and advances the proceeds interest-free to its German subsidiary. Repayment is to be in DM (DM24m) in 5 years' time. On receipt, the German subsidiary converts the £10m into DM24m. The fate of the DM24m is unknown because it is merged with other cash resources raised by the subsidiary from trading and other external sources later in the year. The cash flow statements for the two companies are as follows:

	Parent	Subsidiary
Figures in millions	£	DM
Cash inflow from operating activities	–	6
Returns on investments and servicing of finance	–	(3)
Capital expenditure	–	(48)
Financing		
-loan to subsidiary	(10)	
-loan from parent	–	24
-external bank loans	10	48
Increase in cash	–	27

The year-end exchange rate (£1=DM3.00) is used to translate the results of the subsidiary.

Under FRS 1, the group cash flow statement is required to be drawn up as follows:

	Subsidiary		Parent	Group
Figures in millions	DM	£	£	£
Cash inflow from operating activities	6	2	–	2
Returns on investments and servicing of finance	(3)	(1)	–	(1)
Capital expenditure	(48)	(16)	–	(16)
Financing				
-loan to subsidiary	–	–	(10)	(2)
-loan from parent	24	8	–	–
-external bank loans	48	16	10	26
Increase in cash	27	9	–	9

In the above example, the intra-group cash flows fail to eliminate on consolidation. To balance the group cash flow statement, it is necessary to allocate the £2m difference (which represents the exchange loss in the parent's books and the group accounts) to one of the format headings.

Although this situation is faced by virtually every UK company with intra-group cash flows to and from its foreign subsidiaries, published accounts provide very few clues as to how companies are dealing with the problem. A pragmatic approach would be to net it off against the movement in debtors or creditors in the reconciliation of operating profit to cash inflow from operating activities, effectively including it under the operating activities heading. However, in the example above it might be more appropriate to include it under capital expenditure if the cash was spent immediately after the transfer of the £10m from the UK. The DM48m outflow would become DM24m (or £10m) from the UK parent and DM24m (or £8m) from cash raised in Germany, giving rise to a total of £18m in the group cash flow statement. The US and international accounting standards effectively require an approach similar to this because they stipulate the use of actual exchange rates prevailing at the dates of the cash flows.

Unlike its predecessor, the revised standard contains some (less than helpful) guidance on this point. It proposes that 'where intragroup cash flows are separately identifiable and the actual rate of exchange at which they took place is known, that rate, or an approximation thereto, may be used to translate the cash flows in order to ensure that they cancel on consolidation'.[124] In the example above, the subsidiary should translate the loan from its parent at £1=DM2.40. This converts into £10m and ensures that the intra-group cash flows eliminate. The snag is that the subsidiary's cash flow statement (in £) still fails to balance by £2m! The revised standard is silent on what should be done with this difference (even though this is the problem the guidance set out to solve).

The alternative approach proposed in the revised standard is equally unsatisfactory: 'If the rate used to translate intragroup cash flows is not the actual rate, any exchange rate differences arising should be included in the effect of exchange rate movements shown as part of the reconciliation to net debt.'[125] This appears to be saying that the £2m difference should not be adjusted against any of the standard headings in the cash flow statement. The statement will only balance if the residual increase in cash is increased by £2m to £11m. This is, of course, £2m higher than cash in the closing balance sheet. The difference (or error in the cash flow statement itself) is then required to appear in the reconciliation to net debt as an exchange rate movement.

A more sensible approach would surely have been to require all cash flows to be translated using the exchange rates prevailing at the time of the transaction, as done in the international and US standards. This ensures both that the intra-group cash flows eliminate and that the statement balances. In practice, UK companies will probably be able to continue using the pragmatic approach of including the difference as part of the cash flow from operating activities. This solution is unlikely to produce a material distortion.

2.8.3 Hedging transactions

Where an entity enters into one transaction to hedge another, there is no reason why the underlying nature of the two transactions should be the same. For example, a foreign currency loan taken out to hedge an equity investment denominated in the same currency would normally appear under the financing heading in the cash flow statement. Perhaps inadvertently, the original standard required all cash flows under the hedging transaction (the loan in this example) to appear under the same heading as the transaction that is the subject of the hedge (investing activities under that standard).[126]

The revised standard clarifies that the loan should not be accounted for in the manner described above. It is only cash flows from futures contracts, forward contracts, option contracts or swap contracts that should be accounted for under the same heading as the transaction that is the subject of the hedge.[127] Loans should be accounted for as loans.

An example of an item falling under the hedging requirement in the revised standard is an interest rate swap. An entity wishing to convert an existing fixed rate borrowing into a floating rate equivalent could enter into an interest rate swap under which it will receive fixed rates and pay floating rates. All the cash flows under the swap should be reported under returns on investments and servicing of finance because they are equivalent to interest or are hedges of interest payments.

The requirements in the revised standard are described by the ASB as a pragmatic position that follows the US cash flow standard while awaiting the outcome to the Board's Discussion Paper on derivatives and other financial instruments.[128]

2.9   Notes to the cash flow statement

There are several requirements for the cash flow statement to be supplemented by the disclosure of additional information in a note. Those discussed in earlier sections of this Chapter are summarised below for ease of reference:

- a reconciliation of operating profit to cash flow from operating activities (see 2.4.2 above);

- the reporting entity's policy for determining liquid resources and any changes to it (2.4.8);

- cash flows related to exceptional or extraordinary items and cash flows that are exceptional in their own right because of their size or incidence (2.4.10);

- a reconciliation of the change in cash to the movement in net debt (2.5);

- an analysis of the changes in the opening and closing component amounts of net debt (2.5);

- a summary of the effects of acquisitions and disposals of subsidiary undertakings (2.7.1); and

- a note of the material effects of acquisitions and disposals of subsidiary undertakings on each of the standard headings (2.7.1).

In addition to the above, there are two other disclosure requirements that need to be addressed. These are discussed below.

2.9.1   Restrictions on remittability

Where restrictions (like exchange control) prevent the transfer of cash from one part of the business to another, there should be disclosure of the amounts involved and an explanation of the circumstances.[129]   It would seem that this requirement is referring to the balance sheet amounts, not the cash flows during the period.

The ASB is keen to stress that note disclosure is required only where external factors have a severe effect in practice, rather than where the sole constraint is a special purpose designated by the entity itself. Examples of the former could include cash balances in escrow, deposited with a regulator or held within an employee share ownership trust. The implication is that, whilst these balances still fall within the definition of 'cash', additional disclosure is necessary to provide meaningful information about liquidity, solvency and financial adaptability.

2.9.2 *Material non-cash transactions*

A consequence of the move away from the 'all financial resources' concept inherent in the old funds flow statement is that the cash flow statement reflects fewer transactions, and more limited consequences of those transactions. In order to provide a better understanding of the underlying transactions and a full picture of the change in financial position, the revised standard (like its predecessor) requires material non-cash transactions to be disclosed in the notes.[130] Examples include shares issued for the acquisition of a subsidiary, the exchange of major assets or the inception of finance lease contracts.

In the US, SFAS 95 requires disclosure about non-cash investing and financing transactions.[131] The FRS 1 requirement is theoretically more comprehensive in that it covers all activities, although in practice non-cash operating transactions are likely to be rare.

3 BANKS AND INSURANCE COMPANIES

The revised standard contains a number of specific provisions affecting the preparation of cash flow statements by banks and insurance companies. These are covered in broad outline below.

3.1 Banks

It has been argued that a cash flow statement is not particularly relevant to a bank because cash is its stock in trade. Measures like regulatory capital ratios derived from statements of capital resources may therefore give a better indication of a bank's solvency and financial adaptability. Although the ASB shares this view, banks are not exempted from the requirement to prepare a cash flow statement because the Board believes that the statement contains information on the generation and uses of cash that may be useful to users of the accounts.[132] However, the special nature of banking and its regulation are recognised in certain aspects of the detailed requirements. These apply to 'any entity whose business is to receive deposits or other repayable funds from the public and to grant credits for its own account':[133]

■ definition of cash – because banks do not usually have borrowings with the characteristics of an overdraft, cash for their purposes should normally include only cash and balances at central banks, together with loans and advances to other banks repayable on demand;[134]

■   presentation of interest – to the extent that interest received or paid (and dividends received) are included as part of operating profit, the related cash flows should appear under operating activities. Where interest clearly relates to financing, the cash flows should be included under returns on investments and servicing of finance. Examples include loan capital and other subordinated liabilities;[135]

■   investments held for trading – the related cash flows should be included under operating activities;[136]

■   management of liquid resources – this heading is not required because meaningful identification of cash flows relating to the management of liquid resources is not possible;[137]

■   reconciliation to net debt – this is not required because the change in net debt has very little (if any) meaning in the context of a bank;[138] and

■   notes to the cash flow statement – in the absence of the reconciliation to net debt it would seem that the note which reconciles all items shown under financing to the opening and closing balance sheets (for both years) might still be required.[139]

3.2   Insurance companies

Since insurance premiums are received in advance of the related cash outflows, sometimes long in advance, it has been argued that an insurance company's cash flow statement provides little information about liquidity, viability and financial adaptability, a key objective of the FRS. In its response to FRED 10, the Association of British Insurers pointed out that an insurance transaction reverses the normal sequence of cash flow. The receipt of cash is the commencement of the transaction rather than its completion. The Association proposed that it would accordingly be more appropriate to include a discussion of liquidity, solvency and financial adaptability in the Operating and Financial Review.

Presumably because the provision of information about liquidity, solvency and financial adaptability is no longer the sole objective of the FRS (which has been expanded to include the standardised reporting of cash generation and absorption), insurance companies (other than mutual life assurers) have not been exempted. However, the special nature of their business has been recognised in certain departures from the presentation used by other entities:

■   cash flows relating to long-term business (long-term life, pensions and annuity businesses) should be included only to the extent of cash transferred and available to meet the obligations of the company or group as a whole.[140] This is because the shareholders of an insurance company generally have restricted rights to the profits and associated cash surpluses made by their long-term business. Mutual life assurance companies, which are owned by policy holders, are accordingly exempt from the requirements of the FRS;[141]

■ internal cash flows of the long-term business may be shown as supplementary information in a note to the cash flow statement;[142]

■ an analysis of portfolio investment should replace management of liquid resources and explain how the cash inflow for the period has been invested (including the movement in cash holdings);[143]

■ portfolio investment for the period (as shown in the cash flow statement) should be reconciled to the balance sheet movement in portfolio investments less financing;[144]

■ the note analysing the balance sheet movement in portfolio investment less financing should show the component parts and highlight the movement in long-term business to the extent that these are consolidated in the accounts;[145] and

■ the reconciliation of operating profit to cash flow from operating activities should normally start with profit before tax because returns on investments form part of operating activities.[146]

The revised standard encourages the use of segmentation to reflect the different degrees of access to cash balances.[147]

Appendix I to the revised standard contains an example of a cash flow statement for an insurance company. This reveals a very different statement to that required of other entities in that it shows the net investment of cash flows rather than the net change in cash.

4 COMPARISON WITH US AND IASC PRONOUNCEMENTS

4.1 US

4.1.1 Introduction

In 1980, as part of its conceptual framework project, the FASB issued a Discussion Memorandum – *Reporting Funds Flows, Liquidity, and Financial Flexibility*. The major issues raised in the Memorandum relating to funds flow reporting included (a) the concept of funds that should be adopted as the focus of the funds flow statement, (b) the reporting of transactions that have no direct impact on funds, (c) the approaches for presenting information about funds flows, (d) the presentation of information about funds flows from operations, and (e) the separation of funds flow information about investing activities into outflows for maintenance of operating capacity, expansion of operating capacity, or non-operating purposes.

Although this Discussion Memorandum was followed by an Exposure Draft of a proposed concepts statement – *Reporting Income, Cash Flows, and Financial Position of Business Enterprises* – which suggested that funds flow reporting should focus on cash rather than working capital, the FASB decided not to issue a final statement on the subject. Instead, the FASB chose to consider the subject in connection with its study of recognition and measurement concepts. The outcome was that Concepts Statement No. 5 – *Recognition and Measurement in Financial Statements of Business Enterprises* – concluded that a full set of financial statements should include a statement of cash flows. This led to the FASB setting up a Task Force on Cash Flow Reporting, and ultimately to the publication in November 1987 of SFAS 95 – *Statement of Cash Flows*. In February 1989, SFAS 102 – *Statement of Cash Flows – Exemption of Certain Enterprises and Classification of Cash Flows from Certain Securities Acquired for Resale*, and in December 1989, SFAS 104 – *Statement of Cash Flows–Net Reporting of Certain Cash Receipts and Cash Payments and Classification of Cash Flows from Hedging Transactions* – were issued as amendments to SFAS 95; these amendments have been incorporated in the discussion of SFAS 95 below.

4.1.2 Focus of SFAS 95

SFAS 95 concluded that the primary purpose of a statement of cash flows is to provide relevant information about the cash receipts and cash payments of an enterprise during a period.[148] The information provided by the statement, if used in conjunction with related disclosures in the other financial statements, should assist users to:

(a) assess the enterprise's ability to generate positive future net cash flows;

(b) assess the enterprise's ability to meet its obligations, pay dividends and meet its needs for external financing;

(c) assess the reasons for differences between net income and related cash receipts and payments; and

(d) assess the effects on the enterprise's financial position of both cash and non-cash investing and financing transactions during the period.[149]

In order to achieve these objectives, the statement focuses on the change during the period in *cash* and *cash equivalents*, rather than working capital; ambiguous terms such as 'funds' are not to be used. The total amounts of cash and cash equivalents at the beginning and end of the period shown in the statement of cash flows will be the same amounts as presented in the balance sheets as of those dates. A statement of cash flows is not required for defined benefit pension plans and certain other employee benefit plans or for certain investment companies.[150]

4.1.3 Cash equivalents

SFAS 95 defines cash equivalents as short-term, highly liquid investments that are both:

(a) readily convertible to known amounts of cash; and

(b) so near their maturity that they present insignificant risk of changes in value because of changes in interest rates.[151]

Generally, only an investment with an original maturity (i.e. original maturity to the entity holding the investment) of three months or less qualifies under the above definition.[152]

It is noteworthy that not all investments that qualify are required to be treated as cash equivalents; for example, an enterprise may classify short-term, highly liquid investments as investments rather than cash equivalents. However, a company must disclose its policy for determining cash equivalents, and any change to that policy is considered to be a change in accounting principle, requiring restatement of comparative financial statements.

4.1.4 Form and content of the statement of cash flows

SFAS 95 requires cash receipts and cash payments to be classified as resulting from investing, financing or operating activities.[153] Generally, each receipt or payment is to be classified according to its nature without regard to whether it stems from an item intended as a hedge of another item. For example, the proceeds of a borrowing are a financing cash inflow even though the debt is intended as a hedge of an investment, and the purchase or sale of a futures contract is an investing activity even though the contract is intended as a hedge of a firm commitment to purchase inventory.

However, cash flows from futures contracts, forward contracts, option contracts or swap contracts that are accounted for as hedges of identifiable transactions or events (for example, a cash payment from a futures contract that hedges a purchase or sale of inventory), including anticipatory hedges, may be classified in the same category as the cash flows from the items being hedged provided that the accounting policy is disclosed. If for any reason hedge accounting for an instrument that hedges an identifiable transaction or event is discontinued, then any cash flows subsequent to the date of discontinuance are classified consistent with the nature of the instrument.[154]

4.1.5 Investing activities

Investing activities include:

(a) making and collecting loans; and

(b) acquiring and disposing of

    (i)   securities that are not cash equivalents;

    (ii) property, plant and equipment; and

(iii)   other productive assets, other than inventory materials.[155]

Investing activities exclude acquiring and disposing of certain loans or other debt or equity instruments that are acquired specifically for resale.[156]

Cash inflows from investing activities are:

(a)   receipts from collections or sales of loans made by the enterprise and of other entities' debt instruments (other than cash equivalents and certain debt instruments that are acquired specifically for resale) that were purchased by the enterprise;

(b)   receipts from sales of equity instruments of other enterprises (other than certain equity instruments carried in a trading account), and from returns of investment in those instruments; and

(c)   receipts from sales of property, plant and equipment and other productive assets.[157]

Cash outflows for investing activities are:

(a)   disbursements for loans made by the enterprise, and payments made to acquire debt instruments of other entities (other than cash equivalents and certain debt instruments that are acquired specifically for resale);

(b)   payments to acquire equity instruments of other enterprises (other than certain equity instruments carried in a trading account); and

(c)   payments to acquire property, plant and equipment and other productive assets (including interest capitalised as part of the cost of those assets).[158]

4.1.6   Financing activities

Financing activities include obtaining resources from owners and providing them with a return on, and a return of, their investment; borrowing money and repaying amounts borrowed, or otherwise settling the obligation; and obtaining and paying for other resources obtained from creditors on long-term credit.[159]

Cash inflows from financing activities are:

(a)   proceeds from issuance of equity securities; and

(b)   proceeds from issuing bonds, mortgages, notes and from other short- or long-term borrowing.[160]

Cash outflows for financing activities are:

(a)   payments of dividends to owners;

(b)   cash outlays to repurchase the enterprise's shares;

(c)   repayments of amounts borrowed; and

(d)   other principal payments to creditors who have extended long-term credit.[161]

4.1.7 Operating activities

Operating activities include:

(a) all transactions and other events not defined as investing or financing activities; and

(b) delivering or producing goods for sale and providing services.

Cash flows from operating activities are, generally, the cash effects of transactions and other events that enter into the determination of income.[162]

Cash inflows from operating activities are:

(a) cash receipts from sales of goods or services (the term 'goods' includes certain loans and other debt and equity instruments of other enterprises that are acquired specifically for resale);

(b) cash receipts from returns on loans (interest) and on equity securities (dividends); and

(c) all other cash receipts that do not stem from transactions defined as investing or financing activities, for example amounts received in settlement of lawsuits.[163]

Cash outflows for operating activities are:

(a) cash payments to acquire materials for manufacture or goods for resale (the term 'goods' includes certain loans and other debt and equity instruments of other enterprises that are acquired specifically for resale);

(b) cash payments to other suppliers and employees for other goods or services;

(c) cash payments to governments for taxes, duties, fines etc.;

(d) cash payments to lenders and other creditors for interest; and

(e) all other cash payments that do not stem from transactions defined as investing or financing activities.[164]

4.1.8 Receipts and payments are presented gross

In general, a greater and more meaningful assessment of cash flows can be derived from reporting cash receipts and cash payments gross, rather than net. Nevertheless, SFAS 95 takes the view that, where the turnover is quick, the amounts are large and the maturities are short, the item may be reported net. Examples include receipts and payments relating to investments (other than cash equivalents), loans receivable and debt, provided that the original maturity of the asset or liability is three months or less.[165] SFAS 95 argues that items with these characteristics may be reported net, since knowledge of the related gross receipts and payments is not necessary to understand the enterprise's operating, investing and financing activities.

Banks, savings institutions and credit unions are not required to report gross amounts of cash receipts and cash payments for:

(a)   deposits placed with other financial institutions and withdrawals of deposits;

(b)   time deposits accepted and repayments of deposits; and

(c)   loans made to customers and principal collections of loans.

When these enterprises constitute part of a consolidated enterprise, the net amounts of receipts and payments for deposit or lending activities of these enterprises must be reported separately from the gross amounts of receipts and payments for other investing and financing activities of the consolidated enterprise, including those of a subsidiary of a bank, savings institution or credit union that is not itself a bank, savings institution or credit union.[166]

4.1.9   Non-cash activities are disclosed separately

Information about investing and financing activities that affect recognised assets or liabilities, but that do not result in cash receipts or payments in the period should be disclosed. This disclosure may be in narrative form or summarised in a schedule. Examples include converting debt to equity, acquiring assets by assuming directly related liabilities (e.g. purchasing a building by incurring a mortgage to the seller), or obtaining an asset by entering into a capital lease.[167]

4.1.10   Use of the direct or indirect methods

As is the case under FRS 1 and IAS 7, both the direct and indirect methods of presentation are available for reporting the net cash flow from operating activities. However, regardless of which method is used, SFAS 95 (like FRS 1) requires a reconciliation of net income to net cash flow from operating activities to be presented. In addition, the amounts of interest paid (net of capitalised interest) and income tax paid should be separately disclosed.[168]

4.2   Summary of principal differences between FRS 1 and SFAS 95

The most important difference between the US and UK standards is that the former focuses on the change during the period in cash and cash equivalents, whereas the latter highlights the movement in cash. Cash flows related to cash equivalents are shown under the management of liquid resources heading in the UK.

The categorisation of cash flows under eight headings in the UK compared with three under SFAS 95 naturally results in a number of presentational differences. In the UK, there are separate headings for returns on investments and servicing of finance, taxation, capital expenditure and financial investment, acquisitions and disposals and equity dividends paid, whereas under SFAS 95:

■   interest received and paid as well as dividends received are included in operating activities. Capitalised interest, however, is treated as part of the cost of the asset into which it is capitalised and thus appears in investing activities;

■ taxation cash flows are included in operating activities;

■ cash flows related to capital expenditure and financial investment and acquisitions and disposals are shown in investing activities; and

■ dividends paid are included in financing activities.

Other significant differences between the two standards include the following:

■ SFAS 95 does not require a reconciliation to the movement in net debt;

■ SFAS 95 requires the cash flows of foreign operations to be translated using the exchange rate in effect at the time of the cash flow. FRS 1 generally requires the same rate used in translating the results of the foreign operations to be used in translating their cash flows;

■ SFAS 95 requires information about non-cash investing and financing activities only. FRS 1 requires all material non-cash transactions to be disclosed;

■ where the indirect method of presenting the cash flow from operating activities is used, SFAS 95 allows the reconciliation to operating profit to be shown as part of the cash flow statement itself. FRS 1 stipulates that the reconciliation should be given either adjoining the statement or as a note;

■ SFAS 95 does not require note disclosures dealing with exceptional and extraordinary cash flows or the acquisition or disposal of subsidiaries; and

■ SFAS 95 permits but (unlike FRS 1) does not require cash flows relating to futures contracts, forward contracts, option contracts and swap contracts to be classified along with the cash flows from the item being hedged.

4.3   IASC

In October 1977 the IASC issued IAS 7 – *Statement of Changes in Financial Position* – which required the presentation of a statement of sources and uses of funds. However, the standard was even less prescriptive than SSAP 10, and contained virtually no requirement as to the form or content of the funds statement.

Although the IASC did not deal with IAS 7 in its comparability/improvements project, a separate project on cash flow statements was started in April 1989. This culminated in the publication in 1992 of a revised version of IAS 7 – *Cash Flow Statements*.

The stated objective of IAS 7 is 'to require the provision of information about the historical changes in cash and cash equivalents of an enterprise by means of a cash flow statement which classifies cash flows during the period from operating, investing and financing activities'.[169]

IAS 7 applies to all enterprises including banks, insurance companies and other financial institutions. The reason for this is explained as follows: 'Users of an enterprise's financial statements are interested in how the enterprise generates and uses cash and cash equivalents. This is the case regardless of the nature of the enterprise's activities and irrespective of whether cash can be viewed as the product of the enterprise, as may be the case with a financial institution. Enterprises need cash for essentially the same reasons however different their principal revenue-producing activities might be. They need cash to conduct their operations, to pay their obligations, and to provide returns to their investors. Accordingly, this Standard requires all enterprises to present a cash flow statement.'[170]

It is clear from the stated objective of IAS 7 that the key differences between the international and UK standards are to be found in the definition of cash flows and their categorisation in the cash flow statement. Whereas IAS 7 is concerned with reporting inflows and outflows of cash and cash equivalents (short-term, highly liquid investments that are readily convertible to known amounts of cash and which are subject to an insignificant risk of changes in value),[171] FRS 1 concentrates on changes in cash. Cash flows related to cash equivalents are included under the management of liquid resources section in the UK.

Because IAS 7 does not have separate headings for returns on investments and servicing of finance, taxation, capital expenditure and financial investment, acquisitions and disposals and equity dividends paid:

- interest and dividends received and paid should be separately disclosed and classified in a consistent manner from period to period as either operating, investing or financing activities;[172]

- cash flows arising from taxes on income should be separately disclosed and classified as operating activities, unless they can be specifically identified with financing and investing activities;[173] and

- cash flows arising from the acquisition and disposal of long-term assets and other investments (other than those included in cash equivalents) as well as those arising from the acquisition and disposal of subsidiaries and business units should be classified as investing activities.[174]

Other, more significant, differences between the two standards are that:

- IAS 7 permits both the direct and indirect methods to be used for reporting the net cash flow from operating activities but does not require the reconciliation to operating profit when the direct method is used. Where the indirect method is used, the reconciliation may be shown as part of the cash flow statement itself;

■   IAS 7 does not require a reconciliation to the movement in net debt;

■   IAS 7 requires foreign subsidiary cash flows to be translated at the exchange rates prevailing at the dates of the cash flows. A suitable weighted average may be used as an approximation;[175] and

■   IAS 7 allows net reporting of cash receipts and payments on behalf of customers when the cash flows reflect the activities of the customer rather than those of the entity.[176]

5   CONCLUSION

The introduction of the original FRS 1 was undoubtedly a quantum leap in the ASB's financial reporting reform process. It generally worked well in practice and enhanced the quality of financial reporting considerably. It was clear, though, that certain aspects of the standard were in need of re-examination and the ASB is to be commended for having addressed most of the problem areas.

In particular, the objective of the standard has been tidied up, the definition of cash flow from operating activities improved, the presentation of finance costs associated with certain capital instruments clarified and sensible rules have been introduced for presenting cash flows net rather than gross where appropriate. In addition, the reconciliation to net debt will help considerably in placing the cash flow statement in its proper context.

However, by scrapping the unpopular 'cash equivalents' concept altogether and refocusing the statement on a narrower definition of cash, the ASB has arguably used a sledgehammer to crack a nut. The three month cut-off in the old definition of cash equivalents was clearly unsatisfactory because it bore little resemblance to most companies' treasury maturity horizons. It might have been possible to solve this problem by adopting a more flexible definition, similar to that used in the US and internationally. Whereas the introduction of the management of liquid resources heading was an essential part of the solution to the cash equivalents problem, the other format changes are less easily commended. Splitting the former investing activities into 'capital expenditure and financial investment' and 'acquisitions and disposals' seems little more than tinkering. The same accusation could be levied at the separation of 'equity dividends paid' from returns on investments and servicing of finance. Neither requirement adds any new information nor results in meaningful sub-totals being given. It is highly debatable whether the new layout portrays increasing degrees of discretion in cash flows or anything else.

Our survey of published accounts reveals a high degree of voluntary early implementation of the revised standard. However, early indications are that some of the ASB's hopes are not being borne out in practice. The new section on management of liquid resources was intended to provide improved information on treasury activities. In a number of instances it is being used as the repository for the net difference between two balance sheet amounts. The reconciliation to operating profit was designed to 'place the cash flows of an entity clearly in context, locking them into the profit and loss account and balance sheet'.[177] In some instances it simply highlights that certain cash flows related to items charged in arriving at operating profit (like the reorganisation of acquired subsidiaries and the maintenance of fixed assets) have been excluded from the cash flow from operating activities. In these respects, the revised standard is falling short of its objective of facilitating comparison of the cash flow performances of different businesses.[178]

References

1 There is evidence of companies publishing funds statements as far back as 1862 in the UK and 1863 in the US – see L. S. Rosen and Don T. DeCoster, ' "Funds" Statements: A Historical Perspective'. *The Accounting Review*, January 1969, pp. 124–136. However, it was not until the 1950s (in the US) and the early 1970s (in the UK) that the funds statement was commonly presented in one form or another in annual reports.

2 See Ross M. Skinner, *Accounting Standards in Evolution*, Canada: Holt, Rinehart and Winston of Canada, Limited, 1987, p. 397.

3 The term 'funds statement' has been used throughout this Chapter in preference to the alternatives of 'statement of source and application of funds' or 'statement of changes in financial position'.

4 A review of the 1959 annual reports of the 600 US industrial companies included in the AICPA's publication *Accounting Trends and Techniques* revealed that in 190 cases some form of funds statement was presented.

5 AICPA Accounting Research Study No. 2, *"Cash Flow" Analysis and The Funds Statement*, New York: AICPA, 1963.

6 *Ibid.*, p. xi.

7 APB 19, *Reporting Changes in Financial Position*, AICPA, 1971, para. 7.

8 ED 13, *Statements of Source and Application of Funds*, ASC, April 1974.

9 SSAP 10, *Statements of source and application of funds*, ASC, July 1975.

10 See the foreword to SSAP 10.

11 Accountants International Study Group, *The Funds Statement: Current Practices in Canada, the United Kingdom and the United States*, 1973, para. 8.

12 For a full discussion of the detailed requirements and practical application of SSAP 10, readers should refer to the 2nd Edition of this book which was published by Longman in August 1990.

13 SSAP 10, para. 2.

14 *Ibid.*, para. 1.

15 *Ibid.*, para. 3.

16 *Ibid.*

17 SFAS 95, *Statement of Cash Flows*, FASB, November 1987, para. 2.

18 *Ibid.*

19 Eldon S. Hendriksen, *Accounting Theory*, Fourth Edition, Illinois: Richard D. Irwin, Inc., 1982, p. 236.

20 SFAC No. 1, *Objectives of Financial Reporting by Business Enterprises*, FASB, November 1978, para. 37.

21 SFAC No. 5, *Recognition and Measurement in Financial Statements of Business Enterprises*, FASB, December 1984, para. 13.

22 *Ibid.*, para. 52.

23 See SFAC No. 5, at para. 24.

24 SFAS 95, para. 3.

25 For example, the US, Canada, New Zealand and South Africa.

26 FRS 1, *Cash flow statements*, ASB, September 1991, para. 12.

27 *Ibid.*, paras. 2 and 3.

28 FRS 1 (Revised 1996), *Cash Flow Statements*, ASB, October 1996, Appendix III, para. 6.
29 For a full discussion of the criticisms surrounding the original FRS 1, readers should refer to the 4th Edition of this book which was published by Macmillan in September 1994.
30 ASB, Press Notice PN 6, 26 September 1991.
31 SAS 600, *Auditors' Reports on Financial Statements*, APB, May 1993, Appendix 2, Example 12.
32 FRS 1 (Revised 1996), para. 5.
33 *Ibid.*, Appendix III, para. 12.
34 FRS 1 (Revised 1996), para. 36.
35 *Ibid.*, Appendix III, para. 12.
36 *Ibid.*, para. 22.
37 *Ibid.*
38 *Ibid.*, para. 12.
39 FRS 1 (Revised 1996), para. 2.
40 *Ibid.*
41 *Ibid.*, para. 33.
42 *Ibid.*, para. 7.
43 *Ibid.*
44 *Ibid.*
45 *Ibid.*, Appendix III, para. 13.
46 FRS 1 (Revised 1996), para. 8.
47 *Ibid.*, para. 9
48 FRS 4, *Capital Instruments*, ASB, December 1993, para. 35.
49 FRS 1 (Revised 1996), para. 9.
50 *Ibid.*
51 *Ibid.*, para. 10.
52 See, for example, the 1997 accounts of Severn Trent Plc, South West Water Plc, Thames Water Plc and United Utilities PLC.
53 FRS 1 (Revised 1996), para. 11.
54 *Ibid.*, para. 58.
55 *Ibid.*, para. 11.
56 *Ibid.*, para. 58.
57 FRS 3, *Reporting financial performance*, ASB, October 1992, para. 20.
58 FRED 10, *Revision of FRS 1 'Cash Flow Statements'*, December 1995, para. 60.
59 FRS 1 (Revised 1996), para. 56.
60 *Ibid.*, para. 8.
61 *Ibid.*, para. 56.
62 *Ibid.*, para. 12.
63 *Ibid.*, para. 11.
64 *Ibid.*, para. 12.
65 *Ibid.*
66 *Ibid.*, Appendix III, para. 18.
67 FRS 1 (Revised 1996), para. 58.
68 *Ibid.*, para. 13.
69 *Ibid.*, paras. 8, 14, 15.
70 *Ibid.*, para. 15.
71 *Ibid.*, Appendix III, para. 17.
72 FRS 1 (Revised 1996), para. 16.
73 FRED 10, Appendix III, para. 15.
74 FRS 1 (Revised 1996), Appendix III, para. 14.
75 *Ibid.*
76 FRS 1, para. 81.
77 FRS 1 (Revised 1996), Appendix III, para. 14.
78 FRS 1 (Revised 1996), para. 19.
79 *Ibid.*, para. 22.
80 *Ibid.*, para. 19.
81 Blue Circle Industries PLC, Annual Report & Accounts 1996, p. 64.
82 SFAS 95, para. 17.

83 FRS 1 (Revised 1996), para. 22.
84 *Ibid.*, para. 24.
85 *Ibid.*, para. 23.
86 *Ibid.*, Appendix I, Example 2.
87 *Ibid.*
88 Imperial Chemical Industries PLC, Annual report and accounts, 1996, p. 57.
89 See, for example, the 1996 Annual Report of Emap plc, p. 48.
90 FRS 1 (Revised 1996), para. 25.
91 FRED 10, para. 25.
92 FRS 1 (Revised 1996), para. 2.
93 *Ibid.*
94 *Ibid.*, para. 52.
95 *Ibid.*, para. 26.
96 *Ibid.*, para. 27.
97 *Ibid.*, para. 28.
98 Reuters Holdings PLC, Annual Report 1996, p. 62.
99 FRS 1 (Revised 1996), para. 29.
100 *Ibid.*, paras. 30–31.
101 *Ibid.*, para. 32.
102 Cable and Wireless plc, Report and Accounts 1996, p. 50.
103 FRS 1 (Revised 1996), para. 37.
104 *Ibid.*
105 *Ibid.*, para. 63.
106 *Ibid.*, para. 33.
107 *Ibid.*, para. 53.
108 *Ibid.*, para. 1.
109 *Ibid.*, para. 2.
110 *Ibid.*
111 *Ibid.*, para. 33.
112 *Ibid.*
113 *Ibid.*, para. 48.
114 *Ibid.*
115 *Ibid.*, para. 43.
116 *Ibid.*, para. 15.
117 *Ibid.*, para. 43.
118 *Ibid.*, para. 45.
119 *Ibid.*
120 See, for example, the 1996 Annual Report & Accounts of Wolseley plc, p. 58 and the 1996 Annual Report of Sedgwick Group plc, p. 44.
121 FRS 1 (Revised 1996), para. 45.
122 *Ibid.*, para. 48.
123 *Ibid.*, para. 41.
124 *Ibid.*
125 *Ibid.*
126 FRS 1, para. 37.
127 FRS 1 (Revised 1996), para. 42.
128 *Ibid.*, Appendix III, para. 30.
129 FRS 1 (Revised 1996)., para. 47.
130 *Ibid.*, para. 46.
131 SFAS 95, para. 32.
132 FRS 1 (Revised 1996), Appendix III, para. 20.
133 FRS 1 (Revised 1996), para. 2.
134 *Ibid.*, para. 34.
135 *Ibid.*, para. 60.
136 *Ibid.*, para. 34.
137 *Ibid.*, Appendix III, para. 21.
138 *Ibid.*

139 *Ibid.*, Appendix I, Example 3, Note 3.
140 FRS 1 (Revised 1996), para. 36.
141 *Ibid.*, para. 5.
142 *Ibid.*, Appendix III, para. 24.
143 FRS 1 (Revised 1996), para. 35.
144 *Ibid.*
145 *Ibid.*, para. 36.
146 *Ibid.*, para. 35.
147 *Ibid.*, Appendix III, para. 23.
148 SFAS 95, para. 4.
149 *Ibid.*, para. 5.
150 SFAS 102, *Statement of Cash Flows–Exemption of Certain Enterprises and Classification of Cash Flows from Certain Securities Acquired for Resale*, FASB, February 1989, para. 10.
151 SFAS 95, para. 8.
152 *Ibid.*
153 *Ibid.*, para. 14.
154 SFAS 104, *Statement of Cash Flows–Net Reporting of Certain Cash Receipts and Cash Payments and Classification of Cash Flows from Hedging Transactions*, FASB, December 1989, para. 7b.
155 SFAS 95, para. 15.
156 SFAS 102, para. 10.
157 SFAS 95, para. 16.
158 *Ibid.*, para. 17.
159 *Ibid.*, para. 18.
160 *Ibid.*, para. 19.
161 *Ibid.*, para. 20.
162 *Ibid.*, para. 21.
163 *Ibid.*, para. 22.
164 *Ibid.*, para. 23.
165 *Ibid.*, para. 13.
166 SFAS 104, para. 7a.
167 SFAS 95, para. 32.
168 *Ibid.*, para. 29.
169 IAS 7, *Cash Flow Statements*, IASC, Revised 1992, Objective.
170 *Ibid.*, para. 3.
171 *Ibid.*, para. 6.
172 *Ibid.*, para. 31.
173 *Ibid.*, para. 35.
174 *Ibid.*, paras. 6 and 39.
175 *Ibid.*, paras. 26–27.
176 *Ibid.*, para. 22.
177 ASB, Press Notice PN 84, 31 October 1996.
178 FRS 1 (Revised 1996), para. 1.

Chapter 28   Related parties

1   INTRODUCTION

Related party relationships and transactions between related parties are a normal feature of business; many enterprises carry on their business activities through subsidiaries and associated companies and there will inevitably be transactions between the parties comprising the group. Nevertheless, whilst a number of other countries (including the US, Canada, Australia and New Zealand) have had accounting standards on related party transactions for some time, the relevant UK standard, FRS 8 – *Related Party Disclosures*, was issued only relatively recently.

The ASC had issued ED 46 – *Disclosure of related party transactions* – in April 1989. Nothing ever came from ED 46, though, and the ASB apparently regarded the topic as a relatively low priority when it inherited the ASC's work programme on its formation in 1990. However, in the light of the Robert Maxwell affair, where it is alleged that both the MGN Group and Maxwell Communications suffered seriously as a result of a number of related party transactions, the ASB revived the related party project, issuing FRED 8 – *Related Party Disclosures* – in March 1994, which was converted into FRS 8 in November 1995.

1.1   The related party issue

The problem with related party relationships and transactions is expressed in FRS 8 as follows:

'In the absence of information to the contrary, it is assumed that a reporting entity has independent discretionary power over its resources and transactions and pursues its activities independently of the interests of its individual owners, managers and others. Transactions are presumed to have been undertaken on an arm's length basis, ie on terms such as could have been obtained in a transaction with an external party, in which each side bargained knowledgeably and freely, unaffected by any relationship between them.

'These assumptions may not be justified when related party relationships exist, because the requisite conditions for competitive, free market dealings may not be present. Whilst the parties may endeavour to achieve arm's length bargaining the very nature of the relationship may preclude this occurring. ...

'Even when terms are at arm's length, the reporting of material related party transactions is useful information, because the terms of future transactions are more susceptible to alteration as a result of the nature of the relationship than they would be in transactions with an unrelated party.'[1]

A related party relationship can affect the financial position and operating results of an enterprise in a number of ways:

- Transactions may be entered into with a related party which would not occur if the relationship did not exist. For example, a company may sell a large proportion of its production to its parent company, where it might not find an alternative customer if the parent company had not purchased the goods.

- Transactions may be entered into with a related party on terms different from those applicable to an unrelated party. For example, a subsidiary may lease equipment to a fellow subsidiary on terms imposed by the common parent entirely unrelated to market prices for similar leases; indeed, the terms may be such that no financial consideration passes between the parties.

- Transactions with third parties may be affected by the existence of the relationship; for example, two enterprises in the same line of business may be controlled by a common party that has the ability to increase the volume of business done by each.

1.2   Possible solutions

1.2.1   *Remeasurement of transactions at fair values*

One solution would be to adjust the financial statements to reflect the transaction as if it had occurred with an independent third party and record the transaction at the corresponding arm's length price. However, as a study by the Accountants International Study Group stated, it often is impossible to establish what would have been the terms of any non-arm's length transaction had it been bargained on an arm's length basis, because no comparable transactions may have taken place and, in any event, the transaction might never have taken place at all if it had been bargained using different values.[2]

1.2.2   *Disclosure of transactions*

As a result of the above difficulty, accounting standards internationally have required disclosure of related party transactions and relationships, rather than adjustment of the financial statements. This is the approach adopted by the IASC in its standard on related parties, IAS 24, and by the FASB in its standard, SFAS 57. The ASB has adopted a similar approach in FRS 8 (see 2 below).

The main issues which have to be considered in determining the disclosures to be made are as follows:

- identification of related parties;
- types of transactions and arrangements; and
- information to be disclosed.

1.3 Position in the UK

It was not until the publication of FRS 8 in 1995 that there was a UK accounting standard requiring general related party disclosures in financial statements. Before then, companies legislation introduced disclosures on a piecemeal basis, which are largely restricted to transactions with directors and balances with group companies.

The legal disclosure requirements relating to loans and other transactions with directors, which are now incorporated in the Companies Act 1985, are discussed briefly in 3.1 below and more fully in Chapter 29. They were originally introduced in the Companies Act 1980, largely as a result of reports by DTI Inspectors on their investigations into the affairs of various companies, in which related party matters, particularly transactions with directors, featured prominently. Ironically, one of the earliest examples was the 1969 report on the affairs of Pergamon Press Limited, whose chairman was one Robert Maxwell.

There is also an overriding obligation, under sections 226 and 227 of the Companies Act 1985, for the accounts of the reporting entity to give a true and fair view of the state of affairs and the profit or loss. If the financial statements drawn up in compliance with the detailed requirements of the Act do not contain sufficient information, any necessary additional information must be provided in the balance sheet, or profit and loss account, or in a note to the financial statements.[3] Therefore, if a related party disclosure is necessary to give a true and fair view, it ought to be made, even if it is not specifically required by FRS 8 or the law.

In addition to the requirements of FRS 8 and the Companies Act, the Stock Exchange imposes additional disclosures on listed and AIM companies which impinge on related party issues. These are discussed at 3.3 below.

2 FRS 8

2.1 Contrasted with ED 46 and FRED 8

The objective of FRS 8 is 'to ensure that financial statements contain the disclosures necessary to draw attention to the possibility that the reported financial position and results may have been affected by the existence of related parties and by material transactions with them'.[4]

In FRS 8 the ASB has opted for a more conventional approach than that originally advocated by the ASC in ED 46, which had proposed the disclosure of only 'abnormal' related party transactions, which it defined and illustrated. The logic behind this suggested approach was to attempt to avoid the plethora of disclosures that would inevitably arise if all transactions were to be disclosed. However, not only was this approach contrary to generally accepted international practice, but also it was seen by most commentators to be unworkable. Moreover, as noted above, there is a view that the existence of a related party relationship brings with it the possibility that future transactions may be undertaken on a non-arm's length basis and, accordingly, all material transactions with such parties should be disclosed, whatever their terms.

Accordingly, in FRED 8 the ASB proposed the approach now required in FRS 8 of disclosing all material related party transactions, with the result that there were no differences of substance between FRED and the final FRS. However, there were some major differences of detail, which are noted in the commentary below. FRS 8 is a short standard and its basic requirements are deceptively simple. However, implementation of FRS 8 has often proved it to be far from easy to apply in practice. We address the more common questions of interpretation in the following discussion.

FRS 8 became mandatory for related party transactions first accounted for in accounting periods beginning on or after 23 December 1995.[5] At the time of publication of the FRS the ASB indicated that it would not expect disclosure of earlier transactions other than that required by companies legislation.[6] For this reason, many of the extracts cited in this Chapter have no comparative figures.

2.2 Identification of related parties

FRS 8 sets out four general definitions of 'related party', two of which are based on the concept of 'control', and two on that of 'influence'; these are discussed in 2.2.1 below. These general definitions are supplemented by a list (in paragraph 2.5(b) of the FRS) of entities and individuals that are always to be regarded as related parties and another list (in paragraph 2.5(c)) of entities and individuals that are normally, in the absence of evidence to the contrary, to be so regarded. As a shorthand, the following discussion refers to parties named in paragraph 2.5(b) as 'deemed related parties' and those in paragraph 2.5(c) as 'presumed related parties'.

In many instances it is possible to decide whether or not an entity or individual is a related party purely by reference to the lists of deemed and presumed related parties, which are discussed in 2.2.2 and 2.2.3 below. However, the standard indicates that these examples are not intended to be exhaustive.[7] It will therefore be necessary to refer to the general definitions in other cases.

The explanation section of the FRS clarifies that, where relevant, the definitions are intended to include both natural and legal persons. For example, the party that 'controls' the reporting entity could be either a company (or other vehicle) or an individual. The standard also states that, while all the definitions and examples are framed in terms of single entities or individuals, they are to be read as including entities and/or individuals acting in concert.[8]

2.2.1 General definitions of related party

FRS 8 defines two or more parties as related parties when at any time during the financial period:

(a)   one party has direct or indirect control of the other party; or

(b)   the parties are subject to common control from the same source; or

(c)   one party has influence over the financial and operating policies of the other party to an extent that that other party might be inhibited from pursuing at all times its own separate interests; or

(d)   the parties, in entering a transaction, are subject to influence from the same source to such an extent that one of the parties to the transaction has subordinated its own separate interests.[9]

A   Definitions based on control

The definitions based on 'control' (Definition (a) and Definition (b) above) are relatively easy to understand. Control is defined as 'the ability to direct the financial and operating policies of an undertaking with a view to gaining economic benefits from its activities'.[10] The same definition is used in FRS 5 – *Reporting the substance of transactions* – in respect of 'control of another entity'.[11] It is thus not restricted to voting (i.e. ownership) control, but includes economic control as well.

Definition (a) will most obviously include the reporting entity's parent and subsidiary undertakings and any individuals controlling the entity or its ultimate parent undertaking. However, it can include other relationships, for example those between the reporting entity and its directors or other key management, or its shareholders. The reference to indirect control is simply control exercised through another vehicle (e.g. an intermediate holding company).

Definition (b) has the effect that fellow subsidiary undertakings of the same parent are related parties of each other. It also means that members of so-called 'horizontal' groups (i.e. entities controlled by the same non-corporate shareholders such as individuals, partnerships or trusts) are related parties of each other, even though under UK company law they are not members of the same group.

The explanation section of the standard clarifies that common control is also deemed to exist where two or more parties are subject to control from boards having a 'controlling nucleus' of directors in common.[12] It is thus not open to a reporting entity to argue that common directorships can never give rise to related parties by virtue of the directors' common law duty (in the UK at least) to act in the best interests of each individual company. 'Controlling nucleus' is not defined, but the intention seems reasonably clear.

B *Definitions based on 'influence'*

The definitions of related party based on 'influence' (Definition (c) and Definition (d) above) are far less straightforward than those based on 'control', partly because there is no specific definition of 'influence'. However, the explanation section of the FRS contrasts influence with control on the criterion that the outcome (or potential outcome) of a relationship based on influence is less certain than one based on control.[13]

For example, a company can effectively compel a subsidiary to enter into a particular transaction (control). However, it cannot ensure that a 30%-owned associated undertaking enters into the same transaction, although it may well be able to persuade it to do so (influence). The practical implication of this is that, whereas the existence of a relationship based on control will generally be clear cut, the existence of one based on influence will be open to debate. This is most easily illustrated by considering the definitions themselves.

Definition (c) is similar, but not identical, to the concept of 'significant influence' used in the definition of 'associated undertaking' in SSAP 1 and the Companies Act. Thus, it will clearly capture the relationship between investors and their associated undertakings or joint ventures. However, it also covers situations where one entity influences another without having any ownership interest (e.g. through a 'friendly' director on the other entity's board). Significantly, Definition (c) requires that the party subject to influence '*might be*' (rather than has *actually* been) inhibited from pursuing its own interests. It does not therefore seem possible to contend that Definition (c) does not apply in a particular case by arguing that, although one party (A) is subject to the influence of another (B), A *has not* failed to pursue its own interests. Rather, it would appear to be necessary to argue that A *could never* fail to pursue its own interests as the result of B's influence — a much heavier burden of proof.

There is also the question of what is meant by a party's being 'inhibited from pursuing ... its separate interests'. A narrow view would be that it implies that the party has entered into a transaction on unfavourable terms. A broader view would be that it means simply that the party has entered into a transaction that it would not have undertaken otherwise, whatever its terms. This is not specifically addressed, although it seems clear that the broader view should be taken, since, as noted in 1.1 above, FRS 8 states that related party transactions can occur on arm's length terms. In other words, it is not a necessary condition of a related party transaction that one party has apparently been financially disadvantaged.

Definition (d) above is fundamentally different from all the others, in that its focus is the circumstances of individual transactions rather than the overall relationship between the parties. In contrast to Definition (c), which refers merely to the possibility that one party might influence the other, Definition (d) also requires the transacting parties actually to have been subject to common influence. Furthermore, a much stronger degree of influence is implied by Definition (d) (which requires that one party *has subordinated* its own ... interests') than by Definition (c) (which merely requires that the party subject to influence *might be inhibited* from pursuing ... its own ... interests'). Somewhat confusingly, Definition (d), which refers to the concept of 'influence' uses the same wording ('subordinated its separate interests') as is used in the explanation section of the FRS to describe the concept of 'control' and contrast it with that of 'influence'![14]

In our view, the intention of Definition (d) becomes clearer only when one understands how it has evolved. Originally, FRED 8 proposed that a party subject to control and another subject to influence from the same source would be related parties of each other.[15] This would have had the effect, for example, that a subsidiary and an associated undertaking of the same investor were treated as related parties. In developing FRS 8, the ASB took the view that this was both too wide and too narrow a definition of a related party. On the one hand, a subsidiary and associate of the same investor may happen to transact with each other without any interference from their common shareholder. On the other hand, a common shareholder is clearly in a position to engineer transactions not only between its subsidiaries and associates but also between different associates or joint ventures.

The final version of Definition (d) is intended to resolve this dilemma by requiring the circumstances of each case to be examined. The explanation section of the FRS reinforces this point by stating that the effect of Definition (d) is that two parties are not 'necessarily' related purely because:

(a)   they are both associates (or one is an associate and another a subsidiary) of the same investor; or

(b)   they have a director in common.[16]

That said, however, the great majority of parties related by virtue of Definition (d) will probably fall into one or other of these categories.

Whilst we understand the difficulty facing the ASB in drafting Definition (d), we believe that the final wording is unsatisfactory, since it is clear that in practice it leads to different views being taken of similar situations, as the following example illustrates:

Example 28.1

Mr X is a director of A plc, a listed company, and the owner of B Limited. Both companies are supplied by S Limited. Mr X has negotiated a deal with S Limited to supply goods to B Limited at a discount that would not normally be available to a company of the size of B Limited.

In discussing a virtually identical situation, Wild and Creighton conclude that B Limited and S Limited are related parties under Definition (d) because they have transacted at the instigation of Mr X, who has influenced S Limited 'to subordinate its own separate interests and offer discounts that it would otherwise not have given.'[17] In our view, however, the opposite conclusion is equally valid, on the basis that S's purpose in offering discounts to B is presumably to retain and, possibly expand, its relationship with A. On this construction of the facts, S is promoting, rather than subordinating, its own interests, and therefore Definition (d) does not apply. We also question whether, given the history of Definition (d), it was ever really intended to apply to this type of situation at all.

As noted above, Definition (d) focuses on an individual transaction rather than an ongoing relationship. It would therefore seem logical that, where a party is related to the reporting entity by virtue of a transaction of a type described by Definition (d), it is only that transaction that is disclosable and not, for example, routine sales and purchases of goods. However, the FRS makes it clear that two parties are related when the circumstances giving rise to the relationship exist 'at any time during the financial period'.[18] In other words, even if only one transaction of this type occurs during a financial period, all other transactions with the relevant party in that period are deemed to be related party transactions. This can lead to the slightly strange result that two parties are treated as related in one year but not the next, even though they have transacted a similar amount of business, as the following example shows:

Example 28.2

S is a subsidiary undertaking, and A an associated undertaking, of H. In both 1996 and 1997 S makes sales of £1 million of finished goods to A which, for the purposes of this example, do not fall within Definition (d). However, in 1996 A also buys a freehold property from S for £100,000 at the instigation of H, a transaction that therefore does fall within Definition (d). Thus S and A are related parties in 1996, but not in 1997. Their accounts (subject to the availability of any exemptions, discussed in 2.3.5 below) will therefore disclose related party transactions of £1.1 million in 1996 and nil in 1997 (together with a comparative of £1.1 million). This is arguably misleading, since it confuses the true related party transaction with the ongoing trading relationship.

In our view, the above discussion indicates that reconsideration of Definition (d) should be a high priority for the ASB in any future review of FRS 8.

2.2.2   Deemed related parties

FRS 8 states that 'for the avoidance of doubt, the following are related parties of the reporting entity':

(a) its ultimate and intermediate parent undertakings, subsidiary undertakings, and fellow subsidiary undertakings;

(b) its associates and joint ventures;

(c) the investor or venturer in respect of which the reporting entity is an associate or a joint venture;

(d) directors of the reporting entity and the directors of its ultimate and intermediate parent undertakings; and

(e) pension funds for the benefit of employees of the reporting entity or of any entity that is a related party of the reporting entity.[19]

Entities falling within (a) above have not, in our experience, given rise to any difficulties of interpretation or identification in practice. Issues raised by the other categories are discussed below.

A   *Associates and joint ventures and their investors*

One of the more curious effects of certain of the deemed and presumed related party relationships is that they are not reciprocal. In other words, it may be the case that A and B are deemed or presumed to be related parties when A is the reporting entity, but not when B is the reporting entity. This contradicts the general definitions of related party (discussed in section 2.2.1), which explicitly assume that relationships are reciprocal in all cases. The deemed relationships between associates and their investors are a common case in point, as the following example illustrates:

Example 28.3

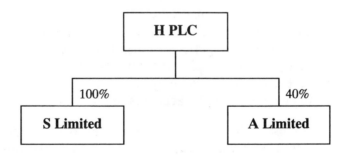

If H is the reporting entity, A is deemed to be a related party of both H and the H group (because it is an associate of both). Thus any transactions between A and either H or S will automatically be disclosed in H's accounts. If, however, A is the reporting entity, H is deemed to be a related party (because it is the investor of which A is an associated undertaking), but S is not. This has the effect that, if A transacts directly with H, those transactions will be disclosed in A's accounts, but, if it undertakes identical transactions with S, disclosure is not *automatically* required. It would be necessary to show that the relationship fell within one of the general definitions based on 'influence' discussed in 2.2.1 above, the more likely being Definition (d).

Another issue is that an investor and investee may have a different perception of the relationship between them. It is not unknown, particularly after an unsuccessful bid, for an investor to equity account for an investee which does not regard itself as being subject to significant influence from the investor. In such cases, it would appear sensible to have regard to the perception of the reporting entity. However, there may still be a related party relationship by virtue of the presumption (discussed in section 2.2.3 B below) that investors owning 20% or more of the reporting entity are related parties.

B   Directors of the reporting entity and its parent undertakings

In treating directors of the reporting entity and its parent undertakings (but not those of its subsidiary undertakings) as related parties, FRS 8 has taken its lead from the Companies Act 1985, rather than the Stock Exchange, which also treats directors of subsidiaries as related parties — see 3.3.3. Again echoing the Companies Act, FRS 8 states that 'directors' for this purpose include shadow directors as defined in the Act[20] (see Chapter 29, section 2.2). However, because the definition of 'materiality' used by FRS 8 is different from that used by the Companies Act, FRS 8 may well require disclosure of some transactions with directors that escape disclosure under the Companies Act. This is discussed more fully in 2.3.2 below.

C   Pension funds

Given the alleged transactions between companies controlled by Robert Maxwell and their pension funds, it was inevitable that FRS 8 would treat pension funds as deemed related parties. However, the ASB was clearly concerned that this might offend the sensitivities of some pension fund trustees. Accordingly, the FRS emphasises that the fact that pension funds are treated as related parties 'is not intended to call into question the independence of trustees with regard to their fiduciary obligations to members of the scheme'. The FRS goes on to say, although without explaining why, that 'transactions between the reporting entity and the pension fund may be in the interest of members but nevertheless need to be reported in the accounts of the reporting entity.'[21]

In any event, as discussed in 2.3.5 D, contributions paid to the scheme are exempt from disclosure. It is only other transactions with the reporting entity (e.g. loans, sales of fixed assets) that must be disclosed. A more common transaction in practice is the recharge of administrative costs by the sponsoring company, examples being Burton and Rank:

Extract 28.1: The Burton Group plc (1996)

23   Related party transactions

The Group recharges the Burton Group Pension Schemes with the costs of administration and independent advisors borne by the Group. The total amount recharged in the period to 31 August 1996 was £1.8 million (1995 - £1.5 million).

Extract 28.2: The Rank Group Plc (1996)

32   RELATED PARTY TRANSACTIONS

The Group recharges The Rank Group UK Pension Schemes with the costs of administration and independent advisers borne by the Group. The total recharged in the year ended 31 December 1996 was £1,112,000 (1995 - £1,016,000).

It is curious that a pension fund and the sponsoring employer are deemed to be related parties when the employer is the reporting entity, but not when the fund is the reporting entity. This is another example of the non-reciprocal nature of some of the deemed and presumed related party relationships referred to above. However, the SORP on accounting for pension schemes requires the sponsoring employer to be treated as a related party.[22]

2.2.3   Presumed related parties

FRS 8 requires that the following should be presumed to be related parties of the reporting entity:

(a)   the key management of the reporting entity and the key management of its parent undertaking or undertakings;

(b)   a person owning or able to exercise control over 20% or more of the voting rights of the reporting entity, whether directly or through nominees;

(c)   each person acting in concert in such a way as to be able to exercise control or influence over the reporting entity; and

(d)   an entity managing or managed by the reporting entity under a management contract.[23]

The presumption that the above are related parties of the reporting entity can be rebutted in a particular case only if 'it can be demonstrated that neither party has influenced the financial and operating policies of the other in such a way as to inhibit the pursuit of separate interests.'[24]

It is far from clear by virtue of which of the general definitions of related party (Definitions (a) to (d), discussed in 2.2.1) these parties are presumed to be related. In particular, the fact that it is possible to rebut the presumption that these parties are related if neither party *'has influenced'* the other contradicts

Definition (c), which defines a relationship as created by the mere ability to exercise, rather than the actual exercise of, influence.

The FRS gives no guidance as to what is meant by the words 'inhibit the pursuit of separate interests'. One interpretation would be that one of the parties has been disadvantaged, financially or otherwise. However, this seems inconsistent with the ASB's view that a related party transaction can be undertaken on an arm's length basis. We therefore interpret this phrase as meaning that one of the parties has entered into a transaction that it would not have entered into in the absence of the relationship, rather than that it has been disadvantaged. On this view, a heavy burden of proof is needed to rebut the presumption that the parties listed above are related parties if they have transacted with the reporting entity. Against that, however, as the following discussion shows, parties falling under most of these headings will be relatively rare.

A   Key management

The FRS defines 'key management' as 'those persons in senior positions having authority or responsibility for directing or controlling the major activities and resources of the reporting entity'.[25] This clearly cannot include directors or shadow directors, since these are treated as related parties in all circumstances, as set out in section 2.2.2 above.

The main intention of the definition is presumably to ensure that transactions with persons with responsibilities similar to those of directors do not escape disclosure simply because they are not directors. This would otherwise have provided an obvious loophole in the FRS. However, it is not clear whether many individuals will fall within this heading. It seems, for example, to be restricted to even fewer persons than the term 'officer' used by the Companies Act to refer to senior persons other than directors.

In the first place, the individual concerned must apparently be in a position to direct or control 'the major activities and resources' of the entity — i.e. all of them, not just one or some of them. It is doubtful whether most board directors would have such power, let alone other staff. It may be that this is a drafting slip and that the ASB's intention was that a member of key management should control '*a* major activity or resource'. This semantic quibble aside, it is still doubtful whether many persons will fall into this category. For example, a purchasing manager may have wide discretion to choose suppliers and negotiate prices, but he will generally be subject to various constraints imposed by the board, so that his authority falls short of an ability to 'direct and control' the purchasing function.

In our view, the type of person most likely to be a 'key manager' is a director of a subsidiary undertaking, but not of the holding company, who nevertheless participates in the management of the group. Companies may argue that, if the individual concerned were truly part of the 'key management' of the group, he would be on the parent company board. However, this would be inconsistent with the view taken by the ASB at the individual company level that 'key management' may be found outside the boardroom. Moreover, a review of the chairman's statement (and the photographs!) in the published accounts of certain groups makes it fairly clear that such individuals do exist.

While 'key management' would normally be employees of the reporting entity (or of a company in the same group), seconded staff and persons engaged under management or outsourcing contracts may well have a level of authority or responsibility such that they should be regarded as 'key management'. However, the wording of the definition of 'key management' appears to restrict its application to natural persons. It is hard to see how corporate entities could be regarded as 'persons in a senior position'.

Perhaps for the various reasons set out above, disclosures relating to key managers (at least, explicitly described as such) are relatively rare. An example is given by Friends Provident, although this effectively aggregates transactions with key management and those with directors:

Extract 28.3: Friends Provident Life Office (1996)

29.   RELATED PARTY TRANSACTIONS [extract]

Key management, their close family and undertakings controlled by them, had various transactions with the Group during the year. Key management consists of all directors and general managers of the Office.

In aggregate these were as set out below:

	£000
Payments during the year by key management* in respect of policies and investments issued or managed by the Group:	
Periodic payments	41
Single payments	291
Payments during the year by the Group to key management* in respect of such policies and contracts	23

* Including close family and undertakings controlled by key management.

B   Shareholders owning 20% or more

There will not normally be any difficulty identifying such persons. The debate will be whether it is possible to rebut the presumption that such persons are related parties. Where the party holding 20% or more is itself a minority shareholder this may be relatively easy. In other cases, however, the issue will not be so clear cut, as the following example shows:

Example 28.4

Company A holds 25% of Company B as the result of a failed takeover bid. It has no representation on the board of Company B and does not account for it as an associated undertaking. On the face of it, it might seem possible to rebut the presumption that A exercises sufficient influence over B to require them to be treated as related parties. On the other hand, if A and B are transacting with each other, the question must be asked as to why those transactions are occurring, and this may lead to the conclusion that they are indeed related parties.

If the transactions are occurring at non-arm's length prices, the presumption must be that A and B are related parties. Even if B is purchasing goods from A on arm's length terms, it begs the question as to why B is choosing to put business in the direction of an unwelcome predator. It may be that B is anxious to maintain a good relationship with A, which could (for example) crash B's share price by suddenly offloading a large part of its shareholding on to the market. In this case B could clearly be construed as acting under the influence (albeit passive) of A. On the other hand if A were a long-standing trading partner, particularly if it were the only available supplier of a particular product, it could be reasonable to rebut the presumption that A and B are related. It would also be possible to rebut the presumption if the transactions arose from contracts entered into before the bid.

A rather curious, and we suspect unintended, side-effect of the presumption that major shareholders are related parties is that participation by those shareholders in share issues and dividends should technically be disclosed as related party transactions. In practice, however, this requirement does not generally appear to be followed strictly, presumably on the view that if both major shareholders and total transactions with shareholders are disclosed, the portion relating to individual shareholders can be readily derived. However, some companies do disclose this information, an example being Associated British Foods (see Extract 28.9 at 2.3.3 below).

C   Each person acting in concert so as to be able to control or influence the reporting entity

'Control' and 'influence' mean the same here as in the context of the general definitions of related party discussed in sections 2.2.1 above.[26] Persons acting in concert 'comprise persons who, pursuant to an agreement or understanding (whether formal or informal), actively co-operate, whether through the ownership by any of them of shares in an undertaking or otherwise, to exercise control or influence over that undertaking'.[27]

The concept is clear enough. An individual who is not able to control or influence the reporting entity on his own may be able to do so by acting with others. The practical difficulty is how to identify concert parties, particularly as the FRS creates a presumed related party relationship where a concert party 'is able to' (rather than actually does) control or influence the reporting entity.

It is very unlikely that a concert party would be constituted under a formal agreement, and in any event such an agreement would be a private matter between the members of the concert party. The fact that a group of shareholders consistently vote together at meetings of the company might be evidence of a concert party; on the other hand, it could simply be coincidental. As in several of the cases discussed above, it would be necessary to look at the circumstances of the case. A group of shareholders who regularly force through controversial resolutions at extraordinary general meetings will probably comprise a concert party, whereas a group who simply vote the same way on routine matters will probably not.

D   *Entities managing or managed by the reporting entity*

The relationship between an entity and one managed by it is not dissimilar to that between a company and its directors and key management. However, related parties falling under this heading may be less common than might appear at first sight, since the requirement, at least if read literally, is that one entity must manage another (i.e. as a whole). In practice, however, many management contracts cover specific assets and functions of an entity, not the entity as a whole.

Suppose that A is a property company that owns a block of flats. Under a management contract, company B manages the flats on a day-to-day basis. B is managing an asset (in fact the sole asset) of A, but is not managing A as a whole, and therefore does not apparently fall within this definition. One would therefore have to consider whether A and B fell within one of the general definitions of related party discussed above. In practice, it is very unlikely that there would be any transactions between A and B, other than the payment of the management fee. The issue would rather be whether B used its influence to initiate transactions between A and another party connected in some way with B.

An example of a disclosure under this heading is given by Associated Nursing Services:

Extract 28.4: Associated Nursing Services plc (1997)

28.   Related Party Transactions [extract]

The following companies are deemed to be related parties by virtue of the fact that Associated Nursing Services plc manages their day to day operations and has influence over the financial and operating policies of the other party.

...

Grosvenor Care plc

Associated Nursing Services plc has a management contract to manage The Haven Nursing Home.

Headingley Homes plc

Associated Nursing Services plc has a management contract to manage the Headingley Nursing Home. Care Haven Ltd., a wholly owned subsidiary of Associated Nursing Services plc, had a contract to build an extension and refurbish the Headingley Nursing Home.

...

During the year [ended 31 March 1997] the following amounts were charged ... for the following services.

	Management fees £000's	Construction fees £000's	Other £000's	Total £000's
...				
Grosvenor Care plc	39	–	4	43
Headingley Homes plc	20	121	8	149
...				

As at 31 March 1997 the following amounts were outstanding ...

	Management fees £000's	Construction fees £000's	Other £000's	Total £000's
...				
Grosvenor Care plc	31	119	–	150
Headingley Homes plc	168	73	55	296
...				

2.2.4   *Close family and controlled entities*

Where an individual is identified as a related party of the reporting entity, there is a presumption that the following are also related parties:

(a)   the 'close family' of that individual; and

(b)   any partnerships, companies, trusts or other entities controlled by that individual or his 'close family'.[28]

A   Close family

'Close family' of an individual is defined as 'those family members, or members of the same household, who may be expected to influence, or be influenced by, that person in their dealings with the reporting entity'.[29] FRED 8 referred to 'immediate' rather than 'close' family and listed the relatives who would normally fall under this heading. FRS 8 abandoned this approach, on the basis that the degree of influence arising from the relationship is more important than its immediacy. However, we assume that 'close family' in FRS 8 is normally intended to include at least those relatives identified as 'immediate family' in FRED 8, i.e. a spouse, parent, child (adult or minor), brother, sister and the spouses of any of these.[30]

The definition refers to the person's 'dealings' with the reporting entity, but it does not make it clear whether the FRS is concerned with dealings in a business capacity only, or also those in a private capacity. We presume that the former only are intended. Otherwise it would, for example, be necessary (subject to considerations of materiality) for a food retailer to disclose details of each director's household shopping at its supermarkets!

An example of a disclosure made as a result of this requirement (and, to some extent, possibly Part II of Schedule 6 to the Companies Act as well) is given by Kwik-Fit (Mr T Farmer being the chairman and chief executive):

Extract 28.5: Kwik-Fit Holdings plc (1997)

Note 9(d) Directors' Interests: Transactions [extract]

Mr and Mrs T. Farmer and family lease certain properties to the Group. The rentals payable on these properties were £341,000 (1996 - £341,000) and the balance owing to Mr and Mrs Farmer at 28 February 1997 was Nil (1996 - Nil).

B   Controlled entities

Although the FRS does not specify whether legal or de facto control is intended in this context, we believe that the broad definition of control used elsewhere in the standard is meant to apply. In other words, controlled entities are not restricted to those subject to legal control. Kwik-Fit provides an example of disclosure that may have been given in pursuance of this provision of FRS 8, although it could equally have been given in order to comply with one or more requirements of Schedule 6 to the Companies Act:

Extract 28.6: Kwik-Fit Holdings plc (1997)

Note 9(d) Directors' Interests: Transactions [extract]

Mr J.R. Padget is a Principal of Padget Associates B.V. who received fees and reimbursement of expenses of £93,317 in relation to services provided to the Group during the year (1996 - £84,000). The balance owing to Padget Associates B.V. at 28 February 1997 was Nil (1996 - Nil).

One effect of the presumption that entities controlled by an individual related party are themselves related parties is to create relationships that are not reciprocal, as the following example illustrates. Suppose that Mr X is a director of A plc and the owner of B Limited. If A is the reporting entity, B is presumed to be a related party (because it is an entity controlled by Mr X, who, being a director of A, is a deemed related party of A). However, if B is the reporting entity, A is not presumed to be a related party (because FRS 8 does not presume that a company, a director of which a related party of the reporting entity, is a related party of the reporting entity).

This seems slightly counter-intuitive, since, if A (a listed company) and B (a small private company) are transacting, the chances are that those transactions are in fact more significant to B than to A. However, this is not the end of the matter, since it could be that A and B are related parties by virtue of one of the general definitions discussed in 2.2.1 above.

C   Rebutting the presumption

We assume that the presumption that close family and controlled entities are related parties is rebuttable, although the FRS provides no guidance as to whether, or on what basis, it may be rebutted. In general, though, it seems very difficult to rebut the presumption where transactions are occurring.

Suppose, for example, that the reporting entity X buys widely available raw materials from Y, a company controlled by Mrs A, the sister of Mr B, a director of X. The transactions are on normal commercial terms, but as has been emphasised elsewhere, the FRS takes the view that this is not relevant. Rather, the basic question that must be addressed is why, out of all of the suppliers in the country, the reporting entity chose Y. Is it really credible that it had nothing to do with the family connection between Mrs A and Mr B?

2.2.5   *Parties presumed not to be related parties*

FRS 8 does not require the following entities to be treated as related parties:

(a)   providers of finance in the ordinary course of business;

(b)   utility companies;

(c)   government departments and their sponsored bodies; or

(d)   parties with whom the reporting entity transacts a significant volume of business.[31]

The reason for this exemption is that, without it, many entities that would not normally be regarded as related parties could fall within the general definitions of related party. For example, a small clothing manufacturer selling 90% of its output to a high street chain could be under the effective control of that customer. The ASB has already (and more appropriately) addressed the issue in its Statement on the *Operating and Financial Review* (OFR), under the heading of 'Dynamics of the business'. Here it is suggested that the OFR should discuss the main factors and influences that may have a major effect on future results, whether or not they were significant in the period under review; for example, dependence on major suppliers or customers.[32]

The exemption is effective only where these parties would be considered as related to the reporting entity 'simply as a result of their role' as providers of finance etc. If there are other reasons why a party would be considered a related party, the exemption does not apply.[33] For example, the water company that supplies the reporting entity is not considered a related party if the only link between the two is the supply of water. If, however, the water company is also an associated undertaking of the reporting entity, the exemption does not apply and the two are considered related parties, in which case transactions relating to the supply of water must be disclosed if material.

2.3   Disclosure of related party transactions

FRS 8 requires disclosure of material related party transactions. A transaction is defined as 'the transfer of assets or liabilities or the performance of services by, to or for a related party irrespective of whether a price is charged'.[34] Read literally, this definition requires many transactions to be disclosed more than once. For example, if a company buys goods on credit from a related party and pays for them 30 days later, both the original sale and the final payment represent a 'transfer of assets ... by [or] to a related party' and should therefore on the face of it be separately disclosed. However, we doubt that this was the ASB's intention, and the nature of the disclosures required by FRS 8 seems to support this view.

2.3.1   Disclosable transactions

The FRS provides a list, not intended to be exhaustive, of the types of transaction which should be disclosed:

(a)   purchases or sales of goods (finished or unfinished);

(b)   purchases or sales of property and other assets;

(c)   rendering or receiving of services;

(d)   agency arrangements;

(e)   leasing arrangements;

(f)   transfer of research and development;

(g)   licence agreements;

(h)   provision of finance (including loans and equity contributions in cash or in kind);

(i)   guarantees and the provision of collateral security; and

(j)   management contracts.[35]

The FRS emphasises that disclosure is required irrespective of whether or not a price is charged.[36] This means that the standard applies to gifts of assets or services and to asset swaps. Common examples of such transactions include:

■   administration by a company of the company pension scheme free of charge;

■   transfer of group relief from one member of a group to another without payment;

■   guarantees by directors of bank loans to the company.

2.3.2   *Materiality*

FRS 8, like all accounting standards, applies only to material items. However, the FRS contains a definition of materiality that goes well beyond the undefined concept in general use, which focuses more on the financial effect on the company's accounts, and is often thought of as a percentage of turnover, profit or net assets.

For the purposes of FRS 8, 'transactions are material when their disclosure might reasonably be expected to influence decisions made by the users of general purpose financial statements'.[37] This has the effect that virtually any related party transaction whose disclosure is sensitive (for tax reasons perhaps) is by definition material, because it is expected by the reporting entity to influence a user of the accounts. It is therefore not possible to avoid disclosing such items on the grounds that they are financially immaterial.

FRS 8 does not clarify whether the materiality of transactions is to be considered individually or in aggregate. Whilst a literal reading of the FRS suggests that they should be considered individually, such an interpretation cannot, in our view, be correct, since it would effectively frustrate the intentions of the FRS, as the following example shows:

Example 28.6

H plc is a small listed company for which transactions of £1 million are regarded as material. Each month it makes sales of £90,000 to its associated undertaking A. If each transaction is considered in isolation no disclosure would be made. If, however, the total transactions for the year (i.e. £1,080,000) are considered together disclosure would be made. In this case, we believe that the latter interpretation is correct.

The situation becomes less clear, however, if for example H had made sales of £90,000 to each of twelve different associates, or to an assortment of associates, joint venture partners and its pension fund. In such cases, it seems more important to focus on the likelihood that disclosure of the transactions will influence a reader of the accounts than on their purely financial materiality.

In addition, where the related party is:

(a)   a director, key manager, or other individual in a position to influence, or accountable for stewardship of, the reporting entity;

(b)   a member of the close family of any individual within (a) above; or

(c)   an entity controlled by any individual within (a) or (b) above,

the FRS requires the materiality of related party transactions with such individuals and entities to be judged 'not only in terms of their significance to the reporting entity, but also in relation to the other related party'.[38]   The intention is clearly to ensure that transactions that could be beneficial to individuals do not escape disclosure on the basis that they are immaterial to the reporting entity.

This requirement impacts mainly on disclosure of transactions with directors and persons or companies connected with them. Such transactions are prima facie disclosable under Part II of Schedule 6 to the Companies Act, except when the interest of the director concerned is not considered material. Prior to FRS 8, there was some debate as to whether materiality should be judged by reference to the circumstances of the company or those of the director (see Chapter 29, section 3.5). FRS 8 now requires materiality to be judged by reference to the circumstances of both parties.

We have considerable doubts as to the wisdom of this aspect of FRS 8. As a matter of principle, it seems wrong that an accounting standard should require disclosure of transactions that are not material to the truth and fairness of the accounts. If it is thought desirable to make such disclosures for other reasons, the proper place to make them is in the report on corporate governance matters, not the financial statements. In addition, strict application of the requirement could lead to anomalies, as the following example shows:

Example 28.5

X PLC sells two company cars to two retiring directors, Mr A and Mr B, for £10,000 and £15,000 respectively, which are their fair market values. Neither transaction is material to the company. Mr A earns £40,000 and Mr B £400,000 a year. The effect of FRS 8 could be that the (lower) £10,000 transaction is disclosed (because it is material to Mr A, but not the company), but that the (higher) £15,000 transaction is not (because it is not material either to the company or to Mr B).

In practice, many companies, perhaps mindful of the spirit of the Cadbury and Greenbury codes, seem to prefer to disclose details of all transactions with which a director is associated, whether they are material or not and even where the third party would not strictly be regarded as a related party by either FRS 8 or the Companies Act. An example is Redland PLC (the 'Braas group companies' referred to being subsidiaries of Redland):

Extract 28.7: Redland PLC (1996)

19   Related Party Transactions [extract]

Mrs H Bruhn-Braas, a non-executive director of Redland PLC, has a controlling interest in BTI. During the year ended 31st December 1996, Braas group companies paid to BTI a total of £16.2 million for transportation services on an arm's length basis. At 31st December 1996, the Braas group owed BTI £0.8 million

Mr DRW Young, an executive director of Redland PLC, is Chairman and a director of Young Samuel Chambers (YSC) Limited, a management consultancy company, which provided Redland companies with services invoiced at a cost of £17,131 during the year ended 31st December 1996. The amount involved is not considered material to either party. Mr Young has no financial interest in, nor received any director's fees from, YSC in 1996.

Whilst we are obviously not privy to the full facts, it is our view that, on the basis of the above descriptions, the transaction involving Mrs Bruhn-Braas does require disclosure, but that involving Mr Young strictly does not and appears to have been given more for the sake of completeness.

Some companies disclose that immaterial transactions have taken place with directors, but do not quantify them. An example is Royal Sun Alliance:

Extract 28.8: Royal & Sun Alliance Insurance Group plc (1996)

35.   Transactions with related parties [extract]

FRS8 also widens the disclosure requirements in respect of material transactions between the Company and its subsidiaries and the directors, other key managers, their close family and entities under their control. A number of these have general and/or long term insurance policies with subsidiary companies of the Group. Such policies are on normal commercial terms except that executive directors and key managers are entitled to special rates which are also available to other members of staff. The Board has considered the financial effect of such insurance policies and other transactions with Group companies and has concluded that they are not material to the Group and, if disclosed, would not influence decisions made by users of these financial statements.

This is quite extensive disclosure of items that are 'not material' and 'would not influence decisions made by users' of the accounts! Perhaps this indicates that the company shares our doubts as to whether FRS 8 really intended to capture transactions such as this, but is concerned not to be seen as ignoring the prima facie requirement for disclosure.

In our view, there is a clear case in any future revision of FRS 8 to exempt from disclosure transactions undertaken on non-preferential terms by individuals in a private (as opposed to a business) capacity with companies whose normal business is trading directly with the general public (e.g. high street banks, certain insurance companies, and retailers).

2.3.3 Disclosures required

FRS 8 requires the following details to be given in respect of related party transactions:

(a)   the names of the related parties;

(b)   a description of the relationship between the parties;

(c)   a description of the transactions;

(d)   the amounts involved;

(e)   any other elements of the transactions necessary for an understanding of the financial statements;

(f)   the amounts due to or from related parties at the balance sheet date and provisions for doubtful debts due from such parties at that date; and

(g)   amounts written off in the period in respect of debts due to or from related parties.[39]

A comprehensive example of the required disclosures, covering various categories of related party, is given by Associated British Foods:

Extract 28.9: Associated British Foods plc (1996)

31.   RELATED PARTY TRANSACTIONS

The Associated British Foods plc group's ("ABF") related parties, as defined by Financial Reporting Standard 8, the nature of the relationship and the extent of transactions with them are summarised below:

	Sub note	1996 £'000
Management charge from Wittington Investments Limited, principally in respect of directors and staff paid by them	1	550
Charges to Wittington Services Limited in respect of services provided by ABF and its subsidiaries	1	(40)
Dividends paid by ABF and received in a beneficial capacity by:		
(i) Trustees of The Garfield Weston Foundation	2	3,221
(ii) Directors of Wittington Investments Limited who are not Trustees of The Foundation		520
(iii) Directors of ABF who are not Trustees of The Foundation and are not directors of Wittington Investments Limited	3	28
(iv) a member of the Weston family employed within the ABF group	4	284

		£m
Sales to fellow subsidiaries on normal trading terms	5	7
Purchases from fellow subsidiaries on normal trading terms	5	–
Amounts due from fellow subsidiary undertakings	5	1
Sales to George Weston Limited on normal trading terms	6	1
Sales to associated undertakings on normal trading terms	7	39
Purchases from associated undertakings on normal trading terms	7	(4)
Amounts due from associated undertakings	7	5
Amounts due to associated undertakings	7	(1)

Sub notes

1.   At 14 September 1996 Wittington Investments Limited held 458,342,290 ordinary shares (1995 – 458,142,290) representing in aggregate 50.9% (1995 – 50.9%) of the total issued ordinary share capital of ABF.

2.   The Garfield Weston Foundation ("The Foundation") is an English charitable trust which was established in 1958 by the late Mr W Garfield Weston. The Foundation has no direct interest in ABF but as at 14 September 1996 held 683,073 shares in Wittington Investments Limited representing 79.2% of that company's issued share capital and is, therefore, ABF's ultimate controlling party. The Trustees of the Foundation comprise six of the late Mr W Garfield Weston's children, including Garry H Weston who acts as Chairman of the Board of Trustees, and four of Garry H Weston's children.

3.   Details of the directors of ABF are given on page 2. Their beneficial interests, including family interests, in ABF and its subsidiaries are given on page 47. ...

4.   A member of the Weston family who is employed by the group and is not a director of ABF or Wittington Investments Limited and is not a Trustee of The Foundation.

5.   Fellow subsidiary companies are Aughton Limited, which was disposed of during the year, and Fortnum & Mason plc.

6.   George Weston Limited is a Canadian listed company in which Mr W G Galen Weston has a controlling interest.

7.   Details of the group's principal associated undertakings are set out on page 46.

None of the disclosures appears to present much practical difficulty, other than, in some cases, sensitivity. In Extract 28.9 above, for instance, the name of the 'member of the Weston family employed within the ABF group' has not been given as strictly required by the FRS (although, in our view, and presumably that of the company, it would add no useful additional information).

One possible problem area is the need to give 'any other elements of the transactions necessary for an understanding of the financial statements'. This is one of the less clear requirements of the FRS. It was proposed in FRED 8, which noted in the explanatory section that 'an example falling within this requirement would be a material difference between the fair value and the transacted amount where material transfers of assets, liabilities or services have taken place'.[40] This provoked some adverse comment, largely because of the difficulties in calculating it.

There was also some concern that the proposals in FRED 8 would have required commercially sensitive transfer pricing information to be given. In fact, such concern was misplaced since nearly all such transactions would have been exempt from disclosure as being between members of the same group (see 2.3.5 below). Be that as it may, the ASB attempted to address these concerns by modifying the final wording in FRS 8 to say that an example of a disclosure falling within this requirement 'would be the need to give an indication that the transfer of a major asset had taken place at an amount materially different from that obtainable on normal commercial terms'.[41]

We consider this somewhat confusing. Either fair value disclosures are required or they are not; and if they are, the requirement should be in the main body of the proposed standard, rather than dealt with almost in passing in the explanation section. Our strong view is that FRS 8 should not require disclosure of the fair value of transactions, since it is often impossible to calculate them meaningfully. We suspect that the underlying objective is to indicate the entity's true economic performance, as if it were unaffected by the influence of related parties. But this may not reflect the reality of the reporting entity's position, since many transactions with related parties would simply not occur at all if the parties were unrelated and it would be misleading to disclose the terms on which they might have been undertaken with third parties.

Example 28.7

A company sells a surplus property whose fair value is said to be £2 million to a related party for £1.5 million. If the financial statements were to disclose the transaction in these bald terms, users would inevitably infer that the company's interests had been prejudiced to the tune of £500,000. However, it may be the case that, in the market conditions at the time, the chances of making any sale were unlikely, and the company is better off with £1.5 million now than the off-chance of £2 million in several months' time. In these circumstances, a case could be made that the property's fair value, on the basis of an immediate sale to a third party, was nearer zero than £2 million, although few would regard a disclosure to this effect as acceptable either.

Perhaps, given the history of this paragraph, there is room to argue that the example in the FRS is a hint that fair value information is required for 'one-off' capital transactions but not for ongoing revenue items. However, this is a frankly unsatisfactory distinction, for which there can be no conceptual justification. On the other hand, from a pragmatic point of view, it would deal with preparers' concerns about giving sensitive pricing information, which is generally more of an issue when the transfer of goods or services is involved.

A further complication arises where assets, liabilities or services are transferred without charge. Where an asset or liability is transferred free of charge, its carrying amount prior to transfer gives at least a starting point for disclosing the value of the transaction. Problems may arise, however, with such items as ceded tax losses which may arguably have markedly different values to the transferor and transferee (e.g. because they can be used by the transferee sooner than by the transferor, or because there is a tax rate difference).

The FRS discourages companies from making 'boiler plate' disclosures to the effect that transactions have been undertaken on normal commercial terms. Such assertions should not be made 'unless the parties have conducted the transactions in an independent manner'. The standard clearly implies that the ASB believes this will rarely be the case, although it gives as a possible example the situation where two fellow subsidiary undertakings deal with each other without interference from their parent.[42] Notwithstanding this hint in the FRS, however, disclosures that transactions have been undertaken on an arm's length basis are very common, as shown by the extracts from Redland (Extract 28.7 at 2.3.2 above), Royal Sun Alliance (Extract 28.8 at 2.3.2 above), Associated British Foods (Extract 28.9 above), and TT Group (Extract 28.12 at 2.3.4 below).

Whilst there is no requirement to state specifically that there have been no material related party transactions, some companies have chosen to do so.[43]

2.3.4 Aggregation

Because of the voluminous disclosures that could result if each related party transaction were shown separately, the FRS permits aggregation of similar transactions with similar parties. However, this should not be done in a way that obscures the importance of significant transactions. For example, purchases or sales of goods with group companies could be aggregated, but any purchases or sales of fixed assets with such companies should be shown as a separate category. Equally, it would not be acceptable to aggregate sales of fixed assets to group companies with sales of fixed assets to key management.[44]

Most companies have taken advantage of the opportunity to aggregate disclosures in this way, very often in relation to transactions with associated undertakings, a typical example being BPB:

Extract 28.10: BPB plc (1997)

12.   Related party transactions

During the year group companies purchased goods from, and sold goods to, associated companies for £5.8 million and £2.3 million respectively; the amounts outstanding at the year end on these purchases and sales were £0.6 million and £0.2 million respectively.

   In addition the group recharged £1.7 million to its associated companies in respect of administrative costs incurred on their behalf; the amount outstanding at the year end was £0.5 million.

However, British Aerospace chose to disclose transactions with its main associates and joint ventures separately, presumably because these transactions form a significant part of its business:

Extract 28.11: British Aerospace Public Limited Company (1996)

30   Related party transactions [extract]

	Sales to related party £m	Purchases from related party £m	Amounts owed by related party £m	Amounts owed to related party £m	Balance of cash advanced to the Group £m	Operating costs funded during the year £m
Related party						
Airbus Industrie GIE	665	-	89	-	160	-
Panavia Aircraft GmbH	92	137	16	-	-	-
Eurofighter Jagdflugzeug GmbH	126	-	9	20	-	-
BAeSEMA Ltd	1	2	1	-	-	-
Matra BAe Dynamics SAS	13	3	3	-	58	-
Aero International (Regional) SAS	1	1	4	5	-	32

Airbus Industrie GIE
The Group shares in the results of Airbus Industrie GIE and participates in Airbus programmes which are effectively carried out on a joint venture basis. Guarantees given by the Group relating to Airbus Finance Company Limited are given in note 21. Amounts owed by, and cash advanced by Airbus Industrie GIE to the Group are shown within trade debtors and creditors respectively.

Panavia Aircraft GmbH
The Group has a 42.5% share in Panavia Aircraft GmbH.

Eurofighter Jagdflugzeug GmbH
The Group has a 33% share in Eurofighter Jagdflugzeug GmbH.

BAeSEMA Ltd
The Group has a 50% share in BAeSEMA Ltd. The Group has guaranteed obligations of BAeSEMA Ltd under a counter indemnity of £12 million.

Matra BAe Dynamics SAS

The Group has a 50% share in Matra BAe Dynamics SAS. Matra BAe Dynamics SAS was set up during the year as a joint venture between Group and the Lagardère Group. ...

Aero International (Regional) SAS

The Group has a 33% share in Aero International (Regional) SAS, which acts as disclosed agent in respect of sales by the group of regional aircraft to third party operators. Guarantees given by the group in respect of Aero International (Regional) SAS are given in note 21.

...

21   Contingent liabilities and commitments [extract]

The Group has guaranteed borrowings of Airbus Finance Company Limited Ltd totalling £36 million (1995 £26 million). The Group has guaranteed borrowings of Aero International (Regional) SAS of £9 million (1995 £nil).

FRS 8 additionally requires that any material transactions with an individual should be shown separately and not aggregated with others.[45]   Thus, if a company sells two assets to two different directors, and the transactions are both material, they cannot be grouped as 'Sales to directors' but must be disclosed individually, as is done by TT Group (Messrs Newman and Shipp being the chairman and deputy chairman respectively):

Extract 28.12: TT Group PLC (1996)

5.   Related party transactions

During the year subsidiary undertakings of the Group in the ordinary course of their respective businesses supplied and purchased goods and services valued at the aggregate of £196,000 (1995 — £91,000) and £33,000 (1995 — £27,000) respectively to companies in which J W Newman and N D Shipp were interested during the year. Such supplies were made on normal credit terms. Additionally, the Company in the ordinary course of its business leased premises and provided normal services in respect of such premises to a company wholly owned by J W Newman and N D Shipp during the year. The annual rental aggregating £6,000 (1995 — £6,000) and the annual service charge aggregating £10,800 (1995 — £9,000) were calculated on open market bases and were paid monthly. Subsidiary undertakings of the Group also in the ordinary course of business leased premises from companies wholly owned by J W Newman and N D Shipp during the year. The annual rentals, including service charges where applicable, aggregating £246,000 (1995 — £239,000) were calculated on open market bases and were paid monthly.

The separate disclosure here in respect of transactions with the parent company is not in fact strictly necessary. They could have been aggregated with those with other group companies and advantage taken of the exemption from disclosing transactions with the parent company when group accounts are presented (see 2.3.5 B).

2.3.5   Exemptions from disclosure

FRS 8 does not require disclosure:

(a)   in consolidated financial statements, of any transactions or balances between group entities that have been eliminated on consolidation;

(b)   in a parent's own financial statements when those statements are presented together with its consolidated financial statements;

(c)   in financial statements of subsidiary undertakings, 90 per cent or more of whose voting rights are controlled within the group, of transactions with entities that are part of the group or investees of the group qualifying as related parties, provided that the consolidated financial statements in which that subsidiary is included are publicly available;

(d)   of contributions paid to a pension fund; or

(e)   of emoluments in respect of services as an employee of the reporting entity.

Reporting entities that take advantage of exemption (c) are required to state that fact.[46] Although these exemptions appear quite extensive, in many cases they are effectively over-ridden by other requirements, as explained in the following discussion.

A   *Transactions eliminated on consolidation*

This is not so much an exemption as a statement of the obvious since, so far as the group accounts are concerned, such items do not exist. The effect is that no related party disclosures relating to subsidiary undertakings are required in group accounts. However, disclosure is still required in respect of transactions or balances with associates or joint ventures since these are not 'eliminated' on consolidation, although they may be subject to consolidation adjustments.

There is no specific guidance on transactions with joint ventures that are proportionally consolidated. However, common sense would suggest that, whilst there may technically be no need to disclose transactions and balances to the extent that they have been eliminated on consolidation, in practice it will be simpler and clearer to disclose the actual sale price and note that some part of this has been eliminated on consolidation.

Where a subsidiary joins or leaves the group during the period, it is treated as a related party for the whole period, not just for the period when it is a subsidiary, because the FRS makes it clear that two parties are related when the circumstances giving rise to the relationship exist 'at any time during the financial period'.[47] Where the reporting entity has transacted with such a company during the part of the period when it was not a member of the group, the transactions during that time will not have been eliminated on consolidation and, accordingly, must be disclosed. An example of such disclosure is given by Thomas Cook:

Extract 28.13: Thomas Cook Limited (1996)

27. Related party disclosures [extract]

On 28 June 1996, Sunworld Limited and its subsidiaries were acquired. Trading between this entity and the Thomas Cook Group post acquisition has been eliminated upon consolidation. However, from 1 January 1996 to the point of acquisition, it is classed as a related party under FRS 8. Sales to the Thomas Cook Group during this period were £23.2 million.

B   *Parent company financial statements when group accounts presented*

This exemption is largely a logical extension of the last. However, this is a case where the requirements of other pronouncements largely negate the FRS 8 exemption. For example:

■   the statutory accounts formats in Schedules 4, 9 and 9A to the Companies Act require separate disclosure in the parent company balance sheet of balances with subsidiary and associated undertakings (see 3 below); and

■   Part II of Schedule 6 to the Companies Act requires disclosure of certain transactions between directors of the parent company and group companies (see Chapter 29, section 3.5).

Also, all related party transactions of the company (other than those eliminated on consolidation) will in any event be disclosed in the group accounts. Parent companies that do not prepare group accounts (e.g. those heading small or medium-sized groups, or subsidiaries of parents complying with the EU Seventh Directive) have to comply with FRS 8 in full in their own accounts, subject to the '90% subsidiary' exemption (see C below).

C   *Transactions with group investees in accounts of 90% (or more) owned subsidiaries*

This exemption covers only transactions with members, or investees (such as associates and joint ventures), of the group. Transactions with other types of related party (e.g. directors or major shareholders) must still be disclosed. In our view, this exemption is unsatisfactory for a number of reasons and should be carefully re-examined by the ASB in any future review of FRS 8.

The choice of 90%-owned subsidiaries as a threshold is odd, since it is unclear whose interest it serves. If the general public is regarded as the main user, it is sufficient for them to be aware that the reporting entity is a subsidiary undertaking, whatever the level of ownership. If, however, the intention is to protect the interests of minority shareholders, a 100% threshold would have been more appropriate. The FRS suggests that the choice of 90% is a pragmatic compromise to deal with subsidiaries with small amounts of voting preference shares, or small numbers of shares held by employees.[48]

Be that as it may, the following examples show how the exemption can lead to plainly anomalous results:

Example 28.8

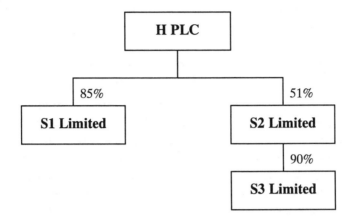

The minority shareholding in S1 Limited is owned by the controlling shareholder of H, whereas those of S2 and S3 are held by completely independent third parties. S1 is not eligible to claim the exemption because only 85% of its voting rights are controlled within the H group. However, S3 can claim the exemption because 90% of its voting rights are controlled by the H group, even though H's effective interest in S3 is only 46%. This means that, if S1 transacts with S3, details of the transactions must, somewhat perversely, be given in the accounts of S1 (whose minority shareholder is presumably fully aware of the transactions), but not those of S3 (whose minority shareholders may not be).

Example 28.9

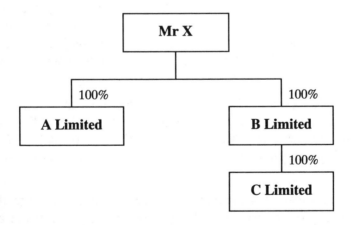

C derives 50% of its profit from transactions with A and 50% from transactions with B. Assuming that B Limited prepares group accounts, C will not have to disclose details of its transactions with B, but will have to disclose details of those with A, even though in substance there is little difference between them. This is because A is a related party of C (both are under the common control of Mr X), but not an investee of the B group.

It should be emphasised, however, that the over-riding requirement for accounts to give a true and fair view may still require disclosure of transactions covered by an exemption under FRS 8.

The FRS does not provide explicit guidance on the situation where the reporting entity seeking to claim the exemption is not a 90% (or more) owned subsidiary for the whole period. However, we interpret the phrase 'in the financial statements of subsidiary undertakings' as indicating that it is the status of the reporting entity at the balance sheet date that is relevant.

The exemption is simply conditional upon group accounts including the reporting entity being 'publicly available', without any further requirement for the group accounts concerned to give related party disclosures comparable to those required by FRS 8 (or, for that matter, to be in English or even the Western alphabet!). A further issue is that, even if the group accounts comply with FRS 8, many of the transactions exempt from disclosure at the subsidiary level will be eliminated on consolidation and will therefore not be disclosed at the group level either.

If the group accounts on which the exemption depends will not provide users with the information omitted from the subsidiary's accounts, it is in practice irrelevant whether or not they are publicly available. Perhaps it is for this reason that the FRS requires companies taking advantage of this exemption to disclose that they have done so.

In our view, for the exemption to be available it is not necessary for the group accounts concerned to be deposited in some central bureau comparable to Companies House in the UK. They could equally be 'publicly available' on request, from the offices of an overseas parent for example. However, companies taking advantage of the exemption will be subject to the Companies Act requirement to disclose the address from which group accounts can be obtained.[49]

In any event, this exemption is largely negated by other requirements. For example, the accounts formats in the Companies Act and SSAP 1 – *Accounting for associated undertakings* – require some information, particularly year-end balances, to be given in respect of transactions with group companies and investees.

All in all, we consider this exemption ill-thought out and urge the ASB to reconsider it in any future review of FRS 8. We broadly prefer the approach of the equivalent exemption in the international standard IAS 24, which applies only to wholly-owned subsidiaries, but covers all related party disclosures (not just those with group companies), provided that a parent in the same country prepares group accounts (see 4.1 below).

D   Pension contributions to a pension fund

This seems a reasonable exemption and, as noted above, may have been granted in order to mitigate the requirement to treat pension funds as related parties in all circumstances. However, the information may well be given more or less directly in the disclosures required by SSAP 24 – *Accounting for pension costs.* Certainly, if the proposed disclosures in the ASB's recent Discussion Paper *Pension costs in the employer's financial statements* are given effect, the information will be given explicitly as part of the reconciliation of the movement in the balance sheet figure for pension costs.[50] The exemption covers only contributions paid to the scheme and not, for example, refunds of surpluses and other transactions with the scheme.

E   Emoluments in respect of services as an employee of the reporting entity

In many cases, this will be over-ridden by the disclosure requirements in respect of directors' emoluments contained in Part I of Schedule 6 to the Companies Act and, for listed companies, the Stock Exchange requirements. It does, however, mean that salaries of key management other than directors do not need to be disclosed. There is no requirement that such amounts must be paid under a contract of employment, so that ex gratia bonuses and similar payments are exempt from disclosure.

Fees paid to directors (particularly non-executive directors) in their capacity as such may not be exempt from disclosure under FRS 8, since they are not 'emoluments is respect of services as an *employee*'. However, this is unlikely to have much practical significance. So far as listed companies are concerned, fees for each director will be disclosed under the Stock Exchange requirements. For other companies, if they have non-executive directors at all, the materiality of the amounts involved will mean that disclosure of fees by individual director will rarely be required.

2.3.6   Transactions subject to a duty of confidentiality

In addition to the types of transaction discussed in 2.3.5 above, FRS 8 does not require any related party transaction to be disclosed where this would involve the reporting entity's breaching a legal duty of confidentiality. It is clear from the explanatory section of the FRS that this concession is aimed principally at banks and similar institutions and covers only those obligations imposed by a generally applicable statute or common law. It does not include the effects of terms in a private contract, for the obvious reason that compliance with the standard would otherwise be voluntary, because companies could insert a confidentiality clause in all related party contracts.[51]

2.4   Disclosure of control

FRS 8 asserts that where a reporting entity is controlled by another party, that fact is relevant information, irrespective of whether transactions have taken place with that party. This is because the control relationship prevents the reporting entity from having independent discretionary power over its resources and transactions. The FRS goes on to suggest that the existence and identity of the controlling party may sometimes be at least as relevant in appraising an entity's prospects as are the performance and financial position presented in its accounts. The reason is that the controlling party may establish the entity's credit standing, determine the source and price of its raw materials, determine the products it sells, to whom and at what price, and may affect the source, calibre and allegiance of its management.[52]

Where the reporting entity is controlled by another party, the FRS requires it to disclose the identity of that controlling party and, if different, of the ultimate controlling party. This disclosure is required irrespective of whether or not the entity has entered into any transactions with the controlling party or parties. If the ultimate controlling party is not known, that fact should be disclosed.[53] The controlling party simply means, in the context of a company, the entity or individual that directly controls the company. The ultimate controlling party means the entity or individual at the top of any 'chain' that controls the immediate controlling party.

For many companies this requirement will be satisfied by disclosing the names of the immediate and ultimate parent companies, the latter being required already by the Companies Act. However, the FRS also requires the identification of non-corporate controlling persons such as trusts, partnerships or individuals. Hitherto these tended to escape disclosure under the Companies Act, although they were highlighted in the accounts of listed companies by the Stock Exchange requirement to disclose major shareholdings. An example of disclosure of control by a trust is given by Associated British Foods (see Extract 28.9 in 2.3.3 above).

Control by directors is disclosed in the directors' report by virtue of the Companies Act requirement to give certain details of directors' interests in the shares of the company and other group companies.[54] It is not clear whether this suffices for the purposes of FRS 8, which requires disclosure of the controlling party to be made in the 'financial statements' (rather than the directors' report). It may be appropriate for the relevant note to the accounts to be cross-referred to the directors' report.

The FRS, obviously, does not supersede the Companies Act requirement to disclose the ultimate parent company and the parent undertaking(s) of the largest and, if different, smallest groups of which the company is a member and for which group accounts are prepared. This means that, potentially, a company may have to disclose as many as five parties further up the 'chain':

(a)   the immediate parent undertaking;[55]

(b)   the parent undertaking of the smallest group for which group accounts are prepared;[56]

(c)   the parent undertaking of the largest group for which group accounts are prepared;[57]

(d)   the ultimate parent company;[58] and;

(e)   the ultimate controlling party (where this is not a company).[59]

2.5   No exemption for small companies

FRS 8 gives no exemptions for disclosure for small companies. The ASB specifically sought commentators' views on this issue in FRED 8, whilst indicating its own preference for granting no exemption. Among the possible reasons for exempting small companies, the FRED cited the following:

■   The external shareholders of all companies already have some protection in the requirements of companies legislation that deal with disclosure of directors' and other officers' transactions.

■   Other users of small companies' accounts may have to rely on an abbreviated balance sheet and notes, which are all that need be filed by small companies and which would not include related party disclosures.

FRED 8 gave the following arguments against granting any exemptions:

■   The disclosure of information about related party transactions is no less important to the user of the accounts of small companies than it is to the user of those of larger entities. Indeed, certain kinds of related party transaction may be more prevalent and of greater significance for the financial statements when the company is small than when it is large (for example, those transactions involving individuals).

■   The confidential nature of such disclosures need not be a cause for concern, since they would be excluded from the abbreviated accounts available to the public.[60]

In the event, the ASB's view prevailed, supported by a majority of commentators, including ourselves. The development section of FRS 8 indicates that there was more than one round of consultation on this issue, the overall effect, if anything, being to harden the ASB's stance. As the FRS puts it: 'Representations from those auditing and using the accounts of small companies reinforced the view that appropriate related party disclosures is particularly important and relevant information in their financial statements, since transactions with related parties are more likely to be material in small companies.'[61]

This position was reinforced in the exposure draft of the *Financial Reporting Standard for Smaller Entities* (FRSSE) published by the ASB in December 1996. The FRSSE in fact envisages slightly more onerous requirements for the disclosure of related party transactions for smaller entities than for the generality of companies, in that it proposes that:

(a) smaller companies should be required to disclose contributions to pension schemes; and

(b) in judging the materiality of transactions, regard should be had to the perspective of the other party in all cases, not just when the other party is an individual or an entity controlled by an individual.[62]

The FRSSE also specifically requires disclosure of guarantees given by directors in respect of borrowings by the reporting entity,[63] although, as noted in 2.3.1 above, disclosure of such transactions is, in our view, clearly required by FRS 8 already.

3 OTHER REQUIREMENTS IN THE UK

In addition to the requirements of FRS 8, the disclosure of some related party matters is dealt with in the Companies Act 1985, existing standards and, for listed and AIM companies, Stock Exchange requirements.

3.1 Legislative requirements

The Companies Act 1985 requires the financial statements (or directors' report) to contain what might be considered as related party disclosures in relation to:

(a) directors;

(b) non-director officers or senior employees; and

(c) group companies (including associated companies).

The disclosures for other related party matters are only regulated by the overriding requirement for the financial statements to give a true and fair view.

The disclosure requirements relating to each of the above categories of related parties are outlined below.

3.1.1 Directors

In general, the Companies Act requires the following information to be disclosed in respect of directors of a company:

(a) names of directors who have served during the year;[64]

(b) interests of each director in the share capital or debentures of the company or of any other group company;[65]

(c) information about directors' emoluments (see Chapter 30); and

(d) loans and other transactions with directors or persons connected with the directors (see Chapter 29).

3.1.2 Non-director officers

The Companies Act also requires disclosure of information relating to loans and other transactions with officers of the company other than directors; these requirements are discussed in Chapter 29 at 6.

3.1.3 Related undertakings

Schedules 4 and 5 to the Companies Act set out detailed disclosure requirements in respect of group companies (including undertakings in which the company has a participating interest),[66] many of which were added by the Companies Act 1989 when the EU Seventh Company Law Directive was incorporated into UK companies legislation. Certain of these disclosures apply to companies which are not required to prepare group accounts and subsidiary undertakings which have been excluded from the consolidated accounts.

A   *Ultimate parent company and parent undertaking(s) drawing up accounts for larger group*

Where a company or parent company is itself a subsidiary undertaking, it must give the name and, if known to the directors, the country of incorporation (if outside Great Britain[67]) of the company (if any) regarded by the directors as the company's ultimate parent company. For this purpose, the term 'company' includes any body corporate (i.e. a UK corporate entity not registered under the Companies Act or an overseas corporate entity).[68]

The Companies Act also requires additional disclosures in relation to the parent undertaking(s) (which need not be a corporate entity) of the largest and smallest group of undertakings for which group accounts are drawn up and of which the reporting company is a member.

The information to be given about each such parent undertaking is:

(a)   name;

(b)   (i)   country of incorporation (if outside Great Britain);

      (ii)   if unincorporated, the address of its principal place of business; and

(c)   if copies of its group accounts are available to the public, the address from which they may be obtained.[69]

B   *Subsidiary undertakings*

A parent company, whether or not it is preparing group accounts, must give the following information about each of its subsidiary undertakings:

(a)   name;

(b)   country of incorporation (if outside Great Britain);

(c)   if it is unincorporated, the address of its principal place of business;[70] and

(d)   the identity of each class of shares held and the proportion of the nominal value of the shares of that class represented by those shares. If applicable, the holdings should be split between those held directly by the parent company, and those held indirectly via other group companies.[71]

A parent company that does not prepare group accounts must disclose, for each subsidiary undertaking, its profit or loss for, and capital and reserves at the end of, its 'relevant financial year' — i.e. its latest financial year coterminous with, or ending before, that of the parent. In a case where a subsidiary's relevant financial year ends before that of the parent, the year-end date must given.

However, this information need not be given if the parent is exempt from preparing accounts under section 228 of the Companies Act 1985 (subsidiary of EU parent — see Chapter 5, section 4.1), or if the group's investment in the undertaking is included in the accounts by way of the equity method of valuation, or if:

(a)   the undertaking is not required by any provision of the Companies Act to deliver a copy of its balance sheet for its relevant financial year and does not otherwise publish its balance sheet in Great Britain or elsewhere; and

(b)   the holding of the group is less than 50% of the nominal value of the shares in the undertaking.[72]

Where a parent company does prepare group accounts it must disclose why each subsidiary is a subsidiary undertaking, unless the reason is (as it typically will be) that the subsidiary's immediate parent holds a majority of voting rights, and the same proportion of the shares, in the subsidiary undertaking.[73] It must also state whether each subsidiary undertaking is included in the consolidation, and give the reason for non-consolidation in any particular case.[74]

In respect of each unconsolidated subsidiary, the parent must disclose its profit or loss for its 'relevant financial year' and its total capital and reserves at the end that year. However, this information need not be given in respect of any subisidiary undertaking if the group's investment in the undertaking is included in the accounts by way of the equity method of valuation or if:

(a)   the undertaking is not required by any provision of the Companies Act to deliver a copy of its balance sheet for its relevant financial year and does not otherwise publish its balance sheet in Great Britain or elsewhere; and

(b)   the holding of the group is less than 50% of the nominal value of the shares in the undertaking.[75]

For each subsidiary undertaking whose financial year did not end with that of the company, the parent must explain why the directors of the parent consider this appropriate, and give the date of its last year-end before that of the reporting company. Alternatively, where there are a number of subsidiary undertakings, the earliest and latest of those dates may be given.[76]

C   Associated undertakings

The following information must be given in group accounts in respect of each associated undertaking:

(a)   name;

(b)   country of incorporation (if outside Great Britain);

(c)   if it is unincorporated, the address of its principal place of business; and

(d)   the identity of each class of shares held and the proportion of the nominal value of the shares of that class represented by those shares. If applicable, the holdings should be split between those held directly by the parent company, and those held indirectly via other group companies.[77]

D   Joint ventures

Where an undertaking is accounted for with in group accounts using proportional consolidation, the following information must be disclosed:

(a)   name;

(b)   principal place of business;

(c)   the factors on which joint management is based;

(d)   the proportion of the capital of the joint venture held by the group; and

(e)   where the financial year end of the joint venture did not coincide with that of the parent company of the reporting group, the date of its last year-end ending before that of the parent.[78]

E   Investments in 'qualifying undertakings'

Where a company or group has an investment in a 'qualifying undertaking' (i.e. a partnership or unlimited company each of whose members is either a limited company or an unlimited company (or Scottish firm), each of whose members is a limited company),[79] it must state the name and legal form of the qualifying undertaking together with its address or that of its head office. This information need not be given if it is not material.

There must also be stated either:

(a)   that a copy of the latest accounts of the undertaking has been, or is to be, appended to the copy of the company's accounts filed with the Registrar of Companies; or

(b)   the name of at least one body corporate (which can be the reporting company) in whose consolidated accounts the qualifying undertaking has been included. This information need not be given if the qualifying undertaking is exempt from preparing accounts.[80] (Somewhat contrarily, the key condition for obtaining such an exemption is that the undertaking has been included in the consolidated accounts of one of its members!)[81]

F   *Other significant holdings of the parent company or group*

Schedule 5 to the Companies Act also requires certain disclosures to be given where a parent company has a significant investment in an undertaking which is not a subsidiary or associated undertaking or joint venture.[82]

A holding is 'significant' for the purposes of these disclosures if either:

(a)   it amounts to 20% or more of the nominal value of any class of shares in the undertaking; or

(b)   the book value of the holding exceeds one-fifth of the company's (or group's) assets as stated in its accounts.

For companies required to prepare group accounts, the disclosures must be given both for investments of the parent company of the reporting group and investments of the group as a whole.

In relation to holdings which amount to 20% or more of the nominal value of the shares in the investee, companies must also disclose (if material):

(a)   the aggregate amount of its capital and reserves of the undertaking at the end of its relevant financial year; and

(b)   its profit or loss for that year.

However, this information need not be given if:

(a)   the undertaking is not required by any provision of the Companies Act to deliver a copy of its balance sheet for its relevant financial year and does not otherwise publish its balance sheet in Great Britain or elsewhere, and the holding of the group is less than 50% of the nominal value of the shares in the undertaking; or

(b)   the company is not required to prepare group accounts because it is an intermediate holding company, and the company's investment in all undertakings in which it has such a holding is shown, in aggregate, in the notes to the accounts by way of the equity method of valuation.

G   *Transactions with group undertakings and undertakings in which the company has a participating interest*

In addition to requiring the amounts in respect of shares in group undertakings and participating interests to be separately disclosed, the balance sheet formats also require separate disclosure of the following inter-company balances involving (i) group undertakings and (ii) undertakings in which the company has a participating interest:

(a)   loans to (under the heading of fixed asset investments);

(b)   amounts owed by (under the heading of current assets, debtors);

(c)   amounts owed to (under both headings for creditors).[83]

The profit and loss account formats contained in the Companies Act require separate disclosure of:

(a)   income from shares in group undertakings;

(b)   income from participating interests;

(c)   income and interest derived from group undertakings; and

(d)   interest and similar charges payable to group undertakings.[84]

The Companies Act requires companies to disclose details of any guarantees and other financial commitments.[85] Where such guarantees or commitments are undertaken on behalf of or for the benefit of:

(a)   any parent undertaking or fellow subsidiary undertaking; or

(b)   any subsidiary undertaking of the company,

they are required to be disclosed separately from any other guarantees and financial commitments; furthermore, guarantees and commitments within (a) above should be disclosed separately from those within (b).[86]

3.2   UK accounting standards other than FRS 8

The main UK accounting standards other than FRS 8 which impinge on the issue of related parties are SSAP 1 – *Accounting for associated companies* – and FRS 2 – *Accounting for Subsidiary Undertakings*, which require certain disclosures to be made in the financial statements of the investing company in addition to those required by Schedule 5 to the Companies Act. These are discussed in detail in Chapters 7 and 5 respectively.

3.3   Stock Exchange requirements

The Stock Exchange requires fully listed and, to a lesser extent, AIM companies to disclose, in their annual reports and accounts, various information relevant to related parties, or which indicate the existence of related parties, in addition to that required by the Companies Act. The specific disclosures relevant to related parties concern either the directors or the shareholders of the company.

3.3.1   *Directors*

A   Emoluments and other benefits

There are extensive requirements for the disclosure of individual directors' emoluments and other benefits, introduced in response to the Cadbury and Greenbury codes. These are discussed in Chapter 30 at 4.

B   Directors' interests in share capital

The requirements extend beyond those contained in the Companies Act 1985 in that they require disclosure of:

(a)   beneficial and non-beneficial interests, separately distinguished. For this purpose a holding is non-beneficial only if neither the director, nor his spouse, nor any of his children under 18 has any beneficial interest; and

(b)   changes in interests between the balance sheet date and a date not more than one month before the date of the notice of the annual general meeting. If there has been no change, then that fact should be disclosed.[87]

C   *Contracts of significance with directors*

Particulars of any contract of significance subsisting during the financial year, to which the company or one of its subsidiary undertakings is a party, and in which a director of the company is or was materially interested are required to be disclosed by listed companies. If there has been no such contract, a statement of that fact is required.[88]

A 'contract of significance' is defined as one which represents in amount or value, a sum equal to 1% or more, calculated on a group basis where relevant, of:

(a)   in the case of a capital transaction or a transaction of which the principal purpose or effect is the granting of credit, the aggregate of the group's share capital and reserves; or

(b)   in other cases, the total annual purchases, sales, payments or receipts, as the case may be, of the group.[89]

(See Chapter 29 at 5 for further discussion of these requirements.)

3.3.2   *Shareholders*

A   *Substantial holdings of the company's shares*

A statement is required to be given showing particulars, as at a date not more than one month prior to the date of the notice of the annual general meeting, of an interest of any person (other than a director), in any substantial part of the share capital of the company. A substantial holding is one which amounts to 3% or more of the nominal value of any class of capital carrying rights to vote in all circumstances at general meetings of the company. If there is no such interest, a statement of that fact is required to be made.[90]

B   *Contracts of significance*

Particulars of any contract of significance between the company, or one of its subsidiaries, and a controlling shareholder are required to be disclosed by listed companies.[91]

A controlling shareholder is one who is entitled to exercise, or control the exercise of, 30% or more of the rights to vote at general meetings, or is able to control the appointment of directors who are able to exercise a majority of votes at board meetings.[92]

In addition, particulars of any contract for the provision of services to the company or any of its subsidiaries by a controlling shareholder are also required to be disclosed. Such a contract need not be disclosed, if it is a contract for the provision of services which it is the principal business of the shareholder to provide and it is not a contract of significance.[93]

C   Waived dividends

Particulars of any arrangement under which a shareholder has waived or agreed to waive any dividends are required to be disclosed. Where a director has agreed to waive future dividends, details should be given of such waiver together with those relating to dividends which are payable during the period under review. Waivers of less than 1% of the total value of any dividend may be disregarded provided that some payment has been made on each share of the relevant class during the relevant calendar year.[94]

In practice, waivers are likely only to arise where the shareholder is a director or has some influence over the company.

D   Purchase by the company of its own shares

The Companies Act contains provisions requiring disclosures of certain information where a company has purchased some of its own shares.[95] The Stock Exchange extends these for listed companies by requiring disclosure of, in the case of purchases made otherwise than through the market or by tender or partial offer to all shareholders, the names of the sellers of such shares purchased.[96]   Again, in most cases, this is likely only to arise where the shareholder is a director or has some influence over the company.

3.3.3   Smaller related party transactions

Under the Listing Rules of the Stock Exchange, listed companies are normally required to issue a circular to shareholders where a related party transaction is contemplated.[97]   In the case of some smaller transactions, however, companies are able instead, subject to various conditions, to disclose details of the transactions in their accounts. The transactions concerned are those where one or more of the following ratios is between 0.25% and 5%:

(a)   net assets the subject of the transaction, to those of listed company;

(b)   profits attributable to net assets the subject of the transaction, to those of listed company;

(c)   consideration, to net assets of listed company;

(d)   consideration, to market capitalisation of equity shares of listed company; and;

(e)   where a business is being acquired, its gross capital, to that of listed company.[98]

'Related party transactions' are defined for this purpose as transactions (other than revenue transactions in the ordinary course of business) between a related party and the company or any company in the same group.[99]

'Related parties' are defined for this purpose as:

(a)   a 'substantial shareholder' (broadly a person able to control, now or at any time during the previous 12 months, 10% of the votes of the company or any other group company);

(b)   any person who is (or was during the previous 12 months) a director or shadow director of the company or any other group company; or

(c)   an associate of any person falling within (a) or (b). An 'associate' is broadly:

> (i)   with respect to an individual: his immediate family; a trust for the benefit of him or his immediate family; or a company in which he and/or his immediate family can either control 30% of the votes or appoint a majority of the board; and

> (ii)   with respect to a company: any company in the same group; any company whose directors are accustomed to act in accordance with its instructions; or any company in which it and/or its other associates can either control 30% of the votes or appoint a majority of the board.[100]

In order to qualify for this exemption a company must, prior to completing the transaction:

(a)   inform the Stock Exchange in writing of the details of the proposed transaction;

(b)   provide the Stock Exchange with written confirmation from an independent adviser acceptable to the Stock Exchange that the terms of the proposed transaction with the related party are fair and reasonable so far as the shareholders of the company are concerned; and

(c)   undertake in writing to the Stock Exchange to include details of the transaction in the company's next published annual accounts, including the identity of the related party, the value of the consideration for the transaction and all other relevant circumstances.[101]

The requirement to include details of small related party transactions in the annual report and accounts of companies which have taken advantage of the facility of not having to issue a circular to shareholders is listed as one of the continuing obligations of the Listing Rules.[102] The following are examples of disclosures which appear to have been made in pursuance of this requirement:

Extract 28.14: EMI Group plc (1997)

32. RELATED PARTY TRANSACTIONS [extract]

EMI Music Publishing acquired the music publishing catalogues of The Entertainment Group of Companies on 31 March 1997 for a total consideration of US$7.8m (£4.8m). These companies were owned by Charles Koppelman and Martin Bandier, directors of certain Group companies.

Extract 28.15: TI Group plc (1996)

31. RELATED PARTY TRANSACTIONS [extract]

On 30th December 1996 Bundy Corporation sold its 20% investment in Usui Bundy Tubing Ltd ('Usui') to Usui Kokusai Sangyo Kaisha Ltd, which already held 60% of Usui, for ¥1,077m (£6m). TI Group retained the rights to use the name 'Bundy' in Japan.

3.3.4 *AIM companies*

AIM companies are required to disclose in their accounts details of any related party transaction (defined as for listed companies in 3.3.3 above)[103] where any one of the following ratios exceeds 0.25%:

(a)   net assets the subject of the transaction, to those of AIM company;

(b)   profits attributable to net assets the subject of the transaction, to those of AIM company;

(c)   consideration, to net assets of AIM company; and

(d)   consideration, to market capitalisation of equity shares of AIM company.

The details given must include the identity of the related party, the value of the consideration and all other relevant circumstances.[104]

4   COMPARISON WITH IASC AND US PRONOUNCEMENTS

4.1   IASC

The relevant international standard which deals with the disclosure of related parties and transactions between a reporting enterprise and its related parties is IAS 24 — *Related Party Disclosures* — which was issued in July 1984. The standard points out that certain other IASs call for disclosures which may also be relevant in respect of related parties.[105]

As is the case with FRS 8, IAS 24's related party definition centres around the concepts of control and influence. However, IAS 24 specifically refers to 'significant influence', which it then discusses in some detail.[106] Nevertheless, the requirements of IAS 24 are such that most related parties under FRS 8 will be related parties under IAS 24.

IAS 24 allows a subsidiary not to give related party disclosures only if it is a wholly-owned subsidiary whose parent is incorporated, and provides consolidated accounts, in the same country. However, this exemption applies to all related party disclosures, whereas FRS 8 exempts 90% (or more) owned subsidiaries only from disclosing information about transactions with other group companies.[107] This is the only major difference between FRS 8 and IAS 24 highlighted in FRS 8 itself.[108]

When it comes to the disclosure of related party transactions, the requirements of IAS 24 are considerably less rigorous than those of FRS 8. For example, IAS 24 does not specifically require disclosure of either the name of the related party or the amounts involved in the transactions.[109]

4.2   US

The main accounting standard in the US dealing with this issue is SFAS 57 – *Related Party Disclosures* – which was issued in March 1982, as a codification into GAAP of SAS 6. While SFAS 57 outlines general US GAAP in this area, there are a number of other pronouncements in the US which impact on the reporting of certain related party transactions. These include SFAS 68 – *Research and Development Arrangements* – and SFAS 13 – *Accounting for Leases* – as well as various Staff Accounting Bulletins issued by the SEC.

The requirements of SFAS 57 are such that related parties under FRS 8 are effectively related parties under SFAS 57[110] and, apart from the following minor differences, FRS 8 is effectively an elaboration of SFAS 57:

- SFAS 57 requires disclosure of all material related party transactions in the financial statements of wholly owned subsidiaries if these are produced,[111] whereas FRS 8 exempts 90% (or more) owned subsidiaries from having to disclose transactions with group companies;

- like IAS 24, SFAS 57 does not specifically require disclosure of the names of the related parties as required by FRS 8; it only requires the nature of the relationship to be disclosed, although it does state that the name should be disclosed if necessary to the understanding of the relationship;[112]

- in addition to requiring disclosure of amounts due to/from the related party, SFAS 57 requires the terms and manner of settlement to be disclosed if not otherwise apparent;[113]

- SFAS 57 does not specifically require disclosure of any material difference between the fair value and the transacted amount of related party transactions as is suggested in certain circumstances by FRS 8. However, SFAS 57 does require 'such other information deemed necessary to an understanding of the effects of the transactions on the financial statements'[114] (much like FRS 8) and 'the effects of any change in the method of establishing the terms from that used in the preceding period' to be disclosed.[115]

5 CONCLUSION

In drafting ED 46, the ASC chose to break away from international practice by proposing that only abnormal transactions be disclosed. This was done so that companies could avoid having to provide over-lengthy disclosures which it was assumed arose under SFAS 57 and IAS 24. However, given the anticipated difficulties that would arise in practice in applying the definitions of normal and abnormal transactions, the ASB decided to abandon the distinction and adopt the more conventional approach.

FRS 8 is a much more complex standard than it appears at a first reading. Initial experience of implementing it in the 1996/7 reporting season indicates, in our view, that the ASB should re-address certain aspects of it sooner rather than later, in particular:

- the definition of related party in paragraph 2.5(a)(iv) of the FRS based on entities transacting on terms such that one has subordinated its own interests (see 2.2.1 above);

- the requirement, in certain cases, to judge materiality by reference to the circumstances of the related party rather than those of the reporting entity (see 2.3.2 above); and

- the exemptions from disclosure for 90% (or more) owned subsidiaries (see 2.3.5 C above).

In addition, whilst we would not advocate a return to an 'abnormal transaction' approach such as that proposed in ED 46, we are concerned that FRS 8 unintentionally embraces certain types of transactions, disclosure of which distracts readers from those related party transactions that are more truly worthy of their attention. We believe that, where possible, such transactions should be removed from the scope of the FRS. Obvious examples include:

- participation by major shareholders in transactions with shareholders as a whole (e.g. dividends, rights issues); and

- where companies trade with the public (e.g. retailers, certain banks and insurance companies), transactions with directors and key managers (and their close family and entities controlled by them) as members of the public on non-preferential terms. However, transactions with such individuals (and persons and entities connected with them) in a business capacity should, in our view, still be disclosed whatever their terms.

Some form of related party disclosure standard was long overdue in the UK. However, users of accounts should be under no illusion that FRS 8 will act as more than a mild deterrent to those intent on corporate fraud on the scale that allegedly occurred in companies connected with Robert Maxwell. Indeed, it is food for thought that, in earlier editions of this book, extracts from the accounts of certain of those companies were included in this chapter as (then) virtually unique examples of good related party disclosures!

References

1 FRS 8, *Related Party Disclosures*, ASB, November 1995, paras. 8-10.
2 Accountants International Study Group, *Related Party Transactions*, para. 15.
3 CA 85, ss 226(4) and 227(5).
4 FRS 8, para. 1.
5 *Ibid.*, para. 7.
6 ASB Press Notice 65, ASB, October 1995.
7 FRS 8, para. 2.5.
8 *Ibid.*, para. 11.
9 *Ibid.*, para. 2.5(a).
10 *Ibid.*, para. 2.2.
11 FRS 5, *Reporting the substance of transactions*, ASB, April 1994, para. 8.
12 FRS 8, para. 13.
13 *Ibid.*, para. 14.
14 *Ibid.*
15 FRED 8, *Related party disclosures*, ASB, March 1994, para. 2(a)(iv).
16 FRS 8, para. 14.
17 *Implementing FRS 8: Some practical aspects*, Ken Wild and Brian Creighton, Accountancy, October 1996, page 128.
18 FRS 8, para 2.5(a).
19 *Ibid.*, para.2.5(b).
20 *Ibid.*, para.2.5(b)(iv), footnote.
21 *Ibid.*, para. 15.
22 Statement of Recommended Practice, *Financial Reports of Pension Schemes*, Pensions Research Accountants Group, July 1996, para. 2.65.
23 FRS 8, para. 2.5(c).
24 *Ibid.*
25 *Ibid.*, para. 2.3.
26 *Ibid.*, paras. 2.2 and 2.5(c)(iii) (foonote).
27 *Ibid.*, para. 2.4.
28 *Ibid.*, para. 2.5.
29 *Ibid.*, para. 2.1.
30 FRED 8, para. 2(d)(iii).
31 FRS 8, para. 4.
32 ASB Statement, *Operating and Financial Review*, ASB, July 1993, para. 12.
33 FRS 8, para. 4.
34 *Ibid.*, para. 2.6.
35 *Ibid.*, para. 19.
36 *Ibid.*, paras. 2.6 and 19.
37 *Ibid.*, para. 20.
38 *Ibid.*
39 *Ibid.*, para. 6.
40 FRED 8, paras. 8(f) and 23.
41 FRS 8, para. 22.
42 *Ibid.*, para. 10.

43 E.g. Bass PLC, Report and Accounts 1996, p. 11 and The BOC Group plc, Report and Accounts 1996, p. 37.
44 FRS 8, paras. 6 and 21.
45 *Ibid.*, para. 21.
46 *Ibid.*, para. 3.
47 *Ibid.*, para 2.5(a).
48 *Ibid.*, Appendix IV, para 12.
49 CA 85, Sch. 5, paras. 11and 30.
50 Discussion Paper, *Pension Costs in the Employer's Financial Statements*, ASB, June 1995, para. 6.2.13.
51 FRS 8, para.16.
52 *Ibid.*, para. 18.
53 *Ibid.*, para. 5.
54 CA 85, Sch. 7, paras. 2-2B.
55 FRS 8., para. 5.
56 CA 85, Sch. 5, paras. 11 and 30.
57 *Ibid.*
58 *Ibid.*, paras. 12 and 31.
59 FRS 8, para. 5.
60 FRED 8, Preface.
61 FRS 8, Appendix IV, para. 14.
62 Exposure draft *Financial Reporting Standard for Smaller Entities*, ASB, December 1996, paras.135-139 and 208.
63 *Ibid.*, para. 138.
64 CA 85, s 234(2).
65 *Ibid.*, Sch. 7, para. 2A.
66 Under the Companies Act, an undertaking in which a participating interest is held and over which significant influence is exercised is an 'associated undertaking'; the term 'associated undertaking' as used in the Companies Act and the term 'associated company' used in SSAP 1 can usually be regarded as synonymous.
67 Throughout section 3.1, references to 'Great Britain' should, where the reporting entity is a company incorporated in Northern Ireland, be read as references to 'Northern Ireland'. The relevant legislation for such companies is the Companies (Northern Ireland) Order 1986, the provisions of which are in substance identical to those of the Companies Act 1985.
68 CA 85, Sch. 5, paras. 12 and 31, section 740.
69 *Ibid.*, paras. 11 and 30.
70 *Ibid.*, para. 15(2) and (3).
71 *Ibid.*, paras. 2(2) and 16(1).
72 *Ibid.*,para.4
73 *Ibid.*, para. 15(5).
74 *Ibid.*, para. 15(4).
75 *Ibid.*, para. 17.
76 *Ibid.*, para. 19.
77 *Ibid.*, para. 22.
78 *Ibid.*, para. 21.
79 SI 1993/1820, *The Partnerships and Unlimited Companies (Accounts) Regulations 1993*, Regulation 3.
80 CA 1985, Sch. 5, paras. 9A and 28A.
81 SI 1993/1820, Regulation 7.
82 CA 85, Sch. 5, paras. 7–9 and 23–28.
83 *Ibid.*, Sch. 4, para. 8, balance sheet formats.
84 *Ibid.*, para. 8, profit and loss account formats.
85 *Ibid.*, para. 50.
86 *Ibid.*, para. 59A.
87 *The Listing Rules*, London Stock Exchange, Chapter 12, para. 12.43(k).
88 *Ibid.*, Chapter 12, para. 12.43(q).
89 *Ibid.*, para. 12.44.

90 *Ibid.*, para. 12.43(l); CA 85, s 199(2).
91 *Ibid.*, para. 12.43(r).
92 *Ibid.*, Chapter 3, para. 3.12.
93 *Ibid.*, Chapter 12, para. 12.43(s).
94 *Ibid.*, para. 12.43(e).
95 CA 85, Sch. 7, para. 8.
96 *The Listing Rules*, London Stock Exchange, Chapter 12, para. 12.43(n).
97 *Ibid.*, Chapter 11.
98 *Ibid.*, Chapter 10, para. 10.5 and Chapter 11, para. 11.8.
99 *Ibid.*, Chapter 11, para. 11.1.
100 *Ibid.*
101 *Ibid.*, para. 11.8.
102 *Ibid.*, Chapter 12, para. 12.43(t).
103 Rules of the London Stock Exchange, Definitions
104 *Ibid.*, Chapter 16, para. 16.24 (for ratios, see para. 16.23(b))
105 IAS 24, *Related Party Disclosures*, IASC, 1984 (reformatted 1994), para. 18.
106 *Ibid.*, para. 5.
107 *Ibid.*, para. 4.
108 FRS 8, Appendix III.
109 IAS 24, paras. 18-25.
110 SFAS 57, *Related Party Disclosures*, FASB, March 1982, para. 24f.
111 *Ibid.*, para. 2, footnote 2.
112 *Ibid.*, footnote 3.
113 *Ibid.*, para. 2(d).
114 *Ibid.*, para. 2(b).
115 *Ibid.*, para. 2(c).

Chapter 29   Directors' and officers' loans and transactions

1   INTRODUCTION

Company directors are treated as fiduciaries[1] and as such must not permit their personal interests and their duty to the company to conflict. In order to avoid such conflicts or potential conflicts arising, transactions between a company and its directors are restricted. Such transactions are regulated in a number of ways, in particular, by means of statutory prohibition, corporate approval and disclosure in the statutory accounts. In this chapter, attention is focused on the Companies Act requirements for disclosure in a company's financial statements of transactions involving directors (except for those relating to directors' remuneration, including share options, which are dealt with in Chapter 30). The provisions determining the legality or otherwise of such transactions are discussed in outline in the Appendix to this chapter.

In considering the disclosures to be made in respect of transactions involving directors (and persons connected with them) it will also be necessary to consider the requirements of FRS 8 – *Related Party Disclosures*, an accounting standard issued by the ASB in November 1995. These are only referred to in passing in this chapter; they are dealt with in their entirety in Chapter 28.

1.1   Outline of historical development in the UK

The Companies Act 1948 provided that a public company could not make a loan to any of its directors or directors of its holding company.[2] Loans to directors of exempt private companies (in essence, companies where the number of members was restricted) were permitted.[3] However, it became apparent over the years that directors could circumvent the restrictions on loans by carefully structuring transactions with their company. Thus, a company could make payments in respect of a director's personal expenditure and seek reimbursement from him without contravening the statutory prohibitions. In such cases, the director would be in substantially the same position as if he had been lent funds to pay off his debts. In an effort to close these loopholes, more extensive requirements were enacted by the Companies Act 1980;[4] for example, the types of unlawful transaction were extended to encompass quasi-loans and credit transactions (see respectively 2.7 and 2.8 below). The relevant legislation is now consolidated in the Companies Act 1985.[5]

2 DEFINITIONS

In order to promote a fuller understanding of this chapter, the following definitions have been included:

2.1 Director

This term includes any person occupying the position of director, by whatever name called;[6] i.e. it is a person's role and duties and not his title which determines whether or not he is a director. Thus, for example, a director's appointment may be defective because the procedure prescribed in the company's articles has not been followed; however, if he performs the functions associated with a person in such a position, he will be regarded as a director for the purposes of the legislation. Conversely, a person may be designated a director yet not be regarded as a director for statutory purposes; for example, it is common for companies to recognise senior managers by conferring titles such as divisional director[7] on them. These persons usually only exercise limited managerial power and hence are unlikely to be subject to the restrictions on directors' transactions, although the disclosure requirements relating to officers may be of relevance (see 2.5 and 6 below).

2.2 Shadow director

This is a person in accordance with whose directions or instructions the directors of the company as a whole (i.e. the board as a collective unit) are accustomed to act. However, if the directors' reason for following a person's advice is that it is given in a professional capacity, that person is not regarded as a shadow director.[8] Clearly, a professional adviser might fall to be treated as a shadow director if the advice which he gives to the board is not given in a professional capacity.

A holding company is not deemed to be a shadow director of a subsidiary even though the directors of the subsidiary act as the holding company directs.[9]

2.3 Alternate director

Broadly, an alternate director is a person who is nominated by another director to act in that director's place during his absence from the company.[10] Alternate directors may only be appointed if the company's articles expressly so provide; for example, Table A[11] provides that: 'any director (other than an alternate director) may appoint any other director or any other person approved by resolution of the directors and willing to act, to be an alternate director and may remove from office an alternate director so appointed by him'.

2.4   Connected person

If the restrictions on directors' transactions extended solely to directors, they could easily be circumvented by the company making, say, a loan to the director's spouse or a company controlled by him. The concept of the connected person seeks to close this loophole.

A person is connected with a director if (not being a director himself) he is:

(a)   that director's spouse, child or step-child (legitimate or otherwise) under the age of 18; or

(b)   a body corporate with which the director is associated.

Broadly speaking, a company is associated with a director if the director and his connected persons are either interested in at least 20% of the company's equity share capital or are entitled to exercise or control more than 20% of the voting power in general meeting.

The director's interest may be direct (i.e. he personally owns the shares or controls the votes) or indirect (i.e. a company that he controls owns the shares or controls the votes). In this latter context, a director will have control of a company (X Co.) if:

(i)   he and his connected persons are interested in X Co.'s equity share capital or are entitled to exercise voting power at a general meeting of X Co.; and

(ii)   he, his connected persons and fellow directors are together interested in more than 50% of X Co.'s share capital or are entitled to exercise more than 50% of the voting power in general meeting.

In order to determine whether or not a company is associated with or controlled by a director, another company with which the director is associated is only deemed to be connected with him if connected by virtue of (c) or (d) below; similarly for these purposes, a trustee of a trust, the beneficiaries of which include another company with which the director is associated, is not thereby deemed to be connected with the director;

(c)   a person acting as trustee of any trust, the beneficiaries of which include the director or his family or a company with which the director is associated. In addition, where the director or his family or an associated company is the object of a discretionary trust, the trustee thereof is also deemed to be a connected person. Trustees of employee share or pension schemes are excluded;

(d)   a partner of the director or any person connected with him by virtue of (a) to (c) above;

(e)   a Scottish firm in which the director or a connected person is a partner, or in which a partner is a Scottish firm in which the director or a connected person is a partner.[12]

These provisions are complex and may be illustrated in the following example:

Example 29.1

Mr A owns 40% of the equity capital of Company X, and his wife and his daughter, aged 17, each hold 6% of the company's equity capital. Company X holds 12% of the equity capital of Company Y. Mr A's partner, Mr B, holds 13% of Company Y's equity capital.

Company X is clearly a connected person of Mr A; he and members of his family are interested in more than 20% of the company's equity capital.

The position of Company Y is more difficult. In order to determine whether Company Y is connected with Mr A, Company X's interest in Company Y's equity capital must initially be disregarded.[13] However, Mr A, by virtue of his family's holdings in Company X, is deemed to control the company (i.e. the total holding of Mr A and his connected persons is 52% of Company X's equity capital).[14] Company Y therefore, is connected with Mr A because he is deemed to have an interest in 25% of the company's equity capital (since Mr B's 13% stake in Company Y is added to Company X's holding of 12%).[15]

It should be noted that FRS 8 presumes that 'close family' members of a director are related parties for the purposes of that standard (see Chapter 28 at 2.2.4 A). The definition of 'close family' is likely to encompass more than just the family members mentioned in (a) above. Thus transactions which may escape disclosure under the Companies Act may need to be disclosed under FRS 8.

2.5   Officer

The statutory definition of officer encompasses directors, managers and company secretaries.[16] This definition is not, however, exhaustive and it would appear that the term extends to any person who exercises a significant degree of managerial power; for example, a financial controller of a company is likely to be an officer, whereas a branch manager of a bank is not.

2.6   Loan

There is no statutory definition of a loan for the purpose of the legislation. However, the term has been judicially defined as 'a sum of money lent for a time, to be returned in money or money's worth'.[17] It is crucial to this definition that the parties to the agreement intend that the amount will be repaid. Recurring problems in this context arise where a director draws remuneration on account or expense advances. Such drawings may constitute a loan depending on the particular circumstances. There is no litmus test which can be applied in determining whether, say, a salary advance is in fact a loan; it is necessary to examine each transaction to decide whether in light of all the facts the director is really receiving an interest free loan. The example below illustrates this problem:

Example 29.2

Mr A, a director of Company Y, draws an expense advance of £9,000, on 1 January 19X0. By the end of the financial year (31 December 19X0), the director has only incurred business expenditure of £2,500 and the outstanding sum is then repaid. Ordinary expense advances would not normally fall within the scope of the legislation because such advances are made on the understanding that the director will apply the funds in performance of his duties to the company. However, in these circumstances the funds have remained outstanding for an unusually long period and, prima facie, the advance appears to have taken on the nature of a loan.

2.7 Quasi-loan

This is a transaction under which one party (the creditor) pays a sum on behalf of another (the borrower) or reimburses expenditure incurred by a third party for the borrower, in circumstances:

(a)   where the borrower (or a person on his behalf) will reimburse the creditor; or

(b)   which gives rise to a liability on the borrower to reimburse the creditor.[18]

A quasi-loan will only arise where the borrower is under an obligation to reimburse the expenditure incurred by the company. Quasi-loans commonly arise where a director is permitted to use a company credit card to pay for private and business expenditure and he undertakes to reimburse the company in respect of personal expenses charged to the card. Likewise, if a company pays a director's household bills on the understanding that the expenses will be recouped by making a deduction from his monthly salary, a quasi-loan will arise.

The following example shows the distinction between a loan and a quasi-loan:

Example 29.3

A director of Company X wishes to buy a painting for £2,000 which is coming up for sale, but will not have the money at that time. If he draws a cheque for £2,000 from the company made payable to himself so that he can buy the painting then, assuming he intends to repay this sum, this will constitute a loan as it is 'a sum of money lent for a time, to be returned in money or money's worth'. If, however, he arranges for the company to pay for the painting on his behalf in the meantime, with the intention that he will repay the company at a later date, then this will be a quasi-loan.

2.8 Credit transaction

This is a transaction whereby a person either:

(a)   supplies any goods or sells any land under a hire-purchase agreement or a conditional sale agreement; or

(b)   leases or hires any land or goods in return for periodical payments; or

(c)   otherwise disposes of land or supplies goods or services on the understanding that payment (whatever form it may take) is to be deferred; i.e. repayment need not be made by means of instalment but could be made by means of a single lump sum.[19]

In this context, services are defined as anything other than goods or land.[20]

The examples below indicate two of the many forms which a credit transaction may assume:

Example 29.4

A property company leases a residence to a director in return for monthly rental payments. This constitutes a credit transaction under (b) above, irrespective of whether the rental payments are made in advance or arrears. Consideration should also be given to whether this arrangement gives rise to a benefit-in-kind which requires disclosure (see 2.3.2 of Chapter 30).

If, however, the lease was rent-free then it would not be a credit transaction as there are no periodical payments.

Alternatively, if the company had granted the director a one year lease but he had made a lump sum payment covering the term of the lease at the outset, then again the transaction would not have constituted a credit transaction, as there would have been no periodical payments.

Example 29.5

A director of a company which repairs motor vehicles has his motor car serviced by the company and payment is to be effected by a single deduction from his following month's salary. The company normally requires payment immediately after the work has been done. This constitutes a credit transaction under (c) above, as payment has been deferred.

However, what if the company's normal procedure was to invoice customers for work done and request payment 30 days after the date of invoice, and the date the amount is to be deducted from the director's salary falls before the date the invoice would be due for payment?

It is unclear whether or not this would constitute a credit transaction, since the legislation does not define what is meant by 'deferred'. It could be argued that this is not a credit transaction as payment is not deferred beyond normal credit terms. However, the legislation makes no reference to normal credit terms and the service would thus appear to require disclosure as a credit transaction.

There is, however, a degree of overlap between credit and material interest transactions and, therefore, those transactions referred to in the above examples which are not credit transactions might require disclosure as material interest transactions (see 3.5 below) or under the requirements of FRS 8 (see generally Chapter 28).

3   DISCLOSURE REQUIREMENTS

3.1   Introduction

A director (including a shadow director) of a company who is interested in a contract with the company must declare the nature of that interest to the board.[21] In this context, transactions include loans, quasi-loans and credit transactions[22] (see E of the Appendix below).

A considerable level of disclosure is required in the notes to both group and individual company financial statements in respect of transactions with directors (including shadow directors).[23] Even where the holding company is not required to produce group accounts by virtue of one of the statutory exemptions (for example, because it is itself a wholly owned subsidiary or the group qualifies as a small or medium-sized group), these requirements still apply in full,[24] and therefore, for example, require disclosure of transactions between the directors and subsidiaries.

If the notes to the financial statements do not disclose the required details of directors' transactions, it is the auditors' duty to include the relevant information in their audit report 'so far as they are reasonably able to do so'.[25]

3.2   Scope

A company's financial statements must disclose transactions between the following:[26]

(a)   the company and its directors and their connected persons;

(b)   the company's subsidiaries (including non-UK subsidiaries) and its directors and connected persons thereof;

(c)   the company, its subsidiaries and the directors (and their connected persons) of any holding company of the company.

A company need not disclose details of transactions entered into between the company or its subsidiaries and directors (and their connected persons) of the subsidiaries (provided the director is not also a director of the company or its holding company).

It should be noted that the term 'subsidiary undertaking' (see Chapter 5 at 1.2.2) does not apply in this context and therefore transactions entered into by such entities, which are not also 'subsidiaries', with a director of the company or any holding company, will not require to be disclosed.

The multiplicity of disclosures which may ensue from a single transaction are detailed below:

Example 29.6

Assume the following group structure:

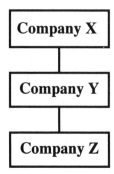

Companies Y and Z are both wholly owned subsidiaries of Company X. Company Z undertakes to guarantee a loan made by a bank to Mr A, a director of company X. The guarantee will be disclosed as follows:

(a)   in the financial statements of Company Z as a guarantee of a loan to a director of its holding company;

(b)   in the financial statements of Company Y as a guarantee of a loan by a subsidiary to a director of its holding company;

(c)   in the financial statements of Company X as a guarantee of a loan by a subsidiary to a director.

These requirements do not apply to banking companies under the Banking Act 1987, which are subject to separate disclosure provisions (see 4 below).[27]

3.3   Transactions requiring disclosure

Broadly, the legislation[28] requires disclosure of two types of transaction involving directors, namely:

(a)   loans, quasi-loans, credit transactions, related guarantees,[29] assignments and arrangements (section 330 type transactions); and

(b)   transactions (other than section 330 type transactions) in which a director has a material interest.

The disclosure provisions apply irrespective of whether:

(a)   the transaction was lawful;

(b)   the person for whom the transaction was made was at the time of its execution a director or a connected person; or

(c)   the company was a subsidiary at the time the transaction was executed.[30]

For example, details of the following transactions would need to be disclosed in a company's financial statements:

(a)   a loan made to an employee who later becomes a director; for example:

Extract 29.1: The BOC Group plc (1996)

Report of the Management Resources Committee [extract]

a)   Directors' remuneration

Dr Stoll has a relocation loan with an overseas Group subsidiary which employs him. This loan was made to him as part of his joining arrangements in 1991, prior to his appointment as a director. It is repayable over the next five years and the balance at 30 September 1996 was £115,000.

(b)   a contract entered into with a director who retired during the financial year; for example:

Extract 29.2: The BOC Group plc (1996)

Report of the Management Resources Committee [extract]

a)   Directors' remuneration

Mr Dyer retired on 19 January 1996 and since that date has received consultancy fees of £193,000. He continues as a consultant until 24 September 1997.

(c)   a credit transaction entered into with a director of another company which then becomes the reporting company's parent.

3.4   Section 330 transactions

3.4.1   Introduction

Details of these transactions must be disclosed in both group and individual company financial statements (subject to various exemptions: see 3.6 below).[31]

Thus, disclosure must be made where any company:

(a)   makes a loan or a quasi-loan to, or enters into a credit transaction with, or enters into a guarantee or provides any security in connection therewith for one of its directors, a director of its holding company or a connected person thereof;

(b)   arranges for the assignment to it, or the assumption by it, of any rights or obligations or liabilities under a transaction that would have contravened section 330 if the company had originally entered into it (see B.3 of the Appendix below);

(c)   takes part in any arrangement such that another person enters into a transaction that would have contravened section 330 had the company entered into it (see B.4 of the Appendix below);

(d)   agrees to enter into any of the above transactions or arrangements.

3.4.2   *Disclosure requirements*

The particulars to be disclosed are the principal terms of the transaction, arrangement or agreement.[32] The principal terms must include, as a minimum:[33]

(a)   a statement of the fact that the transaction was made or existed during the financial year;

(b)   the name of the person for whom it was made and, if this person is connected with a director, that director's name;

(c)   for loans (including agreements and arrangements relating thereto):

   (i)   the principal and interest at the beginning and the end of the financial year,

   (ii)   the maximum amount outstanding during the year,

   (iii) the amount of any interest due but unpaid,

   (iv) the amount of any provision in respect of non-payment of the loan;

(d)   for guarantees and security:

   (i)   the potential liability of the company (or its subsidiary) at the beginning and the end of the financial year,

   (ii)   the maximum potential liability of the company (or its subsidiary),

   (iii) any amount paid and any liability incurred by the company in fulfilling the security or discharging the security;

(e)   for quasi-loans and credit transactions, it is necessary to disclose the value of the transaction. The value of a quasi-loan is defined as the maximum amount which the person to whom the quasi-loan is made is liable to reimburse the creditor. In the case of a credit transaction, value is defined as the price which it is reasonable to expect could be obtained for the goods, land or services to which the transaction or arrangement relates if they had been supplied in the ordinary course of business and on the same terms (apart from price) as they have been supplied, under the transaction or arrangement in question.[34] Although the legislation does not specify the extent of disclosures, given that details of any transaction subsisting during the year must be disclosed, it would be relevant for the disclosures to be similar to those for loans (see (c) above).

In addition to the above, it may be necessary to disclose other principal terms of the transaction; for example, the repayment term in the case of a loan or the credit limit for credit transactions and quasi-loans.

The following extracts illustrate a variety of section 330 type transactions:

A   Loans

Extract 29.3: Friends' Provident Life Office (1996)

10.   LOANS TO DIRECTORS [extract]

	Amount outstanding 1 January 1996 £	Amount outstanding 31 December 1996 £	Maximum outstanding during the year £
K. Satchell House purchase loan (repaid during year)	30,000	-	30,000

The loan was secured by mortgage on the property and by a life assurance policy on the life of the borrower. The rate of interest payable was 4% p.a. on the first £15,000 and 8% p.a. on the remainder. The loan was made by the Office on the same terms as were available to other employees.

Extract 29.4: Cordiant plc (1996)

Remuneration and Nominations Committee report [extract]

On appointment to the Board on 9 January 1995, Mr Bungey already had a loan from the Company which totalled US$261,699 including interest charged at US prime rate. At 31 December 1995, he owed US$79,400 (which included interest of US$4,400) which was repaid in full in April 1996. During 1996, the maximum amount outstanding was US$81,144. There are no outstanding loans granted by any member of the Group to any of the Directors or guarantees provided by any member of the Group for their benefit.

It can be seen from the above extracts that, even though there are no amounts outstanding at the year end, disclosure is required; this is because the transactions *existed* during the period. This would also be the case where there are no amounts outstanding at either the beginning or the end of the year. (An example of this is shown in Extract 29.8 below in respect of a quasi-loan.)

Similarly, even if the individual concerned is no longer a director at the year end, disclosure would be required; this is because the loan was in respect of someone who was a director at some time during the financial year.

B   Guarantees and security

Extract 29.5: The Body Shop International PLC (1996)

7   Directors [extract]

Transactions involving Directors

Prior to her appointment as a Director on 25 July 1994, the Company provided a bank guarantee in respect of J Reid. This guarantee had been cleared to nil by 2 March 1996 (1995: £73,750).

C   *Credit transactions*

Extract 29.6: First Leisure Corporation PLC (1996)

25   Transactions with related parties [extract]

(ii) Directors

Mr J E Bollam, through a company controlled by him, has an interest in a lease of property owned by the Group in Blackpool. Payments under this lease in the year ended 31st October 1996 amounted to £425,000 (1995 £425,000).

Extract 29.7: The Body Shop International PLC (1996)

7   Directors [extract]

Transactions involving Directors

M J Ross owns jointly with his wife all the shares in Craigross Holdings Limited ("Craigross"), subsidiaries of which hold six franchises with the Company.

...

In common with the arrangements with other UK franchisees, the Company has leased the premises relating to three of the franchised outlets to Craigross and has guaranteed the lease commitments on the three other shops. The annual rentals payable in respect of the premises leased to Craigross by the Company were £0.267 million (1995: £0.227 million). ...

D   *Quasi-loans*

Extract 29.8: Chrysalis Group PLC (1996)

24   TRANSACTIONS WITH DIRECTORS [extract]

d   During the year a quasi loan was made to C N Wright. The highest amount outstanding in the year was £23,177. The amount outstanding at 31st August 1996 was nil (1995: nil).

3.5   Material interest transactions

3.5.1   Introduction

The group and individual company financial statements must disclose details of transactions or arrangements in which any person who was a director of the company, its holding company or a connected person thereof had a material interest (subject to various exemptions: see 3.6 below).[35]   Section 330 type transactions are excluded from this category.[36]

It is for the directors to determine whether a transaction is material.[37]   For these purposes, a transaction is not material if the directors of the reporting company (or at least a majority of them), excluding the director whose interest is under review, decide that it is not.[38]   However, if the directors do not consider the question of materiality, it cannot be presumed that the interest was immaterial.[39]

In these circumstances, the question of the materiality of the transaction will be regarded as a matter of fact.

3.5.2 Definition of material interest

The definition of 'material' has proved to be one of the more problematic issues in this area of the law. There are two widely accepted interpretations; namely, that 'material':

(a) should be judged by what is relevant to the users of the financial statements (the relevant view). Rumbelow[40] suggests that the rationale for this disclosure requirement is to ensure that shareholders are better informed about their directors and better able to take any decisions they may have to take as shareholders (particularly as regards those directors). Consequently, he reasons that to decide what is material, one must look to see if the interest is such that its disclosure would be likely to influence a reasonable shareholder in making those decisions;

(b) means substantial in relation to the individual transaction in which the director is interested (the 'Mars Bar' view). Proponents of this view claim that the wording of the provision points to this interpretation.

However, as the following example illustrates, the 'Mars Bar' view may give rise to curious results:

Example 29.7

A director arranges a £50m contract on behalf of his company; the agreement provides for an arrangement fee of ½% of the value of the contract (i.e. commission of £250,000). The director will not need to disclose his interest if the 'Mars Bar' approach is adopted because his interest in the transaction is insignificant in relation to that transaction. However, if a director purchases a bar of chocolate for himself in the staff restaurant, the 'Mars Bar' view would demand disclosure of this transaction (subject to the de minimis exceptions: see 3.6.3 below); in this instance, he has a 100% interest in the transaction.

There is a third possible interpretation; namely, that material must be determined by reference to the director's financial position. Proponents of this view argue that if a transaction is not material vis-à-vis the director's personal position, there will be no conflict of duty and interest. However, the jurisprudence in this area makes it clear that the courts will not look into the merits of a transaction but adhere strictly to the rule that the possible conflict of interest and duty must not be allowed to arise, hence this rationale is somewhat spurious. On a practical note, if this view were adopted curious results could arise, as shown in the following example:

Example 29.8

Mr M, a director of ABC plc, has amassed a personal fortune of £10m. The latest audited accounts of ABC plc show net assets of £50,000 and turnover of £200,000. XYZ plc, a company of which Mr M is the majority shareholder, enters into a contract to buy goods worth £20,000 from ABC plc. Arguably, if the foregoing basis of assessing materiality is used, the transaction would not require disclosure.

On balance, we prefer the relevant view since its application is most likely to satisfy the needs of the users (or potential users) of the accounts, by keeping them informed of the types of dealing between a company and its directors which impact upon investment, credit and other decisions which they may be required to take. Clearly, this test involves the making of a qualitative judgement, that is, whether disclosure of the transaction might make a difference to a business decision. In practice, as Swinson argues,[41] this qualitative assessment may often be answered by establishing whether a director's interest is material in quantitative terms. If an interest is immaterial in quantitative terms, it may be irrelevant to the users of the accounts and vice-versa.

It should be emphasised that the above discussion of 'material' is only in the context of whether the transaction requires disclosure as a result of the Companies Act. However, this will not be the end of the matter in determining whether disclosure is necessary in the accounts because the requirements of FRS 8 also apply. As discussed at 2.3.2 in Chapter 28, FRS 8 requires that in considering whether transactions with individuals (such as directors) need to be disclosed, materiality has to be judged not only in terms of their significance to the reporting entity but also in relation to the other party, which in this case is the director.

The effect of FRS 8 has been that more transactions with directors are now disclosed than hitherto under the Companies Act requirements.

3.5.3   *Disclosure requirements*

The principal terms of material interest transactions must be disclosed;[42] in particular:

(a)   the name of the director who has the material interest and the nature thereof;[43]

(b)   the value of the transaction.[44]

The types of transaction in which a director may have an interest are diverse: the purchase or disposal of residential properties, other arrangements in respect of such property which arise due to the relocation of the directors, purchase or disposal of investments or businesses, provision of professional services and transactions in the ordinary course of business. Some of these are illustrated in the following extracts:

Extract 29.9: The Royal Bank of Scotland Group plc (1996)

50 Transactions with directors, officers and others [extract]

(b) Dr G. R. Mathewson, a director and chief executive of the company and the Bank has a right to repurchase from the Bank his former dwellinghouse which the Bank purchased from him and his wife in May 1988 at a price of £125,000. The right will become exercisable (1) in the event that Dr Mathewson ceases to be an executive director of the company or its subsidiaries; or (2) on 31st May 2008 in the event that he remains an executive director at that date; or (3) on such earlier date as the directors of the company may allow. Any repurchase is to be at the higher of the purchase price paid by the Bank or a price determined by independent professional valuation at the time of repurchase. The dwellinghouse is at present let by the Bank on commercial basis, with any rentals being received wholly by the Bank.

Extract 29.10: Coats Viyella Plc (1996)

Remuneration committee report [extract]

In 1992, the Company through a subsidiary acquired a joint interest in a property with Mr Flower on his taking up permanent residence in England. The subsidiary's investment was £180,000. Under the agreement Mr Flower has the option to purchase the Group's interest at market value. The Group's investment was reduced to £75,000 in January 1994 following partial exercise of Mr Flower's option.

In 1991, the Company through a subsidiary acquired a joint interest in a property with Ms Harrison on her joining the Company as Chief Executive of its Fashion Retail Division. The Group's interest was independently valued in February 1997 at £33,913 and on 5 March 1997 Ms Harrison purchased this interest at valuation.

Extract 29.11: Alfred McAlpine PLC (1996)

14. Fixed Assets – Investments [extract]

During 1996, the Group completed the deferred consideration payments to the Grove family in respect of the acquisition of the minority holding of Alfred McAlpine Homes Holdings Limited (formerly Alfred McAlpine Developments Limited). Mr E W Grove is a former director of both the Company and Alfred McAlpine Homes Holdings Limited. The final element of the deferred consideration was agreed at £15,242,000 and was settled during the year by cash payments of £7,621,000, plus interest of £99,000, and the issue of ordinary shares in the Company to the Grove family to the value of £7,621,000.

(Mr Grove resigned as a non-executive director during the year, on 22 July 1996.)

Extract 29.12: The RTZ Corporation PLC – CRA Limited (1996)

REPORT OF THE REMUNERATION COMMITTEE [extract]

Mr R L Clifford and Mr L A Davis occupied, without payment of rent, accommodation in central London under one year licence agreements granted by a subsidiary company. The values, based on the estimated market rents were respectively £10,000 and £192,000. Mr J C A Leslie occupied, without payment of rent, accommodation in Australia provided by a subsidiary company. The sterling value based on estimated market rent was £25,000.

This extract highlights the fact that the value of the transaction is not necessarily the amount at which the transaction is transacted, but is the amount which could have been obtained in the ordinary course of business.[45]

Where the value of the transaction cannot be expressed as a specific amount of money, then it is deemed to exceed £100,000,[46] as the following extract shows:

Extract 29.13: British Gas plc (1991)

3. Directors and employees [extract]

Norman Blacker was required to relocate during the year ended 31 March 1990 and Cedric Brown during the year ended 31 March 1991. Norman Blacker participated in the Company's relocation scheme throughout the period to December 1991 and Cedric Brown until May 1991. The value of these arrangements cannot be expressed as a specific sum of money and in these circumstances the Companies Act 1985 provides that the value is individually deemed to exceed £100 000. During 1991 approximately 570 employees participated in this scheme, which complies with Inland Revenue guidelines.

Extract 29.14: Wilson Bowden plc (1996)

23   Related party transactions

A number of partners in the firm of solicitors, Fishers (one of whom is Mr T. G. Neiland until his retirement as a partner on 31st March 1996) act for the Group in connection with land acquisitions, planning, conveyancing, commercial contract and general legal matters. During the year ended 31st December 1996 £408,000 (1995 £370,000) was paid to Fishers in respect of these legal services and related expenses.

Other than as noted above no contracts of significance in relation to the Group's business in which the Directors of the Company or other related parties had an interest subsisted at any time during the year.

The above extract illustrates the situation where a professional firm, such as solicitors, in which one of the directors is a partner, provide services to the company in the ordinary course of business.

Disclosure of such transactions is not required where the firm, or company, providing the services is not a connected person as defined by the Act (see 2.4 above); for example, where the director concerned is not a partner in the firm providing the services, but is merely a consultant. Nevertheless some companies disclose information about such transactions within the directors' report, presumably to meet the requirements of the Stock Exchange (see 5 below). One company which disclosed such a transaction, but within the notes to the accounts, as well as numerous other directors' interests in transactions is Chrysalis Group, as shown below:

Extract 29.15: Chrysalis Group PLC (1996)

24 TRANSACTIONS WITH DIRECTORS [extract]

a G H Martin has an interest in a subsidiary undertaking's agreements with Airborn Productions Limited and Airborn Production (Overseas) Limited by virtue of his share interests in those companies. The producer royalties payable to these companies in respect of the year were £37,392 (1995: £25,568).

b G H Martin was paid a royalty advance of £66,000 (1995: £45,000) by Echo Label Limited in connection with a planned future album.

c G H Martin has an interest in the joint venture company Air Studios (Lyndhurst) Limited by virtue of his share interests in the company. He acquired 500 'C' Ordinary Shares of 10p each at par (representing 5 per cent of the issued shares) on incorporation of the Company on 25th January 1991. During the year a capital restructuring of Air Studios (Lyndhurst) Limited took place. This resulted in G H Martin's holding of the share capital being reduced to a negligible percentage of the total issued share capital.

...

e S G Lewis has an interest in a subsidiary company The Echo Label Limited by virtue of his interest in the share capital of Armourvale Limited ("Armourvale") and Lapishaven Limited ("Lapishaven"), two companies which together hold 75 per cent of the share capital of The Echo Label Limited. Mr Lewis' interest in The Echo Label Limited amounts to 18.75 per cent of its capital. Certain put and call option agreements exist between the Group and Mr Lewis in respect of his shares in Armourvale and Lapishaven other than his B shares in Lapishaven, as referred to in note 23(b) [below].

f C J C Levison has, since the 1st August, been a consultant with one of the Group's solicitors, Harbottle & Lewis. Mr Levison received fees from Harbottle & Lewis through his company, Clarion Media Europe Ltd. All fees paid to Harbottle & Lewis are on ordinary commercial terms incurred in the normal course of the Group's business.

g The services of C N Wright and N R A Butterfield were made available to Loftus Road Plc, a company in which Mr Wright has a beneficial of 30 per cent, and of which he, Mr Butterfield and Mr Levison are all non-executive Directors, for an agreed fee of £50,000 for their services prior to Loftus Road Plc's admission to the Alternative Investment Market (AIM). In the year to 31st August 1996 £25,000 of this had been recognised in the profit and loss account.

h From 1 September 1996 C N Wright's services to Loftus Road Plc will be reimbursed to Chrysalis at a rate of £8,000 per month.

23 CAPITAL COMMITMENTS [extract]

b Under the terms of the Option Agreement dated 29th November 1993 between the Group and Steve Lewis, set out in the circular to shareholders dated 30th November 1993 and referred to in note 24 (e) [above], the Group may be required to purchase certain of Mr Lewis' shares in Armourvale Limited and Lapishaven Limited. This put option may be exercised by Mr Lewis at any time after 1st September 1998 whilst he is still employed by the Company, or within 30 days of the subsequent termination of his employment, for a consideration based upon the fair market value of the shares, and capped at £10 million.

3.6 Exemptions from disclosure

The following transactions involving directors do not require disclosure:

3.6.1 General

(a) Transactions between companies in which a director is interested only by virtue of his being a director of both companies;[47]

(b) directors' service contracts.[48] However, details of service contracts of directors of listed companies may require disclosure (see 4.3.11 of Chapter 30);

(c) transactions which were not entered into or which did not subsist during the year.[49] However, transactions which were entered into after the year end will require disclosure if at the year end there was an agreement between the parties to enter into the transaction.[50] In addition, material transactions involving directors post year-end may fall to be disclosed as post balance sheet events in accordance with the provisions of SSAP 17 (see Chapter 24).

3.6.2 Section 330 transactions

(a) Credit transactions and related guarantees, arrangements and agreements where the aggregate amount outstanding for the director and his connected persons did not at any time during the financial year exceed £5,000;[51]

(b) there is a reduced level of disclosure for intra-group loans and quasi-loans,[52] although relief has not been granted for guarantees, credit transactions etc. The only details to be disclosed in respect of such transactions are:

(i) a statement that the transaction etc. was made or subsisted during the financial year;

(ii) the name of the person for whom it was made and in the case of a loan or quasi-loan to a connected person, the name of the director.

This exemption only applies if there are no minority interests involved.

3.6.3 Material interest transactions

(a) Transactions in which the director's interest is not material (as decided by a majority of his fellow directors);[53]

(b) transactions in which a director has a material interest which are entered into at arm's length in the ordinary course of business.[54] This exemption has given rise to particular difficulty. It is sometimes argued that the exemption, as presently drafted, only applies if each party to the transaction is a member of the same group. The explanatory note to the statutory instrument[55] which introduced the exemption indicates that there is no need for the counterparties to the transaction to be group companies. Given that one of the aims of introducing the exemption was to reduce the level of disclosure, it seems logical to interpret the provision as exempting all arm's length material interest transactions involving directors. This view, however, is not universally held.[56]

(c) any material interest transaction between members of a group of companies which would have been disclosable only because of a director being associated (see 2.4 above) with the contracting companies, provided that no minority interests in the reporting company are affected.[57] A higher level of disclosure is required where there are minority interests since minorities can be affected by transfers of value within a group. The wording of this exemption is arcane and the drafting is considered to be defective;

(d) transactions in which a director had a material interest where the value of each transaction (with no reduction in the amount outstanding) in the financial year and the value of transactions in preceding financial years (less the amount by which the director's liabilities have been reduced) did not at any time during the financial year exceed £1,000 or, if more than £1,000, did not exceed £5,000 or 1% of the value of the net assets of the reporting company. Net assets is defined as the aggregate of the company's assets, less the aggregate of its liabilities.[58] It is not clear how this provision interacts with the other exemptions for material interest transactions (see (b) and (c) above). Unless these provisions are discrete, the exemptions are likely to be rendered ineffective.

Whether the effect of any of these exemptions will result in non-disclosure of the relevant transactions in the accounts will depend on whether or not FRS 8 requires disclosure of the transactions. As noted at 3.5.2 above, FRS 8 has a different concept of materiality; it also requires transactions to be disclosed even when the terms are at arm's length. Companies should therefore ensure that, before relying on any of the exemptions above, they have considered the requirements of FRS 8 (see generally Chapter 28).

4 BANKING COMPANIES UNDER THE BANKING ACT 1987

A banking company under the Banking Act 1987 is subject to different disclosure requirements in respect of section 330 type transactions to which the company is a party.[59] Material interest transactions involving directors of banking companies must be disclosed as for other companies (see 3.5 above).[60] Similar requirements apply to a company which is the holding company of a credit institution. References to banking companies below should be read as including such companies.

In brief,[61] banking companies must maintain a register of section 330 type transactions for the current and preceding ten financial years.[62] A statement of such transactions must be:[63]

(a)   made available for members to inspect; and

(b)   examined and reported on by the company's auditor.

4.1   Disclosure of transactions by banking companies

The financial statements must disclose:

(a)   the aggregate amounts of loans, quasi-loans, credit transactions and related transactions outstanding at the end of the financial year; and

(b)   the number of persons for whom the transactions were made.[64]

In this context,[65] amount outstanding means the outstanding liabilities of the person for whom the transaction was made and as respects a guarantee or security, the amount guaranteed or secured.

The following extract provides an illustration of the disclosures of transactions between a banking company and its directors:

Extract 29.16: National Westminster Bank Plc (1996)

49   Transactions with related parties [extract]

(a)   The aggregate amounts outstanding at 31 December under transactions, arrangements and agreements made by institutions authorised under the Banking Act 1987 within the Group for persons who are, or were, directors of the Bank during the year and their connected persons, and with other executive officers of the Bank listed on page 63 and their connected persons comprised the following:–

	Number of directors/ officers of the Bank	Number of connected persons	Aggregate amount £000
Directors and their connected persons			
Loans and credit card transactions	10	8	572
Other executive officers			
Loans and credit card transactions	33	8	2,251

It must be emphasised that these disclosures only apply to section 330 type transactions with the banking company. The disclosure requirements outlined in 3.4.2 above still apply to any such transaction with other companies within the group.

5   STOCK EXCHANGE REQUIREMENTS

In addition to the disclosure provisions imposed by the Companies Act 1985 (and those of FRS 8 – see Chapter 28), the Stock Exchange imposes additional requirements in respect of transactions involving directors of listed companies.[66]

Transactions (other than those of a revenue nature in the ordinary course of business) involving directors, shadow directors, past directors of the company (or other member of the group) and their associates (similar to connected persons) constitute transactions with related parties (formerly known as Class 4 transactions).[67]   Generally, full particulars of the transaction must be given in a circular including the name of the related party concerned and of the nature and extent of the interest of such party in the transaction.[68]

Normally these particulars should be circulated to the company's shareholders prior to obtaining their approval[69] and the Stock Exchange must also be notified of the proposed transaction.[70] A number of exceptions from the requirements are made, one of which is for small transactions provided that an independent adviser expresses the opinion that the terms of the transaction are fair and reasonable. Where this exception applies, the company must also disclose details of the transaction in the next published annual accounts, including the identity of the related party, the value of the consideration for the transaction and all other relevant circumstances.[71]

The annual report and accounts of listed companies must also disclose particulars of any contract of significance to which the company, or one of its subsidiary undertakings, is a party and in which a director of the company is or was materially interested.[72] A contract of significance is defined as one which represents in amount or value, a sum equal to 1% or more, calculated on a group basis where relevant, of:

(a)   in the case of a capital transaction or a transaction the principal purpose of which is the granting of credit, the aggregate of the group's share capital and reserves; or

(b)   in other cases, the total annual purchases, sales, payments or receipts, as the case may be, of the group.[73]

As a result of a change made to the requirements in June 1996, there is now no need to make a statement if there has been no such contract.

The Stock Exchange also imposes additional requirements on companies quoted on the Alternative Investment Market.

Where an AIM company proposes to enter into related party transactions (similar to those for listed companies) which result in specified percentage ratios being 5% or more then it must give particulars to the Stock Exchange and send a copy of the announcement to the shareholders.[74] Where any of the percentage ratios exceed 0.25%, then disclosure of the transaction must be made in the next set of published accounts, including the identity of the related party, the value of the consideration for the transaction and all other relevant circumstances.[75]

6   TRANSACTIONS INVOLVING OFFICERS

6.1   Introduction

The Act requires certain details of transactions between a company and its officers to be disclosed.[76] To this end, group and individual company financial statements must contain particulars in the notes of transactions entered into by officers. A holding company's financial statements must take into account transactions between the company and its subsidiaries with officers of the company; however, transactions between the subsidiaries and their officers do not need to be included in the holding company's financial statements. If a company does not produce group financial statements by virtue of one of the statutory exemptions, these requirements still apply in full.[77]

6.2   Disclosure requirements

The financial statements must disclose the following details in respect of transactions with officers (which, for these purposes, in order to avoid duplication of disclosure excludes directors):[78]

(a)   the aggregate amounts of loans, quasi-loans, credit transactions, guarantees and arrangements outstanding at the end of the financial year; and

(b)   the number of officers for whom the transactions were made.[79]

For these purposes, the amount outstanding is defined as the outstanding liabilities of the person for whom the transaction was made and in the case of a guarantee or security, the amount guaranteed or secured.[80]

Disclosure of such transactions is not, however, necessary for a particular officer if the aggregate amount outstanding under the transactions at the end of the financial year for that officer does not exceed £2,500.[81]

The following extracts illustrate the disclosure of transactions involving officers:

Extract 29.17: British Aerospace Public Limited Company (1996)

6   Directors [extract]

Transactions
At 31st December, 1996 there was an aggregate balance of £148,873 outstanding on house purchase loans made to or arranged for five officers to assist with their relocation at the Company's request.

> *Extract 29.18: Imperial Chemical Industries PLC (1996)*
>
> **39 Statutory and other information** [extract]
>
> Included in debtors are interest-free loans of £50,000 (1995 £81,000) to one officer (1995 two officers) of the Company.

6.3 Banking companies under the Banking Act 1987

Financial statements of banking companies (or companies which are holding companies of credit institutions) do not generally require disclosure of transactions between officers (who were not also directors) and the banking company. However, the information described at 6.2 above is required to be disclosed in respect of transactions between the banking company (or as the case may be the credit institution) and a chief executive or manager of the company or its holding company.[82]

A 'chief executive' means a person who, either alone or jointly with one or more other persons, is responsible under the immediate authority of the directors for the conduct of the business of the company and a 'manager' means a person (other than a chief executive) who, under the immediate authority of a director or chief executive of the financial institution, exercises managerial functions or is responsible for maintaining accounts or other records of the financial institution.[83]

7 CONCLUSION

The provisions of the Companies Act governing the disclosure of transactions between a company and its directors and officers are generally regarded as unsatisfactory. They do not appear to form a coherent whole whereby a director's contractual freedom can be meaningfully regulated; for example, there are de minimis exemptions from disclosure of credit and material interest transactions yet no parallel provisions for loans and quasi-loans. In addition, aspects of the legislation are difficult to comprehend, for example, the material interest transaction exemptions.

Over the years various professional bodies have made representations to the DTI suggesting that the legislation be clarified and simplified. The Companies Act 1989 did make some minor amendments relating to this area, although it was indicated while the Bill was going through the parliamentary process that further changes would be made by Statutory Instrument.[84]

The DTI had indicated that it was the intention to review the legislation in this area, but that it was a long-term task. It did publish in 1991 a consultative document in which it proposed to simplify the rules contained in Schedule 6 to the Act, dealing with the information required to be disclosed in companies' financial statements, but nothing has ever come of it.[85]

More recently it had been planning to issue a further consultation document on the reform of Part X of the Act – *Enforcement of Fair Dealing by Directors* – but this was held back due to concerns and controversy over directors' remuneration. Now that new legislation has been introduced on that issue (see Chapter 30), it remains to be seen if proposals will be put forward to reform Part X of the Act and the related disclosure requirements of directors' loans and transactions.

APPENDIX: LEGAL REQUIREMENTS

A INTRODUCTION

Although the primary objective of this chapter is to discuss how transactions with directors should be disclosed in a company's financial statements, a brief exposition of the statutory provisions determining the legality of such transactions is considered necessary in order to place the disclosure requirements in context.

B PROHIBITED TRANSACTIONS

The Companies Act 1985 contains complex provisions[86] which prohibit or restrict many transactions involving directors (and shadow directors).[87] The legality of a transaction is determined at the time of its execution. Therefore, a loan to a person who subsequently becomes a director is legal because the recipient was not a director at the time of its making.

The basic prohibitions are dealt with in B.1 to B.4 below and the exemptions therefrom are dealt with in C below.

B.1 Loans

A company may not make a loan to its directors or those of its holding company.[88] In addition, a relevant company[89] (i.e. a public company or a company which is part of a group which includes a public company) may not make a loan to a connected person thereof.[90] Likewise, a company may not enter into a guarantee[91] or provide any security in connection with a loan made by another person to its directors or those of its holding company[92] and, in the case of a relevant company, a connected person thereof.[93]

B.2 Quasi-loans and credit transactions

A relevant company may not make a quasi-loan nor enter into a credit transaction with its directors, the directors of its holding company or a connected person thereof. There is a similar restriction on the provision of guarantees or security in connection with such transactions.[94]

B.3 Assignment/assumption of rights, obligations or liabilities

A company may not arrange for the assignment to, or the assumption by it, of any rights, obligations or liabilities in respect of transactions which, if undertaken by the company in the first place, would have been unlawful;[95] for example:

Example 29.9

A bank makes a loan to a director of Company X and thereafter assigns its rights to Company X. The company will have entered into an unlawful assignment.

Example 29.10

The facts are as above, but the loan from the bank is guaranteed by a friend of the director. Subsequently, Company X becomes the guarantor of the loan releasing the director's friend from his obligations. The assumption of the guarantee by Company X is unlawful.

B.4   Arrangements

Schemes whereby a third party enters into an arrangement which if entered into by the company would have been unlawful, in circumstances where the company (or a fellow group company) provides a benefit to the third party, are not permitted;[96] for example:

Example 29.11

Company X arranges for a bank to make a loan to one of its directors on favourable terms in return for which the company places business with the bank. This series of transactions constitutes an unlawful arrangement whereby the bank enters into an arrangement forbidden to Company X and receives a benefit for so doing.

C   EXEMPTED TRANSACTIONS

C.1   Loans of small amounts

A loan to a director of a company or its holding company is not illegal if the aggregate of the sums advanced to the director does not exceed £5,000; in computing the sum of £5,000, amounts already advanced to the director must be taken into account.[97] It should be noted that this exemption does not extend to loans of small amounts to connected persons of directors of a relevant company.

C.2   Short-term quasi-loans

Quasi-loans by a relevant company are permitted if made on the condition that the director reimburses the company within two months and where the aggregate of the sums outstanding under quasi-loans does not exceed £5,000.[98] Again, this exemption does not extend to quasi-loans made to connected persons of directors of a relevant company.

C.3   Minor or business credit transactions

A relevant company may enter in a credit transaction for a person if:

(a)   the aggregate of such amounts does not exceed £10,000;[99] or

(b)   the transaction is entered into by the company in the ordinary course of its business on terms which the company would have extended to a person of the same financial standing unconnected with the company.[100]

It should be noted that this exemption extends to credit transactions for connected persons of directors of a relevant company.

C.4   Inter-company transactions

A relevant company is not prohibited from making loans and quasi-loans to a group company where a director of one company is associated with another.[101] Likewise, a company may make a loan or quasi-loan to or enter into a credit transaction as creditor for its holding company.[102]

Furthermore, a holding company may make a loan to a director of its subsidiary or a connected person thereof; similarly, a subsidiary may make a loan to a director of a fellow subsidiary (provided in both cases that the director is not on the board of the company or the holding company and that the other group company does not thereby obtain some benefit: see B.4 above).

C.5   Directors' business expenditure

A director can be placed in funds to enable him properly to perform his duties as a corporate officer. However, funds may only be advanced:

(a)   if prior approval of the company in general meeting has been obtained; or

(b)   where approval is not obtained at or before the next annual general meeting, the loan is to be repaid within six months of the conclusion of that meeting.[103]

Furthermore, relevant companies may only advance an aggregate of £20,000 to the director for these purposes.[104]

C.6   Money-lending companies

A money-lending company (namely one whose ordinary business includes the making of loans or quasi-loans) may make loans or quasi-loans or enter into related guarantees to its directors, directors of its holding company and connected persons. However, such transactions are only permitted if made by the company in the ordinary course of its business on terms which are no more preferential than are available to persons who have no connection with the company. In addition, relevant companies (excluding banking companies: see 4 above) may make loans or quasi-loans only up to a £100,000 limit.[105]

Loans made for the purpose of facilitating the purchase of or improving a director's house may also be made by money-lending companies if the facility is ordinarily available to employees of the company on equally favourable terms; this exemption is again subject to a £100,000 limit for all companies.[106]

There is some doubt as to the interaction between the monetary limit on housing and 'other' loans to directors of relevant money-lending companies (which are not banking companies under the Banking Act 1987: see 4 above). This problem is compounded by what appears to be a drafting error[107] in references in section 339(1) which impacts upon how previous loans etc. made by money-lending companies are to be aggregated with amounts already advanced to directors and their connected persons. On balance, we believe that the intention of the legislation is that the aggregate value of all loans, whatever their nature, made by money-lending companies to any given director and his connected persons, must not exceed £100,000.

C.7   Companies registered overseas[108]

The following transactions entered into by an overseas company are not subject to the statutory restrictions; transactions entered into by an overseas incorporated subsidiary:

(a)   with a director of its UK incorporated parent; and

(b)   of a UK incorporated parent with a director of the UK parent's overseas incorporated holding company.

D   SANCTIONS

D.1   Civil remedies

A prohibited transaction is voidable at the company's option unless:

(a)   restitution is impossible, for example, where the proceeds of an illegal loan have been used to build an extension to the director's house; or

(b)   the company has been indemnified for the loss suffered by it; or

(c)   rights have been acquired by a bona fide purchaser for value who does not have notice of the contravention.[109]

The director, any connected person for whom the transaction was made and any director who authorised the transaction is liable:

(a)   to account for any gain which he has made; and

(b)   to make good any loss made by the company.[110]

However, where the transaction is made for a person connected with a director, then that director will not be liable if he can demonstrate that he took all reasonable steps to secure the company's compliance with the legislation.[111]

The person connected with the director and any other director who authorised the transaction will not be liable if he can demonstrate that at the time the transaction was entered into he did not know the circumstances constituting the contravention.[112]

D.2   Criminal penalties

A director of a relevant company who authorises or permits the company to enter into a transaction knowing or believing that the transaction was illegal is guilty of an offence and is liable to imprisonment and/or a fine. A relevant company entering into an illegal transaction is also guilty of an offence unless it did not know the circumstances at the time of the transaction. A person who knowingly procures the transaction or arrangement is also guilty of an offence.[113]

E   INTERESTS IN CONTRACTS

A director must, upon pain of a fine,[114] declare any interest (direct or indirect) in a contract with the company at a board meeting.[115] In this context, an interest in a section 330 type transaction requires disclosure[116] (see generally 3 above). If the contract is merely proposed, the director must declare his interest at the board meeting at which the contract is under consideration.[117] The Court of Appeal held in *Guinness plc v Saunders & Ward* [118] that this duty cannot be fulfilled by disclosure to a sub-committee of the board; only disclosure to a properly convened meeting of the full board will suffice. If the director was not interested in the contract at the time it was made, disclosure should be made at the first board meeting after the director becomes interested.[119] For these purposes, a general notice of interest in specific types of contracts given to the board suffices.[120]

Example 29.12

Mr A, a director of Company X is the majority shareholder in Company Y. Company X purchases quantities of stock from Company Y. Mr A must disclose his interest in such contracts to the board of Company X.

These requirements also apply to shadow directors who are required to make disclosure of interests in contracts by means of a written notice addressed to the board.[121]

In addition to the statutory restrictions, the company's articles may amplify the director's ability to enter into contracts. Thus, Table A provides that: 'Subject to the provisions of the Act, and provided that he has disclosed to the directors the nature and extent of any material interest of his, a director notwithstanding his office

(a)   may be a party to, or otherwise interested in, any transaction or arrangement with the company or in which the company is otherwise interested;

(b)   may be a director or other officer of, or employed by, a party to any transaction or arrangement with, or otherwise interested in, any body corporate promoted by the company or in which the company is otherwise interested; and

(c)   shall not, by reason of his office, be accountable to the company for any benefit which he derives from any such office or employment or from any such transaction or arrangement or from any interest in any such body corporate and no such transaction or arrangement shall be liable to be avoided on the ground of any such interest or benefit.'[122]

F   SUBSTANTIAL PROPERTY TRANSACTIONS

A director or connected person may not acquire from or sell to the company a non-cash asset[123] above the requisite value unless the transaction has been approved by the company in general meeting. If the transaction occurs between the company and a director or connected person of its holding company, the holding company's approval is also required.[124]

In this context, the requisite value of transactions is the lower of 10% of the company's net asset value or £100,000. This is subject to a de minimis threshold of £2,000, below which property transactions do not require approval.[125]

There are a number of exemptions from the requirement to obtain approval; for example, an acquisition of an asset of the requisite value:

(a)   by a director from a company which is a wholly owned subsidiary of another company, and

(b)   by a person from a company of which he is a member (i.e. a shareholder acting in his capacity as member), and

(c)   by one group company from another, provided there are no minority interests involved,

do not require approval. In addition, no approval is required for transactions entered into through an independent broker.[126]

A transaction entered into without the necessary approval is voidable at the company's option unless:

(a)   restitution of the property is impossible; or

(b)   rights to the property have been acquired by a bona fide purchaser for value who does not know that approval has not been obtained; or

(c)   the arrangement has been affirmed by the company (and if appropriate its holding company) in general meeting within a reasonable period.[127]

The director, any connected person for whom the transaction was made and any director who authorised the transaction is liable:

(a) to account for any gain which he has made; and

(b) to make good any loss made by the company.[128]

However, where the transaction is made for a person connected with a director, and that director can demonstrate that he took all reasonable steps to secure the company's compliance with these provisions,[129] he will escape liability.

The person connected with the director and any other director who authorised the transaction will not be liable if he can demonstrate that at the time the transaction was entered into he did not know the circumstances constituting the contravention.[130]

G   TRANSACTIONS INVOLVING OFFICERS

Officers, other than directors, are not subject to any statutory restrictions on their ability to transact with their company. A company's articles may address the contractual position of its officers, although Table A[131] is silent on this issue.

References

1 A person who holds anything in trust. A fiduciary relationship arises where a person has rights and powers which he is bound to exercise for the benefit of another. Hence he is not allowed to derive any profit or advantage from the relationship between them, except with the knowledge and consent of the other person: J. Burke, *Jowitt's Dictionary of English Law, Volume I A–K*, p. 788. If a director breaches this duty, a range of remedies is available to the company. The company may, inter alia, seek an injunction, claim damages or compensation, require the director to account for profits made or rescind contracts entered into with him.
2 CA 48, s 190(1).
3 *Ibid.*, s 190(1)(a).
4 CA 80, ss 49–50.
5 CA 85, ss 330–346, Sch. 6, Parts II and III.
6 *Ibid.*, s 741(1).
7 Companies should ensure that they do not allow persons described as divisional directors to hold themselves out as being members of the board. Otherwise there is a danger that contracts entered into by such persons, in excess of their managerial authority, may be binding on the company.
8 CA 85, s 741(2).
9 *Ibid.*, s 741(3).
10 The position of the alternate director is discussed in more detail in R. Pennington, *Company Law*, p. 628, and C. M. Schmithoff (ed.), *Palmer's Company Law Volume I*, p. 879.
11 The Companies (Tables A–F) Regulations 1985 (SI 1985 No. 85), Table A, Article 65.
12 CA 85, s 346.
13 *Ibid.*, s 346(6)(a).
14 *Ibid.*, s 346(7) and Sch. 13, para. 5.
15 *Ibid.*, s 346(8).

16 *Ibid.*, s 744.
17 *Champagne Perrier–Jouet SA v H.H. Finch Ltd* [1982] 1 WLR 1359.
18 CA 85, s 331(3).
19 *Ibid.*, s 331(7).
20 *Ibid.*, s 331(8).
21 *Ibid.*, ss 317(1), (8).
22 *Ibid.*, s 317(6).
23 *Ibid.*, ss 232(1)–(2) and Sch. 6, Part II.
24 *Ibid.*, Sch. 6, para. 15.
25 *Ibid.*, s 237(4).
26 CA 85, s 232(1)–(2) and Sch. 6, paras. 15–16.
27 *Ibid.*, Sch. 9, Part IV.
28 *Ibid.*, s 232(1)–(2), and Sch. 6, paras. 15–16.
29 This includes indemnities: *ibid.*, s 331(2).
30 *Ibid.*, Sch. 6, para. 19.
31 *Ibid.*, ss 232(1)–(2) and Sch. 6, paras. 15(a)–(b) and 16(a)–(b).
32 *Ibid.*, Sch. 6, para. 22(1).
33 *Ibid.*, para. 22(2).
34 *Ibid.*, para. 27(c).
35 *Ibid.*, ss 232(1)–(2) and Sch. 6, paras. 15(c) and 16(c).
36 *Ibid.*, Sch. 6, paras. 15(c) and 16(c) refer to any 'other transaction or arrangement'.
37 *Ibid.*, para. 17(2). Materiality for these purposes should not be confused with the materiality level calculated for the purposes of the audit of the financial statements.
38 *Ibid.* Assuming the directors' opinion is formed in good faith and is not perverse, their view should prevail. However, in extreme circumstances the directors' opinion may need to be overridden in order for the accounts to give a true and fair view.
39 CA 85, Sch. 6, para. 17(2).
40 C. Rumbelow, 'When Directors Must Tell', *The Law Society's Gazette*, Wednesday 3 November 1982, pp. 1390–1392.
41 C. Swinson, 'Director's "Material interest" – just how do you measure it', *Accountancy*, October 1983, p. 110.
42 CA 85, Sch. 6, para. 22(1).
43 *Ibid.*, para. 22(2)(c).
44 *Ibid.*, para 22(2)(f).
45 *Ibid.*, s 340(6).
46 *Ibid.*, s 340(7).
47 *Ibid.*, Sch. 6, para. 18(a).
48 *Ibid.*, para. 18(b).
49 *Ibid.*, para. 18(c).
50 *Ibid.*, paras. 15(b) and 16(b).
51 *Ibid.*, para. 24.
52 *Ibid.*, para. 23.
53 *Ibid.*, para. 17(2).
54 *Ibid.*, para. 20.
55 SI 1984 No. 1860.
56 B. Johnson and M. Patient, *Accounting Provisions of the Companies Act 1985*, p. 270.
57 CA 85, Sch. 6, para. 21.
58 *Ibid.*, para. 25.
59 *Ibid.*, Sch. 9, Part IV, para. 2.
60 *Ibid.*, para. 3.
61 See generally CA 85, ss 343–344.
62 *Ibid.*, s 343(2).
63 *Ibid.*, ss 343(5)–(6).
64 CA 85, Sch. 9, Part IV, para. 3 and Sch. 6, Part III.
65 *Ibid.*, Sch. 6, para. 30.
66 *The Listing Rules*, London Stock Exchange, Chapter 11.
67 *Ibid.*, para. 11.1.

68 *Ibid.*, para. 11.10(c).
69 *Ibid.*, para. 11.4(c).
70 *Ibid.*, para. 11.3.
71 *Ibid.*, paras. 11.7 and 11.8.
72 *Ibid.*, Chapter 12, para. 12.43(q).
73 *Ibid.*, para. 12.44.
74 *Rules of the London Stock Exchange*, London Stock Exchange, Chapter 16: The Alternative Investment Market Admission Rules, rules 16.22–16.24. The percentage ratios are based on assets, profits, consideration to assets and consideration to market capitalisation.
75 *Ibid.*, rule 16.25.
76 CA 85, ss 232(1)–(2) and Sch. 6, Part III.
77 *Ibid.*, ss 232(1)–(2) and Sch. 6, para. 29.
78 *Ibid.*, Sch. 6, para. 29.
79 *Ibid.*, Sch. 6, paras. 28 and 29(1).
80 *Ibid.*, para. 30.
81 *Ibid.*, para. 29(2).
82 *Ibid.*, Sch. 9, Part IV, para. 3(1).
83 Banking Act 1987, ss 105(6)–(7).
84 Hansard, *Parliamentary Debates*, 22 June 1989, Column 507.
85 DTI, *Consultative Document on Amendments to Schedule 6 to the Companies Act 1985: Disclosure by Companies of Dealings in favour of Directors*, October 1991.

Appendix

86 CA 85, ss 317, 320, 330–346.
87 *Ibid.*, ss 317(8), 320(3), 330(5).
88 *Ibid.*, s 330(2).
89 *Ibid.*, s 331(6).
90 *Ibid.*, s 330(2)(b).
91 This includes indemnities: *ibid.*, s 331(2).
92 *Ibid.*, s 330(2)(b).
93 *Ibid.*, s 330(3)(c).
94 *Ibid.*, ss 330(3)–(4).
95 *Ibid.*, s 330(6).
96 *Ibid.*, s 330(7).
97 *Ibid.*, s 334. S 339 determines how the threshold is to be calculated.
98 *Ibid.*, s 332.
99 *Ibid.*, s 335(1). See also s 339.
100 *Ibid.*, s 335(2).
101 *Ibid.*, s 333.
102 *Ibid.*, s 336.
103 *Ibid.*, ss 337(1)–(3).
104 *Ibid.*, s 337(3). See also s 339.
105 *Ibid.*, ss 338(1)–(4). See also s 339.
106 *Ibid.*, s 338(6).
107 If the pre-consolidation legislation is to be reproduced accurately, the reference in s 339(1) to s 338(4) should actually be a reference to s 338(1).
108 The legislation applies to companies; that is, an entity formed and registered under the various Companies Acts: *ibid.*, s 735. This definition applies unless the contrary intention appears: *ibid.*, s 735(4). Since no contrary intention is expressed, a body incorporated overseas is not a company for the purposes of the directors' transactions provisions.
109 *Ibid.*, s 341(1).
110 *Ibid.*, s 341(2).
111 *Ibid.*, s 341(4).
112 *Ibid.*, s 341(5).
113 *Ibid.*, s 342.
114 *Ibid.*, s 317(7).

115 *Ibid.*, s 317(1).
116 *Ibid.*, s 317(6).
117 *Ibid.*, s 317(2).
118 [1988] 1 WLR 863.
119 CA 85, s 317(2).
120 *Ibid.*, s 317(3).
121 *Ibid.*, s 317(8).
122 The Companies (Tables A–F) Regulations 1985, *op. cit*, Article 85.
123 CA 85, s 739(1).
124 *Ibid.*, s 320(1).
125 *Ibid.*, s 320(2).
126 *Ibid.*, s 321.
127 *Ibid.*, ss 322(1)–(2).
128 *Ibid.*, s 322(2).
129 *Ibid.*, s 322(5).
130 *Ibid.*, s 322(6).
131 The Companies (Tables A–F) Regulations 1985, *op. cit.*

Chapter 30   Directors' remuneration

1   INTRODUCTION

This chapter focuses primarily on the disclosure requirements in respect of directors' remuneration. However, preparers of company financial statements should possess an awareness of the law governing the remuneration of directors and their service contracts. Accordingly, a brief exposition of these requirements has been included (see 1.1 to 1.4 below).[1]

Professor Gower reasoned that the need to disclose directors' remuneration was because 'it is too obvious that the system [of remunerating directors] lends itself to abuse, since directors will be encouraged to bleed the company by voting themselves excessive salaries and expense allowances. The latest Act [the Companies Act 1948] attempts to minimise these dangers by providing for full disclosure of the total emoluments received by directors ... '.[2] This requirement is simply a feature of the principle that a fiduciary should not allow his personal interests and duty to the company to conflict.[3]

These original requirements for aggregate information were added to in 1967 by the introduction of a requirement for individual information by the disclosure of the emoluments of the chairman, and of the highest paid director where this was not the chairman, together with the number of directors whose remuneration fell within specified bandings.[4] Although there had been a number of amendments over the years since then (principally revising the amounts of the bandings and when such individual information is required, as well as tightening up some of the potential loopholes), these basic requirements had until recently been in place for 30 years. As a result, they failed to keep up with recent developments in remuneration packages and accounting practice. This had been most evident in the case of listed companies.

In recent years executive remuneration has become a focus of public attention. Controversy surrounding the salaries and benefits of directors of British Gas and some other privatised utility companies in 1995 was simply the most well-publicised expression of public concern as to both the level and the structure of boardroom pay.

This concern was first addressed in 1992 by the Cadbury Committee, which was set up in May 1991 by the Financial Reporting Council, the London Stock Exchange and the accountancy profession, when it issued its report on 'corporate governance'.[5] At the heart of the Committee's recommendations was its Code of Best Practice for the boards of listed companies, paragraph 3.2 of which stated that 'there should be full and clear disclosure of directors' total emoluments and those of the chairman and highest paid UK director, including pension contributions and stock options. Separate figures should be given for salary and performance-related elements and the basis on which performance is measured to be explained.'

In view of increasing debate about share options granted to directors, in September 1994 the UITF issued Abstract 10 – *Disclosure of Directors' Share Options*. This recommends that further information concerning the option prices applicable to individual directors, together with market price information at the year end and at the date of exercise, should be disclosed (see 4.3.10 A below). However, the UITF had received legal advice that the recommended disclosures could not all be construed as being necessary to meet the legal requirements. Consequently, the disclosures are only recommendations and are not mandatory, although as a result of later developments discussed below they are effectively mandatory for listed companies.

The remit of the Cadbury Committee had been corporate governance as a whole, of which executive remuneration was only a part. The comprehensive review of directors' pay as a single issue fell to the Study Group on Directors' Remuneration, commonly known as the Greenbury Committee after its chairman Sir Richard Greenbury, chairman of Marks and Spencer. This Committee was established in January 1995 at the initiative of (but independent from) the CBI, with the remit of identifying good practice in determining directors' remuneration and preparing a Code of such practice for use by UK PLCs.

The Greenbury Committee issued its report in July 1995.[6] This contained a Code of Best Practice, summarised briefly at 4.2 below. In October 1995 and June 1996 the London Stock Exchange gave effect to certain of these recommendations by amending its *Listing Rules* and in May 1997 completed the jigsaw by introducing its requirements on the disclosure of directors' pension entitlements (see 4.3 below). These require listed companies to produce a report to the shareholders on behalf of the Board by the remuneration committee (remuneration committee report), which includes, inter alia, a statement of remuneration policy and for each director an analysis of remuneration, details of share options (in accordance with the recommendations of UITF 10), long-term incentive schemes and pension benefits.

In the light of the detailed disclosures which are now required by listed companies, the Greenbury Committee recommended that the Companies Act requirements should be amended by removing the obligation to give banding information and to change the requirements in respect of disclosure of directors' pensions. Accordingly, the DTI issued a consultative document in January 1996 which aimed to implement the recommendations of the Greenbury Committee, align the Companies Act with the revised *Listing Rules* and, where possible, reduce disclosure requirements for unlisted companies.

Thus in February 1997 the DTI issued The Company Accounts (Disclosure of Directors' Emoluments) Regulations 1997 (SI 1997/570), which changed the requirements for directors' emolument disclosures for accounting periods ending on or after 31 March 1997. The main changes were as follows:

- In addition to total emoluments, listed companies (including companies quoted on the Alternative Investment Market) must disclose total gains on share options and all companies must disclose benefits (in cash or in kind) under long-term incentive schemes.

- Pension contributions are to be given for defined contribution schemes only, but the number of directors qualifying for defined contribution and defined benefit schemes respectively must be given.

- The requirements to give £5,000 bandings and the emoluments of the chairman were abolished.

- The emoluments of the highest paid director need be given only where total emoluments are £200,000 or more (formerly £60,000 and the company must not be member of a group). However, where the highest paid director is a member of a defined contribution pension scheme, the contributions paid must be shown. Where he is a member of a defined benefit pension scheme, his accrued pension and (where applicable) accrued lump sum at the end of the financial year must also be given.

- The exemption for emoluments earned overseas was abolished.

- The requirement to disclose the number of directors who have waived their rights to emoluments, and the amount of such emoluments, was abolished.

The current requirements (as amended by SI 1997/570) are dealt with at 2 below and the Chapter does not discuss in detail the old requirements which apply to accounting periods ending before 31 March 1997.

1.1 Remuneration

Remuneration paid to directors may assume any form and its amount will depend on the terms of the directors' service contracts (if any) and the company's articles of association; for example, Table A[7] provides that 'the directors shall be entitled to such remuneration as the company may by ordinary resolution determine ... '. Accordingly, if the directors do not have service contracts and the articles are silent on this issue, the directors are not *entitled* to receive anything.[8]

Remuneration may not be paid to a director (in whatever capacity he acts) free of income tax nor may a company pay him remuneration of an amount such that, after paying income tax, it will leave a specified sum in his hands.[9] Any provision in a company's articles, or in any contract, or in any resolution for payment to a director of remuneration free of income tax takes effect as if it provided for payment of the gross amount subject to income tax payable by the director.[10]

1.2   Pensions

Pensions are only payable to former directors if the company is authorised to do so by its memorandum or articles of association. Table A[11] contains an express power to provide benefits to former directors and for any member of his family or any dependant and to make contributions to secure such benefits.

1.3   Compensation for loss of office

Payments to a director for loss of office, or as consideration for or in connection with his retirement from office, must be disclosed to and approved by the company in general meeting.[12] It is unclear whether payments to directors in respect of compensation for loss of other offices, for example, the company secretaryship, require approval. Pennington[13] believes that this rule applies irrespective of the office lost, although this view is not universally held. This requirement does not apply to 'any bona fide payment by way of damages for breach of contract or by way of pension in respect of past services'.[14] Thus, for approval purposes, a payment is only treated as compensation for loss of office if the company is under no legal obligation to make it.

1.4   Service contracts

In outline, the provisions of the Companies Act 1985 relating to service contracts are as follows:

(a)   a copy or memorandum of the terms of directors' service contracts must be kept at an appropriate place, e.g. the company's registered office, and be available for inspection. The level of information required for directors who discharge their duties wholly or mainly outside the UK is reduced. These requirements do not apply where the unexpired portion of the contract is less than 12 months or where the company is able to terminate within the ensuing 12 months the director's contract without payment of compensation;[15]

(b)   terms incorporated into a director's service contract for a period of more than five years during which time his employment either cannot be terminated or can only be terminated in special circumstances are void unless approved by the company in general meeting. The resolution is only valid if a written memorandum setting out the proposed agreement is available for inspection for 15 days before and at the meeting itself.[16]

The Stock Exchange imposes additional requirements in relation to service contracts of directors of listed companies. These are discussed at 4.3.11 below.

2 DISCLOSURE OF REMUNERATION UNDER THE COMPANIES ACT 1985

2.1 Introduction

As a result of the changes made by The Company Accounts (Disclosure of Directors' Emoluments) Regulations 1997 (SI 1997/570), the Companies Act 1985 requires the following information in respect of directors to be disclosed in aggregate by way of note to the company's financial statements:[17]

(a) emoluments (see 2.2 to 2.4 below);

(b) gains made on exercise of share options (see 2.5 below);

(c) cash and/or value of other assets (excluding share options) receivable under long-term investment schemes (see 2.6 below);

(d) pension contributions in respect of money purchase benefits (see 2.7 below);

(e) excess retirement benefits (see 2.8 below);

(f) compensation for loss of office (see 2.9 below); and

(g) sums paid to third parties in respect of directors' services (see 2.10 below).

There are exceptions to the requirements under (b) and (c) above for companies which are not listed on the Stock Exchange or quoted on the Alternative Investment Market. Information is also required in respect of the number of directors to whom retirement benefits are accruing (see 2.7 below). In certain circumstances, individual information is required to be given in respect of the highest paid director (see 2.11 below).

In group financial statements, the above requirements only extend to directors of the holding company. It is the duty of each director to give notice to the company of such matters relating to himself as may be necessary for the purposes of these disclosures.[18] If these disclosures are not made in the financial statements, it is the auditors' duty to include in their report, so far as they are 'reasonably able to do so', a statement giving the required particulars.[19]

In view of the fact that companies listed on the Stock Exchange will be giving information in respect of each director, the Companies Act has granted dispensation from providing some of the above information which is to be given on aggregate basis. Accordingly, the Act states that 'any information, other than the aggregate amount of gains made by directors on the exercise of share options [(b) above], shall be treated as shown if it is capable of being readily ascertained from other information which is shown'. Apart from (b) above, this dispensation applies to all of the other disclosures noted above, other than (e) and (g) above. It also extends to the disclosures in respect of the highest paid director (from the information given for each director, users will be able to determine who it is). Accordingly, aggregate information should always be given for gains made on exercise of share options, excess retirement benefits and sums paid to third parties in respect of directors' services.

2.2 Disclosure of aggregate emoluments

2.2.1 Legal requirements

The aggregate amount of emoluments paid to or receivable by directors in respect of qualifying services must be disclosed.[20] Qualifying services mean services:

(a) as director of the company;

(b) as director of any of the company's subsidiary undertakings (whilst a director of the company);

(c) in connection with the management of the affairs of the company or any of its subsidiary undertakings (whilst a director of the company).[21]

In this context, the definition of a subsidiary undertaking is extended to include the situation where the director of the reporting company is nominated by that company to act as its representative on the board of another undertaking (whether or not it is actually a subsidiary undertaking of the reporting company).[22] This extended definition applies for the purposes of all the disclosures discussed in 2.3 to 2.9 below, and is illustrated in Examples 30.1 and 30.2 below:

Example 30.1

Company X has an investment in Company Y. Company X appoints one of its directors, Mr A, to the board of Company Y. Mr A receives fees of £10,000 in respect of this appointment. The financial statements of Company X must include the fees receivable by Mr A in respect of his services as director of Company Y, in the relevant disclosures.

Example 30.2

Company A is a debenture holder of a non-group company, Company B. The trust deed entitles Company A to appoint one of its directors to the board of Company B. The emoluments of the appointee from Company B must be included in the relevant disclosures in Company A's financial statements.

The definition of emoluments and the computation thereof are dealt with at 2.3 and 2.4 below.

Examples of disclosure of aggregate emoluments are shown in Extracts 30.3 and 30.4 at 2.3 below.

2.2.2 Problem areas

A   Other services

The disclosures in respect of directors' remuneration relate to a person's services as director of a company and management services (see 2.2.1 above). In some companies, particularly small private companies, directors may also perform services unrelated to the above and for which they receive remuneration. Such remuneration should be excluded from the directors' emoluments disclosures, as illustrated in the example below:

Example 30.3

A journalist director of a small provincial newspaper is paid a fee for writing a weekly column. Since this fee is quite distinct from his directors' fees or management remuneration, it should be excluded from the remuneration disclosures. However, consideration should be given to disclosing this arrangement as a transaction in which a director has a material interest (see 3.5 of Chapter 29) or as a related party transaction under FRS 8 (see generally Chapter 28).

In practice however, it is often difficult to determine whether or not such services are, in fact, unrelated, since directors are often appointed as a result of the other services which they perform. In such cases where doubt exists, the remuneration for other services is often included with directors' remuneration.

One company which has excluded fees received for services from the aggregate amount of emoluments is Volex Group, as shown below:

Extract 30.1: Volex Group plc (1997)

9   Directors' remuneration, interests and transactions [extract]

§   Total aggregate emoluments for directors during the year comprised £921,072.

In addition to the emoluments shown above:

(iii) Mr. Payzant received consultancy fees of US$11,015 for services rendered to Volex Inc. (the Company's US subsidiary) these fees having been paid to Troubadour Enterprises Inc., a company in which Mr. Payzant holds a controlling interest.

These fees are in addition to fees received as a non-executive director. In many other cases 'consultancy fees' are paid in respect of the person's services as director and management services and are therefore included as part of the emoluments (see Extract 30.14 below).

B   'Golden hellos'

A number of companies offer payments (of varying kinds) as incentives for particular staff to join them (so-called 'golden hellos'). These payments made to directors do not relate to a person's services as director of the company; nor do they pertain to management services and thus, until the Companies Act 1989, were not required to be disclosed as part of directors' remuneration. Previously, such payments were only required to be disclosed as a transaction in which a director has a material interest (see 3.5 of Chapter 29).

However, the Companies Act is now clear that such 'golden hellos' paid to or receivable by a director are to be treated as 'emoluments paid or receivable ... in respect of his services as director'; consequently, such payments have to be included within emoluments disclosed in financial statements.[23]

An example of a golden hello is shown below:

Extract 30.2: J Sainsbury plc (1997)

Report of the Remuneration Committee [extract]

2.   Appointed 19 August 1996. Mr Bremner received £400,000 in respect of acceptance of office and £55,000 guaranteed payments in respect of performance bonus and profit sharing.

The £400,000 was included as part of 'Other salary payments' within the disclosed aggregate emoluments.

There is no specific requirement to disclose the fact that 'golden hellos' are included within the figures or to disclose any details. However, consideration may need to be given as to whether disclosure is still required as a transaction in which a director has a material interest (see 3.5 Chapter 29). In any event, companies may wish to give disclosure in order to explain any distorting effect of including such payments within emoluments in view of their 'one-off' nature.

2.3   Definition of emoluments

2.3.1   *Legal requirements*

Emoluments are defined as including:[24]

- salary;
- fees;
- bonuses;
- any sums paid by way of expenses allowance (insofar as those sums are charged to UK income tax); and

Details of long term bonus earnings which crystallised during the year, excluding bonus relating to periods prior to becoming a director, are as follows:

£000	**Total cash 1997**	Total cash 1996
Lord Blyth	**157**	580
A H Hawksworth	**88**	239
Sir Gordon Hourston	**–**	296
M F Ruddell	**67**	228
S G Russell	**66**	76
D A R Thompson	**81**	265
J J H Watson	**15**	–
B E Whalan	**53**	13
	527	1,697

Each executive director will also be awarded conditional rights to receive ordinary shares in the company having a market value on 20th June 1997 equivalent to the cash bonus shown above, except in the case of Mr A H Hawksworth who has retired. The director will normally become entitled to receive those shares in June 2000 if the conditions are satisfied.

It can be seen from the above example Boots has gone further than the Companies Act requires, by disclosing the amounts for each director. However, this will have been given due to the requirements of the Stock Exchange (see 4.3.10 B).

Such long-term bonuses are to be disclosed in the year in which they become receivable and therefore a similar question arises as with annual bonuses when some or all of the bonus is conditional on the director remaining in employment with the company for a future period (see Example 30.4 at 2.4.1 A above).

In Extract 30.17 above, Boots has clearly regarded the cash element as receivable. However, this only represents half of the bonus. The remainder is to be converted into a certain number of shares with an equivalent value and the director will normally become entitled to these shares only after remaining employed for a further three years. If a director leaves the company during that period then (except in specified circumstances), his conditional entitlement will lapse. Whether such amounts should be included or not will for companies listed on the Stock Exchange normally be of academic interest only, because sufficient information will generally be disclosed to meet the Stock Exchange requirements (see 4.3.10 B below). If that is the case, then the Companies Act requirement (whatever it may be) will have been deemed to have been met under the dispensation that 'information shall be treated as shown if it is capable of being readily ascertained from other information which is shown' (see 2.1 above).

It should be emphasised that the disclosure of the amounts receivable under long-term incentive schemes is completely independent of the charge recognised in the profit and loss account for such schemes. In April 1997, the UITF published its seventeenth Abstract, *Employee share schemes*.[45] This addresses the relatively narrow issue of how companies should recognise and measure the cost of new shares issued as part of an employee share scheme. This is discussed further at 4.7.2 of Chapter 15.

2.7   Pension contributions in respect of money purchase schemes

Under the old legislation, all pension contributions were required to be included within the computation of 'emoluments'. Whilst this gave an accurate indication of the cost of a defined contribution scheme, it was common ground that it inadequately measured the cost of a defined benefit scheme relative to any individual (particularly where companies may have been taking pension holidays). However, given the rest of the requirements for directors' remuneration which were based more on valuing the benefits receivable by the directors, such an approach, particularly in relation to pension rights under defined benefit schemes, clearly did not represent the value of the benefit receivable by the director.

As discussed at 4.3.9 below, the Greenbury Report had recommended that the benefit should be measured as the present value of pension entitlement earned during the year resulting from additional length of service, increases in salary or changes in the terms of the scheme, less any contributions made by the director during the year. In the light of this, the DTI proposed in its Consultative Document that there should be disclosure of the aggregate value of directors' pension entitlements and that this would apply to all companies. However, following comments received on the Consultative Document, this proposal was dropped, although there is a requirement for such information in respect of the highest paid director (see 2.11 below).

Accordingly, all that the Companies Act now requires is disclosure of the aggregate value of any company contributions paid, or treated as paid, to a pension scheme in respect of directors' qualifying services, being contributions by reference to which the rate or amount of any money purchase benefits that may become payable will be calculated.[46] An example of such disclosure is shown in Extract 30.15 at 2.5 above.

For this purpose, the following definitions apply:

- 'Company contributions' mean 'any payments (including insurance premiums) made, or treated to be made, to the scheme in respect of the director by a person other than the director'.[47] The words 'treated to be made' are to cater for disclosure of notional contributions under underpinned schemes (see below).

- 'Pension scheme' has the meaning assigned to 'retirement benefits scheme' by section 611 of the Income and Corporation Taxes Act 1988.[48]

This latter definition is generally interpreted as extending to unfunded pension arrangements.

■ 'Money purchase benefits' are defined as 'retirement benefits payable under a pension scheme the rate or amount of which is calculated by reference to payments made, or treated as made, by the director or by any other person in respect of the director and which are not average salary benefits'.[49]

■ 'Retirement benefits' has the meaning assigned to 'relevant benefits' by section 612(1) of the Income and Corporation Taxes Act 1988.[50]

In most cases the amount to be disclosed will be the contributions to a money purchase scheme (defined contribution scheme) but it will also include contributions to a defined benefit scheme, to the extent that the contributions go to entitling directors to money purchase benefits under that scheme.

The legislation also provides for disclosure of information relating to a pension scheme with an underpin. Such a scheme, although primarily a defined benefit scheme or a money purchase scheme, has a shadow scheme underpinning it with notional contributions and rates. Accordingly the Act states that 'where a pension scheme provides for any benefits that may become payable to or in respect of any director to be whichever are the greater of:

(a) money purchased benefits as determined under the scheme; and

(b) defined benefits as so determined,

the company may assume that those benefits will be money purchased benefits, or defined benefits, according to whichever appears more likely at the end of the financial year'.[51]

As a quid pro quo for not requiring disclosures in respect of the value of pension entitlements under defined benefit schemes (other than in respect of the highest paid director, where applicable – see 2.11 below), the Act also requires disclosure of the number of directors (if any) to whom retirement benefits are accruing in respect of qualifying services under:

(a) money purchase schemes; and

(b) defined benefit schemes.[52]

A 'money purchase scheme' is defined as being a pension scheme under which *all* benefits that may become payable to a director are money purchase benefits.[53] The Act has not used the term 'defined contribution scheme' in order to align the terminology with the definition of money purchase benefits (see above).

A 'defined benefit scheme' means a pension scheme which is not a money purchase scheme.[54] The most obvious example is a final salary scheme.

However, any scheme which is not classified as a money purchase scheme will fall to be regarded as defined benefit scheme. Therefore if a director is a member of a hybrid pension scheme under which both money purchase and defined benefits are payable then it is to be classified as a defined benefit scheme.

For the purpose of determining whether a pension scheme is a money purchase or defined benefit scheme, any death in service benefits provided for by the scheme are disregarded.[55] Thus a scheme in which the only defined benefit element relates to death in service benefits should be classified as a money purchase scheme.

One company which has disclosed this information on the number of directors is Gerrard Group, as shown in Extract 30.15 at 2.5 above.

In our view such information on the number of directors is virtually worthless and should never have been introduced. We would recommend that where companies listed on the Stock Exchange are disclosing information for individual directors (see 4.3.9 below), then they should use the dispensation allowed under the Companies Act referred to at 2.1 above.

2.8 Excess retirement benefits of directors and past directors

The old legislation used to require disclosure of pensions paid by the company to directors or former directors, but this did not include pensions paid by a pension scheme since the company's contributions thereto had already been disclosed as emoluments.

This has now been replaced by a new requirement whereby disclosure should be given of the aggregate amount of retirement benefits paid to or receivable by directors and past directors under pension schemes in excess of the retirement benefits to which they were respectively entitled on the date on which the benefits first became payable or 31 March 1997, whichever is the later.[56]

Amounts paid or receivable under the pension scheme need not be included in the aggregate amount if:

(a) the funding of the scheme was such that the amounts were or, as the case may be, could have been paid without recourse to additional contributions; and

(b) amounts were paid to or receivable by all pensioner members of the scheme on the same basis.[57]

For this purpose, 'pension scheme' and 'retirement benefits' have the same meaning as discussed at 2.7 above and 'pensioner member' means any person who is entitled to the present payment of retirement benefits under the scheme.[58]

The intention of this requirement is to ensure that companies disclose any discretionary increases in pensions of directors or former directors. However, if a former director receives, say, a 3% inflationary increase in his pension and this is given to all pensioner members then this amount, although in excess of his entitlement when benefits first became payable, is not to be disclosed under this provision.

The inclusion of the reference to 31 March 1997 in the requirement is intended to provide the baseline for any future disclosures in respect of pensions in payment at the commencement of the first financial year to which the legislation applies.

The amounts to be disclosed in respect of retirement benefits are to include any benefits in kind given in respect of retirement benefits at the estimated money value of the benefit. In such a case, the nature of the benefit is also required to be disclosed.[59]

2.9 Compensation for loss of office

2.9.1 Legal requirements

The aggregate amount of any compensation payable to directors or past directors in respect of loss of office must be disclosed.[60] An example of such disclosure is given in Extract 30.15 at 2.5 above.

In this context, compensation for loss of office includes compensation in consideration for, or in connection with, a person's retirement from office.[61]

The changes made to the legislation by SI 1997/570 also clarified that it is to include payments made by way of damages for breach of the person's contract with the company or with a subsidiary undertaking of the company or payments made by way of settlement or compromise of any claim in respect of the breach.[62]

Both of these are illustrated in the following extract:

Extract 30.18: Volex Group plc (1997)

9   Directors' remuneration, interests and transactions [extract]

§   Total aggregate emoluments for directors during the year comprised £921,072.

In addition to the emoluments shown above:

(i)   Mr Chapple received payments under the terms of a compromise agreement made upon his resignation from the Board on 21 May 1996 comprising cash payments of £131,429 and contributions to a funded unapproved retirement benefit scheme of £12,850: a further contribution of £17,176 was outstanding at the end of the year. The compromise agreement provides for payments to Mr Chapple throughout the unexpired portion of his service agreement (i.e. to 20 May 1998) net of all income earned by Mr. Chapple from other sources during that period.

(ii)   Mr. Davies received an ex gratia payment of £28,333 upon his retirement on 31 March 1997.

Contributions to a pension scheme made in connection with a director's loss of, or retirement from, office should be included within the aggregate amount of compensation to be disclosed, as illustrated below:

Extract 30.19: Norcros p.l.c. (1997)

REPORT OF THE REMUNERATION COMMITTEE [extract]

Compensation for loss of office and pension rights of Mr M E Doherty and Mr R H Alcock

Mr M E Doherty received compensation for his change of status in May 1996 from executive to non-executive Chairman, as a consequence of the termination with effect from 4 April 1996 of his previous executive employment agreement (which had a two year notice period). A sum of £234,000 was paid into the Norcros Security Plan to augment his pension by £21,781 per annum to give a total of £147,972 per annum payable from his normal retirement age of 60. In addition, an amount of £6,000 was paid to the Norcros Security Plan to provide a lump sum death benefit.

A sum of £250,000 was paid to Mr R H Alcock as compensation for loss of office. In addition he received fees of £102,570 plus VAT under the terms of a consultancy agreement dated 6 May which expired on 31 October 1996.

Although no aggregate amount for compensation for loss of office is disclosed in the above two extracts they are deemed to have been disclosed in view of the dispensation mentioned at 2.1 above.

Another company which has disclosed such pension contributions is Sainsbury, as shown below:

Extract 30.20: J Sainsbury plc (1997)

Report of the Remuneration Committee [extract]

4.   Retired as a Director on 26th April 1996. 1997 pension contributions included £556,000 in respect of compensation for loss of office.

Elsewhere in the report, the amount of compensation for loss of office for 1997 is disclosed as £336,000. Although this method of presentation might not be ideal, it does comply with the requirement for the reason mentioned above in respect of the other extracts.

These requirements extend to the loss of any office or otherwise in connection with the management of the affairs of the company or any of its subsidiary undertakings[63] and apply whether or not the compensation requires company approval (see 1.3 above). For example, if the managing director of a subsidiary company ceases to act in that capacity but remains on the boards of both that company and its parent, any compensation paid by the subsidiary in respect of this loss of office should be disclosed in both the holding company's and subsidiary's financial statements.

The amounts to be disclosed in respect of compensation include any benefits received, or receivable, otherwise than in cash, at the estimated money value of the benefit.[64] In such a case, the nature of the benefit is also required to be disclosed.[65] One company which has made such disclosure is Dalgety in its 1993 accounts, as shown below:

> *Extract 30.21: Dalgety PLC (1993)*
>
> **9 DIRECTORS AND EMPLOYEES** [extract]
>
> d) Compensation of £192,697 was paid in respect of loss of office of a former director, including £17,697 for the provision of a motor car and medical insurance, together with an additional deferred pension of £19,000 per annum payable at normal retirement date.

Although this was given under legislation prevailing at that time, it would still be applicable under the current requirements as this part of the legislation was unchanged by SI 1997/570.

A particular problem associated with non-cash compensation relates to the valuation of such benefits. Ordinarily, the market value of the asset should be disclosed; however, if the book value of the asset is used, an explanatory note should indicate the asset's market value. For example:

Example 30.5

A director is given a motor car upon retirement from the company and the book value of the car is £2,000 and its market value is £3,000. The company should either disclose the market value of the car in the compensation for loss of office disclosure or use the book value of the asset and append an explanatory note to the directors' remuneration note to the following effect: 'the amount for compensation for loss of office includes the written down value of a [description of vehicle] the market value of which was £3,000'.

2.9.2 Problem areas

A Ex-gratia payments

Ex-gratia payments which do not constitute compensation for loss of office and which are not in connection with a person's retirement need not be disclosed. In order to decide whether a payment is ex-gratia, regard should be had to the nature of and all the circumstances surrounding the payment. The donor company's classification of the payment is irrelevant. The following examples distinguish a disguised retirement payment from an ex-gratia payment:

Example 30.6

Mr A retires from the board of Company X. The following week, Company X makes Mr A an ex-gratia payment of £25,000. In these circumstances, the payment, albeit described as ex-gratia, should be disclosed as compensation for loss of office for it would appear to be connected with the director's retirement from the board.

Example 30.7

Mr A is a former director of Company X. After leaving Company X, Mr A sets up his own business, which through no fault of his own, goes into liquidation. Company A learns of Mr A's plight and gifts him the sum of £20,000. In these circumstances, the payment is unrelated to Mr A's retirement from the board of Company X and need not be disclosed in its financial statements as compensation for loss of office.

Where an ex-gratia payment requires to be disclosed as a compensation payment, the note will generally indicate the 'ex-gratia' nature of the payment, as seen in Extract 30.18 above.

Companies listed on the Stock Exchange would require to disclose the payment in Example 30.7 if it was considered significant (see 4.3.8 below).

B   Augmentation of pension rights

As discussed above, contributions to a pension scheme made in connection with a director's loss of, or retirement from, office should be included within the aggregate amount of compensation to be disclosed. However, it may be that in certain situations where there is a surplus on the company's pension scheme, it is agreed with the trustees of the scheme that the augmentation of the pension rights of the retiring director is to be met out of the surplus of the pension scheme, with no specific contribution being made by the company. In these circumstances, we believe that the capital cost of the augmentation of the pension rights should still be disclosed as part of the compensation for loss of office. This is because the amounts to be included within compensation for loss of office are to include non-cash benefits and are also to include payments made not only by the company and its subsidiary undertakings, but any other person (i.e. the pension scheme). One company which appears to have adopted this view was APV in its 1993 accounts, as illustrated below:

Extract 30.22: APV plc (1993)

4   DIRECTORS [extract]

	1993	1992
	£'000	£'000
Compensation for loss of office	332	–

(iv) Compensation of £216,042 was paid in respect of loss of office of a former director, together with an additional deferred pension of £9,875 per annum payable at normal retirement date. The actuarial valuation of this deferred pension has been calculated as £116,400.

However, such an approach is not always followed, as illustrated below:

Extract 30.23: Gerrard Group plc (1997)

Report of the Remuneration Committee [extract]

d) Termination payments

Arrangements for the early termination of contracts are carefully considered by the Committee. When calculating termination payments, the Committee takes into account a variety of factors including age, years of service and the individual director's obligation to mitigate his own loss by seeking new employment.

D A Brayshaw retired from the Board on 31st March 1996. At that date he had a two year rolling contract. The Committee agreed to make a termination payment of £139,000 and not to apply any additional actuarial discount to his pension when he draws it early at age 50 in 1998. R B Williamson retired as executive chairman in December 1996. He received a termination payment of £100,000 and was granted a full pension even although he had not reached the Normal Retirement Age. T W Fellows retired in November 1996 and was granted a full pension even although he had not reached the Normal Retirement Age.

C   *Consultancy agreements*

Over the years, a number of ex-directors have entered into consultancy agreements with the companies on whose boards they have ceased to serve. Typically, these grant the ex-directors a guaranteed fee for a period of time. Whether payments to be made under such agreements should be disclosed as compensation for loss of office will depend on the particular circumstances and the extent to which it is envisaged that consultancy services will be provided by the former director. Where it is unlikely that the director will provide any consultancy service we believe that the amount should be disclosed as compensation for loss of office. However, where it is considered that the ex-director will provide services commensurate with the level of fees which are to be made then it may be appropriate not to include the fees as compensation for loss of office. Nevertheless, in such a situation consideration would need to be given as to whether such a consultancy agreement was a transaction in which the director had a material interest. An example of a company disclosing consultancy fees is Norcros (see Extract 30.19 at 2.9.1 above).

However, companies listed on the Stock Exchange would require to disclose the payments in respect of consultancy agreements if they were considered significant (see 4.3.8 below).

2.10   Payments to third parties

As a result of the Companies Act 1989, financial statements are now required to disclose amounts payable to or receivable by third parties for making available the services of any person:

(a)   as director of the company; or

(b)   as director of any of the company's subsidiary undertakings (whilst a director of the company); or (c)　in connection with the management of the affairs of the company or any of its subsidiary undertakings (whilst a director of the company).[66]

'Third parties' means persons other than:

(a)　the director himself; or

(b)　persons connected with the director or connected with bodies corporate controlled by the director; or

(c)　the company and any of its subsidiary undertakings.[67]

Consequently, payments made to an unconnected organisation, such as a bank, for persons on secondment as a director will have to be disclosed; payments made to a holding company, or fellow subsidiary, for the services of a director will also have to be disclosed. Examples of disclosures in these circumstances are shown in the following extracts:

Extract 30.24: Field Group plc (1997)

		52 weeks ended 30 March 1997	52 weeks ended 31 March 1996
4	**Directors' Emoluments** [extract]		
		£	**£**
a.	Aggregate disclosure:		
	Aggregate emoluments	**962,871**	960,119
	Company pension contributions to money purchase schemes	**12,880**	14,244
	Sums paid to third parties for directors' services	**13,000**	11,330

At 30 March 1997, retirement benefits were accruing to one director under a money purchase scheme and to seven directors under a defined benefit scheme.

The above disclosure in respect of payments to third parties is what is strictly required to comply with the requirement. However, many other companies include such payments within aggregate emoluments, but as long as the amounts paid to third parties are separately identified then they are deemed to meet the requirements under the dispensation noted at 2.1 above. One company which adopts such a treatment is Pilkington, as illustrated below:

Extract 30.25: Pilkington plc (1997)

38　Directors' emoluments [extract]

**　*Sir Nigel Rudd's remuneration as chairman amounting to £120,000 (1996 £80,000) was paid to Williams PLC, his employer.*

The amounts disclosed have to include any benefits in kind given to a third party for the services of a director at the estimated money value of the benefit. In such a case, the nature of the benefit is also required to be disclosed.[68]

2.11 Highest paid director

Although the old Companies Act requirements for disclosure of the chairman's emoluments and directors' bandings have been dispensed with, the new legislation not only continues to require disclosure of information in respect of the highest paid director but has expanded the information which is required.

Where the aggregate amounts shown under 2.2 (emoluments), 2.5 (gains on exercise of share options, where applicable) and 2.6 (long-term incentive schemes) total £200,000 or more, the following shall be shown in respect of the highest paid director:

(a)   the total of such aggregate amounts (there is no need to disclose the separate amounts);[69]

(b)   the value of any pension contributions shown under 2.7 above;[70] and

(c)   where he/she has performed qualifying services during the financial year by reference to which the rate or amount of any defined benefits that may become payable will be calculated;

    (i)   the amount at the end of the year of his/her accrued pension; and

    (ii)   where applicable, the amount at the end of the year of his/her accrued lump sum.[71]

For accounting periods ending before 31 March 1998, comparative figures do not need to be given in respect of the information under (c) above.[72]

An example of such disclosure is shown below:

Extract 30.26: Gerrard Group plc (1997)

4   Directors' emoluments [extract]

Emoluments of the highest paid director are as follows:

	1997 £	1996 £
Aggregate emoluments excluding pension contributions	359,001	404,666
Company pension contributions to money purchase schemes	–	40,500
Defined benefit pension scheme:		
Accrued pension at end of year	103,226	
Accrued lump sum at end of year	–	

As with many of the disclosure requirements, the Act will regard such information as having been disclosed if it can be determined from other information which is shown (see 2.1 above). As companies listed on the Stock Exchange are required to provide information for each director, then they will automatically have complied with this requirement.

The determination of whether disclosure of information in respect of the highest paid director is required excludes the following amounts:

■ pension contributions in respect of money purchase benefits (see 2.7 above);

■ excess retirement benefits (see 2.8 above);

■ compensation for loss of office (see 2.9 above); and

■ sums paid to third parties in respect of directors' services (see 2.10 above).

However, 'Golden hellos' (see 2.2.2 B above) and payments made to persons connected with a director have to be taken into account.

Once it is determined that disclosure of information about the highest paid director is required, the next step is to identify which director this is.

The 'highest paid director' for this purpose means the director to whom is attributable the greatest part of the total of the aggregates under 2.2 (emoluments), 2.5 (gains on exercise of share options, where applicable) and 2.6 (long-term incentive schemes). This therefore excludes the value of any pension contributions shown under 2.7 above (even though such amounts are to be disclosed for whoever is determined to be the highest paid director).

In view of the fact that gains on exercise of share options and amounts receivable under long-term incentive schemes are included in this determination, some companies which are listed on the Stock Exchange may wish to identify the highest paid director and highlight such amounts that are applicable to that director, as it may appear from the remuneration table provided (see 4.3.4 below) that another director is the highest paid director. An example of such disclosure is given by Pilkington, as shown below:

Extract 30.27: Pilkington plc (1997)

38 Directors' emoluments [extract]

	Base salary £000	Performance bonus £000	Taxable benefits £000	1997 Total £000
Directors emoluments were:				
Executive directors				
Roger Leverton	416	–	26	442
Peter Grunwell	472	–	10	482

(a) Roger Leverton was the highest paid director in 1997 after taking into account the gains of £372,000 made on the exercise of share options (1996 Sir Antony Pilkington).

For the purposes of the disclosure of (c) above, 'accrued pension' and 'accrued lump sum' mean respectively the amount of the annual pension, and the amount of the lump sum, which would be payable under the scheme on his/her attaining normal pension age if:

(a)   he/she had left the company's service at the end of the financial year;

(b)   there were no increase in the general level of prices in Great Britain during the period beginning with the end of that year and ending with his/her attaining that age;

(c)   no question arose of any commutation of the pension or inverse commutation of the lump sum; and

(d)   any amounts attributable to voluntary contributions paid by the director to the scheme, and any money purchase benefits which would be payable under the scheme, were disregarded.[73]

'Normal pension age' means the age at which the director will first become entitled to receive a full pension on retirement of an amount determined without reduction to take account of its payment before a later age (but disregarding any entitlement to pension upon retirement in the event of illness, incapacity or redundancy).[74]

Most defined benefit schemes entitle employees to a pension, some of which can be commuted for a lump sum. As a result of (c) above, there is therefore only a need to disclose the accrued pension as done by Gerrard Group in Extract 30.23 at 2.9.2 B above. Both amounts should only be disclosed if the pension scheme benefits are such that the director receives a pension *and* a lump sum. Although the director may be able to commute either some of the pension for an extra lump sum or vice versa, the effect of paragraph (c) is that such a choice should be ignored.

Example 30.8 at 4.3.9 C below illustrates how the accrued pension is calculated.

One issue for companies listed on the Stock Exchange is that the disclosure of the accrued benefit under the Companies Act is to make no adjustment for general inflation during the year, but the disclosures required by the Stock Exchange are to be based excluding the effect of inflation (see 4.3.9 C below). This is illustrated in the following extract:

Extract 30.28: Field Group plc (1997)

		52 weeks ended 30 March 1997	52 weeks ended 31 March 1996

4   Directors' Emoluments [extract]

	£	£
b. Highest paid director: Emoluments	**193,443**	176,822
Defined benefit scheme: Accrued pension at the end of the period	**63,712**	49,744

Report of the Remuneration Committee [extract]

8   Directors' Emoluments

	Base salary 1996/97 £	Benefits 1996/97 £	Annual bonus 1996/97 £	Total emoluments excluding pensions 1996/97 £	1995/96 £	Increase in accrued pension p.a. 1996/97 £	Transfer value of increase 1996/97 £	Accumulated total accrued pension p.a. 1996/97 £
Executive								
K Gilchrist	160,000	5,763	27,680	**193,443**	176,822	**12,297**	**131,552**	**63,712**

The accumulated total accrued pension figures shown in the above table represent the annual amount of accrued pension payable on retirement at normal retirement age, based on the director's service to, and pensionable earnings at, the relevant year end. The transfer value of the increase has been calculated on the basis of actuarial advice and is net of directors' contributions in the year. The increase in accrued pension and transfer value excludes any increase in inflation.

It can be seen that Field Group has disclosed comparative figures for the accrued pension benefits disclosed under the Companies Act requirements (although not required to do so in this year's accounts). The difference between the accrued pension benefits disclosed in note 4 is £13,968 whereas the increase disclosed to meet the Stock Exchange requirements is £12,297, the reason being that the latter has to exclude any increase due to inflation.

For unlisted companies (as defined – see 2.5 above) which have not disclosed amounts in respect of gains made on the exercise of options or share awards under long-term incentive schemes, then there is no requirement to disclose any such amounts in respect of the highest paid director. However, such companies are required to state whether the highest paid director exercised any share options and whether any shares were receivable by that director under a long-term incentive scheme.[75] If the highest paid director has not been involved in any such transactions then that fact need not be stated.[76]

3   EMPLOYEE DISCLOSURES

The Companies Act contains disclosure requirements relating to employees' remuneration which may also impact upon directors.

3.1   Director as an employee

Directors may have a contract of service with the company, in which case they should be included in the detailed employee disclosures. Accordingly, certain of their costs will require disclosure in the wages and salaries note[77] (in addition to the disclosures in the directors' remuneration note), as is illustrated below:

Extract 30.29: John Mowlem & Company PLC (1996)

7   Employees

	1996 **Number**	1995 Number
The average weekly number of persons employed by the Group including Directors during the year was:		
Access Products and Services	**4,141**	4,139
Construction Activities and Services	**6,880**	6,586
Facilities Services	**881**	810
Environmental Services	**419**	343
Project Investment, Property and Corporate activities	**234**	191
Discontinued activities	**–**	115
	12,555	12,184

	1996 **£m**	1995 £m
The aggregate payroll cost of those people was:		
Wages and salaries	**232.9**	229.7
Social security costs	**22.6**	22.9
Other pension costs	**10.2**	9.9
	265.7	262.5

In this context, the employer's national insurance contributions should be included as part of social security costs (that is, any contributions by the company to any state social security or pension scheme, fund or arrangement);[78] however, the value of benefits-in-kind must be excluded.

The emoluments of directors who have a contract only for services as director (i.e. most non-executive directors) should not be included in the wages and salaries note, since such persons are not employees of the company. However, their emoluments will be included in the information disclosed in respect of directors' remuneration.

4   STOCK EXCHANGE REQUIREMENTS

As discussed earlier, in recent years executive remuneration of companies listed on the Stock Exchange has become a focus of public attention with regard to both the level and the structure of boardroom pay.

This concern was first addressed in 1992 by the Cadbury Committee which made various recommendations in respect of directors' remuneration. These are outlined at 4.1 below.

Also in September 1994 the UITF issued an Abstract which recommended various disclosures in respect of directors' share options (see 4.3.10 A below)

The remit of the Cadbury Committee had been corporate governance as a whole, of which executive remuneration was only a part. The comprehensive review of directors' pay as a single issue fell to the Study Group on Directors' Remuneration, commonly known as the Greenbury Committee after its chairman Sir Richard Greenbury, chairman of Marks and Spencer. This Committee was established in January 1995 at the initiative of (but independent from) the CBI, with the remit of identifying good practice in determining directors' remuneration and preparing a Code of such practice for use by UK PLCs.

The Greenbury Committee issued its report in July 1995. This contained a Code of Best Practice, summarised briefly at 4.2 below. In October 1995 and June 1996 the London Stock Exchange gave effect to certain of these recommendations by amending its *Listing Rules* and in May 1997 completed the jigsaw by introducing its requirements on the disclosure of directors' pension entitlements. These requirements (as well as some of the existing requirements in this area) of the Stock Exchange are described at 4.3 below.

4.1   Cadbury Code

In December 1992, the Cadbury Committee, which was set up in May 1991 by the Financial Reporting Council, the London Stock Exchange and the accountancy profession, issued its report on 'corporate governance'.[79] The Committee's purpose was to review those aspects of corporate governance specifically related to financial reporting and accountability, in the light of concern at the perceived low level of confidence both in financial reporting and in the ability of auditors to provide the safeguards which the users of company reports sought and expected.

At the heart of the Committee's recommendations is its Code of Best Practice for the boards of listed companies. Paragraph 3.2 of the Code stated that 'there should be full and clear disclosure of directors' total emoluments and those of the chairman and highest paid UK director, including pension contributions and stock options. Separate figures should be given for salary and performance-related elements and the basis on which performance is measured should be explained.'

This certainly extended the Companies Act disclosures which were required at that time, so as to require further analysis of total emoluments and those of the chairman and the highest paid director. However, there were always going to be differing views as to exactly what disclosures would be required in order to comply with the requirement for 'full and clear disclosure'.

4.2 Greenbury Code

As mentioned above, the comprehensive review of directors' pay as a single issue fell to the Greenbury Committee. Like the Cadbury Committee before it, the Report that it issued contained a Code of Best Practice containing a number of recommendations split into four sections, A to D, which are summarised below.

4.2.1 Section A – The remuneration committee

The remuneration of executive directors should be determined by a remuneration committee consisting entirely of non-executive directors, with no personal financial interest (other than as shareholders) or other potential conflicts of interest. The members of the committee should be named in their annual report to shareholders (see Section B below). They should consult the chairman and/or chief executive on their proposals and should also have access to other advice from inside and outside the company.

4.2.2 Section B – Disclosure and approval provisions

The remuneration committee should make an annual report to shareholders to be included in, or annexed to, the annual report and accounts. This should set out the policies and criteria for determining directors' pay and an analysis of the remuneration of each director by name, together with information on pension entitlements and share options, all of these figures being subject to audit. There should also be a statement that the committee has given full consideration to the recommendations of Sections C and D, as described below. Departures from certain of these recommendations (in particular those relating to length of service contracts and pensionable bonuses) should be explained.

4.2.3 Section C – Remuneration policy

Remuneration packages should pay the rate for the job, but no more. Performance-related pay should be based on genuinely demanding criteria, and in general there should be a move away from short-term cash-based schemes to longer-term share-based schemes. Share-based schemes should be designed to encourage the holding of shares for the longer term rather than realising them for cash. Share-based schemes should aim to measure the company's performance against that of comparator companies using measures such as total shareholder return. The consequences of pay increases on pension entitlements should be carefully considered, and in general annual bonuses should not be pensionable.

4.2.4   Section D – Service contracts and compensation

Companies should generally aim to reduce the notice period of directors' service contracts to one year or less, although in some cases periods of up to two years may be acceptable. Any provision for compensation payments in the event of early termination should not appear to reward failure and should have regard to an outgoing director's obligation to mitigate damages by seeking new employment.

4.3   Stock Exchange requirements in respect of the Greenbury Code

To give effect to the Greenbury recommendations, in October 1995 the Stock Exchange amended the *Listing Rules* by adding a non-mandatory annexe – *Best Practice Provisions: Directors' Remuneration* – and some new mandatory disclosures. The new disclosures can be summarised as follows.

■   A statement that the company has complied with Section A of the Best Practice Provisions (broadly corresponding to Section A of the Greenbury Code).

■   A statement of the company's remuneration policy and a confirmation that, in framing this policy, the remuneration committee has 'given full consideration to' Section B of the Best Practice Provisions (broadly corresponding to Sections C and D of the Greenbury Code).

■   An analysis of the remuneration of each director by name, together with information on share options and long-term incentive schemes other than share options, all of these figures being subject to audit.

■   The unexpired term of the service contract of any director proposed for re-election at the annual general meeting.

The first two items were mandatory for accounting periods beginning, and the other two items for periods ending, on or after 31 December 1995.

These disclosures essentially mirror those proposed in Section B of the Greenbury Code, with the important exception that the *Listing Rules* did not yet require disclosure of individual directors' pension benefits.

A further aspect of the Greenbury Code not specifically dealt with by the October 1995 amendment to the *Listing Rules* was the recommendation that share options should be phased rather than awarded in a large block. In June 1996, however, the Stock Exchange issued a further amendment implementing this recommendation requiring companies to disclose their policy on the granting of options. This was effective for accounting periods ending on or after 30 September 1996.

As mentioned above, the one aspect which was outstanding was the disclosure of individual directors' pension benefits. The Institute of Actuaries and the Faculty of Actuaries published a joint consultation paper on this issue in January 1996, followed in April 1996 by a second paper summarising the comments received on the first and making recommendations on the basis of those comments (see 4.3.9 B below for a discussion of these papers). In May 1996 the Stock Exchange issued a consultative document setting out proposed changes to its requirements so as to give effect to these recommendations. A year later in May 1997 it finally issued its requirements in this regard. These are effective for accounting periods ending on or after 1 July 1997.

Accordingly the Stock Exchange requires all listed companies (other than investment companies, investment trusts, investment property companies and venture capital trusts with no executive directors) to include within their annual report and accounts:

(a)   a statement whether or not the company has complied throughout the accounting period with Section A of the best practice provisions annexed to the *Listing Rules*. A company that has not complied with those provisions, or complied for only part of an accounting period, must explain and justify any areas of non-compliance;[80]

(b)   a report to the shareholders on behalf of the Board by the remuneration committee (or by the Board itself if there is no such committee) containing:[81]

(i)   a statement of the company's policy on executive directors' remuneration;

(ii)   a statement that in framing its remuneration policy full consideration has been given to Section B of the best practice provisions annexed to the *Listing Rules*;

(iii)   the amount of each element in the remuneration package for the period under review of each director by name, including, but not restricted to:

■   basic salary and fees;

■   the estimated money value of benefits in kind;

■   annual bonuses;

■   deferred bonuses;

■   compensation for loss of office and payments for breach of contract or other termination payments;

together with the total for each director for the period under review and for the corresponding prior period, and any significant payments made to former directors during the period under review.

Such details are to be presented in tabular form, unless inappropriate, together with explanatory notes as necessary;

(iv) information on share options, including SAYE options, for each director by name in accordance with the recommendations of UITF 10. Such information to be presented in tabular form together with explanatory notes as necessary;

(v) details of any long-term incentive schemes, other than share options details of which have been disclosed under (iv) above, including:

- the interests of each director by name in the long-term incentive schemes at the start of the period under review;

- entitlements or awards granted and commitments made to each director under such schemes during the period, showing which crystallise either in the same year or subsequent years;

- the money value and number of shares, cash payments or other benefits received by each director under such schemes during the period; and

- the interests of each director in the long-term incentive schemes at the end of the period;

(vi) explanation and justification of any element of remuneration, other than basic salary, which is pensionable;

(vii) details of any directors' service contract with a notice period in excess of one year or with provisions for predetermined compensation on termination which exceeds one year's salary and benefits in kind, giving the reasons for such notice period;

(viii) the unexpired term of any directors' service contract of a director proposed for election or re-election at the forthcoming AGM and, if any director proposed for election or re-election does not have a service contract, a statement to that effect;

(ix) a statement of the company's policy on the granting of options or awards under its employees' share schemes and other long-term incentive schemes, explaining and justifying any departure from that policy in the period under review and any change in the policy from the preceding year;

(x) for defined benefit schemes (as defined in the Companies Act – see 2.7 above):

- details of the amount of the increase during the period under review (excluding inflation) and of the accumulated total amount at the end of the period in respect of the accrued benefit to which each director would be entitled on leaving service or is entitled having left service during the period under review;

- and either:

    (a)   the transfer value (less director's contributions) of the relevant increase in accrued benefit (to be calculated in accordance with Actuarial Guidance Note GN11 but making no deduction for any underfunding) as at the end of the period; or

    (b)   so much of the following information as is necessary to make a reasonable assessment of the transfer value in respect of each director:

- current age;

- normal retirement age;

- the amount of any contributions paid or payable by the director under the terms of the scheme during the period under review;

- details of spouse's and dependants' benefits;

- early retirement rights and options, expectations of pension increases after retirement (whether guaranteed or discretionary); and

- discretionary benefits for which allowance is made in transfer values on leaving and any other relevant information which will significantly affect the value of the benefits.

Voluntary contributions and benefits should not be disclosed; and

(xi)   for money purchase schemes (as defined in the Companies Act – see 2.7 above): details of the contribution or allowance payable or made by the company in respect of each director during the period of review.

Whilst these requirements are closely based on the Greenbury Code, there are some differences of emphasis and detail, which are noted in the relevant sections below. Companies wishing to comply with the spirit of Greenbury rather than merely the letter of the *Listing Rules* should therefore refer to the Greenbury Report itself.

In June 1996 the Stock Exchange also introduced a requirement that where a company (unusually) sets up a long-term incentive scheme for an individual director then certain detailed disclosures about such a scheme have to be disclosed in the next annual report.[82]

In addition to the above disclosure requirements the Stock Exchange has another long-standing requirement relating to directors' remuneration which is to disclose particulars of arrangements under which a director has either waived or agreed to waive any current or future emoluments (this applies in respect of emoluments from the company or any of its subsidiaries).[83] As noted at 1 above, the Companies Act no longer requires information about emoluments which have been waived.

4.3.1 Positioning of Remuneration Committee Report and Disclosures

Item (b) at 4.3 above requires the detailed disclosures to be given in 'a report to the shareholders on behalf of the Board by the remuneration committee', although it is silent as to where this report should appear in the annual report and accounts. As might therefore be expected, there is some variety of treatment among companies. Most companies give all the required information in a separate remuneration committee report presented alongside (or as part of) the directors' report, the chairman's statement and similar sections of the annual report. Where this is done, many such companies do not include any of the information required by the Companies Act in the main body of the accounts, but merely make a statement along the lines of 'Details of directors remuneration are disclosed in the remuneration committee report on pages ...'.

Another treatment is for the report of the remuneration committee to consist of the narrative disclosures only, with the figures being included in the main body of the accounts.

4.3.2 Statement of compliance with Best Practice Provisions

As noted above, the Best Practice Provisions on directors' remuneration annexed to the *Listing Rules* are divided into two sections, A and B, dealing respectively with the composition and terms of reference of the remuneration committee and the policy for setting directors' remuneration. The *Listing Rules* require a company's annual report to contain a statement by the company that it has 'complied with' Section A (together with an explanation and justification of any areas of non-compliance) and a statement by the remuneration committee that it has 'given full consideration to' Section B. An example of a company making an 'unqualified' statement is shown in the following extract:

> *Extract 30.30: Marks and Spencer p.l.c. (1997)*
>
> **Report of the Remuneration Committee** [extract]
>
> The Remuneration Committee's composition, responsibilities and operation comply with the best practice provisions in Section A of the Annex to the Listing Rules of the London Stock Exchange; in implementing its policy, the Committee has given full consideration to the provisions of Section B of the Annex to the Listing Rules.

It should be emphasised that companies are not required to state that they have complied with Section B, only that they have given 'full consideration' to it.

This means that if a company, for whatever reason, does not follow completely the provisions contained in Section B, there is no requirement to explain or justify those areas of non-compliance.

Statements of non-compliance are restricted to the more objective provisions of Section A. The most common non-compliance is in respect of paragraph 2 of the provisions which is that 'remuneration committees should consist exclusively of non-executive directors with no personal financial interest other than as shareholders in the matters to be decided, no potential conflicts of interest arising from cross-directorships and no day-to day involvement in running the business'. Such non-compliance is normally due to executive directors, generally the Chief Executive, being on the committee, as illustrated below:

Extract 30.31: Graseby plc (1996)

Report of the remuneration committee [extract]

The board is mindful of the recommendation of the Greenbury Committee that remuneration committees should consist exclusively of non-executive directors, and will review the committee's composition from time to time. However, the board considers at present that the input of the chief executive is crucial to the assessment of the performance of the other executive directors and senior executives, and therefore to the proper determination of their remuneration packages. It has been decided, therefore, that Mr Lester should remain a member of the committee. As in the past, he will withdraw during discussion of, and play no part in the determination of his own remuneration package. The same applies to Mr Cooper [secretary of the committee]. In all other respects the company has complied with Section A of the best practice provisions annexed to the Listing Rules of the London Stock Exchange (The Listing Rules).

Some companies have taken steps to rectify such non-compliance by the Chief Executive resigning his position on the remuneration committee. However, if this is done during the year, then the non-compliance for the early part of the year must be noted, as was done by Berisford below:

Extract 30.32: Berisford plc (1996)

Remuneration committee report [extract]

The Company has complied throughout the period with Section A of the Best Practice Provisions annexed to the Listing Rules, except, as reported last year, in respect of the membership of the Remuneration Committee up until 23 October 1995 when Alan Bowkett, Chief Executive, ceased to be a member. Since 23 October 1995 the Committee consisted wholly of non-executive Directors.

It has to be said, however, that a number of companies who state they comply with Section A also note that the chairman and/or chief executive attends the meetings of the remuneration committee to assist or advise the committee in its determination of the remuneration of the other executive directors. It could be that a chief executive attending a remuneration committee meeting by invitation sometimes has substantially the same influence as one attending as a member of the committee.

A more unusual statement of compliance is the one disclosed by De La Rue:

Extract 30.33: De La Rue plc (1996)

Remuneration Committee Report [extract]

Compliance   The Company has complied throughout the year with Section A of the best practice provisions annexed to the Listing Rules except that membership of the Remuneration Committee was not indicated on proxy cards issued for the 1996 annual general meeting; membership will be indicated this year. The Committee has given full consideration to Section B of the best practice provisions annexed to the listing rules.

This refers to paragraph 4 of the provisions which states that 'the members of the remuneration committee should be listed each year in the committee's report to shareholders. When they stand for re-election, the proxy cards should indicate their membership of the committee.' This serves as a reminder that companies should not make glib statements about compliance without first checking that they have indeed complied with each of the provisions within Section A.

4.3.3   Statement of remuneration policy

Item (b) (i) at 4.3 above requires the remuneration committee report to include a 'a statement of the company's policy on executive directors' remuneration'. This is a considerably less detailed requirement than that of the corresponding paragraph (B2) of the Greenbury Code, which recommended disclosure of 'the company's policy on executive Directors' remuneration, including levels, comparator groups of companies, individual components, performance criteria and measurement, pension provision, contracts of service and compensation commitments on early termination'.

The Greenbury Report expanded on this recommendation by suggesting that the section on general policy should set out the company's policy on major issues such as:

- the total level of remuneration;

- the main components and the arrangements for determining them, including the division between basic and performance-related components;

- the comparator groups of companies considered;

- the main parameters and rationale for any annual bonus schemes, including caps;

- how performance is measured, how rewards are related to it, how the performance measures relate to longer-term objectives and how the company has performed over time relative to comparator companies;

- the company's policy on allowing executive directors to accept appointments and retain payments from sources outside the company;

- the company's policy on contracts of service and early termination;

- the pension and retirement benefit schemes for directors, including the main types of scheme, the main terms and parameters, what elements of remuneration are pensionable, how the Inland Revenue pensions cap has been accommodated and whether the scheme is part of, or separate from, the main company scheme.[84]

The Report also recommended that the provisions should also apply to non-executive directors and that the report should state how, and by whom, the fees and other benefits of the non-executive directors are determined.[85]

General practice among companies is to give only factual details rather than policies in respect of all these items and to give only a general policy on remuneration, as required by the Stock Exchange. Examples of statements made about particular elements, such as bonuses, share options and long-term incentive schemes, are illustrated in the extracts in the relevant sections below.

4.3.4 Individual directors' emoluments

The remuneration report is to include the amount of each element in the remuneration package for the period under review of each director by name 'including, but not restricted to, basic salary and fees, the estimated money value of benefits in kind, annual bonuses, deferred bonuses, compensation for loss of office and payments for breach of contract or other termination payments, together with the total for each director for the period under review and for the corresponding prior period ...'.

Disclosure of annual bonuses, deferred bonuses and compensation payments is discussed in more detail at 4.3.5, 4.3.6 and 4.3.7 below.

This requirement for a detailed breakdown of each director's remuneration is probably the most sensitive incremental disclosure arising from the implementation of the Greenbury Code. Previously, such analyses had been required (by virtue of the Cadbury Code) in respect only of the pay packages of the chairman and highest paid director (normally the chief executive); the other directors being anonymously included within the bandings formerly required by the Companies Act.

An illustration of the required disclosure is given in the following extract:

Extract 30.34: Allied Colloids plc (1997)

Report of the Remuneration Committee [extract]

Remuneration relating to directors of the Company comprises:

	Fees £'000	Salary £'000	Benefits £'000	Bonus £'000	Compensation for loss of office £'000	Pension contributions £'000	Total 1997 £'000	Total 1996 £'000
Executive Directors								
D. Farrar	–	172	15	15	–	22	**224**	193
J. A. Harnett (from 1.8.96)	–	93	10	9	–	15	**127**	–
B. D. Fisher (to 30.9.96)	–	56	18	–	250	15	**339**	138
P. Flesher (to 30.6.95)	–	–	–	–	–	–	**–**	41
G. McGrow (to 31.7.96)	–	112	9	10	–	–	**131**	135
G. S. Senior (to 31.7.96)	–	37	19	–	113	15	**184**	135
Non-Executive Directors								
Sir Trevor Holdsworth (to 31.12.96)	52	–	–	–	–	–	**52**	70
E. B. Farmer (from 1.8.96)	36	–	–	–	–	–	**36**	–
W. L. Wilkinson	27	–	–	–	–	–	**27**	27
H. Cottam	20	–	–	–	–	–	**20**	20
	135	470	71	34	363	67	**1,140**	759
Totals 1996	117	529	37	–	–	76	759	

It can be seen from the above extract that not only is information given for the executive directors but information is also included in respect of the non-executive directors. However, this is what is required even although the policy statement discussed at 4.3.3 above is only required by the Stock Exchange to be in respect of the executive directors.

The Greenbury Report also recommended that the nature of benefits in kind should be disclosed.[86] Although not required by the Stock Exchange many companies give such disclosure (see extracts at 2.3.2 A above).

A   Comparative figures

The above extract does not include comparatives for each element of the total remuneration package. However, this is all that is necessary as the requirement is just to provide comparatives in respect of the total emoluments for each director; this is the approach followed by many companies. However, other companies disclose comparative amounts for each element, as shown below:

Extract 30.35: Chloride Group PLC (1997)

10   Directors' emoluments [extract]

	Fees/ Basic salary £	Performance related bonus £	Money purchase pension contributions £	Other benefits £	Total £
1997					
Chairman					
R Horrocks	29,000	–	–	3,941	32,941
Chief Executive					
K H Hodgkinson	180,000	90,000	33,061	7,694	310,755
Executive directors					
M L Vass	130,000	65,000	–	28,847	223,847
D J Wright	78,000	39,000	–	4,152	121,152
Non-executive directors					
I F H Davison	15,000	–	–	396	15,396
C W Foreman	19,000	–	–	396	19,396
A S J Fraser	15,000	–	–	396	15,396
Aggregate emoluments	466,000	194,000	33,061	45,822	738,883
1996					
Chairman					
R Horrocks	29,000	–	–	3,806	32,806
Chief Executive					
K H Hodgkinson	159,000	71,438	18,588	7,976	257,002
Executive directors					
M L Vass	118,000	53,017	–	4,081	175,098
D J Wright	71,000	31,900	–	4,057	106,957
Non-executive directors					
I F H Davison	15,000	–	–	396	15,396
C W Foreman	19,000	–	–	396	19,396
A S J Fraser	15,000	–	–	396	15,396
Aggregate emoluments	426,000	156,355	18,588	21,108	622,051

Another company that discloses the comparative elements but in columnar fashion (and also gives further information in respect of non-executive directors) is United Utilities, as shown below:

Extract 30.36: United Utilities PLC (1997)

Remuneration Committee's report [extract]

The remuneration of individual directors was:

Executive directors	Salary		Bonuses		Taxable benefits		Total		Pension contributions	
	1997	1996	**1997**	1996	**1997**	1996	**1997**	1996	**1997**	1996
	£'000	£'000	**£'000**	£'000	**£'000**	£'000	**£'000**	£'000	**£'000**	£'000
Sir Desmond Pitcher	**310.0**	255.6	–	76.7	**16.3**	13.9	**326.3**	346.2	**24.6**	24.2
Brian Staples	**300.0**	235.0	–	142.0	**5.9**	3.7	**305.9**	380.7	**24.6**	24.2
John Beckitt	**162.5**	141.2	–	56.5	**14.4**	12.9	**176.9**	210.6	**19.5**	24.2
Malcolm Faulkner	**116.9**	–	–	–	**9.4**	–	**126.3**	–	**14.0**	–
Bob Ferguson	**179.3**	156.2	–	94.5	**14.2**	9.7	**193.5**	260.4	**21.5**	26.9
Derek Green	**209.0**	185.1	–	92.7	**15.9**	13.3	**224.9**	291.1	**24.6**	24.2

Non-executive directors	Fee		Board committee chairmanship/ membership		Additional responsibility payments		Taxable benefits		Total	
	1997	1996	**1997**	1996	**1997**	1996	**1997**	1996	**1997**	1996
	£'000	£'000	**£'000**	£'000	**£'000**	£'000	**£'000**	£'000	**£'000**	£'000
Eric Clark	**20.0**	20.0	**4.0**	–	–	–	**0.5**	0.1	**24.5**	20.1
Robin Leach	**20.0**	20.0	**6.0**	5.0	–	–	**1.4**	1.2	**27.4**	26.2
Sir Peter Middleton	**20.0**	20.0	–	–	**20.0**	20.0	–	–	**40.0**	40.0
Jane Newell	**11.6**	–	**0.5**	–	–	–	–	–	**12.1**	–
Frank Sanderson	**20.0**	20.0	**4.0**	5.0	**5.0**	5.0	**1.2**	0.9	**30.2**	30.9
John Seed	**20.0**	1.7	**0.5**	–	–	–	**0.9**	–	**21.4**	1.7

A related issue is whether the disclosure of comparative amounts should identify the names of former directors who received remuneration in the previous year but did not receive any remuneration in the current year or indeed whether such payments need to be disclosed at all. The requirement seems to be only in respect of the directors in the period under review, i.e. the current year; this suggests that the amounts in respect of such former directors are not required. However, although the totals of such amounts are not required by the Stock Exchange they will still have to be given, thereby providing sufficient information to enable the company to comply with the requirement of the Companies Act of disclosing comparative figures for aggregate emoluments (unless such an amount is separately disclosed for Companies Act purposes).

Notwithstanding the fact that it is unnecessary to name such former directors and quantify their individual emoluments in the previous year, a number of companies do disclose such information (for example, see Extract 30.43 at 4.3.6 below).

B   Companies Act information

As noted at 2.1 above, the Companies Act deems that the information that it specifies for disclosure is treated as having been given if it can be ascertained from information disclosed elsewhere. Many listed companies appear to take advantage of this dispensation as they do not disclose all of the Companies Act information together as a separately identifiable section of the remuneration committee report or within a note to the accounts.

4.3.5   Annual bonuses

A   Performance criteria

Item (b) (iii) at 4.3 above requires the amount of the annual bonus payment made to each director to be disclosed. This falls a little short of what was apparently envisaged by the Greenbury Report, which also recommended that 'the extent to which any performance criteria have been met should be explained, as should any particular performance criteria on which individual Directors' entitlements depend and any special arrangements for them'.[87]

In practice, however, many companies attempt to comply with the spirit of Greenbury rather than just the letter of the *Listing Rules*. This is hardly surprising given that an explanation of the operation of bonus schemes had been recommended by the Cadbury Code in 1992. Such disclosure is generally given in the policy statement dealing with the annual bonus element of the remuneration package.

Where a bonus scheme is linked to a relatively straightforward accounting measure, it can be clearly summarised in a few lines, as illustrated below:

Extract 30.37: The Boots Company PLC (1997)

Board Remuneration Committee's Report [extract]

Components of emoluments

Short term executive bonus scheme This scheme rewards executive directors for achieving operating efficiencies and profitable growth in the relevant year by reference to challenging but achievable forecasts derived at the beginning of the year from strategic plans.

During 1996/97, the performance criterion was profit after tax. A bonus of 10% of base salary was payable for performance at 95% of profit after tax budget, rising to 25% of salary for performance at budget level and to a maximum of 35% when profit after tax was 110% of budget. In 1996/97 a bonus equal to 35% was earned by executive directors.

Extract 30.38: Imperial Chemical Industries PLC (1996)

Remuneration committee report [extract]

Remuneration package

The level of bonus (if any) under the Annual Performance Related Bonus Scheme is determined by the Remuneration Committee on the basis of criteria established at the beginning of the year to encourage performance in a manner which the Remuneration Committee considers will contribute most to increasing shareholder value for that year.

The maximum bonus available to executive directors is 40% and is not pensionable. For 1996 the bonus for executive directors was again related entirely to increased earnings per share ('EPS'). The trigger point was established at 77.6p compared with the 73.9p achieved EPS in 1995. The 37.9p achieved EPS in 1996 has resulted in no bonus being paid.

However, there remains the basic problem that very few companies state exactly what the relevant performance criteria are and even fewer explain how achievement of those criteria translates into payments to directors. This is not necessarily a criticism of the companies concerned, but in many cases simply reflects the fact that criteria for short-term bonus schemes tend to be more complicated than the more objective yardsticks (such as earnings per share or total shareholder return) used for longer-term schemes.

Performance may be linked to a number of financial measures, some of which may not be apparent from the published accounts (e.g. average daily cash balances), production targets, comparison with peer groups and personal performance; it is therefore more difficult to meet what Greenbury recommended.

In such situations, we would recommend that companies give a general description of the factors that are taken into account in determining the annual bonuses, the maximum bonus which may be payable and the extent to which a bonus has been paid. For example:

Extract 30.39: Allied Colloids plc (1997)

Report of the Remuneration Committee [extract]

Remuneration policy

(ii) Performance-Related Bonus

Senior management participate in a performance related bonus scheme which can pay up to 40% of salary as an annual bonus. The amount of the bonus is determined by achievement of performance targets set by the Committee, in respect of growth in sales, gross profit, profit before interest and tax, cash flow and return on shareholders' funds. The targets are set at demanding levels and are intended to reward substantial improvements in performance. The scheme will pay a bonus of 9% in respect of the year ended 31st March 1997.

B   *Caps*

The Greenbury Report expressed the view that 'bonuses should not be allowed to become, in effect, another guaranteed element of remuneration. They should normally be subject to an upper limit or cap, such as a specified percentage of basic pay'.[88] Each of the extracts shown above disclose the existence of caps. As noted previously, we recommend that disclosure of any such caps should be given as part of the details in respect of the annual bonus scheme.

C *Incentives to take shares*

The Greenbury Report suggested that 'some proportion at least of any bonuses paid to Directors should take the form of shares to be held for a minimum period rather than cash'.[89] One company which has such a bonus scheme is TI Group, as shown below:

Extract 30.40: TI Group plc (1996)

REPORT OF THE ORGANISATION AND REMUNERATION COMMITTEE [extract]

Remuneration package

ii Annual bonus

For headquarters staff executive Directors the annual bonus is based partly on Group performance against plan, and partly on achievement of individual objectives. The annual bonus for executive Directors with line responsibility for operations is based partly on a combination of Group performance and business area performance against annual plan and partly on achievement of individual objectives. The annual plan includes specific cash targets. The maximum potential bonus for executive Directors for 1996 was 60% of basic salary (100% for the Chairman), with the maximum amount normally achievable only if performance attained 112% of plan. The Committee retains the right to exercise an overview with regard to the quality of achievement.

Payments in respect of 1996, comprising cash and shares, are shown in the table on page 33. The share element reflects the general policy of encouraging executives to invest in the Company. For 1997 a similar scheme is in force.

SUMMARY REMUNERATION TABLE

Executive Directors

– Salary, Annual Bonus and Benefits

				Annual Bonus			
	1995 Basic Salary £'000	**1996** Basic Salary £'000	Benefits (Note 1) £'000	Cash £'000	TI Shares (Note 2) £'000	**1996 Total £'000**	1995 Total £'000
Sir Christopher Lewinton	600	625	37	234	235	**1,131**	1,204
L A Edwards	290	300	14	55	55	**424**	414
R J M Fisher	250	260	57	59	58	**434**	386
W J Laule	152	272	16	54	54	**396**	248
J W Potter	246	300	37	55	55	**447**	421
J L Roe	180	190	12	46	45	**293**	285
B A Walsh	290	300	17	67	68	**452**	457

Notes:

2. The bonus award has been allocated between cash and TI shares from the TI Group Employee Share Ownership Trust. The numbers of shares thus acquired, calculated after deduction of an amount in respect of personal tax, are included in the holdings as at 12th March 1997 shown in the summary of Directors' Share Interests on page 48.

Some companies have introduced schemes whereby a director may receive free shares if he uses some of his annual bonus to purchase shares. The receipt of the extra shares are normally conditional upon the director remaining in employment with the company. Such schemes are discussed at 4.3.6 below.

D   *Pensionable bonuses etc.*

The Greenbury Report stated that 'Annual bonuses are a management instrument designed to promote and reward short-term performance. In general neither they nor payments under long-term incentive schemes nor benefits in kind should be pensionable. If such elements are pensionable, the remuneration committee report should explain and justify why.'[90] This has been implemented by the Stock Exchange requirement set out at (b) (vi) at 4.3 above.

4.3.6   *Deferred bonuses*

The Stock Exchange defines a deferred bonus as 'any arrangement pursuant to the terms of which the participant(s) may receive an award of any asset (including cash or any security) in respect of service and/or performance in a period not exceeding the length of the relevant financial year notwithstanding that any such asset may, subject only to the participant(s) remaining a director or employee of the group, be receivable by the participant(s) after the end of the period to which the award relates'.[91]

Such bonuses are identified as one of the elements to be included within the remuneration table under (b) (iii) at 4.3 above. However, it is fair to say that it is unusual to see a heading of 'deferred bonuses' as part of the table; it may be that companies consider it inappropriate to include them, particularly as they generally involve shares, and therefore provide explanatory notes as necessary.

It is unclear from the requirement as to whether the deferred bonuses to be included for the period under review are those bonuses in respect of the current period but which are deferred or whether it is bonuses which relate to previous years, the conditions of which have been fulfilled during the period under review and the award finally given to the director.

A number of companies have introduced bonus schemes whereby the director may apply a proportion of his annual bonus for the purchase of shares in the company with an equivalent value which, generally, will be matched by an equivalent number of shares at nil cost. Such schemes normally involve a condition whereby the director must remain in employment with the company and are therefore 'deferred bonuses'.

Perhaps as a result of differing views of the interpretation of the disclosure requirement, or it may be because of differences between the various schemes, the treatment of such 'deferred bonus plans' varies. One company which has such a scheme is Booker:

Extract 30.41: Booker plc (1996)

Report of the Remuneration Committee [extract]

• **Share based incentives**

In addition to the all-employee SAYE share option scheme, the company has a deferred bonus plan (open to all senior managers on invitation) in order to encourage over the longer term identification with the success of Booker. For those electing to participate in this plan, part (currently one-third) of any performance-related bonus is put into a discretionary employee benefit trust, together with a further payment by the company The trustees of the plan use the funds to purchase Booker shares in the market. After three years the bonus shares plus an equal number of matching shares become distributable, alternatively participants (who remain in the company's employment) can elect to leave them in the plan for a further two years, after which they will receive twice the bonus shares. The company's current policy is to offer executive share options once only when executives join the company.

Directors' remuneration

	Salary (incl. fees) £000	Benefits £000	Annual Bonus £000	1996 Total £000	1995 Total £000	Pension entitlement accrued in: 1996 £000	1995 £000
Chairman							
J F Taylor	122	7	–	129	213	–	2
Executive Directors							
C J Bowen	313	2	–	315	343	11	11
A J Busby	147	3	18 [2]	168	–	10	6
J E Kitson	158	11	–	169	187	2	3
J D Nelson	220	4	18 [2]	242	277	7	7
E C Robinson	151	10	11	172	171	10	12

Notes:

[2] These executive directors have elected to participate in the deferred bonus plan described on page 30 whereby part (currently one-third) of the bonus is put into a discretionary trust. The bonus payments shown above therefore relate solely to the cash element.

It can be seen that Booker has only included the cash element of the bonus. Therefore the one-third of the bonus which the directors are putting into the plan is excluded as well as any of the matching shares to be provided by the company.

Another treatment that is adopted by some companies is to include all of the annual bonus (including that proportion that the director will effectively take in shares by putting them into the plan), but not the matching shares. For example:

Extract 30.42: Cadbury Schweppes p.l.c. (1996)

Report of the Remuneration Committee [extract]

2 Remuneration policy

(b) Annual Incentive Scheme

The Bonus Share Retention Plan ("BSRP") applies for the first time to annual incentive plan awards for 1996. 132 senior executives, including five Directors, are eligible to participate in the BSRP. The BSRP enables participants to defer all or part of their annual incentive plan award and receive such award in the form of Cadbury Schweppes Ordinary Shares ("deferred shares") rather than cash. After a three year period the Company will provide participants with three additional shares for every five deferred shares. All share awards under the BSRP will be purchased in the market and held in trust for such three year period. If a participant leaves the Company during such a three year period, such participant will forfeit part of the additional shares and in certain cases it is possible that all of the additional shares and the deferred shares may be forfeited.

3   Directors' Emoluments

Individual Details   Pay and benefits

	Basic Salary/Fees £000	Incentive Award 1996 see page 39 Cash £000	BSRP award £000	LTIP see pages 39 and 40 £000	Allowances and benefits £000	1996 Total £000	1995 Total £000
N D Cadbury	534	–	–	91	42	**667**	666
J M Sunderland	331	–	174	25	16	**546**	366
J F Brock	283	61	115	7	57	**523**	–
I D Johnston	79	–	32	2	7	**120**	–
D J Kappler	264	–	131	12	16	**423**	344
R J Stack	124	–	59	4	52	**239**	–
R C Stradwick	68	32	–	13	11	**124**	330
F J Swan	36	12	–	21	4	**73**	596
D G Wellings	330	177	–	37	68	**612**	676
D R Williams	377	262	–	26	33	**698**	645
T O Hutchison	55	–	–	–	–	**55**	51
I F H Davison	25	–	–	–	–	**25**	23
K M von der Heyden	32	–	–	–	–	**32**	–
F B Humer	25	–	–	–	–	**25**	23
Mrs A M Vinton	25	–	–	–	–	**25**	23
G H Waddell	25	–	–	–	–	**25**	23
Sir John Whitehead	25	–	–	–	–	**25**	23

The BSRP award will be used to purchase shares which will be held subject to the terms and conditions of the BSRP as described on page 39. At the end of the three year period if the participating Director is still an employee of the Company, he will receive the shares together with the additional shares (in the ratio of three additional shares for every five shares awarded under the BSRP).

By disclosing separately the cash element and the BSRP element of the incentive award for 1996, Cadbury Schweppes has effectively identified the share element of the 'deferred bonus'. This element has been included even although it appears that in some circumstances such deferred shares may be forfeited. Although the additional shares have been excluded, the footnote discloses the relevant ratio and therefore the value of such shares, at the date of the award, can be computed.

One company which goes further and includes the additional shares in quantifying the bonus is Prudential, as shown below:

Extract 30.43: Prudential Corporation plc (1996)

Remuneration Committee Report [extract]

Executive Directors' Remuneration

Annual bonus

Executive directors other than Derek Higgs qualify for awards under the Group's short-term deferred bonus plan, known as the Share Participation Plan. Awards are determined by the Committee based on the performance of the Group against the annual business plan, with particular reference to operating profit and other financial measures and developments. Executive directors may receive an initial cash award which, for 1996, was 15 per cent of salary at the time of the award. Either the net amount of this award must be used to buy shares or an equivalent number of shares must be lodged with the Plan trustee. The Company may then make an award of additional shares, which for 1996 was equivalent to 22.5 per cent of salary at the time of the award, on the basis that both sets of shares are held in trust for five years. If a director leaves prior to this, the additional shares may be released in certain circumstances. The total award, including the additional share award, can range from nil to 45 per cent of salary depending upon actual performance against business plan.

Derek Higgs can be awarded a bonus, payable half in shares and half in cash, which can range from nil to 100 per cent of salary, based on the overall performance of Prudential Portfolio Managers.

Directors' Remuneration

	Salary /Fees £000	Annual Bonus £000	Benefits £000	**Total 1996 £000**	Total 1995 £000
Executive directors					
Keith Bedell-Pearce	208	82	20	**310**	294
Jonathan Bloomer	275	118	29	**422**	383
Sir Peter Davis	425	169	27	**621**	413
(group chief executive from 1/5/95)					
Derek Higgs (appointed 19/2/96)	261	220	14	**495**	–
John Maxwell (resigned 30/11/96, note 1)	193	58	19	**270**	293
Jim Sutcliffe	300	118	19	**437**	368
Hugh Jenkins (retired 31/12/95)	–	–	–	–	377
Mick Newmarch (resigned 23/1/95)	–	–	–	–	59
Total executive directors	1,662	765	128	**2,555**	2,187

Notes

3.   The annual bonus reflects all pre-tax amounts awarded under the Share Participation Plan, including the cost of the additional shares.

On balance we believe that where the only condition is that the director has to remain in employment for a future period, then as the bonus has been earned for the year in question the total value (including that relating to the additional shares) should be disclosed. However, other treatments such as that adopted by Cadbury Schweppes are acceptable. The important issue is that all of the relevant details are disclosed whereby the full value of the bonus can be determined. Such an approach will also meet the Companies Act requirements given that as long as information is disclosed it is deemed to have been disclosed under the Act (see 2.1 above).

To the extent that bonus schemes involve awards which are conditional upon future performance over a longer period than the financial year, then such a scheme is a long-term incentive scheme (see 4.3.10 B below).

4.3.7   Compensation payments

The Greenbury Committee took the view that 'compensation payments to Directors on loss of office have been a cause of public and shareholder concern in recent times'.[92] It is therefore rather surprising that the Greenbury Code contained no recommendation for disclosure of such payments. However, as noted in item (b) (iii) at 4.3 above, the Stock Exchange requires such payments to be disclosed for each director. The Companies Act requires only an aggregate figure for all directors (see 2.9 above).

An example of a company giving the disclosure required by the Stock Exchange within its remuneration table is Allied Colloids, as illustrated in Extract 30.34 at 4.3.4 above.

However, it could be regarded that this is the minimum to be disclosed because the relevant requirement also says that 'such details are to be presented in tabular form, unless inappropriate, together with explanatory notes as necessary'.

Possibly as a result of this, a number of companies go further than just disclosing the amounts by disclosing details of the compensation arrangement. Extracts 30.18 and 30.19 at 2.9 above illustrate such extra disclosures. We believe it is good practice for such disclosures to be made and we would recommend that companies in this situation should provide this extra information.

4.3.8   Payments to former directors

The Greenbury Report recommended disclosure of 'any payments and benefits not previously disclosed, including any additional pension provisions, receivable by Directors who have retired during the accounting period or the previous accounting period'.[93] The intention of this recommendation was that amounts that are in substance compensation payments do not escape disclosure by being dressed up as something else. However, this has been translated into a Stock Exchange requirement to disclose 'any significant payments made to former

63 *Ibid.*, para. 8(2)(b).
64 *Ibid.*, para. 8(3).
65 *Ibid.*
66 *Ibid.*, para. 9(1).
67 *Ibid.*, para. 9(3).
68 *Ibid.*, para. 9(2).
69 *Ibid.*, para. 2(1)(a).
70 *Ibid.*, para. 2(1)(b).
71 *Ibid.*, para. 2(2).
72 The Company Accounts (Disclosure of Directors' Emoluments) Regulations 1997, (SI 1997 No. 570), Regulation 3(2).
73 CA 85, Sch. 6, para. 2(5).
74 *Ibid.*
75 *Ibid.*, para. 2(3).
76 *Ibid.*, para. 2(4).
77 *Ibid.*, Sch. 4, paras. 56(4), 94.
78 *Ibid.*, para. 94(1).
79 The Committee on the Financial Aspects of Corporate Governance, *The Financial Aspects of Corporate Governance*, (The Cadbury Report), December 1992.
80 *The Listing Rules*, London Stock Exchange, Chapter 12, para. 12.43(w).
81 *Ibid.*, para. 12.43(x).
82 *Ibid.*, para. 12.43(u). The detailed requirements are set out in Chapter 13, paras. 13.13A and 13.14.
83 *Ibid.*, para. 12.43(d).
84 The Greenbury Report, para. 5.5.
85 *Ibid.*, para. 5.7.
86 *Ibid.*, para. 5.8.
87 *Ibid.*, para. 5.9.
88 *Ibid.*, para. 6.21.
89 *Ibid.*, para. 6.22.
90 *Ibid.*, para. 6.44.
91 *The Listing Rules*, Definitions.
92 The Greenbury Report, para. 7.2
93 *Ibid.*, para. 5.10.
94 *Ibid.*, para. 5.18.
95 *Ibid.*, para. 5.19.
96 *Note to subscribers to the Listing Rules Amendment No. 10*, London Stock Exchange, May 1997.
97 *Ibid.*
98 The Greenbury Report, paras. 6.23–40.
99 *The Listing Rules*, Chapter 12, para. 12.43(k).
100 UITF 17, *Employee share schemes*, UITF, April 1997.
101 The Greenbury Report, para. 6.29.
102 *The Listing Rules*, Chapter 13, paras. 13.30–31.
103 The Greenbury Report, para. 7.13.
104 *The Listing Rules*, Definitions.
105 *Ibid.*, Chapter 16, para. 16.9.

Chapter 31   Interim reporting

1   INTRODUCTION

The publication of interim financial reports has been a requirement for listed companies for many years, although the Stock Exchange's rules governing their form and content remain sketchy. However, the Accounting Standards Board is in the process of finalising a non-mandatory Statement on the subject, based on work undertaken by the Financial Reporting Committee of the ICAEW.

The most frequently debated issue relating to interim financial reporting is whether the interim period should be regarded as a discrete period in its own right, or whether it should be seen primarily as a mere instalment of the financial year. Under the first perspective, it would be appropriate to apply the same accounting policies and principles as are used for the annual accounts, treating the interim period in just the same way as the full financial year. Under the second, some modifications to these policies and principles are made to allow the interim report to give a better guide to the outcome of the year as a whole. The former approach is generally referred to as the 'discrete' approach, and the latter as the 'integral' approach. In practice, however, these categories are less clear-cut than the above description might suggest, and virtually all companies follow an approach which is a hybrid of these two theoretical extremes.

The integral approach has no clear definition. It implies some pragmatic modification of the inter-period allocation of transactions, so as to match costs more evenly with revenues in the different halves (or quarters) of the year. Critics would say that this is not matching, but smoothing, and that it obscures the results of the interim period rather than presents them more fairly. On the other hand, supporters would say that such modifications are necessary to prevent meaningless distortions arising; an interim period is an even more artificial interval than a financial year, and that to report transactions without trying to relate them to the annual cycle of activity for which they have been incurred would not make sense. Moreover, it can be argued that similar allocations are often necessary in annual accounts. For example, depreciating fixed assets (particularly on a usage basis) necessarily involves deciding how much of the cost of the asset should be related to this year's revenues and how much to those of future years. The debate on this subject is therefore less straightforward than it appears at first sight.

The extent of disclosure in interim reports raises similar issues. If interim reporting is no different in concept from annual reporting, but is simply a more frequent version of the same thing, then one might suppose that the form and content of the report should also be the same. If, however, it is seen as a subsidiary form of reporting which only deals with an instalment of a longer period, then it is easier to justify a different reporting package. Present practice undoubtedly reflects the latter view, although probably more as an expedient compromise than as the result of an attempt to meet a carefully researched need.

In the UK, the normal frequency of reporting is biannual. Relatively few British companies follow the North American practice of reporting every quarter. In this chapter, reference is often made to 'half-yearly' reports, but the discussion applies to interim reports of any duration.

It should be explained that the term 'interim accounts' also appears in the Companies Act, but with quite a different meaning. This refers to the accounts which public companies have to draw up to justify paying a dividend if their last annual accounts show that their distributable reserves were insufficient for this purpose.[1] Such requirements are beyond the scope of this book and are not discussed further here.

2   REQUIREMENTS

2.1   The Stock Exchange Listing Rules

The Stock Exchange requires listed companies to publish a half-yearly report on their activities and profit and loss account information covering the first six months of their financial year. These rules embody the requirements of the EC Interim Reports Directive, which were enacted in UK law in 1984.[2]

The Listing Rules are not demanding. They require only a minimal profit and loss account to be presented, and in a slightly archaic form. They also contain some general injunctions, borrowed from the Directive, concerning the quality of the information presented. In practice, companies tend to go beyond these requirements so as to present a more informative report.

The profit and loss account information which the Stock Exchange requires is as follows:

(a)   net turnover;*

(b)   profit or loss before taxation and extraordinary items;*

(c)   taxation on profits (UK taxation and, if material, overseas and share of associated undertakings' taxation to be shown separately);

Good Group P.L.C.

OPERATING AND FINANCIAL REVIEW

OFR (2),
CBP (Note 10)

INTRODUCTION

This review has been prepared in accordance with the Accounting Standards Board's OFR (38)
statement, issued in July 1993, on the operating and financial review.

OPERATING REVIEW   OFR (8)-(22)

The group's turnover has shown an overall increase of 18.3%. However, this includes the activities of Hose Limited, which manufactures rubber hosepipes, for the eleven months up to its disposal on 30 November 19X4. Hose Limited had been loss-making for a number of years; in the current year it generated an operating loss of £563,000 on turnover of £42,196,000. Consequently, although its disposal may lead to a reduction in the overall level of future turnover in the short term, it should nevertheless result in increased profit figures. Turnover from the remaining activities increased by 28.0% which is made up of a 46.6% increase in sales of fire prevention equipment (excluding the results of Hose Limited) and a 3.2% increase in sales in the electronics division.

Turnover

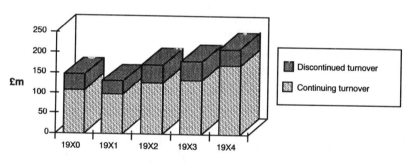

The increase in sales of fire prevention equipment is made up of two elements: a growth of 17.7% in our original operations together with the introduction of the results of Extinguishers, which contributed sales of £21,979,000 in the nine months since its acquisition on 1 April 19X4.

The growth of 17.7% in the fire prevention operations before the acquisition of Extinguishers was particularly pleasing; the year has been yet another difficult one in which to operate. The property market both here and in the United States, despite small signs of recovery periodically being reported, has continued to be depressed, although more recently the property market does appear to have improved marginally. Opportunities for the installation of fire-prevention equipment in new buildings have therefore continued to be low. Nevertheless, the activity in other markets has held up well, safety being an area where cut-backs are more difficult to achieve. With this background it was therefore inevitable that profit margins would be further squeezed despite the cost efficiencies introduced at the start of the year. The margins on Extinguishers' sales were this year lower than those achieved by the rest of the operations. We are looking at ways of improving the margin in future.

Good Group P.L.C.

OPERATING AND FINANCIAL REVIEW

OPERATING REVIEW (continued)

Extinguishers is best known for its fire-retardant fabrics, which are currently sold mainly for commercial use. The company is looking into expanding production to supply manufacturers of domestic products.

Sales in the electronics division have shown only a slight increase this year, although profit margins have held up well. The activity to date has been mainly on defence projects and for the aviation industry.

Expenditure on defence is being cut and the group is moving its focus and reducing work in this area.

The group has made a small move into the electrical safety market and is looking to expand this by means of acquisition. The directors believe that this would be compatible with the fire prevention equipment division and would be part of an overall move to enhance our reputation in the safety market.

Looking at the geographical split of sales, the increases were all generated in the United Kingdom; although sales to the United States showed a slight increase, the sales generated in the United States fell slightly in sterling terms. The US results are even more disappointing given the favourable dollar exchange rates ruling this year.

Action is already being taken to improve the performance in the United States. A new company, Sprinklers Incorporated, has been set up to manufacture the group's new fire-prevention system in the United States. Manufacturing is scheduled to start this Summer.

During the year the signs of recovery in the UK economy were more positive. The directors are hopeful that the construction industry will continue its recent improvements, particularly in the commercial sector. The recovery in the United States was initially ahead of that here. The directors consider that if the construction industry maintains its recent improvements, the current year will see an increase in sales of new fire-protection products in the United Kingdom.

Extinguishers has a strong research and development department, with a long history of introducing new products. With the acquisition, the number of staff employed by the group on research and development has more than doubled. Today's research and development forms the basis of future years' business and therefore is an area in which we place extreme significance. This year we have increased expenditure on research and development by 135% even though the department was not enlarged until three months into the year. We will be increasing the expenditure further in the next few years to enhance further the prospects for the future.

Good Group P.L.C.

REPORT OF THE REMUNERATION COMMITTEE

Greenbury (B1)
YB 12.43(x)

Interests in options

The company has two share option schemes by which executive directors and other executive directors are able to subscribe for ordinary shares in the company and acquire shares in the company from Good Group Employee Trust. The interests of the directors were as follows:

YB 12.43(k)
sch 7.2
Greenbury (B5)
YB 12.43(x)
UITF 10

	Exercise price	At 1 January 19X4	Granted during the year	Exercised during the year	Lapsed during the year	At 31 December 19X4
J N Smith	(a) £2.31	10,000	–	–	–	10,000
	(b) £2.33	10,000	–	(10,000) *	–	–
	(c) £3.80	35,000	–	–	–	35,000
	(d) £3.85	–	10,000	–	–	10,000
		55,000	10,000	(10,000)	–	55,000
J Archer	(a) £2.31	5,000	–	–	–	5,000
	(c) £3.80	35,000	–	–	–	35,000
	(d) £3.85	–	6,500	–	–	6,500
		40,000	6,500	–	–	46,500
F R Brown	(a) £2.31	5,000	–	–	–	5,000
	(d) £3.85	–	6,500	–	–	6,500
		5,000	6,500	–	–	11,500
N O Evans	(d) £3.85	–	6,500	–	–	6,500
R P Jones	(c) £3.80	8,000	–	–	(8,000)	–
P A MacBryde	(c) £3.80	5,000	–	–	–	5,000
	(d) £3.85	–	7,500	–	–	7,500
		5,000	7,500	–	–	12,500

* At the date of exercise, the company's share price was £4.10 per share. Accordingly, J N Smith was able to realise a gain of £17,700. Sch 6.1

The options are exercisable between the following dates:

(a)　1 July 19X5 and 30 June 19X8;
(c)　1 January 19X6 and 31 December 19Y3;
(d)　1 January 19X8 and 31 December 19Y5.

The directors may only exercise any of the above options if the group's earnings per share has increased by 10% more than the increase in the RPI over the period from the date of grant of the options up to the date they first become exercisable and dividends per share have similarly increased by at least the same amount. YB 12.43 (x)

Good Group P.L.C.

REPORT OF THE REMUNERATION COMMITTEE

Greenbury (B1)
YB 12.43(x)

Interests in options (continued)

The market price of the company's shares on 31 December 19X4 was £4.43 per share and the high and low share prices during the year were £4.43 and £3.42 respectively. The company's average share price over the 10 business days prior to the date of grant of options during the year was £3.85.

UITF 10

The interests of the directors to subscribe for or acquire ordinary shares have not changed since the year end.

YB 12.43 (k)

Service contracts

Mrs L B Green, who was appointed a director on 1 March 19X4, retires from the board at the Annual General Meeting and, being eligible, offers herself for re-election.

None of the directors proposed for election or re-election at the forthcoming AGM have service contracts with notice periods, at the date of this report, of one year or more.

The service contracts of J N Smith, J Archer and P A MacBryde, as for all the executive directors, expire on 31 December 19X5, being for one year's duration commencing on   1 January 19X5. None of the non-executive directors have service contracts.

On behalf of the remuneration committee

M C Holman
25 March 19X5

Good Group P.L.C.

DIRECTORS' REPORT

The directors present their report and the group accounts for the year ended　s 234
31 December 19X4.

RESULTS AND DIVIDENDS

The group profit for the year, after taxation and minority interests, amounted to
£7,456,000, an increase of 23.1% from the previous year.

The directors recommend a final ordinary dividend of 8.67 pence per share, amounting　s 234(1)(b)
to £1,061,000, making totals of 15.23 pence and £1,859,000 for the year respectively,
after taking account of dividends waived by Good Group Employee Share Trust (see
note 10). Preference dividends of £175,000 were also paid during the year. The final
ordinary dividend, if approved, will be paid on 3 July 19X5 to ordinary shareholders
whose names were on the register on 13 June 19X5.

PRINCIPAL ACTIVITIES

The group's principal activities during the year continued to be electronics and the　s 234(2)
manufacture and installation of fire-prevention equipment.

REVIEW OF THE BUSINESS

The group has had a satisfactory year with an overall increase in sales. There has been　s 234(1)(a)
a substantial increase in sales of fire-prevention equipment, which have grown in total
by 25.3%. However, this included the results of Hose Limited which was sold during
the year (see below); when the results of Hose Limited have been eliminated, the sales
of the continuing operations of this segment grew by 46.6%. The growth has been
most marked in the home market. Although sales to the United States have shown an
increase from 19X3 levels, the increase was well below that achieved in the home
market and the sales generated in the United States fell slightly. However, a new
company, Sprinklers Incorporated, has been set up to manufacture the group's new
fire-prevention system in the USA.

During the year the group acquired all of the issued share capital of Extinguishers
Limited, a company which is best known for its fire-retardant fabric.

The directors have decided that the group should withdraw from the manufacture of
rubber hosepipes, an activity which has been loss-making for some years. To this end
the directors were successful in completing a sale of the subsidiary, Hose Limited, on
30 November 19X4. The loss on disposal of the subsidiary amounted to £2,437,000,
of which £400,000 represents goodwill previously written off against reserves.

The group's electronics activities have shown only slight growth during the year
although profit margins in this area generally remain good.

FUTURE DEVELOPMENTS

The directors are hopeful that the current year will see an increase in sales of new fire-　sch 7.6(b)
protection products in the United Kingdom. Sprinklers Incorporated is expected to
commence production in June 19X5 and this will lead to an expansion in sales in the
United States. The group is looking for ways of making the electronics business more
profitable by way of acquisitions and new product lines.

Good Group P.L.C.

DIRECTORS' REPORT

RESEARCH AND DEVELOPMENT

With the acquisition of Extinguishers Limited, the number of staff employed by the   sch 7.6(c)
group on research and development has more than doubled.

There are two main fire-prevention research and development projects: improved fire
detection and sprinkler systems and fire-retardant fabrics for vehicles and aircraft.

Research and development in the electronics business is concentrated on the
development of new products capable of generating greater turnover.

EVENTS SINCE THE BALANCE SHEET DATE

On 14 February 19X5 a short leasehold building, with a net book value of £1,695,000,   sch 7.6(a)
was severely damaged by flooding. It is expected that insurance proceeds will fall
short of the costs of rebuilding and loss of profits by some £750,000. No provision has
been made in these accounts for this loss.

POLITICAL AND CHARITABLE CONTRIBUTIONS

During the year the group made a political contribution of £5,500 to the United Party   sch 7.3-5
and various charitable contributions totalling £10,000.

DISABLED EMPLOYEES

The group gives full consideration to applications for employment from disabled   sch 7.9
persons where the requirements of the job can be adequately fulfilled by a handicapped
or disabled person.

Where existing employees become disabled, it is the group's policy wherever
practicable to provide continuing employment under normal terms and conditions and
to provide training and career development and promotion wherever appropriate.

EMPLOYEE INVOLVEMENT

During the year, the policy of providing employees with information about the group   sch 7.11
has been continued through the newsletter 'Good Group News' in which employees
have also been encouraged to present their suggestions and views on the group's
performance. Regular meetings are held between local management and employees to
allow a free flow of information and ideas. Employees are encouraged to participate
directly in the success of the business through the group's profit sharing scheme and
are encouraged to reinvest in the group through participation in share option schemes.

Good Group P.L.C.

NOTES TO THE ACCOUNTS
at 31 December 19X4

24.   NOTES TO THE STATEMENT OF CASH FLOWS (continued)

(b)   Analysis of net debt

	At 1 January 19X4 £000	Cash flow £000	Exchange differences £000	Other non-cash movements £000	At 31 December 19X4 £000	
						FRS 1(33)
Cash at bank and in hand	9,291				7,241	
Bank overdrafts	(3,770)				(760)	
Cash	5,521	695	265	–	6,481	
Short term deposits*	2,019	(528)	(28)	–	1,483	
Loans	(8,900)	(4,110)	(145)	(27)	(13,182)	
Finance leases	(1,415)	370	–	–	(1,045)	
At 31 December 19X4	(2,755)	(3,573)	92	(27)	(6,263)	

* Short term deposits are included within cash at bank and in hand in the balance sheet.

(c)   Major non-cash transactions   FRS 1(46)

See note 14 for an analysis of the acquisition of Extinguishers Limited and the disposal of Hose Limited.

(d)   Exceptional items   FRS 1(37)

Cash flows relating to operating exceptional items
Net cash inflow from operating activities in 19X4 includes £630,000 of cash outflows in respect of professional expenses incurred in respect of the bid defence.

Cash flows relating to non-operating exceptional items
Capital expenditure cash flows include £8,625,000 from the sale of tangible fixed assets (19X3 – £3,965,000) and £125,000 from the sale of fixed asset investments (19X3 – £nil).

25.   POST BALANCE SHEET EVENT
On 14 February 19X5 a short leasehold building with a net book value of £1,695,000   sch 4.12(b)
was severely damaged by flooding. It is expected that insurance proceeds will fall   SSAP 17(23) - (25)
short of the costs of rebuilding and loss of profits by some £750,000. No provision has
been made in these accounts for this loss.

26.   CAPITAL COMMITMENTS
Amounts contracted for but not provided in the accounts amounted to £4,500,000 for   sch 4.50(3)
the group and £1,750,000 for the company (19X3 – £4,250,000 and £950,000
respectively).

Good Group P.L.C.

NOTES TO THE ACCOUNTS
at 31 December 19X4

27.   CONTINGENT LIABILITY

The company has guaranteed the bank overdraft of a subsidiary undertaking to the   sch 4.50(2)
extent of £1,500,000 (19X3 – £1,000,000), of which £760,000 was utilised at 31   sch 4.59A
December 19X4 (19X3 – £375,000).   SSAP 18(18)

28.   PENSION COMMITMENTS

The group operates two defined benefit pension schemes, one in the United Kingdom,   sch 4.50(4)
the Good Group Employee Pension Scheme, and one in the United States, the Good   SSAP 24(88)
Group Employee Pension Plan. Both schemes are funded by the payment of
contributions to separately administered trust funds.

The pension costs are determined with the advice of independent qualified actuaries on
the basis of triennial valuations using the projected unit credit method. The results of
the most recent valuations, which were conducted as at 31 December 19X1, were as
follows:

	UK	United States
Main assumptions:		
Rate of return on investments (% per annum)	10.0	10.0
Rate of salary increases (% per annum)	8.0	7.0
Rate of pension increases (% per annum)	6.0	Nil
Market value of scheme's assets (£000)	4,550	1,450
Level of funding being the actuarial value of assets expressed as a percentage of the benefits accrued to members, after allowing for future salary increases	90%	106%

Further contributions, in addition to the employer's current contribution of 12% of
pensionable earnings, are being made in order to eliminate the deficiency in the UK
scheme by 19X8. The deficit in the UK and the surplus in the US scheme are being
recognised as variations from regular cost over 11 years, the average expected
remaining service lives of both the UK and the US employees.

Since the date of these valuations, the group has acquired Extinguishers Limited and
sold Hose Limited. The group's actuarial advisers have confirmed that these events are
unlikely to have had a significant effect on the position of the UK fund. A valuation as
at 31 December 19X4 is currently being underataken.

29.   POST-RETIREMENT BENEFITS OTHER THAN PENSIONS

The group also operates a plan in the United States which provides employees with   sch 4.50(5)
certain post-retirement benefits other than pensions. The liabilities in respect of these   UITF 6(9)
benefits are assessed by qualified independent actuaries, applying the projected unit
credit method. The charge for the year is £20,000 (19X3 - £19,000). The main
assumptions used in the calculation were:

Rate of inflation in the cost of providing benefits (% per annum)	9.0
Discount rate for obligations (% per annum)	7.0

Good Group P.L.C.

NOTES TO THE ACCOUNTS
at 31 December 19X4

30.   DIRECTORS' LOAN

At the Annual General Meeting held on 15 July 19X4 approval was given for an interest-free loan up to a maximum of £10,000 to be made as necessary to F R Brown to enable him to meet expenditure to be incurred in his capacity as sales director at marketing exhibitions and tours in the USA. During the year £6,500 was advanced to him for this purpose and at 31 December 19X4 £2,432 was outstanding and is included in debtors.

sch 6, part II

31.   OTHER DIRECTORS' INTERESTS

During the year, purchases totalling £510,000 (19X3 – £490,000), at normal market prices have been made by group companies from UK Gnome Industries Limited, of which P A MacBryde's wife is a director and controlling shareholder. £10,000 was outstanding at 31 December 19X4 (19X3 – £9,000).

sch 6, part II
YB 12.43(q)
FRS 8(6)

F R Brown was interested throughout the year, through his 25% equity interest in Homes Fires Limited, in a contract for the supply of fire extinguishers to that company. During the year the company supplied extinguishers to Home Fires Limited to a value of £225,000 at normal market prices. At 31 December 19X4 Home Fires Limited owed £20,000 to the company (19X3 – £nil).

32.   OTHER RELATED PARTY TRANSACTIONS

During the year the group entered into the following transactions, in the ordinary course of business, with other related parties:

Related party	Sales to related party £000	Purchases from related party £000	Amounts owed to related party £000	Amounts owed from related party £000	
International Fires PLC					FRS 8(6)
19X4	6,975	–	–	600	
19X3	6,410	–	–	550	
Power Works Limited					
19X4	–	2,800	230	–	
19X3	–	2,300	145	–	
Showers Limited					
19X4	580	–	–	30	
19X3	430	–	–	12	

International Fires P.L.C.
International Fire P.L.C. owns 31.48% of the shares in the company.

Power Works Limited
The group has a 25% interest in Power Works Limited.

Showers Limited
The group has a 33% interest in Showers Limited.

Good Group P.L.C.

NOTES TO THE ACCOUNTS
at 31 December 19X4

33.   MINORITY INTERESTS

The non-equity minority interests represent a holding of 55% of the preferred shares in   FRS 4(61)
Bright Sparks Limited (see note 14). The holders of those shares have no rights against
any other group company.

Index of Statutes and Standards

This index refers to places in the text where individual paragraphs of accounting standards, exposure drafts, the Companies Act 1985 and the Stock Exchange Listing Rules are discussed.